Visual C++® .NET
Bible

Visual C++® .NET Bible

Tom Archer and Andrew Whitechapel

Wiley Publishing, Inc.

Visual C++° .NET Bible

Published by
Wiley Publishing, Inc.
909 Third Avenue
New York, NY 10022
www.wiley.com

Copyright © 2002 by Wiley Publishing, Inc., Indianapolis, Indiana

Library of Congress Control Number: 2001093476

ISBN: 0-7645-4837-9

Manufactured in the United States of America

10 9 8 7 6 5 4 3 2 1

1B/QZ/QY/QS/IN

Published simultaneously in Canada

Wiley Publishing, Inc. is a trademark of Wiley Publishing

About the Authors

In addition to his hobby of helping fellow developers through his book writing (such as this book and *Inside C#*), **Tom Archer** makes his living programming Visual C++/MFC and .NET/C# projects. His client list includes IBM, AT&T, Equifax, Data General, and Peachtree Software. Tom also enjoys traveling around the world evangelizing about the virtues of .NET development and is available for both corporate and university training sessions. If you have a project that you think Tom can help on either as a developer or as a consultant, he can be reached through his `www.theCodeChannel.com` Web site.

On a personal note, Tom currently has homes in both Atlanta, GA, and Ibiza, Spain, and as an avid pool player (9-ball, 14.1, and one-pocket), he's always looking for a challenging game. So if you're in one of these areas and would like to play seriously or just have fun, be sure to drop him a line. In the meantime, remember Willie Mosconi's response when asked the secret to great pool — "Don't miss!"

Andrew Whitechapel has spent 20 years in the software industry, over 12 of them using C++ at all levels, from embedded systems through to *n*-tier distributed enterprise solutions. He has spent most of the last decade working with the Windows platform, the MFC and ATL, and the suite of Visual Studio tools to produce advanced systems across a range of industry sectors. He firmly believes that .NET will revolutionize the way we design and write software.

In the unmanaged world, Andrew plays rugby for Battersea Ironsides rugby club in London — the best club in the world.

Credits

Senior Acquisitions Editor
Sharon Cox

Project Editor
Chandani Thapa

Development Editor
Brian MacDonald

Technical Editor
Essam Ahmed

Copy Editor
Mildred Sanchez
Kim Cofer

Editorial Manager
Mary Beth Wakefield

Vice President and Executive Group Publisher
Richard Swadley

Vice President and Executive Publisher
Bob Ipsen

Executive Editorial Director
Mary Bednarek

Project Coordinator
Jennifer Bingham

Graphics and Production Specialists
Beth Brooks, Sean Decker, Brian Drumm,
Melanie DesJardins, Joyce Haughey,
Kelly Hardesty, Kristin McMullan,
Jackie Nicholas, Laurie Petrone,
Betty Schulty, Jeremey Unger

Quality Control Technicians
Laura Albert, John Greenough,
Andy Hollandbeck, Susan Moritz,
Carl Pierce, Linda Quigley

Proofreading and Indexing
TECHBOOKS Production Services

*To my beautiful wife, Krista — without your love, support, and strength,
life's never-ending series of trials and tests would simply be unbearable.
Thank you for being there so many times when I've needed you.*

— Tom

To Agatha and Felix.

— Andrew

Preface

I've been designing and writing software using the Visual C++/MFC platform for almost 10 years now, and have thoroughly enjoyed watching this product evolve with the times. However, with each passing year there is always a new class of coders wanting to learn and become productive with Microsoft's flagship C++ development environment. For these soon-to-be MFC gurus and even for those of you who already have a bit of experience using this framework, I wrote this text.

One difficult challenge in writing a book on a tool that you've been using for so many years is ensuring that you don't overlook something that might not be obvious to other people. Therefore, I made it a point during the writing of this book to constantly participate in and monitor the various Visual C++/MFC discussion groups and Web site message boards. This allowed me to gain valuable insight into the issues that needed to be covered. As a result, the material in this book addresses over 75% of the questions posted on an average day, allowing me to present a book specifically designed to teach you MFC in an orderly, logical fashion as well as providing answers for what historically have been the most difficult-to-grasp concepts and tasks.

Who This Book Is For

First, you should note that this book is first and foremost an MFC book, not a .NET book. I have included several chapters at the end of the book on writing managed extensions (the extension to the Visual C++ compiler that allows you to emit code for the .NET runtime). However, these chapters are simply put in as an introductory section to the new .NET framework if you'd like to experiment with .NET before taking the plunge of investing money in a book dedicated to .NET development using managed extensions.

Second, this book can be used by anyone wanting to either learn MFC or extend their already-earned knowledge on MFC. This includes beginner level MFC developers writing their first applications, as well as more advanced users of the language looking for specific tips and techniques. As you'll see in the next section, this book is organized such that it should be easy to jump to the sections that are specifically written for your interest and skill level. Beginners will probably want to start with Chapter 1, where I make no assumptions about your knowledge of creating projects and classes in Visual Studio. In addition, each chapter starts off with an introductory bit of information on the topic of discussion, moves into a fairly easy demo application, and ends with more advanced material on the topic matter. A great example of that is the DLL chapters, where you first learn the basics of writing DLLs and importing and exporting classes. From there, the demos get more elaborate with illustrations on how to place your documents and views into DLLs, how to write Windows hooks, and how to share a single instance of a C++ object across multiple invocations of a DLL using the little-known `placement new` operator.

This book assumes that you're a competent C++ developer. Although I'll teach you MFC, teaching both C++ and MFC from the ground-up in a single book is simply not feasible. Therefore, I will assume that you know and understand such basic C++ as constructors, initializer lists, virtual methods, and so on.

I also assume that you have access to the Visual C++ .NET product, because all the demo projects in this book were created using that environment. Although most of the code in this book is MFC, and should compile with the Visual C++ 6 product, the demos have not been tested in Visual C++ 6.

The database chapters covering ODBC, DAO, ADO, and the MFC Database Classes all include demo applications that use a Microsoft Access database. I chose Access (instead of SQL Server) because it is much easier to distribute, and more people are likely to have Access on their machines. However, nothing in this book requires you to have the actual Microsoft Access product installed—I provide the sample database needed for these demos to function correctly.

The final chapters of this book are an introduction to the .NET world via writing managed extensions. As such, these chapters require that you've installed the .NET Framework SDK.

How This Book is Organized

It's extremely difficult to write a book this large and one that targets both a beginner-level readership as well as more advanced programmers. For this reason, the organization of the book takes on an extremely important role. To that extent, I've done my best to split the different topics of MFC development into distinct and logically ordered categories. This affords the novice a means of sequentially working through the book without becoming overwhelmed while at the same time being organized in such a way that advanced programmers can easily jump to the section they need without having to read through a lot of beginner-level material. Here's how the book is laid out.

The book begins with Part I, "User Interface." As programmers, we're creatures of impulse. Nobody likes to purchase a book, full of enthusiasm and hope, and then see that motivation squelched by endless chapters of theory and syntax before you can even get started writing code! For that reason, this part begins with a chapter whose primary goal is to get you comfortable with the Visual Studio development environment and started writing Visual C++ application immediately. The part then jumps into several chapters that are designed to teach you the user-interface basics of writing MFC applications. This includes chapters on SDI and MDI interfaces, understanding the document/view architecture, working with menus, keyboard and mouse input, and even a couple of chapters on exploring the world of graphics programming.

After you've explored the different aspects of creating user interfaces, Part II "Dialogs" is intended to teach you how to use dialogs effectively in your applications. You begin by learning how DDX enables you to wire dialog controls to control and value member variables, how to display and control modal dialogs, how command routing works, and how to program several of the basic common controls. The next couple of chapters are dedicated to the more advanced issues of dialog box programming such as working with modeless dialog boxes, messaging between dialog boxes, handling accelerators and trapping keyboard input, and working with form views. You'll even learn how to write your own `CCtrlView`-derived class to combine the power of a given control with the flexibility of the document/view architecture. Finally, this part wraps up with a chapter on using the property sheet and page classes in your applications including many advanced tips on disabling tabs, changing tab fonts, and using mnemonics with your property pages.

By this point of the book, you already have most of the basics of programming with the MFC. Therefore, Part III, "Advanced Programming" takes you to the next level. In this section, you begin by learning how to extend the basic functionality of the MFC controls and classes. I start off with a chapter that illustrates how to handle the drawing of your own controls (using *custom draw*) to design and code the types of controls seen with the more advanced Windows applications. From there, you'll learn how to add custom behavior to your controls using a variety of techniques, including standard C++ derivation, multiple inheritance, message maps, and templates. Then you'll learn how to incorporate print and print preview into your applications, program DLLs, and incorporate multi-threading. This part concludes with a full discussion on exception handling and how it enables a much more robust means of error handling in any system, simple or complex.

Obviously, not many applications are useful without some means of saving data. That's where Part IV, "Data I/O" comes in. You begin this part by learning how to use the Windows Clipboard. Most of us use the clipboard as users and never realize how easy it is to add clipboard functionality to our own applications, even those that use proprietary data formats and objects. From there, you get into the serious chapters of database development using ODBC and the MFC database classes. Although you can jump directly into using the MFC database classes, the ordering of the chapters is significant because these classes encapsulate the ODBC API. Therefore, if your intention is to fully understand database programming, I recommend reading both chapters. If you purchased the previous edition of this book, you will notice the removal of the DAO chapter. This chapter has been replaced by a chapter on the Microsoft database API du jour, ADO. The ADO is not just easier to use, it also affords you a truly object-oriented interface to your database programming tasks. Finally, the part wraps up with something brand new to Visual C++ programmers — attributes. Attributes take self-describing, fully-contained components (or objects) to another level, so if you want to ride the wave of the newest and slickest stuff, you'll definitely want to read this chapter.

No book on Visual C++ programming would be complete without a full section on "COM and ATL," and boy, have we loaded up here! In Part V, I take you on a full tour of COM development that some beginner-level books on COM don't aspire to. You begin by learning the basics of interface-based programming, and discovering how to create and consume components. After that, you then get into the advanced areas of understanding COM type libraries and threading models. Once you've got the basics of COM down, you'll start using ATL (Active Template Library). However, unlike many books that stick with Hello World, I've brought in one of the best-known ATL programmers around, Andrew Whitechapel, who takes you through five different chapters designed to teach you the ins and outs of writing real-world, practical ATL applications. This includes the subjects of windowing, eventing, and automation. This part even wraps up with a bonus — a chapter on the WTL (Windows Template Library). If you think ATL makes COM programming easy, just wait till you see how easy the WTL makes ATL programming!

Continuing with the advanced theme of this part of the book, you arrive at a Part VI, entitled "Programming with COM+." Although the first chapter is introductory in nature, do not overlook it if you're new to COM+, because it is not your typical introduction with no code. In fact, you'll almost immediately code a COM+ application to see how stateful applications can be designed and written in C++, and then consumed by script clients. You'll even see this demo used over a network using the DCOM service. The next two chapters then illustrate the two most popular aspects of COM+ development: writing asynchronous events and coding queued components.

Coming off part ATL and COM+, it is only natural to segue into the world of "ATL Server." If you are new to ATL Server, it is a set of extensions to the ATL that enables C++ developers to more easily write Web applications that run on IIS servers. Therefore, this part includes an introductory chapter about this technology, its terminology, and how to start using it. From there, you learn how to create Web services using ATL Server. The part finishes up with a chapter where a "Tip of the Day" application is presented in order to illustrate how easy it is to code a practical Web-based application using C++ and ATL Server.

Finally, Part VIII, "Programming .NET," takes you into the extremely advanced area of writing *managed code* in the .NET environment. You begin your exploration into this brave new world with an introduction to .NET itself (its purpose, the components that make it up, its role in the future of Windows development, and how you can start using it today). From there, you start learning the basics of how to write managed code using Visual C++ to target .NET platforms, writing multi-threaded .NET applications, and using a forms package (Windows Forms).

Conventions used in this book

Like any programmer, I have my own pet terms and programming style. So, let me define a few terms and icons you'll see throughout the book as well as explain why certain things were done the way they were:

+ *Problem domain* — This is a term I learned years ago while using the Coad/Yourdon Object-Oriented Analysis and Design methodology. A problem domain is a generic term that refers to the set of problems to be solved.

+ *Consumers* and *clients* — These terms are used interchangeably to represent any code that uses a class or type.

+ *Server* — This term is used to refer to a piece of code — typically a class — that is used by a client or consumer.

+ *Arguments* and *parameters* — Like most programmers, I use these terms interchangeably when referring to the values passed to a method.

+ *Method prototype* and *method signature* — These terms are used interchangeably in this book.

+ Breaking lines of code — Unfortunately, there are times when the format of the book does not allow a whole line of source code to fit on the page, which requires some odd line breaks. This is regrettable but unavoidable. Please keep this in mind when you see an oddly formatted line of code.

 This icon identifies an interesting point you'll find worth remembering.

 This icon points out a helpful hint or technique you'll find useful in your programming.

 An alert to pay special attention to the section discussed.

Contacting the Author

The best way to contact me is via my Web site, `www.theCodeChannel.com`, where I support all my books and articles.

Acknowledgments

First, I would like to thank Rick Leinecker with whom I co-authored the *Visual C++ 6 Bible* (the predecessor to this edition). Without Rick's support and continued friendship, I would never have made it through my first book. Thanks Rick! Andrew Whitechapel—my coauthor on this edition—was instrumental in producing a quality book. Great work as always, Andrew!

Next, many of you will know the name Roger Onslow. This extremely talented programmer has been freely donating his time in order to help fellow developers for years via the various newsgroups and Web sites. Roger wrote the very fine chapters on custom draw and adding custom behavior to controls.

The very cool Tip of the Day ATL Server application was graciously donated by Erik Thompson. In addition to Erik's help on this chapter, Tom Marshall and Rama Krishna were instrumental in helping me ferret out some sticky issues when migrating it to the release version of Visual Studio .NET. Thanks guys for a great chapter!

Also special thanks goes to Chris Maunder of CodeProject (www.CodeProject.com) for contributing his progress bar control, which I used in several chapters.

Finally, no book can be written in a vacuum. I'd like to thank Wiley's Sharon Cox (project manager) and Chandani Thapa (editor) for their help and great work throughout a process that hit many snags along the way. If it weren't for their patience and continued support, this book would never have been completed. Also, many thanks to my technical editor Essam Ahmed. Essam is an extremely gifted programmer and author in his own right and was an invaluable resource in producing this book.

Contents at a Glance

Contents

Part IV: Data I/O   577

Part V: COM and ATL — 773

User Interface

Writing Your First MFC Application

I'm a believer in learning how to program by writing applications — "trial by fire" as the expression goes. Therefore, I'm not too much into long chapters showing every window and toolbar icon of a development environment. However, the simple fact is that not everyone has years and years of Visual C++ experience and it's sometimes helpful to at least have a quick tour of the environment that can be easily accomplished through the creation of a simple demo application.

Having said that, you should read this chapter if you have little to no experience in Visual Studio. If you are already familiar with using Visual Studio and are eager to begin learning about MFC, I would suggest moving on to Chapter 2. If, however, you are new to Visual C++, or even new to the Visual Studio .NET development environment, I suggest that you read through this chapter because it illustrates many tasks that you will be performing repeatedly throughout this book. These tasks include understanding the new Start Page, creating a dialog-based application, adding an event handler, adding controls to a dialog template resource via the Dialog Editor, using DDX to wire a control to a member variable, correcting build errors, and debugging simple mistakes.

Say Hello to the New Visual Studio

To begin, start the Visual Studio editor (it should be located in your Start menu under Programs ➪ Microsoft Visual Studio .NET). If you're familiar with previous versions of Visual Studio, you're going to be in for many surprises — some good and some not so good. As you can see in Figure 1-1, the first obvious change to the Visual Studio environment is the Start Page.

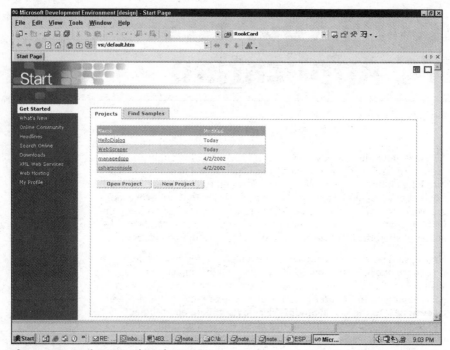

Figure 1-1: Getting started on the Start Page.

Although the Start Page isn't really that great for the experienced developer, it is a great aid to someone either new to programming in general or new to Visual Studio. The Start Page even displays a message alerting you when a new version (or service pack) of Visual Studio is available that supercedes your current version. The first thing you'll notice is that this page is designed with vertical tabs running along the left side of the page. Let's quickly look at some of these tabs and what they offer you.

✦ *Get Started* — This tab will probably be of most importance as you begin your learning curve with Visual Studio because it provides two more tabs that the beginner to this development environment will use quite often: *Projects* and *Find Samples*.

  • As you can see in Figure 1-1, the Projects tab lists the most recent projects that you've worked on. In addition, there are two buttons on this tab that enable you to open existing projects and create new projects. You'll be performing both of these tasks shortly.

  • Probably one of the cooler aspects of this Start Page is the Find Samples tab (shown in Figure 1-2). How many times have you been forced to dig through MSDN (which now fills two CDs!) looking for a specific example? This tab not only allows you to search on article text, but also filter articles by language. You can even select the Type radio button and filter by Controls, Forms, or Web. As you can see, Microsoft has spent a lot of time attempting to make this environment much easier to use, and therefore, more productive. In Figure 1-2, you can see the result of a search for Visual C++ managed extension samples. (Managed extensions are the means by which Visual C++ programmers can write code for the .NET environment. Chapters 41 through 44 address this topic.)

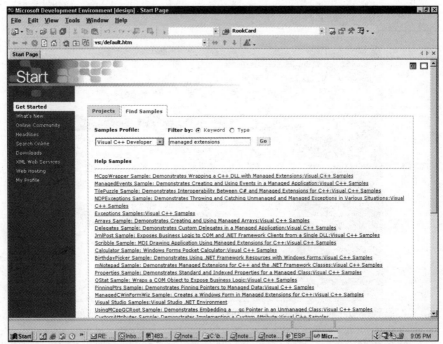

Figure 1-2: The Find Samples tab enables you to quickly locate samples written for the various Microsoft languages.

Note   Most of the tabs on the Start Page require a connection to the Internet because they display and enable you to search for the most current information.

✦ *What's New* — What I really like about this tab is that it connects to the Microsoft Web site and displays only the most current information that a Windows or Web developer would care about. That saves me the time needed to laboriously dig through their overly crowded site. Not only do you get a list of Visual Studio resources, but there are also tabs for Partner Resources, and more importantly to developers, a Product Information tab that contains information about the various Visual Studio development tools and APIs. Also notice that the What's New tab contains a Filter combo box that enables you to specify that you only want to see information associated with a given language or tool.

✦ *Online Community*—Ever have trouble remembering the exact address of that important newsgroup or Web site? We all have, and it only happens when you absolutely need to find an answer to a question *now*. The Online Community tab (as shown in Figure 1-3) lists everything from newsgroups to Web sites and even online chat communities. Once again, you can filter all of these lists via the Filter combo box at the top of the page. You can even see my new site (The Code Channel) listed here. You can find support, demo applications, and latest errata for this book on that site (`http://www.theCodeChannel.com`).

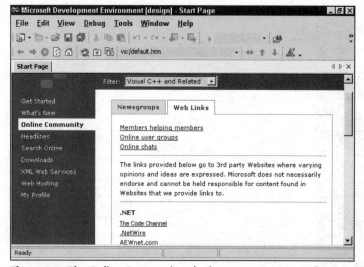

Figure 1-3: The Online Community tab gives you access to Web resources.

✦ *Headlines*—This tab contains the latest news and information from Microsoft. Included here are tabs for Technical Articles and Knowledgebase Articles—no more searching through MSDN for that elusive knowledgebase article!

✦ *Search Online*—This is a simple search page that allows for searching through the MSDN material.

✦ *Downloads*—This page contains three tabs (Downloads, Code Samples, and Reference) of downloadable links. Basically, this is the same information that you'd find if you went to the Microsoft MSDN download page, only it's much easier to find what you want here.

✦ *XML Web Services*—Don't know what a Web Service is? Looking for a Web Service for your company? This tab contains everything you need to know about this new technology, including a tab for registering your own newly created Web Services for other companies to find!

✦ *Web Hosting*—A bit too "markety" for me—this tab contains information for the companies or individuals attempting to create a Web presence by means of a Web site.

✦ *My Profile* – The My Profile page enables you to personalize Visual Studio so that it suits your development tastes. Included in this page are options to select from a base programmer profile (C++, C#, student, and more), keyboard scheme, window layout, and help filter. You can even specify the page that you want displayed when you begin Visual Studio. This can be the Start Page that you're learning about now, the last loaded solution, or even the New Project dialog box.

Creating Your First Visual Studio Project

Let's get started writing some code! You'll begin by creating a very simple, Hello World type application from the (you guessed it) Start Page. Click the Get Started tab. When that page appears, click the Projects tab. From there, click the New Project button. You could also select File ➪ New ➪ Project, or press Ctrl+Shift+N. Whichever way you choose to display the New Project dialog box (shown in Figure 1-4), it enables you to create any type of project supported by Visual Studio.

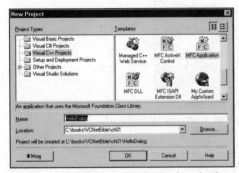

Figure 1-4: There are almost one hundred different project types that can be created from Visual Studio.

1. Select the Project type. In your case, you're going to create a Visual C++ project so select that to begin with. (If you're new to this, don't despair. Figure 1-4 shows the options you should choose.)

2. Scroll down the list of Templates and select the MFC Application template.

3. Type the Name of the project into the Name field. In this case, I've chosen HelloDialog.

4. Confirm or note the location of your project, as shown in the Location field. Your location will depend on where you want to store the project — mine is simply in the folder used to store everything for this chapter.

5. Confirm that the Close Solution option is selected. These two options control where the project you're creating will reside. Simply put, a *solution* is an encapsulation of

one or more projects. Typically, you will create solutions that contain only one project. However, for more experienced programmers and more advanced applications, there will be times when it's convenient to have all of the projects for a given system reside in the same solution. For purposes of this demo, leave the Close Solution option selected — which basically means that you're creating a new solution and not adding this project to the current solution.

6. Click OK. The wizard associated with the selected project type appears — in this case, the MFC Application Wizard (shown in Figure 1-5).

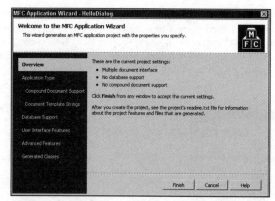

Figure 1-5: The MFC Application Wizard enables you to create a new project with quite a bit of functionality with only a few clicks of the mouse.

The first page that you see with the MFC Application Wizard is the Overview page. This page shows you what settings are currently in place so that you know what type of project you're going to have if you click Finish. The remaining tabs, which appear vertically along the left side of the wizard's dialog box, contain the various options for customizing your new project.

Obviously, its not my intent to bore you to tears by going through every single option as most of these options you either do not need to change, or you will learn them over time as your experience with Visual C++ grows. However, let's look at a few of the key options that you'll be setting from time to time throughout this book.

1. Click the Application Type tab, and then select the Dialog-based radio button that appears under the Application type options (as shown in Figure 1-6). An application type can be one that is based on the famous (or infamous, depending on your viewpoint) MFC document/view model. I discuss this in more detail in Chapters 2 and 3.

   The Project Style (which should be disabled when you select a dialog-based project) is only of interest if you are generating an SDI (single document) or MDI (multiple document) application, and it simply gives you the option of creating an Explorer-like interface. This is an interface where you have a tree view on one side of a splitter window and a list view on the other. Both of these controls are covered in Chapter 7.

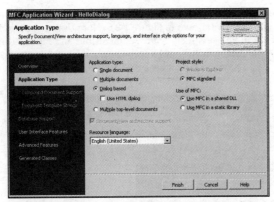

Figure 1-6: There are four basic user interfaces to select from when creating an MFC application using the wizard.

2. Click the User Interface Features tab (shown in Figure 1-7). The settings available to you depend on the project type you select on the Application Type tab. Because the demo is a dialog-based application, the Child frame styles and Toolbars settings are disabled. The only options available are the settings that control the dialog box's border, system menu, and title. As Figure 1-7 shows, the only change I've made is to modify the value in the Dialog title field to read "My First MFC Application."

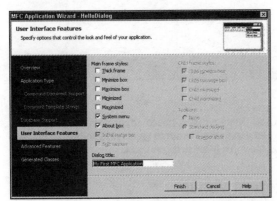

Figure 1-7: When creating a new application via the MFC Application Wizard, you can set many of the frame window's styles that dictate whether the user will see UI elements such as a minimize or maximize button, the system menu, and the About box.

3. Click Finish to create the new project.

When you create a dialog-based application, Visual Studio automatically displays the Resource View, the Dialog Editor, and the Toolbox (shown in Figure 1-8). (Note that these windows might not appear exactly as shown if you've previously used Visual Studio and moved these windows.) I'll discuss how to use the Dialog Editor and Toolbox shortly. First, I want to briefly explain the various views that you have on your new project.

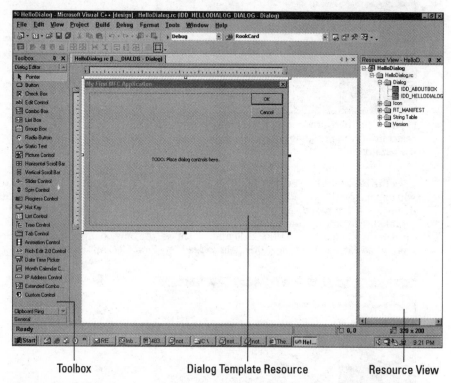

Toolbox   Dialog Template Resource   Resource View

Figure 1-8: By default, when you create a dialog-based application, Visual Studio opens the dialog template resource along with the Resource View and Toolbox so that you can modify the default dialog box (the most likely first task) first.

Exploring the different views

Visual Studio solutions and projects consist of quite a number of different files and classes that are automatically created on your behalf. In this section, you'll take a look at how the various views (available via the View menu) enable you to more quickly and productively navigate your way through them all.

✦ *Resource View*—This view (displayed in Figure 1-8) is represented by a dialog bar on the left side of Visual Studio (by default) and displays the various resources (dialog boxes, menus, strings, and so on) that are associated with the current project.

✦ *Solution Explorer*—A view that you'll be using quite often is the Solution Explorer (shown in Figure 1-9). This window, activated via the View menu, displays all the files associated with the current solution and project. These files are separated into categories of source, header, and resource files to make finding a file easier. To open a specific file, simply double-click that file. Like almost all of the views in Visual Studio, the elements (in this case the file names) support a context menu, which means that you can right-click a given element and a menu specific to that element will appear. As an example, if you want to remove a file from the project, you would simply open Solution Explorer, locate the file you want to remove, right-click that file name (to display the context menu) and select the Delete option. Therefore, from now on when I ask you to select a context menu option, this is the process I'm referring to.

Note Removing a file from a project only removes it from the project and does not delete the actual physical file.

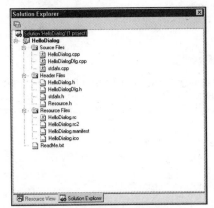

Figure 1-9: The Solution Explorer (shown here by itself) enables you to quickly locate, add, or remove files to or from the current solution's projects.

✦ *Class View*—Another integral view to your development experience in Visual Studio is the Class View (shown in Figure 1-10). In fact, you will be using this view more than any other throughout this book because it provides a very quick and easy means of locating classes and their members as well as performs various functions on them. If the Class View tab isn't available at the bottom of the Window, add the tab by selecting View ➪ Class View from Visual Studio's menu.

Figure 1-10: The Class View (shown here by itself) enables you to quickly locate and manipulate the classes (and their members) of the current solution's projects.

Adding button event handlers

At this point, let's make your little demo application do something. I'll keep it simple by having a message box display a text message when you click a button. In the process, however, you'll learn the following essential tasks that you'll need to perform many, many times as you progress through your Visual C++ career:

✦ Adding an event handler in response to a user action

✦ Displaying a message to the user

✦ Building and executing an application from Visual Studio

Begin by following these steps:

1. Open the Resource View (via the View menu, if necessary), as shown in Figure 1-8.

2. Expand the item labeled Dialog and locate the `IDD_HELLODIALOG_DIALOG` item. This is the resource ID assigned to your application's dialog box. Double-click the `IDD_HELLODIALOG_DIALOG` resource to open it.

3. Visual Studio opens the Dialog Editor and changes the Toolbox to include controls that you can include on the dialog resource. Close the Resource View if it occupies too much space on your monitor.

   As you can see in Figure 1-11, the dialog box that is created automatically for you contains only an OK and Cancel button and a static text control telling you that you can place controls on the dialog box.

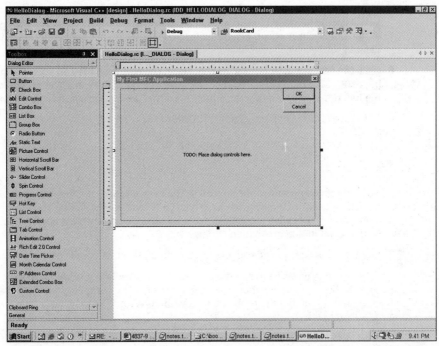

Figure 1-11: The basic, no-frills dialog box created by default by the Visual Studio Wizard.

4. Add an event handler for one of the buttons. You want to add code such that when the user clicks OK, a message appears — the code that executes is called an *event handler*.

There are two ways to add an event handler to a control. The first way is to simply double-click the button for which you want to handle the Click event. This automatically creates a member function to your dialog class that is called whenever the user clicks the button. However, what if you want to handle other events (such as the user clicking with the right mouse button)?

In that case, you need to invoke the Event Handler Wizard. The wizard helps you add event handlers to controls on the dialog box for events like a right-click and a double-click. You can invoke the Event Handler Wizard by right-clicking a control and then selecting the Add Event Wizard item from the context menu that pops up.

Right-click the OK button and select Add Event Handler from the context menu.

5. Select the BN_CLICKED item in the Message type field and confirm that the CHelloDialogDlg class is selected in the Class list field.

The Event Wizard allows you to select the message type you are attempting to handle as well as the function name you wish to have created for you. You can change the name of the function the wizard generates for you if you like, but I generally leave in the name default.

6. Click the Add and Edit button. At this point, the editor opens and you will find yourself in the CHelloDialogDlg::OnBnClickedOk function (assuming you accepted that as the function name). Modify this function so that when finished, it looks as follows:

```
void CHelloDialogDlg::OnBnClickedOk()
{
    AfxMessageBox("You clicked the Ok button");
    // OnOK();
}
```

Notice that I commented out the call to the base class's OnOK function, because the default behavior of a dialog box's OK button is to close the dialog box (via CDialog::EndDialog). Because the dialog box is the main window of this application, that would result in the application ending.

7. Build the application and execute it. You can do this in a couple of ways:

   - You can press F5 to run the application, whereupon you will be asked if you want to build the application. Clicking Yes causes the compiler to build the application and (assuming the project builds without errors) Visual Studio then executes your code.

   - Alternatively, you can do this in two steps: Select the Build ⇨ Build Solution menu option and then press F5.

8. Test the application by clicking OK. You should see a message box like that shown in Figure 1-12.

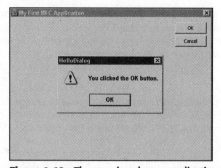

Figure 1-12: The running demo application.

At this point, you can create a dialog-based application and wire an event to a function that displays a message box. Next, you'll learn how to use the Dialog Editor to add controls to the dialog box.

Using the Dialog Editor and Toolbox

You'll continue building onto the simple demo application by adding a couple of controls to the dialog box. This way, you'll learn how to use the different functions of the Dialog Editor. Close the sample application, if it is still running, before you begin these steps.

1. Open the dialog template resource—the `IDD_HELLODIALOG_DIALOG` resource— _(if not already open) and display the Toolbox (press Ctrl+Alt+X).

2. Remove that silly TODO static text control from the dialog box. To do that, simply click the control (click any of the words to select the control) and press Delete.

3. Resize the dialog box by clicking on the dialog box. Several dark-colored boxes appear at the edges of the dialog box called *sizing grippers* (see Figure 1-13). Simply click and drag the lower-right gripper and resize the dialog box to be a bit smaller (it's much too large for your needs).

Gripper

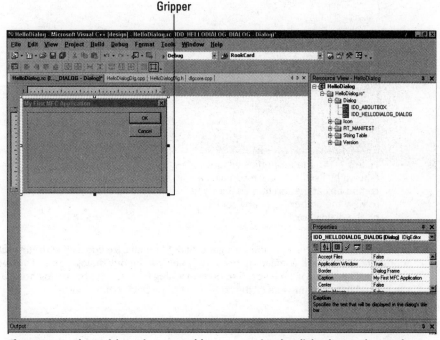

Figure 1-13: The resizing grippers enable you to resize the dialog box and controls.

4. Add a static text control and an edit control from the Toolbox. You can add controls to the dialog box by clicking the control you want to add in the Toolbox, and then clicking on the dialog box approximately where you want to place the control. The controls almost never appear where you want them to, so simply drag them into place once they're on the dialog box. You can also use the arrow buttons on your keyboard for a finer level of control over placement.

5. Change the static text control to "Message text:". You can do this by simply clicking the control and typing the text. This is because the default property for the static text control is its `Caption` property. In order to view all the properties for a control, simply click the desired control and press F4 to view the Properties window (as shown in Figure 1-14).

Figure 1-14: The Properties window (shown by itself here) also contains a combo box at the top that enables you to view the properties of any control on the dialog box.

Before you continue, now would be a good time to familiarize yourself with the Dialog Editor toolbar because it will come in quite handy when you modify dialog boxes. This toolbar (shown in Figure 1-15) can be used to do everything from testing the dialog box, to setting the tab order, to aligning and sizing controls with respect to one another.

Now you have this edit control and the user can type text into it, but how do you use it? The answer is Dynamic Data Exchange (DDX).

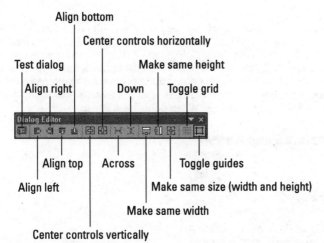

Figure 1-15: The Dialog Editor toolbar enables you to perform many tasks including aligning controls, sizing controls with respect to one another, positioning controls relative to the dialog box, setting the tab order, and testing the dialog box.

Using Dynamic Data Exchange

Dynamic Data Exchange (DDX) is one means by which you can easily move data between the controls on a dialog box and the member variables in your application. In order to create a DDX variable, simply click the control on the dialog template resource and select Add Variable from the context menu. Doing so now for the Edit Control invokes the Add Member Variable Wizard (shown in Figure 1-16).

There are two different types of DDX variables that can be created:

✦ *DDX Control Variables* — A control variable wires a control on a dialog box to a variable that is an MFC class wrapper for the control. An example of this is the CEdit class. Having a member variable of type CEdit that is tied to an edit control gives you the ability to control that edit control through the CEdit member functions instead of having to use the more laborious method of making Windows SDK calls. The various control classes are covered in Chapter 10. Generally, you'll want this type of DDX variable when you want to manipulate the control in some fashion — or example, moving or sizing the control.

✦ *DDX Value Variables* — A value variable wires a control on a dialog box to a variable that is an MFC variable for holding the value of that control. For example, if you have an edit control that will contain a number, you might create a DDX value variable of type CInt to hold the value.

At this point, deselect the Control Variable checkbox because you don't care about manipulating the control itself; you just want its value. From there, select a type of CString from the Variable type combo box. (In the version of Visual Studio I'm working on, CString is not an option, so I had to enter it manually. If the value is not in your list either, simply type it in.) Once you've done that, enter the member variable name that you will use to reference the control's value. In this case, I've used m_strMessageText. You can look back at Figure 1-16 to verify that you enter this information correctly. When done, click Finish.

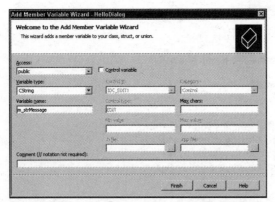

Figure 1-16: Both DDX control and value members can be created with the Add Member Variable Wizard.

Now you have a DDX value variable connected to your edit control. All you need to do is know how to actually get that value at runtime. This is done via the CDialog::UpdateData function. To use this function, you simply pass it a Boolean value of TRUE (the default) when you want to move the data from the dialog box to the variables and FALSE if you're moving data from the variables to the dialog box. Therefore, at this time, edit your dialog's OnBnClickedOk function. If you've closed that window, simply open the Class View, locate the CHelloDialogDlg class, and double-click the OnBnClickedOk function. Once you've located the function, make the following changes:

```
void CHelloDialogDlg::OnBnClickedOk()
{
    UpdateData(TRUE);
    AfxMessageBox(m_strMessageText);
    // OnOK();
}
```

Notice how here you're calling `UpdateData`. This acts to update your DDX variables with the data on the dialog box. This means that the `m_strMessageText` variable will contain the value the user typed into the dialog's edit control, which is subsequently displayed via the call to `AfxMessageBox`. Now build and execute the application. Figure 1-17 shows an example of me running the application.

Figure 1-17: DDX enables you to very quickly add code that wires controls to member variables.

Correcting Build Errors

You now know how Visual Studio runs your programs when everything builds. But what about those times when you make a mistake and the code doesn't build? Let's inject a small syntax error into the code to see that.

Once again, modify the `OnBnClickedOk` function — this time with a very simple, but easy-to-commit error of mistyping the `AfxMessageBox` name. When finished the function should look like this:

```
void CHelloDialogDlg::OnBnClickedOk()
{
    UpdateData(TRUE);
    xAfxMessageBox(m_strMessageText);
    // OnOK();
}
```

Now attempt to build the application. As shown in Figure 1-18, when the compiler (or linker) encounters errors, these errors will be listed in the Task List window.

The Task List window contains several columns, including the description of the error, the file the error was located in, and the line number of the error. In this case, the error message is:

```
error C2065: 'xAfxMessageBox' : undeclared identifier
```

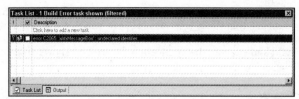

Figure 1-18: You can easily navigate through build-time errors using the Task List.

You obviously know the cause of this particular error, but what if you didn't understand the error message? To get more meaningful assistance in deciphering the error description, simply press F1 to display the help text associated with the error number being displayed (C2065, in this case).

In order to fix the problem, simply double-click the error line and Visual Studio automatically opens the file (if it is not already open) and places the cursor on the offending line. You can then modify the line (by changing xAfxMessageBox to AfxMessageBox) and attempt to build the project again.

Debugging in Visual Studio

The next thing that I cover is how to do some simple debugging in Visual Studio. First I'll introduce a bug into the code. Modify the OnBnClickedOk function such that you pass a value of FALSE to the UpdateData function (instead of TRUE). This line is shown in bold here:

```
void CHelloDialogDlg::OnBnClickedOk()
{
    UpdateData(FALSE);
    AfxMessageBox(m_strMessageText);
    // OnOK();
}
```

You should surmise by now what this will do. Now, instead of DDX moving the data from the control to the m_strMessageText variable, it will move the data from the m_strMessageText variable to the control. The result is that the message box will never be correct. Make this change above and build and execute the application to see this. Note that not only is the message box showing a blank string (what the m_strMessageText is initialized to in the dialog box's constructor), but also each time you click OK, the control is set to this value — the result of calling UpdateData(FALSE). However, you already knew this, so how can you fix it?

Setting breakpoints

You know where the bug is. You just need to stop execution of the application there and check out a few things. Therefore, locate the CHelloDialogDlg::OnBnClickedOk function and place a *breakpoint* on the UpdateData call. To set a breakpoint, simply click in the margin to the left of the text (or select Debug ➪ New Breakpoint, or select New Breakpoint from the context menu for that line of code). I like to simply click the left margin because it's faster and the other methods invoke the New Breakpoint dialog box, which I rarely use. (You can also click the F9 button to set a breakpoint for the current line.)

Once you set a breakpoint, a red dot will appear to mark this line as a breakpoint. Figure 1-19 shows the margin where you have to click and what the breakpoint dot looks like.

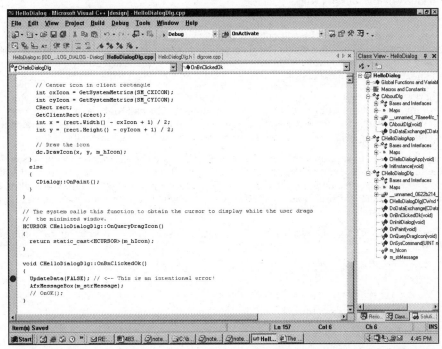

Figure 1-19: You can easily set a place where application execution is to stop with a breakpoint.

Now build and run the application by pressing F5. This time, when you type the text and click OK, execution stops on the `UpdateData` line. (A yellow arrow denotes the current line of execution.)

What you want to do is to inspect the `m_strMessageText` value. You can do this by simply moving your mouse over the variable. Visual Studio automatically shows you the memory address of the variable as well as its value. Currently it is blank.

To move to the next line, simply press F10. Now the current line of execution is the call to `AfxMessageBox`. At this point, you can inspect the variable again and see that for some reason `UpdateData` did not update the variable! Now obviously you know why `UpdateData` is not working. However, remember you're pretending to be in a real debugging situation here. Therefore, the only thing left to do is to step into the MFC source code.

Stepping into the MFC source code

I know I promised to keep this chapter extremely simple, but at some point you're going to be here, so you might as well get your feet wet now. Not only do all MFC developers eventually end up debugging MFC code, but it's incredibly helpful in understanding the internal working of your application—a necessary bit of knowledge to have when you run into those "I have no idea why this doesn't work" scenarios.

To return to your original breakpoint, you just need to click F5> to continue execution, type some more test text into the edit control, and click OK. You could do that, but let's learn something here. When the Visual C++ 6 compiler came out, it introduced the capability of doing something that among Microsoft compilers only Visual Basic could do before—set the next statement of execution.

Therefore, even though the current line of execution is the call to AfxMessageBox, you can literally indicate to Visual Studio that you want to make the call to UpdateData the next line. To do this, invoke the context menu for that line of code and click the Set Next Statement menu option. You will now see a yellow arrow next to the UpdateData call.

So, how do you now "step into" a function? You do this via the F11 key (or Debug ⇨ Step Into menu option). When you do this the first time, you will see that Visual Studio loads the file containing the source code for the UpdateData function (wincore.cpp) into your editor. Note that this assumes you installed the MFC source code when you installed Visual C++. (This is the default installation option.)

The CWnd::UpdateData looks like the following (with some code reformatted to fit the book's layout):

```
BOOL CWnd::UpdateData(BOOL bSaveAndValidate)
{
 // Calling UpdateData before Modal?
 ASSERT(::IsWindow(m_hWnd));

 CDataExchange dx(this, bSaveAndValidate);

 // Prevent control notifications from being
 // dispatched during UpdateData.
 _AFX_THREAD_STATE* pThreadState = AfxGetThreadState();
 HWND hWndOldLockout = pThreadState->m_hLockoutNotifyWindow;
 ASSERT(hWndOldLockout != m_hWnd);   // must not recurse
 pThreadState->m_hLockoutNotifyWindow = m_hWnd;

 BOOL bOK = FALSE;        // assume failure
 TRY
 {
  DoDataExchange(&dx);
  bOK = TRUE;            // it worked
 }
```

```
CATCH(CUserException, e)
{
 // Validation failed--user already alerted, fall through
 ASSERT(!bOK);
 // Note: DELETE_EXCEPTION_(e) not required
}
AND_CATCH_ALL(e)
{
 // Validation failed due to OOM or other resource failure.
 e->ReportError(MB_ICONEXCLAMATION,
                AFX_IDP_INTERNAL_FAILURE);
 ASSERT(!bOK);
 DELETE_EXCEPTION(e);
}
END_CATCH_ALL

 pThreadState->m_hLockoutNotifyWindow = hWndOldLockout;
 return bOK;
}
```

As you can quickly see, nothing here indicates which way the data is being moved (control to variable versus variable to control). However, there are two functions that look suspect: the CDataExchange constructor and the call to DoDataExchange. (I've bolded both in the previous code snippet so that they stand out.)

At this point, you can either set breakpoints on both of these lines of code and press F5 to read them (you don't want to use Set Next Statement in this particular case because necessary local variables will not have been initialized yet) or you can press F10 (which executes one line at a time) until you get to the desired line of execution.

Whichever way you do this, when you reach the CDataExchange constructor, press F11 to step into it.

The CDataExchange constructor is located in the same file and looks like this:

```
CDataExchange::CDataExchange(CWnd* pDlgWnd, BOOL bSaveAndValidate)
{
    ASSERT_VALID(pDlgWnd);
    m_bSaveAndValidate = bSaveAndValidate;
    m_pDlgWnd = pDlgWnd;
    m_idLastControl = 0;
}
```

In other words, it's a dead end. There's nothing here but some variable assignments. So what's the quickest way to get out of here while still executing the code? Press Shift+F11. Doing this will execute the code in the current function and stop execution when it reaches the line of code that follows the call to this function. Now you step down to the call to DoDataExchange. Once you get there, step into that function.

```
void CHelloDialogDlg::DoDataExchange(CDataExchange* pDX)
{
    DDX_Text(pDX, IDC_EDIT1, m_strMessageText);
    CDialog::DoDataExchange(pDX);
}
```

Hmmm. This is your (wizard-generated) code now—notice the class name. You might be onto something because here you can see your m_strMessageText variable referred to for the first time. Now, step into the DDX_Text function and you will see the following (reformatted here):

```
void AFXAPI DDX_Text(CDataExchange* pDX,
                     int nIDC,
                     CString& value)
{
 HWND hWndCtrl = pDX->PrepareEditCtrl(nIDC);
 if (pDX->m_bSaveAndValidate)
 {
  int nLen = ::GetWindowTextLength(hWndCtrl);
  ::GetWindowText(hWndCtrl,
                  value.GetBufferSetLength(nLen),
                  nLen+1);
  value.ReleaseBuffer();
 }
 else
 {
  AfxSetWindowText(hWndCtrl, value);
 }
}
```

Looks like you've hit pay dirt! You can see that the code checks a pDX->m_bSaveAndValidate value, and if it's TRUE, uses the ::GetWindowText function (to retrieve the value from the window into the variable's value). That's what you want. However, if you use F10 to step through the code, you'll see that pDX->m_bSaveAndValidate is set to FALSE, and therefore, the AfxSetWindowText is being called instead. This is why the control is being updated with the m_strMessageText value.

So you figure out why pDX->m_bSaveAndValidate has a value of FALSE and your problem is solved. Suppose you'd really like to take a peak at that first bit of code discussed a few minutes ago, but you don't want to rerun this code to get there. To do this, simply open the Call Stack window by clicking Debug ⇨ Windows ⇨ Call Stack. This window shows you the currently executing stack of functions (as shown in Figure 1-20).

The Call Stack shows the current function as well as all previous functions in the current stack of execution. Here if you click the third function down from the top (the line that begins mfc70d.dll!CWnd::UpdateData) , you'll notice the following line of code:

```
CDataExchange dx(this, bSaveAndValidate);
```

You can easily surmise from here that the bSaveAndValidate value (that you passed from the CHelloDialogDlg::OnBnClickedOk function) is what is being used to update the pDX->m_bSaveAndValidate variable. Therefore, you simply need to update this call to pass a value of TRUE instead of FALSE for your application to work as expected again.

Obviously, in the real world of professional software development, your debugging tasks are sometimes going to be much more difficult. However, no matter how complex the problem you're debugging, you at least know the basics of setting breakpoints, inspecting variable values, stepping over code, stepping into code (including MFC code), setting the next statement of execution, displaying the Call Stack, and jumping to functions in the Call Stack.

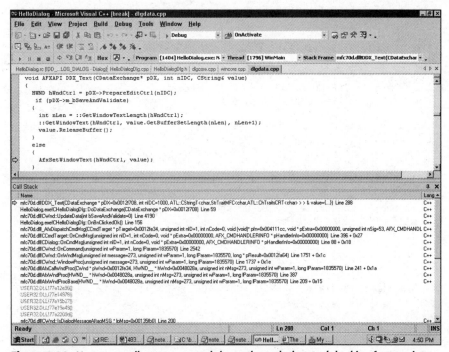

Figure 1-20: You can easily move up and down through the stack looking for a variety of information needed in your debugging via the Call Stack.

Working with MFC Message Handlers

As you know, Windows uses an event-driven programming model. This simply means that instead of an application containing a sequential set of instructions, your application contains a *message loop* that processes messages (or events) that Windows sends to your application. Once a message is received, your message loop is then responsible for handling that message (usually by calling a message handler, or function written to handle the specific message). The message loop continues processing messages until the application is ended (via the

WM_QUIT message). So where is this loop in the demo application? If you dig deep enough into the MFC, you'll find that it's located in the CWnd::RunModalLoop function in the thrdcore.cpp file. Here's what the loop looks like:

```
int CWnd::RunModalLoop(DWORD dwFlags)
{
 ASSERT(::IsWindow(m_hWnd)); // window must be created
 ASSERT(!(m_nFlags & WF_MODALLOOP));

 // for tracking the idle time state
 BOOL bIdle = TRUE;
 LONG lIdleCount = 0;
 BOOL bShowIdle = (dwFlags & MLF_SHOWONIDLE)
  && !(GetStyle() & WS_VISIBLE);
 HWND hWndParent = ::GetParent(m_hWnd);
 m_nFlags |= (WF_MODALLOOP|WF_CONTINUEMODAL);
 MSG *pMsg = AfxGetCurrentMessage();

 // acquire and dispatch messages until the
 // modal state is done
 for (;;)
 {
  ASSERT(ContinueModal());

  // phase1: check to see if we can do idle work
  while (bIdle &&
  !::PeekMessage(pMsg, NULL, NULL, NULL, PM_NOREMOVE))
  {
   ASSERT(ContinueModal());

   // show the dialog when the message queue goes idle
   if (bShowIdle)
   {
    ShowWindow(SW_SHOWNORMAL);
    UpdateWindow();
    bShowIdle = FALSE;
   }

   // call OnIdle while in bIdle state
   if (!(dwFlags & MLF_NOIDLEMSG)
   && hWndParent != NULL && lIdleCount == 0)
   {
    // send WM_ENTERIDLE to the parent
    ::SendMessage(hWndParent,
                  WM_ENTERIDLE,
                  MSGF_DIALOGBOX,
                  (LPARAM)m_hWnd);
   }
```

```
     if ((dwFlags & MLF_NOKICKIDLE) ||
       !SendMessage(WM_KICKIDLE, MSGF_DIALOGBOX, lIdleCount++))
     {
       // stop idle processing next time
       bIdle = FALSE;
     }
   }

   // phase2: pump messages while available
   do
   {
     ASSERT(ContinueModal());

     // pump message, but quit on WM_QUIT
     if (!AfxPumpMessage())
     {
       AfxPostQuitMessage(0);
       return -1;
     }

     // show the window when certain special messages rec'd
     if (bShowIdle &&
     (pMsg->message == 0x118
     || pMsg->message == WM_SYSKEYDOWN))
     {
       ShowWindow(SW_SHOWNORMAL);
       UpdateWindow();
       bShowIdle = FALSE;
     }

     if (!ContinueModal())
       goto ExitModal;

     // reset "no idle" state after pumping "normal" message
     if (AfxIsIdleMessage(pMsg))
     {
       bIdle = TRUE;
       lIdleCount = 0;
     }

   } while (::PeekMessage(pMsg, NULL,
                       NULL, NULL,
                       PM_NOREMOVE));
 }

ExitModal:
 m_nFlags &= ~(WF_MODALLOOP|WF_CONTINUEMODAL);
 return m_nModalResult;
}
```

There's a lot of code here and I don't expect you to understand it all if you're new to MFC. However, the main points to look at here are the following:

✦ After some initialization, an infinite loop — `for (;;)` — is started to process messages.

✦ Within that `for` loop, there is a `while` loop that determines if "idle work" can be done. You see, MFC is constantly handling messages behind the scenes even when your application is seemingly doing nothing. Therefore, this `while` loop first checks the `bIdle` flag to determine if it has time to do some of this background work, and calls the `PeekMessage` function to make sure that the application has not terminated (`PeekMessage` returns 0 when there are no messages in the queue). Therefore, if the `bIdle` flag set to is 1, and there is a message in the queue, the code sends a message to the window stating that it can do some idle processing.

✦ The next (`do`) loop actually processes the messages. This message loop (sometimes called a *message pump*) is what actually processes the messages for your application. Note that after the call to `ContinueModal` (used to verify that the modal state should continue), the code tests for the existence of a `WM_QUIT` message in the queue (via `AfxPumpMessage` returning 0). If that is the case, the function returns and the application ends. If not, the loop continues retrieving and dispatching messages.

While this has been a quick run-through on how MFC processes messages for your application, the main point to take away here is that there is a message pump buried deep within MFC that takes care of this retrieving messages sent to your application from Windows and dispatching them to message handlers for you. The question then becomes, how can you handle specific messages? When you wrote the handler for the OK button being clicked on the dialog box, you were actually handling a message at that time, but you might not have realized it. What happened there is that your MFC created an entry in a *message map* that connected the receipt of the button's `BN_CLICKED` message to the function you wrote (`OnBnClickedOk`). To see that map, open the `HelloDialogDlg.cpp` and search for `BEGIN_MESSAGE_MAP`. You should see the following code:

```
BEGIN_MESSAGE_MAP(CAboutDlg, CDialog)
  ON_BN_CLICKED(IDOK, OnBnClickedOk)
END_MESSAGE_MAP()
```

Note   For most people it is enough to understand that MFC has maps that relate messages to functions and that the various wizards enable you to write these functions. However, for a full dissertation on the internals of how the various MFC macros like `BEGIN_MESSAGE_MAP` work, I recommend Scot Wingo's book, *MFC Internals*.

What you don't know how to do is how to create a message handler for a non-GUI event. In other words, you were able to handle the `BN_CLICKED` message for the OK button simply by double-clicking the OK button in the dialog box editor. However, what about other messages where the dialog box editor can't help? For example what if you wanted to handle anytime the dialog box was moved or sized? To see how this is done, the following steps do something really simple and display a message anytime the user double-clicks the client area.

1. Open the Class View.

2. Locate the class that controls the window whose message you want to code a handler for. In this case, it is the CHelloDialogDlg class.

3. Right-click the class and select the Properties menu option.

4. From the Properties dialog box, click the Messages icon (located near the top of the dialog box). You'll then see two columns. The first column contains a list of all the messages that you can write handlers for, and the second column lists the names of any handlers you've written.

5. Click the column to the right of the WM_LBUTTONDBLCLK message id. The message id will highlight and an arrow will appear in the right side of the second column. Notice that whenever you select a message, you can look at the bottom of the dialog to view a description of that message id. In this case, you can see (in Figure 1-21) that the WM_LBUTTONDBLCLK message "indicates the double-click of left mouse button." Although some messages are more obvious than others, this is definitely helpful if you don't know the exact message id you're searching for.

6. Clicking this arrow will show a list of options that can be performed on this event handler. Because no event handler exists now, the only option you'll see is <Add> OnLButtonDblClk.

7. Simply click that option and Visual Studio will create both a member function called CHelloDialogDlg::OnLButtonDblClk and a message map entry mapping the WM_LBUTTONDBLCLK message to this function. It's that easy.

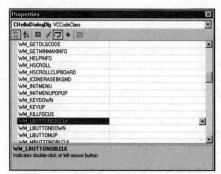

Figure 1-21: You can easily add message handlers through the Properties dialog box.

8. To complete the test, modify it so that when finished it looks as follows:

```
void CHelloDialogDlg::OnLButtonDblClk(UINT nFlags,
CPoint point)
{
   AfxMessageBox("Ouch! Don't touch me there!");

   CDialog::OnLButtonDblClk(nFlags, point);
}
```

9. Building and running this application will result in the application printing out your message if you double-click on the main dialog box's client area.

Obviously, you can edit the handler anytime you want by simply opening the file and directly modifying the function. However, how do you delete a handler? One way is to delete the function prototype from the header file, delete the function definition from the CPP file, and remove the message map entry, but this is kind of a pain. The easiest way is to return to the Properties dialog box, where you'll now see that the WM_LBUTTONDBLCLK entry has two options — one to edit the function, and one to delete it. Selecting the delete option automatically takes care of deleting everything needed to completely remove the event handler.

Note Be very careful with the delete option from the Properties dialog box. In previous versions of Visual Studio, handlers were deleted via the ClassWizard, and not only did you get a confirmation message, but only the prototype and message map entry were deleted, leaving your code in case you had made a mistake or wanted to revert to using the code again at a later date. With the Properties dialog box, there is no confirmation message, and the event handler is completely removed.

Handling Child Events

So now you know how to handle messages for classes that are represented in the Class View. However, what about handling messages for controls on a dialog box (not counting the BN_CLICKED message)? This is also done through the Properties dialog box, but this time with a different view. To see that in action, suppose you wanted to edit the contents of a control anytime the user attempted to leave that control.

1. Open the Class View.

2. Locate the class that controls the window whose message you want to code a handler for. In this case, it is the CHelloDialogDlg class.

3. Right-click the class and select the Properties menu option.

4. From the Properties dialog box, click the Events icon (located near the top of the dialog). As you can see, the view becomes a two-column tree view where the events are categorized by type. Because Control events are the only ones you have at your disposal for a dialog box, it is the only category you'll see.

5. Under the Controls entry, you should see the various controls that have been defined for the current dialog (listed by their resource ids). Expanding the IDOK resource (the OK button) will reveal to you not only the handler you wrote earlier in the chapter, but the other messages that you can write handlers for as well (Figure 1-22).

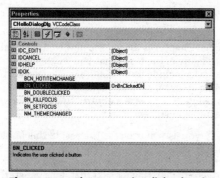

Figure 1-22: The Properties dialog box is used to add Event handlers for dialog child events.

6. Expand the IDC_EDIT1 entry. At this point, it should be intuitive to add the code needed to verify the user's input upon exiting the edit control. You would simply create a handler for the EN_KILLFOCUS event.

Overriding Base Class Functions

The last thing we'll look at in this chapter is how to write an override function. In C++, when you derive one class from another, you automatically inherit the base class's public and protected members (both variables and functions). In order to override the functions of a base class in Visual Studio, you once again use the Properties dialog box. By way of example, the CDialog class has a virtual function called DestroyWindow that is called when the dialog receives the WM_DESTROY message. Therefore, there are many times when you'll want to override this particular function to implement your own cleanup code to do things like close database connections or free memory allocated during the running of the dialog. You can override this class as follows.

1. Open the Class View.

2. Locate the class that controls the window whose message you want to code a handler for. In this case, it is the CHelloDialogDlg class.

3. Right-click the class and select the Properties menu option.

4. From the Properties dialog box, click the Overrides icon (located near the top of the dialog box). As you can see, the view becomes a two-column tree view where the overrides events are categorized as being either "common" or "uncommon" based on your likelihood of needing to implement the override.

5. In this example case, you would simply locate the DestroyWindow entry, click the second column, and then select the Add DestroyWindow option.

Summary

As I mentioned at the outset, this particular chapter is for people new to the Visual Studio environment and is designed to illustrate many of the tasks that you will be performing repeatedly throughout this book. These tasks include understanding the new Start Page, creating a dialog-based application, adding an event handler, adding controls to a dialog template resource via the Dialog Editor, using DDX to wire a control to a member variable, correcting build errors, and debugging simple mistakes.

Hopefully, what you learned here will help you as you traverse the rest of this book. Be forewarned that from this point on, I'm going to assume that you know how to use the various application and class wizards and how to create variables and event handlers. However, this material is always here in case you need a refresher. Having said that, let's get started learning how to program with Visual C++ and MFC.

✦   ✦   ✦

Documents, Views, and SDI

A t the core of an MFC application is the concept of a *document object* and a corresponding *view window*. The document object usually represents a file the application has opened — all the data an application manages. The view window provides a visual presentation of the document's data and accepts user interaction. The view presents only a partial representation of an application's data because an application often manages more data than can be shown on the screen; as a result, there can be many views of a single document. In other words, the relationship between documents and views is a one-to-many relationship — a document can have many views, but you can associate a view with only one document.

Within your applications, you represent document objects with classes that you derive from the MFC `CDocument` base class. You derive your view window classes from the MFC `CView` class. In this chapter, you will learn about `CDocument` and `CView`, and how to use them with single document interface (SDI) applications. You will learn about more complex manipulations of the documents and views in the next chapter.

Document/View Designs

Any MFC Application Wizard (AppWizard)-produced MFC applications that support SDI or the multiple document interface (MDI) use the document/view architecture. AppWizard designs the application such that an instance of the application's document class is created for each file that the application loads. The application then uses an instance of a view class to let the user interact with the application and the data in the document.

 Note Your applications may associate more than one instance of a particular view with a given document, and you may even associate instances of different views with the same document.

The built-in power of the document/view architecture, therefore, is that as users work with the application, they create and destroy instances of the file and user interface management code (and data) that define their very perception of the data with which they work.

A user-friendly application gives views to the application's data that make more sense to the user. For example, for most readers, it is probably difficult to imagine how cold it will be in South Dakota based on tabular temperature data for the entire U.S. However, the common "blue is cold, orange is hot" weather graphs that appear in newspapers make it easy to guess what range of temperatures a traveler might expect with a quick glance at the right part of the map. The tabular data still has value, though. It's an easy way to enter the data in the first place, and it's the only way you might ever find out what the weather is like in South Dakota if you aren't completely sure where it is. The color map and the tabular data are each single views, and an MDI application uses both views, maybe more, of the same data.

Single document interface applications that you produce using the AppWizard use only one document and one view type and only instantiate one of each of these classes. However, this is only true of the AppWizard-generated code — after the AppWizard creates your application, you are free to change the composition of your project as much as you desire, if you decide that it's convenient to use multiple instances of each different view or document.

MDI applications make use of at least one document/view pair, but they may make use of additional documents and views in different combinations to enable the user to work with other files or to represent their data in many different ways. You will learn more about MDI applications in Chapter 3. Figure 2-1 shows which classes may support a simple SDI application that you implement using MFC objects.

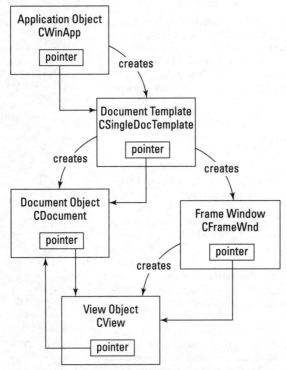

Figure 2-1: The model of the relationship between the five base classes for an SDI application

I'll explain these five main classes as you progress through the chapter. For example, frame windows (indicated in Figure 2-1 by the CFrameWnd base class) are covered in more detail in the section "A word about frame windows." However, there are some things that you'll need to understand about frame windows for the next few sections.

First, a frame window is the window that contains the view. The view is then responsible for the content that the user actually sees and the frame is the parent of that view. You should realize at this point that the frame is the window that is used to attach menus, toolbars, status bars, and title bar (which also contains the system menu and minimize/maximize buttons). Having said that, when the users size an MFC SDI application window, they are actually grabbing the side of a frame window and messages are being sent to that window. The view window, because it is the child of the frame window, also gets these messages and sizes itself accordingly as well.

Second, the frame window is implemented by AppWizard-generated SDI applications via the CMainFrame class. This code is found in the MainFrm.h and MainFrm.cpp source files.

Finally, note that the CMainFrame class derives almost all of its functionality from the CFrameWnd base class, and in the case of SDI applications, doesn't add much. The notable exceptions are when you do things such as adding or manipulating the various frame-window-owned child windows, such as the status bar or toolbars windows. The correlation between status bars, toolbars, and frame windows is covered in Chapter 6.

The CDocument Class

The MFC CDocument class provides the basic behaviors of your application's document objects. The CDocument class can create new documents, serialize document data, provide basic cooperation between a document object and a view window, and more. MFC also includes a series of CDocument-derived classes that implement specialized functionality for certain types of applications. For example, MFC provides the CRecordset and CDAORecordset types to simplify the creation of database views. The relationship between documents and views is shown in Figure 2-2.

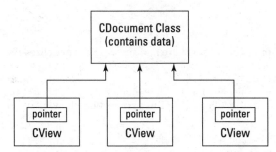

Figure 2-2: The one-to-many relationship between a document and its views

Declaring a document class

When you use the AppWizard to create your applications, you often do not need to worry about declaring your base document class — the AppWizard does it for you. However, it is still useful for you to understand the behavior of the CDocument class — because more complex programs might require multiple instances of multiple derivations from CDocument. In addition, understanding the behavior of CDocument enables you to easily enhance the AppWizard-generated application skeleton.

Note   Whether you create a single document interface application or a multiple document interface application, the AppWizard derives only a single document class for you from the MFC CDocument **base class.**

When you build a simple MFC application, it is often enough for you to make relatively minor modifications to your AppWizard-supplied document class. You often will not need to do much more to the class than add some member variables and some member functions that other portions of the program can use to access those member variables.

For example, the document object for a simple communications program (such as a terminal emulator) might contain member variables for modem settings. Those member variables would probably store information such as telephone number, speed, parity, number of bits in each transmission segment, and so on. You could easily represent the communications settings with a set of simple member variables in the derived document class, as shown in the following code listing:

```
class CSimpleTermDoc : public CDocument
  {
 protected:
    CSimpleTermDoc();
    DECLARE_DYNCREATE(CSimpleTermDoc)
 public:
    CString m_sPhoneNum;
    DWORD m_dwTransSpeed;
    WORD m_nTransParity;
    WORD m_nTransBits;
    DWORD m_dwConnectTime;
```

After you declare the member variables, you must ensure that the program initializes the variables to some default values in the CSimpleTermDoc class' OnNewDocument member function. In addition, you must add code to the Serialize function to ensure that the program properly serializes the variables. The code for the OnNewDocument and Serialize member functions would look similar to the following. In this first section, the various member variables are initialized.

```
// Standard Code for the OnNewDocument() and
// Serialize() Member Functions
BOOL CSimpleTermDoc::OnNewDocument
  {
    if (!CDocument::OnNewDocument())
      return FALSE;
    m_sPhoneNum = _T("555-1212");
    m_dwTransSpeed = 28800;
    m_nTransParity = 0;
```

```
        m_nTransBits = 8;
        m_dwConnectTime = 0;
        return TRUE;
    }
```

As you can see in the following code segment, the CArchive class is used in the serialization process. This class enables you to easily store complex data types to disk and read them back using the C++ << (extraction) and >> (insertion) operators. The first thing the code does is to call the CArchive::IsStoring function to determine if the current process is a read or a write operation. Based on the return value (true if saving, false if reading), the appropriate extraction or insertion operator is used to complete the task.

```
    void CSimpleTermDoc::Serialize(CArchive &ar)
    {
        if (ar.IsStoring())
        {
            ar << m_sPhoneNum;
            ar << m_dwTransSpeed;
            ar << m_nTransParity;
            ar << m_nTransBits;
            ar << m_dwConnectTime;
        }
        else
        {
            ar >> m_sPhoneNum;
            ar >> m_dwTransSpeed;
            ar >> m_nTransParity;
            ar >> m_nTransBits;
            ar >> m_dwConnectTime;
        }
    }
```

For simple applications like this one, you don't need to do anything beyond the initialization and serialization of your member variables to have a complete, fully functioning document class.

CDocument's member functions

The CDocument class has several member functions, in addition to the serialization and initialization member functions that your applications will frequently use. The first set of member functions provides access to the associated view objects. Every document object that you use within your applications will have a list of view objects that you associate with it. You can call the GetFirstViewPosition member function for the document object to obtain an iterator to this list—the iterator will be a POSITION type.

CDocument, in this context, is a collection class; it maintains information about the collection of views associated with the class through a POSITION object. You will use values of type POSITION throughout the MFC, primarily with collection classes. When your applications must traverse a list, you will typically request an iterator that the collection class associates with the first object on the list, and then use an iterator function to access the actual elements the list contains, one by one. Therefore, after you obtain the iterator to the first view in the class with the GetFirstViewPosition member function, you can repeatedly call the GetNextView member function to work through the remaining views in the collection.

In other words, process all the views that your program has associated with a given document object, using code that generally looks similar to the following:

```
POSITION posView = GetFirstViewPosition();
while (posView != NULL)
  {
    CView *pView = GetNextView(posView);
    // Do something with the pointer to the view
  }
```

There is an easier way to do this, however. If your program's code needs to notify all the views for the document that information within the document has changed, you can update the views without using an iterator and an iteration loop. Instead, you can call the document object's UpdateAllViews member function. Furthermore, you can also specify application-specific data that instructs the views to selectively update only portions of the view windows when you call the UpdateAllViews function. You will learn more about selective updates later in this chapter, when you work with the CView::OnUpdate member function.

Some other view-related member functions for the document object that you will use much less frequently include the AddView and RemoveView functions. As their names suggest, the functions let you manually add and remove views from a document's list of views. You will rarely use these functions, because most developers simply use the default MFC implementation with little or no modification.

Whenever the document's data changes (through either a user's action or internal program processing), your program should call the SetModifiedFlag member function. Consistent use of SetModifiedFlag ensures that the MFC framework prompts the user before letting the user destroy a changed, unsaved document. Should you decide to override the framework, you can call the IsModified member function to obtain the status of the flag.

You can use the SetTitle member function to set the document object's title. The application, in turn, displays the title you set in the frame window (the main frame window in an SDI application, and the child frame window for the object in an MDI application).

You can also set the fully qualified pathname for the document with the SetPathName function and obtain the pathname with the GetPathName function. Finally, you can obtain the document template that the program associated with the document at the document's creation through a call to GetDocTemplate.

Documents and message processing

One of the most important features of a document, which you may have inferred from earlier paragraphs in this chapter, is that a CDocument object is not directly associated with a window. However, a CDocument object is a command-target object — which means the object can receive messages from the operating system. The view objects that you associate with a CDocument object are responsible for routing messages from the operating system to the document.

Because the view objects you associate with the document, and the frame window that holds the document, receive messages before passing them through to the document, you have a great deal of control over which messages the frame window, views, and document process. However, some common-sense rules of thumb (as well as some simplicity issues) can provide a good starting point for how to process incoming messages.

When you consider messages, or for that matter any time that you are working with the document/view architecture, you should always keep in mind that a document is an abstract representation of your data — a representation, that is, which is independent of the visual representation of the data that the view window provides. Just as important, a document may have one, many, or no views attached to it — so documents should only respond to messages that are global in nature. That is, a document should only respond to messages that have an immediate effect on the document's data; the effect of such messages should then be reflected by all the views attached to the document. On the other hand, views should respond to messages that are specific to that window's view only.

In practical terms, the division of responsibilities between documents and views generally makes it easier to determine how to process a given command. For example, if your application has a Save command, which the user would select to save the *data* in the object, the document should handle that command, because the command is concerned with the data, not how the user sees the data.

On the other hand, if your application supports a Copy command, which the user would generally select to copy data the user has selected within the display, you would probably want to handle the command in the view. In fact, if a document supports multiple views, the data selected in each view might vary, making it even clearer that you should generally process the Copy command separately for each view attached to a document.

Both scenarios are relatively clean cut — you are saving the data in the first example, and you are copying a representation of the data from within one view to another view in the second example. However, there are some borderline cases. A common example is the Paste command. Determining whether the document class or the view class should handle the Paste command is slightly more complex because it affects the entire document. This is because you are inserting data into the document, not just a single view. On the other hand, the current view may have significant importance when pasting information into a document. For example, the Paste action may replace existing, selected text within the view. In other words, the decision you must make about whether the document object or the view object should handle actions of this type is dependent on your application's design and is generally something you should think through carefully.

Just to keep it interesting, you should not handle certain commands in either the document class or the view class, but rather in the frame window's code. Excellent examples of commands that you should handle within the frame window include commands to hide and display toolbars. The presence or absence of the toolbar is not particularly material to a document or its views. Rather, it is a configuration issue with effects global to the entire application.

Overriding virtual document functions

As you may have noticed earlier in the chapter, both the `OnNewDocument` and `Serialize` are virtual functions and therefore are designed to be overridden as needed. Although the base `CDocument` member functions do provide default processing that is sufficient for most needs, there might be times when your application will need to perform specific processing for a document that the default processing does not provide.

For example, the `CDocument` class and its derivatives call the `OnNewDocument` member function whenever the program initializes a new document object (or when the program reuses an existing document object in an SDI application). Your applications typically call the `OnNewDocument` function when handling a File ➪ New command. Similarly, your `CDocument` calls the `OnCloseDocument` member function when the application is about to close a document. You should override this function within your own document classes if your application must perform any cleanup operations before destroying the document object.

Your document classes will call the `OnOpenDocument` and `OnSaveDocument` functions to read a document from disk or to write a document to disk, respectively. You should override these functions only if the default implementation (which calls the `Serialize` member function) is not sufficient. An excellent example of a situation where you would override `OnOpenDocument` and `OnSaveDocument` is when you are encrypting data before you write it to the disk and decrypting it when you reload it from the disk.

The default implementations of both `OnOpenDocument` and `OnCloseDocument` call the `DeleteContents` member function. The `DeleteContents` member function deletes the document's contents without actually destroying the document object itself. Using `DeleteContents` when opening a new document is more efficient (in terms of both memory usage and application speed) than actually closing and destroying the original document object and creating a new document object.

The `OnFileSendMail` member function sends the document object as an attachment to a mail message. It first calls `OnSaveDocument` to save a copy of the document to a temporary disk file (in the directory set by your `TEMP` environment variable). Next, the program code within the member function attaches the temporary file to a Messaging API (MAPI) message. The member function uses the `OnUpdateFileSendMail` member function to enable the command that you identify with the constant `ID_FILE_SEND_MAIL` in the applications menu, or remove it altogether if MAPI support is not available to the program. Both `OnFileSendMail` and `OnUpdateFileSendMail` are overridable functions, which enables you to implement customized messaging behavior within your applications.

Working with complex document data

Earlier in this chapter you learned how to derive simple document classes from `CDocument`, within which you can store the document's data in a series of simple member variables. However, creating applications that you can use in the real world tends to be more demanding. Most applications you will develop will require significantly more advanced data than what you could ever possibly represent with a few variables of simple data types.

You can use many different approaches to manage complex data types within a document object; however, arguably the best approach is to use a set of classes that you derive from the `CObject` class. Each derived class, then, stores the complex data objects. The document, in turn, uses a standard or custom-created collection class to embed the objects within the document class. For example, you might create data definitions similar to the following for an application:

```
class CAppObject : public CObject
  {
    // definitions
  }
class CAppSubObject1 : public CObject
  {
    // definitions
  }
class CAppSubObject2 : public CObject
  {
    // definitions
  }
```

Then, within the declaration of the document class, you would include a CObList member. The CObList class supports ordered lists of nonunique CObject pointers accessible sequentially or by pointer value. CObList lists behave like doubly linked lists. Your document declaration, therefore, would look similar to the following:

```
class CSampleDoc : public CDocument
  {
    // code here
  public:
    CObList m_DataObjList;
    // code here
  }
```

In a complex situation like this one, it is often not sufficient to simply declare member variables. Your document class is also likely to require member functions that provide methods to let views and other objects that must access the document's data do so. For example, you may not want to let other classes (such as a view class) directly manipulate the m_DataObjList variable. Instead, you should generally provide a member function that the view class can access to iterate through the m_DataObjList object as it needs to.

Such member functions should also ensure that, each time the document's data change, the application properly updates all the document's views. The member functions should also call the document's SetModified member function to indicate to the document that an accessing function or class has changed the document's data. If your application supports an undo-typing capability, you should also place your application's buffered undo data into its correct storage location while inside the member function. To better understand this, consider the following member function, AddNewObj, which adds a new object to the document's object list:

```
BOOL CSampleDoc : AddNewObj(CAppObject *pObject)
  {
    try
      {
        m_DataObjList.AddTail((CObject *)pObject);
        SetModifiedFlag(TRUE);
        UpdateAllViews(NULL, UPDATE_OBJECT, pObject;
        return TRUE;
      }
    catch(CMemoryException *e)
      {
        TRACE("Doc--AddNewObj memory allocation error.\n");
        e->Delete();
        return FALSE;
      }
  }
```

Understanding the importance of the AddNewObj member function is easier when you consider the relationship between the document and its views and how the program passes control back and forth between the two.

First, the user interacts with the view, which might result in a new object being added, an existing object being modified or deleted, or some other action. For now, presume that the user's actions result in the need to add a new object to the document. To add a new object, the view object calls the AddNewObj member function. After the member function successfully adds the new object, the document object calls the UpdateAllViews member function, which, in turn, calls the OnUpdate member function of each view that you have previously associated with the document. The AddNewObj member function passes a *hint value* to the UpdateAllViews member function through the use of the application-defined UPDATE_OBJECT constant and a pointer to a CObject. The hint value instructs the views to repaint only those regions of the view directly and indirectly affected by the addition of the new object. Figure 2-3 shows the control-passing mechanism that the views and the document will use.

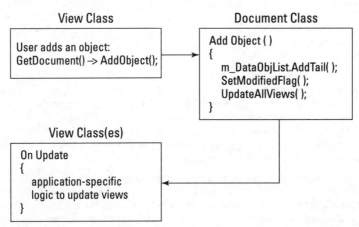

Figure 2-3: Control passes from the view class to the document class and back.

Another advantage of using MFC collection classes within your application is that collection classes support serialization. For example, to load and save your document's data that is stored in CObject objects and referenced through a CObList object, all you need to do is to construct the document's Serialize member function as shown here:

```
void CSampleDoc::Serialize(CArchive &ar)
  {
    if (ar.IsStoring())
      {
        // Store data using the ar << myVar syntax
      }
    else
      {
        // Retrieve data using the ar >> myVar syntax
      }
    m_DataObjList.Serialize(ar);
  }
```

You should be aware, however, that for this technique to work, you must implement the Serialize member function for all your object classes. A CObject-derived class does not serialize itself. If you decide to use one of the general purpose collection templates, serialization is an issue that you must pay close attention to. The collections CArray, CList, and CMap rely on the SerializeElements member function to serialize the objects within the collection. MFC declares this function as shown here:

```
template <class TYPE> void AFXAPI
    SerializeElements(CArchive &ar, TYPE *pElements,
    int nCount);
```

Because the collection class templates do not require that you derive TYPE from CObject, they do not call the Serialize member function for each element (because the Serialize member function is not guaranteed to exist). Instead, the default implementation of SerializeElements performs a *bitwise* read or write action. However, as you can imagine, in most cases, a bitwise read or write is not going to be nearly as easy (or practical) to implement as the ability to serialize the entire value as a single entity. Rather, you should implement your own SerializeElements function for your objects. You might implement such a function as shown here:

```
void SerializeElements(CArchive &ar, CAppObject **pObs,
    int nCount);
{
  for (int i = 0; i < nCount; i++; pObs++)
    (*pObs)->Serialize(ar);
}
```

CCmdTarget and CDocItem

As you learned in the previous section of this chapter, you can use objects that you derive from the CObject class to store data within your documents. Unfortunately, if you want your documents and applications to support OLE automation (now called just *automation*), the CObject class is insufficient. Instead, you must declare your objects as *command targets*. If you want to support automation, you may prefer to derive your data from the MFC CCmdTarget base class. (If you're new to automation, this topic is covered in detail in Chapter 33.)

Alternatively, and generally better, you may want to derive your data objects from the MFC CDocItem class. You can either create a collection of CDocItem objects yourself, or rely on MFC's COleDocument class to create the collection. In other words, instead of deriving your document class from CDocument, derive it from COleDocument. You can use COleDocument in OLE applications where either the COleDocument class or a class previously derived from COleDocument is the base class for the OLE application's document class. Like CDocument, COleDocument is a collection class. COleDocument supports a collection of CDocItem objects, which are derived in turn either from COleServerItem or COleClientItem. However, COleDocument supports CDocItem generically (that is, it doesn't care whether the item is a server or client item). COleDocument's generic implementation means that you can add your own CDocItem-derived objects to the collection without fear that doing so will interfere with normal OLE operations and behavior.

One nice thing about working with COleDocument is that it automatically adds CDocItem members for you. In other words, if you use AddItem, RemoveItem, GetStartPosition, and GetNextItem, you can add, remove, and retrieve document items without further processing. The underlying MFC code handles your other needs (such as serialization) without further programming on your part.

However, working with COleDocument is not without its pitfalls. Because of the way you derive your document items and the OLE COleClientItem and COleServerItem objects, you may need to perform certain special programming actions to add certain functions to a given object. For example, suppose you declare your object items as shown here:

```
class CSampleDocItem : public CDocItem
  {
    //  more code here
    CRect m_Rect;
  };
```

In addition, suppose you also support the `m_Rect` member variable within your OLE client items, as shown here:

```
class CSampleClientItem : public COleClientItem
{
   //  more code here
   CRect m_Rect;
};
```

Given these two declarations, you might suppose that you can create a function that takes an item from your document and manipulates its `m_Rect` member as shown here:

```
void sampFunc(CDocItem *pItem)
{
   samp2Func(pItem->m_Rect);      // Error!
}
```

Because the `CDocItem` class, by itself, does not contain an `m_Rect` member variable, the compiler halts the program's compilation with an error at the function declaration. Unfortunately, using a pointer to your own `CDocItem`-derived class doesn't really solve the problem either:

```
void sampFunc(CSampleDocItem *pItem)
{
   samp2Func(pItem->m_Rect);
}
```

Although declaring the function in this manner supports your derived class, it won't support OLE client items of type `CDocItem`—a significant issue. An obvious solution is to simply create two overridden versions of `sampFunc`, but maintaining two separate, identical versions of the same function is not only lacking in elegance, it makes maintenance all that much more difficult. The best solution is to instead create a wrapper function that takes a pointer to a `CDocItem` object and uses MFC runtime-type information to obtain the member variable, as shown here:

```
CRect GetRect(CDocItem *pDocItem)
{
   if (pDocItem->IsKindOf(RUNTIME_CLASS(CSampleDocItem)))
      return ((CSampleDocItem *)pDocItem)->m_Rect;
   else if
       (pDocItem->IsKindOf(RUNTIME_CLASS(CSampleClientItem)))
      return  ((CSampleClientItem *)pDocItem)->m_Rect;
   ASSERT(FALSE);
   return CRect(0, 0, 0, 0);
}

sampFunc(CDocItem *pItem)
{
    samp2Func(GetRect(pItem));
}
```

This solution, however, requires that you declare and implement both the `CSampleDocItem` and the `CSampleClientItem` classes with the `DECLARE_DYNAMIC` and `IMPLEMENT_DYNAMIC` macros. However, that should not be an issue because your document objects typically support serialization. When you declare and implement a class with the `DECLARE_SERIAL` and `IMPLEMENT_SERIAL` macros, the `DECLARE_DYNAMIC` and `IMPLEMENT_DYNAMIC` macros are implied.

The InitInstance Function

Throughout this chapter, you have learned about deriving document classes for use within your applications. In the next section, you will learn about view classes and how to use them to access the data the document contains. However, before you continue on to views, it is valuable to understand how your SDI-based MFC applications access the starting document for the application.

When you use AppWizard to create a new application, AppWizard implements the InitInstance overridable function according to the options you select within the AppWizard screen. For example, if you select the single document interface (SDI) option, AppWizard creates the following code:

```
BOOL CMyApp::InitInstance()
{
    // Standard initialization
    SetDialogBkColor(); // Set dialog background color to gray
    // Load standard INI file options
    LoadStdProfileSettings();

    // Register the application's document templates.
    // Document templates serve as the connection between
    // documents, frame windows, and views.
    CSingleDocTemplate* pDocTemplate;
    pDocTemplate = new CSingleDocTemplate(IDR_MAINFRAME,
        RUNTIME_CLASS(CMyDoc),
        RUNTIME_CLASS(CMainFrame), // main SDI frame window
        RUNTIME_CLASS(CMyView));
    AddDocTemplate(pDocTemplate);
    OnFileNew();                    // create an empty document
    if (m_lpCmdLine[0] != '\0')
    {
        // TODO: add command line processing here
    }
    return TRUE;
}
```

The InitInstance function that the AppWizard creates first sets the background color of the dialog box to gray. Next, it loads any standard INI file options that may be set. After taking care of this basic housekeeping, the code creates a pointer to a document template, which serves as the connection between the CDocument class, the frame window class, and any views you create for the document. In this case, AppWizard registered the document class as CMyDoc, the frame window as CMainFrame, and the view class as CMyView. The program code then adds the newly created document template to the collection of document templates with the AddDocTemplate member function, and calls the CMyDoc class' OnFileNew member function to create an empty document for the program's startup. The last lines in the function enable you to add stubs within the program to process command-line options (for example, a filename to open within the program).

In Chapter 3 you learn how the InitInstance member function differs within a multiple document interface (MDI) program from within an SDI program. For now, it is sufficient to see how MFC uses the CSingleDocTemplate class to combine a document, view, and window frame class within your programs.

Managing documents and views

Because the document/view architecture is the cornerstone of any document-based application (as you learned earlier, dialog-based applications perform differently than document/view applications), MFC must be capable of creating and destroying objects from the document/view implementation classes. Because your application may handle more than one type of document/view relationship, MFC must have some way of knowing which document, view, and display classes you implement, what the relationships are between the classes, and how to create the implementations of the classes at runtime. After all, although one document might support many different types of views, associating other views with that same document might be nonsensical.

When you create an SDI application, you'll find that AppWizard inserts document template creation code similar to the following in the application object's InitInstance member function (the application here is called SDIApp):

```
BOOL CSDIAppApp::InitInstance()
{
 ...
 CSingleDocTemplate* pDocTemplate;
 pDocTemplate = new CSingleDocTemplate(
  IDR_MAINFRAME,
  RUNTIME_CLASS(CSDIAppDoc),
  RUNTIME_CLASS(CMainFrame),          // main SDI frame window
  RUNTIME_CLASS(CSDIAppView));
 AddDocTemplate(pDocTemplate);
 ...
```

Have a look at what this code does for you. After allocating a CSingleDocTemplate pointer on the stack, the CSingleDocTemplate constructor is called and passed four parameters. The first parameter is a resource ID. You will learn the significance of the resource ID later in this chapter. The second, third, and fourth parameters associated with the CSingleDocTemplate constructor are pointers to runtime class information. The RUNTIME_CLASS macro generates a pointer to the runtime class information for the specified class. Here it's being used to access that data for the application's document, main frame, and view classes. This is done so that the CSingleDocTemplate class can dynamically generate these objects as needed in order to form the complete document/view team.

The CSingleDocTemplate object lives as long as the application continues to execute. MFC uses the object internally and destroys any added document templates when the application's CWinApp object is destroyed. You can find the code that allocates CSingleDocTemplates to your application in its CWinApp::InitInstance function, but you will never write code that deletes the document template objects if you use AddDocTemplate to add the template, because the CWinApp destructor function will automatically clean up that document template allocation.

A word about frame windows

Throughout this chapter you have learned about documents and frames — and you will continue to do so in the remainder of the chapter. However, as you have probably gathered already, understanding the importance of frames in a document/view application is also important, even though you will not work with the frame class(es) anywhere near as frequently as you will work with the document and view classes.

In fact, the view your application implements is a window, but not a pop-up or frame window. Instead, it is a borderless child window that doesn't have a menu of its own, so it must be contained by some sort of frame window. MFC places the view window you create into the client area of the frame window identified in the document template constructor. In an SDI application, the frame window is always the main window for the application. As you will see in Chapter 3, the frame window for views within a multiple document interface application is an MDI child window.

When developing a Windows application, most programmers do not take the extra step of separating the client area of their application from the frame window. Instead, you would typically create a WS_OVERLAPPED-style window and paint right in its client area. To make MFC a little more modular, Microsoft implemented it so that it distinguishes the two types of frame windows that you might use. That is, MFC makes both an internal and an external distinction between an SDI frame window and a MDI frame window. You will learn more about frame windows later, but for now, it's enough to understand that the frame window is the one that receives all of the menu and window frame messages.

Window frame messages are messages that only windows with frames receive. Such messages include messages about resizing the window, maximizing the window, minimizing the window, and so on. The frame window also receives many nonclient area messages because the frame window is responsible for implementing the nonclient area of your application.

Document template resources

As you learned in the section "Managing Documents and Views," the first parameter to the CSingleDocTemplate constructor is a resource ID. This ID identifies the resources used to supply the frame with an accelerator table, a menu, an icon and a toolbar. To see this, you can easily create a test SDI application and open the resource view, revealing that these various resource types all have the same IDR_MAINFRAME ID. Although you don't have to use the default value of IDR_MAINFRAME, your application should use the same resource ID for each of these resource types that will be associated with the application's frame window. This design was implemented by MFC so that a single ID could be passed to the CSingleDocTemplate constructor instead of it requiring an extra set of parameters, one each for the various resource types.

String resources and the document template

A *string resource* is simply a collection of strings that are saved in the resource file. It is always preferable to store your strings this way, as opposed to hard-coding them in your application. The reason for this is improved maintenance and flexibility. One of these strings is crucial to the document/view architecture, and needs to have the same ID as that specified in the CSingleDocTemplate constructor. This string is actually a concatenation of seven substrings, each delimited by a newline character (/n), that identify various settings regarding your application document type. Here is a sample string from an SDI application called SDIApp.

```
STRINGTABLE
BEGIN
IDR_MAINFRAME
"SDIApp\n\nSDIApp\n\n\nSDIApp.Document\nSDIApp.Document"
END
```

The first substring provides a window title for the application's main window when the document type you will be registering is active. Therefore, if you alter this string, you change what the user sees in the title bar. Note that MFC automatically uses this value and appends the name of the open document to it when the user has a document open.

The second substring is a basis for the name of the default document. For example, suppose the second string contains a value of HexDoc. When the user opens the application, the title bar will read "SDIApp – HexDoc." If the user were to open a document, the "HexDoc" would then be replaced with the name of the document. If this value is blank (which is the default, and what is shown in the sample string), the application will display the value Untitled as the document name until a document is opened.

The third substring is the name of the document type. If your application supports more than one document type, when the user selects the New command in the File menu, the user is provided a list of document types to choose from. If you specify an empty string for the third substring entry, the document type that you are registering is not exposed in the New dialog box. You can use this as a technique to hide document types that you don't want the user to be able to create directly.

The fourth string provides a description of the document type and a wildcard filename filter that the application uses to match document files of the type you are registering. The string is added to the List Files Of Type: combo box in the File Open dialog box for your application. You might want to set the string to Pole Maps (*.plm), for instance, if you have a document that maps telephone poles and has the file extension .plm. The text in this string is used only for the benefit of the user — in other words, it doesn't actually determine the wildcards used to find files in the File Open dialog box.

Instead, the fifth string specifies the extension for any files stored by the document type in question. If you don't specify an extension here, the window defaults to the first in the list of filters. Your extension name should include a leading period, but not an asterisk (*). For instance, .xyz is correct, but xyz and *.xyz are not.

The sixth string element identifies the document type for the registration database. This string is used by Windows Explorer, the Registry, and OLE to register your document type. It is not shown to users unless they examine the File Associations dialog box in Windows Explorer or search the Registry itself.

The seventh and final string element is the name of the document as stored in the Windows Registry. Assuming that you are implementing OLE support, this string is used in the Registry (and therefore by OLE itself) to identify the type of document your application implements. For example, both Excel and Word show this string to users when they use the Object option available from the Insert menu to embed an object serviced by your application in the host application's document. You should make this string as short and as meaningful as possible, in order to keep the information from confusing the user.

As you can see, because the string resource is the cornerstone of the document registration process and you can alter many of your application's subtle features using the string resource that your application registers, you should carefully check what you place in the string. Now that I've given you forewarning, have a look at how to modify this string programmatically.

The CDocTemplate class from which MFC derives the CSingleDocTemplate and CMultiDocTemplate classes includes the GetDocString member function. GetDocString, which accepts a reference to a CString object and an index, enables you to query the values of the registered string resource. CDocTemplate implements the GetDocString member function as shown here:

```
virtual BOOL GetDocString( CString& rString,
    enum DocStringIndex index ) const;
```

The second parameter, index, is expressed as a private enum of the CDocTemplate class. Valid values are shown in Table 2-1.

Table 2-1: Valid Values for the Index Parameter

Value	Description
CDocTemplate::windowTitle	Text for the application window's title bar, important only for SDI applications
CDocTemplate::docName	Root for the default document name
CDocTemplate::fileNewName	Name of the document for the File ⇨ New box
CDocTemplate::filterName	Text for the File ⇨ Open dialog's File Type drop-down list box
CDocTemplate::filterExt	Wildcard filename filter matching files for this document type
CDocTemplate::regFileTypeId	Registry database internal name, used by OLE and the File Manager
CDocTemplate::regFileTypeName	Registry database document name, used by all OLE applications and exposed to the user

There's no corresponding CDocTemplate::SetDocString function. You cannot change the attributes of a document template after you create it.

As you have learned, the string resource dictates many subtle aspects of your application, and the default string resource the AppWizard produces gives your application a healthy but basic user interface. You can also change many of the values within the string resource in the Document Template Strings tab of AppWizard's Advanced Options window. All the fields in this tab of the dialog box correspond directly to substrings in the document template string resource. If you know what your application will look like when you finish developing it, you can change the appropriate strings in the Advanced Options dialog box and avoid editing the string resource directly.

However, as you add features, you will certainly have to make adjustments to the string resource. To perform these adjustments, you must edit the string resource directly, using the string table editor (invoked by simply double-clicking the string table resource from the resource view). If you make a mistake, MFC will either blindly put the wrong string in the wrong part of your user interface or generate an Assert Failed error message at runtime. When you change the document template resource string, you should generally test your application immediately to make sure that you have not accidentally disabled or invalidated any other features of your application.

Stock view resources

Many other resources in your application are identified by the resource ID in your document template. All these resources are associated with the document type that your application is currently editing. For the SDI AppWizard application, the ID that is used for the default document template string resource and all of the other resources associated with the template is called IDR_MAINFRAME.

The AppWizard gives your application's main frame a menu that is also identified by IDR_MAINFRAME. In single document interface applications, this means that your menu depends on what kind of document is active. For multiple document interface applications, it means that each individual document type has its own type of menu. If you want all your document types to share a common menu, you can simply change each template type to point at the same menu resource.

The frame also has an icon with the same identifier as the other resources, which indicates that the icon should be used to represent that SDI application. For example, the operating system displays the named icon when the user minimizes the application. For multiple document interface applications, the icon is the icon for minimized MDI child windows. The icon used for the application comes from another source, which you will learn about in Chapter 3.

Your application may also feature a dialog box named after that same template resource ID. Such applications are rare; they are generally applications that have a dialog box as the core interface for the view of their document. You will learn later in this chapter about views that use a dialog as the core of their interface—an important lesson because many of this book's demo applications use this interface.

The application uses the bitmap resource the AppWizard provides to build the default toolbar for the frame window. Although the toolbar seems to be composed of several buttons, the buttons are actually sections of a single bitmap. You will learn more about the CToolbar class, used to make toolbars in MFC, in Chapter 6.

Because the frame implements a window with a menu, it may also provide an *accelerator table*. This table provides translations between keystrokes and WM_COMMAND messages, which the application should send when the operating system detects the keystroke. The framework takes care of searching for the accelerator table and translating and dispatching the messages the operating system generates when the user presses the appropriate key. The default accelerator table that the AppWizard produces has accelerators for the standard user interface elements in the menu.

You should feel free to modify any of these resources to suit the needs of your application. However, you may need to change more than the resource to keep things working. Make sure you read up on the classes that make use of the resources before you change them so that your application stays healthy.

The document template life cycle

As you might imagine, CSingleDocTemplate is a lightweight class—that is, it takes very little memory. You shouldn't worry about keeping document template classes lying about, even if you have dozens of them.

CSingleDocTemplate (and CMultiDocTemplate, which you will learn about in Chapter 3) is used heavily by the application frameworks. After setting them up and getting them started, your application depends on the templates to manage the document, view, and frame windows objects, but you no longer need to manipulate the templates directly. As you saw earlier in this chapter, your application should register all of the document templates that it will use during its `CWinApp::InitInstance` member function. By making them public members of your application object, you can access them later on when you need to juggle documents and views.

When you think about and manipulate document templates, probably the best single perspective to maintain is to let MFC do the work. In other words, you should ask MFC's code in the document template object to create the view and document you need and hook up all of the associations. In a well-designed application, you should almost never have to directly create your own views, documents, and frames. The best applications let the document template do the work.

Advanced work with templates

Now that you understand the basics of templates, you should think about them from the perspective of application design. The way your application works really depends on your point of view. If your users have to do a lot of work to get to a view of the data they are interested in, they'll quickly get frustrated. Worse yet, if the views your application offers do not represent information in a way your users perceive as intuitive, your application will be perceived as awkward, because the users will have to spend too much time thinking about how things should work instead of actually getting work done.

The out-of-the-box application frameworks that the AppWizard produces are too good not to use for most of your applications. Even after some modification, MFC reacts to your changes in ways that are generally perceived by the user as intuitive and consistent with the interfaces they are used to. You'll see an example of this when you get to the Hex Editor demo shortly.

If you register several different document templates, you get the extra dialog box to enable the users to choose their document type after selecting the New option from the File menu. And once you have taken advantage of this simple opportunity, you will soon find that there are several other instances where you might want your application to differ slightly from the mainstream.

Working with multiple templates

You can always use more than one template when you are running an MFC document/view application. Your application will generally create any necessary templates as it handles `CWinApp::InitInstance`. If your application initially came from the AppWizard, you will find that the function has been coded to create and register a template for the document/ view pair that your application uses by default.

If you ever need to use documents or views in any other combination, you should add code to create a template for those particular document/view pairs. Doing so makes it much easier to create instances of the pairs at the user's request. The `CDocTemplate`-derived object you create is just that — an object — and as such, you need to maintain a pointer to it after you use `new` to create it. You generally should keep these pointers to document templates as instance data in your application's `CWinApp`-derived class. If you do, you can reference them at almost anytime during the application's execution.

Each template you register with the frameworks using `CWinApp::AddDocTemplate` is kept in a linked list. MFC uses this list to find templates when the user asks to create a new document or a new view, or performs any operation that requires the application to find an appropriate

document template. For example, if more than one document template exists when
CWinApp::OnFileNew is called, the framework presents a list box that lets the user
select the template for the type of document they wish to create.

The undocumented CDocManager class

The linked list of templates is managed by an internal instance of an MFC collection class
called CDocManager. This class is an undocumented implementation feature of MFC.
Understanding how it works, though, can be quite useful. The CWinApp-derived object in your
application creates an instance of the class. CWinApp holds a pointer to the CDocManager
object. It destroys the object just before your application exits, in CWinApp's destructor function. CWinApp stores this pointer in the m_pDocManager member variable. In fact, you can use
this pointer at any time to gain access to the document manager.

The document manager's main importance derives from its management of that linked list
of template objects. The document manager stores the list in its public m_TemplateList
member. You can then iterate through this list using code similar to the following:

```
void CSampleWinApp::IterateEveryTemplate()
 {
   CDocManager* pManager = AfxGetApp()->m_pDocManager;
   if (pManager == NULL)
      return;
   POSITION pos = pManager->GetFirstDocTemplatePosition();
   while (pos != NULL)
   {
      // get the next template
      CDocTemplate* pTemplate =
          pManager->GetNextDocTemplate(pos);
      // you can now do work with each pointer
      DoSomething(pTemplate);
   }
 }
```

One of the most interesting things you can do with the list of templates is to derive a list of
all active documents. This involves a nested loop; so for each template you find, you can loop
through the documents that the template has created. To do this, you might use some code
similar to the following:

```
void CSampleWinApp::IterateEveryDocument()
 {
   CDocManager* pManager = AfxGetApp()->m_pDocManager;
   if (pManager == NULL)
      return;
   POSITION posTemplate =
       pManager->GetFirstDocTemplatePosition();
   while (posTemplate != NULL)
    {
      // get the next template
      CDocTemplate* pTemplate =
          pManager->GetNextDocTemplate(posTemplate);
      POSITION posDoc = pTemplate->GetFirstDocPosition();
      while (posDoc != NULL)
```

```
        {
          CYourDocument* pThisOne =
              (CSampleDocument*) GetNextDoc(posDoc);
          // do some work with each document
          pThisOne->SomeFunctionCall();
        }
      }
    }
```

In both of these code fragments, you retrieve a pointer to the manager by first getting a pointer to the application object with a call to `AfxGetApp`. Next, you examine the `m_pDocManager` member for the pointer to the template manager. This is, actually, more than a little duplicative because the code fragments are member functions in `CSampleWinApp`; so they're presumably members of the very object that you are obtaining with the call to `AfxGetApp`. Instead, you could have accessed the `m_pDocManager` member directly. However, the inefficiency lets you see the use of `AfxGetApp` to retrieve information about the running application object. More importantly, you have learned how to implement the code in any function of any object in your application because the code does not presume that it is running within the `CWinApp`-derived object.

The code fragments make use of the `CDocManager` member functions `GetFirstDocTemplate-Position` and `GetNextDocTemplate`, which should look familiar to you because they perform similar processing to the `GetFirstViewPosition` and `GetNextView` member functions of the `CDocument` class that you learned about earlier in this chapter. `GetNextDocTemplate` is the one that does the real work — it gets a pointer to the next document of type `POSITION`. As you can see, some runtime casting is also in the code fragments because the second program fragment must promote the pointers to plain `CDocument` objects to pointers to the `CSampleDocument` class. It would be good programming to do `IsKindOf` tests here, or use MFC's `DYNAMIC_DOWNCAST` macro to make sure you get what you really wanted, but the code samples here do not do so for simplicity's sake.

Destroying documents added with AddDocTemplate

If you use `AddDocTemplate` to add your new template to the list that MFC manages for you, you don't need to worry about deleting the template when your application closes. However, in some circumstances, you may want the template hidden from the user, and then you need to make sure your template is deleted. Deleting the template object during the program's execution of the destructor function of your application's `CWinApp` object is too good an opportunity to miss.

When designing your applications, don't worry about keeping templates around as long as you need them; as already mentioned, templates are very lightweight. As with any other object, reasonableness guidelines apply. A thousand templates are probably a little much (and a coding nightmare), but adding ten or twenty templates to an application should not be burdensome, provided you need them.

The CView Class

For every `CDocument`-derived class that presents a visual interface to the user there is a `CView`-derived class that provides the interface. The `CView`-derived class provides the visual presentation of the document's data and handles user interaction through the view window.

The view window, in turn, is a child of a frame window. In an SDI application, the view window is a child of the main frame window. In MDI applications, the view window is a child of a MDI child window. In addition, the frame window can be the in-place frame window during OLE in-place editing (assuming your application supports this feature). A frame window, in turn, may contain several view windows (for example, through the use of splitter windows, which you will learn about in Chapter 3).

Declaring a view class

As earlier sections of this chapter have explained in detail, you should declare all data that is part of a document as part of the document's class. With that overriding precept in mind, however, it is important to recognize that many data elements in your applications will probably pertain to a specific view. More importantly, most of those data elements will be nonpersistent—meaning you will not save them as part of the document.

Suppose, for example, you create an application that is capable of presenting the data within the document at different zoom factors. The zoom factor is specific to each individual view, meaning that different views may use different zoom factors even when the views are presenting information from the same document.

Given these considerations, you are probably best served to declare the zoom factor as a member variable of the view class, as shown here, rather than as a variable in the document class:

```
class CZoomView : public CView
{
protected:
  CZoomView();
  DECLARE_DYNCREATE(CZoomView)
public:
  CZoomableDoc* GetDocument();
  WORD m_wZoomPercent;
}
```

However, much more important than any member variables representing a setting is a member variable that represents the *current selection*. The current selection is the collection of objects within the document that the user has selected for manipulation. The nature and type of manipulation that the user might perform is entirely application-dependent, but it may include such operations as Clipboard cutting and copying or OLE drag-and-drop placement support.

Arguably, the easiest way to implement a current selection is to use a collection class, just as you would in the document class. For example, you might declare the collection that represents the current selection as shown here:

```
class CSelectableView : public CView
{
  //  more code here
  CList <CDocItem *, CDocItem *> m_SelectList;
  //
}
```

In addition to modifying the view class declaration, you must write one or more member functions so that your view class can respond to selection activities, such as filling and emptying the list. However, you must also always override the OnDraw member function. The default implementation of OnDraw performs no processing — you absolutely have to write code that displays your document's data items (even if the view class doesn't contain member variables of its own).

For example, if you derive your document class from COleDocument and use CDocItems to maintain the document's data, your OnDraw member function for your class will probably look similar to the following:

```
void COleCapView::OnDraw(CDC *pDC)
  {
    COLECapDoc *pDoc = GetDocument();
    ASSERT_VALID(pDoc);
    POSITION posDoc = pDoc->GetStartPosition();
    while (posDoc != NULL)
      {
        CDocItem *pObject = pDoc->GetNextItem(posDoc);
        if (pObject->IsKindOf(RUNTIME_CLASS(CNormDocItem)))
          {
            ((CNormDocItem *)pObject)->Draw(pDc);
          }
        else if (pObject->IsKindOf(RUNTIME_CLASS(COleDocItem)))
          {
            ((COleDocItem *)pObject)->Draw(pDc);
          }
        else
          ASSERT(FALSE);
      }
  }
```

Analyzing the CView member functions

Like the CDocument class, the CView class offers a wide variety of member functions that you can use in their default form or override to provide specific functionality within your applications. Among the most commonly used member functions in the CView class is the GetDocument member function, which returns a pointer to the document object that you have previously associated with the view. Another commonly used member function is DoPreparePrinting. The DoPreparePrinting function displays the Print dialog box and creates a printer device context based on the user's selections within the dialog box. You will learn more about the DoPreparePrinting function in Chapter 15.

GetDocument and DoPreparePrinting are the only CView member functions that are not overridable. You can override any of the remaining CView member functions. These member functions supplement the large number of overridable functions that the CWnd class (which is the base class for the CView class) provides. In addition, the member functions handle the vast majority of user interface events. Trying to list all the member functions here is a relatively futile exercise because there are far too many of them to make it worthwhile. However, among the member functions are functions to handle keyboard, mouse, timer, system, and other messages, Clipboard and MDI events, and initialization and termination messages. Your application should override the view class member functions as it needs to. For example, if your application enables the user to place an object in a document by clicking and dragging the mouse, you should override the CWnd::OnLButtonDown member function to support that functionality. In general, you can use the ClassWizard to create the override function and simply add the appropriate code in the section the ClassWizard marks as TODO.

Most applications will override some important functions whenever you work with a `CView` class. You already learned about the first one—overriding `OnDraw` is necessary for any `CView`-derived object to display information at all. In addition, for any application you create that supports OLE (which, in today's development environment, is virtually any application), you must override the `IsSelected` member function. The `IsSelected` member function returns `TRUE` if the object that its argument points to is part of the view's current selection. If you implemented your current selection using the `CList` template collection as a list of `CDocItem` objects (as you learned to earlier in this chapter), you would implement `IsSelected` in a form similar to that shown here:

```
BOOL CSampView::IsSelected(const CObject* pDocItem) const
{
    return (m_SelectList.Find((CDocItem *)pDocItem) != NULL);
}
```

Another important member function that most applications override is the `OnUpdate` member function. As you learned earlier in this chapter, the document class' `UpdateAllViews` member function calls the `OnUpdate` member function for each view associated with a document each time you invoke it. The default implementation of `OnUpdate` simply invalidates the entire client area of the view window (which, in turn, results in redrawing the entire client area). To improve your application's performance, you may wish to override `OnUpdate` and invalidate only the areas of the view window that the application must update. For example, you might implement `OnUpdate` as shown here:

```
void CSampView::OnUpdate(CView *pView,
    LPARAM lHint, CObject *pObj)
{
    if (lHint==UPDATE_OBJECT)       // app-defined constant
        InvalidateRect((CAppObject *)pObj)->m_Rect);
    else
        Invalidate();
}
```

You ordinarily should not do any drawing in the `OnUpdate` member function. Instead, you should do any drawing in the view's `OnDraw` member function.

If your application supports nonstandard mapping modes such as zooming or rotating, the `CView` class `OnPrepareDC` member function acquires special significance. In this function, you will set the view window's mapping mode before the application actually draws anything onto the window. You should always be sure, in the event that you create a device context for your view window, that your application calls `OnPrepareDC` to ensure that the application applies the proper settings to the device context.

Note   If the terms *mapping mode* and *device context* are unfamiliar to you, they are covered in detail in Chapters 8 and 9.

Similarly, your applications may often need to create a device context (DC) for the sole purpose of retrieving the current mapping of the view window. For example, you might need to convert the `POSITION` of a mouse click from physical to logical coordinates within the view's `OnLButtonDown` member function, as shown here:

```
void CSampView::OnLButtonDown(UITN nFlags, Cpoint point)
{
    CClientDC dc(this);
    OnPrepareDC(&dc);
```

```
    dc.DPtoLP(&point);
    // further processing
}
```

Working with views and messages

In addition to those messages for which MFC provides default handlers in either CView or its parent class, CWnd, a typical view class processes many other system messages. Other messages typically include command messages that represent the user's selection of a menu item, toolbar button, or other user interface object.

As discussed earlier in this chapter, whether it is the view or the document (or in some cases, the frame) that should handle a particular message is a decision entirely left up to you. Remember, however, that the most important criteria in making the decision is the scope and the effect of the message or command on the application's processing. If the command affects the entire document or the data stored within it, you should generally handle the command in the document class (except when the command's effect is *through* a specific view, as it might be in some implementations of a Cut or Paste command). If the command affects only a particular view (such as setting a zoom or rotation factor), the view object affected should handle the command.

MFC-derived variants of the CView class

In addition to the basic CView class, MFC provides several derived classes that serve specific purposes and that are intended to simplify handling of complex tasks. Table 2-2 summarizes the MFC-derived CView classes.

Table 2-2: MFC-Derived Variations of the CView Class

Class Name	Description
CCtrlView	Supports views that are directly based on a control (such as a tree control or edit control).
CEditView	Uses an edit control to provide a multiline text editor.
CFormView	Displays dialog box controls. You must base CFormView objects on dialog templates.
CHtmlView	Provides a window in which the user can browse sites on the World Wide Web, as well as folders on the local file system and on a network.
CListView	Displays a list control.
COleDBRecordView	Displays database records using dialog box controls.
CRecordView	Displays database records using dialog box controls. You will learn more about the CRecordView class in Chapter 21.
CRichEditView	Displays a rich-text edit control.
CScrollView	Enables the use of scroll bars for the user to move through the logical data in the document.
CTreeView	Displays a tree control.

Another, rarely overridden variant of the CView class is the CPreviewView class. The MFC framework uses CPreviewView to provide print preview support to your applications. You will learn more about CPreviewView in Chapter 15.

All the CView-derived classes provide member functions that are specific to the class' goal. Member functions of view classes that derive from CCtrlView encapsulate Windows messages specific to the control class they represent.

CFormView and the classes that MFC derives from it (including CDataRecordView, COleDBRecordView, and CRecordView) support Dialog Data Exchange (DDE). You can use all four of these classes as you would use CDialog-derived classes (you will learn about CDialog-derived classes in Chapters 10 and 11).

CForm view versus dialog-based applications

Dialog-based applications represent an exception from the standard MFC document/view model. If you create a dialog-based application using the AppWizard, the resulting program does not have a document or a view class (nor a frame window class, for that matter). Instead, the application implements all its functionality in a single dialog class derived from CDialog.

Although deriving a single dialog class may be sufficient for many simple applications, in doing so you sacrifice support for many MFC features that you can include within a document/view application. A dialog-based application does not have a menu, toolbar, or status bar (all of which reside in the frame window), it will not support OLE or MAPI, and it will not have printing capabilities (at least not without significant additional programming effort on your part).

If you need a dialog-style interface but still want the benefits of the document/view architecture, you can build your application with the CFormView class as the base class for your view window and use the SDI application model. Doing so enables you to retain all the advantages of a full-featured MFC application while still presenting the same dialog-based appearance, using a dialog box template to define the view and take advantage of Dynamic Data Exchange.

Returning to frame windows

So far in this chapter, you have learned what documents, document templates, and views are all about, and you have learned (if only briefly) that a view almost always lives in a frame window. This concept is often overlooked but is an important key to your management of different views within your application.

The only time your applications do not create a view within a real frame window is when the view is active as an embedded OLE object. The view still has a frame in such situations — but the frame is a very different one from the standard frame windows you have learned about.

As this chapter explains, an SDI application usually creates a CFrameWnd instance, while a MDI application typically creates a CMDIFrameWnd instance. Of course, if you've written a dialog-based application, the dialog box is the main window, and your application doesn't have any frame window.

Because of the way command dispatching works, you will find that the frame window often acts as a catchall for choices in your command window. In other words, any command from a menu that isn't handled by your view is offered to your frame window for it to handle.

You should implement handlers, ready for any frame message, no matter which view the user is currently working with. If you have menu choices that should react in different ways for different views, you can implement handlers in both the frame and the view classes. The view handler is executed when the view object is active; otherwise, the frame's handler is called.

The frame window OnCreate function

As you've learned, frame windows are responsible for more than just making sure your application has a menu and a sizable frame. As mentioned earlier, they also serve as an anchor for your window's toolbar and status bar. However, I haven't discussed where these elements get created. Therefore, I'll briefly go over that now.

Most of the frame window's initialization takes place in the virtual OnCreate function. Here's an example OnCreate function for an SDI application generated via the AppWizard.

```
int CMainFrame::OnCreate(LPCREATESTRUCT lpCreateStruct)
{
 if (CFrameWnd::OnCreate(lpCreateStruct) == -1)
  return -1;

 if (!m_wndToolBar.CreateEx(this,
  TBSTYLE_FLAT, WS_CHILD
  | WS_VISIBLE | CBRS_TOP
  | CBRS_GRIPPER | CBRS_TOOLTIPS
  | CBRS_FLYBY | CBRS_SIZE_DYNAMIC)
 || !m_wndToolBar.LoadToolBar(IDR_MAINFRAME))
 {
  TRACE0("Failed to create toolbar\n");
  return -1;       // fail to create
 }

 if (!m_wndStatusBar.Create(this) ||
  !m_wndStatusBar.SetIndicators(indicators,
   sizeof(indicators)/sizeof(UINT)))
 {
 TRACE0("Failed to create status bar\n");
 return -1;       // fail to create
 }

 // TODO: Delete these three lines if you
 // don't want the toolbar to be dockable
 m_wndToolBar.EnableDocking(CBRS_ALIGN_ANY);
 EnableDocking(CBRS_ALIGN_ANY);
 DockControlBar(&m_wndToolBar);

 return 0;
}
```

As you can see, after calling the base class's (CFrameWnd) OnCreate member function, this function creates both a status bar and toolbar window and stores them in the m_wndStatusBar and m_wndToolBar member variables, respectively. However, what I want to point out here are two things. First, notice that the CStatusBar and CToolBar constructors each take a pointer to the frame window. Second, the functions that pertain to docking a toolbar (EnableDocking and DockControlBar) are CFrameWnd functions. These two facts should indicate to you that status bars and toolbars were designed to be put on frame windows and not other types of windows (such as dialog boxes). In fact, that is the case, and it is not a trivial task to get these elements to work outside the scope of a frame window. However, in Chapter 6 you'll learn how to overcome this limitation and place a status bar on a dialog box.

Note   If you need to retrieve an SDI application's frame window (for example, to access its toolbar or status bar elements), this can be done via the global AfxGetMainWnd function. By way of example, the following code retrieves the main frame object and calls its ShowWindow function in order to minimize the window to the appbar.

```
CFrameWnd* pFrame = (CFrameWnd*)AfxGetMainWnd();
ASSERT(pFrame);
if (pFrame)
{
  pFrame->ShowWindow(SW_MINIMIZE);
}
```

Controlling the Title Bar Text

As you've seen, one of the main advantages of the document/view architecture is that it creates a framework that combines the frame window, view window, menu and toolbar resources and document. However, one of the negatives of any framework that does a lot for you is that it is not always obvious how to override default behavior to get what you want. In this section, I'll illustrate an example of that with a task that at first you would think would be very simple but has proved problematic for anyone new to MFC development — controlling the application's title bar text.

Removing the document name

There will no doubt be times when you want to create an application that has many of the user interface benefits of an SDI application without the actual document. Of course, the first thing you'd do in a case where your application has a frame and a view, but no document, is to remove all the file Open and Save options from the menu. However, even when you do that, you end up with a title bar text that shows the name of your application plus the word "Untitled." Where does this come from and how do you get rid of it?

To answer that, you need to realize that anytime you create a document template — such as when an SDI application begins — an empty document is created. This happens by virtue of the framework calling the CWinApp::OnFileNew when the application begins. Once the document is created, the framework ultimately calls the CFrameWnd::OnUpdateFrameTitle function that is reproduced here:

```
void CFrameWnd::OnUpdateFrameTitle(BOOL bAddToTitle)
{
 if ((GetStyle() & FWS_ADDTOTITLE) == 0)
  return;     // leave it alone!

#ifndef _AFX_NO_OLE_SUPPORT
```

```
    // allow hook to set the title (used for OLE support)
    if (m_pNotifyHook != NULL
    && m_pNotifyHook->OnUpdateFrameTitle())
      return;
#endif

    CDocument* pDocument = GetActiveDocument();
    if (bAddToTitle && pDocument != NULL)
      UpdateFrameTitleForDocument(pDocument->GetTitle());
    else
      UpdateFrameTitleForDocument(NULL);
}
```

As you can see, the function first retrieves the frame's style, and using the & operator, determines if the FWS_ADDTOTITLE style bit is turned on before formatting the title bar's text. Therefore, to turn off the framework's well-intentioned attempts to modify the title bar, you need only change the frame window's style.

To modify the style of any window for which you have a CWnd reference, you can simply override its PreCreateWindow function. This function is called by the framework before the actual window is created and attached to the CWnd object. In fact, when you create an SDI application, the MFC Application Wizard inserts an override for you. Therefore, modifying the CMainFrame::PreCreateWindow function as follows will do the trick.

```
BOOL CMainFrame::PreCreateWindow(CREATESTRUCT& cs)
{
   cs.style &= ~FWS_ADDTOTITLE;
   if( !CFrameWnd::PreCreateWindow(cs) )
     return FALSE;

   return TRUE;
}
```

Now, when the OnUpdateFrameTitle is called, it will see that the frame's FWS_ADDTOTITLE style is on and will not append the name of the document to the title bar, leaving only the application name.

Formatting the title bar text

Let's now look at two more issues regarding controlling an application's title bar text. If you look at some of the more popular Windows applications, such as Microsoft Word, you will see that the ordering of the application name and the document name is reversed from that of a wizard-generated application. Oddly, until a couple of versions ago, Visual C++ applications also displayed the order of document name and then application name. For some reason, this was changed, and now the application name is displayed first. To change this behavior, you need only know the name of one little style – FWS_PREFIXTITLE. Knowing this, the following code results in the document name being displayed before the application name. Therefore, an SDI application named SDIApp will display a title bar value of "Untitled – SDIApp" upon startup.

```
BOOL CMainFrame::PreCreateWindow(CREATESTRUCT& cs)
{
   cs.style |= FWS_PREFIXTITLE;
```

```
if( !CFrameWnd::PreCreateWindow(cs) )
 return FALSE;

return TRUE;
}
```

What if, however, you want to format the title bar text in a special way? For example, you might want to format the title like this: "SDIApp – [Document]." Or you might not want the user to see the actual filename, but to see something a little more informational. Let's say your application is called ACME Software and the user can open data files in order to maintain entities such as customers, vendors, and suppliers. When the user opens the customer file (cust.dat), instead of them seeing the file name on the title bar, you'd probably want them to see something like "ACME Software – Maintain Customers."

To see how this is done, simply refer to the CFrameWnd::OnUpdateFrameTitle function you saw earlier. There you'll note that if the FWS_ADDTOTITLE style is on and a document is loaded, the following call is made to the set the title bar text.

```
UpdateFrameTitleForDocument(pDocument->GetTitle());
```

The important part of this is the call to the CDocument::GetTitle function. If you were to set a breakpoint on this call (found in the winfrm.cpp file), you'd see that it leads to the following implementation (found in afxwin2.inl):

```
AFXWIN_INLINE const CString& CDocument::GetTitle() const
 { ASSERT(this != NULL); return m_strTitle; }
```

Therefore, you can either directly set the document's m_strTitle member variable, or you can override its SetTitle member function (the preferred method). Then, you could use any application-specific logic to form the title bar name in just the fashion your application needs.

At this point, you've learned a great deal about the document/view architecture and SDI applications in specific. Now, let's see how that knowledge comes together to create a practical demo application.

The HexViewer SDI Application

In this section you will create an SDI application that enables you to load and display either ASCII or binary files hex format. Please note that this is a very involved, fairly complex demo for this early in the book. However, once you've completed it, not only will you have a practical application for your toolbox, but you will see first-hand that although you're only in Chapter 2, you're already coding realistic applications.

Let's get started by creating a new SDI project called HexViewer. To do that, simply follow these steps:

1. Select File ➪ New Project (or press Ctrl+Shift+N).

2. From there, select the Visual C++ Projects in the left-hand tree view.

3. Once you've done that, select the MFC Application template from the list view on the right-hand side.

4. Now select a location for your new project, type the name of the project in as HexViewer, and click the OK button.

5. When the MFC Application Wizard appears, click the Application Type link on the left and change the Application Type to Single document.

6. Click the Generated Class link on the left.

7. After ensuring that the CHexViewerView is selected in the Generated Classes listbox, change the Base Class to CScrollView. (The CScrollView is simply a CView-derived class that enables you to easily handle horizontal and vertical scrolling.)

8. Click the Finish button to generate the project.

Opening and reading the file

The default AppWizard-generated SDI application framework automatically handles displaying a File Open dialog and retrieving the name of a user-selected file. However, the AppWizard obviously can't know what types of files everyone needs to deal with. Therefore, the first thing you need to do is to add the code necessary to open the user-requested file.

Start by defining the following two member variables in the CHexViewerDoc class (hexviewerdoc.h). These variables (m_pFile and m_lFileSize) will be used to track the open file pointer and the file's size, respectively. (Note that it's always best to define data variables like these as protected, and to provide accessor functions for them. However, I'm defining them here as public for simplicity.)

```
class CHexViewerDoc : public CDocument
{
  ...
public:
    CFile* m_pFile;
    LONG m_lFileSize;
```

Now, update the document class's constructor to initialize these values:

```
CHexViewDoc::CHexViewDoc()
{
    m_pFile = NULL;
    m_lFileSize = 0L;
}
```

While you're coding the initialization of these variables, you might as well add the cleanup as well. Update the document's destructor as follows:

```
CHexViewDoc::~CHexViewDoc()
{
  if (m_pFile != NULL)
  {
    m_pFile->Close();
    delete m_pFile;
    m_pFile = NULL;
    m_lFileSize = 0L;
  }
}
```

When a file is document is opened in an MFC application using the MFC framework, the CDocument::OnOpenDocument virtual function will be called. You might recall that one point

I made back in the "Overriding virtual document functions" section was that you will need to override the CDocument::OnOpenDocument function if you need specific processing for your document type. Therefore, at this point, use the CHexViewerDoc Properties dialog box to override this function. Once you've done that, modify it so that when finished it looks like the following.

```
BOOL CHexViewerDoc::OnOpenDocument(LPCTSTR lpszPathName)
{
 if (!CDocument::OnOpenDocument(lpszPathName))
  return FALSE;

 // Clean up if a file is already open
 if (m_pFile != NULL)
 {
  m_pFile->Close();
  delete m_pFile;
  m_pFile = NULL;
  m_lFileSize = 0L;
 }

 try
 {
  // Open specified file
  m_pFile = new CFile(lpszPathName,
                      CFile::modeRead | CFile::typeBinary);
 }
 catch (CFileException* e)
 {
  CString strError;

  strError.Format(_T("Couldn't open file: %d"),
                  _sys_errlist[e->m_lOsError]);
  AfxMessageBox(strError);
  return FALSE;
 }

 // Set the file size variable - used in determining the
 // scroll size of the view
 m_lFileSize = m_pFile->GetLength();

 return TRUE;
}
```

As you can see here, the first thing that I'm doing is to call the base class's OnOpenDocument function. This is necessary because the base class implementation does any necessary cleanup on any open files and gives the document an opportunity to serialize any data that needs to be kept before the new file is opened.

After that, I verify that the m_pFile pointer is NULL. If not, I know that I already have an open file. If that's the case, I simply close the file, delete the pointer, and reinitialize the member variable.

If you look at the OnOpenDocument signature, you can see that the name of the file is passed to this function from the MFC framework. Therefore, that value is passed to the constructor the MFC wrapper class for performing file I/O—CFile. Notice that I've specified the CFile::modeRead flag (to indicate that I only need read access) and the CFile::typeBinary flag (to indicate that I'm opening the file in binary mode). As you'll learn when I go into the CFile class in more detail in Chapter 24, you can't open a CFile object in ASCII mode and therefore, the second flag isn't technically necessary. However, I personally believe in specifying the CFile::typeBinary flag as a way of better documenting my intentions.

If the file opens successfully, the m_lFileSize value is set using the CFile::GetLength function. If the file open fails, the framework will throw an exception of type CFileException. The catch block for this displays an error message detailing the reason for the file open failure and returns FALSE from the function. Returning FALSE from the OnOpenDocument function indicates to the framework that the document cannot be opened. (Note that the subject of exception handling is covered in Chapter 18.)

The last bit to do to the document class is to add a help member function that the view will call in order to read a line of data from the currently open file. Therefore, add the following function to the Document class.

```
public:
 BOOL ReadLine(CString& strLine,
               int nLength,
               LONG lOffset = -1L);
```

Here's the actual function:

```
BOOL CHexViewerDoc::ReadLine(CString& strLine,
                             int nLength,
                             LONG lOffset /* = -1L */)
{
 LONG lPosition;

 if (lOffset != -1L)
  lPosition = m_pFile->Seek(lOffset, CFile::begin);
 else
  lPosition = m_pFile->GetPosition();

 if (lPosition == -1L)
 {
  TRACE2("CHexViewDoc::ReadLine returns FALSE Seek"
         "(%8.81X, %8.81X)\n",
         lOffset, lPosition);
  return FALSE;
 }

 BYTE* pszBuffer = new BYTE[nLength];
 int nReturned = m_pFile->Read(pszBuffer, nLength);

 if (nReturned <= 0)
 {
  TRACE2("CHexViewDoc::ReadLine returns FALSE Read"
         "(%d, %d)\n",
         nLength,
         nReturned);
  delete pszBuffer;
```

```
 return FALSE;
}

CString strTemp;
CString strCharsIn;

strTemp.Format(_T("%8.8lX - "), lPosition);
strLine = strTemp;

for (int nIndex = 0; nIndex < nReturned; nIndex++)
{
 if (nIndex == 0)
  strTemp.Format(_T("%2.2X"), pszBuffer[nIndex]);
 else if (nIndex % 16 == 0)
  strTemp.Format(_T("=%2.2X"), pszBuffer[nIndex]);
 else if (nIndex % 8 == 0)
  strTemp.Format(_T("-%2.2X"), pszBuffer[nIndex]);
 else
  strTemp.Format(_T(" %2.2X"), pszBuffer[nIndex]);

 if (_istprint(pszBuffer[nIndex]))
  strCharsIn += pszBuffer[nIndex];
 else
  strCharsIn += _T('.');
 strLine += strTemp;
}
if (nReturned < nLength)
{
 CString strPadding(_T(' '), 3*(nLength-nReturned));
 strLine += strPadding;
}
strLine += _T("  ");
strLine += strCharsIn;

delete pszBuffer;

return TRUE;
}
```

Although this code can throw you off at first, I'll walk through it so you understand what's going on. The first thing to notice is that the function takes three parameters. The first of these parameters is a CString value called strLine. This parameter will contain the line of data once it is read and formatted by this function. The second parameter (nLength) indicates the number of bytes to read and the third parameter (lOffset) is used to specify at what byte to begin reading the data from the file.

The first thing the code does is to check the lOffset value. If the value is not equal to –1, the CFile::Seek is called to position the file cursor to the specified offset starting from the beginning of the file (indicated with the CFile::begin flag). If lOffset has a value of –1 (the default), then the CFile::GetPosition function is used to determine the current file position. In both cases, this value is saved in a local variable called lPosition.

The code now knows how many bytes to read (nLength), from what position in the file (lPosition). Therefore, a byte array (pszBuffer) is allocated on the stack that is the same length as the value of nLength. The CFile::Read function is then used to read data into that byte buffer.

After a bit of error checking, you simply need to format the data in a way that the view can handle. Some people would argue that the document should be used as a data repository only and that the data formatting should be left to the individual views. However, either method is fine, especially in an SDI application where there is only one view.

To perform the formatting, a temporary CString variable is allocated on the stack (strTemp). The lPosition value is then formatted into that string (so that the user can see where he is in the file as he scrolls through the data). This value is then copied into the strLine parameter. From there, a for loop is used to format the data in a way that is consistent with most hex viewers.

Coding the view

Now that you've completed the document, it's time to code the view. To get started, you'll need to define a bunch of variables that are going to be used to output the data onto the view's client area. To do that, open the view's header file (HexViewerView.h) and add the following variables (shown in bold). (The CFont and LOGFONT elements are explained in Chapter 8.)

```
class CHexViewerView : public CScrollView
{
...

protected:
 CFont*  m_pFont;
 LOGFONT m_logfont;
 int m_nPointSize;
 int m_nPageHeight;
 int m_nPageWidth;
```

Update the view's construct to initialize these variables and specifically to create the LOGFONT and CFont objects. You'll also notice that you're using the system font in order to display the data. You can either change that to a fancier font now or wait until you've learned more about menus and fonts (Chapters 4 and 8, respectively) and add a menu option to allow the user to specify their own font.

```
CHexViewerView::CHexViewerView()
{
  memset(&m_logfont, 0, sizeof(m_logfont));
  m_nPointSize = 120;
  _tcscpy(m_logfont.lfFaceName, _T("Fixedsys"));

  CWindowDC dc(NULL);
  m_logfont.lfHeight = ::MulDiv(m_nPointSize,
    dc.GetDeviceCaps(LOGPIXELSY), 720);
  m_logfont.lfPitchAndFamily = FIXED_PITCH;

  m_pFont = new CFont;
  m_pFont->CreateFontIndirect(&m_logfont);
}
```

For the cleanup code, modify the view's destructor so that it looks like the following when finished.

```
CHexViewerView::~CHexViewerView()
{
  if (m_pFont != NULL)
  {
    delete m_pFont;
  }
}
```

Upon creation and display of a view, the framework always calls the view class's virtual OnInitialUpdate function. This is where you will put the majority of your view's initialization code. One question that would normally arise for programmers new to MFC is: When do I initialize something in the view's constructor and when do I initialize it in the OnInitialUpdate function? The answer to that is a bit subjective, but here's the pattern I follow in my development. If, in order to perform the initialization, the view's underlying window needs to have been created, then the work must be done in OnInitialUpdate because the window doesn't exist at the point of class construction. In almost any other case, I tend to do the initialization in the constructor. The initialization for this particular view falls into the former category and therefore must be done in the OnInitialUpdate function.

You'll remember that when you created this project, you derived the CHexViewerView class from CScrollView. You'll also recall that I said at the time that the CScrollView made creating a scrollable view easier. Here's one example of that. To set the scroll size so that the user can easily determine how much data the view points to, you need only call the CScrollView::SetScrollSize member function, passing to it the mapping mode and the size of the document. Because you're displaying text, that means specifying the MM_TEXT value, and because the document exposes a public member variable containing the file size (m_lFileSize), this is a snap. Simply modify the view's OnInitialUpdate function as follows (replacing the default sizing code).

```
void CHexViewerView::OnInitialUpdate()
{
  CHexViewerDoc* pDoc = GetDocument();
  ASSERT_VALID(pDoc);

  CSize sizeTotal(0, pDoc->m_lFileSize);
  SetScrollSizes(MM_TEXT, sizeTotal);

  CScrollView::OnInitialUpdate();
}
```

You're almost done, and nothing has been too terribly difficult. Now we need to write the code to actually draw the data onto the client area. This is typically done in the view's OnDraw virtual function, which is called by the framework when the view needs to perform screen display, printing, or print preview. Because almost any drawing involves at least a basic knowledge of GDI (which is covered in Chapter 8) I won't go into a lot of detail here on some issues. However, it is important to at least see how some of this works to get a feeling of satisfaction that you made this cool little demo work. Therefore, locate the view's virtual OnDraw and modify it as shown in Listing 2-1.

The important thing to remember as you read this code is that you can't just dump all the data into the view and expect MFC to scroll it for you. Although it might look that way to the user, it doesn't work that way. Instead, you display a page (or portion of a page) at a time, and you're responsible for determining what part of the file to display based on how much the user has scrolled.

The first thing you do is to retrieve the document object via the virtual GetDocument function. You need this object because the document defines the function (ReadLine) to read data from the user's selected file.

After declaring a few local variables to control how the data is rendered, you then call the CScrollView::GetScrollPosition function.

From there, you call GetClientRect to determine how large the view's client area is on which the file's data will be rendered.

After that, a call to the helper function, MeasureFontHeight, enables you to determine how tall each line will be.

Based on where the user has scrolled to (returned from GetScrollPosition) and the size of the client area and the height of a line of text, you then calculate a starting line and an ending line. Once you've done that, a simple for loop can be used to retrieve each line of data from the document via its ReadLine function.

When the data is returned, a simple call to DrawText is used to render that text onto the view.

Listing 2-1: **The HexViewer OnDraw override**

```
void CHexViewerView::OnDraw(CDC* pDC)
{
CHexViewerDoc* pDoc = GetDocument();
ASSERT_VALID(pDoc);

CString strRender;
CFont*  pOldFont;
CSize   ScrolledSize;
int     nStartLine;
int     nHeight;
CRect   ScrollRect;
CPoint  ScrolledPos = GetScrollPosition();

CRect   rectClient;
GetClientRect(&rectClient);

// Determine how tall each line is
pOldFont = pDC->SelectObject(m_pFont);
nHeight = MeasureFontHeight(m_pFont, pDC);
```

Continued

Listing 2-1 *(continued)*

```
// Find a starting line based on scrolling
// and current client size
ScrolledSize = CSize(rectClient.Width(),
 rectClient.Height());
ScrollRect = CRect(rectClient.left, ScrolledPos.y,
 rectClient.right,
 ScrolledSize.cy + ScrolledPos.y);
nStartLine = ScrolledPos.y/16;

// Verify that we are drawing where we should
ScrollRect.top = nStartLine*nHeight;

if (pDoc->m_pFile != NULL)
{
 int nLine;
 for (nLine = nStartLine;
      ScrollRect.top < ScrollRect.bottom;
      nLine++)
 {
  if (!pDoc->ReadLine(strRender, 16, nLine*16))
   break;

  nHeight = pDC->DrawText(strRender, -1,
          &ScrollRect,
          DT_TOP | DT_NOPREFIX | DT_SINGLELINE);
          ScrollRect.top += nHeight;
 }
}

pDC->SelectObject(pOldFont);
}
```

Finally, add the following help function to the view that is used to measure the font height in pixels for the current device context (DC). Notice that the technique here involves passing a −1 as the value for the string length. This means that nothing is actually drawn. However, the DrawText function still returns the height of the specified text.

```
int CHexViewerView::MeasureFontHeight(CFont* pFont, CDC* pDC)
{
 // how tall is the identified font in the identified DC?

 CFont* pOldFont;
 pOldFont = pDC->SelectObject(pFont);

 CRect rectDummy;
 CString strRender = _T("1234567890ABCDEF- ");
 int nHeight = pDC->DrawText(strRender, -1, rectDummy,
```

```
        DT_TOP | DT_SINGLELINE | DT_CALCRECT);
    pDC->SelectObject(pOldFont);

    return nHeight;
}
```

Finally, build and test your very own hex editor. Figure 2-4 shows an example of running my version and opening the HexViewer.exe file.

Note   You'll learn how to add printing and print preview to this application in Chapter 15.

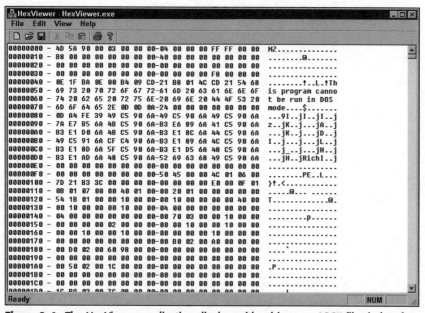

Figure 2-4: The HexViewer application displays either binary or ASCII files in hex format.

Summary

Most MFC applications are based on the document/view model. The document, an abstract object, represents the application's data and typically corresponds to the contents of a file. The view, in turn, provides a presentation of the data and accepts user interface events.

Your applications derive their document classes from the MFC-provided CDocument class. The CDocument class encapsulates much of the basic functionality of a document object. More sophisticated applications generally rely on collection classes to implement the set of objects that comprise a document.

You derive view classes from the MFC CView base class. View windows that CView objects represent are child windows. In an SDI project, the parent window is the main frame window; in a MDI project, the parent window is the controlling MDI child window. A view object, in addition to containing member variables that represent view-specific settings (such as zoom and rotation settings), often implements a current selection. The current selection is the set of document objects that the user has designated or selected within the current view for further manipulation. As with documents, most complex applications use collection classes to manage the current selection.

Finally, document, views, and frame windows all handle messages. Your decision about which of the three classes should handle a particular message is based upon that message's effects.

✦   ✦   ✦

MDI Applications

In Chapter 2, you learned about MFC's document/view model and how it enables the creation of single document interface (SDI) applications. This sets the table nicely for this chapter's topic — multidocument interface (MDI) applications. As you'll soon see, an MDI application is one that allows the user to have multiple files open concurrently with one or more views being used to display each document's data. In fact, most of today's most popular applications are built around the MDI interface, which affords the user more flexibility.

In this chapter, you'll begin by learning about the various MDI classes and how to use them to design and develop your applications. Once I've covered these basics, you'll learn how to program MDI applications, not only to create multiple views of the same document, but also to create multiple views of multiple documents. Once you see how this is done, you'll use this knowledge by developing a very simple MDI paint application that enables you to create and draw as many shapes as memory will allow. Finally, you'll learn about *splitter windows,* a powerful feature that enables you to split a single view into two or more parts so that the user can scroll each part of the view independently.

Comparing MDI and SDI Architectures

Because you just learned about the SDI architecture, it might be helpful to start by explaining how the MDI and SDI architectures differ. The first difference I'll point out is the way frame windows are defined. Take a look at the MDI class layout in Figure 3-1.

If you compare this figure to the SDI architecture class layout figure in Chapter 2 (2-1), you'll see a couple of important differences.

First, whereas a frame window is still used to contain the menu, toolbar, and status bars, it is always derived from the `CMDIFrameWnd` class and it is not used as the frame for the views. Rather, this frame window is only used as the application frame. Second, the frame windows of the MDI views in an MDI application are always derived from `CMDIChildWnd`.

By default, when you use the AppWizard to create an MDI application, the class name for the application frame is called `CMainFrame` (as it is with an SDI application). The default frame window class used to enclose the views in an MDI application is called the `CChildFrame` class.

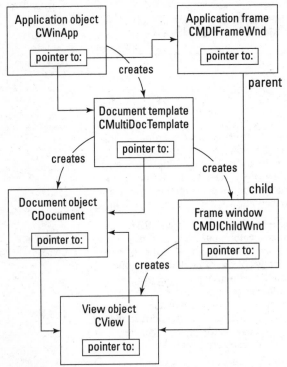

Figure 3-1: The basic class structure layout of the MDI architecture

Combinations of Documents, Views, and Frames

The standard relationship among a document, its view(s), and its frame window(s) is described in a relatively straightforward manner: a one-to-many relationship between documents and views, and a one-to-one relationship between each view and a frame window. Many applications need to support only a single document type (but possibly enable the user to open multiple documents of that type) with a single view on the document and only one frame window per document. However, some applications may need to alter one or more of those defaults — creating multiple views on a single document type, single views on multiple document types, or multiple views on multiple document types. It is worthwhile to consider the different situations that you may encounter when working with documents and views and how you should design your applications to respond appropriately.

Working with multiple document types

Whether you create an SDI or an MDI application, AppWizard creates only a single document class for you. In some cases, though, you may need to support more than one document type. For example, your application may need both worksheet and chart documents. Your application will probably represent each document type with its own document class and typically by its own view class or classes as well. When the user chooses the File ⇨ New option, the framework displays a dialog box that lists the application's supported document types. After the user chooses a document type, the application creates a document of that type. The application then manages each document type with its own document-template object.

To create extra document classes within your own applications, select Project ⇨ Add Class. From there, select the MFC Class template and choose either CDocument or COLEDocument as the base class. To inform the framework about your extra document class, you must then add a second call to AddDocTemplate in your application class' InitInstance member function. For example, an application with two documents would include code within its InitInstance member function similar to the following:

```
CMultiDocTemplate* pDocTemplate;
pDocTemplate = new CMultiDocTemplate(
  IDR_OPAINTTYPE,
  RUNTIME_CLASS(CSample1Doc),
  RUNTIME_CLASS(CMDIChildWnd),  // standard MDI child frame
  RUNTIME_CLASS(CSample1View));
AddDocTemplate(pDocTemplate);
pDocTemplate = new CMultiDocTemplate(
  IDR_OPAINTTYPE,
  RUNTIME_CLASS(CSample2Doc),
  RUNTIME_CLASS(CMDIChildWnd),  // standard MDI child frame
  RUNTIME_CLASS(CSample2View));
AddDocTemplate(pDocTemplate);
```

Using multiple views with documents

As you have learned, many documents require only a single view. However, you also learned that the MFC document/view model enables your applications to support more than one view of a single document. In fact, you can support as many different views on a single document as your application might require. To help you implement multiple views, a document object keeps a list of its views, provides member functions for adding and removing views, and supplies the UpdateAllViews member function for letting multiple views know when the document's data has changed. MFC supports three common user interfaces that you might design within your applications that implement interfaces requiring multiple views on the same document. These three models are described in the following list:

✦ Your application might enable the user to view objects of the same class, each in a separate MDI document frame window (an MDI child window, to be specific). The user would use the New Window option on the Window menu (that the AppWizard supplies automatically within the IDR_MAINFRAME menu resource) to open a second frame with a view of the same document. Then the user could use the two frames to view different portions of the document simultaneously. MFC's default implementation of the New Window option duplicates the initial frame window and view attached to the document (that is, the frame window and view that you attach to the document through its CDocumentTemplate object). Figure 3-2 shows the multiple frame window on a document model.

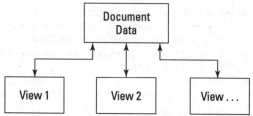

Figure 3-2: The multiple views on the same document model

✦ Your application might enable the user to view objects of the same class in the same document frame window. The application would then use splitter windows to split the view space of a single document window into multiple separate views of the document. The framework, in conjunction with the splitter window, creates multiple view objects from the same view class. You will learn more about the process that splitter windows use to create multiple views and how to implement the CSplitterWnd class later in this chapter. Figure 3-3 shows the splitter windows model that implements only a single view.

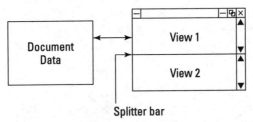

Figure 3-3: The splitter windows document model

✦ Your application might enable the user to view objects of different classes in a single frame window. In this third model (which is a common variation of the splitter window model), the application's multiple views of the document share a single frame window. The application and the framework construct the views from different classes (all of which you derive from CView or one of its derivatives). In this model, each view that you construct provides the user with a different way to view the same document. For example, one view might show a spreadsheet in normal mode while the other view shows the spreadsheet with all the formulas displayed. You would then use a splitter control (which you create with CSplitterWnd) to enable the user to adjust the relative sizes of the views. Figure 3-4 shows the splitter windows model variation that uses multiple views.

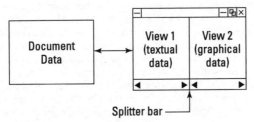

Figure 3-4: The splitter windows model variation

The framework provides the three models to use within your application through the New Window option on the Window menu for the first model and, for the second two models, the CSplitterWnd class. The three models that this section describes are the simplest possible implementations; using the principles that these three models define, you can implement other models using these three models as your starting point.

Understanding the CMDIFrameWnd class

The CMDIFrameWnd class provides the functionality of a Windows multiple document interface (MDI) frame window, along with member functions that you will use within your applications to manage the window. To create a useful MDI frame window for your multiple document interface application, you must derive a class for the main frame window from CMDIFrameWnd. After you derive the class, you add member variables to the derived class to store data specific to your application (but not data specific to an individual document). In addition, you must implement message handler member functions and a message map in the derived class to specify what happens when messages are directed to the window, either by the operating system or by the document template.

You can construct an MDI frame window in two ways: by calling either the Create member function or the LoadFrame member function of CFrameWnd. However, before you call Create or LoadFrame, you must use the C++ new operator to construct the frame window object on the heap. Before calling the Create member function, you can also use the AfxRegisterWnd-Class global function to register the window class and set the icon and class styles for the frame. You should use the Create member function to pass the frame's creation parameters as immediate arguments.

On the other hand, the LoadFrame member function requires fewer arguments than the Create member function and instead retrieves most of its default values from resources that you create within the project, including the frame's caption, icon, accelerator table, and menu. To be accessed by LoadFrame (and loaded into the definition for the new window), all these resources must have the same resource ID (for example, the MFC default resource ID IDR_MAINFRAME or any other resource ID such as IDR_PARENTFRAME).

The CMDIFrameWnd class inherits much of its default implementation from CFrameWnd. The CMDIFrameWnd class has the following additional features that it does not inherit from CFrameWnd:

✦ An MDI frame window manages the child windows within the application, repositioning the child window in conjunction with the user's actions on the child window's control bars and the application window's scroll bars. The MDI client window is the direct parent of every MDI child frame window within the application. The WS_HSCROLL and WS_VSCROLL window styles specified on a CMDIFrameWnd apply to the MDI client window rather than the main frame window so the user can scroll the MDI client area (in other words, the scroll bars will move the child windows within the MDI client area, and not the child windows' client areas themselves).

✦ An MDI frame window owns a default menu that it uses as the menu bar when no MDI child window is active. When an MDI child window is active, the MFC framework automatically replaces the MDI frame window's menu bar with the MDI child window's menu bar.

✦ An MDI frame window works in conjunction with the currently active MDI child window, if there is one. For instance, the currently active MDI child window receives command messages before the MDI frame window.

✦ An MDI frame window has a default implementation of ID_WINDOW_NEW, which creates a new frame and view on the current document. An application can override these default command implementations to customize MDI window handling.

Do not use the C++ `delete` operator to destroy a `CMDIFrameWnd` window object—if you do, it may result in bad reference counts or memory leaks within your application. Instead, you should use the `CWnd::DestroyWindow` member function. The `CFrameWnd` implementation of the `PostNcDestroy` member function deletes the C++ object when the application destroys the window. When the user closes the `CMDIFrameWnd` window object, the default `OnClose` handler function calls the `DestroyWindow` member function (which, in turn, calls the `DestroyWindow` member function for each of the currently open `CMDIChildWnd` window objects).

Although MFC derives the `CMDIFrameWnd` class from the `CFrameWnd` class, you do not need to use the `DECLARE_DYNCREATE` macro when you declare a frame window class that you derive from `CMDIFrameWnd`.

Understanding the CMDIChildWnd class

The `CMDIChildWnd` class provides the functionality of a Windows multiple document interface (MDI) child window, along with members for managing the window. An MDI child window looks much like a typical frame window, except that the MDI child window appears inside an MDI frame window rather than on the desktop. An MDI child window does not have a menu bar of its own but instead shares the menu of the MDI frame window. The framework automatically changes the MDI frame window's menu bar to represent the currently active MDI child window's menu bar.

To create a useful MDI child window for your application, you must derive a class from `CMDIChildWnd` (or, if you do not intend to customize the window's actions, you can simply use the default `CMDIChildWnd` class). You then add member variables to the derived class to store data specific to the document that the child window will be associated with within the application. Furthermore, you must implement message handler member functions and a message map in the derived class to specify what happens when messages are directed to the window. (Otherwise, MFC will use the `CMDIChildWnd` class's default handlers to respond to messages the window receives.) There are three ways to construct an MDI child window:

✦ Directly, using the `Create` member function

✦ Directly, using the `LoadFrame` member function

✦ Indirectly, through a document template

Just as with the `CMDIFrameWnd` class, before you call the `Create` or `LoadFrame` member functions to create a `CMDIChildWnd` object, you must use the C++ `new` operator to construct the frame window object on the heap. Before you call the `Create` member function, you can also use the `AfxRegisterWndClass` global function to register the window class and set the icon and class styles for the frame. As with the `CMDIFrameWnd` class, you should use the `Create` member function to pass the frame's creation parameters as immediate arguments.

Also similar to the `CMDIFrameWnd` class, the `LoadFrame` member function requires fewer arguments than the `Create` member function does and instead retrieves most of its default values from resources, including the frame's caption, icon, accelerator table, and menu. To be accessible by `LoadFrame`, all these resources must have the same resource ID (such as `IDR_CHILDWND`).

When a `CMDIChildWnd` object contains views and documents, they are created indirectly by the framework instead of directly by the programmer. The `CDocTemplate` object orchestrates the creation of the frame, the creation of the containing views, and the connection of the views to the appropriate document. The parameters of the CDocTemplate constructor specify the CRuntimeClass of the three classes involved (document, view, and frame). A CRuntime-Class object is used by the framework to dynamically create new frames when specified by the user (for example, by selecting File ⇨ New or the MDI frame's Window ⇨ New option).

The CMDIChildWnd class inherits much of its default implementation from CFrameWnd. However, the CMDIChildWnd class has the following additional features beyond those it derives from CFrameWnd:

✦ In conjunction with the CMultiDocTemplate class, multiple CMDIChildWnd objects from the same document template share the same menu, saving Windows system resources.

✦ As discussed in the previous section, the currently active MDI child window menu bar entirely replaces the MDI frame window's menu bar, and the caption of the currently active MDI child window is added to the MDI frame window's caption.

Do not use the C++ delete operator to destroy a CMDIChildWnd window object. Doing so may cause reference counter errors. Instead, you should use the CWnd::DestroyWindow member function. The CFrameWnd implementation of the PostNcDestroy member function deletes the C++ object when the application destroys the window. When the user closes the child window, the default OnClose handler function calls the DestroyWindow member function.

Unlike a frame window class that you derive from the CMDIFrameWnd class, a frame window class that you derive from CMDIChildWnd must be declared with the DECLARE_DYNCREATE macro for the RUNTIME_CLASS creation mechanism to work correctly.

Understanding the CMultiDocTemplate class

Much as the CSingleDocTemplate class defines a document template that implements the single document interface, the CMultiDocTemplate class defines a document template that implements the multiple document interface (MDI). An MDI application uses the main frame window as a workspace in which the user can open zero or more document frame windows, each of which displays a document. As you learned in Chapter 2, a document template defines the relationships among three types of classes:

✦ A document class, which you derive from CDocument or COLEDocument.

✦ A view class, which displays data from the document class that you associate with the template. You can derive this class from CView, CScrollView, CFormView, CEditView, or one of the other CView-based classes. You can also use CEditView directly.

✦ A frame window class, which contains the view. For an MDI document template, you can derive this class from CMDIChildWnd, or if you do not need to customize the behavior of the document frame windows, you can use CMDIChildWnd directly without deriving your own class.

An MDI application can support more than one type of document, and documents of different types can be open at the same time. Your application has one document template for each document type that it supports. For example, if your MDI application supports both spreadsheets and text documents, the application will have two CMultiDocTemplate objects.

The application uses the document templates when the user creates a new document. If the application supports more than one type of document, the framework gets the names of the supported document types from the document templates and displays them in a list in the File New dialog box. Once the user has selected a document type, the application creates a document class object, a frame window object, and a view object, and attaches them to each other.

Note   You do not need to call any member functions of `CMultiDocTemplate` except the constructor. The MFC framework handles `CMultiDocTemplate` objects internally.

The overhead of using the CDocument classes

You generally use the document/view architecture when you design your applications. In most applications, in fact, you will use some combination of documents and dialog boxes to design the application interface. One of the most significant benefits of using the document/view architecture is that the `CDocument` class (and its derivatives) is so naturally thin. A single `CDocument` object incurs only a small amount of overhead by itself, plus the small overhead of `CDocument`'s base classes. Both of `CDocument`'s base classes are small.

In fact, the `CDocument` class, without allowance for your own custom data that you will place within each document object, contains only seven members that the MFC framework always places within the class. The `CDocument` class contains the following framework-defined members (all of which the framework uses internally):

✦ Two `CString` objects

✦ Three `BOOL` variables

✦ One `CDocTemplate` pointer

✦ One `CPtrList` object, which contains a list of the document's views

In addition, during execution, the document requires time to create the document object, its view objects, a frame window, and a document template object. On today's faster computers, this time is almost negligible.

MDI applications

Now that you have reviewed the MDI application's components, and noted their differences from the SDI application's components, you should be able to tell that working with an MDI application is essentially the same as working with an SDI application as you did in Chapter 2. In fact, the only significant differences between the two application types are in the differences in frame windows, the need to define additional resources for each of the child windows, and the greater power and flexibility that MDI applications provide. Managing the various documents and views, however, remains fundamentally the same as it was when you were working with only a single document and view. For example, to save the data in a given document, you still use the `Serialize` member function, just as you did in the SDI application, similar to the following:

```
void CSampleObjDoc::Serialize(CArchive& ar)
{
    m_Objects.Serialize(ar);
    if (ar.IsStoring())
    {
        ar << m_size;
    }
    else
```

```
    {
        ar > m_size;
    }
}
```

The difference, of course, is that you have a separate `Serialize` member function for each document you create, and each `Serialize` member function stores and retrieves the data specific to that document.

The PaintObj Program

This demo application program can be found on the book's Web site and is built to use an SDI class, `CPaintobjDoc`. However, the application uses a `CMultiDocTemplate` and a `CMDIChildWnd` to create an MDI application that enables the user to perform simple painting within multiple windows.

You can rebuild the program by loading the `CPaintobjDoc` project file, or just run the `Paintobj.exe` program using Explorer. Figure 3-5 shows the program during execution. Listing 3-1 provides highlights of the program code within the `Paintobj.cpp` and `Paintvw.cpp` source files.

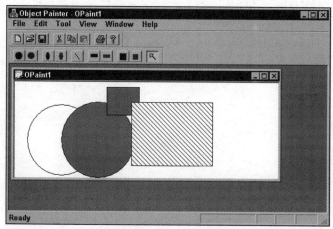

Figure 3-5: The Paintobj.exe program during execution

Listing 3-1: Highlights of the Paintobj.cpp and Paintvw.cpp source code for the Paintobj.exe program

```
// Paintobj.cpp : Defines the class behaviors
// for the application.
//
// CPaintobjApp initialization

BOOL CPaintobjApp::InitInstance()
```

Continued

Listing 3-1 *(continued)*

```
{
    // Standard initialization
    Enable3dControls();
    LoadStdProfileSettings();  // Load standard INI file
                               // options

    // Register the application's document templates, which
    // serve as the connection between documents,
    // frame windows, and views.
    CMultiDocTemplate* pDocTemplate;
    pDocTemplate = new CMultiDocTemplate(
        IDR_OPAINTTYPE,
        RUNTIME_CLASS(CPaintobjDoc),
        RUNTIME_CLASS(CMDIChildWnd),  // MDI child frame
        RUNTIME_CLASS(CPaintobjView));
    AddDocTemplate(pDocTemplate);

    // Create main MDI Frame window.
    CMainFrame* pMainFrame = new CMainFrame;
    if (!pMainFrame->LoadFrame(IDR_MAINFRAME))
        return FALSE;
    m_pMainWnd = pMainFrame;

    // Enable DDE Execute open.
    EnableShellOpen();
    RegisterShellFileTypes();

    // Simple command line parsing
    if (m_lpCmdLine[0] == '\0')
    {
        // Create a new (empty) document.
        OnFileNew();
    }
    else
    {
        // Open an existing document.
        OpenDocumentFile(m_lpCmdLine);
    }

    // Enable drag/drop open.
    m_pMainWnd->DragAcceptFiles();

    // The main window has been initialized,
    // so show and update it.
    pMainFrame->ShowWindow(m_nCmdShow);
    pMainFrame->UpdateWindow();

    return TRUE;
```

```
    }

///////////////////////////////////////////////////////////
// paintvw.cpp : implementation of the CPaintobjView class
//

#include "stdafx.h"
#include "paintobj.h"
#include "mainfrm.h"

#include "paintdoc.h"
#include "paintvw.h"

#ifdef _DEBUG
#undef THIS_FILE
static char BASED_CODE THIS_FILE[] = __FILE__;
#endif

///////////////////////////////////////////////////////////
// CPaintobjView

IMPLEMENT_DYNCREATE(CPaintobjView, CScrollView)

BEGIN_MESSAGE_MAP(CPaintobjView, CScrollView)
    //{{AFX_MSG_MAP(CPaintobjView)
    ON_WM_LBUTTONDOWN()
    ON_WM_LBUTTONUP()
    ON_WM_MOUSEMOVE()
    ON_COMMAND(ID_VIEW_SCROLL, OnViewScroll)
    ON_UPDATE_COMMAND_UI(ID_VIEW_SCROLL, OnUpdateViewScroll)
    ON_UPDATE_COMMAND_UI(ID_VIEW_ZOOMFIT, OnUpdateViewZoomfit)
    ON_COMMAND(ID_VIEW_ZOOMFIT, OnViewZoomfit)
    ON_UPDATE_COMMAND_UI(ID_EDIT_COPY, OnUpdateEditCopy)
    ON_UPDATE_COMMAND_UI(ID_EDIT_CUT, OnUpdateEditCut)
    ON_COMMAND(ID_EDIT_CUT, OnEditCut)
    //}}AFX_MSG_MAP
    // Standard printing commands
    ON_COMMAND(ID_FILE_PRINT, CScrollView::OnFilePrint)
    ON_COMMAND(ID_FILE_PRINT_PREVIEW,
                CScrollView::OnFilePrintPreview)
END_MESSAGE_MAP()

///////////////////////////////////////////////////////////
// CPaintobjView construction/destruction

CPaintobjView::CPaintobjView()
{
    CWinApp* pApp = AfxGetApp();

    m_bZoomMode = FALSE;
    m_bTracking = FALSE;
```

Continued

Listing 3-1 *(continued)*

```
   m_hcurArrow = pApp->LoadStandardCursor(IDC_ARROW);
   m_hcurCross = pApp->LoadStandardCursor(IDC_CROSS);
   m_pActive = NULL;

   ASSERT(m_hcurArrow != NULL);
   ASSERT(m_hcurCross != NULL);

   // Win95 has IDC_SIZEALL, WinNT 3.51/4.0 has IDC_SIZE
   m_hcurSize = pApp->LoadStandardCursor(IDC_SIZEALL);
   if (m_hcurSize == NULL)
      pApp->LoadStandardCursor(IDC_SIZE);
   ASSERT(m_hcurSize != NULL);
}

CPaintobjView::~CPaintobjView()
 {
 }


/////////////////////////////////////////////////////////////
// CPaintobjView drawing

void CPaintobjView::OnDraw(CDC* pDC)
 {
   CPaintobjDoc* pDoc = GetDocument();
   ASSERT_VALID(pDoc);

   POSITION pos;
   pos = pDoc->m_Objects.GetHeadPosition();
   while (pos != NULL)
    {
      CPainted* pPainter =
          (CPainted*) pDoc->m_Objects.GetNext(pos);
      ASSERT(pPainter->IsKindOf(RUNTIME_CLASS(CPainted)));

      if (m_pActive != pPainter)
         pPainter->Draw(pDC);
      else
         pPainter->DrawSelected(pDC);
    }
 }


/////////////////////////////////////////////////////////////
// CPaintobjView diagnostics

#ifdef _DEBUG
void CPaintobjView::AssertValid() const
 {
   CScrollView::AssertValid();
```

```
   }

void CPaintobjView::Dump(CDumpContext& dc) const
 {
    CScrollView::Dump(dc);
 }

CPaintobjDoc* CPaintobjView::GetDocument()
// nondebug version is inline
 {
  ASSERT(m_pDocument->IsKindOf(RUNTIME_CLASS(CPaintobjDoc)));

  return (CPaintobjDoc*)m_pDocument;
 }
#endif //_DEBUG

//////////////////////////////////////////////////////////////
// CPaintobjView message handlers

void CPaintobjView::OnLButtonDown(UINT nFlags, CPoint point)
 {
    CPaintobjDoc* pDoc = (CPaintobjDoc*) GetDocument();

    CClientDC ClientDC(this);
    OnPrepareDC(&ClientDC);
    ClientDC.DPtoLP(&point);

    if (pDoc->m_pSelectedTool == NULL)
     {
        POSITION    pos;
        CPainted*   pPainted;
        CPainted*   pHit;
        pos = pDoc->m_Objects.GetHeadPosition();

        pHit = NULL;
        while (pos != NULL)
         {
            pPainted = (CPainted*) pDoc->m_Objects.GetNext(pos);
            if (pPainted->IsHit(point))
             {
                pHit = pPainted;
                break;
             }
         }
        if (pHit != NULL)
         {
            if (m_pActive != NULL)
             {
                CRect rectInvalid;

                m_pActive->GetBoundingRect(&rectInvalid);
```

Continued

Listing 3-1 *(continued)*

```
                rectInvalid.InflateRect(1, 1);
                InvalidateRect(&rectInvalid);
              }
            m_pActive = pHit;
            m_pActive->DrawSelected(&ClientDC);
          }
        return;
      }
    SetCapture();
    m_bTracking = TRUE;
    pDoc->m_pSelectedTool->OnDown(point);
    CScrollView::OnLButtonDown(nFlags, point);
  }

void CPaintobjView::OnLButtonUp(UINT nFlags, CPoint point)
  {
    CPaintobjDoc* pDoc = (CPaintobjDoc*) GetDocument();
    ASSERT(pDoc != NULL);

    if (m_bTracking)
      {
        ASSERT(pDoc->m_pSelectedTool != NULL);
        pDoc->m_pSelectedTool->OnUp(point, this);

        CRect rect;
        pDoc->m_pSelectedTool->GetBoundingRect(&rect);
        pDoc->ExpandBounds(&rect);
        pDoc->m_Objects.AddTail(pDoc->m_pSelectedTool);
        pDoc->m_pSelectedTool = NULL;
        pDoc->m_nSelectedTool = ID_TOOL_SELECTOR;
        m_bTracking = FALSE;
        ReleaseCapture();
        CMainFrame* pMain =
            (CMainFrame*) AfxGetApp()->m_pMainWnd;
        pMain->ClearPositionText();
      }

    CScrollView::OnLButtonUp(nFlags, point);
  }

void CPaintobjView::OnMouseMove(UINT nFlags, CPoint point)
  {
    CClientDC ClientDC(this);
    OnPrepareDC(&ClientDC);
    ClientDC.DPtoLP(&point);

    CPaintobjDoc* pDoc = (CPaintobjDoc*) GetDocument();
    ASSERT(pDoc != NULL);
    if (pDoc->m_pSelectedTool == NULL)
```

```
    {
      ::SetCursor(m_hcurArrow);
      return;
    }
    ::SetCursor(m_hcurCross);
    if (!m_bTracking)
      return;

    CMainFrame* pMain = (CMainFrame*) AfxGetApp()->m_pMainWnd;
    pMain->SetPositionText(point);
    pDoc->m_pSelectedTool->DragDraw(&ClientDC, point);
    CScrollView::OnMouseMove(nFlags, point);
}

void CPaintobjView::OnInitialUpdate()
{
    CScrollView::OnInitialUpdate();

    CPaintobjDoc* pDoc = GetDocument();
    ASSERT_VALID(pDoc);
    CSize siz;
    pDoc->GetBounds(&siz);

    m_bZoomMode = FALSE;
    SetScrollSizes(MM_TEXT, siz);
    SetScrollSizes(MM_TEXT, siz);
}

void CPaintobjView::OnViewScroll()
{
    CPaintobjDoc* pDoc = GetDocument();
    ASSERT_VALID(pDoc);

    CSize siz;
    pDoc->GetBounds(&siz);
    m_bZoomMode = FALSE;
    SetScrollSizes(MM_TEXT, siz);
}

void CPaintobjView::OnUpdateViewScroll(CCmdUI* pCmdUI)
{
    pCmdUI->SetCheck(!m_bZoomMode);
}

void CPaintobjView::OnUpdateViewZoomfit(CCmdUI* pCmdUI)
{
    CPaintobjDoc* pDoc = GetDocument();
    ASSERT_VALID(pDoc);

    POSITION pos;
    pos = pDoc->m_Objects.GetHeadPosition();
    pCmdUI->SetCheck(m_bZoomMode);
```

Continued

Listing 3-1 *(continued)*

```
    pCmdUI->Enable(pos != NULL);
  }

void CPaintobjView::OnViewZoomfit()
  {
    CPaintobjDoc* pDoc = GetDocument();
    ASSERT_VALID(pDoc);

    CSize siz;
    pDoc->GetBounds(&siz);
    m_bZoomMode = TRUE;
    SetScaleToFitSize(siz);
  }

void CPaintobjView::OnUpdateEditCopy(CCmdUI* pCmdUI)
  {
    pCmdUI->Enable(m_pActive != NULL);
  }

void CPaintobjView::OnUpdateEditCut(CCmdUI* pCmdUI)
  {
    pCmdUI->Enable(m_pActive != NULL);
  }

void CPaintobjView::OnEditCut()
  {
    ASSERT(m_pActive != NULL);

    CPaintobjDoc* pDoc = GetDocument();
    ASSERT_VALID(pDoc);
    POSITION    pos;
    CRect       rectUpdate;
    CPainted*   pPainted;
    BOOL      bFoundIt = FALSE;
    pos = pDoc->m_Objects.GetHeadPosition();

    while (pos != NULL)
      {
        pPainted = (CPainted*) pDoc->m_Objects.GetAt(pos);
        if (pPainted == m_pActive)
         {
           bFoundIt = TRUE;
           break;
         }
        pDoc->m_Objects.GetNext(pos);
      }
    ASSERT(bFoundIt == TRUE);
    if (bFoundIt == TRUE)
```

```
    {
        pDoc->m_Objects.RemoveAt(pos);
        m_pActive->GetBoundingRect(&rectUpdate);
        rectUpdate.InflateRect(1, 1);
        delete m_pActive;
        m_pActive = NULL;
        InvalidateRect(&rectUpdate);
    }
    pDoc->RecalcBoundary();

    if (m_bZoomMode)
        OnViewZoomfit();
    else
        OnViewScroll();
    return;
}
```

Introducing Splitter Windows

In a splitter window, the window is, or can be, split into two or more scrollable panes. A splitter control (or *split box*) in the window frame next to the scroll bars enables the user to adjust the relative sizes of the window panes. Each pane is a view on the same document. In dynamic splitter windows, the views are generally of the same class. In static splitter windows, the views are more often of different classes. You implement splitter windows of both kinds with the CSplitterWnd class.

Dynamic splitter windows enable the user to split a window into multiple panes at will and then scroll different panes to see different parts of the document. The user can also unsplit the window to remove the additional views.

Static splitter windows start with the window split into multiple panes, each with a different purpose. For example, in the Visual C++ bitmap editor, the image window shows two panes side by side. The left pane displays an actual size image of the bitmap. The right pane displays a zoomed or magnified image of the same bitmap. The panes are separated by a *splitter bar* that the user can drag to change the relative sizes of the panes.

Until now, you've learned about applications that present only one main window for their user interface. For some applications, it's interesting or valuable to have two related sections of the application's document visible in the application. Applications that can potentially render wide ranges of information to the user are common candidates for this sort of user interface. Microsoft Excel, for example, enables you to split your view of a spreadsheet and independently scroll over each pane of the window (or over an entirely different portion of the sheet in each window).

Many of the applications that you will design, such as the PaintObj project just presented, could easily present more information than could possibly fit on one screen. Even though the application enables the user to scroll within the window, the user might be interested in seeing two sections of the window simultaneously that are too far apart to ever show in a single window on a screen. By enabling the user to split their view of the window, you can pack more information onto the screen in the same amount of space.

Unfortunately, painting this kind of window without MFC support is tiresome, to say the least. You have to run the paint code twice, essentially fooling it into believing that the window is smaller than it really is, transposing the coordinates painted into each half of the split. Thankfully, MFC provides a simple solution: the CSplitterWnd class. CSplitterWnd is a special window class provided by MFC to live inside your application's frame window. Before you learn how to incorporate a splitter window into the design of your application, it's valuable to briefly review the different types of splitter windows that are available.

Differentiating between splitter windows

Programmers generally call the CSplitterWnd class, and the windows it represents, splitters, so you should be aware of the different terms. Before you implement the CSplitterWnd class, it's worthwhile to take some time to think a little about the way a CSplitterWnd is used within your application and the semantic rules that must be true for the class to make any sense and work properly.

When users split a window, they might decide to add another pane in the window either horizontally or vertically. In other words, the splitter will have to request that another view be created to fill the area to the right of or below the divider. A user can also further divide a window, requiring three new views to be created immediately. This fills the area to the right, beneath, and to the bottom right of the existing window, creating a quartering effect.

The CSplitterWnd class is capable of doing all of this work, because it records contextual information about the document template during its own creation. This enables the splitter to know what document and which view class will be referenced by the new view windows. You can develop code to have the splitter generate different views for each pane in the window, or you can enable it to generate a new instance of the same view type used in the original window. You should first decide how you'd like the user to approach the splitter window in your application. As you learned earlier in this chapter, you have two general choices for your splitter windows: a dynamic splitter or a static splitter.

Specifics of the CSplitterWnd class

You use the CSplitterWnd class within your MFC applications to provide users with the functionality of a splitter window, a window that contains multiple panes. A pane is usually an application-specific object that you derive from CView, but it can be any CWnd object that has the appropriate child window ID.

You usually embed a CSplitterWnd object in a parent CFrameWnd or CMDIChildWnd object. Create a CSplitterWnd object using the following steps:

1. Embed a CSplitterWnd member variable in the parent frame.

2. Override the parent frame's CFrameWnd::OnCreateClient member function.

3. From within the overridden OnCreateClient member function, call the Create or CreateStatic member function of CSplitterWnd (depending on the splitter window type you intend to create).

Call the Create member function to create a dynamic splitter window. A dynamic splitter window typically is used to create and scroll a number of individual panes, or views, of the same document. The framework automatically creates an initial pane for the splitter; then the framework creates, resizes, and disposes of additional panes as the user operates the splitter window's controls. When you call Create, you specify a minimum row height and column width that determine when the panes are too small to be fully displayed. After you call `Create`, you can adjust these minimums by calling the `SetColumnInfo` and `SetRowInfo` member functions.

In addition, you can use the `SetColumnInfo` and `SetRowInfo` member functions to set an ideal width for a column and ideal height for a row. When the framework displays a splitter window, it first displays the parent frame and then the splitter window. The framework then lays out the panes in columns and rows according to their ideal dimensions, working from the upper-left to the lower-right corner of the splitter window's client area.

To create a static splitter window, use the `CreateStatic` member function. The user can change only the size of the panes, not their number or order, in a static splitter window. You must specifically create all the static splitter's panes when you create the static splitter. Make sure you create all the panes before the parent frame's `OnCreateClient` member function returns, or the framework won't display the window correctly.

The `CreateStatic` member function automatically initializes a static splitter with a minimum row height and column width of 0. After you call `CreateStatic`, adjust these minimums (just as you would with a dynamic splitter) by calling the `SetColumnInfo` and `SetRowInfo` member functions.

A splitter window supports special scroll bars (apart from the scroll bars that panes may have). These scroll bars are children of the `CSplitterWnd` object and are shared between the two panes. You create these special scroll bars when you create the splitter window. For example, a `CSplitterWnd` that has one row, two columns, and the `WS_VSCROLL` style displays a vertical scroll bar that is shared by the two panes. When the user moves the scroll bar, `WM_VSCROLL` messages are sent to both panes. When the panes set the scroll bar position, the shared scroll bar is set.

When creating either kind of splitter window, you must specify the maximum number of rows and columns that the splitter will manage. For a static splitter, panes must be created to fill all the rows and columns. For a dynamic splitter, the framework automatically creates the first pane when the application creates the `CSplitterWnd` object.

The maximum number of panes you can specify for static splitters is 16 rows by 16 columns. However, splitting a window into more than two panes generally is confusing to the user, and you are typically better served to create multiple views within multiple frame windows, between which the user switches back and forth. Microsoft's recommended configurations and usage for static splitters are as follows:

✦ One row × two columns for displaying two dissimilar panes side by side (each pane is longer than it is wide)

✦ Two rows × one column for displaying two dissimilar panes, one on top of the other (each pane is wider than it is long)

✦ Two rows × two columns for displaying similar panes, usually in four side-by-side squares (best for displaying graphical data)

The maximum number of panes you can specify for dynamic splitters is two rows by two columns. Microsoft's recommended configurations for dynamic splitters are as follows:

✦ One row × two columns for displaying columnar data

✦ Two rows × one column for displaying textual or other data

✦ Two rows × two columns for displaying grid or table-oriented data

More on dynamic splitters

As you learned earlier in this chapter, dynamic splitters enable users to split the window at their leisure. An application with dynamic splitters has small boxes, one above the vertical scroll bar and one to the left of the horizontal scroll bar. These can be dragged to split the window in one direction or the other: Figure 3-6 shows an application with a dynamic splitter, after the user has split the display into four window panes.

After dragging the box above the vertical bar down a little, the window splits and automatically creates another view. To set up this kind of splitter, you must declare an instance of `CSplitterWnd` in your application's frame window. For SDI applications, this would be the `CMainFrame` class, whereas for MDI applications, it would be within the `CMDIChildWnd` class for each view that implements dynamic splitter windows.

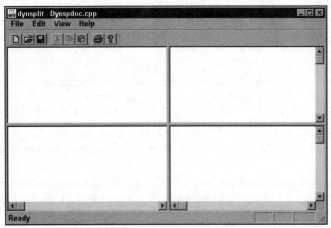

Figure 3-6: This application with dynamic splitter windows shows four user-split panes.

To initialize a dynamic splitter window, create the splitter window when the frame wants to create a client area of the frame window. Normally, the frame window simply creates the view and inserts it into the client area of the frame, but you can have the splitter create and insert itself into the frame. The splitter initializes a single view to populate itself and creates more views when the user splits the window's content.

To get your frame to create the splitter, install an override of the `OnCreateClient` function. For a dynamic splitter in an SDI application, the function just needs code similar to the following:

```
BOOL CMainFrame::OnCreateClient(LPCREATESTRUCT lpcs,
    CCreateContext* pContext)
{
    return m_wndSplitter.Create(this, 2, 2,
        CSize(1,1), pContext);
}
```

The `CSplitterWnd::Create` function accepts a few parameters. The first parameter is a pointer to the parent window of the splitter, which must be the frame. The next two parameters are the maximum number of rows and columns that the splitter supports. You can force it to disallow horizontal splits by passing 1 for the maximum number of rows or vertical splits by passing 1 for the maximum number of columns. Such a splitter window won't have a split box on the appropriate side of the window.

Dynamic splitters in MFC are incapable of supporting more than two rows and two columns. If you try to pass numbers larger than 2 to the Create function, MFC will ASSERT your debug build and not compile the application.

The value of CSize that you pass to the function causes the splitter to enforce lower size limits for the panes it creates. A size of one-by-one, as the previous code fragment uses, effectively makes the splitter allow any window size. If, because of its content, your view has problems painting in very small windows, you may want to enforce a lower limit on your splitter by passing a larger CSize to the creation function.

MFC won't enable your user to create a pane smaller than your passed CSize values. It snaps the pane shut when the user releases the mouse while dragging a new size. Debug builds of MFC display an appropriate warning within the debug window, such as the following:

```
Warning: split too small to create new pane.
```

Given the way all this works, with the splitter creating all of the views, there clearly must be a way for the splitter to know what view to create — and for the splitter to hook up the view to the right document. A pContext parameter gets passed about, from the OnCreateClient parameter to the Create function in CSplitterWnd. The pContext parameter points at the contextual information that tells the CSplitterWnd code who should handle the creation of the new view and its subsequent attachment to a document.

Using different views in dynamic panes

The code snippet from CChildFrame::OnCreateClient shown in the previous section results in a splitter that contains two instances of CView, registered in the document template that created the frame. You can use a different view in the extra panes of your splitter that enables you to convey information in a different manner — side by side with information from the same document in a different view or even a different document in a different view.

When the user creates new panes in a dynamic splitter window, MFC calls the CreateView member function of the CSplitterWnd class to perform the creation. Normally, CreateView simply creates the required view, based on the context information you pass to it through the pContext parameter. If pContext is NULL, the function determines what view is the currently active view and tries to create the same one.

You must derive your own class from CSplitterWnd if you want to have different views in the panes of your application's dynamic splitter window. You will have to override the CreateView function, creating the view of your choice. Fortunately, the overriding code is simple — all you must do is pass the call along to CSplitterWnd::CreateView, naming the RUNTIME_CLASS of the view class you wish to create for the splitter, as shown in the following code:

```
BOOL CMySplitterWnd::CreateView(int row, int col,
   CRuntimeClass* pViewClass, SIZE sizeInit,
   CCreateContext* pContext)
{
   if (row == 0 && col == 0)
   {
      return CSplitterWnd::CreateView(row, col,
         pViewClass, sizeInit, pContext);
```

```
      }
   else
      {
      return CSplitterWnd::CreateView(row, col,
         RUNTIME_CLASS(CSecondView), sizeInit, pContext);
      }
   }
```

The code first checks to determine if the view is being created at row 0, column 0 in the splitter. If this is the case, the splitter is just now being initialized, and you must create a view object of the class requested. If the code is indeed creating the first view for the splitter, it creates whatever view type the splitter originally wanted. However, if the view is being created at a position other than the very first, the code returns the RUNTIME_CLASS of the CSecondView class.

Using a CRuntimeClass object

What the code in the previous section is doing is not necessarily obvious because the calls to CreateView supply a pointer to a CRuntimeClass object. A CRuntimeClass object describes the runtime type information for a class. Given this pointer, the code inside of CreateView can accomplish the construction of whatever object the runtime type information describes.

If you set a breakpoint on the CMySplitterWnd::CreateView function and check the execution stream of an application that uses the code in the previous section, you will learn some important facts about the splitter window class. Most notably, you will find out that the splitter destroys views that are no longer visible and recreates them later. This effectively means that the life cycle of a splitter and its views might be represented as shown in Table 3-1.

If you try this out with an application that uses dynamic splitters as you have implemented them so far, you will end up with four views of the second view class. You can fix this by ensuring that only row or column 1 is ever deleted. You can see that the splitter window does a lot of work to juggle the logical row and column position of the views in the splitter. Behind the scenes, it's also doing a bunch of math to correctly lay out each view window in the client area of the splitter.

Table 3-1: Phases in the Life Cycle of a Splitter and Its Views

User Action	Splitter Response
Start the application (CframeWnd creates CSplitterWnd within it).	Create a view at 0, 0.
Drag the horizontal splitter box down.	Create a view at 1, 0.
Drag the vertical splitter box over.	Create a view at 0, 1. Also create a view at 1, 1, because there are four panes now.
Drag the horizontal splitter box up, erasing the split.	Destroy the panes at 0, 0 and 1, 0.
Drag the horizontal splitter down again, recreating the split.	Create a view at 1, 0 again, and then create the view at 1, 1, because you have four panes again.

Associating splitters and views with multiple documents

The process that the previous section details works fine in situations where your new view references the same document as the existing views. However, if you want the second view to open another document, you have to handle the splitter's creation a bit differently. You have to actually create the splitter and give it a different creation context. You must inform it that it must instantiate new documents and views, as well as move the view window to the correct coordinates, so that it fits with the rest of the window. Believe it or not, this last part is the most difficult portion of the process.

You can avoid doing all of this work by eliminating the call to CSplitterWnd::CreateView. Instead, develop your own creation context to pass along to the CreateView function, which lets it know exactly what it needs to do.

The pContext parameter is a pointer to a CCreateContext object. The CCreateContext object records which frame, object, and document should be used for the newly created document/view pair. The following code fragment builds its own CCreateContext object called ctxSample1. The object is initialized to have the view, document, and template information that the application should create in the new splitter panel:

```
BOOL CYourSplitterWnd::CreateView(int row, int col,
    CRuntimeClass* pViewClass, SIZE sizeInit,
    CCreateContext* pContext)
{
    CCreateContext ctxSample1;
    // If there is no active view, ASSERT.
    CView* pOldView = (CView*)GetActivePane();
    ASSERT(pOldView == NULL);
    // You should test pOldView here and do something
    // reasonable with it.
    // In this fragment, simply find out where the old view is
    ctxSample1.m_pLastView = pOldView;
    ctxSample1.m_pCurrentDoc = pOldView->GetDocument();
    ctxSample1.m_pNewDocTemplate =
        m_pCurrentDoc->GetDocTemplate();
    // Pass call along.
    return CSplitterWnd::CreateView(row, col,
        pOldView->GetRuntimeClass(),
        sizeInit, &ctxSample1);
}
```

Using static splitters

Static splitters are used in applications where dynamic splitters are inadequate or inappropriate. Static splitters can be used when your application needs to show more than two split rows or two split columns. If you are interested in having your window split (no matter what column or row count) but refuse to enable the user to select how and where the splits should occur, you should use a static splitter instead of a dynamic splitter, because it's easier to code what you need using static splitters than it is to write code to negate the actions of MFC.

Static splitters still use the CSplitterWnd class, but require a slightly different creation mechanism. You will still put a CCreateWnd instance in the CFrameWnd or CMDIChildWnd derivative of your application, but your override of the OnCreateClient function will contain quite different code.

Creating a static splitter

When creating a static splitter, you should call CSplitterWnd::CreateStatic instead of CSplitterWnd::Create. The CreateStatic function still creates and wires up the splitter, but you have to create the content for the individual panes yourself. If you do not create the content, MFC will ASSERT the application and stop its execution immediately. To create the pane, call CreateView on the CSplitterWnd object you are using. You have to make one CSplitterWnd call for each splitter pane you add. For example, code to create a static splitter with five rows and three columns would look similar to the following:

```
BOOL CMainFrame::OnCreateClient(LPCREATESTRUCT /*lpcs*/,
    CCreateContext* pContext)
{
  BOOL bRet;
  int nRow;
  int nCol;

  if(!m_wndSplitter.CreateStatic(this, 5, 3))
     return FALSE;
  for (nRow = 0; nRow < 5; nRow++)
     for (nCol = 0; nCol < 3; nCol++)
       {
         bRet = m_wndSplitter.CreateView(nRow, nCol,
             RUNTIME_CLASS(CStaticSplitView),
             CSize(50, 30), pContext);
         if (bRet ==  FALSE)
             return FALSE;
       }
  return TRUE;
}
```

If you wanted to have different views in each pane, you would write the function's code to pass different RUNTIME_CLASS information for each CreateView call.

This chapter outlines ways to manually add a splitter window to your application mainly because a splitter window is most often an afterthought. If you are starting from scratch, you can select the Split window checkbox in your application's MDI Child Frame or Frame Window page. You can reach this checkbox (shown in Figure 3-7) by clicking the User Interface Features link in the MFC AppWizard request application.

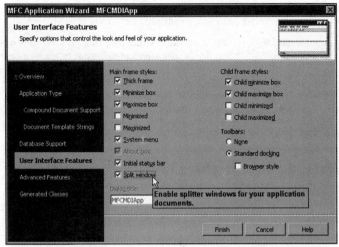

Figure 3-7: If you know beforehand that you'll want a splitter in your SDI or MDI application, you can simply select a checkbox to add the needed classes to your project.

Understanding shared scroll bars

As mentioned earlier in this chapter, the `CSplitterWnd` class also supports shared scroll bars. These scroll bar controls are children of `CSplitterWnd` and are shared with the different panes in the splitter. For example, in a 1-row-by-2-column window, you can specify `WS_VSCROLL` when creating the `CSplitterWnd` class. A special scroll bar control will be created that is shared between the two panes, as shown in Figure 3-8.

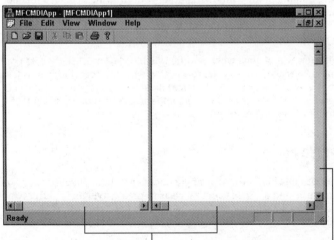

Individual horizontal scroll bars   Shared vertical scroll bar

Figure 3-8: The splitter windows share a single scroll bar.

When the user moves the scroll bar, the framework sends WM_VSCROLL messages to both views. When the views set the scroll bar position, the shared scroll bar is set.

Shared scroll bars are most useful with dynamic or static splits that display two view objects of the same class within their different panes. If you mix views of different types in a splitter, you may have to write special code to coordinate their scroll positions. Any CView-derived class that uses the CWnd scroll bar APIs delegates to the shared scroll bar if it exists. The CScrollView implementation is one example of a CView class that supports shared scroll bars. Non-CView-derived classes, classes that rely on noncontrol scroll bars, or classes that use standard Windows implementations (for example, CEditView) won't work with the shared scroll bar feature of CSplitterWnd.

Determining actual and ideal sizes

The layout of the panes in the splitter window depends on the size of the containing frame window (which in turn resizes CSplitterWnd). CSplitterWnd repositions and resizes the panes within the containing frame so that they fit as ideally as possible.

The row height and column width sizes set by the user, or that the application sets through the CSplitterWnd API calls, represent the ideal size. The actual size can be smaller than the ideal size (if room is insufficient to make that pane the ideal size) or larger than the ideal size (if that pane must be made larger to fill the leftover space on the right or bottom of the splitter window).

Performance issues with splitters

Splitters make it easy to divide the client area of your frame or MDI children to make the frame hold more than one view. However, this means that your view's painting code will be called many more times than before the split. Your view window will necessarily be smaller than it was before you adopted a splitter window, so you must make sure your view does not do any drawing that is not absolutely necessary. Specifically, your view should not do any drawing beyond the bounds of the window. Limiting your drawing in such a manner helps ensure the greatest possible performance for your application. Limiting the amount of redrawing that views must do is by far the most important consideration for applications that paint their views repeatedly in the different panes of a splitter window.

The likelihood that one view will change when another visible view must update its content for the same document is increased when you are working with splitter windows. You should think about the different views in your application and make sure that your UpdateAllViews or UpdateView calls pass enough information to the updating view, thus ensuring that it can do the smallest amount of repainting required.

The Dynsplit Program

The Dynsplit sample program is built around a single document class, CDynsplitDoc, and uses a CSingleDocTemplate and a CSplitterWnd class to create dynamic splitter windows within the application. Listing 3-2 shows code highlights from the Dynsplit.cpp and dynspvw.cpp source code for the Dynsplit.exe program.

Listing 3-2: Highlights of the Dynsplit.cpp and dynspvw.cpp source code for the Dynsplit.exe program

```cpp
// Dynsplit.cpp :
// Defines the class behaviors for the application.
//

#include "stdafx.h"
#include "dynsplit.h"

#include "mainfrm.h"
#include "dynspdoc.h"
#include "dynspvw.h"

#ifdef _DEBUG
#undef THIS_FILE
static char BASED_CODE THIS_FILE[] = __FILE__;
#endif

/////////////////////////////////////////////////////////////
// CDynamicSplitApp

BEGIN_MESSAGE_MAP(CDynamicSplitApp, CWinApp)
    //{{AFX_MSG_MAP(CDynamicSplitApp)
    ON_COMMAND(ID_APP_ABOUT, OnAppAbout)
        // NOTE - ClassWizard adds and removes mapping
        // macros here.
        // DO NOT EDIT these blocks of generated code!
    //}}AFX_MSG_MAP
    // Standard file based document commands
    ON_COMMAND(ID_FILE_NEW, CWinApp::OnFileNew)
    ON_COMMAND(ID_FILE_OPEN, CWinApp::OnFileOpen)
    // Standard print setup command
    ON_COMMAND(ID_FILE_PRINT_SETUP, CWinApp::OnFilePrintSetup)
END_MESSAGE_MAP()

/////////////////////////////////////////////////////////////
// CDynamicSplitApp construction

CDynamicSplitApp::CDynamicSplitApp()
  {
    // TODO: add construction code here.
    // Place all significant initialization in InitInstance.
  }

/////////////////////////////////////////////////////////////
// The one and only CDynamicSplitApp object.

CDynamicSplitApp theApp;
```

Continued

Listing 3-2 *(continued)*

```
/////////////////////////////////////////////////////////
// CDynamicSplitApp initialization

BOOL CDynamicSplitApp::InitInstance()
 {
   // Standard initialization

   Enable3dControls();
   LoadStdProfileSettings();  // Load standard INI file
                             // options
                             //  (including MRU)

   // Register the application's document templates.
   //  Document templates serve as the connection between
   // documents, frame windows, and views.

   CSingleDocTemplate* pDocTemplate;
   pDocTemplate = new CSingleDocTemplate(
      IDR_MAINFRAME,
      RUNTIME_CLASS(CDynamicSplitDoc),
      RUNTIME_CLASS(CMainFrame),    // main SDI frame window
      RUNTIME_CLASS(CDynamicSplitView));
   AddDocTemplate(pDocTemplate);

   // Create a new (empty) document.
   OnFileNew();
   if (m_lpCmdLine[0] != '\0')
    {
      // TODO: add command line processing here.
    }
   return TRUE;
 }

/////////////////////////////////////////////////////////
// CAboutDlg dialog used for App About.

class CAboutDlg : public CDialog
{
public:
   CAboutDlg();

// Dialog Data
   //{{AFX_DATA(CAboutDlg)
   enum { IDD = IDD_ABOUTBOX };
   //}}AFX_DATA

// Implementation
protected:
   virtual void DoDataExchange(CDataExchange* pDX);
```

```
    //{{AFX_MSG(CAboutDlg)
        // No message handlers
    //}}AFX_MSG
    DECLARE_MESSAGE_MAP()
};

CAboutDlg::CAboutDlg() : CDialog(CAboutDlg::IDD)
 {
    //{{AFX_DATA_INIT(CAboutDlg)
    //}}AFX_DATA_INIT
 }

void CAboutDlg::DoDataExchange(CDataExchange* pDX)
 {
    CDialog::DoDataExchange(pDX);
    //{{AFX_DATA_MAP(CAboutDlg)
    //}}AFX_DATA_MAP
 }

BEGIN_MESSAGE_MAP(CAboutDlg, CDialog)
    //{{AFX_MSG_MAP(CAboutDlg)
        // No message handlers
    //}}AFX_MSG_MAP
END_MESSAGE_MAP()

// App command to run the dialog
void CDynamicSplitApp::OnAppAbout()
 {
    CAboutDlg aboutDlg;
    aboutDlg.DoModal();
 }

//////////////////////////////////////////////////////////
// dynspvw.cpp : implementation of the CDynamicSplitView
// class
//

#include "stdafx.h"
#include "dynsplit.h"

#include "dynspdoc.h"
#include "dynspvw.h"

#ifdef _DEBUG
#undef THIS_FILE
static char BASED_CODE THIS_FILE[] = __FILE__;
#endif


//////////////////////////////////////////////////////////
// CDynamicSplitView

IMPLEMENT_DYNCREATE(CDynamicSplitView, CView)
```

Continued

Listing 3-2 *(continued)*

```
BEGIN_MESSAGE_MAP(CDynamicSplitView, CView)
    //{{AFX_MSG_MAP(CDynamicSplitView)
        // NOTE - ClassWizard adds and removes mapping
        // macros here.
        // DO NOT EDIT these blocks of generated code!
    //}}AFX_MSG_MAP
    // Standard printing commands
    ON_COMMAND(ID_FILE_PRINT, CView::OnFilePrint)
    ON_COMMAND(ID_FILE_PRINT_PREVIEW,
                CView::OnFilePrintPreview)
END_MESSAGE_MAP()

/////////////////////////////////////////////////////////
// CDynamicSplitView construction/destruction

CDynamicSplitView::CDynamicSplitView()
 {
    // TODO: add construction code here.

 }

CDynamicSplitView::~CDynamicSplitView()
 {
 }

/////////////////////////////////////////////////////////
// CDynamicSplitView drawing

void CDynamicSplitView::OnDraw(CDC* pDC)
{
    CDynamicSplitDoc* pDoc = GetDocument();
    ASSERT_VALID(pDoc);

    // TODO: add draw code for native data here.
 }

/////////////////////////////////////////////////////////
// CDynamicSplitView printing

BOOL CDynamicSplitView::OnPreparePrinting(CPrintInfo* pInfo)
 {
    // default preparation
    return DoPreparePrinting(pInfo);
 }
```

```
void CDynamicSplitView::OnBeginPrinting(CDC* /*pDC*/,
    CPrintInfo* /*pInfo*/)
{
   // TODO: add extra initialization before printing.
}

void CDynamicSplitView::OnEndPrinting(CDC* /*pDC*/,
    CPrintInfo* /*pInfo*/)
{
   // TODO: add cleanup after printing.
}

/////////////////////////////////////////////////////////////
// CDynamicSplitView diagnostics

#ifdef _DEBUG
void CDynamicSplitView::AssertValid() const
{
   CView::AssertValid();
}

void CDynamicSplitView::Dump(CDumpContext& dc) const
{
   CView::Dump(dc);
}

CDynamicSplitDoc* CDynamicSplitView::GetDocument()
{
 // Note: line split for book formatting
 ASSERT(m_pDocument->IsKindOf(
  RUNTIME_CLASS(CDynamicSplitDoc)));

   return (CDynamicSplitDoc*)m_pDocument;
}
#endif //_DEBUG
```

Summary

In this chapter, I started out by going over the details of the various classes of the MDI architecture and how to use them to design and develop your applications. Once the basics were covered, you learned how to program MDI applications, not only to create multiple views of the same document, but also to create multiple views of multiple documents. After that, you used your newfound knowledge in developing a very simple MDI paint application. Finally, you discovered how to incorporate splitter windows into your application to enable the user to split a single view into two or more parts so that the user can scroll each part of the view independently.

In the past two chapters, you've learned a great deal about the document/view architecture and writing both SDI and MDI applications. As an MFC developer, it is your responsibility to decide exactly what kind of documents and views your application will support, and how your code will interact with the various MFC classes you've learned about. Using what you've learned in these two chapters, you should be on the road to being able to take the skeleton MFC code provided by the AppWizard and produce the type of application framework you need to house your problem domain-specific documents and views. In the next chapter, you'll take the next logical step in your progression through the MFC and learn how to work with the first thing that comes to mind when using a document/view application: menus.

✦ ✦ ✦

Menus

One of the most important user interface objects is a menu because a menu is one of the primary ways that users interact with your application. The emphasis that Microsoft places on menus as a key user interface element is evidenced by the number of menu support functions available in the Win32 API.

In this chapter, I'll cover menus and their close companion, accelerator keys. Menus and accelerator keys are among the most commonly used input mechanisms, so it's important that you have a good understanding of how to work with them. Well-constructed menus serve as the informal documentation for the features and commands of your application.

An *accelerator key* is a keystroke or set of keystrokes, such as Ctrl+C, that a program interprets as a command. From your application's point of view, the events generated by either an accelerator key or a menu selection are the same. In many cases, you'll see menu commands and their corresponding accelerator key displayed in the menu. Application programmers do this to indicate which accelerator keys are bound to which commands.

For example, you'll often see Ctrl+V next to the Paste command in an Edit menu. Interestingly, even though accelerator keys and menu items generate the same messages and events within Windows and MFC, they are separate types of resources that are defined differently. Specifically, menus are defined with menu resources, and accelerators are defined with accelerator resources.

By the end of this discussion, you should have a good grasp of the fundamentals of basic menu and accelerator resource creation and handling. You'll also become familiar with more advanced topics such as generating context menus and dynamically changing a menu's configuration.

Creating and Editing Menus

In Chapter 1, you saw how to work with a dialog box and controls using the resource editor. A menu resource lives in a resource script (`.rc`) file, along with an application's other resources. To access the resource file, click the Resources tab on the bottom of the Project View window. This displays a resource summary in the form of a tree control.

◆ ◆ ◆ ◆

In This Chapter

Creating menus and editing menu resources

Writing menu handlers

Combining menu handlers

Defining and using accelerator resources

Performing on-the-fly menu reconfiguration

Generating context menus

◆ ◆ ◆ ◆

The resource summary list shows all the types of resources available in your application, including bitmaps, dialog boxes, icons, menus, a string table, and a version resource. When you open the Menu node, a list of menu resources is displayed. To start editing a particular menu resource, double-click its name in this list. The selected menu resource is displayed in the menu editor. If you use MFC and the AppWizard to start a new project, you have at least one menu resource. This is the default menu MFC provides, and its name is `IDR_MAINFRAME`.

Using the menu editor, you can open the Menu Item Properties dialog box. This dialog box lists all the details of individual menu items. It also enables you to change any detail of a menu. As you work with the resource editor, you'll find yourself moving between several windows. To make sure that the Menu Item Properties doesn't go into hiding, click the thumbtack button, which "pins" the dialog box and keeps it from moving.

A menu item has three key fields: ID, Caption, and Prompt. The ID field is a numeric constant that uniquely identifies the menu item. As you'll see later on when menu messages are discussed, making sure each menu item has a unique ID is critically important. The Caption field contains the text that is actually displayed on the menu. When users see a menu selection, they are seeing the Caption field. The Prompt field is any text that you'd like to display in the status bar at the bottom of the window when the user browses the menu item. The Prompt field also contains the ToolTip for the menu item. A user can browse a menu item by using either the keyboard to highlight the item or the mouse to hover over the item. The point is that a menu item is browsed when it is highlighted but not selected.

When you are creating a new menu item, you start with one of two fields in the Menu Item Properties dialog box: the ID or the Caption. You start with the ID when creating a menu item using one of MFC's predefined identifier values. You use a predefined value for commands that the MFC framework may handle for you. For example, the ID for New in the File menu is `ID_FILE_NEW`, the ID for Cut in the Edit menu is `ID_EDIT_CUT`, and the ID for New in the Window menu is `ID_WINDOW_NEW`. For a complete list of these predefined identifier values, see `afxres.h`, the MFC include file in which all of its default resource IDs are defined.

To create a brand-new menu item of your own, start by selecting the blank menu item and entering a menu item name in the Caption field. As you start typing the caption, the menu editor instantly modifies the menu to show the results of your changes. You can see the effect of text length on the menu as you type. If you define the caption first, the menu editor defines an ID value for you. If you want to view the automatically created ID, click another menu item, and then click back. If you don't like the name of the ID that the menu editor supplies, you can always define your own name by typing over the supplied name.

When filling in the Caption field, give some thought to a menu item's keyboard mnemonic. A keyboard mnemonic defines the keyboard interface to a menu item. The mnemonic comes into play when the user activates a menu by holding the Alt key while pressing the underlined letter, or mnemonic, for that menu. Take care that you don't duplicate mnemonics. For example, because of keyboard mnemonics, you can select File ➪ Open with the Alt+F+O key combination—that is, by holding down the Alt key and pressing F and then O.

From your user's point of view, keyboard mnemonics are the same as accelerator keystrokes. From a programming perspective, however, they differ in that mnemonic support comes from the menu system. Accelerators, as you'll see later, are defined in an accelerator table. To define a mnemonic, insert an ampersand (&) before the letter that is to be underlined. To insert an ampersand in your menu text, insert two ampersands (&&) in the Caption field.

The third field you should always define for a menu item is the Prompt field. As mentioned earlier, the Prompt field contains the text that is displayed in the status bar when the user browses a menu item. Even though you fill in this field in the menu editor, the string itself isn't stored as part of the menu resource. Instead, an entry is made in the string table resource, with the string ID set to the same value as the menu item command ID. This is yet another benefit of using the resource editor to define menu resources.

The Prompt field has two parts: the status bar string and the ToolTip string. You already know about the status bar string. A ToolTip is a small box that pops up when a user browses a toolbar button with the mouse. As shown in the following example (which shows the prompt value that MFC creates for the Print command), you separate the two parts with a newline character (\n):

```
Print the active document\nPrint
```

Defining menus

There are a couple of ways of defining menus. One way is to do so programmatically when you need to dynamically generate a menu using data only known at runtime. However, the most common way to create a menu is to predefine the menu as a menu resource while you are coding the application. At this point, create an MFC SDI project called **SDIMenus**. Once you've created the project, open the Resource View and expand the Menu item to see the menu associated with your application.

As you learned in Chapter 2, menus are associated with frame windows and are loaded when the frame is created. In addition to that, other resources — such as accelerator keys — are also loaded at this time. Specifically, this all takes place when the framework calls the CFrameWnd::LoadFrame function and passes the resource IDs for each of the interface elements to that function. You'll also recall from Chapter 2 that in the default SDI application, that resource ID is called IDR_MAINFRAME. Therefore, looking at the Resource View, it's easy to find the menu that will be displayed when you execute this application. At this point, double-click the IDR_MAINFRAME menu resource to open it in the editor (Figure 4-1).

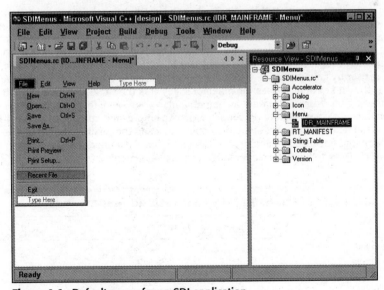

Figure 4-1: Default menu for an SDI application

As you can see, you get many default menu options when creating an SDI application. The first thing to notice is the top-level menus: File, Edit, View, and Help. All of these are called *popup* menu items because they can contain other menu items as children. If you click on one of these menu items, and then view it's Properties dialog box, you'll see that the Popup property is set to true. Under the File menu, you get the standard options to create new documents (files) and open and save the current document. There are also menu items for printing and opening the most recently loaded documents. The Edit menu contains menu items for dealing with the Clipboard (Undo, Copy, Cut, and Paste). The View menu option contains options for toggling the viewing of the toolbar and status bar, and the Help menu contains an option for displaying the About box. The options that the wizard puts on the menu are automatically wired to functions by the framework and will work without you adding any code. As you progress though this chapter, you'll learn how to add your own menu items, how to associate code (event handlers) with those menu items, and in some cases how to override the default event handlers provided by the frame work. For now, let's continue talking about the basics of the menus and how they're supported.

Each menu item has three essential elements: a string name (such as Copy) that the user sees, a numeric value that uniquely identifies the menu item, and a symbolic constant that is used to refer to the item in code. The numeric value should be unique because it is used to associate the menu item with its event handler(s). For this reason, when you add a menu item to a menu, Visual Studio automatically generates the numeric value for you. You'll also find that you can't change this value via the Properties dialog box. This is how Visual Studio helps to ensure that this numeric value stays unique. The only value you need to think about with menus is the symbolic constant. This value is also generated automatically when you add a new menu item to a menu and is formed by combining the popup menu name with the menu item name. To see this, open the Properties dialog box for the File ⇨ New menu item. You'll see that the ID property has a value of ID_FILE_NEW. Therefore, if you ever need to refer to this menu item in code, you can simply use that ID. Shortly, when you see how to add a menu event handler you'll also see that this value is placed in the message map in order to associate a given menu item with the event handler.

Try creating some menu options at this point to learn a few things about menu definition. As you saw in Figure 4-1, the editor gives you a place to type in a menu item to the right of the last defined top-level popup menu (where you see the text "Type here"). Simply click in that area and type the value **My &Menu**. When done, hit the Enter key. The ampersand is used to define a mnemonic for the menu (the second letter M, in this case) and this mnemonic is signified to the user by an underscore under the mnemonic letter. What this means is that if the user holds the Alt key and presses the mnemonic key, it is the same as if the user had clicked that menu item. What if you want an ampersand in your menu text? Although it is not very common, this is easy enough to do. Simply type two ampersand characters. Table 4-1 shows some menu text examples that include ampersands and the resulting text that the user would see. (Note that because two ampersands indicate that the ampersand should be printed, there is no way to have the ampersand itself be a mnemonic.)

Table 4:1: Menu Examples That Include Ampersands

Menu Text	What the user would see
Barnes and &Noble	Barnes and Noble
Barnes && Noble	Barnes & Noble
Barnes && &Noble	Barnes & Noble

Now add an item below My Menu, with the text of **Say Hello**. At this point, if you look at the item's properties, you'll see that its ID is `ID_MYMENU_SAYHELLO` because Visual Studio removes the spaces when forming the constant name for the item. From this point forward, when I refer to a menu item's ID, I'm referring to this value. Also, I'll be referring to menu items by ID from now on because that is the standard way of referring to them.

What if you don't want the menu item where it is? To move an item, simply click it with the left mouse button and drag it to the desired location. For example, because the UI Guidelines for SDI applications state that the left-most two items on the menu should be File and Edit, and that the right-most two items should be View and Help, drag the My Menu item and drop it after the Edit menu.

Now invoke the Properties dialog box again for the Say Hello menu items in order to go over some important options. The first thing to set whenever you create a menu item is the Prompt property. This is the value that displays in the status bar of your application when the item is selected. Therefore, for this item, you can type in something like "Display a message indicating that the event handler was called" (without the quotes). Note that the UI Guidelines state that this value should be an active statement about what the option will do and doesn't have to end in a period. You should know that if you forget to define a prompt for a menu item, MFC will generate an warning message in the output window of Visual Studio when running the application in Debug mode.

The next thing to notice is the `Checked` property. This is used in situations where you want to allow the user to toggle an application setting. You'll see how this works shortly, but for now, add a menu item under the My Menu item with a caption of `Be &Formal` and a prompt value of "Toggle formalities" (without the quotes). Now drag this item over the Say Hello item so that it is first in the menu. For that matter, rename that My Menu menu item to `&Speak`. To do that, you can either invoke the Properties dialog box and change the `Caption` property or simply click the menu and start typing.

A couple more notes on menu item Ids: Popup menus do not have IDs. The reason for this is that the IDs are only used to associate menu items with code, and because clicking a popup menu simply displays its submenu items and can't be associated with any code, there's no need for it to have an ID.

The second thing to note about menu item IDs is that once you've created a menu item and Visual Studio has formed an ID for that item using its caption, even if you change that item's caption, Visual Studio will not automatically create a new menu item. In this case, you would change the ID on the menu item's Properties dialog box for the `ID_MYMENU_BEFORMAL` and `ID_MYMENU_SAYHELLO` items to `ID_SPEAK_BEFORMAL` and `ID_SPEAK_SAYHELLO`, respectively. Some people don't worry about this issue because it doesn't have any impact on your code. However, as you'll see in the next section, when you use the wizard to create event handlers for the menu items, the default names of the event handlers will include the menu ID. Therefore, it's nice to have the menu item IDs have their correct, self-documenting values. At this point you should have a top-level menu of Speak with submenu items of Be Formal and Say Hello (Figure 4-2).

One last thing that I'll cover here is how to open and view the source code of a resource file. First, this code is always maintained in a file that has the same name as the project and an extension of `.rc`. Therefore, in this case, the resource file is `SDIMenus.rc`. However, attempting to open the file from the File ➪ Open menu simply opens the Resource View on the file. In order to open the resource file as you would any other file, you need to know about one extra step. First, select File ➪ Open. When the Open File dialog box appears, select the resource file. Now look at the Open button, and you'll see that it is really two buttons in one. The button to the right enables you to select how you want to open the file. Click that now and select the Open With option. This invokes the Open With dialog box, as shown in Figure 4-3.

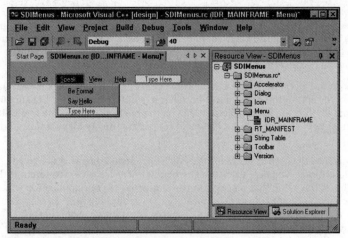

Figure 4-2: Adding menu items with the resource editor

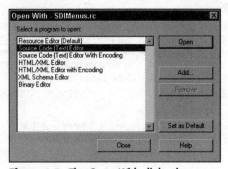

Figure 4-3: The Open With dialog box

What's cool about this dialog box is that not only does it allow you to open a file using the various editors that are built into Visual Studio .NET, but it also enables you to add other editors to this list and set the default editor that will always be used to open that file type.

Select the Source Code (Text) Editor option and then click the Open button. If you're asked if you want to save the currently open resource file, answer yes. Visual Studio then displays the resource file in the standard editor that you're accustomed to editing source code in. If you search this file for the string &Speak, you should see the menu you've created so far as shown in Figure 4-4.

Although teaching the syntax of the resource language is not within the scope of this book, you can easily infer the majority of it. Here you can see that the Speak menu item is defined as a popup and that it doesn't have an ID (as you learned earlier). You can also see that each menu's subitems are listed below the menu within BEGIN and END tags and that each non-popup menu item is identified by the MENUITEM tag and a resource ID. Although it is useful to know how to open this file, you should take great care in editing it. There's a reason it's so difficult to get to, and that's because once you mess around with the IDs, it can sometimes be a pain to correct any mistakes. Also, once your resource file has an error in it, the Resource View will not be able to properly parse it and therefore you won't be able to open the Resource View until you correct the error. Therefore, take care if you plan on manually editing your resource file. Close the resource file now and reopen it with the Resource View.

Now that you know the basics of defining menus, let's now see how to hook up event handlers to your menu items.

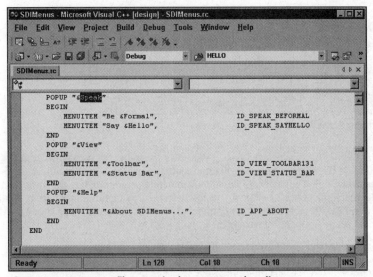

Figure 4-4: Resource file open in the source code editor

Writing menu event handlers

After you've created a menu resource, the next step is to associate code with the various menu item events. To see that in action, right-click the ID_SPEAK_BEFORMAL menu item and select the Add Event Handler option (Figure 4-5).

The first thing you'll notice about the dialog box is the Command name. This is set to the menu item's ID. You'll see where that comes into play in the code shortly. Now take a look at the Message type. As you can see here, there are two messages that you can respond to: COMMAND and UPDATE_COMMAND_UI.

A WM_COMMAND message is sent when a user clicks on the menu item. As such, you simply provide a handler for this message anytime you want code to run as a result of the user clicking a menu item. If MFC cannot find a WM_COMMAND handler for a given menu item, that menu item is automatically disabled and made unavailable to the user.

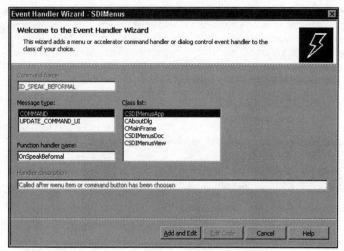

Figure 4-5: Adding event handlers for menu items

The `ON_UPDATE_COMMAND_UI` message is not a Windows message, but a request from the MFC framework to update the appearance of individual menu items. The event handlers for these messages, sometimes called *commandui handlers*, are where your code has the opportunity to do things like placing a check mark next to a menu item, graying out a menu item, or disabling a menu item. Here's an example of a commandui handler that performs those particular tasks based on some application variables.

```
void CMainFrame::OnUpdateCheckedMenuItem(CCmdUI* pCmdUI)
{
  // Set check mark if g_bMenuChecked is TRUE,
  // Otherwise clear check mark.
  pCmdUI->SetCheck( g_bMenuChecked );

  // Enable if g_bMenuEnable is TRUE,
  // Otherwise gray out.
  pCmdUI->Enable( g_bMenuEnable );
}
```

As shown in this code snippet, commandui handlers are passed a pointer to a `CCmdUI` object. You control the menu item state by calling `CCmdUI` member functions. For example, to disable a menu item based on some application logic, you would simply call the `CCmdUI::Enable` function and pass it a value of `FALSE`.

The next thing to notice is the Class list. This is where you tell Visual Studio in which class to insert the event handler. This is a completely subjective choice and really depends on the overall architecture of your application. However, to effectively make this decision you need to know some basics about MFC message routing.

Most of the messages that you handle in an MFC program are directed at one object type: a window. This follows the model used by the Windows API, and, given the types of messages, it seems to make sense. After all, windowing messages such as `WM_CREATE`, `WM_MOVE`, and `WM_SIZE` notify you that a window has been created, moved, or sized. In the Windows API and in MFC, only a window object is interested in such events. In addition, nonwindowing messages — for example, mouse and keyboard messages — direct data to a particular window and therefore cannot be rerouted without creating confusion.

MFC departs from the Windows API in its handling of the two menuing messages. When an application creates a menu command, the frame window holding a menu doesn't have to process every menu message. Instead, the work can be delegated to message handlers (such as your WM_COMMAND handler) within objects that own the resources to which the command applies. Among the candidates for handling menu messages are CCmdTarget-derived classes, which include windows (such as view windows) and application (CWinApp-derived) objects. In a document/view application, document objects and view objects (which are windows) are also candidates for handling menu messages.

Although any CCmdTarget-derived class *can* receive menu messages, in fact, menu messages take a specific path when they are routed. Table 4-2 lists the order that MFC uses to check the message maps when delivering command messages for nondocument/view applications, single-document document/view applications, and multiple-document document/view applications.

Table 4-2: Message Processing Sequences for Command Messages

Base Class	Message Processing Sequence
NonDocument/View Applications	
CFrameWnd	The frame window has first chance to process message.
WinApp	The application object is handled second.
Single Document (SDI) Applications	
CView	The active view has the first shot at messages.
CDocument	The active document is next in message priority after the active view.
CSingleDocTemplate	The document template of the active view follows the active document in processing messages.
CFrameWnd	The frame window is next.
CWinApp	The application object has the last shot at any messages.
Multiple Document (MDI) Applications	
CView	The active view is checked first.
CDocument	The document of the active view comes next.
CMultiDocTemplate	The template for the active view is checked next.
CMDIChildFrame	The child frame comes next.
CMDIFrameWnd	The parent window follows after CMDIChildFrame.
CWinApp	Application object is last.

If MFC's command message routing isn't to your liking, you can define your own priorities and send command messages to any object. However, you must override the OnCmdMsg command message routing functions in several classes. Before doing this, you need to spend some time reviewing the MFC source files to make sure that your changes are in sync with the base classes. In particular, look for the default OnCmdMsg handlers in the following classes: CView, CDocument, CFrameWnd, and CMDIFrameWnd. (You could also override PreTranslateMessage to get the same result.)

For purposes of this demo, select the CMainFrame class, because that is where you'll do all your coding.

Finally, the last thing to note is the function name. Although you can change this value, you'll notice that as mentioned earlier, the default name will be formed from the menu resource ID. In this case, because the ID is ID_SPEAK_BEFORMAL, the function name has defaulted to OnSpeakBeformal, where the On part signifies a handler for the user's having clicked the item, and the remainder represents the menu item resource in mixed case. Not having to change this each time you want to add a handler is one reason that I always make sure that the menu resource IDs are correct.

You should now have a good grounding in the basics of menu programming. This section has defined what a menu resource is, showed how to create a menu resource, and examined the ins and outs of basic menu programming. In order to provide a solid usable menu interface, you need to understand accelerator keys, so that's the next subject.

Writing some simple menu code

At this point, let's see how to put what you've learned this far into action. It's going to be very simple, but it will illustrate how to set up both command and oncommandui event handlers.

1. Add the following member variable to the CSDIMenusView class. This value is used so that you can keep track of whether the option is turned on or not.

```
protected:
  BOOL m_bFormal;
```

2. Now add a command handler for the ID_SPEAK_BEFORMAL menu item to the view class and code it as follows. As you can see, this line of code simply toggles the current value of the m_bFormal member variable.

```
void CSDIMenusView::OnSpeakBeformal()
{
  m_bFormal = !m_bFormal;
}
```

3. Now you need to set the check mark whenever the m_bFormal flag is on. To do that, add a commandui handler and code it as follows. This function uses the CCmdUI::Set-Check command to either turn the check mark on or off based on the member variable.

```
void CSDIMenusView::OnUpdateSpeakBeformal(CCmdUI *pCmdUI)
{
  pCmdUI->SetCheck(m_bFormal);
}
```

4. Now to round out the demo, add a command handler for the `ID_SPEAK_SAYHELLO` function as follows:

```
void CSDIMenusView::OnSpeakSayhello()
{
  CString str;
  str.Format("Hello%s!", m_bFormal ? ", sir" : "");
  AfxMessageBox(str);
}
```

5. That's all there is to most menu handling chores. However, before you build and execute the demo, take a look at the message map created for you in the `CSDIMenusView` class to see where the menu items are being mapped to their respective handlers.

```
BEGIN_MESSAGE_MAP(CSDIMenusView, CView)
 // Standard printing commands
 ON_COMMAND(ID_FILE_PRINT, CView::OnFilePrint)
 ON_COMMAND(ID_FILE_PRINT_DIRECT, CView::OnFilePrint)
 ON_COMMAND(ID_FILE_PRINT_PREVIEW,
  CView::OnFilePrintPreview)
 ON_COMMAND(ID_SPEAK_BEFORMAL, OnSpeakBeformal)
 ON_UPDATE_COMMAND_UI(ID_SPEAK_BEFORMAL,
  OnUpdateSpeakBeformal)
 ON_COMMAND(ID_SPEAK_SAYHELLO, OnSpeakSayhello)
END_MESSAGE_MAP()
```

6. Build and run the application. As you can see (Figure 4-6), the check mark correctly indicates whether formalities are in order, and clicking the Say Hello menu item causes the message box with the appropriate message to be displayed.

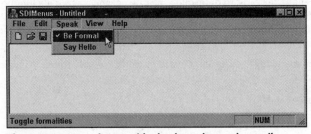

Figure 4-6: Menu items with check marks can be easily maintained via the commandui handler.

Combining menu handlers

Under most circumstances, you will create a single handler for a single menu option. There are valid times when you will want to have a single handler process multiple menu items, however. An example of that would be situations in which you have several menu options where the code to handle each of the options is nearly identical. Instead of duplicating the code, you could simply write one handler and have it determine which exact menu option was selected.

As a very simple example, suppose you have an application that allows the user to select from a menu of predefined WAV files to play. Because the code is going to be almost identical in the case of each option, you could combine the menu handling like this:

1. Create the menu items. For example, you might have a popup menu of Play, and then submenu items for each WAV file—say, Song1, Song2, and Song3.

2. Add a COMMAND handler for the first menu option (ID_PLAY_SONG1) using the Add Event Handler Wizard. The default handler would be named OnPlaySong1. You would change that to OnPlaySong to be more generic.

3. Now the tricky part. If you attempt to use the Add Event Handler to specify the OnPlaySong function as a handler for the other menu options, you will receive an error stating "Overloaded function 'OnPlaySong' already exists."

4. Because the single function you want to use is already defined in the header file, you don't have to worry about that. You simply need to manually update the message map of the class that will contain the handlers for the menu options.

5. Therefore, open that file and locate the message map. Here is an example of that, where I've manually inserted the two map entries shown in bold:

```
BEGIN_MESSAGE_MAP(CSDIAppView, CView)
 // Standard printing commands
 ON_COMMAND(ID_PLAY_SONG1, OnPlaySong)
 ON_COMMAND(ID_PLAY_SONG2, OnPlaySong)
 ON_COMMAND(ID_PLAY_SONG3, OnPlaySong)
END_MESSAGE_MAP()
```

6. If you have a single function handling multiple menu options, how do you know which menu option was selected? At any time in a message handler, you can call CWnd::GetCurrentMessage to determine the current message. This function returns the MSG structure containing the message ID and information specific to that message. For a COMMAND menu message, the wParam structure member will contain the exact menu ID.

   This is how the following OnPlaySong function would be able to tell which exact menu item was selected.

```
void CWaveDemoView::OnSoundsLoadfromdisk()
{
 MSG* pMsg = (MSG*)GetCurrentMessage();
 ASSERT(pMsg);
 if (pMsg)
 {
  if (pMsg->wParam == ID_PLAY_SONG1)
   // play the first song
  else if (pMsg->wParam == ID_PLAY_SONG2)
   // play the first song
  else if (pMsg->wParam == ID_PLAY_SONG3)
   // play the first song
  else ASSERT(TRUE); // should never get here!
 }
}
```

Now that you've learned the basics of defining menus and writing event handlers, let's look at the how accelerator keys work and how they tie into the topic of menus.

Accelerator Keys

An accelerator key, otherwise referred to as a *keyboard shortcut*, enables a user to send a command using the keyboard. The Win32 API provides the accelerator table resource where the accelerator key definitions for your application reside. The AppWizard provides a default table when it generates a document/view application. In addition, if you initialize a frame window by a call to `CFrameWnd::LoadFrame`, the table is automatically loaded and connected to the frame window.

Our exploration of accelerator keys starts with a general examination of keyboard input. To help you determine which keys to use and which ones to avoid, this section provides guidelines for appropriate accelerator key assignment. Next, you'll learn how to create accelerator resources by using the accelerator table editor. Then you'll examine the Windows API mechanisms behind accelerators and learn how to dynamically install an accelerator table.

Examining keyboard input

There are four defined categories of keyboard input: text keys, access keys, mode keys, and shortcut keys. The term *shortcut keys* refers to accelerator keys. Let's take a look at each of these four types of keyboard input, paying special attention to the relationship between accelerator keys and one other category of keys.

The term *text keys* refers to printable characters — that is, uppercase and lowercase letters, numbers, punctuation marks, and other symbols. Nothing in MFC or the Windows API prevents you from using text keys for command keys. If you've spent much time in a character-based, main frame world, you have probably encountered this type of command key. Coming from that background, simple text commands seem natural. However, this practice is inconsistent with the user interface style that has evolved for Windows, and can be frustrating for your users. Put simply, users expect that letter and number keys will generate printable letters and numbers.

The second category of keyboard input is access keys. An access key (which, as mentioned earlier, is sometimes called a *mnemonic*) is an alphanumeric key that, when pressed in combination with the Alt key, accesses a popup menu, a menu item, or a dialog box control. Adding an access key to a menu or a dialog box control isn't difficult; a simple ampersand (&) identifies the access key to the system, and Windows just makes them work. You need to make sure that your accelerator keys don't conflict with access keys. The simplest solution is to avoid defining accelerator keys that take the form of the Alt key plus a letter or number key.

Mode keys, the third category of keyboard input, have a significant effect on possible accelerator key combinations. Mode keys change the actions of other keys (or other input devices). There are two subcategories of mode keys: toggle keys and modifier keys. Toggle keys are somewhat of an artifact from the IBM PC family of computers. A standard Windows-compatible keyboard has three toggle keys: Caps Lock, Num Lock, and Scroll Lock.

The second type of mode keys — modifier keys — is even more important. Although there are a few single-key accelerators (function keys, for example), the presence of modifier keys multiplies the number of key combinations that are available for defining accelerator keys. The standard 101-key keyboard defines three modifier keys: Shift, Ctrl, and Alt. Microsoft has defined a specification for a new, 104-key keyboard in which the basic 101-key layout is enhanced with three new keys: two Windows keys (sporting the Windows logo) and an Applications key. The Windows key is an additional modifier key. Its use is reserved for the operating system.

The final category is the shortcut keys, or accelerators. Any keys that are not included in the other categories are available for use as single-key accelerators. This group includes the function keys (F1, F2, and so on) and the cursor (insertion point) movement keys (Home, the Up arrow key, and so on). With these keys and the modifier-plus key combinations, you have a wide range of choices for creating accelerator keys. Let's look at the mechanics of defining an accelerator key assignment.

Defining accelerator keys

Defining an accelerator key involves two basic steps. First, you must create an accelerator table resource. The accelerator table resource defines the key codes and the command ID that are the result when a user presses the accelerator key. Then you advertise the availability of the key combination to the user. For key combinations that match menu item selections, you do this by modifying the menu item text. Let's look at what's involved in each of these steps.

Creating an accelerator table resource

The Visual C++ IDE has a built-in accelerator table editor. Just like the menu editor, the accelerator table editor provides access to a properties dialog box in which you can edit individual items. To open the Accel Properties dialog box, double-click any accelerator. To make this dialog box stick around, click the thumbtack button.

By clicking the Help button in the Accel Properties dialog box, you can obtain details about each control. The accelerator table itself has three columns: ID, Key, and Type. You probably need only a little experimentation to feel comfortable with creating and editing accelerator entries. To fill in some of the gaps, though, let's look at each set of accelerator properties, starting with the command ID.

The command ID identifies the command code that is passed, via a `WM_COMMAND` message, when a user presses an accelerator key. The command list is filled with values from your program's `resource.h` file, along with a set of MFC's predefined values from `afxres.h`. When you define an accelerator, be sure that its command ID matches the command ID for the corresponding menu item. By doing so, you have to provide only a single command handler function that works for both menu input and accelerator input.

The Key field identifies the keyboard key for the accelerator. For alphanumeric characters, you simply type the number or letter. For nonprintable characters, you use virtual key codes. As you scroll through the combo box that's connected to this field, you'll see that it contains 86 virtual key codes, each with a `VK_` prefix. For example, `VK_F1` is the virtual key code for the F1 function key, and `VK_DOWN` is the virtual key code for the Down arrow key.

If you're not sure which virtual key code to use, the simplest solution is to click the Next Key Typed button. You can then press a modifier-key combination that you want to use for your accelerator, and the accelerator editor will automatically fill in the correct entries for the Key, Modifiers, and Type fields in the Accel Properties dialog box.

You choose the modifier key for your accelerator by clicking one of the checkboxes in the Modifiers field. It's recommended that you use the Ctrl key as a modifier before the others. In addition, you should avoid using the Alt key with an alphanumeric accelerator because it might conflict with a menu access key. Even if you find Alt-alphanumeric-key combinations that don't conflict with your menu access keys, the access keys in internationalized versions often differ.

The Type field gives you a choice between ASCII and VirtKey. Almost every accelerator key should be a virtual key, because these transcend the different types of keyboards used around the world. However, you'll occasionally have to define an ASCII accelerator, most notably for using symbol characters (for example, <, >, or /) as commands. Selecting the ASCII option in the Type field enables you to define character — instead of keyboard key — commands. The ASCII Type enables you to differentiate between uppercase and lowercase letters. However, even though it's possible, for example, to have an *A* command that differs from an *a* command, you should avoid this practice. After all, users expect case-insensitive commands.

Creating accelerator menu hints

To let users know about your accelerator keys, you need to advertise them. The best place for doing this is next to the corresponding menu item. Following the menu item name within a menu resource, you simply insert a tab character (`\t`) and the accelerator key name. For example, the standard accelerator for the Paste menu item is Ctrl+V. The following menu resource entry shows how the hint for this accelerator is included in the Paste menu item:

```
&Paste\tCtrl+V
```

Note In some cases, your accelerator keys don't correspond to menu item selections. To make sure that your users can take advantage of these accelerator keys, you should add a help database entry.

You know how to create accelerator keys and how to add hints within menus, but you still need to figure out which keys to use for keyboard commands. This subject is covered in the following section.

Selecting appropriate accelerator keys

When you define accelerator keys, be sure to use standard accelerator key combinations that are consistent with other Windows applications. Table 4-3 summarizes the standard Windows keyboard commands. Two of the five categories in this table are implemented by the operating system (system commands) or by an MFC class (`CMDIFrameWnd` implements the MDI accelerator keys). The rest are up to you to implement in your own accelerator table. You need to be aware of all of them, however, to avoid defining an accelerator that conflicts with standard Windows keyboard commands.

Table 4-3: Standard Windows Keyboard Commands

Key Combination	*Description*
System Commands	
Ctrl+Alt+Del	For systems enforcing user-level security, invokes a dialog box allowing the user to log out. For other systems, causes the Close Program dialog box to be displayed.
Alt+Tab	Brings the next active application into the foreground.
Alt+Esc	Brings the next active application into the foreground.

Continued

Table 4-3: (continued)

Key Combination	Description
Ctrl+Esc	Displays the Start menu.
Alt+spacebar	Displays the window's system menu.
PrintScrn	Takes a snapshot of the screen and places it on the Clipboard.
Alt+PrintScrn	Takes a snapshot of the active window, and places it on the Clipboard.
Alt	Toggles the application menu bar.
Alt+Enter	Toggles a DOS window in and out of full-screen mode.
Application Commands	
Esc	Cancels the current mode or operation
Tab	Moves the input focus to the next control
Alt+F4	Closes the top-level window (not the desktop)
Shift+F10	Displays a context menu
F1	Summons a help menu
Shift+F1	Summons context help
File Commands	
Ctrl+N	Opens a new document
Ctrl+O	Summons the Open dialog box
Ctrl+P	Summons the Print dialog box
Ctrl+S	Saves the document
Clipboard Commands	
Ctrl+Z	Undoes the last action
Alt+Backspace	Undoes the last action
Ctrl+X	Cuts selected items
Shift+Del	Cuts selected items
Ctrl+C	Copies selected items to the Clipboard
Ctrl+Ins	Copies selected items to the Clipboard
Ctrl+V	Pastes items from Clipboard at the insertion point
Shift+Ins	Pastes items from Clipboard at the insertion point
Multiple Document (MDI) Commands	
Ctrl+F4	Closes the currently active document window
Ctrl+F6	Activates the next document window
Shift+Ctrl+F6	Activates the previous document window

Here are suggestions to help you pick a reasonable set of accelerator keys:

✦ Assign single keys where possible because these keystrokes are the easiest for the user to perform.

✦ Make *modifier+letter* key combinations case-insensitive.

✦ Use Shift+*key* combinations for actions that extend or complement the actions of the key or key combination used without the Shift key. For example, Alt+Tab switches windows in a top-to-bottom order. Shift+Alt+Tab switches windows in reverse order. However, avoid Shift+*text* keys because the effect of the Shift key may differ for some international keyboards.

✦ Use Ctrl+*key* combinations for actions that represent a larger scale effect. For example, in text editing contexts, Home moves to the beginning of a line, Ctrl+Home moves to the beginning of the text. Use Ctrl+*key* combinations for access to commands where a letter key is used — for example, Ctrl+B for bold. Remember that such assignments might be meaningful only for English-speaking users.

✦ Avoid Alt+*key* combinations because they may conflict with the standard keyboard access for menus and controls. The Alt+*key* combinations — Alt+Tab, Alt+Esc, and Alt+spacebar — are reserved for system use. Alt+*numeric-key* combinations enter special characters.

✦ Avoid assigning shortcut keys that are commonly used for other operations in your software. For example, if Ctrl+C is the shortcut for the Copy command and your application supports the standard copy operation, don't assign Ctrl+C to another operation.

✦ Provide support, when possible, for enabling the user to change the shortcut key assignments in your software.

✦ Use the Esc key to terminate a function in process or to cancel a direct manipulation operation. It is also usually interpreted as the shortcut key for a Cancel button.

Once you've selected the accelerator keys for your application, you have to decide whether to put them all in a single accelerator table or spread them out between multiple accelerator tables. For small- to medium-sized applications, a single accelerator table is sufficient. For larger, more complex applications working with several different types of data, you might find that you require several accelerator tables.

The use of multiple accelerator tables enables you to divide the work that's to be done and gives you greater flexibility in enabling different keyboard command sets. Although the MFC document/view classes take advantage of this capability to support multiple accelerator tables, I'm going to avoid the document/view architecture for now so that I can focus on the MFC fundamentals. Let's begin by reviewing how the native Windows API provides accelerator support.

Native Windows API accelerator support

For all that accelerators do for you, the Win32 API has only six accelerator functions. (The scarcity of native API functions is one reason why you don't find a CAccelerators class in MFC.) The most important features are provided by two of these accelerator functions: LoadAccelerators and TranslateAccelerator. LoadAccelerators creates a RAM-resident accelerator table from an accelerator resource. The second function, TranslateAccelerator, tests whether a particular keyboard message corresponds to an accelerator table command entry.

In a Windows program written in C, you call the load function to create the accelerator table and then call the translate function from your program's message loop. As you already know, MFC provides the message loop that every MFC-based program uses. The message loop in the thread class' `CWinThread::Run` function calls `CWinThread::PumpMessage`, which does the following:

```
::GetMessage(&m_msgCur, NULL, NULL, NULL);
if (!PreTranslateMessage(&m_msgCur))
{
   ::TranslateMessage(&m_msgCur);
   ::DispatchMessage(&m_msgCur);
}
```

In this code fragment, the three functions with the global scope operators (`::`) are native Windows API functions. The fourth function, `PreTranslateMessage`, is the name of an over-loaded function that appears in several MFC classes. These functions exist for one primary reason — to check for accelerator keys. To experienced Windows API programmers, this is a familiar message loop, with the exception that `Translate Accelerator` is usually called instead of `PreTranslateMessage`.

By the way, the function's name comes from the fact it is called before `::TranslateMessage`. This latter function takes raw keyboard (virtual key) messages and turns them into cooked ASCII character input. For accelerator keys to be handled properly, they must be raw. In addition, if a particular message is associated with an accelerator, the function returns `TRUE`, and no further processing is required. Otherwise, the normal message loop functions are called.

Although many MFC classes have `PreTranslateMessage` functions, not all can support an accelerator table. In some cases, such as with `CWinApp` and `CWinThread`, the base member function simply calls the corresponding member in the window classes. This implies that accelerator tables can be used only by window classes. However, this limitation is not a design feature of MFC; it is a trait that MFC inherits from the native Windows API.

The basic flow of messages is from the innermost data window to the outermost container window. The command is handled by whichever window first claims it. In a single-document document/view application, the view window gets the first chance to handle an accelerator, followed by the frame window. In a multiple-document document/view application, the sequence progresses from the view window to the child frame, and then to the parent frame. In your document/view-free world, your BASEMENU sample program has only one window — a frame window — which alone among the MFC objects can receive accelerator key commands. Let's take a closer look at the mechanics of providing accelerator tables to MFC's window classes.

Connecting a new accelerator table to a window class

Because an accelerator table by itself doesn't do anything, you need some way of connecting an accelerator table to a window. To connect an accelerator table to a window class, you start by loading the accelerator table into memory. You do this sometime during the initialization of your window — `PreCreateWindow` is generally a good choice. You load an accelerator table into memory by calling `::LoadAccelerators`, which is defined as follows:

```
HACCEL LoadAccelerators(
   HINSTANCE hinst,    // EXE file instance handle
   LPCTSTR lpTableName); // Accelerator table name
```

The first parameter, the instance handle, identifies who you are in this system. This is passed to your program's `WinMain` entry point. The second parameter is the accelerator table name, which you specified in the resource file. The following code fragment loads an accelerator table named `IDR_VIEW_COMMMANDS`:

```
HINSTANCE hInst = AfxGetResourceHandle();
LPCTSTR lpID = MAKEINTRESOURCE(IDR_VIEW_COMMMANDS);
HACCEL g_hAccel = LoadAccelerators( hInst, lpID );
```

The `AfxGetResourceHandle` function helps make sure that you get the correct instance handle—for code in an application as well as in a dynamic link library. The `MAKEINTRESOURCE` macro converts the accelerator table's integer ID into a character string, which is the type required by the function. The return value, `g_hAccel`, is a Windows system handle that gives your program access to the accelerator table in memory.

Once an accelerator table is loaded into memory, the next step is to make sure it is called at the right time. This is a simple matter of overloading the `PreTranslateMessage` function in a `CWnd`-derived class. Here's a sample implementation that does just that:

```
BOOL CWindowingClass::PreTranslateMessage(MSG * pMsg)
{
   if( g_hAccel == NULL )
    return FALSE; // we didn't process

   return ::TranslateAccelerator(m_hWnd, g_hAccel, pMsg);
}
```

The next two sections explore a couple of more advanced programming topics: dynamically created menus and context menus. You'll be introduced to the theory behind each concept and then you'll review practical implementations. Understanding these topics will enable you to add a professional polish to your applications.

Dynamically Changing Menus

In general, any change you can make to a menu in the menu editor can also be made dynamically at runtime. For example, you can create menus from scratch, add menu items, or remove menu items. Certain menu features—for example, owner-drawn menu items and custom bitmap check marks—are accessible *only* at runtime. (An owner-drawn menu item contains a graphic image, such as a bitmap or geometric figure drawn using calls to GDI, instead of a text string.)

Menu command ranges

If you dynamically create menu items, you must provide command handlers. Although you could use ClassWizard to *dummy up* a set, you don't always know how many command handlers you should create. For such situations, MFC enables you to handle a range of command IDs with a single command handler. Because ClassWizard can't deal with a range of command IDs, you must write the code by hand that ClassWizard would otherwise create for you.

Your first concern is picking a range of command IDs that doesn't interfere with existing command IDs. Table 4-4 summarizes how the available command ranges are used by ClassWizard, in particular, and the MFC framework, in general. As shown in this table, what's left for your use is a range of IDs from 0x9000 (36864) to 0xDFFF (57343).

Table 4-4: Available Command Ranges

Range	Description
0x8000–0x8FFF	ClassWizard uses this range for application-defined menus.
0x9000–0xDFFF	This range of command IDs is available for your use.
0xE000–0xFFFF	MFC uses this range for its own purposes.

Next, you need to add a function to the class declaration. ClassWizard creates three pieces of code for every message: an include file declaration, a message map definition, and a function definition. Here's an example of a function declaration for a message-handling function that can handle a range of command IDs:

```
class CMainFrame : public DFrame
{  ...
   void OnCommandRange (UINT id);
   ...
};
```

The next piece is the message map entry, which MFC's message-handling mechanism must have to be capable of finding your function. To create this message map entry, you add an `ON_COMMAND_RANGE` message map macro between the boundaries of a `BEGIN_MESSAGE_MAP` and `END_MESSAGE_MAP` pair. This message map macro takes three parameters: start of range, end of range, and function:

```
ON_COMMAND_RANGE(ID_MIN, ID_MAX, OnCommandRange);
```

The final piece is the function definition itself. It takes a single parameter, which is the command ID for a selected menu item. Here's an example:

```
void CMainFrame::OnCommandRange (UINT id)
{
  switch (id)
  {
    case ID_DYNA_COMMAND_1: ...
    case ID_DYNA_COMMAND_2: ...
    ...
  }
}
```

Changing menus at runtime

By adding menu items on-the-fly, your programs can be responsive to changes in the user's environment. Dynamic menu items are commonly used to update the lists of most recently used files, which often appear in File menus. Sometimes, you know only at runtime how many dynamic menu items you're going to create. To simplify the receipt of command notifications for such items, MFC enables you to create command handlers for a range of command IDs. Unfortunately, ClassWizard doesn't (yet) support this feature. The following section shows you how it's done manually.

Although MFC provides a menu class (`CMenu`), AppWizard's code doesn't use this class to create a menu. Instead, the Windows API supports the simultaneous creation of a window with a menu. When creating a Windows window, MFC's CFrameWnd class requests the creation of a menu. In the process, it also creates a bit of an object-oriented design paradox. Although a CFrameWnd *logically* contains a CMenu, it *physically* contains no CMenu data type.

Although you won't use CMenu to create the menu that is attached to your program's frame window, you'll use it extensively for dynamic menu operations. To get a CMenu pointer to the menu that is connected to a window, you call CWnd::GetMenu:

```
// Fetch pointer to main menu.
CMenu * pmenu = GetMenu();
```

You might notice another twist to this paradox. This line of code fetches a pointer to an object that was never created. What's happening? The short answer, which will soon be elaborated upon, is that MFC creates a CMenu while adding it to a temporary object storage list.

For now, let's examine some of the issues involved in making dynamic modifications to menus, starting with the most common task you probably need: modifying the contents of an existing popup menu.

Changing an existing popup menu

Using a CMenu pointer from CWnd::GetMenu, you can do such things as inserting a new popup menu between the File menu and the Help menu. That's a subject that's explored a bit later in this chapter.

For now, more common operations — adding menu items to and removing menu items from an existing popup menu — are of interest. For this, you need another CMenu * pointer — in this case, to one of the submenus. As shown in the following lines of code, you use CMenu::GetSubMenu to get a submenu pointer:

```
CMenu * pmenu = GetMenu();
CMenu * pmSub = pmenu->GetSubMenu(1);
CMenu::GetSubMenu() is defined as follows:
CMenu* GetSubMenu( int nPos)
```

The sole parameter, nPos, is a zero-based index to the submenu that you want to access. Table 4-5 summarizes common CMenu functions for modifying (or simply querying) the contents of a menu. For example, using the pmSub submenu pointer from the previous example, you can append a new menu item to an existing submenu like this:

```
pmSub->AppendMenu (MF_STRING,        // Menu flag
         ID_MENU_ADDMENUITEM, // Command id.
         "Add Menu &Item");   // Menu string.
```

Table 4-5: Common CMenu Functions

Function	Description
AppendMenu	Adds a new menu item to the end of an existing menu or to a new popup menu.
CheckMenuItem	Sets or clears the menu check mark (rarely used). In place of this function, you should provide an UPDATE_COMMAND_UI handler.

Continued

Table 4-5: *(continued)*

Function	Description
GetMenuItemID	Queries a menu item's command ID.
GetMenuString	Queries a menu item's text label.
EnableMenuItem	Enables and disables menu items (works only if CFrameWnd::m_bAutoMenuEnable = FALSE). In place of this function, you should provide an UPDATE_COMMAND_UI handler.
InsertMenu	Inserts a new menu item at a specified offset within an existing menu.
RemoveMenu	Deletes a specific menu item.

Although the MFC help database describes the parameters, let's take a closer look at the declaration for CMenu::AppendMenu:

```
BOOL AppendMenu( UINT nFlags,
        UINT nIDNewItem = 0,
        LPCTSTR lpszNewItem = NULL);
```

The first parameter, nFlags, is a flag field for specifying the state of the menu item you create. Many menu modification functions use these flags. They're summarized in Table 4-6.

Table 4-6: Menu Modification Flags

Menu Flag	Description
MF_BITMAP	Signifies a menu item with an image rather than a string.
MF_OWNERDRAW	Signifies an application-drawn menu item—more flexible than MF_BITMAP.
MF_POP-UP	Indicates a popup menu.
MF_SEPARATOR	Indicates a visual divider for menu item groups.
MF_STRING	Signifies a menu item, either regular menu or popup menu, with a string.
MF_CHECKED	Displays a check mark on a menu item.
MF_UNCHECKED	Unchecks a checked menu item.
MF_ENABLED	Makes a menu selection available to a user.
M_GRAYED	Makes a menu item unavailable to the user; the item is grayed out.
MF_MENUBREAK	Changes the way the menu item is displayed. At a menu item with this flag, the menu changes direction. For example, a menu bar item, whose text normally is displayed horizontally, wraps to a new line.
MF_MENUBARBREAK	Same as the previous item except that in popup menus, a line is used to separate columns.
MF_BYCOMMAND	Sets the program to pick menu items with the command ID.
MF_BYPOSITION	Sets the program to pick menu items based on their zero-based position.

The meaning of the second parameter, nIDNewItem, depends on whether you're inserting a new menu item or a new popup menu (indicated by MF_POPUP in nFlags). If you're inserting a menu item, this parameter holds an integer command ID for the menu item. If you're inserting a new popup menu, this field is the menu handle of the menu to be inserted. (As you'll see, you use the value of CMenu::m_hMenu for this field.)

The meaning of the last parameter, lpszNewItem, depends on what type of item you're inserting. It's either a pointer to a character string for an MF_STRING item or a unique item identifier for an MF_OWNERDRAW item.

You should note that when you dynamically create menu items, MFC doesn't know how to display help strings in the status window. (Recall that MFC does this automatically for static menu resources, using strings that you enter in the menu editor's Prompt field.) To enable this feature for dynamically created menu items, override CFrameWnd::GetMessageString with your own version of GetMessageString. For dynamically created menu items, you supply the required strings. For statically created menu items, call the default handler that reads in the correct string from the string table.

Although the menu modification techniques that have been described certainly work as advertised, an important issue has been glossed over. Even though it was stated that an MFC program doesn't create a CMenu object for its menu, a CMenu object is clearly being used to change the menu. Where did this object come from? And who will delete the object when it's no longer needed? The answer to these questions lies in structures MFC manages called *handle maps*. Let's take a short detour, and explore how these maps affect menu programming.

Permanent and temporary handle maps

To bridge the gap between MFC objects and Windows API objects, MFC maintains a set of look-up tables, called *handle maps*. In simplest terms, Windows uses handles to identify objects, and MFC uses pointers. The origin of pointer semantics was primarily for maintaining a one-to-one ratio between Windows system objects (windows and menus, for example) and C++/MFC objects (such as CWnd and CMenu objects). And whereas we identify a C++ object with a pointer, a Windows system object is always identified by a *handle*.

Remember, a handle is a number that uniquely identifies a particular object. The meaning of the number is known only to the part of the system that's issued the handle. Internal to the operating system, a handle might be a pointer or an index, but to the outside world it's just a number.

MFC uses handle maps to identify the C++ object that corresponds to a given Windows object handle. After all, when MFC calls Windows API functions, it cannot use the C++ object; MFC must use a handle. And when the Windows system libraries communicate back to MFC, they also use handles. Although MFC can easily figure out the handle from a C++ object (after all, it's usually one of the first data members), a little extra work is required for MFC to convert a system handle to a C++ pointer. To assist in this task, MFC creates handle maps.

MFC creates handle maps for two user interface objects (windows and menus) and for seven graphic output objects (bitmaps, brushes, device contexts, fonts, palettes, pens, and regions). The creation of handle maps and handle map entries is handled transparently most of the time by individual MFC objects as needed.

In a few cases, such as when merging existing Windows API code into an MFC application, you'll find that you have to convert system handles to MFC object pointers. Each of the MFC classes that wrap Windows API objects has member functions that can help with this task. For example, CWnd::Attach connects a CWnd object to an existing system window and creates the proper handle map entry. CWnd::Detach deletes a window handle entry from the MFC handle maps.

MFC creates two types of handle maps: permanent and temporary. A *permanent handle map* exists for Windows API objects that are created via an MFC class. For example, when you initialize a CFrameWnd object by calling CFrameWnd::Create or CFrameWnd::LoadFrame, an entry is made in the permanent handle table. When you delete an MFC object that has a permanent handle table entry, the object knows that it can also destroy the corresponding Windows API object.

Programmers who are experienced with SDK-style programming might wonder why an alternative mechanism wasn't chosen. In particular, why does MFC use handle tables for windows instead of window extra bytes? (Window extra bytes are a fixed number of extra bytes allocated by Windows on a per-window basis.) The reason is that predefined window types, such as dialog box controls, already use window extra bytes. Microsoft designed MFC to be capable of wrapping around preexisting classes. If MFC tried using window extra bytes with a window that already used window extra bytes, a conflict would occur.

MFC's automatic destruction of Windows system objects can cause you untold grief if you don't understand some of the subtler implications. In particular, you should avoid creating CObject-derived objects as local variables. At the end of the function (when the local objects go out of scope) the destructor is called, which destroys the Windows API object. The following code fragment taught this lesson to one of the authors:

```
// DON'T DO THIS!!!-When local variable goes out
// of scope, Windows API object is destroyed.
CMenu cm;
cm.LoadMenu(IDR_POP-UP_MENU);

// The append operation will be short-lived...
CMenu * pmenu = GetMenu();
pmenu->AppendMenu(MF_POP-UP, (UINT)cm.m_hMenu, "Pop-up");
```

With one important change, this code fragment could work properly. The only reason the object is destroyed is because CMenu::~CMenu finds the object in the permanent handle map. By calling CMenu::Detach, you disconnect the handle map entry and avoid this particular headache.

On the other hand, for objects that are not created via an MFC class, MFC has a *temporary handle map*. MFC creates an entry in the temporary handle map for objects that it must create on-the-fly to wrap Windows system objects. Such objects are very short-lived, though, because all entries to the temporary handle map are deleted during idle time processing. For this reason, you'll always reference temporary objects using pointers that are created as local variables. This way, you avoid the problem of having a pointer to an object that has been automatically deleted.

Every MFC function that wraps Windows API objects has the two functions described: Attach and Detach. There's also a third function, FromHandle, which is a universal "get pointer from handle" function. This function first searches a permanent handle map and then the temporary handle map. If no entry is found in either map, an object is created, and an entry is made in the temporary handle map.

Here's an example that clarifies when an entry is made in the temporary handle map. The menu function that has been discussed, CWnd::GetMenu, calls CMenu::FromHandle. When you call this function in an AppWizard-generated program — which loads a menu from a resource — MFC automatically creates a CMenu for you. To ensure that you have complete access to this object, MFC adds an entry to the temporary handle map. Your access to the object lasts at least until your program fetches its next message, because cleanup is handled at idle time.

So how does MFC determine when things are idle? Idle time occurs only when you're not in the middle of handling a message. Idle time is a Windows API artifact that was first created long ago to provide printer spooling support. Idle time occurs whenever the user pauses a moment and allows all message queues to empty. Even the busiest worker on the slowest machine must pause sometime, whether it's to answer a phone, talk to a friend, or just think. A blink is all it takes for an idle moment to occur, at which time MFC frees the C++ objects (but *not* the Windows API objects) that are referenced in temporary handle maps.

Context Menus

Since the debut of Windows 95, Microsoft has promoted the creation of *context menus*. A context menu, sometimes called a *popup menu*, is not connected to the menu bar. Instead, it is displayed when the user selects an object and then clicks the right mouse button. (It's also possible to simultaneously select an object and summon a context menu with just a single click of the right mouse button.) The Visual C++ IDE already makes extensive use of this type of menu, as do many other commercially available applications. Starting with Windows 95, the operating system itself uses context menus for handling numerous routine operations. To fit your applications into this environment, you should consider adding context menus to them as well.

Besides clicking the right mouse button, a user can summon a context menu using a keystroke. The Applications key appears on newer 104-key keyboards, such as the Microsoft Natural keyboard. On keyboards that are so equipped, users can open a context menu by pressing the Applications key. To accommodate users whose keyboards are not equipped with this key, applications should define the Shift+F10 accelerator for summoning context menus.

Like most other MFC objects that wrap Windows API objects, two steps are required for creating a fully functioning object. First, you allocate a C++ object, and then you initialize the object. These lines of code show one way to create and initialize a CMenu object:

```
// Allocate CMenu for context menu.
g_pmenuContext = new CMenu();
if (!g_pmenuContext) return -1;

// Initialize CMenu (connect menu to MFC menu object).
BOOL bSuccess = g_pmenuContext->LoadMenu(IDR_CONTEXT);
if (!bSuccess) return -1;
```

This code fragment is from a function that expects a return value of –1 on failure (the handler function for the WM_CREATE message). Allocation involves the new operator. Initialization involves a call to CMenu::LoadMenu, which takes as its only parameter a menu resource identifier.

Once it's created and initialized, the context menu is ready to appear whenever you want to see it. From the user's perspective, this menu should display when the user clicks the right mouse button. The following WM_RBUTTONDOWN message handler displays the context menu:

```
void CMainFrame::OnRButtonDown(UINT nFlags, CPoint point)
{
  // Convert client coordinate to screen coordinates.
  ClientToScreen(&point);

  // Display context menu at mouse location.
  CMenu * psubmenu = g_pmenuContext->GetSubMenu(0);
```

```
psubmenu->TrackPopupMenu(TPM_LEFTALIGN |  // Flags
               TPM_RIGHTBUTTON,
               point.x,      // x-coordinate
               point.y,      // y-coordinate
               this);        // "this" window

   CFrameWnd::OnRButtonDown(nFlags, point);
}
```

The second of the two parameters to OnRButtonDown gives the location of the mouse in client-area coordinates. However, TrackPopupMenu expects screen coordinates, so you call CWnd::ClientToScreen. This function converts from client-area coordinates (the origin in the top-left corner of the client area) to screen coordinates (the origin in the top-left corner of the screen).

Most of the parameters to CMenu::TrackPopupMenu are reasonably straightforward. However, the last parameter is worth discussing. When the context menu appears, a stream of messages is generated that must be sent to some window or another. The pointer this, in the context of a CFrameWnd-derived class, identifies the window that should receive the menu messages.

The final step that you need to consider is how to clean up a context menu when you're finished with it. The example simply deletes the CMenu object when you're done using it. Like all other entries in the permanent handle map table, when the object is destroyed, the system object is destroyed, and the handle map entry is erased. Although you might delete the menu object in any of several different places, you could do it in the destructor for the window frame object:

```
CMainFrame::~CMainFrame()
{
   if (g_pmenuContext)
      g_pmenuContext->DestroyMenu();
}
```

As part of the Windows user interface standard, Microsoft recommends using the right mouse button for context menus. Users expect this feature, and you put yourself at a disadvantage if you don't make use of it.

Summary

This chapter explored two mechanisms for getting command input from the user: menus and accelerator keys. In both cases, the same command message, WM_COMMAND, is sent when the user requests an action in the form of a command. Menus and acclerator keys also send CN_UPDATE_COMMAND_UI messages to determine the state of commands and menu items. As you have seen, most of the work involved in using these mechanisms is in setting them up.

The next chapter looks at the two most common ways a user interacts with applications: through the keyboard and the mouse. Without keyboard and mouse support, your application, and Windows in general, wouldn't do very much.

✦   ✦   ✦

Mouse and Keyboard Processing

In this chapter, you'll learn how to handle mouse and keyboard input. In the first section, I'll examine the overall system used by Windows to manage input state. I'll also take a look at a concept called *local input state* that made its first debut in Windows NT and is used in all 32-bit versions of Windows.

Next, I'll look at mouse input specifically. Thanks to the Microsoft Foundation Classes (MFC), the days of writing low-level mouse handling code are over (unless you have a lot of free time). In this section I'll examine the methods MFC provides to manage and manipulate the mouse. I'll consider such issues as the shape of the mouse pointer (cursor), the capture of mouse input, and the clipping of the mouse pointer to a specific clipping rectangle.

Finally, I'll look at the various ways that a program can use keyboard input. Using user interface elements such as the edit control, you can allow Windows and MFC to manage the keyboard for you. Many times, however, you might need tighter control over the keyboard. As part of this discussion, I will consider the keyboard focus, the keyboard cursor (insertion point), the selection state, and other user interface constructs that are related to keyboard input.

Event Basics

Many seasoned non-Windows programmers have trouble with the event-driven nature of Windows programming when they first start writing applications. In the context of user input processing, *event-driven* means that rather than polling the system for a key press or a mouse click from the user, Windows sends your application a *windows message* whenever the user hits a key or clicks the mouse.

MFC maps these Windows messages to C++ functions called *message handlers*. The input handling logic of your application resides in these message-handling functions. In the previous chapter, I covered message handlers in relation to menus. Later in this chapter, I'll talk more about message handlers with regards to the handling of keyboard and mouse events. Let's start by looking at the input state of first the mouse, and then the keyboard.

Mouse Input

As mentioned previously, Windows sends input to a program's windows as messages that get stored in a hardware input queue. Table 5-1 lists the main Windows mouse messages to which you'll respond when handling user input.

Table 5-1: Windows Mouse Input Messages

Message	Message Trigger
WM_LBUTTONDOWN	The left mouse button was clicked down while the mouse pointer was over the window's client area.
WM_LBUTTONUP	The left mouse button was released.
WM_RBUTTONDOWN	The right mouse button was clicked down while the mouse pointer was over the window's client area.
WM_RBUTTONUP	The right mouse button was released.
WM_MBUTTONDOWN	The middle mouse button was clicked down while the mouse pointer was over the window's client area.
WM_MBUTTONUP	The middle mouse button was released.
WM_MOUSEMOVE	The mouse pointer was moved over the window's client area.

Creating mouse message handlers

As you learned in Chapter 1, creating message handlers can be done through the Class View. At this point, take a moment and create a mouse message handler that will track (and display) the mouse movement over the view as follows:

1. Create a single-document interface application named HandlerTest.

2. From the Class View, right-click the CHandlerTestView class, and select the Properties menu option from the context menu.

3. Click the Messages icon at the top of the Properties dialog bar. Visual Studio then displays in the Properties dialog bar all messages that this class' window can receive.

4. Locate and click the WM_MOUSEMOVE entry adding a member function called OnMouseMove.

5. Add the following code to the OnMouseMove function:

```
CClientDC ClientDC( this );
CString strInfo;
strInfo.Format( "Current Mouse Position = X:%d Y:%d",
  point.x, point.y );
ClientDC.TextOut(10,10, strInfo, strInfo.GetLength() );
```

6. Compile and run the program. As you move the mouse in the client window, you'll see the mouse position coordinates as they're drawn in the window (shown in Figure 5-1).

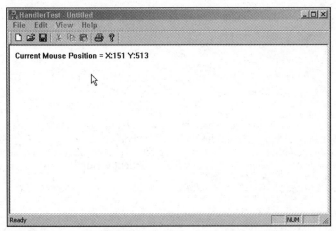

Figure 5-1: Simple application to track (and display) mouse movements

Converting between screen and window coordinates

In the OnMouseMove handler you just created, MFC passes the coordinates of the mouse pointer to the handler function using an MFC class called CPoint. An object of type CPoint is typically used to describe a point on the screen. The CPoint object's *x* and *y* members, accessed as CPoint::x and CPoint::y, respectively, contain the *x* and *y* coordinates for the physical point it represents.

The coordinates that are sent to the OnMouseMove function are in terms of the view window's client area. The lowest value you'll get for both *x* and *y* is zero. The greatest value for the *x* and *y* values will be equal to the width and height of the view window, respectively. The *x* and *y* values may vary depending on the window's mapping mode. For instance, the values when in MM_TEXT mapping mode will be pixels, and the values when in MM_TWIPS will be *twips*. I go into more detail about mapping modes in Chapter 8.

On occasion you might want to know what the mouse coordinates are in terms of the entire screen. The Win32 SDK provides a convenient function called ClientToScreen to translate client *xy* coordinates into screen coordinates. The MFC CWnd class also defines a member function of the same name as a thin wrapper for this function. Additionally, a reciprocal function, ScreenToClient, exists to convert screen *xy* coordinates into client coordinates.

To use the CWnd::ClientToScreen member function, you simply pass the *xy* client coordinates in a CPoint object. As an example, if a window were placed on the screen at position 50, 75, the mouse coordinates returned to OnMouseMove will be in reference to the coordinate pair of 50, 75. If the user is pointing to a location inside of the window that's 15 pixels to the right of the window's top-left corner and 25 pixels down from the window's top-left corner, the coordinates sent to OnMouseMove will be 15, 25. By using the ClientToScreen function, those values are converted to literal screen values by adding the offset into the window to the screen position of the window. In this case, the screen coordinates will be 65, 100. The following code fragment illustrates the use of this function:

```
void CMyClassView::OnMouseMove(UINT nFlags, CPoint point)
{
   CPoint pt;
   pt = point;
```

```
  ClientToScreen( pt );
  CString strInfo;
  strInfo( "Scrn X:%d ScrnY:%d    ",
    pt.x, pt.y );
  CClientDC ClientDC( this );
  ClientDC.TextOut(10,10, strInfo, strInfo.GetLength() );
  CScrollView::OnMouseMove(nFlags, point);
}
```

Another option is to convert from screen coordinates to client coordinates. This is helpful when you get mouse coordinates from the Windows API function GetCursorPos. This function returns coordinate values in terms of the entire screen. Following is an example in which the mouse position is obtained and then converted to client window coordinates:

```
void CMyClassView::TestFunction()
{
  POINT point;
  ::GetCursorPos( &point );
  CPoint pt( point );
  ScreenToClient( pt );
  CString strInfo;
  strInfo( "Scrn X:%d ScrnY:%d ClntX:%d ClntY:%d",
    point.x, point.y, pt.x, pt.y );
  AfxMessageBox( strInfo );
  CScrollView::OnMouseMove(nFlags, point);
}
```

Creating an MFC program that handles mouse events

In this section, you'll see a demo with examples of how an application can respond to the most commonly used mouse events. It handles mouse movement events, mouse button down events, and mouse button up events. One thing I'll quickly note before jumping into coding this demo application is that I make use of certain GDI drawing functions and objects (devices contexts and brushes). Although I'm purposely not going to explain much about them in this chapter in order to stay focused on working with mouse events, the entire subject of working with the GDI is covered in Chapters 8 and 9.

1. Create a new SDI project called MouseDemo1.

2. Add the following code to the view's constructor. This code simply initializes a mode value (keeps track of whether or not it should be displaying information) and a two-dimensional array (used to display either blue or red boxes on the view depending on whether the user left-clicks or right-clicks).

```
CMouseDemo1View::CMouseDemo1View()
{

  // Start in the mode that shows mouse
  // info, not the grid of rectangles.
  m_nInfoMode = MOUSE_SHOWINFO;

  // Clear the two dimensional grid array.
  for( int y=0; y<10; y++ )
```

```
for( int x=0; x<10; x++ )
  m_nGrid[x][y] = 0;
```

}

3. Modify that view's OnDraw function so that when finished it is as follows. Note the m_nInfoMode value initialized in the constructor and the drawing of the red and blue boxes. You'll see shortly how the user specifies whether the application should display the mouse coordinates in text or via these graphics.

```
void CMouseDemo1View::OnDraw(CDC* pDC)
{
  CMouseDemo1Doc* pDoc = GetDocument();
  ASSERT_VALID(pDoc);

  // Only perform a redraw when
  // set to MOUSE_SHOWGRID mode.
  if( m_nInfoMode == MOUSE_SHOWGRID ){

    // Use the client rectangle
    // in order to draw the grid
    // rectangles in a size proportional
    // to the client rectangle.
    RECT Rect;
    GetClientRect( &Rect );

    // Create red, white, and blue brushes.
    CBrush RedBrush( RGB( 255, 0, 0 ) );
    CBrush BlueBrush( RGB( 0, 0, 255 ) );
    CBrush WhiteBrush( RGB( 255, 255, 255 ) );
    CBrush *pUseBrush;

    // The grid has ten horizontal and ten
    // vertical components.
    for( int y=0; y<10; y++ ){
      for( int x=0; x<10; x++ ){

        // Assign DrawRect by calculating
        // one tenth of the client
        // rectangle.
        RECT DrawRect;
        DrawRect.left =
          ( x * Rect.right ) / 10;
        DrawRect.top =
          ( y * Rect.bottom ) / 10;
        DrawRect.right =
          DrawRect.left + ( Rect.right / 10 ) + 1;
        DrawRect.bottom =
          DrawRect.top + ( Rect.bottom / 10 );

        // Select the brush for drawing
        // based on whether the grid
```

```
        // is empty, set to left, or
        // set to right.
        pUseBrush = &WhiteBrush;
        if( m_nGrid[x][y] == 1 )
          pUseBrush = &BlueBrush;
        else if( m_nGrid[x][y] == 2 )
          pUseBrush = &RedBrush;

        // Draw the filled rectangle.
        pDC->FillRect( &DrawRect, pUseBrush );
        }
    }
  }

}
```

4. Now, add the first mouse handler — this one for the WM_LBUTTONDOWN message — and code it as follows. As you can see, the function does little more than call ShowMouseInfo. This is to centralize the code in one function because all of the mouse event handlers need to do the same thing. You'll see the ShowMouseInfo function shortly.

```
void CMouseDemo1View::OnLButtonDown(UINT nFlags,
  CPoint point)
{

  // Call the function that displays the mouse
  // information.
  ShowMouseInfo( "LButtonDown", point, 1 );

  // Call the default OnLButtonDown() function.
  CView::OnLButtonDown(nFlags, point);
}
```

5. Add the following mouse event handlers for the WM_LBUTTONUP, WM_LBUTTONDBLCLK, WM_RBUTTONDOWN, WM_RBUTTONUP, and WM_RBUTTONDBLCLK messages.

```
void CMouseDemo1View::OnLButtonUp(UINT nFlags,
  CPoint point)
{

  // Call the function that displays the mouse
  // information.
  ShowMouseInfo( "LButtonUp", point );

  // Call the default OnLButtonUp() function.
  CView::OnLButtonUp(nFlags, point);
}

void CMouseDemo1View::OnLButtonDblClk(UINT nFlags,
  CPoint point)
{

  // Call the function that displays the mouse
```

```
    // information.
    ShowMouseInfo( "LButtonDblClk", point );

    // Call the default OnLButtonDblClk() function.
    CView::OnLButtonDblClk(nFlags, point);
}

void CMouseDemo1View::OnRButtonDown(UINT nFlags,
    CPoint point)
{

    // Call the function that displays the mouse
    // information.
    ShowMouseInfo( "RButtonDown", point, 2 );

    // Call the default OnRButtonDown() function.
    CView::OnRButtonDown(nFlags, point);
}

void CMouseDemo1View::OnRButtonUp(UINT nFlags,
    CPoint point)
{

    // Call the function that displays the mouse
    // information.
    ShowMouseInfo( "RButtonUp", point );

    // Call the default OnRButtonUp() function.
    CView::OnRButtonUp(nFlags, point);
}

void CMouseDemo1View::OnRButtonDblClk(UINT nFlags,
    CPoint point)
{

    // Call the function that displays the mouse
    // information.
    ShowMouseInfo( "RButtonDblClk", point );

    // Call the default OnRButtonDblClk() function.
    CView::OnRButtonDblClk(nFlags, point);
}
```

6. Now add a handler for the WM_MOUSEMOVE **message.**

```
void CMouseDemo1View::OnMouseMove(UINT nFlags,
    CPoint point)
{
  // Only show the mouse position if
  // you're set to MOUSE_SHOWINFO.
  if( m_nInfoMode == MOUSE_SHOWINFO ){
    CClientDC ClientDC( this );
```

```
        CString strInfo;

        // Copy the CPoint class so
        // that you can convert it to
        // screen coordinates.
        CPoint pt = point;

        // Convert to screen coordinates.
        ClientToScreen( &pt );

        // Format the information.
        strInfo.Format(
          "X:%d Y:%d ScnX:%d ScnY:%d              ",
          point.x, point.y,
          pt.x, pt.y );

        // Draw the information string to
        // the window.
        ClientDC.TextOut( 0, 0,
          strInfo, strInfo.GetLength() );
        }

    // Call the default OnMouseMove() function.
    CView::OnMouseMove(nFlags, point);
  }
```

7. Now that all the mouse event handlers are in place, code the ShowMouseInfo function as follows:

```
void CMouseDemo1View::ShowMouseInfo(
  const char *lpszText, CPoint point, int nFlag )
{

  // Perform the following code if
  // you're set to MOUSE_SHOWGRID.
  if( m_nInfoMode == MOUSE_SHOWGRID ){
    if( nFlag != -1 ){

      // Get the client rectangle
      // so that you can calculate which
      // x and y index the current
      // click position.
      RECT Rect;
      GetClientRect( &Rect );

      // Use the client rectangle
      // and divide by ten to calculate
      // the x and y grid indexes.
      int x = ( point.x * 10 ) / Rect.right;
      int y = ( point.y * 10 ) / Rect.bottom;

      // Either set the grid to left or right
```

```
      // button states, or clear them so that
      // the grid array is empty.
      if( m_nGrid[x][y] == nFlag )
        m_nGrid[x][y] = 0;
      else
        m_nGrid[x][y] = nFlag;

      // Cause the window to redraw.
      InvalidateRect( NULL, FALSE );
      UpdateWindow();
      }
    return;
    }

  // Get a DC to the client window.
  CClientDC ClientDC( this );

  CString strInfo;

  // Format the output string.
  strInfo.Format(
    "X:%d Y:%d %s          ",
    point.x, point.y, lpszText );

  // Draw the output string to the
  // window.
  ClientDC.TextOut( point.x, point.y,
    strInfo, strInfo.GetLength() );

  }
```

8. You're almost there. Now you just need to add the menu entries to allow the user to specify the application's display mode. To do that, add the menu entries shown in Figure 5-2.

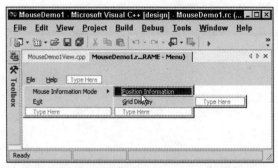

Figure 5-2: Demo application menu to allow the user to specify a display mode that tracks and displays the results of handling the various mouse messages

9. Once you've added the two menu items, you'll need to add the following menu item handlers. (Working with menus is covered in Chapter 4.)

```
void CMouseDemo1View::OnFileMouseGriddisplay()
{

  // Set to MOUSE_SHOWGRID mode.
  if( m_nInfoMode != MOUSE_SHOWGRID ){
    m_nInfoMode = MOUSE_SHOWGRID;
    InvalidateRect( NULL, TRUE );
    UpdateWindow();
    }

}

void CMouseDemo1View::OnUpdateFileMouseGriddisplay(
  CCmdUI* pCmdUI)
{

  // Set the menu check if you're
  // in MOUSE_SHOWGRID mode.
  pCmdUI->SetCheck( m_nInfoMode == MOUSE_SHOWGRID );

}

void CMouseDemo1View::OnFileMousePositioninformation()
{

  // Set to MOUSE_SHOWINFO mode.
  if( m_nInfoMode != MOUSE_SHOWINFO ){
    m_nInfoMode = MOUSE_SHOWINFO;
    InvalidateRect( NULL, TRUE );
    UpdateWindow();
    }

}

void CMouseDemo1View::OnUpdateFileMousePositioninformation
(CCmdUI* pCmdUI)
{

  // Set the menu check if you're
  // in MOUSE_SHOWINFO mode.
  pCmdUI->SetCheck( m_nInfoMode == MOUSE_SHOWINFO );

}
```

10. When finished, run the application and after selecting a mode, move the mouse about the view clicking and right-clicking to see how the application responds. Figure 5-3 shows an example of me testing the application.

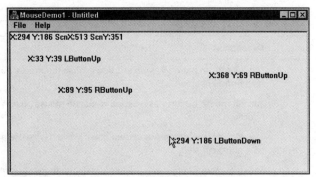

Figure 5-3: This demo application illustrates how easy MFC and Visual Studio .NET make it to incorporate mouse event handling into your applications.

You'll notice that if you minimize the application or in some way cause it to be repainted, the text disappears from the client area. This is because the application is drawing the text as the user clicks the mouse on the client area. Therefore, when the client area is invalidated, the application has no way of repainting this text. As a simple exercise in modifying this application, you could easily store the text strings in an array and print them out to the client area in the view's OnDraw function. That way, the view would always have the correct text — even when it's redrawn.

Nonclient mouse events

At this point you might be asking yourself where the nonclient areas of a window are. The easiest answer is also the most accurate. That is, the nonclient areas are all the areas of the window that surround the client area. As an illustration, open the WordPad application. The client area is the large white area where you can type text. The nonclient areas include all the parts of the window that surround this area. This includes the caption bar, menu bar, scroll bars, and so on.

Windows uses about half of the defined input messages for nonclient area objects. The mouse messages with names that contain the letters NC are messages that Windows handles for the nonclient area components of a window. For example, Windows receives a WM_NCLBUTTONDOWN message when a user selects a menu command, resizes a window frame, or minimizes a window. The differences between these actions depend on the mouse location when the mouse button is clicked.

The nonsystem mouse messages are for application use — that is, they are for your use. With the help of ClassWizard, creating and responding to the basic set of messages is fairly straightforward. Table 5-2 lists the nonclient mouse messages that Windows manages.

Table 5-2: Nonclient Mouse Messages

Message	Description
WM_NCLBUTTONDOWN	The left mouse button was clicked down while the mouse pointer was on a nonclient area.
WM_NCLBUTTONUP	The left mouse button was released while the mouse pointer was on a nonclient area.
WM_NCRBUTTONDOWN	The right mouse button was clicked down while the mouse pointer was on a nonclient area.
WM_NCRBUTTONUP	The right mouse button was released while the mouse pointer was on a nonclient area.
WM_NCMBUTTONDOWN	The middle mouse button was clicked down while the mouse pointer was on a nonclient area.
WM_NCMBUTTONUP	The middle mouse button was released while the mouse pointer was on a nonclient area.
WM_NCMOUSEMOVE	The mouse pointer was moved over a nonclient area of a window.
WM_NCHITTEST	A query message that asks, "Where in the window is the mouse pointer?" The NC in this query message doesn't mean that it's only for the nonclient area, although that is the system's primary interest. Instead, this message returns a hit-test code that identifies the pointer position in the window—for example, over a border, over a menu, or over the client area.

Changing the mouse cursor

One of the most common ways to give feedback to the end user is to change the shape of the mouse pointer. This can be done via the SetCursor function. As an example, the following code snippet loads the standard IDC_CROSS cursor (represented by an I-beam icon).

```
HCURSOR hc = ::LoadCursor(NULL,IDC_CROSS);
ASSERT(hc);
if (hc)
{
   ::SetCursor(hc);
}
```

Note that the code first needs to load a cursor (via the LoadCursor function). This function has the following prototype:

```
HCURSOR LoadCursor(HINSTANCE hInstance,
                   LPCTSTR lpCursorName);
```

The hInstance argument is the instance handle of the module whose executable contains the cursor to be loaded. Because the IDC_CROSS is a standard Windows cursor, this value is set to NULL. The second value is then the cursor name. Windows defines the 16 standard cursors shown in Table 5-3.

Table 5-3: Predefined Windows Mouse Cursors

Value	Meaning
IDC_APPSTARTING	Combination arrow and small hourglass
IDC_ARROW	Standard arrow
IDC_CROSS	Crosshair that you normally see when in a text document or edit control
IDC_HAND	Hand cursor used with Windows 98/Me and Windows 2000/XP
IDC_HELP	Arrow and question mark used to indicate context sensitive help
IDC_IBEAM	Same as IDC_CROSS
IDC_ICON	Obsolete for applications marked version 4.0 or later
IDC_NO	Slashed circle used to denote an invalid drop target for a an attempted drag-and-drop operation
IDC_SIZE	Obsolete for applications marked version 4.0 or later. Use IDC_SIZEALL
IDC_SIZEALL	Four-pointed arrow pointing north, south, east, and west that is used to indicate that the object can be sized in any direction
IDC_SIZENESW	Double-pointed arrow pointing northeast and southwest used to indicate that the object can be sized both horizontally and vertically
IDC_SIZENS	Double-pointed arrow pointing north and south indicating that the object can be sized vertically
IDC_SIZENWSE	Double-pointed arrow pointing northwest and southeast used to indicate that the object can be sized both horizontally and vertically
IDC_SIZEWE	Double-pointed arrow pointing north and south indicating that the object can be sized horizontally
IDC_UPARROW	Vertical arrow
IDC_WAIT	Hourglass to indicate that a lengthy operation is in progress

The ability to specify a module's HINSTANCE and cursor name means that you can create your own cursors and load and set them at runtime. This is typically done through resource-only DLLs and is covered in Chapter 16.

Once a cursor is loaded, a call is then made to the SetCursor function using the HCURSOR (cursor handle) returned from the LoadCursor function. This simple function takes the following form:

```
HCURSOR SetCursor(HCURSOR hCursor);
```

As you can see, the SetCursor function also returns an HCURSOR. This value represents the cursor that was being used by Windows before you issued the call to SetCursor. This enables you to reset the cursor to its original state when finished.

In the preceding code snippet, I used the Win32 LoadCursor and SetCursor functions. You can also use the CWinApp LoadStandardCursor member function to load any of the predefined Windows cursors:

```
HCURSOR hc = theApp.LoadStandardCursor(IDC_CROSS);
```

Aside from the IDC_ARROW cursor, the most commonly used cursor is the IDC_WAIT (hourglass) cursor. Because of its popularity, the MFC provides two functions specifically designed to set this cursor. These functions are called BeginWaitCursor and EndWaitCursor, and are used to display the hourglass cursor and to return the cursor to its previous shape, respectively.

Have a look at a simple application that illustrates how to load and set the various predefined Windows cursors.

Creating an MFC program that changes mouse cursors

To demonstrate how to change mouse cursors within an application, here's a simple application called MouseDemo2.

1. To get things started, create a new SDI project called MouseDemo2.

2. Open the MouseDemoView2.cpp file and add the following static structure to the top of the file (just before IMPLEMENT_DYNCREATE line). The id and szName members will be used in the LoadCursor call and to display in the client area the current cursor, respectively.

```
struct
{
  char* id;
  char szName[255];
} cursors[] = {
  IDC_APPSTARTING, "IDC_APPSTARTING",
  IDC_ARROW, "IDC_ARROW",
  IDC_CROSS, "IDC_CROSS",
  IDC_HAND, "IDC_HAND",
  IDC_HELP, "IDC_HELP",
  IDC_IBEAM, "IDC_IBEAM",
  IDC_ICON, "IDC_ICON",
  IDC_NO, "IDC_NO",
  IDC_SIZE, "IDC_SIZE",
  IDC_SIZEALL, "IDC_SIZEALL",
  IDC_SIZENESW, "IDC_SIZENESW",
  IDC_SIZENS, "IDC_SIZENS",
  IDC_SIZENWSE, "IDC_SIZENWSE",
  IDC_SIZEWE, "IDC_SIZEWE",
  IDC_UPARROW, "IDC_UPARROW",
  IDC_WAIT, "IDC_WAIT"
};
```

3. Add the following code to the view's constructor. This loads the predefined cursors into an array that will be used as the user moves the mouse around the client area.

```
CMouseDemo2View::CMouseDemo2View()
{
  // Load the cursors.
```

```
    for (int i=0; i<16; i++)
      m_hCursor[i] = ::LoadCursor(NULL, cursors[i].id);
}
```

4. At this point, you need a function that sets the current mouse cursor. To make the
   application more interesting, the cursor that is used is determined by calling a function
   (GetCursorRegion) that divides the view into 16 regions and then selects the cursor
   based on what region of the view the mouse is currently over.

```
BOOL CMouseDemo2View::OnSetCursor(CWnd* pWnd,
     UINT nHitTest, UINT message)
{

  // See if this is a HTCLIENT
  // hit test.
  if( nHitTest == HTCLIENT ){

    // Get the mouse position. This
    // will be in terms of the
    // entire screen.
    POINT pt;
    GetCursorPos( &pt );

    // Convert the coordinates to
    // client rectangle coordinates.
    ScreenToClient( &pt );

    // Call the function that you created
    // that gets the cursor region.
    int nCursor = GetCursorRegion( &pt );

    // Set the window cursor.
    ::SetCursor( m_hCursor[nCursor] );

    // Return indicating that you responded
    // to this message.
    return( TRUE );
    }

  // Call the default OnSetCursor() function.
  return CView::OnSetCursor(pWnd, nHitTest, message);
}
```

5. Now for the GetCursorRegion function:

```
int CMouseDemo2View::GetCursorRegion( POINT *lpPt )
{
  // You need the client
  // rectangle so that you can
  // calculate the cursor region.
  // It'll be an x value from 0-3
  // and a y value from 0-3.
  RECT Rect;
  GetClientRect( &Rect );
```

```
// Divide the client rectangle width
// by four to obtain the x region
// index.
int x =
  ( lpPt->x * 4 ) / Rect.right;
if( x > 3 ) x = 3;


// Divide the client rectangle height
// by four to obtain the y region
// index.
int y =
  ( lpPt->y * 4 ) / Rect.bottom;
if( y > 3 ) y = 3;

// Return the index. It'll be a value
// from 0-15.
return( y * 4 + x );

}
```

6. Add a `WM_MOUSEMOVE` handler that ties it all together.

```
void CMouseDemo2View::OnMouseMove(UINT nFlags,
      CPoint point)
{

// Get the cursor region. This
// will be a value from 0-15 and
// will correspond to the 16
// cursors you loaded.
int nCursor =
  GetCursorRegion( &point );

// Get a DC to the client window
// so that you can draw.
CClientDC ClientDC( this );

CString strInfo;
strInfo.Format("Cursor: %s              ",
              cursors[nCursor].szName);

// Draw the string to the client window.
ClientDC.TextOut( 0, 0,
  strInfo, strInfo.GetLength() );

// Call the default OnMouseMove() function.
CView::OnMouseMove(nFlags, point);
}
```

7. After you build and run the application, your results should be similar to those shown in Figure 5-4. Notice the mouse cursor shape.

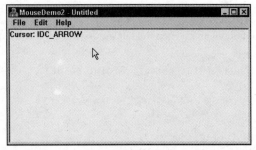

Figure 5-4: Simple demo application that illustrates how to dynamically set the mouse cursor

Capturing the mouse

As you become more experienced with Windows programming, you will need to trap all mouse messages and send them to a particular window. This is called *capturing the mouse*. The most common use of this technique is to trap a matching pair of button down/button up messages. Very weird and hard-to-debug problems can arise if you don't capture the mouse.

For example, suppose you have implemented a message handler for the WM_LBUTTONDOWN. Inside this message handler, you use a Boolean (true/false) variable to track the state of the left mouse button m_bClicked. If the left mouse button is down, that is, if you receive a WM_LBUTTONDOWN message, you set this variable equal to TRUE. If the left mouse button is not clicked, this variable is set equal to FALSE.

Now imagine that the user has clicked the mouse button, and then moves the mouse pointer out of the window before he or she releases the button. If you don't capture the mouse during the WM_LBUTTONDOWN message handler, your application will not receive the WM_LBUTTONUP message. The m_bClicked variable will still set to TRUE even though the button has been released. Your application will be out of synch with the state of the mouse, and all kinds of confusing things can happen.

To understand mouse capture, it helps to see it in action. Run almost any application, and open the File ⇨ Open dialog box. The mouse can be captured by two dialog box controls: list boxes and edit controls. Mouse capture takes place when you click to select an item in a list box or text in the edit control. After clicking in such controls, when you drag the mouse outside the border, you'll see the control scroll its contents. The scrolling is caused by mouse capture.

Another place you can see mouse capture at work is within most text editing windows (including the Visual C++ editor). These windows scroll when you click in a window filled with text and drag beyond the window border. These windows are only able to continue receiving mouse input—in the form of WM_MOUSEMOVE messages—because the mouse has been captured.

Now that you've seen it at work, you probably want to know how you can capture the mouse yourself. It's easy; you just call CWnd::SetCapture. As mentioned, you typically do this in response to a mouse down message. To *release* the capture—something you must be sure to do—call CWnd::ReleaseCapture. A good time to release the mouse capture is in response to a button up message (WM_LBUTTONUP).

Here's some ClassWizard-generated code that shows a typical scenario for mouse capture and release. The mouse is captured when the left mouse button is clicked (in reply to the WM_LBUTTONDOWN message), and it is released when the left mouse button comes up (in reply to the WM_LBUTTONUP message):

```
void CMainFrame::OnLButtonDown(UINT nFlags, CPoint point)
{
  // Grab the mouse.
  SetCapture();

  CFrameWnd::OnLButtonDown(nFlags, point);
}

void CMainFrame::OnLButtonUp(UINT nFlags, CPoint point)
{
  // Release the mouse.
  ReleaseCapture();

  CFrameWnd::OnLButtonUp(nFlags, point);
}
```

Incidentally, when you capture the mouse, Windows doesn't send you any hit-test (WM_NCHITTEST) or pointer-setting (WM_SETCURSOR) messages. The assumption is that you already have complete control of the mouse and that you will change the pointer when you need to. If you want to change the pointer during mouse capture, you would probably do so in response to WM_MOUSEMOVE, the only mouse message you get when the mouse is captured.

Limiting mouse movement

Another facility that Windows lets you control is *mouse pointer clipping*. It's not something you'll do very often, but to complete my discussion of mouse state, I must at least mention it. Mouse pointer clipping involves the definition of a clipping rectangle boundary. The mouse pointer can move only within its defined pointer clipping rectangle.

One example of pointer clipping is obvious when using Windows. Windows itself clips the pointer to the display screen. If it didn't, a user might accidentally send the pointer over the edge of the screen and into oblivion. You've seen some display drivers that have an option that enables the pointer to wrap around the left edge onto the right, and over the top of the screen onto the bottom. Although that's not your preference in mouse pointer, some users undoubtedly appreciate being able to do this.

So why should a program clip the pointer? Obviously, it's necessary to prevent the user from moving the pointer outside a given area. For example, a security program might let the user move the pointer only around the password dialog box. It's tough to come up with good examples of when to use pointer clipping because the few places where it's done, it's disconcerting. For example, the standard Windows PaintBrush application clips the pointer when you're drawing shapes such as *bézier curves*. I personally find this more annoying than useful.

Microsoft's MFC developers apparently agree with my own assessment that this isn't a general-purpose function as they don't include the Windows API function that controls pointer clipping (::ClipCursor) in any MFC class. What's interesting, though, is that although MFC doesn't wrap this function in any of its own classes, it *does* clip the pointer in one specific circumstance. When resizing an OLE toolbar, the pointer is clipped to the parent window's client area. This is one use that makes sense because the size of a child window should be limited by the size of the parent window.

Keyboard Input

Handling keyboard input is fairly simple and straightforward. Once you know which messages to handle, it's merely a matter of creating handlers for each of the desired messages. When working with keyboard input, you can choose to handle one or more of three possible messages. Windows sends three messages for each key press. The first is WM_KEYDOWN, which signals that a key has been pressed. The next message sent is WM_CHAR, along with the virtual key code of the character pressed. The last message sent is WM_KEYUP, which is sent when the key is released. With all of these messages available, you can take complete control of keyboard input.

I'm also going to cover some of the less obvious aspects of keyboard input. I'll start with a look at how the keyboard hardware's scan codes are translated into visible character codes. Next, I'll discuss general user interface issues that relate to keyboard input; namely, what to do when a window gets the keyboard focus.

The physical keyboard

Getting keyboard input to an MS-DOS program often involves an intimate knowledge of how a low-level keyboard code, known as a *scan code*, is generated. Although C-runtime functions translate keyboard input for you, MS-DOS programmers who opt for high performance will grab keyboard scan codes directly. Scan codes are not related to any character set; instead, they are a set of 8-bit codes that indicate which key has been pressed. For example, the key that generates a Y on a U.S.-English keyboard has a scan code of 15 hex. It doesn't take too much imagination — or code — to build a table for converting scan code data to ASCII characters. That's what many MS-DOS programmers must do.

Intimate knowledge of the keyboard was required because MS-DOS programmers have to ignore about half of the scan codes that are generated. Each key on the keyboard actually has *two* scan codes. One indicates that a key has been pressed, and the other indicates that the key has been released. The difference between the two scan codes is 80 hex. For example, the Y key discussed a moment ago sends a scan code of 15 hex when pressed and 95 hex when released. Of these two, the down transition is more interesting. When reading scan codes, the up transition — which has the sign bit set — is usually ignored.

One problem with scan codes is that they are a very hardware-dependent, low-level type of input. To properly perform scan code conversion, you must take into account the keyboard that is currently installed on the system. Most types of keyboards are distinguished on the basis of language or, in some cases, country.

One example, the Swiss-German keyboard, takes into account both language and country. On that keyboard, the Z key and the Y key are reversed from where they are on the U.S.-English keyboard. As a result, an MS-DOS program that relies on scan code conversions according to the U.S.-English keyboard layout won't work correctly in Switzerland without modification.

When I say that keyboard scan codes are hardware dependent, I really mean that they are dependent on the different way keys are laid out to follow various cultural conventions. For a scan code-dependent program that could work worldwide, approximately two dozen different translation tables are required. And that's only taking into account the keyboards that use the Roman alphabet. For other keyboards, such as Russian Cyrillic, Arabic, and the various Asian keyboards, a whole new set of problems arise.

In addition to being hardware dependent, scan codes are so low level that they don't take into account keyboard state, such as the Shift key or the Caps Lock key. As a result, considerable effort is required to simply detect the difference between an upper- and a lowercase letter.

For example, a scan code-dependent program can't tell the difference between *Y* and *y* without a lot of extra work. Scan codes aren't case-sensitive because keyboards aren't case-sensitive.

Windows has different solutions for each of these two problems. To avoid relying on country-specific keyboard layouts, Windows keyboard drivers convert scan codes into a standard set of *virtual key codes*. This set of keys makes up what is sometimes called the Windows *logical keyboard*. To solve the problem of keyboard state, Windows provides a helper function to convert virtual key codes into printable characters. This latter conversion creates the distinction between upper- and lowercase that you rely on when reading text.

The Windows logical keyboard

The logical keyboard is an abstraction that serves to hide differences between keyboards in countries that use Roman characters. You won't see a keyboard layout for the logical keyboard anywhere in the Windows documentation. What you will see, however, are the definitions for virtual key (VK_) codes. It's the job of the keyboard device driver to convert hardware-specific scan codes into virtual key codes.

In particular, Windows calls the keyboard driver to convert raw hardware scan codes into virtual key codes. These virtual key codes are sent to applications as messages. Because there are two scan codes per keyboard key — a key pressed code and a key released code — there are also two messages per key. The WM_KEYDOWN message indicates that a keyboard key has been pressed, and the WM_KEYUP message indicates that a key has been released.

Although virtual key messages solve one problem with scan codes, they don't solve the other problem. The problem they solve is that you don't have to worry about different keyboards. The device driver does whatever translation is necessary to produce a uniform set of key codes.

The problem that still exists, however, is that virtual key codes are fairly low level. In particular, you have to do a lot of work to decide whether letters are upper- or lowercase. And virtual key codes aren't influenced by changes to shift key states, which include the Shift, Ctrl, and Alt keys. Virtual key codes also ignore the state of the Caps Lock, Num Lock, and Scroll Lock keys.

Although they don't provide enough information to get character input, virtual key codes are suitable for use as accelerator key codes. There are two types of accelerators: VIRTKEY and ASCII. I recommend that you always use VIRTKEY, which — as the name suggests — corresponds to virtual keys. The other type of accelerator, ASCII, is created from the other type of keyboard message, which I'm going to discuss next.

An accelerator is a keystroke that a program interprets as a command. From your program's perspective, the results of a menu selection and an accelerator keystroke are identical because Windows generates identical messages for both. You can connect the two in the mind of a user by displaying the accelerator name in the menu, next to the equivalent menu item. For example, you'll often see Ctrl+V next to the Paste command in an Edit menu. Although both types of commands are connected in the user's mind, from a programming perspective the two are defined separately. Specifically, menus are defined with menu resources, and accelerators are defined with accelerator resources.

Cross-Reference   For more information about accelerator keys, see Chapter 4.

Printable character messages

The Windows API contains a function for converting between virtual key code messages and WM_CHAR messages. These are called the *printable character messages* because most are uppercase letters, lowercase letters, numbers, or punctuation marks. That is, they correspond to characters that you can see on the display screen and send to the printer.

The ::TranslateMessage function is the Windows API function that converts virtual key messages into WM_CHAR messages. Unless you've written Windows SDK programs, you've probably never seen this function. And because MFC calls this function for you in its message loop, you don't ever have to worry about it.

What's important is that this function adds WM_CHAR messages to your application's message queue. Every WM_CHAR message that you receive will be preceded by a WM_KEYDOWN message and followed by a WM_KEYUP message. You get printable character input from the WM_CHAR message, and you can safely ignore the associated virtual key messages.

If you ignore WM_KEYDOWN messages, why does Windows bother sending them to you? This message is for all the keys that *don't* have a corresponding printable character. I should mention that such keystrokes seem more like commands than data, and the easiest way to handle keyboard commands is with an accelerator table. However, you can't always use an accelerator table. In particular, it's something of a convention that only one accelerator table is active at any point in time. That accelerator table would be the one for an application's frame window. All other windows must process low-level keyboard input directly, without the benefits that accelerator tables provide.

Table 5-4 lists the virtual key codes for keys that don't create printable characters. When you can't create accelerator table entries, you'll rely on the WM_KEYDOWN message to detect when these keys have been pressed.

To summarize, keyboard input starts as scan codes. A Windows keyboard driver converts these codes to a hardware-independent form: virtual key codes. Typically, Windows applications then send the virtual key code messages to a Windows API function that generates WM_CHAR character messages when printable characters are typed. For nonprintable characters — such as function keys and navigation keys — you must rely on the WM_KEYDOWN virtual key message.

Table 5-4: Virtual Key Codes for Nonprintable Keys

Virtual Key Code	Key
VK_MENU	Menu
VK_APPS	Application
VK_CONTROL	Control
VK_DELETE	Delete
VK_DOWN	Down arrow
VK_END	End
VK_F1 through VK_F12	F1 through F12

Continued

Table 5-4: *(continued)*

Virtual Key Code	Key
VK_HOME	Home
VK_INSERT	Insert
VK_LEFT	Left arrow
VK_PAUSE	Pause
VK_NEXT	Page Down
VK_PRIOR	Page Up
VK_SNAPSHOT	Print Screen
VK_RIGHT	Right arrow
VK_SHIFT	Shift
VK_UP	Up arrow

Now that you understand the types of keyboard input messages that Windows will send you, it's time to address input issues related to application state. Toward that end, the following section describes how an application lets the user know that a window has the keyboard focus. This can be done using several techniques, which I call *echoing the keyboard focus*.

Echoing keyboard focus

When you build support for keyboard input into a window, you must provide a visual cue that lets the user know when that support is enabled. Because a window gets keyboard input when it has the focus, the proper time for displaying those visual cues is when the window gets the focus. It follows, then, that you should disable the visible signs of the focus when the window loses the focus.

To help you build windows that display the proper visual cues, the following sections describe three ways that a window can advertise its ownership of the focus. I'll start with a look at creating insertion points, which are Windows' keyboard pointers. Then, I'll talk about focus rectangles, something you'll see in dialog box controls, but can also be displayed in other types of windows. Finally, I'll talk about the relationship between a window's selection state and the keyboard focus.

Creating and maintaining keyboard cursors

A keyboard cursor or insertion point is a blinking bitmap that lets the user know where keyboard input will have an effect. Table 5-5 lists the eight CWnd member functions that create and manage keyboard cursors. This group of functions is fairly small and easy to understand. The challenge with keyboard cursors revolves around timing issues, such as when to create, show, hide, and destroy the cursors.

Table 5-5: CWnd Member Functions for Creating and Managing Keyboard Cursors

Function	Description
CreateCaret	Creates a keyboard cursor using a bitmap that you provide.
CreateGrayCaret	Creates a solid gray cursor using the size you specify.
CreateSolidCaret	Creates a solid black cursor using the size you specify.
GetCaretPos	Returns the location of the cursor. Because of local input state in the 32-bit versions of Windows, you can find the location of a cursor only if it's contained within a window that's created by the calling thread.
DestroyCaret	Destroys a cursor. To avoid putting your application in an unknown state, destroy the cursor when you lose the keyboard focus (and create a cursor when you gain the keyboard focus).
HideCaret	Makes a cursor invisible.
SetCaretPos	Moves a cursor to a position in a window. When a window containing a cursor is scrolled, the cursor gets scrolled with the window data.
ShowCaret	Makes a cursor visible.

You create a keyboard cursor when a window gets the keyboard focus. Although you might be tempted to create it earlier, you should resist the temptation. After all, you only need a cursor to echo the results of keyboard input, and without the focus, you don't have any keyboard input. In addition to creating the cursor, you need to position it within your window and make it visible. Here's a fragment of code that does the right thing in response to a WM_SETFOCUS message:

```
void CMainFrame::OnSetFocus(CWnd* pOldWnd)
{
  // First call default handler.
  CFrameWnd::OnSetFocus(pOldWnd);

  // Create, position, and make caret appear.
  CreateSolidCaret(0, d_cyLineHeight );
  SetCaretPos( d_ptCaretLocation );
  ShowCaret();
}
```

Just as you create a keyboard cursor when you get the focus, the logical time to destroy the cursor is when you lose the focus. In response to the WM_KILLFOCUS message, you'll first hide the cursor and then destroy it. Here's a code fragment that shows how this is done:

```
void CMainFrame::OnKillFocus(CWnd* pNewWnd)
{
  CFrameWnd::OnKillFocus(pNewWnd);

  // Query and save current caret position.
```

```
    d_ptCaretLocation = GetCaretPos();

    // Eliminate caret.
    HideCaret();
    DestroyCaret();
}
```

The only other keyboard cursor issue involves drawing outside of normal WM_PAINT drawing. If a cursor is in a window, you must hide the cursor before any non-WM_PAINT drawing. Otherwise, you might overwrite the cursor. When the non-WM_PAINT drawing is done, you can restore the cursor. Here's a code fragment that shows what I mean:

```
void CMainFrame::OnChar(UINT nChar, UINT nRepCnt,
  UINT nFlags)
{
  CSize sizeTextBox;

  // Fetch caret position.
  CPoint pt = GetCaretPos();

  // Hide caret before fetching DC.
  HideCaret();

  // Drawing in non-WM_PAINT message.
  // Bracket required to force DC to disappear.
  {
    CClientDC ClientDC( this );
    ClientDC.TextOut(pt.x, pt.y, (LPCTSTR)&nChar, 1);
    sizeTextBox =
      ClientDC.GetTextExtent( (LPCTSTR)&nChar, 1 );
  }

  // Advance caret position.
  pt.x += sizeTextBox.cx;
  SetCaretPos( pt );

  // Display caret.
  ShowCaret();
}
```

This code fragment actually does more than just hide the keyboard cursor. It shows how you respond to the WM_CHAR message to both draw the character that's typed and advance the cursor. Such drawn objects won't be a permanent part of a window's contents unless they are also drawn in response to the WM_PAINT message. Because your code makes no provision for saving the text anywhere, this isn't done. When you understand why this code fragment is *broken*, you truly understand the meaning of the WM_PAINT message. (The WM_PAINT message is covered in detail in Chapter 8.)

To test your cursor-creation code, be sure to force the focus to switch away from your program. Do this by activating the Task Manager (Ctrl+Esc), or by activating any other application that's currently running. When you switch away, the cursor should disappear without a trace. When you switch back, the cursor should be in the same place it was before you switched focus.

The keyboard cursor is called the *insertion point* because it shows users the exact point in a window at which keyboard input will have an effect. Users expect to be able to navigate insertion points around a window through the use of the arrow keys. Another way to echo the keyboard focus is with a focus rectangle, which I discuss next.

Focus rectangles

A focus rectangle provides an alternative to a cursor for signaling the keyboard focus location. Unlike cursors, focus rectangles don't blink. Instead, they provide subtle highlighting that draws a user's eye to a particular part of a window. Whether you use a focus rectangle or a cursor depends on what you are trying to highlight. The most common examples of focus rectangles occur in dialog boxes. For all nonedit controls, focus rectangles are drawn as the user moves the focus, to the different controls in the dialog box, via the Tab key or the mouse.

Focus rectangles aren't solely for dialog box controls, although this is the most obvious and most common use. You can use them anywhere a cursor just doesn't seem right. One difference between focus rectangles and cursors is that cursors are always solid rectangles. Focus rectangles, on the other hand, are hollow, and they wrap around other objects. If you need to echo the focus in a way that is solid or blinking, you want a cursor. For a subtler, hollow pointer, try a focus rectangle instead.

Drawing a focus rectangle is extremely easy. You simply call MFC's `CDC::DrawFocusRect` function. The following example shows how to draw a focus rectangle around a block of text:

```
void CMainFrame::OnLButtonDown(UINT nFlags, CPoint point)
{
   CClientDC ClientDC( this );

   // Draw a line of text at mouse cursor location.
   CString str;
   str.Format("Focus rectangle around this text");
   ClientDC.TextOut(point.x, point.y, str);

   // Calculate width and height of text.
   CSize sizeText =
     ClietnDC.GetTextExtent( str, str.GetLength() );

   // Calculate a margin around the focus rectangle.
   int cxMargin = GetSystemMetrics( SM_CXBORDER ) * 4;
   int cyMargin = GetSystemMetrics( SM_CYBORDER ) * 1;

   // Calculate size of focus rectangle.
   CRect rTextBox;
   rTextBox.left = point.x - cxMargin;
   rTextBox.top = point.y - cyMargin;
   rTextBox.right = point.x + sizeText.cx + cxMargin;
   rTextBox.bottom = point.y + sizeText.cy + cyMargin;

   // Draw a focus rectangle around a block of text.
   ClientDC.DrawFocusRect( &rTextBox );

   CFrameWnd::OnLButtonDown(nFlags, point);
}
```

This code fragment draws a focus rectangle in response to a WM_LBUTTONDOWN message. I show this simply as an example of *how* to call CDC::DrawFocusRect. However, the truth of the matter is that button messages aren't the events that typically trigger the drawing of focus rectangles.

You're more likely to draw the focus rectangle when a window gets the focus. The reason should be obvious: that's when you are certain that your window has the focus. Also, as discussed earlier, this means that you draw a focus rectangle in response to a WM_SETFOCUS message. Here's a fragment of code taken from an MFC program that shows how to do this:

```
void CMainFrame::OnSetFocus(CWnd* pOldWnd)
{
    CFrameWnd::OnSetFocus(pOldWnd);

    CClientDC ClientDC( this );

    // Draw focus rectangle when you get the focus.
    CRect rFocus;
    rFocus.left = d_ptFocusRect.x;
    rFocus.top = d_ptFocusRect.y;
    rFocus.right = d_ptFocusRect.x + d_cxIcon;
    rFocus.bottom = d_ptFocusRect.y + d_cyIcon;
    ClientDC.DrawFocusRect( &rFocus );
}
```

If you draw a focus rectangle, you must be sure to erase it. Because a focus rectangle exists just to show focus ownership, the logical time to erase a focus rectangle is when the window loses the focus. Interestingly enough, a focus rectangle is erased by calling the exact same function that drew it in the first place: CDC::DrawFocusRect. The following code fragment erases the focus rectangle I drew a moment ago. This is done in response to the WM_KILLFOCUS message:

```
void CMainFrame::OnKillFocus(CWnd* pNewWnd)
{
    CFrameWnd::OnKillFocus(pNewWnd);

    CClientDC ClientDC( this );

    // Hide focus rectangle when you lose the focus.
    CRect rFocus;
    rFocus.left = d_ptFocusRect.x;
    rFocus.top = d_ptFocusRect.y;
    rFocus.right = d_ptFocusRect.x + d_cxIcon;
    rFocus.bottom = d_ptFocusRect.y + d_cyIcon;
    ClientDC.DrawFocusRect(&rFocus);
}
```

You might find it a bit puzzling that the same code can erase *and* draw a focus rectangle. To explain how this is possible, I need to describe how CDC::DrawFocusRect works. This function uses Boolean arithmetic to invert a set of pixels. To draw a focus rectangle, pixels are inverted. To erase the same focus rectangle, the same pixels are inverted again, which completely and effectively erases the focus rectangle. This is often referred to as a Boolean operation, and it makes use of GDI's Boolean *raster operations* (or *ROP codes*) that are covered in Chapter 8.

So far, I've described how you make a focus rectangle appear when you get a WM_SETFOCUS message, and how you make it disappear in response to a WM_KILLFOCUS message. However, there's one more message that can affect the health and well being of a focus rectangle. To provide complete support for a focus rectangle, you must redraw the focus rectangle in response to the WM_PAINT message.

You need to draw a focus rectangle when handling a WM_PAINT message for the same reason that you draw any other object in a window's client area. You can't determine ahead of time when some outside event will damage the contents of a window's client area. It might be as simple as a screen saver that automatically starts after 10 minutes of idle time. Whatever the reason, you draw a focus rectangle with the same function described earlier, CDC::DrawFocusRect. With WM_PAINT, however, you must first determine whether the window has the focus. If it doesn't, you don't draw the focus rectangle. Only if it has the focus do you draw the focus rectangle. Here's a WM_PAINT handler that first checks for the presence of the focus before drawing a focus rectangle:

```
void CMainFrame::OnPaint()
{
  CPaintDC PaintDC( this ); // DC for painting

  // Only draw focus rectangle if your window has focus.
  if( GetFocus() == this ){
    // Calculate coordinate
    CRect rFocus;
    rFocus.left = d_ptFocusRect.x;
    rFocus.top = d_ptFocusRect.y;
    rFocus.right = d_ptFocusRect.x + d_cxIcon;
    rFocus.bottom = d_ptFocusRect.y + d_cyIcon;

    // Draw actual focus rectangle.
    PaintDC.DrawFocusRect(&rFocus);
    }
}
```

Both types of focus-echoing mechanisms — keyboard cursors and focus rectangles — are relatively easy to create and use. However, a third issue, the selection state, is closely related to the keyboard focus. By *selection state*, I mean the display of objects selected by a user in a window. To support Windows' standards for user interface activity, selection state must be visible only when a window has focus. At all other times, the selection state of objects must be hidden.

Selection state and keyboard focus

Objects can be selected using either the mouse or the keyboard. Regardless of how it's done, Windows programs change the color of selected objects to help users distinguish them from other objects. I talk about selecting text colors in Chapter 8. For now, suffice it to say that you fetch the colors to use by calling ::GetSysColor with the appropriate color indices, and then you perform a bitwise exclusive OR to determine the color of selected text. This is summarized in the following lines of code:

```
COLORREF d_crForeground = GetSysColor(COLOR_WINDOWTEXT);
COLORREF d_crBackground = GetSysColor( COLOR_WINDOW );
COLORREF d_crSelectFore = d_crForeground ^ 0x00ffffff;
COLORREF d_crSelectBack = d_crBackground ^ 0x00ffffff;
```

In general, when a window loses the keyboard focus, it should hide its selection. When focus is restored, the window should again show the selection. I say "in general" because in a few situations a window will still show its selection state even though it has lost the focus. In particular, two windows might need to simultaneously display the selected state.

To get a sense of when to show selection state and when to hide it, run some of the popular Windows applications. If you watch closely, you'll see that numerous small visual cues indicate changes in activation and focus. Some of these, for example, the change in title bar color, are handled by Windows. Other state changes, such as the three I've discussed here, must be handled by your application. However, instead of dictating hard-and-fast rules, I should point out that the most important criterion is what works for your users.

Summary

In this chapter, you learned quite a bit about the most basic of user interactions — handling mouse and keyboard events. You started about by discovering how to create mouse message handlers to handle events such as the user clicking and double-clicking on the client area. From there, you saw how to convert the current position of the mouse from client to screen coordinates (and vice versa), how to handle nonclient mouse events, how to change the mouse cursor, and even how to capture the mouse. After you completed the section on mouse event handling, you then explored some basic areas of keyboard handling under Windows and MFC. Included in this section were explanations of how the physical keyboard relates to the Windows logical keyboard, the difference between virtual key code messages and printable character messages, and how to echo keyboard focus. At this point in the book, you've learned the basics of a Windows applications — how to create SDI and MDI applications and how to interact with the user using menus, the keyboard, and the mouse. In the next chapter, you'll continue this logical learning path of MFC development by exploring how to use the status bar and toolbar controls.

✦   ✦   ✦

Status Bars and Toolbars

This chapter examines two basic parts of the Windows user interface: status bars and toolbars. A *status bar* is the window positioned (by default) at the bottom of an application's main window that displays in smaller windows (called *panes*) user feedback information such as whether or not the Caps Lock is on, the current page of a document, or the progress of a task the user has initiated. The first part of this chapter examines how to create the status bar for both frame windows and dialog boxes. After you've learned the basics of creating status bars and displaying text, you'll discover some of the more advanced usages of status bars such as displaying progress bars to provide visual feedback to the user on lengthy operations. Finally, you'll learn how to insert a status bar into a dialog box.

Once you've conquered the world of status bars, you'll then take a look at its close cousin, the toolbar. Toolbars are windows (typically aligned to the top of a window or dialog box) with buttons or combo boxes that enable users to issue application commands with a single mouse click. As with status bars, this chapter examines the basic toolbar creation process and describes the AppWizard defaults. Once you've acquired a basic grounding in toolbar creation, more advanced areas such as displaying and hiding toolbars on command, as well as creating your own toolbars, are covered.

Creating and Controlling Status Bars

A status bar is the multifield bar that appears at the bottom of a frame window used to display application-specific data to the user. Almost all Windows SDI and MDI applications have status bars and even some dialog-based applications display them. Figure 6-1 shows the status bar used by Microsoft Word for Windows. Notice all the information displayed about the current page, section, line, and column number as well as several other panes that indicate keyboard status and whether or not the document contains words not found in Word's dictionary (represented by the little book icon with an X on it). In this section, you'll learn how to create the basic, no-frills status bar with the help of MFC.

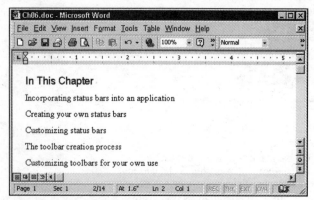

Figure 6-1: Status bars are the standard means of communicating status and other application-specific information to the user.

Default status bar behavior

As you've seen in previous chapters, whenever you use the AppWizard to create either an SDI or an MDI application, a status bar is created for you that contains (from left to right) a very long pane for menu prompt messages and three smaller panes that display the states of the Caps, Num, and Scroll lock keys. In this section, I'll start to look at the underlying code for this control.

A status bar is represented in the MFC framework by the CStatusBar class. The default placement for the status bar code is in the CMainFrame class, so I'll start there. (You can create status bars for dialog boxes, but that takes a bit more work, so I'll do that a little later in the chapter.)

To start, create an SDI application. Once you've done that, you'll see that the AppWizard defines a member variable for the application's status bar in the mainFrm.h file:

```
protected:  // control bar embedded members
 CStatusBar  m_wndStatusBar;
```

Now, open the mainfrm.cpp file and locate the OnCreate function. As the name suggests, this function is called when the framework requests that a window be created. As you learned in Chapter 2, when you create a window in an SDI or MDI application it is contained within a frame. This frame is responsible for such things as the sizing border, status bar, and toolbar. The following code is all that the CMainFrame::OnCreate function does to display the default status bar:

```
if (!m_wndStatusBar.Create(this) ||
    !m_wndStatusBar.SetIndicators(indicators,
     sizeof(indicators)/sizeof(UINT)))
{
 TRACE0("Failed to create status bar\n");
 return -1;      // fail to create
}
```

As you can see, the first thing the code does is to simply call the status bar's Create function (inherited from CWnd). The this pointer is passed to indicate that the CMainFrame object is the parent window of the status bar. There are other parameters to the Create function (window style and status bar resource ID), which I'll discuss shortly. However, in the case of a status bar being displayed on the frame window, the defaults for these parameters are fine for now.

The next call is to the SetIndicators function. With this function, the application passes an array of values that represents the different resource IDs corresponding to each value displayed on the status bar. As you can see, the value being passed here is the array named indicators. This array is defined toward the beginning of the MainFrm.cpp file as follows:

```
static UINT indicators[] =
{
 ID_SEPARATOR,              // status line indicator
 ID_INDICATOR_CAPS,
 ID_INDICATOR_NUM,
 ID_INDICATOR_SCRL,
};
```

A little bit of investigation then reveals that the ID_INDICATOR_CAPS, ID_INDICATOR_NUM, and ID_INDICATOR_SCRL resource IDs are all string resources defined in the application's .rc file as follows (in bold):

```
STRINGTABLE
BEGIN
 ID_INDICATOR_EXT      "EXT"
 ID_INDICATOR_CAPS     "CAP"
 ID_INDICATOR_NUM      "NUM"
 ID_INDICATOR_SCRL     "SCRL"
 ID_INDICATOR_OVR      "OVR"
 ID_INDICATOR_REC      "REC"
END
```

What about the ID_SEPARATOR resource ID? This resource ID is a special value that tells the framework that no string resource is associated with this particular status bar display pane. In fact, if you build and run your AppWizard generated application, you'll see that the pane to the left of the Caps, Num, and Scroll Lock panes displays the text Ready. Then, if you select a menu and mouse over any of its options, you'll see that this pane is updated to display the help text associated with the current menu option. At this point, you know the following very basic information about status bars:

✦ The CMainFrame class contains a member variable of type CStatusBar.

✦ The string resource IDs that will be displayed in the status bar in the indicators array are defined in the MainFrm.cpp file.

✦ The CMainFrame::OnCreate function contains the calls to the CStatusBar::Create function to create the status bar window and CStatusBar::SetIndicators to associate the resource ID array with the newly created status bar.

However, if you're going to make full use of the status bar, you'll probably want to do much more than simply indicate to the user whether or not the Caps Lock key has been pressed. Therefore, let's look at how you can customize the status bar to meet the individual needs of your specific application.

Aligning status bars

As mentioned earlier, by default the status bar window is created in the main frame window's `OnCreate` member function:

```
m_wndStatusBar.Create(this);
```

`CStatusBar::Create` actually takes three parameters; however, two of them have default values, so what you don't see there is that the `CStatusBar::Create` member function takes two additional parameters as follows:

```
virtual BOOL Create(
CWnd* pParentWnd,
DWORD dwStyle = WS_CHILD | WS_VISIBLE | CBRS_BOTTOM,
UINT nID = AFX_IDW_STATUS_BAR
);
```

The first parameter (`pParentWnd`) is the most obvious and the only one that you must specify. It simply represents the parent window of the status bar.

The second parameter (`dwStyle`) is the value that you use to determine things such as whether or not the status bar is visible (`WS_VISIBLE`) and how the status bar is to be aligned relative to its parent window. However, there are some interesting things to note about the `CBRS_` values.

If you look in the `afxres.h` file, you'll see that there are four values that you can use to align a control bar. Each value, shown in Table 6-1, consists of an alignment style and a draw border style. Furthermore, the alignment styles (`CBRS_ALIGN_BOTTOM`, `CBRS_ALIGN_TOP`, `CBRS_ALIGN_RIGHT`, `CBRS_ALIGN_LEFT`) are all mutually exclusive whereas the draw border styles can be combined.

Table 6-1: CBRS_ Values for Aligning the Status Bar

Style Flag	Alignment and Draw Border Combination
CBRS_TOP	CBRS_ALIGN_TOP | CBRS_BORDER_BOTTOM
CBRS_BOTTOM	CBRS_ALIGN_BOTTOM | CBRS_BORDER_TOP
CBRS_LEFT	CBRS_ALIGN_LEFT | CBRS_BORDER_RIGHT
CBRS_RIGHT	CBRS_ALIGN_RIGHT | CBRS_BORDER_LEFT

Caution   One thing that's not documented any place is that only two of these values are valid for a status bar: `CBRS_BOTTOM` and `CBRS_TOP`. If you attempt to align the status bar to either the right or the left, the application will assert in the `CStatusBar::CalcInsideRect` function where a comment states "vertical status bar not supported." Although there aren't too many reasons to create a vertical status bar, it would be nice if information like this were in the online help.

Adding text panes to the status bar

The means by which you update the text of a pane is via the CStatusBar::SetPaneText function. Here's the syntax for that function:

```
BOOL SetPaneText(int nIndex,
                 LPCTSTR lpszNewText,
                 BOOL bUpdate = TRUE);
```

You use the first parameter (nIndex) to specify which pane (relative to zero) is to be updated. I'll make one important point about that shortly. The second parameter (lpszNewText) represents the value to be displayed in that pane, and the third parameter (bUpdate) is used to tell the framework whether or not you want the status bar to be invalidated. Specifying TRUE for this value causes an immediate repaint.

Now that you know the syntax involved, let's look at a concrete example of how to add text panes to a status bar. As you'll see, it's far from obvious and requires a couple of additional steps. Suppose your application has a login procedure and you want to keep the status bar updated to determine whether or not the user is logged in and if so, what user ID is being used.

The first thing you need to do is create a string resource that represents the user not being logged in. To do that, simply open the Resource View and then expand the String Table icon. After that, double-click the String Table entry. When the strings are listed, simply press the Insert key and type the desired value. As an example, you might want the user to see something like <Not logged in>. After that, change the resource ID of your new string to something meaningful such as IDS_LOGIN_STATUS. Now you can add the new pane to the indicators array as follows:

```
static UINT indicators[] =
{
    ID_SEPARATOR,            // status line indicator
    IDS_LOGIN_STATUS,
    ID_INDICATOR_CAPS,
    ID_INDICATOR_NUM,
    ID_INDICATOR_SCRL,
};
```

At this point, if you build and run the application, the pane will show the value <Not logged in>. From here, you need to update your login code to call the status bar object's SetPaneText function as follows:

```
m_wndStatusBar.SetPaneText(1, strUserId);
```

Obviously, because m_wndStatusBar is a member of the CMainFrame class, this code assumes that the code that updated the status bar is in the CMainFrame class as well.

The last thing you need to do is to add a command update handler for the string resource. Since the resource ID in this example is IDS_ LOGIN_STATUS, you must add the following message map entry and function:

```
BEGIN_MESSAGE_MAP(CMainFrame, CFrameWnd)
  ON_WM_CREATE()
  ON_COMMAND(ID_LOG_IN, OnLogIn)
  ON_COMMAND(ID_LOG_OUT, OnLogOut)
```

```
ON_UPDATE_COMMAND_UI (IDS_LOGIN_STATUS, OnLoginStatus)
END_MESSAGE_MAP()
void CMainFrame::OnLoginStatus(CCmdUI *pCmdUI)
{
  pCmdUI->Enable(TRUE);
}
```

That's it. The last thing I'll mention regarding the SetPaneText function's nIndex parameter is that the value you pass includes the separator panes. Therefore, if you were to call SetPaneText as follows, each time the user moved the mouse over a menu item, your text would be replaced with that menu item's help text.

```
m_wndStatusBar.SetPaneText(0, strUserId);
```

Placing a status bar on a dialog box

As you will no doubt discover as you traverse the learning curve of MFC, Microsoft has elected to make the entire document/view architecture its basis for writing MFC applications. To that extent, there are many tasks that are quite trivial when writing SDI or MDI applications but become quite difficult when attempted in a dialog-based application. One such task is using a status bar on a dialog box. In this section, I'll show you what took me hours of digging through MFC source code to discover on my own.

The first thing you need to know is that there is a *second status bar class* in MFC, which is called CStatusBarCtrl. Although both classes wrap the functionality of the standard Windows status bar control, the CStatusBar class is tightly integrated with the entire document/view architecture. The CStatusBarCtrl class, on the other hand, is a very thin wrapper that can more easily be used in applications not integrating with the document/view. Therefore, the CStatusBarCtrl class is much easier to use when you want to place a status bar on a dialog box.

Before you jump into a demo that illustrates how to do this, take a look at the CStatusBarCtrl class and the steps required to use it. Instantiating the CStatusBarCtrl is easy because its constructor requires no parameters. Therefore, a CStatusBarCtrl object can easily be defined as a member variable of the dialog class as follows:

```
class CYourDialog : public CDialog
{
...

protected:
  CStatusBarCtrl    m_wndStatusBar;


...
}
```

Creating a CStatusBarCtrl is a bit different than creating a CStatusBar. The main difference is that you can't simply use one of the CBRS_ style values to tell the framework how you want the status bar aligned with respect to its parent window. With the CStatusBarCtrl::Create function, you are responsible for specifying exactly where you want the status bar placed on a window in terms of position and size. Obviously, this has its advantages because it gives you more control over the status bar placement for cases where you might not want the status bar docked to the edges of a window. Here's the syntax for the CStatusBarCtrl::Create function:

```
virtual BOOL Create(DWORD dwStyle,
                    const RECT& rect,
                    CWnd* pParentWnd,
                    UINT nID
    );
```

The dwStyle parameter specifies the window style to be used. Examples of these are things such as WS_VISIBLE and WS_BORDER. Although these values are not absolutely required, they are generally used. The one style that is required is the WS_CHILD style. Therefore, in most cases you would specify this parameter as follows:

```
m_wndStatusBar.Create(WS_CHILD | WS_BORDER | WS_VISIBLE,
                        // other parameters ...
```

The second parameter (rect) tells the framework exactly where the status bar is to be placed on its parent window and how large it is to be. A standard means of doing this is to first call the GetWindowRect function of the parent window (the dialog box). This returns a value of type RECT (or the thin CRect class wrapper) that has the correct top, left, right, and bottom properties (assuming that you're placing the status bar at the bottom of the dialog box). Then, you simply change the rectangle's top property. This is typically some value that you decide based on the height of your panes. Here's an example where the rect value represents a status bar of 30 pixels and is aligned to the bottom of the dialog box:

```
CRect rect;
GetWindowRect(&rect);
rect.top = rect.bottom - 30;
m_wndStatusBar.Create(WS_CHILD | WS_BORDER | WS_VISIBLE,
                        rect,
                        // other parameters ...
```

The third parameter (pParentWnd) is the pointer to a CWnd object representing the status bar's parent window. Most times you would simply pass the dialog's this pointer to satisfy this requirement. As discussed in Chapter 11, the CDialog class is derived from CWnd, which is why its this pointer can be passed to the CStatusBar::Create member function—it is implicitly upcast.

```
m_wndStatusBar.Create(WS_CHILD | WS_BORDER | WS_VISIBLE,
                        rect,
                        this,
                        // other parameters ...
```

The fourth and final parameter (nID) is one that trips up a few developers. You use this parameter to specify the control's resource ID. The problem is that many developers new to Windows or MFC development get confused because, of course, they're creating this status bar from scratch and don't have a resource. All the function needs is any ID that you create that will be associated with the actual window when the status bar is created. That way, you can handle messages that are sent to the window. Therefore, you need only define a unique ID in your resource.h file (as the resource editor does for any other control) and pass that value. You can, of course, use a value that you've defined locally in your CDialog class. However, I think it's a bit more consistent to use the resource.h file because that file contains all the other resource IDs for your application. Assuming you create an ID called ID_MY_STATUS_BAR, your completed CStatusBarCtrl::Create call now looks like the following:

```
m_wndStatusBar.Create(WS_CHILD | WS_BORDER | WS_VISIBLE,
                      rect,
                      this,
                      ID_MY_STATUS_BAR);
```

Once you've created the status bar window, you should call the CStatusBarCtrl::
SetMinHeight function. Although you can always dynamically size the status bar (as you
can any window), here you are simply stating that the status bar is to be no shorter than the
value passed. The value you pass here should be the same one you used in the call to the
CStatusBarCtrl::Create function. Therefore, combining this function call with the previous Create call results in the following code:

```
const int STATUS_BAR_HEIGHT = 30;

CRect rect;
GetWindowRect(&rect);
rect.top = rect.bottom - STATUS_BAR_HEIGHT;

if (!m_wndStatusBar.Create(WS_CHILD | WS_BORDER | WS_VISIBLE,
                           rect,
                           this,
                           ID_MY_STATUS_BAR))
{
  AfxMessageBox ("Error in creating status bar");
}
else
{
  m_wndStatusBar.SetMinHeight(STATUSBAR_HEIGHT);
  ...
```

Now comes the fun part. Here you need to use the CStatusBarCtrl::SetParts function:

```
BOOL SetParts(int nParts,
              int* pWidths
);
```

This function takes two parameters. The first (nParts) is used to specify how many parts,
or panes, the status bar will contain. The documented limit to this value is 255, although the
practical limit will be much lower depending on the size of your dialog box and the width of
the panes.

The second parameter is a pointer to an integer array. Each element in this array is a value
that represents (in client coordinates) the right edge position of the pane. As an example,
suppose you have three panes on your dialog box and you want each pane to be 100 pixels in
width and aligned to the right of the dialog box. To do that, you simply code the following:

```
const int nPanes = 3;

CRect rect;

GetClientRect(&rect);

// array specifies right edge position of each pane
int iWidths[nPanes] =
{
```

```
      rect.right-200,
      rect.right-100,
      -1
    };

    m_wndStatusBar.SetParts(nPanes, iWidths);
```

As you can see, I first get the rectangle of the dialog box (I really only care about its width) and then use that to create three elements in an integer array where each element is 100 pixels in width. Notice that the last element in the array has a value of –1. This tells the framework to align that pane to the right edge of the status bar.

As another example, if you want to evenly space the panes out, you can write something like the following. This code works for any value you give nPanes from 1 to 255.

```
    const int nPanes = 3;

    CRect rect;
    GetWindowRect(&rect);
    int iDialogWidth = rectDialog.right - rectDialog.left;

    int iPaneWidths[nPanes];

    for (int i = 0; i < (nPanes-1); i++)
     iPaneWidths[i] = (i + 1) * (iDialogWidth / nPanes);

    iPaneWidths[(nPanes-1)] = -1;

    m_wndStatusBar.SetParts(nPanes, iPaneWidths);
```

The last function to cover before you code a demo application is the CStatusBarCtrl::SetText function.

```
    BOOL SetText(LPCTSTR lpszText,
                 int nPane,
                 int nType);
```

The first parameter (lpszText) is simply the text that is displayed in the pane, and the second parameter (nPane) is the zero-based index of the pane. This value should be a number between 0 and the number of panes specified in the call to SetParts minus 1, inclusive. The third and final parameter (nType) is where you specify how the pane is to be drawn. It can be any one of the values shown in Table 6-2.

Table 6-2: SetText Pane Types

nTypeValue	Description
0	This is the most common value and indicates that the pane should be drawn lower than the plane of the status bar to give it a sunken, 3D look.
SBT_NOBORDERS	The pane is drawn without borders.
SBT_OWNERDRAW	If you specify this value, it is your responsibility to draw the pane.
SBT_POPOUT	The opposite of passing 0, this value means that the pane will be drawn on a higher plane than the status bar, giving it a raised, 3D look.

Status bar demo

At this point, let's put what you've learned to task. Create a dialog-based application called DialogStatus. Once the AppWizard has created the project, open the DialogStatusDlg.h file and add the following member variable and function to the DialogStatus class:

```
protected:
 CStatusBarCtrl m_wndStatusBar;

 void CreateStatusBar();
```

At the end of the dialog class' OnInitDialog function, in DialogStatusDlg.cpp, add the call to the CreateStatusBar function:

```
BOOL CDialogStatusDlg::OnInitDialog()
{
 CDialog::OnInitDialog();
 //  .
 // VS.NET-generated code omitted...
 //  .


 // TODO: Add extra initialization here
 CreateStatusBar();

 return TRUE;
}
```

Now, code the CreateStatusBar function, adding it to the bottom of DialogStatusDlg.cpp, as follows. I've interspersed many comments in the code to explain exactly what each step of the code is doing.

```
void CDialogStatusDlg::CreateStatusBar()
{
 // Hard-coded value to represent the status
 // bar's height.
 const int STATUSBAR_HEIGHT = 30;

 // Static structure used to hold each pane's
 // text value and pane style. I simply did it
 // like this so that I could use a for loop
 // when creating the panes.
 static struct
 {
  char szText[25];
  DWORD dwStyle;
 } Panes[] = {
  "Border", 0,
  "No border", SBT_NOBORDERS,
  "Popup", SBT_POPOUT,
 };

 // Set the rect of the status bar based on
```

```
// the dialog. I simply take the dialog's
// coordinates and only change the top value
// since the left, right, and bottom values
// are what I need to align the status bar
// to the bottom of the dialog box.
CRect rect;
GetWindowRect(&rect);
rect.top = rect.bottom - STATUSBAR_HEIGHT;

// Create the status bar using the rect that
// I've defined.
if (!m_wndStatusBar.Create(WS_CHILD
 | WS_BORDER | WS_VISIBLE,
 rect,
 this,
 IDC_STATUSBAR))
{
 AfxMessageBox ("Error in creating status bar");
}
else
{
 // Set the status bar's minimum height to be
 // equal to the value I used to size it
 // earlier.
 m_wndStatusBar.SetMinHeight(STATUSBAR_HEIGHT);

 // Get the size of the window as you'll have to
 // manually do all sizing of the status bar panes.
 CRect rectDialog;
 GetWindowRect(&rectDialog);
 int iDialogWidth = rectDialog.right - rectDialog.left;

 // Simply make each pane of equal size. Obviously,
 // a more advanced usage would have these panes
 // sized according to their data and usage.
 int nPanes = sizeof (Panes) / sizeof (Panes[0]);
 int iPaneWidths[sizeof (Panes) / sizeof (Panes[0])];

 for (int i = 0; i < (nPanes-1); i++)
 iPaneWidths[i] = (i + 1) * (iDialogWidth / nPanes);
 iPaneWidths[(nPanes-1)] = -1;

 m_wndStatusBar.SetParts(nPanes, iPaneWidths);

 // Sample pane data
 for (int i = 0; i < nPanes; i++)
  m_wndStatusBar.SetText(Panes[i].szText,
                         i,
                         Panes[i].dwStyle);
 }
}
```

The final step to making this demo build is to open the `resource.h` file and add a resource ID.

```
#define IDC_STATUSBAR                        1000
```

In my case, I set this value to 1000 because the `_APS_NEXT_CONTROL_VALUE` was 1000. I then changed that value as well to be 1001. If you're creating this demo from scratch, you can do the same. However, if you're using this code to add a status bar to an already existing dialog box, you need to make sure that you set the `IDC_STATUSBAR` value to a unique number to avoid conflict with any other resource IDs.

Now, build and run the application. The results you see should be similar to those shown in Figure 6-2.

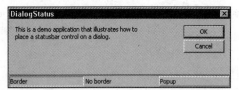

Figure 6-2: Adding a status bar to a dialog box takes some work, but does make the UI just a bit nicer.

While this might seem like a lot of work (and it is), at least you now know how to place a status bar on a dialog box to give your dialog-based applications that extra bit of pizzazz that users are accustomed to.

Adding a progress bar to the status bar

Because the primary focus of the status bar is to present feedback to the user, the most natural control to place on the status bar is the progress bar. Using this control, you can not only provide information on the progress of a lengthy operation to the user, but you can do so without an intrusive dialog. Therefore, I present to you a class called `CProgressBar` that wraps a progress bar control whose features include self-initialization, display, and cleanup as well as the ability to automatically resize itself when its parent window (a status bar in this example) is resized. Finally, the `CProgressBar` class is coded so that it can be instantiated once (say at the application level) and reused multiple times. As you'll soon see, the `CProgressBar` actually has two visual parts — the progress bar and an optional text message displayed to the left of the progress bar. This control can be displayed in any pane of a status bar and its properties (text message, size, and range) can all be changed dynamically as needed by your application logic. Now, let's create the demo application and `CProgressBar` class.

Building the CProgressBar class

Although the progress control class can be used any place, I'll create it within the context of a demo in order to test it. To get started, create an SDI application called `ProgressDemo` and then follow these steps to create the `CProgressBar` class.

1. Once you've created that project, add the new class. To do this, simply choose Project ⇨ Add Class, and select the MFC Class template.

2. When the MFC Class Wizard appears, specify a class name of `CProgressBar` and a base class of `CProgressCtrl`.

3. Update the default constructor like the following:

```
CProgressBar::CProgressBar()
{
   m_Rect.SetRect(0,0,0,0);
}
```

4. Now, add the following constructor to the `CProgressBar` class. Note that along with the default constructor (which will necessitate the separate setting of the values such as size and range) this constructor enables you to initialize these settings when constructing the progress bar control object.

```
CProgressBar::CProgressBar(LPCTSTR strMessage,
                           int nSize /*=100*/,
                           int MaxValue /*=100*/,
                           BOOL bSmooth /*=FALSE*/,
                           int nPane /*=0*/)
{
   Create(strMessage,
          nSize,
          MaxValue,
          bSmooth,
          nPane);
}
```

5. Before coding the `Create` function (called from the second constructor), update the class' destructor as follows and add a `Clear` function whose main objective is to initialize the status bar once the application no longer needs it to display any text.

```
CProgressBar::~CProgressBar()
{
   Clear();
}

void CProgressBar::Clear()
{
   if (!IsWindow(GetSafeHwnd()))
     return;

   // Hide the window. This is necessary so that a cleared
   // window is not redrawn if "Resize" is called
   ModifyStyle(WS_VISIBLE, 0);

   CString str;
   if (m_nPane == 0)
     // Get the IDLE_MESSAGE
     str.LoadString(AFX_IDS_IDLEMESSAGE);
   else
     // Restore previous text
```

```
      str = m_strPrevText;

   // Place the IDLE_MESSAGE in the status bar
   CStatusBar *pStatusBar = GetStatusBar();
   if (pStatusBar)
   {
     pStatusBar->SetPaneText(m_nPane, str);
     pStatusBar->UpdateWindow();
   }
}
```

6. Now for the all-important Create function. This function takes five arguments (the last four of which have defaults). The first argument (strMessage) represents the message to place on the status bar to the left of the progress control. The second argument (nSize) is simply the initial horizontal size to make the progress control. The MaxValue argument is used in setting the progress control's range. Note that the initial value for the starting range value is 0 and initial value for the step value is 1. You can change these values via the public accessor functions that you'll see shortly. The bSmooth argument specifies whether you want the drawing of the progress control to be smooth or chunky. Finally, the nPane argument specifies which pane of the status bar you want the progress bar to appear in.

From there, the code is pretty self-explanatory. It first retrieves the window's status bar. You'll see shortly how that is done. From there, the base class's Create is called and some internal member variables are set pursuant to the values passed as arguments to this function.

```
BOOL CProgressBar::Create(LPCTSTR strMessage,
 int nSize /*=100*/,
 int MaxValue /*=100*/,
 BOOL bSmooth /*=FALSE*/,
 int nPane /*=0*/)
{
   BOOL bSuccess = FALSE;

   CStatusBar *pStatusBar = GetStatusBar();
   if (!pStatusBar)
     return FALSE;

   DWORD dwStyle = WS_CHILD|WS_VISIBLE;
#ifdef PBS_SMOOTH
   if (bSmooth)
     dwStyle |= PBS_SMOOTH;
#endif
   // Get CRect coordinates for requested status bar pane
   CRect PaneRect;
   pStatusBar->GetItemRect(nPane, &PaneRect);

   // Create the progress bar
   bSuccess = CProgressCtrl::Create(dwStyle,
     PaneRect,
     pStatusBar,
```

```
  1);

ASSERT(bSuccess);
if (!bSuccess)
  return FALSE;

// Set range and step
SetRange(0, MaxValue);
SetStep(1);

m_strMessage  = strMessage;
m_nSize       = nSize;
m_nPane       = nPane;
m_strPrevText = pStatusBar->GetPaneText(m_nPane);

// Resize the control to its desired width
Resize();

return TRUE;
}
```

7. Let's look at the GetStatusBar function now. As you can see, this function simply obtains the application main window (typically the main frame in an SDI or MDI application). The status bar is then retrieved from this window via the CFrameWnd::GetMessageBar function. Note that if the main window is not a CFrameWnd-derived class, the code traverses the window's children windows looking for a status bar. This enables you to place the progress bar in a status bar that is on a dialog (as illustrated in the previous demo).

```
CStatusBar* CProgressBar::GetStatusBar()
{
  CWnd *pMainWnd = AfxGetMainWnd();
  if (!pMainWnd)
    return NULL;

  // If main window is a frame window,
  // use normal methods...
  if (pMainWnd->IsKindOf(RUNTIME_CLASS(CFrameWnd)))
  {
    CWnd* pMessageBar =
    ((CFrameWnd*)pMainWnd)->GetMessageBar();

    return DYNAMIC_DOWNCAST(CStatusBar, pMessageBar);
  }
  // otherwise traverse children to try
  // to find the status bar...
  else
    return DYNAMIC_DOWNCAST(CStatusBar,
      pMainWnd->GetDescendantWindow(AFX_IDW_STATUS_BAR));
}
```

8. At this point, you have the creation and clean-up functions coded. Now add the sizing code. To do that, simply add the following `Resize` function to the class. As you can see, there's a bit of work to do here. Mainly, you're concerned with making sure that the progress bar is sized in accordance with its parent window such that the text and progress bar can be viewed in their entirety.

```
BOOL CProgressBar::Resize()
{
  if (!IsWindow(GetSafeHwnd()))
    return FALSE;

  CStatusBar *pStatusBar = GetStatusBar();
  if (!pStatusBar)
    return FALSE;

  // Redraw the window text
  if (IsWindowVisible())
  {
    pStatusBar->SetPaneText(m_nPane,
                            m_strMessage);
    pStatusBar->UpdateWindow();
  }

  // Calculate how much space the text takes up
  CClientDC dc(pStatusBar);

  CFont *pOldFont =
    dc.SelectObject(pStatusBar->GetFont());

  // Length of text
  CSize size = dc.GetTextExtent(m_strMessage);

  // Text margin
  int margin = dc.GetTextExtent(_T(" ")).cx * 2;
  dc.SelectObject(pOldFont);

  // Now calculate the rectangle in which you
  // will draw the progress bar
  CRect rc;
  pStatusBar->GetItemRect(m_nPane, rc);

  // Position left of progress bar after
  // text and right of progress bar
  // to requested percentage of status bar pane
  if (!m_strMessage.IsEmpty())
    rc.left += (size.cx + 2*margin);

  rc.right -= (rc.right - rc.left)
            * (100 - m_nSize) / 100;

  if (rc.right < rc.left)
    rc.right = rc.left;
```

```
// Leave a little vertical margin (10%)
// between the top and bottom of the bar
int Height = rc.bottom - rc.top;
rc.bottom -= Height/10;
rc.top   += Height/10;

// If the window size has changed, resize
// the window
if (rc != m_Rect)
{
  MoveWindow(&rc);
  m_Rect = rc;
}

return TRUE;
}
```

9. So what causes this function to be called? First off, the Create function explicitly calls this function just before returning. Secondly, any publicly called function that would cause the progress bar to change size should call this function. This includes the SetSize and SetText functions that you'll see shortly. Lastly, you want to catch any WM_ERASEBKGND messages and resize the progress bar. Why? Because your control will get this messages if the user resizes the frame window containing the status bar. In response to such an event, the status bar sends the WM_ERASEBKGND message to each of its child windows (which includes this progress control window). Therefore, you need to add a WM_ERASEBKGND message handler called OnEraseBkgnd and code it as follows to ensure that you have a self-sizing control.

```
BOOL CProgressBar::OnEraseBkgnd(CDC* pDC)
{
  Resize();
  return CProgressCtrl::OnEraseBkgnd(pDC);
}
```

10. Add the following accessor functions that enable the client to easily manipulate the status bar after it has been created.

```
BOOL CProgressBar::SetText(LPCTSTR strMessage)
{
  m_strMessage = strMessage;
  return Resize();
}

BOOL CProgressBar::SetSize(int nSize)
{
  m_nSize = nSize;
  return Resize();
}

COLORREF CProgressBar::SetBarColour(COLORREF clrBar)
{
#ifdef PBM_SETBKCOLOR
  if (!IsWindow(GetSafeHwnd()))
    return CLR_DEFAULT;
```

```
      return SendMessage(PBM_SETBARCOLOR, 0, (LPARAM) clrBar);
#else
   UNUSED(clrBar);
   return CLR_DEFAULT;
#endif
}

COLORREF CProgressBar::SetBkColour(COLORREF clrBk)
{
#ifdef PBM_SETBKCOLOR
   if (!IsWindow(GetSafeHwnd()))
     return CLR_DEFAULT;

   return SendMessage(PBM_SETBKCOLOR,
                      0,
                      (LPARAM)
                      clrBk);
#else
   UNUSED(clrBk);
   return CLR_DEFAULT;
#endif
}

BOOL CProgressBar::SetRange(int nLower,
                           int nUpper,
                           int nStep /* = 1 */)
{
   if (!IsWindow(GetSafeHwnd()))
     return FALSE;

   // To take advantage of the Extended
   // Range Values you use the PBM_SETRANGE32
   // message instead of calling
   // CProgressCtrl::SetRange directly.
#ifdef PBM_SETRANGE32
   ASSERT(-0x7FFFFFFF <= nLower && nLower <= 0x7FFFFFFF);
   ASSERT(-0x7FFFFFFF <= nUpper && nUpper <= 0x7FFFFFFF);
   SendMessage(PBM_SETRANGE32,
               (WPARAM) nLower,
               (LPARAM) nUpper);
#else
   ASSERT(0 <= nLower && nLower <= 65535);
   ASSERT(0 <= nUpper && nUpper <= 65535);
   CProgressCtrl::SetRange(nLower, nUpper);
#endif

   CProgressCtrl::SetStep(nStep);
   return TRUE;
}

int CProgressBar::SetPos(int nPos)
{
   if (!IsWindow(GetSafeHwnd()))
```

```
      return 0;

#ifdef PBM_SETRANGE32
   ASSERT(-0x7FFFFFFF <= nPos && nPos <= 0x7FFFFFFF);
#else
   ASSERT(0 <= nPos && nPos <= 65535);
#endif

   ModifyStyle(0,WS_VISIBLE);
   return CProgressCtrl::SetPos(nPos);
}

int CProgressBar::OffsetPos(int nPos)
{
   if (!IsWindow(GetSafeHwnd()))
      return 0;

   ModifyStyle(0,WS_VISIBLE);
   return CProgressCtrl::OffsetPos(nPos);
}

int CProgressBar::SetStep(int nStep)
{
   if (!IsWindow(GetSafeHwnd()))
      return 0;

   ModifyStyle(0,WS_VISIBLE);
   return CProgressCtrl::SetStep(nStep);
}

int CProgressBar::StepIt()
{
   if (!IsWindow(GetSafeHwnd()))
      return 0;

   ModifyStyle(0,WS_VISIBLE);
   return CProgressCtrl::StepIt();
}
```

11. Finally, add the following member variables to the class:

```
class CProgressBar : public CProgressCtrl
{

...

protected:
   int m_nSize; // Percentage size of control
   int m_nPane; // status bar pane for progress bar control
   CString m_strMessage; // message text
   CString m_strPrevText; // Previous text in status bar
   CRect m_Rect; // Dimensions of the whole thing
}
```

That's it! Although it's certainly not a simple class, placing a progress bar on a status bar is not a trivial task. However, as you'll now see in the section on using this class, the little bit of work here is definitely worth it with regards to the feedback you can now give your users.

Using the CProgressBar class

Although using the CProgressBar class is very easy, it's always helpful to quickly go over the basics of initialization and usage and then see a class in a couple of different usage scenarios. To begin with, Table 6-3 shows the basic public member functions at your disposal:

Table 6-3: CProgressBar Public Member Functions

Member Function	Description
`BOOL Success()`	Used to determine if the construction of the class was successful.
`COLORREF SetBarColour(COLORREF clrBar)`	Sets the bar's fill color (returning the previous).
`COLORREF SetBkColour(COLORREF clrBar)`	Sets the background color of the progress bar.
`int SetPos(int nPos)`	Sets the current position of the progress bar to the specified value and redraws the new position.
`int OffsetPos(int nPos)`	Advances the progress bar control's current position by adding the value specified by `nPos` to the current position and redrawing the bar to reflect the new position.
`int SetStep(int nStep)`	Sets the step increment for the progress control (used with the `StepIt` function). This value defaults to 1 upon `CprogressBar` creation.
`int StepIt()`	Advanced the progress bar by the amount specified via the `SetStep` function.
`void Clear()`	Clears the progress bar.
`void SetRange(int nLower, int nUpper, int nStep=1)`	Sets the lower and upper ranges along with a step value.
`void SetText(LPCTSTR strMessage)`	Specifies the text message to appear with the progress control. This is usually something like "x %" where x represents the current position of the progress bar.
`void SetSize(int nSize)`	Sets the progress bar's horizontal size.

Now, let's see some simple example usages to get started. First is an example of creating a progress bar with an initial size of 40 and a max value of 100. The for loop then performs its work and calls the StepIt function periodically to update the progress bar.

```
CProgressBar Bar("Current progress-->", 40, 1000);

for (int i = 0;  i <  1000; i++)
{
  // perform operation
  Bar.StepIt();
}
```

Here's a bit more involved (and realistic) usage. Note that first I'm initializing the progress bar just as I did before. However, now after the first bit of work, I'm setting the progress bar's text to indicate another task being performed, and then during that work I'm calling StepIt and PeekAndPump. The PeekAndPump function pumps messages, thereby allowing user interaction with the window during a lengthy process. Because of its inclusion in this code snippet, if the window size were to change during processing, the progress bar size would automatically change (via the Resize function being called from the WM_ERASEBKGND message handler).

```
CProgressBar bar;

bar.Create("Processing", 40, 1000);
for (int i = 0; i < 1000; i++)
{
  //  perform operation
  bar.StepIt();
}

bar.SetText("Writing");

for  (int i = 0;  i <  1000; i++)
{
  // perform operation
  bar.StepIt();
  PeekAndPump();        // Message pump
}
bar.Clear();
```

On the Web site for this book, you'll find that the ProgressDemo has four menu entries that illustrate these two techniques for using the CProgressBar class as well as two more. Figure 6-3 shows the demo application in progress.

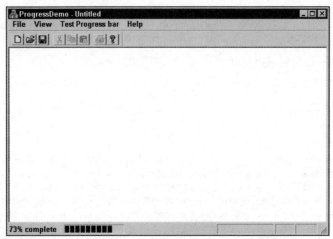

Figure 6-3: Although it is not a trivial task, coding a progress control into your status bar does provide a very important interface element for your user.

Creating and Controlling Toolbars

Toolbars provide instant access to program commands for users. Rather than digging into a menu or remembering a keystroke, users can use toolbars, which are visible on the interface. Because they occupy precious screen real estate, toolbars should include only the most frequently used commands. Large programs tend to have multiple toolbars for different user tasks. Even if your program has only a single toolbar, make sure you give the user the option of hiding it when it gets in the way.

From a programming perspective, a toolbar is a child window that displays a series of bitmap buttons. Once you create a toolbar and make it visible, you can all but ignore it because it generates the same message—WM_COMMAND—that menus and accelerators generate. However, you should synchronize toolbar command IDs with the command IDs in menus and accelerators.

The following sections cover several topics that can help you work with toolbars. Let's start with a quick look at the placement of toolbars in the MFC hierarchy. Then I'll cover some of the details involved in dynamically creating and modifying toolbars.

MFC control bars

MFC's toolbar class, CToolBar, is one of several classes that create windows for receiving some kind of command input and displaying status information to the user. The base class for this group, known collectively as *control bars*, is CControlBar, and it's derived from CWnd.

This inheritance relationship has some very useful implications. For example, because all control bars are derived from CWnd, they are connected to a Windows API window. As a result, all of the functional capabilities of CWnd—creating, moving, showing, and hiding windows—are available when you're working with control bars.

MFC toolbars are *dockable*. When this feature is enabled, a user can drag a toolbar to a different edge of a frame window and have it docked there. It is up to the frame window, however, to indicate which edges are acceptable docking sites. As an alternative, you can also move toolbars away from any frame edge and leave it in a free-floating palette. You'll see how to programmatically control all of this shortly.

MFC toolbars also support *ToolTips,* which are intended to help users understand the purpose of individual toolbar buttons. Users summon ToolTip support—when it's enabled—by moving the mouse cursor over a toolbar button (without clicking the button). After a brief interval, the ToolTip, a word or phrase, appears in a tiny text window that hovers over the toolbar buttons.

To put toolbars to work in your MFC program, you must coordinate several items, including a bitmap resource, the toolbar itself, and the frame window. To help with this effort, the following section shows how to create a toolbar of your own.

Creating and initializing a toolbar

Toolbar creation is a five-step process.

1. Load a bitmap that holds all of the button images. You'll store the bitmap as a bitmap resource, which means you'll first open your project's resource (.RC) file. You create your bitmap button images in a row, using the bitmap editor. The default size of each image is 16 pixels wide by 15 pixels high. When the AppWizard generates the default MFC project that includes a toolbar, the bitmap used for the toolbar is located in the project's \res subdirectory. Although you can use different sizes, a change from the default requires that you inform your toolbar object by calling CToolBar::SetSizes().

2. Define an array of command codes that map button images to command IDs. As shown in the following example, this is an array of unsigned integers (UINT):

```
// toolbar buttons - IDs are command buttons
static UINT BASED_CODE buttons[] =
{
    // same order as in the bitmap 'bitmap1.bmp'
    ID_TOOLBAR_CREATE,
        ID_SEPARATOR,
    ID_TOOLBAR_SHOW
};
```

The two command codes are ID_TOOLBAR_CREATE and ID_TOOLBAR_SHOW. The other item, ID_SEPARATOR, adds a bit of spacing between these two buttons.

3. Create and initialize the toolbar object. As with other windows, you create a toolbar by first instantiating the object, and then calling an initialization function. Here's an example:

```
// Instantiate C++ object and create window.
m_wndToolbar = new CToolBar();
m_wndToolbar.Create(this, WS_CHILD | CBRS_TOP, 0x9100);
```

The initialization function, CToolBar::Create(), overrides the base function CWnd::Create. As with other types of window objects, the style field—that is, the middle field—controls quite a few object attributes. This example has two style flags: WS_CHILD and CBRS_TOP. WS_CHILD is a standard windowing style that makes the toolbar a child window whose parent is pointed to by the pointer variable this. CBRS_TOP is a control bar–specific style that puts the toolbar at the top of the frame window. Table 6-4 lists other style flags that might be useful.

4. Load the button images into the toolbar's buttons. You accomplish this by calling CToolBar::LoadBitmap, as in:

```
m_wndToolbar.LoadBitmap(IDR_TOOLS);
```

5. You also need to associate command IDs with buttons. As shown in the following example, you do this by calling CToolBar::SetButtons, passing in the array of button resource IDs and the number of buttons to set:

```
m_wndToolbar.SetButtons(buttons,
    sizeof(buttons)/sizeof(UINT));
```

At this point, the toolbar is complete. If you followed all the preceding steps, the toolbar should display several buttons, each with a bitmap image from the application's resource file. Once these minimum steps are accomplished, you can take other steps to fine-tune the behavior of your toolbar.

Table 6-4: CToolBar::Create Constants

Flag	Description
WS_VISIBLE	Makes the toolbar window visible initially.
CBRS_BOTTOM	Places the control bar at the bottom of the frame.
CBRS_FLYBY	Causes command descriptions to be displayed in the status window when the mouse cursor pauses over buttons.
CBRS_NOALIGN	Prevents repositioning of the control bar when its parent window is resized.
CBRS_TOOLTIPS	Displays ToolTips when the mouse cursor pauses over the toolbar's buttons.
CBRS_TOP	Places the control bar at the top of the frame.

Docking and floating

By default, a CToolBar toolbar can be moved only by program control. However, you can enable users to move the toolbar to other parts of the frame. To do so, you must notify both the toolbar and the frame window. As shown in the following example, you do this by calling CToolBar::EnableDocking and CFrameWnd::EnableDocking:

```
m_wndToolbar.EnableDocking(CBRS_ALIGN_ANY);
EnableDocking(CBRS_ALIGN_ANY);
```

Users can then dock and undock the toolbar. Alternatively, under program control, you can dock the toolbar by calling CFrameWnd::DockControlBar, and you can undock the toolbar by calling `CFrameWnd::FloatControlBar`. Once you create a toolbar, it remains attached to your frame window and works on its own. There aren't many things you'll have to do, except perhaps hide it or show it on demand, which is discussed in the next section.

Showing and hiding toolbars

The key point to keep in mind when showing or hiding a toolbar is that a toolbar is a window. In practice, this means that you'll rely more on `CWnd` member functions than on `CToolBar` functions.

Before you can show or hide a toolbar, it helps to know the current visibility state of the toolbar window. The `WS_VISIBLE` windowing style is the key to toolbar visibility. To query all of the style bits for a window, you call `CWnd::GetStyle`. To determine the visibility of a toolbar, you simply mask the style flag `WS_VISIBLE` against the results of `GetStyle`. This code fragment sets a Boolean variable based on the visibility of a toolbar window:

```
// Query current visibility.
BOOL bVisible = (m_wndToolbar.GetStyle()
                 & WS_VISIBLE);
```

A call to `CWnd::SetStyle` enables you to change certain window styles; unfortunately, `WS_VISIBLE` is not one of them. Instead, you call `CWnd::ShowWindow` and pass `SW_HIDE` to make the toolbar invisible, and `SW_SHOWNORMAL` to make it reappear. The following code fragment toggles the visibility flag queried in the previous example:

```
// Show or hide.
int nShow = (bVisible) ? SW_HIDE : SW_SHOWNORMAL;
m_wndToolbar.ShowWindow(nShow);
```

Whenever you programmatically change a toolbar, you must inform the frame window about the change. You do this by simply asking it to recalculate the positioning of control bars. You make this request by calling `CFrameWnd::RecalcLayout`, which takes no parameters:

```
// Reconfigure remaining toolbar items.
RecalcLayout();
```

Adding ToolTips and flyby text

In most current applications, toolbars also provide some basic help and hints to the user in the form of ToolTips and *flyby text*. Flyby text is a message that is displayed on the status bar, most commonly in the first pane (denoted by the `ID_SEPARATOR` ID discussed earlier in the chapter). The help text provided in flyby text can be a bit longer than the ToolTips because there is more space to display the text.

When you add a toolbar button or menu selection, Visual C++ stores the resource information in the application's resource table, and a resource ID is assigned. Resource IDs cannot be duplicated within a category of resources, which means that two toolbar buttons cannot share the same resource ID, and two strings cannot share the same ID either. However, it doesn't mean that a toolbar button and a string can't share the same ID. In fact, MFC takes advantage of this fact and uses it to automate displaying ToolTips and flyby text.

Basically, MFC takes the resource ID for a toolbar button or a menu selection and checks to see if the application has a string resource defined in its string table with the same ID. This may sound confusing at first, but just remember that resource IDs must be unique only within their category. For example, let's dissect the resource file excerpt shown in the following snippet:

```
IDR_TOOLBAR 16,15
BEGIN
    BUTTON ID_CUT
    BUTTON ID_COPY
    BUTTON ID_PASTE
    SEPARATOR
    BUTTON ID_PRINT_PREVIEW
    BUTTON ID_PRINT
END
STRINGTABLE
BEGIN
    ID_CUT              "Cut current selection to
                            clipboard\nCut"

    ID_COPY             "Copy current selection to
                            clipboard\nCopy"

    ID_PASTE            "Paste clipboard
                            contents\nPaste"

    ID_PRINT_PREVIEW    "Preview print output\nPrint
                            preview"

    ID_PRINT            "Print document\nPrint"
END
```

Notice how the string table entries have the same ID as the button controls on the toolbar. MFC uses this overlap to match up string table entries with each toolbar control. One string table entry contains both the flyby text and the ToolTip text. Each resource string is simply parsed: all the text before the embedded newline is displayed as flyby text, while the shorter string after the newline is displayed as a ToolTip.

Adding nonbutton controls

Buttons claim the majority of toolbar real estate in comparison to the other control types. However, you can add other types of controls to a toolbar. For example, it would be convenient for a word processor to provide a combo box on a toolbar that enables users to select fonts and font styles.

The first step to adding a nonbutton control is to stake out your real estate claim on the toolbar. You can do so by editing the toolbar resource and inserting a separator as a placeholder for the control:

```
IDR_TOOLBAR 16,15
BEGIN
    BUTTON ID_CUT
    BUTTON ID_COPY
BUTTON ID_PASTE
    SEPARATOR
    SEPARATOR //Placeholder for control
END
```

The second step is to widen the area for the control by using `CToolBar::SetButtonInfo` to increase the width of the area marked by the separator:

```
SetButtonInfo(4, IDC_FONTS, TBBS_SEPARATOR, nWidth);
```

In the preceding snippet, the first argument represents the position of the control on the toolbar, `IDC_FONTS` is the resource ID of the control, `TBBS` is an MFC constant that represents a toolbar separator, and `nWidth` holds the width of the control. After the call to `CToolBar::SetButtonInfo` has completed, the control can be created:

```
CRect rect;
GetItemRect (4, &rect);
rect.bottom = rect.top + nHeight;
m_ctlFonts.Create(WS_CHILD
                  | WS_VISIBLE
                  | WS_VSCROLL
                  | CBS_SORT
                  | CBS_DROPDOWNLIST,
               rect,
               this,
               IDC_FONTS);
```

In practice, the preceding code and the call to `SetButtonInfo` are normally included in the toolbar's `OnCreate` handler function.

Updating nonbutton controls

A toolbar that contains only button controls uses the `CCmdUI` update mechanism to update the states of the toolbar buttons. However, this mechanism is not available for use when nonbutton controls are added to the toolbar. Don't despair though—MFC provides an answer in the form of another toolbar class, `CControlBar` and its update mechanism `CControlBar::OnUpdateCmdUI`.

All you need do is derive the toolbar from `CControlBar` rather than `CToolBar`. Once you've changed your code, the `OnUpdateCmdUI()` function is available. You can override `OnUpdateCmdUI` and update controls that do not have update handlers, such as combo boxes or list boxes.

Using the ReBar control

ReBars are the latest user interface innovation from Microsoft. Before their formal introduction in Visual C++ 6.0, they were referred to as *coolbars*. In the interest of just being different, Microsoft has decided to call them *ReBars*, so you should as well.

ReBars are functionally almost exactly the same as a standard toolbar. A ReBar can host and display other controls in the same way as a toolbar. The main difference lies in their appearance. ReBars appear as a flat strip with its constituent controls drawn flush with no surrounding border. When the mouse pointer is placed over a control, the control appears to pop up from the bar and is drawn with 3D borders. Figure 6-4 displays a ReBar and its parts.

ReBars have one advantage over toolbars. A ReBar can host multiple toolbar strips. The gripper is used to differentiate between toolbar strips on one ReBar. Each continuous line of controls, from gripper to gripper, is one toolbar strip. The user can drag the gripper to dynamically move the toolbar strips. Microsoft has made using ReBars extremely simple.

Rebar Control   Rebar bands

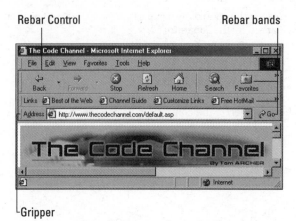

Gripper

Figure 6-4: This example of a ReBar shows the gripper and the ReBar's controls.

Adding ReBar support

Follow these steps to add ReBar support to any MFC application:

1. Add a variable of type `CReBar` to the list of protected variables in `MainFrm.h`. This section of code also contains the variables for the toolbar, `m_wndToolBar`, and the status bar, `m_wndStatusBar`.

2. In `CMainFrame::OnCreate` after the toolbar has been created and initialized, you must attach the ReBar to its parent window. This is accomplished by calling `CReBar::Create` and passing in a pointer to the parent window:

   ```
   m_wndReBar.Create(this);
   ```

3. Once the ReBar is attached to the parent window, you need to add the toolbar to the ReBar so the toolbar's controls are displayed on the ReBar. This is conveniently accomplished using the member function `CReBar::AddBar` and passing to the function the address of the toolbar to be added:

   ```
   m_wndReBar.AddBar(&m_wndToolBar);
   ```

That's all there is to adding ReBars to your application. With an additional three lines of code, your application is now displaying new and improved toolbars.

If you examine the source code for the BarsDemo application that is on the Web site for this book, you'll see that support for ReBars is already included but commented out. Simply uncomment the code and compile to see ReBars in action. Figure 6-5 shows this application in action. Note the use of the status bar to reflect such information as which color is currently being used and the current object count. The toolbar contains buttons for selecting the color to be used in drawing the shapes as well as buttons for drawing the shapes. In addition, the current color selection button remains pressed in for more intuitive feedback to the user.

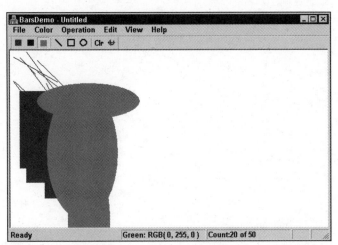

Figure 6-5: The BarsDemo application illustrates many features of using toolbars and status bars in your applications.

Summary

This chapter covered status bars and toolbars. Once you learned the basics of creating status bars and displaying simple text, you discovered some of the more advanced usages of status bars such as displaying progress bars in order to communicate the status of lengthy operations to the user. The section on status bars also showed you how to insert a status bar into a dialog box. From there, you went into the subject of programming toolbars. Once again, you started with the basics of creating and displaying the control. After that, you learned how to programmatically display and hide the toolbar, create your own toolbars, and use nonbuttons (such as combo boxes) on the toolbar. By now, you should feel comfortable adding either of these objects to your applications and using them to make your application that much more polished.

✦ ✦ ✦

Tree View and List View Controls

When Windows 95 was released into the marketplace, it introduced several new common controls. These controls were
packaged in the COMCTL32.DLL file and play an integral part in the
document-centric interface that all the different flavors of Windows
have sported since Windows 95. Among these common controls are
controls designed to provide an easier and more powerful means
of displaying and managing lists of data. When you use Windows
Explorer to browse your system's namespace (the files, folders, and
devices that make up your Windows system), you will see at least
two of these controls: the *tree view control* and the *list view control*.
Although the tree view control is used to display hierarchically structured lists of items, the list view control can display its items in one
of four ways (called *views*). These different views include the Large
Icon view, Small Icon view, List view, and Details (or Report) view.
Each of these different views is explained in detail in "The List View
Control" section of this chapter.

The tree view and list view controls also use the functionality of other
common controls to enhance their appearance as well as their own
functionality. For example, both the tree view and the list view controls use a common control called the *image list control*. As the name
implies, the image list control is used to hold a list of bitmaps or
icons that can then be referenced by index when working with either
the tree view or list view control. As you work your way through this
chapter, you will see how each control uses the image list control to
visually represent its respective data items. In addition to the image
list control, the list view control uses another common control: the
header control. The header control is a single row of column headings
used by the list control to better organize and display the data within
the list control. In advanced applications, the header control enables
the end user of the application to sort the list view control's data by
clicking on the desired column heading. In some applications, the
header control even enables the end user to arrange the columns
of data in a list view control by dragging and dropping the different
columns to their desired positions.

Although the tree view control and list view control have completely
different capabilities, they are often used together to provide two different views of an application's data. As mentioned before, Windows
Explorer is an example of an application that uses the strengths of

both controls to aid in the display of the same data within a single application, as shown in Figure 7-1. In fact, so many developers wanted the capability of mimicking the Windows Explorer look and feel that Visual C++ modified the AppWizard to contain an option for creating an application with the exact same interface as Windows Explorer. Therefore, this chapter focuses on these two very powerful controls and illustrates how you can use them to provide a much more sophisticated user interface for your applications.

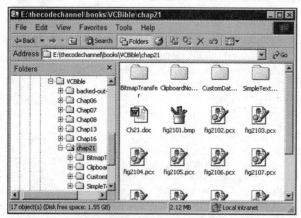

Figure 7-1: Windows Explorer uses the tree view and list view controls to display different views of the same data.

The Tree View Control

As mentioned before, the Windows tree view control is a control that enables you to display data in a hierarchical, or tree-like, fashion. The MFC encapsulation of this functionality is the CTreeCtrl class. However, you should understand that the CTreeCtrl class is only a *very* thin wrapper. In fact, if you look through the MFC source for this class (located in the winctrl2.cpp file), you will find that the majority of the CTreeCtrl member functions do little more than fill out a data structure and send a message to its underlying tree view control. Therefore, before getting into the CTreeCtrl member functions and how to use them, you need a full understanding of the underlying tree view control.

Tree view control basics

The tree view control is used to display hierarchically related data. You've probably seen this hierarchical representation of data in applications such as Windows Explorer, Visual Studio (the project dialog bar), Outlook Express (mail and newsgroup folders), and MSDN (groupings of articles and books by subject). Although each application's utilization of the tree view control is slightly different, some aspects are common to all tree views, such as the roles of root, parent, and child items.

A *parent item* is an item that contains other items, called *child items*. A *child item* can have its own child items, and therefore, a single object can be a parent item and a child item. Any item that does not have a parent item is called a *root item*. (Note that you can have any number of root items.) When the parent is expanded, the child items are always displayed indented below their parent item. Whereas a parent item may contain any number of child items, a child item may only have one parent item. Figure 7-2 shows an example of hierarchical data being displayed in a tree view.

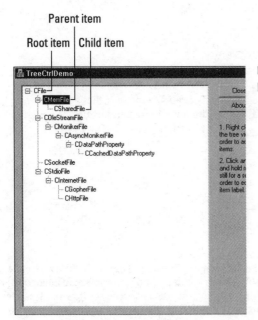

Figure 7-2: Window showing root, parent, and child items

As you can see in Figure 7-2, the item without a parent item (CFile) is the root item. As mentioned already, a single item can be a parent item and a child item. For example, the CAsyncMonikerFile item is a child item of the CMonikerFile item. Yet it is also a parent item to the CDataPathProperty item.

Numerous styles are associated with the tree view control. Figure 7-2, for instance, shows three styles that demonstrate how the different items in the tree view control are visually related. Each of these styles was set in the resource editor via the tree control's properties dialog box. However, the actual style bit constant that you would use if you were to modify these settings in code is in parentheses. These styles (listed here) are covered in more detail when the first tree view control demo is introduced shortly.

✦ Has buttons (TVS_HASBUTTONS)—Displays plus (+) and minus (–) buttons next to parent items.

✦ Has lines (TVS_HASLINES)—Uses lines to show the hierarchy of items.

✦ Lines at root (TVS_LINESATROOT)—Uses lines to link items at the root of the tree view control.

Each item can then optionally have a bitmap (or a pair of bitmaps) associated with it. Many applications choose to associate two images with each item. That way, one image can be displayed when the item is selected and another item can be displayed when an item is not being selected. Figure 7-3 shows an example of the typical images used to represent both selected and unselected items. As you can see, opened folder and closed folder icons are generally used to represent selected and unselected items in a tree view. However, more advanced applications will typically use a set of custom images specific to the data being represented.

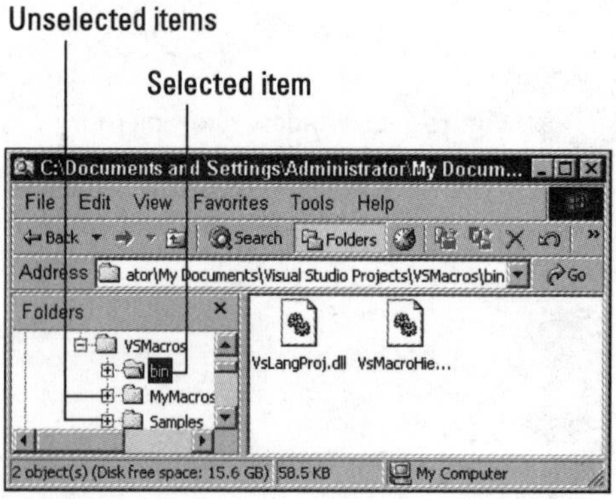

Figure 7-3: An open and closed image indicates to the user that a given tree item is selected and its data is being displayed

The CTreeCtrl class

Although the CTreeCtrl is considered to be a very lightweight wrapper for the tree view control, the CTreeCtrl does considerably lessen the amount of programming needed to manage the tree view control. It does this by hiding the idiosyncrasies of how the tree view control must be managed if it were being programmed in an SDK application and exposing much simpler member functions. For example, to simply insert an item into a tree view control, the application must first create and fill out a TV_INSERTSTRUCT structure and then send a TVM_INSERTITEM message to the tree view. In an SDK application, this looks like the following:

```
TVINSERTSTRUCT tvis;
tvis.hParent = hParent;
tvis.hInsertAfter = hInsertAfter;
tvis.item.mask = nMask;
tvis.item.pszText = (LPTSTR) lpszItem;
tvis.item.iImage = nImage;
tvis.item.iSelectedImage = nSelectedImage;
tvis.item.state = nState;
tvis.item.stateMask = nStateMask;
tvis.item.lParam = lParam;
```

```
HTREEITEM hNewItem =
 ::SendMessage(m_hWnd, TVM_INSERTITEM, 0, (LPARAM)&tvis);
```

By contrast, when you use one of the CTreeCtrl member functions, the code looks like the following:

```
treeControl.InsertItem(_T("My Item"));
```

Therefore, while the CTreeCtrl doesn't add much in terms of functionality to the tree view control, it definitely makes programming the tree view control much less laborious.

Creating a CTreeCtrl object

Although a CTreeCtrl can be created dynamically by using its Create member function, the most common means of creating a CTreeCtrl is via the resource editor. To create a CTreeCtrl object that is associated with a tree view control on your dialog box, you simply follow the same steps that you learned in Chapter 1 regarding creating DDX controls:

1. Drag the iconic representation of a tree view control from the Toolbox toolbar onto a dialog box.

2. Right-click the tree view control and select the Add Variable option from the context menu.

3. When the Add Member Variable Wizard dialog box is displayed, make sure that the Control variable checkbox is checked.

4. Type the name of the member variable (for example, **m_treeCategories**).

5. From the Variable type combo box, select CTreeCtrl.

6. Click the Finish button and a member variable of type CTreeCtrl will automatically be added to the dialog box's class.

Now, when you display the dialog box, DDX (explained in Chapter 1) subclasses the actual tree view control with the MFC CTreeCtrl class you just added to your dialog class. This means that any calls your application makes to the CTreeCtrl member functions result in messages being sent to the class's underlying tree view control.

Handling CTreeCtrl messages

As with other controls, there are two ways of handling messages that are sent to the tree view control (subclassed with your CTreeCtrl class). One way is to handle all messages at the dialog level; the other involves something called *reflection*. Here I'll show you an example of how each technique is used and the advantages and disadvantages of each.

Handling control notification messages at the dialog level

The benefit of handling messages at the dialog level is that it keeps all your code in one place. For example, if you have several controls on a dialog box and the functionality that you're adding to the different controls is very specific to this particular application, it would make sense to simply handle all control notification messages at the dialog level. Additionally, handling messages at the dialog level is less work, faster to implement, and results in fewer files to maintain. Take a look at the following quick demo that simply displays some text in a tree view to illustrate what I mean.

1. Create a dialog-based application called `TreeMessages`. Add the tree view, edit, and static controls as shown in Figure 7-4.

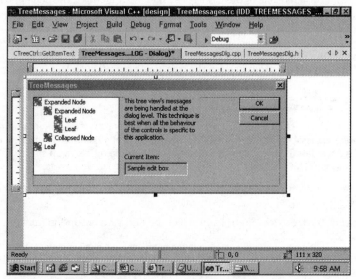

Figure 7-4: The read-only edit control displays the currently selected item text.

2. Add a member variable of type `CTreeCtrl` called `m_treeDialogMessages` to the `CTreeMessagesDlg` class for the tree view control.

3. Set the `Read Only` property of the edit control to `True`.

4. Add a member variable of type `CString` for the edit control named `m_strTree1SelectedItem`.

5. Insert the following code at the end of the dialog box's `OnInitDialog` function, in `TreeMessagesDlg.cpp`, just before the `return` statement. This code simply adds 5 text entries to the tree view control:

```
CString strItem;
for (int i = 0; i < 5; i++)
{
 strItem.Format("Tree 1, Item %d", i + 1);
 m_treeDialogMessages.InsertItem(strItem);
}
```

6. Now return to the dialog resource and add an event handler for the tree view control's `TVN_SELCHANGED` message. This creates a function in the dialog class that is called each time the user selects a different item in the tree view.

7. Finally, modify the selection changed handler so that it looks like the following:

```
void CTreeMessagesDlg::OnTvnSelchangedTree1(NMHDR *pNMHDR,
 LRESULT *pResult)
{
```

```
LPNMTREEVIEW pNMTreeView =
  reinterpret_cast<LPNMTREEVIEW>(pNMHDR);

// Get the selected item and its text value
HTREEITEM ht = m_treeDialogMessages.GetSelectedItem();
CString strSelection =
    m_treeDialogMessages.GetItemText(ht);

// Update the dialog's edit control with the new value
m_strTree1SelectedItem = strSelection;
UpdateData(FALSE);

*pResult = 0;
}
```

8. Build and execute the application. As shown in Figure 7-5, the dialog box is now assuming responsibility for handling the message sent from Windows when the user selects a tree view control item.

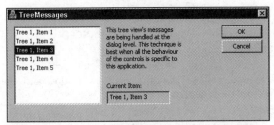

Figure 7-5: Receiving control notification messages at the dialog level can provide the benefits of faster coding, less files to maintain, and is appropriate when the control's behavior is specific to this application.

Using reflection to handle control notification messages

As discussed in Chapter 1, when Windows sends a notification message to a control window, that message is sent to the control's parent window. In the case of the tree view control in the current TreeMessages demo application, that means that the TVN_SELCHANGED message is being sent to the dialog box because technically the dialog box is the parent of the tree view. However, handling messages at the dialog level is not always a good idea, and some object-oriented programming purists would say it's never "correct." An example would be if you want to build a CTreeCtrl-derived class that could be used in several applications. Obviously, if you place all your tree view control behavior in the dialog box, it would be difficult to extract that code and reuse it later. However, by deriving a class from CTreeCtrl and using that class on the dialog box, you can isolate the base class code for easy reuse. Use the following steps to add a second tree view control to the TreeMessages demo to see how this is done:

1. Add the second tree view and static controls to the dialog resource as shown in Figure 7-6. You'll see shortly why I'm omitting the edit control from the first part of the demo.

2. Open the project's Class View window.

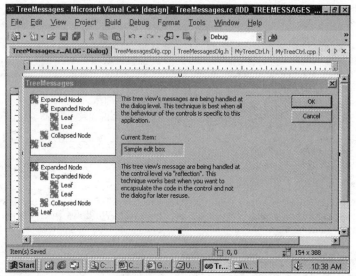

Figure 7-6: The second tree view receives the TVN_SELCHANGED message via message reflection.

3. Right-click the root item (TreeMessages) in the Class View window, and select the Add ➪ Add Class option from its context menu.

4. Click the MFC Class icon and create a CTreeCtrl-derived class using the MFC template. Name this class CMyTreeCtrl and make sure the Base class is CTreeCtrl. Visual Studio automatically creates the needed files (MyTreeCtrl.h and MyTreeCtrl.cpp), adds these files to the project, and even inserts the #include directive for the MyTreeCtrl.h file in the dialog box's header file!

5. Add a member variable of type CMyTreeCtrl to the CTreeMessagesDlg class called m_treeReflection for the tree view control by right-clicking on the CTreeMessagesDlg class in class view and clicking Add ➪ Add Variable. In the Variable type combo box, simply type the name of your newly created base class, CMyTreeCtrl. That's it. Now you have subclassed the dialog box's second tree view control with your own CTreeCtrl-derived class.

6. Insert the following code just before the return statement at the end of the dialog box's OnInitDialog member function in TreeMessagesDlg.cpp.

```
CString strItem;
for (int i = 0; i < 5; i++)
{
 strItem.Format("Tree 2, Item %d", i + 1);
 m_treeReflection.InsertItem(strItem);
}
```

7. Using the CMyTreeCtrl Property dialog box, add a message handler for the TVN_SELCHANGED message. Visual Studio adds an event handler for this message. However, take a look at the message map for the tree control, and you'll see a different message map macro than the one you've used until now:

```
ON_NOTIFY_REFLECT(TVN_SELCHANGED, OnTvnSelchanged)
```

As you can see, instead of the standard ON_NOTIFY macro that was used with the dialog box's handling of the first tree view control's message, you now are using the ON_NOTIFY_REFLECT macro. As you can guess, this macro is what causes the routing (or reflecting) of the message from the control's parent (the dialog box, in this case) back to the control.

8. Now, update the new event handler to simply output a message so that we know which item was selected.

```
void CMyTreeCtrl::OnTvnSelchanged(NMHDR *pNMHDR, LRESULT
   *pResult)
{
  LPNMTREEVIEW pNMTreeView =
  reinterpret_cast<LPNMTREEVIEW>(pNMHDR);

  HTREEITEM hitem = GetSelectedItem();
  if (hitem)
  {
    AfxMessageBox(GetItemText(hitem));
  }

  *pResult = 0;
}
```

If you build and execute the application at this point, you'll see that when you select an item from the first tree control, the dialog box is updated with the current selection. When you select an item from the second tree, a message box appears. The point that I'm illustrating here is that by using reflection, you can place control-specific code in the control class itself instead of the less-object-oriented approach of having the dialog box handle the control's messages.

However, in this application you want the best of both worlds. In other words, you want the second tree control to handle its own messages and for the dialog box's edit control to be updated. So how can you do that? There are several ways. One way would be to define a message ID for the dialog box and a handler for that message that accepts an incoming string. The tree control (upon notification that an item has been selected) could then get a pointer to its parent window (a control can determine its parent window through a call to CWnd::GetParent) and send a message (containing the selected tree view text) to the dialog box. However, that's cumbersome if you had to do it for several different types of notification message.

Thankfully, MFC has a built-in method for the control to get its reflected messages and for the parent to also get a crack at those messages. If the control decides that the parent should have an opportunity to also handle the message, it simply needs to return a value of FALSE. Because the handler technically returns void, this is done by dereferencing the pResult pointer and setting it to 0 as follows:

```
void CMyTreeCtrl::OnTvnSelchanged(NMHDR *pNMHDR,
                                  LRESULT *pResult)
{
  LPNMTREEVIEW pNMTreeView =
  reinterpret_cast<LPNMTREEVIEW>(pNMHDR);

  // your code

  // Tells the framework to let the parent
```

```
  // also handle this message
  *pResult = 0;
}
```

If the control does not want further processing, it simply needs to return TRUE.

```
void CMyTreeCtrl::OnTvnSelchanged(NMHDR *pNMHDR,
                                       LRESULT *pResult)
{
  LPNMTREEVIEW pNMTreeView =
   reinterpret_cast<LPNMTREEVIEW>(pNMHDR);

  // your code

  // Tells the framework that processing
  // for this message is completed
  *pResult = 1;
}
```

Therefore, to have the dialog box's edit control be updated for both tree views, simply comment out the call to AfxMessageBox in the control's selection handler (you know it works now, so there's no need for the message) and add the notification handler to the second tree view just as you did the first tree view. Now, from the user's perspective, the code works exactly the same.

However, I much prefer the more object-oriented approach of encapsulating the functionality of a class in that class itself and using reflection to handle the control's message.

Inserting items into a CTreeCtrl

As you saw in the TreeMessages demo, the CTreeCtrl InsertItem member function is used to insert items into a tree view control. However, depending on the needs of your application, there are four overloaded versions of the InsertItem member function that you need to know about, which are discussed in this section.

The one thing that all of the InsertItem functions have in common is that they return an HTREEITEM value. The HTREEITEM is a handle to a tree item and represents the item once it has been inserted into a tree view control. Once an item is inserted into a tree view control, it is always referred to by this HTREEITEM value. For example, some of the InsertItem functions take an HTREEITEM argument called hParent. That means that if the item being added is a child item of another item already in the tree view control, the hParent argument must be the HTREEITEM handle that represents that parent item in the tree view control.

The following are the four overloads of the InsertItem function and what each function requires in terms of parameters:

```
HTREEITEM InsertItem(LPTVINSERTSTRUCT lpInsertStruct);
```

This function takes as its only argument a pointer to a TV_INSERTSTRUCT structure. This version of the InsertItem function would normally be called only if the application needs to fill out the majority of the TV_INSERTSTRUCT members.

```
HTREEITEM InsertItem(UINT nMask,
                     LPCTSTR lpszItem,
                     int nImage,
```

```
                  int nSelectedImage,
                  UINT nState,
                  UINT nStateMask,
                  LPARAM lParam,
                  HTREEITEM hParent,
                  HTREEITEM hInsertAfter);
```

Like the previous `InsertItem` function, this version of the `InsertItem` function enables the application to specify every `TV_INSERTSTRUCT` structure member. The only difference is that instead of having to allocate the memory for the structure and setting each structure member's value, this function enables your application to pass each value as an argument to the function.

```
HTREEITEM InsertItem(LPCTSTR lpszItem,
                  HTREEITEM hParent = TVI_ROOT,
                  HTREEITEM hInsertAfter = TVI_LAST);
```

This version of the `InsertItem` is by far the simplest. If you use this function, your application need only supply the text of the item that will be displayed in the tree view. Even the item type defaults to a root item. However, this function does not enable you to specify the images associated with the item. The tree view control shown in Figure 7-3 was created using this version of `InsertItem`.

```
HTREEITEM InsertItem(LPCTSTR lpszItem,
                  int nImage,
                  int nSelectedImage,
                  HTREEITEM hParent = TVI_ROOT,
                  HTREEITEM hInsertAfter = TVI_LAST);
```

This last version of the `InsertItem` is the one that you probably find yourself using the most. That is because it enables you to specify the text of the item, the item's parent, where in the tree view control the item should be placed, and the images that are associated with the item. The `nImage` and `nSelectedImage` arguments represent the index. This version of the `InsertItem` function is used in the `TreeCtrlDemo` demo application presented at the end of this section.

Editing labels

When using Windows Explorer, you have no doubt seen that you can edit the text or label of an item in a tree view control simply by clicking the item a second time and then pausing the mouse after the item has been selected. Enabling this feature of the tree view control enables you to give the users of your application the capability of changing an item's text without you having to provide an entire dialog box that contains just a single field for the item's new text. Figure 7-7 shows an example of an item whose text is being edited.

Enabling users to edit text in a tree view control's item requires three simple steps:

1. Set the tree view control's `TVS_EDITLABELS` style.

2. Handle the `TVN_BEGINLABELEDIT` notification message.

3. Handle the `TVN_ENDLABELEDIT` notification message.

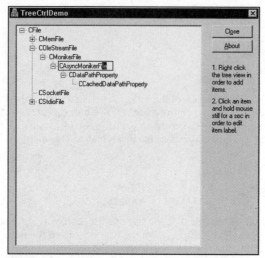

Figure 7-7: The tree view control enables the editing of item labels.

The `TVS_EDITLABELS` style can be set in two different ways. The first method is to modify the tree view control's settings from inside the resource editor. Simply display the dialog box upon which the tree view control exists and invoke the properties dialog box for the tree view control. Once the properties dialog box is displayed, select the Styles tab, and check the Edit labels checkbox. The second method is to programmatically set the tree view's `TVS_EDITLABELS` style with a call to the Win32 SDK `SetWindowLong` function. Here is an example of how to do that:

```
// retrieve the current tree control styles
long lStyle =
  ::GetWindowLong(m_treeCategories.GetSafeHwnd(),
              GWL_STYLE);

// turn the edit label style bit on
lStyle |= TVS_EDITLABELS;

// update the tree view styles
::SetWindowLong(m_treeCategories.GetSafeHwnd(),
              GWL_STYLE,
              lStyle);
```

Once you have set the `TVS_EDITLABELS` style, you need to handle the `TVN_BEGINLABELEDIT` notification message. Actually, the handling of this message is not strictly mandatory. However, many applications choose to handle this message to do such things as limit the length of the text that can be entered for the item. The Event Handler Wizard can be used to add a handler for the `TVN_BEGINLABELEDIT` notification message. Here is an example of one such handler that limits the length of the text entered for the item to 15 characters:

```
void CMyTreeCtrl::OnTvnBeginlabeleditTree1(NMHDR *pNMHDR,
                                       LRESULT *pResult)
{
```

```
LPNMTVDISPINFO pTVDispInfo =
 reinterpret_cast<LPNMTVDISPINFO>(pNMHDR);

*pResult = 1;

CEdit* pEdit = GetEditControl();
ASSERT(pEdit);
if (pEdit)
{
 GetEditControl()->LimitText(15);
 *pResult = 0;
}
}
```

The preceding code snippet is simple; however, a couple of important issues should be pointed out. First, all notification messages return `void`. Therefore, to indicate success or failure, the function must dereference the `LRESULT` pointer (pResult) and set its value to 1 for failure and 0 for success. This is why in the preceding code snippet, pResult is set to zero only if the function succeeds in setting the edit control's length. The second point to note is the call to the `CTreeCtrl` member function `GetEditControl`. To enable the user to edit the text of an item, the tree view control dynamically creates and displays an edit control. The `GetEditControl` function is called in order to get the pointer to a `CEdit` object that represents that edit control. That way, `CEdit` member functions can be used to do such things as limiting the text the user can enter.

Although it is not necessary to handle the `TVN_BEGINLABELEDIT` notification message, it is mandatory to handle the `TVN_ENDLABELEDIT` notification message. Failing to handle this message results in the user's being able to edit the labels, but at the end of the edit, the value of the label will be set to the previous value. This message handler is where you would place code as to whether the text entered for the item is valid. For example, if your application doesn't allow items with duplicate labels, you must validate that in your handler for the `TVN_ENDLABELEDIT` message. The following code snippet shows an example of how a handler might verify that the new text entered by the user does not cause two sibling items to have the same text:

```
// Validating Edited Tree View Item Labels
void CMyTreeCtrl::OnEndlabeledit(NMHDR* pNMHDR,
 LRESULT* pResult)
{
 TV_DISPINFO* pTVDispInfo = (TV_DISPINFO*)pNMHDR;

 BOOL bFoundDuplicate = FALSE;

 if (pTVDispInfo->item.pszText
 && strlen(pTVDispInfo->item.pszText))
 {
  HTREEITEM hParent =
   GetParentItem(pTVDispInfo->item.hItem);

  HTREEITEM hChild =
   GetChildItem(hParent ? hParent : TVI_ROOT);

  while (NULL != hChild && !bFoundDuplicate)
```

```
 {
  if (pTVDispInfo->item.hItem != hChild)
  {
   CString strText = GetItemText(hChild);
   if (0 ==
    strText.CompareNoCase(pTVDispInfo->item.pszText))
    {
     bFoundDuplicate = TRUE;
    }
   else
    {
     hChild = GetNextSiblingItem( hChild );
    }
  }
  else
  {
   hChild = GetNextSiblingItem( hChild );
  }
 }
}

*pResult = (bFoundDuplicate ? 0 : 1);
}
```

If you tried to use the preceding code, you probably discovered that the only way you could finish editing the item's text was to either click somewhere else on the dialog box or to switch to another application. This is because MFC was designed so that the parent window of the tree view control gets first crack at the messages through the PreTranslateMessage virtual function. If the parent window is a CDialog or CFormView object, the Esc and Enter keys are handled by the parent, and they never reach the tree view control. Therefore, in order to enable the tree view control to process the Esc and Enter keys, you must override the PreTranslateMessage function. I'll show you how to do this in the next section.

Handling Enter and Esc while editing CTreeCtrl items

These steps assume that you have created a dialog box with a tree view control on it and that the dialog box's class has a CTreeCtrl member variable (named m_tree) associated via DDX with that tree view control. The Web site for this book contains a demo called TreeCtrlDemo, which illustrates how to do all of this, if you want to play around with an already-working application. If you want to do it from scratch, follow these steps:

1. As in the TreeMessages demo, create a dialog-based application and add a tree view control to the dialog box. I'll assume from this point on that you're using a new project. However, you can also simply add this functionality to the already existing TreeMessages demo if you've already programmed it.

2. Add a new CTreeCtrl-derived class called CMyTreeCtrl to the project.

3. Using the Event Handler Wizard, override the CMyTreeCtrl PreTranslateMessage virtual member function and modify it so that when finished it looks like the following:

```
BOOL CMyTreeCtrl::PreTranslateMessage(MSG* pMsg)
{
 BOOL bHandledMsg = FALSE;
```

```
switch (pMsg->message)
{
 case WM_KEYDOWN:
 {
  switch (pMsg->wParam)
  {
   case VK_ESCAPE:
   case VK_RETURN:
    if (::GetKeyState(VK_CONTROL) & 0x8000)
    {
     break;
    }

    if (GetEditControl())
    {
     ::TranslateMessage(pMsg);
     ::DispatchMessage(pMsg);
     bHandledMsg = TRUE;
    }

   break;

   default: break;
  } // switch (pMsg->wParam)
 } // WM_KEYDOWN
 break;

 default: break;
} // switch (pMsg->message)

// continue normal translation and dispatching
return (bHandledMsg ?
  TRUE : CTreeCtrl::PreTranslateMessage(pMsg));
}
```

Now when you execute the application, pressing Enter while editing an item's text will change the item's text, and hitting the Esc key will abort the change.

Context menus

The last thing to cover before the chapter's next demo is context menus and how to implement them for a tree view control and its items. With the introduction of Windows 95 and its document-centric interface came *context menus*, also called *popup menus*. You can see an example of a context menu by clicking the right-mouse button while pointing at a file or folder in Windows Explorer.

Context menus are popular because they help to simplify the user interface. Before context menus, if an application displayed many different types of items (for example, customers, invoices, receipts, and so on), the application typically had a menu item for every action that the user could invoke for each of these items. Depending upon which type of item was currently selected by the user, the menu items were then enabled or disabled. However, the problem was that this caused large applications to have huge numbers of menu items that the user needed to wade through to find the desired menu items.

This user interface problem helped to bring about the idea of the context menu. Context menus enable the application to define a menu that pertains solely to the item for which it is defined. That way, only the actions that are global to the entire application need be on the application's menu, whereas actions that are specific to a given item can be invoked by displaying that item's context menu.

Context menus have become so popular that it's surprising when an application doesn't support them. In fact, the use of context menus within applications has become so prevalent that most modern keyboards even have a key that imitates a right-mouse button click by sending a message (WM_LBUTTONCLICK) to the current window.

For example, an application that uses context menus for items in a tree view control is Outlook Express. This popular Microsoft e-mail application has a tree view control that contains all of a user's mail and newsgroup folders. Clicking the right-mouse button while pointing at the Inbox folder produces a context menu whose options are specific to the Inbox and are distinct from the context menu options for a newsgroup folder.

Adding a simple context menu to a tree view control entails only two steps. The first step is to create a menu resource that contains the options you want displayed in the menu. Chapter 4 teaches you how to define menu resources for SDI and MDI application. However, defining a context menu is no different. For example, if you want to create a context menu for a customer item in an accounting application, the menu might resemble what you see in Figure 7-8.

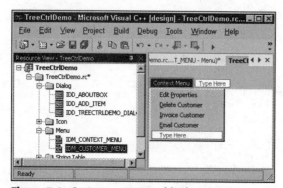

Figure 7-8: Context menus enable the programmer to display a menu that is specific to the currently selected item type, thereby creating a more intuitive interface.

The second step to implementing a context menu is to provide a handler for the WM_RBUTTONDOWN message. The following code example illustrates how to implement the display of a context menu when you right-click a tree view item:

```
// Displaying Context Menus within a Tree View
void CMyTreeCtrl::OnRButtonDown(UINT nFlags,
  CPoint point)
{
// Set focus to the tree control.
SetFocus();

// Map the point that is passed to the
```

```
// function from client coordinates
// to screen coordinates.
ClientToScreen(&point);

// Retrieve the currently selected item.
HTREEITEM hCurrSel = GetSelectedItem();

// Determine which item was right-clicked.
CPoint pt(0, 0);
::GetCursorPos(&pt);
ScreenToClient (&pt);
HTREEITEM hNewSel = HitTest(pt, &nFlags);

// Set the selection to the item that the
// mouse was over when the user right-
// clicked.
if (NULL == hNewSel)
{
 SelectItem(NULL);
}
else if (hCurrSel != hNewSel)
{
 SelectItem(hNewSel);
 SetFocus();
}

// Load the context menu
CMenu Menu;
if (Menu.LoadMenu(IDM_CONTEXT_MENU))
{
 CMenu* pSubMenu = Menu.GetSubMenu(0);

 if (pSubMenu!=NULL)
 {
  // Display the context menu
  pSubMenu->TrackPopupMenu(
   TPM_LEFTALIGN | TPM_RIGHTBUTTON,
   point.x, point.y, AfxGetMainWnd());
 }
 }
}
```

Note that this code listing is very basic and displays the same context menu for all items in the tree view control. However, most applications will have different types of items in their tree view control. Therefore, a single context menu wouldn't be appropriate. In order to implement this, you would simply specify the resource of the menu corresponding to the selected item via the `Menu::LoadMenu` function shown in the code.

Expanding and collapsing tree control branches

Many times you'll fill a tree control with enough information that it will be cumbersome for the user to have to manually expand all the branches in order to see the control's data.

Therefore, it's a good UI design idea to either automatically expand all the branches of a tree when the control is displayed, or to at least have an option that enables the user to do so.

In order to expand (or collapse) an item, you need only call the `CTreeCtrl::Expand` function, passing it the `HTREEITEM` of the item you want to expand (or collapse) and a value indicating whether you're expanding (`TVE_EXPAND`) or collapsing (`TVE_COLLAPSE`) the item. However, there is one limitation here. The Expand function will only work on that item and its children. In other words, it will not continue to its child item's children and so on. Therefore, here is a simple recursive function that enables you to expand or collapse an entire branch downward from the specified `HTREEITEM`. Note that this function assumes a member variable of `m_tree` that is the `CTreeCtrl` object. Obviously, you'll need to modify that part if you're going to implement this in your own `CTreeCtrl`-derived class.

```
void ExpandBranch(HTREEITEM hItem, BOOL bExpand /*= TRUE*/)
{
  if (m_tree.ItemHasChildren(hItem))
  {
    m_tree.Expand(hItem,
      bExpand ? TVE_EXPAND : TVE_COLLAPSE);
    hItem = m_tree.GetChildItem(hItem);
    do
    {
      ExpandBranch(hItem);
    } while ((hItem =
    m_tree.GetNextSiblingItem(hItem)) != NULL);
  }
}
```

As you can see, the function simply determines if the current item has any children, and if so, calls the `CTreeCtrl::Expand` function for that item. The function then uses the `GetChildItem` and `GetNextSiblingItem` functions to retrieve each child of the current item; whereupon the `ExpandBranch` is called recursively for each child.

However, there is one thing to keep in mind when calling this function. You'll recall that a tree control can have any number of root items. Therefore, in order to expand every item of a tree control, you will need to use a loop similar to the one shown here to first get all the root items, and then call `ExpandBranch` for each root item. Here is an additional help function called `ExpandAllBranches` to do that.

```
void ExpandAllBranches(BOOL bExpand /*= TRUE*/)
{
  HTREEITEM hItem = m_tree.GetRootItem();
  do
  {
    ExpandBranch(hItem, bExpand);
  } while ((hItem =
  m_tree.GetNextSiblingItem(hItem)) != NULL);

  m_tree.Select(hItem, TVGN_FIRSTVISIBLE);
}
```

As you can see, the function simply calls `GetRootItem` (which returns the first root item of the tree control), and then `GetNextSiblingItem` to get the other root items. For each item found, the `ExpandBranch` function is called, thereby expanding (or collapsing) the entire tree control. As a bonus, the function also includes a call to `CTreeCtrl::Select` so that when the tree control is expanded, the control is scrolled up to the top of the data and the first item is selected.

Note that like any other recursive function, you can overflow the stack if you have a ridiculously large amount of data in your tree control.

CTreeCtrl demo

In this demo application, I will illustrate the points already covered about the tree view control and the `CTreeCtrl` class so that you can see them working in an actual application.

Creating the demo dialog box

Create a dialog-based application called `TreeCtrlDemo`. Once you have created the project, change the dialog resource so that it looks like the dialog box in Figure 7-9.

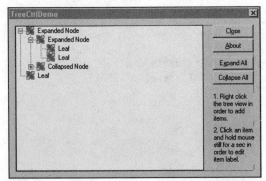

Figure 7-9: The TreeCtrlDemo dialog box after modification

Once you have added the controls, use the Properties dialog box to change the tree view control's styles (in the Appearance category) as follows:

✦ Check the Has buttons style checkbox.

✦ Check the Has lines style checkbox.

✦ Check the Lines at root checkbox.

✦ Check the Edit labels checkbox.

As described in the section "Handling control notification messages at the dialog level," create a new `CTreeCtrl`-derived class called `CMyTreeCtrl`. Once you've done that, create a member variable for the tree view control derived from this `CMyTreeCtrl` class and call it `m_tree`.

Initializing the tree view

You need some dummy data in the tree view to have something to work with when the application starts. Modify the dialog box's `OnInitDialog` function by inserting the following lines of code just before the function's `return` statement. Here I'm simply displaying the MFC `CFile` class hierarchy. (Don't worry about the call to `ExpandAllBranches`. You'll add that function shortly.)

```
BOOL CTreeCtrlDemoDlg::OnInitDialog()
{
  CDialog::OnInitDialog();
  ...

HTREEITEM h1 = m_tree.InsertItem("CFile");
 HTREEITEM h2 = m_tree.InsertItem("CMemFile", h1);
 m_tree.InsertItem("CSharedFile", h2);

 HTREEITEM h3 = m_tree.InsertItem("COleStreamFile",h1);
 HTREEITEM h4 = m_tree.InsertItem("CMonikerFile",h3);
 HTREEITEM h5 = m_tree.InsertItem("CAsyncMonikerFile", h4);
 HTREEITEM h6 = m_tree.InsertItem("CDataPathProperty", h5);
 m_tree.InsertItem("CCachedDataPathProperty", h6);

 m_tree.InsertItem("CSocketFile", h1);

 HTREEITEM h7 = m_tree.InsertItem("CStdioFile", h1);
 HTREEITEM h8 = m_tree.InsertItem("CInternetFile", h7);
 m_tree.InsertItem("CGopherFile", h8);
 m_tree.InsertItem("CHttpFile", h8);

 ExpandAllBranches();

 return TRUE;
}
```

Creating a dialog box to add new items

Because this demo enables the user to add new items to the tree view control, you will need another dialog box. Create a simple dialog box (`IDD_ADD_ITEM`) with a single edit control for the item's text, as shown in Figure 7-10. Once you have added the edit control, create a class for the dialog box, and call that class `CAddItemDlg`.

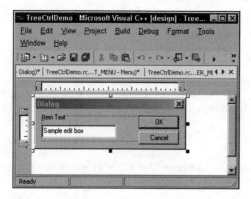

Figure 7-10: Simple dialog box to enable the user to add new items to the tree view control

After the files have been created for this dialog box, create a `CString` member variable for the edit control called `m_strItem`, and add an `OnOK` handler for the dialog box that looks like the following. This handler ensures that the user enters a valid string when attempting to add strings to the tree view control. The context menu (we'll do that next) is responsible for displaying this dialog box.

```
void CAddItemDlg::OnOK()
{
 UpdateData(TRUE);
 if (1 > m_strItem.GetLength())
 {
  AfxMessageBox(_T("Sorry, but you need to "
    "specify a valid string before continuing."));
 }
 else
 {
  CDialog::OnOK();
 }
}
```

Adding the context menu

Now that you have a `CTreeCtrl`-derived class, add a menu resource, a `WM_RBUTTONDOWN` handler to display the context menu, and a handler for the different menu options. In this demo, you'll only have a single menu option because that will suffice in showing you how to add and respond to context menus.

First, create a menu resource called `IDM_CONTEXT_MENU`, and add an item `&Add Item` to the menu, as shown in Figure 7-11.

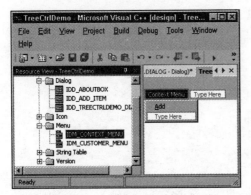

Figure 7-11: Adding context menus to tree controls

Once you have added the menu resource, add a message handler to the `CMyTreeCtrl` class for the `WM_RBUTTONDOWN` message. Modify it as follows:

```
void CMyTreeCtrl::OnRButtonDown(UINT nFlags,
 CPoint point)
{
 // set focus to the tree control
 SetFocus();
```

```
   // map the point that is passed to the
   // function from client coordinates
   // to screen coordinates
   ClientToScreen(&point);

   // Get the currently selected item
   HTREEITEM hCurrSel = GetSelectedItem();

   // Figure out which item was right-clicked
   CPoint pt(0, 0);
   ::GetCursorPos(&pt);
   ScreenToClient (&pt);
   HTREEITEM hNewSel = HitTest(pt, &nFlags);

   // Set the selection to the item that the
   // mouse was over when the user right-
   // clicked
   if (NULL == hNewSel)
   {
    SelectItem(NULL);
   }
   else if (hCurrSel != hNewSel)
   {
    SelectItem(hNewSel);
    SetFocus();
   }

   // Load the context menu
   CMenu Menu;
   if (Menu.LoadMenu(IDM_CONTEXT_MENU))
   {
    CMenu* pSubMenu = Menu.GetSubMenu(0);

    if (pSubMenu!=NULL)
    {
     // Display the context menu
     pSubMenu->TrackPopupMenu(
      TPM_LEFTALIGN | TPM_RIGHTBUTTON,
      point.x, point.y, AfxGetMainWnd());
    }
   }
  }
```

At this point, build and run the application. Clicking the right mouse button while pointing anywhere on the tree view control results in the `IDM_CONTEXT_MENU` being displayed. Now you need to add code to the `CMyTreeCtrl` class so that something happens when an option is selected from that menu. To do this, use the Event Handler Wizard to add a handler to the `CTreeCtrl` class for the `IDD_CONTEXTMENU_ADD` message ID, and modify it as follows:

```
  void CMyTreeCtrl::OnContextmenuAdd()
  {
   HTREEITEM hitemParent = GetSelectedItem();

   // Instantiate and display the Add dialog box
```

```
CAddItemDlg dlg;
if (IDOK == dlg.DoModal())
{
 // Add the new item to the treeview.
 HTREEITEM hitem = InsertItem(dlg.m_strItem,
                              hitemParent);

 // Select the new item. This also causes the
 // item's parent to expand.
 SelectItem(hitem);
 }
}
```

Notice that the selected item's HTREEITEM handle is used as the parent of the newly created item. That is done so that the newly created item is always created as the child of the item that was clicked by the user. If no item is selected, then the item is added as a root item. In addition, the call to the SelectItem function ensures that the newly created item's parent will be expanded and that the new item will be visible.

Avoiding duplicate siblings

Now that the user can add items, the demo application needs to ensure that the user doesn't accidentally add duplicate sibling items. The tree view control doesn't care if it contains duplicate items because it identifies items by their HTREEITEM value; however, having duplicate items in the tree view would be confusing to the user. Therefore, modify the OnContextmenuAdd function you added earlier as follows (where the changes are in bold):

```
void CMyTreeCtrl::OnContextmenuAdd()
{
 HTREEITEM hitemParent = GetSelectedItem();

 // Instantiate and display the Add dialog box
 CAddItemDlg dlg;
 if (IDOK == dlg.DoModal())
 {
  // Only add the item if it is not a duplicate.
  if (!DoesItemExist(hitemParent, dlg.m_strItem))
  {
   // Add the new item to the treeview.
   HTREEITEM hitem = InsertItem(dlg.m_strItem,
                                hitemParent);

   // Select the new item. This also causes the
   // item's parent to expand.
   SelectItem(hitem);
  }
 }
}
```

Next, add the DoesItemExist function. The DoesItemExist function simply uses the GetChildItem and GetNextSiblingItem CTreeCtrl member functions to iterate through the new item siblings to verify if a duplicate entry exists. Notice that the GetItemText function is used to retrieve the text of an item identified by its HTREEITEM handle.

```
BOOL CMyTreeCtrl::DoesItemExist(HTREEITEM hitemParent,
CString const& strItem)
{
BOOL bDoesItemExist = FALSE;

ASSERT(strItem.GetLength());

HTREEITEM hChild =
GetChildItem(hitemParent ? hitemParent : TVI_ROOT);

while (NULL != hChild && !bDoesItemExist)
{
 CString strText = GetItemText(hChild);
 if (0 == strText.CompareNoCase(strItem))
 {
  bDoesItemExist = TRUE;
 }
 else
 {
  hChild = GetNextSiblingItem( hChild );
 }
}

return bDoesItemExist;
}
```

Editing item labels

Now that the user can add items and duplicate items are not allowed, let's add the code necessary to enable editing of an item's text once it has been added to the tree view control. As you saw earlier in the chapter, this is simple once you know which notification messages to handle. At this point, add a message handler for the TVN_ENDLABELEDIT notification message to validate that the new item text is not a duplicate. When you are finished, the handler should look like the following:

```
void CMyTreeCtrl::OnEndlabeledit(NMHDR* pNMHDR,
LRESULT* pResult)
{
TV_DISPINFO* pTVDispInfo = (TV_DISPINFO*)pNMHDR;

BOOL bValidItem = FALSE;

CString strItem = pTVDispInfo->item.pszText;
if (0 < strItem.GetLength())
{
 HTREEITEM hParent =
  GetParentItem(pTVDispInfo->item.hItem);

 CString strItem = pTVDispInfo->item.pszText;

 bValidItem = !DoesItemExist(hParent, strItem);
```

```
  }

  *pResult = bValidItem;
}
```

Add the expanding and collapsing options

Add the following functions to expand and collapse the tree control items. These functions are explained in the section entitled "Expanding and collapsing tree control branches."

```
void CTreeCtrlDemoDlg::ExpandBranch(HTREEITEM hItem,
  BOOL bExpand /*= TRUE*/)
{
  if (m_tree.ItemHasChildren(hItem))
  {
    m_tree.Expand(hItem,
      bExpand ? TVE_EXPAND : TVE_COLLAPSE);
    hItem = m_tree.GetChildItem(hItem);
    do
    {
      ExpandBranch(hItem);
    } while ((hItem =
    m_tree.GetNextSiblingItem(hItem)) != NULL);
  }
}

void CTreeCtrlDemoDlg::ExpandAllBranches(BOOL bExpand
  /*= TRUE*/)
{
  HTREEITEM hItem = m_tree.GetRootItem();
  do
  {
    ExpandBranch(hItem, bExpand);
  } while ((hItem =
  m_tree.GetNextSiblingItem(hItem)) != NULL);

  m_tree.Select(hItem, TVGN_FIRSTVISIBLE);
}
```

Now add the following handlers for the Expand All and Collapse All buttons.

```
void CTreeCtrlDemoDlg::OnBnClickedExpandAll()
{
  ExpandAllBranches();
}

void CTreeCtrlDemoDlg::OnBnClickedCollapseAll()
{
  ExpandAllBranches(FALSE);
}
```

Testing the application

Building and testing the demo at this point should produce a simple tree view that enables the display of context menus, editing of item labels, and insertion of items (with validation that duplicate items are not added). The finished demo is shown in Figure 7-12.

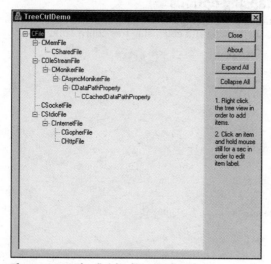

Figure 7-12: The finished TreeCtrlDemo

The List View Control

CListCtrl encapsulates the functionality of the list view control. Like the CTreeCtrl class, CListCtrl serves as a thin wrapper for its underlying Windows common control. Therefore, before getting into the CListCtrl member functions and how to use them, a full understanding of the underlying list view control is required.

The list view control is like the list box control in that it is used to display groups of items. However, that is where the similarity ends in terms of functionality. Whereas the standard list box has no means of displaying a column header row, the list view control does. In fact, the column header row seen in the list view control is itself another Windows common control called the *header control*. An application typically uses this handy control to enable users to sort the list view control's data by clicking the column that the user wants the data sorted by. Because of the header control, list view controls are perfect for displaying multiple columns of data. In addition, the list view control enables its items to be viewed in several different ways: Large Icon view, Small Icon view, List view, and Details or Report view (see Figure 7-13). In the Details view, detailed information about each item is displayed. In the other three views, the details of the items cannot be seen.

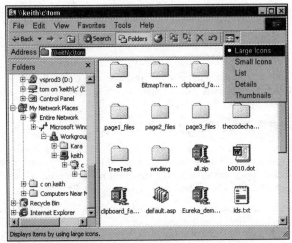

Figure 7-13: Windows Explorer uses the list view to show several different views of the files on your system.

The CListCtrl class

Although CListCtrl is a thin wrapper for the list view control, it considerably lessens the amount of programming required to create and manage the list view control. Like many MFC classes, the CListCtrl class accomplishes this by hiding the idiosyncrasies of how the list view control must be managed if it were being programmed in an SDK application by exposing much simpler member functions. For example, to simply insert an item into a list view control, the application must first create and fill out an LV_ITEM structure and then send an LVM_INSERTITEM message to the list view control. To give you an idea of the difference, here's what inserting an item into a list view control via SDK calls looks like:

```
LV_ITEM item;
item.mask = nMask;
item.iItem = nItem;
item.iSubItem = 0;
item.pszText = (LPTSTR)lpszItem;
item.state = nState;
item.stateMask = nStateMask;
item.iImage = nImage;
item.lParam = lParam;

int iIndex = ::SendMessage(m_hWnd,
                    LVM_INSERTITEM,
                    0,
                    (LPARAM)pItem);
```

This is how to insert an item into a list view control using the `CListCtrl` class. The following line of code inserts an item with the text value of "Test" into the first row of the list view control:

```
listCtrl.InsertItem(0, _T("Test"));
```

As a result, while `CListCtrl` doesn't add much in terms of functionality to the list view control, it definitely makes programming the list view control much easier.

Creating and attaching a CImageList object

If you want your list view control items to have images, you must create and associate an image list control with the list view control. Using the image list control gives you greater control and flexibility over the images associated with the different items in your list view. Follow these steps to create a `CImageList` object and associate it with a `CListCtrl`:

1. Create two bitmap resources. These bitmaps are handled much as the toolbar bitmap resources where the bitmap actually contains one to many images that are referred to in code by their index values. Of these two bitmap resources, one of these bitmaps is used for the Large Icon view, and the other is used for the Small Icon view.

2. Declare two `CImageList` member variables in the dialog box's class. Once again, one image list is for the Large Icon view, and the other is for the Small Icon view.

3. After the list view control has been initialized (usually in the `OnInitDialog` function), call the `CImageList::Create` member function of each `CImageList` object in order create the image list controls. When calling the `Create` member function, you simply specify the bitmap resource and the size of each image in the bitmap resource.

4. Call the `CListCtrl::SetImageList` member function in order to associate the image list objects with the list view control. The first argument of the `SetImageList` function enables you to specify the image list, while the second argument is used to specify which image list is being set (`LVSIL_SMALL` or `LVSIL_NORMAL`).

The following code snippet assumes that you created two bitmap resources named `IDB_LARGE_IMAGES` and `IDB_SMALL_IMAGES`. It also assumes that each image is 17 dialog units wide. Obviously, in a "real" application, the images for the `IDB_LARGE_IMAGES` bitmap resource would be larger than the images in the `IDB_SMALL_IMAGE` bitmap resource so that there's a difference between the "small icon" view and "large icon" view. With those assumptions and information in mind, here is an example of how to create and associate the image list objects with a list view control:

```
// large icon image list
m_imageListLargeIcons.Create(IDB_LARGE_IMAGES,
  17, 1, RGB(255,255,255));
m_listCtrl.SetImageList(&m_imageListLargeIcons,
  LVSIL_NORMAL);

// small icon image list
m_imageListSmallIcons.Create(IDB_SMALL_IMAGES,
  17, 1, RGB(255,255,255));
m_listCtrl.SetImageList(&m_imageListSmallIcons,
  LVSIL_SMALL);
```

Figure 7-14 shows the images used with the list view control of the `ListCtrlDemo` application provided on this book's Web site.

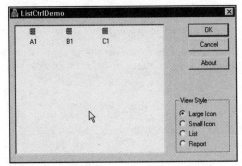

Figure 7-14: The finished image list control

Setting and changing the view style

There are three different ways to set the View style depending on the application's needs. If the list view control is always going to have the same View style, you can set the View style in the resource editor via the list view control's property dialog box.

However, if you need to change the list view control's View style at runtime, then you can use the `CWnd::ModifyStyle` as follows (where `uiDesiredStyle` is LVS_ICON, LVS_SMALLICON, LVS_LIST, or LVS_REPORT). (Note that the LVS_REPORT style is sometimes referred to as the "details view.")

```
ModifyStyle(LVS_TYPEMASK, uiDesiredStyle);
```

A third method is to override the view's `PreCreateWindow` virtual function. This function is called by the framework as the view is being initialized and is passed a CREATESTRUCT structure. One of the members of this CREATESTRUCT is called style. Manipulating this value accomplishes the same thing as calling the `ModifyStyle` function. In the following code snippet, I'm using the bitwise or operator (|) to set the list view's display style to the report view.

```
BOOL CListViewTestView::PreCreateWindow(CREATESTRUCT& cs)
{
  cs.style |= LVS_REPORT;
  return CListView::PreCreateWindow(cs);
}
```

As you can see in Figure 7-14, the demo application includes this functionality by simply giving the user a set of radio buttons that each correspond to a different view type. The event handler for each radio button calls a member function of my `CMyListCtrl` class that then calls the `ModifyStyle` function, passing it the appropriate style value.

Adding columns to a CListCtrl

Before you can add rows to the list view control, you must define the columns that the list view will display. This is accomplished via the `InsertColumn` member function. There are two overloaded versions of the `InsertColumn` function.

```
int InsertColumn(int nCol,
                 LPCTSTR lpszColumnHeading,
                 int nFormat = LVCFMT_LEFT,
                 int nWidth = -1,
                 int nSubItem = -1);
int InsertColumn(int nCol, const LV_COLUMN* pColumn);
```

To illustrate the differences between the two overloaded versions of the `InsertColumn` function, have a look at what it takes to insert the following columns into a list view control:

```
static struct
{
 LPTSTR szColText;
 UINT uiFormat;
} columns[] = {
 _T("Col 1"), LVCFMT_LEFT,
 _T("Col 2"), LVCFMT_CENTER,
 _T("Col 3"), LVCFMT_RIGHT
};
```

The first `InsertColumn` function takes as its arguments the column number (relative to zero) and a pointer to a filled out `LV_COLUMN` structure. Here is an example of inserting three different columns using that function.

```
for (int i = 0;
 i < sizeof columns / sizeof columns [0];
 i++)
{
 LV_COLUMN lvc;
 ::ZeroMemory(&lvc, sizeof lvc);
 lvc.pszText = (LPTSTR)columns[i].szColText;

 lvc.mask = LVCF_TEXT | LVCF_FMT;
 lvc.fmt = columns[i].uiFormat;

 CClientDC dc(this);
 CSize size = dc.GetTextExtent(lvc.pszText);
 lvc.cx = size.cx;

 m_listCtrl.InsertColumn(i, &lvc);
}
```

Notice that each column's text is justified differently. Also, notice how much work is needed to simply insert a column into a list view control. That is because this version of the `InsertColumn` function is almost like using the Win32 SDK to insert a column into the list view control. In fact, this version of the `InsertColumn` function does nothing except send the address of the passed structure to the list view via a message.

The second `InsertColumn` function is definitely much better because it does more for you. With this version, most of the `LV_ITEM` structure members default to a reasonable value. Here is how this `InsertColumn` would look with the same set of three columns:

```
for (int i = 0;
 i < sizeof columns / sizeof columns [0];
 i++)
```

```
{
  m_listCtrl.InsertColumn(i,
    columns[i].szColText, columns[i].uiFormat);
}
```

Obviously, the only reason that you would want to use the first version of InsertColumn is if the application needs to specify one of the LV_ITEM members that is not in the argument list of the second InsertColumn function (for example, mask).

Sizing list view columns

Whenever you add a new column to a list view, you should also resize the new column so that its header text can be seen. You would think this would happen automatically, but it doesn't. I can only assume that the designers of MFC decided to leave this task to the programmer so that you can decide when and if to resize the columns.

To resize a column, you can use the CListCtrl::SetColumnWidth function, where you specify the column to be resized and the size of the column.

```
BOOL CListCtrl::SetColumnWidth(
    int nCol,
    int cx
);
```

Because most times you really only care that the column is wide enough for your data to be visible, MFC provides two constants that can be passed for the cx value. These values are LVSCW_AUTOSIZE and LVSCW_AUTOSIZE_USEHEADER.

The LVSCW_AUTOSIZE_USEHEADER value is used to tell the list view that you want the column sized large enough to display the column heading text. In the following code snippet, I am inserting three columns into a list control and then using a for loop to size each column according to the header text:

```
CListCtrl& list = GetListCtrl();
list.InsertColumn(0, "COLUMN 1");
list.InsertColumn(1, "ANOTHER COLUMN");
list.InsertColumn(2, "A REALLY WIDE COLUMN");

for (int i = 0; i < 3; i++)
{
  list.SetColumnWidth(i,
  LVSCW_AUTOSIZE_USEHEADER);
}
```

However, what if you want a generic function to resize your columns according to header size? Obviously, in that case you couldn't hard-code the number of columns. Instead, you would obtain the header control (via the CListCtrl::GetHeaderCtrl function) and call the CHeaderCtrl::GetItemCount (which returns the number of defined columns). The code to resize all of a list view's columns based on the header text values would then look like the following:

```
CHeaderCtrl* pHeader = list.GetHeaderCtrl();
ASSERT(pHeader);
if (pHeader)
```

```
  {
    for (int i = 0; i < pHeader->GetItemCount(); i++)
    {
      list.SetColumnWidth(i, LVSCW_AUTOSIZE_USEHEADER);
    }
  }
}
```

The LVSCW_AUTOSIZE value indicates that you want the column to be sized according to the widest text value (in terms of pixels needed to display it) in that column. As an example, let's say that you have a list view with a single column and two rows of data. If the first row has a value of "aa," the second column has a value of "WWW," and you call SetColumnWidth(0, LVSCW_AUTOSIZE), then the column will be sized large enough to display the "WWW" string.

Because you now know how to size according to largest text value and header text value, you can write a generic function that can be called to resize all the columns of any list view according to whichever is largest. That way, the function guarantees you that all of the list view's data is always visible. That function follows.

Note that once you've obtained the CListCtrl and the CHeaderCtrl objects, you call the SetRedraw function to stop the drawing of the list view control while you're sizing it. Otherwise, it would result in ugly flickering. After that, you see a for loop that simply iterates through each defined column of the header control object.

For each column, you first set the column width based on the widest value of that column. You then call the CListCtrl::GetColumnWidth to determine and save that width. Next, you set the list view's column width based on the header's text value. Once again, you call the CListCtrl::GetColumnWidth function to retrieve the current column width. Finally, you use the max macro to set the column's width according to whichever value is larger.

```
void CListViewTestView::SizeAllColumns()
{
  CListCtrl& list = GetListCtrl();

  CHeaderCtrl* pHeader = list.GetHeaderCtrl();
  ASSERT(pHeader);
  if (pHeader)
  {
    // Turn off redraw until the columns have all
    // been resized
    list.SetRedraw(FALSE);

    for (int iCurrCol = 0;
        iCurrCol < pHeader->GetItemCount();
        iCurrCol++)
    {
      list.SetColumnWidth(iCurrCol, LVSCW_AUTOSIZE);

      int nCurrWidth = list.GetColumnWidth(iCurrCol);

      list.SetColumnWidth(iCurrCol,
                          LVSCW_AUTOSIZE_USEHEADER);

      int nColHdrWidth = list.GetColumnWidth(iCurrCol);
```

```
        list.SetColumnWidth(iCurrCol,
                            max(nCurrWidth, nColHdrWidth));
    }

    // Now that sizing is finished, turn redraw back on and
    // invalidate so that the control is repainted
    list.SetRedraw(TRUE);
    list.Invalidate();
  }
}
```

Inserting list view items

As you've already seen, the InsertItem member function is used to insert items into a list view control. However, depending on the needs of your application, there are several over-loaded versions of the InsertItem member function:

```
int InsertItem(const LVITEM* pItem);
int InsertItem(int nItem, LPCTSTR lpszItem);
int InsertItem(int nItem, LPCTSTR lpszItem,
  int nImage);
```

The one thing that all of the functions have in common is that they return an int that repre-sents the new item's index (relative to zero) in the list view control. Once an item is inserted into a list view control, it is always referred to by this index.

Although the InsertItem inserts an item into the list view control, it only enables you to specify the first column's text. To specify the text for the other columns, you must use the SetItemText member function.

```
BOOL SetItemText(int nItem, int nSubItem,  LPCTSTR lpszText);
```

The first argument (nItem) in the SetItemText member function represents the index of a list view control's item (returned from the InsertItem function). The second and third argu-ments are used to specify the column number (relative to zero) and the text value to insert into that column. Following is an example (using the three columns defined previously) of how to insert a couple of rows into a list view control:

```
// Inserting Data into a List View Static Struct
{
LPTSTR szCol1;
LPTSTR szCol2;
LPTSTR szCol3;
} rows [] = {
 "A1", "A2", "A3",
 "B1", "B2", "B3",
 "C1", "C2", "C3"
};

for (int iCurrRow = 0;
 iCurrRow < sizeof rows / sizeof rows[0];
 iCurrRow++)
{
```

```
    m_listCtrl.InsertItem(iCurrRow,
     rows[iCurrRow].szCol1, 0);

    m_listCtrl.SetItemText(iCurrRow, 1,
     rows[iCurrRow].szCol2);

    m_listCtrl.SetItemText(iCurrRow, 2,
     rows[iCurrRow].szCol3);
    }
```

Summary

Ever since their inception, the tree view and list view controls have had a reputation as being complex and difficult to program. It is true that the developer has to do more to make these controls work, especially when compared to working with other controls such as the edit control or combo box. However, while these controls might be a bit more difficult to work with, the trade-off in work required on the programmer's part to manage these controls is definitely made worthwhile in terms of the added user interface benefits these controls provide to your application.

✦   ✦   ✦

Programming the GDI

Windows is a graphical-based operating system, and any applications you create for Windows must take advantage of its graphical interface. A graphical interface is easier for users to learn and to use than a text-based interface. The Windows Graphics Device Interface (GDI) relieves programmers from having to know the details involved in drawing a window, displaying a dialog box, or creating a button. Programming in a graphical environment brings about another set of concerns, especially if your application displays visual data such as charts, graphs, and diagrams.

This chapter is about graphical programming under the 32-bit Windows operating systems. As you go through this chapter, you'll learn the basic graphical architecture, called the GDI, and see how each part works to provide the programmer with some tremendous flexibility and power. Once you've learned about things such as device contexts and text manipulation, you'll discover how to use GDI objects such as fonts, pens, and brushes. Finally, the chapter explores the advanced topics of mapping modes, raster operations, and the use of clipping regions.

Introducing the Graphics Device Interface

The GDI forms part of the core of the Windows operating system. The GDI manages all graphics output from a Windows program. This means that no matter if a window is displayed on the screen or a screen saver displays some dazzling graphics or if an application prints a document, the GDI is involved in making it happen.

Although creating dialog boxes and menus is generally something we take for granted, Windows itself uses the functionality of the GDI to draw interface elements. The GDI is even used to display the mouse cursor as it is dragged across the screen.

What's so great about the GDI is its internal architecture. Microsoft created the GDI to decouple rendering graphics from the underlying hardware, thereby providing a layer of abstraction for graphical applications (such as the Windows desktop itself). Because of this, the GDI provides high-level drawing functions that produce generally the same results regardless of the underlying hardware. Decoupling the graphics functions from the hardware enables you to produce interesting graphics with very little effort or concern for the supporting hardware.

Types of graphics

There are three main groupings of GDI functions: text, raster, and vector graphics. At first glance, these categories might seem arbitrary. However, each exists for good reason and provides a much-needed capability. At the device driver level, each type has its own set of entry points and ways of operating. At the higher-level programming interface, an application controls the appearance of each type by using slightly different sets of drawing attributes. Understanding each of these types is the first step on the road to mastering the GDI. The following sections describe each of the different types of graphics in a bit more detail; that knowledge will help later as you explore the more advanced functions provided by the GDI.

Text

An irony of Windows programming is that even though the GDI simplifies graphical rendering, it adds complexity to creating textual output. However, with that added complexity comes added flexibility. One important thing to realize here is that although the text you see on a Word document or in any other application might look like the text you would output from a console application, this text really is graphics. As a result, you can control more aspects of text rendering than you could ever dream of back in the text-based world. Want to create 18-point, red, Helvetica text? No problem. How about 12-point, shadowed, Arial text? Again, no problem at all. You'd have to resort to some pretty intricate programming to get the same effects in a text-based environment. As you'll soon see, you can do all of this (and much more) in Windows with a few GDI calls.

Vector graphics

Within the GDI, the term *vector graphics* refers to the drawing functions that create lines and filled figures, or shapes. The GDI features an entire set of functions that draw straight lines, curves, pie wedges, and polygons. You can mix and match these function calls with the raster functions in any way.

Normally, people think of geometric shapes when they think about vector graphics. However, Windows uses very few of the GDI vector function calls when it draws the user interface. Most applications don't really make much use of GDI vector graphics, except for drawing programs such as CorelDraw or Visio. There's nothing inherently wrong with these functions. However, business applications tend to be more text oriented, and programs that need complex images depend on bitmaps and the raster functions. Exceptions to this are applications that need to do such things as producing graphical reports.

One type of application that does use vector graphics is games. In fact, the images you see on screen during game play are commonly made up of thousands of polygons that are calculated and rendered at runtime. DirectX provides a means of quickly rendering vector graphics.

Raster graphics

The last type of GDI graphic output is *raster* graphics. Raster-type graphics are the most commonly used type of graphics within the Windows environment. A raster graphics function operates on data stored in arrays called *bitmaps*. A standard VGA monitor's 640 × 480 image is simply a bitmap that the display adapter makes visible on the screen. Part of Windows' support for raster graphics is the capability to create off-screen bitmap images. You can render these images off-screen very quickly and then transfer them to the screen. This technique, sometimes called *double-buffering*, makes your images appear to display quickly because you can generate a new image while the user views the on-screen image.

Other examples of raster graphics include icons and cursors that are added to your application by editing the resource file (.rc). Moving windows around the screen is another example of the use of raster graphics. When a window is moved from one part of the screen to another, a raster graphics function picks up the pixels that make up the window and moves them to the destination location on the screen.

Because the data on the display screen is stored in arrays, bitmaps are useful for caching complex graphical objects for quick on-screen rendering. You can create complex objects ahead of time, either during compile time or during the initialization of your application, and then quickly copy them to the screen when needed. The only problem with bitmaps is the space that they require. One bitmap with 640 × 480 pixels and 8-bit color depth requires approximately 300KB of storage space. Obviously, as the image size or color depth (the number of colors in an image) increases, the storage requirement increases as well.

One last point about raster graphics is that they represent the graphics that ultimately get rendered on the screen. That is, text and vector graphics first need to be converted into raster graphics before being displayed. Therefore, vector graphics (a series of coordinate pairs) and text are simply a more efficient means of expressing raster graphics — the system transforms text and vectors into raster graphics and renders them.

GDI devices

A physical graphics device, such as a printer or display adapter, doesn't need to support all three graphics types to be a GDI device. This is the beauty of the GDI. Based on the installed device drivers, the GDI can adapt itself to the hardware installed to provide reasonable graphics results across a wide variety of hardware. In fact, most devices don't have nearly this level of built-in support.

The only requirement for being a GDI device is the capability of turning on a pixel. That's it. For all operations beyond this simple requirement, the GDI can decompose the drawing requests into a simpler form that the hardware can understand. However, it's up to the device driver to tell the GDI exactly what features it supports. The driver communicates this to GDI by passing a set of capability bits that the GDI uses to tune its own drawing requests.

On basic devices with limited capability, the GDI adapts and performs most of the work itself. The GDI can internally convert all text and vector graphics calls into raster data that the device can understand. As you've already seen, even though raster graphics require more storage space, this is offset by the capability of rendering even highly complex graphics on bargain basement hardware.

If a device informs the GDI that it supports more advanced capabilities, the GDI does less of the work. If a hardware device can directly service a drawing request, the GDI passes this request off to the device. This results in overall higher performance in two ways. First, the GDI has less work to do internally and puts less strain on the CPU. Second, higher-level drawing requests take up less memory and disk space than if the same request was broken down into its lower-level components. Having less information to store means less strain on the overall system, which translates into higher performance as well.

This capability of working on a wide range of devices is one reason why the GDI is described as a device-independent graphics interface. If a device does not support a drawing operation itself, the GDI can step in and simulate the request in software. On the other hand, if the device provides native support for the request, the GDI passes the request off to the device and reaps higher system performance.

Types of GDI devices

The types of devices that GDI supports can be divided into two categories: physical devices and pseudodevices. It's a useful distinction because it helps clarify the device-independent nature of the GDI. This section discusses the differences between these different types of devices.

Physical devices

From a programmatic point of view, there are only two basic physical devices: display screens and printers. When an application draws to the screen, it always draws inside a window. The window manager makes sure that one unruly window doesn't overstep its bounds and draw inside another window.

The GDI polices these boundaries by using a technique known as *clipping*. Clipping is the act of drawing boundaries. The most obvious and common boundaries are the borders of windows that the window manager oversees for you. You can create your own clipping regions as well. You might want to use this capability to fill in areas between drawings created by separate parts of an application without incurring the overhead of creating additional windows.

Spooling is another GDI technique that is used to enforce boundaries between drawings produced on the printer. Print jobs are stored, or spooled, until the printer is ready to service them. Without spooling, the printer would intermingle pages of different print jobs.

When writing output to a printer, you must take into consideration things like the size of the paper, the page orientation, and available fonts. You'll still use the same GDI functions to draw on the printer and the display screen.

Pseudodevices

Pseudodevices provide different ways of storing pictures. The term *pseudodevice* means that the operating system gives the same respect to these devices as it does to physical devices. GDI has two types of pseudodevices: *bitmaps* and *metafiles*. Outside of the RAM or disk space used to store them, bitmaps and metafiles have no associated hardware. That is to say, they are software simulations of logical devices.

Metafiles are lists of drawing calls. *Bitmaps* store the results of drawing calls whereas metafiles capture the drawing calls before any pixels are rendered. Think of a metafile as a recording of your program as it draws an image. Metafiles can also be "played back" to the screen to draw the image it stores.

As you've seen before, a bitmap is an array of data that represents a picture. In the same way you can use GDI functions to draw on the screen or to the printer, you can use GDI functions to draw on a bitmap. Even though a bitmap simulates a raster drawing, you aren't limited to using only the raster graphics calls. You can make any text, raster, or vector call to draw on a bitmap.

In this section you've been introduced to the vocabulary of the GDI. You should now understand how the GDI abstracts graphics operations, and how this simplifies Windows programming. The different types of drawing functions have been described and the two categories of devices were investigated. Before you're ready to draw images in Windows, you need to understand one more concept: the device context. That's the subject of the next section.

The Device Context

A device context—also known as a DC—is a data structure that the GDI creates to represent a device connection. For example, to draw on the display screen, a Windows program must have a DC for the display. To create output on a printer, yet another DC is required, created specifically for the printer. If the same program also wants to create output in a metafile and a bitmap, a third and a fourth DC are required. The role of a DC, then, is to provide a connection between a program and either a physical device or a pseudodevice.

In addition to providing a device connection, a DC holds a collection of drawing attribute settings. For example, one drawing attribute in the DC is the text color. When a text drawing function is called, the function refers to the text color attribute to determine the correct color for the text.

You can change any drawing attribute at any time by calling specific GDI functions. For example, the SetTextColor function sets the text color. For every attribute-setting function, there exists a corresponding function to retrieve that attribute. Therefore, in order to determine the current text color settings, you need simply to call the GetTextColor function.

DC drawing attributes

Table 8-1 summarizes the 25 attributes that the GDI stores in a DC. The table indicates which drawing attributes affect each of the three types of graphic objects. The Comments column provides details about default settings and how to change each attribute. The functions that are mentioned in Table 8-1 are member functions of CDC, the MFC class wrapper for the Windows device contexts.

Table 8-1: Attributes of the GDI DC

Attribute	Text	Raster	Vector	Comments
Arc direction			✓	The default is counterclockwise. This can be set with the function SetArcDirection and constants AD_CLOCKWISE or AD_COUNTERCLOCKWISE.
Background color	✓	✓	✓	The default is white. This is used for the background of normal text, color to monochrome conversions, and for the background of styled pens and hatched brushes.
Background mode	✓	✓	✓	The default is OPAQUE. This turns the background color on (OPAQUE) or off (TRANSPARENT). Set this attribute by calling SetBkColor.

Continued

Table 8-1: *(continued)*

Attribute	Text	Raster	Vector	Comments
Bounds rectangle	✓	✓	✓	The default is disabled. When enabled, it tells GDI to keep track of the drawing area. Set this attribute by calling `SetBoundsRect`.
Brush		✓	✓	The default is white. This defines the interior color of closed figures.
Brush origin			✓	The default is 0,0. This sets the point in device space to align a brush, and is necessary for hatched and dithered brushes, because they can have misalignments.
Clipping region	✓	✓	✓	The default is the entire drawing surface. This defines drawing boundaries.
Color adjustment		✓		The default is no adjustment. This defines the changes to bitmaps stretched by the functions `StretchBlt` and `StretchDIBits`. Set this attribute by calling `SetColorAdjustments`.
Current position	✓		✓	The default is 0,0. An *x,y* pair is originally created to assist in line drawing. Enable for text by calling `SetTextAlign` with the `TA_UPDATECP` flag. Set this attribute by calling `SetCurrentPosition`.
Drawing mode			✓	The default is `R2_COPYPEN`. This determines how Boolean operators are used when vector graphics are drawn. Set this attribute by calling `SetROP2`.
Font	✓			The default is system font. This determines which set of graphic figures is used for drawing text.
Graphics mode	✓	✓	✓	The default is `GM_COMPATIBLE`. This determines whether GDI ignores world transform and other Win32 enhancements. Set this attribute by calling `SetGraphicsMode`.
Mapping mode	✓	✓	✓	The default is `MM_TEXT`. This controls much of the coordinate mapping. In the default mode, one logical unit equals one device unit. Set this attribute by calling `SetMapMode`.

Attribute	Text	Raster	Vector	Comments
Miter limit			✓	The default is 10.0. This controls the "pointiness" in a join of a geometric line before capping off the corner.
Palette	✓	✓	✓	The default is system palette. Supported only by certain devices, it gives applications control over how the physical color table, called the palette, is set.
Pen			✓	The default is black pen. This is used by vector graphics functions to draw the borders of geometric figures.
Polygon filling mode			✓	The default is Alternate. This determines how the interior spaces of complex, overlapping polygons are to be filled.
StretchBlt mode		✓		The default is BLACKONWHITE. This determines how pixels are removed when a bitmap is shrunk using StretchBlt. Set this attribute by calling SetStretchBltMode.
Text alignment	✓			The default is TA_LEFT | TA_TOP. This determines the alignment between text drawing coordinates and the resulting textbox. Set this attribute by calling SetTextAlign.
Text color	✓			The default is black. Set this attribute by calling SetTextColor.
Text extra spacing	✓			The default is 0. This determines how many pixels are to be padded into each character cell in a string. Set this attribute by calling SetTextCharacterExtra.
Text justification	✓			The default is 0,0. This determines how many pixels to pad into break characters, spaces, to pad a line of text to fill out a margin. Set this attribute by calling SetTextJustification.
Viewport extent	✓	✓	✓	The default is 1,1. This attribute is used with a mapping mode of MM_ISOTROPIC or MM_ANISOTROPIC. It helps scale a drawing by modifying the device coordinate side of the scaling ratio. Set this attribute by calling SetViewportExt.
Viewport origin	✓	✓	✓	The default is 0,0. This moves the origin around the device space. Set this attribute by calling SetViewportOrg.

Continued

Table 8-1: *(continued)*

Attribute	Text	Raster	Vector	Comments
Window extent	✓	✓	✓	The default is 1,1. This is used with a mapping mode of MM_ISOTROPIC and MM_ANISOTROPIC. It scales a drawing by modifying the world side of the scaling ratio. Set this attribute by calling SetWorldExt.
Window origin	✓	✓	✓	The default is 0,0. This moves the origin around the world coordinate space. Set this attribute by calling SetWindowOrg.

When you create a single or multiple-document application with Visual Studio, you'll find a function in the view class named OnDraw. This function is automatically created by the AppWizard. It receives a message every time your view window gets a WM_PAINT message (more about this message in the next section). A CDC class pointer is passed to the OnDraw function. The CDC pointer can be used to draw to the view window. The following code snippet shows a simple OnDraw function that draws a rectangle to the view window:

```
// An OnDraw function drawing a rectangle
void CMyView::OnDraw(CDC* pDC)
{
  CMyDoc* pDoc = GetDocument();
  ASSERT_VALID(pDoc);

  // Here is where the code you add
  // to draw a rectangle begins.
  RECT Rect;
  Rect.left = Rect.top = 10;
  Rect.right = Rect.bottom = 100;

  // Create a red brush.
  // The RGB macro lets you specify
  // the R, G, and B color components
  // respectively. Their values range
  // from 0 to 255.
  CBrush Brush( RGB( 255, 0, 0 ) );

  // Draw to the window using the GDI
  // FillRect() function.
  pDC->FillRect( &Rect, &Brush );

}
```

The default DC settings provide a good starting place for drawing. The best way to learn about GDI drawing is by writing small programs that draw a few simple objects. As you begin to experiment with new drawing functions, you won't have to make many changes to DC attributes to get reasonable results. Once you have a clearer understanding of how various drawing functions work, you can begin to explore the role of individual drawing attributes.

The WM_PAINT message

For drawing in a window, the most important message is WM_PAINT. In simplest terms, this message asks a window to redraw its contents. You might get this message for many reasons. For example, another window might open on top of your window and overwrite its contents. Or a user might decide to unminimize a previously minimized window. Or you might get this message simply because your program is just starting up.

Whatever the reason for a window getting a WM_PAINT message, the system can't recreate the contents of a window's client area. The original Windows development team considered various ways that the system might be capable of storing window data. One possibility was to take a snapshot of a window before it was covered by other windows. However, the sheer amount of memory required for this approach made it an unworkable solution.

In the character-based world, a screen full of data can be stored in a tiny, 2KB buffer. However, as I mentioned before, the buffer size needed to hold a 256-color, 640 × 480 screen image would be around 300KB. That's 300,000 bytes compared to 2,000 bytes! With several applications running, a megabyte or more would be quickly eaten up. This was too high a price to pay for the first version of Windows, when system memory totaled only 1MB.

Even if memory wasn't a problem, another problem remains. If the system stores window snapshots and any part of a window's data changes, the cache would be worthless. In such a situation, the application would have to redraw the contents of the window anyway. As a result, all of the memory and all of the processor time spent saving the snapshot would be wasted, so the snapshot solution is an inefficient technique at best.

The WM_PAINT message is the solution to the problem of keeping the state of a window up to date. Windows makes every application entirely responsible for maintaining the contents of its windows. The WM_PAINT message provides the mechanism by which the system tells you that it's time to refresh a window. All you have to do is make sure that your program retains whatever state information it needs for accomplishing this task.

Drawing coordinates

When a DC is first created, its default coordinates are pixel, or device, units. You can modify the entire coordinate system to use inches, centimeters, or printer point units. You can also arbitrarily scale your drawings using rubber sheet graphics, but the default units, which are used in this chapter, are device units. In DC attribute terms, this is known as the MM_TEXT mapping mode.

The default origin — that is, coordinate (0,0) — is located in the upper-left corner of the drawing surface. On the display screen, this means the upper-left corner of the window's client area. On the printed page, it means the upper-left corner of whatever would be the top of the page. Just as you can change the coordinate system, you can also change the location of the origin. For the examples in this chapter, though, the default origin is used.

The default direction of movement along the *x*- and *y*-axes is a little different from the *Cartesian coordinate system* you may have studied in school. In a window, the default coordinate system is called *client-area coordinates*. Because the same coordinates are used for mouse input, client-area coordinates make it easy to match mouse clicks to objects you've drawn in your window.

Triggering WM_PAINT

When I introduced the WM_PAINT message, I described it as the most important drawing message. You'll also recall that I mentioned that a window might receive this message for many different reasons. For example, it might be that another window was placed on top of it and now has been removed. Or it might be that a window has been restored after being minimized. Or it could be that the window has been sized. The cause is really unimportant. In all cases, you need to redraw whatever part of the window you're told to redraw.

In some cases, however, the cause of a paint message isn't an external factor such as the user changing a window size. Instead, it's an internal factor that only you can recognize. For example, the user might have entered some additional text in a text input window. Or the user might have added or removed a column of data from a spreadsheet window. Whatever the internal cause, when the data represented in the window changes, you need to generate a paint message.

To generate a paint message, you declare that the contents of the window are invalid. You can do this by calling a few different CWnd member functions. Of these, Invalidate is the simplest because it takes only a single parameter, a Boolean value that specifies whether to erase the background before drawing. This function declares the entire client area to be invalid:

```
// Force redraw of entire window-first erase contents.
Invalidate(TRUE);
```

Another function that generates paint messages is InvalidateRect. This function enables you to identify the specific rectangle to be redrawn. On slower hardware, this helps minimize screen flicker. On any hardware, you'll want to be conservative when you request a redraw, because too much screen flicker can annoy users. From an ergonomic point of view, such flicker causes fatigue—which not only annoys users, but also forces them to take more frequent breaks than might otherwise be necessary when using your software. Here's how to request a paint message for a rectangle that's bounded by the coordinates (10, 10) and (100, 100):

```
// Define invalid rectangle and request paint message.
CRect rect(10, 10, 100, 100);
InvalidateRect(&rect, TRUE);
```

Compared to other messages—for example, those that are associated with mouse or keyboard input—paint messages have a very low priority. After all, if more data comes in, additional paint messages might be necessary. When you declare a window to be invalid, the window might receive other messages before getting the WM_PAINT message.

In some cases, you need to raise the priority of a WM_PAINT message. To force an immediate paint message, you call UpdateWindow. For example, you might need to do this if you've already called Invalidate to request a redraw, but you also want to immediately draw on the updated window. It's not uncommon to declare part of a window invalid and then immediately force a paint message using code like the following:

```
InvalidateRect( &Rect, TRUE );
UpdateWindow();
```

To summarize, when you want the image in a window to be changed, you invalidate the area in which the change will be seen. This area will be drawn during a subsequent WM_PAINT message. The UpdateWindow call does not declare part of a window to be invalid. It simply accelerates repainting for invalidated areas. If no area is invalid, calls to UpdateWindow have no effect on the contents of a window. Windows' conservative paint policy limits the drawing — via clip rectangles — to only the part of a window that is invalid.

As mentioned previously, calling UpdateWindow forces an immediate repaint so that you can draw over a valid window. However, this makes sense only if you're drawing in response to some other message besides WM_PAINT. The next section discusses how you'd do this and explores some of the issues you must address.

Drawing outside WM_PAINT

In some cases, you need to draw in response to messages other than WM_PAINT. One school of thought suggests that you draw only when you get a paint message. This centralizes your drawing code, which helps to make it more robust. This is a worthwhile goal.

However, to enhance a program's performance or its interactivity for the user, you might need to draw in response to other messages. For example, consider a text-editing window. If such a program generated a paint message for every character typed, it would run very slowly (which would be particularly noticeable on slower systems). The overhead associated with continually creating paint messages would use too much processing time.

Or consider a drawing program that enables a user to pick up a graphic object and move it around a window. As the object is moved, it must be redrawn to show the user its new, tentative location. Once again, creating a paint message for each new location would create too much overhead. For both of these cases, you'll want to draw in response to other messages besides the paint message.

However, a word of caution is needed here. If you draw and erase a temporary object — for example, a stretchable rubber rectangle — there's no problem. However, if you draw more permanent objects, your painting code has to know about those objects. After all, you don't know when a user will force a redraw of a window. All the user needs to do to make this happen is to minimize and then maximize your window. The same result occurs when another application's window is maximized over your window. When your application becomes the active application, you'll have to handle a paint message for your entire window. Any lack of synchronization between your paint and nonpaint drawing code will become painfully obvious to your users.

Setting aside these caveats and concerns, it's relatively easy to draw in response to other messages. Instead of using the CDC class, you use a CClientDC object. The clipping for a CClientDC is set to the entire client area of a window. For example, the following code snippet shows how to say "Hello world," which is centered under the cursor, when the user clicks the left mouse button:

```
// Saying "Hello world" using the MFC CClientDC Object
void CMyView::OnLButtonDown(UINT nFlags, CPoint point)
{
  // Create a CClientDC class.
  CClientDC ClientDC( this );

  // Create a CString object with the text.
  CString strText = "Hello world";

  // Get the size of this text string in terms of
```

```
//this DC.
CSize size =
ClientDC.GetTextExtent(strText, strText.GetLength());

// Calculate the coordinates to which you need to draw
// in order to center the text about the mouse point.
int xCentered = point.x - ( size.cx / 2 );
int yCentered = point.y - ( size.cy / 2 );

// Draw the text to the window.
ClientDC.TextOut( xCentered, yCentered, strText );
}
```

So what have you learned so far? You've seen how to get a device context (DC) and draw a line of basic text to the display using the default DC attributes. Although the DC defaults are reasonable and produce good results, you'll eventually want to control the attributes that affect the appearance of text. That's what is covered next.

Manipulating Text

To change the appearance of text, you change one of the DC attributes that affect text. As summarized in Table 8-1, eight attributes affect the appearance or the positioning of text. The most effective way to understand the changes that a DC attribute controls is to see the text change in a real program. If your computer is handy, you might consider generating a tiny SDI AppWizard program so that you can experiment with each attribute, as it is discussed.

GDI color support

Before you can change the color of text, you need to understand how to specify color in GDI. The basic Windows data type for holding color values is COLORREF. The easiest way to define colors is by using the RGB macro, which takes three parameters that define the red, green, and blue color components. For each color component, you specify a value in the range 0–255. For example, here are three color values: one each for red, green, and blue:

```
COLORREF crRed   = RGB( 255, 0, 0 );
COLORREF crGreen = RGB( 0, 255, 0 );
COLORREF crBlue  = RGB( 0, 0, 255 );
```

Although this might seem fairly straightforward, a number of factors make this more complex than it first appears. In GDI, these types of color references are called *logical colors*. In this context, logical doesn't mean Boolean. Instead, this term is used to differentiate between logical colors and physical colors, which are the colors that a physical hardware device can actually display. A high-resolution, 16-million color device shouldn't have a problem displaying various combinations of red, green, and blue, but it's a different story for a black-and-white printer. How are these differences handled?

You should think about logical colors in terms of requests. If you request red and the device can produce red, you get what you asked for. If you request red and the device can't give you what you want, the device provides the closest possible match. That might mean black! To solve the problem of the black-and-white printer, you start by not asking for colors that aren't available. To find out the number of available colors, you call CDC::GetDeviceCaps, as in the following example:

```
int nColors = pDC->GetDeviceCaps( NUMCOLORS );
```

On color display screens, the system creates a default palette with 20 colors. For devices that support only 16 colors, only the first 16 of these 20 colors are used (the rest turn into white or gray). On devices that support more than 16 colors, these 20 form the default set that are available to applications. The following code listing shows the standard RGB values for fetching these colors:

```
// Colors for Common Shades
// 16-color device support
const COLORREF g_crBlack      = RGB(  0,  0,  0);
const COLORREF g_crYellow     = RGB(255,255,  0);
const COLORREF g_crDkYellow   = RGB(128,128,  0);
const COLORREF g_crRed        = RGB(255,  0,  0);
const COLORREF g_crDkRed      = RGB(128,  0,  0);
const COLORREF g_crMagenta    = RGB(255,  0,255);
const COLORREF g_crDkMagenta  = RGB(128,  0,128);
const COLORREF g_crBlue       = RGB(  0,  0,255);
const COLORREF g_crDkBlue     = RGB(  0,  0,128);
const COLORREF g_crCyan       = RGB(  0,255,255);
const COLORREF g_crDkCyan     = RGB(  0,128,128);
const COLORREF g_crGreen      = RGB(  0,255,  0);
const COLORREF g_crDkGreen    = RGB(  0,128,  0);
const COLORREF g_crGray       = RGB(192,192,192);
const COLORREF g_crDkGray     = RGB(128,128,128);
const COLORREF g_crWhite      = RGB(255,255,255);

// Additional four colors for displays with more than
// 16 colors
const COLORREF g_crLtYellow   = RGB(255,251,240);
const COLORREF g_crLtGreen    = RGB(192,220,192);
const COLORREF g_crLtBlue     = RGB(166,202,240);
const COLORREF g_crMedGray    = RGB(160,160,164);
```

On displays that support more than 16 colors, you can always define your own custom palette. When selected into a DC, this gives you access to a much wider range of colors. However, the use of alternate palettes is an advanced topic that is beyond the scope of this book. The default palette serves nicely for all but the most demanding applications.

Text color

Now that you know how to use the RGB macros to pick colors, let's look at the three DC attributes that affect text color. These attributes are text color, background color, and background mode. When you first get a DC, it contains default settings for these three values as shown in Table 8-2.

Table 8-2: Default DC Settings

Text Color Attributes	Default Setting
Text color	RGB (0,0,0): black text
Background color	RGB(255,255,255): white background
Background mode	OPAQUE

To set the color that is to be used for drawing the foreground pixels of text, you call `CDC::SetTextColor`. This function is defined as follows:

```
COLORREF SetTextColor( COLORREF crColor );
```

This function takes a color value as input and returns the previous text color setting. For example, here's how to get red text:

```
pDC->SetTextColor(RGB( 255, 0, 0 ) );
pDC->TextOut ( x, y, "This is red text" );
```

To set the color for background text pixels, call `CDC::SetBkColor`. This function is defined as follows:

```
COLORREF SetBkColor( COLORREF crColor );
```

As you may have surmised, the background pixels are those that are inside the text box but not part of letter strokes. Here's how you set the background color to black:

```
pDC->SetBkColor(RGB( 0, 0, 0));
pDC->TextOut (x, y,
             "This text has a black background",
             32);
```

The final DC attribute that affects the color of text is the background mode. It's basically an on/off toggle for the background mode. The default setting, OPAQUE, tells the GDI to use the background color. The alternate setting, TRANSPARENT, tells the GDI not to use the background color in drawing text. You set the background mode by calling `CDC::SetBkMode`, which is defined as follows:

```
int SetBkMode( int nBkMode );
```

If you're interested in letting your users set the foreground or background colors, you'll probably want to use the Color Selector dialog box. This is one of the common dialog boxes that is included as part of the 32-bit family of Windows operating systems. With just a few lines of code, you get a fully functioning dialog box as follows:

```
CColorDialog ColorDialog;
if( ColorDialog.DoModal() == IDOK ){

    COLORREF Color = ColorDialog.GetColor();

    CString strText;
    strText.Format( "The selected color was RGB( %d, %d,
      %d )", GetRValue( Color ), GetGValue( Color ),
         GetBValue( Color ) );

    AfxMessageBox( strText );
    }
```

You'll see this and the other common dialog boxes covered in more detail in Chapter 10.

Aligning text

Text alignment describes the relationship between the (x,y) text coordinates and the textbox. The default setting aligns the text below and to the right of the text coordinate. To set the text alignment, you call CDC::SetTextAlign. This function takes a single parameter, a combination of the flags listed in Table 8-1. The flags in each column are mutually exclusive — that is, you take one flag from each column. The first row of Table 8-3 lists the default settings, which are in shown in bold.

Table 8-3: Text Alignment Constants

Y-Axis Alignment	X-Axis Alignment	Update Current Position
TA_LEFT	**TA_TOP**	**TA_NOUPDATECP**
TA_CENTER	TA_BASELINE	TA_UPDATECP
TA_RIGHT	TA_BOTTOM	

You might want to change the default settings if you're going to mix text of different sizes (or even the same size and different fonts) on the same line. The *y*-axis default alignment, TA_TOP, would yield strange results if you didn't adjust the *y*-axis values yourself. Here's how you set the text alignment to accommodate multifont drawing:

```
pDC->SetTextAlign( TA_LEFT | TA_BASELINE );
```

It's also convenient to change the text alignment when you are trying to align the right side of text with another graphic object. Although you could tinker with the *x*-axis value, it's easier to set the alignment as follows:

```
pDC->SetTextAlign( TA_RIGHT | TA_TOP );
```

Another situation in which you might want to change the text alignment is when you want to use the DC's current position value for text. The current position is an (*x,y*) coordinate pair that's typically used for vector graphics. However, you can use it for text when you set the TA_UPDATECP flag:

```
pDC->SetTextAlign( TA_UPDATECP );
```

With this setting, the only coordinates used for text drawing are at the current position. As each line of text is drawn, the position is updated so it's ready for the next text. You set the current position by calling CDC::MoveTo. Because it uses the TA_UPDATECP flag, the following code draws its text at 12,92 instead of at the coordinates specified in the TextOut call:

```
// Request that text drawing use current position.
pDC->SetTextAlign( TA_UPDATECP );

// Set current value of current position.
pDC->MoveTo( 12, 92 );

// Even though coordinates are specified here, they are
// ignored.
pDC->TextOut( 100, 200, "This text is not drawn at
 100,200", 33 );
```

Justifying text

There are two final text attributes in the basic set: text justification and text extra spacing. Each of these helps you pad out lines of text. You pad out text lines to produce WYSIWYG (what-you-see-is-what-you-get) output. For the most part, this means that you tweak the display screen output to mimic the printed output.

To adjust the settings of these two attributes, you call `CDC::SetTextJustification` and `CDC::SetTextCharacterExtra`, respectively. `SetTextJustification` enables you to specify the number of pixels to add to each space character. This setting represents additional room beyond what the font would normally use for spaces. If even more padding is needed, you call `SetTextCharacterExtra` instead of `SetTextJustification`. `SetTextCharacterExtra` adds extra pixels to every character (not just the space characters).

I should mention that these two drawing attributes date back to the very first version of Windows and that other techniques for accomplishing the same results have since been added to Windows. For example, the `ExtTextOut` function gives you complete control over the width of individual character cells. If you can take the time for the extra work it requires, it's well worth the results. The addition of TrueType fonts to Windows has also cut down on the differences between display screen fonts and printer fonts. An application that exclusively uses TrueType fonts can get reasonably close to WYSIWYG output with little or no character cell padding.

All the basic text attributes were covered first because they are the simplest. The following section directs your attention to the text attribute that has the greatest effect on the appearance of text — the font.

About Fonts

This section covers the basics for creating and using fonts. The easiest approach for working with fonts is to use the GDI's stock fonts. However, to access a broader range of fonts that are installed in a typical Windows system, you need to create a `CFont` object.

A *font* is a collection of complex graphical images, of a single size and design, which are used to represent character data. Fonts are commonly identified by point size and by name, such as Arial or Times New Roman, and perhaps also by style. To refer to specific fonts, such terms as 18-point Times New Roman or 8-point bold Arial are used.

If you've never been exposed to the world of fonts, it can be quite a shock to learn that literally thousands of different fonts are available. Windows ships with a basic set of fonts, but numerous font packs are sold to add to this set, and it's not at all uncommon for Windows applications to include even more fonts. For example, Corel Corporation's CorelDraw application ships with more than 800 fonts.

Selecting objects into DCs

Anytime you select a nonstock object in a DC, it's a good idea to remember what object was previously selected into the DC. You always get a pointer to the object when you use the `SelectObject` function. For instance, if you use the `SelectObject` function to select a newly created font into the DC, a pointer to a `CFont` object is returned. You can record the font that was selected into the DC before you selected your nonstock font in the following way:

```
CFont *pOldFont;
pOldFont = pDC->SelectObject( &NewFont );
```

After you're done using the nonstock font (or any other GDI object for that matter), you must select the old object back into the DC. If your newly created GDI object is still selected into the DC when you try to delete it (or the object's destructor tries to delete it), the deletion fails, and the memory that the GDI object occupies is locked until your application quits. Following is the final line that you should add once you're done drawing with the nonstock GDI object:

```
pDC->SelectObject( pOldFont );
```

Selecting stock fonts

Before delving into customizing different display fonts, you need to understand how different graphic objects are used within a device context. This process is called *selecting* an object into (or out of) a DC. To select a font, you start by getting your hands on one. In an MFC program, this means having a properly initialized CFont object. The simplest way to get a font is to use one of the predefined stock fonts that Windows provides. The following example shows how to get one of the stock fonts:

```
CFont fontStock;
fontStock.CreateStockObject( ANSI_FIXED_FONT );
```

Like every other drawing attribute, a font must be connected to a DC before it affects the appearance of any output. To connect a font to a DC, you call CDC::SelectObject. For example, this code fragment connects the font that you just created to a DC:

```
pDC->SelectObject( &fontStock );
```

Until you select a different font into the DC, all text that you draw is formatted in this font.

Fonts differ from other drawing attributes in an important way. Most attributes are simply numbers that are stored in the DC. Within the system, however, a font is its own object, and it has its own life separate from the DC. For every font object that you create, you need to make sure that you destroy the object when you're done using it. Otherwise, space is wasted somewhere.

In practical terms, this means simply making sure that you destroy every CFont object that you create. The destructor to this class helps you make sure that no system memory is wasted. But how do you catch those CFont objects that you forget to delete? Fortunately, the Visual C++ tools can help you catch them. Just run the debug build of your program in the debugger that's built into the Visual C++ development environment. When the program shuts down, you'll see a laundry list of objects that haven't been properly cleaned up.

Stock fonts aren't actually cleaned up even when you delete their CFont wrapper. The reason is that the system created those fonts for everyone to use.

Selecting nonstock fonts

To select a font other than a stock font, you have to submit a font request to the GDI. One way to represent a font request is with the LOGFONT (logical font) data structure. To submit a font request to the GDI, you fill in this data structure and pass it to a CFont initialization function, CFont::CreateFontIndirect. The term *Indirect* in this function name refers to the fact that the function takes a pointer parameter. Another initialization function, CFont::CreateFont, takes a series of parameters that, when taken together, match LOGFONT.

A logical font is much like the logical color described earlier in this chapter when setting text color was discussed. A logical font represents a logical request that the GDI and the device driver use to figure out which specific physical font to use. In the same way that you can ask for red and get black, you might ask for 24-point Times New Roman and get 12-point Courier.

The simplest solution would be to always use the device default. A font that you can create using a stock font always provides the device default. It is generally a 10- or 12-point device font. Otherwise, you can limit your choices to the dozen or so fonts that are built into Windows. This is the same general solution that you applied to the red-black color mismatch: Don't ask for something that the system doesn't have. The following code illustrates how to create and use a font in a program's OnDraw function:

```cpp
void CFrameView::OnDraw(CDC* pDC)
{
    CFrameDoc* pDoc = GetDocument();
    ASSERT_VALID(pDoc);

    // Create a CFont object, and then create the
    // font with the CreateFont() function.
    CFont NewFont;
    NewFont.CreateFont( 45, 45,
        0, 0, FW_DONTCARE,
        FALSE, FALSE, FALSE,
        DEFAULT_CHARSET,
        OUT_CHARACTER_PRECIS, CLIP_CHARACTER_PRECIS,
        DEFAULT_QUALITY, DEFAULT_PITCH | FF_DONTCARE,
        "Times New Roman" );

    // Select the newly created font into the
    // DC and remember the old font so that
    // you can restore it later.
    CFont *pOldFont;
    pOldFont = pDC->SelectObject( &NewFont );

    // Draw the text.
    pDC->TextOut( 10, 10, "Hello Fonts!" );

    // Select the old font back into the DC.
    pDC->SelectObject( pOldFont );

}
```

The CreateFont function expects many parameters. Because fonts are such an integral part of graphical programming, let's take a look at the CreateFont function in more detail:

```cpp
BOOL CreateFont(
    int nHeight,
    int nWidth,
    int nEscapement,
    int nOrientation,
    int nWeight,
    BYTE bItalic,
    BYTE bUnderline,
    BYTE cStrikeOut,
    BYTE nCharSet,
```

```
    BYTE nOutPrecision,
    BYTE nClipPrecision,
    BYTE nQuality,
    BYTE nPitchAndFamily,
    LPCTSTR lpszFacename
);
```

I won't go into excruciating detail on each parameter because some are self-explanatory. However, there are a few whose understanding is integral to the effective use of the function. The first parameter is the nHeight. It specifies the desired height (in logical units) of the font. The font height can be specified as a value greater than 0, in which case the height is transformed into device units and matched against the cell height of the available fonts. It can be equal to 0, in which case a reasonable (or average) default size is used. Otherwise, it can be less than 0, in which case the height is transformed into device units and the absolute value is matched against the character height of the available fonts. The absolute value of nHeight must not exceed 16,384 device units after it is converted. For all height comparisons, the font mapper looks for the largest font that does not exceed the requested size or the smallest font if all the fonts exceed the requested size.

The second parameter, nWidth, is used to specify the average width (in logical units) of characters in the font. If the width is 0, the aspect ratio of the device is matched against the digitization aspect ratio of the available fonts to find the closest match, which is determined by the absolute value of the difference.

The third parameter, nEscapement, is used to denote the angle (in 0.1-degree units) between the escapement vector and the x-axis of the display surface. The escapement vector is the line through the origins of the first and last characters on a line. It's important to realize that this angle is measured counterclockwise from the x-axis and is parallel to the base line of a row of text.

The fourth parameter, nOrientation, is used to specify the angle (in 0.1-degree units) between the baseline of a character and the x axis. The angle is measured counterclockwise from the x-axis for coordinate systems in which the y direction is down, and clockwise from the x-axis for coordinate systems in which the y direction is up.

The fifth parameter, nWeight, is used to stipulate the font weight (in inked pixels per 1,000). Although nWeight can be any integer value from 0 to 1,000, the common constants can be as follows:

```
FW_DONTCARE
FW_THIN
FW_EXTRALIGHT
FW_ULTRALIGHT
FW_LIGHT
FW_NORMAL
FW_REGULAR
FW_MEDIUM
FW_SEMIBOLD
FW_DEMIBOLD
FW_BOLD
FW_EXTRABOLD
FW_ULTRABOLD
FW_BLACK
FW_HEAVY
```

These values are approximate; the actual appearance depends on the typeface. Some fonts have only FW_NORMAL, FW_REGULAR, and FW_BOLD weights. If FW_DONTCARE is specified, a default weight is used.

The sixth parameter, bItalic, is a Boolean value that specifies whether the font is italic. The seventh parameter, bUnderline, is a Boolean value that specifies whether the font is underlined, and the eighth parameter, cStrikeout, is a Boolean value that specifies whether characters in the font are struck out.

The ninth parameter (nCharSet) specifies the font's character set. The predefined constants that can be used are as follows:

```
ANSI_CHARSET
DEFAULT_CHARSET
SYMBOL_CHARSET
SHIFTJIS_CHARSET
OEM_CHARSET
```

The OEM character set is system-dependent. Fonts with other character sets may exist in the system. An application that uses a font with an unknown character set must not attempt to translate or interpret strings that are to be rendered with that font. Instead, the strings should be passed directly to the output device driver. The font mapper does not use the DEFAULT_CHARSET value. An application can use this value to enable the name and size of a font to fully describe the logical font. If a font with the specified name does not exist, a font from any character set can be substituted for the specified font. To avoid unexpected results, applications should use the DEFAULT_CHARSET value sparingly.

The tenth parameter, nOutPrecision, defines how closely the output must match the requested font's height, width, character orientation, escapement, and pitch. The values it can be are as follows:

```
OUT_CHARACTER_PRECIS
OUT_STRING_PRECIS
OUT_DEFAULT_PRECIS
OUT_STROKE_PRECIS
OUT_DEVICE_PRECIS
OUT_TT_PRECIS
OUT_RASTER_PRECIS
```

Applications can use the OUT_DEVICE_PRECIS, OUT_RASTER_PRECIS, and OUT_TT_PRECIS values to control how the font mapper chooses a font when the system contains more than one font with a given name. For example, if a system contains a font named Symbol in raster and TrueType form, specifying OUT_TT_PRECIS forces the font mapper to choose the TrueType version. (Specifying OUT_TT_PRECIS forces the font mapper to choose a TrueType font whenever the specified font name matches a device or raster font, even when there is no TrueType font of the same name.)

The eleventh parameter, nClipPrecision, specifies the desired clipping precision. The clipping precision defines how to clip characters that are partially outside the clipping region. The values it can be are as follows:

```
CLIP_CHARACTER_PRECIS
CLIP_MASK
CLIP_DEFAULT_PRECIS
CLIP_STROKE_PRECIS
```

```
CLIP_ENCAPSULATE
CLIP_TT_ALWAYS
CLIP_LH_ANGLES
```

To use an embedded read-only font, an application must specify CLIP_ENCAPSULATE. To achieve consistent rotation of device, TrueType, and vector fonts, an application can use the OR operator to combine the CLIP_LH_ANGLES value with any of the other clip precision values. If the CLIP_LH_ANGLES bit is set, the rotation for all fonts depends on whether the orientation of the coordinate system is left-handed or right-handed. For more information about the orientation of coordinate systems, see the description of the orientation parameter. If CLIP_LH_ANGLES is not set, device fonts always rotate counterclockwise, but the rotation of other fonts is dependent on the orientation of the coordinate system.

The twelfth parameter, nQuality, specifies the font's output quality, which defines how carefully the GDI must attempt to match the logical font attributes to those of an actual physical font. The values it can be are DEFAULT_QUALITY, DRAFT_QUALITY, and PROOF_QUALITY.

The thirteenth parameter specifies the pitch and family of the font. The two low-order bits specify the pitch of the font and can be a combination of either DEFAULT_PITCH, VARIABLE_PITCH, or FIXED_PITCH and FF_DECORATIVE, FF_DONTCARE, FF_MODERN, FF_ROMAN, FF_SCRIPT, or FF_SWISS. An application can specify a value for the pitch and family by using the Boolean OR operator to join a pitch constant with a family constant. Font families describe the look of a font in a general way. They are intended for specifying fonts when the exact typeface desired is not available.

The fourteenth and final parameter is a pointer to a null-terminated string that specifies the typeface name of the font. The length of this string must not exceed 30 characters. The Windows EnumFontFamilies function can be used to enumerate all currently available fonts. If this parameter is NULL, the GDI uses a device-independent typeface.

Working with Pens and Brushes

In the world of GDI, pens and brushes are used to render graphics, text, and images. GDI provides a number of API functions an application can call to create custom pens and brushes, including CreatePen, CreateSolidBrush, CreateHatchBrush, and CreatePatternBrush. MFC wraps these functions in the CPen and CBrush classes so pens and brushes can be dealt with as objects rather than through the raw handles that GDI provides. In this section, we'll take a look at how to work with both pens and brushes.

Pens

Pens are GDI objects that are typically used to draw lines and curves, and to outline shapes. Defining a pen involves specifying three main characteristics: style, width, and color. The CPen defines three overloaded constructors, which each allows you to define these characteristics a bit differently.

```
CPen();
CPen(
    int nPenStyle,
    int nWidth,
    COLORREF crColor
);
```

```
CPen(
    int nPenStyle,
    int nWidth,
    const LOGBRUSH* pLogBrush,
    int nStyleCount = 0,
    const DWORD* lpStyle = NULL
);
```

The simplest way to create a GDI pen is to construct a CPen object and pass it the parameters that define the pen as follows. In the following example, I'm defining a solid pen of pixel width and a color of solid red.

```
CPen pen(PS_SOLID, 1, RGB(255, 0, 0));
```

A second way to create a GDI pen is to use the parameter-less constructor and to then call the CPen::CreatePen, CPen::CreatePenIndirect or CPen::CreateStockObject functions to define the pen's style, width, and color attributes. This technique is typically employed when you define the pen as a member of another class (for example, a view class) and then call the CreatePen function in the containing class's initialization routine (for example, the view's OnInitialUpdate function). In the following code snippet I am using the parameter-less constructor in the instantiation of two separate CPen objects. While both pens will be the same solid, 1-pixel width, red pen as created in the previous code snippet, this shows you two more techniques in creating a pen.

```
CPen pen1;
pen1.CreatePen(PS_SOLID, 1, RGB(255, 0, 0));

CPen Pen2;
LOGPEN logpen;
logpen.lopnStype = PS_SOLID;
logpen.lopnWidth = 1;
logpen.lpenColor = RGB(255, 0, 0);
pen.CreatePenIndirect(&logpen);
```

Note that both the CreatePen and CreatePenIndirect return TRUE if a pen is successfully created and FALSE if it is not. If you enable the object's constructor to create the pen (by calling either of the CPen constructors that take arguments), an exception of type CResourceException is thrown if the pen can't be created. This should happen only if the system is critically low on memory, and should be treated as a catastrophic error, because if your application can't create something as resource-friendly as a single pen, it's doubtful that the application is going to be able to do much.

The last constructor gives you the ability to pass a LOGBRUSH structure. Although I won't be covering brushes until the next section, here's a code snippet that creates a geometric brush.

```
LOGBRUSH logBrush;
logBrush.lbStyle = BS_SOLID;
logBrush.lbColor = RGB(0,255,0);
CPen myPen2(PS_DOT | PS_GEOMETRIC | PS_ENDCAP_ROUND,
            2,
            &logBrush);
```

In the first several examples, the pen's style was defined as PS_SOLID, and in the last example, it was a combination of several styles. To fully understand the options at your disposal, Table 8-4 lists the other available pen styles that can be used when creating a pen.

Table 8-4: Pen Styles

Style	Description
PS_SOLID	Creates a solid pen.
PS_DASH	Creates a dashed pen. This style is only valid with pen widths of 1 device unit or less.
PS_DOT	Creates a dotted pen. This style is valid only with pen widths of 1 device unit or less.
PS_DASHDOT	Creates a pen with alternating dashes and dots. This style is valid only with pen widths of 1 device unit or less.
PS_DASHDOTDOT	Creates a pen with an alternating pattern of one dash and two dots. This style is valid only with pen widths of 1 device unit or less.
PS_NULL	Creates a NULL pen.
PS_INSIDEFRAME	Creates a pen that draws a line inside the frame of closed shapes created by GDI functions that specify a bounding rectangle.

The NULL pen draws nothing, which prompts the question, "Why would you ever want to create a NULL pen?" Believe it or not, a NULL pen does come in handy at times. Suppose you want to draw a solid red circle with no border. If you draw the circle with MFC's CDC::Ellipse function, Windows automatically borders the circle with the pen currently selected into the device context. You can't tell the Ellipse function you don't want a border, but you can select a NULL pen into the device context so that the circle does not have a visible border.

The second parameter passed into CPen object's pen-create functions specifies the pen width—the width of the lines the pen will draw. Pen widths are specified in logical units whose physical meanings depend on the mapping mode. You can create PS_SOLID, PS_NULL, and PS_INSIDEFRAME pens of any logical width, but the other pen styles must be one logical unit in width. Specifying a pen width of zero in any style creates a pen that is one pixel in width, no matter what the mapping mode.

The third and final parameter specified when a pen is created is the pen's color. This is a 24-bit RGB color in which each possible color is defined by red, green, and blue color values ranging from 0 to 255.

Windows predefines three special solid, 1-pixel-wide pens you can use without explicitly creating a pen object. Called *stock pens*, these pens belong to a group of GDI objects known as *stock objects* and are created with the CreateStockObject. The stock pens that are available are defined as WHITE_PEN, BLACK_PEN, and NULL_PEN. The following code creates a stock white pen:

```
CPen Pen;
Pen.CreateStockObject( WHITE_PEN );
```

The following code creates an identical white pen that's not a stock object:

```
CPen Pen;
Pen.CreatePen( PS_SOLID, 1, RGB( 255, 255, 255 ) );
```

In case none of the basic pen styles fits your needs, the CPen class provides a separate constructor for cosmetic and geometric pens that support a wide variety of styling options. You can create a geometric pen, for example, that draws a pattern described by a bitmap image, and you can exercise precise control over endpoints and joins by specifying the end cap style (flat, round, or square) and join style (beveled, mitered, or rounded). The following code creates a geometric pen 16 units wide and draws green solid lines with flat ends. Where two lines meet, the adjoining ends are rounded to form a smooth intersection:

```
LOGBRUSH LogBrush;
LogBrush.lbStyle = BS_SOLID;
LogBrush.lbColor = RGB(0, 255, 0);
CPen Pen(PS_GEOMETRIC | PS_SOLID
        | PS_ENDCAP_FLAT | PS_JOIN_ROUND,
        16, &LogBrush);
```

Windows places several restrictions on the use of cosmetic and geometric pens, not the least of which is that for the endpoint and join styles to work, figures must first be drawn to paths and then rendered with the CDC::StrokePath function. You define a path by enclosing drawing commands between calls to CDC::BeginPath and CDC:EndPath functions as follows:

```
pDC->BeginPath();
pDC->MoveTo( 0, 0 );
pDC->LineTo( 200, 0 );
pDC->LineTo( 200, 200 );
pDC->LineTo( 0, 200 );
pDC->CloseFigure();
pDC->EndPath();
pDC->StrokePath();
```

Brushes

Brushes are GDI objects used to create solid shapes and to render text and are encapsulated by the CBrush class. Brushes come in three basic varieties: solid brushes, hatch brushes, and pattern brushes. Solid brushes paint with solid colors. If your display hardware won't enable a particular solid brush color to be displayed directly, Windows simulates the color by dithering colors that can be displayed. A hatch brush paints with one of six predefined hatch styles modeled after hatching patterns used in engineering and architectural drawings. A pattern brush paints with a bitmap. The CBrush class provides a constructor for each different brush style. You can create a solid brush in one step by passing a COLORRREF value to the CBrush constructor as follows:

```
CBrush Brush( RGB( 255, 0, 0 ) );
```

Or you can create a solid brush in two steps by creating an uninitialized CBrush object and calling CBrush::CreateSolidBrush as follows:

```
CBrush Brush;
Brush.CreateSolidBrush( RGB( 255, 0, 0 ) );
```

Both examples create a solid brush that paints bright red. You can also create a brush by initializing a LOGBRUSH structure and calling CBrush::CreateBrushIndirect. As with CPen constructors, all CBrush constructors that create a brush throw a resource exception if GDI is critically low on memory and a brush can't be created.

Hatch brushes are created by passing the CBrush constructor both a hatch index and a COLORREF value or by calling CBrush::CreateHatchBrushIndirect. Following is an example that creates a hatch brush with perpendicular crosshatch lines that are oriented at 45-degree angles:

```
CBrush Brush( HS_DIAGCROSS, RGB( 255, 0, 0 ) );
```

The next example creates the same hatch brush in two steps:

```
CBrush Brush;
Brush.CreateHatchBrush( HS_DIAGCROSS, RGB( 255, 0, 0 ) );
```

HS_DIAGCROSS is one of six hatch styles you can choose from. Table 8-5 lists all six hatch styles that are available.

Table 8-5: Hatch Styles

Hatch Style	Description
HS_BDIAGONAL	Downward hatch (left to right) at 45 degrees
HS_CROSS	Horizontal and vertical crosshatch
HS_DIAGCROSS	Crosshatch at 45 degrees
HS_FDIAGONAL	Upward hatch (left to right) at 45 degrees
HS_HORIZONTAL	Horizontal hatch
HS_VERTICAL	Vertical hatch

When painting with a hatch brush, Windows fills the space between hatch lines with the default background color unless you change the device context's current background color with CDC::SetBkColor, or turn off background fills by changing the background mode from OPAQUE to TRANSPARENT with CDC::SetBkMode. The following example draws a rectangle 100 units square and fills it with white crosshatch lines drawn against a light gray background::

```
CBrush Brush( HS_DIAGCROSS, RGB( 255, 255, 255 ) );
CBrush *pOldBrush;
pOldBrush = pDC->SelectObject( &Brush );
pDC->SetBkColor( RGB( 192, 192, 192 ) );
pDC->Rectangle( 0, 0, 100, 100 );
pDC->SelectObject( pOldBrush );
```

The next example draws a black crosshatched rectangle against the existing background. The background color mode also determines how Windows fills the gaps in lines drawn with stylized pens and fills between the characters in text strings:

```
CBrush Brush( HS_DIAGCROSS, RGB( 0, 0, 0 ) );
CBrush *pOldBrush
pOldBrush = pDC->SelectObject( &Brush );
pDC->SetBkMode( TRANSPARENT );
pDC->Rectangle( 0, 0, 100, 100 );
pDC->SelectObject( pOldBrush );
```

Windows makes seven stock brushes available:

```
BLACK_BRUSH
DKGRAY_BRUSH
GRAY_BRUSH
LTGRAY_BRUSH
HOLLOW_BRUSH
NULL_BRUSH
WHITE_BRUSH
```

All are solid brushes, and in each case, the identifier is an accurate indicator of the brush's color. HOLLOW_BRUSH and NULL_BRUSH are two different ways of referring to the same thing: a brush that paints nothing. I mentioned the benefits of creating a NULL pen in the previous section. NULL brushes have a similar benefit. For example, if you want to draw a circle, and you don't want the circle to have a border, but you want the interior of the circle to be transparent, you would select a NULL brush into the device context before drawing the circle.

Mapping Modes

When an application draws a line from point A to point B, the coordinates passed to MoveTo and LineTo don't specify physical locations on the screen. Instead, they specify coordinates within a logical coordinate system whose properties are defined by the device context. The GDI translates logical coordinates into physical coordinates on the screen, or device coordinates, using equations that factor in the current mapping mode as well as other attributes of the device context.

In the device coordinate system, the point (0, 0) corresponds to the upper-left corner of the device context's display surface, values of x and y increase as you move to the right and down, and one device unit equals one pixel. In a logical coordinate system, the point (0, 0) defaults to the upper-left corner of the display surface, but can be moved, and the orientation of the x- and y-axes and the physical distance that corresponds to one unit in the x or y direction are governed by the mapping mode. You can change the mapping mode with the CDC::SetMapMode function, and you can move the origin of a logical coordinate system with the CDC:SetViewportOrg and CDC::SetWindowOrg functions. Windows supports eight different mapping modes. They are summarized in Table 8-6.

Table 8-6: Mapping Modes

Mapping Mode	Description
MM_ISOTROPIC	Logical units are converted to arbitrary units with equally scaled axes; that is, 1 unit along the x-axis is equal to 1 unit along the y-axis. Use the SetWindowExt and SetViewportExt member functions to specify the desired units and the orientation of the axes. The GDI makes adjustments as necessary to ensure that the x and y units remain the same size.
MM_ANISOTROPIC	Logical units are converted to arbitrary units with arbitrarily scaled axes. Setting the mapping mode to MM_ANISOTROPIC does not change the current window or viewport settings. To change the units, orientation, and scaling, call the SetWindowExt and SetViewportExt member functions.

Mapping Mode	Description
MM_HIENGLISH	Each logical unit is converted to 0.001 inch. Positive *x* is to the right; positive *y* is up.
MM_LOENGLISH	Each logical unit is converted to 0.01 inch. Positive *x* is to the right; positive *y* is up.
MM_HIMETRIC	Each logical unit is converted to 0.01 millimeter. Positive *x* is to the right; positive *y* is up.
MM_LOMETRIC	Each logical unit is converted to 0.1 millimeter. Positive *x* is to the right; positive *y* is up.
MM_TEXT	Each logical unit is converted to 1 device pixel. Positive *x* is to the right; positive *y* is down.
MM_TWIPS	Each logical unit is converted to 1/20 of a point. (Because a point is 1/72 inch, a twip is 1/1440 inch; however, see the "Font point size" section.) Positive *x* is to the right; positive *y* is up.

The default MM_TEXT mapping mode is the easiest of all the mapping modes to understand because in that mode, logical coordinates translate directly to device coordinates: one logical unit in the *x* or *y* direction equals one pixel on the screen, and values of *x* and *y* increase as you move right and down. In MM_TEXT, as in all of the other mapping modes, the origin of the logical coordinate system coincides with the origin of the device coordinate system unless it is moved with CDC::SetWindowOrg or CDC::SetViewportOrg. For a client-area device context, this means that the pixel in the upper-left corner of the window's client area initially has the logical coordinates (0, 0).

If you'd prefer that the origin of the coordinate system be in the center of the display surface rather than in the upper-left corner, you can move it with CDCLSetWindowOrg or CDC::SetViewportOrg. This option applies to all mapping modes, not just MM_TEXT. If you use CWnd::GetClientRect to initialize a CRect object named Rect with the device coordinates of a window's client area and the DC represents a client-area device context, the following example moves the origin of the coordinate system to the center of the client area:

```
CRect rect;
GetClientRect(rect);
pDC->SetViewportOrg(rect.Width() / 2,
                    rect.Height() / 2);
```

Raster Operations

One thing you can do is change how the draw color combines with the destination. Most of the time, though, drawing to the screen so it appears exactly as you'd expect is what you'll want. For instance, if you draw a red circle, 99 percent of the time you'll want a red circle to be drawn. At other times, a simple draw operation won't do.

You might want to use another raster operation, for example, in some animations. A common technique for moving figures around on the screen is to XOR them before moving them to a new location. XORing one figure over itself completely removes it. That's because when you first draw the figure to the screen using an XOR raster operation, the image source combines with the destination. Anywhere the source has a bit that's set toggles the corresponding bit in the destination to its opposite value. For instance, if the source bit is set (a one) and the destination bit is not set (a zero), the result is a one. If the animation must be moved, XORing the same figure in the same location toggles those same bits, once again restoring them to their original state. The bitmap can then be drawn in a new location using an XOR raster operation. The raster operation codes are defined in Table 8-7.

Table 8-7: Raster Operation Codes

Raster Operation	Description
R2_WHITE	Pixel is always white.
R2_BLACK	Pixel is always black.
R2_NOP	Pixel remains unchanged.
R2_NOT	Pixel is the inverse of the screen color.
R2_COPYPEN	Pixel is the pen color.
R2_NOTCOPYPEN	Pixel is the inverse of the pen color.
R2_MERGEPENNOT	Pixel is a combination of the pen color and the inverse of the screen color (final pixel = (NOT screen pixel) OR pen).
R2_MASKPENNOT	Pixel is a combination of the colors common to both the pen and the inverse of the screen (final pixel = (NOT screen pixel) AND pen).
R2_MERGENOTPEN	Pixel is a combination of the screen color and the inverse of the pen color (final pixel = (NOT pen) OR screen pixel).
R2_MASKNOTPEN	Pixel is a combination of the colors common to both the screen and the inverse of the pen (final pixel = (NOT pen) AND screen pixel).
R2_MERGEPEN	Pixel is a combination of the pen color and the screen color (final pixel = pen OR screen pixel).
R2_NOTMERGEPEN	Pixel is the inverse of the R2_MERGEPEN color (final pixel = NOT(pen OR screen pixel)).
R2_MASKPEN	Pixel is a combination of the colors common to both the pen and the screen (final pixel = pen AND screen pixel).
R2_NOTMASKPEN	Pixel is the inverse of the R2_MASKPEN color (final pixel = NOT(pen AND screen pixel)).
R2_XORPEN	Pixel is a combination of the colors that are in the pen or in the screen, but not in both (final pixel = pen XOR screen pixel).
R2_NOTXORPEN	Pixel is the inverse of the R2_XORPEN color (final pixel = NOT(pen XOR screen pixel)).

Text drawing functions

As summarized in Table 8-8, the GDI provides five text-drawing functions.

Table 8-8: GDI Text Drawing Functions

Function	Description
DrawText	Provides some text formatting while text is drawn. Among the 14 flags that set draw options, some control text alignment (for example, left, right, center, top). Another flag requests that tab characters be expanded to tab stops, and the DT_WORDBREAK flag requests enabling of word wrapping to produce multiple lines of text output.
ExtTextOut	Draws a single line of text with three added features. First, you can specify a clipping rectangle to limit text to an arbitrary rectangle. Second, you can specify an opaque rectangle, which involves filling in a rectangle with the background text color. Third, you can control the spacing of characters by providing an array of character cell width values.
GrayString	Creates mottled text, like that used in menus to show a disabled menu item.
TabbedTextOut	Draws a line of text, just like TextOut. The only difference is that you can define an array of tab stop positions for the support of tab characters.
TextOut	Draws a single line of text.

To draw a single line of text, the easiest function to call is CDC::TextOut. This function is defined in two different ways:

```
BOOL TextOut(int x,
             int y,
             LPCTSTR lpszString,
             int nCount);

BOOL TextOut(int x,
             int y,
             const CString& strText);
```

For the TextOut function, *x* and *y* are coordinates for positioning the text string. By default, text hangs below and to the right of this point. The lpszString parameter is a pointer to a character string. The fourth parameter, nCount, is the count of characters in the string. strText is a CString, which therefore contains both character string and string length information about the text that is to be drawn. Here's an example of a WM_PAINT handling function that calls TextOut to display the text "Hello world" at location (100,100):

```
void CMyView::OnFunction ()
{
  CClientDC ClientCD( this );
  LPCTSTR lpszText = "Hello world";
  ClientDC.TextOut( 100, 100, lpszText, strlen( lpszText ) );
}
```

Here's the same function, rewritten for the second form of TextOut:

```
void CMyView::OnFunction()
{
  CClientDC ClientDC( this );
```

```
    CString strText = "Hello world";
    ClientDC.TextOut( 100, 100, strText );
}
```

Note that when specifying drawing coordinates in GDI drawing functions such as `TextOut`, remember that Windows 95 and Windows 98 recognize only 16 bits of significance. Even though you might pass a 32-bit integer value, the GDI under Windows 95 and Windows 98 operates in only 16 bits (just like the GDI did under Windows 3.*x*). Under Windows NT and Windows 2000, however, all 32 bits of precision are recognized and supported. Unless you want your programs to run only on Windows NT, limit the range of your drawing coordinates to those that fit in 16-bit integers.

`CDC::TextOut` draws a single line of text. In many cases, however, you want to draw multiple lines of text, which requires several calls to `TextOut` with different coordinates for each call. Unlike text drawing in a character-oriented environment, drawing coordinates in the GDI are something other than character cells (for now, pixels). To properly space the text that's drawn by different calls, you need to do some text coordinate calculation. This subject is explored in the following section.

Text coordinate calculations

The GDI provides several functions that are useful in the calculation of text coordinates. You need to use this set of functions because the spacing of text strings depends not only on the font specified by the user, but also on the resolution of the target device. Before drawing any text, you need to ask the GDI for the required text coordinate values.

Table 8-9 lists some of the GDI's more useful text measurement functions. To help you understand these functions, take a look at some of their more common uses. The discussion starts with how to calculate point size, a common concern when working with text. Then how to get to the next string — whether it's on the same line as the current string, or the next line — is described. The last text coordinate topic is centering a line of text around a point.

Table 8-9: Font Measurement Functions

Function	Description
GetCharWidth	Gets a copy of the default character width values for a range of letters in the font currently selected in a DC.
GetDeviceCaps	Gets various bits of device-specific data. In the context of text, LOGPIXELSY provides the number of pixels in a logical vertical inch. This is useful for calculating font point size.
GetTextExtent	Gets the width and height that a given string would occupy when drawn with the font currently selected in a DC.
GetTabbedTextExtent	Like GetTextExtent, this function gets the width and height that a character string would occupy when drawn with the font selected in a DC. This also takes into account tab settings.
GetTextMetrics	Gets a copy of the TEXTMETRIC data for the font currently selected in a DC. This data structure contains basic font measurement information

Font point size

Even a casual user of word processing programs knows that text is measured in *points*. One point is approximately 1/72.54 inches, which makes a point small, but not too small to be seen by the unaided eye. Windows uses a value of 1/72 inch for a point — a reasonable approximation for most uses. Common sizes for regular text range between 8 points and 12 points. Headlines can be anywhere from 14 points up to 24 or 36 points, or even larger. Text is usually measured by its height and not by its width, although in Windows you can request a font using either or both attributes.

As mentioned earlier, the focus here is on device units, which are the simplest to deal with. The basic formula for converting between device units and point size is as follows:

```
PointSize = ( 72 * DeviceUnits ) / LogicalInch
```

Going the other way, here's the formula for converting points to device units:

```
DeviceUnits = ( PointSize * LogicalInch ) / 72
```

Incidentally, you'll probably want to use Windows' MulDiv helper function rather than letting the compiler do the math. This function eliminates rounding and overflow errors that sometimes occur with plain integer arithmetic. Here's the previous formula written to use this function:

```
DeviceUnits = ::MulDiv( PointSize, LogicalInch, 72 );
```

An explanation of a few points about these formulas is required. First, the term *logical inch* refers to the number of pixels in an inch. It's called *logical* because of the way this measurement is defined for display screens. On display screens, a logical inch is usually larger than a physical inch. This helps ensure that 8-point fonts — which are typically the smallest size used — are readable. On printers, logical inches and physical inches are the same.

To obtain the logical inch for a particular device, you call CDC::GetDeviceCaps, the device capabilities function. GetDeviceCaps takes a single parameter, an index of the capability to query. Two indices return logical inch values: LOGPIXELSX for movement in the *x* direction, and LOGPIXELSY for movement in the *y* direction. Because point size refers to the height of text — that is, its size along the *y*-axis — you use LOGPIXELSY to determine the logical inches for a given device:

```
LogicalInch = dc.GetDeviceCaps( LOGPIXELSY );
```

Note   Another point worth mentioning is that these formulas use a ratio of 1:72 instead of the more accurate 1:72.54 ratio of points to inches. This rounding down is done because the GDI in particular — and Windows, in general — doesn't use any floating-point arithmetic. The reason is performance. Intel *x*86 processors prior to the 80486 lacked hardware support for floating-point arithmetic. Because floating-point arithmetic in software can be very slow, Windows uses integer arithmetic, which provides faster operation and a reasonable degree of accuracy. Although this may change in future versions, for now Windows relies solely on integer arithmetic.

Next string, same line

You must sometimes split a single line of text between multiple text-drawing calls — that is, multiple calls to TextOut. This can be necessary for any number of reasons. It might simply be more convenient, given the way your data is stored, or you might want to display a line of text in which parts of the text use different drawing attributes. For example, displaying red text next to blue text requires two calls to TextOut. Using two fonts in the same line of text also requires two text-drawing calls.

To calculate the position for the next string, you call CDC::GetTextExtent. This function tells you both the width and height of a character string for the currently selected font. This function is defined as follows:

```
CSize GetTextExtent(LPCTSTR lpszString,
                     int nCount) const;
```

where lpszString is a pointer to the character string, and nCount is the number of characters to include.

The return value, CSize, is a structure with two members: cx is the width of the character string, and cy is the height. For example, here's how you write "Hello world" on the same line using two calls to TextOut:

```
int x, y;
x = 100;
y = 100;
LPCTSTR lpszHello = "Hello ";
LPCTSTR lpszWorld = "world";

// Draw the first string.
ClientDC.TextOut( x, y, lpszHello, strlen( lpszHello ) );

// Calculate size of first string.
CSize sizeString =
 ClientDC.GetTextExtent(lpszHello, strlen( lpszHello ));

// Adjust x-coordinate.
x += sizeString.cx;

// Draw second string.
ClientDC.TextOut( x, y, lpszWorld, strlen( lpszWorld ) );
```

To preserve the space between the strings, the first string—"Hello"—ends with a space.

Next string, next line

Another common text calculation involves determining how much space to put between two lines of text. As a shortcut, you could use the return value from the function you looked at a moment ago, GetTextExtent. After all, this function provides both the width and the height of a character string. Here's how to use this function to calculate the spacing between two lines of text:

```
// Draw first string.
ClientDC.TextOut(x, y, lpszHello, strlen(lpszHello));

// Calculate size of first string.
CSize sizeString =
   ClientDC.GetTextExtent(lpszHello, strlen(lpszHello));

// Adjust y-coordinate.
```

```
y += sizeString.cy;

// Draw second string.
ClientDC.TextOut(x, y, lpszWorld, strlen(lpszWorld));
```

Although this is workable for many situations, it's not the most accurate calculation. It takes into account the character cell height, but the font designer might have decided that more space is needed between lines of text. And if the font designer went to the trouble of defining additional pixels for interline spacing, it's worthwhile to use that spacing.

The term that font designers use for the space between lines of text is *external leading*. With its origins in the days when type was set by hand as tiny pieces of metal, the term *leading* refers to flat bars of lead that were placed between lines of text. It is considered external leading because it's not included in the character cell height — that is, it's outside. Another term, *internal leading*, refers to intercharacter spacing that's been built into each character cell.

Both the internal and external leading values are stored in a TEXTMETRIC data structure. To get a copy of this data structure for a given font, you call CDC::GetTextMetrics. This function provides text metric data for the font that's currently selected in the DC. Here's an example of calling this function:

```
TEXTMETRIC TmSys;
ClientDC.GetTextMetrics( &TmSys );
```

Caution
Note that the data structure — TEXTMETRIC — is singular, whereas the function call GetTextMetrics is plural. This annoying inconsistency has bubbled up from the native Windows API.

To calculate the space between lines of text, you need to use two TEXTMETRIC members: character cell height and external leading size. For the text metric structure just filled, here's how you calculate the value that must be added to the *y*-coordinate before drawing the next line:

```
int cyLineHeight = TmSys.tmHeight
                 + TmSys.tmExternalLeading;
```

In the earlier example, this would have been added to the *y*-coordinate before drawing the second line of text:

```
// Adjust y-coordinate.
y += cyLineHeight;

// Draw second string.
ClientDC.TextOut(x, y, lpszWorld, strlen(lpszWorld));
```

Two ways to get the height of a character cell have been shown, and you might be wondering how this value relates to a font's point size. Watch out, they are probably not the same — *probably,* because it's possible that they are the same, but to be absolutely sure, you must check another text metric value, the internal leading.

External versus internal leading

As discussed, *leading* is a typesetting word for interline spacing. External leading is the space not included in the character cell height. Internal leading, on the other hand, is the space that is included in the character cell height. To calculate the point size of a font, you subtract the value of the internal leading from the font height. In code terms, that means the following:

```
int DeviceUnits = TmSys.tmHeight
                 - TmSys.tmInternalLeading;
```

The result of this calculation is the height of the character cells in device units. To convert this value to points, you must take into account the device's logical inch. Using the size from the previous formula, here's how you get the font size in points:

```
int LogicalInch = ClientDC.GetDeviceCaps( LOGPIXELSY );
int PointSize = ::MulDiv( 72, DeviceUnits, LogicalInch );
```

Centering text

It's often useful to center a string of text over a particular point. For example, you might want to center a text label over a column of text, or you might want to center a label within another graphic object. Whatever the reason, when you need to solve problems like this, it's helpful to think of text as a graphic object. Like a birthday present, text comes in a box, which is sometimes called a *textbox*.

By default, a character string hangs below and to the right of the text coordinate. As a result, the centering of text requires figuring out how to shift the control point up and to the left. The size of the shift is equal to one-half the size of the textbox—that is, you shift the text up by one-half of the textbox height, and to the left by one-half of the textbox width. To show you what is meant by this, here's a code fragment that centers a text string over a given (x,y) point:

```
// The string.
CString strText = "Centered Line of Text";

// Calculate the shift up and to the left.
CSize size =
  ClientDC.GetTextExtent(strText, strText.GetLength());
int xCentered = x - ( size.cx / 2 );
int yCentered = y - ( size.cy / 2 );

// Draw line of centered text
ClientDC.TextOut( xCentered, yCentered, strText );
```

Clipping Regions

On many occasions you must limit your draw operations to a specific region and prevent anything from being drawn outside of this region. This area is called a *clipping region*, and the SelectClipRgn function is used to create this special GDI object in a particular device context.

The SelectClipRgn function selects the given region as the current clipping region for the device context. Only a copy of the selected region is used. The region itself can be selected for any number of other device contexts, or it can be deleted. The function assumes that the coordinates for the given region are specified in device units.

The CRgn class encapsulates a Windows GDI region. A region is an elliptical or polygonal area within a window. To use regions, you use the member functions of class CRgn with the clipping functions defined as members of class CDC. The following example shows how to create a simple rectangular region bounded by the coordinates (10, 10) and (100, 100):

```
CRgn Rgn;
Rgn.CreateRectRgn( 10, 10, 100, 100 );
```

With a region created, you can then limit the device context's drawing to only the region that's been created as follows:

```
pDC->SelectClipRgn( &Rgn );
```

A more advanced version of SelectClipRgn enables you to choose between five different modes. These modes affect the way the clipping region is combined with regions that are already selected into the device context, and how the region is to be used. The five modes are listed in Table 8-10.

Table 8-10: Clipping Modes

Mode	Description
RGN_AND	The new clipping region combines the overlapping areas of the current clipping region and the region identified by pRgn.
RGN_COPY	The new clipping region is a copy of the region identified by pRgn. This functionality is identical to the first version of SelectClipRgn. If the region identified by pRgn is NULL, the new clipping region becomes the default clipping region (a NULL region).
RGN_DIFF	The new clipping region combines the areas of the current clipping region with those areas excluded from the region identified by pRgn.
RGN_OR	The new clipping region combines the current clipping region and the region identified by pRgn.
RGN_XOR	The new clipping region combines the current clipping region and the region identified by pRgn, but excludes any overlapping areas.

Summary

In this chapter you discovered the basic graphical architecture of Windows (GDI) and, in doing so, learned about things such as device contexts and text manipulation. After those basics were covered, you then became aware of how to use GDI objects such as fonts, pens, and brushes. Finally, the chapter covered several sections on the advanced topics of mapping modes, raster operations, and the use of clipping regions. Although the chapter focused mainly on text output, the concepts of device context, clipping regions, and the like remain constant for all graphical operations. With the knowledge you now possess, you should feel confident tackling all sorts of graphical tasks you once thought intimidating.

✦   ✦   ✦

Bitmaps, Palettes, and DIBs

This chapter shows you how to use bitmaps of several varieties in your applications. You'll be able to display images in many places and in ways that you might have avoided because you thought they were too difficult. This chapter solves your problems. It'll have you displaying images in no time flat.

Bitmap and Video Memory

At the heart of your computer's video system is memory. This memory contains data that represents the patterns that appear on the monitor. Every time the mouse pointer moves, a small amount of data in memory changes. You then see the mouse pointer move across the screen. Each and every graphics operation affects video memory as the GDI (Graphics Device Interface) makes its calculations and alters video memory in an appropriate way.

Bitmaps represent regions of RAM similar to video memory. They're similar because each one represents a memory address that holds data. The difference is that the bitmap memory isn't visually seen, while the video memory is. The RAM that a bitmap allocates represents a rectangular region. In terms of the Windows API, this handle to the allocated memory is known as an HBITMAP. In this memory resides data that, if moved into video memory, would cause a pattern to appear on the monitor. For example, consider a desktop icon. Icons are loaded from disk into memory. This memory is then moved into video memory at the appropriate addresses so that when video memory is rendered on the screen by the video hardware, the icons become visible.

Bitmaps add graphical objects to the screen in a different way than drawn objects such as lines and ellipses. Lines and ellipses are mathematically calculated, and then the pixels in video memory are set in such a way that the object appears. Bitmap data isn't calculated. The pattern already exists in bitmap memory. It's simply a matter of copying a block of memory from the bitmap to video memory. Because of this, using bitmaps is preferable to using a series of draw operations when the end result is a complex graphics image. Imagine how many separate operations it would take to draw your photograph on the screen—possibly thousands. By using a bitmap, the complex photographic image can reside in bitmap memory. Then, with a single operation, the bitmap memory can be quickly copied to a region of video memory.

This chapter discusses two types of bitmap objects. One is wrapped in the MFC CBitmap class. Bitmaps of this type are referred to as *device-dependent bitmaps*. They can be drawn successfully only on a video system that matches their own configuration. For instance, a device-dependent bitmap that has a color depth of 24 bits per pixel draws only to a video system that's 24 bits per pixel. The only exception to this rule is monochrome bitmaps of one bit plane with a color depth of 1 bit per pixel. These can be drawn to video memory of any configuration.

Before starting the discussion, a few words on terminology are in order. In this chapter, the Windows GDI object known as an HBITMAP is referred to as a bitmap. The MFC class that wraps a bitmap is called a CBitmap class. A logical palette is a Windows GDI object, and in this chapter they're called *palettes*. The MFC class that wraps a palette is known as a CPalette object. A device-independent bitmap such as the kind that makes up .bmp files is referred to as a DIB. DIBs can't be found anywhere in the Windows API or MFC as separate items. Instead, this chapter's code loads them into HGLOBAL memory objects. They're still referred to as DIBs, though, so you know what's in the memory. There's a class that's built later on in the chapter that wraps a DIB. It'll be referred to as a CDib object.

No discussion of bitmaps would be complete without including palettes. This chapter uses MFC's CPalette object to perform all of the palette operations. For video adapters with pixel depths (or bit-depths) of 8 bits or less, effective use of palettes is essential for optimizing the appearance of bitmaps.

As mentioned previously, the second type of bitmap covered in this chapter is a device-independent bitmap (DIB). These bitmaps are not wrapped in an MFC class of any kind. Toward the end of this chapter, a class similar to CBitmap will be created that will make it easier to work with DIBs. The advantage that DIBs have over device-dependent bitmaps is that the DIB's configuration doesn't have to match the video configuration for a draw operation to be successful. The bitmap is drawn to the screen taking the configurations of the bitmap and the video into account. For instance, a 24-bit DIB draws successfully to a video system of 8-, 16-, 24-, and 32-bits per pixel. When a color depth mismatch occurs, a color-matching algorithm is used to achieve the best possible match. For instance, a 24-bit DIB that's drawn to an 8-bit video system has to reduce to the 256 colors that are available in the video system. When the DIB is drawn to the screen, the color downsizing is performed during the draw operation. This doesn't affect the DIB data that's in memory. The drawback to this is that performance is greatly reduced. For this reason, if performance is an issue, you should not use DIBs. Instead, device-dependent bitmaps are recommended.

The last thing you'll learn in this chapter is how to use CBitmap objects to reduce or eliminate screen flicker during screen redraws.

Creating CBitmap Objects

CBitmap objects are empty when they're first instantiated. The bitmap that the class wraps must eventually be created for the object to be useful. There are several ways to create bitmaps within a CBitmap class. The first uses the CreateBitmap function and has the following syntax:

```
CBitmap::CreateBitmap(int nWidth, int nHeight,
   int nPlanes, int nBits, const *void lpBits);
```

Bit planes, bits per pixel, and color depth

Back when CGA video was the standard, there were four colors to choose from: black, cyan, magenta, and white. (A seldom-used variation produced black, yellow, green, and red.) CGA video memory stores data for each pixel in two contiguous bits. Each byte of video memory contains enough data for four screen pixels. Oddly enough, the data is stored in two banks of memory. The first bank contains data for the odd scanlines, and the second contains data for the even scanlines.

With the advent of EGA and VGA monitors, the number of possible colors expanded. In EGA/VGA, there are four variables to contend with: the red, blue, and green color bits and the high/low intensity bit. By combining these four bits, you can create 16 colors (high-intensity green, low-intensity green, high-intensity blue and red, and so on). The four variables became known as *bit planes*. It's interesting to note for EGA/VGA video memory that the bits for each of the four color variables reside in different banks of memory. For instance, all of the red memory for an EGA setting of 320 × 200 resides in a bank of memory of 8,000 bytes.

MCGA systems introduced eight bits of information for each pixel. Because the concept of a color plane doesn't describe the capabilities of this type of system, the eight bits of information for each color have become known as the *bits-per-pixel value*. MCGA video memory contains a single byte for each screen pixel. To get the RGB value (RGB is explained later in this chapter) with which the video system will render the pixel, a lookup into a palette is used. MCGA palettes have only 256 entries, so MCGA video can display only 256 simultaneous colors.

All video cards support older modes such as CGA and EGA, but most of them support newer modes in which the actual RGB values are stored in video memory. The most common is 24-bit truecolor video. In this mode, each screen pixel is represented by three consecutive bytes. Each of these bytes has an RGB value for red, green, and blue. Two other common modes in which literal RGB values reside in video memory use 16- and 32-bits of data to represent the RGB color.

To determine the actual bit-depth (the number of bits that make up a pixel) of a given video system, you must check both the bits-per-pixel value and the number of bit planes. You can call the `GetDeviceCaps` API function with the `BITSPIXEL` constant to determine the bits-per-pixel value. To determine the number of color planes, you can call the same API function with the `PLANES` constant.

A simple way to calculate the true bit-depth is to retrieve both of these values and multiply them. This calculation is valid because an EGA/VGA system returns one for the bits-per-pixel value, and a truecolor/highcolor system returns one for the color planes value.

The `nWidth` and `nHeight` parameters specify the size of the bitmap in pixels. The `nPlanes` argument specifies the number of bit planes that the bitmap will be—this is almost always one. The `nBits` argument specifies the number of bits for each pixel. The last argument, `lpBits`, enables you to initialize the bitmap with a bit pattern. The bit pattern is copied into the bitmap memory, but it's still the caller's responsibility to maintain and dispose of the original bit pattern memory. Normally a bit pattern isn't specified when creating a bitmap, and in this case, the `lpBits` parameter is `NULL`. If you don't initialize the bitmap pattern, it will contain meaningless data and look like a jumbled mess. The following example creates a bitmap with a width of 50, a height of 60, 1 bit plane, 24 bits per pixel, and no initial bit pattern:

```
CBitmap Bitmap;
Bitmap.CreateBitmap(50, 60, 1, 24, NULL);
```

Many times, it's important to find out the configuration of a bitmap that has already been created. To do this, you must use the GetObject function to have a BITMAP structure filled in with information about the bitmap. When retrieving information about the CBitmap object, the bmBits member will be NULL because you can't get a direct pointer to bitmap memory. However, if you use CBitmap's CreateBitmapIndirect function, bmBits will be used to initialize the bitmap data if the structure member is not NULL. The bmType member will always be zero. The following BITMAP structure definition is followed by an example of using GetObject to fill in a BITMAP structure:

```
typedef struct tagBITMAP{
    int bmType;
    int bmWidth;
    int bmHeight;
    int bmWidthBytes;
    BYTE bmPlanes;
    BYTE bmBitsPixel;
    void *bmBits;
} BITMAP;

// Bitmap is a CBitmap object.
BITMAP bm;
Bitmap.GetObject(sizeof(BITMAP), &bm);
```

Another way to create a bitmap is with the CreateBitmapIndirect function. To do this, a BITMAP structure must first be filled in with the values for the bitmap that you want to create. A call to CreateBitmapIndirect then uses the members of the structure to create the bitmap. An example that uses the CreateBitmapIndirect function to create a bitmap with a width of 100, a height of 200, 1 bit plane, and 16 bits of color depth follows:

```
BITMAP bm;
bm.bmType = 0;
bm.bmWidth = 100;
bm.bmHeight = 200;
bm.bmWidthBytes = 200;
bm.bmPlanes = 1;
bm.bmBitsPixel = 16;
bm.bmBits = NULL;

CBitmap Bitmap;
Bitmap.CreateBitmapIndirect(&bm);
```

Even though the term *RGB* is commonly used, the order of the RGB triplets in video memory is the reverse of RGB. In other words, if each pixel is represented by three bytes in video memory, the first byte is for blue, the second for green, and the third for red.

Many times you simply want to create a bitmap that's compatible with the video system. You can do this without having to specify the bit planes or bits per pixel by using the CreateCompatibleBitmap function. This function takes a pointer to a device context and uses the device context to figure out how many bit planes and how many bits per pixel the bitmap must be. Following is an example of using this from the OnDraw function:

```
void CBitmapView::OnDraw(CDC* pDC)
{
    CBitmapDoc* pDoc = GetDocument();
```

```
    ASSERT_VALID(pDoc);

    CBitmap Bitmap;
    Bitmap.CreateCompatibleBitmap(pDC);
}
```

Loading and Setting Bitmap Content

Before using a bitmap, you'll want to set its contents with meaningful data. When bitmaps are first created, their memory contains unpredictable data. If you display a bitmap on the screen before setting the data, what you'll see resembles a television that's not set to a station and is just producing random patterns. There are two different ways to set the contents of a bitmap. One uses the SetBitmapBits function, and the other uses the LoadBitmap function.

The SetBitmapBits function copies the contents of a memory buffer into the bitmap memory. The source memory must be created and subsequently managed and deleted by the calling code. There are two reasons you'd want to set bitmap contents from a memory buffer. One is because you want to algorithmically create a pattern in memory and move it into the bitmap. Another is because you want to load bitmap data from disk and then move it into bitmap memory. The following example creates a 24-bit bitmap, creates a memory buffer that produces a red rectangle when copied to memory, and then sets the contents of the bitmap to the red pattern:

```
// Instantiate CBitmap and create the bitmap
CBitmap Bitmap;
Bitmap.CreateBitmap(50, 50, 1, 24, NULL);

// Get the bitmap dimensions and allocate a buffer
// large enough for its contents.
BITMAP bm;
Bitmap.GetObject(sizeof(BITMAP), &bm);
unsigned char pData =
    new unsigned char [bm.bmHeight*bm.bmWidthBytes];
// Loop through and set the buffer values so
// that the pattern will be solid red.
for(int y=0; y<bm.bmHeight; y++){
  for(int x=0; x<bm.bmWidth; x++){
   pData[x*3+y*bm.bmWidthBytes] = 0;
   pData[x*3+1+y*bm.bmWidthBytes] = 0;
   pData[x*3+2+y*bm.bmWidthBytes] = 255;
   }
  }

// Set the bitmap with the red data.
Bitmap.SetBitmapBits(bm.bmHeight * bm.bmWidthBytes,
 pData);

// Delete the data buffer.
delete [] pData;
```

For bitmaps that are 16 colors (four bits per pixel), there's another alternative. You can put the bitmap into your program as a resource and then use the LoadBitmap function to transfer the data into a bitmap. A bonus of using LoadBitmap is that you don't have to use CreateBitmap or any of the other bitmap creation functions; it's done by LoadBitmap. Another advantage is that LoadBitmap creates a bitmap that's compatible with the current video system, regardless of the format of the resource bitmap. Following is an example of loading a bitmap with a resource ID of IDB_BITMAP1 into a CBitmap object:

```
CBitmap Bitmap;
Bitmap.LoadBitmap(IDB_BITMAP1);
```

One other function that you might find useful is LoadMappedBitmap. It takes the same argument that LoadBitmap takes, but converts various colors in the bitmap according to how the user's system colors are set. For instance, it converts black pixels to the color of button text and dark gray to the color of button shadows.

Drawing CBitmaps to the Screen

Once you have a CBitmap object that contains a valid bitmap, you're ready to draw it to the screen. Most of the time, you'll rely on the BitBlt function. This function is *fast*. The BitBlt function is hard to beat when it comes to data transfer between memory and video. It's evident that Microsoft placed a high priority on fast algorithms for blitting operations — and considering the importance of these in such a graphically intensive environment, it's a wise decision. *Blitting* is a generic term that refers to the operation of copying bitmap data to a destination (whether visible video memory or other bitmap data in RAM).

The first thing you must understand is that BitBlt technically copies data from one device context to another. That means a device context must be created for a bitmap before operations to and from it are carried out. In addition, the bitmap must be selected into the device context before performing operations. The BitBlt function is a member of the CDC class and has the following syntax:

```
CDC:BitBlt(int x, int y, int nWidth, int nHeight,
    CDC *pSrcDC, int xSrc, int ySrc, DWORD dwROP);
```

The *x* and *y* parameters are the destination coordinates to which the bitmap will be drawn. The nWidth and nHeight parameters are the width and height of the destination rectangle and must match the source bitmap. The pSrcDC parameter is a pointer to the source device context — the source bitmap must have been selected previously into this device context for the operation to work correctly. The xSrc and ySrc parameters are the upper-left corner of the source bitmap that's to be copied. By changing the xSrc and ySrc and nWidth and nHeight parameters, you can draw partial bitmaps to the screen. The dwROP parameter specifies the raster operation that's to be performed. A more detailed discussion of raster codes appears later in the chapter in the section "Raster Operations."

The following example loads a bitmap with the LoadBitmap function in an application's view class constructor. The example then shows how to draw the bitmap to the screen using the OnDraw function. One important item to note: When selecting the bitmap into the newly created device context, you obtain a pointer to the old bitmap. This enables you to select the old bitmap back into the device context after the bitmap is drawn.

```
CmyView::CmyView()
{

  m_Bitmap.LoadBitmap(IDC_BITMAP1);
```

```
}

CmyView::OnDraw(CDC *pDC)
{
 CBitmapDoc* pDoc = GetDocument();
 ASSERT_VALID(pDoc);

 CDC MemDC;
 MemDC.CreateCompatibleDC(pDC);
 CBitmap *pOldBitmap = MemDC.SelectObject(&m_Bitmap);
 BITMAP bm;
 m_Bitmap.GetObject(sizeof(BITMAP), &bm);
 pDC->BitBlt(10, 10, bm.bmWidth, bm.bmHeight, &MemDC,
  0, 0, SRCCOPY);
 MemDC.SelectObject(pOldBitmap);

}
```

Drawing bitmaps

These steps describe the process necessary to display a CBitmap object:

1. Create a device context for the bitmap that's compatible with the video device context.

2. Select the CBitmap object into the newly created device context, and save a pointer to the old bitmap.

3. Fill in a BITMAP structure using GetObject so that you know what the bitmap's dimensions are. (Skip this step if you already know the dimensions.)

4. Perform the BitBlt function.

5. Select the old bitmap back into the newly created device context.

The examples you've seen so far don't take into account mapping mode (see Chapter 8 for a complete explanation of mapping modes) and the difference between device and logical coordinates. Most applications you write won't change the mapping mode, and most applications have device and logical coordinates that are the same. If you're not sure, though, of the situation in which you'll find yourself, you must add some extra code (and additional overhead). An example using the DrawBitmap function follows in which these additional factors are accounted for:

```
void DrawBitmap(int x, int y, CDC *pDC, CBitmap *pBitmap)
{
 BITMAP bm;
 pBitmap->GetObject(sizeof(BITMAP), &bm);

 CPoint size(bm.bmWidth, bm.bmHeight);
 pDC->DPtoLP(&size);

 CPoint org(0, 0);
 pDC->DPtoLP(&org);

 CDC MemDC;
```

```
MemDC.CreateCompatibleDC(pDC);
CBitmap *pOldBitmap = MemDC.SelectObject(pBitmap);
MemDC.SetMapMode(pDC->GetMapMode());
pDC->BitBlt(x, y, size.x, size.y, &MemDC,
  org.x, org.y, SRCCOPY);
MemDC.SelectObject(pOldBitmap);
}
```

Creating and displaying bitmaps

By creating this application, you'll learn how to create and display bitmaps.

1. Create a single document application.

2. Declare an array of CBitmap objects in the view class.

   ```
   protected:
    CBitmap m_Bitmaps[7];
   ```

3. Import a bitmap as a resource object, and give it an ID of IDB_BITMAP1. I've included a bitmap of the very popular Bob character (the site admin version) from the MFC developer Web site, www.CodeProject.com. This bitmap is included on the book's Web site.

4. In the view's constructor, create bitmaps as follows. As you can see, what I'm doing is creating each bitmap and specifying the bitmap count on each bitmap. The values I'm using are defined in the nBits structure. The last bitmap in the array is then loaded from the resource you just added to the project. As a result of the bitmap count specified, only three of the seven bitmaps in this example will successfully draw to the screen. The first two are the monochrome (1-bit) bitmaps, because they display in all video configurations. The third is the bitmap whose bitmap count matches the number of bits you have defined in your Windows settings. (You can view this by right-clicking the desktop, selecting the Properties menu option, and then clicking the Settings tab. The number of colors for your current configuration are displayed in the combo box on the left of the dialog box.) The third and final bitmap to display will be the last bitmap because it was placed in the array via a call to LoadBitmap. Therefore, it was automatically initialized according to your system color settings. The remaining four bitmaps won't draw because they don't match your system's video configuration. (Note that the first two bitmaps simply display as black rectangles because the first six bitmaps in the array were created as blank bitmaps. However, the point here is to observe which bitmaps display with what bit count settings.

   ```
   CDisplayBitmapsView::CDisplayBitmapsView()
   {
     static int nBits[] = {1, 4, 8, 16, 24, 32};
     for (int i=0; i < 6; i++)
     {
       m_Bitmaps[i].CreateBitmap(54, 64, 1, nBits[i], NULL);
     }
     m_Bitmaps[6].LoadBitmap(IDB_BITMAP1);
   }
   ```

5. Now update the view's OnDraw function as follows. Here you're first allocating a BITMAP structure. (This structure's members are defined in the section entitled "Creating CBitmap Objects.") After that, you're using the TextOut function you learned about

in Chapter 8 to output a heading to the view. After that, a simple `for` loop is used iterate each of the bitmaps (`m_Bitmaps`). You then query each bitmap as to its bit count so that you can see on the view which bitmap was correctly displayed. After that, you print out the bit count for the current bitmap and call the `BitBlt` function to display the actual bitmap.

```
void CDisplayBitmapsView::OnDraw(CDC* pDC)
{
 CDisplayBitmapsDoc* pDoc = GetDocument();
 ASSERT_VALID(pDoc);

 CString strBits;

 BITMAP* pBitmapInfo = new BITMAP;
 pDC->TextOut(100, 5, "Number of bits per bitmap");
 for (int i = 0; i < 7; i++)
 {
  CDC MemDC;
  CBitmap *pOldBitmap;
  MemDC.CreateCompatibleDC(pDC);
  pOldBitmap = MemDC.SelectObject(&m_Bitmaps[i]);

  int iSuccess = m_Bitmaps[i].GetBitmap(pBitmapInfo);
  ASSERT(iSuccess);
  if (iSuccess)
  {
   strBits.Format("%ld", pBitmapInfo->bmBitsPixel);
   pDC->TextOut((20 + i * 50)
                 + (pBitmapInfo->bmWidth / 2),
               20, strBits);

   pDC->BitBlt(20 + i * 50, 50,
               54, 64,
               &MemDC,
               0, 0,
               SRCCOPY);
   MemDC.SelectObject(pOldBitmap);
  }
 }
 delete pBitmapInfo;
}
```

6. If you build and run this application, you should see result similar to those shown in Figure 9-1, where I'm running in 32-color mode.

At times it's necessary to copy video memory into a bitmap. Because `BitBlt` doesn't care what the source and destination are as long as it gets two valid device contexts, it couldn't be easier. All you have to do in order to copy from the screen to a bitmap is reverse the roles of the two device contexts.

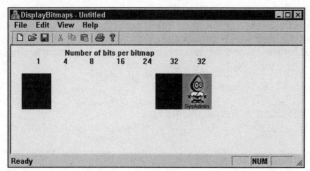

Figure 9-1: The bit count specified when creating a bitmap image needs to coincide with the number of colors defined for the current Windows environment in order for the bitmap to display.

For instance, the previous examples all used the pDC device context pointer as the destination, and the function call was structured as pDC->BitBlt. In order to specify the second device context, the address of MemDC was passed in as a function argument to BitBlt. The destination is MemDC and the function call is structured MemDC.BitBlt. The pDC pointer is passed in as an argument to BitBlt so that it knows what the second device context is from which the source will be obtained. An example follows that uses a function named GetImage that copies from the screen into a bitmap:

```
void GetImage(int x, int y, CDC *pDC, CBitmap *pBitmap)
{

  BITMAP bm;
  pBitmap->GetObject(sizeof(BITMAP), &bm);

  CDC MemDC;
  MemDC.CreateCompatibleDC(pDC);

  CBitmap *pOldBitmap = MemDC.SelectObject(pBitmap);
  MemDC.BitBlt(0, 0, bm.bmWidth, bm.bmHeight, pDC,
   x, y, SRCCOPY);
  MemDC.SelectObject(pOldBitmap);

}
```

Raster Operations

The last argument in the BitBlt function determines how the source combines with the destination. Most of the time, though, you want to copy a bitmap to the screen to have it appear exactly as it does in the bitmap data. At other times, a simple data copy won't do. One example of this is when you want to draw a bitmap to the screen allowing a transparent color to be masked out. The transparent color, when it appears in the source bitmap, would be rejected. Whatever color is in the destination at any pixel location in which the source contains the transparent color would remain unchanged.

This masking technique must be carried out with two separate BitBlt calls. The first part of the process creates a mask based on the source bitmap. It finds the transparent pixels and is created based on them. It then masks the destination in such a way as to eliminate all destination pixels into which the nontransparent source pixels will be drawn. The same mask is then used to mask the source and remove the unwanted transparent-color pixels. The source is then ORed (or XORed) into the destination. The original bitmap must then be restored to its original state; otherwise, the transparent color will no longer exist, and the pair of transparent operations won't work correctly.

A faster way to accomplish this double-masking process is to create a mask ahead of time. That way it doesn't have to be created every time you want to go through the process. If execution time is important, seriously consider this option. The BlitDemo program uses such preformed masks when it draws the fly images. Taking a good look at this demo program will give you a good idea of how it's done.

Another example in which you might want to use another raster operation is in animations. A common technique for moving bitmaps around on the screen is to XOR them before moving them to a new location. XORing one image over itself completely removes it. That's because when you first draw the image to the screen using an XOR raster operation, the image source combines with the destination. Anywhere the source has a bit that's set, XOR toggles the corresponding bit in the destination to its opposite value. For instance, if the source bit is set (a one) and the destination bit is not set (a zero), the result is a one. If the animation must be moved, XORing the same bitmap in the same location toggles those same bits to their previous values, once again restoring them to their original state. The bitmap can then be drawn in a new location using an XOR raster operation. Table 9-1 defines the raster operation codes.

Table 9-1: Raster Operations and Their Definitions

Raster Operation Code	Definition
BLACKNESS	Turns all output black.
DSTINVERT	Inverts the destination bitmap.
MERGECOPY	Combines the pattern and the source bitmap using the Boolean AND operator.
MERGEPAINT	Combines the inverted source bitmap with the destination bitmap using the Boolean OR operator.
NOTSRCCOPY	Copies the inverted source bitmap to the destination.
NOTSRCERASE	Inverts the result of combining the destination and source bitmaps using the Boolean OR operator.
PATCOPY	Copies the pattern to the destination bitmap.
PATINVERT	Combines the destination bitmap with the pattern using the Boolean XOR operator.
PATPAINT	Combines the inverted source bitmap with the pattern using the Boolean OR operator. Combines the result of this operation with the destination bitmap using the Boolean OR operator.

Continued

Table 9-1: *(continued)*

Raster Operation Code	Definition
SRCAND	Combines pixels of the destination and source bitmaps using the Boolean AND operator.
SRCCOPY	Copies the source bitmap to the destination bitmap.
SRCERASE	Inverts the destination bitmap and combines the result with the source bitmap using the Boolean AND operator.
SRCINVERT	Combines pixels of the destination and source bitmaps using the Boolean XOR operator.
SRCPAINT	Combines pixels of the destination and source bitmaps using the Boolean OR operator.
WHITENESS	Turns all output white.

If you need a function that draws a bitmap to the screen and masks a single transparent color, the DrawTransparent function shown here will come in handy. You can add it to your program or, better yet, derive a class from CBitmap that you can always use.

```
void DrawTransparent(int x, int y, CDC *pDC,
  CBitmap *pBitmap, COLORREF Color)
{
BITMAP bm;
pBitmap->GetObject(sizeof(BITMAP), &bm);

CDC ImageDC;
ImageDC.CreateCompatibleDC(pDC);
CBitmap *pOldImageBitmap =
  ImageDC.SelectObject(pBitmap);

CDC MaskDC;
MaskDC.CreateCompatibleDC(pDC);

CBitmap MaskBitmap;
MaskBitmap.CreateBitmap(bm.bmWidth, bm.bmHeight,
  1, 1, NULL);
CBitmap *pOldMaskBitmap =
  MaskDC.SelectObject(&MaskBitmap);

ImageDC.SetBkColor(Color);
MaskDC.BitBlt(0, 0, bm.bmWidth, bm.bmHeight,
  &ImageDC, 0, 0, SRCCOPY);

CDC OrDC;
OrDC.CreateCompatibleDC(pDC);

CBitmap OrBitmap;
```

```
OrBitmap.CreateCompatibleBitmap(&ImageDC,
   bm.bmWidth, bm.bmHeight);
CBitmap *pOldOrBitmap = OrDC.SelectObject(&OrBitmap);

OrDC.BitBlt(0, 0, bm.bmWidth, bm.bmHeight,
   &ImageDC, 0, 0, SRCCOPY);
OrDC.BitBlt(0, 0, bm.bmWidth, bm.bmHeight,
   &MaskDC, 0, 0, 0x220326);

CDC TempDC;
TempDC.CreateCompatibleDC(pDC);

CBitmap TempBitmap;
TempBitmap.CreateCompatibleBitmap(&ImageDC,
   bm.bmWidth, bm.bmHeight);
CBitmap *pOldTempBitmap =
   TempDC.SelectObject(&TempBitmap);

TempDC.BitBlt(0, 0, bm.bmWidth, bm.bmHeight,
   pDC, x, y, SRCCOPY);
TempDC.BitBlt(0, 0, bm.bmWidth, bm.bmHeight,
   &MaskDC, 0, 0, SRCAND);
TempDC.BitBlt(0, 0, bm.bmWidth, bm.bmHeight,
   &OrDC, 0, 0, SRCPAINT);

pDC->BitBlt(x, y, bm.bmWidth, bm.bmHeight,
   &TempDC, 0, 0, SRCCOPY);

TempDC.SelectObject(pOldTempBitmap);
OrDC.SelectObject(pOldOrBitmap);
MaskDC.SelectObject(pOldMaskBitmap);
ImageDC.SelectObject(pOldImageBitmap);

}
```

The BlitDemo Program

The BlitDemo program that's included on the book's Web site shows you how to perform common operations using CBitmap objects. The actual bitmaps are contained as resource objects and are loaded using the LoadBitmap member function.

The program begins by displaying one of the trolley images as shown in Figure 9-2. Clicking the left mouse button with the mouse pointer in the client window displays the next image in the sequence. After the third image has been displayed, the initial image is drawn.

You can use the Operations menu to select one of four different image sequences. The second is a set of four images that show a man on an old-fashioned railroad trolley. The third and fourth image sequences use a set of flies. When the left mouse button is clicked, the fly moves vertically on the screen as if it's flying.

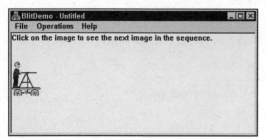

Figure 9-2: The BlitDemo program begins by showing the first of the three bitmaps.

The flies are drawn in two different ways according to your menu selection. The third menu selection causes the flies to be drawn with a combination of an AND operation and an OR operation. There's a mask image for each fly that's loaded at the start of the program. These are used for the AND operation.

The fourth menu selection causes the flies to move across the screen with an XOR operation. You'll notice that the resultant color of the fly depends on the color of the client window. The code shown in Listing 9-1 provides highlights of the BlitDemoView.cpp program:

Listing 9-1: **Highlights of the BlitDemoView.cpp Source Code**

```
// BlitDemoView.cpp:implementation of CBlitDemoView class
//
////////////////////////////////////////////////////////////
// CBlitDemoView construction/destruction

CBlitDemoView::CBlitDemoView()
{

  // Start the program showing bubbles.
  m_nOperation = OPERATION_TROLLEY;

  // Initialize our indexes to the fly,
  // bubble, and trolley.
  m_nCurrentFly = 2;
  m_nCurrentBubble = 0;
  m_nCurrentTrolley = 0;

  // Set the fly's position.
  m_nFlyX = 20;
  m_nFlyY = 10;

  static int nBubble[] = {
  IDB_BUBBLE1, IDB_BUBBLE2, IDB_BUBBLE3 };

  static int nFly[] = {
```

```
    IDB_FLY1, IDB_FLY2, IDB_FLY3, IDB_FLY4 };

    static int nFlyMask[] = {
    IDB_FLYMASK1, IDB_FLYMASK2,
    IDB_FLYMASK3, IDB_FLYMASK4 };

    static int nTrolley[] = {
    IDB_TROLLEY1, IDB_TROLLEY2,
    IDB_TROLLEY3, IDB_TROLLEY4 };

    // Load in the bitmaps using LoadBitmap().
    for(int i=0; i<4; i++){
     if(i < 3)
      m_Bubble[i].LoadBitmap(nBubble[i]);
     m_Fly[i].LoadBitmap(nFly[i]);
     m_FlyMask[i].LoadBitmap(nFlyMask[i]);
     m_Trolley[i].LoadBitmap(nTrolley[i]);
     }

}

CBlitDemoView::~CBlitDemoView()
{
}
//////////////////////////////////////////////////////////
// CBlitDemoView drawing

void CBlitDemoView::OnDraw(CDC* pDC)
{
 CBlitDemoDoc* pDoc = GetDocument();
 ASSERT_VALID(pDoc);

 // When a redraw message comes, just
 // call DrawBitmaps()
 DrawBitmaps(pDC);

}

void CBlitDemoView::DrawBitmaps(CDC *pDC)
{

 // Create a DC into which the bitmap
 // will be selected.
 CDC MemDC;
 MemDC.CreateCompatibleDC(pDC);
 CBitmap *pOldBitmap;

 BITMAP bm;

 pDC->TextOut(0, 0, "Click on the image to see the "
```

Continued

Listing 9-1 *(continued)*

```
                    "next image in the sequence.");
 switch (m_nOperation)
 {
  case OPERATION_BUBBLES:

   // Select the appropriate bitmap into
   // the DC.
   pOldBitmap =
    (CBitmap *) MemDC.SelectObject(
     &m_Bubble[m_nCurrentBubble]);

   // We need the width and height of the
   // bitmap for the BitBlt() function.
   m_Bubble[m_nCurrentBubble].GetObject(
    sizeof(BITMAP), &bm);

   // Perform the BitBlt() function to the destination
   // coordinates 0, 0.
   pDC->BitBlt(0, 50, bm.bmWidth, bm.bmHeight, &MemDC,
    0, 0, SRCCOPY);

   break;

  case OPERATION_TROLLEY:

   // Select the appropriate bitmap into
   // the DC.
   pOldBitmap =
    (CBitmap *) MemDC.SelectObject(
     &m_Trolley[m_nCurrentTrolley]);

   // We need the width and height of the
   // bitmap for the BitBlt() function.
   m_Trolley[m_nCurrentTrolley].GetObject(
    sizeof(BITMAP), &bm);

   // Perform the BitBlt() function to the destination
   // coordinates 0, 0.
   pDC->BitBlt(0, 50, bm.bmWidth, bm.bmHeight, &MemDC,
    0, 0, SRCCOPY);

   break;

  case OPERATION_XORFLY:

   // Select the appropriate bitmap into
   // the DC.
   pOldBitmap =
    (CBitmap *) MemDC.SelectObject(
```

```
      &m_Fly[m_nCurrentFly]);

   // We need the width and height of the
   // bitmap for the BitBlt() function.
   m_Fly[m_nCurrentFly].GetObject(
    sizeof(BITMAP), &bm);

   // Perform the BitBlt() function to the destination
   // coordinates calculated by using m_nFlyX and m_nFlyY
   // as the center of the object. The width and height
   // of the bitmap are then used to draw the object
   // centered on m_nFlyX and m_nFlyY.
   pDC->BitBlt(m_nFlyX - (bm.bmWidth / 2), m_nFlyY + 50,
    bm.bmWidth, bm.bmHeight, &MemDC,
    0, 0, SRCINVERT);

   break;

 case OPERATION_MASKFLY:

   // Select the appropriate bitmap into
   // the DC.
   pOldBitmap =
    (CBitmap *) MemDC.SelectObject(
     &m_FlyMask[m_nCurrentFly]);

   // We need the width and height of the
   // bitmap for the BitBlt() function.
   m_FlyMask[m_nCurrentFly].GetObject(
    sizeof(BITMAP), &bm);

   pDC->BitBlt(m_nFlyX - (bm.bmWidth / 2), m_nFlyY + 50,
    bm.bmWidth, bm.bmHeight, &MemDC,
    0, 0, SRCAND);

   MemDC.SelectObject(&m_Fly[m_nCurrentFly]);

   // Perform the BitBlt() function to the destination
   // coordinates calculated by using m_nFlyX and m_nFlyY
   // as the center of the object. The width and height
   // of the bitmap are then used to draw the object
   // centered on m_nFlyX and m_nFlyY.
   pDC->BitBlt(m_nFlyX - (bm.bmWidth / 2), m_nFlyY,
    bm.bmWidth, bm.bmHeight, &MemDC,
    0, 0, SRCINVERT);

   break;
  }

// Select the old bitmap back
```

Continued

Listing 9-1 *(continued)*

```
// into the DC.
MemDC.SelectObject(pOldBitmap);
}


/////////////////////////////////////////////////////////
// CBlitDemoView message handlers

void CBlitDemoView::OnLButtonDown(UINT nFlags,
CPoint point)
{

  CClientDC ClientDC(this);

  switch(m_nOperation){
   case OPERATION_BUBBLES:
    // Increment to next bubble.
    m_nCurrentBubble++;
    // Make sure the bubble value is in range.
    if(m_nCurrentBubble >= 3)
     m_nCurrentBubble = 0;
    break;
   case OPERATION_TROLLEY:
    // Increment to next trolley.
    m_nCurrentTrolley++;
    // Make sure the trolley value is in range.
    if(m_nCurrentTrolley >= 4)
     m_nCurrentTrolley = 0;
    break;
   case OPERATION_XORFLY:
    // XORFLY uses the same movement calculations
    // as MASKFLY. The only difference is that
    // to erase the previous image, XORFLY
    // calls DrawBitmaps() and MASKFLY draws
    // a rectangle.
    DrawBitmaps(&ClientDC);
   case OPERATION_MASKFLY:
    if(m_nOperation == OPERATION_MASKFLY){
     // Get the bitmap size so that we
     // can calculate the rectangle that
     // we must draw to erase the fly.
     BITMAP bm;
     m_FlyMask[m_nCurrentFly].GetObject(
      sizeof(BITMAP), &bm);
     RECT Rect;
     Rect.left = m_nFlyX - (bm.bmWidth / 2);
     Rect.top = m_nFlyY;
     Rect.right = Rect.left + bm.bmWidth;
     Rect.bottom = Rect.top + bm.bmHeight;
     // Create a brush that's the same as the
```

```
       // window color and then draw a rectangle.
       CBrush Brush(GetSysColor(COLOR_WINDOW));
       ClientDC.FillRect(&Rect, &Brush);
       }
     // We're toggling between 2 and 3 going down
     // and 0 and 1 going up. We can use ^ 1 to
     // accomplish this. If the fly moves past a
     // threshold point, we reverse the direction.
     m_nCurrentFly ^= 1;
     if(m_nCurrentFly >= 2){
      m_nFlyY += 10;
      if(m_nFlyY > 300)
       m_nCurrentFly -= 2;
      }
     else{
      m_nFlyY -= 10;
      if(m_nFlyY <= 10)
       m_nCurrentFly += 2;
      }
     break;
   }
  DrawBitmaps(&ClientDC);

  CView::OnLButtonDown(nFlags, point);
 }

void CBlitDemoView::OnOperationsMaskfly()
{

  // Set the operation to OPERATION_MASKFLY.
  m_nOperation = OPERATION_MASKFLY;
  // Invalidate the client window and force
  // an immediate redraw.
  InvalidateRect(NULL, TRUE);
  UpdateWindow();

}

void CBlitDemoView::OnOperationsShowbubbles()
{

  // Set the operation to OPERATION_BUBBLES.
  m_nOperation = OPERATION_BUBBLES;
  // Invalidate the client window and force
  // an immediate redraw.
  InvalidateRect(NULL, TRUE);
  UpdateWindow();

}

void CBlitDemoView::OnOperationsShowtrolley()
```

Continued

Listing 9-1 *(continued)*

```
{

    // Set the operation to OPERATION_TROLLEY.
    m_nOperation = OPERATION_TROLLEY;
    // Invalidate the client window and force
    // an immediate redraw.
InvalidateRect(NULL, TRUE);
    UpdateWindow();

}

void CBlitDemoView::OnOperationsXorfly()
{

    // Set the operation to OPERATION_XORFLY.
    m_nOperation = OPERATION_XORFLY;
    // Invalidate the client window and force
    // an immediate redraw.
    InvalidateRect(NULL, TRUE);
    UpdateWindow();

}
```

Palettes and Color

The color on IBM-compatible video systems is represented using RGB triplets. Each of the RGB triplets contains a value for the red, green, and blue components of a color. The combination of the three component values determines the color that's seen on the screen.

RGB is a common color space (or color definition). The colors red, green, and blue are considered fundamental and undecomposible. Color systems can be separated into two categories: *additive* color systems and *subtractive* color systems. Colors in additive systems, such as the RGB system, are created by adding colors to black to create new colors. The more color that's added, the more the resulting color tends toward white. The presence of all the primary colors in sufficient amounts creates pure white, whereas the absence of all the primary colors leaves pure black. Colors in subtractive color systems work by reflecting complimentary colors when illuminated; as a result, printers and photographers use subtractive color systems, like CMY, to render colors using an emulsion of ink.

I use the common RGB macro in this section to describe RGB triplets. The RGB macro converts three byte values ranging from 0 to 255 into a COLORREF value. The macro's first argument is the red value, the second green, and the third blue. Values range from 0 to 255. For instance, an RGB value with a red component of 244, a green component of 142, and a blue component of 34 can be notated as RGB(244, 142, 34). Table 9-2 lists some of the common colors found in the default Windows palette.

Table 9-2: RGB Colors in the Default Windows Palette

RGB Values	Color
RGB(0, 0, 0)	Black
RGB(255, 255, 255)	White
RGB(255, 0, 0)	Red
RGB(0, 255, 0)	Green
RGB(0, 0, 255)	Blue
RGB(255, 255, 0)	Yellow
RGB(255, 0, 255)	Magenta
RGB(0, 255, 255)	Cyan
RGB(128, 128, 128)	Dark Gray
RGB(192, 192, 192)	Light Gray

Additional color spaces

Aside from the standard RGB color space, there are two additional color spaces that you might encounter as your exposure to GDI programming increases. These are the CMY and HSV color spaces, and I'll take just a bit of time to talk about them now.

The CMY color space

CMY (cyan, magenta, and yellow) is a subtractive color system used by printers and photographers for the rendering of colors with an emulsion of ink, normally on a white surface. Most hard copy devices that deposit color pigments on white paper, such as laser and ink jet printers, use it. When illuminated, each of the three colors absorbs its complementary light color. Cyan absorbs red, magenta absorbs green, and yellow absorbs blue. By increasing the amount of yellow ink, for instance, the amount of blue in the image is decreased.

The CMY system colors, as in all subtractive systems, are subtracted from white light by pigments to create new colors. The new colors are the wavelengths of light reflected, rather than absorbed, by the CMY pigments. For example, when cyan and magenta are absorbed, the resulting color is yellow. The yellow pigment is said to subtract the cyan and magenta components from the reflected light. When all of the CMY components are subtracted, or absorbed, the resulting color is black.

It is, however, difficult to achieve a good black color in CMY space. A variant of CMY, known as CMYK, has been spawned. CMYK color has a separate component for the color black.

You can calculate a CMY value from an RGB value. To calculate cyan, subtract the RGB red value from 255; for magenta, subtract the RGB green value from 255; and for yellow, subtract the RGB blue from 255. For instance, RGB (240, 12, 135) has equivalent CMY values of 15, 243, and 120.

The HSV color space

HSV, or Hue, Saturation, and Value, color space is one of many color systems that vary the degree of properties of colors to create new colors, rather than using a mixture of the colors themselves. Hue specifies color in the common use of the term, such as red, orange, blue, and so on. Saturation (also called *chroma*) refers to the amount of white in a hue: A fully saturated hue contains no white and appears pure. By extension, a partly saturated hue appears lighter in color because of the admixture of white. Red hue with 50 percent saturation appears pink, for instance. Value (also called *brightness*) is the degree of self-luminescence of a color — that is, how much light it emits. A hue with high intensity is very bright, whereas a hue with low intensity is dark.

HSV most closely resembles the color system used by painters and other artists who create colors by adding white, black, and gray to pure pigments to create tints, shades, and tones. A tint is a pure, fully saturated color combined with white, and a shade is a fully saturated color combined with black. A tone is a fully saturated color with both black and white added to it. Relating HSV to this color mixing, saturation is the amount of white, value is the amount of black, and hue is the color that the black and white are added to.

You can convert a color from RGB space to HSV space with the following function, which you can find in a file named HSV.c on this book's Web site:

```c
#define mid(a, b, c) \
  (a >= b && a <= c ? \
  a : (b >= a && b <= c ? b : c))

void RGB2HSV(int nRed, int nGreen, int nBlue,
  int *nH, int *nS, int *nV)
{
  int nLow, nMid, nHigh;

  if(nRed == nGreen &&
    nGreen == nBlue){
    *nH = 0;
    *nS = 0;
    *nV = nRed;
    return;
  }

  nLow = min(nRed, min(nGreen, nBlue));
  nHigh = max(nRed, max(nGreen, nBlue));
  nMid = mid(nRed, nGreen, nBlue);

  *nV = (nLow + nHigh) / 2;
  *nS = nHigh - nLow;

  int nCommon = (int)
    (60.0 * (double) (nMid - nLow) /

    (double) (nHigh - nLow));

  if(nRed == nLow && nBlue == nHigh)
```

```
    *nH = 240 - nCommon;
  else if(nRed == nLow && nGreen == nHigh)
    *nH = 120 + nCommon;
  else if(nGreen == nLow && nRed == nHigh)
    *nH = 360 - nCommon;
  else if(nGreen == nLow && nBlue == nHigh)
    *nH = 240 - nCommon;
  else if(nBlue == nLow && nGreen == nHigh)
    *nH = 120 - nCommon;
  else if(nBlue == nLow && nRed == nHigh)
    *nH = nCommon;
}
```

Logical palettes

Video systems that are set for 16-, 24-, and 32-bit display determine how individual pixels appear on the screen by storing RGB values into video memory. Video systems that are set for 8-bit display and less operate in a more indirect way, and many times are referred to as *palettized devices*. Images that contain data of depths that are 8 bits or less are referred to as *palettized images*.

Palettized video memory doesn't contain the actual RGB data with which a pixel is rendered. Instead, it contains an index into a table of 256 RGB values. This table resides in a section of video memory known as the Digital Adapter Color (DAC). You can't directly set the DAC table yourself from Windows because it's a shared resource. Instead, you must use GDI to set the hardware palette stored in the DAC.

The GDI palette manager performs many roles as arbitrator of the hardware palette. One important thing it does is it maintains 20 colors (known as *static colors*) with which Windows draws common items such as dialog objects and icons. You can force GDI to override the 20 static colors, but it's not a good idea. More about this subject is provided later in this chapter.

The palette manager prevents duplicate entries from getting into the hardware palette. Duplicate palette entries would diminish the effectiveness of your application if it had to display images in an optimal way. This feature is very valuable for palettized display systems. As with the palette manager's enforcement of the 20 static colors, the rule against duplicate colors can be overridden. This chapter describes later how you can do this.

You can create a logical palette with a LOGPALETTE structure. Within the LOGPALETTE structure is a list of PALETTEENTRY structures. The PALETTEENTRY list contains the RGB values with which Windows can set the hardware palette. The number of PALETTEENTRY structures that can be in the list ranges from 1 to 256. If your video system supports more than 256 palette entries, your logical palette can be more. The real limit to the size of palette entries is the size of your hardware's palette. Most of the time this will be 256. The LOGPALETTE structure definition follows:

```
typedef struct tagLOGPALETTE{
  WORD palVersion;
  WORD palNumEntries;
  PALETTEENTRY palPalEntry[1];
} LOGPALETTE;
```

The palVersion member specifies the LOGPALETTE version. In all current releases of Windows, this value should be 0x300. The palNumEntries member contains the number of palette entries that you can find in the PALETTEENTRY list. The PALETTEENTRY structure definition is as follows:

```
typedef struct tagPALETTEENTRY{
  BYTE peRed;
  BYTE peGreen;
  BYTE peBlue;
  BYTE peFlags;
} PALETTEENTRY;
```

The peRed, peGreen, and peBlue members contain the RGB values. The peFlags member contains a value of one or more flags describing the type of palette entry. Table 9-3 shows these flags.

Table 9-3: Palette Entry Flags

Flag	Description
PC_EXPLICIT	Creates a palette entry that specifies an index into the system palette rather than an RGB color. Used by programs that display the contents of a system palette.
PC_NOCOLLAPSE	Creates a palette entry that's mapped to an unused entry in the system palette even if an entry for that color already exists. Used to ensure the uniqueness of palette colors when two entries map to the same color.
PC_RESERVED	Creates a palette entry that's private to this application. When a PC_RESERVED entry is added to the system palette, it isn't mapped to colors in other logical palettes even if the colors match. Used by programs that perform palette animation.

Here's how you'd create a logical palette with 16 colors in which the RGB colors are calculated based on the loop counter:

```
LOGPALETTE *pLogPal;
pLogPal = (LOGPALETTE *)
 new char [sizeof(LOGPALETTE)+16*sizeof(PALETTEENTRY)];

pLogPal->palVersion = 0x300;
pLogPal->palNumEntries = 16;

for(int i=0; i<16; i++){
 pLogPal->palPalEntry[i].peRed =
  (unsigned char) (i * 16);
 pLogPal->palPalEntry[i].peGreen =
  (unsigned char) (i * 12);
 pLogPal->palPalEntry[i].peBlue =
  (unsigned char) (i * 8);
 pLogPal->palPalEntry[i].peFlags = 0;
}
```

You can use a LOGPALETTE in conjunction with Windows API functions to set the palette. It's better, though, to use the MFC CPalette class. This class makes it more convenient to perform palette operations because the CDC class that wraps the GDI API expects a CPalette object. If you don't use a CPalette class, the CDC class won't be of any use when you set the palette.

Once you have a LOGPALETTE, creating a CPalette object couldn't be easier. The following code takes the LOGPALETTE (named pLogPal) created in the last code fragment and creates a CPalette object with it. Once the CPalette object is created, the LOGPALETTE memory can be deleted.

```
CPalette Palette;
Palette.CreatePalette(pLogPal);
delete [] pLogPal;
```

Once you've created a CPalette object, you must select the palette into the device context and then *realize* it. Realizing a palette occurs when Windows actually copies the palette into the hardware registers. As with most GDI objects, the old object must be selected back into the device context after you're done. Following is code in an OnDraw function that takes the CPalette object created in the last code fragment and uses it to set the Windows palette:

```
CPalette *pOldPalette;
pOldPalette = pDC->SelectPalette(&Palette, FALSE);
pDC->RealizePalette();
pDC->SelectPalette(pOldPalette, FALSE);
```

You can create a CPalette object that contains a generic and fairly uniform distribution of colors. These palettes are known as *halftone palettes*, and can be created with the CreateHalftonePalette function. Following is an example of creating such a CPalette object:

```
CPalette Palette;
Palette.CreateHalftonePalette(pDC);
```

If you pass an argument of NULL to the CreateHalftonePalette function, a 256-color halftone palette is created that's independent of the output device.

Palette events

When you write an application that sets the palette, be aware that other applications may receive the focus and set the palette differently. If this happens, your graphics may not look like what you expect when your application gets the focus back. For this reason, you must add some event handlers so that you can restore the palette when it's appropriate.

The WM_QUERYNEWPALETTE message is sent to an application's top-level window (usually a CMainFrame object for AppWizard-created applications) when a palette realization causes a change in the system palette. Palette realization causes Windows to send the palette data that resides in the selected palette to the video hardware effecting a change. The WM_PALETTECHANGED message is sent to the top-level window when it receives the focus. For multiple document interface applications that maintain different palettes, each child window should look for a WM_GETFOCUS message so that the child window can set its own palette.

The following example assumes that a CPalette object named m_Palette has already been created. It shows how a WM_QUERYNEWPALETTE message should be handled.

```
BOOL CMainFrame::OnQueryNewPalette()
{

 CClientDC ClientDC(this);
 CPalette *pOldPalette =
  ClientDC.SelectPalette(&m_Palette, FALSE);

 if(ClientDC.RealizePalette() > 0)
  Invalidate();

 ClientDC.SelectPalette(pOldPalette, FALSE);

}
BOOL CMainFrame::OnPaletteChanged(CWnd *pFocusWnd)
{

 if(pFocusWnd != this){

  CClientDC ClientDC(this);
  CPalette *pOldPalette =
   ClientDC.SelectPalette(&m_Palette, FALSE);

  if(ClientDC.RealizePalette() > 0)
   Invalidate();

  ClientDC.SelectPalette(pOldPalette, FALSE);
 }

}
```

The SetSystemPaletteUse function

At times you may want access to the entire system palette, including the 20 static colors. If you find yourself in this situation, you can use the SetSystemPaletteUse function to change the number of static colors Windows reserves for itself. The following code reduces the number of static colors to two: one for white and one for black:

```
CClientDC ClientDC(this);
SetSystemPalette(ClientDC.m_hDC, SYSPAL_NOSTATIC);
```

Device-Independent Bitmaps

One of the biggest drawbacks to device-dependent bitmaps is the inability to draw to device contexts with different pixel depths. This problem can be overcome by using a DIB. Unfortunately, DIBs aren't wrapped by any MFC classes. This creates extra work for developers because they must write load, save, draw, manipulation, and support code into their application.

To overcome the lack of a DIB class, this section creates a class named `CDib` that conveniently wraps a DIB. A demo program that uses the class comes next and shows how easy it is to load and display DIBs in programs using the `CDib` class.

The anatomy of a DIB file

Files containing DIBs always start with a `BITMAPFILEHEADER` data structure. This structure doesn't contain much useful information except the size of the file and the offset of the actual DIB data within the file. The *offset* refers to the number of bytes from the beginning of the file at which the actual image data (as opposed to header information) is located. The first two bytes contain a signature of "BM" that can be useful for an initial validity check. (The "BM" signature must be referred to as "MB" because of the way Intel processors swap bytes.) The `BITMAPFILEHEADER` structure follows:

```
typedef struct tagBITMAPFILEHEADER {
  WORD bfType;
  DWORD bfSize;
  WORD bfReserved1;
  WORD bfReserved2;
  DWORD bfOffBits;
} BITMAPFILEHEADER;
```

The `bfType` member is always set to "BM" to indicate that it's a bitmap file. The `bfSize` member contains a value equal to the file size. The reserved members aren't used and should be zero. The `bfOffBits` member contains the offset from the beginning of the file to the actual image date.

The next thing that comes in a DIB file is a `BITMAPINFOHEADER` data structure. In this structure resides essential information about the DIB. It contains such things as width, height, and color depth. The `BITMAPINFOHEADER` structure follows:

```
typedef struct tagBITMAPINFOHEADER{
  DWORD biSize;
  LONG biWidth;
  LONG biHeight;
  WORD biPlanes;
  WORD biBitCount
  DWORD biCompression;
  DWORD biSizeImage;
  LONG biXPelsPerMeter;
  LONG biYPelsPerMeter;
  DWORD biClrUsed;
  DWORD biClrImportant;
} BITMAPINFOHEADER;
```

The `biSize` field is simply the size of the `BITMAPINFOHEADER` structure. The `biWidth` and `biHeight` members refer to the image width and height. The `biPlanes` and `biBitCount` members describe the image color depth. The `biCompression` member is almost always zero but in rare cases may be a value that represents some sort of compression. The `biSizeImage` member contains the size of the image in bytes. The next two members, `biXPelsPerMeter` and `biYPelsPerMeter`, refer to the image resolution and are rarely used. The `biClrUsed` member is usually zero—the only exception is when the number of colors used is actually less than the maximum number of colors for the specified color depth. The `biClrImportant` member indicates how many of the colors are important — zero, which is typically used, means they're all important.

The last information in the file before the actual DIB data is the palette information. For DIBs with bit depths greater than 8, there is no palette data. For DIBs of 8 bits or less, the number of palette entries can be calculated by the following formula:

```
int nNumPaletteEntries =
  1 << BitmapInfoHeader.biBitCount;
```

DIBs can contain fewer palette entries than the maximum allowable. For instance, an 8-bit DIB has a maximum of 256 colors allowed. Applications that save DIBs may choose to save fewer than 256 palette entries in the disk file.

You can use the `BITMAPINFOHEADER` member `biClrUsed` to determine if a DIB has been saved with an explicit number of palette entries. If `biClrUsed` is zero, the DIB file contains the maximum number of palette entries for the DIB's color depth. If it's nonzero, the DIB file contains exactly the number of palette entries in `biClrUsed`. Palette entries are stored in an `RGBQUAD` structure. The format of the `RGBQUAD` structure follows:

```
typedef struct tagRGBQUAD {
  BYTE rgbBlue;
  BYTE rgbGreen;
  BYTE rgbRed;
  BYTE rgbReserved;
} RGBQUAD;
```

Finally, after the `BITMAPFILEHEADER`, the `BITMAPINFOHEADER`, and any palette entries, comes the DIB data. For 8-bit DIBs, each byte represents a pixel; for 16-bit DIBs, every two bytes represents a pixel; for 24-bit DIBs, every three bytes represents a pixel; and for 32-bit DIBs, every four bytes represents a pixel.

If you find yourself needing to calculate an offset into DIB data, heed this warning. To find the number of bytes of each line of a DIB, most programs would multiply the pixel width by the number of bytes per pixel. This may not give you accurate results because the number of bytes for each DIB line must be an even multiple of four. The following code calculates the byte width of a DIB:

```
int nWidthBytes = BitmapInfoHeader.biWidth;
if(BitmapInfoHeader.biBitCount == 16)
  nWidthBytes *= 2;
else if(BitmapInfoHeader.biBitCount == 24)
  nWidthBytes *= 3;
else if(BitmapInfoHeader.biBitCount == 32)
  nWidthBytes *= 4;
while((nWidthBytes & 3) != 0)
  nWidthBytes++;
```

The CDib class

The `CDib` class can save you time and help keep your program tidy. In this section, the class is described one function at a time.

Loading the DIB

The CDib::Load function takes a single argument of a char pointer, which points to a NULL-terminated ASCII string of the filename. If the function is successful, it returns TRUE. If for some reason it fails, it returns FALSE. If a DIB has already been loaded, the Load function deletes the old DIB if the new one is successfully loaded. Listing 9-2 shows the source code for the Load function:

Listing 9-2: **Source Code for the CDib::Load Function**

```
BOOL CDib::Load(const char *pszFilename)
{

  CFile cf;

  // Attempt to open the Dib file for reading.
  if(!cf.Open(pszFilename, CFile::modeRead))
    return(FALSE);

  // Get the size of the file and store
  // in a local variable. Subtract the
  // size of the BITMAPFILEHEADER structure
  // since we won't keep that in memory.
  DWORD dwDibSize;
  dwDibSize =
    cf.GetLength() - sizeof(BITMAPFILEHEADER);

  // Attempt to allocate the Dib memory.
  unsigned char *pDib;
  pDib = new unsigned char [dwDibSize];
  if(pDib == NULL)
    return(FALSE);

  BITMAPFILEHEADER BFH;

  // Read in the Dib header and data.
  try{

    // Did we read in the entire BITMAPFILEHEADER?
    if(cf.Read(&BFH, sizeof(BITMAPFILEHEADER))
      != sizeof(BITMAPFILEHEADER) ||

      // Is the type 'MB'?
      BFH.bfType != 'MB' ||

      // Did we read in the remaining data?
      cf.Read(pDib, dwDibSize) != dwDibSize){

      // Delete the memory if we had any
```

Continued

Listing 9-2 *(continued)*

```
      // errors and return FALSE.
      delete [] pDib;
      return(FALSE);
      }
  }

// If we catch an exception, delete the
// exception, the temporary Dib memory,
// and return FALSE.
catch(CFileException *e){
  e->Delete();
  delete [] pDib;
  return(FALSE);
  }

// If we got to this point, the Dib has been
// loaded. If a Dib was already loaded into
// this class, we must now delete it.
if(m_pDib != NULL)
  delete m_pDib;

// Store the local Dib data pointer and
// Dib size variables in the class member
// variables.
m_pDib = pDib;
m_dwDibSize = dwDibSize;

// Point our BITMAPINFOHEADER and RGBQUAD
// variables to the correct place in the Dib data.
m_pBIH = (BITMAPINFOHEADER *) m_pDib;
m_pPalette =
 (RGBQUAD *) &m_pDib[sizeof(BITMAPINFOHEADER)];

// Calculate the number of palette entries.
m_nPaletteEntries = 1 << m_pBIH->biBitCount;
if(m_pBIH->biBitCount > 8)
  m_nPaletteEntries = 0;
else if(m_pBIH->biClrUsed != 0)
  m_nPaletteEntries = m_pBIH->biClrUsed;

// Point m_pDibBits to the actual Dib bits data.
m_pDibBits =
  &m_pDib[sizeof(BITMAPINFOHEADER)+
    m_nPaletteEntries*sizeof(RGBQUAD)];

// If we have a valid palette, delete it.
if(m_Palette.GetSafeHandle() != NULL)
  m_Palette.DeleteObject();
// If there are palette entries, we'll need
```

```
// to create a LOGPALETTE then create the
// CPalette palette.
if(m_nPaletteEntries != 0){

  // Allocate the LOGPALETTE structure.
  LOGPALETTE *pLogPal = (LOGPALETTE *) new char
     [sizeof(LOGPALETTE)+
      m_nPaletteEntries*sizeof(PALETTEENTRY)];

  if(pLogPal != NULL){

    // Set the LOGPALETTE to version 0x300
    // and store the number of palette
    // entries.
    pLogPal->palVersion = 0x300;
    pLogPal->palNumEntries = m_nPaletteEntries;

    // Store the RGB values into each
    // PALETTEENTRY element.
    for(int i=0; i<m_nPaletteEntries; i++){
      pLogPal->palPalEntry[i].peRed =
        m_pPalette[i].rgbRed;
      pLogPal->palPalEntry[i].peGreen =
        m_pPalette[i].rgbGreen;
      pLogPal->palPalEntry[i].peBlue =
        m_pPalette[i].rgbBlue;
      }

    // Create the CPalette object and
    // delete the LOGPALETTE memory.
    m_Palette.CreatePalette(pLogPal);
    delete [] pLogPal;
    }
  }

  return(TRUE);

}
```

To use the Load function, just call it with a valid filename. If the function successfully loads a valid .bmp file, the function returns TRUE. If for some reason the function fails, it returns FALSE. An example of using the Load function follows:

```
CDib Dib;
BOOL bRet;
bRet = Dib.Load("C:\\Windows\\Clouds.bmp");
if(bRet)
 AfxMessageBox("The Load() function succeeded.");
else
 AfxMessageBox("The Load() function failed.");
```

Saving the DIB

You may find it necessary to save a DIB. This situation arises when you modify the DIB data and want to save it back to disk. The Save function takes the DIB data that's in the CDib memory and saves it to disk. The only argument it takes is a pointer to a filename. It returns TRUE if the save operation is successful, FALSE if it isn't. The source code for the CDib::Save function can be viewed in Listing 9-3:

Listing 9-3: Source Code for the CDib::Save Function

```cpp
BOOL CDib::Save(const char *pszFilename)
{

 // If we have no data, we can't save.
 if(m_pDib == NULL)
  return(FALSE);

 CFile cf;

 // Attempt to create the file.
 if(!cf.Open(pszFilename,
  CFile::modeCreate | CFile::modeWrite))
  return(FALSE);

 // Write the data.
 try{

  // First, create a BITMAPFILEHEADER
  // with the correct data.
  BITMAPFILEHEADER BFH;
  memset(&BFH, 0, sizeof(BITMAPFILEHEADER));
  BFH.bfType = 'MB';
  BFH.bfSize = sizeof(BITMAPFILEHEADER) + m_dwDibSize;
  BFH.bfOffBits = sizeof(BITMAPFILEHEADER) +
   sizeof(BITMAPINFOHEADER) +
   m_nPaletteEntries * sizeof(RGBQUAD);

  // Write the BITMAPFILEHEADER and the
  // Dib data.
  cf.Write(&BFH, sizeof(BITMAPFILEHEADER));
  cf.Write(m_pDib, m_dwDibSize);
  }
 // If we get an exception, delete the exception and
 // return FALSE.
 catch(CFileException *e){
  e->Delete();
  return(FALSE);
  }

 return(TRUE);

}
```

To use the Save function, just call it with a valid filename. A word of caution is in order. If a file exists with the same name as the one that's specified as an argument, that file will be overwritten by the newly created file. It might be a good idea to check for the existence of the file before saving. If the function successfully saves the .bmp file, the function returns TRUE. If for some reason the function fails, it returns FALSE. An example of using the Save function follows:

```
CDib Dib;
BOOL bRet;
bRet = Dib.Save("C:\\Windows\\NewClouds.bmp");
if(bRet)
 AfxMessageBox("The Save() function succeeded.");
else
 AfxMessageBox("The Save() function failed.");
```

Drawing the DIB

Of course, a CDib class isn't much good if you can't draw the DIB to the screen. An essential function for the class is one that draws the DIB to a device context. The Draw function does just this. It has one required parameter, a CDC pointer. The next two arguments, nX and nY (the *x* and *y* coordinates), are optional. If you don't specify the *x* and *y* coordinates, the DIB is drawn to 0, 0. The fourth and fifth arguments, nWidth and nHeight, are also optional. If you don't specify either of them, they default to the width and/or height of the DIB itself. Otherwise, the function takes the DIB data and stretches (or shrinks or both) the data so that it exactly fits the width and height that are specified. The code in Listing 9-4 illustrates how this drawing is done via the CDib::Draw function:

Listing 9-4: **Source Code for the CDib::Draw Function**

```
BOOL CDib::Draw(CDC *pDC, int nX, int nY, int nWidth,
 int nHeight)
{

 // If we have no data we can't draw.
 if(m_pDib == NULL)
  return(FALSE);

 // Check for the default values of -1
 // in the width and height arguments. If
 // we find -1 in either, we'll set them
 // to the value that's in the BITMAPINFOHEADER.
 if(nWidth == -1)
  nWidth = m_pBIH->biWidth;
 if(nHeight == -1)
  nHeight = m_pBIH->biHeight;

 // Use StretchDIBits to draw the Dib.
 StretchDIBits(pDC->m_hDC, nX, nY,
  nWidth, nHeight,
  0, 0,
```

Continued

Listing 9-4 *(continued)*

```
 m_pBIH->biWidth, m_pBIH->biHeight,
 m_pDibBits,
 (BITMAPINFO *) m_pBIH,
 BI_RGB, SRCCOPY);

return(TRUE);


}
```

To use the Draw function in its simplest form, just pass in a CDC pointer. The function returns TRUE if it is successful and FALSE if it is not. Following are three examples of using the CDib::Draw function. The first just passes a CDC pointer. The second passes a CDC pointer and x and y coordinates. The third passes a CDC pointer, x and y coordinates, and width and height values.

```
CDib Dib;
Dib.Load(C:\\Windows\\Clouds.bmp");

// Using a CDC only...
Dib.Draw(pDC);

// Using a CDC and Screen Coordinates:
Dib.Draw(pDC, 10, 25);

// Using a CDC, Screen Coordinates, and Width and Height:
Dib.Draw(pDC, 10, 25, 100, 150);
```

Setting the DIB palette

The last function you need in order to correctly draw the DIBs to the screen is one that sets the palette. For DIBs with pixel depths greater than 8, this function does nothing. For DIBs with pixel depths of 8 bits or less, the palette that is obtained from the DIB data becomes part of the CDib class's CPalette member. Listing 9-5 shows the source code for the SetPalette function:

Listing 9-5: Source Code for the SetPalette Function

```
BOOL CDib::SetPalette(CDC *pDC)
{

// If we have no data we
// won't want to set the palette.
if(m_pDib == NULL)
 return(FALSE);

// Check to see if we have a palette
```

```
// handle. For Dibs greater than 8 bits,
// this will be NULL.
if(m_Palette.GetSafeHandle() == NULL)
 return(TRUE);

// Select the palette, realize the palette,
// then finally restore the old palette.
CPalette *pOldPalette;
pOldPalette = pDC->SelectPalette(&m_Palette, FALSE);
pDC->RealizePalette();
pDC->SelectPalette(pOldPalette, FALSE);

return(TRUE);

}
```

The ShowDIB demo program

A demo program that shows you how to use the CDib class is included on this book's Web site. It's called ShowDIB, and it loads, displays, and saves DIBs. Because the CDib class does most of the work, the source code for the program is limited to the ShowDIBView.cpp source code file and is minimal. Figure 9-3 shows the program running with a DIB loaded.

Figure 9-3: The ShowDIB program enables you to load DIBs from a disk file and display them in the view window.

Now, here's the source code for the ShowDIB program:

```cpp
// ShowDIBView.cpp:implementation of CShowDIBView class
//

#include "stdafx.h"
#include "ShowDIB.h"

#include "ShoswDIBDoc.h"
#include "ShowDIBView.h"

#ifdef _DEBUG
#define new DEBUG_NEW
#undef THIS_FILE
static char THIS_FILE[] = __FILE__;
#endif

/////////////////////////////////////////////////////////////////
// CShowDIBView
IMPLEMENT_DYNCREATE(CShowDIBView, CView)

BEGIN_MESSAGE_MAP(CShowDIBView, CView)
 //{{AFX_MSG_MAP(CShowDIBView)
 ON_COMMAND(ID_FILE_OPEN, OnFileOpen)
 //}}AFX_MSG_MAP
END_MESSAGE_MAP()

/////////////////////////////////////////////////////////////////
// CShowDIBView construction/destruction

CShowDIBView::CShowDIBView()
{
}

CShowDIBView::~CShowDIBView()
{
}

BOOL CShowDIBView::PreCreateWindow(CREATESTRUCT& cs)
{
 return CView::PreCreateWindow(cs);
}

/////////////////////////////////////////////////////////////////
// CShowDIBView drawing

void CShowDIBView::OnDraw(CDC* pDC)
{
 CShowDIBDoc* pDoc = GetDocument();
```

```
    ASSERT_VALID(pDoc);

  RECT Rect;
  GetClientRect(&Rect);
  m_Dib.SetPalette(pDC);
  m_Dib.Draw(pDC, 0, 0,
   Rect.right, Rect.bottom);


}

/////////////////////////////////////////////////////////
// CShowDIBView diagnostics

#ifdef _DEBUG
void CShowDIBView::AssertValid() const
{
 CView::AssertValid();
}

void CShowDIBView::Dump(CDumpContext& dc) const
{
 CView::Dump(dc);
}

CShowDIBDoc* CShowDIBView::GetDocument()
 // nondebug version is inline
 {
 ASSERT(
  m_pDocument->IsKindOf(RUNTIME_CLASS(CShowDIBDoc)));
 return (CShowDIBDoc*)m_pDocument;
}
#endif //_DEBUG

/////////////////////////////////////////////////////////
// CShowDIBView message handlers

void CShowDIBView::OnFileOpen()
{
 static char szFilter[] = "BMP Files(*.BMP)|*.BMP||";

 CFileDialog FileDlg(TRUE, NULL, NULL,
  OFN_HIDEREADONLY, szFilter);

 if(FileDlg.DoModal() == IDOK &&
  m_Dib.Load(FileDlg.GetPathName())){
  InvalidateRect(NULL, TRUE);
  UpdateWindow();
  }


}
```

Double Buffering

When your applications draw to the window with a large number of GDI calls, this often causes a noticeable flicker as the window clears and is then drawn. There's an easy way to eliminate this flicker using the CBitmap class through a concept known as *double buffering*. There are many ways to implement double buffering, but the most common technique is to create a compatible device context, work in that context, and then replace what the window is displaying with the next context. That way, the work you're doing is always in the nonviewable device context, so that the user doesn't see any flicker. They just see an instantaneous change from one image to another. Let's look at the basic steps needed to accomplish this:

1. Create a compatible device context using a CDC object.

2. Create a compatible bitmap using a CBitmap object.

3. Select the CBitmap object into the CDC object, and store the old bitmap so that it can be restored when you're done.

4. Perform all draw operations to the newly created CDC object.

5. Use the BitBlt function to quickly move the newly created CBitmap object to the window's device context.

6. Restore the old bitmap in the newly created CDC object.

7. Clean up the CDC and CBitmap objects in the destructors.

At this point, let's create an application that has a noticeable flicker problem. As always, it's best if you create this project from scratch—you'll learn more. However, if you would rather not, you can find a complete project for this program on the Web site for this book.

1. Begin by creating an SDI application.

2. Set a timer to go off every second.

3. Use the InvalidateRect(NULL, TRUE) and UpdateWindow functions in the timer to cause the view window to redraw.

4. Add the following code to the OnDraw function:

```
RECT Rect;
GetClientRect(&Rect);

static BOOL bColor = FALSE;
if(bColor)
 pDC->SelectStockObject(WHITE_PEN);
else
 pDC->SelectStockObject(BLACK_PEN);
bColor = !bColor;

for(int i=0; i<Rect.right; i++){
pDC->MoveTo(i, 0);
pDC->LineTo(i, Rect.bottom);
}
```

5. Run the program, and maximize it.

When the program is running, you'll see the window flicker every second. That's because there's a delay between the time that the line drawing begins and the time it ends. Because the lines are drawn in alternating colors (white and black), you can easily see the delay and the resulting flicker. Not exactly very pretty, is it?

Now let's see how double buffering eliminates this problem. Open the view's implementation file and locate the OnDraw function. Now, just before the lines are drawn, use CreateCompatibleDC and CreateCompatibleBitmap to create in-memory device context and bitmap objects to which you'll do your drawing. Perform the necessary draw operations. Finally, use BitBlt to move the entire memory bitmap to the visible window. Here's the replacement for the OnDraw function. Here's how this looks in code:

```
void YourView::OnDraw(CDC* pDC)
{
 RECT Rect;
 GetClientRect(&Rect);

 static BOOL bColor = FALSE;

 CDC MemDC;
 MemDC.CreateCompatibleDC(pDC);

 CBitmap MemBitmap;
 MemBitmap.CreateCompatibleBitmap(pDC,
                                  Rect.right,
                                  Rect.bottom);

 CBitmap *pOldBitmap = MemDC.SelectObject(&MemBitmap);

 if(bColor)
 {
  MemDC.SelectStockObject(WHITE_PEN);
 }
 else
 {
  MemDC.SelectStockObject(BLACK_PEN);
 }
 bColor = !bColor;

 for(int i=0; i<Rect.right; i++)
 {
  MemDC.MoveTo(i, 0);
  MemDC.LineTo(i, Rect.bottom);
 }

 pDC->BitBlt(0, 0, Rect.right, Rect.bottom,
  &MemDC, 0, 0, SRCCOPY);

 MemDC.SelectObject(pOldBitmap);
}
```

Now, building and executing your application should result in a noticeable improvement in the drawing of the view's content. Note that the demo application (Flicker) contains a #define statement that enables you to toggle between a flicker-free version and one that flickers. That way you can easily compare and see what double buffering buys you. Simply comment out the following line to run the flicker-free version.

```
#define ALLOW_FLICKER
```

Summary

In this chapter you've learned how to create and use device-dependent bitmaps with the CBitmap class. You've also learned about palettes and the CPalette class, and their importance for images of 8-bit pixel depth. You've also seen how to make DIB manipulation easier by creating a CDib class and how to optimize performance with double buffering.

Bitmaps and DIBs are powerful and flexible tools in your arsenal. In an age of visual applications, it would be difficult to overstate their importance. Now that you've read this chapter, it's a good time to roll up your sleeves and do your own experimentation.

Dialogs

Dialog Basics and Common Controls

In Chapter 1, you learned how to create dialog-based applications. However, in that case the wizard automatically generated the C++ class to use, and the code to load, display, and destroy the dialog box during application execution. Therefore, this chapter starts off by exploring the dialog box basics: how to create dialog template resources, define and associate a CDialog class to control the dialog box, and how to display and manage modal dialog boxes. You'll then discover how the combination of message maps, command routing, and the CCmdTarget class allow you to associate commands (such as the user clicking the OK button) with handler functions.

Once you've finished with the dialog box basics, you'll learn some control basics, learn about the MFC control classes, and see four different ways in which to associate a control class with a control in order to manipulate it. From there, I'll illustrate the use of several key controls in a demo application called ControlsDemo.

Once you're done, this chapter will mesh nicely with Chapter 11, which includes details covering some of the finer points of programming dialog boxes, such as creating and controlling modeless dialog boxes, serializing data from a dialog box, and using dialog template resources as form views for your document/view applications. Once finished with both Chapters 10 and 11, you should feel very comfortable writing almost any application that uses dialog boxes or form views, as well as programming and handling common control events.

Getting Started with Dialog Boxes and Controls

This chapter is split into two distinct sections. This first section illustrates the basics of defining and displaying a modal dialog box, because you can't work with controls unless you at least know these basics. From there, you'll then discover how MFC classes are used to wrap the common controls, how to create your own controls, and how DDX and DDV are used to wire your dialog box's controls to your dialog class's member variables.

Defining a CDialog-derived class

The first thing you need to know is how to define a CDialog-derived class. Because this chapter includes a demo that has a dialog box containing each control covered, go ahead and create that demo now. It should be an SDI application called ControlsDemo. Once the project files have been created, open the Resource View, and expand the entries so that you can see the folder entitled Dialog. Right-click that folder and select the Insert Dialog menu option. Once you've done that, the dialog editor opens and the new dialog template resource is displayed, containing two push buttons with the captions OK and Cancel, respectively. From here on out in this chapter, when I refer to a *template*, I'm talking about the dialog template resource that you see in the dialog editor, and when I mention the *dialog*, I'm referring to the actual window that is displayed at runtime.

To be able to display and write code to handle the various dialog events easily, you could dynamically load the resource, subclass its window procedure, and handle any desired messages. However, you'll rarely need to go to such extremes, and the whole point of MFC is being able to stay away from that kind of Windows SDK-like programming. Instead, MFC provides the CDialog class, which can be used to create, display, and manage dialog boxes easily. Therefore, what you need is to be able to define a CDialog-derived class and associate it with the desired template. That couldn't be easier.

Once you've created a template, simply hold down the Ctrl key and double-click the template (or select Project ⇨ Add Class). This invokes the same MFC Class Wizard that you've used throughout this book. Because you are in the dialog editor, the wizard only shows the base classes that apply to templates. These include the CDHTMLDialog, CDialog, CFormView, COlePropertyPage, and CPropertyPage classes. The CDialog class is covered in this chapter and Chapter 11. The CFormView class is covered in Chapter 11 and the CPropertyPage class is covered in Chapter 12. The CDHTMLDialog and COlePropertyPage classes are not covered in this book.

You need to be careful here because the default base class is the CDHtmlDialog class. Therefore, the first thing you should do is to change that to the CDialog class. Now enter a value for the Class name. For the purposes of this chapter's demo, use a value of CModalTestDlg. (Note that it's a standard MFC programming convention to append the letters Dlg to any CDialog-derived class.) You'll see that the other fields are automatically set based on the class name, and cannot be modified manually. Clicking the Finish button creates your CDialog-based class and associates it with the resource ID of the template. In this case, because you didn't change it (via the template's Properties dialog box) and because it's the first dialog box you've created, the value will be IDD_DIALOG1. You'll see where this value comes into play shortly. Now let's take a look at some of the key functions that the wizard generated.

Key CDialog members

The basic CDialog-derived class that is created for you doesn't contain much because most of the code is in the base CDialog class. However, there are some important functions and member variables to understand now because they'll aid your overall understanding of how dialog boxes are constructed and how they function.

The first thing to look at is the dialog class's constructor. As you can see, the constructor for your CModalTestDlg dialog box takes a single parameter—a CWnd pointer indicating the window that will be the dialog box's parent. You will typically let this default to NULL when you instantiate your dialog boxes, because doing so means that the application's main window will be the dialog box's parent.

```
CModalTestDlg::CModalTestDlg(CWnd* pParent /*=NULL*/)
: CDialog(CModalTestDlg::IDD, pParent)
{
}
```

As you can see, the CModelTestDlg is passing some data to the CDialog constructor in its initializer list, so take a look at the CDialog constructors.

```
CDialog::CDialog(
    LPCTSTR lpszTemplateName,
    CWnd* pParentWnd = NULL
);
CDialog::CDialog(
    UINT nIDTemplate,
    CWnd* pParentWnd = NULL
);
CDialog::CDialog( );
```

The only difference between the first two constructor versions is the way in which you specify the template. The first version is the name of the template. The second version is used when specifying the resource ID. As you can see, in the CModalTestDlg constructor, a value of CModalTestDlg::IDD is being passed. If you open the ModalTestDlg.h file, you'll see that's defined as follows. You can see the resource ID that was created for you in the dialog editor. This is how a dialog template is associated with a CDialog-derived class.

```
enum { IDD = IDD_DIALOG1 };
```

Because you know how to get the resource ID for this second CDialog constructor, you might be wondering how to get the resource name for the first constructor. For this task, the Win32 SDK provides a macro (MAKEINTRESOURCE) that yields the resource name when passed a numeric resource ID. Therefore, in the case of the IDD_DIALOG1, you would use the macro as follows:

```
MAKEINTRESOURCE(IDD_DIALOG1)
```

The third, parameter-less constructor is used for situations where you are constructing a dialog box from a template that is in memory, and therefore does not need the resource ID. It is very rare that you'll use this constructor, and therefore, it is not covered in this book.

Now that you've seen the constructor, the next function to take note of is the DoDataExchange function. Although I briefly explained in Chapter 1 that this function is used for DDX and DDV, I'll go into that in a lot more detail in the section entitled "Using DDX with a dialog template control." For now, it's enough to understand that this is where you associate your dialog box's controls with either MFC control classes or member variables to hold the control's data.

```
void CModalTestDlg::DoDataExchange(CDataExchange* pDX)
{
  CDialog::DoDataExchange(pDX);
}
```

The next thing to take note of is the following message map for the dialog box. This is the code that maps runtime messages and commands to member functions (handlers).

```
BEGIN_MESSAGE_MAP(CModalTestDlg, CDialog)
END_MESSAGE_MAP()
```

Finally, the last function that you'll use on a regular basis is the `OnInitDialog` function. For some reason, whereas previous versions of Visual Studio automatically created this function for you anytime you used the wizard to generate a `CDialog`-derived class, Visual Studio .NET does not. Therefore, in order to create this function, you need to add it via the dialog's Overrides dialog box. If you don't recall how to do this, the steps are outlined in "Overriding Base Class Functions" section of Chapter 1.

Displaying and controlling a modal dialog box

At this point, you have a dialog class. Now let's see how to display and manage it. First, you're only working with modal dialog boxes at this point. Simply put, a *modal dialog* is one that won't allow user interaction with any other windows in the same thread. A *modeless dialog* (covered in the next chapter) does allow for interaction with other windows of the same thread and its construction is a bit different.

Displaying a modal dialog box is a simple two-step process. The first step is to construct the dialog object. From there, you simply call its `DoModal` member function, which will cause the current thread to block until the dialog box has been dismissed.

```
CModalTestDlg dlg;
dlg.DoModal();
```

There are times when you will also see the following, where the dialog box is being constructed and its `DoModal` function called on one line.

```
CModalTestDlg().DoModal();
```

That's fine if you don't need to set any of the dialog box's member variables before calling `DoModal`, or if you don't need to check the `DoModal` return value. However, as you can see with the following prototype, the `DoModal` function does return an `int`, which represents the value that was passed to the `CDialog::EndDialog` function (the proper way to dismiss a dialog box).

```
virtual int CDialog::DoModal();
```

To see how this works, add a popup menu to the `ControlsDemo` application's Main menu called Controls. Under that, add another menu called Modal Dialog. Now, add a `COMMAND` event handler for the menu to the `CMainFrame` class and code it as follows:

```
void CMainFrame::OnControlsModaldialog()
{
  CModalTestDlg dlg;
  int nRet = dlg.DoModal();

  // Handle the return value from DoModal
  switch (nRet)
  {
  case -1:
    AfxMessageBox("Dialog box could not be created!");
    break;
  case IDABORT:
    AfxMessageBox("Dialog aborted");
    break;
```

```
    case IDOK:
        AfxMessageBox("OK button pressed");
        break;
    case IDCANCEL:
        AfxMessageBox("Cancel button pressed");
        break;
    default:
        AfxMessageBox("Unknown result");
        break;
}
```

Since you referenced the CModalTestDlg class, you need to add the following #include directive to the top of the mainframe class's header file:

```
#include "ModalTestDlg.h"
```

If you run the application at this time, you'll see that when you click either the OK or Cancel button, the result will be returned as IDOK or IDCANCEL, respectively, and the appropriate message will be displayed. That brings up the first big question of the chapter: How did MFC map a button's click to an event happening (such as the dialog box's dismissal with a specific return code)? This happens through the magic of message routing that I referred to in Chapter 2 and will go into more detail about here.

Command routing and default processing

Although this is not technically an internals book, it does help to sometimes to go past the superficial to have a better understanding of what's going on under the covers. This enables you to more accurately understand how to both extend your program effectively using MFC, and how to solve problems when they arise in the MFC. Having said that, I'll talk just a bit about how a click on the OK button results in code being called to dismiss a dialog box. Knowing this will enable you to understand how to override that behavior and how to add your own behavior for other buttons.

The CDialog is derived from CWnd, which defines a WindowProc function that handles all incoming messages. The CWnd::WindowProc message calls the CWnd::OnWndMsg function, and based on that function's return value (which signifies if the message was handled or not), it calls the CWnd::DefWindowProc function.

```
LRESULT CWnd::WindowProc(UINT message,
    WPARAM wParam,
    LPARAM lParam)
{
    LRESULT lResult = 0;
    if (!OnWndMsg(message, wParam, lParam, &lResult))
        lResult = DefWindowProc(message, wParam, lParam);
    return lResult;
}
```

The CWnd::OnWndMsg function (a small bit of which is reproduced here from the wincore.cpp file) then determines what type of message has been received. In the case of a button being clicked, Windows always sends a WM_COMMAND message to the button's parent window (the dialog box, in this case).

```
BOOL CWnd::OnWndMsg(UINT message,
  WPARAM wParam,
  LPARAM lParam,
  LRESULT* pResult)
{
  LRESULT lResult = 0;
  union MessageMapFunctions mmf;
  mmf.pfn = 0;

  // special case for commands
  if (message == WM_COMMAND)
  {
    if (OnCommand(wParam, lParam))
    {
      lResult = 1;
      goto LReturnTrue;
    }
    return FALSE;
  }
  ...
```

As you can see, if the message is a WM_COMMAND message, the CWnd::OnCommand function is called and its return value bubbles back up to CWnd::WindowProc so that it can determine if the CWnd::DefWindowProc needs to be called or not.

The CWnd::OnCommand function then cracks the passed message as follows: the wParam variable holds two values where the low-order value is the resource ID of the menu, control, or accelerator, and the high-order value specifies the notification message being sent. (In the case of a button being clicked, this message is the BN_CLICKED message, which stands for *button notification clicked*.) The lParam variable contains the window handle of the control. When you see how to override the CDialog::WindowProc in the next chapter, you'll see the importance of knowing the layout of a WM_COMMAND message's data.

Once the parameters have been cracked, the CWnd::OnCommand function performs some sanity checks, such as making sure that the message values are not 0, and that the control has not been disabled. Once these checks have been done, the function sends the message to the control (it's called *reflection* when the parent sends a message to the control) and only proceeds if the control handles the message and returns a nonzero value. Finally, the CWnd::OnCommand function calls the CDialog::OnCmdMsg function, whereupon it calls the CCmdTarget::OnCmdMsg function. This bit is important.

The CCmdTarget class is the base class for the messaging MFC architecture. This architecture has a documented routing order that it goes through when a command message is sent to a dialog box. First, the message is sent to the dialog box itself. After that, the message is sent to the window that owns the dialog box. Finally, the message is sent to the application object. Therefore, although you probably would never do this, technically you could handle your dialog box's command message in the application object. The point is that by knowing this, it becomes your option.

So how does this routing take place? It's very simple. Remember the following message map macro from earlier?

```
BEGIN_MESSAGE_MAP(CModalTestDlg, CDialog)
END_MESSAGE_MAP()
```

If you look these macros up in the source code, you'll see that they expand to an array of AFX_MSGMAP_ENTRY entries called _messageEntries, an AFX_MSGMAP structure called messageMap (which points to the _messageEntries), and a virtual function called GetMessageMap. So now you can probably guess what the CCmdTarget::OnCmdMsg does. Because, for commands sent to dialog boxes, the dialog box class is first in the routing sequence, it simply calls the dialog box's GetMessageMap and searches that map for an entry (a function) that is defined to handle the particular notification code for the specified control.

Although it appears that CModalTestDlg doesn't have any entries, actually part of the expansion of the BEGIN_MESSAGE_MAP macro is to include the message map entries from the base class (CDialog, in this case). The message map then becomes a linked list of all messages in the current class's hierarchy, which is how MFC implements inheritance in message maps. So now you're almost to understanding how a click on a dialog box button results in your message handlers being called.

Because you know that you didn't add any code to the CModalTestDlg dialog box's message map, there must be a handler in the CDialog message map. If you open the dlgcore.cpp file, and search for BEGIN_MESSAGE_MAP, you'll find the following:

```
BEGIN_MESSAGE_MAP(CDialog, CWnd)
  //{{AFX_MSG_MAP(CDialog)
  ON_COMMAND(IDOK, OnOK)
  ON_COMMAND(IDCANCEL, OnCancel)
  ON_MESSAGE(WM_COMMANDHELP, OnCommandHelp)
  ON_MESSAGE(WM_HELPHITTEST, OnHelpHitTest)
  ON_MESSAGE(WM_INITDIALOG, HandleInitDialog)
  ON_MESSAGE(WM_SETFONT, HandleSetFont)
  ON_WM_PAINT()
  //}}AFX_MSG_MAP
END_MESSAGE_MAP()
```

As you can see, the format of a command entry in the message map is the following:

```
ON_COMMAND(control id, function name)
```

If you check the ID properties of your dialog box's OK and Cancel buttons, you'll find that they are IDOK and IDCANCEL, which is how they get routed through this map. Finally, a search on the two functions CDialog::OnOK and CDialog::OnCancel turns up the following functions (both in dlgcore.cpp):

```
void CDialog::OnOK()
{
 if (!UpdateData(TRUE))
 {
  TRACE(traceAppMsg, 0,
   "UpdateData failed during dialog termination.\n");
  // the UpdateData routine will set focus to correct item
  return;
 }
 EndDialog(IDOK);
}

void CDialog::OnCancel()
{
 EndDialog(IDCANCEL);
}
```

As you can see, both functions finish up by calling EndDialog with the values IDOK and IDCANCEL that you coded in your function to display the dialog box and handle its return value.

So what does knowing all this accomplish? A few things actually:

✦ Knowing the order of the routing chain enables you to more intelligently decide in which class to implement your handler functions.

✦ Now that you know the order of the routing chain and the role that message maps play in associating commands and events to functions, you can more easily search and determine where a command is being processed in either code you inherit from someone else or within the MFC code itself.

✦ Now that you have seen the CDialog message map, you know what commands have built-in handlers that enable you to see how to override default behavior.

At this point, you know enough about dialog templates and the CDialog class to finally get into the discussion of controls and the MFC class wrappers for those controls.

Controls are windows too

To understand how MFC provides support for controls, it's helpful to think about controls and how they're created unrelated to MFC. First, almost any rectangular representation that you see on your screen that accepts input is a window. This includes buttons, edit boxes, and list boxes. As such, these controls are created using the same Win32 CreateWindow and CreateWindowEx functions that are used to create any window.

Note   Because Windows is the name of the operating system, and continually mixing the term *windows* and *Windows* in the same sentence leads to confusing sentences, I'll frequently use the term *control* instead of *control window* or *window* to help avoid any ambiguity.

Take a look at the standard CreateWindow function prototype:

```
HWND CreateWindow(
    LPCTSTR lpClassName,    // registered class name
    LPCTSTR lpWindowName,   // window name
    DWORD dwStyle,          // window style
    int x,                  // horizontal position of window
    int y,                  // vertical position of window
    int nWidth,             // window width
    int nHeight,            // window height
    HWND hWndParent,        // handle to parent or owner window
    HMENU hMenu,            // menu handle or child identifier
    HINSTANCE hInstance,    // handle to application instance
    LPVOID lpParam          // window-creation data
);
```

In the CreateWindow function, the first parameter is a *window class name*. Each of the common controls has a unique class name associated with it. When Windows starts up, the RegisterClass function is called in order to associate a window procedure with the window class of each of the common controls. Then, when a call is made to CreateWindow, Windows knows what window procedure to call to create the window and where to send messages meant for that window. The class names for the common controls are defined in the `CommCtrl.h` file. Here's an excerpt from the `CommCtrl.h` file that defines the class name for the edit control. Note also that there are two versions of the class name for each control: a UNICODE version and an ASCII version.

```
// Edit Class Name
#define WC_EDITA            "Edit"
#define WC_EDITW            L"Edit"

#ifdef UNICODE
#define WC_EDIT             WC_EDITW
#else
#define WC_EDIT             WC_EDITA
#endif

#else
#define WC_EDIT             "Edit"
#endif
```

So, how does all this tie into a discussion of MFC and controls? Because it's important to realize exactly what the MFC control classes do for you to have a better understanding of how to use them effectively.

MFC defines a C++ class for each of the common controls. For example, there is a `CEdit` class to wrap the functionality of the edit control, a `CButton` class to wrap the functionality of the button control, and so on. Each of these control classes is derived from the base `CWnd` class, which defines a member variable (`m_hWnd`) that is the handle to an actual window that can be manipulated through that class's member functions and variables.

In this chapter, I will be covering many of the major common controls and how to perform various tasks with them. Table 10-1 lists the controls that are covered, the window class names of those controls, and the MFC classes that are used to manage those controls and implement event handlers for them. The next section shows you how to associate an MFC control class with a given control at runtime.

Table 10-1: Windows Control Classes

Control	MFC Class	Window Class (WNDCLASS)
Button	CButton	BUTTON
List box	CListBox	LISTBOX
Edit control	CEdit	EDIT
Combo box	CComboBox	COMBOBOX

Associating MFC classes and control windows

The MFC control classes really serve two important jobs. First, they provide a means of sending messages to the underlying window through member functions. As an example, using the

Win32 SDK you would need to send a message to the combo box control in order to add a string value to it. Here's an example of how that would look:

```
HWND hwnd = ::GetDlgItem(hwndDialog, IDC_COMBO1);
::SendMessage(hwnd, CB_ADDSTRING, 0L, (LPARAM)"GetDlgItem");
```

However, with a wrapper control class, such as CComboBox, you could do the same thing with the following code:

```
// assumes that you have already associated
// the combobox variable with a combo box control
combobox.AddString("GetDlgItem");
```

This is the simplest part, because once an MFC class is associated with a given control (remember that its base CWnd class defines a member variable to hold the HWND of the control), calling class member functions to manipulate the control simply results in the class sending the appropriate message to the control. In fact, here's the actual implementation of the CComboBox::AddString member function (found in the afxwin2.inl file).

```
_AFXWIN_INLINE int CComboBox::AddString(LPCTSTR lpszString)
{
 ASSERT(::IsWindow(m_hWnd));
 return (int)::SendMessage(m_hWnd,
                           CB_ADDSTRING,
                           0,
                           (LPARAM)lpszString);
}
```

Here you can see several advantages to using the MFC control classes over Win32 SDK programming:

✦ You don't have to specify the HWND, because the control class has it saved as member variable (once attached to the actual control).

✦ You don't need to memorize the exact message (CB_ADDSTRING, in this case). Instead you can use more descriptive, intuitive member function names (such as AddString).

✦ Parameters that are not used (such as the WPARAM, in this case) are not required in the class member functions. Instead the member function sends the default value.

The second benefit that the control classes provide is the ability for the class to allow you to easily handle control events in your code. With Win32 SDK programming, handling messages meant writing your own message loop, checking the control ID of each message you received, and then for each given ID, coding a handler for the desired message ID. MFC control classes, on the other hand, subclass the control's window procedure, intercept the messages intended for the window, and route those messages through the class's message map, and ultimately to any handlers that the base class implements or that your code overrides.

Now that you know what the MFC control classes do for you, you need to know how to associate a control class with a control. Here are a few of the most common means of doing this:

✦ Using the GetDlgItem function

✦ Using DDX with a dialog template control

✦ Calling the Attach method with a dialog template control

✦ Dynamically creating the control and calling Attach

Before I go into the details of each method, create a dialog-based application called `ControlAttaching`. This will be the demo that you'll use in the next few sections to compare the various means of attaching control classes to controls.

Using the GetDlgItem function

The `CWnd::GetDlgItem` function is typically called from a `CDialog` function in order to retrieve a control class pointer to a control on the dialog box.

```
CWnd* CWnd::GetDlgItem(int nID) const;
void CWnd::GetDlgItem(int nID, HWND* phWnd)const;
```

As you can see, there are two overloaded versions of this function. The first takes as its only parameter the resource ID of the control, and returns a `CWnd` pointer. This pointer can be cast to the desired class. The second version of this function is used in situations where you only care about getting the `HWND` for the control.

Now let's look at how to use this function. In the `ControlAttaching` demo, drag and drop a combo box control onto the application's main dialog template from the Toolbox. Take note of the default control ID, which should default to `IDC_COMBO1`. This is the value that the `GetDlgItem` needs. Now add a button to the dialog box (with an ID of `IDC_GETDLGITEM`) that will be used to add a string to the combo box. Figure 10-1 shows how your dialog box should appear at this point.

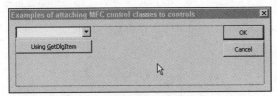

Figure 10-1: Using GetDlgItem to associate a control class with a control.

Now add a handler for the Using GetDlgItem button and code it as follows:

```
void CControlAttachingDlg::OnBnClickedGetDlgItem()
{
  CComboBox* pCbo = (CComboBox*)GetDlgItem(IDC_COMBO1);
  ASSERT(pCbo);
  if (pCbo)
  {
    pCbo->AddString("GetDlgItem-1");
    pCbo->SetCurSel(0);
  }
}
```

Running this code should result in the string `GetDlgItem-1` being placed in the combo box and then that item being selected. Although `GetDlgItem` does give you the ability to manage the control, what about being able to respond to its events? As you'll see in the next section, this can be done with the `Attach` function.

Using the Attach function to subclass controls

Using the `Attach` function is very easy and is used in cases where you want to dynamically associate a control class with a control and be able to respond to that control's events via the class's member functions.

First, add a combo box (`IDC_COMBO2`) and a button control (`IDC_USINGATTACH`) to the dialog template (see Figure 10-2).

Figure 10-2: Using the Attach function to subclass a control.

Using the Add Class Wizard, create a `CComboBox`-derived class called `CMyComboBox`. From the Class View, display the class's Properties dialog box and add a handler for the `CBN_SELCHANGE` notification message. This message is sent by the control when the user changes the selection in the combo box. Update this function as follows to display a message that will verify that your code was called as a result of the message being caught and successfully routed to the class:

```
void CMyComboBox::OnCbnSelchange()
{
  AfxMessageBox("You changed the selection!");
}
```

Add an `include` directive for the `MyComboBox.h` in the `ControlAttachingDlg.h` file just before the class declaration:

```
#include "MyComboBox.h"
```

Define a member variable of type `CMyComboBox` for the `CControlAttachingDlg` as follows:

```
CMyComboBox m_combo2;
```

Add an event handler for the Using Attach button and code it as follows. As you can see, the function first calls the `GetSafeHwnd` function and ensures that the returned `HWND` is `NULL`. This is done because a control can only be subclassed one time. Therefore, if this value is `NULL`, you know that the class is not subclassing a control. Next, the function retrieves the `HWND` of the control via a call to the `GetDlgItem`. After that, a call to the `Attach` function associates the `CMyComboBox` class with the combo box control. Internally, what is happening is that upon the call to `Attach`, MFC will take care of routing messages to the class's event handlers as needed.

```
void CControlAttachingDlg::OnBnClickedUsingattach()
{
  if (NULL == m_combo2.GetSafeHwnd())
  {
    HWND hwnd;
```

```
GetDlgItem(IDC_COMBO2, &hwnd);
if (hwnd)
{
  m_combo2.Attach(hwnd);
  m_combo2.AddString("Using Attach - 1");
  m_combo2.AddString("Using Attach - 2");
  m_combo2.SetCurSel(0);
}
}
}
```

> **Note** When a control is subclassed, the framework always performs a sanity check to ensure that a window has not already been subclassed. This check exists because the framework only saves a single previous window procedure to call when a given message is not processed by the class or a message handler indicates that more processing is needed. In other words, the framework doesn't store a chain of window procedures to call; adding an entry for each subclass. As a result, if this sanity check didn't exist and a given control was subclassed multiple times, the pointer to the original window procedure would be lost and there would be no guarantee that default processing would be done correctly.

The last thing that you need to do is to add code to detach from the control. If you forget this step, MFC will assert when the CComboBox destructor calls DestroyWindow and the framework realizes that the class is still attached to a control. Therefore, add a handler to the dialog box for the WM_DESTROY message and code it as follows:

```
void CControlAttachingDlg::OnDestroy()
{
  CDialog::OnDestroy();

  m_combo2.Detach();
}
```

That's it. If you run the application and click the Using Attach button, two strings will be inserted into the combo box. Changing the selection will result in a message box stating that the event was caught. At this point, you've seen the manual means of associating a control class with a control and even using the Attach function so that messages are properly routed to your class's member functions. Now, let's look at the much easier method of using DDX to accomplish the same tasks.

Using DDX with a dialog template control

The standard way to associate a control class instance with a control in an MFC application is via DDX. I briefly touched on DDX in Chapter 1 where I explained that it has two uses: to wire control classes to controls and to transfer data between controls and class member variables. In this section, I'll explain how the first of those tasks is accomplished here. You'll learn how the second task is used in the section "Using DDX to transfer data."

Because it's always easier to learn about code by looking at code, add a third combo box (IDC_COMBO3) to the demo dialog box now. Now add a button (IDC_USINGDDX) below that combo box as shown in Figure 10-3.

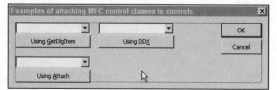

Figure 10-3: Example of using DDX to wire a
control class to a control

After you've added the two controls, right-click the newly added combo box control and
select the Add Member Variable menu option. Make sure that the Control variable option is
selected and that the Variable type is set to CComboBox. Type in a Variable name of m_combo3.
Now, add an event handler for the Using DDX button, and code it as follows:

```
void CControlAttachingDlg::OnBnClickedUsingddx()
{
  m_combo3.AddString("Using DDX");
  m_combo3.SetCurSel(0);
}
```

You've already used DDX in several demos in this book, so this bit is nothing new to
you. However, now you're going to see how simply adding a DDX variable results in an
association between the class and the control. There are two main functions to focus on:
DoDataExchange and UpdateData. When a dialog box is first created, Windows sends that
dialog box a WM_INITDIALOG message. In the case of the CDialog class, this results in the
CDialog::OnInitDialog being called. In this function (located in the dlgcore.cpp file),
a call is made to the UpdateData function. This function instantiates a class called
CDataExchange and calls the dialog box's DoDataExchange function passing it the
CDataExchange object. If you look at your demo's DoDataExchange function, you'll
see the following:

```
void CControlAttachingDlg::DoDataExchange(CDataExchange* pDX)
{
  CDialog::DoDataExchange(pDX);
  DDX_Control(pDX, IDC_COMBO3, m_combo3);
}
```

The default implementation of CDialog::DoDataExchange does nothing, so I'll instead look
at the DDX_Control function, which contains the code that wires a control class to a control.

The first thing that happens is that the function determines if the control class's m_hWnd has
already been set up (meaning that it has already been associated with a window). If not, the
function gets to work by first calling the PrepareCtrl function. This function retrieves the
control's HWND and stores it in the CDataExchange object. After that, the DDX_Control function calls the GetDlgItem itself in order to retrieve the control's HWND. With the HWND, the
CWnd::SubclassWindow function is called. When someone uses the term *subclassing a window*, it simply means that Windows will be instructed to call a different window procedure
with message intended for the control than was originally registered for that window's window class. This is how the MFC control classes are able to "hook into" a control's window
procedure, so messages sent to the control result in your event handlers being called.

```
void AFXAPI DDX_Control(CDataExchange* pDX,
                        int nIDC,
                        CWnd& rControl)
```

```
{
 if ((rControl.m_hWnd == NULL)
 && (rControl.GetControlUnknown() == NULL))
 {
  ASSERT(!pDX->m_bSaveAndValidate);

  pDX->PrepareCtrl(nIDC);
  HWND hWndCtrl;
  pDX->m_pDlgWnd->GetDlgItem(nIDC, &hWndCtrl);
  if ((hWndCtrl != NULL)
  && !rControl.SubclassWindow(hWndCtrl))
  {
   ASSERT(FALSE);  // possibly trying to subclass twice?
   AfxThrowNotSupportedException();
  }
#ifndef _AFX_NO_OCC_SUPPORT
  else
  {
   if (hWndCtrl == NULL)
   {
    if (pDX->m_pDlgWnd->GetOleControlSite(nIDC) != NULL)
    {
     rControl.AttachControlSite(pDX->m_pDlgWnd, nIDC);
    }
   }
   else
   {
    if (pDX->m_pDlgWnd->m_hWnd
    != ::GetParent(rControl.m_hWnd))
     rControl.AttachControlSite(pDX->m_pDlgWnd);
   }
  }
#endif //!_AFX_NO_OCC_SUPPORT
 }
}
```

Needless to say, this is definitely the easiest way to associate a control class with a control.

Creating controls dynamically

Although you will almost certainly use the dialog editor in creating your dialog box's controls most of the time, there are situations where you will want to know how to create a control dynamically. Examples of this are if you need to write a graphical editor or report writer. Another example involves a well-known trick for sorting strings. Because the list box control automatically sorts strings (based on its LBS_SORT style) this trick involves dynamically creating a hidden list box and inserting the data that needs to be sorted into that list box. Then when the data is read back from the list box, it is in the correctly sorted order. Here I'll show you how to create one of the more complicated controls. That way, you can easily modify this code for use in creating the simpler controls.

On the demo's dialog box, add a button that is horizontally adjacent to the Using Attach button. Give this button an ID of IDC_DYNAMICCREATION and a caption of Dynamic Creation.

Right above that and adjacent to the Using Attach combo box is where you'll dynamically create a new combo box.

Now, add the following member variable to the CControlAttachingDlg class:

```
CComboBox m_combo4;
```

Once you've done that, add a handler for the Dynamic Creation button and code it as follows:

```
void CControlAttachingDlg::OnBnClickedDynamiccreation()
{
  if (NULL == m_combo4.GetSafeHwnd())
  {
    CComboBox* pExistingCombo =
    (CComboBox*)GetDlgItem(IDC_COMBO2);
    CWnd* pUsingDynamic = GetDlgItem(IDC_DYNAMICCREATION);
    ASSERT(pExistingCombo && pUsingDynamic);

    if (pExistingCombo && pUsingDynamic)
    {
      CRect rectCombo, rectDropdown;
      pExistingCombo->GetWindowRect(rectCombo);
      ScreenToClient(rectCombo);

      CRect rectButton;
      pUsingDynamic->GetWindowRect(rectButton);
      ScreenToClient(rectButton);

      rectCombo.right = rectButton.left + rectCombo.Width();
      rectCombo.left = rectButton.left;

      pExistingCombo->ShowDropDown();
      pExistingCombo->GetDroppedControlRect(rectDropdown);
      pExistingCombo->ShowDropDown(FALSE);
      ScreenToClient(rectDropdown);
      rectCombo.bottom += rectDropdown.Height();

      DWORD dwStyle = pExistingCombo->GetStyle();
      m_combo4.Create(dwStyle, rectCombo, this, 1222);

      m_combo4.AddString("Dynamic-1");
      m_combo4.AddString("Dynamic-2");
      m_combo4.SetCurSel(0);
      m_combo4.SetFocus();
    }
  }
}
```

As you can see, after verifying that the control class (m_combo4) is not already associated with a control, the function then instantiates a CComboBox object via the GetDlgItem that you've already learned about (using the IDC_COMBO2 ID). It then calls GetDlgItem to also instantiate a CButton object. Because the new combo box will be positioned relative to the existing (Using Attach) combo box and the button, their coordinates are retrieved via calls to GetWindowRect (which returns their top, left, right, and bottom values in a CRect object).

However, this function returns the coordinates relative to the overall screen, so a subsequent call to `ScreenToClient` converts these coordinates to the dialog box's client coordinates. The `rectCombo` object (which will be used in creating the new combo box) is updated to place the new combo box directly to the right of the existing combo box and directly above the Dynamic Creation button.

Next, the existing combo box's drop-down size is determined via a call to its `GetDroppedControlRect` function. Once again the value is translated via `ScreenToClient`. The `rectCombo` bottom value is set to the existing combo box's drop-down value. This might seem strange at first because you would logically think that this would make the combo box's edit control too long. However, the *non*-dropped height of the combo box is always determined by the size of its assigned font; not by the `bottom` member of the `CRect` used to create it. Instead, the `CRect.bottom` value is used to determine the combo box's drop-down height.

Next, the window styles for the existing combo box are retrieved with a call to `GetStyle`, and saved in a local variable called `dwStyle`. At this point, the new combo box can finally be created. This is done via a call to the `CComboBox::Create` function. You'll recall from early in the chapter that I said that windows are created with the `CreateWindow` or `CreateWindowEx` function, and the first parameter is the window class name. If you were to look at the `CComboBox::Create` function, you would see that it calls the `CWnd::Create` function, passing it the window class name of `COMBOBOX`. Further tracing would eventually lead you to the `CWnd::CreateWindowEx` function, which is responsible for calling the Win32 `CreateWindowEx` function. The point to all this spelunking is that while at first the MFC might seem like this mysterious code base where things happen by magic, if you take the time to dig through the labyrinth of functions and macros, you'll discover that the same Win32 SDK functions that have always been used are still being used under the covers. In fact, if your plan is to learn as much as you can about MFC in order to be a productive Windows developer, I recommend that you become very familiar with the MFC code base, because it will not only help you in debugging your applications, but you will also pick up many great programming tips and techniques along the way.

At this point, the function finally has a `CComboBox` object, and so, as in the previous sections, its `AddString` and `SetCurSel` functions can be called.

Once you've finished coding, build and run the application. Figure 10-4 shows the results of running the application and testing the four different methods of interacting with a control via a control class.

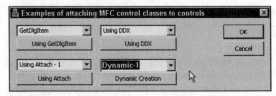

Figure 10-4: Example of dynamically creating a dialog control

One thing that you'll notice is that the font used to render the text in the dynamic combo box control is different than the other combo boxes. This is because when you dynamically create controls you are completely on your own regarding tasks such as setting fonts. You'll see how to manipulate the fonts of controls later on this chapter in the section entitled "Setting a control's font."

Note   You saw where the framework calls the `CreateWindowEx` function to create the control window. However, one thing to note is that when you place controls on a dialog template, you'll never see the code that actually creates those windows at runtime. This is because when you instantiate and display a dialog box in MFC, the framework eventually calls the Win32 SDK `CreateDialogIndirect` function. It's this function that reads the resources for the dialog box and determines the controls to be created.

At this point, you know quite a bit about the dialog box and control basics and how to associate control classes with controls. Now that you can do that, let's look at the controls individually.

 Note   As you work your way through this chapter's demos, you'll see me alternate between using `GetDlgItem` and DDX in order to associate control classes with controls. This is done for two reasons. First, in my own practice I typically use DDX when I know that I'm going to be using the control class in multiple places. On the other hand, if I simply want to perform one task with a given control, I usually just call the `GetDlgItem` and go from there. Second, I like to alternate using different techniques to show you that both methods work equally well.

Using the CButton Class

I'll start with the button class because that is the first control you see anytime you create a dialog box in the dialog editor. You certainly won't be surprised to know that the `CButton` class is used to encapsulate the functionality of the button control. However, it might be surprising to realize that the `CButton` class can create four different button styles: checkboxes, radio buttons, group boxes, and the ever-popular push button. Obviously, if you drag and drop one of these controls onto a dialog template, you'll never have to worry about how the button was created. However, if you ever need to create a button control dynamically, you'll need to know the various style values as you can see from the `CButton::Create` prototype:

```
virtual BOOL Create(LPCTSTR lpszCaption,
    DWORD dwStyle,
    const RECT& rect,
    CWnd* pParentWnd,
    UINT nID);
```

Table 10-2 lists the relevant style flags and a short description of the button type they represent.

For purposes of this section — and from this point forward — I'm going to assume that you are creating your controls via the dialog editor and wiring them to control class member variables in your dialog box via DDX.

At this time, reopen the `ControlsDemo` project you created earlier in the chapter and add a dialog box with an ID of `IDD_BUTTONS` and create a `CDialog`-derived class for it called `CButtonsDlg`. Now add a handler to the `CMainFrame` class for the push button and code it as follows. (Be sure to include the `ButtonsDlg.h` file at the top of the `Mainfrm.cpp` file).

```
void CMainFrame::OnControlsButtons()
{
    CButtonsDlg().DoModal();
}
```

Once you have the dialog box and its display code in place, let's look at the various button types.

Table 10-2: CButton Style Flags

Style	Description
BS_PUSHBUTTON	Garden-variety push button control.
BS_DEFPUSHBUTTON	A push button with a thick border, this is used in dialog boxes to denote the default button.
BS_RADIOBUTTON	A radio button control.
BS_AUTORADIOBUTTON	A radio button that when clicked deselects all other radio buttons in a group.
BS_GROUPBOX	A group box.
BS_CHECKBOX	A standard checkbox.
BS_AUTOCHECKBOX	A checkbox that selects and deselects itself when clicked.
BS_3STATE	A checkbox that has three states: selected, deselected, and indeterminate.
BS_AUTO3STATE	Same as BS_3STATE except that it automatically cycles through the three states when it is clicked.

Push buttons

There really isn't much to talk about regarding push buttons, because they are typically used as an input-only control whose only function is to enable the user to instigate an action in the application. This is why when you find articles on programming buttons it has nothing to do with button functionality; but instead is based on showing how to create fancy buttons with nonrectangular shapes or buttons that contain images. In the section "Bitmap buttons," you'll see how to include buttons on your dialog boxes that contain bitmaps.

With regards to button styles, the most important one to be cognizant of is the BS_DEFPUSHBUTTON style. This style can be set in the control's Properties dialog box by setting the Default property to True. When a push button on a dialog box is defined as the default button, when a user presses the Enter key, a WM_COMMAND message is sent to the dialog box as though the user clicked the default button. Note that this occurs only in cases where another button does not have focus. Pressing the Enter key while a push button has focus (regardless of its style) is the same as clicking that button.

For handling messages to buttons, you already know that in order to handle the WM_COMMAND message for a button, you need only double-click the button in the dialog editor. This automatically creates the handler in the dialog template's associated dialog class, associating the WM_COMMAND message for that push button ID with the function. Also note that if a dialog class is not associated with the dialog template, the MFC Class Wizard will be invoked to allow you to create a dialog class.

Radio buttons

A radio button consists of a round button and an associated text string that describes the option. The control gets its name (and UI) from the old-fashioned car radios that typically sported a horizontal row of buttons, where pushing one of these buttons resulted in any other pushed button being pushed out. Therefore, radio buttons — usually placed within a group box control to visually show their connection with one another — are used in situations where the application is presenting a group of related, but mutually exclusive options. You can see many example usages of this control in the Visual Studio .NET environment. For example, when creating a new MFC project, the Applications Type dialog box contains three sets of radio buttons to allow you to specify Application type (SDI, MDI, or dialog-based), Project style (Windows Explorer or MFC standard) and Use of MFC (in a shared DLL or statically linked). As you can see, within each of these groupings the choices are exclusive of one another and cannot be combined.

Radio button navigation

The next thing you'll look at is how to define a radio button's navigation. To show this, add two groupings of radio buttons to the `CButtonsDlg` template as shown in Figure 10-5.

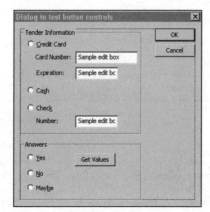

Figure 10-5: Programming radio buttons

You'll notice that I added a group box control around each set of radio buttons. You can see from Table 10-2 that the group box is simply a button control with the `BS_GROUPBOX` style specified and does nothing but visually separate the controls for the user.

After you've added the radio buttons to the dialog box, test the dialog box by pressing Ctrl+T. Once you do, you'll find that your radio buttons are not working as two separate groups. To group your radio buttons correctly, you need to do two things:

1. Press Ctrl-D and set the tab order of the controls on the dialog box.

2. Using the Properties dialog box, set the `Group` property to `True` for the first control in each grouping. This is based on tab order, which is why I recommend that you set the tab order first.

Note that you need to have the radio button tab orders defined to be in sequential order. As an example, in Figure 10-5 you would obviously want the user to tab from the Credit Card radio button to the Card Number edit field. Therefore, you would naturally define the Card Number field to come after the Credit Card radio button in the tab order. However, doing this breaks up the radio button grouping, and thus your radio buttons will not function as a mutually exclusive set of options. Instead you need to set the first tab stop to the group box text (I'll explain why next). Then you need to set the second, third, and fourth tab orders to the

Credit Card, Cash, and Check radio buttons, respectively. Now you can set the tab order for the remaining edit controls in the group box as five, six, and seven, respectively. The reason you can do this is because by default the only tab stop in a group of radio buttons is the first tab defined in the group. Therefore, the tab order you're setting has nothing to do with tabbing, but instead is used to define the radio button group. After setting the first group of radio buttons (the tender information), then do the same for the Answers radio buttons.

Now, if you test the dialog box again, you'll find that the radio button groupings work independently as they should.

One last note about radio button navigation: You might be wondering how the user can use the keyboard to move between radio buttons if only the first radio button in a group is defined as a tab stop. The answer is the arrow keys. The up and left arrow keys enable you to move to the previous radio button in a group, and the down and right arrow keys enable you to move to the next radio button in a group.

Handling radio button events

Although most click handlers for push buttons perform a given task, usually the only time you'll have a click handler for a radio button is for changing the dialog box's UI. This dialog box is a good example of when you would want to handle a radio button's click event, because certain controls should only be enabled when their associated radio button is selected. At this point, add handlers for the three tender radio buttons and code them as follows.

You should take note of a few things here. First, you're using the `GetDlgItem` function to retrieve a `CWnd` object for each control that you want to enable or disable. The reason you're doing that instead of using DDX is that for this demo I don't have any further use for these controls other than to enable or disable them. Therefore, I don't really need a member variable that lasts the lifetime of the dialog box. Second, I've set the controls' IDs to be a bit more intuitive than the defaults of `IDC_EDIT1` and `IDC_EDIT2`. Obviously, I did this to make the code more readable. Third, this is some ugly code! If you run this, it will certainly work. However, I personally detest seeing redundant code like this. So what's the solution when you have three separate event handlers that all need to be coded in a similar fashion? The answer is to combine your event handlers into one. I'll explain two techniques for doing just that later in the chapter in the "Combining Event Handlers" section.

```
void CButtonsDlg::OnBnClickedCreditcard()
{
  CWnd* pWnd;

  pWnd = GetDlgItem(IDC_CARDNUMBER);
  ASSERT(pWnd);
  if (pWnd)
  {
    pWnd->EnableWindow(TRUE);
  }

  pWnd = GetDlgItem(IDC_EXPIRATION);
  ASSERT(pWnd);
  if (pWnd)
  {
    pWnd->EnableWindow(TRUE);
  }
```

```
      pWnd = GetDlgItem(IDC_CHECKNUMBER);
      ASSERT(pWnd);
      if (pWnd)
      {
        pWnd->EnableWindow(FALSE);
      }
    }

    void CButtonsDlg::OnBnClickedCash()
    {
      CWnd* pWnd;

      pWnd = GetDlgItem(IDC_CARDNUMBER);
      ASSERT(pWnd);
      if (pWnd)
      {
        pWnd->EnableWindow(FALSE);
      }

      pWnd = GetDlgItem(IDC_EXPIRATION);
      ASSERT(pWnd);
      if (pWnd)
      {
        pWnd->EnableWindow(FALSE);
      }

      pWnd = GetDlgItem(IDC_CHECKNUMBER);
      ASSERT(pWnd);
      if (pWnd)
      {
        pWnd->EnableWindow(FALSE);
      }
    }

    void CButtonsDlg::OnBnClickedCheck()
    {
      CWnd* pWnd;

      pWnd = GetDlgItem(IDC_CARDNUMBER);
      ASSERT(pWnd);
      if (pWnd)
      {
        pWnd->EnableWindow(FALSE);
      }

      pWnd = GetDlgItem(IDC_EXPIRATION);
      ASSERT(pWnd);
      if (pWnd)
      {
        pWnd->EnableWindow(FALSE);
      }
```

```
   pWnd = GetDlgItem(IDC_CHECKNUMBER);
   ASSERT(pWnd);
   if (pWnd)
   {
     pWnd->EnableWindow(TRUE);
   }
}
```

The last thing you'll do here is to make sure that the dialog box is initialized properly for the tender option. To do that, you simply need to set the desired button to checked. This is done via the CButton::SetCheck function, which takes the parameters shown in Table 10-3.

Table 10-3: CButton::SetCheck Values

Value	Meaning
BST_CHECKED	Sets the button to an unchecked state.
BST_UNCHECKED	Sets the button to a checked state.
BST_INDETERMINATE	Sets the button state to an indeterminate state. This value is only valid if the button has the BS_3STATE or BS_AUTO3STATE style indicating a third (indeterminate state).

At this point, implement the OnInitDialog function in the CButtonsDlg class and add the following code (shown in bold) to check the Credit Card radio button:

```
BOOL CButtonsDlg::OnInitDialog()
{
   CDialog::OnInitDialog();

   CButton* pButton = (CButton*)GetDlgItem(IDC_CREDITCARD);
   ASSERT(pButton);
   if (pButton)
   {
     pButton->SetCheck(BST_CHECKED);
   }
   OnBnClickedCreditcard();

   return TRUE;
}
```

One last thing to note here is that simply calling SetCheck does not result in the same code path as the user clicking the button. In fact, not only will the control class's event handler not be triggered, the other radio buttons in the group won't be unchecked either! Therefore, the OnBnClickedCreditCard function had to be manually invoked as well. Now, if you build and run the demo, you'll see that the controls are enabled and disabled appropriately depending on the selected radio button, as shown in Figure 10-6.

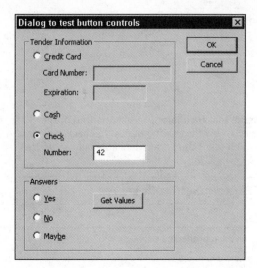

Figure 10-6: Radio buttons are often used to determine which options users have available to them.

As you might have guessed, since the CButton::SetCheck is used to set the value of a radio button, the CButtonGetCheck can be used to determine which button has been set. However, this method is a bit tedious so let's look now at a much easier way to set and retrieve radio button values.

DDX and radio buttons

Just as the DDX_Text function is used to associate a control with a member variable that will contain that control's value, there is a special DDX function used for radio buttons. This function, DDX_Radio is used to associate an int variable with a group of radio buttons. Note that you don't use this function for each radio button—you can only use it for the first radio button in a group of radio buttons. The value of the int will then be the radio button in that group that is selected (relative to zero, and –1 for no selection).

Note   In the version of Visual Studio.NET that I am currently using, adding the DDX_Radio function is a manual process. Hopefully, in the future it will be automated through the Add Member Variable Wizard.

To see this, follow these steps:

1. Add a member variable of type int to the CButtonsDlg class called m_iAnswer.

2. Modify the radio button resource IDs for the Yes, No and Maybe buttons to IDC_BTN_YES, IDC_BTN_NO, and IDC_BTN_MAYBE, respectively. Although this isn't strictly necessary, it does make the code more intuitive.

3. Add the following function call to the CButtonsDlg::DoDataExchange function (new line shown in bold).

```
void CButtonsDlg::DoDataExchange(CDataExchange* pDX)
{
  CDialog::DoDataExchange(pDX);
  DDX_Radio(pDX, IDC_BTN_YES, m_iAnswer);
}
```

4. Change the Get Values button resource ID to IDC_GET_RADIOBUTTON_VALUES, and add an event handler for it. The handler should then be coded as follows to display the current state of the radio buttons whenever they are clicked.

```
void CButtonsDlg::OnBnClickedGetRadiobuttonValues()
{
  if (UpdateData())
  {
    CString str;
    str.Format("Radio button values (%ld):\r\n\r\n"
      "Yes = %s\r\n"
      "No = %s\r\n"
      "Maybe = %s",
      m_iAnswer,
      (0 == m_iAnswer ? "On" : "Off"),
      (1 == m_iAnswer ? "On" : "Off"),
      (2 == m_iAnswer ? "On" : "Off"));
    AfxMessageBox(str);
  }
}
```

Note   If you use the DDX_Radio function for a control that is not defined with the style WS_GROUP (Group = True), the call will assert, because the control must represent the first in a group of radio buttons.

Building and running the application at this point should illustrate that you now know how to handle both push buttons and radio buttons. Let's now look at how to deal with check box controls.

Checkbox controls

A checkbox consists of a square button and an associated text string that describes the option, and is used in situations where you want to display a group of options to the user where any number of those options can be combined. As with radio buttons, most applications group related checkboxes together within a group box control so that users can intuitively see the connection between them. If you look at the Visual Studio .NET Options dialog box, you will see quite a few pages where checkboxes are organized and displayed in this fashion.

A checkbox can be one of four types: standard, automatic, three-state, and automatic three-state. These types are dictated by the BS_CHECKBOX, BS_AUTOCHECKBOX, BS_3STATE, and BS_AUTO3STATE style constants, respectively.

Each style can assume at least two check states: checked (a check mark inside the box) or cleared (no check mark). In addition, a three-state checkbox can assume an indeterminate state, which is signified by the checkbox being colored gray. This is where the BST_INDETERMINATE value that can be used with the CButton::SetCheck function comes into play.

In the chapter's demo application, I've added a group of check boxes and coded a GetValues button for them as I did in the previous section for the radio buttons. However, because you handle both control types in much the same way, I'll skip going step-by-step through the creation of the code. Instead I'll simply make the following points and direct you to the code for any further questions:

✦ Creating a check box event handler is done the usual way — by double-clicking the control in the dialog resource editor.

✦ A CButton object can be associated with a check box control, and its GetCheck and SetCheck functions can be used to retrieve and set the check box's value. Keep in mind is that if the check box is a three-state button, you'll want to make sure to code for all the values shown in Table 10-3.

✦ You can use the special DDX_Check function to associate a variable of type int with the first check box in a group of check boxes. However, whereas the DDX_Radio function associates a single variable with the indexed value of whatever radio button in a group is selected, the DDX_Check function results in the specified variable either being set to 1 or 0 based on whether or not the check box is selected. Therefore, you need to call DDX_Check for each check box for which you need to track or control the selection state.

Bitmap buttons

In addition to customizing a control's behavior, you can also change how the control appears on the screen. In these next two sections, I address how to change the appearance of push buttons and how to dynamically set a button's associated image based on the user action or button state. I'll begin with the CBitmapButton class.

The CBitmapButton class is used to create push buttons that are labeled with bitmapped images instead of text. In defining a CBitmapButton object, you can specify up to four different bitmaps that are used to indicate state. These states are: up (the normal state of the button), down (shown when the button is currently depressed), focused (when the control has focus, although most people use the up/normal bitmap for this value), and disabled. Note that only the first (up/normal state) bitmap is required and that you can use one image to represent multiple states.

Bitmap-button images include the border around the image as well as the image itself. The border typically plays a part in showing the state of the button. For example, the bitmap for the focused state usually is like the one for the up state but with a dashed rectangle inset from the border or a thick solid line at the border. The bitmap for the disabled state usually resembles the one for the up state but has lower contrast (like a dimmed or grayed menu selection).

The bitmaps you choose can be of any size, but all are treated as if they were the same size as the bitmap for the up state. In addition, the CBitmapButton::SizeToContent function enables you to automatically size the button to the size of the bitmap.

As you'll see, creating a CBitmapButton is a very simple process:

1. The first thing you need to do is to acquire or create the images that will represent the various states of the button. On this book's Web site, this demo includes three such bitmaps (up.bmp, down.bmp, and disabled.bmp).

2. If you want to create your own bitmaps, then you have much more artistic ability than I do, and you're on your own. However, I will show you how to import bitmap files that have already been created for you (such as the ones I've done for this demo). To do this, simply open the Resource View, right-click the resources folder, and select the Add Resource menu option. When the Add Resource dialog box appears, click the Import button and select the bitmap file(s) that you wish to import. Because Visual Studio will

give these bitmaps default IDs such as IDB_BITMAP1, you'll want to rename the IDs to something more meaningful. In the demo, I named mine IDB_UP, IDB_DOWN and IDB_DISABLED.

3. Once you have the bitmap resources in place, add a push button to the dialog box. In the demo, I've added a push button control, a static text for instructions, a checkbox control to disable the control (so that you can test that the disabled bitmap is displaying properly) and a group box control to contain them all. You can see all this in Figure 10-7.

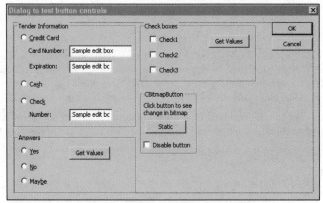

Figure 10-7: Controls added to a dialog box to test a CBitmapButton object

4. Now, set the push button's Owner Draw property to True to indicate that this button will draw itself — actually the CBitmapButton has an OnDraw function that will do the drawing of the bitmaps once you've loaded them and associated them with the various button states.

5. Add a new MFC class to the project of type CBitmapButton, and call it CMyFancyButton. Remember that you need to switch away from the dialog editor when you invoke the Add Class dialog box; otherwise the only options you will have will involve creating dialog classes.

6. Once you've created the CBitmapButton class, add a DDX control variable to the dialog box for the push button of type CButton. Name this variable m_fancyButton. Unfortunately, the CBitmapButton type is not on the Add Member Variable dialog box. Therefore, when finished, you'll need to open the dialog box's header file (ButtonsDlg.h) and change the type of the m_fancyButton member variable to CMyFancyButton. Don't forget to also insert an include directive for the MyFancyButton.h file at the top of the dialog box's header file.

7. You're almost done. In the dialog box's OnInitDialog function, add the following call to the CButton::LoadBitmaps to load the necessary bitmaps and associate them with the desired states. As you can see, the only state I'm leaving as default is the "focus" state, where the "up" bitmap will be used by default. As mentioned earlier, the CBitmapButton::SizeToContent is used to resize the button to the size of the bitmap.

```
BOOL CButtonsDlg::OnInitDialog()
{
  CDialog::OnInitDialog();

  m_fancyButton.LoadBitmaps(IDB_UP,
                            IDB_DOWN,
                            NULL,
                            IDB_DISABLED);
  m_fancyButton.SizeToContent();

  ...
}
```

8. At this point, technically you're done with the bitmap button creation. However, let's add a handler for the disabled checkbox so that you can verify that the disabled state bitmap is being used when appropriate. To do that, first add a DDX control variable called m_btnDisabled for the checkbox.

9. Then add an event handler for that checkbox and code it as follows, where the code simply enables or disables the bitmap button based on the state of the checkbox.

```
void CButtonsDlg::OnBnClickedDisabled()
{
  if (UpdateData())
  {
    m_fancyButton.EnableWindow(BST_CHECKED
    != m_btnDisabled.GetCheck() ? TRUE : FALSE);
  }
}
```

10. Finally, build and run the application to see results similar to those shown in Figure 10-8.

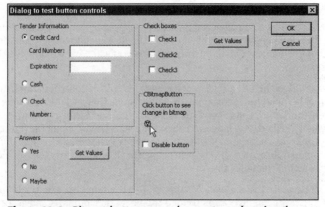

Figure 10-8: Bitmap buttons are a breeze to code using the CBitmapButton class.

Now, let's look at another method of creating bitmap buttons—specifying the BS_BITMAP style.

Using the BS_BITMAP style

Using BS_BITMAP is even easier than using CBitmapButton. You need only provide a single button bitmap. Windows draws the button in its up, down, focus, and disabled states for you. However, with that ease of use comes a bit of inflexibility or convenience, depending on your outlook.

One example of this is the button border. If you look back at Figure 10-8, you'll see that your little bitmap button is missing its border. This is because when you use the CBitmapButton class, you are completely responsible for drawing this button's image (including things like borders). This might be perfect for situations where you either don't want the border or you want to have explicit control over its look.

However, if you don't need this level of control, and you're fine with the buttons that Windows dynamically creates for the different states, then the BS_BUTTON style is definitely the way to go. Something else that bears mentioning is that if you draw your own border (as with the CBitmapButton class), you run the risk of your UI looking out of date as future versions of Windows change how buttons look when depressed or disabled. An example of that is Windows XP. Because it changes the look and feel of the button control, using the BS_BITMAP style keeps your UI looking fresh across all the Windows operating systems.

Take a look at how this would work in the ControlsDemo project.

1. Instead of dynamically creating the button (you've already learned how to create controls dynamically anyway), add the push button that will become the bitmap button to the button's dialog box as well as the other controls in the BS_BITMAP group box control as shown in Figure 10-9. Make sure that the button's ID is IDC_BTSBITMAP.

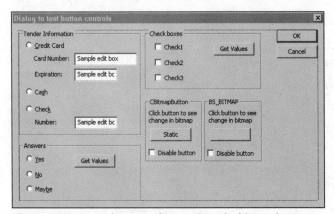

Figure 10-9: Controls to test the creation of a bitmap button using the BS_BITMAP style

2. Change the button's Bitmap property to True. If you simply copied and pasted the other bitmap button to create this button, you'll need to make sure that the Owner Draw property is set to False, because they are mutually exclusive settings.

3. Now add a Bitmap member variable to the CButtonsDlg class.

```
protected:
  CBitmap m_bmpBSBitmap;
```

4. Update the `CButtonsDlg::OnInitDialog` function to include the following code. As you can see, the code first sets a local `CButton` object with the aid of the trusty `GetDlgItem` function. Once you have that, you can load the bitmap into the member bitmap object (`m_bmpBSBitmap`). The code then retrieves that bitmap's handle (using the `CBitmap::GetSafeHandle`) and uses it to call the `CButton::SetBitmap` function. By the way, the reason that the bitmap object was declared as a member object is because if you define it locally and it goes out of scope (and thus destructs), your button won't display anything, because it relies on that bitmap.

```
CButton* pBSBitmapBtn =
 (CButton*)GetDlgItem(IDC_BTSBITMAP);
ASSERT(pBSBitmapBtn);
if (pBSBitmapBtn)
{
 VERIFY(m_bmpBSBitmap.LoadBitmap(IDB_UP));
 HBITMAP hbmp = (HBITMAP)m_bmpBSBitmap.GetSafeHandle();
 pBSBitmapBtn->SetBitmap(hbmp);
}
```

5. Once again, you are done with the bitmap button part, but you should add the disabling code just to test the disabled state of the button. To do that, add a DDX variable called `m_btnDisabledBSButton` for the checkbox.

6. Now add the following event handler for its click event. Once again, I'm using `GetDlgItem` here to alternate techniques; you could just as easily use DDX to get access to the button and checkbox controls.

```
void CButtonsDlg::OnBnClickedDisabled2()
{
 if (UpdateData())
 {
  CButton* pBitmapButton =
  (CButton*)GetDlgItem(IDC_BTSBITMAP);

  CButton* pCheckBox =
  (CButton*)GetDlgItem(IDC_DISABLED2);

  ASSERT(pBitmapButton && pCheckBox);
  if (pBitmapButton && pCheckBox)
  {
   if (BST_CHECKED == pCheckBox->GetCheck())
   {
    pBitmapButton->EnableWindow(FALSE);
   }
   else
   {
    pBitmapButton->EnableWindow(TRUE);
   }
  }
 }
}
```

7. Now build and run the application to see result similar to those shown in Figure 10-10.

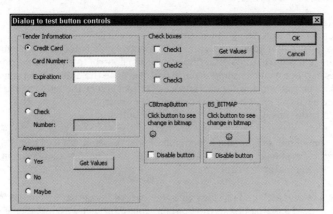

Figure 10-10: Using the BS_BITMAP style had advantages and disadvantages compared to using the CBitmapButton class, depending on your application's needs.

In summary, using the BS_BITMAP style produces a completely different look and feel than providing the various state bitmaps yourself via the CBitmapButton. With BS_BITMAP, you end up with a button that acts just like a push button with your bitmap drawn in the middle. You only provide the one image, so there's no ability to do fancy things like having your image morph based on whether or not the button is depressed or disabled. Instead, it's just the button that is drawn differently and the image remains static. However, the advantages to this technique are that you don't have to either draw or find the various state images for the button and you're insulated from Windows changing the UI if you want a border (something you have to manually draw with the CBitmapButton technique).

Conversely, the CBitmapButton enables you to create fancier buttons where the entire button is the image and that image changes into whatever shape you want based on user interaction. The bottom line here is that choosing between the two is going to come down to personal choice and the specifics of your application.

Note

In addition to the BS_BITMAP style (or selecting the Bitmap style in the dialog editor) there is also a BS_ICON style (specified with the Icon style in the dialog editor). Because creating and programming buttons with these styles is so similar, I'll just note the difference here instead of repeating myself.

The main drawback to using BS_ICON (as opposed to BS_BITMAP) is that the button is limited to the maximum size of an icon, which is 48 × 48 pixels. However, the big advantage to using the BS_ICON style is that icons can use transparent colors, and therefore can adapt to changes in system colors. Using the CBitmapButton class or a BS_BITMAP button, on the other hand, can result in some very ugly buttons depending on the user's display settings.

Other than that, they are programmed in exactly the same way except that the CButton::SetIcon function is used in place of the CButton::SetBitmap function.

Using the CEdit Class

The edit control (encapsulated by the CEdit class) is a rectangular child window in which the user can enter data. It's probably the control that you will find yourself using the most in your applications. By manipulating the styles of this control, you can define everything from a simple single-line edit control to an MLE (multiline edit) control to a password control that displays asterisks in place of the entered data. In fact, because the edit control sends notification messages to its parent window for each user keystroke before the letter is displayed, it is quite easy to write even the most advanced masked edit controls. Therefore, the focus of this section is to get to know this ubiquitous control a little better.

Note   The CEdit control has a maximum upper limit of approximately 60KB of text. This makes CEdit suited to small-to-intermediate text entry tasks. If you need to manipulate more text than 60KB, use the CRichEditCtrl class.

Because you'll be working with code to illustrate the various tasks that can be performed with an edit control, add a dialog box to the ControlsDemo project with an ID of IDD_EDIT. Once done, define a CDialog-derived class called CEditDlg for this template. Now add a menu item to the main menu resource (under the Controls menu) and add an event handler to it that displays the CEditDlg as you did for the Modal Dialog and Buttons dialog boxes.

Using DDX to transfer data

In the section entitled "Using DDX with a dialog template control" you learned that DDX can be used to associate control classes with controls. I also briefly mentioned in that section that DDX can be used to transfer data between controls and control class member variables. Because edit controls are the first control I've mentioned in this chapter that allow user input, this is the perfect place to cover this aspect of DDX.

To get started, modify the IDD_EDIT dialog template so that when finished it looks like that shown in Figure 10-11. You're not going to code all of these controls right now, but because they will all eventually be used you might as well have them all on the dialog box.

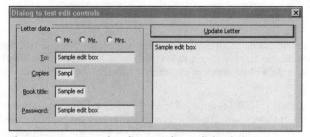

Figure 10-11: Sample edit control test dialog box

Once the controls are in place, right-click the "To" edit control and select the Add member variable menu option. This invokes the Add Member Variable Wizard that you've seen several times already. The first thing to do is to uncheck the Control variable checkbox because that is used to create DDX *control variables,* and you're creating a DDX *value variable* at this point.

Once you've done that, you'll see that the list of possible variable types is much greater. If you drop down this list, you will be able to see the many different types of member variables that can be wired to a control. In my current version of Visual Studio, the CString type is not present in this list. However, if that is the case when the product finally ships, simply type in the name **CString**. From there enter a variable name of m_strTo and click the Finish button.

Now let's see what was done on your behalf. First open the editdlg.h file and search for the defined member variable m_strTo. You'll find that it has been defined as public member variable like this:

```
public:
    CString m_strTo;
```

Next open the editdlg.cpp file and locate the CEditDlg constructor. Here you'll see that the member variable is being initialized in the class's initializer list:

```
CEditDlg::CEditDlg(CWnd* pParent /*=NULL*/)
    : CDialog(CEditDlg::IDD, pParent)
    , m_strTo(L"")
{
}
```

So far, nothing new. However, that's about to change. Now locate the DoDataExchange function. You'll recall that this function is the key to DDX and is called from the UpdateData function, which itself is called when the dialog box initializes and when the dialog box's OnOK handler is called. At this point, you're going to learn about the DoDataExchange function as well as the UpdateData function as it pertains to DDX value variables.

If you look at the DoDataExchange function, you'll see that instead of the DDX_Control function being called as you've seen throughout this chapter, there is a call to DDX_Text as shown here:

```
void CEditDlg::DoDataExchange(CDataExchange* pDX)
{
    CDialog::DoDataExchange(pDX);
    DDX_Text(pDX, IDC_EDIT1, m_strTo);
}
```

Therefore, you'll begin understanding how data is transferred between controls and class members by looking at this function. The first thing you should realize is that DDX_Text has 17 overloads! These various overloaded versions of the function enable you to use every type of variable including byte, short, int, and CString. You can even specify variables of type COleCurrency and COleDataTime.

If you trace into the DDX_Text function, you'll see that after a call to PrepareEditCtrl, the function then inspects a variable called m_bSaveAndValidate. If this value is TRUE, the function retrieves the text from the control (via a call to the Win32 SDK function GetWindowText) and sets the passed variable to that value. If the m_bSaveAndValidate value is FALSE, the opposite happens; the control is updated with the value of the passed variable.

Note   Many times in MFC source code you'll see a call to the function AfxSetWindowText as opposed to the Win32 function ::SetWindowText. The reason for this is that the AfxSetWindowText helper function first checks to see if the specified value is different than the value already contained by the control. If two values are different, then the control is updated. If the two values are the same, the function returns without doing anything. Therefore, this undocumented MFC function should definitely be a part of your toolkit.

```
void AFXAPI DDX_Text(CDataExchange* pDX,
                     int nIDC,
                     CString& value)
{
 HWND hWndCtrl = pDX->PrepareEditCtrl(nIDC);
 if (pDX->m_bSaveAndValidate)
 {
  int nLen = ::GetWindowTextLength(hWndCtrl);
  ::GetWindowText(hWndCtrl,
                  value.GetBufferSetLength(nLen),
                  nLen+1);
  value.ReleaseBuffer();
 }
 else
 {
  AfxSetWindowText(hWndCtrl, value);
 }
}
```

However, you may be wondering what sets the `CDataExchange::m_bSaveAndValidate` variable. The answer is `UpdateData`. The `UpdateData` function takes a single parameter (`bSaveAndValidate`) that is used to determine if the data is being transferred from the class members to the controls (`bSaveAndValidate` = FALSE) or from the controls to the class members (`bSaveAndValidate` = TRUE).

Now that you know how this works, you should realize the following regarding DDX value variables:

✦ If you want to initialize values before the dialog box is initially displayed to the user, you have two options. You can set the values before the call to the base class's `OnInitDialog`, or you can set the values and then manually call `UpdateData(FALSE)`.

✦ Anytime you want to retrieve the values from the dialog box's controls into your dialog class's members, simply call `UpdateData(TRUE)`.

✦ The `CDialog::OnOK` function calls `UpdateData(TRUE)`. Therefore, if the `OnOK` function was called to exit the dialog box, the function that called the dialog box's `DoModal` function will have access to the correct dialog box data.

Working with the edit control

In this section I'll first cover the most common tasks that are performed with the edit control. This includes adding and deleting text from an edit control, creating a multiline edit control, working with a password control, limiting the number of characters that can be typed into an edit, and restricting a user's input to numeric values. Once I've gone through this list, you'll then see the demo application updated to include these features.

Retrieving and setting an edit control's text

There are a number of ways to retrieve the text value of an edit control:

✦ You can attach a `CEdit` object to the control and call `CEdit::GSetWindowText` to set the control's text. As you've already seen in this chapter, you can either do this attachment manually (through the `CWnd::Attach` function) or through the use of a

DDX control variable that calls the `Attach` function when the dialog's `DoDataExchange` function is called. By the way, the `CEdit::GetWindowText` function is simply inherited from `CWnd`, and the `CWnd::GetWindowText` function calls the same Win32 SDK `::GetWindowText` function that the `DDX_Text` function calls. Conversely, to retrieve an edit control's data, you can either use the `CEdit::GetWindowText` function or set up a DDX variable to do that for you.

✦ The second way is to associate a DDX value variable with the edit control. The Add Member Variable Wizard enables you to associate various types such as `CString`, `int`, `bool`, and so on with the control so that you don't have to do the conversion from the desired type to the string type that all edit controls inherently work with.

✦ Finally, you can simply send the `WM_GETTEXT` message to the window. This is what the other methods eventually do, so you might wonder why you'd ever resort to such a non-object oriented technique. The best example I can give you is a password retrieval application (called *Eureka!*) I wrote a couple of years ago. It allows you to "see" the actual value of a password control by moving a mouse over it. (You'll recall that edit controls created with the `ES_PASSWORD` style display, by default, asterisks instead of the actual value.) However, one thing I found out when I wrote that application is that using an attached `CEdit` control and its `GetWindowText` wasn't working. After a few hours of debugging this, I finally found out that the `GetWindowText` function takes shortcuts when then target window is in another process. Specifically, this function attempts to pass a `WM_GETTEXT` message directly to the target window's window function instead of calling `SendMessage` or `PostMessage`. This technique simply won't work across process boundaries. Therefore, if you need to retrieve the value of an edit control that is in another process, you should send the `WM_GETTEXT` message to that window using the `SendMessage` or `PostMessage` function.

Just as the `GetWindowText` and `WM_GETTEXT` message can be used to retrieve an edit control's data, so too can the `SetWindowText` and `WM_SETTEXT` message be used to set the control's value.

Defining a multiline edit control

By default all edit controls are single line. To create a multiline edit control, you need to either specify the `ES_MULTILINE` style for the control, or set the `Multiline` property to `True` in the dialog editor. This is simple enough. However, there are a few other styles that are extremely important if the control is to provide the interface you want to your users.

The first thing to realize is that if the user is entering data into a multiline edit, the default manner for entering a new line is by pressing Ctrl+Enter. As you learned earlier, this is because when a user presses the Enter key while on a dialog box, and if a button does not have focus, it is the same as the user clicking the OK button. In the next chapter, you'll see how to override this.

Now, let's talk about those other styles. If a user is entering data into a multiline edit control, and the control already displays as much data as can be displayed, and the user presses Ctrl+Enter, the control will beep and the new line will not be entered. However, if the control has the `ES_AUTOVSCROLL` style specified (Auto VScroll property set to `True`), the edit control will automatically scroll vertically in this situation.

If the user attempts to type past the right edge of the control and the `ES_AUTOHSCROLL` style is specified (Auto HScroll property set to `True`), the multi-line edit control automatically scrolls horizontally. In this case, the user must manually start a new line by pressing

Ctrl+Enter. If ES_AUTOHSCROLL style is not specified (AutoHScroll property set to False), the control automatically wraps words to the beginning of the next line when necessary. Note that the position of the word wrap is determined by the window size. If the window size changes, the word wrap position changes and the text is redisplayed.

Finally, multi-line edit controls can have scroll bars. An edit control with scroll bars can process its own scroll-bar messages. Edit controls without scroll bars scroll as described, and process any scroll messages sent by the parent window. Scroll bars are specified with the WS_VSCROLL and WS_HSCROLL styles (Vertical Scroll and Horizontal Scroll properties).

Setting and retrieving multiline edit control data

Although the techniques described in the section "Adding and deleting text" can be used for multiline as well as single-line edit controls, they do have the limitation that they return all the text of an edit control or it completely replace the text currently in the edit control. The problem is that many times with a multiline edit control you are only interested in retrieving or modifying part of an edit control's text. To address that need there is a set of functions, starting with the CEdit::GetLine function:

```
int GetLine(int nIndex, LPTSTR lpszBuffer) const;
int GetLine(int nIndex,
            LPTSTR lpszBuffer,
            int nMaxLength) const;
```

As you can see, there are two overloaded versions of the GetLine function. In both cases, the first parameter is the zero-based index of the line position you want to retrieve. The second parameter is then a pointer to a string buffer that the control uses to store the text. Finally, the last parameter in the second overload is the maximum size of the buffer.

In addition to the GetLine function, another useful function to know about is CEdit::LineLength. This function is used to determine how much space to allocate in your buffer. When GetLine copies text to the buffer, it does not have a null terminator. In order to use the buffer once GetLine fills it, you must have some way of determining where in the buffer the string ends. GetLine returns the size of the buffer it used to copy text. You can then use this information to find the end of the string.

If you need to know the total number of lines in a CEdit control, use CEdit::GetLineCount, which returns the current line count for the target control. However, GetLineCount returns a line count of 1 even if the control is empty. This detail is overlooked by many beginning Windows C++ programmers.

Defining an edit control as a password control

I'm sure you've seen many applications that display asterisks as the user is typing in a password. This feature is supported by the edit control by simply setting the ES_PASSWORD style (or the Password property). However, not only can you specify that a user's text is to be protected in this fashion as they type it in, but you can also set the password character to be used instead of accepting the default asterisk character. Using the CEdit class, this is done via the CEdit::SetPasswordChar function. In the following code snippet, the password character is set to a plus sign. The code then verifies that the edit control has the ES_PASSWORD style on and then verifies that the plus sign is the set password character.

```
pmyEdit->SetPasswordChar('+*');
VERIFY(pmyEdit->GetStyle() & ES_PASSWORD);
VERIFY(pmyEdit->GetPasswordChar() == '+');
```

Setting the edit control maximum length

As I mentioned earlier, the maximum length of an edit control is approximately 60KB of text. That's certainly more than most people will want to use, and you can always use the rich edit control if you need more. However, there are times when you will want to limit the number of characters entered into an edit control. For example, if the data being entered will be used to populate a database, and the database column is a fixed length, then you should probably set a maximum length for the edit control so that the user doesn't waste time entering data that will be truncated and not saved. This is done simply by calling the `CEdit::SetLimitText` function and specifying the maximum number of characters that can be entered.

Restricting input to numeric values

Restricting input to just numbers is actually simpler than you probably thought and doesn't require any sort of subclassing with your own `CEdit`-derived class. The first thing you need to do is to set the `ES_NUMBER` style (Number property). That ensures that the user will not be allowed to enter anything but numeric characters into the edit control.

Now, to retrieve the data into a numeric dialog class member variable, simply use the Add Member Variable dialog box and specify a numeric type, such as `int` or `double`. The correct overloaded version of the `DDX_Text` function will be inserted into the `DoDataExchange`, and it will ensure that the data is properly formatted.

Setting the tab stops

Another important function of multiline edit controls is the ability to set its tab stops. This is done via the `CEdit::SetTabStops`, which measures the distance in *dialog units*. A dialog unit is approximately equal to one-quarter the average width of the system font. The default distance between tab stops in an edit control is 32 dialog units. With the `SetTabStops` function you can set the distance between tab stops or set each tab stop individually with an absolute position. This example demonstrates both of these concepts. In the first example, I'm setting the tab stops to 16 dialog units. In the second example, I'm explicitly setting a series of tab stops with absolute values.

```
m_Edit1.SetTabStops(16);

int nTabStops[]={5,10,30,45,52 };
m_Edit1.SetTabStops(5,nTabStops);
```

Updating the demo application

Now it's time to code the `CEditDlg` part of the demo application. First create `CString` DDX variables for all the edit controls as shown in Table 10-4 with two important notes. First, if you've already defined the `m_strTo` member variable, you can ignore that one. Second, the first radio button needs to use the `DDX_Radio` function explained earlier in this chapter.

Once you've created the member variables, you'll need to set the following control properties:

✦ First radio button (Mr.): Set the Group property to True.

✦ Copies edit control: Set the Number property to True.

✦ Password edit control: Set the Password property to True.

✦ Letter edit control: Set the Multiline, Readonly, and Auto VScroll properties to True. Set the Auto HScroll property to False.

Table 10-4: CEditDlg DDX Value Variables

Control	Variable Type	Variable Name
To edit control	CString	m_strTo
Copies edit control	int	m_nCopies
Book title edit control	CString	m_strBookTitle
Password edit control	CString	m_strPassword
Letter multiline edit control	CString	m_edtLetter
First radio button	int	m_iTitle

After you've finished with the dialog box, all that is left is to code the event handler for the Update Letter button. Here's the code for that. The first thing to notice is the call to UpdateData to get the control values into the dialog box's member variables. From there you can then check to make sure that all values have been entered. If that is the case, you then format the m_strLetter (the DDX variable used for the multiline edit control) using the value. Notice that although the password edit control's value cannot be seen on the dialog box, there is no special processing needed to retrieve its value. Instead its value is retrieved just like any other edit control. Also note that the extra blank lines in the Format call are my own doing in order to make the code a bit more readable. Finally, take note of the formatting characters used here. Specifically, the tab character is represented by the escape character followed by a *t* (\t), and the newline character is represented in a multiline edit control by a carriage return/line feed combination (\r\n). Lastly, note that once the m_strLetter member variable is set, a call to UpdateData(FALSE) updates its associated multiline control on the dialog box.

```
void CEditDlg::OnBnClickedOk()
{
 if (UpdateData())
 {
  if (0 < m_strTo.GetLength()
  && 0 < m_strBookTitle.GetLength()
  && 0 < m_nCopies
  && 0 < m_strPassword.GetLength())
  {
   CString strTitle;
   GetTitle(strTitle);

   m_strLetter.Format("Dear %s %s,"

   "\r\n\r\n"

   "\tAs my way of saying thanks for the great job in "
   "helping me write this book, I am sending you %ld "
   "copies of the book, '%s'.\r\n"

   "\tThis book does include a password protected site "
```

```
       "where you can download all source code. Your password "
       "is '%s'."

       "\r\n\r\n"

       "Sincerely, "
       "\r\n"
       "Tom Archer",

       strTitle, m_strTo,
       m_nCopies, m_strBookTitle,
       m_strPassword);

       UpdateData(FALSE);
    }
    else
    {
      AfxMessageBox("You must enter all values");
    }
  }
}
```

Now, add the GetTitle helper function to the CEditDlg class and code it as follows. As you can see, this function determines which radio button is currently checked by looking at the m_iTitle member variable. Based on that, it calls the GetDlgItem function to get a CWnd pointer for that radio button, and then retrieves that radio button's caption via a call to GetWindowText.

```
    void CEditDlg::GetTitle(CString& strTitle)
    {
      CWnd* pWnd = NULL;

      switch (m_iTitle)
      {
        case 0:
          pWnd = GetDlgItem(IDC_RADIO1);
          break;
        case 1:
          pWnd = GetDlgItem(IDC_RADIO2);
          break;
        case 2:
          pWnd = GetDlgItem(IDC_RADIO3);
          break;
        default: ASSERT(FALSE);
      }

      ASSERT(pWnd);
      if (pWnd)
      {
        pWnd->GetWindowText(strTitle);
      }
    }
```

When you've finished coding these two functions, build and run the application to see results similar to those shown in Figure 10-12.

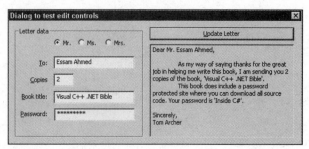

Figure 10-12: Example of basic edit control programming

Using the CListBox Class

The list box control (encapsulated by the CListBox class) is used to display a list of strings, generally referred to as *items*. List boxes are useful for displaying information that is organized in a flat, single-dimensional manner, such as lists of states or zip codes. In fact, a list box can display anything that can be represented by a string. Note that although you can create an owner-drawn list box that contains multiple columns, list boxes are generally used in situations where you have only a single column of items to display. For situations where you want to display multiple columns, the vastly more robust list view control should be used (covered in Chapter 7).

Because you'll be working with code to illustrate the various tasks that can be performed with an edit control, add a dialog box to the ControlsDemo project with an ID of IDD_LISTBOX. Once you're done, define a CDialog-derived class called CListBoxDlg for this template. Now, add a menu item to the main menu resource (under the Controls menu) and add an event handler to it that displays the CListBoxDlg as you've done for the previous dialog boxes.

At this point, I'll use the same format that I did in covering the edit control where I first introduce the basic tasks associated with working with the list box control, and then when I'm finished, incorporate this into the ControlsDemo application.

Adding and deleting items

The most basic task in dealing with the list box is adding items to it. There are actually two CListBox member functions for doing this: AddString and InsertString.

The AddString function takes a pointer to a string and adds that string to the list box. If the list box is not sorted (specified via the LBS_SORT style or the Sort property), the string is added to the end of the list box. If the list box is sorted, the string is added and the sort routine is called. The return value is the zero-based index of the list box where the item was eventually stored.

```
int CListBox::AddString(LPCTSTR value);
```

The InsertString function takes two parameters. The first indicates the zero-based index where the string is to be inserted into the list box. The second parameter is the string pointer for the value to be inserted. Note that using the InsertString function to insert a string a specific index overrides the sort style — that is, once the string is inserted, the sort routine is not called. As with the AddString function, the return value will be the index of the list box where the string was inserted.

```
int CListBox::InsertString(int index, LPCTSTR value);
```

Regardless of how a string is inserted into a list box, they are deleted individually from the list box with the CListBox::DeleteString function. The DeleteString function takes as its sole argument the zero-based index of the item to be removed and returns the number of items left in the list box after the removal.

To remove all the items from a list box at one time, you can call the CListBox::ResetContent function.

Note Almost all of the CListBox member functions return LB_ERR on failure. Therefore, you should always check for this value after an attempt is made to modify the list box control's contents.

Selecting items and searching

CListBox has several functions that enable you to get information about and manipulate the current selection. For single-selection list boxes, use GetCurSel. This function returns the zero-based index of the currently selected item. GetCurSel returns the value LB_ERR when nothing is selected.

Conversely, setting a list box's selection is done by passing the index of the item to be selected to the SetCurSel function To clear all selections in a list box, pass SetCurSel with the value –1.

You can also set the selection based on a string using the function SelectString.

```
int SelectString(
    int nStartAfter,
    LPCTSTR lpszItem
);
```

As you can see, the SelectString function takes two arguments. The first argument (nStartAfter) indicates the zero-based index of the item before the first item to be searched. Therefore, to search the entire list box, you need to specify a value of –1. The second argument (lpszItem) is a string representing the starting text of the item to be selected. Using the data shown in Figure 10-13, the following function call would highlight (select) the Jean Valjean entry because it is the first string after the third entry (remember that the nStartAfter value is zero-based) that begins with a J.

```
m_lbx.SelectString(2, "J");
```

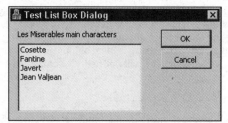

Figure 10-13: The SelectString function is a powerful means of searching through a list box for a given string or substring.

Note also that the `SelectString` function wraps around to the beginning of the list if it receives a value other than –1. Once again, using the data shown in Figure 10-13, this means that the following function call would highlight the Cosette entry even though the `nStartAfter` value is 2. This is because the list box searches from the third entry forward until the end of the list box's entries and then starts over (wraps) from the beginning; ultimately finding the Cosette entry at index 0.

```
m_lbx.SelectString(2, "Cosette");
```

To search a list box for a string without selecting any items, use either `FindString` or `FindStringExact`. `FindString` uses the same starting text search as `SelectString`, while `FindStringExact` searches for the exact text specified. Both functions return the index of the item found or `LB_ERR` if no items are located.

Multiple selection list boxes work a bit differently. Items can be selected with `SetSel`, for a single selection, or `SelItemRange`. These functions can be combined to create multiple selections:

```
m_ListBox1.SetSel(5);
m_ListBox1.SelItemRange(TRUE,7,12);
m_ListBox1.SelItemRange(FALSE,1,4);
```

This code selects items 5 and 7 through 12 and deselects items 1 through 4.

Working with item data

Although many developers don't realize it, there is a style associated with every window called `GWL_USERDATA`. Using this data, the application can define a numeric value (or typically a pointer to a structure of data) that contains information that is be associated with the window. This style was used quite frequently back in the days when SDK programming was the standard means of writing Windows applications. Now, of course, with C++ and MFC, programmers can simply create `CWnd`-derived classes and define member variables to hold this data. However, a very similar concept is the *item data* of the list box control. Here, instead of associating data with an entire window, you have the ability to associate data with specific items in the list box.

As an example, suppose your application reads vendor records from a database table and populates a list box with the vendor names. When the user clicks a vendor in the list box, how will the application be able to keep track of the rest of the data for that vendor? One way would be to use the list box control's item data property as follows:

1. Upon dialog box initialization, for all vendor records:

    a. Instantiate a CVendor object

    b. Add the vendor name to the list box

    c. For the just added item, set that index's item's data to the CVendor address

2. When an item is selected:

    a. Retrieve the index of the list box using GetCurSel

    b. Using that index value, retrieve the item data

    c. Cast the item data to a CVendor object

    d. You now have the CVendor object associated with the list box selected item

3. Upon dialog box destruction, for each item in the list box, retrieve the item data and delete the underlying CVendor object from memory

Although this is a fair bit of work, it does present a very common means of associating objects with list box items. Let's look at the two functions that allow you to set and retrieve item data as well as an example of how they would be used in actual C++ code.

```
CVendor* pVendor = new CVendor();
// populate pVendor object

int idx = m_lbx.AddString("Vendor 1");
if (LB_ERR != idx)
{
 m_lbx.SetItemData((DWORD)pVendor);
}
```

As you can see from this code, the CListBox::SetItemData function takes a DWORD value. Therefore, you can store a simple numeric value with the item or a cast a struct or class pointer and use it.

Now if the user selects an item, the CVendor object can easily be retrieved with the CListBox::GetItemData function:

```
int idx = m_lbx.GetCurSel();
if (LB_ERR != idx)
{
 CVendor* pVendor = (CVendor*)m_lbx.GetItemData();
 // use the pVendor object
}
```

Finally, the C++ code to cycle through a list box deleting all item data pointers would look like this:

```
CVendor* pVendor;
int nItems = m_lbx.GetCount();
for (int i = 0; i < nItems; i++)
{
 pVendor = (CVendor*)m_lbx.GetItemData(i);
 ASSERT(pVendor);
```

```
    if (pVendor)
    {
      delete pVendor;
    }
}
```

You should also note at this point that all Windows controls that store multiple items (list box, combo box, list view, and tree view) support the item data field.

Using the CComboBox Class

A combo box (encapsulated by the CComboBox class) is a unique control in that it is actually two controls in one. The rectangular portion that you see when the combo box is not dropped down is in fact an edit control and the drop-down portion is a list box control. In fact, if you enumerate the child windows of a combo box, you'll find that the combo box contains a single child window, and that its window class name is EDIT.

There are actually three different types of combo boxes based on the style that is specified upon its creation. Table 10-5 lists three different combo box types (by the Type property that would be set in the dialog editor), the window style (used to create the combo box via the CreateWindow function), and the descriptions of just what type of control the user would see.

Table 10-5: Windows Control Classes

Combo Box Type Property	Windows Style Used with CreateWindow	Description
Simple	CBS_SIMPLE	Text can be entered into the edit control, and the drop-down is always visible.
Drop-down	CBS_DROPDOWN	Text can be entered into the edit control, and the drop-down is only visible when the user clicks the drop-down arrow.
Drop-down list	CBS_DROPDOWNLIST	Text cannot be entered into the edit control, and the drop-down is only visible when the user clicks the drop-down arrow.

An example using these styles is a case where the user is being presented with a list of items, but they can only select a valid item already in the list. The drop-down list is probably best for that scenario because its edit control is read-only. For situations where the user is presented with a list, but they can enter textual values not in the list, either the Simple or the Drop-down style would work.

Because the combo box consists of an edit control and a list box control, you've already seen the major functions that can be used with this control. For example, in order to retrieve or set the data of the edit portion of the combo box, you would use the CComboBox::GetWindowText and CComboBox::SetWindowText functions, respectively.

Additionally, the CComboBox class supports the adding and removing of strings via the CComboBox::AddString, CComboBox::InsertString, CComboBox::DeleteString, and CComboBox::ResetContent functions.

Here are a few of the functions that are unique to the CComboBox class:

✦ CComboBox::ShowDropDown — Displays or hides the drop-down list

✦ CComboBox::GetDroppedState — Queries the state of the drop-down list

✦ CComboBox::GetLBText — Retrieves a list entry given a zero-based index value

✦ CComboBox::GetLBTextLen — Gets the length of a specified entry given a zero-based index value

Another important CComboBox function is SetExtendedUI. This enables the extended user interface for the drop-down portion of the combo box. By default, the drop-down list is displayed whenever the combo box is clicked, regardless of combo box type. If the extended user interface is enabled, the drop-down list is displayed only for combo boxes created with the CBS_DROPDOWNLIST style. In addition, normal settings cause Alt+F4 to display the drop-down list when the control has focus. The down arrow is then used to scroll through the list. If the extended user interface is enabled, only the down arrow is needed to display and scroll through the drop-down list. Most users expect combo boxes to exhibit this extended behavior. Therefore, it's best to use the SetExtendedUI function wherever possible.

Modifying Control Attributes at Runtime

There will be many times when you'll want to dynamically modify certain control attributes at runtime. Examples of this are changing a control's color and setting the font of a given control. In this section, I'll illustrate how to perform each of these tasks. Afterwards, I'll cover one last item in this chapter — how to iterate through all the controls on a dialog box — setting the font of each control as you go.

Changing a control's color

One of the most obvious omissions in the design of controls is the lack of a member function that changes the color of the control. You can change a control's font with SetFont, but there is not an equivalent member function to change colors such as SetColor. Therefore, in this section I'll show you how this is done.

Using MFC, there are two ways to change a control's color. Both take advantage of the fact that controls send a WM_CTLCOLOR message to the parent window before they paint themselves. This message contains a handle to the device context used to paint the control. Because you have access to the device context, you can call member functions such as CDC::SetTextColor or CDC::SetBkColor to change the colors on the control. With this knowledge, you can write a message handler to select different colors. The message handler must return a brush handler (HBRUSH) that the control will use to paint its background. The prototype of the message handler looks like this:

```
afx_msg HBRUSH OnCtlColor(CDC* pDC,
                          CWnd* pWnd,
                          UINT nCtlColor)
```

MFC passes this handler three values. The first, pDC, is a pointer to the control's device context. The second parameter, pWnd, is a pointer to the control itself. Finally, the third parameter, nCtlColor, describes the type of WM_CTLCOLOR message that triggered the message handler. These message types are summarized in Table 10-6.

Table 10-6: WM_CTLCOLOR Message Types

nCtlColor Value	Type of Control
CTLCOLOR_STATIC	Static text control, all button styles except push buttons, read-only, or disabled edit controls, and the edit portion of a disabled combo box.
CTLCOLOR_EDIT	Edit control and the edit portion of a combo box.
CTLCOLOR_LISTBOX	List box and the list box portion of a combo box.
CTLCOLOR_BTN	Push button — note that processing this message has no effect in Windows 95.
CTLCOLOR_SCROLLBAR	Scroll bar.
CTLCOLOR_DLG	Dialog box.
CTLCOLOR_MSGBOX	Message box.

The following code sample illustrates a basic message handler for WM_CTLCOLOR. Assume that m_edtName is an edit control and m_brGreenBrush is a CBrush object, both being member variables of the dialog class (CMyDialog).

```
HBRUSH CMyDialog::OnCtlColor(CDC* pDC,
                            CWnd* pWnd,
                            UINT nCtlColor)
{
 if (m_edtName.GetSafeHwnd() == pWnd->GetSafeHwnd())
 {
  pDC->SetTextColor(RGB(255,255,255));
  pDC->SetBkColor(RGB(255,0,0));
  return (HBRUSH) m_brGreenBrush;
 }

 CDialog::OnCtlColor(pDC, pWnd, nCtlColor);
}
```

This code changes the color of the m_edtName control to white with a red background. This is one way to change a control's color. The only disadvantage of using this technique is that the parent window is responsible for changing each control's color. It would be better if you could encapsulate this behavior inside each control. This way, each control becomes a separate entity that can be reused. Because the controls send messages to their parent windows before they paint themselves, you need some way of "reflecting" these messages back to the child window, or control, that originated the message.

MFC provides such a mechanism. By using the ON_WM_CTLCOLOR_REFLECT message map macro, you can cause the parent window to send all unprocessed WM_CTLCOLOR messages back to the child window that originated the message. Now you can write customized controls that change their colors without relying on their parent window. The following code sample describes a custom control that changes its background, text, and text background:

```
class CMyStatic : public CStatic
{
public:
    CMyStatic();
protected:
    CBrush m_Brush;
afx_msg HBRUSH CtrlColr(CDC*, UINT);
    DECLARE_MESSAGE_MAP()
};

BEGIN_MESSAGE_MAP(CMyStatic, CStatic)
    ON_WM_CTLCOLOR_REFLECT()
END_MESSAGE_MAP()

CMyStatic::CMyStatic()
{
    m_Brush.CreateSolidBrush (RGB(255,255,255));
}

HBRUSH CMyStatic::CtlColor (CDC* pDC, UINT nCtlColor)
{
    pDC->SetTextColor(RGB(nRed,nGreen,nBlue));
    pDC->SetBkColor(RGB(255,0,0);
    return (HBRUSH) m_Brush;
}
```

Now you could simply derive your CStatic controls from CMyStatic instead of CStatic and they would automatically have this coloring in effect for them.

Setting a control's font

To set the font of a control, you simply need to define the desired font, attach an MFC control window class to the control, and then call that class's SetFont member function (derived from CWnd). Because the SetFont function will ultimately send a WM_SETFONT message to the window, you can do that as well. Here's the step-by-step instructions on setting the fonts for every single control on a dialog box.

1. Declare the font object (m_font). I typically do this at the dialog class level.

```
class CMyDialog : public CDialog
{
  ...
  CFont m_font;
  ...
};
```

2. Define the font. I typically do this in the dialog box's `OnInitDialog` because I use the dialog box's device context in defining the font, and it won't be available until this function is called.

Note that I first define the `LOGFONT` structure on the stack and them initialize that block of memory to all zeroes with a call to `ZeroMemory`.

After acquiring the dialog's device context, I use a helper function (`PointSizeToHeight`) to convert the desired font point size to the height value that the `CreateFontIndirect` function will expect. I set the font's weight to `FW_BOLD` (as opposed to `FW_NORMAL`) and set the font name to MS Sans Serif. Finally, a call to `CFont::CreateFontIndirect`, which takes as its only parameter the `LOGFONT` structure, is used to define the font object's characteristics.

```
LOGFONT lf;
ZeroMemory(&lf, sizeof LOGFONT);

CClientDC clientDC(this);
lf.lfHeight = PointSizeToHeight(8, clientDC.m_hDC );
lf.lfWeight = FW_BOLD;
strcpy(lf.lfFaceName, "MS Sans Serif");
VERIFY(m_font.CreateFontIndirect(&lf));
```

3. Here is the `PointSizeToHeight` helper function. It is a very standard formula for converting a font point size for a given device context to a font height value needed to create the font.

```
int PointSizeToHeight(int iPointSize, HDC hDC)
{
 int iRetVal = 0;
 ASSERT(hDC != NULL);
 if (hDC != NULL)
 {
  iRetVal = -(MulDiv(iPointSize,
              ::GetDeviceCaps(hDC, LOGPIXELSY), 72));
 }

 return (iRetVal);
}
```

4. Finally, in the dialog's `OnInitDialog` function, you can set the font of the desired control with code like the following (where `m_edit` is assumed to be a `CEdit` object associated with an edit control on the dialog box):

```
m_edit.SetFont(&m_font);
```

Now, let's look at how to cycle through all the controls on a dialog box ,setting the font for each control.

Iterating through the controls on a dialog box

Iterating through all the controls on a dialog box is actually very easy. You simply need to use the `CDialog` class's derived (from `CWnd`) `GetTopWindow` and `GetNextWindow` functions. The `GetTopWindow` function is specifically designed to examine the *Z order* of the child windows associated with the specified parent window, and retrieves a handle to the child window at the top of that Z order. In the case of a dialog box, that means that it will return the topmost child control. From there, you can start a `while` loop, calling the `GetNextWindow` function (passing it a value of `GW_HWNDNEXT`) to retrieve the remaining windows. The `GetNextWindow` function returns a null value when there are no more windows to enumerate.

Using the code from the previous section on defining a font, here's a code snippet that would set the font of each control on the dialog box to that defined by the `m_font` object.

```
CWnd* pChildWnd = NULL;
pChildWnd = GetTopWindow();
while (NULL != pChildWnd)
{
 pChildWnd->SetFont(&m_font);
 pChildWnd = pChildWnd->GetNextWindow(GW_HWNDNEXT);
}
```

Note that the `GetNextWindow` is also used to iterate through the windows in reverse order except that you would pass it the value of `GW_HWNDPREV`.

Summary

This chapter began by exploring the dialog box basics by illustrating how to create dialog template resources, how to define and associate a `Cdialog` class to control the dialog box, and how to display and manage modal dialog boxes. From there, you discovered how the combination of message maps, command routing, and the `CCmdTarget` class allows you to associate commands (such as the user clicking the OK button) with handler functions.

Once you finished with the dialog box basics, you then learned some control basics; including four different ways in which to associate a control class with a control in order to manipulate it. Finally, you saw how to program several key controls including buttons, edit controls, list boxes, and combo boxes.

This chapter should provide a nice segue into the next chapter, because that chapter includes details covering some of the finer points of programming dialog boxes, such as creating and controlling modeless dialog boxes, serializing data from a dialog box, and using dialog template resources as form views for your document/view applications. Once finished with both of these chapters, you should feel very comfortable writing almost any application that uses dialog boxes or form views as well as programming and handling common control events.

✦ ✦ ✦

Dialog Boxes and Form Views

In Chapter 10, you learned quite a bit about the basics of working with dialog boxes and DDX, as well as a few of the Windows common controls. With the basics out of the way, this chapter focuses on the more advanced tasks for dialog boxes. This includes creating and managing modeless dialog boxes, messaging between dialog boxes, implementing CommandUI in a dialog box, and keyboard processing. Once you've finished that, you'll then see how to create view classes based on dialog templates for use in SDI and MDI applications via the `CFormView` class and how to programmatically switch between a document's attached views. Finally, the chapter wraps up with a cool demonstration of how to define `CCtrlView`-derived classes in order to combine the power of that control with the flexibility of the document/view architecture.

Modeless Dialog Boxes

You've already learned about modal dialog boxes in the previous chapters. Therefore, I'll begin this chapter by discussing how to incorporate modeless dialog boxes into your MFC applications. As opposed to modal dialog boxes, when a modeless dialog box is displayed, Windows enables user input to the dialog box's parent window. When the user attempts to interact with the parent window, the modeless dialog box is still shown over top of the parent window in the Z-order. However, the parent has focus. (The Z-order of a window indicates the window's position in a stack of overlapping windows.)

Here are the seven basic steps to defining, creating, and managing the lifetime of a modeless dialog box. Note that many of these steps you already know and therefore won't be explained in detail. The steps specific to modeless dialog boxes are explained in the following sections leading up to a full demo application illustrating these steps in action.

1. Create the dialog template resource — As with modal dialog boxes, the first step is to create the dialog template resource and add the desired controls, setting the styles of both. Note that there are no special styles that need to be set for a dialog box to be used in a modeless fashion.

2. Create the `CDialog`-derived class for the template — As with modal dialog boxes, you need to use the ClassWizard to generate a `CDialog`-derived class.

3. **Declare an instance of the parent class** — When you decide what class will be the parent of the modeless dialog box — typically a view or another dialog — define as a member variable of the parent class either an instance of the modeless dialog class or a pointer to the modeless dialog class.

4. **Instantiate the dialog box in the parent class** — The parameters you define in the modeless dialog box's constructor are typically predicated on how the modeless dialog box will communicate with the parent window. One common technique is to pass the parent window's `this` pointer to the dialog box so that it can use that to communicate data back to the parent.

5. **The parent displays the modeless dialog box** — In order to display a modeless dialog box, the parent window calls the `CDialog::Create` function (and possibly the `CWnd::ShowWindow` function). I'll cover this in more detail in the next section, "Creating and displaying modeless dialog boxes."

6. **Code communications between the parent and the modeless dialog box** — Most modeless dialog boxes need to have a means of communicating data between the modeless dialog box and the parent window. There are two common techniques for doing this. One is to have the parent window pass its `this` pointer to the dialog box's constructor, where the dialog box could directly call the parent window class's member functions. Another method is to also pass the parent window's `this` pointer and for the dialog box to post messages to the parent window. I'll explain both techniques in more detail in the section "Communicating data and state."

7. **The parent manages the modeless dialog box** — This has to do with the fact that modeless dialog boxes cannot be destructed simply by calling the `CDialog::OnOK` or `CDialog::OnCancel` functions. These functions are meant for modal dialog boxes only. Therefore, the modeless dialog box communicates back to the parent that it needs to be destructed. This is what I mean by *communicating state*. Because the technique used to communicate this information is the same as that used to communicate any other data to the parent, this is also covered in the section "Communicating data and state."

Creating and displaying modeless dialog boxes

Once the modeless dialog box class has been instantiated, call the `Create` function to both create and display the dialog box. As you can see here, the `Create` function has two overloads:

```
BOOL Create(LPCTSTR lpszTemplateName,
            CWnd* pParentWnd = NULL);

BOOL Create(UINT nIDTemplate,
            CWnd* pParentWnd = NULL);
```

As you might have noticed, the two `Create` functions mimic exactly the two overloaded `CDialog` constructors for instantiating a modal dialog box. This is for a very logical reason. When an application constructs and displays a modal dialog box, the calling function is *blocked* until the `DoModal` function returns. Therefore, the construction and display of the dialog box can occur within the same function. However, the display of a modeless dialog box is asynchronous. When the calling function calls the `Create` function and the modeless dialog box is displayed, the `Create` function returns immediately after displaying the dialog box. This means that the calling function will almost certainly terminate while the dialog box is still visible. The problem is that if the `CDialog` object had been created on the stack, it would go out of scope and destruct. The result would be a dialog box that, after being displayed for mere milliseconds, would disappear because the destructor would destroy it. Therefore, it is common to see applications create a `CDialog`-derived object in one function, store a pointer to that dialog object, and call `Create` in another function. You will see how to do this when we get to the demo application for this section.

> **Note** Although the `Create` function will normally cause a modeless dialog box to be displayed, there is one situation where that is not the case. If the dialog template has the `Visible` style (`WS_VISIBLE`) off, the modeless dialog box technically will be executing, but won't be visible to the user. Therefore, in order to either ensure that this isn't the case, or to display a modeless dialog box whose `Visible` style is set to `False`, call the `ShowWindow` function with a value of `SW_NORMAL`.

```
dlg.Create(IDD_MY_MODELESS_DIALOG);
dlg.ShowWindow(SW_NORMAL);
```

As you know, you typically don't have to specify the dialog template resource for a modal dialog box. The reason for this is because when you use the ClassWizard to create a `CDialog`-derived class based on a template, the code is automatically generated to call the `CDialog` constructor with the dialog box's associated template ID. This is good for a couple of reasons. First, it's one less task that you have to worry about in your code, and second, it allows you to code a dialog box such that the user can't make a mistake in instantiating the dialog box. For the same benefits, it's very common for programmers using modeless dialog boxes to define the derived `Create` function as a protected (or private) function, and to overload it with a parameter-less version. This second version then calls the first version with the correct ID. This is also the method employed in the demo application.

One last thing to be cognizant of in a modeless dialog box environment is that the user might attempt to return to the parent window and invoke the modeless dialog box again. There are two ways to solve this. The first thing would be to disable the UI element that displays the modeless dialog box when that dialog box is already being viewed. For example, if you have a menu item on a view to display a Find dialog box, you could then add code to that menu item's CommandUI handler like the following:

```
void CMyView::OnUpdateEditFind(CCmdUI *pCmdUI)
{
    pCmdUI->Enable(!m_pDlg->GetSafeHwnd()};
}
```

In this function, you have a view class (the modeless dialog box's parent window) that defines a member variable used to hold a pointer to the modeless dialog box (`m_pDlg`). Because you know that after the `Create` function is executed, and until the dialog box is destroyed, the dialog class will contain a valid `HWND` value, you can simply call the class's `GetSafeHwnd` and use it to determine if the dialog is still active. Therefore, you can easily disable the menu item in that case.

However, I personally dislike this approach. I prefer the method of simply setting the focus to the dialog box if the user clicks the option again:

```
void CMyView::OnEditFind()
{
 ASSERT(m_pDlg);
 if (m_pDlg)
 {
  if (!m_pDlg->GetSafeHwnd())
  {
    m_pDlg->Create(IDD_FIND, this);
    m_pDlg->ShowWindow(SW_SHOW);
```

```
    }
    else
    {
      m_pDlg->SetFocus();
    }
  }
}
```

Communicating data and state

There are two issues in communicating data and state. First, most of the time that a modeless dialog box is being used, there is data to communicate between the dialog box and its parent window. For example, a Find dialog box might want to communicate back to the parent window the search parameters selected by the user when the user clicks the Find button. Second, if you look at the code for the base `CDialog OnOK` and `OnCancel` handlers, you'll see that they are both are designed to only work with modal dialog boxes. As a result, these functions should never be used to terminate a modeless dialog box, and you should always override them in your own code. So how do you terminate a modeless dialog box? The modeless dialog box should communicate its desire to be terminated back to the parent. Because the information sent to the parent window should indicate whether the user has asked to complete the operation or cancel the operation, I refer to this as *communicating state*.

To begin with, any time you want to communicate between two windows, you have several choices. However, because both windows exist in the same process, you're generally going to pick between two options: calling member functions or sending messages. Because you certainly know how to call C++ class functions and using messaging is the more flexible solution, I'll focus on the latter technique in this section. Say you've defined a modeless dialog box called `CMyDialog` that is constructed and displayed from a parent window, and the dialog box needs to send data back to the parent window. These are the steps you need to accomplish that:

1. You must define a message and place it in a commonly shared header file (typically the dialog class's header file). Using the aforementioned modeless Find dialog box, here's how you could define a message that would be used to communicate back to the parent window that the user has chosen his search criteria and is requesting that the search be carried out.

   ```
   #define WM_FINDDATA (WM_APP + 1)
   ```

Note

Many programmers who realize that messages numbered 0 through (WM_USER − 1) are reserved for the system believe that it is valid to define values for use in their applications staring with WM_USER. Technically, this is incorrect and can in some circumstances cause problems in your code that are extremely difficult to track down. The reason is that while the next block of numbers (WM_USER through 0x7FFF) are specifically defined to be used by an application to send messages within a private window class, these values should never be used to define messages that are meaningful throughout an application because some predefined window classes already define values in this range. For example, predefined control classes such as BUTTON, EDIT, and LISTBOX may use these values. Messages in this range should not be sent to other applications unless the applications have been designed to exchange messages and to attach the same meaning to the message numbers.

As a result, it is always safe to use the next block of messages, which are defined as WM_APP through 0xBFFF. The Microsoft documentation specifically states that this range is reserved for private application messaging and that no numbers in this range conflict with any system message IDs. In the name of completeness, I'll also add that the last two blocks of defined numbers are 0xCCC through 0xFFFF (used for string messages) and values greater than 0xFFFF (reserved for Windows).

2. Define an event handler in the parent window for the new message ID. Unfortunately, Visual Studio doesn't provide a wizard-like means of doing this so you'll have to manually enter the map entries yourself. To do this, first define the message handler in the header file using the afx_msg keyword, returning a long, and taking as parameters a UINT (for the WPARAM) and a LONG (for the LPARAM):

```
afx_msg long OnFindData(UINT wParam, LONG lParam);
```

Note

If you compile a file that uses the afx_msg keyword, you'll find that this keyword actually resolves to white space in the latest release of Visual C++. However, it is always safe to use this defined keyword to abstract you from any future changes to Visual C++ and how this keyword is defined.

Once you define the prototype for the function, you then need to add the map entry. Here I've defined a message map entry for the WM_FINDDATA message that will map to the OnFindData function in my modeless dialog box's parent window class (a CView-derived class called CMyView).

```
BEGIN_MESSAGE_MAP(CMyView, CView)
ON_MESSAGE(WM_FINDDATA, OnFindData)
...
END_MESSAGE_MAP()
```

3. Implement the parent window handler. Here's the OnFindData handler:

```
long CMyView::OnFindData(UINT wParam, LONG lParam)
{
 // Retrieve application specific data from wParam
 // and/or lParam parameters.

 // When finished...
 return 0L;
}
```

4. Now you need to make sure that the modeless dialog box can communicate back to the parent. I've already mentioned a few times that you can simply pass the parent window's this pointer to the modal dialog box upon instantiation of the dialog box class. However, you might be wondering why that's needed, because the dialog box constructor specifically states that a default parameter is the parent window.

The problem is that when you do not specify the parent window yourself, MFC will automatically set the modal dialog box's parent window to the main application window. From a dialog-based application this is not a problem, and therefore, you can get away with simply instantiating a modal dialog box without specifying a parent window. It can then call GetParent and communicate with the parent dialog box. However, if the parent of the modeless dialog box is a view class, you've got some issues to deal with. Specifically, not passing the view's pointer as the parent window will cause the MFC to pass the frame window as the parent, because that technically is the main application window. As a result, if a view constructs a modeless dialog box and doesn't pass its this pointer, and the modeless dialog box calls the GetParent function in an attempt to communicate with the view, it will never succeed because all messages will be sent to the view's frame (which is the application's main window).

So to summarize, if the parent is the main dialog box in a dialog-based application, you do not have to pass the parent window pointer to the modeless dialog box. For most other cases, you do need to pass the parent window's this pointer. As a result, I always pass the pointer to make my dialog box code more reusable.

Therefore, modify the dialog box's constructor to remove the default part of the parameter and to specifically dictate that the parent window be explicitly specified by the parent. Here's a before and after example of this change:

```
// before
CFindDlg(CWnd* pParent = NULL);

// after
CFindDlg(CWnd* pParent);
```

5. Now the modeless dialog box can easily communicate back to the parent window using the GetParent function and the agreed-upon message IDs:

```
void CFindDlg::OnBnClickedOk()
{
 if (UpdateData())
 {
  CWnd* pParent = GetParent();
  ASSERT(pParent);
  if (pParent)
  {
   pParent->SendMessage(WM_FINDDATA, 0, 0);
  }
 }
}
```

Obviously the data passed in the LPARAM and WPARAM is application-specific, and is something that both the parent window and modeless dialog box understand. Typically if you are passing anything other than a simple number (which can be cast to either LPARAM or WPARAM), the modeless dialog box will construct a structure understood by both windows (typically defined in the dialog box's header file) and pass that structure's pointer to the parent window.

Note   When one window is allocating data to send to another there is always the question of who is responsible for deleting that memory. That depends on the scope of the data's use. You'll recall that there are two ways to send messages in windows: via the SendMessage and PostMessage functions. The SendMessage function is analogous to me walking up to you and handing you a letter, where I've decided that I'm not leaving until you receive the letter from me. Therefore, in this case, the function calling SendMessage is blocked until the message is received and the message handler returns. The PostMessage function, on the other hand, is analogous to me sticking the letter in the mail. You'll either get it or you won't; I'm trusting the post office to take care of that, and I'm not hanging around. Therefore, in this situation, the messaging is asynchronous.

So, who cleans up then? In the SendMessage scenario, it depends on whether the receiving window will be saving the data for later use. Because you already know that the calling function is blocked until the message handler returns, if the message handler is the only code on the end that alters the data, then the calling function can delete the memory upon return. On the other hand, if the window receiving the message is going to store the data for later use, then it needs to clean up the memory because the sending window won't know when the data is no longer needed. In the case of the PostMessage, it's very easy. Since the messaging is asynchronous, the only function that can clean up the memory must be on the callee side.

So now that you know how to send data from a modeless dialog box to its parent, how do you send state data? The exact same way as you would any data. You simply define messages that the parent would respond to in order to destruct the window. Typically in my applications, I handle `OnOK` in the modeless dialog box to perform some sort of function. In the modeless Find dialog box example, that results in me sending the `WM_FINDDATA` message to the parent. If the user clicks the Close button on this dialog box, I then send a `WM_DIALOGCLOSE` (which I define) to the parent. The parent then destructs the window as follows:

```
long CMyView::OnDialogClose(UINT wParam, LONG lParam)
{
 // using member variable that identifies
 // modeless dialog box
 m_pDlg->DestroyWindow();
 return OL;
}
```

This way, the modeless dialog box is destroyed properly.

However, in your specific application, you might want to send both `OnOK`- and `OnCancel`-like states to the parent. In this case, you have two choices. You can either create two separate windows messages, or you can create a single message to handle both cases. You already know how to create individual messages, so I'll focus on the latter. Because you know you can send data in the message to the parent, you could simply pass the `IDOK` or `IDCANCEL` Windows constants to the parent window using a single message ID. For example, let's say you've defined the `WM_DIALOGCLOSE` message. The modeless dialog box could then send this message in either of the following ways:

```
// get parent window; send OK message
pParent->PostMessage(WM_DIALOGCLOSE, IDOK);
// get parent window; send CANCEL message
pParent->PostMessage(WM_DIALOGCLOSE, IDCANCEL);
```

Now the parent class's `WM_DIALOGCLOSE` handler would look something like the following:

```
long CMyView::OnDialogClose(UINT wParam, LONG lParam)
{
  if (wParam == IDOK)
   ...
  else if (wParam == IDCLOSE)
   ...
  else ASSERT(FALSE); // sanity check

  m_pDlg->DestroyWindow();
  return OL;
}
```

At this point, I've talked quite a bit about modeless dialog boxes and how to program them. Therefore, a demo application would definitely help to solidify and illustrate how all this works in a practical application.

Modeless demo application

Because I always like to punctuate sections with a demo application demonstrating the key points presented, let's walk through a very practical situation where a modal dialog box would be used. You've probably seen that most Find dialog boxes are modeless; allowing the user to move the cursor around the text to look for a subsequent search attempt, or to modify the text. Therefore, in this demo, you are going to create a dialog-based application that contains a rich edit control that allows you to open and display RTF files. The application's Find dialog box will then provide the ability to search the opened RTF document and will highlight the found text.

1. At this point, create a dialog-based application called ModelessDemo.

2. When the project has been created, open the dialog editor and add controls so that when finished it looks like that shown in Figure 11-1.

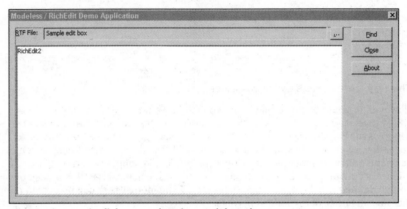

Figure 11-1: Main dialog template for modeless demo

3. Set the Read Only styles of both the edit control and rich edit control to True.

4. Create a value member variable called m_strFileName of type CString for the edit control.

5. Create a control member variable called m_edtRTFDocument of type CRichEdit for the rich edit control.

6. Because the demo uses the rich edit control, you need to add a call to the rich edit initialization routine in your application's InitInstance function:

```
BOOL CModelessDemoApp::InitInstance()
{
  InitCommonControls();
  AfxInitRichEdit2();
  ...
```

Note   The fact that an application needs to call AfxInitRichEdit ties together several things I mentioned back in Chapter 10. You'll recall that I stated that all controls are simply windows that when registered cause Windows to associate a class name with a window procedure. Subsequent calls passing that class name to CreateWindow or CreateWindowEx can then be resolved to the correct window procedure. In the case of the common controls, this happens automatically because these controls live in the CommCtrl.DLL file, which is loaded automatically when Windows loads.

However, with the rich edit control this is not the case. Instead, the rich edit control lives in a separate file. (I'm using the 2.0 rich edit, which resides in the `riched20.dll` file.) Therefore, this DLL needs to be explicitly loaded so that it can register the rich edit class name (`RICHEDIT`) so that rich edit controls can be successfully created. It's the `AfxInitRichEdit2` function that does this. If you forget to call this function, MFC will attempt to load the dialog via the `CreateDialogIndirect` function. That function will attempt to create all the controls defined on the dialog box's template and when it fails to create the rich edit control, the `CreateDialogIndirect` will return failure, causing your application to end even before it begins.

7. Add the following handler for the dialog box button with the ellipsis. Here the code is simply invoking the common File Open dialog box and having it display by default only RTF files. Upon return from this function, the selected filename is verified via a helper function you'll see next. If the filename is valid, the read-only filename edit control is updated and the `ReadRTFDocument` function is called.

```
void CModelessDemoDlg::OnBnClickedFileOpen()
{
 CFileDialog fileDlg(TRUE);
 fileDlg.m_ofn.lpstrFilter = "RTF Documents"
  " (*.RTF)\0*.rtf\0\0";
 if (IDOK == fileDlg.DoModal())
 {
  if (IsValidFilename(fileDlg.GetFileName()))
  {
   m_strFilename = fileDlg.GetPathName();
   UpdateData(FALSE);
   ReadRTFDocument(m_strFilename);
  }
  else
  {
   AfxMessageBox("Invalid file name");
  }
 }
}
```

8. Now add the simple filename validation function:

```
BOOL CModelessDemoDlg::IsValidFilename(CString const&
                                      strFilename)
{
  BOOL bSuccess = FALSE;
  if (4 < strFilename.GetLength())
  {
    CString str = strFilename.Right(4);
    if (0 == str.CompareNoCase(".RTF"))
      bSuccess = TRUE;
  }
  return bSuccess;
}
```

9. The following function opens the user-specified file and calls the `CRichEdit::StreamIn` function, passing it a callback function you'll see next. Note here that I'm bypassing a bit of error checking in order to focus on the demo. You should definitely implement error checking for any `CFile` operations as discussed in Chapter 24.

```
void CModelessDemoDlg::ReadRTFDocument(
 CString const& strFilename)
{
  CFile file(strFilename, CFile::modeRead);
  EDITSTREAM es;
  es.dwCookie = (DWORD) &file;
  es.pfnCallback = MyStreamInCallback;
  m_edtRTFDocument.StreamIn(SF_RTF, es);
}
```

10. Now add the callback function that does the actual update of the rich edit control from the data read:

```
static DWORD CALLBACK MyStreamInCallback(DWORD dwCookie, LPBYTE
pbBuff, LONG cb, LONG *pcb)
{
  CFile* pFile = (CFile*) dwCookie;
  *pcb = pFile->Read(pbBuff, cb);
  return 0;
}
```

11. Create the dialog template (with an ID of `IDD_FIND`) for the modeless dialog box as shown in Figure 11-2.

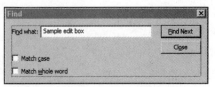

Figure 11-2: Main dialog template for modeless demo

12. Create two `int` member variables (using `DDX_Check`) for the checkbox controls. Call them `m_iMatchCase` and `m_iMatchWholeWord`. Add a `CString` member variable called `m_strFindWhat` for the edit control.

13. Create a `CDialog`-derived class for the dialog box called `CFindDlg`.

14. Define a `CFindDlg` member variable for the `CModelessDemoDlg` class:

```
class CModelessDemoDlg : public CDialog
{
  ...
  CFindDlg m_findDlg;
```

15. Initialize the `m_findDlg` member variable in the `CModelessDemoDlg` constructor's initializer list:

```
CModelessDemoDlg::CModelessDemoDlg(CWnd* pParent)
 : CDialog(CModelessDemoDlg::IDD, pParent)
 , m_findDlg(this)
```

```
, m_strFilename(_T(""))
{
  ...
}
```

16. Add a handler to the CModelessDemoDlg class for the Find button to display the modeless Find dialog box. Notice the check to see if the dialog box is already constructed, in which case the focus is set to it.

```
void CModelessDemoDlg::OnBnClickedFind()
{
  if (!m_findDlg.GetSafeHwnd())
  {
    m_findDlg.Create(IDD_FIND, this);
    m_findDlg.ShowWindow(SW_SHOW);
  }
  else
  {
    m_findDlg.SetFocus();
  }
}
```

17. Change the CFindDlg constructor so that its pParent parameter is not a default parameter:

```
class CFindDlg : public CDialog
{
 CFindDlg(CWnd* pParent);
  ...
```

18. Define the following message IDs in the FindDlg.h file:

```
#define WM_FINDDATA (WM_APP + 1)
#define WM_DIALOGCLOSE (WM_APP + 2)
```

19. Define the following data structure in the FindDlg.h file:

```
struct
{
  CString m_strFindWhat;
  BOOL m_fMatchCase;
  BOOL m_fMatchWholeWord;
} FINDDATA;
```

20. Code an event handler for the Find dialog box's Find Next button. As in the previous sections, I'm allocating a data structure in order to communicate data back to the parent window and sending it via the PostMessage function and the defined WM_FINDDATA message ID.

```
void CFindDlg::OnBnClickedOk()
{
 if (UpdateData())
  {
  if (0 < m_strFindWhat.GetLength())
   {
   CWnd* pParent = GetParent();
   ASSERT(pParent);
   if (pParent)
```

```
    {
      FINDDATA* pfd = new FINDDATA;
      pfd->m_strFindWhat = m_strFindWhat;
      pfd->m_fMatchCase = m_iMatchCase;
      pfd->m_fMatchWholeWord = m_iMatchWholeWord;

      pParent->PostMessage(WM_FINDDATA, 0, (WPARAM)pfd);
    }
  }
  else
  {
    AfxMessageBox("You need to enter the search text");
  }
 }
}
```

21. Now code the parent's side of this message. This part will, of course, be specific to your own application. In this demo, I'm casting the lParam to a FINDDATA structure pointer, and then using that structure's members to fill out the FINDTEXTEX structure needed to search a rich edit control. If data is found, I set focus to the rich edit control and highlight the found text. Finally, the FINDDATA structure is deleted because the dialog box sent this message asynchronously.

```
long CModelessDemoDlg::OnFindData(UINT wParam,
                                  LONG lParam)
{
 ASSERT(lParam);
 if (lParam)
 {
   FINDDATA* fd = (FINDDATA*)lParam;

   DWORD style = FR_DOWN;
   if (fd->m_fMatchCase) style |= FR_MATCHCASE;
   if (fd->m_fMatchWholeWord) style |= FR_WHOLEWORD;

   CPoint pos = m_edtRTFDocument.GetCaretPos();
   int currCh = m_edtRTFDocument.CharFromPos(pos);

   FINDTEXTEX fte;
   fte.chrg.cpMin = currCh;
   fte.chrg.cpMax = -1;

   fte.lpstrText = fd->m_strFindWhat ;

   long lResult = m_edtRTFDocument.FindText(style, &fte);
   if (-1 != lResult)
   {
    m_edtRTFDocument.SetFocus();
    m_edtRTFDocument.SetSel(fte.chrgText);
   }

   delete fd;
```

```
    }

    return 0;
}
```

Note

One thing that I should mention here, even though it's a bit out of context in terms of dialog boxes, is the style bits being set for the rich edit control, because this took me a couple of hours to figure out. The current rich edit control is the 2.0 version. According to the documentation, and the way searches worked with the 1.0 rich edit control, the search always defaults to a "search down" style. However, with the 2.0 control, if you attempt a search it will not default correctly and will fail. Thus, you need to explicitly specify the FR_DOWN style when searching a rich edit control.

22. Now add the following handler to the modeless dialog box for its Close button:

```
void CFindDlg::OnBnClickedCancel()
{
  CWnd* pParent = GetParent();
  ASSERT(pParent);
  if (pParent)
  {
    pParent->PostMessage(WM_DIALOGCLOSE, 0, 0);
  }
}
```

23. Finally, add the parent window handler for the WM_DIALOGCLOSE message that simply destructs the modeless dialog box:

```
long CModelessDemoDlg::OnDialogClose(UINT wParam,
                                     LONG lParam)
{
  ASSERT(m_findDlg.GetSafeHwnd());
  m_findDlg.DestroyWindow();
  return 0L;
}
```

Now build and run the application. As you can see in Figure 11-3, you now have a practical application of using the modeless dialog box where you can open RTF files and search through them for specified text.

Obviously, you could do all kinds of cool things to this application to make it even more practical. For example, it would be nice if the Find dialog box displayed a message if the text was not found. Nicer still would be the ability to search selected text; if the search is unsuccessful the user could then send a message, like in Microsoft Word, where a message box states that the search failed and asks the user if they want to perform the search from the beginning of the document (if the user had unintentionally performed a search only on the selected text). Because all of these things are outside the scope of programming modeless dialog boxes, I'll leave their implementation to you. However, this book's Web site does contain a version of this demo with all these bells and whistles.

CommandUI and KickIdle

One advantage to coding a practical demo application is that it can easily be extended to illustrate many common programming tasks. One such task involves the concept of *CommandUI* that I introduced in Chapter 4. This feature involves writing a *CommandUI handler* for controls and menu items. When the processor is idle, MFC calls each window's CommandUI handlers, passing it a `CCmdUI` object whose member functions allow the application to perform such tasks as enabling or disabling the control based on your application-specific logic. The demo modeless application definitely has a need for that feature because it doesn't make sense for the Find button to be enabled if a file has not been read. In fact, I'm often surprised at how many dialog-based applications exist that do not disable buttons when the button's functionality is not available. Instead, the programmer simply displays a message stating that the function cannot be carried out. Since the natural response of most users is "Then why is the button enabled if I can't push it?" you'll learn in this section how to implement CommandUI within a dialog box.

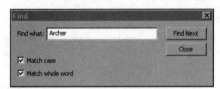

Figure 11-3: A Find dialog box makes a very practical example of when and how to use modeless dialog boxes in your application.

However, there's a problem. If you simply add a CommandUI handler to your dialog box for the various controls, they never get called! That's because idle processing is different for views than for dialog boxes. Instead you have to know about a very special, undocumented message and a helper function. Here are the steps to implementing CommandUI in a dialog:

1. Write the CommandUI handler for the control. This can be any control that you need to enable or disable at various times when the application is run.

2. Implement a message handler for the `WM_KICKIDLE` message. If you dig into the MFC source code, you'll see that this message is sent during the idle processing code block of the `CWnd::RunModalLoop` function (`wincore.cpp`).

3. Call the `CWnd::UpdateDialogControls` function in the `WM_KICKIDLE` handler. This will explicitly cause the window's CommandUI handlers to be called.

That's it! Now you'll implement this into the demo application with a bit of a twist. Instead of hard-coding this into the `CModalDemoDlg`, you'll create a `CDialog`-derived base class (`CIdleDlg`) that can be used for all your dialog box needs so that any class derived from this class can enjoy CommandUI benefits.

1. Using the ClassWizard, generate a new `CDialog`-derived class called `CIdleDlg`.

2. Open the `IdleDlg.h` code and modify it as follows (in bold). Note that I also changed the constructors because, as a base class, this dialog box isn't associated with a specific template ID. Therefore, the constructors here mimic exactly the base `CDialog` constructors. In addition, the `enum` and `DoDataExchange` functions that the ClassWizard generated were deleted.

   ```
   #pragma once

   class CIdleDlg : public CDialog
   ```

```
{
public:
 CIdleDlg(UINT nIDTemplate, CWnd* pParent = NULL);
 CIdleDlg(LPCTSTR lpszTemplateName, CWnd* pParent = NULL);

protected:
   afx_msg LRESULT OnKickIdle(WPARAM wParam,
                                   LPARAM lParam);
   DECLARE_MESSAGE_MAP()
};
```

3. Modify that `IdlDlg.cpp` so that when finished it looks like the following. The key things here to notice are the inclusion of the `afxpriv.h` file, the message handler for the `WM_KICKIDLE` message, and the call to `UpdateDialogControls`.

   This `afxpriv.h` file defines the `WM_KICKIDLE` message and specifically contains many classes and definitions of values that are only documented in the MFC Technical Notes found in your online help.

```
#include "stdafx.h"
#include "afxpriv.h"
#include "IdleDlg.h"

BEGIN_MESSAGE_MAP(CIdleDlg, CDialog)
 ON_MESSAGE(WM_KICKIDLE, OnKickIdle)
END_MESSAGE_MAP()

CIdleDlg::CIdleDlg(UINT nIDTemplate, CWnd* pParent)
: CDialog(nIDTemplate, pParent) { }

CIdleDlg::CIdleDlg(LPCTSTR lpszTemplateName,
                   CWnd* pParent)
: CDialog(lpszTemplateName, pParent) { }

LRESULT CIdleDlg::OnKickIdle(WPARAM, LPARAM)
{
   UpdateDialogControls(this, TRUE);
   return FALSE;
}
```

4. Insert an `include` directive for the `IdleDlg.h` file in the `stdafx.h` file. I like to place any header `include`s in this file that I know I'm going to be using throughout my project, because it saves me having to remember to include it in each needed case.

```
#include "IdleDlg.h"
```

5. Manually search and replace all occurrences of `CDialog` with `CIdleDlg` in the following files. Yes, it's a pain, but it's worth it to have more control over the UI.

```
ModalDemoDlg.h
ModelDemoDlg.cpp
FindDlg.h
FindDlg.cpp
```

6. Add the following CommandUI handler definition in the `CModalDemoDlg` class.

```
class CModalDemoDlg
{
...
 afx_msg void OnUpdateFind(CCmdUI* pCmdUI);
}
```

7. Now add the map entry to the `CModalDemoDlg` message map.

```
BEGIN_MESSAGE_MAP(CModelessDemoDlg, CIdleDlg)

 ...
 ON_UPDATE_COMMAND_UI(IDC_FIND, OnUpdateOk)
END_MESSAGE_MAP()
```

8. Finally, code the handler to only enable the file. As you can see, I'm simply checking that the filename edit control DDX variable has a value. That's fairly safe to use because it's read-only and only set if a file has been successfully read.

```
void CModelessDemoDlg::OnUpdateFind(CCmdUI* pCmdUI)
{
 pCmdUI->Enable(0 < m_strFilename.GetLength());
}
```

Now build and run the application. As you can see from the side-by-side comparison in Figure 11-4, the top instance of the application has no file open, and therefore, the Find button is correctly disabled. The bottom instance, on the other hand, is displaying a file, and thus the Find button is enabled.

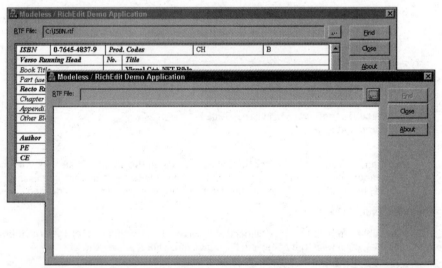

Figure 11-4: By knowing a couple of tricks, you can present the same intuitive interface with dialog boxes that you can with SDI/MDI applications with regards to CommandUI handlers.

Keyboard Accelerators

You will find as you work with dialog boxes in MFC that there are many features that, while trivial to implement in an SDI or MDI application, require a fair bit of understanding of MFC internals to them get to work with dialog boxes. One such example is getting accelerators to work on dialog boxes.

Accelerators — discussed at length in Chapter 4 — can be defined in two ways. From the user perspective, accelerators are keyboard shortcuts that cause the application to do something, much like pressing a button or selecting a menu item. From a programmer's perspective, accelerators, which are defined in the accelerator table in the resource file, are key combinations that, when pressed by the user, result in a WM_COMMAND message being sent to a given window, just like buttons and menu items. Figure 11-5 shows the accelerator table for a newly created SDI application. Notice that it contains the familiar combinations to perform such tasks as open files, use the clipboard, and print the current document.

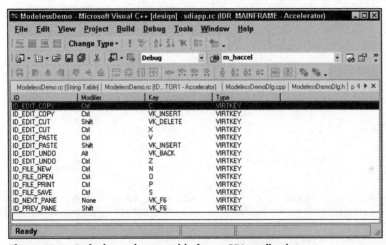

Figure 11-5: Default accelerator table for an SDI application

Now take a look at the accelerator table for the ModelessDemo application. It shouldn't take you too long because it's not there! Instead you'll have to create your own. Assuming you have added an accelerator table to your project, the accelerator keys still do not function as you would expect.

So, why don't accelerators work on dialog boxes? To answer that you need to know about the TranslateAccelerator function. This function translates a WM_KEYDOWN or WM_SYSKEYDOWN message to a WM_COMMAND or WM_SYSCOMMAND message (if there is an entry for the key in the specified accelerator table) and then sends that message to the appropriate window procedure. However, the modal dialog box application's message loop does not call TranslateAccelerator, and therein lies the problem. Therefore, you simply need to mimic this ability in your dialog boxes using the following steps:

1. As dialog-based applications by default do not contain an accelerator table, you need to add one. To do this, simply open the Resource View, right-click the ModelessDemo.rc folder, and click the Add Resource menu option. When the Add Resource dialog box is displayed, double-click the Accelerator entry to create an empty accelerator table and have it added to the current project's resource table.

2. Add your accelerators to the table. For this demo, create an accelerator for the Ctrl+X key. Therefore, the Modifier should be set to Ctrl, the Key should be the letter X, and the Type should specify VIRTKEY. (The ID is unimportant, but you do need to remember it.)

3. Add an accelerator handler (HACCEL) as a member variable of the application class (CModelessDemo, in this case). You can name this member variable m_hAccel.

4. Locate the application object's InitInstance method. Just before the instantiation of the dialog box, insert the following code to load the module's accelerator table. Note that the ID used is IDR_ACCELERATOR1. This is the default ID used when you create the first table for a project. If you change this value in the Resource View (or project's .rc file), you'll need to make sure that you use the appropriate ID in this function call.

```
m_haccel=LoadAccelerators(AfxGetInstanceHandle(),
  MAKEINTRESOURCE(IDR_ACCELERATOR1));
```

5. With the accelerator table now loaded, you need to override the application object's ProcessMessageFiler function to call the TranslateAcclerator function:

```
BOOL CModelessDemoApp::ProcessMessageFilter(int code,
                                            LPMSG lpMsg)
{
 if (m_haccel)
 {
  if (::TranslateAccelerator(m_pMainWnd->m_hWnd,
                      m_haccel, lpMsg))
   return(TRUE);
 }

 return CWinApp::ProcessMessageFilter(code, lpMsg);
}
```

6. Now you're set up. All you need to do is to map an accelerator to a command. Add a message map entry to the dialog box's message map like the following. You'll need to use the accelerator ID that was generated when you added the accelerator in Step 2. As you can see, I'm simply mapping this accelerator the same function that is called when the user clicks the Find button.

```
BEGIN_MESSAGE_MAP(CModelessDemoDlg, CIdleDlg)
 ...
 ON_COMMAND(ID_ACCELERATOR32771, OnBnClickedFind)
END_MESSAGE_MAP()
```

At this point, you can build and test your application. Upon pressing the Ctrl+F combination you should see your Find modeless dialog box.

Intercepting Keyboard Input

Another very common question that I hear is "How can I trap a certain keystroke in my dialog box?" Actually, this solution also applies to views. In what situations is this a valid need? One example is user interfaces where you want the Enter key to be treated like a Tab character. As you know, hitting Enter on a dialog causes a WM_COMMAND message to be sent to the dialog box (either for the button currently having focus or for the IDOK message in cases where a button is not in focus). Another example is if you have special subclassed controls on the dialog box and you need to ensure that those controls receive their keyboard input. Whatever the reason, the way to handle this is to override the PreTranslateMessage function in the dialog or view class.

Because returning TRUE from the PreTranslateMessage function causes the message to stop being processed, there are two ways to implement this function. For example, in the following function, I am trapping the Enter key (VK_RETURN) and determining if the Shift key is also being held down. Based on that, I set the focus to the previous or next control on the dialog box and set a local Boolean value (bHandledMsg) to TRUE. In the last line, I then either call the base class's implementation of this function or I return bHandledMsg (if it is equal to TRUE) in order to stop further processing. Your code will look very similar to this if you are processing many different keys:

```
BOOL CModelessDemoDlg::PreTranslateMessage(MSG* pMsg)
{
 BOOL bHandledMsg = FALSE;

 if (WM_KEYDOWN == pMsg->message
 && VK_RETURN == pMsg->wParam)
 {
  CWnd* pwndCurrent = NULL;
  pwndCurrent = GetFocus();

  if (pwndCurrent)
  {
   CWnd* pwndNext = NULL;
   if (::GetKeyState(VK_SHIFT) & 0x8000)
   {
    pwndNext = GetNextDlgTabItem(pwndCurrent,TRUE);
   }
   else // move to the NEXT control
   {
    pwndNext = GetNextDlgTabItem(pwndCurrent);
   }
   pwndNext->SetFocus();

   bHandledMsg = TRUE;
  }
 }

 return (bHandledMsg ? bHandledMsg
                     : CIdleDlg::PreTranslateMessage(pMsg));
}
```

However, if you are processing a key that can easily be translated into another key (as is the case here), then your code can be greatly simplified by changing the variable that indicates the key being pressed by the user (pMsg->wParam) to the desired key and allowing the default processing to take place. In the following code snippet that's all I'm doing. I'm trapping the Enter key and then basically telling Windows that it was really a Tab key that was pressed.

```
BOOL CModelessDemoDlg::PreTranslateMessage(MSG* pMsg)
{
 BOOL bHandledMsg = FALSE;

 if (WM_KEYDOWN == pMsg->message
```

```
    && VK_RETURN == pMsg->wParam)
    {
      pMsg->wParam = VK_TAB;
    }

    return CIdleDlg::PreTranslateMessage(pMsg);
}
```

Serialization from Dialog-Based Applications

Object persistence is the process of reading and writing objects to and from disk. MFC implements object persistence via a mechanism called *serialization*. With serialization, the capability of saving data can easily and quickly be incorporated into an MFC application with a minimum of coding and expense (no need to purchase an expensive DMBS). However, like other features that you've seen so far in this chapter, support for serialization is built into the document/view framework and as such is not very intuitive to implement in dialog-based applications.

Before we continue I would like to say that the basics of serialization are covered in Chapter 2. Therefore, I will assume that you've either read that chapter or already know the basics of serialization. That way, I can focus this section on what is needed to serialize data from a dialog-based application.

Having said that, the main difference between serializing data from a document-based application and a dialog-based application is that in the latter case, the programmer is responsible for creating the CArchive object (and its underlying CFile object) that will be used to serialize the data to and from disk. Here are the steps involved in adding serialization to a dialog-based application. Each step is discussed in more detail subsequently.

1. Make each class that is to be written to and read from disk *serializable*.

2. Implement the dialog class' Serialize virtual member function.

3. Add code to the dialog object to read the objects from disk.

4. Add code to the dialog object to save the objects to disk.

Making each class serializable

In order to make a class serializable, you must use the DECLARE_SERIAL macro in the class's declaration and the IMPLEMENT_SERIAL macro in the class's implementation file. Both of these macros are fully described in the online documentation. However, it is important to note that the class being serialized *must* be derived from CObject. You will see exactly how to do this when serialization is implemented in a demo application at the end of this section.

Implementing the Serialize virtual function

After adding the DECLARE_SERIAL and IMPLEMENT_SERIAL macros to the classes that you want to be serializable, you need to override the Serialize virtual member function for each class that will be serialized. The Serialize function takes as its only argument a reference to a CArchive object. The CArchive object is based on a CFile object, which in turn is based on a physical disk file. In order to serialize an object to disk, the CArchive << operator function is used. Conversely, to restore an object from disk, the >> operator function is used. The CArchive object has several overridden versions of the operator>> and operator<<

member functions so that almost any C/C++ type can be serialized with a single line of code. Here's an example of a class (CEmployee) that needs to serialize three fields (m_strName, m_iAge, and m_dtBirthdate). Notice the CArchive IsStoring member function. This function is used to determine if the data is being written to disk (stored) or read from disk (loaded).

```
void CEmployee::Serialize(CArchive& ar)
{
 if (ar.IsStoring())
 { // storing code
  ar << m_strName;
  ar << m_iAge;
  ar << m_dtBirthdate;
 }
 else
 { // loading code
  ar > m_strName;
  ar > m_iAge;
  ar > m_dtBirthdate;
 }
}
```

Reading data from disk

The most logical place to place the code necessary for reading objects from disk is in the OnInitDialog member function. Here you would add code to check for the existence of the data file and, if that data file exists, create a CFile object. The newly created CFile object would then be used to create a CArchive object that would be passed to the dialog box's Serialize function.

Saving data to disk

Whereas the reading of objects from disk would logically be done in the OnInitDialog function, deciding from what function to save the data is application-specific. For example, you might have a button on your dialog box called Commit that, upon being pressed, saves all the work done up to that point to disk. On the other hand, your application might simply save the data only when the user exits the application (the demo application will take this approach). In order to save the object to disk, the application would need to check for the existence of the data file, and create the file if it didn't already exist. Once the file existed, a CFile object would be instantiated and used to construct a CArchive object that would then be passed to the dialog box's Serialize function.

Dialog-based serialization demo

1. Create a new dialog-based application called DialogSerialize.

2. Update the application's main dialog template by adding the controls shown in Figure 11-6.

3. Add DDX member variables to the dialog box for the edit controls. All of these variables need to be of type CString and named m_strAcademic, m_strArtist, m_strAuthor, m_strBook, m_strMovie, m_strPoet, and m_strScientist.

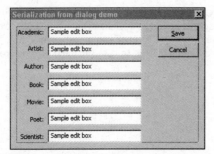

Figure 11-6: Serialization demo dialog template

4. Using the ClassWizard, generate a new CObject-derived class called CMyFavorites.

5. Add the following member variables to the CMyFavorites class and initialize each variable to a blank string in the class's constructor:

```
class CMyFavorites : public CObject
{
 ...
 CString m_strAcademic;
 CString m_strArtist;
 CString m_strAuthor;
 CString m_strBook;
 CString m_strMovie;
 CString m_strPoet;
 CString m_strScientist;
};
```

6. Override the CMyFavorites class's Serialize function and modify it as follows:

```
void CMyFavorites::Serialize(CArchive& ar)
{
  if (ar.IsStoring())
  {   // storing code
    ar << m_strAcademic;
    ar << m_strArtist;
    ar << m_strAuthor;
    ar << m_strBook;
    ar << m_strMovie;
    ar << m_strPoet;
    ar << m_strScientist;
  }
  else
  {   // loading code
    ar >> m_strAcademic;
    ar >> m_strArtist;
    ar >> m_strAuthor;
    ar >> m_strBook;
    ar >> m_strMovie;
    ar >> m_strPoet;
    ar >> m_strScientist;
  }
}
```

7. At this point, you're finished on the object side. Now you just need to code the UI so that you can view and modify the data. To get started, open the `DialogSerializeDlg.cpp` file and add the following statement to define the name of the data file:

```
#define DATA_FILE _T("demo.dat")
```

8. Add the following helper function that will be used to determine if the data file exists and if it can be accessed for reading and writing:

```
BOOL CDialogSerializeDlg::CanSerialize()
{
 return (0 == _access(DATA_FILE, 6));
}
```

9. Add the following `include` directive to the top of the `DialogSerializeDlg.cpp` file:

```
#include <io.h>
#include "MyFavorites.h"
```

10. Declare a `CMyFavorites` member variable in the `CDialogSerializeDlg` (also including the necessary `MyFavorites.h` header file):

```
#include "MyFavorites.h"

class CDialogSerializeDlg : public CDialog
{
 ...

 CMyFavorites m_myFavorites;

 ...
}
```

11. Add the following code to the `CDialogSerializeDlg::OnInitInstance` function (just before the `return` statement). After verifying that the file exists and can be opened for reading, the first thing this code snippet does is to create a `CFile` object based on the data file (`demo.dat`). The newly instantiated `CFile` object is then used to construct a `CArchive` object. Notice the second argument to the `CArchive` constructor. This value is used by the `Serialize` function to determine whether data is being read in or written out.

Note that you're not updating the DDX variable yet. That's because you're going to use a shortcut in getting the data to the dialog box. You'll see that shortly.

```
BOOL CDialogSerializeDlg::OnInitDialog()
{
 ...

 if (CanSerialize())
 {
  CFile file;
  CFileException fe;

  if (file.Open(DATA_FILE,
  CFile::typeBinary | CFile::modeRead, &fe))
  {
   CArchive ar(&file, CArchive::load);
```

```
      Serialize(ar);

      UpdateData(FALSE); // update controls
    }
  }

  return TRUE;
}
```

12. Add the following event handler for the Save button. The majority of this function is spent attempting to open the data file and verify if the application can obtain write access to it. If it can, the function calls the dialog box's Serialize function.

```
void CDialogSerializeDlg::OnBnClickedOk()
{
  BOOL bCanSave = FALSE;

  if (UpdateData())
  {
    UINT nFlags = CFile::typeBinary | CFile::modeWrite;

    // File doesn't exist, so create it
    if (_access(DATA_FILE, 0))
    {
      nFlags |= CFile::modeCreate;
      bCanSave = TRUE;
    }
    else
    {
      bCanSave = CanSerialize();
    }

    if (bCanSave)
    {
      CFile file;
      CFileException fe;

      // File exists with read & write permissions
      if (file.Open(DATA_FILE, nFlags, &fe))
      {
        CArchive ar(&file, CArchive::store);
        Serialize(ar);
      }
    }
  }
}
```

13. Now, add an override of the Serialize function to the CDialogSerializeDlg class and modify it to call the m_myFavorites Serialize function:

```
void CDialogSerializeDlg::Serialize(CArchive& ar)
{
  m_myFavorites.Serialize(ar);

  if (ar.IsStoring())
```

```
    {   // storing code
    }
    else
    {   // loading code
    }
}
```

14. Finally, all you need to do is to move the data from the CMyFavorites object into the dialog box's controls. As a shortcut, simply replace all the DDX_Text calls referencing the DDX member variables to reference instead the m_myFavorites member variables. When you go through one object to update another using DDX the first object, it is called a *foreign object*. In case you're wondering why this wasn't done earlier, it's because the current Visual Studio ClassWizard does not have the foreign object support that Visual Studio 6 had. After you've updated the DoDataExchange function, remember to delete the DDX member variables from the header file.

```
void CDialogSerializeDlg::DoDataExchange(CDataExchange* pDX)
{
    CDialog::DoDataExchange(pDX);
    DDX_Text(pDX, IDC_EDIT1, m_myFavorites.m_strAcademic);
    DDX_Text(pDX, IDC_EDIT2, m_myFavorites.m_strArtist);
    DDX_Text(pDX, IDC_EDIT3, m_myFavorites.m_strAuthor);
    DDX_Text(pDX, IDC_EDIT7, m_myFavorites.m_strBook);
    DDX_Text(pDX, IDC_EDIT4, m_myFavorites.m_strMovie);
    DDX_Text(pDX, IDC_EDIT5, m_myFavorites.m_strPoet);
    DDX_Text(pDX, IDC_EDIT6, m_myFavorites.m_strScientist);
}
```

When you are done, build and execute the application. Try typing in some data and clicking the Save button. Exit the application and you should see that upon return (Figure 11-7), your data has indeed been serialized to disk and read back in.

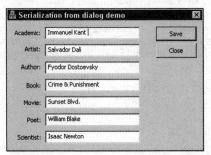

Figure 11-7: Demo application that illustrates how to serialize data from a dialog-based application

Creating Form Views for SDI and MDI Applications

In Chapters 2 and 3 you saw how to create SDI and MDI applications with regards to documents, views, and frames. However, one thing I didn't touch on in those chapters is the notion of the form view (encapsulated by the CFormView class). Basically, a form view is the combination of a view and a dialog template resource. With a form view, it's much easier to place controls on your view in the dialog editor, and because the form view is dialog-based you get all the benefits of DDX that you saw in the previous chapter.

Before I get into some demos showing you how to use the CFormView class with both SDI and MDI applications, I want to go over a few facts about this class that will help you in using it.

CFormView objects receive notification messages directly from their controls and they receive command messages from the application framework. As you'll see in the demo application, this makes it easy to control the views from the frame's menu or toolbar.

Although the CFormView (like CDialog) is associated with a dialog template resource, the CFormView is technically derived from CScrollView (which is then derived from CView). I note this because many beginners make the mistake of assuming that the same CDialog functions such as OnInitDialog, OnOK, and OnCancel must also be available with the CFormView class; they're not.

There is no mechanism built into the CFormView class to automatically call the UpdateData function to facilitate DDX data transfer between controls and member variables. As a result, you must call the UpdateData function manually each time you need to invoke the data transfer.

Although the CFormView is not directly derived from CDialog, you can cast the CFormView to CDialog to call certain functions. For example, you saw earlier that you can very easily determine the next or previous control in the tab order and can then move focus to that control. However, those are technically CWnd functions inherited by CDialog. One control navigation function that is specific to CDialog is the GotoDlgCtrl function. Having said that, the following code will work from a CformView:

```
CDialog* pDlg = (CDialog*)this;
pDlg->GotoDlgCtrl(GetDlgItem(IDC_CHECK3));
```

You might be wondering how you can cast one type to another completely different type and have them work. The answer lies in the fact that they are not that different. Because both the CFormView and CDialog classes are derived from CWnd, they do share the same memory layout (at least the CWnd part). Therefore, as long as you're not calling a CDialog function that is specific to CDialog (or a base class that is not part of the CFormView definition) you can get away with this common C++ trick. You can see this if you look at the definition for the CDialog::GotoDlgCtrl function (found in the afxwin2.inl file):

```
_AFXWIN_INLINE void CDialog::GotoDlgCtrl(CWnd* pWndCtrl)
{
 ASSERT(::IsWindow(m_hWnd));
 ::SendMessage(m_hWnd,
          WM_NEXTDLGCTL,
          (WPARAM)pWndCtrl->m_hWnd, 1L);
}
```

If you look at this function closely, you see that the first thing it does is to use the m_hWnd member variable in a call to a Win32 SDK function. It can access this member variable because this m_hWnd is defined in the base class for both the CFormView and CDialog classes. As a result, that part of the memory layout for both classes is the same. From there, the Win32 SendMessage function with the pWndCtrl pointer this function received as a parameter being passed. So, as you can see, there's nothing going on here that is specific to the CDialog class, which is why this works. Effectively, what is happening then is that the cast is taking place to appease the C++ compiler that this can be done. Remember that the entire concept of casting in C++ is built on the fact that you're basically telling the compiler to not worry about the fact that the classes seem dissimilar because you know what you're doing. You'll see in the next section that this casting trick is a big part of the `CCtrlView` class.

Creating an SDI form view application

At this point, let's create a simple SDI application that will illustrate to you how form views are defined, how to manage their controls, and respond to control notification messages.

1. Select the New Project option. After selecting the MFC Application template, type in a name of `SDIFormViewDemo` and click OK.

2. Specify the Application type as SDI

3. On the Generated Classes tab, select the `SDIFormViewDemoView` class and then change its Base class to `CFormView`.

4. Click the Finish button to create the SDI form view-based project.

5. When the project has been created, open the Resource View. You should see that along with the standard About box dialog template, the wizard has also generated an additional dialog template (`IDD_SDIFORMVIEWDEMO_FORM`, in the case of this demo) that will be the UI for the application's form view.

6. Open that dialog template and take note that the `Visible` property is set to `False`, the `Style` property is set to `Child` and the `Border` property is set to `none`. This is significant because the dialog template associated with a `CFormView` class must have these setting or your code will assert upon startup. Although the wizard does define these settings for you automatically, there might be times when you'll want to manually create a dialog template and then associate it with a `CFormView`.

7. To test the application, place some controls on the dialog template as shown in Figure 11-8.

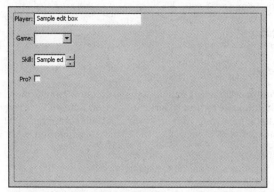

Figure 11-8: Dialog template for simple form view test application

You'll wire the controls to handlers shortly. For now the purpose of this application is to see that the form views are presented correctly. That's all there is to writing a form-view based SDI application.

Switching between a document's views

Once you have multiple forms in an application, it will be necessary to provide the user some way of both creating and activating these forms from the menu. Here are the basic steps to accomplishing this task.

The trick to doing this is knowing a little about how and where document templates are stored. You'll recall from Chapter 2 that document templates are objects that tie together a view, frame, document, and the resources for these elements (including menus, icons, and strings), and that in the InitInstance function of the application object, these templates are created and added to the undocumented application's internal CDocManager object. However, this object maintains a list of all documents and views. Although that's useful information in certain contexts you only need to know about the views associated with a given document.

As it turns out, CDocument has a couple of functions that aid in that endeavor: GetFirstViewPosition and GetNextView. As you can tell by the function names, these functions are especially useful in enumerating through all the views of a given document. But how can you determine an exact view? For example, say you have an accounting application with many views, such as a customer view and a vendor view. How can you programmatically display the correct view when the user clicks the Maintain Customers view, for example? One way is to use runtime information.

Each CObject-derived class is associated with a CRuntimeClass class structure that can be used to query an object (or its base class) at runtime. To accomplish that, the CObject base class also includes a member function called IsKindOf that allows you to dynamically determine if an instance is of a given class. For example, suppose you have two CObject-derived classes called CVender and CSupplier. If at runtime you have a collection containing objects of both types and you want to determine if an object is one type or the other, you can simply use the RUNTIME_CLASS macro (which returns the CRuntimeClass structure for a given class), and pass that to the object's IsKindOf function call. A return value of TRUE indicates that the object is of the specified type.

```
// pCurrObj is either CVendor or CSupplier
CRuntimeClass* pInfo = RUNTIME_CLASS(CVendor);
if (pCurrObj->IsKindOf(pInfo))
  // I have a vendor
else
  // I have a supplier
```

As you can see in the following function, this ability plays in nicely with your need to check a view's type. Using this technique allows you to write a function (shown here) where the runtime class information can be passed to that function and then compared against each of the document's views using the view object's IsKindOf member function.

```
// Note that this function uses CDocument functions
// and therefore needs to be a member function of a
// CDocument-derived class.
void CreateOrActivateFrame(CDocTemplate* pTemplate,
                           CRuntimeClass* pViewClass)
{
 // Search through document's attatched views
 CView* pView;
 POSITION pos = GetFirstViewPosition();
 while (pos != NULL)
```

```
{
 pView = GetNextView(pos);
 // If the kind found matches kind
 // passed as parameter, activate it
 if (pView->IsKindOf(pViewClass))
 {
  pView->GetParentFrame()->ActivateFrame(SW_RESTORE);
  return;
 }
}
// Did not find the correct active, so create
// and initialize one
CFrameWnd* pFrame = pTemplate->CreateNewFrame(this, NULL);
ASSERT(pFrame);
pTemplate->InitialUpdateFrame(pFrame, this);
}
```

As you can see, along with the view class's runtime information, a document template pointer is also passed. You'll see why shortly.

The first thing the function does is to iterate through the document's view collection. For each view, the function calls the IsKindOf function to determine if the view is of the desired type. If this match is successful, the code then attempts to display the view. Remember that the view is a child of the frame, and typically any time you need to size or move the view, you do so through its parent frame. Therefore, a call to the CView::GetParentFrame retrieves the current view's parent frame window. From there, the code calls the frame's ActivateFrame function, which moves the view to the top of the z-order so that the user can see it. Note also that the code also passes a value of SW_RESTORE. I did this in case the user has minimized the view.

So what happens if you don't find a view matching the specified type? If you dig into the bowels of the MFC view creation code, you'll find that a call to the document template's CreateNewFrame and InitialUpdateFrame functions are actually what causes a view to be created and displayed. Seeing how MFC creates and displays views and frames teaches you the required steps to perform this task. As a result, the CreateOrActivate function uses the same technique to create an instance of the specified view type.

Let's put this function into a demo application to see how it would work. Note that if you already have an MDI application with dialog templates and their associated CFormView classes defined, you can skip to Step 7.

1. Create an MDI application called CreateOrActivate. When creating an MDI application whose views will all be based on different dialog templates, I don't bother changing the default view's base class in the wizard because I won't be using it anyway.

2. Add a dialog template to the project and place some controls on it.

3. Add a second dialog template and add some controls to the new template to distinguish it from the first dialog template.

4. For both templates, set the Style property to Child and the Visible property to False.

5. Create CFormView-derived classes for each dialog template called CFormView1 and CFormView2, respectively.

6. Create a popup menu for the `IDR_CreateOrActivateTYPE` menu resource with a caption of My Views. Add two menu options to that popup menu with the captions View 1 and View 2, respectively.

7. Add `COMMAND` event handlers for both menu options the document class. I prefer adding my handlers to the document class in an MDI application because logically all the views are based on the data in the document.

8. Define a `CMultiDocTemplate` member variable in the document for each form view. Here are the document template pointers for the two form views in the demo:

```
class CCreateOrActivateDoc : public CDocument
{
 ...

 CMultiDocTemplate* m_pFormView1Template;
 CMultiDocTemplate* m_pFormView2Template;


 ...
}
```

9. Add the following `include` directives to the document's header file (`createoractivatedoc.h`). The first is the frame header file that is used by default for your views, and the other two are the view header files:

```
#include "ChildFrm.h"
#include "FormView1.h"
#include "FormView2.h"
```

10. Create and add the template to the application's doc manager in the document's constructor:

```
CMDIFormViewTestDoc::CMDIFormViewTestDoc()
{
 CWinApp* pApp = AfxGetApp();
 ASSERT(pApp);

 if (pApp)
 {
  m_pFormView1Template =
   new CMultiDocTemplate(IDR_CreateOrActivatTYPE,
    RUNTIME_CLASS(CCreateOrActivateDoc),
    RUNTIME_CLASS(CChildFrame),
    RUNTIME_CLASS(CFormView1));
  pApp->AddDocTemplate(m_pFormView1Template);

  m_pFormView2Template =
   new CMultiDocTemplate(IDR_CreateOrActivatTYPE,
    RUNTIME_CLASS(CCreateOrActivateDoc),
    RUNTIME_CLASS(CChildFrame),
    RUNTIME_CLASS(CFormView2));
  pApp->AddDocTemplate(m_pFormView2Template);
 }
}
```

11. Define the following function in your document class. This is the function that will either create the view (if it is not present) or activate it (bring it to the foreground).

```
void CCreateOrActivateDoc::CreateOrActivateFrame(
 CDocTemplate* pTemplate,
 CRuntimeClass* pViewClass)
{
 CView* pView;

 // Search through document's attatched views
 POSITION pos = GetFirstViewPosition();
 while (pos != NULL)
 {
  pView = GetNextView(pos);

  // If the kind found matches kind passed as
  // parameter, activate it
  if (pView->IsKindOf(pViewClass))
  {
   pView->GetParentFrame()->ActivateFrame(SW_RESTORE);
   return;
  }
 }

 // Did not find the correct active, so
 // create and initialize one
 CFrameWnd* pFrame = pTemplate->CreateNewFrame(this,
                                               NULL);
 ASSERT(pFrame);
 pTemplate->InitialUpdateFrame(pFrame, this);
}
```

12. Finally, update each place where you want to display a child view with a call to the CreateOrActivate function. In this demo, the handlers, when finished, would look like the following. As you can see, all you have to do is pass the document template pointer and the runtime information for the view's CFormView-derived class.

```
void CCreateOrActivateDoc::OnMyviewsView1()
{
   CreateOrActivateFrame(m_pFormView1Template,
                         RUNTIME_CLASS(CFormView1));
}

void CCreateOrActivateDoc::OnMyviewsView2()
{
   CreateOrActivateFrame(m_pFormView2Template,
                         RUNTIME_CLASS(CFormView2));
}
```

When finished, build and run the application. After you open each view from the menu, you application should resemble that shown in Figure 11-9.

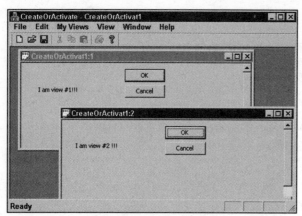

Figure 11-9: Demo application illustrating how to display multiple views in an MDI application

MFC Control Views

One very handy feature of MFC is the `CCtrlView` class. This class enables you to combine a common control with the document/view architecture. Note that `CCtrlView` is an abstract class (its destructor is pure virtual) and therefore cannot be instantiated directly. Therefore, to take advantage of this functionality, you must either use predefined `CCtrlView`-derived classes (such as `CTreeView`, `CListView`, `CEditView`, or `CRichEditView`), or derive your own class from `CCtrlView`. Up to this point, you've already learned how to work with both controls and views. You've even worked with both the `CTreeView` and `CListView` classes in Chapter 7. Therefore, I won't rehash any of that; instead, I'll focus here on something a bit more interesting.

In Chapter 7, you saw that by calling `CTreeView::GetTreeCtrl` and `CListView::GetListCtrl`, you were able to retrieve the view's associated control and work with it. However, this has resulted in a lot of misconceptions about how the `CCtrlView` works. For example, some people assume that because you can call a control view function to retrieve a control, the control must be an embedded member of the view. Others see that the function to get the control does nothing more than return the view's `this` pointer cast to the control class, and therefore, think that somehow the control must be in the view's inheritance tree. Both assumptions are incorrect. Therefore, I'll first look to clear up on some common misconceptions about the `CCtrlView` class and illustrate how it does work. Once I've done that, you'll then see how to define your own `CCtrlView`-derived class using a standard control (a list box).

General misconceptions

Because you've already seen the `CListView` class, I'll use it as an example. The first misconception that I hear revolves around the fact that there are two MFC classes that deal with the Explorer-like listing of objects: `CListCtrl` and `CListView`. Contrary to what a lot of beginners might logically think, these two classes do not encapsulate two different Windows classes. They both deal with one and only one Windows class called a `ListView`. In fact, the

CListCtrl is the encapsulation of the ListView. So why didn't the MFC designers call it a CListView? Because even though the common controls team decided to call their window class a ListView, the suffix "View" has a very specific meaning to MFC developers and conjures up images of working within the context of the document/view architecture. Therefore, the MFC team decided to instead call it a CListCtrl since to them it is a "control" and not a "view" (in the MFC way of thinking of views).

The next misconception is that the CListView is a CView-derived class that contains an embedded CListCtrl object. This misconception is certainly the result of two things: first, it would be natural to think of a view as containing a control, and second, the CListView has a member function called GetListCtrl, which returns a (seemingly contained) CListCtrl reference.

However, what is happening here (and you'll see this code shortly) is that when you open a view with MFC (typically associated with a given SDI or MDI document template), the MFC framework creates a frame for you and then within that frame creates a window. It is that window that serves as your view and what you perceive as the window's client area. However, with the CCtrlView-derived classes (such as CListView) what is happening is that you can specify any type of window to be used as the client area! In the case of the CListView class, that class's author simply specified that a ListView window class be used, and when the view comes up its entire client area is taken up by a ListView and the framework automatically handles the different things such as making sure that the ListView resizes appropriately when the frame is resized.

How it works

Take a look at the code for how the CListView gets created so that you can see how this thing works. The first thing to look at is the CListView constructor (found in AFXCVIEW.INL). As you can see, the CListView constructor simply calls the CCtrlView constructor and passes it a value of WC_LISTVIEW.

```
_AFXCVIEW_INLINE CListView::CListView()
: CCtrlView(WC_LISTVIEW, AFX_WS_DEFAULT_VIEW)
{ }
```

As you saw in the previous chapter, these window class names are defined in the COMMCTRL.H file like this:

```
#ifdef _WIN32

#define WC_LISTVIEWA            "SysListView32"
#define WC_LISTVIEWW            L"SysListView32"

#ifdef UNICODE
#define WC_LISTVIEW             WC_LISTVIEWW
#else
#define WC_LISTVIEW             WC_LISTVIEWA
#endif

#else
#define WC_LISTVIEW             "SysListView"
#endif
```

Now, all you know is that the `CListView` constructor is going to pass a value of `SysListView32` to the `CCtrlView` constructor. From there, dig a bit deeper to see how simple this whole thing really is.

```
CCtrlView::CCtrlView(LPCTSTR lpszClass, DWORD dwStyle)
{
 m_strClass = lpszClass;
 m_dwDefaultStyle = dwStyle;
}

BOOL CCtrlView::PreCreateWindow(CREATESTRUCT& cs)
{
 ASSERT(cs.lpszClass == NULL);
 cs.lpszClass = m_strClass;

 // initialize common controls
 VERIFY(AfxDeferRegisterClass(AFX_WNDCOMMCTLS_REG));
 AfxDeferRegisterClass(AFX_WNDCOMMCTLSNEW_REG);

 // map default CView style to default style
 // WS_BORDER is insignificant
 if ((cs.style | WS_BORDER) == AFX_WS_DEFAULT_VIEW)
  cs.style = m_dwDefaultStyle & (cs.style | ~WS_BORDER);

 return CView::PreCreateWindow(cs);
}
```

Thus the `CCtrlView` class creates a window using the class name that is passed to its constructor. Because this class is derived from `CView`, the window in question will have a frame placed around it automatically when the view is created as part of an SDI or MDI document template. It will also automatically be resized to always encompass the entire frame when the frame is resized (relieving you from writing the sizing code to handle that event).

Creating CListBoxView classes

So now that you know that bit of MFC trivia, how does that help you in the real world? Now that you know how this works, you can see that MFC has only used a handful of controls with `CCtrlView` (`CListView`, `CTreeView`, `CEditView`, and so on). Imagine that you have another control that you want to act similarly. For example, suppose you wanted a list box to cover the entire client area and you didn't want to muck around with the sizing code when the view gets resized. Using the `CCtrlView` class this is incredibly easy. (Note that I'm using the standard list box control in this example because it is very easy to program and use in this context. However, you can easily apply these same rules to your own custom `CWnd`-derived classes as well.) To create something we'll call a `CListBoxView`, simply declare the class as follows:

```
#pragma once

class CListBoxView : public CCtrlView
{
 DECLARE_DYNCREATE(CListBoxView)

// constructor
public:
```

```
CListBoxView();

// Attributes
public:
 CListBox& GetListBox() const;

 //{{AFX_MSG(CListBoxView)
 //}}AFX_MSG
DECLARE_MESSAGE_MAP()
};
```

Next, implement the source as follows:

```
#include "stdafx.h"
#include "ListBoxView.h"

IMPLEMENT_DYNCREATE(CListBoxView, CCtrlView)

CListBoxView::CListBoxView() :
 CCtrlView(_T("LISTBOX"), AFX_WS_DEFAULT_VIEW) { };

CListBox& CListBoxView::GetListBox() const
{ return *(CListBox*)this; }

BEGIN_MESSAGE_MAP(CListBoxView, CCtrlView)
 //{{AFX_MSG_MAP(CListBoxView)
 ON_WM_NCDESTROY()
 //}}AFX_MSG_MAP
END_MESSAGE_MAP()
```

Take note of the constructor's initializer list and the fact that it passes the class name of the list box control to the CCtrlView constructor. By doing so, this class we call a CCtrlView reveals that it's a list box control at heart.

The only function of any interest is the GetListBox function. As you can see, this function simply returns a casted pointer to itself. How can you return a view pointer when the function requested a list box pointer? Remember that almost all MFC control classes are really nothing more than very thin wrappers for their associated Windows classes. As an example, when you call the CListBox::AddString member function, the CListBox object simply sends a Windows message to its associated window to add the specified string:

```
_AFXWIN_INLINE int CListBox::AddString(LPCTSTR lpszItem)
 { ASSERT(::IsWindow(m_hWnd));
    return (int)::SendMessage(m_hWnd,
                             LB_ADDSTRING,
                             0,
                             (LPARAM)lpszItem); }
```

Therefore, if a user of a CListBoxView requests a CListBox pointer to call CListBox member functions this will work because even though they are not the same object in memory, they do both have similar layouts in memory (both being derived from CWnd and therefore, having m_hWnd member variables). Because of this fact, the AddString function will work because the message is simply being sent to the m_hWnd associated with the CListBoxView. Needless to say, you have to be very careful, because if you attempted to call a CListBox member function that dealt with instance data not associated with your CListBoxView you will certainly get a GPF.

Using the CListBoxView class

When you've finished you'll see how easy it is to use any CWnd-derived class as a view in your MFC applications. Testing this class is as easy as writing it. Simply follow these steps:

1. Add the ListBoxView.cpp and ListBoxView.h files to your new project.

2. Open the LbxViewTestView.h file and include the ListBoxView.h file.

3. Replace all occurrences of CView with CListBoxView.

4. Open the LbxViewTestView.cpp file and replace all occurrences of CView with CListBoxView.

5. Add the view's OnInitialUpdate member function as follows:

```
void CLbxViewTestView::OnInitialUpdate()
{
 CListBoxView::OnInitialUpdate();

 CListBox* pLbx = (CListBox*)this;
 if (pLbx)
 {
  CString str;
  for (int i = 0; i < 10; i++)
  {
   str.Format("Test %ld", i);
   pLbx->AddString(str);
  }
 }
}
```

Now if you run the application, you should see results similar to those shown in Figure 11-10.

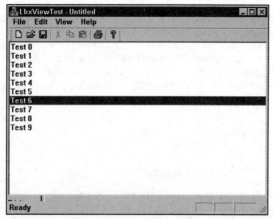

Figure 11-10: Once you know how, it's very easy to create your own CCtrlView-derived classes that combine the power of almost any control with the flexibility of the document/ view architecture.

Summary

In this chapter you learned several advanced tasks for dialog boxes. This included creating and managing modeless dialog boxes, messaging between dialog boxes, implementing CommandUI in a dialog, and keyboard processing. You also saw how to create view classes based on dialog templates for use in SDI and MDI applications via the `CFormView` class and how to programmatically switch between a document's attached views. Finally, the chapter wound up with a demonstration on how to create `CCtrlView`-derived classes in order to combine the power of that control with the flexibility of the document/view architecture.

✦ ✦ ✦

Property Sheets and Pages

As applications become more feature-rich, a common problem to deal with is the lack of screen real estate available when attempting to display numerous controls on a single dialog box. One example is the Visual Studio .NET Customize dialog box, where you can select from over 20 toolbars to view, control over a hundred commands, and set about a dozen options. Another example might be an accounting application where your users can define a customer or vendor, and the controls needed would be too many to fit nicely on a single dialog box. There are two controls that help with this problem.

The first way to solve this problem is via the tab control. However, the tab control is not generally used within a dialog box for the simple reason that it was designed to be used alongside other controls instead of strictly being the parent of other controls. Instead a better solution is actually a combination of two classes — CPropertySheet and CPropertyPage.

In this chapter, you will learn about these two MFC classes and how to implement them in both modal and modeless environments. Once you have learned the different options and ways in which to implement these classes, a demo with several variations will be presented. While working your way through the demo, you will learn how to do many tasks that are necessary with property sheets and property pages. These tasks include property-sheet-level functions such as removing, renaming, and repositioning the standard property sheet buttons. In addition, property-page-level topics such as changing the tabs' Caption and font as well as implementing mnemonics on tabs are covered.

CPropertySheet and CPropertyPage

Before I jump into how to create and use property sheets and property pages, you should first get at least a firm understanding of the classes involved and how they're defined. When you're creating a tabbed interface using the CPropertySheet and CPropertyPage classes, the CPropertyPage class represents the individual tabs and the CPropertySheet class represents the window on which those tabs are displayed. However, it's surprising to most people new to these classes that although the CPropertySheet looks like a dialog box, it is actually derived from CWnd. and it's the tabs (CPropertyPage objects) that are derived from CDialog.

This is further obfuscated due to the fact that many of the functions used to manage `CPropertySheet` objects are very similar to the functions used to manage `CDialog` objects. For example, construction of both a `CPropertySheet` and a `CDialog` object is done in a two-part process. Modal property sheets and dialog boxes are both displayed by first constructing the object and then calling its `DoModal` member function. Modeless property sheets and dialog boxes are both displayed by first constructing the object and then calling the object's `Create` function.

However, aside from their similarities in appearance and the functions used to display them, property sheets and dialog boxes are different from an MFC standpoint. For example, the dialog object maintains the data viewed on a dialog box. By contrast, the data viewed on a property sheet is usually maintained in the different property pages. Because the separate property pages are used to represent each tab and usually maintain the data that is displayed on that page, it's the `CPropertyPage` class that is derived from `CDialog`; not the `CPropertySheet` class.

Now, let's look at what's entailed in creating property pages.

Creating property page resources

The reason this chapter follows the two chapters about dialog boxes is very simple. Once you know how to create dialog boxes, you pretty much know most of what's needed to work with property pages. Whether you're defining a dialog template for use as a dialog box or as a property page, the resource editor is used to create a dialog template resource upon which controls are positioned and sized. However, the property page settings differ from those of a dialog box with regards to the following:

✦ The value of the `Caption` property appears on the tab instead of on the title bar of the dialog box.

✦ The `Style` property of a property page must be set to `Child`.

✦ The `Border` property of a property page must be set to `Thin`.

✦ The `Disabled` checkbox of a property page must be checked.

Luckily, you don't need to remember these different styles every time you create a property page, because the Add Resource dialog box (shown in Figure 12-1) has three different options for creating property pages. To display this dialog box, simply right-click anywhere in the Resource View and select the Add Resource context menu item.

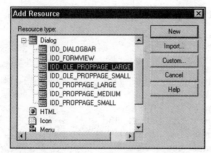

Figure 12-1: You can use the Add Resource dialog box to create the dialog template resources for property pages.

As indicated by the control ID names, the only difference between the various property pages is their initial sizes. When a property sheet is created from the Add Resource dialog box, the settings previously listed are preset automatically.

Creating the CPropertyPage class

Once a property page has been designed in the resource editor, a CPropertyPage-derived class can be created via the ClassWizard. Once again, this is done much the same way as creating a CDialog-derived class. The only difference is that instead of selecting CDialog as the base class, you should select CPropertyPage. Be careful about the last part. If you invoke the ClassWizard to create a new class of a dialog template resource, ClassWizard always defaults the base class to CDHtmlDialog. Unfortunately, ClassWizard doesn't look at the styles to determine that a CPropertyPage is probably the correct way to go in some cases.

Displaying a modal CPropertySheet

As mentioned earlier, the CPropertySheet class is not derived from CDialog although CPropertySheet objects are constructed and displayed in the same manner that CDialog objects are constructed and displayed. For example, to create and display a modal property sheet, you would normally declare a CPropertySheet object on the stack and call its DoModal function (just as you'd do with a CDialog object). However, in the case of a property page, you need to add the relevant property pages to the property sheet before calling the property sheet's DoModal function.

Following is an example of how to do this. As you can see, CPropertyPage objects are added to a CPropertySheet object via the CPropertySheet::AddPage function:

```
#include "MyPropertyPage1.h"
#include "MyPropertyPage2.h"

...

void ShowModalPropertySheet()
{
 CPropertySheet sheet;
 CMyPropertyPage1 pageMyPage1;
 CMyPropertyPage2 pageMyPage2;

 sheet.AddPage(&pageMyPage1);
 sheet.AddPage(&pageMyPage2);
 sheet.DoModal();
}
```

Pretty simple, huh? Now let's look at what it takes to display the property sheet in a modeless setting.

Displaying a modeless CPropertySheet

Displaying a modeless property sheet is almost identical to displaying a modal property sheet. The main difference is instead of using the DoModal function to display the property sheet, the CPropertySheet::Create function is used. In addition, you should take a couple of important points into account when dealing with modeless property sheets and property pages.

Modal property sheets are displayed in a synchronous manner. This means that when a function calls the property sheet's DoModal function, control does not return to the calling function until the property sheet has been dismissed. Therefore, the property sheet and property page objects can be allocated on the stack within the function that called the property sheet's DoModal function.

Modeless property sheets, however, are displayed in an asynchronous manner because the call to display the property sheet returns while the property sheet is still visible. As a result, if you were to allocate the property sheet on the stack, display the property sheet in a modeless fashion, and then exit the function, the property sheet object would destruct and the window would disappear. In addition, if you were to declare the property sheet in a different scope (for example, as a member variable of a view class responsible for displaying the sheet), and declare the property pages on the stack within the same function responsible for displaying the modeless property sheet, the page objects would destruct on function exit. This results in some nasty GPF (General Protection Fault) errors when the user attempts to click on the page that is still viewable on the screen, but whose underlying data structure has been deleted.

As a result, you must take great care regarding how and when to allocate the property sheet and property page objects when dealing with modeless property sheets. One such technique would involve the following steps:

1. Using the ClassWizard, create a CPropertySheet-derived class. For purposes of this example, I'll refer to this as CMyPropertySheet.

2. Declare an instance of the CMyPropertySheet as a member variable or global variable of the class that will display the sheet (such as the view, dialog, or document class).

3. In the function responsible for displaying the sheet, determine if the sheet has already been constructed by checking its HWND member variable. If it has not been constructed, instantiate the page objects, add them to the sheet via the AddPage function and then call Create to display the sheet. If the sheet has already constructed (and by definition is somewhere on the desktop) a nicety for the user would be to call the BringWindowToTop function so that the user can easily locate the wayward property sheet.

```
void CPropertySheetDemoDlg::OnBnClickedButton1()
{
  HWND hwnd = g_sheet.GetSafeHwnd();
  if (!hwnd)
  {
    CPropPage1* p1 = new CPropPage1();
    CPropPage2* p2 = new CPropPage2();
    g_sheet.AddPage(p1);
    g_sheet.AddPage(p2);

    g_sheet.Create();
  }
  else
  {
    g_sheet.BringWindowToTop();
  }
}
```

4. Now you need to make sure the pages are removed from memory when appropriate. To do that, override the property sheet class's `PostNcDestroy` virtual function like the following. Note that because I'm removing the pages from the sheet as their associated `CPropertyPage` objects are being deleted from memory, I need to iterate through the sheet's pages in reverse order.

```
void CMyPropertySheet::PostNcDestroy()
{
 int nPages = GetPageCount();
 for (int i = (nPages - 1); i >= 0; i--)
 {
  CPropertyPage* pPage = GetPage(i);
  ASSERT(pPage);
  if (pPage)
  {
   delete pPage;
   RemovePage(i);
   TRACE("[CMyPropertySheet::OnDestroy] Removing page "
     "%ld\n", i);
  }
 }

 CPropertySheet::PostNcDestroy();
}
```

As you can see, there's a lot more work to do with modeless property sheets, but knowing how to work with both modal and modeless situations enables you to decide which one to use based on what's best for your application.

Note Although you'll be creating a demo that shows some of the more advanced uses of property sheets and pages later on in this chapter, the `PropertySheetDemo` project on the book's Web site contains an absolute minimum, no frills dialog-based application that displays both a modal and modeless property sheet.

One last difference between modal and modeless property sheets to note is that unlike modal property sheets, modeless property sheets are not automatically displayed with an OK and Cancel button; your program has to create these buttons manually. You will see how to do this in the next section as you delve into `CPropertySheet` a little further.

Displaying a property sheet within a dialog box

So far, you've seen how to create and display both modal and modeless property sheets. However, at times you will need to display a property sheet within another dialog box. If you are in need of this rather advanced user interface functionality, it can be accomplished by following some easy steps. (This demo can be found on the book's Web site as `PSheetWithinADialog`.)

1. Create the dialog templates for the property pages.

2. Create `CPropertyPage`-derived classes for the pages. (In the demo I called mine `CMyPropertyPage1` and `CMyPropertyPage2`.)

3. Include the header files for these pages in the dialog box's header file:

```
#include "MyPropertyPage1.h"
#include "MyPropertyPage2.h"
```

4. Declare the CPropertySheet and CMyPropertyPage objects as member variables of the dialog class:

```
class CPSheetWithinADialogDlg : public CDialog
{
...

protected:
CPropertySheet m_sheet;
CMyPropertyPage1 m_pageMyPage1;
CMyPropertyPage2 m_pageMyPage2;


...
```

5. In the dialog box's OnInitDialog function, call the CPropertySheet::AddPage function to add the CMyPropertyPage objects:

```
BOOL CPSheetWithinADialogDlg::OnInitDialog()
{
CDialog::OnInitDialog();


...


m_sheet.AddPage(&m_pageMyPage1);
m_sheet.AddPage(&m_pageMyPage2);
```

6. So far, this is nothing new. However, that's going to change at this point because now the sheet will be contained by another window. Therefore, you need to specify that fact on the Create call with the WS_CHILD style. In addition, a call to set the extended style WS_EX_CONTROLPARENT is needed or the parent dialog box's keyboard input (Tab, Esc) won't be processed correctly. In addition, you need a call to SetWindowPos to manually position the sheet. Note that the cx and cy values are being ignored here (as a result of specifying SWP_NOSIZE). This means that the dialog template size will dictate the runtime size of the sheet. Here's the code that follows the previous step's AddPage calls:

```
// add page code
...

m_sheet.Create(this, WS_CHILD | WS_VISIBLE);
m_sheet.ModifyStyleEx (0, WS_EX_CONTROLPARENT);
m_sheet.SetWindowPos(NULL, 5, 5, 50, 50,
SWP_NOZORDER | SWP_NOSIZE | SWP_NOACTIVATE);

return TRUE;
}
```

Building and executing this code results in a dialog box similar to what you see in Figure 12-2.

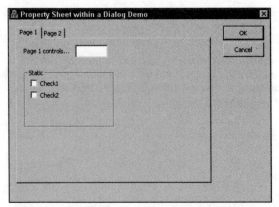

Figure 12-2: Displaying property sheets and pages inside a dialog box is much easier than you might think.

Although this certainly works, there's one problem that I personally have with this technique, and that is I cannot stand hard-coded values such as the x and y value specified in the call to the SetWindowPos function. Therefore, a much more elegant approach would be to drop a static control on the dialog template where you want the property sheet to appear and to base the sheet's positioning on that static control at runtime. Here's the modified OnInitDialog function that illustrates that (I've bolded the changes):

```
BOOL CPSheetWithinADialogDlg::OnInitDialog()
{
  CDialog::OnInitDialog();

  ...

  m_sheet.AddPage(&m_pageMyPage1);
  m_sheet.AddPage(&m_pageMyPage2);

  m_sheet.Create(this, WS_CHILD | WS_VISIBLE);
  m_sheet.ModifyStyleEx (0, WS_EX_CONTROLPARENT);

  CWnd* pWnd = GetDlgItem(IDC_PROPSHEET_WINDOW);
  ASSERT(pWnd);
  if (pWnd)
  {
   CRect rect;
   pWnd->GetWindowRect(&rect);
   ScreenToClient(&rect);

   m_sheet.SetWindowPos(NULL, rect.left, rect.top, 0, 0,
     SWP_NOZORDER | SWP_NOSIZE | SWP_NOACTIVATE);
  }
```

As you can see, my static control has an ID of IDC_PROPSHEET_WINDOW. I simply call GetDlgItem to retrieve a CWnd pointer for the static control and then query its size with a call to GetWindowRect. After converting the returned size to client coordinates, I then use the x and y values of the `rect` to dynamically position the sheet as the static control is positioned on the template. Also, if you use this technique you'll want to remember to set the static control's `Visible` property to `False`.

One last note is that if you're concerned about instantiating a `CWnd` object for the sole purpose of getting a control's position on the screen, you can also use code like the following, which accomplishes the exact same thing but is probably a bit more efficient:

```
RECT rect;
HWND hwnd;
GetDlgItem(IDC_PROPSHEET_WINDOW, &hwnd);
ASSERT(hwnd);
if (hwnd)
{
 ::GetWindowRect(hwnd, &rect);
 ScreenToClient(&rect);

 m_sheet.SetWindowPos(NULL, rect.left, rect.top, 0, 0,
 SWP_NOZORDER | SWP_NOSIZE | SWP_NOACTIVATE);
}
```

Now that you've seen the basics of working with property sheets and pages, let's look a demo using these controls, and after that, I'll cover some of the more advanced issues.

A Modal Property Sheet Demo

This demo (`ModalDemo`) teaches many aspects of using modal property sheets by writing a Find dialog box. The Find dialog box is like those in other applications with one exception: Once a search has been completed, the results are displayed on a second tab. This handles scenarios in which a search results in more than one hit.

This demo will enable you to deal with many realistic scenarios concerning programming property sheets. For example, in a Find dialog box, you wouldn't want the Results tab enabled unless matches are found. Therefore, after you get the basic property sheet up and running, you will learn to enable and disable tabs. In addition, it's a nice touch for the end user to see the number of matches on the Results tab. To accomplish that task, you will learn to dynamically change a tab's caption. Like all of the demo applications in this book, the full source for this demo can be found on the book's Web site.

The main objective of this demo is to teach the different aspects of the `CPropertySheet` and `CPropertyPage` classes. Therefore, many aspects of this demo will be faked so that the demo doesn't go on a five-page tangent on how to deal with issues that have nothing to do with property sheets or property pages. So, without further ado, let's get started.

1. Create a new MFC SDI project named `ModalDemo`.

Note   The naming convention I employ for my property page resource IDs involves using the standard dialog template prefix of `IDD`, plus the name of the property sheet, plus the name of this page. Therefore, in the case of a "find" property sheet with two property pages ("find" and "results"), my two property page template IDs would be `IDD_FINDBOOK_FIND` and `IDD_FINDBOOK_RESULTS`. This can sometimes lead to IDs that are a bit redundant. However, in large projects, it also results in your related IDs being grouped together properly in the Resource View.

2. Create a property page resource called `IDD_FINDBOOK_FIND` and add the necessary controls to make it look like the property page in Figure 12-3. Make sure to disable the Author and Publisher edit controls, set the combo box Type to Drop List, and add some dummy data to it (in semicolon-delimited strings such as **Visual C++/MFC;C#/.NET; JScript.NET;**).

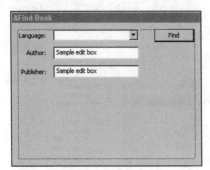

Figure 12-3: Find Book property page dialog template

3. Once the controls have been placed on the `IDP_FINDBOOK_FIND` dialog box, use the ClassWizard to create a `CPropertyPage` class called `CFindPage`.

4. Create DDX control member variables for the Language combo box and the Find button. Name them `m_cboLanguages` and `m_btnFind`, respectively.

5. After the Find property page is complete, create a second property page called `IDD_FINDBOOK_RESULTS`, and modify it so that when finished, it looks like the property sheet in Figure 12-4.

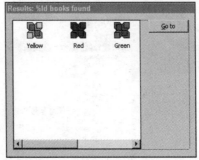

Figure 12-4: The Results property page after the controls have been added.

6. Once again, use the ClassWizard to create a `CPropertyPage`-derived class — this one called `CResultsPage`.

7. After the ClassWizard creates the `CResultsPage` class, create two DDX control member variables for the list control and the button. Name them `m_lstResults` and `m_btnGoto`, respectively.

8. Add a string resource with the ID of IDS_FIND. The value for this string should be Find Book. This string resource will be passed to the CPropertySheet constructor. Figure 12-5 shows the end result of this operation with the string already created in my projects string table.

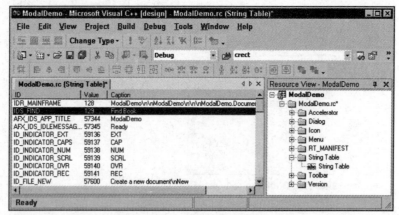

Figure 12-5: String resources can easily be added to a project simply by opening the string table (from the Resource View) and typing in the desired values.

9. After you create the two property pages, locate the IDR_MAINFRAME menu resource. First remove all the File options except Exit. Then add a new popup menu item called Books and under that a menu item called Find Book (as shown in Figure 12-6).

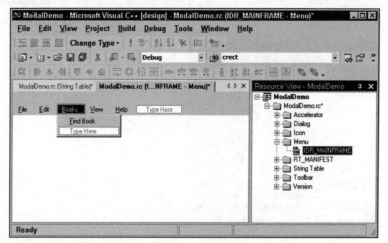

Figure 12-6: The user views the Property Sheet from this menu option.

10. Add a COMMAND event handler for the Find Book menu item to the CModalView class.

11. Edit the handler so that when finished it looks as follows. Make sure to also add the include directives for the `FindPage.h` and `ResultsPage.h` header files at the top of the `ModalDemoView.cpp` file.

```
void CModalDemoView::OnBooksFindbook()
{
    CPropertySheet sheet(IDS_FIND);
    CFindPage pageFind;
    CResultsPage pageResults;

    sheet.AddPage(&pageFind);
    sheet.AddPage(&pageResults);
    sheet.DoModal();
}
```

In the preceding code, a `CPropertySheet` is created on the stack using the constructor that takes as its only argument a string resource ID. This is why you added the `IDS_FIND` resource string earlier, because it saves you from having to hard-code the string in the source code.

Next, two `CPropertyPage` objects are instantiated. After the property pages are created, they are both added to the `CPropertySheet` via the `CPropertySheet::AddPage` function, and the `CPropertySheet::DoModal` function is called to display the property sheet.

12. At this point, build and run the application. Once you select the Find Book option from the Edit menu, your modal property sheet should look like that shown in Figure 12-7.

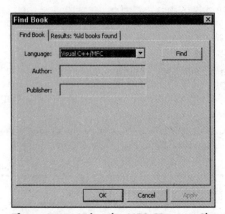

Figure 12-7: Using the MFC CPropertySheet and CPropertyPage classes, you can create dialog boxes like this in minutes.

Most of what you've just done you already know. However, this sets the demo up for the more advanced property sheet and property page programming tasks that I'll cover in the next section.

Advanced Tips and Techniques

As you have seen, it is very easy to create and display both modal and modeless property sheets. Unfortunately, this is the point where the Visual C++ online documentation and most books leave off. However, you aren't reading this chapter to learn something that can be covered in just a few pages. So roll up your sleeves, and let's start doing some real work with property sheets and property pages.

Note that this section involves making changes to the modal property sheet demo (ModalDemo). Unless otherwise noted, all the tips and techniques presented in this section are valid for both modal and modeless property sheets.

Removing standard buttons

When a modal CPropertySheet is displayed, several buttons are automatically created. However, there may be situations where your application doesn't have a need for all of these standard buttons. For example, the Apply button is certainly not applicable for every application. So the question is, "If the buttons are displayed automatically, how does the programmer specify that they are not needed?" Actually, as you are about to see, removing any or all of the standard buttons from a CPropertySheet is not difficult.

Suppose you want to remove the Cancel and Apply buttons. Users select the Cancel button when they have changed their minds and want to back out of the dialog box without affecting any changes. The Apply button gives users the capability of applying the changes while remaining on the property sheet. In other words, when using a dialog box, it is customary to expect that changes will only be made once the dialog box has been dismissed. However, with property sheets, you can use the Apply button to enable users to view their changes while the property sheet remains displayed. This enables users to continue making changes and, depending on the application, see the effects as they work their way through the property sheet's pages.

However, this demo is about a Find Book property sheet, and because no data will be changed, neither of these buttons is applicable to this application. The question now becomes, "How do you remove these buttons when you don't have the dialog template resource for the property sheet?"

Because MFC is creating these buttons automatically for you, they are all created with static, nonchanging resource IDs. Their IDs are listed in Table 12-1.

Table 12-1: Resource IDs for Buttons

Button	Resource ID
OK	IDOK
Cancel	IDCANCEL
Help	IDHELP
Apply	ID_APPLY_NOW

In order to remove the standard buttons, you only need to do the following for each control (where *id* is one of the IDs listed in Table 12-1):

```
CWnd* pWnd = GetDlgItem(id);
if (pWnd)
{
 pWnd->ShowWindow(FALSE);
}
```

Therefore, to remove the Cancel and Apply buttons from the demo's property sheet, you need to make only the following modifications to the demo:

1. Using the ClassWizard, create a CPropertySheet-derived class called CFindSheet.

2. Place an #include directive for the FindSheet.h file in the ModalDemoView.cpp file.

   ```
   #include "FindSheet.h"
   ```

3. Modify the CModalDemoView::OnBooksFindbook function to instantiate this new CFindSheet class instead of the standard CPropertySheet. (The altered line is shown in bold.)

   ```
   void CMainFrame::OnEditFindbook()
   {
    CFindSheet sheet(IDS_FIND);
    CFindPage pageFind;
    ...
   ```

4. Using the ClassWizard, override the CFindSheet::OnInitDialog function to hide the unwanted buttons (IDCANCEL and ID_APPLY_NOW):

   ```
   BOOL CFindSheet::OnInitDialog()
   {
    BOOL bResult = CPropertySheet::OnInitDialog();

    int ids[] = {ID_APPLY_NOW, IDCANCEL};
    for (int i = 0; i < sizeof ids / sizeof ids[0]; i++)
    {
     CWnd* pWnd = GetDlgItem(ids[i]);
     ASSERT(pWnd);
     if (pWnd) pWnd->ShowWindow(FALSE);
    }

    return bResult;
   }
   ```

If you build and run the application, you can verify that the unwanted Apply and Cancel buttons are no longer present on your property sheet (Figure 12-8).

However, there is one very untidy result to what you just did. The only remaining button (IDOK) appears as if it has been marooned in the middle of the dialog box. The next section shows how to move that button or any other of the standard buttons. You might like it in the middle, but let's see how to reposition buttons just in case you don't.

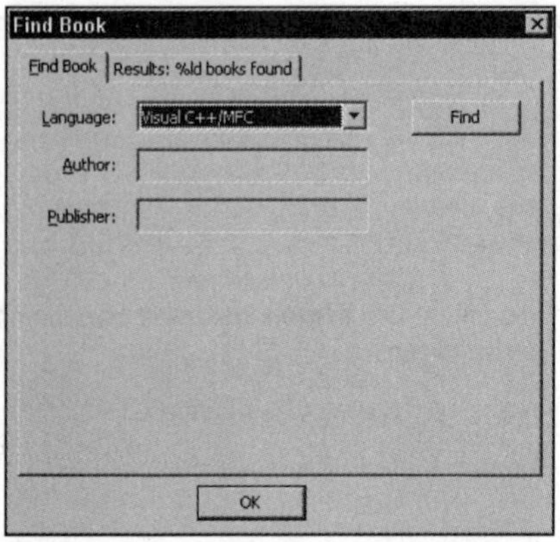

Figure 12-8: Property sheet after having had the Cancel and Apply buttons removed; however note the ugly positioning of the OK button.

Repositioning standard buttons

At this point, the property sheet looks a little strange because it only has one button and that button is horizontally positioned almost in the middle of the dialog box. In addition, both property pages have buttons that are aligned along the right side of the property page. Therefore, it would certainly look a lot more appealing if the OK button were also aligned along the right side of the property sheet. Unfortunately, there is no single member function along the lines of AlignButtons. As a result, you have to do this the old-fashioned way: using the MoveWindow function. The code shown in Listing 12-1 should be added to the bottom of the CFindSheet::OnInitDialog function (just before the return statement).

Here's a brief explanation of the code. First, a CWnd object (pbtnOK) is associated with the OK button. Then, the property sheet is shortened by the height of a button and widened by the width of a button. After the property sheet is properly sized, the screen position of the first property page is used to properly align the OK button with the property page.

Listing 12-1: **Moving buttons in a property sheet**

```
CWnd* pbtnOk = GetDlgItem(IDOK);
ASSERT(pbtnOk);

CRect rectSheet;
GetWindowRect(rectSheet);

// Get size of OK button.
CRect rectOkBtn;
pbtnOk->GetWindowRect(rectOkBtn);

// Get border space between btn bottom and sheet bottom.
int iBorder = rectSheet.bottom - rectOkBtn.bottom;

// Resize sheet.
```

```
rectSheet.right += rectOkBtn.Width() + iBorder;
rectSheet.bottom = rectOkBtn.top;
MoveWindow(rectSheet);

// Find first page.
CPropertyPage* pPage = GetPage(0);
ASSERT(pPage);
CRect rectPage;
pPage->GetWindowRect(rectPage);

// Save width and height.
int cxOk = rectOkBtn.Width();
int cyOk = rectOkBtn.Height();

// Move OK button.
rectOkBtn.top = rectPage.top;
rectOkBtn.bottom = rectOkBtn.top + cyOk;
rectOkBtn.left = rectSheet.right -
 (cxOk + iBorder);
rectOkBtn.right = rectOkBtn.left + cxOk;
ScreenToClient(rectOkBtn);
pbtnOk->MoveWindow(rectOkBtn);
```

After you have inserted the code in Listing 12-1 in the `CFindSheet OnInitDialog` member function, build the project and run it. You should see results similar to Figure 12-9.

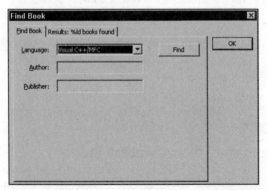

Figure 12-9: Moving and resizing a property sheet's standard buttons is not very intuitive, but can be done via the standard GetWindowRect and MoveWindow functions.

Changing the standard button's caption

A button's caption should reflect what will happen if the button is clicked. If someone is using this Find Book dialog box and sees an OK button, he or she would naturally be confused as to what will happen once that button is clicked. Will clicking the OK button close the dialog box or perform the search? Therefore, the next task is to illustrate how to change the text of a property sheet button.

Because the `CPropertySheet` and its standard buttons are created dynamically, changing a standard button's caption must be done in your application code. The following is all that is needed to change the OK button's caption. Once again, any of the property sheet's standard button IDs could be used (as listed previously), as well as any IDs for controls that you have added to the property sheet. Here's how you would change a button's caption at runtime (include its mnemonic, which we'll discuss in more detail later in the chapter):

```
CWnd* pWnd = GetDlgItem(IDOK);
pWnd->SetWindowText(_T("Cl&ose"));
```

Obviously, this code is generic, and can be used on any property sheet that has not removed the `IDOK` button. However, in the current `ModalDemo` application, the `IDOK` button is already associated with the `m_btnOK` `CButton` class. Therefore, simply add the following line of code to the end of the `OnInitDialog` function (just before the `return` statement):

```
pWnd->SetWindowText(_T("Cl&ose"));
```

Note   When you run this application, the mnemonic may not show up until after you hold down the Alt key depending on the version of Windows you are running.

Disabling tabs

You might need to disable a given tab within a property sheet at times. For example, suppose that the application needs certain fields on one page to be entered before it can display another page. Unfortunately, at the time of this writing, no elegant means of disabling a tab exists. Therefore, in lieu of a `CPropertySheet` member function, here's an outline of the steps required to disable a property page. After the numbered steps, each step is expanded so that you can see exactly what is required to implement this functionality in code.

1. Create a member variable to store the current tab index.

2. Create an array member variable to hold all of the index values for the currently disabled tabs.

3. Handle the `TCN_SELCHANGING` notification message to set the current tab index.

4. Handle the `TCN_SELCHANGED` notification message to decide if you want to enable the tab to be activated. If you don't, you must post a `PSM_SETCURSEL` message. In this message, the last active tab index is specified.

Creating a member variable to store the current tab index

Add a member variable to the `CFindSheet` class to hold the current tab index. When a user attempts to access a disabled tab, this index value represents the tab that will be activated. Actually, it happens so fast that the user will only perceive not being able to switch to the disabled tab.

```
protected:
  int m_iLastActivePage;
```

Creating a member variable to hold currently disabled tabs

The next step is to add a member variable of type `CUIntArray` to the `CFindSheet` class. This array will hold all of the indexes to the currently disabled tabs on the property sheet:

```
CUIntArray m_arrDisabledPages;
```

Adding member functions to disable specified tabs

Next, add the function declaration to the CFindSheet class to enable the disabling of property pages (see Listing 12-2). The property pages that need to be disabled are specified in a variable argument (*vararg*) list that is terminated with the standard value of –1. This function adds the specified tab indexes to the m_arrDisabledPages array. After that, the SetDisabledText function is called to append the " – Disabled" text to the tab's Caption.

In addition to having to do all of this work to simply disable a tab, there is also no way to change the font for a specific tab. In other words, you cannot gray out the text of the specific tab so that the user can intuitively see that the tab is not accessible. Therefore, Microsoft recommends that you simply append the text "– Disabled" to the tab's Caption. Bogus? Absolutely. Unfortunately, at this time, it's all there is.

Listing 12-2: Adding the function declaration to the CFindSheet class

```
void CFindSheet::DisablePage(int iFirstPage, ...)
{
 int iPage = iFirstPage;

 va_list marker;
 va_start (marker, iFirstPage);
 int nArgs = 0;

 while (iPage != -1)
 {
  // Add page to disabled page index array.
  m_arrDisabledPages.Add(iPage);

  SetDisabledText(iPage);

  // Get next page index.
  iPage = va_arg(marker, UINT);

  // The list MUST end with a -1!!!
  ASSERT(nArgs++ < 100);
 }
}
```

Adding member functions to set captions of disabled tabs

Once you have added the DisablePage function, add the following #define directive and SetDisabledText function. This function appends the DISABLED_TEXT value to the tab's Caption so that the user knows that the tab cannot be activated.

```
#define DISABLED_TEXT " - Disabled"

void CFindSheet::SetDisabledText(int iPage)
{
 CTabCtrl* pTab = GetTabControl();
 ASSERT(pTab);
 TC_ITEM ti;
```

```
char szText[100];
ti.mask = TCIF_TEXT;
ti.pszText = szText;
ti.cchTextMax = 100;
VERIFY(pTab->GetItem(iPage, &ti));
strcat(szText, DISABLED_TEXT);
VERIFY(pTab->SetItem(iPage, &ti));
}
```

Handling tab notification messages for disabled tabs

Now that you have everything in place to know if a tab should be disabled or not, you need to add the function that actually disables user activation of a disabled tab. Use the ClassWizard to implement the OnNotify virtual function, and edit it to look like Listing 12-3.

As mentioned earlier, any time the user attempts to activate a property page, this function checks to see if the desired property page is disabled. If it is, the OnNotify function resets the current property page to the last active property page by posting a PSM_SETCURSEL message to the object's underlying property sheet.

Listing 12-3: **Implementing the OnNotify virtual function**

```
BOOL CFindSheet::OnNotify(WPARAM wParam,
 LPARAM lParam, LRESULT* pResult)
{
NMHDR* pnmh = (NMHDR*)lParam;
ASSERT(pnmh);
if (TCN_SELCHANGING == pnmh->code)
 {
 m_iLastActivePage = GetActiveIndex();
 }
else if (TCN_SELCHANGE == pnmh->code)
 {
 int iCurrPage = GetActiveIndex();
 if (IsPageDisabled(iCurrPage))
  {
  PostMessage(PSM_SETCURSEL, m_iLastActivePage);
  }
 }

 return CPropertySheet::OnNotify(wParam,
  lParam, pResult);
}
```

Adding a function that verifies if a tab is disabled

Add the function shown in Listing 12-4 to verify if a specified property page is disabled. This function simply iterates through the m_arrDisabledPages array to see if the specified property page has been disabled and returns a BOOL value indicating if it is disabled or not.

Listing 12-4: Verifying if a property page is disabled

```
BOOL CFindSheet::IsPageDisabled(int iPage)
{
 BOOL bFoundEntry = FALSE;
 int iSize = m_arrDisabledPages.GetSize();

 int i = 0;
 while (i < iSize && !bFoundEntry)
 {
  if (m_arrDisabledPages.GetAt(i) == (UINT)iPage)
  {
   bFoundEntry = TRUE;
  }
  else
  {
   i++;
  }
 }

 return bFoundEntry;
}
```

Testing the capability of disabling tabs

The Find Book property sheet has a property page for the search criteria and a property page for the search results. Therefore, it would be logical to assume that the Results property page would be disabled until the user has initiated a search that successfully found books that matched the criteria specified on the Find Books property page.

Therefore, locate the `CFindSheet OnInitDialog` function, and place the following line of code just before the `return` statement. Notice that with any function that takes a variable argument list, you must send a value that is recognized as the terminating value to the list. In this case, the standard value of –1 is being used. Testing and running the application at this point should produce a property sheet in which the Results property page is not accessible. Because you want to reenable this tab once the user initiates a search, the next section will show how to reenable tabs.

```
DisablePage(1, -1);
```

Reenabling property pages

Now that you disabled the property page(s), you need to be able to reenable it. To accomplish this, simply add the following functions to both enable a given property page and to remove the " – Disabled" text from the tab's `caption`.

Understanding the EnablePage function

Because the code is in place to add a property page to an array (`m_arrDisabledPages`) when it is disabled, the `EnablePage` function simply needs to search the `m_arrDisabledPages` array for the specified page (see Listing 12-5). If the page is found, it is removed from the array, and the `SetEnabledText` function is called.

> **Listing 12-5: Searching the m_arrDisabledPages array for a specified page**

```
void CFindSheet::EnablePage(int iPage)
{
 BOOL bFoundEntry = FALSE;
 int iSize = m_arrDisabledPages.GetSize();

 int i = 0;
 while (i < iSize && !bFoundEntry)
 {
  if (m_arrDisabledPages.GetAt(i) == (UINT)iPage)
  {
   bFoundEntry = TRUE;
  }
  else
  {
   i++;
  }
 }

 if (bFoundEntry)
 {
  m_arrDisabledPages.RemoveAt(i);
  SetEnabledText(iPage);
 }
}
```

Examining the SetEnabledText function

Once a page has been reenabled, the SetEnabledText function must be called to strip the " – Disabled" string from the end of the tab's Caption. The EnableTab function calls this function when it has removed a property page from the m_arrDisabledPages array:

```
void CFindSheet::SetEnabledText(int iPage)
{
 CTabCtrl* pTab = GetTabControl();
 ASSERT(pTab);
 TC_ITEM ti;
 char szText[100];
 ti.mask = TCIF_TEXT;
 ti.pszText = szText;
 ti.cchTextMax = 100;
 VERIFY(pTab->GetItem(iPage, &ti));
 char* pFound = strstr(szText, DISABLED_TEXT);
 if (pFound)
 {
  *pFound = '\0';
  VERIFY(pTab->SetItem(iPage, &ti));
 }
}
```

Testing the EnableTab function

To test the capability of reenabling a tab, use the ClassWizard to add a message handler for the Find button on the CFindPage property page. This function gets a pointer to the property page's parent window (the property sheet) and calls the CFindSheet::EnablePage function. You must add an #include directive for the FindSheet.h file at the top of the FindPage.cpp file for this function to compile. In addition, you need to ensure that the CFindSheet::EnablePage is a public member function, or that the CFindPage is a friend class of the CFindSheet class. Personally, I prefer the latter, because these classes are designed to work together and no other class should be calling this function.

```
void CFindPage::OnBtnFind()
{
 CFindSheet* pParentSheet = (CFindSheet*)GetParent();

 ASSERT(pParentSheet-IsKindOf(
  RUNTIME_CLASS(CFindSheet)));

 pParentSheet->EnablePage(1);
}
```

Finally! I told you this stuff isn't easy at times.

Now, build and run the application. When you do, you should see that the Find Book property page is enabled and the Results property page is disabled. Upon clicking the Find button, however, the Results property page should become enabled.

Note that in a real application, you would not enable the tab until you've actually performed a successful search. However, with this code you can now enable/disable tabs in a manner consistent with your specific application's needs. You've probably been wondering about the printf-like caption on the Results property page ("Results: %ld books found"). In the next section, you'll see not only how to set a property page's caption, but also how to include formatting like this in the dialog template.

Dynamically setting CPropertyPage tab captions

When you created the dialog template resources for the two property pages, you specified a Caption property. However, what happens when you want to change a tab's caption at runtime? This demo provides an example of when you would want to do so. Because the Results property page contains a list of the items found, it would be helpful for the user if the tab also indicated the number of items found.

Using the SetItem function to set a tab's caption

To set a tab's Caption, you get a pointer to the property sheet's underlying tab control (CTabCtrl) object, retrieve the current text (CTabCtrl::GetItem), and then set the text with the CTabCtrl::SetItem function call. At its simplest, this can be performed as follows:

```
CTabCtrl* pTab = GetTabControl();
ASSERT(pTab);
TC_ITEM ti;
char szText[100];
ti.mask = TCIF_TEXT;
ti.pszText = szText;
ti.cchTextMax = 100;
```

```
VERIFY(pTab->GetItem(iIndexOfDesiredTab, &ti));

strcpy(szText, "Your new tab Caption");
VERIFY(pTab->SetItem(iIndexOfDesiredTab, &ti));
```

Testing the SetItem function to set a tab's caption

The preceding example is simple. However, what if you want to format the caption? For example, what if you needed to show the caption as "Results: 5 books found"? Let's see the changes that would be necessary with the demo application to make that happen.

1. Add these #define directives to the top of the FindSheet.cpp file:

```
#define RESULTS_TAB_INDEX 1
#define RESULTS_TAB_CAPTION "Results: %ld books found"
```

2. After the #define directives are in place, add the following functions to the CFindSheet class. As you can see, the SetResults function simply calls a function to alter the Results tab's caption and then enables or disables the tab based on the value of nHits. After all, why enable the property page if the search turned up nothing? Because CFindPage will be calling the SetResults function, declare the SetResults function as being public:

```
void CFindSheet::SetResults(int nHits)
{
 SetResultsTabCaption(nHits);
 if (0 == nHits)
 {
  DisablePage(1, -1);
 }
 else
 {
  EnablePage(1);
 }
}
```

3. After retrieving the tab's caption via the CTabCtrl::GetItem function call, the RESULTS_TAB_CAPTION is used to format the new caption:

```
void CFindSheet::SetResultsTabCaption(int nHits)
{
 CTabCtrl* pTab = GetTabControl();
 ASSERT(pTab);
 TC_ITEM ti;
 char szText[100];
 ti.mask = TCIF_TEXT;
 ti.pszText = szText;
 ti.cchTextMax = 100;
 VERIFY(pTab->GetItem(RESULTS_TAB_INDEX, &ti));

 sprintf(szText, RESULTS_TAB_CAPTION, nHits);
 VERIFY(pTab->SetItem(RESULTS_TAB_INDEX, &ti));
}
```

4. Once these two functions are defined, you just need to update the `CFileSheet::` `OnInitDialog` by removing the call to `DisablePage` and replacing it with a call to the `SetResults` function. You no longer have to disable the tab because the `SetResults` function does that automatically if a value of 0 (indicating no hits) is passed to it:

```
SetResults(0);
```

5. Assuming you added some dummy test entries into combo box, you can test this caption setting code by updating the `CFindPage::OnBtnFind` function to fake finding books based on the language selected. Obviously, this is being hard-coded so that you can concentrate on simply testing the code that implements dynamically changing a tab's caption.

```
void CFindPage::OnBtnFind()
{
CFindSheet* pParentSheet = (CFindSheet*)GetParent();
ASSERT(pParentSheet->IsKindOf(
  RUNTIME_CLASS(CFindSheet)));

int iIndex;
if (0 == (iIndex = m_cboLanguages.GetCurSel()))
{
pParentSheet->SetResults(2);
}
else
{
pParentSheet->SetResults(0);
}
}
```

If you build and test this demo application at this point, you will see that the number of books "found" is equal to the index of the combo box entry selected. However, more importantly, you've just learned how to dynamically change a tab's caption based on runtime data and to enable or disable tabs accordingly.

Let's continue looking at some more advanced property page tasks by examining how to change a tab's font.

Changing a tab's font

You may recall that a specific tab's font cannot be changed. However, you can change the font for all tabs contained within a property sheet. If you take a close look at the different tabs you added to the demo application, one thing that is obvious is that the tab captions don't stand out. In other words, they fade into the background. Here are the basic steps required to change the tab caption's font:

1. Create the desired font.

2. Acquire a pointer to the property sheet's underlying `CTabCtrl` object.

3. Call the `CTabCtrl::SetFont` function.

Actually, this demo was going to change the font for the active tab, but unfortunately, this doesn't appear to be possible. In other words, all of the tab's captions are displayed with the same font, and that font is changed with the `CTabCtrl::SetFont` function. To change the font in the demo application, declare a member variable of type `CFont` in the `CFindSheet` class called `m_fontTab`. Next, add the following lines of code to the end of the `CFindSheet::OnInitDialog` function:

```
m_fontTab.CreateFont(-8, 0, 0, 0, FW_BOLD, 0, 0,
 0, 1, 0, 0, 0, 0, _T("MS Sans Serif"));
CTabCtrl* pTab = GetTabControl();
ASSERT(pTab);
if (pTab)
{
 pTab->SetFont(&m_fontTab);
}
```

Using mnemonics with CPropertyPage tabs

One advantage the Windows interface has over other operating systems is its sense of user interface consistency. Take the example of a mnemonic. Whenever you see static text on the screen with one of the letters underlined, the underlined letter is known as a *mnemonic*. Holding down the Alt key and pressing the mnemonic usually results in that field getting focus. Actually, if the control is read-only, the next input-capable control in the tab order receives focus.

However, just when you get comfortable with the concept of putting mnemonics in all of your dialog boxes, along comes the `CPropertyPage` class, which completely ignores them. If, for example, you set a `CPropertyPage`'s tab caption to "&Result", and press Alt+R, nothing happens. To get around this glaring shortcoming of the `CPropertyPage` class, you have to override the `CPropertySheet::PreTranslateMessage` that you learned about in Chapter 11. Every single keystroke is filtered through this function for every property page owned by the property sheet.

Use the ClassWizard to create the `PreTranslateMessage` function. The demo's implementation of this function is shown in Listing 12-6. As you can see, `WM_SYSKEYDOWN` messages are the only concern because that is the message that is sent when the user is holding down the Alt key. The `pMsg->wParam` value is then evaluated to make sure that the key that was pressed is a number or a letter. After that, the function simply iterates through the property sheet's property pages and compares the mnemonic that was typed to the mnemonic (if any) for each property page. If a matching property page is found, the `SetActivePage` function is called only if the page is not disabled. Figure 12-10 shows the demo after having implemented the changes outlined in this section.

Listing 12-6: **Implementation of CFindSheet::PreTranslateMessage**

```
BOOL CFindSheet::PreTranslateMessage(MSG* pMsg)
{
 BOOL bHandledMsg = FALSE;

 switch(pMsg->message)
 {
  case WM_SYSKEYDOWN:
  {
```

```cpp
    // You only want 0-9 and letters.
    if ((0x2f < pMsg->wParam)
      && (0x5b > pMsg->wParam))
    {
      CTabCtrl *pTab = GetTabControl();
      ASSERT(pTab);

      TC_ITEM ti;
      char szText[100];
      ti.mask = TCIF_TEXT;
      ti.pszText = szText;

      char szMnemonic[3];
      sprintf(szMnemonic, "&%c", pMsg->wParam);

      BOOL bFoundMatchingPage = FALSE;
      int iCurrPage = 0;
      while ((iCurrPage < pTab->GetItemCount())
        && (!bFoundMatchingPage))
      {
        ti.cchTextMax = 99;
        pTab->GetItem(iCurrPage, &ti);

        CString strText = szText;
        strText.MakeUpper();
        if (-1 != strText.Find(szMnemonic))
        {
          bFoundMatchingPage = TRUE;
          if (!IsPageDisabled(iCurrPage))
          {
            SetActivePage(iCurrPage);
            bHandledMsg = TRUE;
          }
        }
        else
        {
          iCurrPage++;
        }
      }
    }
    break;

  default: break;
  }

  return (TRUE == bHandledMsg ?
    TRUE : CPropertySheet::PreTranslateMessage(pMsg));
}
```

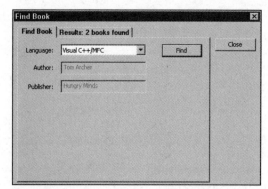

Figure 12-10: Although the CPropertySheet class offers a good deal of functionality, certain tasks require a bit of manual coding that is not very intuitive.

Summary

You're now at the end of Part II, and you've been exposed to quite a bit about dialog boxes, controls, form views, control views, property sheets, and property pages. You began in Chapter 10 by learning how to create dialog templates resources, define and associate a CDialog-class to control the dialog box, and how to display and manage modal dialog boxes. You also discovered how the combination of message maps, command routing, and the CCmdTarget class allows you to associate commands (such as the user clicking the OK button) with handler functions. Once you were finished with the dialog basics, you then learned some control basics; including four different ways in which to associate a control class with a control in order to manipulate it. Finally, you saw how to program several key controls including buttons, edit controls, list boxes, and combo boxes.

In Chapter 11, you learned many of the finer, more advanced issue of programming with dialog boxes, including displaying and controlling modeless dialog boxes, overriding the PreTranslateMessage function to hook the dialog box's message procedure, serializing data without the document/view architecture, and iterating through all the controls on a dialog box in order to perform tasks such as setting their fonts. In that chapter, you also discovered how to create form views from dialog templates for your SDI and MDI applications, and the wonders of control views; including seeing how to create your own specialized CCtrlView-derived class.

Finally, in this chapter, you learned about the CPropertySheet and CPropertyPage classes and how to use them in both modal and modeless environments. You learned that although these classes are good at encapsulating their intended functionality, they fall somewhat short of expectations when it comes to providing basic functions. However, you also learned how to circumvent these classes' shortcomings and to provide your own support for the enabling and disabling of property pages, property page navigation through keyboard mnemonics, and setting a specific property page tab's font and caption. Hopefully, the code in this chapter and this Part overall will make your programming tasks involving dialog boxes and controls much easier than they might have otherwise been.

✦   ✦   ✦

Advanced Programming

Custom Draw Controls

Have you ever wondered how some applications have these really cool looking controls that act just like standard Windows controls, but have really cool looking interfaces? For example, consider accounting applications that have check register-like list view controls where every other line alternates in a background color or Microsoft Outlook-like controls that combine the capabilities of a tree view and list view in a single control. In this chapter, you'll learn the ins and outs of writing reusable custom draw controls so that you too can start designing and writing your own cool controls. I'll start out by briefly going over the three main ways in which custom controls are normally written and then comparing these different techniques. Once I've done that, I'll dive directly into the technique that is the focus of this chapter — a method known as *custom draw*. Once I've covered the basics of using custom draw to do your own drawing for your controls, I'll present a base class list control that shows how easy it is to start building your own library of custom draw controls for your applications.

Owner Draw versus Custom Draw

There are three very common means of customizing standard Windows controls. The first is the most extreme and involves manually handling the WM_PAINT messages and performing all the painting yourself. With this solution, you get no help at all from Windows. You have to create a device context, determine where and how big your control is, what state it is in, and then draw it all yourself. Because of the time it takes to write all this code as well as its inherent complexity; most programmers tend to shy away from this method.

The second common method of creating custom controls is via owner-draw (or self-draw) controls. These are a bit easier to write. Here, Windows sets up the device context for you. It also fills in a structure that gives you the rectangle that the control occupies, the state the control is in, and flags to say how much drawing you need to do. You still need to do all the drawing yourself, but with all this information handed to you, it is not such a chore. In particular, for controls like list boxes and list view controls, Windows will go line by line through the control and ask you to draw each individual item; you don't need to know how to draw the entire control. To make things easy for owner-draw control writers, Windows also provides special drawing functions, like DrawFrameControl. Owner-draw is available for static, button, combo box, and list box controls, but not for edit controls. It is also available for the list view and tab common controls. However, for list view controls, *owner draw* only works in report mode and you have to draw the entire item (including all the subitems) in one go.

For standard Windows controls (buttons, edit boxes, and so on), you can also use the WM_CTLCOLOR family of notification messages to make some simple changes, usually just to the colors used. Windows sends WM_CTLCOLOR messages during the actual painting cycle of the control to give you the chance to make changes to the device context and nominate a brush to use for the background. You are somewhat limited in what you can do here, but the big advantage is that the control still does most of the work itself; you do not need to tell it how to draw itself. However, these messages are only available for the standard Windows controls; the Windows common controls do not support WM_CTLCOLOR.

The third and final means of creating custom controls is with *custom draw*. This is different from owner draw, although some programmers confuse the two. It is available for the list view, tree view, tooltip, header, trackbar, toolbar, and rebar controls. Custom draw lets you hook into the paint cycle of the control in one or more stages of the drawing process. At each draw stage you can make changes to the drawing context and choose to either do your own drawing, let the control do the drawing, or combine the two. You also get to control what further notifications you will receive during the paint cycle.

Handling NM_CUSTOMDRAW notifications

When the control first starts to paint itself, in response to a WM_PAINT message, you receive an NM_CUSTOMDRAW notification message, with the draw stage set to CDDS_PREPAINT. If you don't handle this yourself, that will be the end of it, because the default message handler will just tell the control to carry on with default drawing and not to interrupt you again.

If you do handle the message, you have a chance to do a bit of painting yourself if you want. You can then set a flag in the return result that says whether you want the control to do its default painting. (You typically will want the default painting, because doing it yourself is not a trivial task.) You can also set flags to say whether you want to receive further notifications. You can ask the control to send you a NM_CUSTOMDRAW notification for the CDDS_POSTPAINT draw stage when the control has finished drawing (you can then do some extra drawing yourself). You can also say that you want to get notifications for the CDDS_ITEMPREPAINT draw stage for each item drawn.

Similarly, when you get each NM_CUSTOMDRAW notification for the CDDS_ITEMPREPAINT draw stage, you can set up the colors to use, make changes to the device context including font changes, and maybe do some drawing yourself. You can then say whether you want the default painting for the item and whether you want to receive a CDDS_ITEMPOSTPAINT when the item drawing is finished.

If you are in report mode, you can also ask for individual notifications for each subitem. These have the draw stage set to (CDDS_ITEMPREPAINT | CDDS_SUBITEM), and again you can fiddle with the device context, do your own drawing, or let the control do some drawing and optionally receive a (CDDS_ITEMPOSTPAINT | CDDS_SUBITEM) drawing stage message at the end of each subitem.

Note   Subitem notifications are only available for custom controls V4.71 (that is, for IE4.0 or Windows 98) or later, so ensure that you check the version of COMCTL32 you have on your machine if you intend to use custom draw controls.

Figure 13-1 shows the general flow of NM_CUSTOMDRAW notification messages for a list control with two items, each with two subitems (columns). At first glance, the flow of NM_CUSTOMDRAW notification message can seem a bit daunting. However, with time you'll discover that having all these messages is to your benefit.

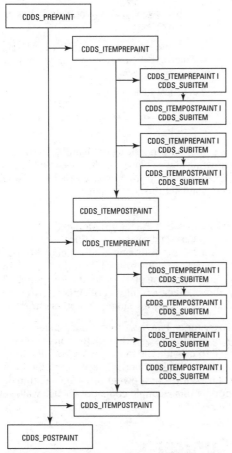

Figure 13-1: Sequence of NM_CUSTOMDRAW notification messages

Why custom draw

Figure 13-1 shows a lot of notification messages. So your question might very well be: What's in it for me in return for dealing with all that? Table 13-1 compares the advantages of custom draw to owner draw for list view controls. I think you'll see that custom draw provides you with greater flexibility and ease of use when drawing controls.

Table 13-1: Benefits of Owner Draw versus Custom Draw

Owner Draw	Custom Draw
This only works with report-view style.	This works for any style.
You must do all the drawing yourself.	You can choose your own drawing, default drawing, or a combination of both.
You can change colors and fonts for default drawing.	You can choose your own drawing, default drawing, or a combination of both. You can also change colors and fonts for default drawing.
You must draw the entire line (including subitems) in one go.	You can handle subitems individually.

The price you pay for this flexibility is some complexity in writing the handler for the NM_CUSTOMDRAW messages. All the various drawing stages come through the one handler. The handler has to understand how to behave for each of the draw stages, extract the required information from the NMLVCUSTOMDRAW struct, and set the correct flags so that it receives subsequent notification messages correctly.

However, things are more complicated than this. Some of the information in the NMLVCUSTOMDRAW struct is only relevant during certain draw-stage notifications. For example, Windows only sets the iSubItem value for the subitems notifications; it has bogus values for the other notifications message. Similarly, Windows only fills in the RECT in the struct with valid values for some draw stages (depending on the version of common controls you have). Experimental evidence shows that even this is not completely correct; in fact only some of the values are valid during some drawing stages and others are not.

To ease the burden on the working class programmer, I have written a class called CListCtrlWithCustomDraw that does a lot of the housekeeping work for you and uses simple virtual functions that you can override to provide the functionality you require. You do not need to worry about setting the correct flags, or unpacking information from structures and so on. Now that you've seen for yourself how owner draw and custom draw compare, in the next section, I'll present not only this example code, but I'll also walk you through the specifics on how exactly it all works.

Creating a Custom Draw Control

Now that you understand the custom draw facility of the Windows common controls, I will take you through the creation of a class that should ease a great deal of the burden required in writing custom draw controls. This code can be found on the Web site for this book. The class that you'll see here (CListCtrlWithCustomDraw) does a lot of the housekeeping work for you and uses simple virtual functions that are easily overridden to provide the functionality you require. As you'll see, the class automatically takes care of the generic housekeeping chores such as setting the correct flags and unpacking information from structures.

Creating the class

Get the ball rolling by creating a dialog-based application called ListCtrlColor. From there, add a new CListCtrl-derived class called CListCtrlWithCustomDraw. The first thing you'll do to your new class is to add a handler for the NM_CUSTOMDRAW notification message called OnCustomDraw. Once you've done that you should have a message map with the following entry:

```
ON_NOTIFY_REFLECT(NM_CUSTOMDRAW, OnCustomDraw)
```

The resulting OnCustomDraw function has two arguments: pNMHDR and pResult. The pResult value is where you set the flags that indicate when you want further custom draw messages and whether or not to use the default painting. For a list view control, the pNMHDR is actually a pointer to a NMLVCUSTOMDRAW structure (notification message for list view custom draw) that tells you about the current drawing stage, what item or subitems you are looking at, and so forth.

You could edit the function declaration so it passes an NMLVCUSTOMDRAW*, but instead you can safely cast the pNMHDR from NMHDR* to NMLVCUSTOMDRAW* to give access to the data, even though these are distinct and separate structures.

If you have a C++ background, you may ask why NMLVCUSTOMDRAW does not simply derive from NMHDR in the first place. Well, that sort of thing just does not happen in the Windows SDK API. Because Microsoft designed the SDK API to work with both C and C++, it cannot use any language features specific to C++. That means all the structures in the SDK are PODs (plain old data structures) with no member functions, inheritance, and so on.

However, all is not lost. To get a similar effect to inheritance, the SDK uses a C technique; the first member of a derived struct is an instance of the base struct. In this particular case, you have (with simplified declarations) the following:

```
typedef struct {
  HWND hwndFrom;
  UINT idFrom;
  UINT code;
} NMHDR;

typedef struct {
  NMHDR   hdr;
  DWORD   dwDrawStage;
} NMCUSTOMDRAW;

typedef struct {
  NMCUSTOMDRAW nmcd;
  COLORREF clrText;
} NMLVCUSTOMDRAW;
```

Because NMLVCUSTOMDRAW is a POD, a pointer to an NMLVCUSTOMDRAW is also a pointer to its first member (nmcd). In other words, it is a pointer to an NMCUSTOMDRAW. This, in turn, is a pointer to the first member of NMCUSTOMDRAW (hdr), which is an NMHDR. Therefore, it is quite legitimate to pass a pointer to an NMCUSTOMDRAW structure using a pointer to an NMHDR and cast it as required. Now, on with the show.

The CListCtrlWithCustomDraw class

In the OnCustomDraw for CListCtrlWithCustomDraw, you provide a generic handler for custom draw notifications. The bulk of the code is a switch statement on the draw stage you are up to. At each of the prepaint stages, you call virtual functions to get color information, fonts required, and to take over (or augment) the drawing process. You also allow for extra drawing during the postpaint stages.

Listing 13-1 shows the fleshed-out OnCustomDraw function for CListCtrlWithCustomDraw.
I've been quite liberal with the sprinkling of comments throughout so that the code is easy to
understand.

Listing 13-1: **The OnCustomDraw function**

```
void CListCtrlWithCustomDraw::OnCustomDraw (NMHDR* pNMHDR,
                                            LRESULT* pResult)
{
  // First, extract data from
  // the message for ease of use later.
  NMLVCUSTOMDRAW* pNMLVCUSTOMDRAW = (NMLVCUSTOMDRAW*)pNMHDR;

  // You'll copy the device context into hdc
  // but won't convert it to a pDC* until (and if)
  // you need it because this requires a bit of work
  // internally for MFC to create temporary CDC
  // objects.
  HDC hdc = pNMLVCUSTOMDRAW->nmcd.hdc;
  CDC* pDC = NULL;

  // Here is the item info.
  // Note that you don't get the subitem
  // number here, because this may not be
  // valid data except when you are
  // handling a subitem notification.
  // So you'll do that separately in
  // the appropriate case statements
  // below.
  int nItem = pNMLVCUSTOMDRAW->nmcd.dwItemSpec;
  UINT nState = pNMLVCUSTOMDRAW->nmcd.uItemState;
  LPARAM lParam = pNMLVCUSTOMDRAW->nmcd.lItemlParam;

  // Next, you set up flags that will control
  // the return value for *pResult.
  bool bNotifyPostPaint = false;
  bool bNotifyItemDraw = false;
  bool bNotifySubItemDraw = false;
  bool bSkipDefault = false;
  bool bNewFont = false;

  // What you do next depends on the
  // drawing stage you are processing.
  switch (pNMLVCUSTOMDRAW->nmcd.dwDrawStage) {
   case CDDS_PREPAINT:
   {
    // PrePaint
    m_pOldItemFont = NULL;
    m_pOldSubItemFont = NULL;

    bNotifyPostPaint = IsNotifyPostPaint();
```

```
   bNotifyItemDraw = IsNotifyItemDraw();

   // Do you want to draw the control yourself?
   if (IsDraw()) {
    if (! pDC) pDC = CDC::FromHandle(hdc);
     CRect r(pNMLVCUSTOMDRAW->nmcd.rc);

    // Do the drawing.
    if (OnDraw(pDC,r)) {
     // You drew it all yourself
     // so don't do default.
     bSkipDefault = true;
    }
   }
  }
break;

case CDDS_ITEMPREPAINT:
{
 // Item PrePaint
 m_pOldItemFont = NULL;

 bNotifyPostPaint =
    IsNotifyItemPostPaint(nItem,nState,lParam);
 bNotifySubItemDraw =
    IsNotifySubItemDraw(nItem,nState,lParam);

 // Set up the colors to use.
 pNMLVCUSTOMDRAW->clrText =
  TextColorForItem(nItem,nState,lParam);

 pNMLVCUSTOMDRAW->clrTextBk =
  BkColorForItem(nItem,nState,lParam);

 // Set up a different font to use, if any.
 CFont* pNewFont = FontForItem(nItem,nState,lParam);
 if (pNewFont) {
  if (! pDC) pDC = CDC::FromHandle(hdc);
   m_pOldItemFont = pDC->SelectObject(pNewFont);

  bNotifyPostPaint = true; // need to restore font
 }

 // Do you want to draw the item yourself?
 if (IsItemDraw(nItem,nState,lParam)) {
  if (! pDC) pDC = CDC::FromHandle(hdc);

  if (OnItemDraw(pDC,nItem,nState,lParam)) {
   // You drew it all yourself.
   // So don't do default.
   bSkipDefault = true;
  }
```

Continued

Listing 13-1 *(continued)*

```
  }
 }
 break;

 case CDDS_ITEMPREPAINT|CDDS_SUBITEM:
 {
 // SubItem PrePaint
 // Set subitem number (data will be valid now).
 int nSubItem = pNMLVCUSTOMDRAW->iSubItem;

 m_pOldSubItemFont = NULL;

 bNotifyPostPaint =
  IsNotifySubItemPostPaint(nItem, nSubItem, nState,
                           lParam);

 // Set up the colors to use.
 pNMLVCUSTOMDRAW->clrText =
  TextColorForSubItem(nItem,nSubItem,nState,lParam);

 pNMLVCUSTOMDRAW->clrTextBk =
  BkColorForSubItem(nItem,nSubItem,nState,lParam);

 // Set up a different font to use, if any.
 CFont* pNewFont =
  FontForSubItem(nItem, nSubItem, nState, lParam);

 if (pNewFont) {
  if (! pDC) pDC = CDC::FromHandle(hdc);
   m_pOldSubItemFont = pDC->SelectObject(pNewFont);

   bNotifyPostPaint = true;    // need to restore font
  }

  // Do you want to draw the item yourself?
  if (IsSubItemDraw(nItem,nSubItem,nState,lParam)) {
   if (! pDC) pDC = CDC::FromHandle(hdc);
    if (OnSubItemDraw(pDC,nItem,nSubItem,nState,lParam)) {

    // You drew it all yourself
    // so don't do default.
    bSkipDefault = true;
   }
  }
 }
 break;

 case CDDS_ITEMPOSTPAINT|CDDS_SUBITEM:
 {
 // SubItem PostPaint
 // Set subitem number (data will be valid now).
```

```
  int nSubItem = pNMLVCUSTOMDRAW->iSubItem;

 // Restore old font if any.
 if (m_pOldSubItemFont) {
  if (! pDC) pDC = CDC::FromHandle(hdc);
   pDC->SelectObject(m_pOldSubItemFont);

  m_pOldSubItemFont = NULL;
 }

 // Do you want to do any extra drawing?
 if (IsSubItemPostDraw()) {
  if (! pDC) pDC = CDC::FromHandle(hdc);
  OnSubItemPostDraw(pDC,nItem,nSubItem,nState,lParam);
 }
}
break;

case CDDS_ITEMPOSTPAINT:
{
 // Item PostPaint
 // Restore old font if any.
 if (m_pOldItemFont) {
  if (! pDC) pDC = CDC::FromHandle(hdc);
  pDC->SelectObject(m_pOldItemFont);
  m_pOldItemFont = NULL;
 }

 // Do you want to do any extra drawing?
 if (IsItemPostDraw()) {
  if (! pDC) pDC = CDC::FromHandle(hdc);
   OnItemPostDraw(pDC,nItem,nState,lParam);
 }
}
break;

case CDDS_POSTPAINT:
{
 // Item PostPaint
 // Do you want to do any extra drawing?
 if (IsPostDraw()) {
  if (! pDC) pDC = CDC::FromHandle(hdc);
   CRect r(pNMLVCUSTOMDRAW->nmcd.rc);

  OnPostDraw(pDC,r);
 }
}
break;
}

ASSERT(CDRF_DODEFAULT==0);
*pResult = 0;
```

Continued

Listing 13-1 *(continued)*

```
 if (bNotifyPostPaint) {
  *pResult |= CDRF_NOTIFYPOSTPAINT;
 }

 if (bNotifyItemDraw) {
  *pResult |= CDRF_NOTIFYITEMDRAW;
 }

 if (bNotifySubItemDraw) {
  *pResult |= CDRF_NOTIFYSUBITEMDRAW;
 }

 if (bNewFont) {
  *pResult |= CDRF_NEWFONT;
 }

 if (bSkipDefault) {
  *pResult |= CDRF_SKIPDEFAULT;
 }

 if (*pResult == 0) {
  // Redundant as CDRF_DODEFAULT==0 anyway
  // but shouldn't depend on this in your code.
  *pResult = CDRF_DODEFAULT;
 }
}
```

That's a fair bit of code. The good news is, there's less code left for you to write when you derive from CListCtrlWithCustomDraw. After all, one of the main benefits of object-oriented code is that the most complex code is in the class so that client code (which should constitute the majority of your application) has an easier time of it.

To make this code work, the virtual functions from the prepaint stages need to be defined. The defaults for these functions are to do nothing; so using the CListCtrlWithCustomDraw on its own works the same as a standard list control. It is only when you derive from this class and override some of the virtual functions that the list view control changes appearance. If you do not override them, you get the standard behavior.

To start with, here are the additions to the class declaration for ListCtrlWithCustomDraw. Because this code is lengthy, my remarks describing the various members and functions are interspersed as comments.

Listing 13-2: Additions to ListCtrlWithCustomDraw

```
protected:
 CFont* m_pOldItemFont;
 CFont* m_pOldSubItemFont;

 //
```

```
// Callbacks for whole control
//

// Do you want to do the drawing yourself?
virtual bool IsDraw() { return false; }

// If you are doing the drawing yourself,
// override and put the code in here
// and return TRUE if you did indeed do
// all the drawing yourself.
virtual bool OnDraw(CDC* /*pDC*/, const CRect& /*r*/)
{ return false; }

// Do you want to handle custom draw for
// individual items?
virtual bool IsNotifyItemDraw() { return false; }

// Do you want to be notified when the
// painting has finished?
virtual bool IsNotifyPostPaint() { return false; }

// Do you want to do any drawing after
// the list control is finished?
virtual bool IsPostDraw() { return false; }

// If you are doing the drawing afterwards yourself,
// override and put the code in here.
// The return value is not used here.
virtual bool OnPostDraw(CDC* /*pDC*/, const CRect& /*r*/)
{ return false; }

//
// Callbacks for each item
//

// Return a pointer to the font to use for this item.
// Return NULL to use default.
virtual CFont* FontForItem(int /*nItem*/,
                           UINT /*nState*/,
                           LPARAM /*lParam*/)
{ return NULL; }

// Return the text color to use for this item.
// Return CLR_DEFAULT to use default.
virtual COLORREF TextColorForItem(int /*nItem*/,
                                  UINT /*nState*/,
                                  LPARAM /*lParam*/)
{ return CLR_DEFAULT; }

// Return the background color to use for this item.
// Return CLR_DEFAULT to use default.
virtual COLORREF BkColorForItem(int /*nItem*/,
```

Continued

Listing 13-2 *(continued)*

```
                                    UINT /*nState*/,
                                    LPARAM /*lParam*/)
{ return CLR_DEFAULT; }

// Do you want to do the drawing for this item yourself?
virtual bool IsItemDraw(int /*nItem*/,
                        UINT /*nState*/,
                        LPARAM /*lParam*/)
{ return false; }

// If you are doing the drawing yourself,
// override and put the code in here
// and return TRUE if you did indeed do
// all the drawing yourself.
virtual bool OnItemDraw(CDC* /*pDC*/,
                        int /*nItem*/,
                        UINT /*nState*/,
                        LPARAM /*lParam*/)
{ return false; }

// Do you want to handle custom draw for
// individual subitems?
virtual bool IsNotifySubItemDraw(int /*nItem*/,
                                 UINT /*nState*/,
                                 LPARAM /*lParam*/)
{ return false; }

// Do you want to be notified when the
// painting has finished?
virtual bool IsNotifyItemPostPaint(int /*nItem*/,
                                   UINT /*nState*/,
                                   LPARAM /*lParam*/)
{ return false; }

// Do you want to do any drawing after
// the list control is finished?
virtual bool IsItemPostDraw() { return false; }

// If you are doing the drawing afterwards yourself,
// override and put the code in here.
// The return value is not used here.
virtual bool OnItemPostDraw(CDC* /*pDC*/,
                            int /*nItem*/,
                            UINT /*nState*/,
                            LPARAM /*lParam*/)
{ return false; }

//
// Callbacks for each subitem
```

```
        //

        // Return a pointer to the font to use for this subitem.
        // Return NULL to use default.
        virtual CFont* FontForSubItem(int /*nItem*/,
                                      int /*nSubItem*/,
                                      UINT /*nState*/,
                                      LPARAM /*lParam*/)
        { return NULL; }

        // Return the text color to use for this subitem.
        // Return CLR_DEFAULT to use default.
        virtual COLORREF TextColorForSubItem(int /*nItem*/,
                                             int /*nSubItem*/,
                                             UINT /*nState*/,
                                             LPARAM /*lParam*/)
        { return CLR_DEFAULT; }

        // Return the background color to use for this subitem.
        // Return CLR_DEFAULT to use default.
        virtual COLORREF BkColorForSubItem(int /*nItem*/,
                                           int /*nSubItem*/,
                                           UINT /*nState*/,
                                           LPARAM /*lParam*/)
        { return CLR_DEFAULT; }

        // Do you want to do the drawing for this subitem yourself?
        virtual bool IsSubItemDraw(int /*nItem*/,
                                   int /*nSubItem*/,
                                   UINT /*nState*/,
                                   LPARAM /*lParam*/)
        { return false; }

        // If you are doing the drawing yourself,
        // override and put the code in here
        // and return TRUE if you did indeed do
        // all the drawing yourself.
        virtual bool OnSubItemDraw(CDC* /*pDC*/,
                                   int /*nItem*/,
                                   int /*nSubItem*/,
                                   UINT /*nState*/,
                                   LPARAM /*lParam*/)
        { return false; }

        // Do you want to be notified when the
        // painting has finished?
        virtual bool IsNotifySubItemPostPaint(int /*nItem*/,
                                              int /*nSubItem*/,
                                              UINT /*nState*/,
                                              LPARAM /*lParam*/)
```

Continued

Listing 13-2 *(continued)*

```
{ return false; }

// Do you want to do any drawing after
// the list control is finished?
virtual bool IsSubItemPostDraw() { return false; }

// If you are doing the drawing afterwards yourself,
// override and put the code in here.
// The return value is not used here.
virtual bool OnSubItemPostDraw(CDC* /*pDC*/,
                               int /*nItem*/,
                               int /*nSubItem*/,
                               UINT /*nState*/,
                               LPARAM /*lParam*/)
{ return false; }
```

There is quite a bit of code here as well. Again, there is good news. Each of the virtual functions performs a simple and well-defined task; a programming technique known as *tight cohesion*. As you can see, however, it's the OnCustomDraw function that does all the heavy lifting.

Using the CListCtrlWithCustomDraw class

The final step is to derive a class from CListCtrlWithCustomDraw and put this new class to work. To do that, create a new class and derive it from the new CListCtrlWithCustomDraw class. In order to do that, you might need to do a bit of hacking. First derive the new class from CListCtrl and then globally search and replace all occurrences of CListCtrl with CListCtrlWithCustomDraw. Once you've done that, you can start to override some of the virtual functions to change the appearance of the control.

For this example, you will paint the entire control in *cyan*, and then make the individual cells in the list control alternate in colors to give a checkerboard appearance. It's not very pretty, but it does illustrate some of the possibilities.

Here are the virtual functions you will override in CmyListCtrl:

```
virtual bool IsDraw();

virtual bool OnDraw(CDC* pDC, const CRect& r);

virtual bool IsNotifyItemDraw();

virtual bool IsNotifySubItemDraw(int nItem,
                                 UINT nState,
                                 LPARAM lParam);

virtual COLORREF TextColorForSubItem(int nItem,
                                      int nSubItem,
                                      UINT nState,
```

```
                                    LPARAM lParam);

virtual COLORREF BkColorForSubItem(int nItem,
                                   int nSubItem,
                                   UINT nState,
                                   LPARAM lParam);
```

And here are their implementations:

```
bool CMyListCtrl::IsDraw() {
 return true;
}
bool CMyListCtrl::OnDraw(CDC* pDC, const CRect& r) {
 CBrush brush(RGB(0,255,255));       // cyan
 pDC->FillRect(r,&brush);
 return false; // Do default drawing as well.
}


bool CMyListCtrl::IsNotifyItemDraw() {
 return true;
}
bool CMyListCtrl::IsNotifySubItemDraw(int /*nItem*/,
                                     UINT /*nState*/,
                                     LPARAM /*lParam*/) {
 return true;
}
COLORREF CMyListCtrl::TextColorForSubItem(int nItem,
                                          int nSubItem,
                                          UINT /*nState*/,
                                          LPARAM /*lParam*/)
{
 if (0 == (nItem+nSubItem)%2) {
  return RGB(255,255,0);      // yellow
 } else {
  return CLR_DEFAULT;
 }
}
COLORREF CMyListCtrl::BkColorForSubItem(int nItem,
                                        int nSubItem,
                                        UINT /*nState*/,
                                        LPARAM /*lParam*/) {
 if (0 == (nItem+nSubItem)%2) {
  return RGB(255,0,255); // magenta
 } else {
  return CLR_DEFAULT;
 }
}
```

One thing to keep in mind is that overriding IsDraw and OnDraw enables you to either draw the entire control yourself or just to do some extra work before the default drawing process. In this case, the OnDraw function fills the control with cyan and then returns FALSE to indicate that you still want the default drawing process to continue.

If you want to individually change the colors of each cell, simply override the IsNotifyItemDraw and IsNotifySubItemDraw member functions. If you want the subitems to be custom drawn by returning a value of TRUE from IsNotifySubItemDraw, then you also need to return TRUE from IsNotifyItemDraw. If IsNotifyItemDraw returns FALSE, then there will be no subitem custom drawing either.

In the TextColorForSubItem function, simply do some arithmetic with the item and subitem number to select either a different color or the default color for the control. Finally, to test this out, add a list control to the main dialog box for this application as shown in Figure 13-2.

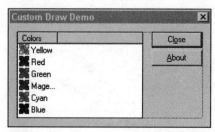

Figure 13-2: Once you have a custom control, using it is a snap.

In the Dialog Editor, create a member variable of type CMyListCtrl called m_listctrl. Once you've done that, edit the list control properties in the dialog box and set the style to use the *report view*. Then, add the following code to the OnInitDialog member function in order to define the columns and fill in some test data:

```
m_listctrl.InsertColumn(0,"label",LVCFMT_LEFT,60,0);
m_listctrl.InsertColumn(1,"first",LVCFMT_LEFT,40,1);
m_listctrl.InsertColumn(2,"second",LVCFMT_LEFT,30,2);
m_listctrl.InsertColumn(3,"third",LVCFMT_LEFT,20,3);

int row;
row = m_listctrl.InsertItem(0,"row1");
m_listctrl.SetItem(row,1,LVIF_TEXT,"aaa",0,0,0,0);
m_listctrl.SetItem(row,2,LVIF_TEXT,"bbb",0,0,0,0);
m_listctrl.SetItem(row,3,LVIF_TEXT,"ccc",0,0,0,0);
row = m_listctrl.InsertItem(1,"row2");
m_listctrl.SetItem(row,1,LVIF_TEXT,"AAA",0,0,0,0);
m_listctrl.SetItem(row,2,LVIF_TEXT,"BBB",0,0,0,0);
m_listctrl.SetItem(row,3,LVIF_TEXT,"CCC",0,0,0,0);
row = m_listctrl.InsertItem(2,"row3");
m_listctrl.SetItem(row,1,LVIF_TEXT,"X",0,0,0,0);
m_listctrl.SetItem(row,2,LVIF_TEXT,"YY",0,0,0,0);
m_listctrl.SetItem(row,3,LVIF_TEXT,"ZZZ",0,0,0,0);
```

Now, simply build and execute the application. The result (shown in Figure 13-3) is a dialog box with the cyan background and checkerboard. (Obviously, this figure is in black and white, but hopefully you'll be able to distinguish between the colors used for the cells and background. If not, running the demo application will illustrate this.)

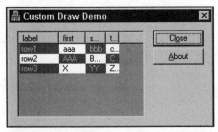

Figure 13-3: A list view dialog box showing custom draw controls

Summary

In this chapter, you learned the ins and outs of writing reusable custom draw controls. I started out by briefly going over the three main ways in which custom controls are normally written and compared these different techniques. Once that was done, I dove directly into the technique of custom draw where you learned the basics of using custom draw to do your own drawing for your controls. Finally, I presented a base class list control that illustrated how easy it is to start building your own library of custom draw controls for your applications.

You should realize that you've just scratched the surface with what can be done with custom draw. However, because you now know the basics of what messages to handle, how to handle the information passed from Windows, and what information Windows wants back to write your own cool controls, you are limited only by your imagination. At this point, I suggest looking at some advanced user interfaces such as Microsoft Outlook or Visual Studio .NET, and taking a swing at creating your own custom draw controls. I think you'll find that what you've learned in this chapter gives you a great jump on doing some things you might not have thought possible before. In the next chapter, I'll take this a step further and you'll see how to apply new behaviors to these custom draw controls.

✦　　✦　　✦

Adding Custom Behavior to Controls

CHAPTER

14

◆ ◆ ◆ ◆

◆ ◆ ◆ ◆

This chapter continues showing you how to customize your applications by explaining how to add customized behavior to your controls. We'll start out by comparing some of the more common techniques of extending behavior such as straight C++ inheritance, multiple inheritance, templates, and message maps. Once I show you the different benefits and hidden pitfalls of each, I'll then show you which technique I believe to be the best and why. As you've seen so far in this book, I believe the best teacher is good working examples. Therefore, the latter half of the chapter will show a complete practical example of extending the addition of resizing abilities to dialog boxes and property sheets that employ what you've learned throughout the chapter.

When I started writing this chapter, I had planned on illustrating the best and most productive way to extend the behavior of your C++ classes, but I encountered a bug in the Microsoft C++ compiler that caused me to utter more than a few choice words. Therefore, in this chapter, not only will you learn how to extend your custom drawn controls, but you will also see first-hand how I managed to sidestep a bug that had me climbing the walls for days. After all, you learn much more by resolving the inevitable showstopper bug than any other means.

Adding Behavior

From Chapter 13 you know that by deriving from `CListCtrlWithCustomDraw` and overriding appropriate virtual functions, you can achieve all sorts of results — everything from simple color or font changes to completely drawing all or part of the list control yourself. The `CListCtrlWithCustomDraw` class simplifies custom draw processing by splitting the monolithic handler for `WM_CUSTOMDRAW` into a number of virtual function calls that you can override individually to give the behavior you require. The next logical step is to add the same sort of behavior to other common control classes, such as `CTreeCtrl`. There are five ways to add behavior to common control classes:

+ Modifying the base class

+ Multiple inheritance

✦ Message maps

✦ Template classes

✦ Multiple inheritance and templates

Modifying the base class

First, consider how you can go about adding new functionality to a group of classes. The most obvious, brute-force way to add the same functionality to a number of classes is to simply copy and paste the code into each one. While I have had the misfortune of working in some shops where the "programmers" must have thought that the CPP extension on C++ files stood for "copy and paste programming," this is obviously far from an ideal solution.

If you were creating your own class hierarchy and wanted to add some functionality to all of your derived classes, then the obvious place to add it is the base class. If the details of how to implement the behavior need to be different for the derived classes, then you would use virtual functions to override the required implementation. For example, consider a simple class hierarchy as shown in Figure 14-1.

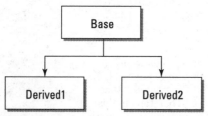

Figure 14-1: A simple class hierarchy

This gives you pseudocode that is something like this:

```
class Base {};
class Derived1 : public Base {};
class Derived2 : public Base {};
```

Add a virtual NewFunction to the base class:

```
class Base {
public:
 virtual void NewFunction();
};

class Derived1 : public Base {
 // no change, just gets Base::NewFunction()
};

class Derived2 : public Base {
public:
// override the new member function
 virtual void NewFunction();
};
```

NewFunction is now available in both class Derived1 and class Derived2. Furthermore, the implementation of NewFunction has been overridden for class Derived2.

This is fine if you are writing the entire class hierarchy yourself and can change the source code as you see fit. However, when it comes to MFC, you are working with an existing class library. You cannot go adding new member functions to the CWnd base class. You cannot even change the other classes in the existing hierarchy. That means that modifying the base class will not work in this case.

Multiple inheritance

Another way of adding functionality is to use multiple inheritance so you can add functionality to derived classes without modifying the base class. You put the new functionality into a separate base class and then change the declarations of the derived classes so they derive from this new class.

To make things more familiar, I will use MFC class names in the diagrams and code snippets. The base class will be CWnd, and your two derived classes are CListCtrl and CTreeCtrl. You cannot change any of these classes directly because they are part of the MFC class library. However, you can derive your own classes from them as shown in Figure 14-2.

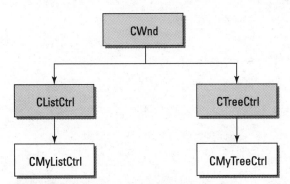

Figure 14-2: Deriving user-defined classes from MFC classes

This gives you code that is something like this:

```
// library classes .. you don't touch these
class CWnd {};
class CListCtrl : public CWnd {};
class CTreeCtrl : public CWnd {};

// my classes
class CMyListCtrl : public CListCtrl {};
class CMyTreeCtrl : public CTreeCtrl {};
```

To add extra functionality, you create a new class called CAddBehavior and use multiple inheritance for your own derived classes, as shown in Figure 14-3. You do not need to make any changes to the library classes.

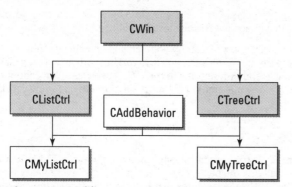

Figure 14-3: Adding a new class with multiple inheritance

```
// library classes .. you don't touch these
class CWnd {};
class CListCtrl : public CWnd {};
class CTreeCtrl : public CWnd {};

// new behavior
class CAddBehavior {
public:
 virtual void NewFunction();
};

// my classes
class CMyListCtrl : public CListCtrl, public CAddBehavior {};

class CMyTreeCtrl : public CTreeCtrl, public CAddBehavior {
public:
 virtual void NewFunction();
};
```

There is a slight catch here, however. If the implementation of CAddBehavior::NewFunction requires access to the members of CWnd—to do anything useful, it probably will—then you are out of luck as things stand because you cannot derive CAddBehavior from CWnd. There is a trick you can use here to help get around this obstacle. You can store a pointer to a CWnd object in the CAddBehavior class. That way, the CAddBehavior class has access to the necessary CWnd members when needed.

```
class CAddBehavior {
public:
 CAddBehavior(CWnd* pWnd)
 : m_pWnd(pWnd) {
 // body of constructor
 }
virtual void NewFunction();
protected:
 CWnd* m_pWnd;
};
```

```
class CMyListCtrl : public CListCtrl, public CAddBehavior {
public:
 // change the constructor for CMyListCtrl
 CMyListCtrl()
 : Base()
 , CAddBehavior(this) {
  // body of constructor
 }
};
// similarly for CMyTreeControl
```

Figure 14-4 shows how a CMyListCtrl object would conceptually be laid out in memory. In addition to the specific data for CMyListCtrl, there is a CListCtrl part (which includes the CWnd base class) and a CAddBehavior part.

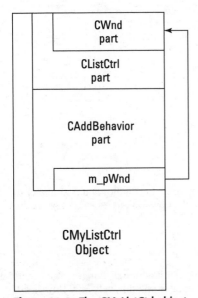

Figure 14-4: The CMyListCtrl object

When an object of CMyListCtrl is constructed, both its CListCtrl part and its CAddBehavior parts are also constructed. The constructor initializes the pointer in the CAddBehavior part to point to itself; in particular, to its CWnd part. This means that CAddBehavior::NewFunction can use m_pWnd to call public members of CWnd.

The only remaining catch is that NewFunction can only access public members of CWnd. If you could change CWnd and declare CAddBehavior to be a friend class of CWnd, then all would be well, but you can't do that because the whole reason for using multiple inheritance in the first place is so that you do not need to change the base CWnd class.

As always, though, there is a solution: Derive a class from CWnd that does have CAddBehavior as a friend. Then you can use that to access protected members of CWnd. That would make your code look like this:

```
class CAddBehaviorFriend : public CWnd {
friend class CAddBehavior;
};

class CAddBehavior {
public:
 CAddBehavior(CWnd* pWnd)
 : m_pWnd((CAddBehaviorFriend*)pWnd) {
 // body of constructor
 }
virtual void NewFunction();
protected:
 CAddBehaviorFriend* m_pWnd;
};

class CMyListCtrl : public CListCtrl, public CAddBehavior {
public:
 // change the constructor for CMyListCtrl
 CMyListCtrl()
 : Base()
  , CAddBehavior(this) {
  // body of constructor
 }
};
// similarly for CMyTreeControl
```

As you can see, multiple inheritance provides a robust means of adding functionality to derived classes without modifying the base class. Let's now look at how message maps can be used to add behavior to classes.

Message maps

Multiple inheritance seems like a reasonable solution. With minimal changes you can add new functionality to any or all of your derived classes, but all is still not well. MFC throws a big wrench in the works with message maps. Now, don't get me wrong; message maps are wonderful things, but there are some limitations. There can be only a single message map at each level of the hierarchy, and the functions called and the class that owns the message map must have CWnd ancestry. That means you cannot put up a message map in your CAddBehavior class. Nor can you put a message map in the CMyListCtrl class and have it directly call member functions of CAddBehavior.

This problem is fairly easy to get around. You put the message map in the CMyListCtrl class and call member functions of CMyListCtrl, which in turn call member functions of CAddBehavior such as NewFunction. The resulting code looks something like this:

```
class CMyListCtrl : public CListCtrl, public CAddBehavior {
public:
 // change the constructor for CMyListCtrl
 CMyListCtrl()
 : Base()
 , CAddBehavior(this) {
```

```
  // body of constructor
  }

protected:
  //{{AFX_MSG(CMyListCtrl)
  afx_msg void OnSomeMe ssage();
  //}}AFX_MSG
DECLARE_MESSAGE_MAP()
};

BEGIN_MESSAGE_MAP(CMyListCtrl, CListCtrl)
  //{{AFX_MSG_MAP(CMyListCtrl)
    ON_COMMAND(ID_SOMETHING,OnSomeMessage);
  //}}AFX_MSG_MAP
END_MESSAGE_MAP();

void CMyListCtrl::OnSomeMessage() {
  NewFunction();
  }

  // similarly for CMyTreeControl
```

The only problem now is that you need to add multiple inheritance, a new constructor, a message map, and some wrapper functions that call CAddBehavior for every class that you want to have your new behavior. This is almost as much work to get right as manually adding the behavior to each class individually. So, it doesn't look like all this has helped much.

Template classes

There is another method of adding behavior that doesn't involve multiple inheritance. In fact it is very much like manually adding code to each class. This method is *templates*. To add functionality using a template, one usually slots a template class between a base class and a derived class. The template class has a template parameter that specifies a base class and adds extra functionality to it. You then derive your class from an instance of the template class with the appropriate base class filled in. This is somewhat different from multiple inheritance. The multiple-inheritance method looks something like this:

```
class Base {};

class Extra {
public:
  virtual void NewFunction();
};

class Derived : public Base, public Extra {
  // gets Extra::NewFunction()
};
```

The template class method, on the other hand, looks like this:

```
class Base {};

template <class BASE>
class Extra : public BASE {
public:
```

```
virtual void NewFunction();
};

class Derived : public Extra<Base> {
 // gets Extra<Base>::NewFunction()
};
```

This is illustrated in the class diagram shown in Figure 14-5.

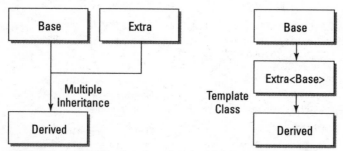

Figure 14-5: The difference between multiple inheritance and templates

One problem with templates is that their implementation usually has to be exposed to the world with inline member function definitions. Also, you end up with separate instances of each function for every different base class you use, which can result in larger binaries and code that is generally slower to load and execute.

The best of both worlds

You can combine the shared code and encapsulation of multiple inheritance with the ease of use of templates to get a good solution that uses the advantages of both methods. It's also worth mentioning that the Microsoft ATL (ActiveX Template Library) also uses this technique. There are four separate chapters on ATL, beginning with Chapter 30.

```
// Multiple inheritance...

class Base {};

class ExtraBase {
public:
 virtual void NewFunction();
};

template <class BASE>
class Extra : public BASE, public ExtraBase {
};

class Derived : public Extra<Base> {
 // gets Extra<Base>::NewFunction()
};
```

This is illustrated in Figure 14-6.

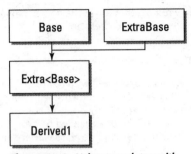

Figure 14-6: Using templates with multiple inheritance

By using the combination of multiple inheritance and templates you should be able to improve on your previous solution. The template class can do the work of adding multiple inheritance, fixing constructors, and adding wrapper functions and message maps for you at compile time so you don't need to do this for every derived class.

This means you end up with code something like this:

```
template <class BASE>
class TAddBehavior : public BASE, public CAddBehavior {
public:
 // change the constructor for TAddBehavior
 TAddBehavior ()
 : BASE()
 , CAddBehavior(this) {
 // body of constructor
 }

protected:
 //{{AFX_MSG(TAddBehavior)
  afx_msg void OnSomeMessage();
 //}}AFX_MSG
 DECLARE_MESSAGE_MAP()
};

BEGIN_MESSAGE_MAP(TAddBehavior, BASE)
 //{{AFX_MSG_MAP(TAddBehavior)
  ON_COMMAND(ID_SOMETHING,OnSomeMessage);
 //}}AFX_MSG_MAP
END_MESSAGE_MAP();

void TAddBehavior::OnSomeMessage() {
 NewFunction();
}

class CMyListCtrl : public TAddBehavior<CListCtrl> {
};

// similarly for CMyTreeControl
```

You can see that the template class now does all the work of stitching in the new behavior for you. All you have to do is derive from it and the problem is solved; well, not quite.

The problem with message maps

The problem would be solved if the MFC message map macros worked with template classes. Unfortunately they don't. In particular, BEGIN_MESSAGE_MAP just will not work with template classes. The reason is that this macro actually defines and initializes a couple of static members and functions. Syntactically, each of the definitions needs to be preceded by template, but they are not, because the macro is written to work with nontemplate classes. Here are the definitions for the message map macros:

```
#ifdef _AFXDLL
#define DECLARE_MESSAGE_MAP() \
private: \
  static const AFX_MSGMAP_ENTRY _messageEntries[]; \
protected: \
  static AFX_DATA const AFX_MSGMAP messageMap; \
  static const AFX_MSGMAP* PASCAL _GetBaseMessageMap(); \
  virtual const AFX_MSGMAP* GetMessageMap() const; \

#else
#define DECLARE_MESSAGE_MAP() \
private: \
  static const AFX_MSGMAP_ENTRY _messageEntries[]; \
protected: \
  static AFX_DATA const AFX_MSGMAP messageMap; \
  virtual const AFX_MSGMAP* GetMessageMap() const; \

#endif

#ifdef _AFXDLL
#define BEGIN_MESSAGE_MAP(theClass, baseClass) \
  const AFX_MSGMAP* PASCAL theClass::_GetBaseMessageMap() \
  { return &baseClass::messageMap; } \
  const AFX_MSGMAP* theClass::GetMessageMap() const \
  { return &theClass::messageMap; } \
    AFX_COMDAT AFX_DATADEF const AFX_MSGMAP \
    theClass::messageMap = \
    { &theClass::_GetBaseMessageMap, \
      &theClass::_messageEntries[0] }; \
    AFX_COMDAT const AFX_MSGMAP_ENTRY \
      theClass::_messageEntries[] = \
  { \

#else
#define BEGIN_MESSAGE_MAP(theClass, baseClass) \
  const AFX_MSGMAP* theClass::GetMessageMap() const \
  { return &theClass::messageMap; } \
  AFX_COMDAT AFX_DATADEF const AFX_MSGMAP \
   theClass::messageMap = \
  { &baseClass::messageMap, &theClass::_messageEntries[0] }; \
```

```
   AFX_COMDAT const AFX_MSGMAP_ENTRY \
    theClass::_messageEntries[] = \
   { \

#endif

#define END_MESSAGE_MAP() \
   {0, 0, 0, 0, AfxSig_end, (AFX_PMSG)0 } \
   }; \
```

Notice that the macros are slightly different depending on whether or not they are being used within an MFC Extension DLL. (This type of DLL and "regular" DLLs are covered in Chapter 16.)

The DECLARE_MESSAGE_MAP and END_MESSAGE_MAP are both fine as they are. DECLARE_MESSAGE_MAP is used within the class declaration itself, and so doesn't need template prefixed. END_MESSAGE_MAP is also fine because it just adds the last line of initialization to the message map data.

So you only need to make a special version of BEGIN_MESSAGE_MAP macro that includes the required template syntax. This is pretty straightforward and is shown in the following example:

```
#ifdef _AFXDLL
#define BEGIN_MESSAGE_MAP_FOR_TEMPLATE(theClass, baseClass) \
   template <class baseClass> const \
    AFX_MSGMAP* PASCAL theClass::_GetBaseMessageMap() \
   { return &baseClass::messageMap; } \
   template <class baseClass> const AFX_MSGMAP* \
    theClass::GetMessageMap() const \
   { return &theClass::messageMap; } \
   template <class baseClass> AFX_COMDAT AFX_DATADEF \
    const AFX_MSGMAP theClass::messageMap = \
   { &theClass::_GetBaseMessageMap, \
    &theClass::_messageEntries[0] }; \
   template <class baseClass> AFX_COMDAT const \
    AFX_MSGMAP_ENTRY theClass::_messageEntries[] = \
   { \

#else
#define BEGIN_MESSAGE_MAP_FOR_TEMPLATE(theClass, baseClass) \
   template <class baseClass> const \
    AFX_MSGMAP* theClass::GetMessageMap() const \
   { return &theClass::messageMap; } \
   template <class baseClass> AFX_COMDAT AFX_DATADEF \
    const AFX_MSGMAP theClass::messageMap = \
   { &baseClass::messageMap, &theClass::_messageEntries[0] }; \
    template <class baseClass> AFX_COMDAT const \
     AFX_MSGMAP_ENTRY theClass::_messageEntries[] = \
   { \
#endif
```

That should do it . . . you can now use BEGIN_MESSAGE_MAP_FOR_TEMPLATE when you define the message map and all should work just fine.

The bug

That is, everything should work just fine if it were not for an unexpected error message. Please note that I'm building with the error-level set to level 4; I don't let my code build with even warning messages. (You'll recall that warning levels were discussed back in Chapter 1.)

When I first built sample code that used this special version of the message map macro, I got the following message within the macro line:

```
warning C4211: nonstandard extension used : redefined extern to static
```

What's going on here? For a start, because I am using a macro, I cannot see the exact line of the macro that is causing the problem. The first step in such a case is to expand the macro by hand and use that instead of the macro call.

After I did that (it is not too hard when you use find and replace in the text editor), I tried compiling again to see if it was more obvious where the error is. This time I saw that the error is in the definition of theClass::messageMap. That is, the error is in the following line from the original macro:

```
template <class baseClass> AFX_COMDAT AFX_DATADEF \
  const AFX_MSGMAP theClass::messageMap = \
  { &baseClass::messageMap, &theClass::_messageEntries[0] }; \
```

No matter how many times I looked at that code, I just could not see anything wrong with it.

Time for the next step: Try to reproduce the problem in a simpler context and cut it down until you get the simplest code possible that still exhibits the bug. This is pretty much a binary search process. I started with the existing code and removed whatever code doesn't look like it would affect the bug, one at a time. After each step, I recompiled and verified that either the bug is still there or has disappeared. If it was still there, I carried on, otherwise I needed to reinstate the section of code I removed and either try something else or split the removal into smaller steps. Some of the things that I tried first include removing the AFX_COMDAT and AFX_DATADEF macros (they made no difference); I also changed from the more complicated AFX_MSGMAP structure to just using a simple int. Still the bug persisted.

I won't bore you (any further) with all the intermediate steps and false trails, but instead show you the code that demonstrates when the error happens and when it doesn't.

```
#include "stdafx.h"

template <class T> class X1 {
  /* virtual */ const int* f() const { return &i; }
  static const int i;
};
template <class T> const int X1<T>::i = 1;
X1<double> x1;

template <class T> class X2 {
  virtual const int* f() const { return &i; }
  static /* const */ int i;
};
template <class T> int X2<T>::i = 2;
X2<double> x2;
```

```
template <class T> class X3 {
 virtual const int* f() const { return &i; }
 static const int i;
};
template <class T> const int X3<T>::i = 3;
X3<double> x3;

class X4 {
 virtual const int* f() const { return &i; }
 static const int i;
};
const int X4::i = 3;
X4 x4;

int main()
{
 return 0;
}
```

Look at the three template classes: X1, X2, and X3. X1 and X2 are both similar to X3, except that X1 makes function f nonvirtual and X2 makes the static data value nonconst. X4 is a nontemplate version. X1, X2, and X4 all compile just fine. However, X3 gives the same error message:

```
D:\SOURCE\TEST\Test.cpp(21) : warning C4211: nonstandard
extension used : redefined extern to static

D:\SOURCE\TEST \Test.cpp(11) : while compiling class-template
static data member 'const int X3::i'
```

This error message seems to make no sense at all. It seems that the compiler gets confused with a combination of template classes, virtual functions, and static const data. In other words, it is a compiler bug!

I always have mixed feelings about compiler bugs. I get some satisfaction from knowing that the programmers at Microsoft are just as human as the rest of us and I feel relieved that it wasn't something I did wrong after all (this time). On the other hand, I'm annoyed that I had to spend so much time tracking down an error that was someone else's fault. And I then think...how am I going to work around it?

In this case there is a fairly simple solution. Although I cannot make the functions nonvirtual functions, I can get rid of the const-ness of the static data. To do this, I need to change the definition of my special version of BEGIN_MESSAGE_MAP as well as DECLARE_MESSAGE_MAP (where the static data is declared). While I'm at it, I'll also make an exact copy of the END_MESSAGE_MAP macro so the names are all consistent. This is what I ended up with:

```
#ifndef _MESSAGEMAPSFORTEMPLATES_
#define _MESSAGEMAPSFORTEMPLATES_

#if _MSC_VER > 1000
#pragma once
#endif // _MSC_VER > 1000
```

```
#ifdef _AFXDLL
#define DECLARE_MESSAGE_MAP_FOR_TEMPLATE() \
private: \
 static /*const*/ AFX_MSGMAP_ENTRY _messageEntries[]; \
protected: \
 static AFX_DATA /*const*/ AFX_MSGMAP messageMap; \
 static const AFX_MSGMAP* PASCAL _GetBaseMessageMap(); \
 virtual const AFX_MSGMAP* GetMessageMap() const; \

#else
#define DECLARE_MESSAGE_MAP_FOR_TEMPLATE() \
private: \
 static /*const*/ AFX_MSGMAP_ENTRY _messageEntries[]; \
protected: \
 static AFX_DATA /*const*/ AFX_MSGMAP messageMap; \
 virtual const AFX_MSGMAP* GetMessageMap() const; \

#endif

#ifdef _AFXDLL
#define BEGIN_MESSAGE_MAP_FOR_TEMPLATE(theClass, baseClass) \
 template <class baseClass> const AFX_MSGMAP* \
  PASCAL theClass::_GetBaseMessageMap() \
   { return &baseClass::messageMap; } \
 template <class baseClass> const AFX_MSGMAP* \
  theClass::GetMessageMap() const \
   { return &theClass::messageMap; } \
 template <class baseClass> AFX_COMDAT AFX_DATADEF \
  AFX_MSGMAP theClass::messageMap = \
  { &theClass::_GetBaseMessageMap,\
   &theClass::_messageEntries[0] }; \
 template <class baseClass> AFX_COMDAT \
  AFX_MSGMAP_ENTRY theClass::_messageEntries[] = \
   { \

#else
#define BEGIN_MESSAGE_MAP_FOR_TEMPLATE(theClass, baseClass) \
 template <class baseClass> const AFX_MSGMAP* \
  theClass::GetMessageMap() const \
   { return &theClass::messageMap; } \
 template <class baseClass> AFX_COMDAT AFX_DATADEF \
  AFX_MSGMAP theClass::messageMap = \
  { &baseClass::messageMap, &theClass::_messageEntries[0]}; \
  template <class baseClass> AFX_COMDAT \
  AFX_MSGMAP_ENTRY theClass::_messageEntries[] = \
   { \

#endif
#define END_MESSAGE_MAP_FOR_TEMPLATE() END_MESSAGE_MAP()

#endif
```

I can now use these macros as direct replacements for the original macros when I write a template class.

Phew! Now, take a deep breath before you see how you can combine the custom draw class presented earlier in Chapter 13 with the techniques and bug workarounds I've just shown you in this section to come up with a set of classes that helps with custom draw for common controls.

Resizing Dialogs and Property Pages

In the previous section, you looked at various ways that you can add behavior to classes, in particular those derived from MFC classes. This time, you will look at a practical example of adding resizing behavior to dialog boxes and property pages.

The problem

Dialog boxes and property pages are quite similar. In fact, CPropertyPage derives directly from CDialog. This is, of course, a good thing. It means that you do essentially the same things in dialog boxes as property pages. You can create both from dialog resources; both have DDX, and so on.

However, that is not entirely good news. Suppose you have written class CMyDialog derived from CDialog that implements some handy features. You derive all your own dialog boxes from CMyDialog instead of CDialog, so they all have your new features, as shown in Figure 14-7. So far, this works fine.

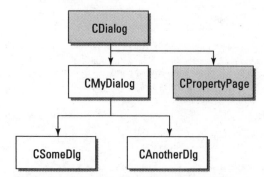

Figure 14-7: Deriving CMyDialog from CDialog

Now you want to add those same nice features to your property pages. After all, dialog boxes and property pages are very similar. Unfortunately, you cannot simply change the MFC CPropertyPage class so it derives from your CMyDialog instead. So what do you do?

You could duplicate your code and write a CMyPropertyPage class derived from CPropertyPage. However, as discussed earlier, that is not good form. More important, it is the start of a maintenance nightmare because you'd have to make the same fixes and changes to both classes.

The next obvious choice is to use a template, so you only have to write the code once; but as you found out earlier, the MFC message map macros do not work well with templates. You can make your own versions of the macros that do work in a template class, but that method has its limitations as well.

Templates are only a good solution for trivial extensions. Templates expose their internal workings to the world as inline functions. This defeats the purpose of encapsulation and increases dependencies within a project. Therefore, you use multiple inheritance to neatly wrap up the internals of the class.

Template-friendly message maps

First, have a quick look at the template-friendly message-map macros again. I copied the MFC message-map macros and added template <class baseClass> in front of the variable and function definition lines in the new BEGIN_MESSAGE_MAP_FOR_TEMPLATE. I also removed the const declarations to get around a compiler bug described earlier in this chapter. Yes, it looks ugly, but then, it is an MFC macro.

```
File "XMessageMapsForTemplates.h":
#ifndef _XMESSAGEMAPSFORTEMPLATES_
#define _XMESSAGEMAPSFORTEMPLATES_

#if _MSC_VER > 1000
#pragma once
#endif // _MSC_VER > 1000

#ifdef _AFXDLL
#define DECLARE_MESSAGE_MAP_FOR_TEMPLATE() \
private: \
    static /*const*/ AFX_MSGMAP_ENTRY _messageEntries[]; \
protected: \
    static AFX_DATA /*const*/ AFX_MSGMAP messageMap; \
    static const AFX_MSGMAP* PASCAL _GetBaseMessageMap(); \
    virtual const AFX_MSGMAP* GetMessageMap() const; \

#else
#define DECLARE_MESSAGE_MAP_FOR_TEMPLATE() \
private: \
    static /*const*/ AFX_MSGMAP_ENTRY _messageEntries[]; \
protected: \
    static AFX_DATA /*const*/ AFX_MSGMAP messageMap; \
    virtual const AFX_MSGMAP* GetMessageMap() const; \

#endif

#ifdef _AFXDLL
#define BEGIN_MESSAGE_MAP_FOR_TEMPLATE(theClass, baseClass) \
  template <class baseClass> const AFX_MSGMAP* PASCAL \
  theClass::_GetBaseMessageMap() \
```

```
            { return &baseClass::messageMap; } \
        template <class baseClass> const AFX_MSGMAP* \
         theClass::GetMessageMap() const \
         { return &theClass::messageMap; } \
        template <class baseClass> AFX_COMDAT AFX_DATADEF \
         /*const*/ AFX_MSGMAP theClass::messageMap = \
         { &theClass::_GetBaseMessageMap, \
           &theClass::_messageEntries[0] }; \
        template <class baseClass> AFX_COMDAT /*const*/ \
         AFX_MSGMAP_ENTRY theClass::_messageEntries[] = \
             { \

    #else
    #define BEGIN_MESSAGE_MAP_FOR_TEMPLATE(theClass, baseClass) \
     template <class baseClass> const AFX_MSGMAP* \
      theClass::GetMessageMap() const \
         { return &theClass::messageMap; } \
     template <class baseClass> AFX_COMDAT AFX_DATADEF \
      /*const*/ AFX_MSGMAP theClass::messageMap = \
      { &baseClass::messageMap, &theClass::_messageEntries[0]}; \
     template <class baseClass> AFX_COMDAT /*const*/ \
      AFX_MSGMAP_ENTRY theClass::_messageEntries[] = \
      { \

    #endif
    #define END_MESSAGE_MAP_FOR_TEMPLATE() END_MESSAGE_MAP()

    #endif
```

Something I failed to mention before is how to make these macros work. The trick is in calling the BEGIN_MESSAGE_MAP_FOR_TEMPLATE. The first argument should be the template class name with a dummy parameter within angle brackets. You use the same parameter name as the second parameter. For example, suppose you declare your class like this:

```
template <class TBASE> class TMyClass : public TBASE {
    ...
    DECLARE_MESSAGE_MAP_FOR_TEMPLATE()
};
```

Then you can write the following definition for the message map (usually in the same header file):

```
BEGIN_MESSAGE_MAP_FOR_TEMPLATE(TMyClass<TBASE>, TBASE)
```

Multiple inheritance

You use multiple inheritance to neatly encapsulate and share the implementation of the template. The template class behaves primarily as a CDialog but also inherits from your new class to add the required behavior as shown in Figure 14-8.

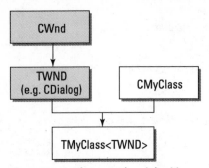

Figure 14-8: The new class inheriting from the template and the base class

The corresponding C++ code looks like this:

```
template <class TWND> // TWND will be derived from CWND
class TMyClass : public TWND, public CMyClass {
...
};

class CMyClass {
    ...
private:
    CWnd* m_pWnd;
};
```

CMyClass has all the implementation details hidden away in its .cpp file. TMyClass forwards its calls to the corresponding CMyClass functions.

Note Notice that I name my template classes with a capital T (for template) rather than a C (for class). You should adopt conventions and, if needed, make up your own. In a way, it does not really matter which conventions you adopt, as long as you use them consistently. When working with MFC, you should try to adopt conventions that fit well with MFC's conventions; otherwise your code ends up with a mixture of the two.

Take a look at Figure 14-9. It would be nice if you could derive CMyClass from CWnd as well. However, MFC limitations mean you cannot make calls to CWnd member functions, or use message maps and so on. As always, there is a way out. In CMyClass, you can store a pointer to your CWnd-derived template object, and make CWnd calls through that pointer.

This assumes that the class with which you instantiate TMyClass is derived from CWnd. If it is not, then you will get compilation errors.

Although you strive to not have compilation errors in the first place, it is always preferable to catch them as early as possible in the development process. It is best to catch them while you are writing code. MS Intellisense helps here. The next best way to catch errors is during compile time, then link time, and finally at runtime via checking error codes and invoking the ASSERT macro at the appropriate time. The worst way to find errors is to let your program compile, link, build, run, and then crash.

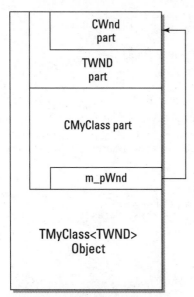

Figure 14-9: Many times, if you can visualize your hierarchy, you can come up with elegant solutions to difficult problems.

In the following example, I have encapsulated storing the pointer to a CWnd in a separate class. I will use this class as the base class for my implementation classes.

```
File "XWndMultipleInheritance.h":

// XWndMultipleInheritance.h : header file
//

#ifndef _XWNDMULTIPLEINHERITANCE_
#define _XWNDMULTIPLEINHERITANCE_

#if _MSC_VER > 1000
#pragma once
#endif // _MSC_VER > 1000

class CXWndMultipleInheritance {
    // Construction
public:
    CXWndMultipleInheritance(CWnd* pWnd) : m_pWnd(pWnd) {}
    // Casting operators etc
public:
    operator CWnd&() { return *m_pWnd; }
    operator const CWnd&() const { return *m_pWnd; }
```

```
        operator CWnd*() { return m_pWnd; }
        operator const CWnd*() const { return m_pWnd; }
        CWnd* operator->() { return m_pWnd; }
        const CWnd* operator->() const { return m_pWnd; }
        // Encapsulate some common calls
        // (add to this later if required)
    public:
        LRESULT CWnd_SendMessage(UINT message,
                                 WPARAM wParam = 0,
                                 LPARAM lParam = 0) {
            return (*this)->SendMessage(message,wParam,lParam);
        }
        LRESULT CWnd_PostMessage(UINT message,
                                 WPARAM wParam = 0,
                                 LPARAM lParam = 0) {
            return (*this)->PostMessage(message,wParam,lParam);
        }
        HWND CWnd_GetSafeHwnd() const {
            return (*this)->GetSafeHwnd();
        }
        void CWnd_ScreenToClient(LPPOINT lpPoint) const {
            (*this)->ScreenToClient(lpPoint);
        }
        void CWnd_ScreenToClient(LPRECT lpRect) const {
            (*this)->ScreenToClient(lpRect);
        }
        void CWnd_ClientToScreen(LPPOINT lpPoint) const {
            (*this)->ClientToScreen(lpPoint);
        }
        void CWnd_ClientToScreen(LPRECT lpRect) const {
            (*this)->ClientToScreen(lpRect);
        }
        // the pointer to the actual window
    private:
        CWnd* m_pWnd;
    };

    #endif
```

As you can see, the pointer is set up in the constructor. You gain access to it via the casting operators. I also added some shortcuts for some commonly used functions.

The template class

With that out of the way, you can start fleshing out the template class using the following steps:

1. Create a new CWnd-derived MFC class called TXResizable.

2. Change the class declaration to be a template (with multiple inheritance as described previously).

3. Move the body of the generated `.cpp` file near the end of the header file.

4. Make all the functions inline by either prepending the function with the `inline` keyword in the implementation file (`.cpp`) or by moving the function to inside the class's definition (in the header file).

5. Fix the default constructor so that it correctly initializes both base classes.

6. Add a `#pragma` to prevent the Visual C++ compiler from emitting warnings about using `this` in the base member initializer list.

7. Add `#include XMessageMapsForTemplates.h` and change the message map declarations and definitions to use your template-friendly macros.

8. Delete the now unused `.cpp` file.

You end up with a class that looks consistent with Visual Studio Wizard–generated code. The result of all that tweaking is the following header file:

```
File: "TXREsizable.h":

#ifndef _TXRESIZABLE_H_
#define _TXRESIZABLE_H_

#if _MSC_VER > 1000
#pragma once
#endif // _MSC_VER > 1000
// TXResizable.h : header file
//

#include "XMessageMapsForTemplates.h"

/////////////////////////////////////////////////////////////////
// TXResizable window

template <class TDIALOGORPAGE>
class TXResizable : public TDIALOGORPAGE,
                    public CXResizable {
    // Construction
public:
    TXResizable();

    // Attributes
public:

    // Operations
public:

    // Overrides
    // ClassWizard generated virtual function overrides
    //{{AFX_VIRTUAL(TXResizable)
    //}}AFX_VIRTUAL
```

```
        // Implementation
public:
    virtual ~TXResizable();

        // Generated message map functions
protected:
    //{{AFX_MSG(TXResizable)
    // NOTE:  The ClassWizard will add and remove
    // member functions here.
    //}}AFX_MSG
    DECLARE_MESSAGE_MAP_FOR_TEMPLATE()
};

/////////////////////////////////////////////////////////////
//{{AFX_INSERT_LOCATION}}
// Microsoft Visual C++ will insert additional
// declarations immediately before the previous line.


/////////////////////////////////////////////////////////////
// TXResizable

#pragma warning (disable: 4355)
// 'this' : used in base member initializer list
TXResizable::TXResizable()
: TDIALOGORPAGE()
, CXResizable(this)
{
}

// 'this' : used in base member initializer list
#pragma warning (default: 4355)
TXResizable::~TXResizable()
{
}


BEGIN_MESSAGE_MAP_FOR_TEMPLATE(TXResizable<TDIALOGORPAGE>,
                              TDIALOGORPAGE)
//{{AFX_MSG_MAP(TXResizable)
// NOTE: The ClassWizard will add and remove
// mapping macros here.
//}}AFX_MSG_MAP
END_MESSAGE_MAP()


/////////////////////////////////////////////////////////////
// TXResizable message handlers

#endif
```

You may be surprised to learn that you can still use the wizard to add message handlers to this code. ClassWizard appears to be smart enough to handle this because it is actually quite dumb. ClassWizard doesn't care what macro names are used, or that you are working with templates; all it looks for are the //{{ AFX_XXX comments. The only catch is that you have to move any ClassWizard-generated functions to just before the #endif that is at the end of the header file and edit it to be a legitimate inline member-function definition. For example, here is the function that ClassWizard generates if you add a WM_SIZE handler:

```
void TXResizable::OnSize(UINT nType, int cx, int cy)
{
    C???::OnSize(nType, cx, cy);
    // TODO: Add your message handler code here
}
```

Because ClassWizard cannot determine what the base class is, it just uses the letter C. This is good because it forces you to correct the code. Again, compilation errors are a good thing. You then hand-edit the preceding code to look like this:

```
template <class TDIALOGORPAGE>
void TXResizable<TDIALOGORPAGE>::OnSize(UINT nType,
                                        int cx,
                                        int cy)
{
    TDIALOGORPAGE::OnSize(nType, cx, cy);
    // TODO: Add your message handler code here
}
```

Putting it all together

Now all you need to do is combine all this with some actual code that performs dialog and property page resizing. This means you need to write your CXResizable class (it had to happen sooner or later).

You derive CXResizable from CXWndMultipleInheritance (described earlier). This class has all the logic for resizing. You also add the appropriate message handlers to the TXResizable class (using ClassWizard) and edit them so they call the appropriate functions of CXResizable.

There is quite a bit of code here, so I will not reproduce it all here. The full source is available on the Web site for this book in the form of a demo project. However, I will discuss some of the main points of interest. I'll start at the very beginning of the header file.

Resizing controls in a dialog

There are many ways a control can resize itself when you resize the dialog box or property page in which it lives. Some controls stay positioned relative to the edges of the dialog box or page, whereas others move in proportion with the change in size. Some controls will keep their size, whereas others will grow in one direction or both.

enum EResizeFlags specifies resizing options for each of the four coordinates that comprise the rectangle for the control position within a dialog box or page. By combining these flags, you can determine how the control moves or resizes.

```
enum EResizeFlags {
   RESIZE_LEFT_LFIX = 00000,
   RESIZE_LEFT_LPROP = 00001,
   RESIZE_LEFT_RPROP = 00002,
   RESIZE_LEFT_CPROP = RESIZE_LEFT_LPROP|RESIZE_LEFT_RPROP,
   RESIZE_LEFT_RFIX = 00004,
   RESIZE_LEFT_FLAGS = RESIZE_LEFT_LPROP
                       |RESIZE_LEFT_RPROP
                       |RESIZE_LEFT_RFIX,
... etc for other coordinates and useful combinations

};
```

The flags with _LFIX (and _TFIX) suffixes anchor the control relative to the left (or top) of the dialog box; there is no change in the coordinate. _RFIX and _BFIX anchor the control relative to the right (or bottom) of the dialog box. For example, if the dialog box width increases by 100 pixels, then the left coordinate will also move 100 pixels to the right. _LPROP, _RPROP, and _CPROP move the coordinate in proportion to the position of the control across the dialog box. LPROP bases that proportion on the left-hand side of the control, CPROP on the center, and RPROP on the right-hand side. _TPROP, _BPROP, and _CPROP are the equivalent for the top and bottom coordinate.

I used three bits to encode the options for each of the four coordinates for 12 bits total. This fits quite nicely into an integer. I will show you the algorithm for resizing using this flag, and its implementation, shortly.

Now look at the CXResizable class itself. Notice that most of the functions are virtual, so you can override them in your derived classes to add to or replace their default implementations.

IsResizable determines whether the dialog box or page will be resizable. By default, it looks at the border style bits of the dialog box or page to see if it has a modal dialog frame style (DS_MODALFRAME). If not, then it is resizable.

```
bool CXResizable::IsResizable() const
{
 // is this dialog/page resizable?
 bool bResizable = true;
 if (::IsWindow(CWnd_GetSafeHwnd()))
 {
  // only if it doesn't have a modal frame
  bResizable = ((*this)->GetStyle() & DS_MODALFRAME)
           != DS_MODALFRAME;
 }
 return bResizable;
}
```

The GetClientRectWas/Now/Ini set of functions return the client rectangles before and after sizing, and for the initial dialog box size. The GetWindowRectWas/Now/Init do the same for the window rectangle.

```
void GetClientRectWas(CRect& rc) const { rc = m_rcWas; }
void GetClientRectNow(CRect& rc) const { rc = m_rcNow; }
void GetClientRectIni(CRect& rc) const { rc = m_rcIni; }
void GetWindowRectWas(CRect& rc) const { rc = m_rwWas; }
void GetWindowRectNow(CRect& rc) const { rc = m_rwNow; }
void GetWindowRectIni(CRect& rc) const { rc = m_rwIni; }
```

To make it obvious that a dialog box is resizable, you draw a gripper in the bottom-right corner. `GetGripperRect` gives the position of the gripper for hit testing and painting. It uses `GetSystemMetrics` to make the gripper the same dimensions as the scroll bar width. You should always use `GetSystemMetrics`, `GetSysColor`, and so on, rather than hard-coding sizes.

```
void CXResizable::GetGripperRect(CRect& rcGripper)
{
// the gripper is at the bottom right and is
// the same size asa scroll bar
GetClientRectNow(rcGripper);

rcGripper.left = rcGripper.right
               - ::GetSystemMetrics(SM_CXVSCROLL);

rcGripper.top = rcGripper.bottom
              - ::GetSystemMetrics(SM_CYVSCROLL);
}
```

`DrawGripper` does the work of drawing the gripper. I use the very handy `DrawFrameControl` to do this; there is no need to reinvent this particular wheel. If you ever have to draw your own user-interface elements, look at `DrawFrameControl` first.

```
void CXResizable::DrawGripper(CDC* pDC)
{
// draw the gripper in the appropriate position
CRect rcGripper;
GetGripperRect(rcGripper);
pDC->DrawFrameControl(rcGripper,
                      DFC_SCROLL,
                      DFCS_SCROLLSIZEGRIP);
}
```

`IsResizeDirectly` determines whether a dialog box or page has resized indirectly, because its container changed size, or has been resized directly, by the user. A property page usually only changes size when the property sheet changes size. However, you can directly resize a modeless dialog box by dragging its edges. `IsResizeDirectly` stops the gripper from appearing and being active.

```
bool CXResizable::IsResizeDirectly() const
{
// property pages cannot be sized directly
// (the property sheet will resize them instead)
bool bIsDialog = (*this)->IsKindOf(RUNTIME_CLASS(CDialog));

bool bIsPropertyPage =
(*this)- >IsKindOf(RUNTIME_CLASS(CPropertyPage));

return bIsDialog && ! bIsPropertyPage;
}
```

`OnSize`, `OnNcHitTest`, and so on, in `CXResizable` may look like message handlers, but strictly speaking, they're not, because `CXResizable` does not derive from `CWnd`. However, the message handlers in the `TXResizable` template call these member functions of the same name.

`OnPaint` fills the background to avoid repaint problems and draws the gripper if required. Note that the logic for determining when to draw the gripper is here instead of in `DrawGripper`. That way, you can override `DrawGripper` to change the gripper's appearance without having to rewrite the logic that determines when to draw it.

```
bool CXResizable::OnPaint()
{
 if (::IsWindow(CWnd_GetSafeHwnd())
 && IsResizable())
 {
  CPaintDC dc(*this); // device context for painting
  CRect rc;
  GetClientRectNow(rc);
  dc.FillSolidRect(rc,::GetSysColor(COLOR_3DFACE));

  // draw the gripper if required
  if (IsResizeDirectly()
  && ! (*this)->IsZoomed())
  {
   DrawGripper(&dc);
   return true;
  }
 }
 return false;
}
```

`OnGetMinMaxInfo` looks at the `GetWindowRectIni` to determine the minimum drag size. During resizing, MFC calls `OnGetMinMaxInfo`, which fills the `MINMAXINFO` structure to indicate maximum and minimum sizes for the window.

```
void CXResizable::OnGetMinMaxInfo(MINMAXINFO FAR* lpMMI)
{
 if (::IsWindow(CWnd_GetSafeHwnd()))
 {
  // the smallest size is the original dialog/page size
  CRect rw;
  GetWindowRectIni(rw);
  lpMMI->ptMinTrackSize.x = rw.Width();
  lpMMI->ptMinTrackSize.y = rw.Height();
 }
}
```

`OnNcHitText` handles dragging by the gripper. Note that if it returns `HTNOWHERE`, then the `TXResizable` handler code will call the default `OnNcHitTest`.

```
UINT CXResizable::OnNcHitTest(CPoint point)
{
 if (::IsWindow(CWnd_GetSafeHwnd())
 && IsResizeDirectly())
 {
  if (IsResizable()
  && ! (*this)->IsZoomed())
  {
```

```
      // check for a hit in the gripper
      CPoint pointScreen = point;
      CWnd_ScreenToClient(&pointScreen);
      CRect rcGripper;
      GetGripperRect(rcGripper);
      if (rcGripper.PtInRect(pointScreen))
      {
       return HTBOTTOMRIGHT;
      }
     }
    }
   return HTNOWHERE;
  }
```

OnSize **is where the real work happens. It updates the cached client and screen rectangles. If the size actually changes, it calls** ResizeControls **to do the actual resizing.** ResizeControls **uses** EnumChildWindows **to iterate through all the child windows (controls) in the dialog box or page and resize (and reposition) each one appropriately.**

```
  void CXResizable::OnSize(UINT /*nType*/,
   int /*cx*/, int /*cy*/)
  {
   if (::IsWindow(CWnd_GetSafeHwnd()))
   {
    CRect rc, rw;
    (*this)->GetClientRect(rc);
    (*this)->GetWindowRect(rw);
    // do we have a valid rectangle?
    if (! rc.IsRectEmpty())
    {
     // copy the previous rectangle into m_rcWas
     // if there was one .. otherwise just set it
     if (m_rcNow.IsRectEmpty())
     {
      m_rcWas = rc;
      m_rwWas = rw;
     }
     else
     {
      m_rcWas = m_rcNow;
      m_rwWas = m_rwNow;
     }

     m_rcNow = rc;
     m_rwNow = rw;

     // if we haven't already set up the initial
     // rectangle, do it now
     if (m_rcIni.IsRectEmpty())
     {
      m_rcIni = rc;
      m_rwIni = rw;
```

```
    }

    // if the size has changed, resize ourselves
    if (m_rcNow != m_rcWas)
    {
     ResizeControls();
    }
   }
  }
 }
```

You need to pass quite a bit of information to be able to resize each child window intelligently. However, there is only room for passing a single LPARAM to the enumerating function. I shove all the information I need into a struct, and pass a pointer to that struct in the LPARAM.

The EnumChildWindows call tells Windows to call EnumChildProc_ResizeControls for each control. This function unpacks the data from the struct, calls a virtual function to work out the new rectangle for the control, and then moves and resizes it. For cleaner repainting, you can use the Begin/End/DeferWindowPos APIs. These accumulate all the window size and position changes you make and apply them in one go at the end.

For each control you call the virtual ResizeControl function. This in turn calls the appropriately named ResizeControlUsingFlags. However, you can override ResizeControl for any other method of resizing you choose.

ResizeControlUsingFlags uses the flags defined in EResizeFlags. Although there are quite a few lines of code, it is basically just a bunch of simple switch statements.

```
    void CXResizable::ResizeControlUsingFlags(UINT id,
     CWnd* pControl, CRect& rcControl, const CSize& szNow,
     const CSize& szWas, const CSize& szIni,
     const CSize& szDelta)
    {
       UINT nFlags = GetResizeFlags(id,
                                    pControl,rcControl,
                                    szNow,
                                    szWas,
                                    szIni,
                                    szDelta);
       if (nFlags != RESIZE_LFIX) {
         {
             int l = rcControl.left;
             int r = rcControl.right;
             int c = (l+r+1)/2;
             int dlprop = ::MulDiv3(l,szNow.cx,
                                      szWas.cx,
                                      szIni.cx)-l;
             int drprop = ::MulDiv3(r,szNow.cx,
                                      szWas.cx,
                                      szIni.cx)-r;
             int dcprop = ::MulDiv3(c,szNow.cx,
                                      szWas.cx,
                                      szIni.cx)-c;
```

```
        int dfull = szDelta.cx;
        switch (nFlags & RESIZE_LEFT_FLAGS) {
        case RESIZE_LEFT_LFIX:
           break;
        case RESIZE_LEFT_LPROP:
           rcControl.left += dlprop;
           break;
        case RESIZE_LEFT_RPROP:
           rcControl.left += drprop;
           break;
        case RESIZE_LEFT_CPROP:
           rcControl.left += dcprop;
           break;
        case RESIZE_LEFT_RFIX:
           rcControl.left += dfull;
           break;
        }
        switch (nFlags & RESIZE_RIGHT_FLAGS) {
        case RESIZE_RIGHT_LFIX:
           break;
        case RESIZE_RIGHT_LPROP:
           rcControl.right += dlprop;
           break;
        case RESIZE_RIGHT_RPROP:
           rcControl.right += drprop;
           break;
        case RESIZE_RIGHT_CPROP:
           rcControl.right += dcprop;
           break;
        case RESIZE_RIGHT_RFIX:
           rcControl.right += dfull;
           break;
        }
    }
    {
        int t = rcControl.top;
        int b = rcControl.bottom;
        int c = (t+b+1)/2;
        int dtprop = ::MulDiv3(t,szNow.cy,
                               szWas.cy,
                               szIni.cy)-t;
        int dbprop = ::MulDiv3(b,szNow.cy,
                               szWas.cy,
                               szIni.cy)-b;
        int dcprop = ::MulDiv3(c,szNow.cy,
                               szWas.cy,
                               szIni.cy)-c;
        int dfull = szDelta.cy;
        switch (nFlags & RESIZE_TOP_FLAGS) {
        case RESIZE_TOP_TFIX:
           break;
```

```
            case RESIZE_TOP_TPROP:
               rcControl.top += dtprop;
               break;
            case RESIZE_TOP_BPROP:
               rcControl.top += dbprop;
               break;
            case RESIZE_TOP_CPROP:
               rcControl.top += dcprop;
               break;
            case RESIZE_TOP_BFIX:
               rcControl.top += dfull;
               break;
            }
            switch (nFlags & RESIZE_BOTTOM_FLAGS) {
            case RESIZE_BOTTOM_TFIX:
               break;
            case RESIZE_BOTTOM_TPROP:
               rcControl.bottom += dtprop;
               break;
            case RESIZE_BOTTOM_BPROP:
               rcControl.bottom += dbprop;
               break;
            case RESIZE_BOTTOM_CPROP:
               rcControl.bottom += dcprop;
               break;
            case RESIZE_BOTTOM_BFIX:
               rcControl.bottom += dfull;
               break;
            }
         }
      }
   }
```

Although this function is virtual, you would probably not want to override it because it is highly dependent on `EResizeFlags`. However, `ResizeControlUsingFlags` does call the virtual function `GetResizeFlags` that you probably will override in your own class.

`GetResizeFlags` is where the dialog box or property page specifies how each of its controls is to be resized. The default implementation of `GetResizeFlags` returns `RESIZE_NONE` for all controls; all the controls stay huddled up in the top-left corner of the dialog box or page when you resize it.

I often replace this simple `GetResizeFlags` function with a smart version that looks at the Window class and position of the controls, and use that to work out what resize flag to return.

Using TXResizable

Now you can derive your own dialog boxes from `TXResizable<CDialog>` (and your property pages from `TXResizable<CPropertyPage>`). Indeed, you can use a `typedef` for these and derive from that:

```
typedef TXResizable<CDialog> CXResizableDialog;
typedef TXResizable<CPropertyPage> CXResizablePropertyPage;
```

To use these classes with your own application, you need to change the dialog resources and select a border style of Resizing from the Style tab of the dialog properties.

To see any real resizing of controls, provide your own `GetResizeFlags` function that says how to resize each control. The sample application shows some simple resizing for both the main application and the about box. Figure 14-10 shows what the application looks like when you first start (before any resizing).

Figure 14-10: The demo application upon startup (before any resizing)

However, the real magic occurs when you attempt to resize the dialog box. Take a look at Figure 14-11 and you can see what you've created. Now the controls on your dialog box stretch proportionately to the size of the dialog box (as per their settings).

Figure 14-11: A resizable (elastic) dialog box at work

Summary

In this chapter, you started out by comparing some of the more common techniques of extending behavior such as straight C++ inheritance, multiple inheritance, templates, and message maps. Once you learned the different advantages and disadvantages associated with each technique, I showed you which technique I believe to be the best and why. This point was illustrated with a full, practical example, which extended the behavior of the standard dialog box and property sheet control by enabling its controls to resize as the user resizes the parent window. Hopefully, all of this has shown you that with a combination of a little knowledge, a little work, and some imagination, you can extend your controls to do just about anything you desire.

✦   ✦   ✦

Print and Print Preview

You can go years in your Windows development career without ever having to incorporate printing into your application and then one day, wham! Your supervisor comes in and explains that he needs a "2-up" report for the company's accounting application that has three level breaks with subtotals on the first two breaks and totals on the third. While you're trying to remember the last time you ever coded a control-break, he then comes upon another idea. "Hey! Why don't we just include a full-blown report writer in our application? That way the users can customize their own applications!" As you babble something about integration with a third-party report writer, he gives you this look that screams "You are a (very well paid) Windows developer, right?" That's when it hits you. How many times have you ditched the idea of learning the intricacies of the Windows printing model in lieu of the newer and cooler technologies to brag about?

Well, fear not. In this chapter you'll discover that although some of the Windows printing architecture is a bit archaic by today's standards, it's not nearly as difficult as it seems at first. In fact, if you've done even a little graphics device interface (GDI) development, you'll feel right at home with printing under Windows. And even if you haven't done any true GDI development, you'll still find that once you pick up the lingo and learn a few concepts, you'll be writing even the most sophisticated reports and print preview dialog boxes possible.

To aid in your quest to learn the necessary basics about printing in the least amount of time possible (every consultant's objective), I'll begin this chapter by explaining the fundamentals of printing using the Windows SDK including printing from a dialog-based application (something that the MFC technique is not built for) and allowing the user to abort print jobs. From there, the next section will illustrate how the MFC framework does much of the heavy lifting for you regarding the printing process. In this section, you'll discover the ins and outs of the MFC print architecture, what your role is when using MFC support for printing, and what MFC does for you. You'll also see a demo application that combines the lessons taught in this chapter with some of the GDI material you learned in Chapters 8 and 9 to create a WYSIWYG view printing application. Finally, the chapter wraps up with coverage of overriding the basic print preview functionality and using the `CPrintDialog` class.

Printing with the Win32 SDK

There are two reasons for starting out this chapter by using the Win32 SDK to print. The first is that, many times, in order to fully understand what MFC does for you regarding a given task, it's helpful to see how that task is realized without MFC. Second, printing with MFC is accomplished via the document/view architecture. Therefore, knowing how to print without MFC enables you to incorporate printing into applications that are either dialog-based or do not strictly adhere to the document/view paradigm.

First, I'll list the basic steps to print a document using the Win32 SDK and then explain each one. After that, you'll see a demo application illustrating these steps.

1. Acquire a device context.

2. Allocate and fill a `DOCINFO` structure.

3. Call the `::StartDoc` function to create a new document, or print job.

4. Call the `::StartPage` function for each page within the document.

5. Print the desired data, using GDI calls such as `::TextOut` or `::DrawText`.

6. Call `::EndPage` to signal the end to individual pages.

7. Call `::EndDoc` to end the current print job.

8. Delete the device context.

Now, I'll look at each step in more detail before showing you these steps at work in a simple print demo application. First, in order to print data from a Windows application, your code must obtain a device context for the target printer. Although device contexts are covered in more detail in Chapter 8, it's enough to understand here that a device context provides a layer of abstraction between an application and a physical device such that device-specific code does not have to be written. When using the Win32 SDK, you can acquire a device context for a given device with a call to the `CreateDC` function. After the application acquires a device context for a printer, the application can start the printing process by calling the `StartDoc` function. Besides the device context handler returned by the `CreateDC` function, the `StartDoc` function requires as a pointer to a `DOCINFO` structure. This structure describes the document that the application is about to print.

After you start to print, your application must call the `StartPage` function to begin each page and the `EndPage` function to end each page. You can think of a page as a drawing screen. The application must complete all the drawing for each page it prints before the application begins to draw on the next page. Although this might seem obvious, you'd be surprised how many people want to go back to a previous page and print something there that is based on a value not known until a later page is printed. Unfortunately, it can't be done. When the application finishes printing the entire document, the application should call the `EndDoc` function.

Now, let's see a printer version of the canonical Hello World application.

Simple print demo

Create a dialog-based application called `PrintHello`. After the project has been created, open the application's main dialog box resource and modify it so that when finished it looks like that shown in Figure 15-1.

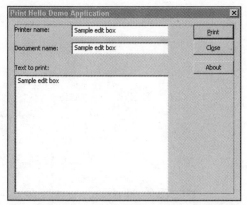

Figure 15-1: Basic demo application that prints user-supplied text to a printer

As you can see, the demo enables you to specify the printer to print to. That way, you can test the application directly off the CD-ROM and not have to change the printer name I used on my own network and then recompile everything. Once you've added the controls to the dialog box, you'll need to make the following changes and additions:

✦ Set the Text to print control's Multi-line, VScroll, and Auto-VScroll properties to True. Set Auto HScroll to False.

✦ Add a member variable of type CString for the Printer Name edit control called m_strPrinterName.

✦ Add a member variable of type CString for the Document Name edit control called m_strDocumentName.

✦ Add a member variable of type CString for the Text to print edit control called m_strText.

After you've modified the dialog box controls and created the appropriate DDX member variables, add an event handler for the Print button's BN_CLICKED message and define it as follows:

```
void CPrintHelloDlg::OnBnClickedOk()
{
 if (UpdateData(TRUE))
 {
  HDC hDC;
  DOCINFO di;

  // Create a device context for the printer.
  hDC = ::CreateDC("WINSPOOL",
                   m_strPrinterName,
                   NULL,
                   NULL);

  if (hDC)
  {
```

```
// Set up DOCINFO structure.
ZeroMemory(&di, sizeof(DOCINFO));
di.cbSize = sizeof(DOCINFO);
di.lpszDocName = m_strDocumentName;

// Start the printing.
if (SP_ERROR != ::StartDoc(hDC,&di))
{
 // Signal a new page.
 ::StartPage(hDC);

 // Print text to print DC just as you
 // would to a display DC.
 ::TextOut(hDC,
           10, 10,
           m_strText,
           m_strText.GetLength());

 // Signal end of page.
 ::EndPage(hDC);

 // End printing.
 ::EndDoc(hDC);
}
else
{
 AfxMessageBox("Could not start the printing "
               "process (::StartDoc).");
}

 // Delete the DC.
 ::DeleteDC(hDC);
}
else
{
 AfxMessageBox("Could not acquire a printer DC. "
               "Do you have a printer installed? "
               "If so, check the name and make sure "
               "you entered it correctly.");
}
}
}
```

Now build and run the application. Figure 15-2 shows an example of running this demo application on my network. Note that I'm using the unified naming convention (UNC) for my printer because it's on a different machine. This convention simply takes the following general form:

```
\\<server name>\<resource>
```

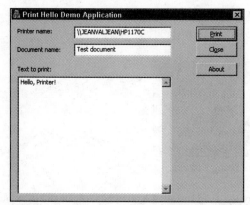

Figure 15-2: Simple demo to illustrate printing text to a printer specified by the user

Note   To see the names of the installed printers in your system, run the Printers applet from the Control Panel.

Clearly, this type of simple implementation is suitable only for very small print jobs. For example, an application with larger print jobs should provide a way for the user to pause, or even stop, a print job currently in progress. I'll look at the issue of aborting print jobs next.

Aborting print Jobs

In this section, I'll cover the two techniques for aborting jobs and explain how they differ so that you know when to implement each one. The first technique involves calling the ::AbortProc function. You use this function when your code needs to explicitly cancel the print operation. One example of that is if your code encounters an application-specific error, such as not being able to read the necessary data to print. Another example is if your application displays a progress dialog box that also contains a Cancel button to allow the user to abort the print. I'll look at that technique first as well as a demo application illustrating its implementation.

The second technique involves coding an abort procedure and passing its address to the ::SetAbortProc function as a callback. As you'll see, this technique is used to abort a print job asynchronously as a result of a print spooler error, such as the spooler running out of disk space while creating the temporary files necessary to complete the print job.

Aborting print jobs via AbortDoc

As I mentioned, the ::AbortDoc function is used when the application either encounters an application error and needs to abort, or if the user has indicated that he wants to stop the current printing job. To see this in action, you'll code a demo application that prints a user-specified number of pages at a rate of one per second until all pages have been printed or until the user has clicked a Stop button.

1. Create an MFC dialog-based application called `AbortDocDemo`.

2. Create a dialog resource similar to Figure 15-3.

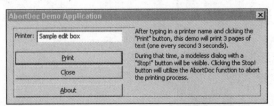

Figure 15-3: AbortDoc demo main dialog box

3. Create a DDX member variable of type `CString` called `m_strPrinter` for the printer control. Create a DDX member variable of type `int` called `m_nPages` for the Pages control.

4. The next few steps use the progress dialog box presented in Chapter 11. First, create the dialog template that will display the progress of the current print job and allow the user to cancel the print operation (Figure 15-4). As you can see, the dialog box has an ID of `IDD_PROGRESS` and contains a simple progress control.

Figure 15-4: AbortDoc progress dialog box template

5. Add a DDX member variable of type `CProgressCtrl` called `m_progress` based on the template's progress control.

6. Create a `CDialog`-derived class based on the template and call it `CProgressDlg`.

7. Add a `BOOL` member variable to the `CProgressDlg` class and initialize it in the class's constructor to `FALSE`.

8. Add the following function to the `CProgressDlg`. This function is called periodically by the main dialog box to ensure that the progress dialog box processes messages (such as the user clicking the Stop! button).

```
BOOL CProgressDlg::PeekAndPump()
{
 static MSG msg;

 while (::PeekMessage(&msg,NULL,0,0,PM_NOREMOVE))
 {
  if (!AfxGetApp()->PumpMessage())
  {
   ::PostQuitMessage(0);
   return FALSE;
  }
}
```

```
        }

    return TRUE;
}
```

9. Add a helper function to allow the main dialog box to update the progress dialog box's title bar:

```
void CProgressDlg::SetCaption(CString str)
{
    SetWindowText(str);
    Invalidate();
}
```

10. Add a handler for the Stop! Button, coded as follows:

```
void CProgressDlg::OnBnClickedStop()
{
    m_bAborted = TRUE;
    OnOK();
}
```

11. With the progress dialog box coded, add a member variable to the CAbortDocDemoDlg of type CProgressDlg. (Remember to add the include directive for the ProgressDlg.h file at the top of the AbortDocDemoDlg.h file.)

12. Add a handler for the Print button as follows. The main difference between this application and the previous demo is the addition of a progress dialog box—the relevant changes are shown in bold. After calling the helper function StartPrintJob, which acquires the device context, you then call another helper function (StartProgressDlg) that is responsible for displaying the modeless dialog box. You'll see that shortly. Next notice the for loop, where you can see that after the document has started (via a call to StartDocument), the number of pages printed is controlled by the number input on the dialog box and the CProgressDlg::m_bAborted flag being FALSE. Within the loop, you call StartPage, and update the progress dialog box's caption. You then call a Print function to output data to the printer. After that, you update the progress dialog box's progress bar, end the page, and call the CProgressDlg::PeekAndPump function. This last step allows the modeless dialog box to process its UI. If the user clicks (or has clicked) the Stop! button, the CProgressDlg::m_bAborted flag will be set to TRUE, causing the for loop to terminate. After that, the document is ended and the dialog box is cleaned up.

```
void CAbortDocDemoDlg::OnBnClickedOk()
{
    if (UpdateData())
    {
        try
        {
            HDC hdc = StartPrintJob();
            StartProgressDlg();

            DOCINFO di;
            ZeroMemory(&di, sizeof(DOCINFO));
            di.cbSize = sizeof(DOCINFO);
            di.lpszDocName = "AbortDoc Test";
            StartDocument(hdc, di);
```

```
    for (int i = 0;
         i < m_nPages && !g_dlgStop.m_bAborted;
         i++)
    {
      StartPage(hdc);

      CString str;
      str.Format("Printing page %ld of %ld", (i+1),
                 m_nPages);
      g_dlgStop.SetCaption(str);

      Print(hdc, (i+1));

      g_dlgStop.m_progress.SetPos(i + 1);

      EndPage(hdc);

      g_dlgStop.PeekAndPump();
    }

    EndDocument(hdc);
    EndProgressDlg();
    EndPrintJob(hdc);
  }
  catch(char* pz)
  {
    AfxMessageBox(pz);
  }
 }
}
```

13. Add the various helper functions. These functions perform the tasks that you've already learned about, but now are simply put into helper functions, and throw exceptions upon error in order to make the code cleaner.

```
HDC CAbortDocDemoDlg::StartPrintJob()
{
  HDC hdc = ::CreateDC("WINSPOOL",
                       m_strPrinter,
                       NULL,
                       NULL);
  if (!hdc)
  {
    throw "Could not acquire a printer dc. "
          "Do you have a printer installed? "
          "If so, check the name and make sure "
          "you entered it correctly.";
  }

  return hdc;
}
```

```
void CAbortDocDemoDlg::StartProgressDlg()
{
  if (!m_dlgStop.GetSafeHwnd())
  {
    m_dlgStop.Create(IDD_PROGRESS);
  }
  m_dlgStop.m_bAborted = FALSE;
  m_dlgStop.ShowWindow(SW_SHOW);

  // Set the dialog box's progress bar.
  m_dlgStop.m_progress.SetRange(0, m_nPages);

  // Disable the main window.
  EnableWindow(FALSE);
}

void CAbortDocDemoDlg::StartDocument(HDC const& hdc,
                                     DOCINFO const& di)

{
  if (SP_ERROR == ::StartDoc(hdc,&di))
    throw "Could not start the printing "
          "process (::StartDoc).";
}

void CAbortDocDemoDlg::StartPage(HDC const& hdc)
{
  if (!::StartPage(hdc))
    throw "Error calling ::StartPage";
}

void CAbortDocDemoDlg::Print(HDC const& hdc, int counter)
{
  // Simulate getting data to print
  ::Sleep(1000);

  CString strText;
  strText.Format("Page %ld - AbortDoc Test",  counter);

  ::TextOut(hdc,
            10, 10,
            strText,
            strText.GetLength());
}

void CAbortDocDemoDlg::EndPage(HDC const& hdc)
{
  if (!::EndPage(hdc))
    throw "Error calling::EndPage";
}
```

```
void CAbortDocDemoDlg::EndDocument(HDC const& hdc)
{
  if (!::EndDoc(hdc))
    throw "Error calling ::EndDoc";
}

void CAbortDocDemoDlg::EndProgressDlg()
{
  // Destroy the "Stop" dialog box.
  m_dlgStop.DestroyWindow();

  // Re-enable the main dialog box and
  // set focus to it.
  EnableWindow(TRUE);
  SetFocus();
}

void CAbortDocDemoDlg::EndPrintJob(HDC const& hdc)
{
  if (!::DeleteDC(hdc))
    throw "Error calling ::DeleteDC";
}
```

Note   When testing printing applications that print many pages, it's always beneficial to pause the printer queue. You can do this by running the Printers applet in Control Panel, right-clicking the printer that you're using, and selecting the Pause Printing menu option.

Building and running the application should yield results similar to those shown in Figure 15-5.

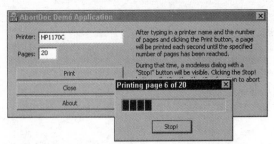

Figure 15-5: Allowing your users to cancel a print operation is easy with the aid of a modeless dialog box.

Aborting print jobs via SetAbortProc

Although the ::AbortDoc function is great for situations where the application is instigating the print job cancellation, it does no good for handling errors discovered by the print spooler. For situations where you want to include print spooler error handling, you'll need to call the ::SetAbortProc function and provide it a callback function that is called when each page is started, and if an error occurs in the print process. Here is the prototype for the ::SetAbortProc function:

```
int SetAbortProc(
  HDC hdc,                    // handle to DC
  ABORTPROC lpAbortProc      // abort function
);
```

The abort function must then take the following form:

```
BOOL CALLBACK AbortProc(
  HDC hdc,        // handle to DC
  int iError      // error value
);
```

As you can see, the abort function takes a handle to the device context and an error code. The valid values to check for are the following:

- ✦ SP_ERROR

- ✦ SP_OUTOFDISK

- ✦ SP_OUTOFMEMORY

- ✦ SP_USERABORT

It's really impossible to present a demo on this topic without being able to duplicate one of these error conditions. However, it's simple enough to describe. You simply test the iError parameter for each of these values, and if you decide that printing can continue, you return a value of TRUE. If, on the other hand, you want printing to stop, return a value of FALSE. This obviously means that you'll need to handle the case of there not being an error (iError = 0), in which case you return TRUE.

One last thing that I should mention is that in the past, the AbortProc function has been used to enable the user to cancel a print job. The way this was done was to code a message loop in the AbortProc function and have that loop also check that a global flag indicating that printing needed to be cancelled was not set. In other words, it was basically the same thing you saw in the previous section, except that checking to continue printing occurred in AbortProc instead of in the function responsible for printing.

In my opinion, the AbortDoc function should be used to allow users to cancel print jobs and the abort function should be used to handle print spooler errors.

Printing with MFC

After everything you have learned thus far, it should not be surprising that Visual C++ provides a set of MFC wrappers that you can use within your programs to support printing and device output. As you know, Microsoft Windows implements device-independent display via the GDI. In MFC, this means that the same drawing calls in the OnDraw member function of your view class are responsible for drawing on the display and on other devices, such as printers. For print preview, the target device is a simulated printer output to the display.

Understanding your role and the framework's role in printing

Because you are using MFC wrapper classes, your responsibilities when programming MFC applications are not quite so broad as they are when you write printing code within a Windows program that does not use MFC. Specifically, it is your responsibility to ensure that your view class performs the following tasks:

1. Inform the framework how many pages are in the document.

2. When asked to print a specified page, draw that portion of the document.

3. Allocate and deallocate any fonts or other GDI resources needed for printing.

4. If necessary, send any escape codes needed to change the printer mode before printing a given page — for example, to change the printing orientation on a per-page basis.

The MFC framework, in turn, handles the following tasks that are necessary for printing:

1. Display the Print dialog box.

2. Create a CDC object for the printer.

3. Call the StartDoc and EndDoc member functions of the CDC object.

4. Repeatedly call the StartPage member function of the CDC object, inform the view class which page should be printed, and call the EndPage member function of the CDC object.

5. Call overridable functions in the view at the appropriate times.

The remainder of this chapter discusses how your programs should work with the MFC framework to support printing and print preview.

Understanding the MFC printing sequence

As you will learn later in this chapter, you will find that you often override member functions in the view class(es) of your applications to correctly support printing from those classes. You will generally overload, at a minimum, three member functions to support printing within your class: OnDraw, OnBeginPrinting, and OnPrepareDC. These functions are critically important to the printing and print previewing processes. However, other functions are also available that enable you to add even more printing power to your applications. The functions important to the printing process are listed in Table 15-1.

Table 15-1: Printing Functions of a View Class

Function	Description
OnBeginPrinting	Override this function to create resources, such as fonts, that you need for printing the document. You can also set the maximum page count here.
OnDraw	Displays data in a frame window, a print preview window, or on the printer, depending on the device context sent as the function's parameter.

Function	Description
OnEndPrinting	Override this function to release resources created in OnBeginPrinting.
OnPrepareDC	Override this function to modify the device context that is used to display or print the document. You can, for example, handle pagination here.
OnPreparePrinting	Override this function to provide a maximum page count for the document. If you don't set the page count here, you should set it in OnBeginPrinting.
OnPrint	Override this function to provide additional printing services, such as printing headers and footers, not provided in OnDraw.

To print a document, MFC calls the functions in Table 15-1 in a specific order. First, it calls OnPreparePrinting, which simply calls DoPreparePrinting. DoPreparePrinting, in turn, is responsible for displaying the Print dialog box and creating the printer DC. The AppWizard implements the OnPreparePrinting function as shown here:

```
BOOL CYourView::OnPreparePrinting(CPrintInfo* pInfo)
  {
    // default preparation
    return DoPreparePrinting(pInfo);
  }
```

As you can see, OnPreparePrinting receives as a parameter a pointer to a CPrintInfo object. Using this object, you can obtain information about the print job, as well as initialize attributes such as the maximum page number. Table 15-2 lists the most useful data and function members of the CPrintInfo class.

Table 15-2: Members of the CPrintInfo Class

Member	Description
SetMaxPage	Sets the document's maximum page number.
SetMinPage	Sets the document's minimum page number.
GetFromPage	Gets the number of the first page that the user selected for printing.
GetMaxPage	Gets the document's maximum page number, which may be changed in OnBeginPrinting.
GetMinPage	Gets the document's minimum page number, which may be changed in OnBeginPrinting.
GetToPage	Gets the number of the last page the user selected for printing.
m_bContinuePrinting	Controls the printing process. Setting the flag to FALSE ends the print job.

Continued

Table 15-2: *(continued)*

Member	Description
m_bDirect	Indicates whether the document is being directly printed (as opposed to through the Windows spooler).
m_bPreview	Indicates whether the document is in print preview.
m_nCurPage	Holds the current number of the page being printed.
m_nNumPreviewPages	Holds the number of pages (1 or 2) that are being displayed in print preview.
m_pPD	Holds a pointer to the print job's CPrintDialog object.
m_rectDraw	Holds a rectangle that defines the usable area for the current page.
m_strPageDesc	Holds a page-number format string.

When the DoPreparePrinting function displays the Print dialog box, the user can set the value of many of the data members of the CPrintInfo class. Your program then can use or set any of these values. Usually, you at least call SetMaxPage, which sets the document's maximum page number, before DoPreparePrinting, so that the maximum page number displays in the Print dialog box. If you cannot determine the number of pages until you calculate a page length based on the selected printer, you have to wait until you have a printer DC for the printer.

After OnPreparePrinting, MFC calls the OnBeginPrinting member function, which is not only another place where you can set the maximum page count, but also the function in which you should create resources, such as fonts, that you need to complete the print job. The OnPreparePrinting member function receives, as parameters, a pointer to the printer DC and a pointer to the associated CPrintInfo object.

```
virtual void CView::OnBeginPrinting(CDC* pDC,
                                    CPrintInfo* pInfo);
```

Next, MFC calls the OnPrepareDC member function for the first page in the document. The call to OnPrepareDC is the beginning of a print loop that the framework executes once for each page in the document. OnPrepareDC is the function in which you should control what part of the whole document prints on the current page. As you will learn, you handle this task by setting the document's viewport origin.

After OnPrepareDC, MFC calls OnPrint to print the actual page. Normally, OnPrint calls OnDraw with the printer DC, which automatically directs OnDraw's output to the printer rather than to the screen. Therefore, the natural question would be "Why would I override OnPrint as opposed to just putting all my print/display code in the same OnDraw function?" The answer is that OnPrint is the place where you can insert printer-specific code such as the printing of headers and footers as shown here:

```
void CPrint1View::OnPrint(CDC* pDC, CPrintInfo* pInfo)
{
    PrintHeader();
    OnDraw(pDC);
    PrintFooter();
}
```

As long as there are more pages to print, MFC continues to call `OnPrepareDC` and `OnPrint` for each page in the document. After the last page is printed, MFC calls `OnEndPrinting`, where you can destroy any resources you created in `OnBeginPrinting`. Figure 15-6 summarizes the entire printing process.

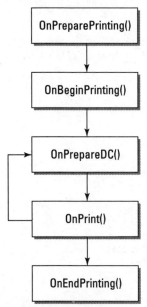

Figure 15-6: The MFC printing process uses a specific series of steps when printing any document type.

WYSIWYG demo print application

At this point, you're probably thinking that the MFC way is much more complicated than the older Win32 SDK way. Actually, it only appears that way because there are so many different things that you can do with MFC that it takes a bit of explaining just to introduce the basics. Therefore, in this section you'll see a WYSIWYG demo application that will both print and display data from the view's `OnDraw` virtual function. When you're finished, I think you'll agree that printing with MFC requires far less work than with the Win32 SDK.

1. Create a new MFC MDI application called `MFCPrintDemo`, and make sure to change the view's base class to `CScrollView` in the Generated Classes tab in the MFC Application Wizard.

2. To simulate an actual application, you'll place the data in the document where it should be for a document/view application. Add the following `CStringArray` member to the `CMFCPrintDemoDoc` class. This will hold an array of strings to display and print.

```
class CMFCPrintDemoDoc : public CDocument
{
...
public:
  CStringArray m_data;
...
}
```

3. Update the `CMFCPrintDemoDoc::OnNewDocument` function to load the array with our hard-coded data. (Note that the line breaks are shown here because of book formatting.)

```
BOOL CMFCPrintDemoDoc::OnNewDocument()
{
 if (!CDocument::OnNewDocument())
  return FALSE;

 m_data.Add(T("      The Aeneid by Virgil"));
 m_data.Add(T("      ===================="));
m_data.Add(T("Of arms I sing and of the "
             "man who first"));
 m_data.Add(T("from Trojan shores beneath "
             "the ban of fate"));
 m_data.Add(T("To Italy and coasts Lavanian came"));
 m_data.Add(T("Much tossed about on land and ocean"));
 m_data.Add(T("He by violence of the Gods above"));
 m_data.Add(T("to sate relentless Juno's ever-"
             "rankling ire"));

 return TRUE;
}
```

4. You have your data; now code the view. You're probably wondering why the view was derived from `CScrollView`. I had you do that so that the page being displayed would mimic exactly a standard 8.5- by 11-inch piece of paper and be able to scroll vertically and horizontally to view the entire page. In fact, you're going to use some of the GDI you learned in Chapters 8 and 9 and center a block of text on both the view and the printed page.

To get started, define the following member variables in the `CMFCPrintDemoView` class. The `m_rectPrint` variable will define the area that will be printed (the page) while the other three variables will be used to determine the height and width of the view.

```
protected:
  CRect m_rectPrint;
  CSize m_sizePage;
  CSize m_sizePageScroll;
  CSize m_sizeLineScroll;
```

5. Initialize the member variables in the view's constructor. Note that these calculations will actually give you an 8- by 10.5-inch drawing surface so that your drawing is a quarter inch inside the edge of an 8.5- by 11-inch sheet of paper.

```
CMFCPrintDemoView::CMFCPrintDemoView()
: m_rectPrint(0,0,11505,-15105)
, m_sizePage(11520, 15120)
, m_sizePageScroll(m_sizePage.cx/2, m_sizePage.cy/2)
```

```
   , m_sizeLineScroll(m_sizePage.cx/100, m_sizePage.cy/100)
   {
   }
```

6. Update the `CMFCPrintDemoView::OnInitialUpdate` function as follows:

```
void CMFCPrintDemoView::OnInitialUpdate()
{
 CScrollView::OnInitialUpdate();

 SetScrollSizes(MM_TWIPS,
    m_sizePage,
    m_sizePageScroll,
    m_sizeLineScroll);
}
```

7. As mentioned earlier, you generally insert code into the `OnPreparePrinting` function to set the maximum page count. Therefore, do that now in setting the page count for this document to one:

```
BOOL CMFCPrintDemoView::OnPreparePrinting(
CPrintInfo* pInfo)
{
 pInfo->SetMaxPage(1);

 return DoPreparePrinting(pInfo);
}
```

8. Update the `OnDraw` function to call two helper functions: one to draw the rulers around the page and one to draw the data:

```
void CMFCPrintDemoView::OnDraw(CDC* pDC)
{
   DrawRulers(*pDC);
   DrawData(*pDC);
}
```

9. Now draw the rulers. Nothing real fancy going on here, you're just using the `m_rectPrint` to draw a border around the page. After that, two simple loops provide numbering around the top and left edges of the page. Finally, a line is drawn through the middle of the page to prove that you are indeed centering the text correctly:

```
void CMFCPrintDemoView::DrawRulers(CDC& dc)
{
   // Draw a border around the page
   dc.Rectangle(m_rectPrint);

   CString str;

   // Draw horizontal and vertical rulers
   for (int i = 0; i <= 8; i++)
   {
     str.Format("%02d", i);
     dc.TextOut(i * 1440, 0, str);
   }

   for (int i = 0; i <= 10; i++)
```

```
      {
        str.Format("%02d", i);
        dc.TextOut(0, -i * 1440, str);
      }

      dc.MoveTo(0, -(m_sizePage.cy / 2));
      dc.LineTo(m_sizePage.cx, -(m_sizePage.cy / 2));
    }
```

10. Finally, code the `DrawData` function. Because there's a bit going on here, let's briefly walk through it. First, the code obtains a pointer to the document, because that object contains the data to be printed. Next, it creates a new font object and obtains the height for that font (storing it in the local variable `nHeight`). Once the new font has been created, it is selected into the current device context, and the previous font is saved (to be restored when the function exits).

    The function then retrieves the data array size (storing it in the local variable `dataSize`) and determines the starting point for drawing the text. As you can see, that is done by simply getting the page size, dividing it in half, and setting it to a negative value. This will result in `cy` being the vertical middle of the page.

    Once the starting vertical place has been established, the function can start a `for` loop to read all of the strings from the data array. For each string, a call to `GetTextExtent` (passing the string) lets you determine the exact width of that string. You'll notice that you don't use this function to get the height because that can be determined via the font metrics. However, the width is very much dependent on the exact string value. Once this value has been determined, you then calculate the starting horizontal position of the text (`cx`) by subtracting the width of the text from the width of the page and dividing by two. Then, you can finally call `TextOut` passing it the `cx` and `cy` values, knowing that all the text will be perfectly centered on the page. The last thing the function does is to select the previous font into the device context.

```
void CMFCPrintDemoView::DrawData(CDC& dc)
{
  CMFCPrintDemoDoc* pDoc =
    (CMFCPrintDemoDoc*)GetDocument();
  ASSERT_VALID(pDoc);

  CFont font;
  font.CreateFont(-200, 0, 0, 0, 400,
                  FALSE, FALSE, 0, ANSI_CHARSET,
                  OUT_DEFAULT_PRECIS, CLIP_DEFAULT_PRECIS,
                  DEFAULT_QUALITY,
                  DEFAULT_PITCH | FF_ROMAN,
                  "Arial");
  CFont* pOldFont = (CFont*) dc.SelectObject(&font);
  TEXTMETRIC tm;
  dc.GetTextMetrics(&tm);
  int nHeight = tm.tmHeight + tm.tmExternalLeading;

  int i;
  int dataSize = pDoc->m_data.GetSize();

  int cy = -(m_sizePage.cy / 2);
  cy += (dataSize / 2) * nHeight;
```

```
int cx;

for (i = 0; i < dataSize; i++)
{
 CSize size = dc.GetTextExtent(pDoc->m_data[i]);

 cx = (m_sizePage.cx - size.cx) / 2;
 dc.TextOut(cx, cy - (i * nHeight), pDoc->m_data[i]);
}

dc.SelectObject(pOldFont);
}
```

Building and running the application should result in what you see in Figure 15-7.

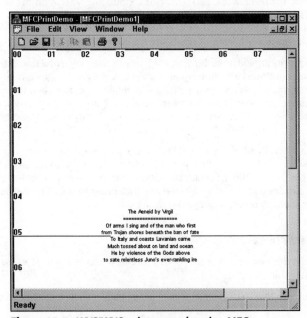

Figure 15-7: WYSIWYG print example using MFC

Now print the view and you'll see that it also displays on paper just as it does on the screen.

Note

This application hard-coded the various values used to work with 8.5- by 11-inch paper. In order to adapt this application to use other paper sizes (such as legal or A4), you need only make a few minor adjustments. Principally, you need to modify how the m_rectPrint is set. Instead of setting it in the class's constructor, it needs to be set in the virtual OnPrint function. You'll recall that one of the OnPrint parameters is a CPrintInfo object and that Table 15-2 listed the m_rectDraw member as being a member of that class. Therefore, the first step would be to update the OnPrint function to set the view's m_rectDraw member variable equal to the CPrintInfo::m_rectDraw member variable. After that, you simply need to modify the other member variables accordingly.

The Print Preview Architecture

Print preview is somewhat different from screen display and printing because, instead of directly drawing an image on a device, the application must simulate the printer using the screen. To accommodate this, MFC defines a special (undocumented) class derived from CDC, called CPreviewDC. All CDC objects contain two device contexts, but usually they are identical. In a CPreviewDC object, the two device contexts are different, with the first context representing the printer being simulated and the second context representing the screen on which output is actually displayed.

The print preview process

When the user selects the Print Preview command from the File menu, the framework creates a CPreviewDC object. Whenever your application performs an operation that sets a characteristic of the printer device context, the framework also performs a similar operation on the screen device context. For example, if your application selects a font for printing, the framework selects a font for screen display that simulates the printer font. Whenever your application sends output to the printer, the framework instead sends the output to the screen.

Print preview also differs from printing in the order that each draws the pages of a document. During printing, the framework continues a print loop until a certain range of pages has been rendered. During print preview, one or two pages are displayed at any time, and then the application waits; no further pages are displayed until the user responds. During print preview, the application must also respond to WM_PAINT messages, just as it does during ordinary screen display.

The OnPreparePrinting function is called when preview mode is invoked, just as it is at the beginning of a print job. The CPrintInfo structure passed to the function contains several members whose values you can set to adjust certain characteristics of the print preview operation. For example, you can set the m_nNumPreviewPages member to specify whether you want to preview the document in one-page or two-page mode.

Modifying print preview

You can easily modify the behavior and appearance of print preview in a number of ways. For example, you can, among other things:

✦ Cause the print preview window to display a scroll bar for easy access to any page of the document.

✦ Cause print preview to maintain the user's position in the document by beginning its display at the current page.

✦ Cause different initialization to be performed for print preview and printing.

✦ Cause print preview to display page numbers in your own formats.

If you know how long the document is and call SetMaxPage with the appropriate value, the framework can use this information in preview mode as well as during printing. Once the framework knows the length of the document, it can provide the preview window with a scroll bar, enabling the user to page back and forth through the document in preview mode. If you haven't set the length of the document, the framework cannot position the scroll box to indicate the current position, so the framework doesn't add a scroll bar. In this case, the user must use the Next Page and Previous Page buttons on the preview window's control bar to page through the document.

For print preview, you may find it useful to assign a value to the m_nCurPage member of CPrintInfo, even though you would never do so for ordinary printing. During ordinary printing, this member carries information from the framework to your view class. This is how the framework tells the view which page should be printed.

By contrast, when print preview mode is started, the m_nCurPage member carries information in the opposite direction: from the view to the framework. The framework uses the value of this member to determine which page should be previewed first. The default value of this member is 1, so the first page of the document is displayed initially. You can override OnPreparePrinting to set this member to the number of the page being viewed at the time the Print Preview command was invoked. This way, the application maintains the user's current position when moving from normal display mode to print preview mode.

Sometimes you may want OnPreparePrinting to perform different initialization depending on whether it is called for a print job or for print preview. You can determine this by examining the m_bPreview member variable in the CPrintInfo structure. This member is set to TRUE when print preview is invoked.

The CPrintInfo structure also contains a member named m_strPageDesc, which is used to format the strings displayed at the bottom of the screen in single-page and multiple-page modes. By default these strings are of the form "Page n" and "Pages n - m," but you can modify m_strPageDesc from within OnPreparePrinting and set the strings to something more elaborate. See CPrintInfo in the Class Library Reference for more information.

Enhancing an application's print preview

The default print preview capabilities are almost sufficient for most applications' needs. To some extent, most of your application's print preview capabilities are enhanced when you enhance printing capabilities. Recall that in the override of OnPreparePrinting earlier in this chapter, you called the SetMaxPages function to specify the length of the application document. Specifying the application's pages, for example, enables the framework to automatically add a scroll bar to the preview window.

Another enhancement you can make is to change the number of pages displayed when the user invokes the preview mode. To set the number of pages displayed in preview mode, modify the OnPreparePrinting function so that it appears as shown here:

```
BOOL CYourView::OnPreparePrinting(CPrintInfo* pInfo)
{
  BOOL bResult;
  CWinApp* pApp = AfxGetApp();

  // Ask the app what the default printer is. If there
  //isn't any, punt to MFC so it will generate an error

  if (!pApp->GetPrinterDeviceDefaults(
   &pInfo->m_pPD->m_pd)
  || pInfo->m_pPD->m_pd.hDevMode == NULL)
    return DoPreparePrinting(pInfo);

  HGLOBAL hDevMode = pInfo->m_pPD->m_pd.hDevMode;
  HGLOBAL hDevNames = pInfo->m_pPD->m_pd.hDevNames;
  DEVMODE* pDevMode = (DEVMODE*) ::GlobalLock(hDevMode);
  DEVNAMES* pDevNames =
   (DEVNAMES*) ::GlobalLock(hDevNames);
```

```
        LPCSTR pstrDriverName = ((LPCSTR) pDevNames)+
            pDevNames->wDriverOffset;
        LPCSTR pstrDeviceName = ((LPCSTR) pDevNames)+
            pDevNames->wDeviceOffset;
        LPCSTR pstrOutputPort = ((LPCSTR) pDevNames)+
            pDevNames->wOutputOffset;

        CDC dcPrinter;
        if (dcPrinter.CreateDC(pstrDriverName, pstrDeviceName,
            pstrOutputPort, NULL))
        {
            pInfo->SetMaxPage(2);  // the document is two
                                   // pages long:
            dcPrinter.DeleteDC();
            bResult = DoPreparePrinting(pInfo);

//   New Lines
            /* Preview 2 pages at a time
               Set this value after calling DoPreparePrinting to
               Override value read from registry */
            pInfo->m_nNumPreviewPages = 2;
//   End New Lines

        }
        else
        {
            MessageBox("Could not create printer DC");
            bResult = FALSE;
        }
        ::GlobalUnlock(hDevMode);
        ::GlobalUnlock(hDevNames);
        return bResult;

    }
```

The new lines assign the value 2 to m_nNumPreviewPages. This causes the application to preview both pages of the document at once—the title page (page 1) and the drawing page (page 2). Note the value for m_nNumPreviewPages must be assigned after calling DoPreparePrinting, because DoPreparePrinting sets m_nNumPreviewPages to the number of preview pages used the last time the program was executed; this value is stored in the application's Registry entry.

Understanding the CPrintDialog Class

The CPrintDialog class encapsulates the services provided by the Windows common dialog box for printing. Common print dialog boxes provide an easy way to implement Print and Print Setup dialog boxes in a manner consistent with Windows standards.

If you wish, you can rely on the framework to handle many aspects of the printing process for your application. In this case, the framework automatically displays the Windows common dialog box for printing. You can also have the framework handle printing for your application but override the common Print dialog box with your own Print dialog box.

If you want your application to handle printing without the framework's involvement, you can use the `CPrintDialog` class as is with the constructor provided, or you can derive your own dialog class from `CPrintDialog` and write a constructor to suit your needs. In either case, these dialog boxes behave like standard MFC dialog boxes because they are derived from class `CCommonDialog`.

To use a `CPrintDialog` object, first create the object using the `CPrintDialog` constructor. Once the dialog box has been constructed, you can set or modify any values in the `m_pd` structure to initialize the values of the dialog box's controls. The `m_pd` structure is of type `PRINTDLG`. For more information on this structure, see the Win32 SDK documentation.

If you do not supply your own handles in `m_pd` for the `hDevMode` and `hDevNames` members, be sure to call the Windows function `GlobalFree` for these handles when you are done with the dialog box. When using the framework's Print Setup implementation provided by `CWinApp::OnFilePrintSetup`, you do not have to free these handles. The handles are maintained by `CWinApp` and are freed in `CWinApp`'s destructor. It is only necessary to free these handles when using `CPrintDialog` alone.

After initializing the dialog box controls, call the `DoModal` member function to display the dialog box and enable the user to select print options. `DoModal` returns whether the user selects the OK (`IDOK`) or Cancel (`IDCANCEL`) button.

If `DoModal` returns `IDOK`, you can use one of `CPrintDialog`'s member functions to retrieve the information input by the user. The `CPrintDialog::GetDefaults` member function is useful for retrieving the current printer defaults without displaying a dialog box. This member function requires no user interaction.

You can use the Windows `CommDlgExtendedError` function to determine whether an error occurred during initialization of the dialog box and to learn more about the error. For more information on this function, see the Win32 SDK documentation.

`CPrintDialog` relies on the `commdlg.dll` file that ships with Windows versions 3.1 and later. To customize the dialog box, derive a class from `CPrintDialog`, provide a custom dialog template, and add a message map to process the notification messages from the extended controls. Any unprocessed messages should be passed on to the base class. Customizing the hook function is not required.

To process the same message differently depending on whether the dialog box is Print or Print Setup, you must derive a class for each dialog box. You must also override the Windows `AttachOnSetup` function, which handles the creation of a new dialog box when the Print Setup button is selected within a Print dialog box.

Summary

In this chapter, you learned two distinct means of incorporating printing into your applications. You began by exploring the fundamentals of printing using the Windows SDK including printing from a dialog-based application (something that the MFC technique is not built for) and allowing the user to abort print jobs. From there, you then discovered how the MFC framework does much of the work for you in the printing process. In that section, I illustrated the details of the MFC print architecture, what your role is when using MFC support for printing, and what MFC does for you. You also worked through a demo application that combines the lessons taught in this chapter and the GDI chapters in order to create a WYSIWYG view printing application. Finally, the chapter wrapped up with coverage of overriding the basic print preview functionality and using the `CPrintDialog` class.

✦　　✦　　✦

Working with DLLs

From the very first 16-bit version of Windows, every flavor and version of Windows has relied heavily on the functions and data stored in dynamic link libraries (DLLs). In fact, when you look at your Windows system, almost everything you see is represented in one form or another by a DLL. The fonts and icons on your display are stored in a DLL. The code necessary to display the Windows desktop and process your input is stored in a DLL. Even the Windows API is contained in DLLs. This chapter explains what DLLs are and how to develop and use them with a Visual C++ application.

Because Visual C++ defines two types of DLLs (*regular DLLs* and *extension DLLs*), this chapter is split into two sections. In the first section, you will learn the advantages of using what Visual C++ calls a regular DLL and how to create them with the MFC DLL Wizard. You will also learn how to dynamically load a DLL and call its exported functions. In addition, you will see three demos in this section. The first demo illustrates how to design and code a Control Panel-like interface where an application will interact with any DLL exporting certain predefined functions. The second demo illustrates Windows hooks and how to develop a Windows (keyboard) hook procedure. Finally, the third demo illustrates the advanced task of sharing C++ objects across multiple invocations of a DLL.

In the second section of this chapter, you will discover MFC extension DLLs, how they are constructed, and their uses and benefits. Specifically, the goal of this part of the chapter is to show how you can export whole MFC-derived classes from a DLL or even specific member functions of a given class. Once you have learned the basics of MFC extension DLLs, two demos will be presented. The first demo illustrates a very practical solution to the problem associated with using nested MFC extension DLLs in an MFC application. The second and last demo is something I'm asked for quite a bit. Here, you'll learn how to use a DLL to encapsulate a document template, document, and view so that it can be used by other applications. That's quite a bit of work, so let's get started!

DLL Overview

DLLs are built on the concept of *client/server* communications. Functions and data are stored in a DLL (the server) and are exported for use by one or more clients. These clients can be applications or other DLLs. Therefore, when the term *client* is used in this chapter it signifies any client of the DLL, whether it is an application or another DLL.

Static and dynamic libraries

In a *static library*, the functions and data are compiled into a binary file (usually with a .LIB extension). The linker then copies these functions and data from the library and combines them with the other modules of the application to create the final executable (an .EXE file). The linker is also responsible for something called *fixup*. Fixup is the process in which calls from other modules in the executable are mapped to functions in the library. When an application links to a static library, the process is called *static linking*. Because everything the application needs from the library is copied into the executable, the library does not have to be shipped with the executable. The main benefit of static libraries is easier deployment because fewer files are being shipped. However, the obvious drawback is that if the library needs to be changed, all dependent files must be rebuilt.

In the case of dynamic linking, a library's functions and data are not copied into a client executable. Instead, two files are created: an *import library* and a *dynamic library* (a DLL). The import library contains the names and locations of the functions being exported by the DLL, and the DLL contains the actual functions and data. An application that wants to use the exported functions of a given DLL then links to the import library. Actually, this is the case only if the application is *implicitly linking* to the DLL. The issues of implicit linking versus *explicit linking* are covered in the next section. However, regardless of how a client is linking to a DLL, the DLL is a separate file from the client and therefore must be deployed as part of the application (unless the correct version is already present on the target machine).

The process of creating a DLL is very similar to that used in creating an executable. The library's functions are compiled into an .OBJ file (module), and a linker creates the final binary output file by linking the different modules together. However, in the case of a DLL, a special linker switch (/DLL) is used to tell the linker that a DLL is being created instead of an EXE.

Loading DLLs

There are two ways for a client to load a DLL: implicitly and explicitly. DLL clients implicitly load a DLL by either linking with the DLL's import library or by listing the desired exported functions of the DLL in the IMPORTS section of the client's .DEF file. Implicit loading of a DLL is by far the most common means of loading DLLs for the simple reason that it requires no extra coding on the part of the client. The application programmer simply includes the necessary header file(s), makes the desired function calls, and links with the DLL. However, implicitly linking to a DLL has a couple of limitations that make it unattractive for certain situations:

✦ The DLL file must have an extension of .DLL.

✦ The client incurs the overhead of loading the DLL, even if no functions in the DLL are ever called.

When a client implicitly loads one or more DLLs, the DLLs are loaded into memory when the client is loaded. In order for Windows to load a given DLL, it must first find the actual physical file. Windows uses the following order when attempting to load a DLL:

✦ The current folder

✦ The Windows folder

✦ The Windows system folder

✦ The folder where the client resides

✦ The folders listed in the PATH environment variable

✦ Mapped network folders

Although implicit linking is the easiest manner for a client to link to a DLL, there are times when explicit linking has its advantages. Explicit linking involves specifically telling the Windows operating system which file to load and when to load it. Although explicitly loading a DLL requires a little more work on the application programmer's part, it has several advantages over implicit linking:

✦ The library can have any extension.

✦ The DLL is loaded only if the client actually uses it.

✦ The client has the option at runtime of choosing between loading different libraries based on runtime information.

A DLL is loaded explicitly as follows:

1. The client calls the Win32 function LoadLibrary. This function returns a handle to the library. If the function fails, a NULL value is returned, and the Win32 function GetLastError must be called to determine the cause of the failure.

2. The client uses the handle returned by the LoadLibrary function to call the Win32 function GetProcAddress, passing to it the name of the desired function. The GetProcAddress function returns the address of function, which can then be used to call the function.

3. Now the client can call the function via the pointer to it returned from the call to GetProcAddress.

4. When the client is finished using the DLL, it should call the Win32 function FreeLibrary in order to unload the library from memory and free any associated resources.

Figure 16-1 shows these steps in a standard UML Sequence Diagram.

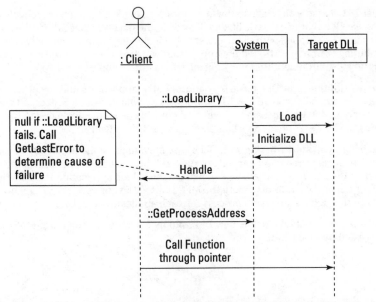

Figure 16-1: Once you load a DLL via LoadLibrary and obtain a function pointer via GetProcAddress, you can then call the function through a pointer.

Visual C++ Regular DLLs

Visual C++ defines two types of DLLs: regular DLLs and extension DLLs. Regular DLLs are used when the functions being exported are C functions, C++ classes, or C++ member functions. Note that the term *C++ classes* is not to be confused with MFC C++ classes. If your DLL needs to export an MFC class, you should look into writing and managing MFC extension DLLs, which is covered later in this chapter. The advantages of using a regular DLL as opposed to an MFC extension DLL include the following:

✦ The client does not have to be an MFC application. It simply has to be capable of calling C-like functions. This could be anything from an MFC application to a Delphi or Visual Basic application. You can even have .NET code call into this type of DLL.

✦ A regular DLL can use C++ classes internally (including MFC) and then export only the C function wrappers. That way, any changes to these C++ classes will not affect the calling application or DLL.

Creating a regular DLL

You can create regular DLLs using Visual C++ with the aid of the MFC DLL Wizard. After invoking the New Project dialog box, select Win32 Projects as the project type. Then select the MFC DLL template and type the name of the desired DLL (RegDll, in this case)

Once you've typed the location and name of the DLL project, click the OK button to invoke the MFC DLL Wizard. When the DLL Wizard is displayed, click the Application Settings link. As you can see, this dialog box enables you to specify whether or not you want to statically or dynamically link with the MFC libraries.

Just as there are advantages to using regular DLLs over MFC extension DLLs, there are advantages and disadvantages regarding how you choose to link MFC support into your DLL:

✦ If a regular DLL dynamically links to the MFC libraries, its file size will be much smaller than a regular DLL that uses static linking. However, the disadvantage is that the MFC DLLs must now be shipped with the product. Obviously, this is a problem only if you are distributing your application. If the application you are developing will run on only one PC or in an environment that you control, this is not a liability.

✦ If you are distributing your DLL for use by another MFC application and the other application dynamically links to the MFC libraries, you will always be concerned about which version of MFC each is using. However, if your DLL is statically linking to the MFC libraries, you won't question which version your DLL is using.

As you can see, before you start working with DLLs, you must make some decisions. These decisions, by and large, are predicated on factors such as whether or not you control the environment where the DLL will be used, what language the calling application will be written in, and whether or not you want to distribute the MFC DLLs with your code. In all likelihood, you will have to go through this decision process for each application and DLL that you write.

Once you've selected your options for the new DLL, simply click the Finish button to have your new DLL created by Visual Studio.

Understanding the regular DLL internals

Once you've created the new DLL, the only main header file (RegDll.h) will contain the class (CRegDllApp) that represents your DLL.

```
// RegDll.h : main header file for the RegDll DLL
...
class CRegDllApp : public CWinApp
{
public:
    CRegDllApp();

// Overrides
public:
    virtual BOOL InitInstance();

    DECLARE_MESSAGE_MAP()
};
```

The first thing you should notice is that the DLL class is derived from the familiar CWinApp MFC class and implements the InitInstance member function. As you can probably guess, this is where you would provide any needed initialization code for your DLL.

If you are already familiar with creating DLLs with C or C++, you might be wondering where the DllMain function is. After all, every Win32 DLL must have a DllMain entry point. Well, the answer is that MFC DLL Wizard automatically creates a DllMain function, much like the WinMain function for Win32 applications. The advantage to having a CWinApp class is that you can program your DLL as you would any other CWinApp-derived class. For example, because initialization for CWinApp classes usually takes place in the InitInstance function, you can also override the CWinApp::InitInstance function for the DLL and provide global initialization there. In addition, deinitialization should be placed in the ExistInstance function derived from your DLL's CWinApp-derived class.

Implementing your own DllMain function

While MFC provides a default DllMain implementation and the MFC documentation generally advises you to do your initialization in the InitInstance function of your DLL's CWinApp-derived class, there may be times when you must implement your own DllMain function. One potential problem with using the MFC-provided DllMain function in conjunction with an InitInstance function override is that the InitInstance function is called only when a process attaches to the DLL or detaches from the DLL. This is fine in most cases, but at times your DLL may need to perform initialization and deinitialization when a thread attaches or detaches. In order to handle this scenario, it might be necessary to implement your own DllMain.

The reason you have a DllMain function automatically compiled into your DLL is because the MFC source code links code into your DLL from the Dllmodul.cpp file. In fact, if you browse to the folder on your hard disk that contains the MFC source code, you will not only find this file, but inside it you will find the definition of the DllMain function. In addition to the DllMain function, the Dllmodul.cpp file contains most of the code that is used to support a regular DLL. Unfortunately, there is no object-oriented means of overriding this function in your project. The Microsoft-recommended way to override or alter this function is to copy this file into the DLL's source code folder and include it in the DLL's project. Now you can make the changes you deem necessary, and the local, modified copy of the Dllmodul.cpp file will be compiled and linked into your DLL.

Dynamically loading DLLs

As mentioned earlier, to dynamically load and use a DLL at runtime, the application need only call the LoadLibrary function followed by subsequent calls to GetProcAddress for each function. In this section, I'll talk a bit about some scenarios where you would want to design your application to take advantage of this capability and then you'll be presented with a demo that will illustrate how this is done.

Programming function seams

A *function seam* is a layer of abstraction between a function and its caller. Its purpose is to insulate the caller from the internals of the function to be called. As an example, suppose you have an application that supports multiple communications protocols. The application might support APPC, NetBIOS, and Named Pipes, to name a few. How can your application support all of these completely different communications APIs without your changing the main module's source code for each one?

One way is to implement a function seam where each communications API is placed in a separate DLL. Each DLL then exports the exact same set of functions. For example, each DLL would export a generic Read function with a universally agreed-upon function definition. When you use this technique, the calling function can load the appropriate DLL and call its Read function without having to worry about what the DLL is doing internally to satisfy the read request.

An example of using function seams is ODBC (which is covered in Chapter 20). After an application makes a request of the ODBC Driver Manager, that request must be passed on to the specified ODBC driver. Because the ODBC Driver Manager can't be modified to support each ODBC driver, ODBC provides the layer of abstraction by mandating that all ODBC drivers export a specific set of functions per a published specification. That way, the ODBC Driver Manager never has to have any understanding of how the request is being carried out and doesn't require any special coding for the different ODBC drivers.

Writing multilingual applications

Another common example of dynamically loading a DLL is when programming multilingual applications. There are a couple of different ways to support more than one language, but one popular technique is to use resource-only DLLs. A resource-only DLL is one that only contains resources such as menus, images, and dialog boxes.

As an example, suppose you want to create an application that supports both Spanish and English. The business logic is the same for both languages. The only difference is in the resources. Therefore, you simply create two distinct DLLs containing only the resources (menus, dialog boxes, and so on) needed by the application. You only need to make sure that the resource ID values are identical in both DLLs and that you moved any hard-coded strings from your code into a string table.

Once you have done this, the calling program calls LoadLibrary to load the desired DLL (representing the user's language) and then passes the returned HINSTANCE to the AfxSetResourceHandle function call. This function enables you to specify the source of the resources that the application will use. After this, any code referring to a given resource ID will result in the desired resource-only DLL being used.

When the header file or import library is not available

At times your application must call a function provided by a DLL, but the header file or import library for the DLL is not available. You can call the DLL's exported functions from your application, but without the header file, you won't be able to compile your application, and without the import library you won't be able to link your application. However, if you can dump a list of the functions the DLL exports (via dumpbin or QuickView) and you know the function's prototype, you can have your application dynamically load the library and get the address of the functions you need to call. At that point, you can call the desired functions.

Retrieving resources from a binary file

Another popular reason for dynamically loading a library is to retrieve its resources. Because the resource compiler binds the resources to the application or DLL when it is built, the resources are located in the binary file (application's executable or DLL) itself. A very common trick is to use the different mouse cursors that are standard with Windows. These cursors are retrieved from the USER32.DLL, which is a resource DLL, by dynamically loading the DLL, calling the LoadCursor function, and passing the resource ID of the desired cursor.

Note   You can view the resource of any binary file by simply opening it in Visual Studio .NET as you would any other file. Visual Studio will automatically load the resources and display them in the Resource View.

In Figure 16-2, I've opened the USER32.DLL file and have determined that the resource ID for the "application busy" icon is 111. At this point, I can use this icon in my code by following the aforementioned steps.

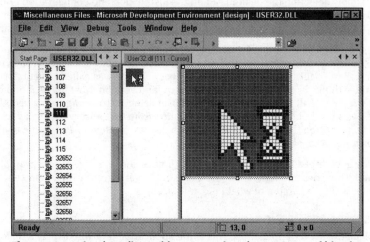

Figure 16-2: Visual Studio enables you to view the resources of binaries.

Coding a Control Panel-like Programming Model

As a Windows user, you are probably very familiar with the Control Panel, and the fact that it allows you to see and manage all the system's applets (which are generally system-level maintenance or monitoring applications). Because Microsoft wanted users to be able to write their own applets and to be able to plug them into the Control Panel, they used a programming model that is very common for these scenarios where one piece of software (the Control Panel) must be able to communicate with subsequently written client modules (the applets). This is accomplished by the definition of a set of functions that each applet must export so that it can be dynamically recognized by the Control Panel.

It works like this: When the Control Panel is displayed, it reads the Windows system folder looking for DLLs with a specific extension (.cpl), loads each file found (via a call to LoadLibrary), and then calls GetProcAddress on the documented initialization function (CPlApplet) that each applet must export. The Control Panel then interacts with the applet by continuously calling this function and passing it the different predefined messages that indicate the type of interaction. For example, a CPL_INIT message is sent to indicate that the applet needs to initialize itself, the CPL_DBLCLK message indicates that the user wants to display the applet, and the CPL_EXIT message is sent to indicate that the applet needs to shut itself down. This model has proved very popular over the years before COM became the de facto standard for writing these types of applications. In fact, before Visual Studio supported COM interfaces to allow users to write Add-Ins, this model was used for that task as well.

In this section, you'll see first-hand how to design and develop such a system using this programming model. The demo application is actually designed after a real-world application I wrote while at IBM. While on the IBM/World Book team, it was decided that the end-user needed to be able to add support for different communications APIs (for use in connecting to the Internet) by simply selecting the desired API off the installation and configuration utility. However, how would the main application know which APIs were present so that the user could configure those APIs for their unique needs? We used the Control Panel-like approach.

Whenever the user selected the option to modify their communications protocols, the code would look in a predefined folder for any files with a certain extension. One by one, each file was loaded via a call to LoadLibrary. After that, GetProcAddress was called to get information about the API—things like short name, descriptions, and version. Now the user could be presented with a list box of all loaded APIs. When the user selected to configure a given API, GetProcAddress was used once again to load the function from that library to display its dialog box. Calling that function then caused the library to display whatever API-specific configuration dialog box it defined.

Although you may never need this kind of application, it does serve as a very cool example of dynamically loading libraries and function addresses, so let's get started with a demo application that illustrates a simple version of what I did at IBM.

Writing the server application

To get started, code the server application. This is the application that will display a dialog box to the user, listing all the available client APIs that can be loaded and whose dialog boxes can displayed to configure them.

1. Create an MFC dialog-based application called DynServer.

2. Update the dialog box with controls, so that when finished it looks like that shown in Figure 16-3. (Note that the control to hold the API names is a list box and not a list view.)

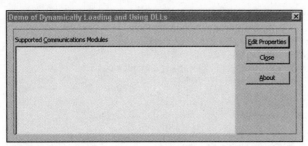

Figure 16-3: Main server dialog box for the dynamic DLL loading demo application.

3. Create a DDX control variable for the list box control called `m_lbxApis`.

4. In this demo, I'm going to assume that two functions will be documented for any DLL that wants to work with this main application. These functions will be named `GetDescription` and `DisplayProperties`. Therefore, you'll need to create a header file to define the prototypes for these functions. Create a file called `DynServerXface.h` and define it as follows.

```
#pragma once

typedef void (* DYNDLL_INFORMATION)(LPSTR lpszDesc);
#define DYNDLL_INFORMATION_FCN "GetDescription"

typedef void (* DYNDLL_EDITPROPS)();
#define DYNDLL_EDITPROPS_FCN "DisplayEditPropertiesDlg"
```

5. Insert an `include` directive for the `DynServerXface.h` file at the top of the `DynServerDlg.cpp` file.

```
#include "DynServerXface.h"
```

6. Insert the following code to the end of the dialog box's `OnInitDialog` function just before the `return` statement. As you can see, I've bolded the especially salient function calls in this code snippet. The first thing to notice is that the code uses the Win32 functions `FindFirstFile` and `FindNextFile` in a do/while loop to search for all DLL files whose file names begin with the string "DynClient." For each DLL found, the code loads that DLL using the `LoadLibrary` function. From there, a call to `GetProcAddress` returns the pointer to the function that can be used to retrieve a textual description of the API from the DLL. That function is called, the description is inserted into the list box, and the DLL's handle is saved with the list box entry as its item data.

```
BOOL CDynServerDlg::OnInitDialog()
{
  ...
  WIN32_FIND_DATA findData;
  HANDLE hFile;
  CString strFileMask = "DynClient*.DLL";

  char szCurrentDirectory[CHAR_MAX];
```

```
GetCurrentDirectory(sizeof(szCurrentDirectory),
                    szCurrentDirectory);

ZeroMemory(&findData, sizeof(findData));
hFile = FindFirstFile(strFileMask, &findData);
if (INVALID_HANDLE_VALUE != hFile)
{
 do
 {
  if ((findData.dwFileAttributes
      & FILE_ATTRIBUTE_NORMAL)
  || (findData.dwFileAttributes
      & FILE_ATTRIBUTE_ARCHIVE))
  {
   HINSTANCE hInst = NULL;
   hInst = LoadLibrary(findData.cFileName);

   if (hInst)
   {
    DYNDLL_INFORMATION pfnCommApiDllInfo =
    (DYNDLL_INFORMATION)::GetProcAddress(hInst,
    DYNDLL_INFORMATION_FCN);

    if (pfnCommApiDllInfo)
    {
     char szDesc[255];
     pfnCommApiDllInfo(szDesc);

     int iIndex = m_lbxApis.AddString(szDesc);

     m_lbxApis.SetItemData(iIndex, (DWORD)hInst);
    }
   }
  }
 } while (FindNextFile(hFile, &findData));
}
FindClose(hFile);

return
}
```

7. Now you need to insert code so that when the user selects an entry in the list box, that
associated API's configuration dialog box is displayed. To do that, add an event handler
for the Edit Properties button. This will be easy to code because each list box entry has
as its item data a handle to the associated DLL, and you've already seen how to use the
GetProcAddress to load a function pointer and then call that function.

```
void CDynServerDlg::OnBnClickedOk()
{
 int iIndex = m_lbxApis.GetCurSel();
 if (CB_ERR == iIndex)
 {
```

```
   AfxMessageBox("You must first select an API");
  }
  else
  {
   HINSTANCE hInst =
    (HINSTANCE)m_lbxApis.GetItemData(iIndex);
   if (NULL == hInst)
   {
    AfxMessageBox("Invalid HINSTANCE");
   }
   else
   {
    DYNDLL_DISPLAYPROPS pfnEditProps =
     (DYNDLL_DISPLAYPROPS)::GetProcAddress(hInst,
      DYNDLL_DISPLAYPROPS_FCN);

    if (pfnEditProps)
    {
     pfnEditProps();
    }
   }
  }
 }
}
```

8. The last thing you need to do for this application is simply clean up all these loaded DLL handles. To do that, add a handler for the dialog box's WM_DESTROY message and code it as follows:

```
void CDynServerDlg::OnDestroy()
{
 CDialog::OnDestroy();

 HINSTANCE hInst;
 CString strCommApiDll;
 BOOL bSuccess;

 for (int i = 0; i < m_lbxApis.GetCount(); i++)
 {
  m_lbxApis.GetText(i, strCommApiDll);

  hInst = (HINSTANCE)m_lbxApis.GetItemData(i);
  if (hInst)
  {
   bSuccess = ::FreeLibrary(hInst);
  }
 }
}
```

That's all there is to writing an extendable server application that publishes the functions it needs to interact with clients. Now let's code the client modules.

Writing the client modules

As a client, you know there are two rules to interacting with the DynServer application. First, the file must be a DLL whose filename begins with the string DynClient. So for example, a DLL to support configuring the TCP/IP protocol might be called DynClientTCPIP.dll. Next, the DLL must export two functions adhering to the prototypes defined in the DynServerXface.h file. Now that you know the rules, let's get started.

1. Create a regular DLL called DynClientTcpIp where you also select the Add to Solution option on the New Project dialog box. In a real-world application, your client modules might be provided by a third-party; therefore, it wouldn't be a good idea to put all the projects in the same solution. However, in this demo application, it makes building the entire solution a one-step process.

2. Open the Resource View and expand the DynClientTcpIp project entry.

3. Now, right-click the DynClientTcpIp.rc file and select the Add Resource menu option.

4. When the Add Resource dialog box appears, select Dialog resource type, and click New to create a new dialog box for this DLL.

5. Add some controls on the dialog box so that you can recognize it as being the TCP/IP dialog box. Obviously, the dialog box won't contain any real functionality, because you're simply testing the ability to invoke the correct dialog box when the user selects an API from the application's list box. Figure 16-4 shows the dummy dialog box I created for the TCP/IP module.

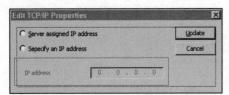

Figure 16-4: Test properties dialog box for a communications module

6. Create a new dialog class called CEditPropsDlg based on the resource.

7. Open the DynClientTcpIp.cpp file and add the following include directives. Note that I'm using an explicit path to the DynServerXface header to simplify things here. This will work if you create these projects as shown. However, you can also add the DynServer directory to the project's Additional Include Directories (found on the project's Properties dialog box) so that you don't need to fully qualify the path as I'm doing here.

```
#include "..\DynServer\DynServerXface.h"
#include "EditPropsDlg.h"
```

8. Now add the two functions to the same file as follows. As you can see, the GetDescription function sets the incoming string pointer to the value the user will see in the main application's list box, and the DisplayPropertiesDlg simply displays the dialog box you just created.

```
void GetDescription(LPSTR lpszDesc)
{
  strcpy(lpszDesc, _T("TCP/IP Support"));
```

```
}

void DisplayProperties()
{
  CEditPropsDlg().DoModal();
}
```

9. Finally, you need to export the two functions by adding them to the `DynClientTcpIp.def` like this:

```
; DynClientTcpIp.def : Declares the module parameters for the DLL.

LIBRARY        "DynClientTcpIp"

EXPORTS
    ; Explicit exports can go here
       GetDescription @1
       DisplayProperties @2
```

10. That's it. You can use these steps to create as many modules as you wish, but the general process is always going to be the same whether you're adding modules for this demo or using the Control Panel-like programming model for your own applications. Figure 16-5 shows the results of running the demo (available on the book's Web site) where I've loaded two modules (TCP/IP and APPC) and have selected to edit the TCP/IP properties.

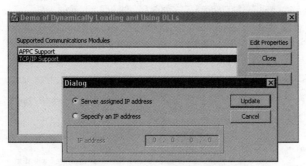

Figure 16-5: The test properties dialog box in the completed demo

Now that you've seen one example of writing regular DLLs that involved dynamically loading and querying libraries in order to call their exported functions, let's see another popular use for DLLs — writing Windows hook functions.

Writing Windows hooks

Because Windows hooks are written using DLLs, you will now learn about Windows *hooks* and how to write hook procedures. At a high level, hooks are used by applications that need to monitor other applications or system (keyboard or mouse) activity. At a lower level, hooks are points in the Windows messaging path where functions are injected, or attached, to filter certain types of messages before they reach their target destinations. Once these messages are caught, they can be modified, logged, or simply discarded. The functions themselves are called *filters*. These filters are classified according to the types of events they are filtering. For example, the hook that you will see in this section is known as a *keyboard hook*. When a filter function is attached to a hook, this is known as *setting a hook*. As you might imagine, there will be times when more than one hook of the same type has been set. In order to deal with this situation, Windows keeps track of the chain of filter functions. A very important point is that the most recently added filter function is the first function in that chain, and therefore, it has the first opportunity to filter any message traffic. That function can then perform its work and send the message on to the next hook procedure in the chain or discard the message completely.

Table 16-1 lists the hook functions that are supported in Windows along with their brief descriptions.

Table 16-1: Windows Hook Functions

Function	Description
WH_CALLWNDPROC	Monitors all Windows messages before the message is sent to its destination window procedure (see WH_CALLWNDPROCRET).
WH_CALLWNDPROCRET	Monitors messages after they have been processed by the destination window procedure.
WH_CBT	Monitors messages used by Computer-Based-Training applications.
WH_DEBUG	Aids in debugging other hook functions.
WH_GETMESSAGE	Monitors Windows messages posted to a message queue.
WH_JOURNALPLAYBACK	Posts messages previously recorded by a WH_JOURNALRECORD hook procedure.
WH_JOURNALRECORD	Records input messages posted to the system message queue.
WH_KEYBOARD	Monitors keyboard activity.
WH_KEYBOARD_LL	Monitors low-level keyboard input events (Windows NT/2000/XP only).
WH_MOUSE	Monitors mouse messages.
WH_MOUSE_LL	Monitors low-level mouse input events (Windows NT/2000/XP only).
WH_MSGFILTER	Monitors messages generated as a result of an input event in a dialog box, message box, menu, or scroll bar.
WH_SHELL	Receives notification of events meaningful to shell applications.
WH_SYSMSGFILTER	Similar to the WH_MSGFILTER, monitors messages generated as a result of an input event in a dialog box, message box, menu, or scroll bar. However, WH_SYSMSGFILTER monitors these messages for all active applications.

The SetWindowsHookEx function

In order to set a hook, the SetWindowsHookEx function must be called. Its prototype looks like this:

```
SetWindowsHookEx(int idHook,
                 HOOKPROC lpfn,
                 HINSTANCE hMod,
                 DWORD dwThreadId)
```

The first argument, idHook, represents a constant that identifies what type of hook is being set. Table 16-1 lists these various types of hooks. Note that the value used in the demo application is the WH_KEYBOARD constant, which specifies that a keyboard hook is being set.

The second argument, lpfn, is simply a pointer to a function of type HOOKPROC. For a keyboard hook, the function that is passed to the SetWindowsHookEx function must have the following prototype. If you're not accustomed to defining functions like this and then using them as arguments to functions, don't worry. This function will be explained in more detail when the demo is covered.

```
LRESULT CALLBACK KeyboardProc(int code, WPARAM, LPARAM);
```

The third argument, hMod, is the HINSTANCE of the module that contains the filter function.

The fourth and last argument to the SetWindowsHookEx function enables the application to specify the thread for which the hook is being set. For example, the application can set a hook for one single thread or for all threads that are currently active. For the latter, simply specify a value of NULL for this argument.

Threads are discussed in more detail in Chapter 17.

When the SetWindowsHookEx function returns, it returns a value of type HHOOK (handle to a hook). If the hook was not successfully set, this returned value is NULL, and you would need to call the GetLastError function in order to determine the cause of its failure.

The UnhookWindowsHookEx function

If an application sets a Windows hook, it is also obliged to remove a hook from the hook chain before terminating. This can be done via a call to the UnhookWindowsHookEx function. This function (see the following syntax) simply takes the HHOOK value returned by successfully setting a hook via the SetWindowsHookEx function. The UnhookWindowsHookEx function returns a Boolean value, which can be used to test for the success or failure of this function. Once again, should the function fail, a call to GetLastError is required to determine the cause of failure.

```
BOOL UnhookWindowsHookEx(HHOOK hHook);
```

The CallNextHook function

When a filter function is set for a given hook type, the filter function is placed at the head of a chain (first in line) of the filter functions for that hook type. Once a filter function completes its task, it has the option of calling the next filter function in the chain via the CallNextHook function. There are times, however, when you won't want processing to continue. As an example, if you are writing a keyboard hook and want to discard the keystroke, you would not call this function. However, if you are simply logging an event and you want the message to continue along its intended messaging path, the application would need to call the CallNextHook function once it is finished processing the message. Otherwise, the message would never be processed! If there are no other filter functions for this type of hook, Windows delivers the message to the appropriate message queue.

Demo Application: The keyboard hook DLL

As an example Windows hook, suppose you wanted to filter for certain keys being pressed. For example, you might want to capture all F1 keystrokes because you've implemented your own Help system that you want to be used system-wide. Another example might be if you're logging all keyboard activity for a system to audit that system's use. In this demo application, you'll simply be filtering for the F10 key being pressed. However, the process would be same regardless of the exact keys your own application would need to capture.

To get things started, create the DLL that will contain the filter function for the keyboard hook. To do that, create a regular DLL named KeybdHook.

Now, open the KeybdHook.h file, and add the following lines before the CKeybdHookApp class declaration. The first #define simply provides an easy way of exporting functions that have the __stdcall calling mechanism. The second function is the actual filter function. It is the function that will be called for every single keystroke that Windows processes. Its arguments will be explained shortly.

```
#define EXPORTED_DLL_FUNCTION \
  __declspec(dllexport) __stdcall

LRESULT EXPORTED_DLL_FUNCTION KbdHookProc (int nCode,
  WPARAM  wParam, LPARAM lParam);
```

Next, open the KeybdHook.cpp file, and add the following lines to the top of the file. This creates a shared data segment across all uses of this DLL. That way, the values defined within it are global for all uses of this DLL. When global variables are declared, they must be initialized.

```
#pragma data_seg(".SHARDAT")
static HWND      ghWndMain  = 0;
static HHOOK     ghKeyHook = NULL ;
#pragma data_seg()

HINSTANCE ghInstance = 0;
HOOKPROC  glpfnHookProc = 0;
```

After declaring the global variables that will be used in this DLL, add the filter function shown in the following example to KeybdHook.cpp. This function will be called every time Windows processes a keystroke. As you can see, the function is simply catching the F10 keystroke (characterized by the VK_F10 constant).

This demo is a very simple example of catching a keystroke to show you how this task is accomplished. Therefore, I simply display a message box to prove that the keystroke was caught, regardless of the application that the user is running at the time. Once the filter function catches the keystrokes it is filtering, you are then free to run whatever application-specific logic you require.

Notice that if the keystroke is handled and you do not want Windows to continue processing the keystroke, simply return a value of TRUE instead of calling the CallNextHookEx function.

```
LRESULT EXPORTED_DLL_FUNCTION KbdHookProc
(int nCode, WPARAM  wParam, LPARAM lParam)
{
  BOOL bHandledKeystroke = FALSE;

  if (((DWORD)lParam & 0x40000000)
  && (HC_ACTION == nCode))
  {
```

```
  switch (wParam)
  {
   case VK_F10:
    AfxMessageBox("Caught the F10 key!");
    bHandledKeystroke = TRUE;
   break;

   default :
   break ;
  }
 }

 return (bHandledKeystroke ?
  TRUE :
  ::CallNextHookEx (ghKeyHook, nCode, wParam, lParam));
 }
```

Let's do a quick run-through of the different arguments that are passed to a keyboard hook function like the one just used.

One of the values that the first argument, nCode, might contain is the HC_ACTION constant. Actually, this argument can have only one of two values: HC_ACTION and HC_NOREMOVE. In both cases, the WPARAM and LPARAM variables will contain information about the keystroke. However, in the case where nCode has a value of HC_NOREMOVE, the destination application for this keystroke has used the PeekMessage function, specifying the PM_NOREMOVE flag. In addition, if the value of nCode is less than zero, the filter function should not attempt to process the keystroke and instead should call the CallNextHookEx function.

Note   When you call either the PeekMessage or GetMessage functions, the message is typically removed from the queues because each message is returned to the application. However, there are times when an application might need to filter a message queue for certain messages without preventing that message from reaching its final destination. For example, a hook procedure might want to simply log an event, but let the message continue along its normal route. Another example would be if an application scanning a queue for a messages finds that it can't handle the message it retrieved. It might then need to send that message on to be processed. In situations like these, applications should call PeekMessage with PM_NOREMOVE value in the uRemove parameter. If PM_NOREMOVE is used, PeekMessage will return messages as normal but will not remove them from their queues.

The WPARAM value contains the virtual keycode of the generated keystroke and is used to verify which key was pressed. Finally, the LPARAM value is used to find out more information about the keystroke, such as the repeat count and whether the key was down or up before the message was sent.

Exporting the DLL functions

The DLL has to export a couple of functions to enable a client to set and release the keyboard hook. To do this, first open the KeybdHook.h file, and declare the following function that will be used to install or set the keyboard hook:

```
BOOL EXPORTED_DLL_FUNCTION InstallKeyboardHook
  (HWND hWnd);
```

Once you have declared the function, define it as follows in the KeybdHook.cpp file. If this function works successfully and the keyboard hook is set, the ghKeyHook variable will be set to the HHOOK value returned from the SetWindowsHookEx function. Therefore, the first thing the `InstallKeyboardHook` function does is to check this variable to see if it has a value. If it does, then the hook has already been set, and this function simply returns without doing anything. If the `ghKeyHook` variable does not have a value, this function attempts to set the keyboard hook. You already defined the `glpfnHookProc` variable in the previous global data segment, but what about the `ghInstance` variable being set? This variable will be set in the `InitInstance` function for this DLL. This will be covered shortly. This function then returns success or failure based on whether or not `SetWindowsHookEx` successfully set the hook.

```
BOOL EXPORTED_DLL_FUNCTION InstallKeyboardHook
 (HWND hWnd)
{
 BOOL bSuccess = FALSE;

 if (!ghKeyHook)
 {
  ghWndMain     = hWnd ;
  glpfnHookProc = (HOOKPROC) KbdHookProc ;

  bSuccess = (NULL != (ghKeyHook =
   ::SetWindowsHookEx (WH_KEYBOARD, glpfnHookProc,
   ghInstance, NULL)));
 }

 return bSuccess;
}
```

Now that you have exported a function to set the keyboard hook, you must also export a function to release the keyboard hook. Declare the following function above the `InstallKeyboardHook` function declaration in the `KeybdHook.h` file:

```
BOOL EXPORTED_DLL_FUNCTION DeInstallKeyboardHook();
```

After declaring the function to remove the keyboard hook, place the following function definition in the `KeybdHook.cpp` file. Note that the `ghKeyHook` variable is reset to `NULL` if the `UnHookWindowsHookEx` function works successfully. That is so the client of this DLL can call `InstallKeyboardHook` again to reset the hook if needed.

```
BOOL EXPORTED_DLL_FUNCTION DeInstallKeyboardHook()
{
 if (ghKeyHook)
 {
  if (TRUE == (0 != ::UnhookWindowsHookEx(ghKeyHook)))
  {
   ghKeyHook = NULL;
  }
 }

 return (NULL == ghKeyHook);
}
```

Now that all the code for setting and removing a keyboard hook is in place, add the following `InitInstance` and `ExitInstance` functions to the `CKeybdHookApp` object. They should be defined as follows:

```
BOOL CKeybdHookApp::InitInstance()
{
```

```
    AFX_MANAGE_STATE(AfxGetStaticModuleState());
    ghInstance = AfxGetInstanceHandle();
    return TRUE;
}

int CKeybdHookApp::ExitInstance()
{
    DeInstallKeyboardHook();
    return CWinApp::ExitInstance();
}
```

After you have finished adding the `InitInstance` and `ExitInstance` member functions, build the DLL, and copy it to a folder where it will be found by the client application that you will build next.

Building a client for the keyboard hook DLL

Now that you have written the hook function, it is time to do the easy part: testing it. To test your new keyboard hook, simply create a new dialog-based application called `KeybdHookClient`. After the project has been created, add a message handler for when the OK button is clicked. In the handler, simply call the DLL's exported `InstallKeyboardHook` function. Your function should look like this:

```
void CKeybdHookClientDlg::OnOK()
{
    InstallKeyboardHook(GetSafeHwnd());
}
```

Next, override the dialog box's `OnCancel` function. This function simply ensures that the keyboard hook is removed before the application terminates. When finished, the `OnCancel` function should look like the following:

```
void CKeybdHookClientDlg::OnCancel()
{
    DeInstallKeyboardHook();
    CDialog::OnCancel();
}
```

As with any DLL, now all you have to do is include the header file that contains the declarations for the functions you want to call. Add the following `#include` at the top of the `KeybdHookClientDlg.cpp` file. Obviously, you have to either fully qualify this name or place the folder where this file resides in your include folder path.

```
#include "KeybdHook.h"
```

The only thing left to do before building and running the test application is to include the keyboard hook DLL's import library, `KeybdHook.lib`.

Testing the keyboard hook DLL

To test the keyboard hook, simply find a product that uses the F10 key to do something. That way, you can verify that your filter function is catching the event *before* the application receives the Windows message and does anything. Because the F10 key is defined by CUA (Common User Access) to provide keyboard access to the menu, plenty of applications implement this keystroke. Therefore, upon pressing F10, if your filter function's message appears before the application's menu is highlighted, you know that the filter function worked properly.

In order to test this, I chose the standard Notepad application because it is installed with every copy of Windows. To test the keyboard hook DLL in Notepad, simply do the following:

1. Start the Notepad application. Your cursor will originally be placed in the body of the document (actually a multiline edit control).

2. Press the F10 key, which places you on the File menu.

3. Press the Esc key to return from the menu to the document.

4. Run the `KeybdHookClient` application, and press the Enter key, which sets the keyboard hook.

5. Return to the Notepad application and press the F10 key.

   Instead of being placed on Notepad's File menu, you will see a message box that states that the F10 key was successfully filtered. Because the keyboard hook filter function did not call the `CallNextHook` function, this key will not be sent to the Notepad application, and you will not be able to get to the Notepad menu via this keystroke. In other words, you have effectively disabled the F10 key from working in any application.

6. Close the `KeybdHookClient` application. This releases the keyboard hook.

7. Return to the Notepad application, and press the F10 key again. You should see that the F10 key now works as it originally did because the keyboard hook has been released.

Figure 16-6 shows the result of this demo. Notice that although the Notepad application was the current application when the F10 key was pressed, the filter function caught it and displayed its own message instead of enabling the Notepad application to process it.

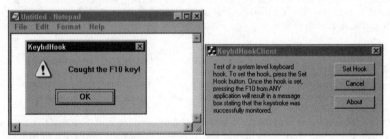

Figure 16-6: The KeybdHook DLL illustrates how easy it is to write a system-wide keyboard hook.

Global C++ objects with DLLs

Win32 DLLs are mapped into the address space of the calling process, with each invocation of the DLL getting a fresh copy of its data. However, a DLL will often want to manage data that is not specific to any one invocation, requiring the definition of global data in the DLL. As you saw in the keyboard hook demo, sharing global data across multiple invocations of a DLL is not difficult. You simply use the `#pragma` directive to name a data segment, and declare and initialize the desired global variable within that data segment. This enables the application to maintain data without regard to any one specific invocation of a DLL. Global data is useful for keeping track of things such as how many clients are attached to the DLL. Another example is a database server. The server would probably have tables and lists of currently attached clients, locked and cached records, and database handles. As you can see, declaring a global variable of a simple type (for example, `long` or `WORD`) can be used to keep track of how many clients are attached to a DLL. Unfortunately, managing more elaborate data structures such as C++ objects involves quite a bit more work on the part of the DLL.

The problem with using the previous approach to globalize C++ objects in a DLL is that each time a process attaches to the DLL, the constructor for that object is called. Here's an example of the problem:

```
#pragma  data_seg(".SHARDAT")
  _declspec(dllexport) CCounter counter;
  _declspec(dllexport) WORD wCounter = 0;
#pragma data_seg()

class CCounter
{
public:
 Ccounter() { m_wCounter = 0; }
};
```

In the preceding code snippet, the DLL must keep track of how many clients are currently attached to it. Both lines of code attempt to do this. The first line of code uses an object that contains a member variable to keep track of the number of attached clients, while the second line uses a simple variable of type WORD. Assume that both counters should be incremented every time a client attaches to the DLL and decremented every time a client detaches from the DLL. If you use the preceding code, the wCounter variable would function as expected. However, the CCounter object would not function correctly. This is because each time a client attaches to the DLL, the constructor for CCounter would be called, which would reinitialize its member variable counter back to zero.

If you scan the MSDN in search of a resolution to this problem, you will find the following advice:

> In order to share [C++ objects], you must use a memory-mapped file. For more information about memory-mapped files, see File Mapping in the Win32 SDK documentation.

If you have ever worked with memory-mapped files, this advice is not exactly the kind of answer you're looking for. Although memory-mapped files can be a very powerful tool, using them to share simple objects is a little like using a shotgun to kill flies. Luckily, an alternative is available, and it involves using the placement new operator.

Placement new operator

Although a thorough explanation of placement new is outside the scope of this chapter, I will explain it sufficiently to show how and why it is used to share global objects in a DLL.

Objects are normally allocated on the heap, on the stack, or in static memory. These allocations are realized via dynamic allocation, automatic allocation, and static allocation, respectively. However, at times you might need to specify the exact address where an object should be created. For example, a piece of hardware may need to share data with an application. This is accomplished with the placement new operator. Here's an example where the object CRegisters is being allocated at a specific hard-coded address in memory:

```
void* pMemory = (void)0xDEADBEEF;
CRegisters* pRegisters = new (pMemory) CRegisters();
```

The storage that is allocated at the address pointed to by pMemory must be large enough to hold a CRegisters object, and it must be properly aligned to hold a CRegisters object. Note that the numeric value of pRegisters is the same as pMemory. However, the pRegisters is of type CRegisters whereas pMemory is a void pointer.

Obviously, you probably don't want to explicitly state at what address the object should be created. However, using `placement new`, you can allocate a buffer of memory and then pass the address of that buffer to the `placement new` operator, which would look like the following in a `data_seq` in your DLL:

```
#pragma data_seg(".SHARDAT")
static char lpszMemory[sizeof(CRegisters)];
CRegisters* g_pRegisters = NULL;
int g_nClients = 0;
#pragma data_seg()
```

At this point, you have a buffer of memory (`lpszMemory`) that is the size of a `CRegisters` object. In addition, a `CRegisters` object pointer is initialized to `NULL` and a counter (`g_nClients`) is used to keep track of the number of attached clients. Now all the DLL has to do is allocate the memory and construct the `CRegisters` object when the first client attaches (you'll know it's the first attachment to the DLL because the value of `g_pRegisters` will be `NULL`) and delete the allocated memory when the last client detaches (the value of `g_nClients` will be zero when no clients are attached to the DLL). This will be shown in more detail in a demo called `GlobalDllObjects`.

GlobalDllObjects demo

Let's put what you've learned global C++ object, shared data and placement new to work with a demo that will share a C++ object across multiple invocations of that DLL. To get started, create a regular DLL called `GlobalDllObjects`. Once you've created the project, open the `GlobalDllObjects.h` file, and add the following code just before the declaration of the `CGlobalDllObjectsApp` class. These directives ensure that although any module can include this header file, the `GLOBALDLLOBJECTS_API` macro will resolve only to `declspec(dllexport)` if the module has defined `GLOBALDLLOBJECTS_EXPORTS`.

```
#ifdef GLOBALDLLOBJECTS_EXPORTS
#define GLOBALDLLOBJECTS_API __declspec(dllexport)
#else
#define GLOBALDLLOBJECTS_API __declspec(dllimport)
#endif
```

Next, add the declaration of the `CTest` class to the `GlobalDllObjects.h` file that will be instantiated and shared by the DLL (see the following code). The new operators have been overridden so that this class cannot be constructed using anything else but the placement new operator. In addition, both the class constructor and destructor display messages when they are invoked. This is done so that when you execute this DLL's test client, you can verify that the `CTest` object's constructor and destructor are called only once regardless of how many clients attach to the DLL.

```
class GLOBALDLLOBJECTS_API CTest
{
public:
 // the only construction of the object
 // that is allowed is via the placement
 // new operator
 void* operator new(size_t) { return NULL; }
 void* operator new(size_t, void* p) { return p; }
 void operator delete(void*) {};

 // display message box during object c'tor and d'tor
 // to show that object is only being constructed
```

```
// when first client attaches and destructed when
// last client detaches
CTest() {
 ::MessageBox(NULL,"CTest c'tor",
 "CTest.DLL", MB_OK);
 }

 ~CTest() {
 ::MessageBox(NULL,"CTest d'tor",
 "CTest.DLL", MB_OK);
 }

 CTest(const CTest&);
};
```

Add the following function declarations after the `CTest` class declaration. These functions enable a DLL's client to retrieve the pointer to the global `CTest` object and to inquire as to how many clients are currently attached to the DLL.

```
#define EXPORTED_DLL_FUNCTION \
 __declspec(dllexport) __stdcall

void EXPORTED_DLL_FUNCTION GetTestPtr(CTest*& rpTest);
int EXPORTED_DLL_FUNCTION GetNbrOfClients();
```

Next, open the `GlobalDllObjects.cpp` file, and add the following `#include` directive for the `new.h` file immediately after the `#include` of `stdafx.h`:

```
#include <new.h>
```

As mentioned previously, the DLL's main module will have to define `GLOBALDLLOBJECTS_EXPORTS`. Therefore, place the following `#define` directive before the `#include` directive for the `GlobalDllObject.h` file:

```
#define GLOBALDLLOBJECTS_EXPORTS
```

Now, add the following code to create a global mutex for the DLL. This mutex enables the DLL to synchronize the access to the global data that the DLL will have to allocate and deallocate.

```
// inter-process locking
HANDLE g_hMutex = ::CreateMutex(NULL, FALSE, "CTest");
```

Next, add the following `data_seg` to the `GlobalDllObjects.cpp` file. As you can see, the `data_seg` is named `.SHARDAT` and consists of three global variables. The first variable is a block of memory that is the size of a `CTest` object. The second variable is a `CTest` object pointer that is initialized to `NULL`. The third and last variable is a counter that keeps track of the number of currently attached clients.

```
#pragma data_seg(".SHARDAT")
static char lpszMemory[sizeof(CTest)];
CTest* g_pTest = NULL;
int g_nClients = 0;
#pragma data_seg()
```

Cross-Reference The subject of mutexes and other system-level synchronization objects are covered in Chapter 17.

Now that you have declared your global variables, the CTest object must be constructed. As you learned earlier, initialization of a regular DLL can be performed in the InitInstance member function. Therefore, implement the InitInstance function as follows:

```
BOOL CGlobalDllObjectsApp::InitInstance()
{
```

The first thing the InitInstance function does is to call the WaitForSingleObject function so that multiple clients attaching to the DLL at the same time won't cause memory for the CTest object to be allocated twice. In effect, access to the DLL's InitInstance function (where the CTest object is allocated) is being serialized via this mutex.

```
::WaitForSingleObject(g_hMutex,INFINITE);
```

After the mutex has been acquired, the g_pTest pointer is tested. If it does not have a value, then the current client must be the first client to attach to the DLL.

```
if (!g_pTest)
{
 ::MessageBox(NULL,
  "CGlobalDllObjectsApp::InitInstance - "
  "constructing global CTest",
  "CTest.DLL", MB_OK);
```

In the case of the first client attaching to the DLL, the CTest object is constructed into the address pointed at by the lpszMemory global variable as shown in the following example.

```
g_pTest = ::new (lpszMemory) CTest;
ASSERT(g_pTest);
}
```

The last thing the function does is increment the global variable g_nCount to reflect that another client has attached and released the locked mutex with a call to the ReleaseMutex function.

```
g_nClients++;
::ReleaseMutex(g_hMutex);

return CWinApp::InitInstance();
}
```

After you have implemented the InitInstance function, implement the ExitInstance function as follows:

```
int CGlobalDllObjectsApp::ExitInstance()
{
```

Once again, before anything is done to alter the global variables, the global mutex is acquired to ensure serialized access to the variables.

```
::WaitForSingleObject(g_hMutex,INFINITE);
```

Once the mutex has been acquired, the global variable that represents the current number of attached clients (g_nClients) is tested. If the value of g_nClients is zero, the allocated memory for the CTest object is freed.

```
if (0 ==--g_nClients)
{
```

```
MSG msg;

::PeekMessage(&msg, NULL,
WM_QUIT, WM_QUIT, PM_REMOVE);

::MessageBox(NULL,
"CGlobalDllObjectsApp::ExitInstance - "
"destructing global CTest",
"CTest.DLL", MB_OK);
```

The following line deletes the global `CTest` pointer and sets the pointer to `NULL` so that if another process attaches before this DLL is unloaded from memory, the pointer is reallocated.

```
delete g_pTest;
g_pTest = NULL;
}
```

Release and close the handle to the global mutex used to serialize access to the global variables as follows.

```
::ReleaseMutex(g_hMutex);
::CloseHandle(g_hMutex);

return CWinApp::ExitInstance();
}
```

The last change you need to make to the DLL's code is to implement two functions that will be exported to the DLL's clients. The first function, `GetTestPtr`, is used to retrieve the global `CTest` pointer. The second function, `GetNbrOfClients`, retrieves the number of currently attached clients.

```
void EXPORTED_DLL_FUNCTION GetTestPtr(CTest*& rpTest)
{
rpTest = g_pTest;
}

int EXPORTED_DLL_FUNCTION GetNbrOfClients()
{
return g_nClients;
}
```

Now that the code has been completed for the DLL, you need to define the named section to the linker. To do that, follow these steps:

1. Select the project in the Solution Explorer.

2. Select the Properties option from the Visual Studio Project menu.

3. Locate the Command Line option within the Linker settings as shown in Figure 16-7.

4. Add the following to the end of the edit control:

   ```
   /SECTION:.SHARDAT,RWS
   ```

5. Do the same thing for any other configurations (see the combo box in the upper-left corner of the dialog box) that you plan to use.

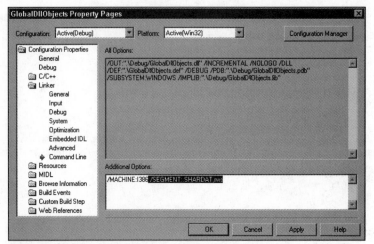

Figure 16-7: The Project Properties dialog box enables you to do things like define shared data segments for DLLs.

That's it. Now build the DLL, and copy it to a folder where Windows will load it.

Tip

In the `ExitInstance` function, you might have noticed a call to the `PeekMessage` function immediately before the `MessageBox` function call. This is done for a couple of reasons. First, the client application (`GlobalDllObjectsClient`) is implicitly linking to the DLL. Therefore, if the DLL's `ExitInstance` is running, it is because a client application is terminating. Second, when the main dialog box of an MFC dialog-based application is closed, MFC posts a `WM_QUIT` message. Message boxes are not displayed if a pending `WM_QUIT` message is in the queue. However, calling `PeekMessage` with the `PM_REMOVE` flag removes the message from the queue and enables the message box to be displayed. Here's an example of how to call the `PeekMessage` function for this purpose:

```
MSG msg;
::PeekMessage(&msg, NULL,
  WM_QUIT, WM_QUIT, PM_REMOVE);
```

The GlobalDllObjectsClient test application

Now that the DLL is built, you must build a test application to verify that it works as planned. To do this, create a dialog-based MFC application called `GlobalDllObjectClient`. As with all the source code in this chapter, this application can be located on the book's Web site in the Chapter 16 folder. Once the project has been created, open the `GlobalDllObjectClientDlg.cpp` file, and add the following `#include` directive:

```
#include "GlobalDllObjects.h"
```

Add a handler for the `BN_CLICKED` notification message for the main dialog box's OK button. This function calls the `GlobalObjectDll`'s `GetTestPtr` function to retrieve the DLL's global pointer to the `CTest` object. In addition, the `GetNbrOfClients` function is called in order to retrieve the number of currently attached clients. These values are then both displayed in a message box. That way, you can truly verify if the DLL's C++ object is being shared across multiple concurrent usages of the DLL. When you are finished, the OnOK function should appear as follows:

```
void CGlobalDllObjectClientDlg::OnOK()
{
 CTest* pTest;
 GetTestPtr(pTest);
 ASSERT(pTest);
 if (pTest)
 {
  CString str;

  str.Format("CTest address = 0x%08x, "
   "Attached clients = %ld\n",
   pTest, GetNbrOfClients());

  AfxMessageBox(str);
 }
}
```

The last thing you must do is to add the GlobalDllObjects import library to the GlobalDllObjectsClient project. After that, simply build the application.

Testing the GlobalDllObjects DLL

Start a copy of the GlobalDllObjectsClient application. You should see two message boxes. The first message box is displayed as a result of the DLL's InitInstance function creating the DLL's global CTest object. The second message box is displayed from the constructor of the CTest object. You should see these two message boxes only when the first client is attached to the DLL because all subsequent clients should be using the same CTest object that was created when the first client attached.

To prove that everything is working according to plan, invoke a second copy of the application (keep the first one running). Clicking the second application's OK button should result in a message box that displays the same address for CTest as the first application is displaying and now the number of users should be displayed as 2. Figure 16-8 illustrates an example of two concurrent users of the DLL. Notice that the first dialog box indicates one user because that message box was displayed before the second application was invoked.

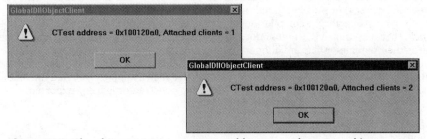

Figure 16-8: The placement new operator enables you to share C++ objects across multiple invocations of a DLL.

MFC Extension DLLs

So far, I've spent the entirety of this chapter discussing regular DLLs. Now, it's time to turn our attention to the MFC extension DLLs. MFC extension DLLs are used to export classes (or functions of classes) that derive from the MFC framework. As an example of that, say that you have created a new toolbar that is derived from the MFC CToolbar class. To share this class from a DLL, it must be exported from an MFC extension DLL. Another example of when to use an MFC extension DLL is if your application is an MDI application, and you want to encapsulate each view or logical group of views in a separate DLL. Because these are two very common needs, I'll address each of these tasks with a demo in this section.

Understanding the MFC extension DLL internals

Although both MFC extension DLLs and regular DLLs can be created with the MFC DLL Wizard and, therefore, can be built in a similar fashion, there are a number of fundamental differences between the two DLL types:

✦ Clients of an MFC extension DLL *must* be MFC applications.

✦ Unlike a regular DLL, an MFC extension DLL does not have a CWinApp-derived object.

✦ When writing a regular DLL, you typically do the DLL's initialization and cleanup in the InitInstance and ExitInstance routines, respectively. However, since you don't have a CWinApp-derived class with the MFC extension DLLs, you perform this work in the DllMain function.

✦ MFC extension DLLs introduce a new class, CDynLinkLibrary, to enable the export of resources or objects of type CRuntimeClass.

Exporting classes via MFC extension DLLs

The most common reason for creating an MFC extension DLL is when you need to export one or more classes based on the MFC framework. Classes and their functions are exported in one of two ways, depending on whether an entire class is being exported or a subset of the classes' member functions.

In the previous section on regular DLLs, you saw that in order to export functions from a regular DLL, the .DEF file is normally used. The inconvenience this causes with C++ classes (such as the MFC classes) or member functions is that if you want to use the .DEF file to export them, you must specify the compiler-dependent mangled or decorated name. The name is *mangled* because, unlike C, C++ functions can have the same name within the same scope as long as their parameter lists are different. Therefore, the compiler creates a unique name based on replacing the parameter types of the function signature with symbols that represent that type to that compiler. As an example of a mangled name, suppose you had the following class defined in an MFC DLL where the CDllTestApp constructor is being exported.

```
class CDllTestApp : public CWinApp
{
public:
    __declspec( dllexport) CDllTestApp();

// Overrides
public:
    virtual BOOL InitInstance();
```

```
    DECLARE_MESSAGE_MAP()
};
```

If you were to compile this DLL and then dump its export table using DUMPBIN /EXPORTS DllTestApp.dll, you would see the following output. Note specifically the renaming (mangling) of the CDllTestAp function (shown in bold).

```
Microsoft (R) COFF/PE Dumper Version 7.00.9466
Copyright (C) Microsoft Corporation.  All rights reserved.

Dump of file dlltest.dll

File Type: DLL

  Section contains the following exports for DllTest.dll

    00000000 characteristics
    3CBF80D2 time date stamp Thu Apr 18 22:28:34 2002
        0.00 version
           1 ordinal base
           1 number of functions
           1 number of names

    ordinal hint RVA       name

          1    0 00077D13 ??0CDllTestApp@@QAE@XZ

Summary

       34000 .data
        6000 .idata
       1B000 .rdata
       10000 .reloc
        5000 .rsrc
      109000 .text
       73000 .textbss
```

As you can see, the CDllTestApp function has been renamed to ??0CDllTestApp@@QAE@XZ. This is the name you'd need to specify. You could take the time to determine all the different characters the Visual C++ compilers uses for the different parameters, and that way you'd know how each mangled name is formed. However, this would take a great deal of time (because these parameters are not documented) and would be subject to breaking in future releases of the compiler (the reason they're not documented is so that the compiler team can change them without worrying about breaking existing user code).

Therefore, this is obviously not the way to export your functions. Instead, MFC has a couple of macros that make this job much easier. When exporting entire classes from a DLL, the AFX_EXT_CLASS macro is used in the classes' declaration like this:

```
class AFX_EXT_CLASS CMyFancyToolbar : public CToolbar
{
  ...
}
```

Exporting parts of a class is just as easy. Instead of placing the AFX_EXT_CLASS macro in front of the class name, simply place the macro in front of the function being defined that you wish to export.

```
class CMyFancyDialog : public CDialog
{
public:
 AFX_EXT_CLASS CMyFancyDialog();
 AFX_EXT_CLASS int DoModal();
public:
    BOOL Create(LPCTSTR lpszTemplateName,
        CWnd* pParentWnd = NULL);
    BOOL Create(UINT nIDTemplate, CWnd* pParentWnd = NULL);
...
```

Note that in the CMyFancyDialog class, the class constructor and DoModal functions are exported while the two overloaded Create functions aren't. This means that a client can construct the class and call its DoModal function. However, if calls to the two overloaded Create functions are placed in the client's code, the client won't build and the linker wills state that the calls to CMyFancyDialog::Create could not be resolved.

More on the AFX_EXT_CLASS

As you just saw, the AFX_EXT_CLASS macro can be used to export either entire classes or parts of classes. However, when a client application includes the header file that contains the declaration of the classes that the DLL is exporting, a problem is going to arise from the fact that both modules are stating to the linker that they are responsible for exporting the class. This potential problem is resolved by the way the AFX_EXT_CLASS macro is defined, which depends on the following preprocessor definitions for the project:

✦ If _AFXDLL and _AFXEXT are defined for the project, the AFX_EXT_CLASS macro resolves to the following:

```
__declspec(dllexport)
```

✦ If _AFXEXT is not defined, the AFX_EXT_CLASS macro resolves to the following for import purposes:

```
__declspec(dllimport)
```

Therefore, when the MFC DLL Wizard is used to create an MFC extension DLL, both _AFXDLL and _AFXEXT are defined. Anytime the DLL's source code refers to the AFX_EXT_CLASS, the class is being exported.

Using nested MFC extension DLLs

As mentioned previously, the AFX_EXT_CLASS macro is used to export an entire class or parts of a class from a DLL. However, problems may arise if your application needs to use nested MFC extension DLLs. As an example, suppose you have an MFC extension DLL of common routines and classes that you use on all projects. I'll call this DLL the "global DLL." You may then have another MFC extension DLL that contains common routines and classes for a specific project, which I'll call the "project DLL." The project DLL would almost certainly use the common DLL. This is a standard example of nested MFC extension DLLs.

When you attempt to link the project DLL, you will receive linker errors. This is because of the following:

1. When you build the common DLL, it has certain functions and classes that are defined as being exported.

2. When you build the project DLL and it imports the common DLL, the linker thinks that you are attempting to export those same functions and classes again from this new DLL when in fact, you want to import them from the common DLL, not export them.

Here's the workaround to this problem. Instead of using the AFX_EXT_CLASS macro, you should use a macro that takes into consideration the project that is using it. For example, you could create a common macro called COMMON_IMPORT_EXPORT and define it as follows.

```
#ifdef _COMMON_DLL
  #define COMMON_IMPORT_EXPORT  _declspec(dllexport)
#else
  #define COMMON_IMPORT_EXPORT  _declspec(dllimport)
#endif
```

Now, the common DLL files that include the header file that defines the exported functions and classes simply add the following #define directive before the #include directive. That way, the COMMON_IMPORT_EXPORT define will resolve to an export. Any other modules including the header file will not have the _COMM_DLL defined, and therefore, the COMMON_IMPORT_EXPORT define will resolve to imports for them.

```
#define _COMMON_DLL
```

Another means of defining _COMMON_DLL is by setting it in the project's Properties Pages dialog box.

Exporting resources

Each MFC application contains a linked list of CDynLinkLibrary objects. If your code in an MFC application requests that MFC load a resource on its behalf, MFC first attempts to load the requested resource from the current module. MFC locates this module's resources by calling the AfxGetResourceHandle function. If the requested resource cannot be located, MFC iterates the application's linked list of CDynLinkLibrary objects in an attempt to locate the resource. To set the default module that MFC uses to first locate requested resources, you must use the AfxSetResourceHandle function to specify the HINSTANCE of the module.

Demo Application: Encapsulating documents and views in a DLL

Because this is the age of component-based reusable software, the MFC extension DLL demo will illustrate how to place document/view support into a DLL. Suppose you have written a document and view to support the reading of .JPG files. Maybe you had to write an application that, among many other things, needed to display these files. You would normally create the document and view classes to support these files within the scope of the main application. However, what happens if tomorrow you need to provide the same JPG viewing functionality for another application? It would obviously be a much better practice to place application-independent logic (such as the viewing of JPG files) into a DLL. That way, any MFC client would be able to include that functionality simply by linking to the DLL and calling the appropriate exported functions.

Creating the MFC extension DLL for the image document and view

First, create an MFC extension DLL named `ImageViewer`. Once you have created the project, create a form view in the resource editor called `IDD_IMAGE_VIEWER`. This form view will be used to display images. Then create a `CFormView`-derived class called `CImageViewerView` based on the `IDD_IMAGE_VIEWER` dialog template resource. Now, create a `CDocument`-derived class called `CImageViewerDoc`.

Once you have created the DLL's document and view classes, open the `ImageViewerView.h` file, and add the following `#include` directives.

```
#include "resource.h"
#include "imageobject.h"
```

Note This demo will use Infinite Vision's *ImageObject* library to display the images. You can find a demo of this imaging library on the book's Web site in the `ImageObject` directory . The `imageobject.h` file is the main include file for that library.

After inserting the `#include` directives, add the following member variable to the `CImageViewer` class. This object is all you need to display a graphics file in the view.

```
protected:
 CImageObject* m_pImageObject;
```

Now open the `ImageViewerView.cpp` file, and make the following changes to the constructor and destructor:

```
CImageViewerView::CImageViewerView()
 : CFormView(CImageViewerView::IDD)
{
 m_pImageObject = NULL;
}

CImageViewerView::~CImageViewerView()
{
 delete m_pImageObject;
 m_pImageObject = NULL;
}
```

Because the purpose of this demo is placing documents and views in a DLL and not the specifics of what the document or view does, the view will simply display the requested image. To do that, override the `OnDraw` function as follows:

```
void CImageViewerView::OnDraw(CDC* pDC)
{
 if (!m_pImageObject)
 {
  CDocument* pDoc = GetDocument();
  ASSERT_VALID(pDoc);

  CString strPathName = pDoc->GetPathName();
  ASSERT(0 < strPathName.GetLength());
  if (0 < strPathName.GetLength())
  {
```

```
    m_pImageObject = new CImageObject(strPathName);
   }
  }

  if (m_pImageObject)
  {
   m_pImageObject->SetPalette(pDC);
   m_pImageObject->Draw(pDC);
  }
 }
```

Encapsulating the image document and view in a class

Now that you have the document and view created and coded, it's time to concentrate on the important part of this demo: encapsulating the document and view in a DLL. First, create a file called ImageViewer.h. The file will be a very simple one used to expose a CImageViewer class with a single function, CImageViewer::Init. This Init function is what an application calls in order to use the document and view that are coded in this DLL.

The ImageViewer.h file should look like the following. Once you have created and saved this file, add a #include to the top of the ImageViewer.cpp file for it.

```
#pragma once

class AFX_EXT_CLASS CImageViewer
{
public:
 BOOL Init();
};
```

Now that you already have the ImageViewer.cpp file open in the editor, add the following #include directives after the #include directive of the ImageViewer.h file:

```
#include "ImageViewerView.h"
#include "ImageViewerDoc.h"
```

Add the Init function, as shown in the following example. This function takes as its only argument a pointer to the application object, because that value is required by the AddDocTemplate function call. After that, this function creates a CMultiDocTemplate and adds it to the application object's list of document templates via the AddDocTemplate function.

```
 BOOL CImageViewer::Init()
 {
  BOOL bSuccess = FALSE;

  CWinApp* pApp = AfxGetApp();
  ASSERT(pApp);
  if (pApp)
  {
   CMultiDocTemplate* pDocTemplate;

   pDocTemplate = new CMultiDocTemplate(
    IDR_IMAGEDOCTYPE,
```

```
      RUNTIME_CLASS(CImageViewerDoc),
      RUNTIME_CLASS(CMDIChildWnd),
      RUNTIME_CLASS(CImageViewerView));

  ASSERT(pDocTemplate);
  if (pDocTemplate)
  {
   pApp->AddDocTemplate(pDocTemplate);
   bSuccess = TRUE;
  }
 }

 return bSuccess;
}
```

In order for the document template to be created, you must create a string table in the DLL's resource file and add a document entry. It should have an ID of IDR_IMAGEDOCTYPE and a value of "\nImageV\nImageV\nImage Files (*.jpg, *.gif, *.bmp)\n.jpg;.gif;.bmp;\nImage Viewer.Document\nImageV Document".

The last step before building the DLL is to link with the ImageObject import library. Don't forget that in order to run the test application, you not only have to copy the DLL you are coding now to the appropriate folder, but you also must install the ImageObject library from the Web site.

Building a test for the image document and view DLL

Now that you have written the MFC extension DLL to house the document and view for the types of files you will enable the users to open, it's time to do the easy part: Create the application.

Create an MDI application named ImageViewerClient, making sure that the Document/View option is selected. Then open the ImageViewerClient.h file, and add the following #include directive before the declaration of the CImageViewerClientApp class. This is the include file for the DLL's CImageViewer class; therefore, you must either point the #include directive to the folder where the ImageViewer.h file resides, or set this project's include files setting to include it.

```
#include "ImageViewer.h"
```

Add the following member variable to the application class:

```
protected:
 CImageViewer* m_pImageViewer;
```

Now, open the ImageViewerClient.cpp file, and add the following line to the application object's constructor:

```
m_pImageViewer = new CImageViewer();
```

Locate the InitInstance function. Replace the entire function body with the following code:

```
BOOL CImageViewerClientApp::InitInstance()
{
```

```
Enable3dControls();
LoadStdProfileSettings();

CMainFrame* pMainFrame = new CMainFrame;
if (!pMainFrame->LoadFrame(IDR_MAINFRAME))
 return FALSE;

pMainFrame->ShowWindow(m_nCmdShow);
pMainFrame->UpdateWindow();
m_pMainWnd = pMainFrame;

ASSERT(m_pImageViewer != NULL);
m_pImageViewer->Init();

return TRUE;
}
```

Finally, create a destructor for `CImageViewerClient` to delete the `m_pImageViewer` object, as follows:

```
CImageViewerClientApp::~CImageViewerClientApp()
{
 delete m_pImageViewer;
}
```

The last thing you do before you can test your new application is to simply add the import library for your MFC extension DLL to this application's project.

Figure 16-9 shows the result of running this application and opening a couple of .JPG files.

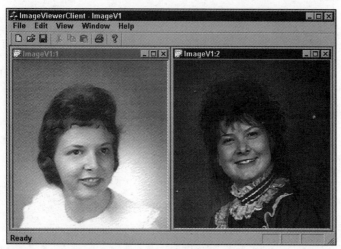

Figure 16-9: The ImageViewer DLL illustrates how to encapsulate an MFC document and view in a DLL for reuse across multiple applications.

When you use this demo, any application can easily have image-viewing capability simply by linking with the ImageViewer import library and calling a single exported C++ function (`CImageViewer::Init`).

Summary

Throughout this chapter you've seen just how easy it is to implement both regular DLLs and MFC extension DLLs to solve different programmatic problems. With regards to regular DLLs, you were presented with three demos. The first demo illustrated a practical use of dynamically loading and querying a DLL for exported function by way of using the Control Panel-like programming model. The second demos then illustrated how to write a system-level keyboard hook, and the third demo showed how to share C++ objects across multiple invocations of a DLL. For MFC extension DLLs, you learned how to export whole classes or specific member functions of a class from a DLL, as well as how to place documents and views in a separate DLL from the main application. As you can see, DLLs can be used to solve many everyday development problems, and using Visual C++ to develop these DLLs makes this work that much easier. In the next chapter, you'll learn how to write applications that perform concurrent tasks via multithreading.

✦   ✦   ✦

Multithreaded Programming

In the Win32 environment, each running application constitutes a *process* and each process consists of one or more threads of execution. A *thread* is a path of execution through a process' code. One fundamental difference between 16- and 32-bit Windows is that 32-bit Windows doesn't limit its applications to just one thread each. A process in a 32-bit Windows application begins its life as a single thread, but that thread can spawn additional threads. A preemptive scheduler inside the operating system divides CPU time among active threads so that they appear to run simultaneously. Secondary threads are ideal for performing background tasks such as paginating documents and performing garbage collection. They can also play more visible roles by creating windows and processing messages to those windows, just as the primary thread processes messages sent to an application's main window.

Multithreading is not for everyone. Multithreaded applications are difficult to write and debug because the parallelism of the concurrently running threads adds an extra layer of complexity to the code. Used properly though, multiple threads can dramatically improve an application's responsiveness. A word processor that does its spell-checking in a dedicated thread, for example, can continue to process input in the primary thread so that the user doesn't have to wait for the spell checker to finish. What makes writing a threaded spell checker difficult is that the spell-checking thread invariably has to synchronize its actions with other threads in the application.

Most programmers have been conditioned to think about their code in synchronous terms — function A calls function B, function B initializes variable C and returns to A, and so on. However, threads are asynchronous by nature in a multithreaded application; you have to think about what happens if, for example, two threads call function B at the same time or one thread reads a variable while another writes it. If function A launches function B in a separate thread, you also must anticipate what problems could occur if function A continues to run while function B executes. For example, it's common to pass the address of a variable created on the stack in function A to function B for processing. But if function B is in another thread, the variable may no longer exist when function B gets around to accessing it. Even the most innocent-looking code can be fatally flawed when it involves the use of multiple threads.

MFC encapsulates threads of execution in the CWinThread class. It also includes synchronization classes encapsulating events, mutexes, and other thread synchronization objects found in the Windows kernel. Does MFC make multithreading easier? Not exactly. Developers who have written multithreaded Windows applications in C are often surprised to learn that MFC adds complexities all its own. The key to writing multithreaded programs in MFC is having a keen understanding of what you're doing and knowing where the potholes are. This chapter is designed to help you do both.

Working with Threads

As far as Windows is concerned, all threads are alike. MFC, however, distinguishes between two types of threads: *user interface threads* (called *UI threads*) and *worker threads*. The difference between the two is that UI threads have message loops and worker threads do not. UI threads can create windows and process messages sent to those windows. Worker threads perform background tasks that receive no direct input from the user and therefore don't need windows and message loops. Another major difference between worker threads and UI threads has to do with *affinity*. A UI thread has a very high degree of affinity, which means that the thread that creates a window is the only thread that can directly interact with it. Worker threads, on the other hand, have no affinity, and thus are suited for a greater number of tasks. You'll see that exemplified in the section entitled "Sharing MFC Objects Among Threads."

When you open a folder in the Windows shell, the shell launches a UI thread that creates a window showing the folder's contents. If you drag-copy a group of files to the newly opened folder, that folder's thread performs the file transfers. (Sometimes the UI thread creates yet another thread — this time a worker thread — that does the actual file copy.) The benefit of this multithreaded architecture is that once the copy operation has begun, you can switch to windows opened onto other folders and continue working while the files are copied in the background. Launching a UI thread that creates a window is conceptually similar to launching an application within an application in that the outer application, or parent, continues to run in an asynchronous manner from the inner application, or child. The most common use for UI threads is to create multiple windows serviced by separate threads of execution.

Worker threads are ideal for performing isolated tasks that can be broken off from the rest of the application and performed in the background while other processing takes place in the foreground. A classic example of a worker thread is the thread an animation control uses to play AVI clips. Basically all the thread does is draw a frame, put itself to sleep for a fraction of a second, wake up, and start again. It adds little to the processor's workload because it spends most of its life suspended between frames, and yet it also provides a valuable service. This is a great example of multithreaded design because the background thread is given a specific task to do and then allowed to perform that task over and over until the primary thread signals that it's time to end.

Creating worker threads

There are two ways to create a thread in an MFC application. You can construct a CWinThread object and call that object's CreateThread function to create the thread, or you can use AfxBeginThread, which constructs a CWinThread object and creates the thread in one step. As you might have guessed, MFC defines two different versions of AfxBeginThread: one for creating UI threads and one for worker threads.

One thing to note is that AfxBeginThread and CWinThread::CreateThread are not merely wrappers around the ::CreateThread function. In addition to launching threads of execution, they also initialize internal variables used by the framework, perform sanity checks at various points during the thread creation process, and take steps to ensure that functions in the C runtime library are accessed in a thread-safe way. For this reason, you should never use the Win32 ::CreateThread function to create a thread in an MFC program unless the thread will not be using MFC.

AfxBeginThread makes it simple — almost trivial, in fact — to create a worker thread. The following are what it takes to spawn a thread, passing it a simple data structure:

1. Define thread function. This is the function that will be called when you spawn the new thread.

2. Spawn the thread, passing it the pointer to the thread function and a pointer to any application-specific data that you want the thread to process (cast to LPVOID).

Here's an example of what I'm talking about. Here I've defined a simple data structure to hold a customer number and name value:

```
// define data to be passed to thread function
struct CustomerInfo
{
 int m_iCustomerNbr;
 char m_szCustomerName[25];
};
```

From there, I've added code to a dialog's OK button handler to instantiate a CustomerInfo object and call the AfxBeginThread function, passing to it the thread function (you'll see that next) and a pointer to the CustomerInfo object that is constructed from the data on the dialog. Note that AfxBeginThread function returns a pointer to a CWinThread object so that your application can manage the thread once it's been spawned. I'll discuss the different things that can be done with this object shortly.

```
void CWorkerThread1Dlg::OnBnClickedOk()
{
  if (UpdateData())
  {
    CustomerInfo* pCustomerInfo = new CustomerInfo;
    strcpy(pCustomerInfo->m_szCustomerName,
           m_strCustomerName);
    pCustomerInfo->m_iCustomerNbr = m_iCustomerNumber;

    CWinThread *pThread = ::AfxBeginThread(ThreadFunc,
                 static_cast<LPVOID>(pCustomerInfo));
  }
}
```

As you can see, the prototype for the thread function calls for the passing of an LPVOID and returns a UINT.

```
UINT ThreadFunc(LPVOID pParams);
```

Having said that, let's look at how the thread function for our example could be coded.

```
UINT ThreadFunc(LPVOID pParam)
{
  // Cast the incoming LPVOID to the correct type.
  CustomerInfo* pCustomerInfo =
   static_cast<CustomerInfo*>(pParam);

  // Format a string to display that the data arrived
```

```
            // safely.
            CString str;
            str.Format("Processing customer %ld - %s\n",
                       pCustomerInfo->m_iCustomerNbr,
                       pCustomerInfo->m_szCustomerName);
            AfxMessageBox(str);

            // Delete the data when finished.
            delete pCustomerInfo;

            return(0);
        }
```

In the previous example, you saw the minimum amount of information that must be supplied to the AfxBeginThread function. The worker thread form of AfxBeginThread actually accepts as many as four additional parameters that specify the thread's priority, stack size, creation flags, and security attributes. The complete prototype for this function is as follows:

```
        CWinThread *AfxBeginThread(AFX_THREADPROC pfnThreadPro,
          LPVOID pParam,
          int nPriority = THREAD_PRIORITY_NORMAL,
          UINT nStackSize = 0,
          DWORD dwCreateFlags = 0,
          LPSECUTIRY_ATTRIBUTES lpSecutiryAttrs = NULL);
```

The nPriority parameter specifies the thread's execution priority. High priority threads are always scheduled for CPU time before low priority threads, but in practice even threads with extremely low priorities usually get all the processor time they need. It's important to realize that the nPriority parameter does not specify an absolute priority level. It specifies a priority level relative to the priority level of the process to which the thread belongs. The default is THREAD_PRIORITY_NORMAL, which assigns the thread the same priority as the process that owns it. Other priority values are covered later in the chapter. Additionally, you can modify a thread's priority level via a call to the CWinThread object's SetThreadPriority member function.

The nStackSize parameter passed to AfxBeginThread specifies the thread's maximum stack size. In the Win32 environment, each thread receives its own stack. The 0 default nStackSize value allows the stack to grow as large as 1MB. This doesn't mean that every thread receives a minimum of 1MB of memory; it means that each thread is assigned 1MB of address space in the larger 4GB address space in which 32-bit Windows applications execute. Memory isn't committed (assigned) to the stack's address space until it's needed, so most thread stacks never use more than a few kilobytes of physical memory. Placing a limit on the stack size allows the operating system to trap runaway functions that recurse endlessly and eventually consume the stack. The default limit of 1MB is fine for almost all applications.

The dwCreateFlags parameter can be one of two values. The default value 0 tells the system to start executing the thread immediately. If CREATE_SUSPENDED is specified instead, the thread starts out in a suspended state and doesn't begin executing until another thread (usually the thread that created it) calls the CWinThread object's ResumeThread member function as shown in the following example:

```
        // Create a suspended thread
        CWinThread *pThread =
```

```
AfxBeginThread(ThreadFunc,
               &ThreadInfo,
               THREAD_PRIORITY_NORMAL,
               0,
               CREATE_SUSPENDED);
...
// Resume execution of thread
pThread->ResumeThread();
```

Sometimes it's useful to create a thread but defer its execution until later. As you'll see later, it's also possible to create a thread that suspends itself until a specified event occurs.

The final parameter in the `AfxBeginThread` argument list, `lpSecurityAttrs`, is a pointer to a `SECURITY_ATTRIBUTES` structure that specifies the new thread's security attributes and also tells the system whether child processes should inherit the thread handle. The `NULL` default value assigns the new thread the same properties as the thread that created it has.

Coding the thread function

As you saw, a worker thread's thread function must take the following form:

```
UINT ThreadFunc (LPVOID pParam);
```

You can declare the function outside a class (as I did earlier), but if you are going to define it as a member function of a class, it must be declared as `static`. The reason is that all non-static C++ member functions have as a hidden first parameter a pointer to the object's instance (a `this` pointer). Therefore, the function's prolog (compiler-generated initialization code) expects `this` to be on the stack when the function is called. However, when the thread is started and the thread function is called, the `this` pointer is not passed and very nasty things start to happen (usually GPFs and blue screens). The way around this problem is to define the member function as `static`. That way, the function's prolog will know not to expect a `this` pointer as the first four bytes on the stack.

Getting back to the thread function's prototype, the `pParam` argument is a 32-bit value (cast to `LPVOID`) that can be any information that you want to pass to the thread. Very often `pParam` is the address of an application-defined data structure containing information that is to be processed. However, it can also be a scalar value, a handle, or even a pointer to an MFC object. It doesn't really matter as long as you cast it when you pass it to the `AfxBeginThread` function and the thread function knows how to deal with it on its end. In the following example, instead of passing a simple scalar value, I'm defining a `CustomerInfo` structure that can then be cast to `void*` and passed to a thread function.

```
struct CustomerInfo
{
  int m_iCustomerNbr;
  char m_szCustomerName[25];
};

UINT ThreadFunc(LPVOID pParam)
{
  CustomerInfo* pCustomerInfo =
    static_cast<CustomerInfo*>(pParam);
```

```
    CString str;
    str.Format("Processing customer %ld - %s\n",
               pCustomerInfo->m_iCustomerNbr,
               pCustomerInfo->m_szCustomerName);
    AfxMessageBox(str);

    delete pCustomerInfo;

    return(0);
}
```

Once the thread function is invoked, the incoming void pointer can be cast back to the original data structure and used. This code (taken from the WorkerThread1 demo) when built and run will yield results similar to that shown in Figure 17-1.

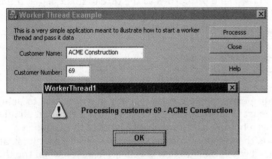

Figure 17-1: Like most programmatic tasks, starting a worker thread and passing it data so that concurrent work can be accomplished is incredibly simple once you know how.

One last point about thread functions is that it's perfectly legal to use the same thread function for two or more concurrent threads. However, you must be sensitive to reentrancy problems caused by global and static variables. As long as the variables (and objects) a thread uses are created on the stack (local variables), no reentrancy problems occur because each thread gets its own stack (therefore all local variables' values are unique to each thread).

Creating UI threads

Creating a UI thread is an altogether different process than creating a worker thread. A worker thread's behavior is defined by its thread function, but a UI thread's behavior is governed by a dynamically createable class derived from CWinThread. The CWinThread class resembles an application class derived from CWinApp. The UI thread class shown in the following code sample creates a top-level frame window that closes itself when clicked with the left mouse button. Closing the window terminates the thread, too, because CWnd::OnNcDestroy posts a WM_QUIT message to the thread's message queue. Posting a WM_QUIT message to a secondary thread ends the thread. Posting a WM_QUIT message to a primary thread ends the thread and ends the application, too.

```
// The CUIThread class
class CUIThread : public CWinThread
{
```

```
    DECLARE_DYNCREATE( CUIThread )

public:
  virtual BOOL InitInstance();

};

IMPLEMENT_DYNCREATE( CUIThread, CWinThread );

BOOL CUIThread::InitInstance()
{
  m_pMainWnd = new CMainWindow();
  m_pMainWnd->ShowWindow( SW_SHOW );
  m_pMainWnd->UpdateWindow();

  return( TRUE );

}

// The CmainWindow class
class CMainWindow : public CFrameWnd
{

public:
  CMainWindow();

protected:
  afx_msg void OnLButtonDown( UINT, CPoint );
  DECLARE_MESSAGE_MAP()

};

BEGIN_MESSAGE_MAP( CMainWindow, CFrameWnd )
  ON_WM_LBUTTONDOWN()
END_MESSAGE_MAP()

CMainWindow::CMainWindow()
{
  Create( NULL, "UI Thread Window" );
}

void CMainWindow::OnLButtonDown( UINT nFlags,
  CPoint Point )
{

  PostMessage( WM_CLOSE, 0, 0 );

}
```

Note the SW_SHOW parameter passed to ShowWindow in place of the normal m_nCmdShow parameter. m_nCmdShow is a CWinApp data member, so when you create a top-level window from a UI thread, it's up to you to specify the window's initial show state.

A CUIThread is launched by calling the form of AfxBeginThread that accepts a CRuntimeClass pointer to the thread class as follows:

```
CWinThread *pThread =
  AfxBeginThread( RUNTIME_CLASS ( CUIThread ) );
```

The UI thread version of AfxBeginThread accepts the same four optional parameters as the worker thread version, but it doesn't accept a pParam value. Once started, a UI thread runs asynchronously with respect to the thread that created it, almost as if it belonged to another application.

Suspending and resuming threads

A running thread can be suspended with CWinThread::SuspendThread and started again with CWinThread::ResumeThread. A thread can call SuspendThread on itself, or another thread can call SuspendThread for it. However, a suspended thread can't call ResumeThread to wake itself up; someone else must call ResumeThread on its behalf. A suspended thread consumes next to no processor time and imposes essentially zero overhead on the system.

For each thread, Windows maintains a suspend count that's incremented by SuspendThread and decremented by ResumeThread. A thread is scheduled for processor time only when its suspend count is 0. If SuspendThread is called twice in succession, ResumeThread must be called twice also. A thread created without a CREATE_SUSPENDED flag is assigned an initial suspend count of 0. A thread created with a CREATE_SUSPENDED flag begins with a suspend count of 1. Both SuspendThread and ResumeThread return the thread's previous suspend count, so you can make sure a thread gets resumed no matter how high its suspend count is by calling ResumeThread repeatedly until it returns 1. ResumeThread returns 0 if the thread it's called on is not currently suspended.

Putting threads to sleep

A thread can put itself to sleep by calling the ::Sleep function. A sleeping thread uses no processor time and is automatically awakened after the number of milliseconds you provide through Sleep's single parameter. The following statement suspends the current thread for ten seconds (10,000 milliseconds):

```
::Sleep(10000);
```

One use for ::Sleep is for implementing threads whose actions are inherently time-based, such as the background thread in an animation control or a thread that moves the hands of a clock. Another use for ::Sleep is for relinquishing the remainder of a thread's timeslice to other threads waiting to execute. The following statement suspends the current thread and allows the scheduler to run other threads of equal priority:

```
::Sleep(0);
```

If no other equal priority threads are awaiting execution time, the function call returns immediately, and the scheduler resumes executing the current thread. If you write an application that uses multiple threads to draw to a display surface, a few strategically placed ::Sleep statements can do wonders for the quality of the output.

Terminating a thread

Once a thread begins, it can terminate in two ways. A worker thread ends when the thread function executes a `return` statement or calls `AfxEndThread`. A UI thread terminates when a `WM_QUIT` message is posted to its message queue or a function within the thread calls `AfxEndThread`. A thread can post a `WM_QUIT` message to itself with the API function `::PostQuitMessage`. `AfxEndThread`, `::PostQuitMessage`, and `return` all accept a 32-bit exit code that can be retrieved with `::GetExitCodeThread` after the thread has terminated. The statement that follows copies the exit code of the thread referenced by `pThread` to the `DWORD` variable `dwExitCode`:

```
DWORD dwExitCode;
::GetExitCodeThread( pThread->m_hThread, &dwExitCode );
```

If called for a thread that's still executing, `::GetExitCodeThread` sets `dwExitCode` equal to `STILL_ACTIVE` (0x103).

Terminating a thread with a thread handle

One complication in calling `::GetExitCode` in an MFC application is that by default a `CWinThread` object automatically deletes itself when the corresponding thread terminates. Therefore, a `::GetExitCodeThread` statement such as the one in the preceding code sample will probably generate an access violation if the thread has terminated because `pThread` will no longer be valid. You can avoid such problems by setting the thread object's `m_bAutoDelete` data member to `FALSE` so that the `CWinThread` object won't be deleted automatically upon thread termination. (Don't forget to delete the `CWinThread` object yourself to avoid memory leaks.)

An alternative approach is to save the thread handle stored in the `CWinThread` object's `m_hThread` data member and pass it to `::GetExitCodeThread` directly. Thread handles passed to `::GetExitCodeThread` can identify existing threads or threads that once existed but have since terminated.

Terminating a thread from another thread

Generally speaking, threads can terminate only themselves. If you want thread A to terminate thread B, you must set up a signaling mechanism that allows thread A to tell thread B to terminate itself. In most cases, a simple variable can serve as a flag that signals a thread to terminate, as demonstrated here:

```
// Thread A
static BOOL bContinue = TRUE;

CWinThread *pThread =
  AfxBeginThread( ThreadFunc, bContinue );

// Do some work

// Tell thread B to terminate
bContinue = FALSE;

// Thread B
UINT ThreadFunc( LPVOID pParam )
```

```
{
  BOOL *pContinue = (BOOL*) pParam;

  while( *pContinue ){
    // Do some work
    }

  return( 0 );

}
```

Conventional wisdom says that this is a poor way for threads to communicate, but in fact it's just as effective as using a thread synchronization object. Of course, to prevent access violations, you need to ensure that bContinue doesn't go out of scope while thread B is running. That's why bContinue is declared static in the example. Even if the function that sets bContinue to FALSE in thread A returns before thread B terminates, the variable will still be valid because it's located in the application's data segment, not on the stack.

Now suppose that you'd like to modify this example so that once it sets bContinue to FALSE, thread A stops what it's doing until thread B is no longer running. Here's the proper way to do it:

```
// Thread A
static BOOL bContinue = TRUE;
CWinThread *pThread =
  AfxBeginThread( ThreadFunc, &bContinue );

// Do some work

// Save the thread handle
HANDLE hThread = pThread->m_hThread;

// Tell thread B to terminate
bContinue = FALSE;

::WaitForSingleObject( hThread, INFINITE );


// Thread B
UINT ThreadFunc( LPVOID pParam )
{
  BOOL *pContinue = (BOOL *) pParam;
  while( *pContinue ){
    // Do some work
    }
  return( 0 );
}
```

::WaitForSingleObject waits until the specified object — in this case, another thread — enters a signaled state. A thread object goes from nonsignaled to signaled when the thread terminates. The first parameter passed to ::WaitForSingleObject is the handle of the object you want to wait on. (It can also be a process handle, the handle of a synchronization object, or a file-change notification handle, among other things.) The handle is retrieved from the CWinThread object before bContinue is set to FALSE because the CWinThread object may no longer exist when the call to ::WaitForSingleObject is executed.

The second parameter is the length of time the thread that calls ::WaitForSingleObject is willing to wait. INFINITE means waiting as long as it takes. When you specify INFINITE, you take the chance that the calling thread could lock up if the object it's waiting on never becomes signaled. You can specify a number of milliseconds instead, as in the following example:

```
::WaitForSingleObject( hThread, 5000 ), WaitForSingleObject()
```

This call returns after the specified time—5 seconds, in this case—has elapsed even if the object still hasn't become signaled. You can check the return value to determine why the function returned. WAIT_OBJECT_0 means that the object became signaled, and WAIT_TIMEOUT means that it did not.

Given a thread handle or a CWinThread object wrapping a thread handle, you can quickly determine whether the thread is still running by calling ::WaitForSingleObject and specifying 0 for the timeout period, as shown here:

```
if (::WaitForSingleObject( hThread, 0 ) ==WAIT_OBJECT_0 )
  // The thread no longer exists
else
  // The thread still exists
```

Called this way, ::WaitForSingleObject doesn't wait; it returns immediately. A return value equal to WAIT_OBJECT_0 means that the thread is signaled (no longer exists), and a return value equal to WAIT_TIMEOUT means that the thread is nonsignaled (still exists). Remember, because a CWinThread object is automatically deleted when a thread terminates, it doesn't make sense to call ::WaitForSingleObject to find out whether a CWinThread is signaled or nonsignaled unless the CWinThread object's m_bAutoDelete data member is set to FALSE. Don't make the mistake of waiting for a thread to terminate by writing code like this:

```
// Thread A (don't do this!)

static BOOL bContinue = TRUE;

CWinThread *pThread =
  AfxBeginThread( ThreadFunc, bContinue );

// Do some work
HANDLE hThread = pThread->m_hThread;

// Save the thread handle
bContinue = FALSE;

// Tell thread B to terminate
DWORD dwExitCode;
do{
  ::GetExitCodeThread( hThread, &dwExitCode );
  } while( dwExitCode == STILL_ACTIVE );

// Thread B
UINT ThreadFunc( LPVOID pParam )
{
  BOOL *pContinue = (BOOL*) pParam;

  while( *pContinue ){
    // Do some work
```

```
    }

  return( 0 );

  }
```

In addition to spending CPU time needlessly by forcing the primary thread to spin in a do-while loop, this code will probably cause the application to lock up. When a thread calls ::WaitForSingleObject, it waits very efficiently because it is effectively suspended until the function call returns. The thread is said "to be blocked" or "to block" until ::WaitForSingleObject returns.

A thread can kill another directly, but you should use this method only as a last resort. The statement ::TerminateThread(pThread -> m_hThread, 0); terminates pThread and assigns it an exit code of 0. The Win32 API Reference documents some of the many problems ::TerminateThread can cause, which range from orphaned thread synchronization objects to DLLs that don't get a chance to execute normal thread-shutdown code.

Threads, processes, and priorities

The thread scheduler is the component of the operating system that decides which threads run when and for how long. Thread scheduling is a complex task whose goal is to divide CPU time among multiple threads of execution as efficiently as possible to create the illusion that all of them are running at once. On machines with multiple CPUs, Windows NT (and above) really does run two or more threads at the same time by assigning different threads to different processors. This feature is known as *symmetric multiprocessing*, or SMP. Windows 98 is not an SMP system, so it schedules all of its threads on the same CPU even if several CPUs are present.

The Windows 98 thread scheduler uses a variety of techniques to improve multitasking performance and to try to ensure that each thread in the system gets an ample amount of CPU time, but ultimately the decision about which thread should execute next boils down to the thread with the highest priority. At any given moment, each thread is assigned a priority level from 0 through 31, with higher numbers indicating higher priorities. If a priority-16 thread is waiting to execute and all of the other threads vying for CPU time have priority levels of 15 or less, the priority-16 thread gets scheduled next. If two priority-16 threads are waiting to execute, the scheduler executes the one that has executed before the other. When that thread's timeslice is up, the other priority-16 thread gets executed, if all of the other threads still have lower priorities. As a rule, the scheduler always gives the next timeslice to the thread waiting to execute that has the highest priority.

Does this mean that lower priority threads never get executed? Not at all. First, remember that Windows is a message-based operating system. If a thread's message queue is empty when the thread calls ::GetMessage to retrieve a message, the thread blocks until a message becomes available. This gives lower priority threads a chance to execute because blocked threads receive no timeslices. Most UI threads spend the major part of their time blocked on the message queue waiting for input, so as long as a high priority worker thread doesn't monopolize the CPU, even very low priority threads typically get all the CPU time they need. A worker thread never blocks on the message queue because it doesn't process messages.

The thread scheduler also plays a lot of tricks with threads' priority levels to enhance the overall responsiveness of the system and reduce the chance that any thread is starved for CPU time. A thread may have a priority level of 7, but if that thread goes for too long without receiving a timeslice, the scheduler may temporarily boost the thread's priority level to 8 or 9 or even higher to give it a chance to execute. Windows boosts the priorities of all threads that belong to the foreground process to improve the responsiveness of the application in which the user is working, and it boosts a thread's priority even further when the thread has an input message to process.

The system also uses a technique called *priority inheritance* to prevent high priority threads from blocking for too long on synchronization objects owned by low priority threads. For example, if a priority-16 thread tries to access a critical section owned by a priority-10 thread, the scheduler treats the priority-10 thread as if it had priority 16 until the thread releases the critical section. This way, the critical section comes free faster, and the priority-16 thread won't get stuck waiting on a lower priority thread.

How do thread priorities get assigned in the first place? When you call `AfxBeginThread` or `CWinThread::SetThreadPriority`, you specify the relative thread priority value. The `::CreateThread` API function that starts a thread doesn't accept a relative thread priority value. When `AfxBeginThread` starts a thread for you, it calls `SetThreadPriority` after it creates the thread to set the thread's relative priority. The operating system combines the relative priority level with the priority class of the process that owns the thread to compute a base priority level for the thread. The thread's actual priority level — a number from 0 through 31 — varies from moment to moment depending on whether the process that owns it is running in the foreground or the background. The actual priority level is also subject to change from the system's dynamic boosting, but most of the time it stays within 2 or 3 of the base priority level. You can't control boosting (and you wouldn't want to even if you could), but you can control the base priority level by setting the process priority class and the relative thread priority level.

Process priority classes

Most processes begin life with the priority class `NORMAL_PRIORITY_CLASS`. Once started, however, a process can change its priority class by calling `::SetPriorityClass`, which accepts a process handle (obtainable with `::GetCurrentProcess`) and one of the specifiers shown in Table 17-1.

Table 17-1: Relative Thread Priorities

Priority Class	Description
ABOVE_NORMAL_PRIORITY_CLASS	Valid only in Windows 2000, this value specifies that the thread should have a priority above NORMAL_PRIORITY_CLASS, but below HIGH_PRIORITY_CLASS.
BELOW_NORMAL_PRIORITY_CLASS	This priority is valid only on Windows 2000 and indicates a thread priority that is below NORMAL_PRIORITY_CLASS, but above IDLE_PRIORITY_CLASS.
HIGH_PRIORITY_CLASS	The process should receive priority over IDLE_PRIORITY CLASS and NORMAL_ PRIORITY_CLASS processes as well as the Windows 2000-specific ABOVE_NORMAL_PRIORITY_CLASS and BELOW_NORMAL_PRIORITY_CLASS values.

Continued

Table 17-1: *(continued)*

Priority Class	Description
IDLE_PRIORITY CLASS	About as low as it gets, this value specifies that the thread be run only when the processor is in idle mode. An example of this value's usage would be the thread to control a screen saver.
NORMAL_PRIORITY_CLASS	The default process priority class. The process has no special scheduling needs.
REALTIME_PRIORITY_CLASS	The process must have the highest possible priority, and its threads should preempt even threads belonging to HIGH_PRIORITY_CLASS processes.

Most applications don't need to change their priority classes. HIGH_PRIORITY_CLASS and REALTIME_PRIORITY_CLASS processes can severely inhibit the responsiveness of the system and even delay critical system activities, such as flushing of the disk cache, which execute at high priority. One legitimate use for HIGH_PRIORITY_CLASS is for system applications that remain hidden most of the time but pop up a window when a certain input event occurs. These applications impose little overhead on the system while they're blocked waiting for input, but once the input appears, they receive priority over normal applications. REALTIME_PRIORITY_CLASS is provided primarily for the benefit of real-time data acquisition programs that must have the lion's share of the CPU time in order to work properly. IDLE_PRIORITY_CLASS is ideal for screen savers, system monitors, and other low priority applications that operate unobtrusively in the background.

Sharing MFC Objects Among Threads

There are some disadvantages about writing multithreaded MFC applications. As long as threads are written so that they don't call member functions belonging to objects created by other threads, there are few restrictions on what they can do. However, if thread A passes a CWnd pointer to thread B, and thread B calls a member function of that CWnd object, MFC is likely to halt a debug build of the application with an assertion error. A release build might work fine, but then again, it might not. There's also a possibility in this situation that a debug build won't assert, but that it won't work properly, either. It all depends on what goes on inside the framework when that particular CWnd member function is called. You can avoid a potential minefield of problems by compartmentalizing your threads and having each thread create the objects it uses rather than rely on objects created by other threads. However, for cases in which that's simply not practical, here are a few rules to go by.

First, many MFC member functions can be safely called on objects in other threads. Most of the inline functions defined in the .inl files in MFCs include directory can be called through object pointers passed in from other threads because they are little more than wrappers around API functions. However, calling a non-inline member function is asking for trouble. For example, the following code, which passes a CWnd pointer named pWnd from thread A to thread B and has B call CWnd::GetParent through the pointer, works without problems:

```
CWinThread *pThread =
  AfxBeginThread( ThreadFunc, (LPVOID) pWnd );

UINT ThreadFunc( LPVOID pParam )
{
```

```
   CWnd *pWnd = (CWnd *) pParam;
   CWnd *pParent = pWnd->GetParent();

   return( 0 );

}

CWinThread *pThread =
  AfxBeginThread( ThreadFunc, pWnd);

UINT ThreadFunc( LPVOID pParam )
{
   CWnd *pWnd = (CWnd *) pParam;
   // Get ready for an assertion error!
   CWnd *pParent = pWnd->GetParentFrame();

   return( ) );
}
```

Why does `GetParent` work when `GetParentFrame` doesn't? Because `GetParent` calls through almost directly to the `::GetParent` function in the API. No problem there; `m_hWnd` is valid because it's part of the `CWnd` object that pWnd points to, and `FromHandle` converts the HWND returned by `GetParent` into a CWnd pointer.

Now consider what happens when you call `GetParentFrame`. The line that causes the assertion error is `ASSERT_VALID(this)`. `ASSERT_VALID` calls `CWnd::AssertValid`, which performs a sanity check by making sure that the HWND associated with `this` appears in the permanent or temporary handle map the framework uses to convert HWNDs into CWnds. Going from a CWnd to a HWND is easy because the HWND is a data member of the class, but going from an HWND to a CWnd can be done only through the handle maps. Here's the problem: Handle maps are local to each thread and are not visible to other threads. If the CWnd whose address is passed to `ASSERT_VALID` was created by another thread, the corresponding HWND won't appear in the current thread's permanent or temporary handle map and MFC will assert. Many of MFC's non-inline member functions call `ASSERT_VALID`, but inline functions do not — at least not in current releases.

MFC's assertions frequently protect you from calling functions that wouldn't work anyway. In a release build, `GetParentFrame` returns NULL when called from a thread other than the one in which the parent frame was created. However, in cases in which assertion errors are spurious — that is, in cases in which the function would work okay despite the per-thread handle tables — you can avoid assertions by passing real handles instead of object pointers. For example, it's safe to call `CWnd::GetTopLevelParent` in a secondary thread if `FromHandle` is called first to create an entry in the thread's temporary handle map, as shown here:

```
CWinThread *pThread =
  AfxEeginThread( ThreadFunc, (LPVOID) pWnd->m_hWnd );

UINT ThreadFunc( LPVOID pParam )
{
   CWnd *pWnd = CWnd::FromHandle( (HWND) pParam );
   CWnd *pParent = pWnd->GetTopLevelParent();

   return( ) );

}
```

That's why the MFC documentation warns that windows, GDI objects, and other objects should be passed between threads by means of handles instead of by means of pointers to MFC objects. In general, you'll have fewer problems if you pass handles instead of object pointers and then use `FromHandle` to *re-create* objects in the temporary handle map of the current thread. But don't take that to mean that just any function will work. It won't.

What about calling member functions belonging to objects created from pure MFC classes such as `CDocument` and `CRect`—classes that don't wrap the `HWND`, `HDC`, or other handle types and therefore don't rely on handle maps? Just what you wanted to hear: Some work and some don't. There's no problem with this code:

```
CWinThread *pThread =
  AfxBeginThread( ThreadFunc, pRect );

UINT ThreadFunc( LPVOID pParam )
{
  CRect *pRect = (CRect *) pParam;
  int nArea = pRect->Width() * pRect->Height();

  return( 0 );

}
```

The following code will assert on you:

```
CWinThread *pThread =
  AfxBeginThread( ThreadFunc, pDoc );

UINT ThreadFunc( LPVOID pParam )
{
  CMyDocument *pDoc = (CMyDocument *) pParam;
  PDoc->UpdateAllViews( NULL );

  return( 0 );

}
```

Even seemingly innocuous functions frequently don't work when they're called from secondary threads. The bottom line is that before you call member functions of MFC objects created in other threads, you must understand the implications. The only way to understand the implications is to study the MFC source code to see how a particular member function behaves. Also keep in mind that MFC isn't *thread-safe,* a subject discussed later in this chapter. So even if a member function appears to be safe, ask yourself what might happen if an object created by thread A were accessed by thread B and thread A preempted thread B in the middle of the access. This is incredibly difficult stuff to sort out and only adds to the complexity of writing multithreaded applications. Avoid crossing thread boundaries with calls to MFC member functions, and you'll avoid a lot of problems, too.

Using C Runtime Functions in Multithreaded Applications

Certain functions in the standard C runtime library pose problems for multithreaded applications. `strtok`, `time`, and many other C runtime functions use global variables to store intermediate data. If thread A calls one of these functions, and thread B preempts thread A and calls the same function, global data stored by thread A could be overwritten by global data stored by thread B. Most modern C and C++ compilers come with two versions of the C runtime library: one that's thread-safe (can be called into by multiple concurrent threads) and one that isn't. The thread-safe versions of the runtime library typically won't rely on thread synchronization objects. Instead, they store intermediate values in per-thread data structures. Visual C++ comes with six versions of the C runtime library. Which one your application uses will be predicated on a combination of factors, including whether you're compiling a debug build or a release build, whether you want to link with the C runtime library statically or dynamically, and, of course, whether your application is single threaded or multithreaded.

Multithreaded Demo Application

In this demo application, I'm going to show you how to use threads in an MDI application where each view will have its own thread draw a spirograph pattern in the view's client area. Therefore, if you open four windows, you will see four simultaneously running threads all drawing these designs in their respective threads. Therefore, create a new MDI project called MTSpirograph and let's get started.

First, create a couple of member variables for the view to keep track of its child thread. Open the MTSpirograph.h file and add the following member variables:

```
class CMTSpirographView : public CView
{
...
public:
 CWinThread *m_pThread;
 BOOL m_bKillThread;
...
}
```

Now modify the view's constructor to initialize those variables as follows:

```
CMTSpirographView::CMTSpirographView()
{
 // NULL the pointer to the thread so
 // you know it hasn't been created.
 m_pThread = NULL;

 // This is the flag that tells the
 // thread to quit.
 m_bKillThread = FALSE;
}
```

As you learned in Chapter 2, view classes have a virtual function called OnDraw that enables you to draw your content to the client area of the view if needed. Therefore, at this time, locate the CMTSpirographView::OnDraw function and add the following code to create a data structure (more on how this is used shortly) and to spawn a new worker thread, passing it the data structure. Notice that because OnDraw is called each time the client area has been invalidated, you need to make sure that the thread is only spawned once.

```
void CMTSpirographView::OnDraw(CDC* pDC)
{
 CMTSpirographDoc* pDoc = GetDocument();
 ASSERT_VALID(pDoc);
 if (pDoc)
 {
```

```
// If the m_pThread is NULL, you need to kick
// off the thread.
if (NULL == m_pThread)
{
  // Store the window handle and the Kill flag.
  m_ThreadInfo.hWnd = m_hWnd;
  m_ThreadInfo.lpKillThread = &m_bKillThread;

  // Start the thread.
  m_pThread = AfxBeginThread(ThreadProc,
                             (LPVOID)&m_ThreadInfo);
}
}
}
```

Before you get into the actual thread function (which is a bit complex because of the GDI drawing of the spirograph), modify the view's destructor so that when the view is destroyed, the thread will also be terminated. Notice that the thread function is monitoring a value (m_BKillThread) that you set to TRUE. When the thread function sees this value is true, it will return, thereby terminating the thread. In order to give it time to end gracefully, I employ use of the ::WaitForSingleObject function that you learned about earlier.

```
CMTSpirographView::~CMTSpirographView()
{
  // Get the thread handle into local space since
  // the thread will delete itself.
  HANDLE hThread = m_pThread->m_hThread;

  // Set the flag to kill the thread to TRUE;
  m_bKillThread = TRUE;

  // Wait for the thread to end.
  ::WaitForSingleObject(hThread, 5000);
}
```

Now, you need only to code the actual thread function itself. Because you'll be using functions from the C math library such as cos and sin, add the following include directive to the top of the MTSpirographView.cpp file.

```
#include <math.h>
```

At this point, you can add the code that draws the pattern in the view. Make sure to place this function before it is referenced in the view's OnDraw function, or define a prototype for it. As I've done throughout this book, I've tried to be quite liberal with my comments throughout the function in order to explain the code.

```
UINT ThreadProc(LPVOID lpParam)
{
  // Get a THREAD_INFO pointer from the
  // parameter that was passed in.
  THREAD_INFO *lpThreadInfo = (THREAD_INFO*)lpParam;

  // The next six variables represent
  // values used to draw the spirograph;
  unsigned char red, green, blue;
  int nFixedRadius = 80;
```

```
int nMovingRadius = 10;
int nMovingOffset = 70;

// Begin colors based on the system time. This
// makes the color somewhat random.
red = (unsigned char)(GetTickCount() & 0x000000ff);
green = (unsigned char)((GetTickCount() & 0x00000ff0) >> 4);
blue = (unsigned char)((GetTickCount() & 0x0000ff00) >> 8);

while (FALSE == *lpThreadInfo->lpKillThread)
{
 // Get a DC for the window.
 HDC hdc = ::GetDC(lpThreadInfo->hWnd);

 // Get the client rect so you can
 // calculate the center point.
 RECT rect;
 ::GetClientRect(lpThreadInfo->hWnd, &rect);
 int nMidx = rect.right / 2;
 int nMidy = rect.bottom / 2;

 // Clear the window.
 ::InvalidateRect(lpThreadInfo->hWnd, NULL, TRUE);
 ::UpdateWindow(lpThreadInfo->hWnd);

 // Create a pen based on the color. Select it
 // into the DC and remember the old pen so
 // you can select it back in later.
 HPEN hPen, hOldPen;
 hPen = ::CreatePen(PS_SOLID, 1, RGB(red, green, blue));
 hOldPen = (HPEN)::SelectObject(hdc, hPen);

 // Iterate through a bunch of times and
 // draw the spirograph.
 int prevx, prevy, x = 0, y = 0;
 for(int i=0; i<=500; i++)
 {
  // Remember x and y.
  prevx = x;
  prevy = y;

  // Calculate the new x and y.
  x = (int) ((nFixedRadius + nMovingRadius)
    * cos((double) i) - (nMovingRadius + nMovingOffset)
    * cos((double)(((nFixedRadius + nMovingRadius)
    / nMovingRadius) * i)));

  y = (int) ((nFixedRadius + nMovingRadius)
    * sin((double) i) - (nMovingRadius + nMovingOffset)
    * sin((double)(((nFixedRadius + nMovingRadius)
    / nMovingRadius) * i)));

  // Draw the line (or move to the first
  // point if this is the first time through).
```

```
  if (i > 0)
  {
   ::LineTo(hdc, x + nMidx, y + nMidy);
  }
  else
  {
   ::MoveToEx(hdc, x + nMidx, y + nMidy, NULL);
  }
 }

 // Increment the color variables so
 // that the colors move around.
 red += 6;
 green += 5;
 blue += 4;

 // Increase the fixed radius and
 // limit it to a max of 150.
 nFixedRadius++;
 if(nFixedRadius > 170)
 {
  nFixedRadius = 90;
 }

 // Increase the moving radius and
 // limit it to a max of 120.
 nMovingRadius++;
 if(nMovingRadius > 40)
 {
  nMovingRadius = 10;
 }

 // Increase the moving offset and
 // limit it to a max of 90.
 nMovingOffset++;
 if(nMovingOffset > 100)
 {
  nMovingOffset = 70;
 }

 // Select the old pen into the DC,
 // delete the pen you created, and
 // release the DC you got.
 ::SelectObject(hdc, hOldPen);
 ::DeleteObject(hPen);
 ::ReleaseDC(lpThreadInfo->hWnd, hdc);

 // Sleep so you don't chew up too
 // much CPU time.
 Sleep(200);
 }

 return(0);
}
```

Now build and execute your multithreaded, spirograph-drawing application. If all goes well, your results should look similar to those shown in Figure 17-2.

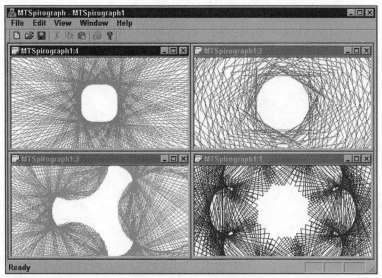

Figure 17-2: This multithreaded spirograph-drawing demo application shows some of the basics of starting and controlling threads.

One of the things you can learn from the spirograph demo application is that there's no such thing as a free lunch — at least not when doing multithreaded programming. When several threads are running, the designs are drawn much more slowly. Any thread that performs a task consumes CPU cycles. The more threads you have running, the more processor time required.

With clever planning, however, you can avoid unnecessary system slowdowns as discussed earlier. Using ::Sleep to yield to other threads is a polite and efficient way of making sure a thread doesn't hog CPU time.

Summary

In this chapter, you went from a basic crash course on the use of threads to learning how to spawn and control both UI and worker threads. Hopefully along the way, you've also discovered that while threads might seem daunting at first, once you've take care to ensure that you know what you're doing when using them, they can aid you tremendously in making your applications run smoother and more efficiently.

✦   ✦   ✦

Exception Handling

Exceptions are error conditions that arise when the normal flow of a program is impractical. Both hardware and software can generate exceptions. Hardware exceptions include dividing by zero and the overflow of a numeric type. Software exceptions include the inability of an application to allocate memory or open a disk file. An example of a software exception can be seen with the `CFile` class. If the `CFile` class is used to open a disk file and the file cannot be opened, an exception of type `CFileException` is *thrown*, and the `CFileException` object contains the specific information as to why the opening of the file failed. The function that called the `CFile::Open` function is then responsible for deciding what to do based on the information contained within the exception object. Therefore, *exception handling* is the handling of these scenarios in an orderly and controlled manner. Because the Microsoft Visual C++ compiler implements the C++ exception-handling model based on ISO WG21/ANSI X3J16, the term exception handling in this chapter should be understood as referring to C++ exception handling.

One important thing to note here is that exception handling should not be used to handle "normal" or "expected" errors that the application should be capable of recovering from quite easily. Because functions exist to test for the existence of a file before attempting to open it, the programmer in the example mentioned previously would naturally have expected to be able to open the specified file. The fact that the file could not be opened represents an unexpected or abnormal condition, and in all likelihood, the function that attempted to open the file in the first place would not be capable of continuing with its task. Therefore, exception handling should be used in this case. Software exceptions and C++ exception handling within the context of a Visual C++ application are the topics of this chapter.

After you learn the syntax of exception handling, exception handling will be compared to the more standard method of using return codes to signal error conditions. Once you have seen the benefits that exception handling has over other error-handling techniques, I'll introduce the `CException` class, as well as a demo that illustrates how to handle exceptions returned from the `CFileException` class. Because some functions can throw many exception types, I use several examples to fully cover the subject of how to define and implement a single exception class. The chapter then finishes by presenting several advanced exception-handling issues and techniques.

Structured Exception Handling

All 32-bit versions of Windows support a form of exception handling at the operating system level called *structured exception handling* (SEH). SEH provides exception handling for almost any programming language, even when the language itself does not directly support it. However, in the documentation concerning exception handling that is provided on MSDN, Microsoft states the following regarding C++ exception handling versus SEH:

> Although structured exception handling can also be used with C++, the new C++ exception-handling method should be used for C++ programs.

For more information on structured exception handling, you can refer to the "Adding Program Functionality" section of the *Visual C++ Programmer's Guide*. This guide can be found in the library edition of the MSDN.

Exception-Handling Syntax

Exception-handling syntax consists of only three keywords: try, catch, and throw. In exception handling, there are two participants: a server function that is *throwing* the exception, and a client function that is *catching* the exception.

Throwing the exception

When a function reports the fact that an exception has occurred, it throws an exception using the following syntax:

```
throw assignment-expression
```

The manner in which the throw statement is called is similar to the C/C++ return statement. In C++, the preceding *assignment-expression* can be any type. For example, a function can throw a char pointer as follows:

```
void GetBuffer(char** ppBuffer, unsigned int uiSize)
{
 *ppBuffer = NULL;
 *ppBuffer = new char(uiSize);
 if (NULL == *ppBuffer)
 {
  throw "Memory Error: Could not allocate memory";
 }
}
```

However, because MFC provides a base class called CException, this chapter will concentrate on throwing and catching exceptions of type CException as well as classes that are derived from CException. Using the CException class and developing your own CException-derived classes will be covered shortly.

Catching the exception

Because a called function can throw an exception, the calling function must be capable of responding to this event. This is done via the catch statement. In order to catch an exception, you need to bracket your code in a `try` block and specify which types of exceptions the code within that `try` block is capable of handling. All of the statements in the `try` block will be processed in order as usual unless an exception is thrown by one of the functions being called. If that happens, control is passed to the first line of the appropriate `catch` block. Using the previous example, this is how a calling function might appear:

```
#include <iostream.h>

int main()
{
 char* pBuffer;
 try
 {
  GetBuffer(&pBuffer, 512);
  cout << pBuffer;
 }
 catch(char* szException)
 {
  cout << szException;
 }

 return 0;
}
```

As you are aware, if your function attempted to call the `cout` function with an invalid `char` pointer, your application would probably receive some type of Access Validation error. However, in the preceding example, if the string buffer could not be allocated by the `GetBuffer` function, an exception would have been thrown by `GetBuffer` and caught in main's `catch` block. Therefore, in the event that the memory could not be allocated, the `cout` function would not be executed.

So what happens if a called function throws an exception, and it is not caught by the calling function? This depends on the design of the application. When an exception is thrown, control is passed back up the call stack until a function is located that has a `catch` block for the type of exception being thrown. If a function with the appropriate `catch` block is not located, the application aborts. Therefore, if you write a function that calls another function that can throw an exception and your function doesn't catch that exception, you must be sure that some function in the call stack does handle the exception.

Another important point about catching exceptions is how to catch multiple types of exceptions. Simply adding a `catch` block for every exception type that will be caught accomplishes this. Another way to handle catching multiple exceptions types in C++ is to define a `catch` block for the base class of all the exceptions that can be thrown and use C++ RTTI (runtime type information) to figure out which exception was thrown. That way, your function needs to contain only a single `catch` block. Because the MFC exception classes have special support for the runtime checking of MFC class types, this topic is covered in more detail in the section "The CException Class," later in this chapter.

Now that you know how easy it is to syntactically implement exception handling, let's take a look at why you would want to use exception handling as opposed to the more familiar approach of returning error codes to signal error conditions.

Comparing Error-Handling Techniques

The standard approach to error handling typically has been to return an error code to the calling function. The calling function is then left with the responsibility of deciphering the returned value and acting accordingly. The return value can be as simple as a basic C/C++ type or a pointer to a C++ class. More elaborately designed error-handling techniques involve the called function returning a simple value that signifies that an error has occurred. These systems then also incorporate a global function to retrieve the error information about the error. However, the concept is still the same: The calling function in some way calls a function and must inspect a returned value to verify the success or failure of the function that was called. This approach is severely flawed in a number of important ways. What follows are a few of the areas where exception handling provides tremendous benefits over using return codes.

Dealing with error codes

When you use return codes, the called function returns an error code, and the error condition is handled by the calling function. Because the error handling occurs outside the scope of the called function, there is no guarantee that the caller will check the returned error code. As an example, suppose you write a class called `CCommaDelimitedFile` that wraps the functionality of reading and writing comma-delimited files. Among other things, your class would have to expose functions to open the file and read data from the file. When you use the older return code method of reporting errors, these functions would return some variable type that would have to be checked by the caller in order to verify the success of the function call. If the user of your class calls the `CCommaDelimitedFile::Open` function and then attempts to call the `CCommaDelimitedFile::Read` function without checking whether or not the open succeeded, this could lead to undesired results. However, if the class's `Open` function throws an exception, the caller would be forced to deal with the fact that the open failed. This is because anytime a function throws an exception, control is passed back up the call stack until it is caught. Here's an example of what that code might look like:

```
try
{
  CCommaDelimitedFile file;
  file.Open("c:\\test.csv");

  CString strFirstLine;
  file.Read(strFirstLine);
}
catch(CException* pe)
{
  AfxMessageBox("Exception caught");
}
```

As you can see, if either the `CCommaDelimitedFile::Open` or the `CCommaDelimitedFile::Read` function throws an exception, the calling function is forced to deal with it. If this function does not catch the exception and no other function in the current code path attempts to catch an exception of this type, the application aborts. Pay particular attention to the fact that because both the `Open` and `Read` functions were placed in the same `try` block, an invalid read would not be attempted if an exception was thrown. This is because programmatic control is passed from the `Open` call `try` block to the first line of the `catch` block. Therefore, exception handling ensures that a failure in a called function cannot be ignored.

Handling errors in the correct context

The calling function often does not have enough information to handle the error. This is perhaps the biggest advantage to using exception handling. If Function A calls Function B to carry out a very simple task, it is easy to deal with an error code. However, what if Function B calls Function C, which then calls Function D and Function E? How can Function A deal with the fact that an error occurred several function layers down? Let's take a look at an example that better illustrates the problem.

In this example, a class (CAccessDb) is used to generate and manipulate Microsoft Access databases. Suppose this class has a static function called GenerateDb. Because the GenerateDb function would be used to create new Microsoft Access databases, it would have to perform several tasks to create the database. For example, it would have to create the physical database file, the specified tables (including any rows and columns), and define any necessary indexes and relations. The GenerateDb function may even have to create some default users and permissions. Figure 18-1 illustrates the number of function levels that would be traversed in this example.

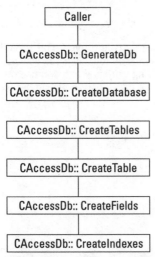

Figure 18-1: Without exception handling, long code paths make it extremely difficult for the calling function to handle returned errors.

The programmatic design problem is that if an error were to occur in the CreateIndexes function, which function would handle it and how? Obviously at some point, the function that originally called the GenerateDb function would have to handle the error, but how could it? It would have no idea how to handle an error that occurred several function calls deep in the code path. The calling function would not be in the correct "context" to handle the error. In other words, the only function that could logically create any meaningful error information about the error is the function that failed. Having said that, if return codes were used in this example, each function in the code path would have to check for every single error code that every single function below it could return. One obvious problem with this is that the calling function would have to handle a ridiculously large number of error codes. In addition, maintenance would be extremely difficult because every time an error condition is added to any of the functions in the code path, every other instance in the application where a function calls it would have to be updated to handle the new error code.

Exception handling resolves all of these issues by enabling the calling function to trap for a given type of exception. In this example, if a class called CAccessDbException was derived from CException, it could be used for any types of errors that occur within any of the CAccessDb member functions. (The CException class will be covered shortly.) Then if the CreateIndexes function failed, it would construct and throw an exception of type CAccessDbException. The calling function would catch that exception and would be capable of inspecting the exception object in order to decipher what exactly went wrong. Therefore, instead of handling every possible type of return code that the GenerateDb and any of its called functions could return, the calling function would be assured that if *any* of the functions in that code path failed, the proper error information would be returned. An additional bonus is that because the error information is contained with a class, new error conditions can be added, and the calling function would remain unchanged.

Improving code readability

When you use exception-handling code, code readability is greatly improved. This directly relates to reduced costs in terms of code maintenance. The reason for this is the way in which return codes are handled versus the exception-handling syntax. When you use return codes with the CAccessDb::GenerateDb function mentioned previously, code similar to the following is required in order to handle error conditions:

```
void CCallingClass::CallingFunction()
{
 if (CAccessDb::GenerateDb())
 {
  ...
 }
 else
 {
   // Somehow figure out which function in the
   // code path failed and why
 }
}

RETURN_CODE CAccessDb::GenerateDb()
{
 if (CreatePhysicalDb())
 {
  if (CreateTables())
  {
   if (CreateIndexes())
   {
    return SUCCESS;
   }
   else
```

```
        {
          // handle error
        }
      }
      else
      {
        // handle error
      }
    }
    else
    {
      // handle error
    }
  }
```

Add a few pointer validations to the preceding code, and you have a tremendous amount of error validation code mixed in with the rest of the code. If you have your editor set to display tabs instead of spaces and the tab value is set to 4 (the Visual Studio default), the first character of a line of code will start around column 20 at times! Although none of this is disastrous for your code, it does make the code more difficult to maintain. Code that is difficult to maintain is code that invites bugs. Let's look at how this same example would look if exception handling was used:

```cpp
void CCallingClass::CallingFunction()
{
  try
  {
    CAccessDb::GenerateDb();
    ...
  }
  catch(CAccessDbException* pe)
  {
    pe->DisplayError();
    pe->Delete();
  }
}

void CAccessDb::GenerateDb() // throws CAccessDbException
{
  CreatePhysicalDb();
  CreateTables();
  CreateIndexes();
}
```

Notice how much cleaner and elegant the second solution is. This is because error detection and recovery code are no longer mixed with the logic of the calling code itself. As you can see, because exception handling has made this code much more straightforward, maintaining this code has been made easier.

Throwing exceptions from constructors

Because constructors cannot return values, exceptions are a great way of signaling that an error has occurred during the construction of an object. Therefore, if you know that the class you are attempting to instantiate throws an exception, you must bracket its construction in a `try` block. This includes scenarios in which you are constructing the object on the stack. Here are two examples of catching exceptions that are thrown during object construction. The first example shows an attempt to construct an object on the heap:

```
try
{
 CTest pTest = new CTest;
}
catch(someexceptiontype)
{
 // handle exception
}
```

The second example shows an attempt to construct an object on the stack:

```
try
{
 CTest Test;
}
catch(someexceptiontype)
{
 // handle exception
}
```

The CException Class

As mentioned earlier, C++ exception handling enables you to catch exceptions of almost any type. However, using C++ classes gives you the benefit of catching an object that includes the information necessary to describe the error condition as well as functions to retrieve that information. MFC provides a set of classes for just this purpose. The base class for all MFC exception classes is called `CException`. The base `CException` class is not very complex at all. In fact, aside from the constructor, the class includes just three functions: `GetErrorMessage`, `ReportError`, and `Delete`.

Creating and deleting CException objects

Although the `CException` class does define functions for *retrieving* information about a specific exception, it does not contain any member variables for *defining* that information. This is because you would normally never instantiate a `CException` object directly. You should use instead one of the MFC `CException`-derived classes, or derive your own exception classes from `CException` and implement the `GetErrorMessage` and `ReportError` virtual member functions.

The `CException` constructor takes as its only argument a `BOOL` value (`m_bAutoDelete`) that represents whether the exception object should automatically be deleted. Setting this value to `TRUE` specifies that the exception object was created on the heap. This causes the exception object to be deleted when the `Delete` member function is called. The only time you should set `m_bAutoDelete` to `FALSE` is when the exception object is created on the stack or when the exception object is a global object. In all but a very few cases, you will set this value to `TRUE`.

As mentioned previously, the CException class provides a member function called Delete for deleting an exception object. Calling this function is very straightforward; however, here are a few guidelines to follow when deleting an exception object:

✦ Never delete an exception object directly using the C++ delete operator. Instead use the CException::Delete function.

✦ If an exception is caught and will be thrown or somehow still used outside the scope of the current catch block, do not delete it.

✦ If an exception is caught and will not be used outside the current catch block, it should be deleted (using the Delete function). This includes scenarios in which an exception of one type is caught and an exception of another type is being thrown. The caught exception should still be deleted if it will no longer be referenced.

Tip   If you are new to the C++ try/catch mechanism and are familiar instead with the MFC TRY/CATCH macros, you are probably wondering why you have to delete the exceptions that your function catches. Actually, you have always had to delete any caught exceptions that were not rethrown. The MFC macros deleted the exception for you "under the hood." However, if you are going to use the C++ try/catch mechanism, you are now responsible for this cleanup.

Retrieving error information from a CException object

The CException class has two functions for retrieving information about the cause of the exception: ReportError and GetErrorMessage. The ReportError function displays a message box indicating the cause of the exception. Because most applications have to format any messages that are displayed to the end user, the ReportError function is normally only used when debugging the application. Here's an example of the ReportError function in use:

```
CStdioFile file;
CFileException fe;

try
{
 file.Open("IKnowThisFileDoesNotExist.txt",
  CFile::typeText | CFile::modeReadWrite,
  &fe);
 file.Close();
}
catch(CFileException* pe)
{
 pe->ReportError();
}
```

In the preceding example, the CFileException class was used. The CFileException class is used for exceptions when dealing with the CFile class and any of its derived classes. This class will be covered in more detail shortly. Also notice that the exception was not deleted. That is because the exception object was constructed on the stack. Therefore, the exception object will be destructed automatically when it goes out of scope.

While the ReportError function displays the exception's description, the GetErrorMessage function returns a textual description of the error that occurred. When calling this function, the application needs to supply an LPTSTR for the description's buffer and a maximum length for the description that will be returned. When the function returns, the description can then be used to do such things as formatting an error message for display or logging the error condition to a file. Using the previous example, here's how you might format a `CFileException` description and display the result to the user:

```
CStdioFile file;
CFileException fe;

try
{
 file.Open("IKnowThisFileDoesNotExist.txt",
  CFile::typeText | CFile::modeReadWrite,
  &fe);
 file.Close();
}
catch(CFileException* pe)
{
 TCHAR szErrorMessage [CHAR_MAX];
 if (pe->GetErrorMessage(szErrorMessage,
  _countof(szErrorMessage)))
 {
  CString strErrorMessage;
  strErrorMessage.Format("File error encountered: %s",
   szErrorMessage);
  AfxMessageBox(strErrorMessage);
 }
}
```

Catching multiple exception types

The functions in a `try` block at times have to catch exceptions that are different from one another. For example, suppose you create a class called `CValidatePtr` that validates pointers. If this class throws an exception, the calling function has to catch it. However, what if in the same `try` block another function is being called that can throw an exception that is not an exception of type `CValidatePtrException`? This scenario can be handled in two ways. The first method, shown in the following example, is to declare multiple `catch` blocks, where each `catch` block exists for the exception type that it is prepared to handle.

```
CTestDlg::OnOk()
{
 try
 {
  CValidatePtrException::ValidatePtr(m_pTestPtr,
   RUNTIME_CLASS(CTestPtr));

  m_pTestPtr->DoSomeThing();
 }
 catch(CValidatePtrException* pe)
 {
  // Do something with this type of exception.
  pe->Delete();
 }
 catch(CTestPtrException* pe)
 {
```

```
   // Do something else with this exception.
   pe->Delete();
  }
```

A second method used to catch multiple exception types from the same try block is to use the IsKindOf function. Because the CException class specifies the DECLARE_DYNAMIC and IMPLEMENT_DYNAMIC macros, the CObject::IsKindOf function can be used to determine what type of exception is thrown. Here is an example of how the IsKindOf function is implemented:

```
CTestDlg::OnOk()
{
 try
 {
  CValidatePtrException::ValidatePtr(m_pTestPtr,
   RUNTIME_CLASS(CTestPtr));

  m_pTestPtr->DoSomeThing();
 }
 catch(CException* pe)
 {
  if (pe->IsKindOf(RUNTIME_CLASS(CValidatePtrException)))
  {
   // Do something with this type of exception.
   pe->Delete();
  }
   else if (pe->IsKindOf(CTestPtrException))
  {
   // Do something else with this exception.
   pe->Delete();
  }
 }
}
```

Defining CException-Derived Classes

As explained earlier, because the CException class does not expose a method of defining the cause of the exception, you must derive a class from CException. The following list shows the MFC-provided exception classes that are derived from CException:

- ✦ CSimpleException
- ✦ CArchiveException
- ✦ CFileException
- ✦ CDaoException
- ✦ CDBException
- ✦ COleException
- ✦ COleDispatchException
- ✦ CInternetException

Although defining your own CException class is not difficult, one of the greatest benefits of using MFC is that you have the MFC source code readily available. And who better to take tips from about deriving a class from an MFC base class than an MFC-derived class! Therefore, before taking a look at how to derive your own class from CException, let's look at how MFC did the same thing with the CFileException class.

Discovering the CFileException class

The CFileException class is used when dealing with the errors associated with the CFile class or any of its derived classes. A CFileException can be thrown as a result of several different error conditions. Among these are conditions such as the specified file not being found, an invalid directory path, and a sharing violation when attempting to access a file.

The CFileException class has to associate a string value for each exception for use in the CFileException::Dump and AfxThrowFileException functions. However, the designers of the CFileException class wanted to make sure that the function instantiating the CFileException would be capable of specifying a numeric value that would represent the cause of the exception. These numeric values are defined in an enum within the CFileException class itself. Because each enum automatically has a number associated with it, a static string array is defined for the CFileException class. That way the textual description of any given CFileException can be found by using the enum value as an index into this static string array. Because this is a good technique for using in your own CException-derived classes, the enum structure and the static string array are listed here:

```
enum {
  none,
  generic,
  fileNotFound,
  badPath,
  tooManyOpenFiles,
  accessDenied,
  invalidFile,
  removeCurrentDir,
  directoryFull,
  badSeek,
  hardIO,
  sharingViolation,
  lockViolation,
  diskFull,
  endOfFile
};

static const LPCSTR rgszCFileExceptionCause[] =
{
  "none",
  "generic",
  "fileNotFound",
  "badPath",
  "tooManyOpenFiles",
  "accessDenied",
  "invalidFile",
```

```
          "removeCurrentDir",
          "directoryFull",
          "badSeek",
          "hardIO",
          "sharingViolation",
          "lockViolation",
          "diskFull",
          "endOfFile",
        };
```

As you can see, each `enum` value matches a specific textual description in the `rgszCFileExceptionCause` static string array. Therefore, when a `CFileException` object is constructed and thrown, it can be done in the following manner:

```
    throw new CFileException(CFileException::fileNotFound);
```

This is a very good example of how to implement specific error types with your exception classes. Actually, however, there is an even better way to deal with situations in which you have to associate a text value with an exception. One point you might have missed in the preceding definition of the static string array was that it is defined only for debug builds. In other words, the `rgszCFileExceptionCause` array is defined only within an `#ifdef _DEBUG/#endif` block. So where does the `CFileException` class get its error descriptions, and how are they associated with the `int` value that is passed to its constructor? The answer is the resource file. Because it has to localize all messages that the user will see, the `CFileException` class stores its error descriptions in the resource file. If you take a peek at how the `CFileException::GetErrorMessage` function is defined, you will see the following:

```
    BOOL CFileException::GetErrorMessage(LPTSTR lpszError,
    UINT nMaxError, PUINT pnHelpContext)
    {
     ASSERT(lpszError != NULL
     && AfxIsValidString(lpszError, nMaxError));

     if (pnHelpContext != NULL)
      *pnHelpContext = m_cause + AFX_IDP_FILE_NONE;

     CString strMessage;
     CString strFileName = m_strFileName;
     if (strFileName.IsEmpty())
      strFileName.LoadString(AFX_IDS_UNNAMED_FILE);
     AfxFormatString1(strMessage,
      m_cause + AFX_IDP_FILE_NONE, strFileName);
     lstrcpyn(lpszError, strMessage, nMaxError);

     return TRUE;
    }
```

The first couple of lines validate the `lpszError` argument's address and set the help context. Next, the filename that was specified when the `CFileException` was constructed is retrieved. If a filename was not passed to the constructor, a string value of "unnamed file" is loaded from the resource file.

Notice the line that calls `AfxFormatString1`. This function formats a `CString` using a string resource identified by the resource ID in the second argument. As you can see, a value identified as `AFX_IDP_FILE_NONE` is used. Actually what is happening here in a release build is much like what happens in a debug build. The only difference is that when you build a debug version of your application, the `enum` value is used as an index into a static string array. In the release build of your application, however, the `enum` value is added to the `AFX_IDP_FILE_NONE` value and used as a string resource ID. That way all of the `CFileException` error descriptions are kept in the MFC DLL for release builds that use the MFC in a shared DLL. For release builds that statically link MFC into their applications, the same resources are compiled into the application.

A CFileException demo program

Here is a demo application that shows the `CFileException` class in action. This demo can be found on the Web site for this book. Because you have seen how the `CFileException` class is defined, the purpose of this demo is to illustrate how easy it is to throw and catch exceptions of this type.

1. Start by using AppWizard to create a dialog-based application called FileExceptionTest. Once the project files have been created, modify `IDD_FILEEXCEPTIONTEST_DIALOG` so that when you are finished it looks like the dialog box in Figure 18-2.

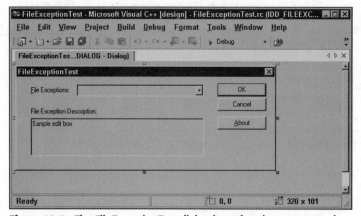

Figure 18-2: The FileExceptionTest dialog box after the new controls have been added

2. After creating the controls on the application's dialog box, use ClassWizard to create a `CString` variable named `m_strFileExceptionDescription` for the File Exception Description edit control. Then create a `CComboBox` variable named `m_cboFileExceptions` for the File Exceptions combo box.

3. Open the `FileExceptionTestDlg.cpp` file, and add the code to the end of the `OnInitDialog` function right before the `return` statement as shown in the following example:

```
static struct
{
int iException;
char szException[25];
```

```
} FILE_EXCEPTIONS[] = {
CFileException::none, "None",
CFileException::generic, "Generic",
CFileException::fileNotFound, "File Not Found",
CFileException::badPath, "Bad Path",
CFileException::tooManyOpenFiles, "Too many open files",
CFileException::accessDenied, "Access denied",
CFileException::invalidFile, "Invalid File",
CFileException::removeCurrentDir, "Remove Current Dir",
CFileException::directoryFull, "Directory Full",
CFileException::badSeek, "Bad Seek",
CFileException::hardIO, "Hard I/O",
CFileException::sharingViolation, "Sharing Violation",
CFileException::lockViolation, "Lock Violation",
CFileException::diskFull, "Disk Full",
CFileException::endOfFile, "End of File",
};

int iIndex;
for (int i = 0; i < sizeof FILE_EXCEPTIONS /
 sizeof FILE_EXCEPTIONS[0]; i++)
{
 iIndex = m_cboFileExceptions.AddString(
  FILE_EXCEPTIONS[i].szException);
 m_cboFileExceptions.SetItemData(iIndex,
  (DWORD)FILE_EXCEPTIONS[i].iException);
}
```

4. Next, use ClassWizard to add a handler for the CBN_SELCHANGE notification message for the combo box (IDC_COMBO1). This function calls the DisplayFileException function every time a file exception cause is selected from the combo box:

```
void CFileExceptionTestDlg::OnSelchangeCombo1()
{
 try
 {
  DisplayFileException();
  AfxMessageBox("We should never get here!");
 }
 catch(CFileException* pe)
 {
  char sz[255];
  pe->GetErrorMessage(sz, 255);

  m_strFileExceptionDescription = sz;
  UpdateData(FALSE);

  pe->Delete();
 }
}
```

5. Now implement the DisplayFileException function as follows. As you can see, this function simply uses the selected combo box entry's item data (set in the OnInitDialog function) to determine which type of exception should be thrown.

```
void CFileExceptionTestDlg::DisplayFileException()
{
 int iIndex;
 if (CB_ERR != (iIndex =
 m_cboFileExceptions.GetCurSel()))
 {
 int iFileException =
 m_cboFileExceptions.GetItemData(iIndex);
 throw new CFileException(iFileException);
 }
}
```

6. Building and running the demo application at this point should show results similar to Figure 18-3.

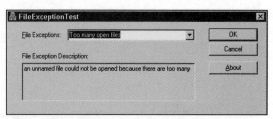

Figure 18-3: The FileExceptionTest demo application demonstrates throwing and catching exceptions of type CFileException.

Defining your own CException-derived classes

Now that you know how CFileException is designed, it's time to see how to derive your own exception classes from CException. Begin by imagining a real-life scenario in which you would use exceptions. Suppose you are developing a distribution system that has a few maintenance dialog boxes such as a dialog box for maintaining customers. According to the principles of effective object-oriented design, the customer maintenance dialog box would contain a pointer to the customer being created or edited on the dialog box. When the user chooses to save the customer, the dialog box would call UpdateData(TRUE) and then call the CCustomer::Save function.

In keeping with the MFC technique of having a CFileException class that is used for all exceptions that occur with CFile objects, create an exception class called CCustomerException (derived from CException) that is used in conjunction with the CCustomer class.

Notice the const int CUSTOMER_EXCEPTION_STRING_RESOURCE definition. This would be used just like the AFX_IDP_FILE_NONE value is used in the CFileException::GetError Message function. In other words, the m_iCause member variable would be added to this value, and the result would be used as the string resource ID in order to retrieve the exception description at runtime.

```
const int CUSTOMER_EXCEPTION_STRING_RESOURCE = 1000;

class CCustomerException : public CException
{
DECLARE_DYNAMIC(CCustomerException)
```

```
public:
 CCustomerException(int iCause);
protected:
 int m_iCause;

public:
 enum
 {
  causeDuplicateCustomer = 0,
  causeInvalidTermsCode,
  causeInvalidSupplierCode
 }
public:
 virtual BOOL GetErrorMessage(LPTSTR lpszError,
   UINT nMaxError, PUINT pnHelpContext = NULL);
};
```

Functions that use the CCustomer class can now simply catch exceptions of type
CCustomerException and call its member functions in order to display or retrieve the
cause of the error.

```
CCustomerMaintenanceDlg::OnOK()
{
 try
 {
  if (UpdateData(TRUE))
  {
   m_pCustomer->Save();
   CDialog::OnOK();
  }
 }
 catch(CCustomerException* pe)
 {
  TCHAR szErrorMessage[CHAR_MAX];
  if (pe->GetErrorMessage(szErrorMessage,
  _countof(szErrorMessage)))
  {
   AfxMessageBox(strErrorMessage);
  }

  pe->Delete();
 }
}
```

However, now a couple of problems with this approach arise. First, you would need to create
a new exception class for every class in the system that would have to signal an exception. In
a very large system, this could be a ridiculously large number of classes and files to maintain.
The second problem is that if you created a different class for every exception with the only
difference in their class declarations being the values of an enum structure, you definitely
would not be following effective object-oriented design techniques. In other words, you
should declare a new class type only when a class does not exist that exhibits the same
behavior that is needed. Therefore, there must be a better way of defining exceptions for the
entire system without having an exception class for each one. Actually, there is a very simple
way to do this.

Start by examining a class that is itself derived from CException: the CSimpleException class. This class is said to be a "resource critical" exception because it is based on string resources. Actually, yet another level of abstraction has to be traversed. Although the CSimpleException class does declare a member variable to hold a string resource ID, it does not declare a function to set that resource ID. However, the CUserException class (derived from CSimpleException) does provide a constructor that takes as one of its arguments the string resource ID. That way, when the GetErrorMessage function (inherited from the CSimpleException base class) is called, the appropriate string resource that represents the cause of the exception is loaded. This is how the CSimpleException::GetErrorMessage function is implemented:

```
BOOL CSimpleException::GetErrorMessage(LPTSTR lpszError,
  UINT nMaxError, PUINT pnHelpContext)
{
ASSERT(lpszError != NULL
&& AfxIsValidString(lpszError, nMaxError));

if (pnHelpContext != NULL)
 *pnHelpContext = 0;

// If you didn't load your string (eg, you're a
// console app) return a null string and FALSE.

if (!m_bInitialized)
 InitString();

if (m_bLoaded)
 lstrcpyn(lpszError, m_szMessage, nMaxError);
else
 lpszError[0] = '\0';

return m_bLoaded;
}

void CSimpleException::InitString()
{
m_bInitialized = TRUE;
m_bLoaded = (AfxLoadString(m_nResourceID,
m_szMessage, _countof(m_szMessage)) != 0);
}
```

Now instead of creating a new exception class for every class that needs to throw an exception, your application can construct a CUserException object with the correct string resource ID and throw it. To see just how easy this is to implement, let's take a look at some code that illustrates two example classes that can throw exceptions: CCustomer and CSupplier. Because the CUserException does most of the work, all you have to do is define the exception causes in the CCustomer and CSupplier class declarations. The code looks like this:

```
class CCustomer : public CObject
{
...
public:
 enum
 {
```

```
  causeDuplicateCustomer = 1000,
  causeInvalidTermsCode = 1001,
  causeInvalidSupplierCode = 1002
...
};

class CSupplier : public CObject
{
enum
 {
  causeDuplicateSupplier = 2000,
  causeInvalidDiscountRate = 2001
};
```

Using this approach, you have to catch only one exception class for all of the error conditions in your application. At this point, you only have to create the string resources with the IDs that you specify in the different class's enum structures. The CCustomerMaintenanceDlg::OnOK function from the preceding code would now look as follows:

```
CCustomerMaintenanceDlg::OnOK()
{
 try
 {
  if (UpdateData(TRUE))
  {
   m_pCustomer->Save();
   CDialog::OnOK();
  }
 }
 catch(CUserException* pe)
 {
  TCHAR szErrorMessage[CHAR_MAX];
  if (pe->GetErrorMessage(szErrorMessage,
   _countof(szErrorMessage)))
  {
   AfxMessageBox(szErrorMessage);
  }

  pe->Delete();
 }
}
```

Advanced Exception-Handling Techniques

So far the basic concepts of using exception handling and the semantics related to throwing and catching exceptions have been covered, and a few of the MFC classes that make doing all of this very easy were discovered. However, now that you understand the basics, some very important questions still remain.

Suppose Function A calls Function B, which in turn calls Function C. If Function C can advertise the fact that it can throw a particular kind of exception, does Function B have to catch it even though it won't, or can't, do anything with it? How should code be split with regards to the try and catch blocks? Are there special considerations for throwing exceptions from virtual functions? Let's take a look at these issues while delving a little more deeply into how to make exception handling work and deliver on its promise of making your code tighter.

Deciding what function should catch an exception

Now you know how to catch an exception that a called function may throw, and you know that control passes up the call stack until an appropriate catch block is found. The question is, Should a try block catch every possible exception that a function within it may throw? The answer to that is no. As mentioned earlier, two of the biggest benefits of using exception handling in your application are reduced coding and lower maintenance cost. Here's an example to illustrate that point:

```cpp
#include <iostream.h>

int main()
{
 try
 {
  PerformWork()
  cout << "Program terminated without any problems";
 }
 catch(char* szException)
 {
  cout << szException;
 }

 return 0;
}
void PerformWork()
{
 try
 {
  char* pBuffer;
  GetBuffer(&pBuffer, 512);
  cout << pBuffer;
 }
 catch(char* szException)
 {
  throw szException;
 }
}
void GetBuffer(char** ppBuffer, unsigned int uiSize)
{
 *ppBuffer = NULL;
 *ppBuffer = new char(uiSize);
 if (NULL == *ppBuffer)
 {
  throw "Memory Error: Could not allocate memory";
 }
}
```

As you can see, the `PerformWork` function catches the exception that `GetBuffer` might throw even though it doesn't do anything with the exception except rethrow it. The `main` function then catches the rethrown exception and truly handles it by doing something (in this case displaying an error message). Following are a few reasons why functions that simply rethrow an exception shouldn't catch the exception to begin with:

✦ Because the function doesn't do anything with the exception, you would be left with a `catch` block in the function that is at best superfluous. Obviously, it's never a good idea to have code in a function simply for the sake of its existence.

✦ If the exception type being thrown by the `GetBuffer` function changes, you would have to go back and change both the `main` function and the `PerformWork` function. This results in an increased maintenance cost for the system.

✦ Doing this enough times in a large application can degrade your system performance. This is because during the process of an exception being handled, every function in the stack would be returned to in order for it to simply rethrow the exception back up the call stack.

Because C++ automatically continues up the call stack until a function catches the exception, intermediate functions can ignore the exceptions that it cannot process. Recall that if a function with the appropriate `catch` block is not located, the application aborts.

Deciding what code to put in a try block

Determining what code to put in a `try` block is often really a stylistic issue. Normally you would only put code in a `try` block whose operation could result in an exception being thrown. However, many programmers tend to put almost the entire function in a `try` block for reasons of readability. Therefore, you will routinely see code like the following:

```
void SomeClass::SomeFunction(CWnd* pWnd)
{
 try
 {
  CString strWindowText;
  pWnd->GetWindowText(strWindowText);

  m_pRecord->Save(strWindowText);

  ...
 }
 catch(CException* pe)
 {
  pe->ReportError();
  pe->Delete();
 }
}
```

As you can see in the `SomeClass::SomeFunction` function, the first two lines of code to define a `CString` object and to retrieve text from a window don't have anything to do with the possibility of the Save function throwing an exception. Therefore, these two lines of code could have been placed before the `try` block like this:

```
void SomeClass::SomeFunction(CWnd* pWnd)
{
 CString strWindowText;
 pWnd->GetWindowText(strWindowText);

 try
 {
  m_pRecord->Save(strWindowText);

  ...
 }
 catch(CException* pe)
 {
  pe->ReportError();
  pe->Delete();
 }
}
```

As mentioned earlier, this really comes down to a stylistic choice. Although placing all of the code in the try block can make it more readable, both techniques are perfectly valid.

Deciding what code to put in a catch block

The only code that should ever appear in a catch block is code that will at least partially process the exception. For example, at times a function will catch an exception, do what it can to process the exception, and then rethrow the exception so that further exception handling can be done. Here is a scenario that illustrates this:

```
CMyDialog::OnOk()
{
 try
 {
  m_pDoc->SaveInvoice(*m_pInvoice);
  CDialog::OnOK();
 }
 catch(CException* pe)
 {
  pe->ReportError();
  pe->Delete();
 }
}

CMyDoc::Save(CInvoice const& rInvoice)
{
 try
 {
  m_pDB->Commit();

  m_pDB->SaveInvoiceHdr(rInvoice->GetHeader());
  m_pDB->SaveInvoiceDtl(rInvoice->GetDetail());

  m_pDB->Commit();
```

```
    SetModifiedFlag(TRUE);
  }
catch(CDBException* pe)
  {
   m_pDB->Rollback();

   throw pe;
  }
}
```

In this code a dialog box called `CMyDialog` is used to enter invoices. Upon handling the `OnOK` function, the dialog box attempts to use its embedded document object (`m_pDoc`) to save the invoice. If the `SaveInvoice` function throws an exception, `CMyDialog::OnOK` catches it and displays an error message. Otherwise, the dialog box is dismissed (because the invoice has been saved).

You've already seen this type of "call and catch" done several times in this chapter. However, take a look at the `CMyDoc::Save` function. This function calls the `Commit` function, saves the data, and then calls the `Commit` function again before exiting. Now look at its `catch` block. Before this function rethrows the exception, it calls the `Rollback` function to undo any uncompleted changes from the database. This is an example of a function that catches an exception, performs some internal cleanup, and then rethrows the exception it caught.

Throwing exceptions from virtual functions

Throwing exceptions from virtual functions can definitely be tricky. As is always the case when overriding a virtual function, you should never do anything that previously written code cannot handle. Here's an example of that where I have a class that derived from the `CException` base class. This class adds the functionality of logging an exception to a file when the `LogException` function is called. Therefore, `CSomeClass::SomeFunction` places the `DoSomething` function call in a `try` block in order to catch the `CTestException` exception if it is thrown.

```
class CTest
{
 ...

public:
virtual void DoSomething(); // throws CTestException

 ...
};

class CTestException : public CException
{
 ...

public:
 void LogException ();

 ...
};
```

```
CSomeClass::SomeFunction(CTest* pTest)
{
...
 try
 {
  pTest->DoSomething();
 }
 catch(CTestException* pe)
 {
  pe->LogException();
  pe->Delete();
 }
...
}
```

What happens now if another programmer derives a new class from CTest, overrides its DoSomething virtual member function, and wants to throw a different type of exception? The answer is simple. If the exception is derived from a class that the SomeFunction function is documented as throwing, there is no problem. In other words, all previous code continues to work as before. However, if the new class's implementation of the DoSomething function throws an exception that was not documented when code was developed using the DoSomething function, you will have to go back and modify all of the existing code that calls the DoSomething function. Otherwise, you run the risk of breaking existing code if exceptions of the new type are thrown. Listing 18-1 shows an example of how that would fail.

Listing 18-1: **Throwing an undocumented exception**

```
class CNewTest : public CTest
{
 ...

public:
 // throws CNewTestException
 virtual void DoSomething();
 ...
};

CSomeClass::SomeFunction(CTest* pTest)
{
 try
 {
  pTest->DoSomething();
 }
 catch(CTestException* pe)
 {
  pe->LogException();
  pe->Delete();
 }
}
```

Now if the `CSomeClass::SomeFunction` function is called with a pointer to a `CNewTest` object and the `DoSomething` function throws an exception, it will not be caught. One of the biggest selling points of C++ is the capability of adding new code to a system without having to rewrite existing code. In this case, however, existing code has been broken. The reason is that the `DoSomething` function was documented as throwing an exception of one type and then an overridden version of this function threw an exception of another type. Luckily, there are two ways to solve this problem.

If you override a function documented as throwing a specific type of exception and you need to throw a different type of exception, throw an exception derived from the originally documented exception type. In Listing 18-1, that means because the `DoSomething` function was originally documented as throwing an exception of type `CTestException`, the `CNewTest::DoSomething` override should only throw exceptions of that type or a class that is derived from that type.

Another way to solve this problem is for the calling function to generically catch an exception type that represents the base class to all of the exception types in the system. Then the calling function can use the `IsKindOf` function to check for specific exception types. This type of approach should definitely be used when you are designing a class that has functions that you know will be overridden. Listing 18-2 shows a better way of handling the example shown in Listing 18-1.

Listing 18-2: Catching an exception that represents a base class to all exception types

```
class CTest
{
  ...

 // Upon failure, DoSomething() throws
 // CTestException (derived from CException).
 virtual void DoSomething(); // throws CException

  ...
};

class CTestException : public CException
{
  ...

public:
 void LogException ();

  ...
};

class CNewTest : public CTest
{
  ...

  // Upon failure, DoSomething() throws
```

Continued

Listing 18-2 *(continued)*

```
  // CNewTestException (NOT derived from CException).
  virtual void DoSomething();

  ...
}

CSomeClass::SomeFunction(CTest* pTest)
{
 try
 {
  pTest->DoSomething();
 }
 catch(CTestException* pe)
 {
  pe->LogException();
  pe->Delete();
 }
 catch(CException* pe)
 {
  TCHAR szErroMessage[512];
  if (pe->GetErrorMessage(szErrorMessage,
   _countof(szErrorMessage)))
  {
  // Call global logging function
  // passing szErrorMessage so that
  // all exceptions get logged.
  }

  pe->Delete();
 }
}
```

Summary

In this chapter you started out by learning the C++ exception-handling syntax. You then saw a brief comparison of the various error handling techniques and how they compared to exception handling. After that, I introduced to you the MFC CException class, and you discovered how to use it to better design your code with more robust error handling in mind. Once you had learned the basics, you then learned how to judge which functions should catch exceptions, what code to place in try and catch blocks, and how to throw exceptions from virtual functions.

As you saw throughout this chapter, exception-handling syntax is simple, the MFC exception classes are straightforward, and implementing exception handling in your application is as easy as designing your functions ahead of time. What makes exception handling so powerful is not obtuse syntax or a complex lattice of C++ classes. It is the overall use of exceptions in your application and the benefits derived therein that make exception handling an important tool to developing dependable applications with robust and complete error checking.

This chapter concludes the "Advanced Programming" Part, which started out with a chapter where you discovered how to design and program custom controls. From there, you then saw how to incorporate printing and print preview into your applications and how to design and write both DLLs and multithreaded applications. Finally, the section ended with this chapter that explained how to incorporate handle errors in your applications via exception handling. At this point, you know quite a good deal about writing MFC applications in terms of user interface and application design. However, one thing I haven't covered yet is how to save data. Therefore, the next section will cover many different techniques for saving and reading data using everything from standard database access technologies like ODBC and ADO to using the data access technique *du jour*, XML.

✦   ✦   ✦

Data I/O

Clipboard

The Windows Clipboard is the standard Windows method for transferring data between two applications. This can be done programmatically, as when a programmer uses the Clipboard as a very simple—albeit limited—interprocess communications protocol (IPC), or by the user when there is a need to easily copy data from one application to another. In this chapter, you will start out by learning the basics of programming with the Clipboard. This includes some basic uses of the Clipboard, how the user normally accesses the Clipboard functionality, and the support MFC has for programming the Clipboard. Once I've covered these basics, you'll see a demo that illustrates how to exchange the simplest type of data—text—between two applications. Most applications need to be capable of transferring more than simple text, however. Therefore, in the subsequent demos, you will discover how to copy bitmap data as well as application-specific data to and from the Clipboard. Once you've seen how to allow your users to exchange data between applications, the next logical step is to be able to programmatically determine (via notifications messages) when the Clipboard has new data.

Using the Windows Clipboard API

There are actually two distinct mechanisms for interfacing to the Clipboard. The first involves using the Windows Clipboard API and the second uses OLE. Because the Clipboard API is by far the most common method used, most of this chapter's demos will use this technique. If you're familiar with the Windows API, especially the means by which memory is allocated via the `GlobalAlloc` and `GlobalLock` functions, the steps needed to use the Clipboard will be all the easier to learn. Another thing to realize at this point is that regardless of the type of data being transferred, you take the same basic programmatic steps anytime you are transferring data to or from the Clipboard. Figure 19-1 shows these steps in a standard UML Sequence Diagram. The following sections go into more detail about each step.

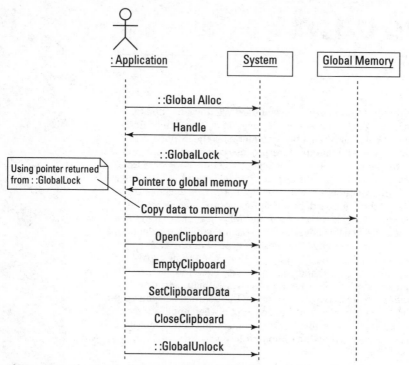

Figure 19-1: The standard steps used to transfer data to and from the Clipboard using the Windows Clipboard API

Allocating memory for your data

The phrase "placing data on the Clipboard" is really a misnomer as the Clipboard is not some sort of global data buffer. Actually, the Clipboard is little more than a handle to a data buffer that is created and maintained by the application that is making this data available for other applications. Because the data must be accessible from all processes, the Clipboard uses the Windows API functions GlobalAlloc and GlobalLock.

As a quick refresher, here is the syntax for these two functions and how they work. The GlobalAlloc function is used to allocate a global block of memory that holds the entirety of the data being made available via the Clipboard, as shown in the following example:

```
HGLOBAL GlobalAlloc(UINT uFlags, SIZE_T dwBytes)
```

The uFlags parameter is used to specify to Windows how the memory is to be allocated. If you specify a value of 0 (or NULL), then a value of GMEM_FIXED is assumed. The valid values for this parameter are in Table 19-1 and can be combined with the logical OR operator.

Table 19-1: Valid GlobalAlloc Values

uFlag Value	Description
GHND	This value is the same as GMEM_MOVEABLE | GMEM_ZEROINT.
GME_FIXED	This default value allocates a block of fixed (nonmoveable) memory. It's also the return value from GlobalAlloc when specifying GMEM_FIXED is a pointer.
GMEM_MOVEABLE	In Windows, memory blocks are never moved in physical memory. However, they can be moved within the default heap. Therefore, the return value when specifying GMEM_MOVEABLE is a handle to the memory.
GPTR	This value combines GMEM_FIXED and GMEM_ZEROINT, the latter simply initializing the allocated memory to all zeroes.

Note Because specifying a value of GMEM_FIXED for the uFlag parameter to the GlobalAlloc call will return a pointer, whereas specifying GMEM_MOVEABLE will return a handle, these two values are mutually exclusive.

The parameter dwBytes is a double-word (DWORD) value that enables you to specify how large a buffer you wish to allocate.

The second function that you need to call to allocate the memory for your data is the Windows API function, GlobalLock, as shown in the following example:

```
LPVOID GlobalLock(HGLOBAL hMem)
```

This function is very straightforward and takes as its only parameter a handle returned from the GlobalAlloc function.

Copying the data into the global memory

Once you've allocated the global memory and have obtained a pointer to it, you can copy the desired data into that global memory buffer. How you do this depends on what type of data you're transferring, so I'll go into more detail about this step in the three demos that follow in this chapter.

Unlocking the global memory

Unlocking global memory is a very important, yet often overlooked step in the process. According to the Windows documentation, once you've allocated the memory and inserted the data to be made public to other processes, you are not to touch this memory again. The reason is simple. Once you've made the Clipboard mechanism aware of the new data (in the next step), Windows will now have control over that memory and any further tampering with it on your end might very well invalidate the integrity of the data.

To unlock the global memory block, make a call to the `GlobalUnlock` API function. Here's the very simple syntax for this function:

```
BOOL GlobalUnlock(HGLOBAL hMem)
```

The `hMem` parameter is the handle returned from the `GlobalAlloc` function.

Opening the Clipboard

To open the clipboard for use, you must call the `OpenClipboard` function. Note that this function locks the clipboard for the current process so that other applications cannot modify the clipboard's contents while you're working with it.

```
BOOL OpenClipboard(HWND hWndNewOwner)
```

The `hWndNewOwner` simply allows you to associate the open Clipboard with a given window. If you don't need to do this (most don't), simply specify a value of `NULL` for this parameter, in which case Windows will associate the open Clipboard with the current task. All of the demos in this book use this technique, as I personally haven't seen too many situations where an association with a specific window was needed.

Emptying the Clipboard

The `EmptyClipboard` function empties the clipboard and frees the handles to any data that are on the clipboard. As a result, it is the responsibility of any application using the Clipboard to call this function in order to prevent memory leaks.

```
BOOL EmptyClipboard()
```

Note that you do not need to call a function to determine if any data exists prior to calling this function. `EmptyClipboard` will only return a nonzero value if the function fails. If it succeeds or if the Clipboard doesn't contain any data, the function returns zero (representing success).

Setting the Clipboard data

Finally, at this step, you set the Clipboard data. As mentioned earlier, the Clipboard really doesn't contain data but simply maintains a global handle obtained (and populated) by your application. The function to perform this step is the `SetClipboardData` function. This is also the function that enables you to specify the format of the data being transferred:

```
HANDLE SetClipboardData(UINT uFormat, HANDLE hMem)
```

The value you specify for the `uFormat` parameter must be either a standard Clipboard format, listed in Table 19-2, or a registered format. Registered formats are user-defined formats that enable you to specify formats for application-specific data. These formats are discussed later on.

Table 19-2: Standard Clipboard Formats

uFormat Value	hMem Value
CF_BITMAP	Handle to a bitmap; you'll see how to use this format in this chapter's second demo.

uFormat Value	hMem Value
CF_DIB	Handle to a BITMAPINFO structure followed by the bits that constitute the bitmap.
CF_DIBV5	Used in Windows 2000 only, this is also a handle to a BITMAPINFO structure where the subsequent bits represent the bitmap color information and the bitmap image.
CF_DIF	Handle to a Software Arts' Data Interchange Format (SADIF) buffer.
CF_DSPBITMAP	Handle to a bitmap display format associated with an application-specific format. The data being pointed to must be data that can be displayed in bitmap format.
CF_DSPENHMETAFILE	Handle to an enhanced metafile display format associated with a private format. In this case, the data must be displayable in enhanced metafile format in lieu of the privately formatted data.
CF_DSPMETAFILEPICT	Handle to a metafile picture display format associated with a private format. The data being pointed to must be displayable in metafile picture format in lieu of the privately formatted data.
CF_DSPTEXT	Handle to text display format associated with a private format. The data must be displayable in text format in lieu of the privately formatted data.
CF_ENHMETAFILE	Handle to an enhanced metafile (HENHMETAFILE).
CF_GDIOBJFIRST through CF_GDIOBJLAST	This range of integers represents application-defined GDI object clipboard formats. Note that the handles represented by these values are not automatically deleted using the GlobalFree function when the Clipboard is emptied. Additionally, the hMem parameter is not a handle to a GDI object, but is a handle allocated by the GlobalAlloc function with the GMEM_MOVEABLE flag.
CF_HDROP	Handle to type HDROP that identifies a list of files being transferred via the Clipboard—typically used in drag-and-drop operations. The DragQueryFiles function is used to retrieve information about these files.
CF_LOCALE	Handle to the locale identifier associated with the text in the Clipboard.
CF_METAFILEPICT	Handle to a metafile picture format (METAFILEPICT) structure.
CF_OEMTEXT	Handle to a text format containing characters in the OEM character set. In this format, each line must be terminated with a carriage return/linefeed (CR/LF) combination. A null character represents end of data (EOD) using this format.
CF_OWNERDISPLAY	If an application specifies a uFormat value of CF_OWNERDISPLAY, the hMem value must be NULL. In addition, the application is then responsible for displaying and updating the Clipboard viewer window and handling the following messages: WM_ASKCBFORMATNAME, WM_HSCROLLCLIPBOARD, WM_PAINTCLIPBOARD, WM_SIZECLIPBOARD, WM_VSCROLLCLIPBOARD.
CF_PALETTE	Handle to a color palette.
CF_PENDATA	Handle to data representing pen extensions for the Microsoft Windows for Pen Computing.

Continued

Table 19-2: *(continued)*

uFormat Value	hMem Value
CF_PRIVATEFIRST through CF_PRIVATELAST	Much like using the CF_GDIOBJFIRST through CF_GDIOBJLAST range, these integers represent a series of values for private Clipboard formats. Note that the data associated with these handles is not freed automatically and as such it is the application's responsibility to do so.
CF_RIFF	Handle to an audio data format that is more complex than can be represented with the standard (WAV) format where the uFormat parameter is set to CF_WAVE.
CF_SYLK	Handle to Microsoft Symbolic Link (SYLK) formatted data.
CF_TEXT	Handle to standard text. With this format, each line must be terminated with a carriage return/linefeed (CR/LF) combination. A null character represents end of data (EOD). This is used for ANSI text whereas CF_UNICODETEXT is used for UNICODE text.
CF_WAVE	Handle to the audio data in one of the standard wave formats such as 11 kHz or 22 kHz pulse code modulation (PCM).
CF_TIFF	Handle to tagged image file (TIFF) formatted data
CF_UNICODETEXT	For use with Windows NT/2000 or later, this format is used for UNICODE data as opposed to ANSI text (which is represented by the CF_TEXT value).

Closing the Clipboard

When an application has finished examining or modifying the Clipboard data, the CloseClipboard function is called. This has the effect of unlocking the Clipboard so that other applications can have access to it.

```
BOOL CloseClipboard()
```

Transferring Simple Text Demo

The first demo illustrates how to transfer text to and from the Clipboard. Although this is not needed as much as it once was because of the Windows context menu (right-clicking over any edit control will result in a menu containing the standard Clipboard functions), there are still some very valid uses for this capability. One example is if you want to pass simple text-based data to another application. However, in order to keep the example as clean as possible, this demo will consist of a dialog box with two edit controls. One edit control will enable you to type text into it and copy that text to the Clipboard. The second edit control will be a read-only control. A button will enable you to paste text from the Clipboard into this second control. By keeping the demo relatively simple, it's much easier for you to focus on the specifics of working with the Clipboard and it's also more convenient when you want to copy and paste the relevant code from this demo into your own project files.

Creating the SimpleTextTransfer demo project

First, create a dialog-based application called `SimpleTextTransfer`. Once you've done that, modify the default dialog box so that it looks like the one shown in Figure 19-2.

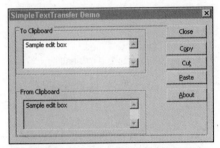

Figure 19-2: Simple dialog box to test using the Clipboard to transfer standard ANSI text

After you've modified the dialog box, you need to make the following changes to the dialog box controls:

✦ Set the Multiline property for both edit controls to True.

✦ Set the AutoVScroll property for both edit controls to True.

✦ Set the Vertical Scroll property for both edit controls to True.

✦ Set the Read Only property for "from Clipboard" edit control to True.

✦ Create a control member variable for each of the two edit controls. Name them `m_edtToClipboard` and `m_edtFromClipboard`, respectively.

Copying text to the Clipboard

Once you've finished with the dialog box controls' properties, add an event handler for the Copy button's `BN_CLICKED` message and modify it so that it looks like the following example. I've placed comments throughout the code to make the code easy to understand.

```
void CSimpleTextTransferDlg::OnBnClickedBtncopy()
{
 if (UpdateData())
 {
  CString strData;
  m_edtToClipboard.GetWindowText(strData);

  // Test to see if you can open the clipboard first before
  // wasting any cycles with the memory allocation
  if (OpenClipboard())
  {
   // Empty the Clipboard. This also has the effect
```

```
        // of allowing Windows to free the memory associated
        // with any data that is in the Clipboard
        EmptyClipboard();

        // Ok. You have the Clipboard locked and it's empty.
        // Now allocate the global memory for your data.

        // Here you simply use the GlobalAlloc function to
        // allocate a block of data equal to the text in the
        // "to clipboard" edit control plus one character for the
        // terminating null character required when sending
        // ANSI text to the Clipboard.
        HGLOBAL hClipboardData;
        hClipboardData = GlobalAlloc(GMEM_DDESHARE,
                                    strData.GetLength()+1);

        // Calling GlobalLock returns to you a pointer to the
        // data associated with the handle returned from
        // GlobalAlloc
        char * pchData;
        pchData = (char*)GlobalLock(hClipboardData);

        // At this point, all you need to do is use the standard
        // C/C++ strcpy function to copy the data from the local
        // variable to the global memory.
        strcpy(pchData, LPCSTR(strData));

        // Once done, you unlock the memory--remember you
        // don't call GlobalFree because Windows will free the
        // memory automatically when EmptyClipboard is next
        // called.
        GlobalUnlock(hClipboardData);

        // Now, set the Clipboard data by specifying that
        // ANSI text is being used and passing the handle to
        // the global memory.
        SetClipboardData(CF_TEXT,hClipboardData);

        // Finally, when finished, simply close the Clipboard
        // which has the effect of unlocking it so that other
        // applications can examine or modify its contents.
        CloseClipboard();
    }
  }
}
```

Cutting text to the Clipboard

As you might have guessed, the only difference between copying data to the Clipboard and cutting it to the Clipboard is that in the latter case, the data is removed from the edit control after the transfer takes place. Therefore, at this point, add an event handler for the Cut button's BN_CLICKED message. Once you've done that, modify that handler so that it looks as follows:

```
void CSimpleTextTransferDlg::OnBnClickedBtncut()
{
 OnBnClickedBtncopy();
 m_edtToClipboard.SetWindowText("");
}
```

Pasting text from the Clipboard

At this point, the application can place data on the Clipboard, but it doesn't yet allow for the pasting of that data to the dialog box. Therefore, you'll take care of that now. As with the Copy and Cut buttons, add an event handler for the Paste button's BN_CLICKED message as follows:

```
void CSimpleTextTransferDlg::OnBnClickedBtnpaste()
{
 // Test to see if you can open the Clipboard first.
 if (OpenClipboard())
 {
  // Retrieve the Clipboard data (specifying that
  // you want ANSI text (via the CF_TEXT value).
  HANDLE hClipboardData = GetClipboardData(CF_TEXT);

  // Call GlobalLock to retrieve a pointer
  // to the data associated with the handle returned
  // from GetClipboardData.
  char *pchData = (char*)GlobalLock(hClipboardData);

  // Set a local CString variable to the data
  // and then update the dialog box with the Clipboard data
  CString strFromClipboard = pchData;
  m_edtFromClipboard.SetWindowText(strFromClipboard);

  // Unlock the global memory.
  GlobalUnlock(hClipboardData);

  // Finally, when finished, simply close the Clipboard
  // which has the effect of unlocking it so that other
  // applications can examine or modify its contents.
  CloseClipboard();
 }
}
```

Testing the SimpleTextTransfer demo

At this point, compile and test the application. Your results should be similar to what you see in Figure 19-3.

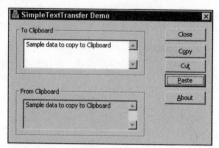

Figure 19-3: With just a few lines of code, you can easily add Clipboard functionality to your application.

However, there is just one problem with your little test. Pressing the Alt+Print Screen key combination copies a bitmap of the current window to the Clipboard. You can test this by opening the Paint application and pasting the image into a new bitmap image. However, if you copy an image to the Clipboard and then click the Paste button on the demo application, the text in the "to clipboard" edit control is wiped out, and nothing appears. This is because the demo is attempting to use the data on the Clipboard without first determining if the data is valid for this application.

In order to check the format of the data on the Clipboard, simply use the IsClipboardAvailable function as shown in the following example:

```
BOOL IsClipboardFormatAvailable(UINT format)
```

The format parameter can be any value listed in Table 19-2. Here's the modified BN_CLICKED handler for the dialog box's Paste button. I've bolded the lines that have changed from the previous incarnation of this function.

```
void CSimpleTextTransferDlg::OnBnClickedBtnpaste()
{
  // Test to see if you can open the Clipboard first.
  if (OpenClipboard())
  {
    if (::IsClipboardFormatAvailable(CF_TEXT)
    || ::IsClipboardFormatAvailable(CF_OEMTEXT))
    {
      // Retrieve the Clipboard data (specifying that
      // you want ANSI text (via the CF_TEXT value).
      HANDLE hClipboardData = GetClipboardData(CF_TEXT);

      // Call GlobalLock to retrieve a pointer
      // to the data associated with the handle returned
      // from GetClipboardData.
      char *pchData = (char*)GlobalLock(hClipboardData);

      // Set a local CString variable to the data
      // and then update the dialog box with the Clipboard data
```

```
    CString strFromClipboard = pchData;
    m_edtFromClipboard.SetWindowText(strFromClipboard);

    // Unlock the global memory.
    GlobalUnlock(hClipboardData);
}
else
{
    AfxMessageBox("The data on the clipboard is "
                  "not (ANSI) text");
}

// Finally, when finished, simply close the Clipboard
// which has the effect of unlocking it so that other
// applications can examine or modify its contents.
CloseClipboard();
    }
}
```

Now, if you run this application, copy a bitmap (or any data that is not defined as CF_TEXT or CF_OEMTEXT) and press the demo's Paste button, you will see the message shown in Figure 19-4.

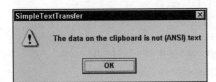

Figure 19-4: Checking the format of the data on the Clipboard before attempting to use it

Transferring Bitmap Images Demo

As mentioned earlier, the steps required to use the Clipboard are largely the same regardless of the type of data being transferred. However, in the case of images, there are some extra steps needed for displaying the image itself. Although this is not strictly a Clipboard function, this task is something that is quite commonly requested. Therefore, in this section, I'll walk you through the steps required to both paste a bitmap image from the Clipboard and to also copy an image to the Clipboard for use by other applications.

Creating the BitmapTransfer demo project

Create a dialog-based application called BitmapTransfer. Once you've done that, modify the default dialog box so that it looks like the one shown in Figure 19-5.

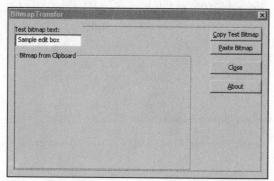

Figure 19-5: Dialog box to test using the Clipboard to transfer bitmap images

Once you've created the dialog box, add a member variable (m_grpBitmapFromClipboard) of type CStatic for the group box. This will be used to position (and size) the bitmap that is copied from the Clipboard.

Pasting a bitmap from the Clipboard

Create an event handler for the dialog box's Paste Button's BN_CLICKED message and modify it so that when finished it appears as follows. As before, I've included remarks within the code as comments to explain what each function does and why it's being used.

```
void CBitmapTransferDlg::OnBnClickedBtnpastebitmap()
{
// Test to see if you can open the clipboard first.
if (OpenClipboard())
{
 // Determine if the data on the Clipboard is a bitmap.
 // Failure to do so will almost certainly lead to a
 // GPF if the data on the Clipboard is not a bitmap
 // but is treated as such.
 if (::IsClipboardFormatAvailable(CF_BITMAP))
 {
  //Get the clipboard data. Notice the CF_BITMAP value
  // being passed.
  HBITMAP handle = (HBITMAP)GetClipboardData(CF_BITMAP);

  // At this point, you can assume that you have a handle
  // to a bitmap object since you've checked the Clipboard
  // data type first. Now, using the CBitmap::FromHandle
  // static member function will return a pointer to
  // a CBitmap object wrapper for that bitmap data.
  CBitmap* bm = CBitmap::FromHandle(handle);

  // Since you are going to manually place the bitmap
  // on the dialog box, you need to create a device context.
```

```
    // First, you get the current client device context (cdc).
    CClientDC cdc(this);

    // Now, you create a memory device context that is
    // compatible with the client device context.

    CDC dc;
    dc.CreateCompatibleDC(&cdc);

    // The CDC.SelectObject member function enables you to
    // select a GDI object into the memory device context.
    dc.SelectObject(bm);

    // Because you want to display the bitmap
    // inside the dialog box's group control,
    // you simply retrieve its coordinates using
    // its GetWindowRect member function, which then copies
    // its size and position into a structure of type RECT.
    RECT rect;
    m_grpBitmapFromClipboard.GetWindowRect(&rect);

    // The ScreenToClient function will translate the
    // positioning values from screen coordinates to the
    // dialog box's client coordinates.
    ScreenToClient(&rect);

    // Now you "bit-blit" the image onto the device context.
    // Notice that the group control's values are used to
    // both position and size the bitmap.
    cdc.BitBlt(rect.left + 10, rect.top + 20,
               (rect.right - rect.left) - 10,
               (rect.bottom - rect.top) - 40,
               &dc,
               0,0,
               SRCCOPY);

  }
  else
  {
   // Basic message stating that the data on the Clipboard
   // is not a bitmap image.
   AfxMessageBox("There is no BITMAP data on the
                 Clipboard.");
  }

  // Finally, when finished, simply close the Clipboard
  // which has the effect of unlocking it so that other
  // applications can examine or modify its contents.
  CloseClipboard();
 }
}
```

Testing the Paste Bitmap functionality

Now that you've coded the Paste button functionality, you need to test it. To do so, simply press the Alt+Print Screen key combination in order to copy a bitmap image of the current window to the Clipboard. Now, return to the demo application and click the Paste Bitmap button. You should see the bitmap displayed within the dialog's group box. Figure 19-6 shows an example of displaying a part of a UML diagram copied to the Clipboard.

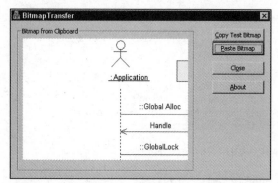

Figure 19-6: Bitmaps can easily be pasted from the Clipboard with a minimum of knowledge of both GDI concepts and Clipboard functions.

Copying bitmap data to the Clipboard

Instead of doing something like copying a bitmap from a resource, let's do something just a bit more fun. Here the demo will actually draw the bitmap image and then copy that image to the Clipboard. To prove that the image is being dynamically created, I'll use text that the user supplies on the dialog box as the image. Start by adding a static text prompt and an edit control to the dialog box as shown in Figure 19-7.

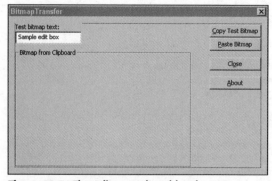

Figure 19-7: The edit control enables the user to specify the text that is included in the bitmap image written to the Clipboard.

Once you've added the edit control to the dialog box, create a DDX member variable for it named m_edtBitmapText. Now, add an event handler for the Copy Bitmap button's BN_CLICKED message and modify it so that when finished it looks as follows:

```
void CBitmapTransferDlg::OnBnClickedBtncopybitmap()
{
// Test to see if you can open the clipboard first.
if (OpenClipboard())
{
  // Empty the Clipboard. This also has the effect
  // of allowing Windows to free the memory associated
  // with any data that is in the Clipboard
  EmptyClipboard();

  //Create a new bitmap object.
  CBitmap* pNewBitmap = new CBitmap();

  // Obtain the client device context.
  CClientDC cdc(this);

  // Create a compatible memory device context
  // onto which you'll draw the new image.
  CDC dc;
  dc.CreateCompatibleDC(&cdc);

  // Arbitrary size and positioning of the image.
  CRect client(0, 0, 200, 200);

  // Initialize a bitmap that is compatible with
  // the client device context.
  pNewBitmap->CreateCompatibleBitmap(&cdc,
                                     client.Width(),
                                     client.Height());

  // Select your new bitmap image into the memory
  // device context.
  dc.SelectObject(pNewBitmap);

  // Obtain the user text from the dialog box's edit control.
  CString strBitmapText;
  m_edtBitmapText.GetWindowText(strBitmapText);

  // The DrawImage function makes the actual GDI calls
  // to do all the drawing. This way the function
  // is abstracted from this code and can be used
  // in other contexts. All you have to pass it is the
  // device context to use and the text to draw.
  DrawImage(&dc, strBitmapText);

  // Once the image has been created, simply copy the image
  // to the Clipboard using the SetClipboard function.
```

```
// Notice that you need only specify the format as
// CF_BITMAP and pass a handle to the bitmap. This handle
// is a member variable of the CBitmap object.
SetClipboardData(CF_BITMAP, pNewBitmap->m_hObject);

// Finally, when finished, simply close the Clipboard
// which has the effect of unlocking it so that other
// applications can examine or modify its contents.
CloseClipboard();

// Once the data has been copied to the Clipboard and
// the Clipboard has been closed, it is safe to delete the
//locally allocated memory for the CBitmap object.
delete pNewBitmap;
}

// Display a confirmation message that the bitmap is on
// the Clipboard.
MessageBox("The bitmap has been copied to clipboard. "
           "Click the Paste Bitmap button to display "
           "the bitmap on this dialog",
           NULL,
           MB_OK);
}
```

As mentioned in the comment of the OnBnClickedBtncopybitmap function, the actual GDI calls are in the DrawImage function. Therefore, you need to create a new member function for the dialog box called DrawImage and code it as follows:

```
void CBitmapTransferDlg::DrawImage(CDC * pDC, CString pText)
{
// Here you simply pick an arbitrary size for the new image
CRect rectDrawingArea(0,0,200,200);

// First, you fill the area with a light gray color
pDC->FillSolidRect(rectDrawingArea,RGB(212,208,200));

// Now, create a pen object, which will be used
// to draw the lines on the image. The parameters
// being passed simply indicate that you want a
// a solid pen (PS_SOLID) as opposed to dashed
// or dotted lines, a width of 3 pixels and the
// color blue (RGB=0,0,255).
CPen pen;
pen.CreatePen(PS_SOLID, 3, RGB(0,0,255));

// As you saw in the Paste Bitmap code, in order to
// use this new GDI object (the pen), you need to
// select that object into the device context. Save the
// current pen so that when finished you can restore the
// current pen.
CPen * oldpen = pDC->SelectObject(&pen);

// These are simple GDI calls to draw a tic-tac-toe
// type diagram.
```

```
pDC->MoveTo(70, 10);
pDC->LineTo(70, 190);

pDC->MoveTo(130, 10);
pDC->LineTo(130, 190);

pDC->MoveTo(10, 70);
pDC->LineTo(190, 70);

pDC->MoveTo(10, 130);
pDC->LineTo(190, 130);

// When finished using the pen, simply select the previous
// pen back into the current device context.
pDC->SelectObject(oldpen);

// Now delete the pen that was used to draw the image.
pen.DeleteObject();

// Using the device context object's TextOut
// member function, draw the text over the image
// at three arbitrary positions.
pDC->TextOut(10, 10, pText);
pDC->TextOut(20, 50, pText);
pDC->TextOut(50, 100, pText);
}
```

Testing the bitmap to Clipboard functionality

Once you've coded the aforementioned functions, rebuild the demo application and run it. You can test the copy functionality by typing text into the edit control and clicking the Copy Bitmap button. After you receive the confirmation message that the bitmap has been created and copied to the Clipboard, click the Paste Button to display the bitmap in the dialog box. Your results should be very similar to those shown in Figure 19-8.

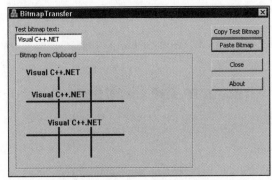

Figure 19-8: The edit control enables the user to specify the text that is included in the bitmap image written to the Clipboard.

Transferring Custom Data Demo

There are many cases when it would be appropriate to use the Clipboard to transfer a custom, or application-specific, data format between applications or different windows in the same application. One such example would be if you had a view that displayed a list of customers. You might very well want the user to be capable of using the standard Clipboard functions to copy and paste their customer objects from one part of the application to another or even between applications (assuming that both applications understand your customer object). Although this might seem to be a difficult task, in this section I'll show you how easy it is to register your own format and use that format when dealing with the Clipboard.

Creating the CustomDataTransfer demo project

As with the previous demos in this chapter, create a dialog-based application. This time the project should be named CustomDataTransfer. Once the project files have been created, modify the dialog box so that when finished it looks like the one presented in Figure 19-9.

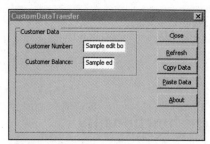

Figure 19-9: Sample dialog box to test the transfer of custom data to and from the Clipboard

Once you've modified the dialog box, add the following DDX member variables:

✦ Add a variable of type int (m_iCustomerNumber) for the Customer Number edit control.

✦ Add a variable of type double (m_dCustomerBalance) for the Customer Balance edit control.

Copying custom data formats to the Clipboard

The first step in copying custom data to the Clipboard is to register that format with Windows. This is done via the RegisterClipboardFormat function as follows:

```
UINT RegisterClipboardFormat(LPCTSTR lpszFormat);
```

As you can see, this is a very simple function that takes the name of the format being registered. The name itself can be any valid string representing what you want to call your data format as long as the code responsible for pasting this data from the Clipboard also knows the format name.

If the registration succeeds, the return value will be an integer in the range of 0xC000 to 0xFFFF, which represents the data format. This is the value that is then used when the SetClipboardFormat function is called. You'll see how this all works together shortly.

One last important point to make is that if the data format name specified in the lpszFormat parameter is already being used, a new format will not be registered. Rather, the Register ClipboardFormat function will return the value representing the existing format.

Copying the custom data to the Clipboard

First, open the CustomDataTransferDlg.h file and add the following definition for a CCustomer class. This class holds the data the user types into the dialog box controls.

```
class CCustomer
{
public:
  int iCustomerNumber;
  double dCustomerBalance;
};
```

Next, add an event handler for the Copy Data button's BN_CLICKED message. Once the function has been added, simply modify it to look like the following:

```
void CCustomDataTransferDlg::OnBnClickedBtnCopydata()
{
    // Update the member variables from the dialog box
    // controls.
  if (UpdateData())
  {
  // Register the new data uiCustomerDataFormat.
  UINT uiCustomerDataFormat =
   RegisterClipboardFormat("CUSTOMER_DATA");

  // Test to see if you can open the Clipboard first.
  if (OpenClipboard())
  {
  // Empty the Clipboard. This also has the effect
  // of allowing Windows to free the memory associated
  // with any data that is in the Clipboard.
  EmptyClipboard();

  // Allocate a CCustomer object on the stack.
  CCustomer customer;

  // Retrieve the customer data from the dialog box.
  customer.iCustomerNumber = m_iCustomerNumber;
  customer.dCustomerBalance = m_dCustomerBalance;

  // Allocate the global memory to hold the CCustomer data.
  HGLOBAL hClipboardData;

  // Here you simply use the GlobalAlloc function to
```

```
// allocate a block of data equal to the size of the
// CCustomer object.
hClipboardData = GlobalAlloc(GMEM_DDESHARE,
                            sizeof(CCustomer));

// Calling GlobalLock returns to you a pointer to the
// data associated with the handle returned
// from GlobalAlloc
CCustomer * pchCustomerData =
 (CCustomer*)GlobalLock(hClipboardData);

// Put the customer into the allocated global memory.
*pchCustomerData = customer;

// Once done, you unlock the memory--remember you don't
// call GlobalFree because Windows will free the memory
// automatically when EmptyClipboard is next called.
GlobalUnlock(hClipboardData);

// Now, set the Clipboard data by specifying that
// ANSI text is being used and passing the handle to
// the global memory. Notice that the value returned
// from the RegisterClipboardData is used.
SetClipboardData(uiCustomerDataFormat, hClipboardData);

// Finally, when finished, you simply close the Clipboard
// which has the effect of unlocking it so that other
// applications can examine or modify its contents.
CloseClipboard();
}

// Let the user know that the data has been copied to the
// Clipboard.
MessageBox("Custom written to clipboard. "
           "Click the Paste Data button to view the data.",
           NULL,
           MB_OK);
  }
}
```

Pasting the custom data from the Clipboard

As the last step of this demo, you insert the code needed to paste the custom data from the Clipboard. First, you add a handler that initializes the dialog box. That way, it's a bit easier to test that the values being pasted from the Clipboard are actually coming from the Clipboard. To do so, simply add an event handler for the BN_CLICKED message of the Refresh button and insert the following code:

```
void CCustomDataTransferDlg::OnBnClickedBtnRefresh()
{
  m_iCustomerNumber = 0;
```

```
    m_dCustomerBalance = 0;

    UpdateData(FALSE);
}
```

As you can see, this code simply initializes the two member variables representing the customer data and then calls the `CDialog::UpdateData` member function to update the dialog box controls with these values.

Now here is the actual code that you use to paste the custom data from the Clipboard. As before, add an event handler for the `BN_CLICKED` message of the Paste Data button.

```
void CCustomDataTransferDlg::OnBnClickedBtnPastedata()
{
 // Calling the RegisterClipboardFormat function passing
 // a format name that has already been registered
 // will result in that format's id being returned.
 UINT uiCustomerDataFormat =
  RegisterClipboardFormat("CUSTOMER_DATA");

 // Test to see if you can open the Clipboard first.
 if (OpenClipboard())
 {
  // Determine if the data on the Clipboard is in the
  // format of the Customer custom data.
  if (::IsClipboardFormatAvailable(uiCustomerDataFormat))
  {
   // Retrieve a handle to the customer data from the
   // Clipboard.
   HANDLE hData = GetClipboardData(uiCustomerDataFormat);

   // Call GlobalLock to retrieve a pointer
   // to the data associated with the handle returned
   // from GetClipboardData and cast that pointer to
   // a CCustomer pointer.
   CCustomer* pchCustomerData =
     (CCustomer*)GlobalLock(hData);

   // Instantiate a local copy of the CCustomer object
   CCustomer customer = *pchCustomerData;

   // Set the dialog's DDX member variables from
   // the CCustomer object.
   m_iCustomerNumber = customer.iCustomerNumber;
   m_dCustomerBalance = customer.dCustomerBalance;

   // Update the dialog box from the DDX member variables.
   UpdateData(FALSE);

   // Unlock the global memory.
   GlobalUnlock( hData );
```

```
//When finished, simply close the Clipboard
// which has the effect of unlocking it so that other
// applications can examine or modify its contents.
CloseClipboard();
}
else
{
// Basic message stating that the data on the Clipboard
// is not in the correct format.
AfxMessageBox("There is no Customer data on the
             Clipboard");
}
}
else
{
// Display a message if the Clipboard couldn't be opened
// so that the user realizes why the dialog box values
// didn't change.
AfxMessageBox("The Clipboard could not be opened");
}
}
```

The last thing that to make note of before you look at this demo in action is the call to RegisterClipboardFormat in order to retrieve the Clipboard id for the Customer custom data format. I used this technique to show how the RegisterClipboardFormat function can be used to obtain the id of an already existing format. Although this is a valid technique, when a second application needs to access the id of a format, you would generally store the id in a member variable if all access is going to be via a single application.

Testing the CustomDataTransfer demo

At this point, build the application and run it. The customer number and balance should default to values of 1005 and 150.36, respectively. Clicking the Copy Data button to copy these values to the Clipboard will result in a confirmation message. After clicking OK to that message, click the Refresh button to initialize the customer values to zero. Finally, click the Paste Data button to see the original customer values pasted from the Clipboard (Figure 19-10).

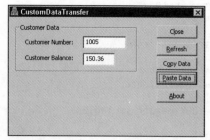

Figure 19-10: Using custom data formats on the Clipboard is as easy as registering the format and using the returned id in subsequent Clipboard API calls.

Receiving Clipboard Change Notification

The last thing I cover in this chapter is how to receive programmatic notification that the Clipboard has changed. This feature can be extremely useful when using the Clipboard to synchronize two views or applications. To receive notification that the Clipboard has changed, simply follow these steps:

1. Call `SetClipboardViewer` to add the window to the chain of windows that are notified of any Clipboard changes.

2. Add a handler for the `WM_DRAWCLIPBOARD` message.

3. Write your code to perform whatever functions you need to as a result of the Clipboard changing.

To see this in action, create a dialog-based application called `ClipboardNotification`. Once the project files have been created, open the dialog box resource and modify it so that it looks like the one shown in Figure 19-11.

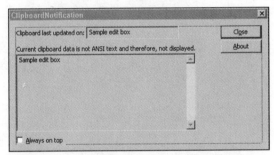

Figure 19-11: Sample dialog box used to capture Clipboard change notifications

After you have created the controls for the dialog box, do the following:

✦ Set the Clipboard last updated edit control's Readonly property to True.

✦ Set the Clipboard data edit control's Multiline property to True.

✦ Set the Clipboard data edit control's Vertical Scroll property to True.

✦ Set the Clipboard data edit control's AutoVScroll property to True.

✦ Set the Clipboard data edit control's Read Only property to True.

✦ Create a `CString` member variable called `m_strLastUpdated` for the "Clipboard last updated on" edit control.

✦ Change the "Current clipboard data" static control name to `IDC_STC_NOTEXT`. You need to do this because the demo uses a DDX member variable to show and hide this control and you cannot add DDX member variables for controls with an id of `IDC_STATIC` — the default id used when creating a static control in the Visual Studio dialog editor.

✦ Create a `CStatic` member variable called `m_stcNotText` for the static control whose caption starts "Current clipboard."

✦ Create a `CString` member variable called `m_strClipboardText` for the Clipboard text edit control.

Add the following function declaration to the ClipboardNotification.h **file:**

```
protected:
 void DisplayClipboardData();
```

Once you've added the prototype, add the actual DispalyClipboardData **function as follows:**

```
void CClipboardNotificationDlg::DisplayClipboardData()
{
// Initialize the Clipboard data controls.
m_strClipboardText = "";

// Test to see if you can open the Clipboard first.
if (OpenClipboard())
{
 // Application will only display ANSI text data.
 if (::IsClipboardFormatAvailable(CF_TEXT)
 || ::IsClipboardFormatAvailable(CF_OEMTEXT))
 {
   // Since the data is ANSI text, hide the "not
   // ANSI text" message.
   m_stcNotText.ShowWindow(SW_HIDE);

   // Retrieve the Clipboard data (specifying that
   // you want ANSI text (via the CF_TEXT value).
   HANDLE hClipboardData = GetClipboardData(CF_TEXT);

   // Call GlobalLock to retrieve a pointer
   // to the data associated with the handle returned
   // from GetClipboardData.
   char *pchData = (char*)GlobalLock(hClipboardData);

   // Set a local CString variable to the data
   // and then update the dialog box with the Clipboard data
   m_strClipboardText = pchData;

   // Unlock the global memory.
   GlobalUnlock(hClipboardData);
 }
 else
 {
   // Need to let the user know that the app is working,
   // but that there is no ANSI text on the Clipboard
   // to display.
   m_stcNotText.ShowWindow(SW_SHOW);
 }

 //When finished, simply close the Clipboard
 // which has the effect of unlocking it so that other
 // applications can examine or modify its contents.
 CloseClipboard();

 // Update the dialog box controls with the new data.
 UpdateData(FALSE);
 }
}
```

One thing to notice about the DisplayClipboardData function is that the Last Updated value is not changed here. This is because this function is called when the application starts up and when the application receives notification messages that the Clipboard has changed. In the first case, the application won't know the date and time of that change so the Clipboard notification message handler will have to be responsible for setting the dialog box's time-stamp value and calling this function for the display of the actual data. However, you do want to display something when the application first starts so that the user doesn't think that the timestamp is just not working. Therefore, locate the dialog box constructor and modify it so that when finished it looks as follows (the changed part of the constructor's initializer list is in bold):

```
CClipboardNotificationDlg::CClipboardNotificationDlg(CWnd* pParent
/*=NULL*/)
  : CDialog(CClipboardNotificationDlg::IDD, pParent)
  , m_strLastUpdated("<Unknown>")
  , m_strClipboardText("")
{
  m_hIcon = AfxGetApp()->LoadIcon(IDR_MAINFRAME);
}
```

Once you've coded the DisplayClipboardData function and initialized the m_strLastUpdated member variable, add a call to it from the OnInitDialog function as follows (noted in bold):

```
BOOL CClipboardNotificationDlg::OnInitDialog()
{
  Dialog::OnInitDialog();

  ...

  // Display the Clipboard data upon initialization.
  DisplayClipboardData();

  return TRUE;
}
```

Now the application needs to tell Windows that it wants to be included in the notification chain for Clipboard changes. You do this by adding the following code (shown in bold) to the end of the dialog box's OnInitDialog function:

```
BOOL CClipboardNotificationDlg::OnInitDialog()
{
  Dialog::OnInitDialog();

  ...

  // Display the Clipboard data upon initialization.
  DisplayClipboardData();

  // Tell Windows that this window is to receive notification
  // messages whenever the Clipboard is changed.
  SetClipboardViewer();

  return TRUE;
}
```

Unfortunately, the next bit has to be done manually. Open the `ClipboardNotificationDlg.h` file and add the following prototype to the dialog box class:

```
afx_msg LRESULT OnClipboardChange(WPARAM, LPARAM);
```

After that, open the `ClipboardNotificationDlg.cpp` file and add the following entry to the dialog's message map:

```
ON_MESSAGE(WM_DRAWCLIPBOARD, OnClipboardChange)
```

At this point, code the message handler (`OnClipboardChange`) as follows. Notice that the function doesn't need to call `UpdateData` after setting the `m_strLastUpdated` value, because the call to `DisplayClipboardData` takes care of this.

```
LRESULT CClipboardNotificationDlg::OnClipboardChange(
  WPARAM w, LPARAM l)
{
  // Get the current time.
  CTime time = CTime::GetCurrentTime();

  // Format the time as you update the dialog's Last
  // Updated value.
  m_strLastUpdated = time.Format("%a, %b %d, %Y -- %H:%M:%S");

  // Call the function to display the Clipboard data.
  DisplayClipboardText();

  return 0L;
}
```

If you build and run the application at this time, you should see results similar to those shown in Figure 19-12. For fun, simply copy a few things to the Clipboard and watch the Clipboard change automatically! This includes copying bitmaps, in which case the dialog box will display a message stating that the Clipboard contains non-text data.

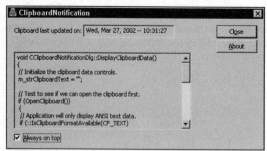

Figure 19-12: Hooking into the Clipboard change notification chain is as easy as making an API call and then handling a single Windows message.

You might want to also add an "Always on top" checkbox to the dialog box. That way, you can more easily see that the data on the dialog box is being changed. To do that, simply add a checkbox control to the bottom of the dialog box with the text "Always on top" and create a member variable of type `int` for it called `m_bAlwaysOnTop`. In the dialog box's initializer list, set the value of this variable to `TRUE`, as shown in bold in the following example:

```
CClipboardNotificationDlg::CClipboardNotificationDlg(CWnd*
  pParent /*=NULL*/)
  : CDialog(CClipboardNotificationDlg::IDD, pParent)
  , m_strLastUpdated("<Unknown>")
  , m_strClipboardText("")
  , m_bAlwaysOnTop(1)
{
  m_hIcon = AfxGetApp()->LoadIcon(IDR_MAINFRAME);
}
```

Now, add a message handler for the button's BN_CLICKED message:

```
void CClipboardNotificationDlg::OnBnClickedCheck1()
{
// Get the m_bAlwaysOnTop value.
UpdateData();

if (m_bAlwaysOnTop == 1)
{
// Set to always on top.
SetWindowPos(&wndTopMost,
             0, 0, 0, 0,
             SWP_NOMOVE
             | SWP_NOSIZE
             | WS_EX_TOPMOST);
}
else
{
  ::SetWindowPos(GetSafeHwnd(),
             HWND_NOTOPMOST,
             0, 0, 0, 0,
             SWP_NOMOVE | SWP_NOSIZE);
}
}
```

Finally, add a call to the OnBnClickedCheck1 function at the end of the dialog box's OnInitDialog function.

Summary

In this chapter, you learned just about everything there is to know about working with the Clipboard. The first steps showed you how to transfer data to and from the Clipboard using the Clipboard API and then launched into several demos to show you how to transfer specific data types. Along the way, you learned how to transfer simple text, bitmap data, and even your own custom data formats. The chapter then wrapped up with a demo on how to receive notification of when the Clipboard has been changed. At this point, you should be extremely comfortable with using the Clipboard as either a means of transferring data to and from other applications or within a single application.

✦   ✦   ✦

ODBC

You might be wondering what an ODBC (Open Database Connectivity) chapter is doing in a book on Visual C++.NET. After all, hasn't ODBC outlived its usefulness with the subsequent introduction of higher level encapsulations (MFC Database Classes) and database access technologies (ADO and OLEDB)? As with many difficult questions, the answer is "yes" and "no." As I explain in the next three chapters, the MFC Database Classes, ADO and DAO interfaces all provide a much easier means of adding database connectivity to your applications. However, there are two very good reasons for my inclusion of an ODBC chapter in this book.

First, the MFC Database Classes are an abstraction of the ODBC SDK. Therefore, if you decide to go that route, you will still need to have a basic understanding of its ODBC underpinnings for times when things don't work as planned. Second, as you'll see in this chapter's last demo, there are times when you need the raw power and flexibility that only ODBC can provide.

This chapter begins by describing what ODBC is and how it provides a level of indirection to your data sources such that you can focus on database programming without becoming mired in the details and idiosyncrasies of a particular Database Management System (DBMS). Once you have learned some basic tasks — such as how to connect to an ODBC data source, how to retrieve data, and how to execute an SQL request — two demos are introduced. In the first demo, you will learn how to use ODBC SDK functions to connect to, fetch data from, and disconnect from a data source. After reviewing these basic ODBC functions, you will be introduced to a C++ class (`CODBCDynamic`) that can dynamically read data from any ODBC data source. This class uses the ODBC SDK to dynamically query the data source so that you don't have to know the data source's schema until runtime. Because the source code is encapsulated in a C++ class with a very thin interface, it can be plugged easily into any Visual C++ application.

Defining ODBC and Database Terms

Before continuing, I want to clarify some terms that I use in this chapter. In some cases, these are standard terms with universally recognized definitions (for example, DBMS and SQL). In other cases, an otherwise ambiguous term will be defined and an explanation provided of how that term will be used in this chapter's text.

✦ *Database Management System (DBMS)* — A DBMS is the software that provides access to and manipulation of structured data. Examples of some of the more popular PC DBMSs are Microsoft Access, Microsoft SQL Server, Oracle Server, and Sybase SQL Server. Most DBMSs (including all of the aforementioned databases) provide a SQL interface. Note that all the demo applications in this chapter have been tested with both Microsoft Access and Microsoft SQL Server. However, the source code for this and the other database chapters all work with the Microsoft Access database file found on this book's Web site.

✦ *Structured Query Language (SQL)* — This is the language used to access and manipulate data in a DBMS. SQL statements are divided into two categories: Data Definition Language (DDL) and Data Manipulation Language (DML) statements. DML statements are used to manipulate the structure of the database itself, for example, you can use DDL statements to create tables, indexes, and perform database maintenance tasks.

✦ *ODBC SDK* — The ODBC Software Development Kit (SDK) is the Application Programming Interface (API) that database applications use to access ODBC services, such as interfacing to DBMSs, for which an ODBC driver exists. The ODBC SDK is also used to develop ODBC drivers; however, the development of ODBC drivers is not a simple undertaking and is outside the scope of this book.

✦ *ODBC Driver Manager* — The ODBC Driver Manager is a DLL (ODBC32.DLL) that is the gateway through which the application interfaces with the DBMS. The entire ODBC SDK API is exported from this DLL.

✦ *ODBC Cursor Library* — This is a DLL (ODBCCR32.DLL) that logically resides between the ODBC Driver Manager and the ODBC drivers. Once a request to a data source has returned data, this DLL is responsible for handling the scrolling through that data.

✦ *ODBC Driver* — As mentioned previously, the ODBC driver is the component that actually interfaces to the DBMS once the ODBC Driver Manager makes a request to it on your behalf. Any information or response is also passed back through the ODBC Driver Manager to you. For you to be able to use a particular DBMS with ODBC, you must acquire an ODBC driver for it. Note that this chapter assumes that you are an application developer and are not developing an ODBC driver. Visual C++.NET provides ODBC drivers for the following:

  • SQL Server

  • Microsoft Access

  • Microsoft FoxPro

  • Microsoft Excel

  • dBASE

  • Paradox

  • Text files

Note   Don't worry if you don't yet understand how all these different pieces of the ODBC subsystem fit together. I'm just going over terms at this point. In the next section, I go into more detail about how all this works.

✦ *Data source*—The term *data source* is used in this chapter to represent a specific instance of a DBMS that you are using. For example, suppose a demo application uses a Microsoft Access database called `Test`. When the text refers to the DBMS, it is referring to the Microsoft Access product and when the term data source is used, it is referring to the actual `Test` database (`test.mdb` in this case).

✦ *Data Source Name (DSN)*—For ODBC to be able to work with a data source, that data source must be *registered* with the ODBC Driver Manager. Creating a DSN accomplishes this task. Microsoft provides a utility called the ODBC Data Source Administrator for this purpose (Figure 20-1). You'll see how to configure new DSNs a bit later in the section called "Creating an ODBC DSN."

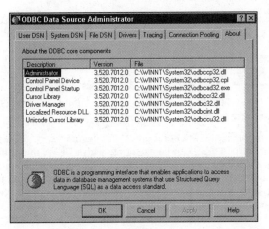

Figure 20-1: The ODBC Data Source Administrator enables the creation and modification of ODBC data source names (DSNs).

ODBC: The Need for a Standard

In the early days of the PC, database applications were developed to run on only one workstation (standalone) and support only one data source. The DBMS the application supported typically provided a proprietary API that the application used to interface to that database; as a result, applications became tightly coupled to databases. Because very little PC development was being done (most applications were still being written on larger mid-range or mainframe computers) and DBMSs were rarely, if ever, changed, this worked very well for many years. However, as more companies began accepting the PC as a viable platform on which to develop their software, the following problems arose:

✦ *Scalability*—With PCs becoming more common on every employee's desk, at some point the application had to become client/server capable. In other words, each desktop would have a copy of the application while the data source would exist only on the server. If the application had been written as a standalone application, it usually meant switching to another DBMS (one that supported multiple concurrent users). This almost always meant incurring the cost of rewriting large parts of the application as a result of the close relationship between the application and the database.

✦ *Interoperability*—If a company developed software to sell, the software was typically written to interface to a specific DBMS. If the decision was later made to interface to additional DBMSs, either the software went through massive design and coding changes, or the company developed a special version of the software for each DBMS it wished to support. Obviously, both "solutions" were costly propositions. Companies needed the capability of writing the software so that a single code base could interface to any DBMS.

✦ *Software development costs* — Because the APIs used to interface to the different DBMSs were almost always proprietary, if a company wanted to develop software to use a particular DBMS, the company had to hire developers who were proficient with that specific DBMS and its idiosyncrasies. If the company wanted support for additional DBMS systems, it had to hire experts for those systems as well. Here again, the need was clear: A standard API that would enable programmers to generically interface to a data source without regard to the specific DBMS implementation.

As a result of these problems (and many more), Microsoft and several other companies set out to create a standard API in which to communicate with the various DBMSs. The result of this collaboration was ODBC.

Understanding how ODBC works

Although ODBC itself is comprised of several pieces, a single sentence definition is that ODBC *provides a standard means of communicating with data sources using a SQL-like syntax.*

Before continuing, let me make one important distinction here. Many beginners to ODBC see the SQL part of that definition and think that ODBC can be used only with a DBMS that utilizes SQL. In reality, the ODBC API provides a SQL-like interface to *any data format for which an ODBC driver exists.* A great example of this is ASCII text. Suppose you have your data in text format. Normally, you would have to write your own routines to access and manipulate your data. However, because Microsoft provides a free ODBC driver for text files, you can use ODBC and write SQL statements just as if your data was in a *true* DBMS such as SQL Server or Oracle.

At this point, you know what ODBC does. Now, here's a look at how it works from an application developer's perspective.

In order to provide a layer of programmatic abstraction such that a single code base can access multiple data sources, the original designers of ODBC had two problems to solve. First, ODBC needed to provide database developers with a generic API that would be used to issue database requests to the underlying DBMS. Second, ODBC needed a standard means of communicating with any DBMS. These goals are addressed with the ODBC Driver Manager and ODBC drivers as follows: When an application makes an ODBC function call, it is actually calling an exported function of the ODBC Driver Manager. The ODBC Driver Manager then calls an exported function of the ODBC driver (usually provided by the DBMS vendor). It is the responsibility of the ODBC driver's vendor to respond to the ODBC Driver Manager. Therefore, the only layer of code that has any knowledge of the inner workings of the DBMS is the ODBC driver. You can see these components at work in Figure 20-2.

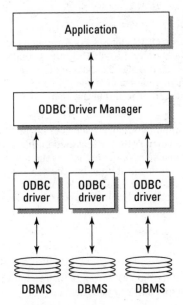

Figure 20-2: ODBC provides a layer of abstraction so that database applications can use a single code base to interface to a wide variety of DBMSs.

ODBC API conformance levels

In order to provide an API that can work with all DBMSs, ODBC defines certain minimum requirements that every ODBC-compliant driver is required to meet. This level of conformity is called *Core Level* and it is defined by the X/Open SQL Access Group (SAG) Call Level Interface (CLI) specification. Although ODBC defines a minimum conformance level, ODBC also gives more robust DBMSs to make their services available by defining several levels of conformance. ODBC drivers are then defined, or categorized, by the level of conformance to which they adhere.

It is important to understand that for an ODBC driver's manufacturer to claim that its driver corresponds to a given conformance level, the driver must implement all of the functionality defined within that level (whether or not the underlying data source does). However, drivers are not limited to implementing functions that are defined within the level of conformance to which they adhere. An ODBC driver can, for example, be defined as a Core Level driver and still implement functionality from other levels.

Because all ODBC drivers must implement the functions defined in the Core Level, database applications do not have to check a driver's conformance level before calling a Core Level function. However, if a database application has to make an ODBC call that is not defined in the Core Level, it is the database application's responsibility to ensure that the driver supports the desired function. There are two ways to accomplish this. The simplest and least flexible way is to find out from the driver's manufacturer if the driver supports the function(s) in question. Obviously, this is not an acceptable approach if the application is being written to work in a heterogeneous manner. In order to verify whether a driver supports a specific function, ODBC provides the `SQLGetFunctions` function.

ODBC SQL conformance levels

In addition to the different ODBC API conformance levels, ODBC defines conformance levels for the SQL grammar and SQL data types that are supported by the ODBC driver. Actually, you can find the definition for these conformance levels in the SQL-92 specification. As with the ODBC API conformance levels, a minimum ODBC SQL conformance level is defined. This minimum level is called the *SQL minimum grammar* and can be found in the *Microsoft ODBC 3.0 Programmer's Reference*.

All ODBC-compliant drivers must support the SQL minimum grammar. If a driver purports to conform to a given SQL-92 level, then it must support all syntax that is included in that level. However, if a driver supports a given SQL-92 level, it can also support higher-level functionality. For example, suppose a driver only supports the minimum grammar, but the driver's developers also want to support some higher-level functionality. They can do this as long as they advertise the driver as simply being compliant with the minimum grammar. Now, let's look at how to implement ODBC in your applications.

Implementing ODBC

The best way to proceed from this point is to split the different ODBC functions into logical groups that correspond to the order in which you are most likely to use them in your application:

✦ Configuring ODBC

✦ Connecting to a data source

✦ Querying the data and the data source

✦ Preparing and executing SQL requests

✦ Retrieving data

✦ Disconnecting from a data source

Configuring ODBC

As discussed earlier, ODBC provides a utility called the ODBC Data Source Administrator which is used to configure ODBC. If you are running Windows NT, this application can be accessed via a Control Panel applet. If you're running Windows 2000, you can select Start ➪ Programs ➪ Administrative Tools ➪ Data Sources (ODBC). If you have trouble locating this application (I've seen some installations where this was the case), simply type the following at the Start ➪ Run command line:

```
odbcad32
```

Once you've started the application, you'll see a list of installed ODBC drivers, defined DSNs, and tabs for configuring the tracing and connection pooling options. Figure 20-3 shows an example list of configured ODBC drivers.

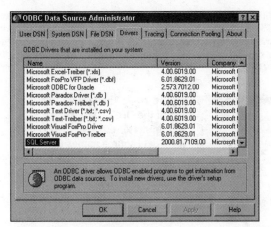

Figure 20-3: The Drivers tab of the ODBC Data Source Administrator displays installed ODBC drivers.

The ODBC drivers shown in Figure 20-3 are sometimes referred to as the *desktop drivers* because they support some of the more popular desktop DBMSs. You will sometimes hear these drivers incorrectly referred to as the "Access drivers." This is because the many developers using these drivers are using them with the Microsoft Access DBMS. However, as you can see, several DBMSs are supported with these drivers.

You install ODBC support for a DBMS by defining the ODBC driver with the ODBC Data Source Administrator. You generally don't have to worry about this task because it is typically carried out by an installation program provided by the driver's manufacturer.

Once the ODBC driver has been installed and a database created, you have to create a DSN. DSNs are used to map a specific data source to an ODBC driver. Following are the three valid types of DSNs supported:

   ✦ *User data source* — This data source is local to the computer on which it is created and can be used only by the user who creates it.

   ✦ *System data source* — This data source belongs to the computer on which it is created and belongs to that computer rather than the user who created it. Any users can access this data source as long as they have the correct privileges.

   ✦ *File data source* — This data source is specific to the underlying database file. In other words, any user that has the appropriate driver installed can use the data source.

Each ODBC driver defines what information is needed to create a DSN for a data source that the driver supports. Once the ODBC driver is selected, the ODBC Data Source Administrator, when adding a DSN, instructs the driver to display its configuration dialog box. At a minimum, most ODBC drivers require the physical filename that represents the data source, whether the system is local or remote, and the folder where the file resides.

Because the information needed to create a DSN is driver specific, you must consult the documentation for that driver in order to create a DSN for it. For example, if you're creating a DSN for a Microsoft Access database, you have the capability of specifying a system database file, a username, and a password.

Figure 20-4 shows the System DSNs on a PC running Windows 2000. As you can see, I've already added a System DSN called VCNET Bible. This DSN is used for the demo applications in this chapter as well as in Chapter 21. You'll see how to create this DSN when I discuss the first demo application later in this chapter. For now, however, take a look at how to programmatically perform some basic tasks using the ODBC API.

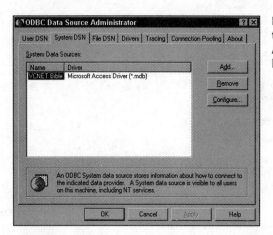

Figure 20-4: The System DSN tab of the ODBC Data Source Administrator displays all system-level data source names (DSNs).

Let's now take a look at what is required to programmatically connect to a data source. From there you'll get into the chapter's first demo where you'll learn how to both create and configure a DSN as well as use the ODBC SDK to retrieve and update data.

Connecting to a data source

Once a DSN has been configured via the ODBC Data Source Administrator, the database that was specified when the DSN was created can be accessed via the ODBC API. The first programmatic step to using ODBC is to connect to the data source. You do this via a series of function calls. The general flow of connecting to a data source is as follows:

1. Initialize ODBC and acquire a unique environment handle, or `henv`. This handle uniquely represents the thread's use of ODBC. To retrieve a handle for the current thread, call the `SQLAllocHandle` function.

   As you can see in the code snippet that follows, the application first declares a variable of type `SQLHENV`. Next, the `SQLAllocHandle` function is called specifying that a `henv` is desired and passes the address of the locally declared `henv` variable.

   ```
   SQLHENV henv;
   SQLRETURN rc = SQLAllocHandle(SQL_HANDLE_ENV,
                                 SQL_NULL_HANDLE,
                                 &henv);
   ```

2. Once you've obtained an environment handle, you need to set the ODBC version to which the application conforms. This is done via a call to `SQLSetEnvAttr`. The application calls this function and passes the `SQL_ATTR_ODBC_VERSION` constant to indicate

the supported ODBC version. In the following example, the fact that the constant `SQL_OV_ODBC3` is being passed indicates that ODBC 3.0 is the version that the application supports:

```
SQLSetEnvAttr(henv,
              SQL_ATTR_ODBC_VERSION,
              (SQLPOINTER) SQL_OV_ODBC3,
              SQL_IS_INTEGER);
```

3. Before an application can connect to a data source, it must acquire a database connection handle, or `hdbc`, from ODBC. This is accomplished by calling the `SQLAllocHandle` function using the `SQL_HANDLE_HDBC` constant as its first argument. The second argument must be a valid `henv` that was acquired using Step 1. The third and last argument must be a pointer to a variable of type `SQLHDBC`. The following code snippet shows a standard-looking call to retrieve the database handle:

```
SQLHDBC hdbc;
SQLRETURN  rc = SQLAllocHandle(SQL_HANDLE_ENV,
                              henv,
                              &hdbc);
```

4. Once you have an `hdbc`, you can finally connect to the data source by using any of three different ODBC functions: `SQLConnect`, `SQLDriverConnect`, or `SQLBrowseConnect`.

   - The `SQLConnect` function is a straightforward and simple way of connecting to a data source. Using this function, you simply pass the DSN, user id, and password to ODBC to connect to the data source.

   - The `SQLDriverConnect` function is an alternative for ODBC drivers and requires more information than can be passed using `SQLConnect`.

   - Finally, the `SQLBrowseConnect` function is an even more advanced means of connecting to a data source. Using one or more calls to `SQLBrowseConnect`, you can iteratively request the information needed to connect to a data source. The way this works is that the `SQLBrowseConnect` function returns the value `SQL_NEEDS_DATA` until the application has provided all of the information needed to connect to the data source, at which time the function returns `SQL_SUCCESS`.

   - To concentrate on more important topics of ODBC functionality, I'll use the basic `SQLConnect` function in the upcoming demos. Here is an example of using the `SQLConnect` function to connect to a data source named VCNET Bible. Note that the `SQL_NTS` constants simply tell ODBC that the previous argument passed was a null terminated string.

```
SQLRETURN rc = SQLConnect(hdbc,
                         (SQLCHAR*)"VCNET Bible",
                         SQL_NTS,
                         (SQLCHAR*)"", SQL_NTS,
                         (SQLCHAR*)"", SQL_NTS);
```

Once you've connected to a DSN using one of the various ODBC connect commands, the next logical step is to query for data, so let's take a look at how that is done next.

Querying the data and the data source

One of the most powerful aspects of ODBC is that it enables you to query an ODBC driver's capabilities. The functions that allow querying for this information are SQLGetFunctions, SQLGetInfo, and SQLGetTypeInfo.

✦ *SQLGetFunctions* is used to query an ODBC driver to determine the different functions, or groups of functions, the driver supports. In order to use this function, the application simply calls this function, passing it a valid hdbc and a numeric value that identifies either a specific ODBC function or group of ODBC functions. The values are defined in the SQLEXT.H file, which is installed with Microsoft SQL Server, the ODBC SDK, and Visual Studio .NET.

The following code snippet attempts to determine if the SQLTables and SQLColumns functions are available for the DBMS associated with the specified DSN:

```
SQLUSMALLINT bSQLTablesFunctionExists;
SQLUSMALLINT bSQLColumnsFunctionExists;

SQLGetFunctions(hdbc,
                SQL_API_SQLTABLES,
                &bSQLTablesFunctionExists);
SQLGetFunctions(hdbc,
                SQL_API_SQLTABLES,
                & bSQLColumnsFunctionExists);

if (bSQLTablesFunctionExists
&& bSQLColumnsFunctionExists)
{
    // both functions exist
}
```

The benefit of the SQLGetFunctions function is that it enables your application to determine beforehand if the driver supports a given function before attempting to call it. Therefore, you might be wondering at this point, "Does this mean I need a bunch of conditional logic in that single code base?" The answer is that it depends on your ODBC drivers and what you want to do with the data sources. As discussed in the section on conformance levels early in this chapter, if the only functions you're going to call are defined as Core Level functions or if you are working with a known set of drivers, you won't need this function. However, if you need your code to work with all ODBC drivers and you're attempting to use functions that might not be implemented in all drivers, the SQLGetFunctions function is invaluable.

✦ *SQLGetInfo* returns information about the ODBC driver and its capabilities. For example, you can use it to ascertain an ODBC driver's version and name as well as its level of ODBC API conformance and ODBC SQL conformance.

✦ An application calls *SQLGetTypeInfo* when seeking information regarding what SQL data types are supported by the data source as well as certain information about the data type. The tricky part about this function is that it does not directly return a value. Instead, the driver returns the information in the form of a result set, which works in much the same way a retrieval of data from a data source would. Therefore, once the function returns, the application must retrieve the results accordingly. You will see how to retrieve data in the next section as well as in the demo applications introduced later in the chapter.

Preparing and executing SQL requests

Once you have connected to a data source, the last thing the application must do before executing SQL requests against the data source is to acquire a statement handle, or hstmt. To allocate the hstmt, simply declare a variable of type SQLHSTMT and call the SQLAllocHandle function to specify that an hstmt is desired (using the SQL_HANDLE_STMT constant) and to pass the address of a declared hstmt variable. Here's a code snippet showing how this works:

```
SQLSTMT hstmt;
SQLRETURN  rc = SQLAllocHandle(SQL_HANDLE_STMT,
                               hdbc,
                               &hstmt);
```

Once the application acquires an hstmt, it can issue SQL statements against the data source. There are two different ways of executing a SQL query against a data source. One way is to call the SQLExecDirect function to specify the SQL statement in the function's second argument as shown in the following example. This function inserts a row of data into the UserMaster table:

```
SQLRETURN rc = ::SQLExecDirect(hstmt,
                               (unsigned char*)"INSERT INTO "
                               "UserMaster VALUES('UserID',"
                               "'User Name', 0)",
                               SQL_NTS))
```

Another means of executing a statement is to first prepare the statement using the SQLPrepare function and to then execute that statement using the SQLExecute function as shown here.

```
SQLRETURN rc;
LPCSTR szSQL = "INSERT INTO UserMaster "
               "values('UserID2', 'Just Another User', 0)";

if (SQL_SUCCESS == (rc = ::SQLPrepare(hstmt,
                                      (unsigned char*)szSQL,
                                      SQL_NTS)))
{
  if (SQL_SUCCESS == (rc = ::SQLExecute(hstmt)))
  ...
```

This SQLPrepare/SQLExecuteDirect function combination is much more efficient than simply calling ExecuteDirect when executing an SQL statement multiple times. This is because each time you call the ExecuteDirect function, the expression must be compiled by the underlying DBMS. However, if you call SQLPrepare first, then the expression is compiled a single time and then used each time the SQLExecuteDirect function is called.

Retrieving data

In the previous section you saw two different methods of using a SQL statement to insert data into a table. However, what do you do if the SQL statement returns data, and how do you map that data to your application's variables? That's where the next group of ODBC functions comes into play. When an ODBC function is said to have returned a result set, you need to *bind* your variables to the different columns of data that are returned. ODBC provides a great deal of flexibility in retrieving the data, depending on the type of application you are developing.

If one of your application's design goals is flexibility, using the SQLNumResultCols, SQLDescribeCol, and SQLGetData functions can be a tremendous benefit. These functions enable the database developer to develop the application without knowing how many columns and data types are going to be returned. For example, these functions might be used in an ad-hoc query tool in which end users can define their own queries. Because of the dynamic nature of this application, the application won't know the number of columns and their respective data types until runtime.

So how does the application know what data was returned from a query that wasn't defined until runtime? The application uses the functions you learned in the previous section to build and run the user-defined SQL statement. ODBC then returns a handle to a result set. However, the application doesn't know anything about the result set in terms of how many columns have been returned or what the data type of each column is. Therefore, the application calls the SQLNumResultCols function to determine how many columns had been returned in the result set. After that, a call to SQLDescribeCol for each column yields the data type for each specified column. Once a specific column's data type is known, the SQLGetData function can be used to retrieve the value for that column. Obviously, this is a simplistic description, but it provides a general overview of what is involved. These functions are illustrated in all their gory detail in the second and third demos covered in this chapter.

Obviously, not everyone needs the level of flexibility previously described. The majority of database developers issue SQL statements that they code in their applications and, therefore, do not need to query ODBC to determine the type of data being returned in the result set. In these situations, you can use the SQLBindCol and SQLFetch functions to retrieve the data from an ODBC result set into your application's variables. The SQLBindCol function enables you to specify the column number in the result set that you are binding, the type of data at that column position, and the address of a variable to hold the data once SQLFetch is called to retrieve the data.

Note that you do not have to bind every column. You need only bind the columns whose data you wish to map into your variables. Once you have called SQLBindCol for each desired column, you can call SQLFetch as many times as necessary, or until you have read the entire result set. Here is an example of how to use these two functions to retrieve your data from a result set. This code segment assumes that a SQL statement has already been run to retrieve the data into a result set:

```
#define LEN_USERID 16

SDWORD cb;
char szUserID[LEN_USERID];

if (SQL_SUCCESS == (rc = SQLBindCol(hstmt, 1,
  SQL_C_CHAR, szUserID, LEN_USERID, &cb)))
{
  if (SQL_SUCCESS == (rc = SQLFetch(hstmt)))
  {
    // szUserID now contains the value from
    // the first row of the returned result set
    ...
```

Disconnecting from a data source

Once you have finished using a connection to a data source, you must disconnect from the data source (via the SQLDisconnect function) and release any handles that have been allocated. Here is an example of what your "cleanup" code might look like:

```
if (henv)
{
  if (hdbc)
  {
    if (bIsConnected)
    {
      if (hstmt)
      {
       ::SQLFreeHandle(SQL_HANDLE_STMT, hstmt);
      }
      ::SQLDisconnect(hdbc);
      bIsConnected = FALSE;
    }
    ::SQLFreeHandle(SQL_HANDLE_DBC, hdbc);
    hdbc = NULL;
  }
  ::SQLFreeHandle(SQL_HANDLE_ENV, henv);
  henv = NULL;
}
```

Now that you've seen the basics of using ODBC, look at a demo application in the next section.

Using ODBC to Fetch Data

The demo in this section (ODBCDemo) is a simple ODBC application that uses many of the functions that you have read about up to now: allocating the different ODBC handles, connecting to a data source, fetching data, de-allocating the ODBC handles, and disconnecting from the data source. Although this application is very simple, you can use these same functions in your own application regardless of its scope or complexity.

To start, create a new Visual C++ dialog-based application called ODBCDemo. While in the MFC Application Wizard, select the SDI, MDI, or Multiple top-level documents application type. Then click the Database Support link. As you can see in Figure 20-5, each of these application types offers varying database support in terms of the wizard generating code for you.

Let's briefly look at each of the Database support options as this set of radio buttons controls which of the other options on the dialog box can be selected.

✦ The first option (None) is obvious. Selecting it disables all other options, and the wizard does not generate any database related code in your project.

✦ Selecting the Header files only option, this enables you to select which database access technology your application is going to use. From there, if you select the ODBC option, the wizard includes in your project file the ODBC header file AFXDB.H. It also automatically adds the necessary link libraries to the project. If you select the OLEDB option, the necessary OLEDB header files will be included: ATLBASE.H, AFXOLEDB.H, and ATLPLUS.H.

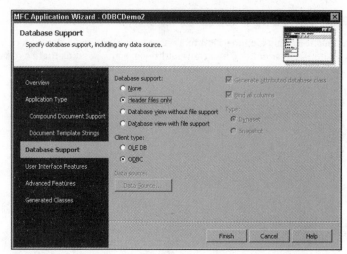

Figure 20-5: The MFC Application Wizard offers several database support options.

✦ The Database view without file support option is only available if you are using the document/view architecture. This option includes the header files, link libraries, a record view, and a recordset class. The way this works is that you first choose this option and then the Data Source button becomes enabled. From there, you can select the ODBC DSN (or OLEDB Provider) and table or view that you want to use. In addition, you also have the opportunity to specify if you want a dynaset or snapshot cursor (explained in Chapter 21), and if you want to "bind the columns." This simply means that RFX will be used to associate fields in the table or view with the class members of the recordset created for you. Put simply, RFX is the database equivalent of DDX that you learned about in Chapter 1. Finally, the Generate attributed database class option is used if you want the recordset class to use attributes. Attributes are only available if you choose an OLEDB Provider.

✦ The Database view support with file support option works exactly like the Database view support without file support, except that it also includes support document serialization.

From the fact that the last two options create views for you, and can involve other document/view related features (such as RFX), it's understandable that these options can't be used with dialog-based applications. If you read the documentation it certainly implies that these are the only options not available to you if you choose a dialog-based application. However, if you choose to create a dialog-based application, all database support options are grayed out. I can only assume this is a bug in Visual Studio.NET and will be resolved. However, given that it's only a minor annoyance to have to manually include the proper header files and link libraries for database support, I don't think this will be a bug with a high priority.

Having said all that—and because I like to do things manually to see how they work—create this application as a dialog-based application. After you create the DSN in the next step, you'll see how to manually add ODBC support to your project.

Creating an ODBC DSN

To create an ODBC System DSN perform the following steps:

1. Open the ODBC Data Source Administrator and select the System DSN tab.

2. Click the Add button on the right side of the dialog box.

3. Select the appropriate ODBC driver. (For the demos in this chapter, you should select the Microsoft Access Driver (*.mdb) driver.) When you have selected the desired driver, click the Finish button in the lower-right corner of the dialog box.

4. In the Data Source Name text box, type the name of the DSN. (For the demos in this chapter, set the DSN name to **VCNet Bible**.) Once you have typed the DSN (and option-ally, a description), click the Select button on the left side of the dialog box.

5. Using the File dialog box, select the database that will represent the data source for the new DSN. (For the database demo applications of this book, you'll need to use the VCNetBible.mdb Access file provided on the Web site for this book.)

Note   Although you do not need the Microsoft Access product to run this demo, you will need it if you want to open and modify the contents of demo database.

6. Once you have selected the database and returned to the Setup dialog box, click the OK button in the upper-right corner of the dialog box.

7. The System Data Sources list view control will now contain your newly created VCNET Bible DSN. Click the OK button in the lower-left corner of the dialog box to end the application.

Adding ODBC support to a Visual C++ project

You need to include the appropriate header files and link library in order to use the ODBC SDK in an application. Most times, I simply add the needed `include` directives to the `stdafx.h` file so that every file in the project has access to the necessary ODBC functions.

There are actually two methods of adding ODBC support. The first method is to include the following header files:

```
#include <sql.h>
#include <sqlext.h>
#include <sqltypes.h>
```

Note that if you are adding these to the `stdafx.h` file, you need to add them at the end of the file to ensure that the necessary Windows header files are included, because some Windows constructs (such as HWND) are referenced in the ODBC header files.

Now, you need to add the ODBC import library (`odbc32.lib`) to your project. To do this, select Project ➪ Add Existing Item, and browse to the import library. The default Visual Studio .NET installation will locate this file in the `\program files\microsoft visual studio.net\ vc7\platformsdk\lib` folder. Simply select it, and it will automatically be added to your project and will appear in your project's Solution View.

This is not too terribly difficult. However, the easiest method of adding ODBC support is to simply add the following include directive to a file in your project.

```
#include <afxdb.h>
```

This file includes the necessary Windows header files (if not already included) so there's no need to worry about include file ordering and this file also uses the #pragma comment directive so that the necessary ODBC import libraries are linked into your application. Needless to say, this last method is the one I personally prefer.

Modifying the ODBCDemo dialog box

Because this is a dialog-based application, your project already contains a dialog box to use for displaying the customer data. At this point, locate the IDD_ODBCDEMO_DIALOG dialog template resource in the project's Resource dialog bar and make the following modifications:

1. Add the controls to the dialog box as shown in Figure 20-6. Note that the control under the Term Codes static text is a list box and that you do not need to add the About button.

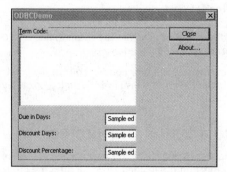

Figure 20-6: The ODBCDemo dialog box looks similar to this after the new controls have been added.

2. You should now have four input controls (a list box for the Term Code list and three Edit fields for the Due in Days, Discount Days, and Discount Percentage). For these controls, create the DDX member variables shown in Table 20-1.

Table 20-1: Member Variables for ODBCDemo

Control	Category	Variable Type	Variable Name
Term Code	Control	CListbox	m_lbxTermCodes
Due in Days	Value	long	m_lDueInDays
Discount Days	Value	long	m_lDiscountDays
Discount Percentage	Value	double	m_dDiscountPctg

Adding the initialization and database code

After modifying the ODBCDemo main dialog box, add the following code to retrieve the data from the Access database and populate the list box:

1. Add the following function declaration to the CODBCDemoDlg class:

```
public:
  void FillTermCodesListbox();
```

2. Now add the following struct definition to the top of the ODBCDemoDlg.cpp file:

```
struct TERM_CODE
{
  CString m_strTermCode;
  long m_lDueInDays;
  long m_lDiscountDays;
  double m_dDiscountPctg;
};
```

3. Add the following #define directive after the term code struct definition:

```
#define LEN_TERM_CODE 20
```

4. Locate the OnInitDialog function and add the following function call just before the return statement. This call loads the list box upon initialization of the dialog box:

```
FillTermCodesListbox();
```

5. Add the following function at the end of the ODBCDemoDlg.cpp file (the code listing is a bit long so I've interspersed text throughout the code in order to explain exactly what the different parts of the code are doing):

```
void CODBCDemoDlg::FillTermCodesListbox()
{
```

Declare and initialize the following variables to be used in this function. The ODBC handles are set to NULL so that upon exiting the function, it is easier to tell which handles were successfully allocated (the ones that are not NULL).

```
BOOL bSuccess = FALSE;

CString strFunction;

SQLHENV henv = NULL;
SQLHDBC hdbc = NULL;
BOOL bIsConnected = FALSE;
SQLHSTMT hstmt = NULL;

SQLRETURN rc;

SWORD    sMsgNum = 0;
char     szState[7]="";
SDWORD   pfNative=0;
```

The following function calls (SQLAllocHandle, SQLSetEnvAttr, and SQLAllocHandle) initialize the ODBC and return handles to use in subsequent ODBC function calls:

```
if (SQL_SUCCESS == (rc =
::SQLAllocHandle(SQL_HANDLE_ENV, SQL_NULL_HANDLE,
&henv)))
{
 if (SQL_SUCCESS == (rc = ::SQLSetEnvAttr(henv,
 SQL_ATTR_ODBC_VERSION, (SQLPOINTER) SQL_OV_ODBC3,
 SQL_IS_INTEGER)))
 {
  if (SQL_SUCCESS == (rc =
  ::SQLAllocHandle(SQL_HANDLE_DBC, henv, &hdbc)))
  {
```

The call to SQLConnect connects this application to the DSN that was created in the section "Creating an ODBC DSN" earlier in the chapter.

```
rc = ::SQLConnect(hdbc,
                  (SQLCHAR*)"VCNet Bible",
                  SQL_NTS,
                  (SQLCHAR*)"", SQL_NTS, (SQLCHAR*)"",
                  SQL_NTS);
if ((SQL_SUCCESS == rc)
|| (SQL_SUCCESS_WITH_INFO == rc))
{
 bIsConnected = TRUE;
```

Once you have connected to the DSN, allocate a statement handle to use when you submit your SQL to the data source.

```
if (SQL_SUCCESS == (rc =
::SQLAllocHandle(SQL_HANDLE_STMT, hdbc, &hstmt)))
{
```

The following code builds a SQL SELECT string, prepares it (via SQLPrepare), and executes it (via SQLExecute):

```
LPCSTR szSQL = "SELECT * FROM TermCodeMaster";
if (SQL_SUCCESS == (rc = ::SQLPrepare(hstmt,
(unsigned char*)szSQL, SQL_NTS)))
{
 if (SQL_SUCCESS == (rc = ::SQLExecute(hstmt)))
 {
```

After the SQL statement has been executed, bind the local variables to their corresponding columns by calling SQLBindCol for each desired column. Next, call SQLFetch to retrieve the data into the bound variables.

```
SDWORD cb;
char szTermCode[LEN_TERM_CODE];
long lDueInDays;
long lDiscountDays;
double dDiscountPctg;

SQLBindCol(hstmt, 1, SQL_C_CHAR, szTermCode,
```

```
      LEN_TERM_CODE, &cb);

   SQLBindCol(hstmt, 2, SQL_C_LONG, &lDueInDays,
      0, &cb);

   SQLBindCol(hstmt, 3, SQL_C_LONG,
      &lDiscountDays, 0, &cb);

   SQLBindCol(hstmt, 4, SQL_C_DOUBLE,
      &dDiscountPctg, 0, &cb);

   int iIndex;

   rc = SQLFetch(hstmt);
   while (SQL_SUCCESS == rc)
   {
```

So that the database does not have to be accessed each time a term code is selected from the list box in order to retrieve that term code's information, allocate a TERM_CODE struct that will contain all of the information for each term code that is read from the database. That way, when each term code is added to the list box, that list box entry's item data is set to the TERM_CODE pointer, making the retrieval of each term code's information much more efficient.

```
      TERM_CODE* pTermCode = new TERM_CODE;
      pTermCode->m_strTermCode = szTermCode;
      pTermCode->m_lDueInDays = lDueInDays;
      pTermCode->m_lDiscountDays = lDiscountDays;
      pTermCode->m_dDiscountPctg = dDiscountPctg;

      iIndex=m_lbxTermCodes.AddString(szTermCode);
      m_lbxTermCodes.SetItemData(iIndex,
      (DWORD)pTermCode);

      rc = SQLFetch(hstmt);
    }
   }
  }
 }
}
}
}
}
```

Once all of the records have been read from the data source, all that is left to do is to clean up and de-initialize ODBC by disconnecting from the data source and releasing any acquired ODBC handles.

```
if (henv)
 {
  if (hdbc)
  {
   if (bIsConnected)
   {
```

```
    if (hstmt)
    {
      ::SQLFreeHandle(SQL_HANDLE_STMT, hstmt);
    }
    ::SQLDisconnect(hdbc);
    bIsConnected = FALSE;
  }
  ::SQLFreeHandle(SQL_HANDLE_DBC, hdbc);
  hdbc = NULL;
  }
  ::SQLFreeHandle(SQL_HANDLE_ENV, henv);
  henv = NULL;
  }
}
```

6. You now must add a function so that when a term code is selected from the list box, the proper information is displayed in the dialog box. To do this, add an event handler for the list box's `LBN_SELCHANGE` message. Once Visual Studio opens the `ODBCDemoDlg.Cpp` file and places the cursor in the newly created `OnLbnSelchangeLbxTermCodes` function, code the handler as follows.

```
void CODBCDemoDlg::OnLbnSelchangeLbxTermCodes()
{
  int iIndex = m_lbxTermCodes.GetCurSel();
  if (LB_ERR != iIndex)
  {
    TERM_CODE* pTermCode =
      (TERM_CODE*)m_lbxTermCodes.GetItemData(iIndex);

    if (pTermCode)
    {
      m_lDueInDays = pTermCode->m_lDueInDays;
      m_lDiscountDays = pTermCode->m_lDiscountDays;
      m_dDiscountPctg = pTermCode->m_dDiscountPctg;

      UpdateData(FALSE);
    }
  }
}
```

Here's what the `OnLbnSelchangeLbxTermCodes` function does. When an item (a term code) in the list box is selected, this function will be called. The function then retrieves the index of the item that was selected (via the `CListbox::GetCurSel` function). If there was not an error in retrieving this index (–1 is returned on error or if no item is currently selected), the current item's item data is retrieved. This is the same item data that was set in the `FillTermCodesListbox` function earlier. This item data, therefore, is a pointer to the information about this specific term code data that was read from the data source upon initialization of the dialog box and stored in a `TERM_CODE` structure. The member variables that correspond to the different dialog box controls are changed to reflect the current term code's information. The `UpdateData` function is then called to move the data from these member variables to the controls in the dialog box.

7. Now add a function so that when the dialog box is closed, the `TERM_CODE` structures that were created need to be deleted. To do this, add the following virtual function override to the `CODBCDemoDlg`. As the name suggests, the MFC framework calls this function when dialog box is closed. When executed, this code iterates through every term code in the list box, and after retrieving its item data, calls the C++ delete operator to free the structure's associated memory.

```
BOOL CODBCDemoDlg::DestroyWindow()
{
 TERM_CODE* pTermCode;
 int nTermCodes = m_lbxTermCodes.GetCount();
 for (int i = 0; i < nTermCodes; i++)
 {
  pTermCode =
    (TERM_CODE*)m_lbxTermCodes.GetItemData(i);

  if (pTermCode)
  {
   delete pTermCode;
  }
 }

 return CDialog::DestroyWindow();
}
```

8. Now, build and run the application. The results should be similar to what you see in Figure 20-7. Simply click the different term codes in the list box to view its associated data.

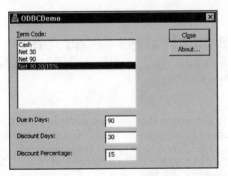

Figure 20-7: The ODBCDemo application demonstrates how to use the ODBC SDK to execute SQL queries against an ODBC data source and fetch the returned data.

Now that you've seen the basics of opening a data source and reading data, let's move on to more of the tasks that make ODBC special — the ability to dynamically query a data store.

Using ODBC to Dynamically Query a Data Source

At times you will be faced with scenarios in which you do not know the schema of a database until runtime — for example, in ad-hoc query and reporting tools. In both cases, end users can build their own SQL from a list of tables. As shown in the previous demo, it is extremely easy to pass ODBC a SQL string, have it executed, and retrieve the resulting data. However, how can you do this when you don't know the SQL string until runtime?

Luckily, ODBC provides several functions that you can use for this very purpose. After connecting to the data source, the next steps required are the following:

1. Prepare the SQL statement with the `SQLPrepare` function.

2. Execute the SQL statement with the `SQLExecute` function.

3. Call `SQLNumResultCols` to find out how many columns were returned in the result set.

4. Call the `SQLDescribeCol` function for each column to get the column type.

5. Convert the SQL type returned from `SQLDescribeCol` to a C type for each column.

6. Allocate memory for the data (depending on the C type) for each row in the result set.

7. Call `SQLGetData` to read the data into the allocated memory for each row/column.

Did I say "luckily"? Well, it may not be easy, but at least it can be done in ODBC whereas most database APIs don't even come close to allowing this sort of flexibility. Therefore, in this demo, you will not only learn how to do everything previously mentioned, but you will also put all this code into a reusable C++ class called `CODBCDynamic` so that you can reduce the 400+ lines of required client code to two lines!

Note   Unlike the first tutorial-style demo, this demo won't be hands-on. This is because the code necessary to create this class is so long that it would result in a demo that many people would not want to take the time to manually key in. Therefore, instead of dumping a 20-page listing of code on you, I'm going to present only the salient classes and functions that illustrate how to use some of the more advanced ODBC functions to dynamically query and manipulate a data source.

Looking at the CODBCDynamic class declaration

First take a look at the `ODBCDynamic.h` file (with comments sprinkled). Here you have just the standard `pragma` directive to get things started:

```
#pragma once
```

Next, take a look at a couple of `typedef` definitions that are used with the `CODBCDynamic` class. The `CODBCDynamic` class contains an `ExecuteSQL` member function that will be covered shortly. After the class' `ExecuteSQL` function has been called, the class' `CODBCRecordArray` array (m_ODBCRecordArray) will contain an entry of type `CODBCRecord` for each record returned by the SQL statement. Each of these `CODBCRecord` objects is simply a `CMapStringToOb` object, where the string is a column name and the object is a `CDBVariant` pointer whose value represents the database value for that record/column combination. Using a map for the record enables the programmer to either iterate through the entire map to get each column's value for that record or request a specific column's value if the column name is known. Here is that code (I used templatized maps to ensure type safety):

```
typedef CTypedPtrMap<CMapStringToPtr, \
 CString /* column name */, \
 CDBVariantEx* /* value */> CODBCRecord;

typedef CTypedPtrArray<CObArray, \
 CODBCRecord*> CODBCRecordArray;
```

The following example shows a basic constructor and destructor as well as some member variables used to hold the different ODBC handles. Note that the constructor takes as its only argument the ODBC DSN that the SQL statements will be executed against.

```
class AFX_EXT_CLASS CODBCDynamic
{
public:
 CODBCDynamic(LPCSTR lpszDSN);
 ~CODBCDynamic();
 protected:
 void CleanOutRecordArray();

protected:
 SQLHENV m_henv;
 SQLHDBC m_hdbc;
 BOOL m_bIsConnected;

public:
 SQLHDBC GetHDBC ()
 {
   return m_hdbc;
 }
```

This is the member variable representing the array of records returned from the ExecuteSQL member function:

```
public:
 CODBCRecordArray m_ODBCRecordArray;
```

These are internal helper functions that are explained shortly:

```
protected:
 short GetFieldTypeFromSQLType(short nSQLType);

 void* GetDataBuffer(CDBVariantEx* pvarValue,
   short nFieldType, int* pnLen, short nSQLType,
   UDWORD nPrecision);

 long GetData(SQLHSTMT hstmt, short nFieldIndex,
   short nFieldType, LPVOID pvData, int nLen,
   short nSQLType);
```

These are the only two functions that the class' clients need to use.

```
public:
 long ExecuteSQL(LPCTSTR lpszSQL);
 long FetchData(HSTMT hstmt);
};
```

The ExecuteSQL function enables the client to pass any valid SQL string and have it executed. The resulting data is then placed in the m_ODBCRecordArray seen earlier.

The FetchData function is for those cases when you have a result set and still want to use this class' code to dynamically map the data into an easy-to-use array. An example is the

SQLGetTypeInfo function, which enables you to query the ODBC driver for information concerning the different types that the data source supports. When you call this function, you need to supply an hstmt and the information returned from the driver is placed in the cursor associated with this hstmt. Your code then needs to read through this cursor. Therefore, as an added bonus to this class, I added the FetchData function, which takes an hstmt that already contains a cursor with data. As you'll see shortly, both functions go through the same code path to build the internal data array and maps.

You may have noticed that after a call to ExecuteSQL the programmer has no way to initialize the class before making another call. That is because this initialization code is in a protected member function called CleanOutRecordArray, and it is one of the first things the class calls when the ExecuteSQL member function is called. Therefore, each time the client calls the ExecuteSQL member function, it is guaranteed that the memory associated with the previously executed SQL statement is initialized. For this reason, you must make sure that you copy to a new location any data that you want to reference across multiple calls to ExecuteSQL.

Understanding how the CODBCDynamic class works

As I mentioned earlier, although displaying the entire CODBCDynamic class wouldn't really serve any purpose, it is helpful to show some of the more relevant functions (in the order they are called) so that you understand just how this class dynamically retrieves data from a data source without knowing anything about the database's schema. In the process, you will learn some of the more advanced features of using the ODBC API.

Connecting to the DSN

To connect to the DSN, you begin with the CODBCDynamic constructor. You may recall from the description of the class' header file that when a user of your class instantiates this class, they do so by passing it a DSN. The appropriate handles are then allocated, and the DSN is connected to using the basic connection functions you learned about in this chapter's first demo application.

```
CODBCDynamic::CODBCDynamic(LPCSTR lpszDSN)
{
 SQLRETURN rc;

 m_henv = NULL;
 m_hdbc = NULL;
 m_bIsConnected = FALSE;

 if (SQL_SUCCESS == (rc =
 ::SQLAllocHandle(SQL_HANDLE_ENV,
  SQL_NULL_HANDLE, &m_henv)))
 {
  if (SQL_SUCCESS == (rc = ::SQLSetEnvAttr(m_henv,
    SQL_ATTR_ODBC_VERSION, (SQLPOINTER) SQL_OV_ODBC3,
    SQL_IS_INTEGER)))
  {
   if (SQL_SUCCESS == (rc =
   ::SQLAllocHandle(SQL_HANDLE_DBC, m_henv, &m_hdbc)))
   {
    rc = ::SQLConnect(m_hdbc,
```

```
        (unsigned char*)lpszDSN, SQL_NTS,
        (unsigned char*)"", SQL_NTS, (unsigned char*)"",
        SQL_NTS);
      if ((SQL_SUCCESS == rc)
      || (SQL_SUCCESS_WITH_INFO == rc))
      {
        m_bIsConnected = TRUE;
      }
    }
  }
 }
}
```

Fetching the returned data from a SQL statement

After constructing an instance of the CODBCDynamic class, the ExecuteSQL function can be called:

```
long CODBCDynamic::ExecuteSQL(LPCTSTR lpszSQL)
{
  long lRecordsRead = 0;
```

As mentioned previously, the CleanOutRecordArray function is used to initialize the record array. This function uses a couple of simple for loops to iterate through the record array and column/value map and releases the previously allocated memory.

```
CleanOutRecordArray();

BOOL bSuccess = FALSE;
SQLRETURN rc;
SQLHSTMT hstmt = NULL;

if (SQL_SUCCESS == (rc =
::SQLAllocHandle(SQL_HANDLE_STMT, m_hdbc, &hstmt)))
{
```

The class then uses the SQLPrepare and SQLExecute functions to have the data source execute the SQL that was passed to this function. Remember that when you execute a SQL function, a result set is returned and is represented by an hstmt.

```
  if (SQL_SUCCESS == (rc = ::SQLPrepare(hstmt,
  (unsigned char*)lpszSQL, SQL_NTS)))
  {
    if (SQL_SUCCESS == (rc = ::SQLExecute(hstmt)))
    {
```

Once the result set has been retrieved, another member function (FetchData) is called to retrieve the data into local memory. This function is called internally so that the same code path is used whether you are calling the ExecuteSQL function with a SQL string or the FetchData function with an hstmt representing a result set.

```
    lRecordsRead = FetchData(hstmt);
    }
    ::SQLFreeHandle(SQL_HANDLE_STMT, &hstmt);
  }
}
```

When the function returns, the return value will be the total number of records that were retrieved for the SQL statement that was passed to this function.

```
return lRecordsRead;
}
```

Now things start to get interesting. The FetchData function is the function that really does the stuff you, as an aspiring ODBC guru, should care about.

```
long CODBCDynamic::FetchData(HSTMT hstmt)
{
  SQLRETURN rc;

  long lRecordsRead = 0;
  CODBCRecord* pODBCRecord;

  SWORD FAR iNumResultCols = 0;
  CObArray arrODBCColumns;
```

This class is nothing more than a placeholder for the information that defines a given column. Its use is explained next.

```
  CODBCColumnInfo* pODBCColumnInfo;
```

The first record is fetched from the result set.

```
  rc = SQLFetch(hstmt);
  while (SQL_SUCCESS == rc)
  {
```

Because you wouldn't want to get the column information every time a record is fetched from the result set, some first-time processing has to occur. Here, the number of columns in this result set is ascertained via the SQLNumResultCols function. A for loop is then used so that, for each column, the SQLDescribeCol function is called to retrieve information about the column that will be needed to allocate the proper amount of memory when the data is retrieved.

Next, an object of type CODBCColumnInfo is created. The pointer to this object is then saved into an array where the index of the array is equal to the index of the column in the result set. That way, for example, when the function is reading the data for record x, column y, the column information can be located in this column information array at index y.

```
    if (1 == ++lRecordsRead)
    {
    if (SQL_SUCCESS == (rc = ::SQLNumResultCols(hstmt,
    &iNumResultCols)))
    {
      for (int i = 1; i <= iNumResultCols; i++)
      {
      char lpszColName[MAX_COLNAME + 1];
      SWORD nLen;
      SWORD nSQLType;
      UDWORD nPrecision;
      SWORD nScale;
      SWORD nNullability;

      if (SQL_SUCCESS == (rc = ::SQLDescribeCol(hstmt,
```

```
      i, (UCHAR*)lpszColName, MAX_COLNAME, &nLen,
      &nSQLType, &nPrecision, &nScale, &nNullability)))
      {
```

The `GetFieldTypeFromSQLType` function simply uses a `switch` statement to determine the correct type to be used for the column's SQL type. The type is needed so that when the `SQLGetData` function is called to retrieve the data into the local variables, the correct type can be passed for the column whose data is being retrieved.

```
      // Determine the default field type and
      // get the data buffer
      short nFieldType =
        GetFieldTypeFromSQLType(nSQLType);

      pODBCColumnInfo =
        new CODBCColumnInfo(lpszColName,
        nLen, nFieldType, nSQLType, nPrecision);

      arrODBCColumns.Add((CObject*)pODBCColumnInfo);
    }
   }
  }
}
```

At this point, the column information has been retrieved. A new `CODBCRecord` object is created. Recall that this is simply a `CObArray`.

```
      pODBCRecord = new CODBCRecord();
```

For each of the result set's columns, a `CDBVariantEx` object is created. The `CDBVariant` class is a simple derived class of type `CDBVariant`. The base class is used to hold virtually any type of data. It accomplishes this by having a member variable for a number of different types. This class is used by examining the object's `m_dwType` member variable. The value of that member variable indicates which member variable to retrieve the data from.

An example might be in order to clarify things. If the `m_dwType` member variable is equal to `DBVT_BOOL` (`boolean` value type), then the data is retrieved by referencing the object's `m_bVal` member variable. If you want to see a complete list of all the types that this class supports, it is documented in online help.

The `CDBVariantEx` class then simply adds one member function, `GetStringValue`, which enables a calling function to retrieve the object's data value into a `CString` regardless of the actual type. This makes it easier for clients to retrieve data when printing or displaying that data.

```
      for (int j = 0; j < iNumResultCols; j++)
      {
      CDBVariantEx* pvarValue = new CDBVariantEx();
      pvarValue->Clear();

      int nGetDataBufferLen = 0;
```

The column's data type, `GetDataBuffer`, is called to allocate the necessary memory. You may be wondering why there's a `void` pointer called `pvData` when the data can be copied into the `CDBVariantEx` object. This is because ODBC isn't designed to copy data into C++ classes such as my `CDBVariantEx` class. In other words, ODBC simply takes an address of memory where the data is to be copied. Therefore, the `GetDataBuffer` function sets the address of the `pvData` pointer to the appropriate member variable of the `CDBVariantEx` object, depending on the type.

For example, suppose you have a column whose type is `short`. The `pvData` pointer would be set to the address of the `CDBVariantEx` object's `m_iVal` member variable. This way, in effect, the data is being read directly into the `CDBVariantEx` object, and you don't have to go through the extra step of copying it there.

```
void* pvData = GetDataBuffer(pvarValue,
  ((CODBCColumnInfo*)arrODBCColumns[j])->
  m_nFieldType, &nGetDataBufferLen,
  ((CODBCColumnInfo*)arrODBCColumns[j])->m_nSQLType,
  ((CODBCColumnInfo*)arrODBCColumns[j])->
  m_nPrecision);
```

At this point, you finally know the column type and have allocated the appropriate amount of memory to hold the data for that type. Now the `GetData` member function is called. This function basically just calls the ODBC `SQLGetData` function passing it the `pvData` pointer retrieved earlier. Notice the second argument (`j+1`). This is the column number that represents the column whose data is being retrieved. When this function returns, the class will finally have the data for this record and column combination.

```
long nActualSize = GetData(hstmt, j+1,
  ((CODBCColumnInfo*)arrODBCColumns[j])->
  m_nFieldType, pvData, nGetDataBufferLen,
  ((CODBCColumnInfo*)arrODBCColumns[j])->
  m_nSQLType);

// deal with NULLs
if (-1 == nActualSize)
{
  pvarValue->Clear();
  pvarValue->m_dwType = DBVT_NULL;
}
```

Now that the data for this column has been retrieved, the column name and its `CDBVariant` value (for the current record) are added to the column/value map for the current record.

```
pODBCRecord->
  SetAt(((CODBCColumnInfo*)arrODBCColumns[j])->
  m_lpszColName, pvarValue);

if ((-1 != nActualSize)
&& (((CODBCColumnInfo*)arrODBCColumns[j])->
m_nFieldType == SQL_C_CHAR))
{

  // Release the string buffer
  CString strValue = (CString)*pvarValue->m_pstring;
  strValue.ReleaseBuffer(nActualSize <
  ((CODBCColumnInfo*)arrODBCColumns[j])->m_nLen
  ? nActualSize :
  ((CODBCColumnInfo*)arrODBCColumns[j])->m_nLen);
}
}
```

Once all of the columns/values have been added to the map for the current record, the record is added to the record array, and the next record is fetched from the data source.

```
m_ODBCRecordArray.Add(pODBCRecord);
rc = SQLFetch(hstmt);
}
```

After all of the records have been fetched from the result set, a little cleanup is necessary for the column type objects that were created when the first record was retrieved.

```
for (int iColumn = arrODBCColumns.GetUpperBound();
iColumn >= 0; iColumn--)
{
  CODBCColumnInfo* pODBCColumnInfo =
   (CODBCColumnInfo*)arrODBCColumns[iColumn];

  if (pODBCColumnInfo)
  {
   delete pODBCColumnInfo;
  }
  arrODBCColumns.RemoveAt(iColumn);
}
ASSERT(0 == arrODBCColumns.GetSize());
```

Return the number of records read to this function's caller.

```
  return lRecordsRead;
}
```

Using the CODBCDynamic class

Now that you have seen what's involved in writing a class like this, here's a look at what it takes to use it.

```
CODBCDynamic odbcDynamic(m_strDSN);
odbcDynamic.ExecuteSQL(CString(_T("Your SQL "
                                 "statement goes here)));
```

That's it; you only need two lines of client code to replace the more than 400 lines it took to write the CODBCDynamic class! At this point, simply iterating through the record array yields a CMapStringToOb that represents all of the columns and their values for each record. The client can then iterate through that map to get every column's value, or it can use the CMapStringToOb::Lookup function to retrieve a specific column's data (provided column's name is known).

Figure 20-8 shows an example that uses the CODBCDynamic class.

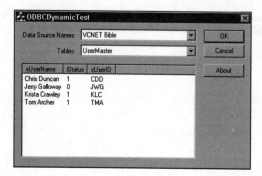

Figure 20-8: The CODBCDynamicTest application demonstrates how to use the CODBCDynamic class to query any ODBC DSN without knowing the database's schema.

As you can see, the sample application fills a combo box with all of the DSNs in the system. Once a DSN is selected, a second combo box is filled with all of the tables that exist in the data source pointed to by the DSN. After the user selects a table, the `CODBCDynamic::ExecuteSQL` function is called to retrieve all of the records from the table, which are then displayed in the list control.

Summary

In this chapter you learned about ODBC and how it provides a single API that you can use to interface to any DBMS from a single code base provided that DBMS has an ODBC driver. In addition, you learned how to use the ODBC SDK to connect to, fetch data from, and disconnect from a data source. You also learned how to use a C++ class to encapsulate some of the more advanced ODBC SDK functions that enable you to access a data source without knowing the database's schema until runtime.

However, writing database applications using the ODBC SDK is not without its drawbacks. One trade-off to having the power and flexibility of a robust API such as the ODBC SDK is that the programming is more difficult, both in terms of what you as a programmer are responsible for, and the number of lines of code necessary to carry out a given task. As shown in the `ODBCDemo` application, even the simple task of writing a loop to read and display all of the records in a single table requires about a dozen different ODBC function calls and almost 100 lines of code. Luckily, Microsoft recognized this fact and released a set of MFC classes, collectively known as the MFC database classes. These classes, covered in the next chapter, give the database developer a much simpler object-oriented interface to the ODBC functionality that you have learned about throughout this chapter.

✦　　✦　　✦

MFC Database Classes

Chapter 20 introduced ODBC (Open Database Connectivity) and illustrated how ODBC was created to provide a means by which programmers could utilize a single code base to interface to multiple DBMSs. Although ODBC certainly has its advantages in terms of flexibility, it is not without its drawbacks. One obvious drawback is the amount of code required to perform even the simplest database operations. As an example, suppose you want your application to do something as simple as read every row from a given table. Before a database application using ODBC can even begin reading the data from the table, the application must first acquire an *environment handle*, tell ODBC which version of ODBC the application conforms to, acquire a "database connection handle," and acquire a "statement handle." Throw in the releasing of all those handles and some error checking, and you have about 100 lines of source code — and you haven't even started reading data yet!

Therefore, no sooner had Microsoft introduced ODBC than programmers started asking the logical question, "This is great, but when are you going to wrap this new functionality with some of the MFC classes?" Thankfully, starting with version 1.5 of MFC, Microsoft did just that by introducing a set of MFC classes that encapsulates the ODBC functionality. These classes are generally referred to as the *MFC database classes* and are the subject of this chapter. Note that because the MFC database classes do encapsulate the rather robust ODBC SDK API, if you are not already familiar with ODBC, you might want to take a look at Chapter 20 to at least familiarize yourself with the concepts and terminology that will be used throughout this chapter.

In this chapter, you will begin by learning about the four principal database classes, `CDatabase`, `CRecordset`, `CRecordView`, and `CDatabaseException`. Once you have finished learning about these classes and their functionality, two demos will be presented. The first demo is a fully functional maintenance application using the MFC database classes. This application has all the capabilities of a traditional maintenance application (creating, reading, updating, and deleting) for maintaining a "user master" table. The second demo is actually two demos in one. In the first part, you will learn how to use *parameterized recordsets* to retrieve data from a Microsoft Access database, and in the second part of the demo, you will learn how to call a parameterized Microsoft Access query that returns data.

The CDatabase Object

A CDatabase object represents a connection to a data source. After a CDatabase object is constructed, a *data source name* (DSN) is specified with a call to either the Open or the OpenEx member function. The connection to the DSN's underlying data source is made once one of these functions is called. A CDatabase object is typically used in conjunction with one or more CRecordset objects. These CRecordset objects represent the data returned from a query against the data source, and are explained in more detail in the following section. However, there are times when you'll use a CDatabase object without an associated CRecordset object. One example is if your application needs to issue a SQL statement against a data source that does not return any data. The CDatabase::ExecuteSQL function exists for just this purpose. Here's a code snippet that illustrates how easy it is to insert a record into a table using the CDatabase class:

```
try
{
 // Allocate a CDatabase object on the stack.
 CDatabase db;

 // Call the Open function with a valid DSN.
 if (db.Open("VCNET Bible"))
 {
  // Call the ExecuteSQL function passing
  // any valid SQL command that does not
  // return any data.
  db.ExecuteSQL("INSERT INTO UserMaster
                "VALUES('TestID', "
                "'Test User Name', 0)");

  // Close the connection when finished.
  db.Close();
 }
}
catch(CDBException* pe)
{
 AfxMessageBox(pe->m_strError);
 pe->Delete;
}
```

Compare this code segment to the more than 50 lines of ODBC SDK code that was needed to accomplish this exact task in Chapter 20. The database classes, while not as powerful as using the ODBC SDK directly, are much easier and faster to use in terms of programmer productivity than the ODBC SDK. Take a minute and look at the preceding code in more detail. The first thing you see in the code snippet is a try/catch block as shown in the following example:

```
try
{
 ...
}
catch(CDBException* pe)
{
```

```
      AfxMessageBox(pe->m_strError);
      pe->Delete;
   }
```

Almost all of the CDatabase classes' member functions throw an exception of type CDBException if an abnormal condition occurs. The CDBException class, which is derived from CException, provides almost nothing above and beyond what its base class defines. The three member variables that are inherited serve to tell the application what went wrong at the time the exception was thrown.

✦ m_nRetCode—Cause of the exception in the form of the ODBC return code (of type SQLRETURN)

✦ m_strError—String that describes the error that causes the exception to be thrown

✦ m_strStateNativeOrigin—String that describes the error that causes the exception to be thrown in terms of the ODBC error codes

Because most of the CDatabase classes' member functions throw exceptions of type CDBException, it is prudent to verify that exceptions of type CDBException (or its base class, CException) are being caught somewhere in the code path.

The next part of the code snippet to examine is the construction of the CDatabase object and the opening of the DSN's underlying data source. As you can see, the DSN name is "VCNET Bible." This value has been hard-coded in order to keep the example simple. In normal practice this value would be specified as a typedef, const, string resource, or maybe even stored in the Windows Registry.

```
CDatabase db;
if (db.Open("VCNET Bible"))
...
```

The CDatabase constructor doesn't do very much at all. As mentioned previously, a connection to the data source isn't made until either the Open or the OpenEx function is called so let's take a look at how to open a database connection using the Open function.

Using the CDatabase::Open function

At this point, let's focus on the Open function by examining its prototype (including the type of exception it can throw).

```
virtual BOOL Open( LPCTSTR lpszDSN,
  BOOL bExclusive = FALSE, BOOL bReadOnly = FALSE,
  LPCTSTR lpszConnect = "ODBC;",
  BOOL bUseCursorLib = TRUE );

throw( CDBException, CMemoryException );
```

As you can see in this prototype, the application can specify several options when opening a database connection using the CDatabase::Open function. However, only the first argument is explicitly required. In the example provided earlier, this first argument was the only argument that was passed and represented the DSN.

The bExclusive argument specifies whether to allow other concurrent connections to the specified data source. If you need an exclusive connection, simply pass a value of TRUE.

The bReadOnly argument allows the application to specify whether or not updates to the data source will be allowed once a connection is made. The default value for this argument is FALSE, meaning that updates to the data source can be made through this connection. Any CRecordset objects that are created and attached to this CDatabase automatically inherit this value.

The lpszConnect argument allows the application to specify the ODBC connect string to use when the CDatabase's underlying MFC code attempts to connect to the specified DSN via ODBC. If this argument is to be used, a value of NULL must be specified for the lpszDSN argument. The benefit of using this argument is flexibility. For example, if the application must specify a user ID and password, it can be done via the lpszConnect argument. The ODBC driver that is being used dictates the format of this argument.

The last argument to the CDatabase::Open member function is the bUseCursorLib flag. If this value is set to TRUE (the default value), only *static snapshot* or *forward-only cursors* are allowed for the connection. If a value of FALSE is used, then *dynasets* can be used.

After opening the recordset, the next line executes a SQL statement and closes the database:

```
db.ExecuteSQL("INSERT INTO UserMaster "
  "VALUES('TestID', 'Test User Name', 0)");

db.Close;
```

The CDatabase::ExecuteSQL function has a very straightforward syntax. The application need do nothing more than simply specify the SQL statement that needs to be executed by the underlying data source. Note that this function should be used only when the application does not anticipate that data will be returned as a result of executing the SQL statement.

Using the CDatabase::OpenEx function

As mentioned earlier, an alternative method of opening a database connection using the CDatabase class is via the CDatabase::OpenEx function. Actually, according to the MFC documentation, this is now the preferred way of opening a database connection:

```
virtual BOOL OpenEx(LPCTSTR lpszConnectString,
  DWORD dwOptions = 0 );

throw( CDBException, CMemoryException );
```

As you can see, the CDatabase::OpenEx function takes only two arguments. The first argument, lpszConnectString, is an LPCTSTR used to pass the ODBC connect string. The second argument, dwOptions, is used to specify the different options that are to be used when the connection is opened. This value is composed from a combination of the following values combined using the logical OR operator:

```
CDatabase::openExclusive
CDatabase::openReadOnly
CDatabase::useCursorLib
CDatabase::noODBCDialog
CDatabase::forceODBCDialog
```

Most of these values are holdovers from the CDatabase::Open function, with the addition of the CDatabase::noODBCDialog and CDatabase::forceODBCDialog flags. These flags indicate whether an application wants the ODBC Driver Manager to present the user with the ODBC connection dialog box when the connection is attempted.

Transactions and the CDatabase object

Another useful set of member functions that the `CDatabase` class supports are the functions that support *transactions* (sometimes called *commitment control*). Transactions give you the capability to specify that multiple database operations be treated as a logical group. That way, if any operation in the grouping should fail, the database reverses, or undoes, the transactions defined in this group, thereby leaving the data in the database in a consistent state.

As an example, suppose an accounting application must move an amount from one account to another. What would happen if after removing the amount from one account, the attempt to update the second account's balance failed? The integrity of the database would be compromised because the money was removed from one account but was not added to the second account. That is where transactions are useful. By using transactions, the application can specify that either both of these functions must complete successfully or neither of them should. Therefore, transactions are one means of ensuring data integrity. Here's the way a transaction works:

✦ The application calls the `CDatabase::CanTransact` member function to determine if the data source supports transactions. Obviously, if this function returns false, any calls to the transaction functions will have no impact. Therefore, applications should call this function to ensure the transactional capabilities of the data store.

✦ The calls the `CDatabase::BeginTrans` member function. This action sets a *transaction boundary*.

✦ The application requests the different operations that are all part of a logical grouping of database tasks. Using the accounting example, an application might attempt to first debit one account a certain amount of money and then, in a separate step, attempt to credit the second account with that amount.

✦ When the last operation of this logical group is performed, the application then calls the `CDatabase::CommitTrans` member function. At this point, any changes that were made to the database since the last `BeginTrans` call are made permanent.

✦ If for some reason the application wants to undo, or roll back, the changes to the database to the point of the `BeginTrans` call, the application need only call the `CDatabase::Rollback` function. Note that all changes from the point of the call to `Rollback` back until the last call to `Commit` will be reversed. Therefore, calling `Commit` and then calling `Rollback` will have no effect.

The CRecordset Object

Whereas a `CDatabase` object represents a connection to a data source, a `CRecordset` object (known as a *recordset*) represents a set of records retrieved from a data source. Although the `CRecordset` class does support several types of recordsets, two types of recordsets are generally used: dynasets and snapshots. A *dynaset,* or keyset-driven recordset, is a dynamic set of data that supports bi-directional scrolling and stays synchronized with the updates made by other users of the data source. A *snapshot,* on the other hand, is a static picture of the data taken at the time the recordset was filled. This set of data is not affected by changes made by other users. In order for an application using a snapshot recordset to see changes made by other users, the recordset must be closed and reopened. The snapshot recordset also supports bi-directional scrolling.

The fastest way to illustrate using recordsets is to create one using Visual Studio's Add Class dialog box. The recordset you will use is based on the `UserMaster` table that exists in the `VCNetBible.mdb` Microsoft Access database. This file is located on the Web site for this book. Figure 21-1 shows the `UserMaster` table in Microsoft Access 2000.

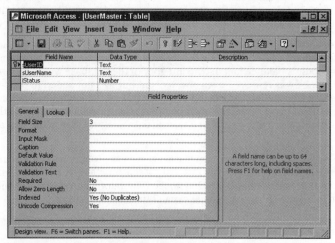

Figure 21-1: The UserMaster table (shown here in Microsoft Access 2000) is used throughout this chapter and in the demo application.

Begin by clicking Project ➪ Add Class. Once the Add Class dialog box is displayed (Figure 21-2), click the MFC category, select the MFC ODBC Consumer template, and click Open.

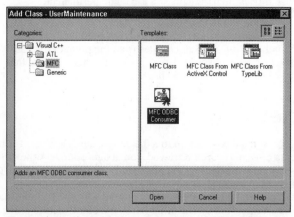

Figure 21-2: The Add Class dialog box enables you to create classes that represent connections to your ODBC data sources.

Note

If you attempt to open the Add Class dialog box while you have the dialog template resource open, you will find that your options are very limited. This is because the Add Class code in Visual Studio is context sensitive. In other words, because you have a dialog resource open, and you have selected the Add Class menu option, Visual Studio assumes that you are attempting to add a class that will be a subclass of the dialog, and therefore any classes not having to do with dialogs will not appear. In fact, you won't even get the same interface as shown in Figure 21-2. Therefore, make sure that you have a source file open when you click Project-⇨Add Class when creating a record set class.

The next dialog box you see is the MFC ODBC Consumer Wizard (Figure 21-3). This dialog box is where you select the ODBC DSN and specify the type of recordset you are creating (dynaset or snapshot) as well as whether or not you want the wizard to automatically bind the columns of the recordset to variables in your application. For purposes of this demo, click the Snapshot radio button and the Bind all columns checkbox. Then, click the Data Source button.

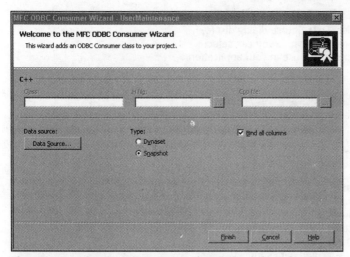

Figure 21-3: When creating a CRecordset-derived class, the ODBC Consumer dialog box enables you to specify many of the characteristics used to define the new class.

At this point, the Select Data Source dialog box is displayed. Simply click the Machine Data Source tab and select the "VCNET Bible" DSN as shown in Figure 21-4.

After selecting the DSN, a dialog box (Figure 21-5) asking you for a Login name (user ID) and Password appears. Because the demo database does not have any sort of security defined, simply click OK without entering any data.

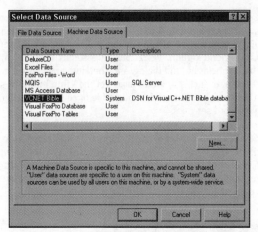

Figure 21-4: The Select Data Source dialog displays all defined ODBC DSNs from which you can select the one you are attempting to use in your application.

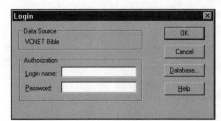

Figure 21-5: For more secure environments, the MFC ODBC Consumer Wizard allows you to specify the user ID and password credentials needed to access the specified data source.

As the last step in this process, you are presented with a list of tables and views (queries) that exist in the data source (Figure 21-6). For purposes of this demo, select the UserMaster table and click OK.

Finally, you return to the original MFC ODBC Consumer Wizard dialog box where the class name as well as its implementation and header file names have been automatically generated (Figure 21-7) based on the database object. Simply click Finish to complete the task of creating your CRecordset-derived class (called CUserMaster, in this case).

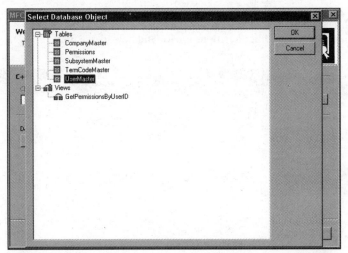

Figure 21-6: When creating a CRecordset class, the Select Database Object dialog box is used to select the table or view (query) that the recordset will be based on.

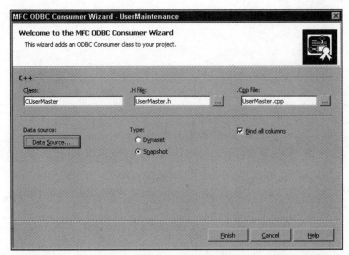

Figure 21-7: Creating a CRecordset class might seem like several steps, but once you realize that a few clicks results in a couple of hundred lines, you'll appreciate the work Visual Studio does for you.

Listings 21-1 and 21-2 show the amount of work the ClassWizard has done, with some comments removed for brevity. Throughout this part of the chapter you will learn what these different member variables and member functions are for and how to use them.

Listing 21-1: **UserMasterSet.h**

```
#pragma once

class CUserMasterSet : public CRecordset
{
public:
 CUserMasterSet(CDatabase* pDatabase = NULL);
 DECLARE_DYNAMIC(CUserMasterSet)

 CString     m_sUserID;
 CString     m_sUserName;
 int         m_iStatus;


public:
 virtual CString GetDefaultConnect();
 virtual CString GetDefaultSQL();
 virtual void DoFieldExchange(CFieldExchange* pFX);

#ifdef _DEBUG
  virtual void AssertValid() const;
  virtual void Dump(CDumpContext& dc) const;
#endif
};
```

Listing 21-2: **UserMasterSet.cpp**

```
#include "stdafx.h"
#include "dbtest.h"
#include "UserMasterSet.h"

#ifdef _DEBUG
#define new DEBUG_NEW
#undef THIS_FILE
static char THIS_FILE[] = __FILE__;
#endif

// CUserMasterSet

IMPLEMENT_DYNAMIC(CUserMasterSet, CRecordset)

CUserMasterSet::CUserMasterSet(CDatabase* pdb)
: CRecordset(pdb)
```

```
{
 m_sUserID = L"";
 m_sUserName = L"";
 m_iStatus = 0;
 m_nFields = 3;
 m_nDefaultType = snapshot;
}

CString CUserMasterSet::GetDefaultConnect()
{
 return _T("DSN=VCNet Bible");
}

CString CUserMasterSet::GetDefaultSQL()
{
 return _T("[UserMaster]");
}

void CUserMasterSet::DoFieldExchange(
 CFieldExchange* pFX)
{
 //{{AFX_FIELD_MAP(CUserMasterSet)
 pFX->SetFieldType(CFieldExchange::outputColumn);
 RFX_Text(pFX, _T("[sUserID]"), m_sUserID);
 RFX_Text(pFX, _T("[sUserName]"), m_sUserName);
 RFX_Int(pFX, _T("[iStatus]"), m_iStatus);
 //}}AFX_FIELD_MAP
}

// CUserMasterSet diagnostics

#ifdef _DEBUG
void CUserMasterSet::AssertValid() const
{
 CRecordset::AssertValid();
}

void CUserMasterSet::Dump(CDumpContext& dc) const
{
 CRecordset::Dump(dc);
}
#endif //_DEBUG
```

Once you have a CRecordset-derived class, your application can use it to perform any of the following tasks:

✦ Construct a recordset

✦ Open a recordset

✦ Read and write data using RFX (record field exchange)

✦ Filter records

✦ Sort records returned as a result of a SQL statement

✦ Navigate through a result set (returned data)

✦ Save records

✦ Delete records

Constructing a recordset

The CRecordset constructor takes as its only argument a pointer to a CDatabase object. This argument has a default value of NULL. If the application instantiates a CRecordset object and specifies this value as NULL, MFC automatically creates a temporary CDatabase object using the information specified when the recordset class was created via the ClassWizard. This information can be found in the CRecordset::GetDefaultConnect and CRecordset::GetDefaultSQL functions. However, if the application is going to use several recordsets, it is much more efficient to create one CDatabase object and use that object when creating the recordsets. That way, only one CDatabase object is created for all of the recordsets instead of a CDatabase object being created for every recordset.

Opening a recordset

Once the recordset has been constructed, it is opened via the CRecordset::Open function. The syntax for this function is as follows:

```
virtual BOOL Open(
 UINT nOpenType = AFX_DB_USE_DEFAULT_TYPE,
 LPCTSTR lpszSQL = NULL,
 DWORD dwOptions = none );

throw( CDBException, CMemoryException );
```

The first argument is used to specify the type of recordset being opened: *dynaset*, *snapshot*, *forward-only*, or *dynamic*. Each of these recordset types is represented by an enum value in the CRecordset class. The default recordset type for the nOpenType argument is CRecordset::snapshot.

```
class CRecordset : CObject
{
. . .
public:
 enum OpenType
 {
  dynaset,
  snapshot,
  forwardOnly,
  dynamic
};
```

The lpszSQL argument allows the application to specify the SQL statement that will be executed against the data source when the recordset is opened. If this argument is allowed to default to NULL, the code in the CRecordset::GetDefaultSQL function is used. In most cases, you will see only the name of a table or query being returned from this function. In this situation, the recordset retrieves all of the columns from the specified table or query without filtering the data or sorting it in any way. The topic of filtering and sorting the data returned via a recordset is covered shortly.

Reading and writing data using RFX

As mentioned earlier, to retrieve all of the records from a table without regard to order, the application can simply instantiate a CRecordset-derived class that was created via ClassWizard and call its CRecordset::Open function. However, you also need to know how the data gets from the data source into the application's variables. The answer lies in something called RFX (record field exchange). When a CRecordset-derived class is created using the ClassWizard, ClassWizard enumerates all of the columns in the selected table or query and declares variables of the appropriate type in the new class's header file. ClassWizard also generates a function called DoFieldExchange that serves to tie these member variables to their corresponding columns in the data source. This DoFieldExchange function is then called when MFC needs to move data from the data source to your member variables or vice versa.

The underlying MFC code actually does all the nitty-gritty ODBC SDK functions (for example, binding the columns, fetching the data, and so on) that are covered in Chapter 20. However, now it all happens automatically for you! When an application opens a recordset, the CRecordset::Open function moves to the first record. The application can then start navigating through the data using the CRecordset::MoveFirst, CRecordset::MovePrev, CRecordset::MoveNext, and CRecordset::MoveLast member functions. These functions are explained shortly.

Filtering records

Now that you know how to use the CDatabase and CRecordset classes to open and retrieve data from a data source, the next step is to learn how to filter that data to get just the records your application needs. Actually, you can accomplish this in several ways. As you saw in the previous section, an application can specify the SQL to be executed against a data source in the lpszSQL argument of the CRecordset::Open function. Following is an example of filtering records with the CRecordset::Open function. This code snippet reads only the records from the UserMaster table whose iStatus value is equal to zero:

```
try
{
 CDatabase db;
 if (db.Open("VCNET Bible"))
 {
  CUserMasterSet* pUserMasterSet =
   new CUserMasterSet();

  pUserMasterSet->Open(CRecordset::snapshot,
   "SELECT * from usermaster where iStatus = 0");

  // Use the data that was returned.

  pUserMasterSet->Close();
  db.Close();
```

```
    }
  }
catch(CDBException* pe)
{
 AfxMessageBox(pe->m_strError);
 pe->Delete();
}
```

A second way of filtering the data returned in a recordset is to use a *parameterized recordset*. Using the `CUserMasterSet` (see Listings 21-1 and 21-2) that was created earlier in the chapter, take a look at what changes would be necessary to modify the `CUserMasterSet` class so that when its `Open` function is called, only records from the `UserMaster` table whose `iStatus` value is equal to 0 are retrieved.

1. The first step is to declare the variable(s) that will hold the *parameter data*. Parameter data is data that is used in the `WHERE` clause of the SQL statement that MFC builds when the recordset is opened. Because this recordset is filtered by the value of the `iStatus` column, a variable should be created for this column. A common naming standard when doing this is to simply add Param to the end of the column name that is being filtered on, as shown in the following block of code:

```
// Field/Param Data
//{{AFX_FIELD(CUserMasterSet, CRecordset)
CString    m_sUserID;
CString    m_sUserName;
int        m_iStatus;
//}}AFX_FIELD
```

Next, add the following variable declaration:

```
int        m_iStatusParam;
```

2. Initialize the variable in the recordset's constructor, and set the `m_nParams` value to the number of parameters that will be used. This is extremely important. If you attempt to use a parameterized recordset and do not set this value, the recordset's `Open` will `ASSERT` during the call to `DoFieldExchange`.

```
m_sUserID = L"";
m_sUserName = L"";
m_iStatus = 0;
m_nFields = 3;
```

When you finish it should look like the following code:

```
m_sUserID = L"";
m_sUserName = L"";
m_iStatus = 0;
m_nFields = 3;
m_iStatusParam = 0;
m_nParams = 1;
```

3. Update the `DoFieldExchange` function such that when finished, it looks like the following code. The `CFieldExchange::SetFieldType` must be called with the `CFieldExchange::param` argument. This tells MFC that the `m_iStatusParam` variable (specified in the second argument) holds the data on which `iStatus` should be filtered.

```
pFX->SetFieldType(CFieldExchange::outputColumn);
RFX_Text(pFX, _T("[sUserID]"), m_sUserID);
RFX_Text(pFX, _T("[sUserName]"), m_sUserName);
RFX_Int(pFX, _T("[iStatus]"), m_iStatus);
pFX->SetFieldType(CFieldExchange::param);
RFX_Int(pFX, _T("[iStatus]"), m_iStatusParam);
```

4. Once these changes have been made, the only other changes necessary are to the code that actually opens the recordset. When opening a parameterized recordset, the application needs to set the CRecordset::m_strFilter as follows. Once that is done, it can set the parameter variable to the value it wants to filter on. Finally, a call to the CRecordset::Open function returns only the desired records as dictated by the value of the parameter variables.

```
try
{
 CDatabase db;
 if (db.Open("VCNET Bible"))
 {
  CUserMasterSet* pUserMasterSet =
   new CUserMasterSet();

  pUserMasterSet->m_strFilter = "iStatus = ?";
  pUserMasterSet->m_iStatusParam = 0;
  pUserMasterSet->Open();

  // Use the data that was returned.

  pUserMasterSet->Close();
  db.Close();
 }
}
catch(CDBException* pe)
{
 AfxMessageBox(pe->m_strError);
 pe->Delete();
}
```

As you can see, using parameterized recordsets is not very difficult. The biggest hassle is that, unfortunately, it is a very manual process, and if you forget to do any of the steps involved you can end up losing a lot of time tracking down why your application's recordset open isn't working properly.

Sorting records returned with a recordset

As you just saw in the previous section, the CRecordset class provides a member variable (m_strFilter) that allows the filtering of records. The CRecordset class also provides another member variable to specify the order in which records are returned when the recordset is opened. This member variable is called m_strSort. To use it, your application simply needs to set it to the name of the column by which the data will be sorted. For example, in the preceding code, if you wanted the application to sort the data by sUserId, the resulting code would look like the following:

```
try
{
 CDatabase db;
 if (db.Open("VCNET Bible"))
 {
  CUserMasterSet* pUserMasterSet =
   new CUserMasterSet();

  pUserMasterSet->m_strFilter = "iStatus = ?";
  pUserMasterSet->m_iStatusParam = 0;

  pUserMasterSet->m_strSort = "sUserID";
  pUserMasterSet->Open();

  // Use the data that was returned.

  pUserMasterSet->Close();
  db.Close();
 }
}
catch(CDBException* pe)
{
 AfxMessageBox(pe->m_strError);
 pe->Delete();
}
```

If your application must sort the data by more than one column, just separate each column name with a comma.

Using wildcards in your search

Besides the standard operators (=, <>, >=, <=), you can also use *wildcards* with the SQL SELECT statement to search for records. This feature, sometimes referred to as *pattern matching*, enables you to search for records where either you don't know the exact value of the key being used or you want to find all records matching a given pattern. To use these wildcards, you simply use the LIKE keyword instead of an operator.

There are two such wildcards define in SQL-92. The first is the * character, which signifies all characters from that point of the string forward. The following SQL statement returns all user records from the UserMaster table where the User ID starts with the letters "TM."

```
SELECT UserName from UserMaster WHERE UserId LIKE "TM*"
```

If you run this query against the following user IDs, the TMA and TMB records would be returned.

```
TAB
TMA
TMB
TNO
```

Note that any characters after the * are ignored. Therefore, supplying a value of TM*X is the same as specifying TM*.

The second wildcard is for a single character. This wildcard is represented by the ? character. An example of using that wildcard would be the following:

```
SELECT UserName from UserMaster WHERE UserId LIKE "T?B"
```

Executed against the four user IDs presented before, this statement would return the TAB and TMB records.

Note that these wildcards can be combined as long as you understand that once the * is reached, the rest of the search string is ignored (whether or not it contains more wildcards). Here's an example of a string containing multiple wildcards:

```
SELECT UserName from UserMaster WHERE UserId LIKE "?M*"
```

This would result in the return of all records that have a second character of M, regardless of length. Speaking of length, note that the following two statements are *not* equal.

```
SELECT UserName from UserMaster WHERE UserId LIKE "?"
SELECT UserName from UserMaster WHERE UserId LIKE "*"
```

Because the ? character is a wildcard for a single character, this statement will only return records with a length of 1, regardless of that column's value. The second statement, on the other hand, will return all records.

Now for the bad news. Not all databases support the same wildcards. For example, in the case of Microsoft Access, the SQL standard * character is not used — it is replaced by the % character. Also, instead of the ? character, the _ character is used. Therefore, if you're using wildcards with a Microsoft Access database, you'll need to keep this in mind.

Finally, in order to use these wildcards with the CRecordset::m_strFilter member variable, simply replace the operator with the word like (not case sensitive). Therefore, the following would be valid (against an Access database).

```
pUserMasterSet->m_strFilter = "sUserID like TM%";
```

Now let's look at how to iterate through result sets once they are returned from executing an SQL statement.

Moving through the result set

Now that you know how to retrieve a set of filtered and sorted records, take a look at how to navigate through the resulting records. The CRecordset class actually makes this extremely easy using the MoveFirst, MovePrev, MoveNext, and MoveLast functions. You can tell from the function names what each function does. However, you should know the following when implementing these functions in your code:

✦ If the application attempts to call any of the move functions, they will throw a CDBException if the recordset did not return any records. Therefore, the application should always call the CRecordset::IsBOF or CRecordset::IsEOF before attempting to call one of the move functions.

✦ The MoveFirst and MovePrev functions are not supported for recordsets that were defined as forward-only.

✦ If an application is navigating through a recordset and the possibility exists that other users can delete records in that recordset, the application should call the CRecordset::IsDeleted function to verify that the record is still valid.

✦ If an application has moved to the last record in a recordset and calls MoveNext, a CDBException is thrown. Therefore, when using MoveNext to move sequentially through a recordset, applications should always call the IsEOF function before calling MoveNext.

Here is a simple example of moving through a recordset with a while loop:

```
pUserMasterSet->Open();
while (!pUserMasterSet->IsEOF())
{
 AfxMessageBox(pUserMasterSet->m_sUserID);
 pUserMasterSet->MoveNext();
}
```

As you can see, CRecordset::IsEOF is called after every move so that an invalid call to CRecordset::MoveNext is not made once the end of the recordset has been reached.

Saving records

Using the CRecordset class to save records is easy. There are basically two different ways of saving data: adding new records and updating existing records. To add a new record, an application simply needs to do the following:

1. Call the CRecordset::AddNew function. This prepares a new, blank record.

2. Move the data into the recordset's member variables.

3. Call the CRecordset::Update function to create the new record in the data source.

To update an existing record, an application must do the following:

1. Call the CRecordset::Edit function.

2. Move the data into the recordset's member variables.

3. Call the CRecordset::Update function to update the current record in the data source.

It is very important to note the order in which you call these functions. The data must be moved into the member variables *after* calling the Edit function. Otherwise, MFC does not update the data source. The reason for this is that the MFC database classes cache, or buffer, the data and do a memory compare when the Update function is called. If no changes have been made to the member variables since the Edit function was called, the data source is not updated with the new data even though the application explicitly called the Update function.

Deleting records

To delete a record from a recordset, the record must be the current record in the recordset. The application then has to call the CRecordset::Delete function. After deleting the record, one of the CRecordset move functions must be called in order to move to another record because the current record is no longer valid.

Programming with the MFC Database Classes

Now that you've learned the basics of using the MFC database classes, you'll get a chance to put that knowledge to work in a pair of demos. The first demo (a user maintenance demo) will be a simple dialog-based application that loads all the users from the book's sample Access database and allows the user to edit and delete the user data. The second demo then illustrates how to define and execute parameterized queries against an Access database.

The UserMaintenance demo

The `UserMaintenance` demo illustrates how you can use the MFC database classes to perform the basic database operations of reading, writing, and deleting records. You can find the source code for this application on the Web site for this book. However, if you are going to either download this demo or type the code as you follow along in the book, you must create the appropriate DSN first. The DSN is called VCNET Bible. If you don't recall how to create a DSN, refer to the section "Creating an ODBC DSN" in Chapter 20. Start by using ClassWizard to create a dialog-based application called UserMaintenance.

Adding support for the MFC database classes

After you have created the application, you must add the `include` directive for the `afxdb.h` header file. This header file contains the declarations of the MFC database classes. Although the #`include` directive can be placed in any file that is going to reference any of the database classes, it is usually more convenient to place it in the `stdafx.h` file.

Creating the UI for the demo

1. Because this demo is a dialog-based application, all of the UI is done on the dialog box that was created automatically by AppWizard when the project was created. The project should have a dialog box called `IDD_USERMAINTENANCE_DIALOG`. Locate that dialog box, and edit it so that when finished it resembles the one shown in Figure 21-8. (Make sure that the IDs for the Save and Close buttons are `IDOK` and `IDCANCEL`, respectively.)

Figure 21-8: The UserMaintenance dialog box should look similar to this after the new controls have been added.

2. After the resource IDs have been set, create member variables with the following properties for each of the dialog box controls:

Control	Category	Variable Type	Variable Name
Users list box	Control	CListbox	m_lbxUsers
User ID edit	Value	CString	m_strUserID
User Name edit	Value	CString	m_strUserName
Status edit	Value	int	m_iStatus
Save button	Control	CButton	m_btnSave
Delete button	Control	CButton	m_btnDelete
Close button	Control	CButton	m_btnClose

Adding a utility class to encapsulate the user's data

A utility, or helper, class is needed to encapsulate each record's data. As you will see later, once a record is read, an object of type CUser is created. A string (UserID) is then inserted into the Users list box that represents that record. Each list box entry's item data, in turn, then points back to the CUser object that holds User's data.

```
#pragma once

class CUser
{
public:
  CString m_strUserID;
  CString m_strUserName;
  int m_iStatus;
};
```

Creating a CRecordset class for the UserMaster table

You now must create a recordset class to access the data in the UserMaster table. Call this class CUserMasterSet. Follow the directions given previously in this chapter in the section "The CRecordset Object" if you don't remember how to create a CRecordset-derived class to create a snapshot record set with column binding.

If you create a recordset based on a data store that supports users and passwords, your recordset implementation file might end up with a #error directive like the following: (Line wrapped for formatting.)

```
#error Security Issue: The connection string may contain
a password
```

This is a security precaution to allow you to remove the user ID and password you supplied when creating the record set from the file. So you question might be, Why did I have to specify a user ID and password that I then have to delete afterward? The answer is that the Select Data Source dialog box needed this information in order to open the data store so you could select the table or view upon which to base your record set. So how do you hide this information from the source code, but still use it programmatically? The answer would be that you could store this information in another form (for example, in an encrypted file) and then retrieve it at runtime. Then you could use your user ID/password information when calling the `CDatabase::Open` or `CDatabase::OpenEx` functions.

For purposes of this demo, simply delete the `#error` directive because the demo database is not protected with a password.

Modifying the dialog box header file

You must make a couple of minor changes to the dialog box header file for this program:

1. Open the `UserMaintenanceDlg.h` file, and add the following `include` directive before the declaration of the `CUserMaintenanceDlg` class:

   ```
   #include "User.h"
   ```

2. Add the following member function declarations:

   ```
   protected:
     void FillListboxWithUsers();
     BOOL GetSelectedUser(int* piIndex, CUser** ppUser);
     void InitControls();
     BOOL SaveUser(CUser* pUser);
     BOOL DeleteUser(CUser* pUser);
   ```

Modifying the dialog box implementation file

The last thing that you should do for this program is to modify the dialog box code in order to perform the database I/O.

1. Open the `UserMaintenanceDlg.cpp` file, and add the following `#include` directive. This is the header file for the record set you created.

   ```
   #include "UserMasterSet.h"
   ```

2. Locate the `OnInitDialog` function and place the following code at the end of the function before the `return` statement. The `FillListboxWithUsers` function fills the Users list box with all of the users found in the `UserMaster` table. The `InitControls` function initializes the state of the command buttons.

   ```
   FillListboxWithUsers();
   InitControls();
   ```

3. At the end of the file, add the following function. As you can see, this function first opens a database connection to the DSN VCNET Bible and then opens the user recordset. From there, it uses a `while` loop and the `CRecordSet::MoveNext` function to iterate over all of the user records. For each record found, a `CUser` object is instantiated, the username is added to the list box, and that list box item's item data is set to the address of the `CUser` address. This is done so that when the user selects a given user (in the list box), the application can retrieve that item's item data (the `CUser` object pointer) and have all the data defining that user. After the `while` loop, the function closes the recordset and database connections.

   ```
   void CUserMaintenanceDlg::FillListboxWithUsers()
   {
   ```

```
        int iIndex;

        CUserMasterSet* pUserMasterSet = NULL;
        try
        {
         pUserMasterSet = new CUserMasterSet();
         pUserMasterSet->Open();

         while (!pUserMasterSet->IsEOF())
         {
          CUser* pUser = new CUser();
          pUser->m_strUserID = pUserMasterSet->m_sUserID;
          pUser->m_strUserName =
           pUserMasterSet->m_sUserName;
          pUser->m_iStatus = pUserMasterSet->m_iStatus;

            // Convert from the record set UNICODE
            // string to a form acceptable to the
            // CListBox::AddString function.
            CString str(pUserMasterSet->m_sUserName);

            // Add the user name to the list box.
            iIndex = m_lbxUsers.AddString(str);

          m_lbxUsers.SetItemData(iIndex, (DWORD)pUser);

          pUserMasterSet->MoveNext();
         }

         pUserMasterSet->Close();
         delete pUserMasterSet;
        }
        catch(CDBException* pe)
        {
         AfxMessageBox(pe->m_strError);

         if (pUserMasterSet)
         {
          if (pUserMasterSet->IsOpen())
          {
           pUserMasterSet->Close();
          }
          delete pUserMasterSet;
         }

         if (db.IsOpen())
         {
          db.Close();
         }

         pe->Delete();
        }
        }
```

4. Once the `FillListboxWithUsers` function has been defined, add the following initialization function. Here I'm simply setting the user field values to blank (and –1 in the case of the status field) and disabling the buttons that shouldn't be clickable until a user is being modified.

```
void CUserMaintenanceDlg::InitControls()
{
 m_lbxUsers.SetCurSel(-1);

 m_strUserID = "";
 m_strUserName = "";
 m_iStatus = -1;

 m_btnSave.EnableWindow(FALSE);
 m_btnDelete.EnableWindow(FALSE);
 m_btnClose.EnableWindow(TRUE);

 m_lbxUsers.SetFocus();

 UpdateData(FALSE);
}
```

5. You must now add a function so that when a user is selected from the list box, the proper information is displayed in the dialog box. To do this, implement a message handler for the `LBN_SELCHANGE` notification message for the Users list box. Once you are finished, make sure the code looks as follows:

```
void CUserMaintenanceDlg::OnLbnSelchangeList1()
{
 int iIndex;
 CUser* pUser;

 if (GetSelectedUser(&iIndex, &pUser))
 {
  m_strUserID = pUser->m_strUserID;
  m_strUserName = pUser->m_strUserName;
  m_iStatus = pUser->m_iStatus;

  m_btnSave.EnableWindow(TRUE);
  m_btnDelete.EnableWindow(TRUE);

  UpdateData(FALSE);
 }
}
```

6. Add the following helper function. This function is called to retrieve the currently selected User in the list box when either the Update or Delete button is clicked.

```
BOOL CUserMaintenanceDlg::GetSelectedUser(
 int* piIndex, CUser** ppUser)
{
 BOOL bSuccess = FALSE;

 int iIndex;
 if (LB_ERR != (iIndex = m_lbxUsers.GetCurSel()))
```

```
  {
   *piIndex = iIndex;
   *ppUser = (CUser*)m_lbxUsers.GetItemData(iIndex);
    bSuccess = TRUE;
  }

  return bSuccess;
}
```

7. At this point, the application has the functions necessary to read all of the Users from the UserMaster table and display their respective information on the dialog box. Now it's time to add update capability to the application. Add a message handler for the Save button's BN_CLICKED notification message, and implement it as follows:

```
void CUserMaintenanceDlg::OnBnClickedOk ()
{
 int iCurrIndex;

 CUser* pUser = NULL;
 if (GetSelectedUser(&iCurrIndex, &pUser))
 {
  ASSERT(pUser);
  if (pUser)
  {
   UpdateData();

   CString strPrevUserID;
   strPrevUserID = m_strUserID;
   CString strPrevUserName;
   strPrevUserName = m_strUserName;
   int iPrevStatus = m_iStatus;

   pUser->m_strUserID = m_strUserID;
   pUser->m_strUserName = m_strUserName;
   pUser->m_iStatus = m_iStatus;

   if (SaveUser(pUser))
   {

    if (LB_ERR == m_lbxUsers.DeleteString(iCurrIndex))
    {
     AfxMessageBox("The User ID was Saved, "
      "but the previous User ID could not be "
      "removed from the listbox.");
    }
    else
    {
     int iNewIndex = m_lbxUsers.AddString(
      pUser->m_strUserName);
     if ((LB_ERR == iNewIndex) || (LB_ERRSPACE ==
      iNewIndex))
     {
```

```
        AfxMessageBox("The User ID was Saved, but "
          "the new User ID could not "
          "be added to the listbox.");
      }
      if (LB_ERR == m_lbxUsers.SetItemData(iNewIndex,
      (DWORD)pUser))
      {
        AfxMessageBox("SetItemData returned LB_ERR. "
          "This will probably cause "
          "serious problems if you attempt to update "
          "or delete this item from the listbox");
      }
    }

    InitControls();

    UpdateData(FALSE);
  }
  else
  {
    pUser->m_strUserID = strPrevUserID;
    pUser->m_strUserName = strPrevUserName;
    pUser->m_iStatus = iPrevStatus;
    AfxMessageBox("SaveUser failed");
  }
 }
}
else
{
 // should never get here because of
 // enabling/disabling button on lbx selection
 AfxMessageBox("You must first select a "
  "User ID to Save");
 }
}
```

8. Add the following helper function. This function is called when the information on the dialog box must be saved. As you can see, the function takes a User object as its only parameter, and based on that User object's data, builds an SQL UPDATE string to use with the CDatabase::ExecuteSQL function. (By the way, this could have been done through the record set, but I did it this way simply to show you alternative ways of working with the database classes.)

```
BOOL CUserMaintenanceDlg::SaveUser(CUser* pUser)
{
 BOOL bSuccess = FALSE;
 CDatabase db;

 try
 {
  if (db.Open("VCNet Bible"))
  {
```

```
          CString strSQL = CString("UPDATE UserMaster SET ");
          strSQL += CString("sUserName = '") +
           pUser->m_strUserName + CString("', ");

          strSQL += CString("iStatus = ");
          char szStatus[10];
          itoa(pUser->m_iStatus, szStatus, 10);
          strSQL += szStatus;

          strSQL += CString(" WHERE sUserID = ");
          strSQL += CString("'") + pUser->m_strUserID +
           CString("'");

          db.ExecuteSQL(strSQL);

          bSuccess = TRUE;
        }
      }
    catch(CDBException* pe)
    {
     AfxMessageBox(pe->m_strError);

     if (db.IsOpen())
     {
      db.Close();
     }

     pe->Delete();
    }

    return bSuccess;
  }
```

9. Add a message handler for the Delete button's `BN_CLICKED` notification message, and implement it as follows. (Note that your function name might be different because it will be based on the resource ID you gave the button.) The code first determines which user is currently selected in the list box. From there, a confirmation message box is displayed to ensure that the user does want to delete the selected user record. If the user confirms the delete request, the `DeleteUser` helper function is called, the item is removed from the list box, and the `InitControls` function is called to initialize the dialog box.

```
void CUserMaintenanceDlg::OnBtnDelete()
{
 int iIndex;
 CUser* pUser = NULL;
 if (GetSelectedUser(&iIndex, &pUser))
 {
  ASSERT(pUser);
  if (pUser)
  {
   UpdateData();
```

```
    CString strMsg;

    strMsg = "Are you sure that you want to delete "
      "the User ";
    strMsg += "'";
    strMsg += pUser->m_strUserName;
    strMsg += "'?";
    if (IDYES == AfxMessageBox(strMsg, MB_YESNOCANCEL))
    {
     if (DeleteUser(pUser))
     {
      if (LB_ERR == m_lbxUsers.DeleteString(iIndex))
      {
       AfxMessageBox("The User was successfully "
         "Deleted, but there was an error in "
         "removing it from the listbox.");
      }

      InitControls();

      UpdateData(FALSE);
     }
     else
     {
      AfxMessageBox("DeleteUser failed");
     }
    }
   }
  }
  else
  {
   // should never get here because of
   // enabling/disabling button on lbx selection
   AfxMessageBox("You must first select a User "
     "ID to Delete");
  }
 }
}
```

10. Add the following helper function at the end of `UserMaintenanceDlg.cpp` that is called when a record needs to be deleted:

```
BOOL CUserMaintenanceDlg::DeleteUser(CUser* pUser)
{
 BOOL bSuccess = FALSE;
 CDatabase db;

 try
 {
  if (db.Open("VCNET Bible"))
  {
   CString strSQL = CString("DELETE FROM UserMaster "
     "WHERE ");
```

```
      strSQL += CString("sUserID = '") +
       pUser->m_strUserID + CString("'");

      db.ExecuteSQL(strSQL);

      bSuccess = TRUE;
     }
    }
    catch(CDBException* pe)
    {
     AfxMessageBox(pe->m_strError);

     if (db.IsOpen())
     {
      db.Close();
     }
    }

    return bSuccess;
    }
```

11. Now, add an override of the dialog box's `DestroyWindow` function to delete the User objects allocated in the `FillListboxWithUsers` function.

```
    BOOL CUserMaintenanceDlg::DestroyWindow()
    {
     CUser* pUser;
     int nUsers = m_lbxUsers.GetCount();
     for (int i = 0; i < nUsers; i++)
     {
      pUser=
       (CUser*)m_lbxUsers.GetItemData(i);

      if (pUser)
      {
       delete pUser;
      }
     }

     return CDialog::DestroyWindow();
    }
```

12. Now, build and execute the application. Your results should be similar to what you see in Figure 21-9.

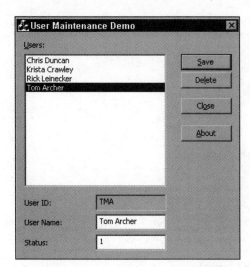

Figure 21-9: The UserMaintenance application demonstrates how to read and write data using the MFC database classes.

Parameterized recordsets and queries

This demo, a dialog-based application called Parameterized, is split into two parts. The first part illustrates the use of a parameterized recordset in a practical application. Earlier in the chapter, you learned that parameterized recordsets are recordsets that enable you to filter the records that are returned when the recordset is opened. Like this chapter's first demo application, this demo contains a dialog box that displays information about Users from the UserMaster table. However, this demo has one very important difference. In the first demo, all of the Users were read from the UserMaster table upon initialization of the dialog box and inserted into a list box from which the user selected one and performed various database operations, such as update, delete, and so on. In this demo, however, the dialog box enables the user to enter a UserID, whereupon a parameterized recordset is used to search the UserMaster table for the specified User. If the UserID is located, its information is displayed on the dialog box. If the UserID cannot be located, a message box to that effect is displayed.

The second part of the demo illustrates the use of a parameterized query that returns data. This query is based on a join of multiple tables in the demo Access database. This query takes only one argument: the UserID. If a UserID is entered into the dialog box and is found in the UserMaster table, this query is called to retrieve other information about the User. This information is then also displayed on the dialog box.

To get started, create a dialog-based application called Parameterized. Once AppWizard has created the project and its files, add an #include directive for the afxdb.h file to stdafx.h.

Creating the UI for the demo

Because this demo is a dialog-based application, all of the UI is done on the dialog box that was created automatically by AppWizard when the project was created. The project should have a dialog box called IDD_PARAMETERIZED_DIALOG.

1. Locate the `IDD_PARAMETERIZED_DIALOG` dialog box, and edit it so that when finished, it resembles the one shown in Figure 21-10.

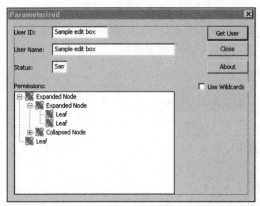

Figure 21-10: The dialog box for the Parameterized CRecordset and query demo after the new controls have been added

2. Turn on the following styles for the Permissions tree:

   • Has buttons

   • Has lines

   • Lines at root

   * Scroll

3. Create member variables with the following properties for the dialog box controls:

Control	Category	Variable Type	Variable Name
User ID edit	Value	CString	m_strUserID
User Name edit	Value	CString	m_strUserName
Status edit	Value	int	m_iStatus
Use Wildcards	Value	int	m_iUseWildcards
Permissions tree	Control	CTreeCtrl	m_treePermissions

Note that you might have to modify the `CParameterizedDlg::DoDataExchange` function to ensure that the `DDX_Check` function is called for the `m_iUseWildcards` member variable (instead of `DDX_Text`).

```
void CParameterizedDlg::DoDataExchange(CDataExchange* pDX)
{
  CDialog::DoDataExchange(pDX);
```

```
    DDX_Control(pDX, IDC_TREE1, m_treePermissions);
    DDX_Text(pDX, IDC_EDIT1, m_strUserID);
    DDX_Text(pDX, IDC_EDIT2, m_strUserName);
    DDX_Text(pDX, IDC_EDIT3, m_iStatus);
    DDX_Check(pDX, IDC_CHECK1, m_iUseWildcards);
}
```

Creating the UserMaster recordset

You now need a recordset class to access the data in the UserMaster table. Call this class CUserMasterSet. Follow the directions in the section "The CRecordset Object" presented earlier in the chapter if needed. Don't forget to remove the #error directive in the UserMasterSet.cpp file.

Modifying the CRecordset class to accept parameters

Once you have created the CRecordset-derived class, you need to modify it so that it can accept parameters.

1. Add the following member variable to the CUserMasterSet class. This variable's value is used to filter the UserMaster records when the recordset is opened.

   ```
   CString m_sUserIDParam;
   ```

2. Place the following initialization code in the CUserMasterSet constructor. The first line simply initializes the parameter variable you just declared in the header file. The second line is extremely important because it specifies how many parameters you have in this recordset. If you omit this line, you will receive an ASSERT when you call the CRecordset::Open function.

   ```
   m_sUserIDParam = _T("");
   m_nParams = 1;
   ```

3. Now, locate the CUserMasterSet::DoFieldExchange function, and add the following lines immediately before the end of the function. These lines associate the parameter variable with the correct column in the UserMaster table. Take special note that the column name is the sUserID column. In the case of a parameterized recordset, you generally have two variables pointing to the same column for each parameter defined for that recordset. One of the variables is used to send data to and receive data from the column in your table (m_sUserID in this demo), and the other is used only as the key to search on (m_sUserIDParam in this demo).

   ```
   pFX->SetFieldType(CFieldExchange::param);
   RFX_Text(pFX, _T("[sUserID]"), m_sUserIDParam);
   ```

Adding search capability to the application

Now it's time to add the functionality necessary to allow the user to search the UserMaster table for specific users.

1. Open the ParameterizedDlg.cpp file, and add the following #include directive:

   ```
   #include "UserMasterSet.h"
   ```

2. You now must add a function so that when the Get User button is clicked, the proper information is displayed in the dialog box. To do this, add a message handler for the Get User button's BN_CLICKED notification message. Make sure that the function looks

like the following. As you can see, I'm simply setting the recordset's m_strFilter to filter based on the sUserID column having a value equal to that of the m_strUserID value specified by the user. From there I call the Open method, which applies the filter and returns only records matching the search criteria. If a record is found, I update the dialog controls accordingly. If a matching record is not found, a message box is presented stating such.

As an added bonus the application does allow for wildcard usage as explained in the section "Using wildcards in your search.". However, because this dialog box only displays a single user, if the user supplies a search criteria that results in more than one record being returned only, the first record will be displayed.

```
void CParameterizedDlg::OnBnClickedOk()
{
 CUserMasterSet* pUserMasterSet = NULL;

 try
 {
  pUserMasterSet = new CUserMasterSet();
 }
 catch(CMemoryException* pe)
 {
  TRACE("CParameterizedDlg::OnOk - Memory "
   "Exception creating recordset\n");

  pUserMasterSet = NULL;

  pe->Delete();
 }

 if (pUserMasterSet)
 {
  UpdateData(TRUE);

  try
  {
   // Format filter based on whether or not the
   // user wants to use SQL wildcards in the
   // search.
   pUserMasterSet->m_strFilter.Format("sUserID %s ?",
    m_iUseWildcards == 0 ? "=" : "like");

   pUserMasterSet->m_sUserIDParam = m_strUserID;
   if (pUserMasterSet->Open())
   {
    if (!pUserMasterSet->IsEOF())
    {
     m_strUserName = pUserMasterSet->m_sUserName;
     m_iStatus = pUserMasterSet->m_iStatus;

     UpdateData(FALSE);
    }
```

```
          else
          {
           CString str = m_strUserID + CString(" was not "
             "found");

           AfxMessageBox(str);
          }
          pUserMasterSet->Close();
         }
        delete pUserMasterSet;
       }
      catch(CDBException* pe)
      {
       if (pUserMasterSet->IsOpen())
       {
        pUserMasterSet->Close();
       }
       delete pUserMasterSet;

       TRACE("CParameterizedDlg::OnOk - Database "
        "Exception - %s\n", pe->m_strError);

       pe->Delete();
      }
     }
   }
```

Building the application

Now that the code has been entered to search the database for a specific record, simply build the application and run it. Building the application at this point and running it should give results similar to what you see in Figure 21-11.

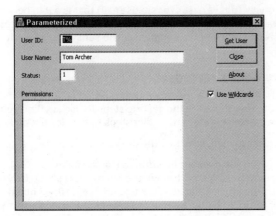

Figure 21-11: The Parameterized demo illustrates how to use parameterized recordsets.

Creating parameterized queries

Now that you have completed the first part of the demo, it is time to add the parameterized query code. Use the `UserMaster` table that has been seen throughout this chapter, as well as some new tables. In this example, pretend that you are writing a large system that includes multiple subsystems — for example, a distribution system that supports subsystems such as Order Entry, Invoicing, Receiving, Purchasing, and so on. This system might also need to support multiple companies.

Many larger corporations are broken into smaller companies or divisions. Because every User would probably not have access to every subsystem for every company, the system would need to support some type of security. User Bob might have access to Order Entry and Invoicing in Company A, but he might not have any permissions in Company B. A Permissions table could be used to limit access to different parts of the system. In the example just mentioned, Bob would have two records in the Permissions table (one for each company/subsystem pair to which he has access). This scenario is the basis for the second part of this demo.

The demo database

Aside from the `UserMaster` table that has been used in the demos throughout this chapter, three new tables (already in the demo database) are required for this demo:

✦ **Company Master table** — This table lists all of the companies for the system. The only columns are for the Company ID and Company Name.

✦ **Subsystem Master table** — This table lists all of the subsystems for the system (for example, Order Entry, Receiving, and so on). The only columns are for the Subsystem ID and Subsystem Name.

✦ **Permissions table** — Because a User can have permissions for any number of companies/ subsystems, an intersection table is required to handle this many-to-many scenario. This table only has three columns: the User ID, Company ID, and Subsystem ID. These columns represent the primary keys for their respective tables. A record exists in this table for every User/Company/Subsystem for which the User has permissions.

The demo database also includes a query (`GetPermissionsByUserID`) that is a join between all four of the tables in the database. The query takes a User ID as an argument and returns the Company Name and Subsystem Name for all of the companies and subsystems for which this User has permissions.

Using a parameterized query with a recordset

The following are the steps necessary to generate a recordset that is based on a view (or query) that requires parameters. (Note that these are the generic steps to use anytime you are creating such a recordset. The next section details the exact steps to take for the demo.)

1. Create a `CRecordset`-derived class named, selecting the desired view (query).

2. Change the recordset's `GetDefaultSQL` member function to use the following `CALL` syntax. When accessing a parameterized query through the Microsoft Desktop Drivers, you must use this syntax. When the application calls the `CRecordset::Open` function, MFC checks to see if the string returned by the `CRecordset::GetDefaultSQL` starts with the string `{CALL`. If it does not, MFC attempts to build a SQL `SELECT` statement. A question mark represents the parameter that is passed. For multiple parameters, simply add a question mark for each parameter and separate each parameter with a comma.

```
{CALL QueryName(?[,?])}
```

3. Define a variable for each parameter in the recordset class.

4. Initialize the parameter variable(s) in the recordset's constructor and set the CRecordSet::m_nParams member variable to the number of parameters that will be passed to the query.

5. Update the recordset's DoFieldExchange using the standard RFX_Text functions. However, you must call the CFieldExchange::SetFieldType first (passing a value of CFieldExchange::param) so that MFC knows you are setting up a parameter. Here's an example of doing that where the member variable m_sUserIDParam will be used as the parameter and associated with the sUserID column.

```
pFX->SetFieldType(CFieldExchange::param);
RFX_Text(pFX, _T("[sUserID]"), m_sUserIDParam);
```

Note that when using a parameterized query, you do not need to set the m_strFilter variable.

6. Assign a value to the recordset's parameter variable(s).

7. Call the recordset's Open function in read-only mode.

Creating the permissions recordset

Now that you have seen the generic steps used to create a recordset that is based on a parameterized query, create one for the demo application. This recordset is based on the demo database's sole query: GetPermissionsByUserID.

1. Create a CRecordset-derived class called CPermissionsQry based on the GetPermissionsByUserID query. Make sure you remember to remove the #error directive from the PermissionQry.cpp file when finished.

2. Open the PermissionsQry.cpp file and locate the GetDefaultSQL member function. Modify the GetPermissionsByUserID function so that it looks like the following when you are done:

```
CString CPermissionsQry::GetDefaultSQL()
{
   return _T("{CALL GetPermissionsByUserID(?)}");
}
```

3. Define the following variable in the CPermissionsQry class.

```
CString m_sUserIDParam;
```

4. Append the following two lines of code to the CPermissionsQry constructor:

```
m_sUserIDParam = _T("");
m_nParams = 1;
```

5. Add the following two lines of code at the end of the DoFieldExchange function:

```
pFX->SetFieldType(CFieldExchange::param);
RFX_Text(pFX, _T("[sUserID]"), m_sUserIDParam);
```

6. Declare the following member variable in the CParameterizedDlg class. This function is called to read all of the permissions for the User. The permissions are then displayed in the dialog box's CTreeCtrl control.

```
protected:
 void ShowPermissions();
```

7. Add the following `include` directive to the top of the `ParameterizedDlg.cpp` file.

```
#include "PermissionsQry.h"
```

8. In the `CParameterizedDlg::OnBnClickedOk` function, just before the call to `UpdateData(FALSE)`, add the following call to update the dialog box's permissions tree view.

```
ShowPermissions();
```

9. Now code the `CParameterizedDlg::ShowPermissions` function as follows. This function first removes all entries from the tree view (via the `CTreeCtrl::DeleteAllItems` function). Then it sets the parameter variable created earlier (`m_sUserIDParam`) equal to the user ID value on the dialog box. The recordset is then opened. This results in the underlying query being run, which will cause the recordset to contain the records returned from this query.

```
void CParameterizedDlg::ShowPermissions()
{
 m_treePermissions.SetRedraw(FALSE);
 m_treePermissions.DeleteAllItems();

 CPermissionsQry* pPermissionsQry = NULL;

 try
 {
  pPermissionsQry = new CPermissionsQry();
 }
 catch(CMemoryException* pe)
 {
  TRACE("CParameterizedDlg::OnOk - Memory Exception "
   "creating recordset\n");

  pPermissionsQry = NULL;

  pe->Delete();
 }

 if (pPermissionsQry)
 {
  try
  {
   pPermissionsQry->m_sUserIDParam = m_strUserID;
   if (pPermissionsQry->Open())
   {
    if (!pPermissionsQry->IsEOF())
    {
     HTREEITEM hCompany;

     CString strPrevCompanyID;
     while (!pPermissionsQry->IsEOF())
     {
```

```
     CString
      strCompanyName(pPermissionsQry->m_sCompanyName);

     hCompany =
      m_treePermissions.InsertItem(strCompanyName);

     strPrevCompanyID =
      pPermissionsQry->m_sCompanyID;

     while ((!pPermissionsQry->IsEOF())
     && (strPrevCompanyID
         == (CString)pPermissionsQry->m_sCompanyID))
     {
      ASSERT(hCompany);
      if (hCompany)
      {
       CString
        strSubsystemName(pPermissionsQry->
                         m_sSubsystemName);
       m_treePermissions.InsertItem(strSubsystemName,
                                    hCompany);
      }

      pPermissionsQry->MoveNext();
     }
    }
   }
   else
   {
    CString str;
    str.Format("No permissions found for %s",
     m_strUserID);
    m_treePermissions.InsertItem(str);
    str = "Note that wildcards will not work "
     "with the parameterized query!";
    m_treePermissions.InsertItem(str);
   }

   pPermissionsQry->Close();
  }
  delete pPermissionsQry;
}
catch(CDBException* pe)
{
 if (pPermissionsQry->IsOpen())
 {
  pPermissionsQry->Close();
 }
 delete pPermissionsQry;
 TRACE("CParameterizedDlg::OnOk - Database "
```

```
        "Exception "
        "- %s\n", pe->m_strError);
    }
  }

  ExpandAllBranches();
  m_treePermissions.SetRedraw(TRUE);
}
```

10. Finally, add the following two functions that are used to expand the tree view's items once the tree view has been filled.

```
void CParameterizedDlg::ExpandAllBranches()
{
 HTREEITEM hRoot = NULL;
 HTREEITEM hItem;
 for (HTREEITEM hItem = m_treePermissions.GetRootItem();
   hItem != NULL;
   hItem = m_treePermissions.GetNextSiblingItem(hItem))
 {
  if (!hRoot) hRoot = hItem;
  ExpandBranch(hItem);
 }
 m_treePermissions.Select(hRoot, TVGN_FIRSTVISIBLE);
}

void CParameterizedDlg::ExpandBranch(HTREEITEM hItem,
                                     BOOL bExpand /* = TRUE */)
{
  if (m_treePermissions.ItemHasChildren(hItem))
  {
    m_treePermissions.Expand(hItem,
      bExpand ? TVE_EXPAND : TVE_COLLAPSE);
    hItem = m_treePermissions.GetChildItem(hItem);
    do
    {
        ExpandBranch(hItem);
    } while ((hItem =
    m_treePermissions.GetNextSiblingItem(hItem)) != NULL);
  }
}
```

11. Build and run the demo application. Running the demo should produce results similar to what you see in Figure 21-12.

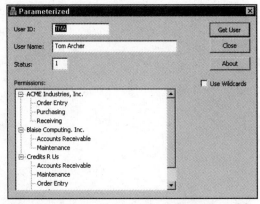

Figure 21-12: The Parameterized demo illustrates how to use parameterized Microsoft Access queries that return data.

Summary

Chapters 20 and 21 have introduced the ODBC SDK and the MFC database classes as well as described each technology's respective strengths and weaknesses. At this point, one very important question should be addressed. Which is better—the MFC database classes or the ODBC SDK? As you have seen, having both the ODBC SDK and the MFC database classes gives the database developer two technologies with differing strengths. The advantage to using the ODBC SDK is realized in terms of power and flexibility, whereas the main advantage of the MFC database classes is derived from ease of use. Although the ODBC SDK is a good choice for developing robust, scalable systems that interface with different DBMSs, the MFC database classes are the clear-cut winner for smaller systems that interface only to one DBMS. Therefore, choosing between these technologies comes down to a matter of priorities and, hence, is a personal choice that only the database developer can make.

ADO

In the previous two chapters, you've learned how to use ODBC (Open Database Connectivity) to access your data via the ODBC SDK and the MFC Database Classes. Although ODBC obviously gets the job done, it does have some rather major drawbacks. First, it is accessed via a DLL interface. This means that late binding clients such as scripting languages cannot use it. Second, ODBC is not object-oriented. Finally, it is obvious that ODBC will not be getting any significant upgrades in the foreseeable future. For all of these reasons, this chapter will introduce you to a new database access methodology called ADO (ActiveX Data Objects).

By the time you've finished this chapter, you will have learned how to use the ADO object hierarchy to perform almost all of the basic database application tasks of reading data, sorting and filtering recordsets, and updating data. Along the way, you will also discover how to read and write data in batch mode for better performance as well as set database sharing permissions and record-level locking levels in order to ensure data integrity when running in multiuser environments. Finally, the chapter will end with a demo application that illustrates how to code basic CRUD (create, read, update, and delete) functionality using ADO.

ADO Overview

As you've seen throughout this book, I'm the type of programmer that likes to get straight to the point and show code immediately instead of simply showing a bunch of diagrams and flow charts. However, in the case of Microsoft database access technologies, I thought it would be best to take just a second to sort out this alphabet soup of abbreviations.

The Universal Data Access initiative

First a little background might help you to understand the chronology of events that has led me to include an ADO chapter in this book.

In the fall of 1997, Microsoft first announced something called the Universal Data Access (UDA). However, at this time Microsoft was seemingly playing its own little game of "musical database access technologies." First it was ODBC. Developers needed to use ODBC because it supported a means of accessing heterogeneous data sources from a single code base. Then the combination of DAO and RDO (Remote Data Objects) was announced as the more object-oriented and efficient way to go. After all, DAO would use the Jet engine directly for cases where you were accessing a Microsoft Access database, and RDO would go through ODBC for other RDBMs. After that, Microsoft had yet another announcement: DAO now supported two *workspaces*. One was the Jet workspace for using Access and the other was called *ODBCDirect*. This meant you could once again use DAO as a single code base to access all your data sources and simply change the workspace according to whether or not you were using Access or some other DBMS (with an ODBC driver). Needless to say, when Microsoft once again announced a new strategy, ADO, not too many people were buying into it — especially when DAO (which has MFC support) was not a part of it. The Visual C++ market's reluctance to seriously consider switching from ODBC or DAO to ADO was a prime reason that the previous edition of this book included a chapter on DAO, but not ADO.

However, as of the release of Visual Studio .NET, there is no longer any IDE (via the various wizards) support for DAO. Although DAO classes have not been removed from MFC (in order to support legacy code), if you want to code your applications using DAO, you will have to do all the coding manually. This means manually writing in the RFX and DFX calls yourself as well as creating the actual recordset classes. Therefore, it is obvious that Microsoft is serious about DAO coming to an end and developers making a choice between ODBC and OLE DB/ADO.

UDA is Microsoft's attempt at creating a single noncompeting grouping of data access technologies that enable efficient, heterogeneous access to almost any popular database on almost any platform. These complimentary tools are the Microsoft Data Access Components (MDAC), ADO, OLE DB, and ODBC. The stated goal is that regardless of the type of application being written (2-tier client/server, distributed, stand-alone, or Web-based), the developer will have a choice of "best-of-breed" tools, applications, and data sources to drive that application. Figure 22-1 shows the UDA architecture.

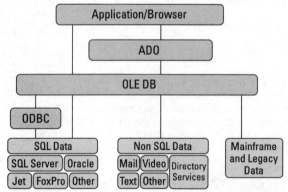

Figure 22-1: The UDA architecture provides a grouping of complimentary database technologies that enable any type of application to access any database.

ADO architecture

One of the major advantages that ADO does have over DAO is that while DAO is composed of 13 collections and 17 objects, the ADO represents a relatively flat object hierarchy. It's this lack of a complex lattice design that makes for an API that is much more flexible and easy to use. Figure 22-2 shows the ADO object model.

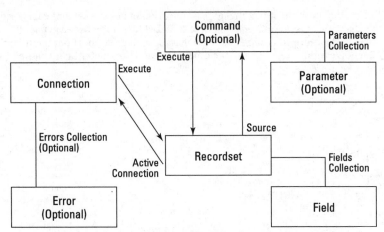

Figure 22-2: In comparison to other object-oriented database access technologies, ADO is represented by a flat, yet powerful object hierarchy.

As you can see, the whole of ADO is built around just six objects, which are explained in the following sections:

✦ Connection

✦ Command

✦ Parameter

✦ Recordset

✦ Field

✦ Error

The Connection object

The Connection object is used to present a connection to a data source. The Open method (explained in the section "Connecting to a data source") of this object takes several parameters such as connection information, database location, user ID, password, and the permission level that the user of the connection will have to modify data. All high-level connection functionality is controlled through this object. This includes transaction control, the setting of the isolation level, and the execution of SQL statements that don't return data.

The Command object

The Command object is used to execute commands in the database. You can use this object to run SQL statements or call stored procedures (named SQL functions that are stored in the database). Anytime that a command returns data, the Recordset object must be used to retrieve that data. You'll see this shortly in the section "Executing commands that return data."

The Command object is optional because not all databases support commands. However, if the database does support command execution, then you should be able to use the ADO Command object when executing those commands.

Another note is that the Command object includes a collection of Parameter objects. Once again, the Parameter object is an optional object in the ADO hierarchy because not all databases support parameterized commands. If the database does support parameters, the Parameters collection contains one Parameter object for each parameter being passed to the command (see Figure 22-3).

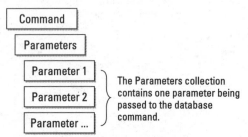

Figure 22-3: If the database supports parameterized commands, you can use the Command object's Parameters collection to create a Parameter object for each one.

The Parameter object

As mentioned, the Parameter object is used for passing variables and for calling stored procedures or parameterized queries. These objects are contained in the Command object's Parameters collection and have properties such as Name, Value, Type, and Size that indicate the column being addressed and the value being passed.

The Recordset object

Although you can technically program ADO without using the Recordset object, you're really not going to do much without it. This is because the Recordset object contains the data returned from a SQL statement. Navigating through the Recordset object is done very much like navigating a recordset in other database access technologies such as ODBC and DAO, with methods like MoveFirst, MovePrevious, MoveNext, and MoveLast. There are over 50 methods to this object so I won't cover all of them. However, the demo applications show you the basic recordset functions such as iterating returned data rows and updating those rows.

The Field object

The Field object represents a single column in the recordset and includes properties such as Name (column name), Type, Precision (for numeric types), and Value. The most important thing to keep in mind here is that ADO is designed to be used with a multitude of languages including late binding languages such as JScript and VBScript. This cross-language usage where every language has its own type system results in the Field object always containing a data value of type Variant. It is, therefore, the responsibility of the programmer to convert the value from a Variant to the necessary data type for usage as well as converting it back to Variant when updating the database.

The Error object

The last object that I'll touch briefly on before discussing how to program using ADO is the Error object. This is an optional object because it is only needed by databases that support returning multiple errors for a single command. When a database only returns a single error for each command attempted, it generally uses the standard COM error mechanism for raising error conditions. As you go through the demo applications, you'll see how these COM error exceptions are caught and examined.

If the database does support the Error object, the error information is not sent from ADO, but is sent from the database. That's an important distinction. The reason this is important to understand now is that when you receive errors (and you will), you will need to look up the specified error codes in the documentation that comes with your database and not the ADO online help.

The many (inter)faces of ADO

ADO is supplied in the form of a COM server. In fact, one rather ironic issue regarding the whole ADO versus DAO issue is that although Microsoft wants developers to use ADO from now on, there are no MFC classes for using ADO! Oh well; maybe in the next release. For now, in order to use ADO you must use its COM interface. Because ADO is used through COM, you have three options of using it from Visual C++:

✦ Use the #import directive to import the ADO type library (typelib).

✦ Use the wizard to import the ADO type library and generate C++ wrapper classes for the different interfaces.

✦ Use the COM API to access the ADO COM components and interfaces directly.

Perusing the ADO type library

If you're familiar with COM (or have already jumped ahead to Chapter 26), you know that COM servers can have the following attributes:

✦ A COM server can be housed in a DLL so that it executes in the client's address space. This is called an *in-proc server* and it greatly improves performance.

✦ COM components can provide an automation interface (sometimes referred to as a *dispinterface*) so that late binding languages can use their services.

✦ COM servers can ship with a type library (sometimes called a *typelib*) so that their components and interfaces can easily be discovered by client applications.

The ADO COM server does all of the following:

✦ It is housed in a file called msado15.dll.

✦ It has a *dual interface* (meaning that it supports the vtable interface usually used in languages like Visual C++ and it supports automation clients like Visual Basic).

✦ It ships with a type library for easy discovery of its components and interfaces.

One example of an application that can discover type libraries is the OLEVIEW application, which ships with Visual Studio .NET. The great thing about this application is that sometimes the documentation on the different components and interfaces exposed by the ADO COM server is a bit sparse to say the least. However, with the OLEVIEW product, you can do a bit of spelunking on your own. To see what I mean, run the OLEVIEW application (you can simply type **oleview** at the Run prompt). When the application starts up, select File ➪ View Typelib and browse to the msado15.dll file—it is stored in C:\Program Files\Common Files\ System\ADO by default. Voila! Now you can peruse all of the library's enum values and interfaces.

As you can see in Figure 22-4, I've opened the ADO type library and selected the Connection interface's Execute method (left pane). Upon selection of a method, the right pane is used to display the IDL that was used to define that method. If you're new to COM, IDL is the language used to define interfaces and methods when creating a type library. I go into more detail on this subject in Chapter 26.

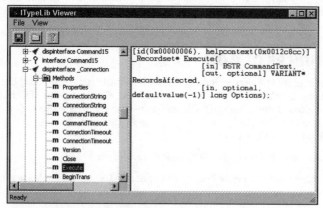

Figure 22-4: Because the ADO ships as an in-proc COM server supporting dual interfaces, you can use the OLEVIEW utility to peruse its interfaces and methods.

Tip   One last thing to be aware of is that even though the name of the file is `msado15.dll`, it is actually the DLL for version 1.5 and greater.

Programming with ADO

You're finally up to the good part! Now that I've covered why you should consider using ADO for your database work, the ADO object hierarchy, and the ADO COM server, let's start writing some code.

One thing I do want to interject about the demo applications is that although there are three different means of using COM components from Visual C++, the demos in this chapter use the `#import` method. I simply chose this technique because from my experience, it is the mechanism used by most Visual C++ developers.

Importing the ADO type library

Because the MFC does not provide a set of classes for use with ADO, you must create your own. This is automated through the use of the `#import` precompiler directive. This directive, introduced with Visual C++ 5.0, enables you to import a type library that was built with the automation interface I mentioned earlier. When the compiler encounters an `#import` directive, it reads through the type library and generates two header files that are then automatically included in the build. These header files, created with the extensions `.tlh` and `.tli`, are placed in the project's build folder along with any binary files that are also created.

Therefore, adding the following #import to your project will result in two files named msado15.tlh and msado15.tli being created automatically. (Depending on your installation, your ADO typelib might be in a different folder. If that is the case, simply locate the file and adjust the #import line accordingly.)

```
#import "c:\program files\common files\system\ado\msado15.dll"
```

The .tlh file is the source code equivalent of a header file for the type library. For example, the Connection object is represented by the _Connection smart pointer. Once you locate that in the msado15.tlh file, you find the following where you can see that _Connection is derived from Connection15:

```
struct __declspec(uuid("00000550-0000-0010-8000-00aa006d2ea4"))
_Connection : Connection15
{
 ...
```

If you then locate Connection15, you'll see its definition and its members (including the Execute method you saw in the OLEVIEW utility earlier):

```
struct __declspec(uuid("00000515-0000-0010-8000-00aa006d2ea4"))
Connection15 : _ADO
{
 ...
_RecordsetPtr Execute (
 VARIANT * RecordsAffected,
 VARIANT * Parameters,
 long Options );
 ...
}
```

The .tli file is then the source code equivalent of an implementation file for the type library. Once again, searching through the code in the msado15.tli file for the _Connection15:: Execute method reveals this (formatted here for clarity):

```
 inline _RecordsetPtr Command15::Execute (
  VARIANT * RecordsAffected,
  VARIANT * Parameters,
  long Options )
 {
  struct _Recordset * _result = 0;
  HRESULT _hr = raw_Execute(RecordsAffected,
                            Parameters,
                            Options,
                            &_result);
  if (FAILED(_hr))
   _com_issue_errorex(_hr,
                       this,
                       __uuidof(this));

  return _RecordsetPtr(_result, false);
 }
```

When importing the ADO COM type library it is standard to place the `#import` directive in the `stdafx.h` file (so that it's included for all files) and to use the following syntax:

```
#import "c:\program files\common files\system\ado\msado15.dll" \
no_namespace \
rename("EOF", "adoEOF")
```

You'll notice a couple of things here. First, if any part of the `#import` directive is split onto a separate line, you must use the standard C++ line continuation character (\). Second, there are two new bits I've added. The first is the `no_namespace` attribute. This is used because when a type library is imported it is automatically imported into a namespace by default. Although namespaces are good for avoiding naming conflicts, their inclusion here would mean having to qualify the different types defined in the `.tlh` file, which would make coding very tedious (because you'd have to do a lot more typing). I added the `rename` attribute because it turns out that there is indeed one naming conflict between the `.tlh` file and MFC. Because there's only one conflict, you just use the `rename` attribute to resolve that. As you can see on the last line, that one conflict that gets resolved is the `EOF` constant. Because EOF is already defined, using the `rename` attribute tells the precompiler that when it generates the `.tlh` and `.tli` files, it should replace all occurrences of `EOF` with `adoEOF`. Then in your code, you simply refer to `adoEOF` when you want to test for end-of-file. I named the constant `adoEOF` to make my code more readable—when someone else reads my code, there should be no question that I'm referring to the EOF constant ADO requires, and not some other random EOF constant.

Initializing and uninitializing COM

Because you are using COM to interact with ADO, you must first initialize COM somewhere in your code. This can be at application startup or just before you create an instance of an ADO `Connection` object. The easiest way to initialize COM is by calling the COM SDK `::CoInitialize` function as shown in the following example. The only parameter to this function is reserved and always passed as a `NULL`.

```
HRESULT CoInitialize(LPVOID pvVoid)
```

As `::CoInitialize` is used to initialize COM, the `::CoUninitialize` function is used to end your COM session:

```
void CoUninitialize()
```

For more information on these two functions, including how to handle the returned `HRESULT` as well as `::CoInitialize` versus `::CoInitializeEx` and `::CoUninitialize` versus `::CoUninitializeEx`, please refer to Chapter 29 of this book where I go into much more detail regarding these and other COM programming issues.

Connecting to a data source

Now it's time to connect to a data source. As mentioned earlier, the Connect interface is used for this purpose. In order to acquire this interface using the imported ADO type library, you simply instantiate the `_ConnectionPtr` object and call its `Open` method as follows:

```
HRESULT hr;
_ConnectionPtr myConnection;
myConnection.CreateInstance(__uuidof(Connection));
hr = myConnection->Open ( "connection string", "user ID",
    "pswd", 0);
```

```
HRESULT Open(_bstr_t ConnectionString,
             _bstr_t UserID,
             _bstr_t Password,
             long Options);
```

The first parameter (ConnectionString) is the connection definition string. There are several options here depending on the data source you are connecting to and how you're connecting to it. For example, you can pass the name of an ODBC OLE DB driver where OLE DB is being used to access an ODBC data source, or you can pass the name of an ODBC DSN. I'll show you both examples after I've gone through the other three parameters.

The second parameter (UserID) is an optional parameter that represents a user that is defined to the database. If you were using an ODBC DSN you would pass the user ID as part of the connection string.

The third parameter (Password) is also an optional parameter and represents the password defined for the user specified in the UserID parameter. Once again, if you specify an ODBC DSN in the connection string, then that connection string should also include the password.

Finally, the fourth and last parameter (Options) dictates the level of permissions for modifying the data in the connection. These values are defined in the ConnectModeEnum enum. These values can be found in the msado15.tlh file and are described in Table 22-1.

Table 22-1: Valid Values for the Connect Mode

Constant	Value	Meaning
adModeUnknown	0 (0x00)	Indicates that permissions have not been set or cannot be determined. It is the default value.
adModeRead	1 (0x01)	Indicates read-only permissions.
adModeWrite	2 (0x02)	Indicates write permissions.
adModeReadWrite	3 (0x03)	Combines adModeRead and adModeWrite to open the connection with read/write permission.
adModeShareDenyRead	4 (0x04)	Denies others from opening a connection with read permission.
adModeShareDenyWrite	8 (0x08)	Denies others from opening a connection with write permission.
adModeShareExclusive	12 (0x0C)	Combines adModeShareDenyRead and adModeShareDenyWrite to prevent others from opening the connection.
adModeShareDenyNone	16 (0x10)	Allows all others to open and share this connection with any permissions.
adModeRecursive	4,194,304 (0x400000)	Propagates the specified mode to all subrecords of the current record; it is used in conjunction with the adModeShareDenyXXX constants.

As promised, here are a couple of examples of connecting to a data source using ADO. In the first example, I've created an instance of the `_ConnectionPtr` using the C++ `__uuidof` operator, which retrieves the GUID of the Connection interface. The GUID for this and all other ADO interfaces can be found in the `.tlh` file.

In the `Open` method's connection string parameter, I've specified an OLE DB provider that connects to a Microsoft Access database. The actual physical file is a local copy of the same database provided on the book's Web site and is used in all the database demo applications in this book. Because this is an unsecured Microsoft Access database, there is no need to pass any user ID and password information. I also used the default permission option of `adModeUnknown` because I know that I'm using this database in a single-user environment and don't have to worry about other connections.

```
_ConnectionPtr pConnection1;
pConnection1.CreateInstance(__uuidof(Connection))

pConnection1->Open(_bstr_t("Provider=Microsoft.Jet."
                   "OLEDB.4.0;"
                   "Data Source = c:\\VCNETBIBLE.MDB"),
                   _bstr_t(""),
                   _bstr_t(""),
                   adModeUnknown);
```

The only difference in the second example is the connection string. Here I use an ODBC DSN that points to the same physical file as the first `Open` example. If you need a refresher on creating ODBC DSNs, please refer to Chapter 20.

```
_ConnectionPtr pConnection2;
pConnection2.CreateInstance(__uuidof(Connection))

pConnection2->Open("DSN=VCNetBible;",
                   _bstr_t(""),
                   _bstr_t(""),
                   adModeUnknown);
```

Creating commands

Although there are different ways of creating SQL statements to execute against a data source, the most common is by using the Command interface. The following example shows how to create an instance of a `Command` object using the `pConnection1` interface pointer created earlier.

```
_CommandPtr pCommand;
pCommand.CreateInstance (__uuidof (Command));
pCommand->ActiveConnection = pConnection;
pCommand->CommandText = "Select * From UserMaster";
```

As you can see, first you do the usual instantiation of the smart pointer and retrieval of the interface pointer using the `CreateInstance` method. After that, simply point the `Command` at the current `Connection` by setting the Command interface's `ActiveConnection` property. Next, use the Command interface's `CommandText` property to specify the SQL that will be executed against the data source. Using the `Command` object to execute SQL commands is useful in cases where you don't want or care about the result of the SQL command. (Some SQL commands, like `INSERT`, don't return a result, or a set of rows from the database. Therefore, executing an `INSERT` statement using the `Command` object is ideal.) I'll show you how to execute SQL commands that return a set of rows from the database in the following section.

Executing commands that return data

Once you're prepared to execute a command, there are a couple of ways to do it. You can use the Command interface's Execute method, as described in the previous section, or you can use the Recordset interface's Open method where you pass it the Command interface pointer. Here's an example of the latter of those two:

```
_RecordsetPtr pRecordset;
pRecordset.CreateInstance(__uuidof (Recordset));
pRecordset->CursorLocation = adUseClient;
pRecordset->Open((IDispatch*)pCommand,
                 vtMissing,
                 adOpenStatic,
                 adLockBatchOptimistic,
                 adCmdUnknown);
```

After acquiring a pointer to the Recordset interface, its CursorLocation property is set to adUseClient. This value specifies the location of the cursor services (the previous example uses a local cursor as opposed to a remote one). The valid values are listed in Table 22-2.

Table 22-2: CursorLocationEnum Values

Constant	Value	Meaning
adUseNone	1	Specifies that cursor services are not to be used.
adUseServer	2	Indicates that data provider or driver supplied cursors are to be used; it is the default value.
adUseClient	3	Uses client-side cursors.

A cursor represents a pointer to a specific record in the result set that the Recordset object manages. In this example, your only choice is to store the cursor's data locally because you're using a Microsoft Access database on your system. If you were to open the Recordset object while connected to a SQL Server, you could use a client cursor or server (adUseServer) cursor. When working with a SQL Server, which usually resides on another system, using a client-side cursor offers better performance at the cost of increased memory requirements because all of the results from a SQL command need to be downloaded to the client's system. Server-side cursors are great for clients that don't have a lot of memory or processing power because the cursor actually resides on the SQL Server system. The cost is an increase in network traffic because each request for a record results in a trip to the SQL server and back to the client; as a result, it is common to find server-side cursors in environments where there's a fast connection to the SQL Server (such as within a corporate network).

The next call is then to the Recordset interface's Open method. This method's first parameter is a variant that can be a Command object, a SQL statement, the name of a table, the name of a stored procedure, or even a URL. In this case, I passed the Command object (cast to IDispatch) created earlier.

The second parameter is a variant representing the active connection in the Command object. Because this property is optional and I've already set the Command object's ActiveConnection property, I simply pass a value of vtMissing. In Visual C++, whenever you want to specify a missing parameter whose type is variant, you can either use the vtMissing constant that is defined in the comutil.h file (included as result of the #import). Alternatively, you can also specify a _variant_t value of DSP_E_PARAMNOTFOUND and type VT_ERROR.

The third parameter is the cursor type, defined here as static.

The fourth parameter is the lock type. I used adLockBatchOptimistic because you'll be using batch processing in the demo to improve performance. Table 22-3 shows the different valid LockType constants that you can use.

Table 22-3: LockType Values

Constant	Value	Meaning
AdLockUnspecified	−1	When you use this value, no lock type is specified. If the recordset is created via the Clone method (a means of copying a recordset), the second recordset (destination) will have the same lock characteristics as the first recordset (source).
AdLockReadOnly	1	This value indicates that the recordset's data cannot be modified.
AdLockPessimistic	2	By specifying this value, you are indicating that you want the provider to ensure that the data that exists during editing is still the same when you update it. Therefore, the provider typically locks the records signaled for edit until the update is requested. The downside is possibly holding locks for too long a period of time, thereby not allowing others to edit the same data. However, the upside is that you are assured of not overwriting data that was changed between the time that you read the data and the time you updated it.
AdLockOptimistic	3	The opposite of pessimistic locking, specifying that you want optimistic locking means that the records will only be locked when they are being updated. Once again, the downside here is that the data could be changed between the time you read the data for update (edit mode) and the time you updated the data. The upside is that the other users can read and update the data without having to wait for you to release the lock (via an explicit unlock request or via an update).
adLockBatchOptimistic	4	The value is used for batch updating where only optimistic locking is allowed. Note that the OLE DB providers for the AS/400 and DB/2 do not support this lock type.

Finally, the last parameter indicates to ADO how the provider should evaluate the first parameter if it is not a `Command` object. However, because I am passing a `Command` object in the first parameter, I simply pass a value of `adCmdUnknown`.

Filtering and sorting the data

Now that you can see how easy it is to execute a statement like `SELECT * FROM UserMaster` against the data source, let's look at how you can accomplish filtering and sorting. Think of the `Recordset` object as a representation of the results that are returned as a result of executing a SQL Statement (like the `SELECT` statement). The `Recordset` object has several methods and properties you can use, regardless of where the results reside (on the client or the server, as described in the previous section). Suppose you have a `UserMaster` table and you want to retrieve all users whose names begin with the letter K. You might be tempted to think, "Well, I could just change my `Command` object's SQL to":

```
SELECT * FROM UserMaster where sUserName like K*
```

You could do that if all you ever want in your recordset are the rows corresponding to that filter. However, that wouldn't necessarily be the best solution in all cases.

Suppose you have a dialog box that allows the user to continually filter their data. If you use the first technique (filtering via the `Command` object), your code would have to recreate a `Command` object and re-execute the SQL against the data store (potentially against a distributed server) each time the user sets the filter. This is fine if the user only sets the filter once. However, this technique is expensive both in terms of time and resources if the user can set the filter continually.

In addition, what if the application allowed for nested filtering? For example, your application might use the `Command` object's `CommandText` method to retrieve all users that the current user has permissions to view. With that returned data set, the user may want to filter and sort those rows.

These are just a couple of examples, but as you can see there are times when you'll want your application to be capable of filtering a recordset that has already been read from the server. In order to do this, you use the `Recordset` object's `Filter` method.

The following code snippet filters the `UserMaster` table for all users whose names begin with the letter K. (I've omitted all the error checking code in the name of brevity):

```
// Get the Fields collection from the recordset.
FieldsPtr pFields = pRecordset->Fields;

// From the Fields collection, get the desired Field.
FieldPtr pField = pFields->GetItem("sUserName");

// From the Field, get that field's properties collection.
PropertiesPtr pProperties = pField->Properties;

// From the Properties collection, get the desired property.
PropertyPtr pProperty = pProperties->GetItem("Optimize");

// Finally, set the desired property's value.
pProperty->Value = VARIANT_TRUE;

pRecordset->Filter = "sUserName LIKE 'K*'";
pRecordset->Sort = "sUserName";
```

```
// loop to read recordset data...

pRecordset->Filter = (long) adFilterNone;
```

As you can see, there's a lot of code here. However, almost all of it retrieves objects from deeply nested collections. The only real work being done here is the setting of the `FieldPtr` object's `Optimize` property and the setting of the `Recordset` object's `Sort` and `Filter` properties.

Let's look at the `Optimize` property first. As the name suggests, this property enables you to optimize a sort or filter based on a particular field. How you implement this depends on your particular database. However, most of the time you will enable your database to select the most appropriate index to use for the ensuing database operations.

After that, the following lines tell the database that you want only the rows where the `sUserName` column begins with the letter K, and you want to sort those returned rows by the `sUserName` column:

```
pRecordset->Filter = "sUserName LIKE 'K*'";
pRecordset->Sort = "sUserName";
```

The last thing that you'll need to do when you're finished using the data that was filtered is to reset the `Filter` property so that subsequent operations are once again using the entire data set. Notice that ADO provides a constant (`adFilterNone`) for doing this.

```
pRecordset->Filter = (long)adFilterNone;
```

Now you finally have some data to work with.

Iterating through a recordset

In order to iterate through a recordset, you simply use a `for` loop and check the `adoEOF` property. Remember that you renamed that property (and method) name during the `#import`, earlier in the chapter. The following are two examples of a simple loop to read through all of a `Recordset` object's rows.

The first example uses the `Recordset` object's `GetCollect` method to return the field in a `Variant` (`column`) type. After that, simply check to ensure that the field does not contain a null value. If not, display the value in a message box. Notice that the data value has to be converted before the data can be displayed (from `Variant` to `BSTR` to `char*`). This is what I was referring to earlier in the chapter when I said that because ADO uses variants in order to support late-binding languages, it is up to the developer to make the appropriate data conversions when using that data.

```
_variant_t column;
while (!pRecordset->adoEOF)
{
 // METHOD #1 : Using GetCollect
 column = pRecordset->GetCollect("sUserName");

 if (column.vt != VT_NULL)
 {
  AfxMessageBox((char*)_bstr_t(column));
 }

 pRecordset->MoveNext();
}
```

The second example uses the `Field` object's `Value` property to retrieve the field's value:

```
_variant_t column;
while (!pRecordset->adoEOF)
{
  // METHOD #2 : Using the Field object's Value
  column = pField->Value;

  if (column.vt != VT_NULL)
  {
    AfxMessageBox((char*)_bstr_t(column));
  }

  pRecordset->MoveNext();
}
```

At first glance it might look obvious that the `Field` object's `Value` property is quicker to write. However, remember you only have the `Field` pointer because you acquired it to do the sort and filter. Therefore, if you don't already have the `Field` pointer, you have to write something like the following (along with all the error correction code for each attempted acquisition of an object's pointer):

```
FieldsPtr pFields2 = pRecordset->Fields;
if (pFields2)
{
  FieldPtr pField2 = pFields2->GetItem("sUserName")
  if (pField2)
  {
    column = pField2->Value;
  }
  else
  {
    // error
  }
}
else
{
  // error
}
```

I personally only use the `Field` object's `Value` property when I already have the `Field` object. Otherwise, I prefer the `Recordset` object's `GetCollect` method.

Updating the data

Now that you know how to execute SQL statements against a data source and even filter the returning rows via the `Recordset` object's `Filter` property, the next logical step after reading data is to be able to update that data. This can be done quite easily using the `Recordset` object. There are actually two different ways of updating data via ADO: batch updates and single-record updates. I'll touch briefly on each one here.

Batch updates

The batch update is the form used in this chapter's demo application. You are in batch update mode if a value of `adLockBatchOptimistic` is specified for the `LockType` parameter of the `Recordset` object's `Open` method. As an example of how you could use this mode, suppose you have an application that allows the user to scroll through the records one record at a time. You might have the standard forward and back data controls on your dialog box. As the user navigates through each record, that record is saved to a *save buffer*. That way the user doesn't need to explicitly save each record. To the user, the data just seems to automatically update as they move from one record to the next. However, the changes are not actually made in the database until the application calls the Recordset object's UpdateBatch method. Another point to make is that the application can explicitly call the Recordset object's Update method. However, in batch update mode, the changes will not be made permanent until UpdateBatch is called.

```
HRESULT UpdateBatch(enum AffectEnum AffectRecords)
```

Table 22-4 lists and explains the different values that can be passed for the AffectRecords parameter.

Table 22-4: AffectEnum Values

Constant	Value	Meaning
AdAffectCurrent	1	Specifies that only the current record's changes will be written to the database.
AdAffectGroup	2	Specifies that only the records that satisfy the current filter settings will be written. This is a very powerful value.
adAffectAll	3	Specifies that all pending changes will be written. This is the default value.

This automatic updating begs one obvious question. What if you want to abort a particular update? You do this via the Recordset object's CancelUpdate method.

Single-record updates

The second way to update records via the Recordset object is by using the object's Update method as follows:

```
HRESULT Update(const _variant_t& Fields = vtMissing,
               const _variant_t& Values = vtMissing)
```

As you can see, the Update method takes only two parameters. The first (Fields) is a Variant that represents a single column name or a Variant array representing either column names (or their ordinal values) that are to be updated. The second parameter (Values) is then used to specify either a single value of a Variant array of values.

As an example of how to use this, suppose you want to change the user name of the current record. You could simply do the following:

```
// Declare the two variants (column name and value).
_variant_t vColumn, vValue;

// Set the column name.
vColumn.SetString("sUserName");
```

```
// Set the column's new value.
vValue.SetString("Test Name");

// Update the column via the Recordset Update method.
pRecordSet->Update(vColumn, vValue);
```

Demo ADO Application

Now let's put all you've learned so far to work in the form of a demo application. This demo application will display a filtered list of users in a list view control. The information displayed will include the user's ID, name, and status. Once you've coded the bits necessary to filter, sort, and list this data, you then add a dialog box that will enable the user to modify their name and update the database accordingly. To get started, create an MFC dialog-based application called ADODemo.

Initializing the connection

The first coding you need to do is to create a member variable in the dialog class of type _ConnectionPtr. This variable (shown in bold in the following code) will be used to both fill the list view control as well as update the database.

```
class CADODemoDlg : public CDialog
{
...
protected:
 _ConnectionPtr m_pConnection;
...
}
```

Now, add the following code to the dialog box's OnInitDialog function just before the return statement. As you can see, this code simply initializes COM, creates an ADO Connection object (pointing to the demo database), and then calls the DisplayUsers function.

Note   You'll notice that this demo refers to an ODBC DSN in the Connection.Open function call. I'm doing this for variety because you've already seen how to create a DSN-less ODBC connection. However, if you want to use this code as shown, you need to create the DSN (named VCNet Bible) based on the book's sample database. If you haven't done this before, please refer to the section "Creating an ODBC DSN" in Chapter 20. If you want to use (or test) a DSN-less connection, simply comment out the first Open call and uncomment the second. (Make sure you change the Data Source to point to the location where you've copied the database.)

```
LONG lStyle =
 m_lstUsers.SendMessage(LVM_GETEXTENDEDLISTVIEWSTYLE);

lStyle |= LVS_EX_FULLROWSELECT;

m_lstUsers.SendMessage(LVM_SETEXTENDEDLISTVIEWSTYLE,
                   0, (LPARAM)lStyle);
try
{
 // Initialize COM.
 CoInitialize(NULL);
```

```
     // Connecting to the database via a
     // _ConnectionPtr interface
     m_pConnection.CreateInstance(__uuidof(Connection));
     m_pConnection->Open("DSN=VCNet Bible;",
                         _bstr_t(""),
                         _bstr_t(""),
                         adModeUnknown);

 /* Uncomment this for a DSN-less connection
  m_pConnection->Open(_bstr_t("Provider=Microsoft.Jet."
                      "OLEDB.4.0;"
                      "Data Source = c:\\VCNETBIBLE.MDB"),
                      _bstr_t(""),
                      _bstr_t(""),
                      adModeUnknown);
 */

  if (NULL != m_pConnection)
  {
   DisplayUsers();
   SizeAllColumns();
  }
  else
  {
   AfxMessageBox("Could not acquire a Connection interface.");
  }
 }
 catch(_com_error &e)
 {
  _bstr_t bstrError(e.ErrorMessage());
  CString strError = (char*)bstrError;
  AfxMessageBox(strError);
 }
 catch (...)
 {
  AfxMessageBox("Unknown Error!");
 }
```

Displaying the users

Now you need to modify the application's main dialog box to display the users. To do that, modify the default dialog box so that when finished it looks like the one shown in Figure 22-5.

When you've placed the controls on the dialog box, change the list view control's View property to Report and the Single Selection property to True.

Once you've finished updating the OnInitDialog function, create a new member function for the dialog box called DisplayUsers. This function is a bit long (because it does include some error handling) so I've interspersed comments throughout the code to explain what I'm doing each step of the way. However, the main gist of the function is to accomplish the following steps:

1. Insert the columns in the list view control.

2. Create a Command object that selects the records from the UserMaster table.

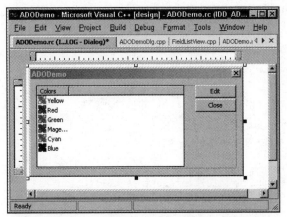

Figure 22-5: The ADODemo application illustrates the basic functionality of reading, filtering, and updating data using ADO from a Visual C++ application.

3. Create and open a `Recordset` object.

4. Create a `Field` object for each column in the table.

5. Set the `Recordset` object's `Filter` property to retrieve records only where the `sUserId` begins with the letter K.

6. Iterate the records of the `Recordset` object, inserting each one into the list view control.

```
void CADODemoDlg::DisplayUsers()
{
 if (NULL != m_pConnection)
 {
  // Create columns for listview control.
  m_lstUsers.InsertColumn(0, "User ID");
  m_lstUsers.InsertColumn(1, "User Name");
  m_lstUsers.InsertColumn(2, "Status");

  try
  {
   _CommandPtr pCommand;
   pCommand.CreateInstance (__uuidof (Command));
   pCommand->ActiveConnection = m_pConnection;
   pCommand->CommandText = "Select * From UserMaster";

   _RecordsetPtr pRecordset;
   pRecordset.CreateInstance (__uuidof (Recordset));
   pRecordset->CursorLocation = adUseClient;
   pRecordset->Open((IDispatch *) pCommand,
                    vtMissing,
                    adOpenStatic,
                    adLockBatchOptimistic,
                    adCmdUnknown);
```

```cpp
// Get the Fields collection from the recordset.
FieldsPtr pFields = pRecordset->Fields;

// From the Fields collection, get the desired Field.
   FieldPtr pUserId = pFields->GetItem("sUserId");
   ASSERT(NULL != pUserId);

   FieldPtr pUserName = pFields->GetItem("sUserName");
   ASSERT(NULL != pUserName);

   FieldPtr pStatus = pFields->GetItem("iStatus");
ASSERT(NULL != pStatus);

// From the Field, get that field's properties collection.
PropertiesPtr pProperties = pUserName->Properties;

// From the Properties collection,
// get the desired property.
PropertyPtr pProperty = pProperties->GetItem("Optimize");

// Finally, set the desired property's value.
pProperty->Value = VARIANT_TRUE;

pRecordset->Sort = "sUserName";
pRecordset->Filter = "sUserName LIKE 'K*'";

_variant_t vUserId;
_variant_t vUserName;
_variant_t vStatus;

int nUsers = 0;
while (!pRecordset->adoEOF)
{
 vUserId = pUserId->Value;
 vUserName = pUserName->Value;
 vStatus = pStatus->Value;

 if (vUserId.vt != VT_NULL)
 {
  CString strUserId =   (char*)_bstr_t(vUserId);
  int iIndex = m_lstUsers.InsertItem(nUsers++,
                                     strUserId,
                                     0);

  CString strUserName = (char*)_bstr_t(vUserName);
  m_lstUsers.SetItemText(iIndex, 1, strUserName);

  m_lstUsers.SetItemText(iIndex,
                         2,
                         ( 1 == vStatus.iVal
                             ? "Active" : "Inactive"));
 }
```

```
    pRecordset->MoveNext();
  }

  pRecordset->Filter = (long) adFilterNone;
 }
 catch(_com_error &e)
 {
  _bstr_t bstrError(e.ErrorMessage());
  CString strError = (char*)bstrError;
  AfxMessageBox(strError);
 }
 catch (...)
 {
  AfxMessageBox("Uknown Error!");
 }
 }
 else
 {
  AfxMessageBox("No Connection interface was created "
               "in OnInitDialog");
 }
}
```

At this point, building and running the application should yield results similar to those seen in Figure 22-6.

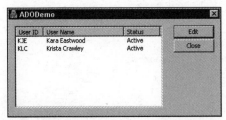

Figure 22-6: Once you get over the COM work involved with interfacing to ADO, the actual objects and methods are very easy to use.

Updating the user information

As a finishing touch on this demo, add a dialog box that will enable the user of this application to update data. To do that, add a new dialog box resource as shown in Figure 22-7.

After you create the dialog box resource, set the User Id control's Read only property to True. Next, create a new CDialog-based class called CUpdateDlg and add DDX value member variables of type CString for the two controls called m_strUserId and m_strUserName, respectively.

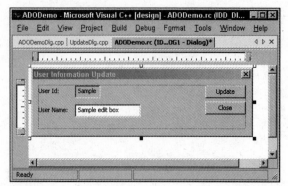

Figure 22-7: Sample dialog box to test updating data via ADO.

This dialog box won't do much except verify that the user types in a user name if he or she wants to update the database. To do that, add an event handler for the Update button's BN_CLICKED message and modify it as follows:

```
void CUpdateDlg::OnBnClickedOk()
{
 // Retrieve dialog box values into DDX variables.
 if (UpdateData())
 {
  // Make sure that you have a user ID and name.
  if (0 < m_strUserId.GetLength()
  &&  0 < m_strUserName.GetLength())
  {
   // If so, end dialog box. Parent dialog box will
   // retrieve values.
   CDialog::OnOK();
  }
  else
  {
   // If not, tell user that you need these
   // values in order to update the database.
   AfxMessageBox("You must specify a user name to continue");
  }
 }
}
```

Once you've done that, you need only add the following event handler for the main dialog box's Edit button.

```
void CADODemoDlg::OnBnClickedOk()
{
 // Get selected item index from listview.
 POSITION pos = m_lstUsers.GetFirstSelectedItemPosition();
 if (NULL != pos)
 {
  // Code assumes one selection only.
  int nItem = m_lstUsers.GetNextSelectedItem(pos);
  ASSERT(-1 < nItem);
```

```
if (-1 < nItem)
{
 try
 {
  HRESULT hr;

  _CommandPtr pCommand;
  hr = pCommand.CreateInstance (__uuidof (Command));
  if (SUCCEEDED(hr))
  {
   pCommand->ActiveConnection = m_pConnection;

   CString strUserId =
    m_lstUsers.GetItemText(nItem, 0 /* first column */);

   CString strQuery;
   strQuery.Format("SELECT * FROM UserMaster WHERE "
                   "sUserId = \'%s\'", strUserId);

   pCommand->CommandText = (_bstr_t) strQuery;

   _RecordsetPtr pRecordset;
   hr = pRecordset.CreateInstance (__uuidof (Recordset));
   if (SUCCEEDED(hr))
   {
    pRecordset->CursorLocation = adUseClient;
    pRecordset->Open((IDispatch *) pCommand,
                     vtMissing,
                     adOpenStatic,
                     adLockOptimistic,
                     adCmdUnknown);

    // Instantiate the dialog box and initialize
    // its DDX variables from the database.
    CUpdateDlg dlg;

    // Get the Fields collection from the recordset.
    FieldsPtr pFields = pRecordset->Fields;

    // From the Fields collection, get the desired Field.
    FieldPtr pUserId = pFields->GetItem("sUserId");
    ASSERT(NULL != pUserId);

    FieldPtr pUserName = pFields->GetItem("sUserName");
    ASSERT(NULL != pUserName);

    dlg.m_strUserId = (char*)(_bstr_t)pUserId->Value;
    dlg.m_strUserName = (char*)(_bstr_t)pUserName->Value;

    if (IDOK == dlg.DoModal())
    {
     // Declare the two variants (column name and value).
```

```
                    _variant_t vColumn, vValue;

                    // Set the column name.
                    vColumn.SetString("sUserName");

                    // Set the sUserName column's new value.
                    vValue.SetString(dlg.m_strUserName);

                    // Update the column via the Recordset Update method.
                    pRecordset->Update(vColumn, vValue);

                    // Update main dialog box with new changes.
                    m_lstUsers.SetItemText(nItem, 1, dlg.m_strUserName);
                  }

                  pRecordset->Close();
                }
                else
                {
                  AfxMessageBox("Failed to instantiate a "
                                "Recordset interface");
                }
              }
              else
              {
                AfxMessageBox("Failed to instantiate a "
                              "Command interface");
              }
            }
            catch(_com_error &e)
            {
              _bstr_t bstrError(e.ErrorMessage());
              CString strError = (char*)bstrError;
              AfxMessageBox(strError);
            }
            catch(...)
            {
              AfxMessageBox("Uknown Error!");
            }
          }
          else
          {
            AfxMessageBox("Could not retrieve index of selected user");
          }
        }
        else
        {
          AfxMessageBox("Please select a user to edit.");
        }
      }
```

Adding some UI niceties

If you've read Chapter 7, you'll recall that I introduced a simple function that enables you to size all the columns of a list view control. This definitely comes in handy because the default behavior of the list view control is to originally display with minimum column sizing, meaning that you'd have to manually size each column upon application startup in order to see your data. Therefore, add the following function to your CADODemoDlg class. (For a further explanation of this code please refer to the section "Sizing list view columns" in Chapter 7.)

```
void CADODemoDlg::SizeAllColumns()
{
  CHeaderCtrl* pHeader = m_lstUsers.GetHeaderCtrl();
  ASSERT(pHeader);
  if (pHeader)
  {
    // Turn off redraw until the columns have all
    // been resized.
    m_lstUsers.SetRedraw(FALSE);

    for (int iCurrCol = 0;
        iCurrCol < pHeader->GetItemCount();
        iCurrCol++)
    {
      m_lstUsers.SetColumnWidth(iCurrCol, LVSCW_AUTOSIZE);

      int nCurrWidth = m_lstUsers.GetColumnWidth(iCurrCol);

      m_lstUsers.SetColumnWidth(iCurrCol,
                          LVSCW_AUTOSIZE_USEHEADER);

      int nColHdrWidth = m_lstUsers.GetColumnWidth(iCurrCol);

      m_lstUsers.SetColumnWidth(iCurrCol,
                      max(nCurrWidth, nColHdrWidth));
    }

    // Now that sizing is finished, turn redraw back on and
    // invalidate so that the control is repainted.
    m_lstUsers.SetRedraw(TRUE);
    m_lstUsers.Invalidate();
  }
}
```

Once you've finished, build and run the application as shown in Figure 22-8. To test your new ADO application, select a user, click the Update button, change the user's name, and then click the Update button. Not only will the main dialog box reflect the new changes, but if you open the demo database in Access, you should also see the changed data there as well.

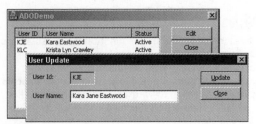

Figure 22-8: Once you learn the basics of ADO, writing database applications is very easy.

Summary

In this chapter, you learned how to use the ADO object hierarchy to perform almost all of the basic database application tasks of reading data, sorting and filtering recordsets, and updating data. Along the way, you also discovered how to read and write data in batch mode for better performance as well as set database sharing permissions and record-level locking levels in order to ensure data integrity when running in multiuser environments. Finally, the chapter ended with a demo application that illustrates how to code basic CRUD (create, read, update, and delete) functionality using ADO. So far, in this Data I/O section, you've seen chapters that have illustrated database programming using ODBC, the MFC Database Classes, and ADO. In the next chapter, I'll continue with the coverage of the various database access technologies with a lesson on programming with DAO.

✦   ✦   ✦

DAO

In the previous chapter, I briefly mentioned that the DAO (Data Access Objects) was designed as an efficient means of connecting to Microsoft Access databases. Because the Microsoft Access database engine is referred to as the *Jet engine*, you'll often hear the terms *DAO* and *Jet* used interchangeably. DAO was originally designed for Microsoft Access and later Visual Basic, and Visual Basic for Applications. For several years this meant that database programmers that needed to interface their applications to an Access database from any other language had only one option: ODBC. Although ODBC (which is covered in Chapter 20) is certainly a very powerful tool for accessing heterogeneous databases, it is not the appropriate API for all database applications. This is especially true for database applications that need only to interface to Access databases.

As you learned in Chapter 20, one of the advantages of ODBC over other database technologies is its capability of enabling a single code base to interface to different databases. Unfortunately, this results in "least common denominator" code. In other words, if you are writing a single code base to work with multiple databases, you will not be able to take advantage of any specific database's capabilities without writing special case code for each database. When you start writing this special case code, you have deviated from the goal of a single code base. In addition, some of the functionality of the Access DBMS is simply not supported through the Access ODBC driver (Microsoft Desktop Drivers).

Microsoft addressed this issue with version 3.0 of DAO by exposing the full functionality of the Jet engine through *automation* (formerly called *OLE automation*). You'll learn much more about the world of automation in Chapter 33. However, for now it's enough to understand that automation enables a sever application to allow client applications to access its functions programmatically. In version 3.0 of DAO, an automation in-process server was included that contains an embedded *type library*. As with any automation type library, this enables a client application to query the automation server for descriptions of exposed objects via the OLE IDispatch interface. This capability opened up an entirely new paradigm to database development involving the Access DBMS. With DAO 3.0, any language that supports automation can access almost every facet of the Jet's functionality through the DAO automation interfaces. Writing Visual C++ applications that use DAO to interface to Access databases is the subject of this chapter.

In this chapter, you will learn about the different objects that constitute the DAO object hierarchy. From there, you'll be exposed to the different DAO APIs that enable you to programmatically manipulate DAO objects from your own client applications. Once these APIs have been covered, a demo will be introduced that uses the MFC DAO classes to write a maintenance application. Although this demo is fairly simple in scope, it does teach the fundamentals necessary for writing larger, more robust database applications using the MFC DAO classes.

The DAO hierarchy

As stated earlier, DAO is an API that can be used to interface to Access databases. More specifically stated, DAO is a hierarchy of objects and collections of objects packaged in a DLL. At the top of this hierarchy is the DBEngine object. Every other object is, in turn, a subobject of the DBEngine object. Before describing some of the more important objects in detail, take a look at Figure 23-1. This figure illustrates the complete DAO object hierarchy for the Jet Workspace (workspaces are covered shortly).

The DBEngine object

The DBEngine is the top-level object in the DAO object hierarchy. Therefore, the DBEngine object contains and controls all of the other objects in the DAO object model. Although many of the other DAO objects have an associated collection object, the DBEngine does not. That means that there is one and only one DBEngine object, and it is not an element of any collection.

The DBEngine object contains numerous methods and properties as well as two collections: the Workspaces collection and the Errors collection. The DBEngine object is used to do such high-level tasks as create Workspace objects and carry out database maintenance tasks such as compacting and repairing Access databases.

The Workspaces collection object

The Workspaces collection object is a nonordered collection of all active Workspace objects. One way to think of a Workspace is as a session between your application and the Jet engine. The Workspaces object is used to start new sessions or manage existing sessions.

As with any DAO collection object, you can retrieve any of the contained objects either by name or ordinal number. Like C/C++ arrays, DAO collection indexes are relative to zero. This means that to retrieve the first Workspace object from the Workspaces collection by ordinal number, you have to specify a value of 0.

The Workspace object

The Workspace object specifies an active, named session with the Jet engine. You can use the Workspace object for managing transactions, creating and opening databases, and performing security-level functions such as creating users and groups.

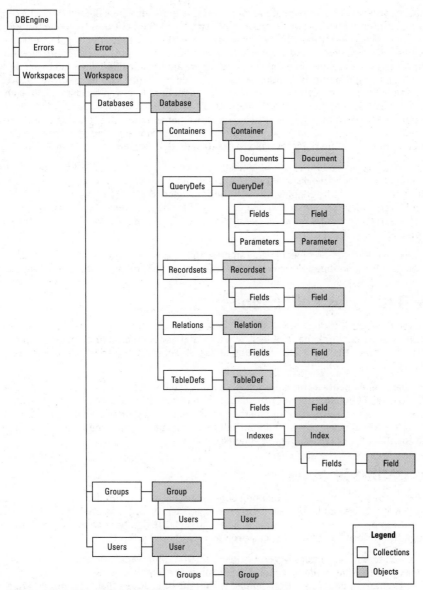

Figure 23-1: The DAO object hierarchy (Jet Workspace) is used to expose the full functionality of the Jet engine.

In general, you won't have to create an object of this type because a default `Workspace` object is created for you. However, your application may need at times to create unique `Workspace` objects — for example, when using the `Workspace` methods to manage transactions (`BeginTrans`, `CommitTrans`, and `Rollback`). When multiple databases are opened within a single `Workspace`, *all* databases opened within the specified `Workspace` are affected by the transactions methods. Suppose you've opened two databases using the `Workspace` `OpenDatabase` method. If you call the `BeginTrans` method followed by changes to each database, and then call the `Rollback` method, all changes to both databases will be lost. If your application requires that these two databases manage their transactions independently, the application must create `Workspace` objects for each database. The `CreateWorkspace` method of the `DBEngine` object is used to create a unique, named `Workspace` object.

There are two types of `Workspace` objects: `Jet` and `ODBCDirect`. In DAO 3.5, Microsoft introduced the `ODBCDirect` workspace type. This enabled programmers using DAO to also access ODBC data sources without going through the Jet engine. Figure 23-1 illustrates the DAO object hierarchy for the `Jet` workspace. Because this chapter concentrates solely on the `Jet` workspace, refer to the *Microsoft Jet Database Engine Programmer's Guide* for more information on using ODBCDirect.

Whereas each `Workspace` object is contained within the `Workspaces` collection, each `Workspace` object contains three collections of its own: `Databases`, `Users`, and `Groups`.

The Databases collection

The `Databases` collection contains all the open `Database` objects that were created or opened in its parent `Workspace` object. When a database is created or changed via the `Workspace` object, the associated DAO `Database` object is appended to that `Workspace` object's `Databases` collection.

Other than simply being a container for all of a `Workspace` object's open `Database` objects, the `Databases` collection doesn't provide much in terms of functionality. About the only `Database` collection properties and methods you might find yourself needing are the `Count` method (used to retrieve the total number of open `Databases`) and the `Refresh` method (used to reflect the current database schema).

The Database object

The `Database` object represents an open connection between an application and a database. A physical database can be managed only through DAO via an associated `Database` object. Once the application has created the `Database` object, the database can then be manipulated through the various `Database` object's properties and methods.

The `Database` object contains several collections that directly correlate to the database schema of its associated database file. For example, the `QueryDefs`, `TableDefs`, `Relations`, and `Containers` collections are all defined within the `Database` object and directly relate to Access entities.

It's important to realize that creating a `Database` object doesn't automatically establish a link with associated database's tables or queries. To do this, you must use the `TableDefs` collection or the `Recordsets` collection. However, creating a `Database` object is a prerequisite to accessing a database's tables or queries.

A database's schema can be changed through the `Database` object via its `CreateQueryDef`, `CreateTableDef`, `CreateRelation`, and `CreateProperty` methods. In addition, the `MakeReplica`, `Synchronize`, and `PopulatePartial` methods can be used to create and synchronize full or partial replicas of the database file associated with a `Database` object.

The Recordsets collection

The Recordsets collection contains all of the open Recordset objects for a given Database object. The Recordset object is most often how you will deal with data using DAO. Much like the Databases collection, the Recordsets collection doesn't provide much functionality beyond the Count property and Refresh method provided by all DAO collection objects.

The Recordset object

The Recordset object represents the data that is returned from executing a query. The major difference between the Recordset object and most of the other DAO objects is that it is not persistent. In other words, while other DAO objects such as the Database, TableDef, and QueryDef objects relate to a part of a physical database, the Recordset object represents only the set of records produced by running a query against one or more tables or queries. There are five types of supported DAO Recordsets, as follows:

✦ *Table* — An Access table that you can manipulate by adding, changing, and deleting records.

✦ *Dynaset* — A dynamic set of records that can also be manipulated by adding, changing, and deleting records.

✦ *Snapshot* — A static set of records (this type of recordset is not updateable).

✦ *Forward-Only* — Identical to the Snapshot recordset type except that you can only proceed forward through the recordset. (This newly defined recordset is ideal for a situation in which you need to traverse a recordset only once.)

✦ *Dynamic* — Similar to a Dynaset recordset, with one very important difference: After you run the query that results in a recordset of this type, if another user adds or deletes records that would have been included in this recordset, the changes are reflected in this recordset automatically.

The Recordset type is specified when the OpenRecordset method is called. The default Recordset type is a table-type recordset. Because the Recordset object represents a set of records that were produced as a result of a query, the Recordset object also exposes methods to navigate this set of records. These methods include MoveFirst, MoveNext, MovePrevious, and MoveLast. Creating and updating records is accomplished via the AddNew, Edit, and Update methods. The Move and Seek methods provide additional means of traversing the records.

The many (inter)faces of DAO

Although the capability of communicating with the Jet engine through an industry standard mechanism like automation was a much-heralded announcement, programming with DAO through automation is generally thought to be a somewhat tedious task. In answer to these complaints, Microsoft released another interface to DAO called the *DAO SDK*. Actually, the DAO SDK includes a set of C++ classes called the *dbDAO classes*.

However, you will often see the terms *DAO SDK* and *dbDAO* used interchangeably. In addition to the DAO SDK, Microsoft also released a set of DAO classes specifically for use with MFC. These classes, the MFC DAO classes, are almost identical in terms of interface to the MFC database classes used for ODBC data sources.

DAO automation interfaces

Because DAO provides a standard vtable-based implementation of automation, the DAO SDK was released to provide C++ header files that define the DAO vtable interfaces. This, in turn, eliminated the need to use the IDispatch interface. With the DAO SDK, once an application creates an instance of the DBEngine object, instances of objects can be created through their parent objects using the DAO hierarchy previously shown in Figure 23-1. Otherwise, these objects are standard COM objects and as such, must be explicitly released when the application has finished using them. If you are familiar with COM or automation programming, this interface may be perfect for your application. However, if you are programming in C++ and would rather use a more C++ friendly method of interfacing to the Jet engine, two other methods may be more appealing.

dbDAO C++ classes

The dbDAO C++ classes (included as a part of the DAO SDK) were the first alternatives to using the DAO automation interface directly. These classes not only provide C++ programmers with the convenience of encapsulating the DAO in C++ classes, but they also provide a Visual Basic-like syntax to database programming. The decision to use a Visual Basic-like syntax for the dbDAO functions was made for two reasons. First, most programmers familiar with Access databases had at least started using the Access database with Visual Basic. Second, because the ratio of Visual Basic programmers to Visual C++ programmers at the time was estimated at about five to one, it only made sense to cater to the majority. Therefore, with dbDAO, Microsoft killed two birds with one stone.

Another major advantage that dbDAO has over the native DAO automation interface is that with dbDAO, only a limited amount of COM and automation knowledge is necessary to use the classes effectively. This is because the dbDAO classes abstract the developer from many of the underlying details of dealing directly with the DAO automation interface. For example, dbDAO automatically handles reference counting (using the AddRef and Release methods), dynamic allocation and deallocation of objects, and many lower-level automation details that the programmer would normally have to deal with.

In short, the dbDAO classes afford the database developer the same benefits as the DAO automation interface, with the lowest possible overhead short of programming directly to the DAO automation interfaces.

MFC DAO classes

Not to be outdone, the developers of MFC released their own DAO interface with Visual C++ 4.0. The MFC DAO classes have a hierarchy that's similar to the MFC Database classes that utilize ODBC. The advantage to this is that developers with experience with the ODBC-based MFC Database classes have a shorter learning curve with the MFC DAO classes. In addition, the MFC DAO classes are fully integrated with the MFC wizards and the MFC class hierarchy.

It should be noted that even though the syntax of the MFC DAO classes is very distinct from the dbDAO classes, both class hierarchies simply wrap the DAO automation interface. Hence, if something can't be done using the DAO automation interface, it's a good bet it can't be done at all with either dbDAO or MFC.

Using the MFC DAO Classes

The MFC DAO classes are composed of eight classes: `CDaoDatabase`, `CDaoWorkspace`, `CDaoRecordset`, `CDaoTableDef`, `CDaoQueryDef`, `CDaoException`, `CDaoRecordView`, and `CDaoFieldExchange`. With the exception of the MFC document/view-specific `CDaoRecordView` and `CDaoFieldExchange` classes and the `CDaoException` class, each of the MFC DAO classes relates to a DAO object.

In terms of class hierarchy and member function interfaces, the MFC DAO classes are designed in a very similar manner to the MFC Database classes. However, besides the fact that the MFC Database classes use the ODBC SDK internally to carry out their work (as opposed to DAO automation), the major difference between the two sets of database access classes is that the MFC DAO classes are much more robust in terms of functionality. For example, DDL operations are supported by the MFC DAO classes whereas the MFC Database classes do not support them.

As mentioned previously, there are only eight MFC DAO classes, as opposed to almost thirty objects defined in the DAO object model (Jet Workspace). This disparity in the number of classes is because of several factors:

✦ The MFC DAO class hierarchy is a "flat" version of the DAO object model. In the DAO object model, if an object can contain a collection of another type of object, separate objects represent both the collection and the contained object type. For example, because a `Database` object can contain multiple `TableDef` objects, a `TableDefs` collection object and a `TableDef` object are defined in the DAO object model. However, because most DAO collection objects simply provide a method that returns the number of objects contained within the collection, the MFC DAO classes represent most DAO collections with a `CMapPtrToPtr` map.

✦ The MFC DAO classes do not support all of the DAO functionality. For example, the MFC DAO classes do not support any of the Jet security operations. This means that the DAO `Users` and `Groups` objects have no corollary classes in MFC. Therefore, in order to manage security for an Access database using DAO from a Visual C++ application, you have to use either the dbDAO classes or the DAO automation interfaces.

Of the eight MFC DAO classes, this section will concentrate on the classes a typical database application is most likely to use: `CDaoDatabase`, `CDaoWorkspace`, `CDaoRecordset`, and `CDaoException`. The reason that the `CDaoRecordView` class is not included in this chapter is because it is nothing more than a view with an embedded `CDaoRecordset` object. Therefore, once you have learned about the `CDaoRecordset` class, using the `CDaoRecordView` class is a very straightforward proposition.

CDaoDatabase

The `CDaoDatabase` class represents a connection between an application and a database. After constructing a `CDaoDatabase` object, the application must specify the database name as the first argument in the `CDaoDatabase::Open` member function. The `CDaoDatabase` class can be used in conjunction with one or more `CDaoRecordset` objects (the `CDaoRecordset` class will be covered shortly), or it can be used without a `CDaoRecordset`. For example, you would want to use the `CDaoDatabase` class by itself if the application needs to issue a SQL statement that does not return any data against a database. The `CDaoDatabase::Execute` function exists for just this purpose. The following is an example of how easy it is to insert a record into a table using the `Execute` function.

Note   The table being used in this chapter is a simple demo Access database that can be found on the Web site for this book.

```
try
{
  CDaoDatabase db;
  db.Open("VCNetBible.mdb");

  db.Execute("INSERT INTO UserMaster "
    "VALUES('TST', 'Test User Name', 0)");

  db.Close();
}
catch(CDaoException* pe)
{
  AfxMessageBox(pe->m_pErrorInfo->m_strDescription,
   MB_ICONEXCLAMATION );
  pe->Delete();
}
```

Note that when you use the AppWizard to create an application, one of the options provided is whether or not you will want DAO support. If you elect to use this support, the appropriate header files are included in your project. However, if you need to add DAO support to an existing project, you simply have to add the #include directive for the DAO header file (afxdao.h) to the appropriate files in your project.

Let's look at the previous code in more detail. The first thing you see in the code snippet is a C++ try/catch block.

```
try
{
  . . .
}
CATCH(CDaoException* pe)
{
  AfxMessageBox(pe->m_pErrorInfo->m_strDescription,
   MB_ICONEXCLAMATION );
  pe->Delete();
}
```

When using the MFC DAO classes, all DAO errors are expressed as exceptions of type CDaoException. Because the DAO object model supports the existence of an Errors collection, the CDaoException class defines member functions to retrieve any information from multiple DAO Error objects stored in the DBEngine Errors collection. When a DAO error occurs, one or more Error objects are added to the DBEngine Errors collection. However, if a DAO operation results in one or more of the Error objects being created and added to the Errors collection, the previous Error objects are discarded first. If a DAO operation does not produce an error of any kind, the Errors collection retains its previous content. Here are a couple of the more important member functions and variables that you will use when dealing with the CDaoException class:

✦ m_nAfxDaoError — This member variable is set when a DAO component error has occurred, such as the Jet engine not being initialized.

✦ m_pErrorInfo — This is a pointer to a CDaoErrorInfo structure that includes, among other things, a member variable containing the textual representation of the error.

✦ GetErrorCount—This member function returns the number of Error objects in the database engine's Errors collection.

Because all of the MFC DAO classes' member functions can throw exceptions of type CDaoException, it is wise to wrap all code using these functions in try/catch blocks. The first thing the example is attempting to do in the try block is to construct a CDaoDatabase object and open it. Obviously, the name and location of the database file have been hard-coded in order to simplify the example.

```
CDaoDatabase db;
db.Open("VCNetBible.mdb"))
...
```

The CDaoDatabase constructor doesn't do anything special. You must call the CDaoDatabase ::Open member function to actually connect to a database. Here is the prototype for the CDaoDatabase::Open member function:

```
virtual void Open(LPCTSTR lpszName,
 BOOL bExclusive = FALSE, BOOL bReadOnly = FALSE,
 LPCTSTR lpszConnect = _T("") );
  throw( CDaoException, CMemoryException );
```

As you can see in this prototype, an application can set several options when opening a database using the CDaoDatabase::Open function. However, only the first argument is explicitly required for this function, and it was the only one passed in the preceding example. This first argument represents the fully qualified name of the database being opened. The remaining arguments are as follows:

✦ The bExclusive flag is used to specify if the database is to be opened for exclusive access. If the specified file is already opened and this flag is set to TRUE, an exception of type CDaoException is thrown by the Open function.

✦ The bReadOnly flag specifies whether or not updates to the data source are enabled. The default value is FALSE. Any recordsets that are created and attached to a CDaoDatabase object inherit this flag.

✦ The lpszConnect argument specifies the ODBC connect string. However, if the application is using an Access database, this argument must be an empty string.

After opening the CDaoDatabase object, the next lines execute the SQL statement and close the database:

```
db.Execute("INSERT INTO UserMaster "
 "VALUES('TST', 'Test User Name', 0)");

db.Close();
```

As you can see, CDaoDatabase::Execute has a very straightforward syntax. The first argument (and the only required one) for this function takes a SQL statement or the name of an action query to be run. Note that this function is only used when the SQL statement or action query being run won't result in the return of data from the data source. In fact, calling an action query that returns a value results in an exception of type CDaoException being thrown by the Execute function.

A second argument can also be specified in the Execute function that specifies options relating to the integrity of the query. For example, this argument can be used to stipulate options such as the database performing a rollback on any updates if an error occurs during the execution of the SQL statement or action query.

CDaoWorkspace

The `CDaoWorkspace` class is used to manage a named database session. As mentioned previously in the section describing DAO objects, an application does not ordinarily require multiple workspaces, because when the database and its associated recordset objects are opened via the MFC DAO classes, a default DAO workspace is used. However, the capability does exist to create additional workspaces for performing such tasks as logically grouping transactions. Remember that the transaction operations (like `BeginTrans` and `CommitTrans`) are performed at the workspace level. This means that in order to manage transactions independently across `CDaoDatabase` objects, the application must explicitly create additional `CDaoWorkspace` objects for each database that requires its transactions be handled independently.

The `CDaoWorkspace` object, therefore, provides access to the default workspace that is created when the `DBEngine` is initialized. In addition, when a workspace is opened or created (or one of its static member functions is called), the `DBEngine` is initialized, which then creates the default workspace for that instance of the database engine.

As alluded to earlier, another useful set of member functions that the `CDaoWorkspace` class supports are the functions for supporting transactions. Transactions give the application the capability of bracketing a set of functions in a logical group so that if any one of those functions fail, no changes are made. For those of you not familiar with transactions, an example might be in order here. Suppose an accounting application needs to transfer an amount from one account to another. What would happen if after removing the amount from one account, the attempt to update the second account's balance failed? The integrity of the database would be compromised because the amount would not be in either account. With transactions, an application can specify that both of these financial transactions must complete successfully. If either of these transactions fails, then both accounts revert to their previous balances, and no changes are made.

Here's the way it works. An application first sets a transaction boundary by calling the `CDaoWorkspace::BeginTrans` function. Anything done after this point is subject to being rolled back, or undone. Once the application calls the `CDaoWorkspace::CommitTrans` function, all changes made since the last transaction boundary are committed, or made permanent. If for some reason the application needs to roll back or undo any changes since the last transaction boundary, the `CDaoWorkspace::Rollback` function is called. Note that before attempting to call the `CommitTrans` function, an application must first call the `BeginTrans` function.

CDaoRecordset

Whereas a `CDaoDatabase` object represents a connection to a database, a `CDaoRecordset` object represents a set of records from one of those connections. As you may recall from earlier in the chapter, the DAO `Recordset` object supports five different types of recordsets. The MFC `CDaoRecordset`, however, only supports three of those: table-type, dynaset, and snapshot. A table-type recordset represents a single base table whose data can be altered by the application. A dynaset recordset is the outcome of a query whose results can also be updated by the application. Finally, a snapshot recordset is a static picture of data taken at the time the recordset was filled. This data cannot be updated.

As you can see from the following list, the principal DAO class that you'll do much of your database work with is the `CDaoRecordset` class. Take a look at this list, and then I'll go into each task individually.

✦ Construct a recordset.

✦ Open a recordset.

✦ Read and write data using DFX (DAO field exchange).

✦ Filter records.

✦ Sort records returned with a recordset.

✦ Move through the recordset.

✦ Save records.

✦ Delete records.

Defining a CDaoRecordset-derived class

Now things get a bit ugly. For whatever reasons, Microsoft has deemed it necessary to remove ClassWizard support for the creation of classes deriving from the MFC DAO classes. Therefore, you need to do a bit of manual work here if you want to use DAO. This will include creating an ODBC consumer class and then modifying it to work with DAO instead of ODBC.

To see how this is done, create a new MFC project. You're not going to do anything other than learn how to generate DAO recordsets with this project, so you can name it anything you like.

Once you've created the project, select the Add Class option from the Project menu. This displays the Add Class dialog box you've seen many times by now. From here, click the MFC category and then the MFC ODBC Consumer template. Once you've done that, click OK. From there, you should see the MFC ODBC Consumer Wizard (shown in Figure 23-2).

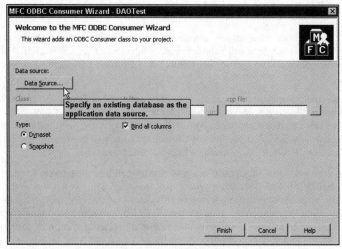

Figure 23-2: The ODBC Consumer Wizard allows you to select a DSN and name the recordset class (and its header/implementation) files.

Click the Data Source button to invoke the ODBC Administration application. If you've already created an ODBC DSN for the book's database, you can simply select the "VCNet Bible" DSN (on the Machine Data Source tab) and then click OK. If you haven't created the DSN, create it now using the Access database (VCNetBible.mdb) from this book's Web site. Also, if you're unfamiliar with creating ODBC DSNs, please refer to the section "Creating an ODBC DSN" in Chapter 20.

Once you've selected your DSN, the wizard will require you to supply a Login name and Password for the database. The sample database is not protected, so simply click OK without entering any information. From there, you will be presented with a list of all the tables and views defined in the database (Figure 23-3).

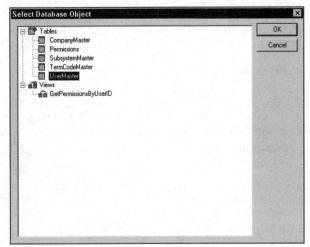

Figure 23-3: The Select Database Object dialog box

From here, you select the table or view on which you want to base your recordset. For this demo, select the UserMaster table. You will then be returned to the ODBC Consumer Wizard, where the various values (class name, header file name, and CPP file name) will have been entered for you.

You'll probably get a security warning because the Login name and Password (blank in this case) are going to be copied into your recordset's implementation file (in the GetDefault Connect function). You can see this warning in Figure 23-4. This is only an issue if you have a database that uses passwords, and you don't want those passwords to be viewed by anyone who can view the source code. Click OK to dismiss that warning message.

Now open the UserMaster.cpp file, and you'll see that the wizard has inserted a #error directive into the file just before the GetDefaultConnect function. This was done so to make sure that you realize the risks involved. Simply delete this #error directive. In cases where you do care about this situation, you could simply store your Login name and password in another format (for example, in an encrypted file) and retrieve that information at runtime when the GetDefaultConnect function is called. Actually, as you'll see next, GetDefault Connect is for ODBC recordsets, and GetDefaultDBName is for DAO recordsets.

Now for the changes that will turn this ODBC class into a DAO class. (In each of these steps I am referring to both the header file and the CPP file unless stated otherwise.)

1. Place the following include directive in the recordset's header file.

   ```
   #include <afxdao.h>
   ```

2. Replace all occurrences of CRecordset with CDaoRecordset.

Figure 23-4: Security confirmation error about clear-text user password information

3. Replace all occurrences of `CDatabase` with `CDaoDatabase`.

4. Replace all occurrences of `CFieldExchange` with `CDaoFieldExchange`.

5. Locate the virtual member function `GetDefaultConnect` and rename it `GetDefaultDBName`.

6. In the `GetDefaultDBName` function, return the fully qualified file name of the Microsoft Access database that you're using instead of the ODBC connect string. (In the ODBC connect string inserted by the wizard, this will be the value of the `DBQ` attribute.)

7. In the recordset's constructor, find the following line of code:

   `m_nDefaultType = dynaset;`

   Replace it with the following:

   `m_nDefaultType = dbOpenSnapshot;`

8. In the implementation file, replace all occurrences of `RFX_` with `DFX_`.

9. In the implementation file, replace all occurrences of `DFX_Int` with `DFX_Short`.

10. In the header file, change any member variables that are bound to data columns and are of type `int` to type `short`.

11. In the header file, change any member variables that are bound to data columns and are of type `CStringW` to type `CString`.

Voila! You now have a DAO recordset class to work with.

Constructing a CDaoRecordset object

The `CDaoRecordset` constructor takes only one argument: a pointer to a `CDaoDatabase` object. This argument has a default value of `NULL`. If the application does not specify a `CDaoDatabase` object when constructing a `CDaoRecordset`, MFC automatically creates a temporary `CDaoDatabase` object using the information specified when the recordset was created with the ClassWizard. The information that will be used can be found in the `CDaoRecordset::GetDefaultDBName` function.

However, if your application must use multiple recordsets, it is much more efficient for the application to create one `CDaoDatabase` object and use that object for subsequently created `CDaoRecordset` objects. That way, a temporary `CDaoDatabase` does not have to be created for each `CDaoRecordset` object. One way of doing this is to create a `CDaoDatabase` object when the application initializes and stores the pointer in the application or document object. Then, whenever the application needs to construct a `CDaoRecordset` object, the global `CDaoDatabase` object can be used.

Opening a recordset

Once a `CDaoRecordset` object has been constructed, it can be opened using its `Open` member function. One of the arguments for this function is the recordset type. This argument is used to specify whether the recordset being opened is a dynaset, table, or snapshot recordset type. These types are represented by the `dbOpenDynaset`, `dbOpenTable`, and `dbOpenSnapshot` constants, respectively. All of these constants are defined in the `afxdao.h` header file. If the application does not specify a recordset type, the type of recordset opened is dictated by the value entered when the class was created with ClassWizard. This value is stored in the `m_nDefaultType` member variable and is initialized in the class constructor. If the application calls the `Open` function without specifying a SQL string to be executed, the `GetDefaultSQL` member function is used to determine which records end up in the recordset after the `Open` function returns.

Reading and writing data using DFX

In order to retrieve all of the records from a table without regard to order, the application simply must create a `CDaoRecordset`-derived class (as shown previously) and call its `CDaoRecordset::Open` member function. However, at this point you may be wondering how the data gets from the data source into the application's variables. The answer is DFX (DAO field exchange).

When a `CDaoRecordset`-derived class is created using ClassWizard, ClassWizard enumerates all of the columns in the selected table or query and declares variables of the appropriate type in the recordset's header file. ClassWizard also generates code for a function called `DoFieldExchange` that serves to tie the member variables to their corresponding columns in the database. The `DoFieldExchange` function is called when MFC needs to move data from the database to the class's member variables or vice versa. The underlying MFC code actually does all the low-level DAO work, such as binding the columns and fetching the data, that the application would have had to do manually if it weren't for this *helper* function.

When a `CDaoRecordset` object is opened with its `Open` member function, it moves to the first record in the recordset so that the application can immediately start using the data. The application can then start navigating through the resulting data using the `CDaoRecordset::MoveFirst`, `CDaoRecordset::MovePrev`, `CDaoRecordset::MoveNext`, and `CDaoRecordset::MoveLast` member functions. (These functions will be explained shortly.)

Filtering records

Now that you know how to open and retrieve data from a data source, you need to learn how to filter that data to get just the records you desire. Actually, there are several ways to accomplish this. As you saw in the section "Opening a recordset," one way is to specify the SQL in the `CDaoRecordset::Open` function. The following code is an example of using that function to filter the desired records from the `UserMaster` table. This code reads only the records that represent users whose status code is equal to zero.

```
CDaoDatabase db;
CUserMaster rs;
try
{
 rs.Open(AFX_DAO_USE_DEFAULT_TYPE,
  "SELECT * from UserMaster where iStatus = 0");
```

```
while (!rs.IsEOF())
{
AfxMessageBox(rs.m_sUserName);
rs.MoveNext();
}
}
catch(CDaoException* pe)
{
AfxMessageBox(pe->m_pErrorInfo->m_strDescription,
 MB_ICONEXCLAMATION);
pe->Delete();
}
```

A second way to filter the data returned in a recordset is to use a *parameterized recordset*. Using the CDaoUserMaster class created earlier in the chapter, you would make the following changes such that only records whose iStatus has a value of zero are retrieved.

1. In the recordset header file, define a member variable for each parameter you are going to use. It's a standard naming convention to take the name of the member variable representing the column you want to filter on and append the word Param to it. For example, if you were going to filter the recordset by the iStatus column, which is associated with the m_iStatus member, you would define the following parameter variable.

   ```
   short m_iStatusParam;
   ```

2. Initialize the parameters variables in the recordset's constructor, and set the m_nParams value to the number of parameters that will be used. Once again, following that example would mean doing the following, where the new lines are shown in bold:

   ```
   //{{AFX_FIELD_INIT(CDaoUserMasterSet)
   m_sUserID = _T("");
   m_sUserName = _T("");
   m_iStatus = 0;
   m_nFields = 3;
   m_iStatusParam = 0;
   m_nParams = 1;
   //}}AFX_FIELD_INIT
   m_nDefaultType = dbOpenDynaset;
   ```

Note   If you attempt to use a parameterized recordset and do not set the m_nParams member variable, the recordset's Open will fail, and you will receive an ASSERT when the framework calls DoFieldExchange.

3. Now you would update the DoFieldExchange function to call the appropriate DFX_ function for the parameter variable. In this example, the following bold lines would be added. Note that the CDaoFieldExchange::SetFieldType must be called with the CDaoFieldExchange::param argument. As you can see, you now have two member variables associated with the iStatus column — the m_iStatus field that will contain the column's value and the m_iStatusParam that will be used to filter the recordset.

```
void CDaoUserMasterSet::DoFieldExchange(
 CDaoFieldExchange* pFX)
{
 //{{AFX_FIELD_MAP(CDaoUserMasterSet)
 pFX->SetFieldType(
 CDaoFieldExchange::outputColumn);

 DFX_Text(pFX, _T("[sUserID]"), m_sUserID);
 DFX_Text(pFX, _T("[sUserName]"), m_sUserName);
 DFX_Short(pFX, _T("[iStatus]"), m_iStatus);

 pFX->SetFieldType(CDaoFieldExchange::param);
 DFX_Short(pFX, _T("[iStatus]"), m_iStatusParam);
 //}}AFX_FIELD_MAP
}
```

4. Initialize the CDaoRecordset::m_strFilter member variable using the ? character as a placeholder for each parameter you are going to pass. Then set the different parameter member values. Finally, open the recordset. The framework will automatically take the specified parameter data and generate an SQL SELECT statement using the placeholders in the m_strFilter string.

Once again, using the filtering on the iStatus column as an example, this would look like the following in practice.

```
CUserMaster rs;
try
{
 rs.m_strFilter = "iStatus = ?";
 rs.m_iStatusParam = 0;
 rs.Open();

 while (!rs.IsEOF())
 {
  AfxMessageBox(rs.m_sUserName);
  rs.MoveNext();
 }
}
catch(CDaoException* pe)
{
 AfxMessageBox(pe->m_pErrorInfo->m_strDescription,
  MB_ICONEXCLAMATION );
 pe->Delete();
}
```

As you can see, using parameterized recordsets is not complex, but if you forget to do any of the steps involved, you can end up losing a lot of time tracking down why your Open function call is not working.

Sorting records returned with a recordset

As you just saw in the previous section, the CDaoRecordset class provides a member variable (m_strFilter) to filter the records that a recordset represents. The CDaoRecordset class also provides a member variable to specify the order in which the records are returned. This member variable is named m_strSort. To use this member variable, simply set its value to the name of the column that you want the recordset sorted by. For example, in the sample code previously used, if you wanted to sort by the iStatus column in the UserMaster table, your code would look like the following:

```
CDaoDatabase db;
CUserMaster rs;
try
{
 rs.m_strSort = _T("iStatus");
 rs.Open();

 while (!rs.IsEOF())
 {
 AfxMessageBox(rs.m_sUserName);
 rs.MoveNext();
 }
}
catch(CDaoException* pe)
{
 AfxMessageBox(pe->m_pErrorInfo->m_strDescription,
  MB_ICONEXCLAMATION);
 pe->Delete();
}
```

If you need to sort by more than one column, simply separate each column name with a comma.

Moving through the result set

Once a recordset has been opened and the desired data has been retrieved (via the m_strFilter member variable) in the desired sequence (via the m_strSort member variable), you must know how to move through the resulting records. The CDaoRecordset class makes this easy with the MoveFirst, MovePrev, MoveNext, and MoveLast member functions. It's not difficult to figure out from the function names what each function does. However, you should know the following when attempting to navigate through a recordset:

✦ All of the move functions throw an exception if the recordset does not return any records. Therefore, the application should always call CDaoRecordset::IsBOF or CDaoRecordset::IsEOF before attempting to call one of the move functions.

✦ The MoveFirst and MovePrev functions are not supported for recordsets that are defined as forward-only. Note that this particular rule is applicable only to ODBCDirect workspaces.

✦ If the application calls one of the move functions and retrieves a record that may have been deleted by another user, the application should call the CDaoRecordset::IsDeleted function to verify that the record is still valid.

Saving records

Saving data using the CDaoRecordset class is very easy and straightforward. There are basically two different ways to save data: by adding new records and by updating existing records. To add a new record, the application simply must do the following:

1. Call the CDaoRecordset::AddNew function, which prepares a new, blank record for use.

2. Move the new data into the recordset's member variables.

3. Call the CDaoRecordset::Update function.

For an application to update an existing record, do the following:

1. Call the CDaoRecordset::Edit function.

2. Move the new data into the recordset's member variables.

3. Call the CDaoRecordset::Update function.

It's important to note the order in which you call these functions. When updating an existing record, the data must be moved into the member variables *after* calling the Edit function. Otherwise, MFC does not update the data. The reason for this is that the MFC DAO classes cache the recordset's data when the Edit function is called and do a memory compare when the Update function is called to see if the data has changed. If no changes have been made to the member variables since the Edit function was called, the data will not be saved even though the Update function was explicitly called.

Deleting records

To delete a record from a recordset, the current record must be the record your application needs to delete. The application then simply calls the CDaoRecordset::Delete function. After deleting the record, the current record in the recordset is not a valid record, and the application must call one of the move functions until a valid record in the recordset is reached.

Writing the DAO Demo Application

This demo (DaoUserMaintenance) has all the create, read, update, and delete capabilities of a traditional maintenance application for maintaining users. Although this demo is fairly simple in scope, it does teach the fundamentals necessary for writing larger, more robust database applications. Note that in the following demo (which can be found on this book's Web site), you will develop a fully functional maintenance application using the MFC DAO classes.

To get started, create a dialog-based application called DaoUserMaintenance. Once the AppWizard generates the project, add the following #include directive to the stdafx.h file.

```
#include <afxdao.h>
```

Now open the resource view and modify the application's main dialog box (IDD_ DAOUSERMAINTENANCE_DIALOG) so that when finished it looks like that shown in Figure 23-5.

Figure 23-5: Demo application dialog box in the resource editor

Once you have created the controls onto the dialog box, create the DDX member for the different controls using the value shown in Table 23-1.

Table 23-1: Member Variables for DDX

Control	Category	Variable Type	Variable Name
User list box	Control	`CListbox`	`m_lbxUsers`
User ID edit	Value	`CString`	`m_strUserID`
User Name edit	Value	`CString`	`m_strUserName`
Status edit	Value	`int`	`m_iStatus`
Save button	Control	`CButton`	`m_btnSave`
Delete button	Control	`CButton`	`m_btnDelete`

Adding a utility class to encapsulate the user's data

A utility class is required to encapsulate each record's data. As you will see later, when the application reads a record from the recordset, a `CUser` object is created. An entry is then made into the list box that represents that record. This list box entry's item data contains a pointer to the `CUser` object. At this point, define the following class just before the `CDaoUserMaintenanceDlg` class in the `daousermaintenancedlg.h` file.

```
class CUser
{
public:
 CString m_strUserID;
 CString m_strUserName;
 int m_iStatus;
};
```

Creating a CDaoRecordset class for the UserMaster table

Now create a `CDaoRecordset`-derived class that is based on the demo database's `UserMaster` table. If necessary, refer back to the steps in the section "Defining a CDaoRecordset-derived class" presented earlier in this chapter.

Initializing the dialog box

Locate the `CDaoUserMaintenanceDlg ::OnInitDialog` function, and add the following function calls (shown in bold) just before the `return` statement. The `FillListboxWithUsers` function fills the list box with all of the users found in the database. The `InitControls` function does such things as initialize the state of the buttons (disabling the Save and Delete buttons when a user is not selected, enabling the Save and Delete buttons when a user is selected, and so on).

```
BOOL CDaoUserMaintenanceDlg::OnInitDialog()
{
 CDialog::OnInitDialog();
```

```
...

FillListboxWithUsers();
InitControls();

return TRUE;
}
```

Filling the list box with users

Add the following include directive to the top of the DaoUserMaintenanceDlg.cpp file:

```
#include "UserMaster.h"
```

Now, define a function called FillListboxWithUsers for the CDaoUserMaintenanceDlg class and code it as follows. Because the MFC DAO classes throw exceptions upon encountering unexpected conditions, it's always best to wrap your DAO calls in a try block. After instantiating and opening the user recordset (which automatically retrieves all user records), the code goes into a while loop in order to read all users until end of file is reached (verified by calling CRecordset::IsEOF). Within the while loop (and for each user), the function instantiates a CUser object and sets its members to the data returned from the recordset. The user name is then added to the list box, the new list box entry's item data is set to the address of the CUser object, and the next user is retrieved from the recordset.

```
void CDaoUserMaintenanceDlg::FillListboxWithUsers()
{
 try
 {
  int iIndex;

  CUserMaster rs;
  rs.Open();

  while (!rs.IsEOF())
  {
   CUser* pUser = new CUser();
   pUser->m_strUserID = rs.m_sUserID;
   pUser->m_strUserName = rs.m_sUserName;
   pUser->m_iStatus = rs.m_iStatus;

   iIndex = m_lbxUsers.AddString(rs.m_sUserName);
   m_lbxUsers.SetItemData(iIndex, (DWORD)pUser);
   rs.MoveNext();
  }
 }
 catch(CDaoException* pe)
 {
  AfxMessageBox(pe->m_pErrorInfo->m_strDescription,
   MB_ICONEXCLAMATION );
 }
}
```

Initializing the dialog box's controls

Define a function called `InitControls` for the `CDaoUserMaintenanceDlg` class and code it as follows. As you can see, this function merely initializes the various controls on the dialog box and disables the Save and Delete buttons, because they shouldn't be active unless a user is selected in the list box.

```
void CDaoUserMaintenanceDlg::InitControls()
{
 m_lbxUsers.SetCurSel(-1);

 m_strUserID = "";
 m_strUserName = "";
 m_iStatus = -1;

 m_btnSave.EnableWindow(FALSE);
 m_btnDelete.EnableWindow(FALSE);

 m_lbxUsers.SetFocus();

 UpdateData(FALSE);
}
```

List box item selection event handler

You now must add a function so that when a user is selected from the list box, the proper information is displayed in the dialog box. To do this, implement a message handler for the `LBN_SELCHANGE` notification message, and code it as follows (your function may have a different name, depending on the resource ID of the list box). As you can see, the function simply calls a helper function that returns the `CUser` object associated with the selected list box entry. From there, the dialog box's controls are updated with that object's data. Note that once a user is selected, the Save and Delete buttons are enabled via a call to `CWnd::EnableWindow(TRUE)`.

```
void CDaoUserMaintenanceDlg::OnSelchangeLbxUsers()
{
 int iIndex;
 CUser* pUser;

 if (GetSelectedUser(&iIndex, &pUser))
 {
  m_strUserID = pUser->m_strUserID;
  m_strUserName = pUser->m_strUserName;
  m_iStatus = pUser->m_iStatus;
  m_btnSave.EnableWindow(TRUE);
  m_btnDelete.EnableWindow(TRUE);
  UpdateData(FALSE);
 }
}
```

Now add the `GetSelectedUser` helper function. It simply calls the `CListBox::GetCurSel` function to determine the index of the selected list box item. Once it has that index value, it can then call the `CListBox::GetItemData` to retrieve that item's item data. The item data is cast to a `CUser` object pointer and returned to the caller.

```
BOOL CDaoUserMaintenanceDlg::GetSelectedUser(int* piIndex,
                                             CUser** ppUser)
{
 BOOL bSuccess = FALSE;

 int iIndex;
 if (LB_ERR != (iIndex = m_lbxUsers.GetCurSel()))
 {
  *piIndex = iIndex;
  *ppUser = (CUser*)m_lbxUsers.GetItemData(iIndex);
   bSuccess = TRUE;
 }

 return bSuccess;
}
```

Saving user data

At this point, if you were to build the application, you would see that it can already read and display all defined users, and displays a user's data on the dialog box when the user is selected in the list box. Now it's time to write the code that will allow you to save changes to a user's data. To do that, implement the following handler for the Save button's BN_CLICKED message.

The first thing the function does is to call the GetSelectedUser help function you coded earlier to obtain the CUser object associated with the selected user. Once that's done, a call to UpdateData updates the dialog box's member variables with the data from the dialog box. Note that the function makes a copy of the user data. You'll see why shortly. Next, the CUser object's variables are updated with the dialog box's data and the SaveUser help function is called. If the SaveUser function returns TRUE (indicating success), the function removes the user from the list box and adds it back (setting its item data). Finally, the dialog box is initialized (via a call to InitControls). Now, if the SaveUser function fails, the saved copy of the original user values is used to reset the CUser object, and a message is displayed indicating the save failure.

```
void CDaoUserMaintenanceDlg::OnBtnSave()
{
 int iCurrIndex;

 CUser* pUser = NULL;
 if (GetSelectedUser(&iCurrIndex, &pUser))
 {
  ASSERT(pUser);
  if (pUser)
  {
   UpdateData();

   CString strPrevUserID;
   strPrevUserID = m_strUserID;

   CString strPrevUserName;
   strPrevUserName = m_strUserName;

   int iPrevStatus = m_iStatus;

   pUser->m_strUserID = m_strUserID;
```

```
    pUser->m_strUserName = m_strUserName;
    pUser->m_iStatus = m_iStatus;
    if (SaveUser(pUser))
    {
     if (LB_ERR == m_lbxUsers.DeleteString(iCurrIndex))
     {
      AfxMessageBox("The User ID was Saved, "
       "but the previous User ID could not be "
       "removed from the listbox.");
     }
     else
     {
      int iNewIndex = m_lbxUsers.AddString(
       pUser->m_strUserName);
      if ((LB_ERR == iNewIndex) || (LB_ERRSPACE ==
       iNewIndex))
      {
       AfxMessageBox("The User ID was Saved, but "
        "the new User ID could not "
        "be added to the listbox.");
      }
      if (LB_ERR == m_lbxUsers.SetItemData(iNewIndex,
      (DWORD)pUser))
      {
       AfxMessageBox("SetItemData returned LB_ERR. "
        "This will probably cause "
        "serious problems if you attempt to update "
        "or delete this item from the listbox");
      }
     }

     InitControls();

     UpdateData(FALSE);
    }
    else
    {
     pUser->m_strUserID = strPrevUserID;
     pUser->m_strUserName = strPrevUserName;
     pUser->m_iStatus = iPrevStatus;
     AfxMessageBox("SaveUser failed");
    }
   }
  }
 else
 {
  // should never get here because of
  // enabling/disabling button on lbx selection
  AfxMessageBox("You must first select a "
   "User ID to Save");
 }
}
```

Now add the SaveUser helper function that actually does the work necessary to save a given record. In cases where you know you are going to issue a SQL statement (as in the following SQL UPDATE) against a database and you do not already have a current record, it is more efficient to use the CDaoDatabase::Execute function than to instantiate and use a recordset. The following code formats an SQL UPDATE statement using the CUser object, and passes it to the Execute function for processing. Notice that although I'm using the CDaoDatabase object instead of a CDaoRecordset object, instantiating the CUserMaster class enables me to call its GetDefaultDBName in order to determine the name of the database. That way I don't have to hard-code the name of the database in my application.

```
BOOL CDaoUserMaintenanceDlg::SaveUser(CUser* pUser)
{
 BOOL bSuccess = FALSE;
 CDaoDatabase db;

 try
 {
  CUserMaster rs;
  db.Open(rs.GetDefaultDBName());

  CString strSQL = CString("UPDATE UserMaster SET ");
  strSQL += CString("sUserName = '") +
   pUser->m_strUserName + CString("', ");

  strSQL += CString("iStatus = ");
  char szStatus[10];
  itoa(pUser->m_iStatus, szStatus, 10);
  strSQL += szStatus;

  strSQL += CString(" WHERE sUserID = ");
  strSQL += CString("'") + pUser->m_strUserID +
   CString("'");

  db.Execute(strSQL);

  bSuccess = TRUE;
 }
 catch(CDaoException* pe)
 {
  AfxMessageBox(pe->m_pErrorInfo->m_strDescription,
   MB_ICONEXCLAMATION );

  pe->Delete();
 }

 return bSuccess;
}
```

Deleting users

Finally, it's time to see how to delete a record using DAO. To do this, add a BN_CLICKED handler for the Delete button, and modify it so that when finished, it looks like the following. As you can see, this code first obtains the currently selected user (via GetSelectedUser) and then displays a confirmation message to verify that the user does intend to delete the selected record. If the answer is yes, the DeleteUser helper function is called and the item is removed from the list box upon successful deletion.

```
void CDaoUserMaintenanceDlg::OnBtnDelete()
{
 int iIndex;
 CUser* pUser = NULL;
 if (GetSelectedUser(&iIndex, &pUser))
 {
  ASSERT(pUser);
  if (pUser)
  {
   UpdateData();
   CString strMsg;

   strMsg = "Are you sure that you want to delete "
    "the User ";
   strMsg += "'";
   strMsg += pUser->m_strUserName;
   strMsg += "'?";
   if (IDYES == AfxMessageBox(strMsg, MB_YESNOCANCEL))
   {
    if (DeleteUser(pUser))
    {
     if (LB_ERR == m_lbxUsers.DeleteString(iIndex))
     {
      AfxMessageBox("The User was successfully "
       "Deleted, but there was an error in "
       "removing it from the listbox.");
     }

             InitControls();

     UpdateData(FALSE);
    }
    else
    {
     AfxMessageBox("DeleteUser failed");
    }
   }
  }
 }
 else
 {
  // should never get here because of
  // enabling/disabling button on lbx selection
  AfxMessageBox("You must first select a User "
   "ID to Delete");
 }
}
```

Now, add the following helper function (DeleteUser) to do the actual work of deleting a record. Once again, you are instantiating a CDatabase object. With the code using this object so much, in a real application, a pointer to a database object with dialog-level scope would have been created for efficiency. The code here is fairly simple. It formats an SQL DELETE statement and uses the CDatabase::ExecuteSQL function to run it against the data store, returning TRUE to the caller upon success.

```
BOOL CDaoUserMaintenanceDlg::DeleteUser(CUser* pUser)
{
 BOOL bSuccess = FALSE;
 CDaoDatabase db;

 try
 {
  CUserMaster rs;
  db.Open(rs.GetDefaultDBName());

  CString strSQL;
  strSQL.Format("DELETE FROM UserMaster WHERE "
   "sUserID = '%s'", pUser->m_strUserID);

  db.Execute(strSQL);

  bSuccess = TRUE;
 }
 catch(CDaoException* pe)
 {
  AfxMessageBox(pe->m_pErrorInfo->m_strDescription,
   MB_ICONEXCLAMATION );

  pe->Delete();
 }

 return bSuccess;
}
```

Cleaning up

Finally, add one last function to free up the memory allocated when the CUser objects were created. Override the dialog box's virtual DestroyWindow function and code it as follows to iterate through the list box, retrieving and deleting the CUser objects from memory.

```
void CDaoUserMaintenanceDlg::DestroyWindow()
{
 CDialog::OnDestroy();

 CUser* pUser;

 for (int i = 0; i < m_lbxUsers.GetCount(); i++)
 {
  pUser = (CUser*)m_lbxUsers.GetItemData(i);
  if (pUser)
  {
   delete pUser;
  }
 }
}
```

Testing the demo application

It's time to finally build and test the application. If you do, you should see results like those shown in Figure 23-6. You can view all user records, modify them and save the changes, and even delete the records. As an exercise, you might want to try and incorporate the ability to add records at this point. From what you've learned in this chapter, it should be a snap.

Figure 23-6: The demo application illustrates reading, updating, and deleting data using DAO.

Summary

In this chapter, you learned about the basics of DAO, the different objects that constitute the DAO object hierarchy, and the different DAO APIs that enable you to programmatically manipulate the Microsoft Jet engine from your application. In addition, you learned how to use the MFC DAO classes to write a maintenance application. Although no one can argue with the fact that you don't have the programmatic level of control using DAO as you do with the ODBC SDK, a simple, clean database API such as DAO is all you need at times.

In the past several chapters, you've learned a great deal about adding database access methodologies to your applications, starting with ODBC in Chapter 20. This was then followed by chapters illustrating database access via the MFC Database Classes, ADO and, with this chapter, DAO. In the next chapter, I'll continue looking at data I/O techniques, but this time a lower level. Chapter 24 illustrates how to use the CFile and CStdioFile classes to open, read, and write binary and ASCII files.

✦   ✦   ✦

CFile and File I/O in MFC

In This Chapter

Using the CFile class

Demo to read and display binary files

Using the CStdioFile class

Writing a comma-delimited file class

Working with compressed files

Writing a compressed file class

L oading information from and saving information to disk files is important for almost all applications. The data that's saved can range from binary image data to a body of text to specialized data files. In this chapter, you'll look at the subject of reading and writing data using the CFile and the CStdioFile classes. You'll start out with an overview of using the CFile class and see how its members enable you to read and write binary data. Once you're done with that, you'll see a demo application that allows you to open and display binary files. After the demo, you'll then get an overview of the CStdioFile class and see it extended via a set of classes that let you read comma-delimited files. Finally, the chapter finishes up with a data compression class library that extends the basic capabilities of the CFile classes to enable you to read and write compressed data using any of three different compression standards: Huffman, LZSS, and LZW.

The CFile Class

The CFile class is the MFC base class for file handling and directly provides unbuffered, binary disk input/output services. From this class are derived several other classes (shown in Figure 24-1), including the support of text files (through its derived CStdioFile class) and serialization (through the derived CArchive class).

Note The CArchive class—while used to serialize data and objects to disk—is not shown in Figure 24-1 because it does not derive from CFile. The CArchive file and serialization are covered in Chapter 2.

The hierarchical relationship between the CFile class and its derived classes allows your program to operate on all file objects through the polymorphic CFile interface. This means your code can be written so that it makes calls to the CFile virtual functions, and depending on the actual object being used, the calls might resolve to physical files being read or written, or even a memory file being used. First, let's see how to instantiate a file object.

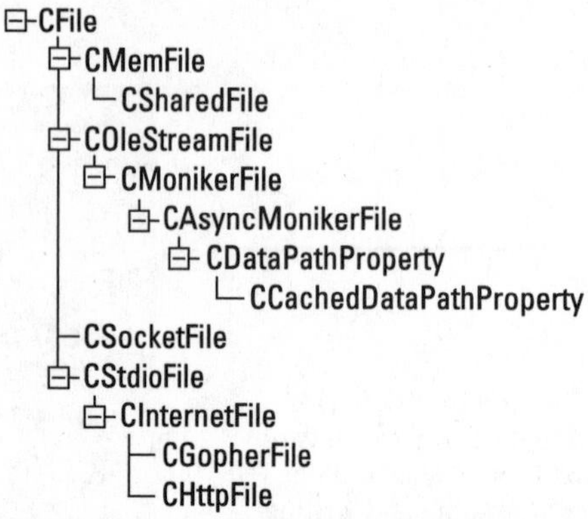

```
┌─CFile
│  ┌─CMemFile
│  │  └─CSharedFile
│  ┌─COleStreamFile
│  │  ┌─CMonikerFile
│  │  │  ┌─CAsyncMonikerFile
│  │  │  │  ┌─CDataPathProperty
│  │  │  │  │  └─CCachedDataPathProperty
│  ┌─CSocketFile
│  ┌─CStdioFile
│  │  ┌─CInternetFile
│  │  │  ├─CGopherFile
│  │  │  └─CHttpFile
```

Figure 24-1: The CFile class hierarchy

Instantiating a CFile object

The first thing you must do is to create a CFile object. There are three constructors for the CFile class:

```
CFile::CFile();
CFile::CFile(HANDLE hFile);
CFile::CFile(LPCTSTR lpszFileName, UINT nOpenFlags);
```

The first (parameter-less) constructor is used in situations where you are not ready to specify the file at the time that you construct the CFile object — such as if you are declaring a CFile member variable of a class. If you use this constructor, you must then call the CFile::Open function (covered shortly) to associate a physical file with the CFile object and to open that file. The following are valid ways of using this constructor:

```
CFile file1;

CFile* pFile2 = new CFile();
...
delete pFile2;
```

The second constructor — the one with only the hFile parameter — is used in cases where you have a valid file handle to a file that has already been created (via CreateFile). Therefore, this has the effect of associating a CFile object with a file that is already open. As a result, there is no need to call the CFile::Open function if you use this constructor as in the following code.

Note also that despite its misleading name, the CreateFile function is also used to open existing files. Here I'm simply opening a file called text.txt in read mode. If the open is successful (the hFile will be NULL if not), I then construct a CFile object using the file handle.

```
HANDLE hFile = ::CreateFile("test.txt",
                    GENERIC_READ,
                    FILE_SHARE_READ,
                    0,
                    OPEN_EXISTING,
                    FILE_ATTRIBUTE_NORMAL,
                    NULL);
```

```
if (hFile)
{
 CFile file(hFile);
 ...
}
```

The third, and last, constructor is used in cases where you are specifying the physical file to be associated with this `CFile` object. Note that the `lpszFileName` parameter can be a relative or absolute path. The `nOpenFlags` parameter is then used to specify how the file is to be opened. The `nOpenFlags` options are listed in the next section. Using this constructor is the equivalent of instantiating a `CFile` object with the parameter-less constructor and then calling the `CFile::Open` function.

Opening a file

Because two of the three `CFile` constructors either associate the newly created `CFile` object with an already open file, or open a specified file, the `CFile::Open` function is designed to work with the parameter-less `CFile` constructor.

```
virtual BOOL CFile::Open(LPCTSTR lpszFileName,
                         UINT nOpenFlags,
                         CFileException* pError = NULL);
```

As you can surmise from the syntax, the `lpszFileName` is used to specify either a relative or absolute path to a filename.

The `nOpenFlags` parameter (which can also be specified when constructing a `CFile` object) is a value that defines the file's sharing and access modes. Table 24-1 lists the valid values that can be combined using the bitwise OR (/) operator. Note that you must combine at least one sharing value and one access mode value.

Table 24-1: File Open Flags

Flag	Description
CFile::modeCreate	Directs the constructor to create a new file. If the file exists already, it is truncated to 0 length.
CFile::modeNoTruncate	Combine this value with `modeCreate`. If the file being created already exists, it is not truncated to 0 length. Thus, the file is guaranteed to open, either as a newly created file or as an existing file. This might be useful, for example, when opening a settings file that may or may not exist already. This option applies to `CStdioFile` as well.
CFile::modeRead	Opens the file for reading only.
CFile::modeReadWrite	Opens the file for reading and writing.
CFile::modeWrite	Opens the file for writing only.
CFile::modeNoInherit	Prevents the file from being inherited by child processes.
CFile::shareDenyNone	Opens the file without denying other processes read or write access to the file. Create fails if the file has been opened in compatibility mode by any other process.

Continued

Table 24-1: *(continued)*

Flag	Description
CFile::shareDenyRead	Opens the file and denies other processes read access to the file. Create fails if the file has been opened in compatibility mode or for read access by any other process.
CFile::shareDenyWrite	Opens the file and denies other processes write access to the file. Create fails if the file has been opened in compatibility mode or for write access by any other process.
CFile::shareExclusive	Opens the file with exclusive mode, denying other processes both read and write access to the file. Construction fails if the file has been opened in any other mode for read or write access, even by the current process.
CFile::shareCompat	This flag is not available in 32-bit MFC. This flag maps to CFile::shareExclusive when used in CFile::Open.
CFile::typeText	Sets text mode with special processing for carriage return/linefeed pairs (used in derived classes only).
CFile::typeBinary	Sets binary mode (used in derived classes only).

One of the interesting things about the CFile::Open function is that, unlike most CFile functions, it does not throw an exception upon failure. (Exception handling is covered in Chapter 18.) Instead, you have two choices when it comes to handling file open failures. The first is to simply specify a NULL value for the pError parameter (the default). In this case, you can tell if the open failed or not, but you cannot determine why:

```
CFile file;
if (file.Open("notfound.txt", CFile::readOnly))
{
    AfxMessageBox("File could not be opened");
}
```

In order to determine the exact cause as to why the file could not be opened, simply instantiate a CFileException object and pass its address to the CFile::Open function like this:

```
CFile file;
CFileException e;
if (!file.Open("notfound.txt", CFile::readOnly, &e))
{
e.ReportError();
}
```

Reading data from a file

Once a file has been successfully opened, you can begin reading data from that file. Keep in mind that at this point, I'm referring to the CFile class. Therefore, any reading done with an object of this type will only be for binary files. As you can see from the following syntax, the Read function takes two parameters:

```
UINT CFile::Read(void* lpBuf, UINT nCount);
```

The lpBuf parameter first is a pointer to a buffer into which the data will be read. This buffer must be allocated before calling the Read function. As you'll soon see, this function is typically called in a while loop in order to read through the entire file. The second parameter (nCount) indicates the number of bytes to read. In cases where you don't know the amount of bytes to read, you simply set this value to the length of the buffer. The returned value from this function is the total number of bytes read during the operation.

```
try
{
   CFile* pFile = new CFile("test.txt",
                           CFile::modeRead
                           | CFile::typeBinary);

   UINT count;
   BYTE* pBuffer = new BYTE[255];
   while (0 < (count = pFile->Read(pBuffer, 255)))
   {
      // process file
   }
   pFile->Close();
   delete pFile;
}
catch(CFileException* pe)
{
   pe->ReportError();
   if (pFile)
   {
      delete pFile;
   }
}
```

Note that the CFile::typeBinary is not strictly necessary and some people include it simply as documentation. If you attempt to use the CFile::typeText value with a CFile object, the Open will assert. Now let's look at the Write function, and then I'll discuss the first demo application.

Writing data to a file

In order to write data to a CFile object, you must specify the CFile::modeWrite value. The CFile::Write function, as with the CFile::Read function, has no overloads and takes two arguments:

```
void CFile::Write(void* lpBuf, UINT nCount);
```

The first parameter (lpBuf) is the data buffer holding the information that will be written. The second parameter (nCount) is the number of bytes to write. Note that the Write function returns no value indicating the number of bytes successfully written. The function will throw an exception if an error occurs. The following example shows how to write data to an open disk file:

```
CFile file;
if (file.Open("test.txt", CFile::modeWrite))
{
   char szData[] = "This is a test";
   try
   {
```

```
      // Go to end of file so as to not
      // overwrite existing data.
      file.SeekToEnd();

      file.Write(szData, strlen(szData));

      file.Close();
    }
  catch(CFileException* pe)
  {
    pe->ReportError();
    if (pFile)
    {
      delete pFile;
    }
  }
}
```

Positioning in a file

There will be times when you need to position to a specific place in the file. In the previous example, notice that the SeekToEnd function was used to move to the end of the file so that any existing data was not overwritten. The syntax for the SeekToEnd function is as follows (where the return value is the total number of bytes in the file):

```
ULONGLONG CFile::SeekToEnd();
```

The counterpart to the SeekToEnd function is the SeekToBegin function. As the name implies, this obviously has the effect of moving to the beginning of the file. In addition, this function doesn't return a value and doesn't take any parameters.

```
void CFile::SeekToBegin();
```

Finally, another navigation function that is useful is the CFile::Seek function. Using this function, you can specify an offset into the file that you want as the current offset for reading or writing purposes:

```
ULONGLONG Seek(LONGLONG lOff, UINT nFrom);
```

The lOff parameter is used to specify the number of bytes to move the file pointer from the position specified by the nFrom parameter. Along with a number indicating the exact byte position, the nFrom value can be any one of the values shown in Table 24-2.

Table 24-2: Seek Function Pointer Movement Modes

Mode	Description
CFile::begin	Move the file pointer the specified number of bytes forward from the beginning of the file.
CFile::current	Move the file pointer the specified number of bytes from the current position in the file.
CFile::end	Move the file pointer the specified number of bytes from the end of the file. Note that the number of bytes must be negative to seek into the existing file; positive values will seek past the end of the file.

Note that `CFile::Seek(0L, CFile::end)` has the same effect as `CFile::SeekToEnd`. Now that you know the basics of the `CFile` class, let's code some demos to see how this new knowledge can be used to your advantage.

Demo to Open and Display Binary Files

The first demo you'll see is one that illustrates how to open and display a binary file. Doing this will allow you to use `CFile` class as well as several of the member functions you've read about up to this point. To get started, create a new dialog-based application called ViewBinary. When you've created the application, create a new dialog box and controls like that shown in Figure 24-2. Note that the dialog box is sized to 370 by 210 pixels.

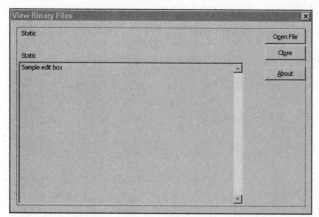

Figure 24-2: Dialog template resource for the ViewBinary demo

With regards to the two static controls, name the top static control on the dialog box `IDC_STC_FILE_NAME` and create a `CString` member variable for it named `m_strFileName`. For the second static control (directly above the edit control), give it an ID of `IDC_STC_FILE_HEADER` and create two DDX member variables for it. The first is a static control variable called `m_stcFileHeader`, whereas the second is a `CString` variable called `m_strFileHeader`.

Once you've taken care of the static controls, set the following properties for the edit control:

✦ ID = IDC_EDT_FILE_CONTENTS

✦ AutoVScroll = true

✦ Multiline = true

✦ Read only = true

✦ Vertical Scroll = true

Once you've set these properties, create both a control and a value member variable for the edit control. Name these variables `m_edtFileContents` and `m_strFileContents`, respectively. Now you're ready to add the code. Start by adding an event handler for the Open File button's `BN_CLICKED` message as follows:

```
void CViewBinaryDlg::OnBnClickedOk()
{
```

```
// Present the file open dialog box so that the
// user can select a file to be displayed.
CFileDialog dlg(true);

// If the user selects a file...
if (IDOK == dlg.DoModal())
{
  CFile* pFile;
  try
  {
    // Display name of open file.
    m_strFileContents = "";
    m_strFileName = dlg.GetPathName();
    UpdateData(FALSE);

    // Create a CFile object and open the
    // selected file.
    pFile = new CFile(dlg.GetPathName(), CFile::modeRead);

    // Allocate a buffer to hold the data read
    // from the file.
    BYTE* pBuffer = new BYTE[255];

    UINT nBytesRead;
    CString strHex;

    // Simple while loop to read every 255 bytes
    // from the file.
    while (0 < (nBytesRead = pFile->Read(pBuffer, 255)))
    {
      // For every byte in the buffer...
      for (int nIndex = 0; nIndex < nBytesRead; nIndex++)
      {
        // Determine how to format it (e.g., every 17th
        // byte is preceded by a carriage return/line feed)
        // and format the strHex string accordingly.
        if (nIndex == 0)
          strHex.Format(_T("%2.2X"), pBuffer[nIndex]);
        else if (nIndex % 16 == 0)
          strHex.Format(_T("\r\n%2.2X"), pBuffer[nIndex]);
        else if (nIndex % 8 == 0)
          strHex.Format(_T("-%2.2X"), pBuffer[nIndex]);
        else
          strHex.Format(_T(" %2.2X"), pBuffer[nIndex]);

        // Add the new (formatted) character to the
        // string that is associated with the edit
        // control.
        m_strFileContents += strHex;
      }
    }
```

```
        pFile->Close();
        delete pFile;

        // Tell the dialog box to update the edit control
        // from the DDX member variables.
        UpdateData(FALSE);
      }
      catch(CFileException* pe)
      {
        pe->ReportError();
        if (pFile)
        {
          delete pFile;
          m_pFile = NULL;
        }
      }
    }
  }
```

Now that you've seen the code to open, read, and display a file's contents, add just a couple of lines to make the display a bit more readable. To do that, add the following CFont member declaration to the dialog box's header file:

```
protected:
  CFont m_font;
```

Then, modify the dialog box's OnInitDialog member function as follows. Here you're creating a fixed-system font and setting both the file header static control and the file contents edit control to use that font. Doing so will make the file display much easier to read. After that, the code simply prints out a header.

```
m_stcFileHeader.SetFont(&m_font);
m_edtFileContents.SetFont(&m_font);

CString strTemp;
for (int i = 1; i < 17; i++)
{
  if (i == 1) strTemp = "01";
  else if (i == 9) strTemp = "-09";
  else if (i < 9) strTemp.Format(" 0%ld", i);
  else strTemp.Format(" %ld", i);

  m_strFileHeader += strTemp;
}
UpdateData(FALSE);
```

At this point, build and execute the application, and you should see results similar to those shown in Figure 24-3.

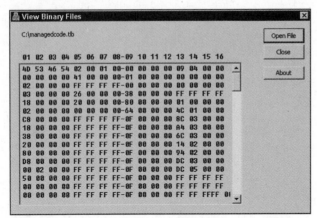

Figure 24-3: Using the CFile class, you can write an application to read and display binary files very easily.

Working with Text-based Files

Up until now, you have only worked with the CFile class and its support of reading and writing binary files. In this section, you'll look at how to work with text files using the CStdioFile class and then a class that you'll write (CCsvFile) that enables you to easily work with comma-delimited files.

Let's begin by discussing some differences between CFile and CStdioFile. The first thing to note is that the CStdioFile can be used to read both binary and text (ASCII) files whereas the CFile class is used only for binary access. In addition, the CFile member functions Duplicate, LockRange, and UnlockRange are not supported for the CStdioFile. If you do attempt to call these functions, a CNotSupportedException will be raised. Another thing to note is that when writing a new-line character (0x0A) to a CStdioFile (in text mode), two characters are actually written (0x0D and 0x0A). However, when reading a line-feed from a CStdioFile, the pair is translated to one character (0x0A).

Finally, the CStdioFile class adds only two methods to the members inherited from CFile. These methods enable you to write (CStdioFile::ReadString) and read (CStdioFile::WriteString) data to and from text files. The WriteString function takes the following form:

```
void CStdioFile::WriteString(LPCTSTR lpsz);
```

The only parameter that this function takes (lpsz) is a pointer to a null-terminated string. Note that the null is *not* written to the file. The ReadString function has the following overloads:

```
LPTSTR CStdioFile::ReadString(LPTSTR lpsz, UINT nMax);
BOOL CStdioFile::ReadString(CString& rString);
```

The first version works a bit like the CFile::Read function in that you pass it a pointer to an allocated buffer (lpsz) and a value (nMax) indicating the number of bytes to read. However, there are some important differences. First, the buffer is terminated with a NULL character. Second, the ReadString function stops reading when a new-line character is found regardless of the nMax value. If less than nMax – 1 characters have been read, a line-feed character is automatically inserted into the buffer. To see an example of this, consider the following file content:

```
abcdefg
hijklmn
opqrstu
vwxyz
```

As you can see, there are four lines to this data. Assuming this data was in a file named c:\test.txt, you could attempt to read data from it as follows:

```
try
{
    CStdioFile file("c:\\test.txt",
        CFile::modeRead | CFile::typeText);

    char buf[26];
    file.ReadString(buf, 26);

    CString s;
    s.Format("BEFORE%sAFTER", buf);
    AfxMessageBox(s);

    file.Close();
}
catch(CFileException* pe)
{
    pe->ReportError();
}
```

Running this code would result in the output shown in Figure 24-4. You should note two things. First, even though I specified that I wanted to read 26 characters, the ReadString returned after reaching the first line-feed character (after the g). Second, the text AFTER that appears on the second line of the message box confirms that a NULL value is indeed inserted into the buffer upon return from the ReadString function. Finally, the function not only updates the passed buffer, but also returns a pointer to the buffer. If the returned value is NULL, then no data was read from the file (usually indicating end-of-file).

Figure 24-4: Simple read test using the CStdioFile::ReadString function

Note   Figure 24-4 doesn't refer to a demo application on the book's Web site. This is just a dialog box to show you an example of how CStdioFile::ReadString parses text.

The second version of the ReadString function simply takes a reference to a CString as its only parameter. In this case, there is no attempt to read a certain number of bytes. Here you are stating that you want an entire line of text. Note that a line-feed is not inserted into the returned string. This function returns TRUE if data has been read and FALSE if no data was read. Here's a code snippet where a file called c:\test.txt is being read and displayed one record (line) at a time in a message box:

```
try
{
    CStdioFile file("c:\\test.txt",
        CFile::modeRead | CFile::typeText);

    CString strRecord;
    while (file.ReadString(strRecord))
    {
        AfxMessageBox(strRecord);
    }

    file.Close();
}
catch(CFileException* pe)
{
    pe->ReportError();
}
```

Now let's see how you use what you've learned thus far to create a usable, practical set of classes to read comma-delimited files.

Comma Delimited Files Class

When storing small amounts of text-only data, comma-delimited files (CSV format) are a very handy and useful format. The reason for this is that it's a simple format, it doesn't require a relational database product, and it's supported by numerous applications. For example, Excel has an option to output a file in CSV format. In fact, if you do a search on the Web for the term *comma-delimited file*, you'll find that many companies provide their data in this easy-to-use format.

As the name implies, each record's columns are delimited by a comma. As an example, suppose you want to store data consisting of a first name, last name, occupation, gender, and state of residence. The following shows what the data would look like for two sample records:

```
Tom,Archer,Programmer,M,GA
Krista,Crawley,housewife,F,GA
```

Some applications even allow you to specify that the first row is a header row containing the column names of the data:

```
First name,Last name,Job description,Gender,State
Tom,Archer,Programmer,M,GA
Krista,Crawley,housewife,F,GA
```

In this section, you'll see how easy the CStdioFile makes it to code a very basic class to read data from a CSV file. To get started, you need two classes. The first class, which you'll name CcsvFile, will be derived from CStdioFile and is the one used to read data from the physical file. The second class (CCsvRecord) will contain the actual data for a given row. As you can guess, the CCsvFile class will contain a collection of CCsvRecord objects, one for each row in the file.

To get started, define the lowest level of granularity—the CCsvRecord class. Define the class as follows—derived from CObject so that it fits nicely into an Object map member of the CCsvFile class:

```
class CCsvRecord : public CObject
{
}
```

Because a CSV record consists of columns, add a `CStringArray` member called `m_arrColumns` that will contain the actual data for the record:

```
protected:
    CStringArray m_arrColumns;
```

Now you can code the `CCsvRecord` constructor. As you can see, the constructor simply takes a string value that holds the comma-delimited record. The constructor uses the C `strtok` function and iterates through the string looking for a comma. Each time a comma is found, the `token` variable contains the preceding value. This value is then added to the `m_arrColumns` array. The end result is that once this constructor has executed for a comma-delimited string, each column's data is stored in an array element in `m_arrColumns`.

```
char DELIMITERS[] = ",";

CCsvRecord::CCsvRecord(LPTSTR lpszRecord)
{
    char *token;
    token = strtok(lpszRecord, DELIMITERS);

    while(NULL != token)
    {
        m_arrColumns.Add(token);
        token = strtok(NULL, DELIMITERS);
    }
}
```

The next thing you add is the ability for a client to easily loop through the array without directly accessing the `m_arrColumns` member. You do this by adding a method called `GetNbrOfColumns` that simply returns the size of the `m_arrColumns` array as shown in the following example:

```
UINT CCsvRecord::GetNbrOfColumns()
{
    return m_arrColumns.GetSize();
}
```

Next, you add the function (`CCsvRecord::GetColumn`) to retrieve the actual data associated with a column. As you can see, the interface to this function requires the client to simply specify a column number. The function verifies that the column number is valid and if so, returns the value requested.

```
CString CCsvRecord::GetColumn(UINT uiColumn)
{
  CString strColumn;

  if (((uiColumn >= 0)
  && (uiColumn <= (GetNbrOfColumns() - 1))))
  {
    strColumn = m_arrColumns[uiColumn];
  }

  return strColumn;
}
```

That's it for the CSVRecord class. Now, define the CSVFile class. Start by declaring the class as being derived from CStdioFile because doing so will mean inheriting a very easy means of reading data from a text file into a string one record at a time — exactly what you need for this class:

```
class CCsvFile : public CStdioFile
{
}
```

The next thing you need to do is to define the collection of CCsvRecord objects. Use a *templatized collection* to ensure type safety. Here's the type definition for the record array:

```
#include "afxtempl.h"

typedef CTypedPtrArray<CObArray, CCsvRecord*> CCsvRecordArray;
```

Now, define a CCsvFile member variable of the CCsvRecordArray type. This array holds CCsvRecord objects:

```
protected:
    CCsvRecordArray m_CsvRecordArray;
```

Just like the CStdioFile class, the CCsvFile constructor takes a single parameter that is the filename to be opened. As you can see, the constructor does not in its initializer list call the CStdioFile constructor that takes a filename. This is because I wanted to first verify that the name passed was valid and that the specified file exists. Therefore, the parameter-less CStdioFile constructor is being used. Once the code determines that the file exists (you'll see that function shortly), the file is opened (via a call to CStdioFile::Open) in read mode. After the file is opened, the records are loaded via a call to LoadRecords as shown in the following example:

```
CCsvFile::CCsvFile(LPSTR lpszFileName)
{
    m_dwNumberOfRecords = 0;

    ASSERT(lpszFileName != NULL);
    ASSERT(AfxIsValidString(lpszFileName));

    if (CCsvFile::FileExists(lpszFileName))
    {
        if (Open(lpszFileName, CFile::modeRead))
        {
            m_dwNumberOfRecords = LoadRecords();
        }
    }
}
```

Although the FileExists function doesn't do much, I'll quickly look at it for completeness. The "magic number" 4 being passed to the C runtime function _access indicates that I'm attempting to determine if the file can be opened with read permission:

```
static BOOL FileExists(LPCTSTR lpszFileName)
{
    return (0 == (_access(lpszFileName, 4)));
}
```

Now, look at the LoadRecords function. The function returns the total number of records found in the file, so this value is initialized to zero. The function then simply reads through the file using the CStdioFile-inherited ReadString function. Note that the ReadString function returns FALSE when no data was read into the string. For each string that is returned from the ReadString function, a CCsvRecord is instantiated and added to the m_CsvRecordArray array. When finished, the function simply returns the size of this array indicating the number of records that the file contains:

```
DWORD CCsvFile::LoadRecords()
{
    m_dwNumberOfRecords = 0;

    CCsvRecord* pCsvRecord;
    CString strRecord;
    while (ReadString(strRecord))
    {
        pCsvRecord = new CCsvRecord(strRecord.GetBuffer(0));

        ASSERT(pCsvRecord);
        if (pCsvRecord)
        {
            m_CsvRecordArray.Add(pCsvRecord);
        }
        strRecord.ReleaseBuffer();
    }

    return m_CsvRecordArray.GetSize();
}
```

At this point, the classes are pretty much done. The only thing you need to add is the ability to iterate through the record array. Do that by implementing the GetStartPosition and GetNextAssoc functions common to the MFC collection classes as shown in the following example:

```
UINT CCsvFile::GetStartPosition()
{
    UINT uiPosition;

    if (0 < m_CsvRecordArray.GetSize())
    {
        uiPosition = 0;
    }
    else
    {
        uiPosition = CCsvFile::EndOfFile;
    }

    return uiPosition;
}

void CCsvFile::GetNextAssoc(UINT& uiPosition,
                            CCsvRecord** ppCsvRecord)
{
    UINT uiNewPosition = CCsvFile::EndOfFile;
    *ppCsvRecord = NULL;
```

```
        UINT nRecords = m_CsvRecordArray.GetSize();
        if (uiPosition >= 0 && uiPosition <= (nRecords - 1))
        {
            *ppCsvRecord = m_CsvRecordArray[uiPosition];
            if ( (uiPosition + 1) <= (nRecords - 1) )
            {
                uiNewPosition = uiPosition + 1;
            }
        }

        uiPosition = uiNewPosition;
    }
```

The `CCsvFile::EndOfFile` value is just an `enum` that the client can use to determine if the end of file has been reached:

```
    public:
        enum
        {
            EndOfFile = -1
        };
```

Finally, you can code the `CCsvFile` destructor to clean up the allocated `CCsvRecord` objects:

```
    CCsvFile::~CCsvFile()
    {
        CCsvRecord* pCsvRecord;
        for (int i = m_CsvRecordArray.GetUpperBound(); i > -1; i--)
        {
            pCsvRecord = m_CsvRecordArray[i];
            m_CsvRecordArray.RemoveAt(i);

            ASSERT(pCsvRecord);
            if (pCsvRecord)
            {
                delete pCsvRecord;
            }
        }
        VERIFY(0 == m_CsvRecordArray.GetSize());
    }
```

That's it! To summarize, these classes, although extremely useful, really do almost nothing except open a specified file, read in each record (using `CStdioFile::ReadLine`), create an object for that record, and store each column of data in a data array within the record object. This is all very easy thanks to the `CStdioFile` class. Now let's look at a text version of the earlier ViewBinary demo.

Demo to Open and Display CSV Files

Now that you have a couple of classes that allow for the opening and reading of CSV files, this demo should be extremely easy. To get started, create a new dialog-based application called ViewCSV. Once you've created the project, open the Project Explorer and add the following files to your project. (These files are located on this book's Web site.)

- ✦ CsvFile.h

- ✦ CsvFile.cpp

- ✦ CsvRecord.h

- ✦ CsvRecord.cpp

Once you've added the CSV support classes, open the main dialog box and modify it so that when finished, it looks like that shown in Figure 24-5.

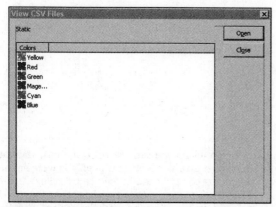

Figure 24-5: Dialog template for the ViewCSV demo application

Note that the list view control's View property is set to Report. Once you've created these controls, rename the static control's ID to IDC_STC_FILE_NAME and create a CString member variable for it called m_strFileName. Then create a CListCtrl member called m_lstFileContents for the list view control.

When finished with the dialog box, open the ViewCSV.h file and add the following #include directive and member function:

```
#include "CsvFile.h"

protected:
    void InsertDataIntoListView(UINT uiRow,
                                CCsvRecord& csvRecord);
```

Now, add an event handler for the Open File button's BN_CLICKED message and modify it so that when finished it looks like the following:

```
void CViewCSVDlg::OnBnClickedOk()
{
    CFileDialog dlg(true);
    if (IDOK == dlg.DoModal())
    {
        try
        {
            m_strFileName = dlg.GetPathName();
            UpdateData(FALSE);
```

```
CCsvFile file(dlg.GetPathName());

CCsvRecord* pCsvRecord;
for (UINT uiRow = file.GetStartPosition();
        CCsvFile::EndOfFile != uiRow;)
{
    // Get the actual record.
    file.GetNextAssoc(uiRow, &pCsvRecord);
    if (pCsvRecord)
    {
        InsertDataIntoListView(uiRow, *pCsvRecord);
    }
}
}
catch(CFileException* pe)
{
    pe->ReportError();
}
}
}
```

In particular, notice the code that is shown in bold. As you can see, once you've instantiated a CCsvFile, it is incredibly easy to use. Simply set up a for loop as though you were enumerating a collection using the CCsvFile::GetStartPosition and CCsvFile::GetNextAssoc to retrieve the file's CCsvRecord objects. Note that the CCsv::GetStartPosition function will return CCsv::EndOfFile when there are no more records to be read. For each record, the code calls the InsertDataIntoListView function—shown here:

```
void CViewCSVDlg::InsertDataIntoListView(UINT uiRow,
                            CCsvRecord& csvRecord)
{
// For each column in the passed record...
for (int iCol = 0;
        iCol < csvRecord.GetNbrOfColumns();
        iCol++)
{
// If this is the first row in the list view...
if (uiRow == 1)
{
// Create the list view columns.
CString strColumnName;
strColumnName.Format("Col %ld", iCol);
m_lstFileContents.InsertColumn(iCol, strColumnName);
}

// Lines broken to format properly for book
if (iCol == 0)
 m_lstFileContents.InsertItem(
  m_lstFileContents.GetItemCount(),

  csvRecord.GetColumn(iCol));
else
 m_lstFileContents.SetItemText(
  m_lstFileContents.GetItemCount()-1,
```

```
        iCol,csvRecord.GetColumn(iCol));
    }
  }
```

At this point, build and execute the application. Doing so should produce the results like those shown in Figure 24-6 where you can see that we've successfully read in and displayed our textual data.

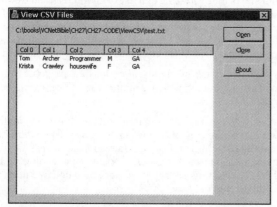

Figure 24-6: The CCsvFile and CCsvRecord classes enable very easy access to comma-delimited files.

Working with Compressed Data

In the early 1980s, when most applications were shipped via floppy disk, developers went to great lengths to compress their data to a size small enough to fit on a single floppy. After all, more disks meant extra costs both in terms of manufacturing and in terms of shipping. Additionally, it was generally thought that an application requiring too many disks was a turn-off to users who had to sit at their machines playing "feed the monkey" in order to install the software. There was no question about whether to compress data; the only question was which method to use.

Nowadays, most developers don't think about disk space when it comes to compressing data because the hard drives of today are hundreds of times larger than their predecessors. However, whereas the reasoning behind compressing data in the past might have been to ship a product on fewer floppies or to make more efficient use of disk space, the principal factor driving the need to compress data today is the Internet. Today, most people expect to be able to download applications, data files, and even service packs from the Internet, and to do so without waiting for downloads that take hours to complete. Therefore, I submit to you that data compression is just as vital today, if not more so, than in days past. To that extent, this section is focused on explaining the various compression options and formats. At the end of this section I'll even present to you a complete class library that gives you all the tools you need to compress and decompress data.

Data compression standards

As you'll soon see, my compression library supports the three major data compression standards: Huffman, LZSS, and LZW. Therefore, before you get into the code of how these standards are supported, let's look at a brief overview of each one.

Huffman

Huffman coding takes a probabilistic approach to data compression. It depends on knowing the probability of each symbol's appearance in a message. Given the probabilities, a table of codes is constructed with different codes having a different number of bits. The codes with the greater probability have the least number of bits, and the codes with the lesser probability have the most number of bits.

The Huffman compression algorithm starts off by looking at a list of characters and developing a corresponding list of probabilities (or frequency counts). This way the frequency of occurrence is known for each character. The list is sorted by frequency count so that the most probable characters are at the top of the list and the least probable at the bottom. A binary tree is developed with which the binary token for each character can be accessed.

The individual symbols in the tree are laid out as a string of leaf nodes that are going to be connected by a binary tree. Each node has a weight, which is simply the frequency or probability of the symbol's appearance.

The two free nodes with the lowest weights are located. A parent node for these two nodes is created, and it is assigned a weight equal to the sum of the two child nodes. The parent node is added to the list of free nodes, and the two child nodes are removed from the list. One of the child nodes is designated as the path taken from the parent node when decoding a 0 bit. The other is arbitrarily set to the 1 bit. These steps are repeated until only one free node is left. This free node is designated as the root of the tree.

LZSS

LZSS compression uses previously seen text as a dictionary. It replaces phrases in the input text with pointers into the dictionary to achieve compression. The amount of compression depends on how long the dictionary phrases are, how large the window into previously seen text is, and the entropy of the source text with respect to the LZSS model.

The main data structure in LZSS is a text window divided into two parts. The first part consists of a large block of recently decoded text. The second part, normally much smaller, is a look-ahead buffer. The look-ahead buffer has characters read in from the input stream but not yet encoded.

The normal size of the text window is several thousand characters. The look-ahead buffer is generally much smaller — maybe 10 to 100 characters. The algorithm tries to match the contents of the look-ahead buffer to a string in the dictionary.

The code that implements this compression algorithm is fairly simple. It merely has to look through the entire text window for the longest match, encode it, and then shift.

The decompression algorithm is even simpler because it doesn't have to do comparisons. It reads in a token, outputs the indicated phrase, outputs the following character, shifts, and repeats. It maintains the window, but it does not work with string comparisons.

LZW

LZW is also a dictionary-based compression scheme. It stores phrases in a potentially unlimited dictionary. It is different than LZSS in that it abandons the concept of a text window. LZW does output a series of tokens similar to LZSS. Each LZW token has two components: a phrase location and a character that follows the phrase. Each token consists of a code that selects a given phrase and a single character that follows the phrase. The phrase length is already known by the decoder and doesn't have to be part of the token.

When you use the LZW algorithm, both the encoder and decoder start off with a very small dictionary consisting of 256 phrases, each a single character. As each character is read in, it is added to the current string. As long as the current string matches some phrase in the dictionary, this process continues.

Eventually the string will no longer have a corresponding phrase in the dictionary. This is when LZW outputs a token and a character. Remember that the string did have a match in the dictionary until the last character was read in. The current string, therefore, is defined as that last match with one new character added on.

The compression algorithm outputs the index for the previous match, and the character that broke the match. It then takes an additional step. The new phrase, consisting of the dictionary match and the new character, is added to the dictionary. The next time the phrase appears, it can be used to build an even longer phrase.

LZW can arbitrarily set the size of the phrase dictionary. This may cause two effects that must be dealt with. First, you have to consider the number of bits allocated in the output token for the phrase code. Second, and more importantly, you have to consider how much CPU time managing the dictionary will take.

The CompressDemo program

The CompressDemo application (available on the book's Web site) illustrates what the class library can do. The first thing you need to do when you run the application is to select a file for compression. Any file or file type will do, but text, BMP, and WAV files compress well, so you might want to try one of those file types as they'll show the best compression ration numbers on the screen.

To load a file, select File ⇨ Open, and then use the standard Windows file selector to select a file. The file loads, and a window appears with some relevant information about the file. Unless the file you load has been compressed with the data compression library, it will be labeled as "no compression" in the window, because it wasn't compressed with the data compression libraries (also available on this book's Web site). Figure 24-7 shows the window with a file loaded.

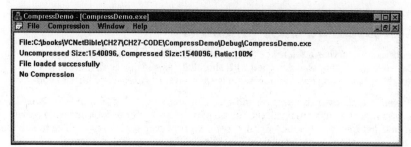

Figure 24-7: When a file is loaded, a window displays information about the file.

The next thing to do to test the program is select a compression type from the Compression menu. The choices offered are Huffman, LZSS, LZW, and None. LZW is the default choice and usually produces the best results. Leave this choice selected for now as shown in Figure 24-8.

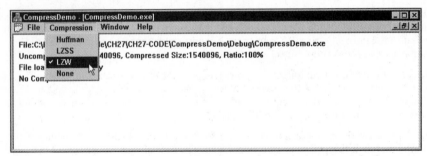

Figure 24-8: You can select from three different data compression standards.

To save the file with the chosen compression method, select File ➪ Save As. A standard Windows file selector appears. Type a filename and click OK. This example saves your file as TEST.CMP using LZW compression. After the file is saved, the information in the window is updated to reflect the saved file size and the compression type as shown in Figure 24-9.

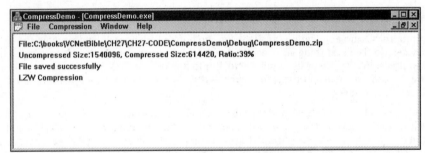

Figure 24-9: Once you save the compressed file, the window is updated with key compression statistics.

CCompressedFile class functions

This section is provided as a reference to the public function calls the data compression library offers. Because the library was designed with simplicity as a major goal, there aren't many calls. That's good because using data compression is easy—it just takes a few lines of code.

You may want to skip over this section and read the section entitled "Behind CompressDemo," which shows how the calls are used. (For some people, it's better to look at the usage of function calls before actually studying their syntax.) However, for those who like to see the syntax first, here are the more important functions of the compression library.

✦ CCompressedFile::MakeNewFile—This is the static function that creates CompressedFile objects. The first argument is the existing filename that's to be opened. The second argument (which defaults to LZW) determines the data compression type that will be used. Note that if you give the function a filename, the object created carries the compression type of that file, regardless of the compression type that's given in the second argument. Here is an example of creating a CCompressedFile object for LZW compression:

```
CCompressedFile *pFile = MakeNewFile( NULL, LZW );
```

✦ `CCompressedFile::Open`—This function is almost exactly like the `CFile::Open` function. It opens a file for reading or writing. At the same time, it initializes all arrays and variables for the data compression or decompression. The following code snippet illustrates how to use this function to open a file for reading:

```
CCompressedFile *pFile = MakeNewFile( "Filename" );
if( pFile->Open( "Filename", CFile::modeRead ) )
  AfxMessageBox( "File open success." );
else
  AfxMessageBox( "File open failure." );
delete pFile;
```

✦ `CCompressedFile::Close`—This function closes the file and flushes all buffers.

✦ `CCompressedFile::GetPosition`—This function returns the position to which the file pointer points. If 500 bytes have been written to a newly created file, the value returned will be 500. If 2,048 bytes have been read from a newly opened file, the value returned will be 2048. Following is an example that reads 500 bytes and then displays the position in a message box:

```
CCompressedFile *pFile = MakeNewFile( "Filename" );
if( pFile->Open( "Filename", CFile::modeRead ) ){
  char cbBuffer[500];
  pFile->Read( cbBuffer, 500 );
  CString strText;
  strText.Format( "The current position is %ld",
    pFile->GetPosition() );
  AfxMessageBox( strText );
  }
else
  AfxMessageBox( "File open failure." );
delete pFile;
```

✦ `CCompressedFile::GetLength`—This function returns the byte length of the file.

✦ `CCompressedFile::FindFileInArchive`—Compressed archive files that are created with the `CompressedFile` class library can have more than one file stored in each archive file. Before this function is called, the compressed file must be opened with the `Open` function. The `FindFileInArchive` function then searches the file list up to the file specified by `nIndex`. If five files are in the archive and an argument of 2 is passed in, the file at index 2 is sought. This is the third file in the archive, and that's the one that will be decompressed. Following is an example that opens a file with multiple files stored inside, finds the second file (index 1), and reads 500 bytes:

```
CCompressedFile *pFile = MakeNewFile( "Filename" );
if( pFile->Open( "Filename", CFile::modeRead ) ){
  if( pFile->FindFileInArchive( 1 ) ){
    char cbBuffer[500];
    pFile->Read( cbBuffer, 500 );
    AfxMessageBox( "FindFileInArchive() successful." );
    }
  else
    AfxMessageBox( "FindFileInArchive() failed." );
  }
```

```
    else
      AfxMessageBox( "File open failure." );
    delete pFile;
```

✦ CCompressedFile::ReadByte — This function reads a single byte from an opened file. Here is an example:

```
CCompressedFile *pFile = MakeNewFile( "Filename" );
if( pFile->Open( "Filename", CFile::modeRead ) ){
  int nData = pFile->ReadByte();
  if( nData == -1 ){
    // There was a read error.
    }
  }
delete pFile;
```

✦ CCompressedFile::WriteByte — This function writes a single byte to an opened file as shown here:

```
CCompressedFile *pFile = MakeNewFile( NULL, HUFFMAN );
if( pFile->Open( "Filename",
  CFile::modeWrite | CFile::modeCreate ) ){
  pFile->WriteByte( 'C' );
  }
delete pFile;
```

✦ CCompressedFile::Read — This function reads a specified number of bytes into a buffer. It returns the number of bytes actually read. This functions almost exactly like the CFile::Read function:

```
CCompressedFile *pFile = MakeNewFile( "Filename" );
if( pFile->Open( "Filename", CFile::modeRead ) ){
  char cbBuffer[500];
  pFile->Read( cbBuffer, 500 );
  }
delete pFile;
```

✦ CCompressedFile::Write — This function writes a specified number of bytes that are in a buffer to the file. This functions almost exactly like the CFile::Write function. An example follows:

```
CCompressedFile *pFile = MakeNewFile( NULL, HUFFMAN );
if( pFile->Open( "Filename",
  CFile::modeWrite | CFile::modeCreate ) ){
  static char szString[] = "This is a test";
  pFile->Write( szString, strlen( szString ) );
  }
delete pFile;
```

Behind CompressDemo

This section explores the ways in which the CCompressedFile class member functions are used by showing them in a sample application: CompressDemo.

Opening a file

The code that loads a file from disk into memory can be found in the `CCompressDemoView` class. The function in which it's placed is the `OnDraw` function. Every time a file is opened, a new MDI window is opened and drawn. The file can then be loaded the first time the `OnDraw` function is called.

Once the file is loaded, information about it is drawn to the child window. That way the user can see the details about the file, its compression method, its size, and its compression ratio. The first thing that happens in the `OnDraw` function is to see whether or not the file has been loaded. The Boolean variable `m_bLoaded` is FALSE if the file hasn't been loaded, or TRUE if it has been loaded.

After obtaining the filename from the document class, a `CCompressedFile` class object is created with the `MakeNewFile` static function. When the file is loaded, a determination is made whether or not the file has been compressed with the `CCompressedFile` compression class. This is transparent to the programmer, but it's nice to know that you don't have to worry about it.

A buffer is allocated for the data that will be read. The size that's needed for the uncompressed data can be obtained by examining the `CCompressedFile` member variable named `m_dwUncompressedSize`. Once the buffer is allocated, a single call to the `Read` function is made. The `Read` function looks exactly like the `Read` function of the `CFile` class. It takes two arguments: a pointer to a buffer and the size to read.

The compressed and uncompressed sizes are stored into the view class from the `CCompressedFile` class. This is just so the information can be displayed in the view window after the `CCompressedFile` object is deleted. The file is closed, and then deleted. No further `CCompressedFile` read operations are performed in the application.

Information about the file is displayed at the end of the `OnDraw` function. The filename, compression type, compressed and uncompressed sizes, the compression ratio, and the status of the read operation are all drawn. Follow these steps to open a compressed file:

1. Start off by creating a `CCompressedFile` object by calling the static `MakeNewFile` function. The first parameter is not necessary. It's the filename of the file, but you'll usually give the filename when you open the file. The second argument is the compression type. This can be HUFF, LZSS, LZW, or UNCOMP. The second argument defaults to LZW if you don't pass it a value:

   ```
   CCompressedFile *pFile = MakeNewFile( "TEST.TXT" );
   ```

2. Next, you have to open the file. Here's the code to open a file named TEST.TXT:

   ```
   pFile->Open( "TEST.TXT", CFile::modeRead );
   ```

   If you're dynamically allocating a buffer into which the data will be read, use the `m_dwUncompressedSize` variable to obtain the size of the buffer. The following code allocates a buffer for reading:

   ```
   char *pBuffer = new char[pFile->m_dwUncompressedSize];
   ```

3. Now you can read the data with a call to the `Read` function. The code to do this follows:

   ```
   pFile->Read( pBuffer, pFile->m_dwUncompressedSize );
   ```

4. Finally, you must close the file. Here's the code for that:

   ```
   pFile->Close();
   ```

Saving a file

Saving files is done in the CCompressDemoView class, with the OnFileSaveAs function. The first things that happen in the OnSaveAs function are checks to make sure there is an allocated buffer, and that the size of the data is not zero. Either one of these situations creates an unsuccessful write operation.

The next thing the code does is create a CCompressedFile object with the static MakeNewFile function. This function takes as its second argument the compression type for the file.

The Open function is then called. It is called in the same way as the Open function of the CFile class. It takes a filename as its first argument and the file attributes as its second argument. It returns TRUE if successful or FALSE if unsuccessful.

A single call to the Write function is made. Doing this causes the CCompressedFile to write all of the data to disk. This Write function is called exactly as the Write function of the CFile class. It takes a buffer pointer as its first argument and an integer value representing the number of bytes to write to disk. The display variables are all updated so that any change in file status, size, or compression type is reflected in the view window. Follow these steps to save a compressed file:

1. Once again, start off by creating a CCompressedFile object by calling the static MakeNewFile function:

```
CCompressedFile *pFile = MakeNewFile( NULL, LZW );
```

2. Next, you have to open the file. Here's the code to open a file named TEST.CMP:

```
pFile->Open("TEST.CMP",
            CFile::modeWrite | CFile::modeCreate);
```

3. Now you can write the data with a call to the Write function. The code to do this follows:

```
char szBuffer[] =
  "This is a test of this compression class.";
pFile->Write( szBuffer, strlen( szBuffer ) );
```

4. Finally, you must close the file. Here's the code for that:

```
pFile->Close();
```

Summary

In this chapter, you learned the basic syntax of using the CFile class and you worked your way through a simple demo that illustrates the reading and displaying of binary data. From there, you then learned how the CStdioFile supports the reading and writing of ASCII (text) data and developed a couple of classes to enable you to easily read a comma-delimited file. Finally, the chapter finished up with a data compression class library that extends the basic capabilities of the CFile classes to enable you to read and write compressed data using any of three different compression standards: Huffman, LZSS, and LZW. In the next chapter, the final one in the Data I/O section, you'll see how to use XML as a storage medium from Visual C++ applications.

✦ ✦ ✦

Using XML from Visual C++

◆ ◆ ◆ ◆

XML is one of those technologies whose name has been bandied around for so long and in so many distinct contexts that if you were to ask two programmers for a definition, you'd likely get three answers. One of the reasons for the confusion is that XML doesn't do anything. In other words, it's not a language that you can download or a product that you can buy. Instead, it is a standard for structuring, storing, and transmitting data. In fact, that's the best way to describe XML—it is a standard for creating self-describing data. Therefore, in this, the last Data I/O chapter, I'll explore what XML is, what it isn't, and why you, as a Visual C++ programmer, should even care about it.

I'll start off with some fundamental benefits XML affords both Web developers and anyone wanting to package their data in a format that is quickly becoming the standard. Once I've gone over the introduction to XML, you'll then learn the lingo of XML. I know. I know. Not another set of terms to learn. Sorry, but yes. If you're going to play the XML game, you're going to have to get to know the players. Afterward, I'll discuss how XML documents are structured and what tools are available for creating XML documents. At this point, it will be time to work with this technology. Here you'll learn about the object model specifically designed to access XML data. You'll write your very own XML viewer that will enable you to load, read, and display your XML documents via the Internet Explorer (IE) XML COM interfaces.

This chapter is split into two distinct parts. You should read the first part if you are completely new to XML. Read the second part if you know XML pretty well and want to jump into using it from C++. In that case, jump ahead to the section "Introducing the XML DOM."

XML Overview

XML stands for eXtensible Markup Language, and as the name implies is a bit like HTML in that both are standards used to mark up (or define) a document. However, there are some important distinctions between the two. Even if you don't specifically develop Web sites, chances are high that you know about HTML and its purpose. Put simply, HTML is a markup language designed to display information, usually on the Web. The various HTML tags allow you to specify exactly how an *agent* (typically a browser) should present that data to a user. XML, on the other hand, has been designed to *describe* data, that is, to give you a means of creating *self-describing data*. Therefore, the XML tags that you'll learn about don't focus on the presentation of data, but instead focus on the structure of data.

Another difference between HTML and XML is that HTML has predefined tags that you use to mark up your Web pages. Using XML, you define your own data-specific tags. Also, XML uses something called a *Document Type Definition* (DTD) to describe the data to applications that want to use that data. Therefore, XML is not a replacement or competitor to HTML. In fact, XML is meant to compliment HTML in that while HTML is used to display information, XML is used to describe information. So now that you know what XML is, what is it used for? Let's look at that now.

XML Terminology and Syntax

Although the rules that define a properly formed XML document are simple, understand that they are very strict. With HTML, you can sometimes do things like incorrectly nest tags, but if you try that with XML, no *parser* (described shortly) is going to be capable of reading the document. Therefore, let's go over the terminology and syntax associated with XML documents and XML in general.

The first term you'll look at is *XML parser*. As the name implies, an XML parser is simply code that can read and understand XML formatted documents. IE uses a parser that enables you to view XML documents in the browser. You'll see this and Visual Studio's capability of doing the same shortly.

To understand XML syntax, let's look at a sample XML document:

```
<?xml version="1.0" encoding="utf-8" ?>
<email language="EN">
  <from>tarcher@mindspring.com</from>
  <to>editor@hungryminds.com</to>
  <subject>Chapter status </subject>
  <message>I expect to be finished today!!</message>
</email>
```

Now let's look at some more terminology:

✦ The first line of the document is called the *XML declaration* and includes information such as the XML version number and the character encoding method.

```
<?xml version="1.0" encoding="utf-8"?>
```

✦ Each tag in XML, beginning with a < and ending with a > denotes an *element*.

✦ The <email> line denotes the *root element* in the document. It is like saying "this document is an e-mail."

✦ The next four elements (from, to, subject, and message) all describe *child elements* of the root element.

✦ The word language, in the <email> element, is the name of an attribute used to further describe the element.

✦ Finally, the </email> tag denotes the end of the <email> (root) element.

If you're new to XML, you're probably beginning to understand why so many people like this standard of describing and formatting data. Because it's so easy! Now take a look at some syntax rules regarding what is termed a *well-formed* XML document.

First off, all elements must have a closing tag. In HTML, there are tags such as `<IMG>` that do not have closing tags. Additionally, many people have become accustomed to using HTML tags like `<P>` and `<LI>` without the closing tags and getting away with it because the browser lets them. With XML, however, there is no such lenience. The only (seemingly) exception to this rule is the declaration line (the first line of the XML document that describes the version number and character encoding). I say *seemingly* because this is not technically a part of the XML document itself, and therefore is not an XML element.

Empty elements can be defined. Suppose you're using the e-mail XML document shown previously, but no subject was specified for this record. This can be represented in one of two ways, where the first method is called an *empty element*:

```
<subject/>
<subject></subject>
```

All XML documents must have a single root element. Every other element in the XML document is then a child of this root. Therefore, the following XML would be incorrect because it has defined more than one root:

```
<?xml version="1.0" encoding="utf-8" ?>
<book>
   <title>Inside C#</title>
   <author>Tom Archer</author>
</book>
<book>
   <title>Visual C++ .NET Bible</title>
   <author>Tom Archer</author>
</book>
```

In this case (where you have multiple books) you would need to define your root element as though it were a collection:

```
<?xml version="1.0" encoding="utf-8" ?>
<books>
   <book>
      <title>Inside C#</title>
      <author>Tom Archer</author>
   </book>
   <book>
      <title>Visual C++ .NET Bible</title>
      <author>Tom Archer</author>
   </book>
</books>
```

XML tags are case-sensitive. This is not a big deal if you program in C++. However, it's worth mentioning because if you also do any coding in VB or Web scripting, then you're accustomed to those environments not caring about case. Therefore, the element `<email>` is a completely different element than `<Email>`. In addition, this also means that the following would result in an invalid XML file because the two tags are different in terms of case—meaning that the element has no closing tag:

```
<subject>Chapter status</Subject>
```

All elements must be properly nested. Yet another example of where the browsers let you get away with incorrectly formed HTML is in the nesting of elements. Take the following example:

```
<b><i>My bold, italic text</b></i>
```

Logically, you know as a programmer that the closing tags are reversed. However, the browser does let you get away with this. XML parsers, on the other hand, will not. As a result, the following is an error:

```
<email language="EN">
  <from>
    <emailAddr>
      tarcher@mindspring.com
    </from>
  </emailAddr>
</email>
```

The reason for this is simple. When a browser is interpreting the line of HTML, it realizes that everything after the `<i>` tag is going to be bold and italic so it really doesn't matter which tag is ended first. However, XML is used to represent data. Therefore, in this incorrectly formed XML, the parser treats the `<emailAddr>` element as though it's a table within the `<from>` table. When the parser reaches the end marker for the parent table `</from>`, it has no idea how to read your data.

Attributes must always be quoted. Modify the books example to add an `edition` attribute to the `<book>` element. Here are three books with different edition values:

```
<?xml version="1.0" encoding="utf-8" ?>
<books>
  <book edition="2">
    <title>Inside C#</title>
    <author>Tom Archer</author>
  </book>
  <book edition='3'>
    <title>Visual C++ .NET Bible</title>
    <author>Tom Archer</author>
  </book>
  <book edition=1>
    <title>JScript .NET Programming</title>
    <author>Essam Ahmed</author>
  </book>
</books>
```

In this case, the first two book elements are valid because you can use either the single quote or double quotes when specifying an attribute's value. However, the last book element is an error because its value is not quoted.

You can place comments in your data. Just like code (or script), you can insert comments into your XML data with the following syntax:

```
<myRootElement>
  <!--this is a comment about my data-->
  <childElement>
  </childElement>
</myRootElement>
```

There are several reserved characters to look out for. These characters are used as a part of the XML document syntax and cannot be used as data. Table 25-1 lists those characters and the substitutes that you must use.

Table 25-1: Reserved XML Characters and Their Substitutes

Character	Substitute
<	&lt;
>	&gt;
&	&amp;
"	&quot;
'	&apos;

As mentioned, I don't want to turn this into a full-fledged tutorial on XML because such a tutorial could take several chapters and is outside the scope of this chapter. However, I wanted to provide a quick overview of what XML is and the syntax and terminology used. Now, I'll discuss how to create some XML documents and how to utilize the DOM to load and view XML data.

Introducing the XML DOM

The XML document object model, or DOM, is a very powerful and robust programmatic interface that not only enables you to programmatically load and parse an XML file, or document, it also can be used to traverse XML data. Using objects defined in the DOM, you can even manipulate that data and then save your changes back to the XML document. In fact, a full and comprehensive look at all the DOM's functionality would be impossible in a single chapter. Therefore, what I'd like to do here is to hit on the high notes of using the DOM to load an XML document and to iterate through its elements.

The key to understanding how to use the DOM is realizing that the DOM exposes (through its COM interface) XML documents as a hierarchical tree of nodes. Here's a more fleshed out XML document that will be used in this chapter's demo applications:

```xml
<?xml version="1.0" encoding="utf-8"?>
<autos>
  <manufacturer name="Chevrolet">
    <make name="Corvette">
      <model>2000 Convertible
        <price currency="usd">60,000</price>
        <horsePower>420</horsePower>
        <fuelCapacity units="gallons">18.5</fuelCapacity>
      </model>
      <model>2002 Convertible
        <price currency="usd">62,000</price>
        <horsePower>422</horsePower>
        <fuelCapacity units="gallons">22.2</fuelCapacity>
      </model>
    </make>
  </manufacturer>
  <manufacturer name="Mazda">
```

```
      <make name="RX-7">
        <model>test model
          <price currency="usd">30,000</price>
            <horsePower>350</horsePower>
            <fuelCapacity units="gallons">15.5</fuelCapacity>
        </model>
      </make>
    </manufacturer>
  </autos>
```

The following shows how the DOM interprets this document:

✦ <Autos> — This is a NODE_ELEMENT (more on this later) and is referred to as the documentElement because it is the top-level node in the document.

✦ <manufacturer>, <make>, <model>, <price>, <horsePower>, and <fuelCapacity> — Each one of these is also a NODE_ELEMENT.

✦ currency="usd", units="gallons" — When a NODE_ELEMENT contains an attribute/value pair like this, the value is referred to as a NODE_TEXT.

As you will see shortly, there are a number of COM components that are part of the XML DOM. Here's a list of some of the more interesting components and their purpose:

✦ XMLDOMDocument — The top node of the XML document tree

✦ XMLDOMNode — Any single node in the XML document tree

✦ XMLDOMNodeList — The collection of all XMLDOMNode objects

✦ XMLDOMNamedNodeMap — The collection of all the XML document tree attributes

Loading and Viewing XML Documents

I'm a firm believer in a tutorial-style, "let's walk through the code" approach, so I'll discuss just what the COM can do for you by cranking up the Visual C++ development environment and writing some code to load an XML document and navigate through its elements.

Create the Visual C++ project and dialog box

Although you can create the Visual C++ project and dialog box with MFC or ATL, I'll keep things simple and use MFC. Therefore, create an MFC dialog-based project called XMLViewer. When the AppWizard finishes creating the project, open the Resource View and modify the dialog box so that when finished it looks like that featured in Figure 25-1.

Now, make the following changes to the dialog boxes and controls:

1. Give the static control an ID of ID_STC_DOC_NAME.

2. Create a CString DDX member variable for the static control called m_strDocName.

3. Give the edit control an ID of IDC_EDT_DOC_CONTENTS.

4. Set the edit control's Multiline, Vertical Scroll, Auto-VScroll, and Read-Only properties to TRUE.

5. Create a CString DDX member variable for the edit control called m_strDocContents.

Now incorporate the IE XML support into your application.

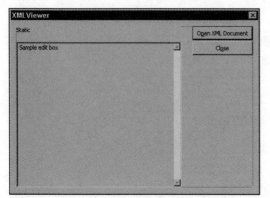

Figure 25-1: The dialog template for the first version of the XMLViewer

Incorporating XML support

Once you have finished with the dialog template, it's time to do some coding. First, you need to import the Microsoft XML Parser typelib (OLE type library). The simplest way to do this is to use the C++ #import directive. Simply open your project's stdafx.h file and add the following lines at the end of the file:

```
#import <msxml.dll> named_guids
using namespace MSXML;
```

Now you can start declaring some variables to use with the DOM. Open your dialog class's header file (XMLViewerDlg.h) and add the following smart pointer member variables, where the IXMLDOMDocumentPtr is the pointer to the XML document itself and the IXMLDOMElement is a pointer to the XML document root (as explained previously). The MSXML:: prefix is used to denote the namespace that these types are defined in so that you don't get compile-time errors because of name ambiguity.

```
class CXMLViewerDlg : public CDialog
{

...

protected:
  MSXML::IXMLDOMDocumentPtr m_plDomDocument;
  MSXML::IXMLDOMElementPtr m_pDocRoot;

...

}
```

Once you've declared the XML smart pointers, insert the following code in your dialog class's OnInitDialog member function (just before the return statement). This code simply sets up your XML document smart pointer (m_plDomDocument):

```
BOOL CXMLViewerDlg::OnInitDialog()
{
```

```
CDialog::OnInitDialog();

...

// Initialize COM
::CoInitialize(NULL);

HRESULT hr =
  m_plDomDocument.CreateInstance(MSXML::CLSID_DOMDocument);
if (FAILED(hr))
{
  _com_error er(hr);
  AfxMessageBox(er.ErrorMessage());
  EndDialog(1);
}

return TRUE;
}
```

Now, load and display an XML document in the viewer.

Loading an XML document

Once you've done the preliminary work for including XML support into your Visual C++ applications, you're ready to do something useful like actually loading an XML document. To do that, first rename the OK button on the application's main dialog box to "Open XML Document." Then add an event handler for its BN_CLICKED message called OnBnClickedOpenDoc. Here you're simply going to give the user a means of selecting an XML document to open, after which you'll open and display the contents of the selected document:

```
void CXMLViewerDlg::OnBnClickedOpenDoc()
{
  // Display file open dialog box and let user specify
  // XML file.
  CFileDialog fileDlg(TRUE);
  if (IDOK == fileDlg.DoModal())
  {
    m_strDocName = fileDlg.GetPathName();
    m_strDocContents = "Empty document";

    // Just in case you don't get anything
    UpdateData(FALSE);

      // Specify XML file name.
    CString strFileName(m_strDocName);

    // Convert XML file name string to something
    // COM can handle (bstr).
    _bstr_t bstrFileName;
    bstrFileName = strFileName.AllocSysString();

    // Call the IXMLDOMDocumentPtr's load function
```

```
  // to load the XML document.
  variant_t vResult;
  vResult = m_plDomDocument->load(bstrFileName);

  if (((bool)vResult) == TRUE) // success!
  {
    // Convert bstr to something you can use in Visual C++
    _bstr_t bstrDocContents = m_plDomDocument->xml;
    m_strDocContents = (LPCTSTR)bstrDocContents;
  }
  else
  {
    m_strDocContents = "Document FAILED to load!";
  }

  UpdateData(FALSE);
}
```

That's it! The XML document is now loaded *and* displayed. Don't believe it's that easy? Build and run the application and (assuming you open the sample cars.xml file) you should see the results shown in Figure 25-2.

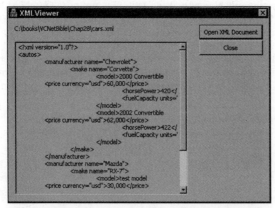

Figure 25-2: Using the IE typelib's COM interfaces to the XML DOM, you can write code that will allow you to easily open and load XML documents.

As you can see, loading and displaying an XML document can be done from Visual C++ with just a few lines of code using the IE-provided COM interfaces to the XML DOM.

OK, this doesn't really count as reading through an XML document, but I wanted to show you that you can successfully load a document and that you can easily get the entire document's contents with a single line of code (the IXMLDOMDocumentPtr::load function). In the next section, you'll see how to manually iterate through XML elements.

Iterating through an XML document

In this section, you're going to update the demo to display each element of the document in a tree view, because XML data is hierarchical in nature. The first step is to alter the dialog box as follows:

1. Remove the edit control from the dialog box.

2. Add a tree control in its place (same height and width).

3. Give the tree control an ID of ID_TREE_DOC_CONTENTS.

4. Set the control's Has Buttons, Has Lines, Lines at Root, and Scroll properties to TRUE.

5. Add a CTreeCtrl DDX member variable called m_treeDocContents for the tree control.

Now that you've replaced the edit control with a tree control on the dialog box, you need to remove some code that worked on the edit control. Open the XMLViewerDlg.h file and remove the m_strDocContents member. Then delete its entry in the CXMLViewerDlg::DoDataExchange function. Finally, delete the three lines that reference it in the CXMLViewerDlg::OnBnClickedOpenDoc function. At this point, you have your tree control in place and can fill it out with the XML document's contents.

When iterating through an XML document's elements, the IXMLDOMNodePtr::firstChild and IXMLDOMNodePtr::nextSibling functions are used quite extensively. To see this in action, define two functions. The first function is a reentrant function (DisplayChildren) that calls another function (DisplayChild) to display the element that is passed to it. DisplayChild inserts the element's node name into the tree view and returns that tree item's handle. After the call to DisplayChild, the DisplayChildren function implements a simple for loop using the firstChild and nextSibling functions to retrieve all of the children of the current element.

```
void CXMLViewerDlg::DisplayChildren(HTREEITEM hParent,
MSXML::IXMLDOMNodePtr pParent)
{
    // Display the current node's name.
    HTREEITEM hItem = DisplayChild(hParent, pParent);

    // Simple for loop to get all children
    for (MSXML::IXMLDOMNodePtr pChild = pParent->firstChild;
        NULL != pChild;
        pChild = pChild->nextSibling)
    {
        // For each child, call this function so that you get
        // its children as well.
        DisplayChildren(hItem, pChild);
    }
}

HTREEITEM CXMLViewerDlg::DisplayChild(HTREEITEM hParent,
    MSXML::IXMLDOMNodePtr pChild)
{
    // Add the element's node name to the tree view
```

```
    // and return the hItem.
    CString strElement((LPCTSTR)pChild->nodeName);
    return m_treeDocContents.InsertItem(strElement, hParent);
}
```

Now, modify `OnBnClickedOpenDoc` by placing the following code in the conditional `if` statement that follows the call to `m_plDomDocument->load`. (The changes are in bold.)

```
if (((bool)vResult) == TRUE) // success!
{
    m_pDocRoot = m_plDomDocument->documentElement;
    DisplayChildren(TVI_ROOT, m_pDocRoot);
    if (0 == m_treeDocContents.GetCount())
    {
        m_treeDocContents.InsertItem("Empty document");
    }
}
else
{
    m_treeDocContents.InsertItem("Document FAILED to load!");
}
```

Finally, add a call to the `CTreeCtrl::DeleteAllItems` function to clear out the tree view each time you load a new XML document:

```
void CXMLViewerDlg::OnBnClickedOpenDoc()
{
    // Display file open dialog box and let user specify
    // XML file.
    CFileDialog fileDlg(TRUE);
    if (IDOK == fileDlg.DoModal())
    {
        m_strDocName = fileDlg.GetPathName();
        m_treeDocContents.DeleteAllItems();
        ...
```

If you build and run the project at this point, you will see the document listed hierarchically in the tree (as you would expect). However, you will also notice something peculiar. As Figure 25-3 illustrates, the first few elements look fine. However, the first item under the item labeled "model" shows a value of "#text."

Now the question would naturally be "What is #text, and why is it being displayed when I thought I was enumerating nodes?" To answer that, look at an excerpt from the XML document:

```
<manufacturer name="Chevrolet">
  <make name="Corvette">
    <model>2000 Convertible</model>
    <price currency="usd">60,000</price>
    <horsePower>420</horsePower>
    <fuelCapacity units="gallons">18.5</fuelCapacity>
  </make>
</manufacturer>
```

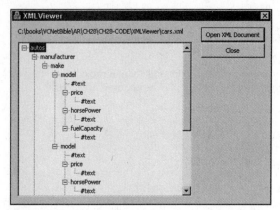

Figure 25-3: The nodeName returns a value of #text for the value of an element.

As you can see, in the `<model>` element, a *value* follows the `<model>` tag. These values are still treated as nodes in XML when using the `IXMLDOMNodePtr::firstChild` and `IXMLDOMNodePtr::nextSibling` enumeration methods. In other words, the values 2000 Convertible, price, horsePower, and fuelCapacity are all considered to be children of the `<make>` element, and by definition, siblings of one another. However, because price, horsePower, and fuelCapacity all are named elements, the DOM can tell you their names. In the case of 2000 Convertible value, it doesn't have a name. Therefore, the DOM returns a value of #text to indicate that this element is a text element. So the question becomes, "How can I tell one node type from another?" I'm glad you asked.

You do this by using the `IXMLDOMNodePtr::nodeType` property. This property will always have one of the values listed here:

```
enum tagDOMNodeType
{
    NODE_INVALID = 0,
    NODE_ELEMENT = 1,
    NODE_ATTRIBUTE = 2,
    NODE_TEXT = 3,
    NODE_CDATA_SECTION = 4,
    NODE_ENTITY_REFERENCE = 5,
    NODE_ENTITY = 6,
    NODE_PROCESSING_INSTRUCTION = 7,
    NODE_COMMENT = 8,
    NODE_DOCUMENT = 9,
    NODE_DOCUMENT_TYPE = 10,
    NODE_DOCUMENT_FRAGMENT = 11,
    NODE_NOTATION = 12
};
```

Therefore, what you care about is determining if the node type is equal to `NODE_TEXT`, and then retrieving its value accordingly. Simply modify the `CXMLViewerDlg::DisplayChild` member function as shown here. When you're done, you will see the expected values instead of the literal "#text."

```
HTREEITEM CXMLViewerDlg::DisplayChild(HTREEITEM hParent,
    MSXML::IXMLDOMNodePtr pChild)
```

```
  {
    // Determine the node type and based on that type
    // retrieve the value you want in the tree view.
    CString strElement;
    if (MSXML::NODE_TEXT == pChild->nodeType)
    {
      strElement = (LPCTSTR)pChild->text;
    }
    else
    {
      strElement = (LPCTSTR)pChild->nodeName;
    }

    // Add the element's node name to the tree view
    // and return the hItem.
    return m_treeDocContents.InsertItem(strElement, hParent);
  }
```

Now, if you build and run the application, you should see the expected output as shown in Figure 25-4.

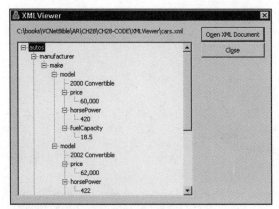

Figure 25-4: You need to evaluate the IXMLDOMNodePtr::nodeType property in order to determine the type of element with which you are working.

Adding UI niceties

One last thing you should take care of is the annoying fact that you have to expand every single branch manually to see the data. Therefore, add the following function to expand (or collapse, depending on the bExpand parameter's value) the branch, as specified by the hItem parameter. As you can see, this is another reentrant function that expands the current item and then executes a do/while loop calling itself for all children of that item. The result is that all items below the item represented by hItem will ultimately be expanded or collapsed as shown in the following example:

```
void CXMLViewerDlg::ExpandBranch(HTREEITEM hItem,
  BOOL bExpand /* = TRUE */)
{
```

```
    if (m_treeDocContents.ItemHasChildren(hItem))
    {
      m_treeDocContents.Expand(hItem,
        bExpand ? TVE_EXPAND : TVE_COLLAPSE);
      hItem = m_treeDocContents.GetChildItem(hItem);
      do
      {
          ExpandBranch(hItem);
      } while ((hItem =
      m_treeDocContents.GetNextSiblingItem(hItem)) != NULL);
    }
}
```

Now, you just need to plug this in somewhere. Open the Dialog Editor and add two buttons—one each for expanding and collapsing all tree branches (shown in Figure 25-5).

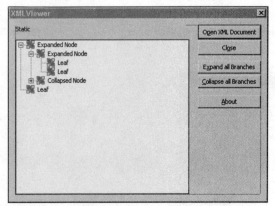

Figure 25-5: Adding buttons to ease use of XMLViewer application

Once you've added the button controls, add an event handler for each button's BN_CLICKED message called OnBnClickedExpandAll and OnBnClickedCollapseAll, respectively.

Now, modify these functions to look like these:

```
void CXMLViewerDlg::OnBnClickedExpandAll()
{
  HTREEITEM hItem = m_treeDocContents.GetRootItem();
  ExpandBranch(hItem);
  m_treeDocContents.Select(hItem, TVGN_FIRSTVISIBLE);
}

void CXMLViewerDlg::OnBnClickedCollapseAll()
{
   ExpandBranch(m_treeDocContents.GetRootItem(), FALSE);
}
```

As you can see, the OnBnClickedExpandAll function gets the root element's HTREEITEM, passes it to ExpandBranch (allowing the bExpand parameter to default to TRUE) and then calls the CTreeCtrl::Select function. Passing the value TVGN_FIRSTVISIBLE to the

`CTreeCtrl::Select` function has the effect of scrolling the specified item into view such that it is the top item displayed in the tree view.

The `OnBnClickedCollapseAll` simply calls the `ExpandBranch` function, also passing the root item, but specifying a value of `FALSE` to indicate that all branches should be collapsed. Obviously, because all branches will collapse to the XML root level element, there is no need to scroll the tree view. Finally, modify the `OnBnClickedOpenDoc` to automatically expand all branches after the call to `DisplayChildren` as shown in the following example:

```
void CXMLViewerDlg::OnBnClickedOpenDoc()
{

    ...

    DisplayChildren(m_pDocRoot);
    if (0 == m_treeDocContents.GetCount())
    {
      m_treeDocContents.InsertItem("Empty document");
    }
    else
    {
      OnBnClickedExpandAll();
    }

    ...

}
```

Now, if you build and run this application, it will not only load any valid XML document, but will do so in a nice little viewer application.

Summary

In this chapter, you discovered the XML DOM and learned how to access its features from Visual C++ / COM via the Microsoft XML Parser COM typelib. You started out by building a simple application to load and display the contents of an XML document. From there you learned how to iterate through a document's XML elements, determine each node's type, and display a node's name and text values. There is obviously much more to DOM than what you've seen here, but hopefully what you've learned will whet your appetite to dig into the documentation and to see all the great things you can do with XML documents using the DOM.

At this point, you have completed the Data I/O section of this book. This part started with a chapter illustrating how to use the Clipboard to transfer data between applications. From there you then saw a series of chapters that covered various database access technologies. These technologies included ODBC, the MFC database classes, ADO, and DAO. From there, you then discovered the MFC classes—`CFile` and `CStdioFile`—that are used to access binary and ASCII files. Finally, the part wound up with this chapter illustrating how to load and view XML documents from your Visual C++ applications. In the next part, you'll dive into COM and ATL development starting with chapters illustrating the benefits of component-based and interface-based development and proceeding to the more advanced topics of COM threading and eventing and windowing with ATL.

✦   ✦   ✦

COM and ATL

◆ ◆ ◆ ◆

◆ ◆ ◆ ◆

Introduction to Interface-Based Programming

Now that you have a good background in working with Visual Studio, the MFC, and a range of user interface features, it's time to consider the interface-based programming model. The Microsoft Component Object Model (COM) is based on interfaces. Basing your code on interfaces is what allows you to develop component-based systems, including distributed component-based systems.

In this chapter I'll explain what is meant by interface-based programming, and how this relates to COM and distributed component-based architectures such as the new Microsoft .NET initiative.

I'll incrementally build up a picture of why the interface model is useful, and how you can design and use interfaces in your code, along with the internal concrete implementation of your component objects. I'll use a simple order-processing and credit-verification scenario to flesh out the concepts with some real code. You'll see how interface-based programming is such an elegant solution, and how the COM model depends on it. You'll also see how the COM-standard interface, `IUnknown`, fits into the picture, and why it is designed the way it is. In passing, I'll also look at support techniques such as HRESULTs and GUIDs.

To show that interface-based programming really is open-ended and flexible, I'll show how to extend an interface with new functionality through interface inheritance. Finally, you'll explore IDL, the Interface Definition Language, which was evolved specifically to define interfaces.

Component-Based Software

What is *interface-based programming*? The question assumes that you understand what is meant by the term *interface*. Let's first consider a brief (very brief, I promise) history of component-based software.

The first step along this evolutionary path was the introduction of subroutines to FORTRAN. This was a revolutionary step because it moved from a monolithic software model to a modularized model. You could write subroutines, which could then be re-used in other parts of your system.

Other languages followed this pattern, and you're probably familiar with the library of functions available for the C language in the form of the C Runtime Library (CRT).

Object-oriented languages took matters a step further along the path by encapsulating functions and data within classes. Classes can be re-used in their entirety, so that instead of just single isolated global functions, your re-usable library contains small parcels of functions that each form a cohesive unit and also provide for some degree of self-maintenance (in the form of constructors/destructors and access restrictions to protect sensitive internal data). Libraries like the Standard Template Library (STL) and the Microsoft Foundation Classes (MFC) have become almost standard for C++ and especially Windows-based development.

You could say that component-based software is just another step along from object-oriented programming—what it brings to the party is the idea of the complete separation of internal component functionality from its external access. That is, when you call into a component, you don't need to know how it works inside, you only need to know how to call its functions. In other words, you only need to know how to interface to it.

So, an *interface* in software has the same meaning as in general use: an interface is what exists between two things, and how two things react to each other. Interface-based programming, then, is an approach to software development, which is strongly focused on the interface. You start your development by designing the interface first, and you make sure at each stage that the interface is adhered to.

n-Tier systems

Since the mid 1990s developers have been devising software systems that split different general areas of functionality into several tiers. Consider the generalized example illustrated in Figure 26-1.

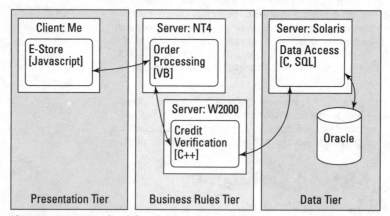

Figure 26-1: Example of the classic 3-tier model.

Key features of this design include:

✦ Logically distinct areas of functionality such as front-end presentation, middle-tier calculations and data processing, and back-end data storage are formally separated.

✦ The logical tiers can often be directly mapped to physical implementations. That is, implementing each logical tier on a different physical platform (although this is not necessary, nor always necessarily appropriate).

✦ The physical platforms do not need to be of the same type. In this example there are different versions of Windows and non-Windows platforms.

✦ The various components that make up the total system do not each need to be written in the same source-code language.

So where does the interface come into all this? Well, if you have cleanly separated the interface from the implementation for each of your components, it means that the only thing that any component depends upon is its interface with other components. No component in the system depends on any internal implementation of any functionality. It follows logically that this is an extremely flexible, open-ended and scalable design. For example, if you decide you need to change the credit verification logic, you only need to rebuild or replace the credit verification component. So long as you don't change the interface that the credit verification component exposes, you won't break any clients, and in fact the rest of the system will continue oblivious to the fact that you've changed the component.

You could unplug the existing component and plug in a replacement that you've bought from some other software vendor. As an extreme example, suppose you want to change from Solaris/Oracle to Windows XP/SQL-Server for your database? With interface-based programming, you could even drop out your entire database, including the machine that it sits on, and plug in a replacement — *dynamically*, while the system is running. No downtime, no recompilation of the system, just plug-and-play. This example is somewhat extreme, and I wouldn't recommend it, but it is entirely possible in a land where the interface is king.

Interface versus implementation

Although COM components do not have to be written in C++, it is convenient to consider the low-level mechanics of such components using C++ because the low-level mechanics of C++ itself are (not coincidentally) very similar.

So, if you're writing in C++, how do you code an interface? Recall that an interface is how clients call into your component, not the internal implementation of the functionality. So one overriding consideration is that you must not expose any internal implementation. You could specify private/protected for any data members and only expose certain carefully-chosen public functions. And you could put the server in a DLL for modular re-use. Let's try to do this with the credit-verification component from Figure 26-1.

First, you set up a DLL project, and declare the class in a header file as an exported class, being careful to hide the data member(s):

```
// CreditVerification.h
#ifdef _DLL
#define DLLSPEC __declspec (dllexport)
#else
#define DLLSPEC __declspec (dllimport)
#endif

class DLLSPEC CCreditVerification
{
private:
    num CardType {Visa, MasterCard, Amex} m_type;
public:
    void SetCardType(char* s);
    bool VerifyCardNumber(long n);
};
```

Next, implement the class in a separate CPP file:

```
// CreditVerification.cpp
#include "stdafx.h"

#define _DLL
#include "creditverification.h"

void CCreditVerification::SetCardType(char* s)
{
   if (0 == strcmp("Visa", s))
      m_type = Visa;
   else if (0 == strcmp("MasterCard", s))
      m_type = MasterCard;
   else m_type = Amex;
}

bool CCreditVerification::VerifyCardNumber(long n)
{
   if (m_type == Visa)
      return (n % 2);
   else if (m_type == MasterCard)
      return (n % 3);
   else if (m_type == Amex)
      return (n % 5);
   else return false;
}
```

Once you've built the server DLL, you turn to the client. Suppose you have a simple console application; to keep the compiler and linker happy, you could use the server DLL's header file (making use of the conditionally-defined __declspec(dllimport)). You'd be trying to hide the internal implementation from the client, and you have separated the class declaration in the header file from its definition in the CPP file, so the client can see the header but not the CPP.

```
// TestCCV.cpp
#include "stdafx.h"
#include "..\CreditVerification\CreditVerification.h"

int _tmain(int argc, _TCHAR* argv[])
{
   CCreditVerification* c = new CCreditVerification;
   c->SetCardType("MasterCard");
   if (c->VerifyCardNumber(1234))
      MessageBox(0, "Card Verified", "OK", 0);
   else
      MessageBox(0, "Card Rejected", 0, 0);

   return 0;
}
```

Now you've hidden the internal implementation of the server component from the client, right? No, not really. Yes, the data is declared private, and the client doesn't use the server's CPP file. However, the client is explicitly instantiating the class, so in memory in the client's process there is an instance of the CCreditVerification class including all its data and its internal implementation. The data is still private, so using C++ the client can't access it, but with a little pointer arithmetic it would be simple enough to walk through memory accessing anything you like.

So the client is not just dependent on the interface. If you change the internal implementation of the server (say you add some other data members, or change the type of the existing data, or add some functions, or re-arrange the members), you break the client. Also, both client and server are currently written in the same language, and built with the same version of the same vendor's compiler and linker. If any of these things change, you break the client. Consider, for example, name decoration — different compilers decorate names differently. How would you cope if the client were written in VB, which is not case-sensitive? This first attempt might work as a single system, but none of it is particularly re-usable, and certainly not dynamically re-usable.

Abstract classes and interfaces

You want C++ code that defines only an interface, without exposing any implementation at all. The construct in C++ that offers only declaration and not definition is an abstract class. An abstract class in C++ is a class with one or more pure virtual functions, and a pure virtual function has no body. You could extend this and declare an abstract class that has *only* pure virtual functions — no implementation, no data. This is the essence of an interface: a list of functions that defines the parameters and return types but no implementation.

Your next version of the code may work like this. In the server project, you no longer export the implemented class. Instead, you only list the interface (as a `struct`, so everything's public, with only pure virtual functions). You only export a global function that will internally instantiate an implementation of the interface, but you'll notice it returns an interface pointer, not a concrete class pointer. This means the client can use this pointer to access only those functions in the interface — they can't use it to walk through memory to get to any internal implementation, because they don't know how it's implemented internally.

```
// CreditVerification.h
#pragma once

#ifdef _DLL
#define DLLSPEC __declspec (dllexport)
#else
#define DLLSPEC __declspec (dllimport)
#endif

struct ICreditVerification
{
    virtual void SetCardType(char* s) = 0;
    virtual bool VerifyCardNumber(long n) = 0;
};

DLLSPEC ICreditVerification* GetCreditVerificationObject();


// CreditVerification.cpp
#include "stdafx.h"
#define _DLL
#include "creditverification.h"

class CCreditVerification : public ICreditVerification
```

```
    {
    private:
        enum CardType {Visa, MasterCard, Amex} m_type;
    public:
        void SetCardType(char* s)
        {
            if (0 == strcmp("Visa", s))
                m_type = Visa;
            else if (0 == strcmp("MasterCard", s))
                m_type = MasterCard;
            else m_type = Amex;
        }
        bool VerifyCardNumber(long n)
        {
            if (m_type == Visa)
                return (n % 2);
            else if (m_type == MasterCard)
                return (n % 3);
            else if (m_type == Amex)
                return (n % 5);
            else return false;
        }
    };

    DLLSPEC ICreditVerification* GetCreditVerificationObject()
    {
        return new CCreditVerification;
    }
```

On the client side, the client now uses an interface pointer, not a concrete class pointer. This way, if you change the internal implementation of the class on the server—or completely replace this server and plug in a replacement—it has no impact on the client. The client is now only dependent on the interface, not on any internal implementation.

```
// TestCCV.cpp
#include "stdafx.h"
#include "..\CreditVerification\CreditVerification.h"

int _tmain(int argc, _TCHAR* argv[])
{
    ICreditVerification* c = GetCreditVerificationObject();
    c->SetCardType("MasterCard");
    if (c->VerifyCardNumber(1234))
        MessageBox(0, "Card Verified", "OK", 0);
    else
        MessageBox(0, "Card Rejected", 0, 0);

    return 0;
}
```

The C++ VTBL

When you instantiate a new CCreditVerification class object on the server, the very first thing in the memory allocated for the object is the VPTR. When you instantiate a class that implements inherited virtual functions, the beginning of the memory for the object is actually the address of the VTBL. The VTBL is a list of addresses of the virtual functions that have been implemented somewhere in memory, as shown in Figure 26-2.

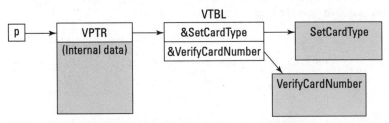

Figure 26-2: VPTRs, VTBLs, and implemented virtual functions.

The pointer returned back to the client by your GetCreditVerificationObject function is a pointer to a pointer to a pointer to a function. If you think about this for a moment, you'll realize that, in addition to hiding internal implementation from the client, this also provides language independence. If the client is using indirection to invoke some code at some location on the server, the name of the function (and issues of name-decoration, case-sensitivity, and so on) no longer matter. You're no longer invoking the function by its name, but by its address.

Object management

Now, the primary goal of separating interface from implementation is largely achieved, but there are a few minor administrative details to clean up. For instance, although the client calls GetCreditVerificationObject to indirectly instantiate the server-side component object, how does it clean up memory afterwards? The client doesn't use new — because that would assume knowledge of the concrete class — so it can't use delete. One solution might be to export a DeleteCreditVerificationObject function from the server, like this:

```
DLLSPEC
void DeleteCreditVerificationObject(ICreditVerification* p)

{
    delete p;
}
```

It would be somewhat dangerous to allow clients to force the server to delete arbitrary memory, however. Another solution might be to expose another function from the interface to do the cleanup, like this:

```
void DeleteMe() { delete this; }
```

This would be okay, but what if you have multiple clients using the same object, such as multiple threads in the same client process? You could impose some reference-counting architecture on the client to keep track of when the last client-side thread is done with the server object. However, all clients would have to do this, and because it forms a standard part of the component-based architecture, you should implement this on the server instead. You can make each server object responsible for tracking its own lifetime and deleting itself when no client is using it. This is in fact the approach taken by COM. All COM objects include three standard functions, two of which are purely for lifetime management, and these functions are part of the IUknown interface, discussed in the following section.

Working with IUnknown

The IUnknown interface is the core interface of all of COM. This is defined in objbase.h (or unknwn.h) as shown here (with some macros expanded):

```
interface IUnknown
{
  virtual long QueryInterface(IID& iid, void** pp) = 0;
  virtual long AddRef() = 0;
  virtual long Release() = 0;
};
```

Note that early versions of these header files also included this definition, before interface became an extended keyword in the C/C++ language:

```
#define interface struct
```

All other COM interfaces are derived from IUnknown, and the three IUnknown members are universally the first three members of any interface. This allows all COM interfaces to be treated polymorphically as IUnknown interfaces:

✦ AddRef increments the object's reference count.

✦ Release decrements the object's reference count, freeing the object if the count becomes zero.

✦ QueryInterface returns (as an out-parameter) a pointer to another interface on the same object, given the IID (interface ID).

The AddRef and Release members together provide for lifetime management of an object. This allows multiple clients to independently use the same instance of an object. Only when all clients have released their reference counts will the object destroy itself and free its resources. I'll discuss QueryInterface a bit later on, in the "Discovering identity" section.

Lifetime management

To adopt the COM-standard lifetime management mechanism, you would revise your interface declaration to derive from IUnknown:

```
// CreditVerification.h
#pragma once

#ifdef _DLL
#define DLLSPEC __declspec (dllexport)
#else
#define DLLSPEC __declspec (dllimport)
#endif

#define interface struct

interface IUnknown
{
        virtual long QueryInterface(IID& iid, void** pp) = 0;
        virtual long AddRef() = 0;
        virtual long Release() = 0;
```

```
};

interface ICreditVerification : IUnknown
{
    virtual void SetCardType(char* s) = 0;
    virtual bool VerifyCardNumber(long n) = 0;
};

DLLSPEC ICreditVerification* GetCreditVerificationObject();
```

In the internal implementation, you add a new data member to keep track of the number of clients using the object. You have to initialize this, so you need a constructor. AddRef merely increments the reference count (and returns it). Release decrements the reference count, and if it falls to zero, deletes the current object before returning:

```
// CreditVerification.cpp
class CCreditVerification : public ICreditVerification
{
private:
    enum CardType {Visa, MasterCard, Amex} m_type;
    long m_refCount;
public:
    CCreditVerification() : m_refCount(0) {}
    virtual long QueryInterface(IID& iid,
                                void** pp)
    {
        return 0;
    }

    virtual long AddRef() { return ++m_refCount; }
    virtual long Release()
    {
        if (--m_refCount == 0)
        {
            delete this;
            return 0;
        }
        return m_refCount;
    }

    void SetCardType(char* s) {...}
    bool VerifyCardNumber(long n) {...}
};
```

You also need to enhance the exported global GetCreditVerificationObject to increment the reference count (because if you're returning an object, you must have a client):

```
DLLSPEC ICreditVerification* GetCreditVerificationObject()
{
    ICreditVerification* p = new CCreditVerification;
    p->AddRef();
    return p;
}
```

On the client side, you just need to call Release when you're done with the object. Note that there's a little asymmetry here: The server calls AddRef (because it knows when its returning a pointer to a client), but the client calls Release (because only the client knows when its done with the pointer):

```cpp
// TestCCV.cpp
#include "stdafx.h"
#include "..\CreditVerification\CreditVerification.h"

int _tmain(int argc, _TCHAR* argv[])
{
    ICreditVerification* c = GetCreditVerificationObject();
    c->SetCardType("MasterCard");
    if (c->VerifyCardNumber(1234))
        MessageBox(0, "Card Verified", "OK", 0);
    else
        MessageBox(0, "Card Rejected", 0, 0);

    c->Release();
    return 0;
}
```

The interface/object now has the IUnknown functions at the top of the VTBL, as shown in Figure 26-3.

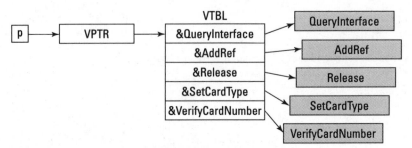

Figure 26-3: A true COM IUnknown-based component.

GUIDs, CLSIDs, and IIDs

You'll have noticed that QueryInterface takes a reference to an IID as its first parameter. So, what is an IID? The Open Software Foundation created an algorithm for generating GUIDs for their Distributed Computing Environment (DCE), where remote procedure calls (RPCs) need to travel around distributed networks and still manage to identify a specific piece of code to call. The algorithm uses a machine's network card address (unique in space) and the current date/time when the algorithm is run (unique in time). This will always (theoretically) produce a unique value (called a UUID in RPC parlance) because these numbers are 16-byte values (128 bits), in which you can create 3.4×10^{38} combinations.

There are two basic formats for listing GUIDs. The first is as a series of hex digits like this:

```
{01234567-1234-1234-1234-012345678ABC}
```

The second is as a (slightly differently formatted, but equivalent) `struct`, like this:

```
typedef struct GUIID
{
    unsigned long x;
    unsigned short s1;
    unsigned short s2;
    unsigned char c[8];
} GUID;
```

For Windows, the algorithm itself is implemented in a tool called UUIDGEN, and Visual Studio ships with a dialog-based front-end called GUIDGEN, as shown in Figure 26-4). You can use this to generate one GUID at a time in a variety of text formats that are more directly useful in source code. From the GUIDGEN utility (located in the Visual Studio.NET Tools menu), you simply select the format you want and click Copy to copy the generated string to the Clipboard. Then paste it into your source code.

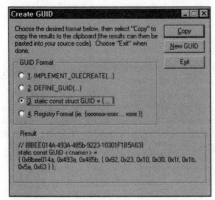

Figure 26-4: Visual Studio GUIDGEN dialog box.

Therefore, an IID is a GUID that uniquely identifies an interface. So, what then is a CLSID? A CLSID is simply a GUID that uniquely identifies a class, or component. As you'll see over the next several chapters, it's important to have at least a basic understanding of these constructs, because you'll be working with them a lot in your COM development.

Discovering identity

`QueryInterface` is the function that allows a COM object to support multiple interfaces. Once a client gets the initial interface pointer to any object, it can get another interface pointer to the same object through `QueryInterface`. To do a query, pass the IID of the interface you want. In return, you get back the interface pointer, if it is available, or an error code that says, "That interface is not supported." If you get a pointer, you can call the member functions of that interface, calling `Release` when you're through with it.

To complete the set, you'll now implement `QueryInterface` for the component. First, in the header, include the standard `objbase.h` where such things as the IID type are declared. Then you can use GUIDGEN to generate a couple of IIDs, and add a new interface:

```
// CreditVerification.h
#include <objbase.h>

GUID IID_ICreditVerification = { 0xcbb27840, 0x836d, 0x11d1,
{ 0xb9, 0x90, 0x0, 0x80, 0xc8, 0x24, 0xb3, 0x23 } };

GUID IID_ISomethingElse = { 0xd6925520, 0x8505, 0x11d1,
{ 0xb9, 0x90, 0x0, 0x80, 0xc8, 0x24, 0xb3, 0x23 } };

interface ISomethingElse : IUnknown
{
    virtual void Foo() = 0;
};
```

In the server's implementation, you can add the new interface to the list of supported interfaces by specifying multiple inheritance:

```
// CreditVerification.cpp

class CCreditVerification :
    public ICreditVerification, public ISomethingElse
{
...
public:
    void Foo() { }
```

Finally, you can implement QueryInterface as it's meant to be. Note that you're changing the formal declaration very slightly to make it conform to the declaration of IUnknown you pulled in when you included objbase.h (this pulled in unknwn.h where IUnknown is declared):

```
long __stdcall QueryInterface(REFIID iid, void**pp)
{
    if (NULL == pp)
        return E_INVALIDARG;
    *pp = NULL;

    if (iid == IID_IUnknown)
        *pp = this;
    else if (iid == IID_ICreditVerification)
        *pp = static_cast<ICreditVerification*>(this);
    else if (iid == IID_ISomethingElse)
        *pp = static_cast<ISomethingElse*>(this);

    if (*pp)
    {
        AddRef();
        return S_OK;
    }
    return E_NOINTERFACE;

    return 0;
}
```

As you can see, all you're really doing is testing the incoming IID. If it's something you support, you fill in the pointer out-parameter with the address of the appropriate VTBL; otherwise you return a suitable error code. I'll discuss error codes like E_INVALIDARG a little later.

All this allows you to offer the client multiple sets of VTBLs, that is, multiple interfaces, from a single COM object:

```
// TestCCV.cpp
#include "stdafx.h"
#include "..\CreditVerification\CreditVerification.h"

int _tmain(int argc, _TCHAR* argv[])
{
    ICreditVerification* c = GetCreditVerificationObject();
    c->SetCardType("MasterCard");
    if (c->VerifyCardNumber(1234))
        MessageBox(0, "Card Verified", "OK", 0);
    else
        MessageBox(0, "Card Rejected", 0, 0);

    ISomethingElse* s;
    c->QueryInterface(IID_ISomethingElse, (void**)&s);
    s->Foo();

    s->Release();
    c->Release();
    return 0;
}
```

Note Because QueryInterface is calling AddRef, you must be careful on the client-side to call Release for each interface pointer you have successfully filled in.

Working with HRESULT values

Recall that you changed the declaration of QueryInterface to the one you pulled in from unknwn.h. You specified a return type of long, but strictly speaking QueryInterface is defined to return an HRESULT. This is defined in wtypes.h as:

```
typedef long HRESULT;
```

Almost all COM functions and interface methods return a value of the type HRESULT. The HRESULT is a way of returning success, warning, and error values. HRESULT values are not handles to anything; they are only 32-bit values with several fields encoded in the value. A zero or positive result indicates success, and a negative result indicates failure. The composition of an HRESULT is listed in the standard header winerror.h, and is shown in Figure 26-5.

S	R	C	N	r					Facility									Code													
31	30	29	28	27	26											16	15														0

Figure 26-5: HRESULT bits.

The high-order `Severity` bit in the `HRESULT` represents success or failure:

#define identifier (winerror.h)	Value	Example
SEVERITY_SUCCESS	0	32 bits +ve, hence SUCCEEDED test >= 0
SEVERITY_ERROR	1	32 bits -ve, hence FAILED tests < 0

The `R`, `C`, `N`, and `r` bits are reserved.

The `Facility` field indicates the system service responsible for the error. There are currently five facilities: `FACILITY_NULL`, `FACILITY_ITF`, `FACILITY_DISPATCH`, `FACILITY_RPC`, and `FACILITY_STORAGE`.

The `Code` field is a unique number that is assigned to represent the error or warning.

As an example, the error `STG_E_MEDIUMFULL` would be represented as follows with regards to the `Facility`, `Severity`, and `Code` bits:

```
Facility = Storage
Severity = Error
Code = Out of disk space
```

COM defines a number of macros that make it easier to work with `HRESULT` values, listed in the following example (extracted from `winerror.h`):

```
// Generic test for success on any status
// value (non-negative numbers
// indicate success).
#define SUCCEEDED(Status) ((HRESULT)(Status) >= 0)

// and the inverse
#define FAILED(Status) ((HRESULT)(Status)<0)

// Generic test for error on any status value.
#define IS_ERROR(Status) \
  ((unsigned long)(Status) >> 31 == SEVERITY_ERROR)

// Return the code
#define HRESULT_CODE(hr)    ((hr) & 0xFFFF)
#define SCODE_CODE(sc)      ((sc) & 0xFFFF)

//  Return the facility
#define HRESULT_FACILITY(hr) (((hr) >> 16) & 0x1fff)
#define SCODE_FACILITY(sc)   (((sc) >> 16) & 0x1fff)

//  Return the severity
#define HRESULT_SEVERITY(hr) (((hr) >> 31) & 0x1)
#define SCODE_SEVERITY(sc)   (((sc) >> 31) & 0x1)

// Create an HRESULT value from component pieces
#define MAKE_HRESULT(sev,fac,code) \
    ((HRESULT) (((unsigned long)(sev)<<31) \
    | ((unsigned long)(fac)<<16) | ((unsigned long)(code))) )
```

```
#define MAKE_SCODE(sev,fac,code) \
    ((SCODE) (((unsigned long)(sev)<<31) \
    | ((unsigned long)(fac)<<16) \
    | ((unsigned long)(code))) )
```

So, strictly speaking, the `QueryInterface` should be written like this:

```
HRESULT __stdcall QueryInterface(REFIID iid, void**pp)
```

You should also be using appropriate tests on the client side. Note that if you're abandoning your work, you must be careful to clean up on the way out:

```
HRESULT hr = c->QueryInterface(IID_ISomethingElse,
                               (void**)&s);
if (FAILED(hr))
{
    MessageBox(0, "QI failed on ISomethingElse", 0, 0);
    c->Release();
    return 1;
}
```

Immutability of interfaces

Recall that you're separating the interface from the implementation so that any change to the implementation cannot break any client. A necessary corollary of this is that once you've published an interface, you cannot change it. An interface is an immutable contract between client and component (or between component and component). Clients don't depend on anything internal to the component, but they do depend on the interface. At the lowest level, clients depend on the VTBL, so you cannot do anything that risks changing the VTBL. That means you cannot add functions, change the number or type of any parameters or return types, remove functions, or rearrange the order of functions.

Suppose you merely change the order of the functions in the interface. For example, suppose the original order is like this:

```
interface ICreditVerification : IUnknown
{
    virtual void SetCardType(char* s) = 0;
    virtual bool VerifyCardNumber(long n) = 0;
};
```

And you change it to this:

```
interface ICreditVerification : IUnknown
{
    virtual bool VerifyCardNumber(long n) = 0;
    virtual void SetCardType(char* s) = 0;
};
```

How can this break the client? Well, recall that the client code has been compiled and built to expect a particular VTBL layout. As Figure 26-6 illustrates, the client holds a pointer to a VTBL that is inconsistent with the VTBL on the server.

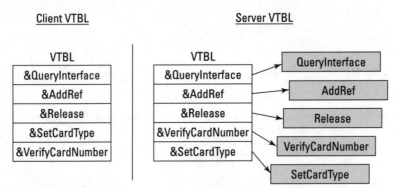

Figure 26-6: The expected client VTBL (on the left) and server VTBL (on the right)

Of course, the built client code is not using function names, but function addresses. So the poor client is following a chain of pointers to ultimately invoke some code at some address, which it thinks is the SetCardType function code, but is in fact the VerifyCardNumber function. So, they'll be passing the wrong parameters, and you'll blow the stack.

Suppose you add a function at the end that doesn't change the order; so all the existing calls should work, shouldn't they? Well, maybe. It depends on whether the client's language compiler builds code that depends on the size of the VTBL. If it does, and if you increase the size of the VTBL, again you have a problem.

The right way to enhance functionality over time as requirements change and new technologies appear is through interface inheritance.

Interface inheritance

You can't change an interface once you've published it, so you can't enhance it. What you can do, however, is write another interface, perhaps making it inherit from the original interface, to expose the additional functionality. For instance, suppose you want to add a function to your ICreditVerification interface/. This section explains the way to do it.

Use GUIDGEN to generate a new IID, and put this in the header file:

```
GUID IID_ICreditVerification2 = { 0xd6925522, 0x8505, 0x11d1,
{ 0xb9, 0x90, 0x0, 0x80, 0xc8, 0x24, 0xb3, 0x23 } };
```

Derive the new interface from your old one:

```
interface ICreditVerification2 : ICreditVerification
{
    virtual char* GetCardType(int i) = 0;
};
```

In the component's internal implementation, you can simply derive from the new (extended) interface in place of the old one. This will be fine for both old and new clients, because if you implement all the extended interface functions, you implement by default all the original interface functions.

```
class CCreditVerification :
    public ICreditVerification2, public ISomethingElse
{
```

```
public:
...
   char* GetCardType(int i)
   {
      switch(i)
      {
      case 0: return "Visa";
      case 1: return "MasterCard";
      case 2: return "Amex";
      }
      return NULL;
   }
```

Of course, you need to enhance the `QueryInterface` also, to correctly report that it supports both old and new interfaces:

```
HRESULT __stdcall QueryInterface(REFIID iid, void**pp)
{
   if (NULL == pp)
      return E_INVALIDARG;
   *pp = NULL;

   if (iid == IID_IUnknown)
      *pp = this;
   else if (iid == IID_ICreditVerification)
      *pp = static_cast<ICreditVerification*>(this);
   else if (iid == IID_ISomethingElse)
      *pp = static_cast<ISomethingElse*>(this);
   else if (iid == IID_ICreditVerification2)
      *pp = static_cast<ICreditVerification2*>(this);

   if (*pp)
   {
      AddRef();
      return S_OK;
   }
   return E_NOINTERFACE;

   return 0;
}
```

Then, on the client, you can test for any of the three (or four, counting `IUnknown`) interfaces the object implements. Again, note that you must be careful in cases of failure to clean up correctly:

```
// TestCCV.cpp

int _tmain(int argc, _TCHAR* argv[])
{
   ICreditVerification* c = GetCreditVerificationObject();
...

   ISomethingElse* s;
   HRESULT hr =
    c->QueryInterface(IID_ISomethingElse, (void**)&s);
   if (FAILED(hr))
```

```
    {
        MessageBox(0, "QI failed on ISomethingElse", 0, 0);
        c->Release();
        return 1;
    }
    s->Foo();

    ICreditVerification2* v;
    hr = s->QueryInterface(IID_ICreditVerification2,
                           (void**)&v);
    if (FAILED(hr))
    {
        MessageBox(0, "QI failed on ICreditVerification2",
                   0, 0);
        s->Release();
        c->Release();
        return 1;
    }
    MessageBox(0, v->GetCardType(2), "Card Type", 0);

    v->Release();
    s->Release();
    c->Release();
    return 0;
}
```

IDL Overview

Many years ago, the Open Software Foundation Distributed Computing Environment (OSF DCE) people came up with the idea of a language that could be used to precisely describe interfaces that would be used for RPCs (Remote Procedure Calls). They wanted to ensure that you could correctly describe interfaces for calls made across heterogeneous networks from one process to another. This language had to be robust enough to cope with the possibility that the processes at either end of the communication were sitting on different hardware and OS platforms, with all the attendant conflicts of different integer sizes such as "little endian" versus "big-endian." The solution was IDL, the Interface Definition Language. Microsoft extended OSF DCE IDL very slightly, and in a sense, COM is merely a very slight extension of RPC.

An RPC interface describes the remote functions that the server program implements. The interface ensures that the client and server programs communicate using the same rules when the client invokes a remote procedure that the server offers. An interface consists of an interface name, some attributes, optional type or constant definitions, and a set of procedure declarations. Each procedure declaration must contain a procedure name, return type, and parameter list.

Interfaces are defined in the Microsoft Interface Definition Language (MIDL). Again, Microsoft IDL is based on DCE IDL. So, your first task is to create the interface definition in IDL code, and save it in a file with an `.idl` extension. Next, you pass this source file to the MIDL compiler to generate a header file that your program includes in the client and server source files. The MIDL compiler also generates two C source files. You compile and link one of these to your client program, and the other to your server program. These two C source files are the client and server stubs. For example, if your IDL file is called `Bill.idl`, MIDL generates `Bill.h`, `Bill_c.c`, and `Bill_s.c`.

The C/C++ code generated as targets when you compile an IDL file can then be used as source-code on both the server and client side. For example, you could remove all the COM interface code (everything except the global `GetCreditVerificationObject` function) from the original server header file, and instead use the .h file generated by the following IDL:

```
import "oaidl.idl";
import "ocidl.idl";

[uuid (cbb27840-836d-11d1-b990-0080c824b323)]
interface ICreditVerification : IUnknown
{
    HRESULT SetCardType([in] char* s);
    HRESULT VerifyCardNumber([in] long n);
};

[uuid (d6925520-8505-11d1-b990-0080c824b323)]
interface ISomethingElse : IUnknown
{
    HRESULT Foo();
};

[uuid (d6925522-8505-11d1-b990-0080c824b323)]
interface ICreditVerification2 : ICreditVerification
{
    HRESULT GetCardType([in] int i, [out] char*);
};

[uuid(CCE10873-6FE8-40a1-98EA-0CC3CDC07883)]
library CreditLibrary
{
        importlib("stdole2.tlb");

        [ uuid(9D438627-F0F5-4212-91F2-9DDD4A45FA57) ]
        coclass CreditVerification
        {
            [default] interface ICreditVerification;
            interface ICreditVerification2;
            interface ISomethingElse;
        };
};
```

The file is divided into three parts. The outermost scope of the entire file is the library block — this is the source of the binary type library built as one of the MIDL targets. There will be a maximum of one library in any IDL file. Within the library block, you can list one or more `coclass`es — these are the IDL equivalent of a C++ concrete component class. Each `coclass` can list that it implements one or more interfaces, and one of the interfaces can be marked as the default interface.

The square brackets before each section delimit a set of attributes that apply to the block of code that follows them, that is, an interface, library, or `coclass`. Unlike C/C++, IDL supports the capability of tightly associating a GUID with an interface.

The additional square-bracket-delimited attributes that may be applied to each parameter allow the RPC DLLs to compose network packets in the most efficient and platform-independent manner. For instance, a parameter flagged as an [in] parameter needs to be parceled up into a network packet only when sent in to the component, whereas an [out] parameter is put in the packet on the way out.

Note that to conform to COM standards, I've had to change the signatures of the interface functions so that they return HRESULT values. This is reflected in the implemented code in the concrete class:

```cpp
// CreditVerification.cpp
#include "creditverification_h.h"
#include "creditverification.h"

class CCreditVerification :
    public ICreditVerification2, public ISomethingElse
{
public:
    HRESULT __stdcall GetCardType(int i, unsigned char* s)
    {
        switch(i)
        {
        case 0: strcpy((char*)s, "Visa");
            return S_OK;
        case 1: strcpy((char*)s, "MasterCard");
            return S_OK;
        case 2: strcpy((char*)s, "Amex");
            return S_OK;
        default: strcpy((char*)s, "Unrecognized");
            return E_INVALIDARG;
        }
    }

    HRESULT __stdcall SetCardType(unsigned char* s)
    {
        if (0 == strcmp("Visa", (const char*)s))
            m_type = Visa;
        else if (0 == strcmp("MasterCard", (const char*)s))
            m_type = MasterCard;
        else m_type = Amex;
        return S_OK;
    }
    HRESULT __stdcall VerifyCardNumber(long n)
    {
        if (m_type == Visa && (n % 2))
            return S_OK;
        else if (m_type == MasterCard && (n % 3))
            return S_OK;
        else if (m_type == Amex && (n % 5))
            return S_OK;
        else return E_INVALIDARG;
    }

    HRESULT __stdcall Foo() { return S_OK; }
    ...
```

This is also reflected, of course, in the client-side code:

```cpp
// TestCCV.cpp
#include "stdafx.h"
#include "..\CreditVerification\CreditVerification_h.h"
#include "..\CreditVerification\CreditVerification.h"

int _tmain(int argc, _TCHAR* argv[])
{
    ICreditVerification* c = GetCreditVerificationObject();
    c->SetCardType((unsigned char*)"MasterCard");
    if (c->VerifyCardNumber(1234) == S_OK)
        MessageBox(0, "Card Verified", "OK", 0);
    else
        MessageBox(0, "Card Rejected", 0, 0);

    ISomethingElse* s;
    HRESULT hr = c->QueryInterface(IID_ISomethingElse,
                                   (void**)&s);
    if (FAILED(hr))
    {
        MessageBox(0, "QI failed on ISomethingElse", 0, 0);
        c->Release();
        return 1;
    }
    s->Foo();

    ICreditVerification2* v;
    hr = s->QueryInterface(IID_ICreditVerification2,
                           (void**)&v);
    if (FAILED(hr))
    {
        MessageBox(0, "QI failed on ICreditVerification2",
                   0, 0);
        s->Release();
        c->Release();
        return 1;
    }
    char buf[32] = {0};

    hr = v->GetCardType(2, (unsigned char*)buf);
    if (SUCCEEDED(hr))
        MessageBox(0, buf, "Card Type", 0);

    v->Release();
    s->Release();
    c->Release();
    return 0;
}
```

Summary

This chapter might have seemed like hard work. For many people, using the various developer wizards to generate code for them is a reasonable level to work at. However, if you seriously want to understand the code that is generated, and to develop in the knowledge that you've really got a handle on the underlying mechanisms and architecture, you need to understand the point of interfaces.

If you don't want to make basic errors in lifetime management of your COM components, you need to know why and how the IUnknown interface works. If you want to develop systems that will scale, and write scalable, distributed *n*-tier application, you need to understand the VTBL indirection model. So, although this is hard work, it is worth it. And you only have to understand the model once: it's like riding a bicycle — once you get the point of COM, you don't ever forget it. Now that I've explained many of the benefits of interface-based programming, the next chapter will illustrate how to create and consume components using COM.

✦   ✦   ✦

Creating and Consuming Components

◆   ◆   ◆   ◆

In This Chapter

Aims and benefits of COM

Objects and servers

Creating COM objects

COM and registry

Using a class factory to create objects

Registering COM components

◆   ◆   ◆   ◆

In the previous chapter, you saw how important it is to separate the internal implementation of a component from its exposed interface. All significant component-based architectures — from RPC to COM and CORBA — depend on this separation. In this chapter, you'll see how this separation leads to even more benefits, including compile and language independence, location transparency, and increased scalability.

Given such an architecture where clients and component servers have limited knowledge of each other's internal workings, how is it that they can still interact with each other? Exactly how does a client create and consume a component? What are the underlying mechanics, and how does the runtime support this? How, in the first place, does a component make itself known to the system? This chapter answers all these questions, and provides a detailed explanation of class factories and the use of the registry in component systems.

Aims and Benefits of COM

To fully understand the COM model and implementation, you need to consider the reason that COM was developed. COM lost quite a lot of ground in the early days of its existence simply because Microsoft didn't make it clear to the developer community exactly what it was and what it was for. They mistakenly promoted it as an upgrade to OLE, an older technology based on Dynamic Data Exchange (DDE) aimed squarely at Object-Linking and Embedding for integrating the Office products. COM was actually introduced as OLE2, a supposed upgrade for the problems with the original OLE. It took a little while before everyone realized that you could do so much more with COM, and that it was in fact a true interface-based paradigm for developing component-based systems. COM successfully addresses all the following issues:

> ◆ *Software reuse* — COM is an object-oriented model and has the additional benefit of achieving binary reuse, that is, reuse of built code, not source code.

✦ *Language independence*—You can write a COM object server in one language and a client that uses the object in another language. As long as the source code language compiler (or the supporting runtime library) can achieve object code that conforms to the COM binary standard, you can do COM with it. The binary standard is the VTBL, which was discussed in the last chapter. In this chapter you'll see how you can use a VTBL from languages other than C++.

✦ *Vendor/Compiler independence*—Consider the problems of using DLLs written by different vendors using different compilers, such as C++ name decoration. With COM, these problems disappear. If you have language independence, you must also have compiler/vendor independence.

✦ *Location transparency*—The client does not need to know where the server is—it could be hosted in an in-process DLL, a local EXE server, or a remote DLL or EXE server.

✦ *Scalability*—With COM, you can deploy the various components that make up a distributed system in the most efficient configuration, and upgrade the system on a component-by-component basis as and when required (even dynamically).

✦ *Versioning*—What happens if you install an older version of a DLL on top of a newer version? With COM, this is not (so much of) a problem.

Now that you've seen what interface-based programming is all about, you only need to see how the COM runtime supports component-based systems in order to see how all these benefits accrue. The missing piece of the puzzle is how the COM runtime allows clients to create component objects. In the classic *n*-tier architecture, there is a logical and often physical separation of clients (or consumers) and component servers. As you have seen, this separation gives you software reuse and scalability. How COM uses this model to achieve compiler/language independence and location transparency is the subject of the rest of this chapter.

Objects and Servers

Before you can proceed with this discussion, you need to be clear on some terms, specifically, how a COM server relates to a COM object. COM offers a standard way to organize COM object hosting servers, COM objects, interfaces, and interface functions (methods). An *interface* can expose one or more functions. A component or *COM Object* can implement one or more interfaces. A *server* (be that an EXE or DLL module) can host one or more COM objects. This relationship is shown in Figure 27-1.

Exactly how many functions you expose in an interface, or how many interfaces you implement in an object, or how many objects you host in your server, are a matter for individual design. For example, Microsoft Word is a full COM EXE server that also acts as an automation server, an OLE container/server, and a standalone user-interface desktop application. Word exposes seven COM objects, offering a total of nearly 200 interfaces. Word interfaces may offer as many as 100 functions. At the other extreme, a typical ActiveX Control server is likely to host only one control object, which implements about 15 interfaces, each with up to 10 functions.

Note that it is a convention to represent COM objects with a stylized jack socket to represent each exposed interface, and with the IUnknown interface given pride of place at the top, as shown in Figure 27-2.

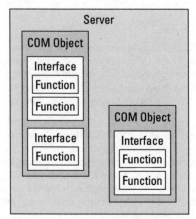

Figure 27-1: Objects and servers

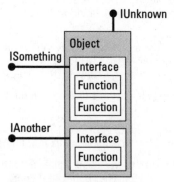

Figure 27-2: Interface jacks

If you want to implement the COM object model successfully, there are two main requirements:

✦ COM objects must link dynamically. As the user's requirements change, or new versions of constituent COM objects are released, the user must be able to connect to the new COM objects at runtime. Note that this does not mean that COM objects have to reside in DLL servers.

✦ COM objects must hide, or *encapsulate* the details of how they were implemented. If you want to replace a COM object with another, the new COM object must connect in the same manner as the old COM object. This imposes important constraints:

   • Any client should be capable of using any COM object regardless of the programming language in which either the client or the COM object is written.

   • COM objects must be shipped in binary form.

   • COM objects must be upgradeable without breaking existing users. New versions of a COM object should work with both old and new clients.

✦ COM objects must be transparently relocatable on a network. The client should be capable of treating a remote COM object the same way it treats a local COM object.

COM Object Creation

The previous chapter incrementally built up a picture of a component system, focusing on the reasoning behind interface-based programming. The final component code was complete as far as separating interface from implementation was concerned. It was almost a true COM component, correctly implementing interfaces derived from IUnknown, and therefore taking part in the interface-identification mechanism and the lifetime management mechanism standard in COM.

However, it fell a little short of a true COM component because it didn't address the issue of how the client could cleanly create an instance of the component. The clients relied on being capable of using a GetCreditVerificationObject function known to them from using the component's header file. This was clearly server-specific, and in a true COM environment would not be acceptable. To build a true COM component, you must somehow set things up such that any client, written in any language, can create an instance of your component using only generic functions offered by the COM runtime, and without any use of server source code.

The COM runtime support is provided through a series of system DLLs, notably OLE32.DLL and OLEAUT32.DLL. These in turn make use of the lower-level RPC services offered in RPCRT4.DLL and RPCNS4.DLL. So, in a true COM scenario, the client would make use of the functions in these DLLs to create the component.

Fortunately, the steps required for a client to create and use a COM object are very straight-forward. Specifically, OLE32.DLL offers two crucial functions: CoInitialize and CoCreateInstance, which the client calls to create a COM object, following these steps:

1. The client notifies the COM runtime of its intent to take part in a COM communication, by calling CoInitialize.

2. The client creates the COM object it wants through a call to CoCreateInstance, specifying both the interface it wants and the object that it thinks implements that interface.

3. Assuming CoCreateInstance succeeded, it will return to the client a pointer to the requested interface implemented on the requested object. The client can then use the interface pointer to access the functions of the interface.

4. When the client has finished working with the object, it must release the interface (by calling the object's Release function).

5. The client indicates it has no further interest in COM, by calling CoUninitialize.

Graphically, much of this can be seen in Figure 27-3.

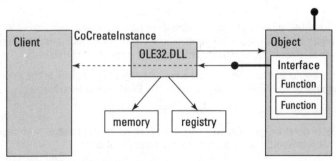

Figure 27-3: COM object creation

Figure 27-3 also illustrates the significant processing internal to CoCreateInstance. This function performs the following steps:

1. Checks to see if the COM object server is already in memory offering its services.

2. If not, COM scans the registry to find the hosting server module location specified by the COM object's CLSID, and loads the server.

3. (For a DLL server) Calls the exported DllGetClassObject function to create an instance of the object.

4. Returns a pointer to the requested interface on that object back to the client.

This is what typical client-side COM code looks like:

```
// TestCreditObject.cpp
#include "stdafx.h"
#include "..\CreditServer\CreditServer\CreditServer_h.h"

int _tmain(int argc, _TCHAR* argv[])
{
    CoInitialize(NULL);
    ICreditVerification* p = NULL;

    HRESULT hr = CoCreateInstance(CLSID_CreditVerification,
                                  NULL,
        CLSCTX_SERVER, IID_ICreditVerification, (void**)&p);
    if (FAILED(hr))
        cout << "Failed to create server\n";
    else
    {
        p->SetCardType((unsigned char*)"MasterCard");
        if (p->VerifyCardNumber(1234) == S_OK)
            MessageBox(0, "Card Verified", "OK", 0);
        else
            MessageBox(0, "Card Rejected", 0, 0);

        p->Release();
    }

    CoUninitialize();
}
```

As you can see from this code, the client must specify two GUIDS: the CLSID of the object that implements the interface, and the IID of the interface itself. Note that the client does not make any mention of the hosting server. This follows that aim of location transparency; the client doesn't need to know the name or location of the server that hosts the object. In this way, you can plug-and-play, substituting the server with another at any time. This clearly lends itself to a very open-ended and scalable solution architecture.

The second parameter to CoCreateInstance is NULL in this simple example, and is most often NULL in practice. Only in an aggregation situation is this ever non-NULL (that is, where one COM object creates, or aggregates with, another COM object). The third parameter is CLSCTX_SERVER in this example. This is a flag value indicating the nature of the hosting server to which you wish to connect. Your choices are:

✦ CLSCTX_INPROC — In-process, or DLL server

✦ CLSCTX_LOCAL — Local, or out-of-process EXE server

✦ CLSCTX_REMOTE—A remote server, on another machine

✦ CLSCTX_SERVER—Any of CLSCTX_INPROC, CLSCTX_LOCAL, or CLSCTX_REMOTE

If you specify CLSCTX_SERVER, as in this example, you're indicating to the COM runtime that you don't care what the nature of the hosting server is, as long as it gets the object you've asked for.

The client doesn't specify the server name or location. Instead, the client makes a call into the COM runtime (the ole32.dll). It is the responsibility of the COM runtime to locate and load the hosting server module (EXE or DLL), run whatever server-side code is necessary to create the object, query the object for the requested interface, and return the interface pointer back to the client. CoCreateInstance finds the server that hosts the object by using the registry, which is the subject of the next section.

The Registry

I mentioned that CoCreateInstance finds the server by performing a registry lookup. All COM objects must be registered in the registry—this includes objects hosted in servers such as Word and Excel as well as ActiveX Controls and remote servers.

When you build a COM server, you can register all kinds of information against it, but there is only one crucial requirement: a registry entry that maps the object's CLSID against the pathname of its hosting server. All the COM entries in the registry are to be found under HKEY_CLASSES_ROOT. For example, consider the entry for the primary Word application object shown in Figure 27-4.

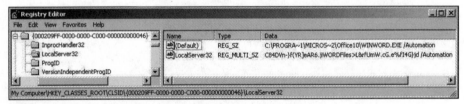

Figure 27-4: Word application object registration

The minimum requirement is illustrated by your CreditVerification object's entry in Figure 27-5:

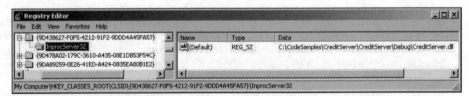

Figure 27-5: CreditVerification object registration

So how do you get this information into the registry? The best solution is to write code to make calls to the registry API using calls such as RegOpenKeyEx and RegSetValue. Alternatively, a simple strategy is to use a .REG file. This is a simple text file that you can merge into the registry using the Registry ➪ Import Registry File menu option in Regedit. Here's an example of that (line broken for formatting purposes only):

```
REGEDIT4

[HKEY_CLASSES_ROOT\CLSID\
{9D438627-F0F5-4212-91F2-9DDD4A45FA57}
\InprocServer32]@=
"C:\\ CodeSamples\\CreditServer\\CreditServer\\Debug\\
CreditServer.dll"
```

`CoCreateInstance` looks up the registry and finds the path to the hosting server module. What happens next? If you just focus on DLL servers for now, the next thing to happen is that `CoCreateInstance` calls `LoadLibrary` to load the DLL. It then calls `GetProcAddress` to find a specific exported function. So far, these steps are simply standard runtime dynamic linking behavior. The specific exported function that `CoCreateInstance` needs to get is `DllGetClassObject`.

At certain points, for example triggered by a client calling `CoUninitialize`, the COM runtime also calls into the server DLL to a function called `DllCanUnloadNow` to see if the DLL can be completely removed from memory. So, when you write a COM server, you need to export at least these two standard functions.

Required DLL exports

The two required DLL exports for the CreditVerification server follow the general pattern indicated in the following code. First, `DllCanUnloadNow` simply keeps track of a global count of all the objects in the server currently in use by clients. You can increment this count by simply incrementing an internal number value whenever you successfully return an interface pointer to a client.

```
STDAPI DllCanUnloadNow()
{
    if (g_cComponents == 0)
        return S_OK;
    else
        return S_FALSE;
}
```

The `DllGetClassObject` export is a little more interesting. COM calls into this in order to create the object that the client has requested. However, this function doesn't create the object. Instead, it returns the address of what is called a *class factory*. The class factory is actually another COM object hosted by the server. In fact, the server will have a different class factory object for every COM object that it exposes.

```
STDAPI DllGetClassObject(const CLSID& clsid,
    const IID& riid, void** ppv)
{
    if (clsid != CLSID_CreditVerification)
        return CLASS_E_CLASSNOTAVAILABLE;

    CCreditObjectFactory* pFactory = new CCreditObjectFactory;
    if (pFactory == NULL)
        return E_OUTOFMEMORY;

    HRESULT hr = pFactory->QueryInterface(riid, ppv);
```

```
    pFactory->Release();
    return hr;
}
```

You can export these two standard functions from your DLL using a module definition file (DEF), for example:

```
; CreditServer.def
LIBRARY         CreditServer.dll
EXPORTS
                DllGetClassObject   PRIVATE
                DllCanUnloadNow     PRIVATE
```

In Visual Studio, this needs to be set up so that the linker builds this properly, as shown in Figure 27-6.

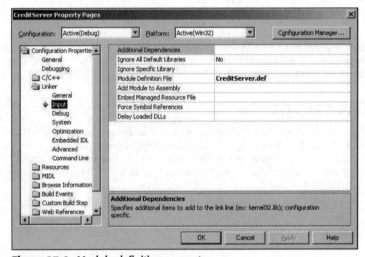

Figure 27-6: Module definition property

IClassFactory

As I stated, behind the scenes, CoCreateInstance doesn't create COM objects directly. Instead, it creates an intermediary COM object called a class factory. The standard interface for creating COM objects is IClassFactory. It is the class factory that then creates the required COM object. Each class factory is itself a COM object whose sole purpose is to create instances of a client-useable COM object specified by a CLSID. DllGetClassObject is typically implemented as follows:

```
interface IClassFactory : IUnknown
{
    HRESULT __stdcall CreateInstance (IUnknown* pUnknownOuter,
        const IID& riid, void** ppv);
    HRESULT __stdcall LockServer (BOOL bLock);
};
```

In order to create your own class factory, you would simply define a class that implements the IClassFactory interface. Here's an example of that, where I'm defining a credit verification class factory that will be responsible for creating credit verification components.

```
class CCreditObjectFactory : public IClassFactory
{
private:
    long m_refCount;
public:
    CCreditObjectFactory();

    // IUnknown
    HRESULT __stdcall QueryInterface(
        const IID& riid, void** ppv);
    ULONG __stdcall AddRef(void);
    ULONG __stdcall Release(void);

    // IClassFactory
    HRESULT STDMETHODCALLTYPE CreateInstance(
        IUnknown * pUnkOuter, REFIID riid, void ** ppv);
    HRESULT __stdcall LockServer (BOOL bLock);
};
```

AddRef and Release are implemented in the usual way. So is QueryInterface, although, of course, it will be testing for IUnknown and IClassFactory only.

```
HRESULT __stdcall CCreditObjectFactory::QueryInterface(
    const IID& riid, void** ppv)
{
    if (riid == IID_IUnknown || riid == IID_IClassFactory)
        *ppv = static_cast<IClassFactory*>(this);
    else
    {
        *ppv = NULL;
        return E_NOINTERFACE;
    }
    static_cast<IUnknown*>(*ppv)->AddRef();
    return S_OK;
}
```

The LockServer function does a very similar job to AddRef and Release, but for the entire DLL. It makes sure the DLL that contains the class factory is not unloaded from memory until all clients have finished using it. To achieve this, you might keep a count of client locks (separate from the global count of hosted components in use). LockServer is often implemented as a simple stub, like this:

```
HRESULT __stdcall CCreditObjectFactory::LockServer (BOOL bLock)
{
    return S_OK;
}
```

The first parameter to IClassFactory::CreateInstance is a pointer to an IUnknown interface—the same pointer that's passed to CoCreateInstance. The other two parameters are the same as the parameters to QueryInterface, and with these the client can request an interface in the COM object at the same time that it creates the COM object. Note, however, that `CreateInstance` doesn't take a CLSID parameter; this is because it can only create a COM object corresponding to one specific CLSID — the one passed to `CoCreateInstance`:

```
HRESULT STDMETHODCALLTYPE CCreditObjectFactory::CreateInstance(
    IUnknown * pUnkOuter, REFIID riid, void ** ppv)
{
    CCreditVerification * pCV;
    HRESULT hr;

    if (NULL == ppv)
        return E_INVALIDARG;
    *ppv = NULL;

    if (NULL != pUnkOuter)
        return CLASS_E_NOAGGREGATION;

    pCV = new CCreditVerification;
    if (NULL == pCV)
        return E_OUTOFMEMORY;

    hr = pCV->QueryInterface(riid, ppv);
    if (FAILED(hr))
        delete pCV;

    pCV->Release();
    return hr;
}
```

As you can see, the class factory code actually does whatever language-specific operations are necessary to get the interface pointer (in the case of C++, by instantiating the object class and calling its `QueryInterface`). `CoCreateInstance`, having got hold of the class factory and made use of it to get the component object interface pointer, then releases the class factory. The class factory is thus normally destroyed after it has created its object. A simplified implementation of `CoCreateInstance` is listed in the following example:

```
HRESULT CoCreateInstance (const CLSID& clsid,
                          IUnknown* pUnknownOuter,
        DWORD dwClsContext, const IID& iid, void** ppv)
{
    // Set the out parameter to NULL.
    *ppv = NULL;

    // Create the class factory, and
    // get an IClassFactory pointer.
    IClassFactory* pIFactory = NULL;
    HRESULT hr = CoGetClassObject (clsid, dwClsContext, NULL,
        IID_IClassFactory, (void**)&pIFactory);
    if (SUCCEEDED(hr))
    {
        // Create the COM object.
        hr = pIFactory->CreateInstance(pUnknownOuter,
                                       iid, ppv);
        // Release the class factory.
        pIFactory->Release();
    }
```

```
    return hr;
}
```

The COM library offers the `CoGetClassObject` function, which takes a CLSID and returns a pointer to an interface belonging to the class factory for that CLSID:

```
HRESULT __stdcall CoGetClassObject (const CLSID& clsid,
DWORD dwClsContext, COSERVERINFO* pServerInfo,
const IID& riid, void** ppv);
```

As you can see, `CoGetClassObject` is very similar to `CoCreateInstance`. One difference is that `CoGetClassObject` takes a `COSERVERINFO` pointer, which is used by DCOM to control accessing remote COM objects. Another difference is that `CoCreateInstance` returns a pointer to the COM object, whereas `CoGetClassObject` returns a pointer to the COM object's class factory.

A newer creation interface, `IClassFactory2`, released by Microsoft in 1996, adds licensing functionality to `IClassFactory` — the client must pass the correct license key to the class factory before it will create the COM object. If you want to create an object using a creation interface other than `IClassFactory` (that is, if you want to use `IClassFactory2`), you have to use `CoGetClassObject` directly rather than using the `CoCreateInstance` wrapper. There are other reasons why you might want to use `CoGetClassObject` directly, for example, if you want to create several COM objects all at once, it's not efficient to create and release the class factory for every instance of the COM object.

You may wonder why you need to go to all the bother of having a separate COM object to create a COM object. COM can call `IClassFactory::CreateInstance` as a standard API for all objects, without having to know anything about the specifics of creating each object. For example, the COM runtime doesn't need to know to instantiate the object with the C++ `new` operator. You could have each object expose its own `CreateInstance`, instead of having a separate object, but then you'd have that creation code sitting around for the life of the object, whereas once the class factory has done its `CreateInstance` job, it can be removed from memory. You could also have a global function in the server that would accept a CLSID and create the corresponding object, but that would only work exported from a DLL, not from an EXE.

Using RegSvr32

I mentioned earlier in the chapter that REG files are a simple way to get information into the system's registry. REG files have several drawbacks, however: they're text, so susceptible to corruption by users, and they're separate from the server binary, so they could get misplaced or deleted. A better solution is to write the code to register your server using the registry API, and build this code into the server itself. Then you can use a utility such as RegSvr32 to call this server code to update the registry.

If you want to write the code to register your server from the binary, the DLL must export these two functions — used for registering and unregistering the objects in the server:

```
// registry.h

HRESULT RegisterServer(HMODULE hModule, const CLSID& clsid,
    const char* szFriendlyName, const char* szVerIndProgID,
    const char* szProgID) ;

HRESULT UnregisterServer(const CLSID& clsid,
    const char* szVerIndProgID,   const char* szProgID) ;
```

Implementing these two functions is straightforward API code, using such functions as RegOpenKeyEx, RegCreateKeyEx, RegSetValueEx, RegEnumKeyEx, RegDeleteKeyEx, and RegCloseKey.

Recall that the minimum requirement is a mapping between the CLSID of the object and the pathname of the server. You can also register a ProgID, which is a human-readable string mapping to the CLSID. ProgIDs can be versioned, and the convention is to use a core ProgID string suffixed with a version number, like this:

```
const char g_szNiceName[] =
  "Simplest Credit Verification Object";
const char g_szVerIndProgID[] = "CreditServer.CreditObject";
const char g_szProgID[] = "CreditServer.CreditObject.1";
```

You could then write functions such as the following to support both registration and unregistration. Note this code is very standard registry API code — there's nothing COM-specific about any of this, so I won't explain it beyond the liberal comments supplied:

```
BOOL setKeyAndValue(const char* pszPath,
                    const char* szSubkey,
                    const char* szValue);
void CLSIDtochar(const CLSID& clsid,
                 char* szCLSID,
                 int length);
LONG recursiveDeleteKey(HKEY hKeyParent,
                        const char* szKeyChild);

// Size of a CLSID as a string
const int CLSID_STRING_SIZE = 39;

// Register the component in the registry.
HRESULT RegisterServer(HMODULE hModule, const CLSID& clsid,

const char* szNiceName, const char* szVerIndProgID,
const char* szProgID)
{
    char szModule[512];  // get server location
    DWORD dwResult = ::GetModuleFileName(hModule, szModule,
    sizeof(szModule)/sizeof(char));
    assert(dwResult != 0);


    // Convert the CLSID into a char.
    char szCLSID[CLSID_STRING_SIZE];
    CLSIDtochar(clsid, szCLSID, sizeof(szCLSID));

    char szKey[64];     // Build the key CLSID\\{...}
    strcpy(szKey, "CLSID\\");
    strcat(szKey, szCLSID);

    // Add the CLSID to the registry.
    setKeyAndValue(szKey, NULL, szNiceName);
    // Add the server filename, ProgID and version-independent
// subkeys under the CLSID key.
    setKeyAndValue(szKey, "InprocServer32", szModule);
```

```
   setKeyAndValue(szKey, "ProgID", szProgID);
   setKeyAndValue(szKey, "VersionIndependentProgID",
szVerIndProgID);

   // Add the version-independent ProgID subkey under
// HKEY_CLASSES_ROOT.
   setKeyAndValue(szVerIndProgID, NULL, szNiceName);
   setKeyAndValue(szVerIndProgID, "CLSID", szCLSID);
   setKeyAndValue(szVerIndProgID, "CurVer", szProgID);

   // Add the versioned ProgID subkey
   // under HKEY_CLASSES_ROOT.
   setKeyAndValue(szProgID, NULL, szNiceName);
   setKeyAndValue(szProgID, "CLSID", szCLSID);

   return S_OK;
}

// Remove the component from the registry.
LONG UnregisterServer(const CLSID& clsid,
const char* szVerIndProgID, const char* szProgID)
{
   // Convert the CLSID into a char.
   char szCLSID[CLSID_STRING_SIZE];
CLSIDtochar(clsid, szCLSID, sizeof(szCLSID));

   char szKey[64];   // Build the key CLSID\\{...}
   strcpy(szKey, "CLSID\\");
   strcat(szKey, szCLSID);

// Delete the CLSID Key - CLSID\{...}
   LONG lResult = recursiveDeleteKey(HKEY_CLASSES_ROOT,
                                     szKey);
   assert((lResult == ERROR_SUCCESS) ||
(lResult == ERROR_FILE_NOT_FOUND));

   // Delete the version-independent ProgID Key.
   lResult = recursiveDeleteKey(HKEY_CLASSES_ROOT,
                                szVerIndProgID);
   assert((lResult == ERROR_SUCCESS) ||
(lResult == ERROR_FILE_NOT_FOUND));

   // Delete the ProgID key.
   lResult = recursiveDeleteKey(HKEY_CLASSES_ROOT, szProgID);
   assert((lResult == ERROR_SUCCESS) ||
(lResult == ERROR_FILE_NOT_FOUND));

   return S_OK;
}

// Convert a CLSID to a char string.
void CLSIDtochar(const CLSID& clsid,
                 char* szCLSID,
                 int length)
```

```
{
    assert(length >= CLSID_STRING_SIZE);

    LPOLESTR wszCLSID = NULL;

    // get CLSID
    HRESULT hr = StringFromCLSID(clsid,
                                 &wszCLSID);

    assert(SUCCEEDED(hr));

    // convert wide to non-wide
    wcstombs(szCLSID, wszCLSID, length);

    // Free memory
    CoTaskMemFree(wszCLSID);
}

// Delete a key and all of its descendents.
LONG recursiveDeleteKey(HKEY hKeyParent,
                        const char* lpszKeyChild)
{
    HKEY hKeyChild;   // Open the child key.
    LONG lRes = RegOpenKeyEx(hKeyParent, lpszKeyChild,
0, KEY_ALL_ACCESS, &hKeyChild);
    if (lRes != ERROR_SUCCESS)
        return lRes;

    FILETIME time;
    char szBuffer[256];
DWORD dwSize = 256;

// Enumerate all descendents of this child.
while (RegEnumKeyEx(hKeyChild, 0,
                    szBuffer,
                    &dwSize,
                    NULL,
                    NULL,
                    NULL,
                    &time) == S_OK)
{
    // Delete this child's descendents.
    lRes = recursiveDeleteKey(hKeyChild, szBuffer);
    if (lRes != ERROR_SUCCESS)
    {
        RegCloseKey(hKeyChild);
        return lRes;
    }
    dwSize = 256;
}
RegCloseKey(hKeyChild);

// Delete this child.
```

```
        return RegDeleteKey(hKeyParent, lpszKeyChild); }

// Create a key and set its value.
BOOL setKeyAndValue(const char* szKey, const char* szSubkey,
                    const char* szValue)
{
    HKEY hKey;
    char szKeyBuf[1024];

    strcpy(szKeyBuf, szKey);    // Copy keyname into buffer.
    if (szSubkey != NULL)
    {                                   // append subkey name
        strcat(szKeyBuf, "\\");
        strcat(szKeyBuf, szSubkey );
    }

                            // Create and open key and subkey.
    long lResult = RegCreateKeyEx(HKEY_CLASSES_ROOT,
szKeyBuf, 0, NULL, REG_OPTION_NON_VOLATILE,
KEY_ALL_ACCESS, NULL, &hKey, NULL);
    if (lResult != ERROR_SUCCESS)
        return FALSE;

    if (szValue != NULL)    // Set the value.
        RegSetValueEx(hKey, NULL, 0, REG_SZ,
(BYTE *)szValue, strlen(szValue)+1);

    RegCloseKey(hKey);
    return TRUE;
}
```

Then, you could wrap these internal calls into the standard exports:

```
STDAPI DllRegisterServer()
{
    return RegisterServer(g_hModule, CLSID_CreditVerification,
g_szNiceName, g_szVerIndProgID, g_szProgID);
}

STDAPI DllUnregisterServer()
{
    return UnregisterServer(CLSID_CreditVerification,
g_szVerIndProgID, g_szProgID);
}
```

In order to register the correct path to the server, DllRegisterServer must internally call GetModuleFilename, which needs the module handle of the DLL containing it so that it can get the DLL's filename and register it. This module handle is passed to DllMain, so you need to make a minor change to DllMain also. Here's an example:

```
BOOL APIENTRY DllMain(HMODULE hModule, DWORD dwReason,
    void* lpReserved)
{
    if (dwReason == DLL_PROCESS_ATTACH)
        g_hModule = hModule;
```

```
    return TRUE;
}
```

When all the code is correct, you can set RegSvr32 to run as a post-build step in Visual Studio, as shown in Figure 27-7.

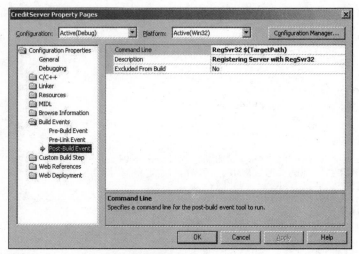

Figure 27-7: RegSvr32 post-build step

The net result in the registry is shown in Figure 27-8.

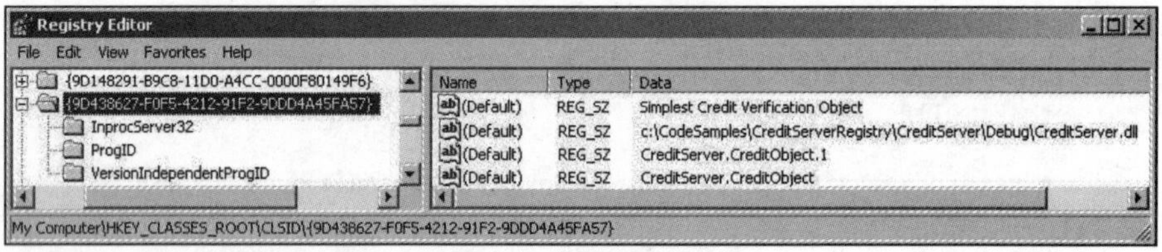

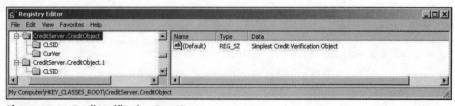

Figure 27-8: Updated CreditVerification registry entry

Note that there would also be two further entries in HKEY_CLASSES_ROOT (not under the CLSID subkey), for the ProgID and version-independent ProgID, as shown in Figure 27-9. These would also map against the CLSID.

Figure 27-9: CreditVerification ProgID

This strategy allows clients to use the ProgID in place of the CLSID if they choose, using the following code:

```
int _tmain(int argc, _TCHAR* argv[])
{
    CoInitialize(NULL);
    ICreditVerification* p = NULL;

    CLSID clsid;
    HRESULT hr = CLSIDFromProgID(
L"CreditServer.CreditObject", &clsid);

    hr = CoCreateInstance(clsid, NULL,
        CLSCTX_SERVER, IID_ICreditVerification, (void**)&p);
```

Summary

Building on your understanding of interface-based programming, you saw how the COM runtime supports language/compiler independence and location transparency. The client and server are separated, with the ole32.dll sitting between them. The COM runtime locates the server module that hosts the required component, and the client doesn't need to know where it is, or even what the filename is.

The COM runtime also protects the clients from knowing how to directly instantiate the code that implements the interface, and this gives you language/compiler independence. Even the COM runtime is protected from any language-specific knowledge of the internals of the component server. All of this naturally lends itself to increased scalability. Anytime you need to replace a component with a bigger, faster, different one on a different machine somewhere across the network, you just unplug the old one and plug in the new one. You saw how the registry is used to track the name and location of the server, so when you replace something, you just have to make sure the registry is updated.

I focused on DLL servers in this chapter because they're simpler. The same underlying mechanics are also used for EXE servers. However, EXE servers introduce another possible issue—marshaling, which you'll come to grips with in the next chapter.

✦　　✦　　✦

Type Libraries

By now, you recognize the importance of interface-based programming, and the particular place that IDL has in the scheme of things. You've also seen how the COM environment supports dynamic runtime object creation and language and location independence. However, consider this: Your client and server are written in different source code languages with different built-in data types; also the server may be running in a separate process space from the client, or possibly on a different machine (and even perhaps on a different operating system and hardware platform). How can you be sure that the right parameters are passed to a component in the right way, and that you will get the right return values back (as out-parameters)? How does a client know in the first place what the component's functions are, and what the parameters are?

In this chapter, you'll see how the COM runtime solves these problems, and (not coincidentally) consider another aspect of IDL — type libraries. After an introduction to type libraries, you'll learn about marshaling and how it allows for the managing of communicating data between client and server address spaces. After a brief introduction to the MkTypLib utility, you'll discover some C++ compiler extensions introduced specifically to allow your code to easily integrate type libraries. Finally, the chapter will wrap up with sections on how to marshal data with EXE servers and how to write your own proxy-stub marshaling code for custom interfaces.

Type Libraries

A *type library* is a binary file that stores information about a COM object's properties and methods. A client application, either directly or through the COM runtime, can read such a type library to determine what interfaces an object supports, what the methods on these interfaces are, and the number and type of each parameter in each method. This is possible even if the COM object and client applications were written in different source code languages.

When you are writing a COM object server, you are encouraged to write and register a type library. The type library can be in a separate binary .tlb file, or it can be built into the server's EXE or DLL module. It is possible to write code in C++ for a type library, but it is more common to use IDL.

You can use tools like the OLE/COM Object Viewer (oleview.exe) to view binary type libraries. For example, Figure 28-1 shows oleview.exe viewing the Word 2000 type library.

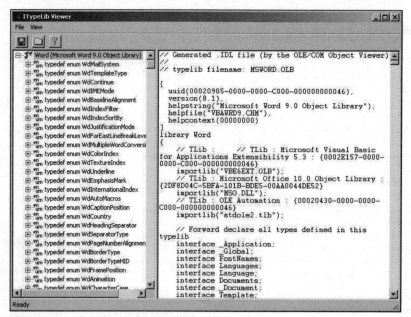

Figure 28-1: The OLE/COM object viewer

There are actually two main uses of type libraries: one is for clients to discover the supported interfaces and methods; and the second is for the COM runtime to discover the supported interfaces and methods. The COM runtime can use a type library at runtime to work out how to pass parameters correctly between a client and a COM component. This operation is called *marshaling*, and the COM runtime DLLs can use type libraries to provide automatic marshaling for interfaces described in type libraries.

Marshaling

DLLs are mapped into the memory space of the loading process, and if a DLL is used by several applications simultaneously, it is loaded into memory and mapped into each application's virtual address space. The reason this is worth mentioning here is to remind you that if a client application and the COM object that it's using are in the same process space, it follows that they share the same virtual memory address mappings, so (all other things being equal) a pointer value in the client will be mapped to the same thing in the COM object. (This isn't necessarily always so, as you will see later, but for now it's a reasonable assumption.)

However, your COM object might be hosted in an EXE not a DLL. Every EXE runs in a different process, and every process has a separate logical address space. The logical address 0x0000ABCD in one process maps to a different physical memory location than the address 0x0000ABCD in another process.

So, if you have a pointer in your client's address space, and this pointer needs to point to a COM object in the server's address space, you need to be sure that the address is valid at both ends. The answer is *marshaling*: the process of managing the communication between client and server address spaces. Fortunately, COM usually does the marshaling for you. The way it does this is by intercepting calls between client and COM object. This interception is a transparent mechanism of the COM runtime.

The basic mechanism is as follows: For out-of-process server objects, COM creates an object proxy in the client's address space. The proxy exposes the same functions and accepts the same parameters as the real object, but doesn't actually contain the real object's internal functionality. Instead, the proxy communicates via RPC with a stub in the server's address space, as indicated in Figure 28-2.

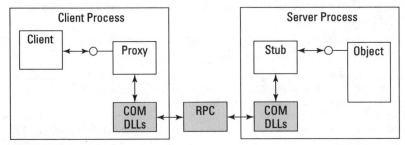

Figure 28-2: Marshaling

The COM DLLs provide marshaling support for all the Microsoft-standard interfaces. If you want to write your own custom interface to be hosted in an EXE (out-of-process) server, you need to do a bit more work to support the marshaling process, which is why you need type libraries. You describe your interface(s) — including their methods and the parameters of these methods — in IDL, and then build this IDL into a type library.

Type-library marshaling

If your interface restricts itself to a certain predefined set of known data types, the COM DLLs will be capable of providing marshaling at runtime on the basis of the type library alone. This is because the COM DLLs must provide the necessary marshaling code for automation (because automation clients are not using the VTBL). So, if your interface restricts itself to automation types, it can make use of COM's standard marshaling.

Proxies and stubs are created by COM when the client calls a method that returns an interface pointer, such as CoCreateInstance. After getting the pointer to the class factory from the server, but before returning it to the client, COM looks in the HKCR\Interface section of the registry for a key containing the interface's IID. Under that key, COM finds a subkey ProxyStubClsid32, containing the CLSID of the server that produces the proxies and stubs.

For standard (and automation-conformant custom) interfaces, this is {00020424-0000-0000-C000-000000000046}, which is the CLSID for an object called PSOAInterface, an in-process object implemented in oleaut32.dll. This object is the *Universal Marshaler*, and it uses the information in the type library to determine how interface methods are marshaled. A second subkey under your interface key is the TypeLib key, which must be set to the GUID of the type library describing the interface.

Now let's take a look at the MkTypeLib and how it takes IDL/ODL input and creates binary type library output.

IDL, ODL, and MkTypLib

The MkTyplib.exe utility was a Microsoft product for producing type libraries from source code written in Microsoft's Object Definition Language (ODL). Microsoft took the OSF DCE RPC Interface Definition Language (IDL) and merged it with ODL, specifically for use with COM. You now write source code in IDL and compile with MIDL to produce a type library and ancillary output code. The C++ source code files generated by MIDL are as follows:

✦ *Interface header file* (name.H) — Contains both C and C++ equivalents of the interface definitions and interface function prototypes described in the IDL file, that is, enough information to describe the VTBL.

✦ *Interface UUID file* (name_i.C) — Provides the C/C++ const definition of the interface, COM object, and type library GUIDs specified in the IDL file.

✦ *Interface proxy file* (name_p.C) — Contains C implementations of the functions in the interface(s) described in the IDL. For example, for an interface IMotion that has Walk and GetPath methods, this file would implement IMotion_Walk_Proxy, IMotion_Walk_Stub, IMotion_GetPath_Proxy, and IMotion_GetPath_Stub functions. These functions form both the proxy (client-side) and stub (server-side) parts of the marshaling DLL.

The proxy functions marshal the input arguments into NDR format (transmittable across a network), transmit the marshaled arguments together with information that identifies the interface and the operation, and then unmarshal the return value and any output arguments when the transmitted operation returns.

The stub functions unmarshal the input arguments, invoke the server's implementation of the interface function, and then marshal and transmit the return value and any output arguments.

The file also contains marshaling and unmarshaling support routines for complex data types.

✦ *DLL data file* (dlldata.c) — Contains a series of macros that expand out to entry points and data structures required by the class factory for the proxy DLL. These data structures specify the object interfaces contained in the proxy DLL. This file also specifies the class ID of the class factory for the proxy DLL. This is always the UUID (IID) of the first interface of the first proxy file (alphabetically).

The CreditVerification COM object from the previous chapter was built with an IDL file, so, although I didn't discuss it before, when you build the IDL file with MIDL, as well as the generated C++ source code files, you also get a .tlb file. You can examine this .tlb in OLE-VIEW, as shown in Figure 28-3.

Note   You haven't registered this type library, so it won't be listed in the OLEVIEW tree view, but you can open it by using the File ➪ View TypeLib menu option.

You could, of course, register your type library. To do this, you just need to add another global function to the registry.h file like this:

```
HRESULT RegisterTypeLibrary(HMODULE hModule, REFGUID rguid,
    unsigned short wvMaj, unsigned short wvMin,
    LCID localeID, const char* szTypeLib);
```

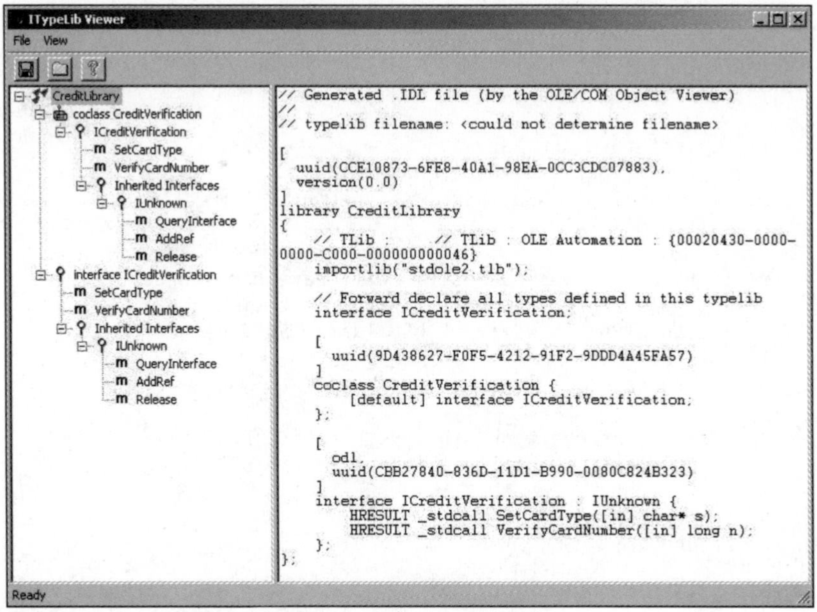

Figure 28-3: Viewing the CreditVerification type library

Then you can implement the function like this:

```
// Register the Type Library
HRESULT RegisterTypeLibrary(HMODULE hModule, REFGUID rguid,
unsigned short wvMaj, unsigned short wvMin,
LCID localeID, const char* szTypeLib)
{
    HRESULT hr;
    ITypeInfo* pITypeInfo = NULL;
    ITypeLib* pITypeLib = NULL;

    hr = ::LoadRegTypeLib(rguid, wvMaj, wvMin,
                          localeID, &pITypeLib);
    if (FAILED(hr))
    {
        // If it wasn't registered, try to load
        // it from the path.
        // Get the fullname of the server's executable.
        char szModule[512];
        DWORD dwResult = ::GetModuleFileName(hModule,
szModule, 512);

        // Split the fullname to get the pathname.
        char szDrive[_MAX_DRIVE];
        char szDir[_MAX_DIR];
        _splitpath(szModule, szDrive, szDir, NULL, NULL);
```

```
        // Append name of registry.
        char szTypeLibFullName[_MAX_PATH];
        wsprintf(szTypeLibFullName, "%s%s%s", szDrive,
szDir, szTypeLib);

        // Convert to wide char.
        wchar_t wszTypeLibFullName[_MAX_PATH];
        mbstowcs(wszTypeLibFullName, szTypeLibFullName,
                _MAX_PATH);

        // If LoadTypeLib succeeds, it will have registered
        // the type library for us, for the next time.
        hr = ::LoadTypeLib(wszTypeLibFullName, &pITypeLib);
        if (FAILED(hr))
           return hr;

        // Ensure that the type library is registered.
        hr = RegisterTypeLib(pITypeLib, szTypeLibFullName,
                          NULL);
        if (FAILED(hr))
           return hr;
    }
    return hr;
}
```

Next, call this function when you register or unregister the server:

```
STDAPI DllRegisterServer()
{
    RegisterTypeLibrary (g_hModule, LIBID_CreditLibrary,
        1,0, 0x00, "CreditServer.tlb");
    return RegisterServer(g_hModule, CLSID_CreditVerification,
        g_szNiceName, g_szVerIndProgID, g_szProgID);
}

STDAPI DllUnregisterServer()
{
    UnRegisterTypeLib(LIBID_CreditLibrary, 1, 0, 0x00,
                    SYS_WIN32);
    return UnregisterServer(CLSID_CreditVerification,
        g_szVerIndProgID, g_szProgID);
}
```

Rebuild the server project, and refresh OLEVIEW, and you should see the type library in the tree view, as shown in Figure 28-4.

So far you've seen how you can build and register a type library, and how tools such as OLEVIEW can read a type library; but what about a regular client? Well, those gallant folk at Redmond came up with a few extensions to the Microsoft C++ compiler to support client-side use of type libraries.

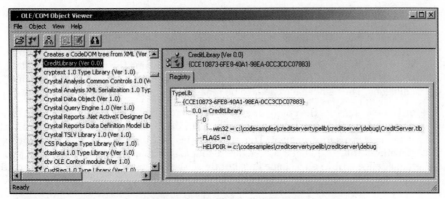

Figure 28-4: Showing the registered type library in OLEVIEW

C++ Compiler Extensions

From version 5 onward, the Visual C++ compiler can directly read COM type libraries and translate the contents into C++ source code that can be included in the compilation. Language extensions are available to facilitate COM programming on the client side:

✦ the #import preprocessor directive

✦ __declspec extended attributes: uuid and property

✦ __uuidof

A set of COM support classes are provided to support the VARIANT and BSTR types, implement smart pointers, and encapsulate the error objects thrown by _com_raise_error. They are:

✦ _com_error

✦ _com_ptr_t

✦ _variant_t

✦ _bstr_t

✦ #import — With the #import preprocessor directive, you can make the compiler import, or read, a specified binary type library and generate C++ header files that describe the COM interfaces found in the type library as C++ classes. You can control the content of these generated files with a set of optional #import attributes. When you use #import, you specify the name of the file containing the type library information (TLB, EXE, DLL).

#import creates two header files: the primary file with a .tlh extension, and a secondary file with the .tli extension. The primary header file is similar to the _i.c and .h files produced by the MIDL compiler, but with additional compiler-generated code and data. The secondary header file contains the implementations for compiler-generated member functions and is included in the primary header file. The most important code in the primary TLH is a set of smart pointer declarations. The TLH also contains initializations of the named GUID constants. These are names of the form CLSID_CoClass and IID_Interface, similar to those generated by the MIDL compiler.

The bulk of the code in the TLH is enclosed in a namespace with its name specified by the library statement in the original IDL file. You can use the names from the type library header either by an explicit qualification with the namespace name or by including a `namespace` statement immediately after the `#import` statement in the source code. The namespace can be suppressed by using the `no_namespace` attribute of the `#import` directive. However, suppressing the namespace may lead to name collisions. The namespace can also be renamed with the `rename_namespace` attribute.

✦ `uuid` — This makes the compiler attach a GUID to a class or structure declared or defined (full COM object definitions only) with the `uuid` attribute. The `uuid` attribute takes a string as its argument. This string names a GUID in normal registry format with or without the { } delimiters. Here are a couple of examples of that. (Note that you must define a GUID on a single line, but these are line-broken here for book formatting purposes.)

```
struct declspec(uuid("00000000-0000-0000-
c000-000000000046")) IUnknown;

struct __declspec(uuid("{00020400-0000-0000-
c000-000000000046}")) IDispatch;
```

This attribute can be applied in a redeclaration. This allows the system headers to supply the definitions of interfaces such as `IUnknown`, and the redeclaration in some other header (such as `comdef.h`) to supply the GUID.

✦ `property` — This attribute can be applied to nonstatic virtual data members in a class or structure definition. The compiler treats these virtual data members as data members by changing their references into function calls.

When the compiler sees a data member declared with this attribute on the right of a member-selection operator, it converts the operation to a `get` or `put` function, depending on whether such an expression is an l-value or an r-value. In more complicated contexts, such as +=, a rewrite is performed by doing both `get` and `put`. For example, if you have a property called `price` in your COM object, the TLH would include code like this. (Note once again that the line is broken due to the formatting restrictions of the book.)

```
declspec(property(get=GetPrice,put=PutPrice))
short Price;
```

This could then be used in the client code like this:

```
TheObject.Price = 3;    // translated to:
// TheObject.PutPrice(3);
x = TheObject.Price;    // translated to:
// x = TheObject.GetPrice();
```

✦ `__uuidof` — The `__uuidof` keyword retrieves the GUID attached to the expression. The expression can be a type name, a pointer, reference, or array of that type, a template specialized on these types, or a variable of these types. The argument is valid as long as the compiler can use it to find the attached GUID. A special case is when either 0 or `NULL` is supplied as argument. In this case, `__uuidof` returns a GUID made up of zeros.

✦ `_com_error` — A `_com_error` object represents an exception condition detected by the error-handling wrapper functions in the header files generated from the type library or by one of the COM support classes. The `_com_error` class encapsulates the `HRESULT` error code and any associated `IErrorInfo` object.

✦ _com_ptr_t—The template class _com_ptr_t is a smart-pointer implementation that encapsulates interface pointers and eliminates the need to call AddRef, Release, or QueryInterface. In addition, it hides the CoCreateInstance call in creating a new COM object. These smart pointer classes are generated via the _COM_SMARTPTR_TYPEDEF macro. For example, for interface IFoo, the .tlh file will contain:

```
__COM_SMARTPTR_TYPEDEF(IFoo, __uuidof(IFoo));
```

The compiler expands this to the following (split into two lines for book formatting):

```
typedef _com_ptr_t<com_IIID<IFoo, __
    uuidof(IFoo)> > IFooPtr;
```

Type IFooPtr can then be used in place of the raw interface pointer IFoo*.

✦ _variant_t—A _variant_t object encapsulates the VARIANT data type. The class manages resource allocation and deallocation, and makes function calls to VariantInit and VariantClear as appropriate.

✦ _bstr_t—A _bstr_t object encapsulates the BSTR data type. The class manages resource allocation and deallocation, via function calls to SysAllocString and SysFreeString, and other BSTR APIs when appropriate. The _bstr_t class uses reference counting to avoid excessive overhead.

So, you could change the client to read the server's binary type library, thus finally eliminating all source code dependencies.

First, remove the CreditServer_i.c from the client project, and remove the #include for the server's header file. Replace this with an #import for the server's binary type library:

```
// TestCreditObject.cpp
#include "stdafx.h"
// #include "..\CreditServer\CreditServer\CreditServer_h.h"
#import
"..\CreditServerTypeLib\CreditServer\Debug\CreditServer.tlb"
\
    no_namespace named_guids
```

Then, in the _tmain function, remove the raw ICreditVerification pointer, and all code that uses it, and replace it with an #import-generated ICreditVerificationPtr smart pointer object:

```
int _tmain(int argc, _TCHAR* argv[])
{
  CoInitialize(NULL);
/*  ICreditVerification* p = NULL;

  HRESULT hr = CoCreateInstance(CLSID_CreditVerification,
                                NULL,
                                CLSCTX_SERVER,
                                IID_ICreditVerification,
                                (void**)&p);
  if (FAILED(hr))
    cout << "Failed to create server\n";
  else
  {
    p->SetCardType((unsigned char*)"MasterCard");
    if (p->VerifyCardNumber(1234) == S_OK)
```

```
            MessageBox(0, "Card Verified", "OK", 0);
        else
            MessageBox(0, "Card Rejected", 0, 0);

        p->Release();
    }
*/
    try
    {
        ICreditVerificationPtr p(CLSID_CreditVerification);
        p->SetCardType("MasterCard");
        if (p->VerifyCardNumber(1234) == S_OK)
            MessageBox(0, "Card Verified", "OK", 0);
        else
            MessageBox(0, "Card Rejected", 0, 0);
    }
    catch(_com_error& e)
    {
        MessageBox(0, e.ErrorMessage(), 0, 0);
    }

    CoUninitialize();
}
```

Note The smart pointer code is placed within a `try` block because any failed HRESULT values are converted to `_com_error` exceptions.

As you can see, the Microsoft C++ compiler extensions — especially the `#import` and the `_com_ptr_t` smartpointer class — make client-side COM code a breeze.

EXE Servers and marshaling

That's two pieces of the puzzle: You now know how to build a type library on the server side, and how to use it on the client side. The third piece is how the COM runtime DLLs make use of the type library during marshaling. To explore how this works, you'll write an EXE version of your COM object server — this way, you'll force the runtime to use marshaling, because the client and server will now reside in different process spaces. The only differences between the DLL version and the EXE version are explained in the following paragraphs.

The EXE version doesn't need a `.def` file, or any of the exported DLL functions. You'll retain the internal registry functions, however, and there'll be one small change to your internal `RegisterServer` function:

```
    setKeyAndValue(szKey, "LocalServer32", szModule);
```

Because you don't need `DllCanUnloadNow`, you also don't need a global count of objects, so the `g_cComponents` variable and all references to it can be removed. On the other hand, you'll use the object destructor to terminate the server (this is somewhat draconian, but it'll serve your purposes here):

```
    // long g_cComponents = 0;

    CCreditVerification::CCreditVerification() : m_refCount(1)
    {
```

```
// InterlockedIncrement(&g_cComponents);
}

CCreditVerification::~CCreditVerification()
{
// InterlockedDecrement(&g_cComponents);
   PostQuitMessage(0);
}
```

If you want the COM runtime to be capable of using type library marshaling, you have to restrict your interface methods to parameters that are known in the standard marshaler (oleaut32.dll), and enforce this in your IDL code by flagging the interface as automation-conformant:

```
[uuid (cbb27840-836d-11d1-b990-0080c824b323), oleautomation]
interface ICreditVerification : IUnknown
{
...
```

Now for the WinMain. As an out-of-process server, you have to call CoInitialize and CoUninitialize. You also need to instantiate and register a class factory (with COM runtime, not in the registry), and then continue about your normal business (with a regular message pump), and finally revoke the registration of the class factory as shown in the following example:

```
// CreditServerOP.cpp
int APIENTRY WinMain(HINSTANCE hInstance,
                     HINSTANCE hPrevInstance,
                     LPSTR lpCmdLine,
                     int nCmdShow)
{
   MSG msg;
   HRESULT hr;
   DWORD dw;
   CCreditObjectFactory f;

   CoInitialize(NULL);

   hr = CoRegisterClassObject(CLSID_CreditVerification, &f,
      CLSCTX_SERVER, REGCLS_MULTIPLEUSE, &dw);
   if (FAILED(hr))
      exit(hr);

   while (GetMessage(&msg,NULL,0,0))
   {
      TranslateMessage(&msg);
      DispatchMessage(&msg);
   }

   CoRevokeClassObject(dw);
   CoUninitialize();

   return 0;
}
```

To provide for registering and unregistering, the normal behavior is to take in command-line arguments such as /RegServer and /UnregServer. To accommodate these, you can add this function:

```
LPCTSTR FindOneOf(LPCTSTR p1, LPCTSTR p2)
{
    while (p1 != NULL && *p1 != NULL)
    {
        LPCTSTR p = p2;
        while (p != NULL && *p != NULL)
        {
            if (*p1 == *p)
                return CharNext(p1);
            p = CharNext(p);
        }
        p1 = CharNext(p1);
    }
    return NULL;
}
```

You can then call this function in WinMain:

```
int APIENTRY WinMain(HINSTANCE hInstance,
                     HINSTANCE hPrevInstance,
                     LPSTR lpCmdLine,
                     int nCmdShow)
{
    MSG msg;
    HRESULT hr;
    DWORD dw;
    CCreditObjectFactory f;

    // Have you been invoked just to update the registry?
    TCHAR szTokens[] = _T("-/");
    BOOL bRun = TRUE;
    LPCTSTR lpszToken = FindOneOf(lpCmdLine, szTokens);

    while (lpszToken != NULL)
    {
        if (lstrcmpi(lpszToken, _T("UnregServer"))==0)
        {
            UnRegisterTypeLib(LIBID_CreditLibrary,
1,0, 0x00, SYS_WIN32);
            UnregisterServer(CLSID_CreditVerification,
                g_szVerIndProgID, g_szProgID);
            bRun = FALSE;
            break;
        }
        if (lstrcmpi(lpszToken, _T("RegServer"))==0)
        {
            RegisterTypeLibrary (hInstance, LIBID_CreditLibrary,
                1,0, 0x00, "CreditServer.tlb");
            RegisterServer(hInstance, CLSID_CreditVerification,
                g_szNiceName, g_szVerIndProgID, g_szProgID);
```

```
            bRun = FALSE;
            break;
        }
        lpszToken = FindOneOf(lpszToken, szTokens);
    }

    if (bRun)
    {
        CoInitialize(NULL);

        hr = CoRegisterClassObject(CLSID_CreditVerification,
                                    &f,
                                    CLSCTX_SERVER,
                                    REGCLS_MULTIPLEUSE,
                                    &dw);

        if (FAILED(hr))
            exit(hr);

        while (GetMessage(&msg,NULL,0,0))
        {
            TranslateMessage(&msg);
            DispatchMessage(&msg);
        }

        CoRevokeClassObject(dw);
        CoUninitialize();
    }

    return 0;
}
```

You can test this again with your client, and everything should work as before. On the other hand, if you don't register the server's type library, you'll get an "Invalid pointer" exception thrown from the client's `try` block when you try to use the `ICreditVerificationPtr` smart pointer, because it won't have succeeded in instantiating the server.

Custom interfaces and proxy-stub DLLs

Recall that you were careful to flag your interface as `oleautomation` in the IDL, so that the COM runtime reading the type library knows that it can use the standard marshaling code in `oleaut32.dll`. But what happens if you remove the `oleautomation` attribute? You'd be back to an "Invalid pointer" exception — the object won't be instantiated, because COM decides that it can't use the standard marshaler, and because it's an out-of-process server, marshaling is mandatory, so COM just fails to instantiate the object.

Does this mean you can only ever use automation-conformant parameters in your interface methods? No, it doesn't. You can use any parameters you like, as long as you build your own proxy-stub marshaling code. You can build this code either into your main server module or in a separate DLL, and this DLL must be registered against the custom interface(s) you want to use it for. You'll be relieved to hear that although the marshaling code is not completely trivial and does make use of lower-level RPC functions, it is relatively easy to produce.

Recall that when you submit a COM IDL file to MIDL you get a binary `.tlb` file, and C/C++ source code in a `.h` and an `_i.c` file. Although I haven't mentioned it before, you also get two other C/C++ source files: a _p.c file and a file called dlldata.c. To build a custom proxy-stub DLL, all you have to do is build all four C++ source files together, and register the resulting DLL.

For simplicity, you can create a new Win32 DLL project (and perhaps add it to the server solution workspace, although this is optional). Then, add all four C++ source files to the project. You also need a .def file with these entries:

```
LIBRARY        CSProxyStubDLL
EXPORTS
    DllGetClassObject       PRIVATE
    DllCanUnloadNow         PRIVATE
    GetProxyDllInfo         PRIVATE
    DllRegisterServer       PRIVATE
    DllUnregisterServer     PRIVATE
```

The properties for the proxy-stub DLL project should include the additional preprocessor definitions shown in Figure 28-5.

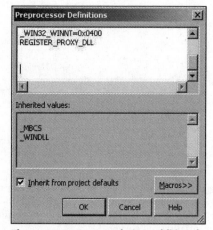

Figure 28-5: Proxy-stub DLL additional definitions

You also need to link with the RPC and OLEAUT32 import libraries, as shown in Figure 28-6.

After building the proxy-stub DLL, don't forget to register it. When you check in the registry for this, you need to be looking under CLSID for the ID of the custom interface, because it's the interface that needs the custom proxy-stub marshaling, not the object as a whole.

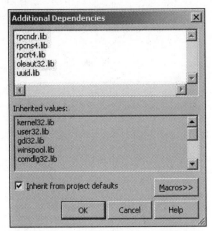

Figure 28-6: Proxy-stub DLL additional imports

Summary

In this chapter you saw how the COM runtime supports the notion of language independence and location transparency by allowing clients written in any language to correctly invoke functions on server objects written in any other language.

For your server, you can build and register a type library that clients can then read in a language-neutral fashion to discover the interfaces supported by your server, and the signatures of those interfaces.

The primary mechanism for ensuring that parameters (including out-parameter return values) are correctly passed back and forth is called marshaling. For certain known data types (such as the automation-conformant types), the COM DLLs contain standard marshaling code. The COM DLLs can also make use of a registered type library to work out how to marshal parameters. Finally, you can build and register your own custom marshaling code for your interface using C++ source code generated as targets from your IDL.

✦   ✦   ✦

Threading in COM

Armed with knowledge of COM marshaling, you can now turn your attention to COM threading and the apartment model. The creation, termination, and synchronization of threads is a standard Win32 pattern, and the functions you call to achieve this (CreateThread or _beginthreadex) are no different in a COM environment. However, remember that a COM environment features extreme disconnection between client and server — each has only very limited knowledge of the other. Therefore, you have to be a little more careful when using multiple threads under COM.

In the following pages, you'll see how the apartment model has been designed to optimize performance and scalability when using COM objects from multiple threads. I'll explain the different types of apartments and how DLL and EXE servers specify which type of apartment they wish to use. Finally, you'll learn about the Free-Theaded Marshaler and discover why you probably shouldn't use it.

The Apartment Model

In COM, the threading architecture divides COM objects contained in a process into logical groups called *apartments*. An apartment is a logical boundary that contains COM object instances and one or more threads. When a thread initializes COM with a call to CoInitialize or CoInitializeEx, an apartment is created.

The threads in an apartment that create and call COM objects are considered to be in the same apartment. Only those threads can have direct access to the COM objects. Threads in different apartments must access the COM objects through *marshaling*.

Out-of-process servers explicitly decide their apartment type by calling CoInitializeEx with either COINIT_APARTMENTTHREADED or COINIT_MULTITHREADED. This doesn't work for in-process servers, because the client will have already called CoInitializeEx by the time the new object is created. To allow in-process servers to control their apartment type, COM allows each CLSID to have its own distinct threading model that is advertised in the local registry using the ThreadingModel named value. COM supports four *Threading Models*, as described in Table 29-1.

Table 29-1: COM's Threading Models

Registry Key	Description
(None)	The absence of a `ThreadingModel` value implies that the class is completely thread-ignorant and can only run in the main single-threaded apartment (STA) in a process. The main STA is defined as the first STA to be created in the process via a call to `CoInitializeEx` with `COINIT_APARTMENTTHREADED`. This is the case for older servers that existed before apartment threading models were introduced. The single-threading model is essentially one STA.
Apartment	Supports the STA model: The class can execute in any STA in the process (not just the main STA), but cannot execute in the multithreaded apartment (MTA).
Free	Supports the MTA model only: The class can execute only in an MTA and can never execute in an STA. A free-threaded model, also known as a *multithreaded apartment model,* provides the most benefits, but it requires more work to create thread-safe objects.
Both	Supports the STA and MTA models: The class can execute in either an MTA or any STA in the process. If the client thread that calls `CoCreateInstance` is an STA thread type, the server will be used under the STA model. If the client thread is an MTA thread type, the server will be used under the MTA model. The server avoids marshaling for mixed models, but more work is required to create thread-safe objects.

The `ThreadingModel` registry entry for the `CreditVerification` object is shown in Figure 29-1. (The CreditVerification project was first introduced in Chapter 27 and is augmented in this chapter.) As you can see, the threading model is set to Apartment.

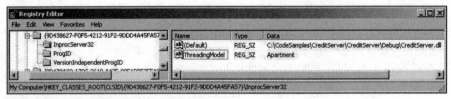

Figure 29-1: ThreadingModel Registry entry

STAs and MTAs

A single-threaded apartment has only one thread that creates and calls objects. Because there is only one thread that can access those objects in the apartment, the objects are effectively synchronized.

STAs provide better throughput than single-threaded applications. You can use the STA model to write more efficient code. At the same time as a thread in one STA waits for an operation to finish, another STA can allow the interim execution of a thread in another STA.

When a thread calls `CoInitialize` or `CoInitializeEx` with `COINIT_APARTMENTTHREADED`, it is a single-threaded apartment. A thread that is initialized as an STA is known as an *STA thread type*. COM objects that are instantiated by an STA thread type can only be accessed by that thread. This protects COM objects from being accessed by multiple threads simultaneously.

A multithreaded apartment is also referred to as the *free-threading model*. In this model, multiple threads can reside in one apartment. Multithreaded apartments provide the highest performance.

All threads that call CoInitalizeEx with COINIT_MULTITHREADED live in a single MTA, and are known as *MTA thread types*. Unlike the STA model, there is only one MTA per process. When additional MTA threads are initialized as MTA thread types, they live in the same apartment. In addition, there is no need to marshal between threads.

COM objects that are created by MTA thread types must be thread-safe, and must provide their own synchronization code. By removing the bottleneck that is created by marshaling, MTAs provide the highest performance and throughput on the server side.

MTA objects can receive concurrent calls from multiple out-of-process clients through a pool of COM-created threads that belong to the object's process.

In the MTA model, any thread can call a COM object concurrently, and COM does not synchronize the calls. Because synchronization is not provided, COM objects written for an MTA must be thread-safe. Therefore, static, global, and other shared variables must be protected by using synchronization objects such as events, mutexes, and semaphores.

Client/Server threading

In practical terms, specifying STA or MTA for your client or server thread has the consequences listed in Table 29-2.

Table 29-2: Specifying STA or MTA

	STA (Apartment)	MTA (Free)	Both
Client Thread	The thread declares that it will not allow any COM objects that it uses to be accessed directly from other threads. Therefore it is safe to use nonthread-safe COM objects.	The thread declares that it will allow any COM objects it uses to be accessed directly from other threads. Therefore these COM objects must be thread-safe.	n/a
COM Object	The object assumes that it can only be accessed through one thread. Therefore it is not necessarily thread-safe.	The object assumes that it might be accessed through multiple threads "simultaneously." Therefore the object must be thread-safe.	When acting as a client to other COM objects, the object does not allow any COM objects that it uses to be accessed directly from other threads. Therefore these other objects don't need to be thread-safe. When acting as a server, the object assumes that it can be accessed through multiple threads simultaneously. Therefore the object must itself be thread-safe.

Note that threading models still apply to local (out-of-process) servers, even though communication with objects in these servers will always be marshaled because of the process boundary. A local server object will have an inproc client, which is its standard marshaling stub. If the local object is thread-safe, COM can allow multiple (out-of-proc) clients to access the same interface through stubs on separate threads (for speed). It then follows that the Both model does not apply to out-of-proc objects.

Mixed-model threading

For in-process servers, if a client thread initializes as an STA thread type, and the server supports only a single STA (that is, the ThreadingModel value is absent), the main thread that creates objects on the server will have direct access to all of those objects. However, only one object can be accessed at a time; multiple objects cannot run concurrently, nor will multiple accesses to a single object be concurrent. COM will automatically serialize all calls into the STA through a hidden window message queue, as shown in Figure 29-2.

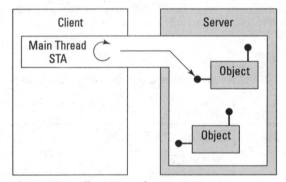

Figure 29-2: Client STA and server STA

If the client creates additional MTA threads, COM will automatically marshal their object calls through a proxy-stub to the main STA thread. This ensures that the objects in the STA are synchronized, because the main thread can receive only one method call at a time from the caller. Simultaneous calls from multiple threads are queued by the marshaling code until the main thread can process them, as shown in Figure 29-3.

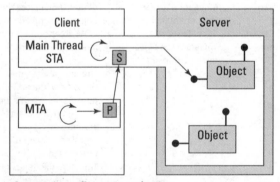

Figure 29-3: Client STA and MTA

If a server supports multiple STAs (that is, the `ThreadingModel` has a value of Apartment), each client thread that is initialized as an STA thread type will be capable of creating and accessing objects on the server directly. Each STA thread will have its own apartment, and each object in each apartment will still be synchronized. Again, if additional MTA threads are created, COM will automatically marshal their object calls through a proxy-stub to the main STA thread, as shown in Figure 29-4.

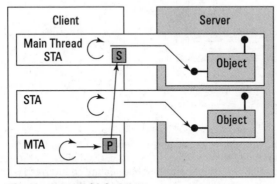

Figure 29-4: Multiple STAs

If a client thread initializes as an STA thread type, but the server supports only MTA threads (that is, the `ThreadingModel` has a value of Free), COM will automatically marshal calls by the STA thread through a proxy-stub. This is necessary because the server might report events or make callbacks. Any server callbacks to the client must be synchronized because the objects in the client exist in a single-threaded apartment, as shown in Figure 29-5.

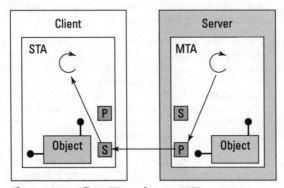

Figure 29-5: Client STA and server MTA

Note   The same would be true if the server initializes as STA and the client as MTA; you would still have a pair of proxy-stubs marshaling between them.

If a client thread initializes as an MTA thread type, and the server supports MTA, COM does not provide any synchronization. Because any thread that is initialized as an MTA type can call any object on the server directly, the server must synchronize its COM objects to prevent data corruption, as shown in Figure 29-6.

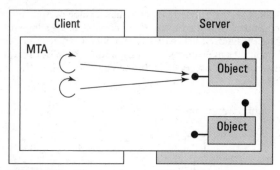

Figure 29-6: Client and server MTA

Thread Marshaling

Threads that want to use a COM object that resides in another apartment must have the interface pointers of the object marshaled to them. To support this, COM allows interfaces to be exported from one apartment and imported into another. Marshaling an interface pointer transforms it into a transmissible byte stream whose contents uniquely identify the interface (IPID), the implementing object (OID), and its exporting apartment (OXID). When an interface is imported, the result is a pointer to a proxy that can be legally accessed by any thread in the importing apartment.

COM uses window messages to synchronize multiple threads to marshal an interface pointer to other threads. Each STA thread type has a message loop that receives marshaled calls from other processes and other apartments in the same process. When a client makes a call to a server object, the marshaling code places a corresponding window message in the server thread's message queue. Multiple thread calls are queued in the message queue while the object's STA thread type processes each message, one at a time.

Normally, interface pointers are marshaled automatically by the COM DLLs. For example, if a client thread initializes as an MTA thread type, but the server supports only STA, COM automatically marshals calls by the client through a proxy-stub. However, sometimes you might want to marshal interfaces explicitly from one apartment to another. For example, if the client creates additional STA threads, and wants to use the same server object with these threads as well as the main MTA thread, the interface pointer will need marshaling. The COM API supplies a small set of functions to support explicit marshaling. You would use `CoMarshalInterThreadInterfaceInStream` to marshal an interface pointer into a stream object. This stream object can then be passed to another thread. The second thread can call `CoGetInterfaceAndReleaseStream` to unmarshal the stream and obtain an apartment-relative interface pointer appropriate for use in the second thread, as shown in Figure 29-7.

Note　The function `CoMarshalInterThreadInterfaceInStream` is actually a thin wrapper to `CreateStreamOnHGlobal` and `CoMarshalInterface`, whereas `CoGetInterfaceAndReleaseStream` is a wrapper to `CoUnmarshalInterface`.

For example, using a DLL (and ole automation-conformant) version of the CreditVerification server (which registers as STA) you first saw in Chapter 27, you could write a client that initializes its main thread as MTA, and then creates a second STA thread. The client's main MTA thread could instantiate a `CreditVerification` object on the server. Then, the client chooses to share its COM object interface pointer with its second (STA) thread. In order to do this safely, the client uses `CoMarshalInterThreadInterfaceInStream`.

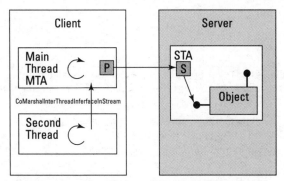

Figure 29-7: CoMarshalInterThreadInterfaceInStream

You need to make the following changes to your earlier client. First, in the Project properties (or at the top of the CPP file with `main` in it), define the preprocessor symbol `_WIN32_DCOM`— this gives you access to `CoInitializeEx` (shown in Figure 29-8).

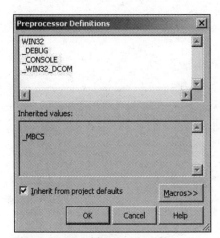

Figure 29-8: Adding support for CoInitializeEx

In `main`, declare a handle for the second thread, and an `IStream` pointer:

```
HANDLE tH;
IStream* pIS;
```

Then call `CoInitializeEx` with `COINIT_MULTITHREADED`, instead of `CoInitialize`. Next, having declared and initialized the `ICreditVerification` smart pointer, create the second thread and marshal the interface to it (you'll write the `AnotherThread` function in a minute):

```
HRESULT hr = CoMarshalInterThreadInterfaceInStream(
  IID_ICreditVerification, p, &pIS);
if (FAILED(hr))
  _com_issue_error(hr);

DWORD tID;
```

```
tH = CreateThread(0,
   0,
   (LPTHREAD_START_ROUTINE)AnotherThread,
   (void*)pIS, 0, &tID);
```

Next, continue in `main`, and use the `ICreditVerification` pointer as normal. Finally, just before the call to `CoUninitialize`, call `WaitForSingleObject(tH, INFINITE)` to ensure the second thread has stopped before exiting.

Now write the second thread's controlling function, `AnotherThread`. First, call `CoInitializeEx` with `COINIT_APARTMENTTHREADED`. Then call `CoGetInterfaceAndReleaseStream` to extract the `ICreditVerification` pointer from the stream passed in to the function:

```
void __stdcall AnotherThread(IStream* pIS)
{
   // STA second thread
   HRESULT hr = CoInitializeEx(NULL,
                 COINIT_APARTMENTTHREADED);
   try
   {
      ICreditVerificationPtr p;
      hr = CoGetInterfaceAndReleaseStream(pIS,
         IID_ICreditVerification, (void**)&p);
      if (FAILED(hr))
         _com_issue_error(hr);

      p->SetCardType("Visa");
      if (p->VerifyCardNumber(5678) == S_OK)
         MessageBox(0, "AnotherThread: Card Verified",
"OK", 0);
      else
         MessageBox(0, "AnotherThread: Card Rejected", 0, 0);
   }
   catch (_com_error &e)
   {
      cout << "AnotherThread: " << e.ErrorMessage() << "\n";
   }

   CoUninitialize();
}
```

MEOW packets

When you use `CoMarshalInterThreadInterfaceInStream`, a MEOW packet is what gets put into the stream. Once marshaled into an NDR (Network Data Representation) data packet, an interface pointer is a symbolic representation of access to an object, and thus is simply an object reference. The wire representation of a marshaled interface pointer uses the `MInterfacePointer` struct:

```
typedef struct tagMInterfacePointer {
   ULONG          ulCntData; // size of data
   byte           abData[];  // [size_is(ulCntData)]
                             // data
} MInterfacePointer, *PMInterfacePointer;
```

The second member of this struct contains the actual object reference in a struct called an OBJREF. The OBJREF struct assumes one of three forms, depending on the type of marshaling being employed: standard, handler, or custom:

```
typedef struct tagOBJREF {
  unsigned long  signature; // Always MEOW
  unsigned long  flags;     // OBJREF flags
  GUID           iid;       // interface identifier

  union
  {
  // [switch_is(flags), switch_type(unsigned long)]
   struct { // [case(OBJREF_STANDARD)]
    STDOBJREF std; // standard objref
    DUALSTRINGARRAY saResAddr; // resolver address
   } u_standard;

   struct { // [case(OBJREF_HANDLER)]
    STDOBJREF std; // standard objref
    CLSID clsid; // Clsid of handler code
    DUALSTRINGARRAY saResAddr; // resolver address
   } u_handler;

   struct { // [case(OBJREF_CUSTOM)]
    CLSID clsid; // Clsid of unmarshaling code
    unsigned long cbExtension; // size of extension data
    unsigned long size; // size of data that follows
    byte  *pData; // extension + class specific data
    // [size_is(size), ref]
   } u_custom;
  } u_objref;
} OBJREF;
```

Note that the OBJREF structure begins with a signature field defined as the unsigned long hexadecimal value 0x574F454D. If you arrange this value in little-endian format (4D 45 4F 57), and then convert each byte to its ASCII equivalent, the resulting characters spell MEOW. Some people think that this is why the data packet is called MEOW. Others believe that MEOW stands for Microsoft Extended Object Wire representation. However, no one knows for sure. The important thing is how it's defined and what it represents.

For standard marshaling (the simplest case), the inner struct within the OBJREF consists of a struct of type STDOBJREF and a struct of type DUALSTRINGARRAY. Here's the STDOBJREF struct:

```
typedef struct tagSTDOBJREF {
  unsigned long flags; // SORF_ flags
  unsigned long cPublicRefs; // count of references passed
  OXID oxid; // oxid of server with this oid
  OID oid; // oid of object with this ipid
  IPID ipid; // ipid of Interface
} STDOBJREF;
```

Of primary interest is the third field. This is a hyper (64-bit integer): the OXID (Object Exporter Identifer) identifies the server that owns the object (and, effectively, the apartment).

So, with a bit of tinkering in memory, you ought to be able to find out the apartment ID for any thread. Although this information is not normally of any use to you, there is in fact an API that pulls the contents of an IStream into a block of global memory—which certainly makes it easy to examine in the debugger at runtime. This API is GetHGlobalFromStream. In the following example, you will continue with your CoMarshalInterThreadInterfaceInStream project to experiment with this information. First, you need to add a new member variable to the CCreditVerification class:

```
ULARGE_INTEGER m_uliOXID;
```

Initialize this in the constructor:

```
CCreditVerification::CCreditVerification() : m_refCount(1)
{
    InterlockedIncrement(&g_cComponents);

    HGLOBAL hG = 0;
    CComPtr<IStream> pS;
    HRESULT hr = CoMarshalInterThreadInterfaceInStream(
        IID_IUnknown, this, &pS);
  if (SUCCEEDED(hr))
  {
        hr = GetHGlobalFromStream(pS, &hG);
        if (SUCCEEDED(hr))
        {
            BYTE* pG = (BYTE*)GlobalLock(hG);

            WORD w1 = MAKEWORD(pG[32], pG[33]);
            WORD w2 = MAKEWORD(pG[34], pG[35]);
            m_uliOXID.LowPart = MAKELONG(w1, w2);

            w1 = MAKEWORD(pG[36], pG[37]);
            w2 = MAKEWORD(pG[38], pG[39]);
            m_uliOXID.HighPart = MAKELONG(w1, w2);

            GlobalUnlock(hG);
        }
    }
}
```

You could add a method to access the OXID, called GetApartmentID for example, and others for the OID, IPID, and perhaps ThreadID. For now, just examine the contents of the global memory block that contains the MEOW packet. Set a breakpoint on the constructor and step in until the pG pointer to global memory has a value. Then examine the Locals window (shown in Figure 29-9).

The frumious FTM

One of the least understood and potentially most problematic features offered by the COM runtime support is the Free-Threaded Marshaler (FTM). This is a Microsoft-supplied COM object that allows an object to marshal interface pointers between threads in the same process. This is intended for use by free-threaded DLL servers that must be accessed directly by all threads in a process, even those threads associated with STAs. It custom-marshals the real memory pointer into other apartments as a fake proxy to give direct access to all callers, even if they are not free-threaded.

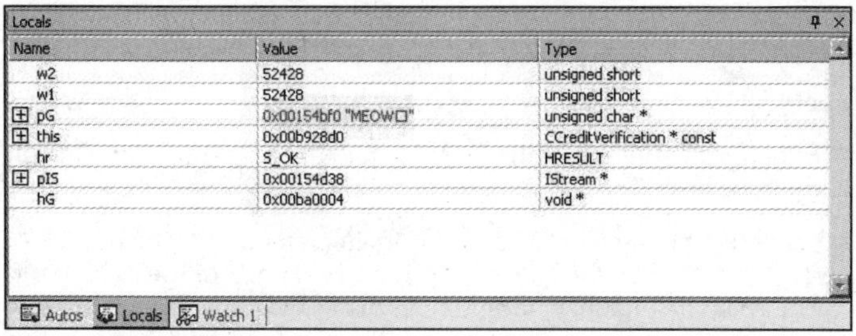

Figure 29-9: MEOW packets

The purpose of the FTM is to allow thread-safe objects to bypass the standard marshaling that occurs whenever cross-apartment interface functions are invoked. To achieve this, the FTM implements `IMarshal`, and you aggregate the FTM to your object. That is, you set up your COM object such that when it is created it also creates the FTM behind the scenes and exposes the FTM's interfaces as if they were your object's interfaces. The COM runtime DLLs query all objects for `IMarshal` up front to see if the object wants to do its own marshaling in place of the system-supplied marshaling. So, aggregating the FTM (and updating your `QueryInterface` to list `IMarshal` as a supported interface) allows you to make use of the custom marshaling inside the FTM. The designed result is that the FTM's custom marshaling can sometimes be faster than standard marshaling.

This is how it works: When a client asks the object for an interface, the COM runtime queries the object for `IMarshal`. If the object implements `IMarshal`, and the marshaling request is in process, the FTM copies the actual interface pointer into the marshaling packet. So the client actually gets a raw pointer to the object instead of a pointer to a proxy, as would normally be the case, thereby eliminating the proxy-stub performance overhead. Naturally, this strategy assumes you have made your object thread-safe, because multiple threads will potentially be accessing it without the benefit of any proxy-stub interception and synchronization. On receiving a call, the FTM performs the following tasks:

✦ Checks the destination context specified by the `CoMarshalInterface` function's `dwDestContext` parameter.

✦ If the destination context is `MSHCTX_INPROC`, the FTM copies the interface pointer into the marshaling stream.

✦ If the destination context is any other value, the FTM finds or creates an instance of COM's default (standard) marshaler and delegates marshaling to it.

Great care should be exercised in using the FTM because its basic behavior in fact breaks the rules of COM, allowing raw pointers to be used across apartments. This can be like a time bomb waiting to go off unless you make sure your object restricts its operations as follows:

✦ An object aggregating the FTM must not hold direct pointers to interfaces on an object that does not aggregate the FTM. If the object were to use direct references to ordinary single-threaded aggregate objects, it could break their single-threaded nature. If the object were to use direct references to ordinary multithreaded aggregate objects, these objects can behave in ways that show no sensitivity to the needs of direct single-threaded aggregate clients.

✦ An object aggregating the FTM must not hold references to proxies to objects in other apartments. Proxies are sensitive to the threading model and can return `RPC_E_WRONG_THREAD` if called by the wrong client.

If you do decide to aggregate the FTM, you can do so with the function `CoCreateFreeThreadedMarshaler`. This function performs the following tasks:

✦ Creates an FTM object.

✦ Aggregates this FTM to the object specified by the `punkOuter` parameter. This object is normally the one whose interface pointers are to be marshaled.

If the (outer) aggregating object implements `IMarshal`, its implementation of `IMarshal` should delegate `QueryInterface` calls for `IMarshal` to the `IUnknown` of the FTM. If the outer object doesn't implement `IMarshal` itself, it should nonetheless expose `IMarshal` as supported through its implementation of `QueryInterface`. The `CreditVerification` object aggregating the FTM would look like this:

```
class CCreditVerification : public ICreditVerification
{
private:
    IUnknown* m_pUnkMarshaler;
...

CCreditVerification::CCreditVerification() : m_refCount(1)
{
    InterlockedIncrement(&g_cComponents);
    CoCreateFreeThreadedMarshaler(this, &m_pUnkMarshaler);
}

HRESULT __stdcall CCreditVerification::QueryInterface(
REFIID iid, void**pp)
{
    HRESULT hr = E_NOINTERFACE;

    if (NULL == pp)
        return E_INVALIDARG;
    *pp = NULL;

    if (iid == IID_IUnknown)
        *pp = this;
    else if (iid == IID_ICreditVerification)
        *pp = static_cast<ICreditVerification*>(this);
    else if (iid == IID_IMarshal)
        hr = m_pUnkMarshaler->QueryInterface(IID_IMarshal, pp);

    if (*pp)
    {
        AddRef();
        return S_OK;
    }
    return hr;
}
```

You should also change the apartment type to Free or Both, because it doesn't make any sense to aggregate the FTM for an STA-model object:

```
    setKeyAndValue(szKey, "InprocServer32",
"ThreadingModel", "Free");
```

If you test this revised server object with your existing client, you should find that everything works fine, even though the client initializes as STA and the server as MTA.

Summary

If you've survived to the end of this chapter, you should now have a good understanding of the COM apartment threading model, including the reasons underlying the model, and how the model is implemented. You can now set the threading model type for each of your COM objects and client applications in the most appropriate way, given their intended usage.

You also learned how to marshal interface pointers from one client thread to another using `CoMarshalInterface` and the longest-named function in the API, `CoMarshalInterThreadInterfaceInStream`. Finally, you now also have an understanding of the Free-Threaded Marshaler — that bane of distributed componentized system developers — sufficient to determine when its use is sensible and safe, and when to leave it well alone.

✦　　✦　　✦

Introduction to ATL

Now that you've considered the purpose and design of the COM model, and the underlying mechanics of its implementation, you will probably recognize that manually coding all the necessary plumbing is likely to be tedious, repetitive, and error-prone. If you're not convinced of that, ponder for a moment the details of `QueryInterface`, `AddRef`, `Release`, class factory objects, DLL required exports, registry updating, factory and module locking, apartment threading models, aggregation support, error information propagation, and so on.

Convinced? Well, of course help is at hand. The *Active Template Library* is a library of template classes, implemented interfaces, macros, and the like designed specifically to support the developer in producing COM objects. This chapter discusses the two main ATL wizards (the ATL COM AppWizard and the ATL Object Wizard), and what they can do for you. I'll compare the wizard-generated code for both attributed and unattributed code, and I'll examine the relationships between your code and the various ATL library classes.

I'll also discuss how to extend the code generated by the wizards, how to support multiple objects within a server, and how to support multiple interfaces within an object. Finally, I'll work with the debugging and run-time error-propagation support provided by the ATL.

The Active Template Library

The ATL is a set of template-based C++ classes designed to allow the developer to easily create small, fast COM objects. It has special support for key COM features including standard server hosting code for both DLL and EXE servers; stock implementations of `IUnknown`, `IClassFactory`, and `IDispatch`; support for automation and dual interfaces; standard COM enumerator interfaces; connection points; tear-off interfaces; ActiveX controls; and a comprehensive set of support for all threading models.

The ATL is shipped both as source code that you include in your application, and as a DLL (`atl70.dll`), which you can link to dynamically if you prefer. There are two main wizards shipped with the ATL:

+ The ATL COM AppWizard, which generates code for a server host, according to a range of options you select

+ The ATL Object Wizard, which generates code for a wide range of COM objects, including standard objects, ActiveX controls, property pages, OLEDB consumers, and so on

Creating an ATL COM Application

You use the ATL COM AppWizard to create the skeleton code and necessary project files for an ATL project. The wizard also implements the code for the options you select. At this point, select File ➪ New ➪ Project. When the New Project dialog box is displayed (Figure 30-1), select the Visual C++ Projects project type and the ATL Project template. Enter a project name (such as SimpleServer), and click the OK button.

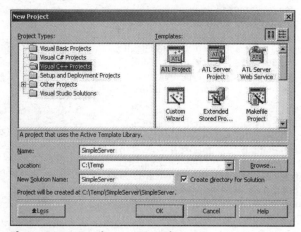

Figure 30-1: Creating an ATL project

The ATL Project Wizard will be invoked and its main dialog box will be displayed, showing an overview of the settings that will be used to create the project. As you can see on the left-hand side of the dialog box, there is only one set of options that you can modify—Application Settings. Click this link now to view the Application Settings you see in Figure 30-2.

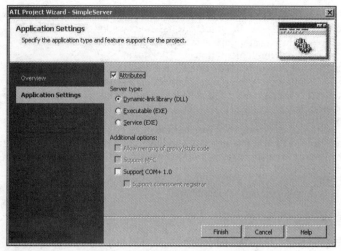

Figure 30-2: Accept the default application settings.

Although you should accept all the defaults for this chapter's first demo, I'll briefly outline the various settings here:

✦ *Attributed*—This setting is used to determine if the project will contain attributed code. Note that there's a bit of a trade-off here involving attributes. Attributes are an extremely useful feature introduced in Visual C++ .NET that greatly simplify COM and ATL development by enabling you to attach textual annotations to classes and members that define their runtime characteristics. The way this works is that when you include attributes in your source files, the compiler works with provider dynamic-link libraries (DLL) to insert code or modify the code in the generated object files. Because the demo will use attributes, you'll see that as we progress through the chapter. Now for the bad news. If you do choose to use attributes, you must be cognizant of the fact that an attributed project does not allow support for MFC code or the merging of proxy/stub code. I'll talk about the significance of these two options shortly. *Nonattributed* code is discussed in the section "Working with nonattributed code."

✦ *Server Type*—The next option is the server type option, which allows you to define the binary that will be output when you build your project. The following are the mutually exclusive settings for this option.

  • *Dynamic Link Library (DLL)*—Creates an in-process COM object server. This creates the fastest ATL code, and COM+ requires the object to be hosted in a DLL server.

  • *Executable (EXE)*—Creates an out-of-process COM object server. This is appropriate if, for instance, your server can be launched stand-alone by a user as well as act as a server to COM client applications.

  • *Service (EXE)*—Creates a Windows NT service maintained by the Service Control Manager.

✦ *Allow merging of proxy/stub code*—As mentioned earlier, attributed projects do not include support for the merging of proxy/stub code. Therefore, the only way to enable this option is to turn off Attributed option. Simply put, this option means that the MIDL-generated proxy and stub code will reside in the same DLL as the server. This is done as a convenience for situations where marshaling interfaces is required.

✦ *Support MFC*—The most obvious option to you at this point of the book, selecting this simply means that the project will include linkage to the MFC libraries so that your code can have access to the MFC classes and types that you've worked with throughout this book. Once again, you can only set this option if you turn off the Attributed option.

✦ *Support COM+ 1.0*—Selecting this option causes the wizard to add the `mtxguid.lib` and `comsvcs.lib` libraries to the project. In addition, if you select this option, you can also ask for your component to be capable of getting a list of components, and register or unregister components via the COM+ Component Registrar. This is done by selecting the Support component registrar option.

Click the Finish button to create your new ATL project. Next, you'll examine the code that the wizard generated in order to begin understanding the lay of the land with regards to ATL applications.

Examining the ATL application code

If you examine the ClassView pane in Visual Studio after the wizard has generated the code, you'll see that as with any COM DLL server, there are five exported functions: DllMain, DllCanUnloadNow, DllGetClassObject, DllRegisterServer, and DllUnregisterServer (see Figure 30-3).

Figure 30-3: ATL AppWizard-generated DLL project

At this point, open the CSimpleServerModule.cpp file to view the following code. What you see here is an example of attributed programming. The particular attributes cause the automatic generation of the DllMain, DllRegisterServer, and DllUnregisterServer functions for you.

```
// SimpleServer.cpp : Implementation of DLL Exports.

#include "stdafx.h"
#include "resource.h"

[ module(dll,
    uuid = "{29185547-E5E8-4D76-A56F-2D1273E2225A}",
  name = "SimpleServer",
  helpstring = "SimpleServer 1.0 Type Library",
  resource_name = "IDR_SIMPLESERVER") ];
```

Now, let's look at the five global exports that I referred to. In the Class View, if you double-click one of the entries under the Global Functions and Variables item, you'll find that the Visual Studio Object Browser is displayed. This tool, while useful in other scenarios, really doesn't do anything for you here because it's simply another way to present the same information already viewable in the Class View. Therefore, if you've opened the Object Browser, you can close it now.

Instead, what you want to do is to expand the module class in the Class View (called `CSimpleServerModule` in this demo). From there, expand the Bases and Interfaces item, and then the `CAtlDllModuleT<CSimpleServerModule>` entry. At this point, you will see the five global functions (along with a constructor, a destructor, and an implementation of the `GetClassObject` function). Double-clicking one of these functions will open that function in the editor. Let's briefly look at each function to see what's going on under the hood to set up your ATL component.

The first thing I'll look at is the `DllMain` function. This function has the standard code blocks that handle processes attaching and detaching from the DLL (represented by the handling of the `dwReason` argument having a value of either `DLL_PROCESS_ATTACH` or `DLL_PROCESS_DETACH`). There are really only two main things to note here. First, the code verifies that the ATL module initialization successfully occurred. If not, the application asserts (via a call to `ATLASSERT`) and the `DllMain` aborts (returns `FALSE`). On the `DLL_PROCESS_DETACH` side of things, `DllMain` calls the `_AtlWinModule.Term` function, which releases all module data members. So, nothing exceptional here. Just some initialization and cleanup code.

The second thing to notice is the call to the `DisableThreadLibraryCalls` function. This function enables a DLL to disable the standard `DLL_THREAD_ATTACH` and `DLL_THREAD_DETACH` notification calls (which is why you don't see those events being handled in this function). This can be a useful optimization for multithreaded applications that have many DLLs, frequently create and delete threads, and whose DLLs do not need these thread-level notifications of attachment or detachment. In these sorts of applications, DLL initialization routines often remain in memory to service `DLL_THREAD_ATTACH` and `DLL_THREAD_DETACH` notifications. By disabling the notifications, the DLL initialization code is not paged in because a thread is created or deleted, thus reducing the size of the application's working code set.

```
BOOL WINAPI DllMain(DWORD dwReason,
  LPVOID /* lpReserved */) throw()
{
 if (dwReason == DLL_PROCESS_ATTACH)
 {
  if (CAtlBaseModule::m_bInitFailed)
  {
   ATLASSERT(0);
   return FALSE;
  }
 #ifdef _ATL_MIN_CRT
  DisableThreadLibraryCalls
                 (AtlBaseModule.GetModuleInstance());
 #endif
 }
#ifdef _DEBUG
 else if (dwReason == DLL_PROCESS_DETACH)
 {
  // Prevent false memory leak reporting.
  // ~CAtlWinModule may be too late.
  _AtlWinModule.Term();
 }
#endif    // _DEBUG
 return TRUE;
}
```

All in all, there doesn't seem to be all that much going on in DllMain; mostly because much of the crucial work is actually done in the CAtlComModule constructor and destructor (from atlbase.h). I'll look at those functions next.

If you continue drilling down through the call path, you will see that the module's Init function walks the object map to call ObjectMain on each object, and the Term function performs the usual cleanup.

The object map is used by the _AtlModule class to maintain a set of class object definitions. The object map is implemented as an array of _ATL_OBJMAP_ENTRY structures. Each time you add a COM object to an ATL project, an entry is made in the object map. The object map contains information for the following:

✦ Entering and removing object descriptions in the system registry

✦ Instantiating objects through a class factory

✦ Establishing communication between a client and the root object of the component

✦ Performing lifetime management of class objects

The CAtlDllModuleT class maintains a global reference count on the server that keeps the DLL loaded as long as the count is nonzero. The lock count is incremented and decremented using Lock and Unlock. Typically, Lock is called when an object in the server is created, and Unlock is called when the object is destroyed.

```
CAtlComModule::CAtlComModule() throw()
{
 cbSize = sizeof(_ATL_COM_MODULE);

 m_hInstTypeLib = reinterpret_cast<HINSTANCE>(&_ImageBase);

 m_ppAutoObjMapFirst = &__pobjMapEntryFirst + 1;
 m_ppAutoObjMapLast = &__pobjMapEntryLast;

 if (FAILED(m_csObjMap.Init()))
 {
  ATLTRACE(atlTraceCOM, 0,
  _T("ERROR : Unable to initialize critical section "
     "in CAtlComModule\n"));
  ATLASSERT(0);
  CAtlBaseModule::m_bInitFailed = true;
 }
}

CAtlComModule::~CAtlComModule()
{
 Term();
}
```

The next function, DllCanUnloadNow, is fairly straightforward. This function, called in order to determine if the DLL can be unloaded from memory, simply determines if any objects are currently in use. If no objects are in use, the function returns S_OK indicating that the DLL can be unloaded. Conversely, if any objects are locked, the function returns S_FALSE, meaning that it is not safe to remove the DLL from memory.

```
HRESULT CAtlDllModuleT::DllCanUnloadNow() throw()
{
```

```
    T* pT = static_cast<T*>(this);
    return (pT->GetLockCount()==0) ? S_OK : S_FALSE;
}
```

When a client requests an object from the DLL, COM loads the DLL and calls DllMain with DLL_PROCESS_ATTACH as the dwReason argument. Among other things, the object gets cached in an object map. Once the DllMain function has returned, COM calls the DllGetClassObject function to get the class factory object for the requested COM object. DllGetClassObject then uses the cached object map pointer to iterate over the object map, scanning for the requested CLSID and returning that object.

```
HRESULT CAtlDllModuleT::DllGetClassObject(REFCLSID rclsid,
  REFIID riid,
  LPVOID* ppv) throw()
{
  T* pT = static_cast<T*>(this);

  return pT->GetClassObject(rclsid, riid, ppv);
}
```

If you follow the call sequence through the ATL source code, you'll see that the DllRegisterServer and DllUnregisterServer call into the CAtlComModule functions to register and unregister the server's objects, type library, and interfaces. The first (TRUE) parameter indicates that the type library will be registered or unregistered. The second optional parameter is the CLSID of a single object to register (as opposed to all objects). These functions use the registry script resources of the server's COM objects (to be created separately by the ATL Object Wizard).

```
HRESULT RegisterServer(BOOL bRegTypeLib = FALSE,
  const CLSID* pCLSID = NULL)
{
  return AtlComModuleRegisterServer(this,
                                    bRegTypeLib, pCLSID);
}

HRESULT UnregisterServer(BOOL bRegTypeLib = FALSE,
  const CLSID* pCLSID = NULL)
{
  return AtlComModuleUnregisterServer(this,
                                      bRegTypeLib, pCLSID);
}
```

Note that RegisterServer and UnregisterServer use the ATL registrar component to parse the registry scripts. The registrar is available prebuilt in the ATL DLL, or as statically linked code. Which one you're using depends on whether you have _ATL_STATIC_REGISTRY or _ATL_DLL defined. If you don't have _ATL_STATIC_REGISTRY defined, you default to using the DLL, which means you must distribute ATL DLL with your application and register it during installation.

Note that because you have not created any objects or interfaces, your project will not contain an IDL file as of yet. That will change in the next section when you add an object to the project.

Creating new ATL objects

After you generate an ATL project with the ATL COM AppWizard, you can add a COM object by using the ATL Object Wizard. For each COM object you add to your project, the ATL Object Wizard generates .cpp and .h files, as well as an .rgs file for script-based registry support.

At this point, add an ATL simple object to the project by invoking the Add Class dialog box and selecting the ATL entry in the Categories tree view. From there, select the ATL Simple Object template and click Open. The ATL Simple Object Wizard appears (Figure 30-4).

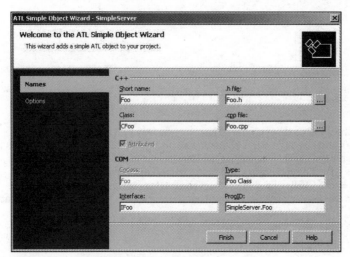

Figure 30-4: Naming the simple object

The first page of the ATL Simple Object Wizard allows you to specify the various names that define your object. For example, you can specify the C++ name that you'll use internally in your code, the Coclass name used by COM, the interface name used by the object's COM clients, and the filenames (header and implementation).

The first thing to notice is that the Attributed checkbox is disabled. This is because you selected the Attributed option when creating the project. Therefore, any objects you create for this project are going to be attributed. If you had selected not to use attributes in this project, this option would be available on an object-by-object basis.

Because you're just getting started with ATL, I'll keep the demo extremely simple. Type in a name of **Foo** for the Short name field. As you can see, the value entered here becomes the root for the other fields, including the C++ class name, the file names, and the COM information (such as interface and ProgID).

Note   The COM Coclass name cannot be modified if the object is attributed for the simple reason that the current implementation of ATL does not support the coclass attribute.

Now click the Options tab (Figure 30-5) to set the value that will be used to specify threading model, interface type, and any additional interface to support.

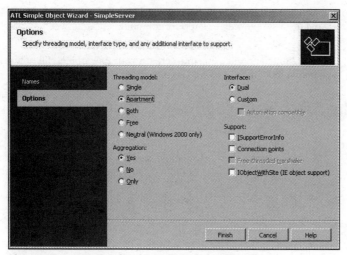

Figure 30-5: ATL Simple Object Wizard Options tab

The various options on this page are as follows:

✦ *Threading*—Because ATL is built on top of COM, the various threading models are the same as those covered in Chapter 29. The only thing specific to note about this section is that if you select the Neutral option (which is valid for Windows 2000 only) it means that the object follows the guidelines for multithreaded apartments, but it can execute on any kind of thread.

✦ *Aggregation*—The Aggregation option is used for objects that will choose which interfaces to expose to clients. The interfaces are then exposed as if the aggregate object implemented them. Clients of the aggregate object communicate only with the aggregate object. A value of No indicates that aggregation is not supported, whereas Yes (the default) means that aggregation is supported, but the object does not need to implement it. Selecting the Only option is done to specify that the object will be an aggregate object.

✦ *Interface*—The Interface option enables you to specify whether the object will support a dual-interface so that agnostic clients such as scripting languages can use your object through Automation. The subject of ATL Automation is covered in Chapter 33.

✦ *Support*—As you can see, this is a catchall group for several options. The first of these options is used to govern whether you want the object to support the ISupportErrorInfo interface. This interface enables objects to return error information to the client and is covered in the section "Implementing the ATL ISupportErrorInfo Interface."

The Connection points option deals with defining how your object will work with raising events with its clients. The topics of connection points and eventing are covered in Chapter 32.

Selecting the Free-threaded marshaler (FTM) option creates an FTM object to marshal interface pointers efficiently between threads in the same process. This option is only available if you specify either Both or Free in the Threading option. Once again, because ATL doesn't change anything about the underlying COM threading models, you can read about threading and the FTM in Chapter 29.

Finally, the IObjectWithState option is used to implement the IObjectWithSiteImpl interface, which provides a simple way to support communication between an object and its site in a container.

At this point, accept all the defaults and click Finish to create your new object. I'll now go into the detail of looking at the code that was created to support your Foo ATL object.

Examining the ATL object code

As with the code generated by the ATL AppWizard, the ATL Object Wizard generates heavily attributed code (assuming you selected the Attributed option). There are two main parts: an interface and a coclass. If you examine the interface code, you'll see that much of it is exactly what you would expect to see for an IDL interface definition, but it is in fact C++ code (with attribute extensions, of course):

```
// IFoo
[
  object,
  uuid("C06D95D1-708A-4768-9E14-2B29923EBADD"),
  dual,   helpstring("IFoo Interface"),
  pointer_default(unique)
]
__interface IFoo : IDispatch
{
};
```

Similarly, the C++ class is tagged as a coclass, and has other IDL-like attributes. The threading, ProgId, version-independent ProgId, and uuid attributes are registered in the registry as shown in the following example:

```
// CFoo
[
  coclass,
  threading("apartment"),
  vi_progid("SimpleServer.Foo"),
  progid("SimpleServer.Foo.1"),
  version(1.0),
  uuid("A1F1E7D9-1C00-468F-898A-054AE9EF76AB"),
  helpstring("Foo Class")
]
class ATL_NO_VTABLE CFoo : public IFoo
{
public:
  CFoo()
  {
  }

  DECLARE_PROTECT_FINAL_CONSTRUCT()

  HRESULT FinalConstruct()
  {
    return S_OK;
  }

  void FinalRelease()
```

```
    {
    }
};
```

The only traditional C++ code is an empty constructor, two inherited overrides `FinalConstruct` and `FinalRelease`, and a macro. The macro `DECLARE_PROTECT_FINAL_CONSTRUCT` protects your object from being deleted if (during `FinalConstruct`) an internal aggregated object decrements the reference count to zero. To delve a little deeper into this code, you can expand the hierarchy of the class in the ClassView pane, as shown in Figure 30-6.

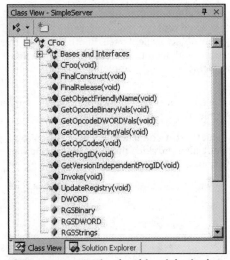

Figure 30-6: ATL Simple Object inherited members

When you create a COM object with ATL, it derives from the base classes that are provided by ATL. The specific base classes that are added to your ATL project depend on which options you specify in the ATL COM AppWizard. At a minimum, an ATL COM object will derive from the base classes `CComObjectRootEx` and `CComCoClass`, as shown in Figure 30-7.

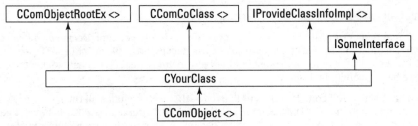

Figure 30-7: ATL object classes

These classes have the following purposes:

✦ CComObjectRootEx manages the reference count, and provides internal versions of the IUnknown methods. This is also where the threading model is specified, in this case via CComSingleThreadModel.

✦ CComCoClass defines the default class factory, the aggregation model, and methods for retrieving an object's CLSID and setting error information.

✦ IProvideClassInfoImpl is the class that implements the IProvideClassInfo interface that defines a single method GetClassInfo for accessing the type information for an object's coclass entry in its type library.

✦ IYourInterface – In this example, this would be IFoo, and represents the base class for your C++ class, CFoo. This is what your object's clients see. In other words, this is the contract between your object and the client such that when you define a method or property for this interface, it is then implemented in the implementing class (shown next).

✦ CYourClass – In this example, this is the CFoo class that is based on the IFoo interface. This is where you'll provide the implementation code for your ATL object.

✦ CComObject implements the IUnknown methods (which actually delegate to the ComObjectRootEx methods). CComObject also provides the code for locking the module while the object is loaded in memory.

ATL derives a COM object from a CYourClass with the CComObject template class. The CComObject definition starts like this:

```
template <class Base>
class CComObject : public Base
{
```

Base is the placeholder for CYourClass. So, CYourClass is used to specialize the CComObject template, mainly by being the parent class for the specialization.

Also note the ATL_NO_VTABLE symbol that was used in declaring the CFoo class. COM objects of CYourClass are never separately instantiated. Instead, the class factory creates the COM objects of the CComObject class. The CComObject class provides the VTBL. CYourClass does not need a VTBL because it is never separately instantiated. ATL ensures there is no VTBL by using the ATL_NO_VTABLE macro as part of the class declaration. The ATL_NO_VTABLE macro is defined (in atldef.h) like this:

```
#define ATL_NO_VTABLE __declspec(novtable)
```

This is also tied in with the FinalConstruct/FinalRelease concept: Because you can't call any virtual functions from a constructor of a class declared ATL_NO_VTABLE, ATL provides the FinalConstruct function. You should put any virtual calls in here instead, because the vtable has been fully built now.

This wizard-generated code is sufficient in itself — that is, it contains all the necessary default plumbing to function as a COM object in a COM server. Of course, the wizards haven't generated anything except the standard plumbing because they don't know what your business requirements are for the object. So, your next task is to add a method to the object. To do this, right-click the IFoo interface in ClassView. Select Add ⇨ Add Method. In the Add Method dialog box, type the method name, such as Something, with no parameters, as shown in Figure 30-8.

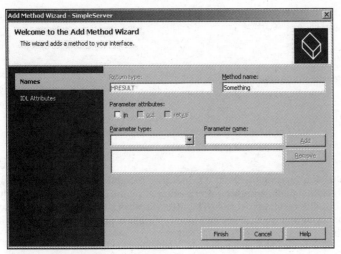

Figure 30-8: Adding a method

This adds the `Something` method to your `IFoo` interface, and adds a new file `Foo.cpp` with a skeleton function `CFoo::Something`. For example, implement this function to do something trivial, such as:

```
STDMETHODIMP CFoo::Something(void)
{
    MessageBox(NULL, "Something", "Message", 0);
    return S_OK;
}
```

You can now build the server, and one of the wizard-generated build settings will be to register the object(s) it contains in the registry, so you're all set on the server-side.

Note After building the server, you'll notice that the ATL template class `IDispatchImpl` is added to the ClassView pane as an inherited class for your `CFoo` class — this is because the interface was defined to derive from `IDispatch`.

The proof of the pudding, of course, is in the client. So, you'll now create a simple client to test the ATL object. To do that, create a new Win32 project and add it to the currently solution by making sure that the Add to Solution radio button is selected on the New Project dialog box. Note that this step isn't necessary, but putting both projects into a single solution means that you can build both at the same time instead of continually loading and unloading a project to switch back and forth between them. On the Application Settings tab, select a Console Application — you'll deliberately create the simplest possible client, just to show that there's nothing mysterious going on behind the scenes. The wizard generates a simple `_tain` function. Add the following code noted in bold.

```
#import "..\SimpleServer\_SimpleServer.tlb" no_namespace named_guids
int _tmain(int argc, _TCHAR* argv[])
{
    CoInitialize(NULL);

    try
    {
```

```
        IFooPtr p(CLSID_CFoo);
        p->Something();
    }
    catch (_com_error& e)
    {
        printf(e.ErrorMessage());
    }

    CoUninitialize();

    return 0;
}
```

As you can see, you're simply using the #import directive to create the necessary include files from the ATL object's typelib, and then, after instantiating the IFooPtr interface, calling its Something method. The result is that the ATL object displays a message box. Once again, the demo is intentionally simple so that you can focus on what is needed to both create and consume ATL objects.

Working with nonattributed code

Recall that one of the checkboxes in the very first ATL AppWizard dialog box was labeled "Attributed." This is checked by default, and for good reason — you are encouraged to use attributes to describe your code configuration because it's a much cleaner and more maintainable approach than the equivalent traditional C++ hard-coding. But, just for the exercise, duplicate (or rather, parallel) your simple server with nonattributed code.

If you create a new ATL project with all the settings as before, but clear the attributed checkbox, you'll end up with code that's more accessible (but carries with it the burden of maintenance):

```
class CUnattServerModule :
        public CAtlDllModuleT< CUnattServerModule >
{
public :
 DECLARE_LIBID(LIBID_UnattServerLib)
 DECLARE_REGISTRY_APPID_RESOURCEID(IDR_UNATTSERVER,
  "{579B6205-A4FC-48F8-806C-E0A735189581}")
};

CUnattServerModule _AtlModule;

// DLL Entry Point
extern "C" BOOL WINAPI DllMain(HINSTANCE hInstance,
                          DWORD dwReason, LPVOID lpReserved)
{
    hInstance;
    return _AtlModule.DllMain(dwReason, lpReserved);
}


// Used to determine whether the DLL can be unloaded by OLE
STDAPI DllCanUnloadNow(void)
{
```

```
    return _AtlModule.DllCanUnloadNow();
}


// Returns a class factory to create an object
// of the requested type
STDAPI DllGetClassObject(REFCLSID rclsid,
                         REFIID riid, LPVOID* ppv)
{
    return _AtlModule.DllGetClassObject(rclsid, riid, ppv);
}

// DllRegisterServer -- Adds entries to the system registry
STDAPI DllRegisterServer(void)
{
    // registers object, typelib, and
    // all interfaces in typelib
    HRESULT hr = _AtlModule.DllRegisterServer();
    return hr;
}


// DllUnregisterServer -- Removes entries
// from the system registry
STDAPI DllUnregisterServer(void)
{
    HRESULT hr = _AtlModule.DllUnregisterServer();
    return hr;
}
```

Notice that the accompanying wizard-generated IDL file is no longer hidden with a leading underscore, and contains traditional IDL code:

```
// UnattServer.idl
import "oaidl.idl";
import "ocidl.idl";

[
    uuid(C9F01851-4004-4650-9C51-CD8043DD77E5),
    version(1.0),
    helpstring("UnattServer 1.0 Type Library")
]
library UnattServerLib
{
    importlib("stdole2.tlb");
};
```

Adding the same Foo ATL Simple Object as before now generates the following code:

```
// CFoo

class ATL_NO_VTABLE CFoo :
 public CComObjectRootEx<CComSingleThreadModel>,
 public CComCoClass<CFoo, &CLSID_Foo>,
 public IDispatchImpl<IFoo, &IID_IFoo,
```

```
&LIBID_UnattServerLib, /*wMajor =*/ 1, /*wMinor =*/ 0>
{
public:
 CFoo()
 {
 }

DECLARE_REGISTRY_RESOURCEID(IDR_FOO)

BEGIN_COM_MAP(CFoo)
 COM_INTERFACE_ENTRY(IFoo)
 COM_INTERFACE_ENTRY(IDispatch)
END_COM_MAP()

DECLARE_PROTECT_FINAL_CONSTRUCT()

HRESULT FinalConstruct()
{
 return S_OK;
}

void FinalRelease()
{
}

public:

};

OBJECT_ENTRY_AUTO(__uuidof(Foo), CFoo)
```

The significant differences are that you no longer support IProvideClassInfo, the registry resource is now visible, and you have both a visible COM map and a visible object map.

Now take a look at the registry resource. As you can probably surmise, the HKCR stands for HKEY_CLASSES_ROOT, and the entries within it specify the keys and values that will be added to the registry in that husk.

```
HKCR
{
 UnattServer.Foo.1 = s 'Foo Class'
 {
  CLSID = s '{491D7C63-2B81-4CAD-B851-F97C469D950F}'
 }
 UnattServer.Foo = s 'Foo Class'
 {
  CLSID = s '{491D7C63-2B81-4CAD-B851-F97C469D950F}'
  CurVer = s 'UnattServer.Foo.1'
 }
 NoRemove CLSID
 {
  ForceRemove {491D7C63-2B81-4CAD-B851-F97C469D950F} = s 'Foo Class'
  {
   ProgID = s 'UnattServer.Foo.1'
   VersionIndependentProgID = s 'UnattServer.Foo'
```

```
    ForceRemove 'Programmable'
    InprocServer32 = s '%MODULE%'
    {
     val ThreadingModel = s 'Apartment'
    }
    val AppID = s '%APPID%'
    'TypeLib' = s '{C9F01851-4004-4650-9C51-CD8043DD77E5}'
   }
  }
 }
```

The COM map is the mechanism that exposes interfaces on an object to a client through `QueryInterface`. `CComObjectRootEx::InternalQueryInterface` only returns pointers for interfaces in the COM map.

The wizards generate unattributed code according to slightly different rules for naming and location, so, for instance, the client-side #import statement would need to look like this:

```
#import "..\UnattServer\debug\UnattServer.tlb" no_namespace named_guids
```

And the generated named guid omits the leading C, so the smart pointer instantiation looks like this:

```
    IFooPtr p(CLSID_Foo);
```

In summary, the decision to use or not use attributes really comes down to some decisions that you have to make on a case-by-case basis. If you choose attributed code, then you can't use the MFC in your ATL object or merge proxy/stub code in the same DLL. You also can't rename the default coclass name of a wizard-created ATL object. If these restrictions aren't a big deal to you, then I would suggest using attributes for the simple reason that attributes make programming simpler because they afford you the ability to create self-contained, self-describing objects. In addition, it's also worth noting that many of Microsoft's newer technologies (for example Visual C++ .NET with Managed Extensions, and C#) support the attributed programming model, so it might be best to start at least becoming familiar with what attributes are and how to use them, because you'll be seeing them quite a bit in the future.

Extending the Wizards

The ATL AppWizard and ATL Object Wizard offer a reasonable set of options for the type of server and objects you want to generate, but there are some limitations. Clearly, the wizard-writers had to draw the line somewhere. Two questions immediately come to mind:

   ✦ How can you get code for multiple objects in a server?

   ✦ How can you get code for a single object to support multiple interfaces?

These two issues are discussed in the following sections.

Multiple objects

Remember that the ATL COM AppWizard generates the server code (DLL or EXE), while the ATL Object Wizard generates code for a COM object to be hosted in the server. Because of this separation of functionality, you can use the Object Wizard to create multiple objects for the same server.

For example, taking one of your existing SimpleServer projects as the starting point, you can simply right-click on SimpleServer classes in ClassView, and select New ATL Object. If you use the short name Bar, and accept all the defaults, the wizard generates code for the IBar interface and CBar coclass. You can then add a method to the IBar interface: an HRESULT method called Another, with no parameters, and implement this in the C++ code to call MessageBox as before.

You can then enhance your test client to use both objects: In addition to using the IFoo pointer, you can use the IBar pointer as well; for example:

```
try
{
    IFooPtr p(CLSID_CFoo);
    p->Something();

    IBarPtr p2(CLSID_CBar);
    p2->Another();
}
```

Now let's see how to add multiple interfaces to a single ATL object.

Multiple interfaces

Multiple objects are easy enough, but what about multiple interfaces in one object? The ATL Object Wizard generates code for an object that implements either a dual or custom interface, but no more. If you want to support additional interfaces, your approach will depend on whether you've asked for attributed code or not.

If you don't have attributed code, to add an interface to a COM object that was created with ATL, you can add the appropriate interface information to the COM object header file and implement the methods of the interface. These are the steps required to modify the COM object header file:

1. Add the interface to the multiple-inheritance table.

2. Add the interface to the COM map by using the *COM_INTERFACE_ENTRY macro.

3. Add the necessary definitions for each method of the interface. In the following example, I've added a function called Mango (implemented by the IMango interface) where the changes are in bold.

```
class ATL_NO_VTABLE CBanana :
    public CComObjectRootEx<CComSingleThreadModel>,
    public CComCoClass<CBanana, &CLSID_Banana>,
    public IDispatchImpl<IBanana, &IID_IBanana,
&LIBID_SIMPLESERVERLib>,
    public IMango;
{
public:
    CBanana()
    {
    }

DECLARE_REGISTRY_RESOURCEID(IDR_BANANA)

DECLARE_PROTECT_FINAL_CONSTRUCT()
```

```
BEGIN_COM_MAP(CBanana)
    COM_INTERFACE_ENTRY(IBanana)
    COM_INTERFACE_ENTRY(IDispatch)
    COM_INTERFACE_ENTRY(IMango)
END_COM_MAP()

public:
  virtual HRESULT STDMETHODCALLTYPE BananaFunc( void)
  {
   return E_NOTIMPL;
  }

  virtual HRESULT STDMETHODCALLTYPE MangoFunc( void)
  {
   return E_NOTIMPL;
  }
};
```

Alternatively, and whether you have attributed or unattributed code, you can use the Implement Interface wizard. To do this, right-click on the coclass in ClassView (such as CFoo), and select Add ⇨ Implement Interface.

You then have another set of choices, which boil down to one question: Do you have a built (and registered) COM server available that exposes the interface you want to implement on your object? If so, you can scroll through the list of registered servers and make your selection. For example, suppose you want to implement the ICalendar interface exposed by the Microsoft Calendar control (see Figure 30-9).

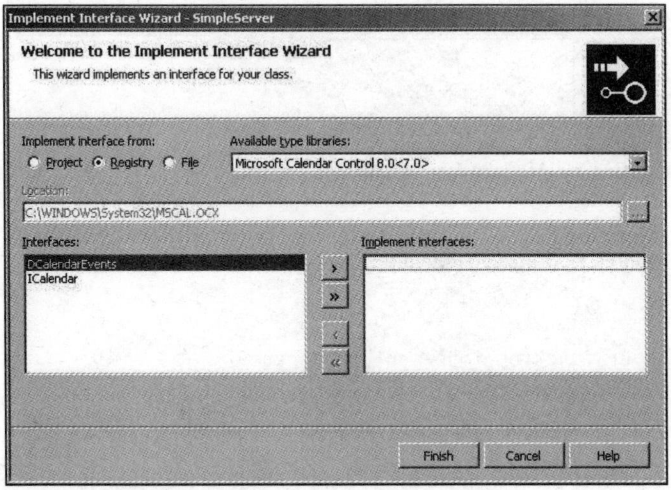

Figure 30-9: Implementing an exposed interface

This is useful, but you're more likely to want to define and implement a completely new interface. In this case, you can manually type a new interface definition into your Foo.h file, with whatever attributes you want and a new guid; for example:

```
// IGoo
[
```

```
            object,
            uuid("DB3C94F8-5C8D-4aec-93EC-526DB67CD1F8"),
            dual,    helpstring("IGoo Interface"),
            pointer_default(unique)
        ]
        __interface IGoo : IDispatch
        {
        };
```

After you have saved this revised code, you can right-click the IGoo interface in ClassView, and add a method as normal. Next, right-click the CFoo coclass and select Add ➪ Implement Interface again, but this time, select the Project radio button, and Embedded IDL as the source. You will be offered a list of all interfaces defined in the project's IDL that have not yet been implemented by this coclass (see Figure 30-10). Select IGoo and click Finish.

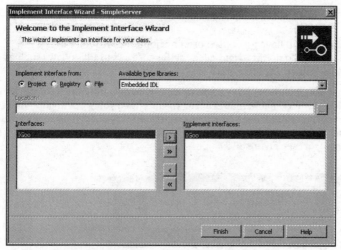

Figure 30-10: Implementing an interface from an embedded IDL

You then implement the method(s) on the interface in some appropriate manner, (don't forget to change the return to some sensible HRESULT value). For example:

```
        STDMETHOD(Banana)()
        {
            // Add your function implementation here.
            MessageBox(0, "Banana", "Msg", 0);
            return S_OK;
        }
```

You can then enhance the test client to make use of both interfaces; for example:

```
        try
        {
            IFooPtr p(CLSID_CFoo);
            p->Something();

            IGooPtr p2;
            HRESULT hr = p->QueryInterface(IID_IGoo,
```

```
                                            (void**)&p2);
        if (SUCCEEDED(hr))
        {
            p2->Banana();
        }
    }
```

ATL Debugging Support

ATL-specific debugging support is provided through two macros:

✦ _ATL_DEBUG_QI for debugging QueryInterface calls

✦ _ATL_DEBUG_INTERFACES for debugging reference counts

You should insert one or both of these into the stdafx.h file and then rebuild your server.

The _ATL_DEBUG_QI macro

The _ATL_DEBUG_QI macro must be defined before the #include for <atlcom.h>. A debug string is sent to the output window for every call to QueryInterface on the server. The string contains the name of the class, followed by the name of the interface on which QueryInterface was called. If the interface name isn't found in the registry, the interface ID is shown instead. If the QueryInterface call fails, the string "failed" is added to the output.

The _ATL_DEBUG_INTERFACES macro

The _ATL_DEBUG_INTERFACES macro must be defined before the #include for <atlbase.h>. Anytime AddRef or Release is called on an interface, the reference count, class name, and interface name are sent to the output window. Output with a > symbol indicates AddRef, and a < symbol indicates Release. Figure 30-11 shows how you can use these macros.

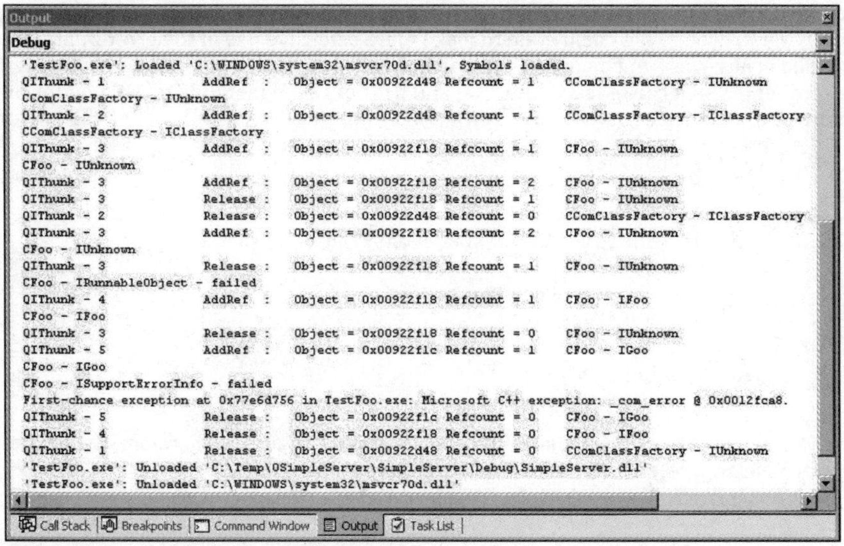

Figure 30-11: Using the ATL debugging macros

ATL build configurations

The ATL COM AppWizard creates a project file that contains two main build configurations, each tuned to a different set of goals and needs, as listed in Table 30-1.

Table 30-1: ATL COM Project Build Configurations

Build Configuration	Description	Preprocessor Symbols	Dependencies
Win32 Debug	Compiler optimizations are disabled, and the linker generates debug information	_DEBUG	Implicit link to the ATL registrar component in ATL.DLL
Win32 Release	Aims to reduce external dependencies: compiler optimizations are set to Minimum Size	NDEBUG, _ATL_ STATIC_REGISTRY	None

Note Earlier versions of the ATL wizards offered additional configurations, and you can emulate these if you wish by adding a new build configuration with the settings you want.

Implementing the ATL ISupportErrorInfo interface

The ISupportErrorInfo interface ensures that error information can be propagated up the call chain correctly. The ATL Object Wizard offers you the option to incorporate support for this interface when you generate the object code. The ATL has an implementation of this interface in the ISupportErrorInfoImpl template class.

In the following walkthrough exercise, you will enhance your previous ATL SimpleServer and client applications to take advantage of extended error information and ATL debugging macros. First, change the client code to make more extensive use of the error information provided in any _com_error object that might be thrown. Here you're doing that by calling the error object's ErrorMessage, Source, and Description methods to get a better overall picture of what failed and why.

```
catch (_com_error& e)
{
char buf[120];
wsprintf(buf, "Code = %08lx\nCode meaning = %s\n"
        "Source = %S\nDescription = %S\n",
        e.Error(), e.ErrorMessage(),
        (wchar_t*)e.Source(),
        (wchar_t*)e.Description());
MessageBox(0, buf, 0, 0);
}
```

Now, to test your error code, you need to cause an error to occur. Therefore, deliberately request an unsupported interface, and attempt to use the pointer.

```
try
{
 IFooPtr p(CLSID_CFoo);
 p->Something();

 IPersistFilePtr pp = p;
 CLSID clsid;
 pp->GetClassID(&clsid);
}
```

When you're done, build and run the solution. The `MessageBox` call in your client-side catch block should produce a simple error message as shown in Figure 30-12.

Figure 30-12: Default error information

That's what you get by default. Now, build in more support for error information. Remember that the ATL Object Wizard gives you the option to support `ISupportErrorInfo`. If you want this support now, you can simply add the ATL implementation class `ISupportErrorInfoImpl` to the multiple inheritance for your `CFoo` class:

```
class ATL_NO_VTABLE CFoo :
    public IFoo,
    public ISupportErrorInfoImpl< &__uuidof(IFoo) >
```

To fully test this, add a new method to the `IFoo` interface. Call the method `Buggy` and implement it as shown in the following code, and then build and test.

```
STDMETHODIMP CFoo::Buggy(void)
{
    return Error("A nice error message",
        __uuidof(IFoo), E_UNEXPECTED);
}
```

When your client calls this method, it should produce a more comprehensive error message as shown in Figure 30-13.

Figure 30-13: Error information with ISupportErrorInfo

Summary

Because we're in the business of code reuse, it is only common sense to reuse all the standard COM plumbing, and that's exactly what the ATL is designed for. In this chapter, you've seen how the two main ATL wizards generate the bulk of the code you need for any COM object. You've also seen that we have choices about how this code should be generated, not only in terms of the nature of the required server and objects, but also in terms of the source code itself. You've had some exposure to attribute-based code.

Behind the scenes, much of the standard plumbing is provided by templated classes including `CComObjectRootEx`, `CcomCoClass`, and `_AtlModule`, and you delved a little into these to see how the ATL makes life so easy.

You also considered how to extend the code generated by the wizards, to support multiple objects within a server, and to support multiple interfaces within an object. Finally, you saw that the ATL supports both debugging and run-time error-propagation through a series of macros and implementation of `ISupportErrorInfo`.

✦   ✦   ✦

Windowing with ATL

◆ ◆ ◆ ◆

In This Chapter

Alternate message maps

Chained message maps

Reflected messages

Writing an ATL
Windows app

Creating an ATL
Frame/View app

Writing Scribble with
ATL

Adding menu support

◆ ◆ ◆ ◆

As you learned in the previous chapter, the original intent of ATL was to enable C++ programmers to create faster and more lightweight COM components than is generally possible using MFC. This chapter builds on that by delving into how to write Windows applications using ATL. At this point, you might be asking (and correctly so), why would you want to learn yet another means of writing Windows applications when MFC has all this robust functionality for doing just that built-in. Therefore, before continuing, I will go over the advantages of programming windows with ATL to see if this chapter is what you need.

Determining whether or not to use ATL to program windows depends on a couple of factors and how important they are to your overall system design. First, just as ATL components are faster and more lightweight than their MFC/COM equivalents, ATL Windows applications tend to be much more efficient in their resource utilization (both runtime and binary file size). Second, you are tied to using the document/view architecture when writing MFC SDI or MDI applications, but ATL has no such restrictions. Therefore, if you're looking to create high-performing, lightweight Windows applications that don't rely on the MFC document/view architecture, then this chapter is definitely for you.

The ATL windowing classes are not difficult to learn. In fact, you could probably skip the chapter on creating ATL components altogether and still be able to go through this chapter, creating the demo applications, without any problem. In this chapter, I'll provide an introduction to the ATL windowing classes and describe how message maps are implemented in order to control message processing. Once I've gone over the basics, I'll then present a series of demo applications so that you can see for yourself that the learning curve with ATL windowing is much less steep and much shorter than learning the MFC. The first demo application illustrates that creating a Windows application (albeit a simple one) with ATL is probably much easier than you thought. Once you've done that, you'll then see how to code a simple Scribble-like application that allows the user to draw on the client area. Finally, you'll end the chapter by discovering how to add menus and respond to menu events using ATL.

ATL Window Classes

Although the ATL is designed primarily to support COM, it does contain a range of classes for modeling windows. You can use these classes for COM objects that have windows, such as ActiveX Controls, and for Windows applications that do not necessarily involve COM. The most important ATL windowing classes are the following:

✦ CWindow—Very much like the MFC CWnd class, the CWindow class is a thin wrapper for creating and controlling a window. The class includes a window handle and an HWND operator that converts a CWindow object to an HWND. This enables you to pass a CWindow object to any function that requires a handle to a window.

✦ CWindowImpl —The CWindowImpl class, which inherits from CWindow, enables you to define message-handling behavior. You'll see how this is done in this chapter's first demo application.

✦ CContainedWindow—As its name indicates, the CContainedWindow class implements a window that routes messages to the message map of another class. This architecture enables you to centralize message processing.

✦ CAxWindow—The CAxWindow class is used to control a window that hosts ActiveX controls. Using this class, you can create an ActiveX control or attach to an existing control.

✦ CDialogImpl —The CDialogImpl class is used for both modal and modeless dialog boxes. CDialogImpl also provides a dialog box procedure that routes messages to the default message map in your derived class. The CDialogImpl class does not support the hosting of ActiveX controls.

✦ CSimpleDialog—A scaled down version of the CDialogImpl class, the CSimpleDialog class only supports modal dialog boxes and can only host Windows common controls. Like the CDialogImpl class, it also provides a dialog box procedure that routes messages to the default message map in your derived class.

✦ CAxDialogImpl —Like CDialogImpl, the CAxDialogImpl class is used as a base class for implementing a modal or modeless dialog box. However, the major difference here is that the CAxDialogImpl does support the hosting of ActiveX controls.

✦ CWndClassInfo—The CWndClassInfo class encapsulates the information of a window class.

✦ CWinTraits and CWinTraitsOR—Encapsulate the *traits* (WS_ window styles) of an ATL window object. ATL window traits give you the ability to define a set of default window styles for a newly created window.

Message Maps

Just like MFC, the mechanism for controlling messaging routing is based on message maps and macros. Therefore, although they are a bit different in implementation, if you're at all familiar with MFC message maps, you should have no problem understanding how to code message maps in ATL. In the previous section, I briefly mentioned a class called CWindowImpl that enables you to define message-handling behavior. This is because CWindowImpl is also derived from an abstract class called CMessageMap. CMessageMap then declares a single pure virtual function called ProcessWindowMessage, which you are responsible for implementing in your CWindowImpl-derived class via the BEGIN_MSG_MAP and END_MSG_MAP macros.

In addition to the familiar format of MFC message handlers that you learned about in Chapter 1, ATL message handler functions accept an additional argument of type BOOL&. This argument indicates whether a message has been processed. This argument is set to TRUE by default, but your handler function can set the argument to FALSE to indicate that the message was not handled and needs further processing. In this case, ATL will continue to look for a handler function further in the message map. By setting this argument to FALSE, you can first perform some action in response to a message and then allow the default processing or another handler function to continue processing the message. There are three categories of message map macros:

✦ Message handlers for all messages

✦ Command handlers for WM_COMMAND messages

✦ Notification handlers for WM_NOTIFY messages

The full list of message map macros is found in Table 31-1.

Table 31-1: Message Map Macros

Macro	Description
MESSAGE_HANDLER	Maps a window message to a handler function.
COMMAND_HANDLER	Maps a WM_COMMAND message to a handler function based on the notification code and the ID of the menu item, control, or accelerator.
COMMAND_ID_HANDLER	Maps a WM_COMMAND message to a handler function based on the ID of the menu item, control, or accelerator.
COMMAND_CODE_HANDLER	Maps a WM_COMMAND message to a handler function based on the notification code.
NOTIFY_HANDLER	Maps a WM_NOTIFY message to a handler based on the notification code and the control identifier.
NOTIFY_ID_HANDLER	Maps a WM_NOTIFY message to a handler based on the control identifier.
NOTIFY_CODE_HANDLER	Maps a WM_NOTIFY message to a handler based on the notification code.

For example, if you have an ATL dialog class with child controls on the form, you might have a message map like the one shown in the following example:

```
BEGIN_MSG_MAP(CMyDialog)
  MESSAGE_HANDLER(WM_INITDIALOG, OnInitDialog)
  COMMAND_HANDLER(IDC_EDIT1, EN_CHANGE, OnChangeEdit1)
  COMMAND_ID_HANDLER(IDOK, OnOK)
  COMMAND_CODE_HANDLER(EN_ERRSPACE, OnErrEdits)
  NOTIFY_HANDLER(IDC_LIST1, NM_CLICK, OnClickList1)
  NOTIFY_ID_HANDLER(IDC_LIST2, OnSomethingList2)
  NOTIFY_CODE_HANDLER(NM_DBLCLK, OnDblClkLists)
END_MSG_MAP()
```

As you learned in Chapter 1, the MFC message routing architecture works in two distinct ways depending on the type of message being delivered. Windows messages are routed up through the class hierarchy, whereas command messages are routed across the document/view class lattice. The first scheme is not very appropriate for ATL because ATL has a much looser hierarchy of partially implemented template classes as opposed to the strict C++ inheritance framework employed by MFC. The second scheme is not applicable at all because the ATL does not rigidly impose anything equivalent to the MFC document/view architecture.

Therefore, the ATL has its own means of routing messages. Actually, like MFC, it has two distinct routing methods: *alternate message maps* and *chained message maps*. In addition, a parent window can also handle messages sent to it by a child control by sending the message back as a *reflected message*. In the following sections I'll touch on each of these issues and how they relate to ATL windowing and then I'll write some demo applications that illustrate how it all works in practice.

Alternate message maps

Earlier I mentioned the CContainedWindow class enables you to centralize message processing by providing a means of implementing a window that routes messages to the message map of another class. *Alternate message maps* are primarily designed to be used with this CContainedWindow class. These alternate message maps are a mechanism by which you can consolidate message handlers within a single BEGIN_MSG_MAP and END_MSG_MAP macro pair.

In order to construct a CContainedWindow, you need only to pass it the address of the class that contains the message map to be used, and the ID of the alternate message map within the message map (or zero for the default message map).

For example, suppose you use the Object Wizard to generate a class based on a Windows control. When you do this, the Object Wizard embeds a CContainedWindow member to represent the actual control window. If you look at the following code you can see this in action. Here, I've simply created an ATL object based on a standard Windows button control. The m_ctlButton member is, in effect, superclassing the actual button control window that the user will see.

```
class ATL_NO_VTABLE CMyButton :
 public CComObjectRootEx<CComSingleThreadModel>,
 public CComCoClass<CMyButton, &CLSID_MyButton>,
 public CComControl<CMyButton>,
 //...
 {
public:
 CContainedWindow m_ctlButton;
 CMyButton() : m_ctlButton(_T("Button"), this, 1) { }

BEGIN_MSG_MAP(CMyButton)
 MESSAGE_HANDLER(WM_CREATE, OnCreate)
 MESSAGE_HANDLER(WM_SETFOCUS, OnSetFocus)
 CHAIN_MSG_MAP(CComControl<CMyButton>)
 ALT_MSG_MAP(1)
END_MSG_MAP()
 //...
```

Note also in the preceding code that the string being passed to the CContainedWindow constructor is the WNDCLASS style (not the window caption) and determines the type of control window being created. The this pointer being passed as the second parameter simply tells the CContainedWindow constructor that the CMyButton class contains the message map for processing any messages sent to the button control window. Finally, the last parameter specifies the message map that processes the contained window's messages. In this case, you pass a value of 1. If you look at the BEGIN_MESSAGE_MAP macro (shown here again for convenience) you'll see that the last entry defines something called an ALT_MSG_MAP. This is the alternate message map, and its identifying ID is 1. Therefore, by passing a value of 1 to the CContainedWindow constructor, you specify exactly which message map to use.

```
BEGIN_MSG_MAP(CMyButton)
 MESSAGE_HANDLER(WM_CREATE, OnCreate)
 MESSAGE_HANDLER(WM_SETFOCUS, OnSetFocus)
 CHAIN_MSG_MAP(CComControl<CMyButton>)
 ALT_MSG_MAP(1)
END_MSG_MAP()
```

Now, suppose you want to handle the button control window's WM_LBUTTONDOWN message in a function called OnLButtonDown. All you need to do is to update the alternate message map (via the ALT_MSG_MAP macro) as follows:

```
BEGIN_MSG_MAP(CMyButton)
 MESSAGE_HANDLER(WM_CREATE, OnCreate)
 MESSAGE_HANDLER(WM_SETFOCUS, OnSetFocus)
 CHAIN_MSG_MAP(CComControl<CMyButton>)
ALT_MSG_MAP(1)
 MESSAGE_HANDLER(WM_LBUTTONDOWN, OnLButtonDown)
END_MSG_MAP()
```

Now, the WM_LBUTTONDOWN message is routed to the parent window's message map, and then routed to the correct alternate part of that message map.

Chained message maps

Chaining message maps enables you to specify that you want messages routed through to the message map in another class or object. In order to accomplish this, ATL supplies the following macros (all of which begin with CHAIN_MSG):

- ✦ CHAIN_MSG_MAP(*theBaseClass*) — This macro causes messages to be routed to the default message map of the specified base class.

- ✦ CHAIN_MSG_MAP_ALT(*theBaseClass, mapID*) — Use this macro if you want messages routed to an alternate map of a class. Simply supply the base class containing the alternate map and that map's ID.

- ✦ CHAIN_MSG_MAP_MEMBER(*theMember*) — Similar to CHAIN_MSG_MAP, this macro enables you to route message to the default message map of the specified data member. The only restriction is that the specified member must be derived from CMessageMap.

- ✦ CHAIN_MSG_MAP_ALT_MEMBER(*theMember, mapID*) — Similar to CHAN_MSG_MAP_ALT, this macro enables you to route messages to the alternate message map of a specified data member. Once again, you specify the member name (which must be derived from CMessageMap) and that member's alternate message map ID.

Let's take a look at an example to illustrate what I'm talking about. Once again, you take the Object Wizard generated code for a class used to control a standard Windows button, this time using a CHAIN_MSG_MAP.

```
BEGIN_MSG_MAP(CMyButton)
 MESSAGE_HANDLER(WM_CREATE, OnCreate)
 MESSAGE_HANDLER(WM_SETFOCUS, OnSetFocus)
 CHAIN_MSG_MAP(CComControl<CMyButton>)
 ALT_MSG_MAP(1)
END_MSG_MAP()
```

Although this might look strange at first, the code simply specifies that the WM_CREATE and WM_SETFOCUS messages will be handled in this class, as specified by the MESSAGE_HANDLER macros, and that any other message will be routed to the message map in the CComControl<> base class. In addition, if the message handlers for the WM_CREATE or WM_SETFOCUS messages set bHandled to FALSE, these messages will also be passed to the CComControl<> base class for further handling.

That was a simple usage of the CHAIN_MSG_MAP macro. The following example shows how the CHAIN_MSG_MAP_MEMBER is used:

```
BEGIN_MSG_MAP(CMyButton)
 MESSAGE_HANDLER(WM_CREATE, OnCreate)
 MESSAGE_HANDLER(WM_SETFOCUS, OnSetFocus)
 CHAIN_MSG_MAP(CComControl<CMyButton>)
ALT_MSG_MAP(1)
 CHAIN_MSG_MAP_MEMBER(m_ctlButton)
END_MSG_MAP()
```

This assumes that m_ctlButton is a member of the container window and is an instance of a class derived from CContainedWindow (which ultimately derives from CMessageMap) where you have an entry in the message map for the messages you're interested in.

```
class ATL_NO_VTABLE CMyButton :
 public CComObjectRootEx<CComSingleThreadModel>,
 public CComCoClass<CMyButton, &CLSID_MyButton>,
 public CComControl<CMyButton>,
 //...
{

BEGIN_MSG_MAP(CMyButton)
 MESSAGE_HANDLER(WM_CREATE, OnCreate)
 MESSAGE_HANDLER(WM_SETFOCUS, OnSetFocus)
 CHAIN_MSG_MAP(CComControl<CMyButton>)
ALT_MSG_MAP(1)
 CHAIN_MSG_MAP_MEMBER(m_ctlButton)
END_MSG_MAP()
   //...
   CMyButtonControl m_ctlButton;
   //...
}

class CMyButtonControl : public CContainedWindow
{
 //...
 BEGIN_MSG_MAP(CMyButtonControl)
  MESSAGE_HANDLER(WM_LBUTTONDOWN, OnLButtonDown)
 END_MSG_MAP()
```

Chained message maps allow you to daisy chain message maps from one map to another, which is very similar to the approach taken by the message routing mechanism used in MFC.

Reflected messages

Now that you know about alternate message maps and chained message maps, let's look at reflected messages. As in MFC, a parent window can handle Windows messages sent to it by a child control by sending the message back as a reflected message. When the control receives these reflected messages (with an additional flag), it can identify them as being reflected from the container and handle them appropriately.

As an example, suppose you want a child control to handle its own WM_DRAWITEM messages. For this to work, REFLECT_NOTIFICATIONS must be present in the parent window's message map, because the message will first be sent to the child's parent window. Look at the following code snippet where a dialog box (CMyDialog) has a REFLECT_NOTIFICATIONS entry in its message map:

```
BEGIN_MSG_MAP(CMyDialog)
 MESSAGE_HANDLER(WM_INITDIALOG, OnInitDialog)
 COMMAND_ID_HANDLER(IDOK, OnOk)
 NOTIFY_HANDLER(IDC_EDIT1, EN_CHANGE, OnChangeEdit1)
 REFLECT_NOTIFICATIONS()
END_MSG_MAP()
```

If you dig just a bit deeper, you'll see that the REFLECT_NOTIFICATIONS macro expands to a call to CWindowImpl::ReflectNotifications, which has the following prototype:

```
template <class TBase>
LRESULT CWindowImplRoot<TBase>::ReflectNotifications(
 UINT uMsg,
 WPARAM wParam,
 LPARAM lParam,
 BOOL& bHandled);
```

The function extracts the window handle to the child control that sent the message from the wParam or lParam (depending on the type of message), and then sends the message to the child window as shown in the following example (notice how the message ID is sent):

```
::SendMessage(hWndChild,
              OCM__BASE + uMsg,
              wParam,
              lParam);
```

The child window then uses the standard MESSAGE_HANDLER macros in order to process the message:

```
BEGIN_MSG_MAP(CMyContainedControl)
 MESSAGE_HANDLER(OCM_DRAWITEM, OnDrawItem)
 DEFAULT_REFLECTION_HANDLER()
END_MSG_MAP()
```

The message IDs (OCM_XXX) are defined in olectrl.h. In this case, the OCM_DRAWITEM value is defined as OCM_BASE + WM_DRAWITEM. Here's an excerpt from the olectrl.h file showing that:

```
#define OCM__BASE         (WM_USER+0x1c00)
#define OCM_COMMAND       (OCM__BASE + WM_COMMAND)
...
#define OCM_DRAWITEM      (OCM__BASE + WM_DRAWITEM)
#define OCM_MEASUREITEM   (OCM__BASE + WM_MEASUREITEM)
...
```

ATL Window Application Demo

Now that you've seen the very basics of the ATL classes that are used to support creating Windows applications and the different ways in which to route messages, let's do some demo applications to see this at work. The first demo application is the standard Hello World type application. However, instead of letting the AppWizard have all the fun, I'm going to walk you through the steps required to manually create an ATL Windows application. That way, you can better see for yourself exactly what steps are involved. Additionally, because you're ostensibly using ATL in order to create the most lightweight application possible, it doesn't make sense to allow a wizard to create a project with (possibly) gratuitous code that the application doesn't need.

Creating a Win32 application project

Create a simple Win32 application called HelloATL. To do this, open the New Project dialog box, select the Visual C++ Projects project type, and click the Win32 Project Template. Now, type the name of the project (HelloATL) and select the destination folder. At this point, you should see the Win32 Application Wizard shown in Figure 31-1.

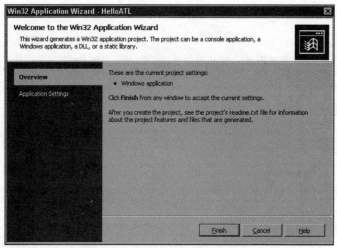

Figure 31-1: Building an ATL Windows application from a Win32 application lets you better see exactly what it takes to incorporate ATL support.

If you click Application Settings as shown in Figure 31-2, you will see that you also have the ability to specify Application type (Console, Windows, Static library, or DLL) as well as a few additional properties. Of those properties, the setting to note here is that as of the time of this writing (Beta 2), the ability to automatically add support for ATL (or MFC) had not been implemented. However, it doesn't really matter to us for purposes of this particular demo application, because I want you to see how to manually add ATL support anyway.

You're not going to change anything here, so click the Finish button in order to have the new project's files created.

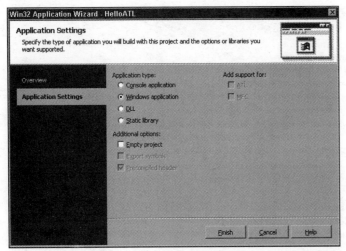

Figure 31-2: As of Beta 2, ATL support could not be added to a newly created Win32 application through the Win32 Application Wizard.

Manually adding ATL support

At this point, you have a bona fide Windows application but you don't yet have any ATL support. You can get ATL support, including support of the ATL wizards, by making a few additions to the project you just created. Open the stdafx.h file and (at the end of the file) add the following include directives (for the necessary ATL header files) and define a variable of type CComModule:

```
#include <atlbase.h>
extern CComModule _Module;
#include <atlcom.h>
#include <atlwin.h>
```

Next, you need to declare an instance of the CComModule object. Also declare the global CComModule object in your application's main file (HelloATL.cpp) and add an empty object map. You won't be using the object map (hence its emptiness). However, the CComModule class expects it and your project won't compile without it.

```
CComModule _Module;

BEGIN_OBJECT_MAP(ObjectMap)
END_OBJECT_MAP()
```

That's it! You now have ATL support.

Creating an ATL window

Once again, at the time of this writing, there is no wizard support for creating classes specifically using the ATL window classes. Therefore, you need to do some manual work to create a CWindowImpl-derived class.

Open the Class View, right-click the root, and select the Add Class option from the context menu to display the standard Add Class dialog box shown in Figure 31-3.

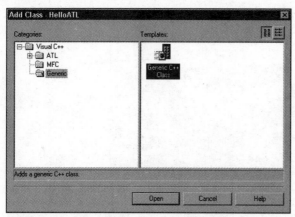

Figure 31-3: As of Beta 2, you could not create
CWindowImpl-derived classes with the Wizard.

Select the Generic C++ Class item and then click the Open button. Here's where things get a
little tricky. For the Class Name, specify `CMyWindow` and for the base class specify
`CWindowImpl<CMyWindow>` as shown in Figure 31-4.

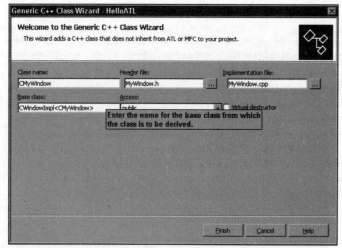

Figure 31-4: Without direct support for creating a CWindowImpl-
derived class, you have to know a couple of tricks.

Now, click the Finish button. At this point, you will receive a warning message (shown in
Figure 31-5) that simply tells you that the wizard could not locate the specified base class.
You'll fix that next. For now, simply click the Yes button indicating that you want the wizard
to continue creating the class files.

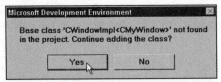

Figure 31-5: The Wizard displays a warning about the use of an undefined base class, but that's to be expected and not a problem.

Once the files have been created, Visual Studio should automatically open the `MyWindow.h` file. Add the following include directive (in bold) to the top of the file. Now when you build the project, this file will compile because the ATL headers defining the `CWindowImpl` class are included from the `stdafx.h` file.

```
#pragma once
#include "stdafx.h"

class CMyWindow : public CWindowImpl<CMyWindow>
...
```

In the `CMyWindow` class declare a message map containing a handler for the `WM_DESTROY` and `WM_PAINT` messages:

```
BEGIN_MSG_MAP(CMyWindow)
 MESSAGE_HANDLER(WM_DESTROY, OnDestroy)
 MESSAGE_HANDLER(WM_PAINT, OnPaint)
END_MSG_MAP()
```

Next, add the two message prototypes:

```
LRESULT OnDestroy(UINT uMsg,
                  WPARAM wParam,
                  LPARAM lParam,
                  BOOL& bHandled);
LRESULT OnPaint(UINT uMsg,
                WPARAM wParam,
                LPARAM lParam,
                BOOL& bHandled);
```

Now, code something very simple just to make sure it all works. First, open the `MyWindow.cpp` file and add the following `OnDestroy` function:

```
LRESULT CMyWindow::OnDestroy(UINT uMsg,
                             WPARAM wParam,
                             LPARAM lParam,
                             BOOL& bHandled)
{
  PostQuitMessage(0);
  return 0;
}
```

Next, code the `OnPaint` function. As you can see, this function merely uses some simple GDI functions to print a string to the client area of the window. As is normal with ATL, there are no classes to encapsulate this.

Note Coincidentally, there is such a class in WTL, a very nice framework that combines the power of MFC with the elegance of ATL. I've provided an introduction similar to this chapter in Chapter 34.

```
LRESULT CMyWindow::OnPaint(UINT uMsg,
                           WPARAM wParam,
                           LPARAM lParam,
                           BOOL& bHandled)
{
HDC hDC = GetDC();

PAINTSTRUCT ps;
BeginPaint(&ps);

TextOut(hDC, 10, 10, _T("Hello ATL"), 9);

EndPaint(&ps);

return 0;
}
```

Tweaking WinMain to create the ATL module

And now here is the final piece of the puzzle. Open the `HelloATL.cpp` file and replace the `_tWinMain` function with the following:

```
int APIENTRY _tWinMain(HINSTANCE hInstance,
                       HINSTANCE hPrevInstance,
                       LPSTR     lpCmdLine,
                       int       nCmdShow)
{
_Module.Init(NULL, hInstance);

CMyWindow wnd;
wnd.Create(NULL,
           CWindow::rcDefault,
           _T("Hello"),
           WS_OVERLAPPEDWINDOW|WS_VISIBLE);

MSG msg;
while(GetMessage(&msg, NULL, 0, 0))
 {
 TranslateMessage(&msg);
 DispatchMessage(&msg);
 }
}
```

What you're doing here is simply initializing the `CComModule`, creating and processing the application's message queue, and de-initializing the `CComModule` upon application exit. (Don't forget to include the `MyWindow.h` file as well.)

Testing the HelloATL application

Now, simply build and run the demo application. You should see a window displaying a simple Hello ATL message in the client area, as shown in Figure 31-6.

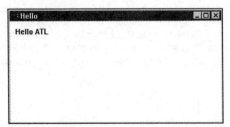

Figure 31-6: Creating a simple Hello World type application with ATL is probably much easier than you thought.

Easy, eh? Now let's take this a step further with another demo in the next section.

ATL Frame-View Application Demo

Now that you've seen how to create a basic Windows application using ATL, let's take this up a notch and use ATL to create an application that is modeled on the MFC SDK frame-view architecture. Actually, you'll create a couple of versions of this application with each version adding functionality to the preceding version.

The first version of this demo application is a simple version of the famed MFC Scribble application. In this demo application, you learn several key aspects of ATL windows. First, you see how to include into an ATL application a main frame and view class that most MFC developers are accustomed to seeing and then you learn how to handle mouse messages as you allow the user to draw on the client area of the view. Once you've done that, the second and third versions of this demo illustrate how to add menus and dialog boxes to an application.

Creating the Scribble project

Create a Win32 Application, as you did in the previous example, called ATLScribble. Next, add the following include directives for the ATL headers as well as a reference to a global CComModule object in your stdafx.h file.

```
#include <atlbase.h>
extern CComModule _Module;
#include <atlcom.h>
#include <atlwin.h>
```

Now, open the ATLScribble.cpp file and add the following global declaration of the CComModule object and the object map to the top of the file (after the include directives).

```
CComModule _Module;

BEGIN_OBJECT_MAP(ObjectMap)
END_OBJECT_MAP()
```

Adding a mainframe window

So far, you've added the ATL support exactly as you did in the first demo. Now, you add a main frame window. Right-click the root node in Class View and select the Add Class option from the context menu. Select the Generic C++ Class template and click Open. When the Generic C++ Class Wizard dialog box appears, type a Class Name of CMainFrame and a base class of CWindowImpl<CMainFrame, CWindow, CFrameWinTraits>. Once again, you will receive a warning message because the Wizard cannot locate the CWindowImpl class in the current project. Click Yes at the message box asking you if you want to continue adding the class. In this newly created MainFrame.h file, declare the following window class name and message map as follows:

```
DECLARE_WND_CLASS(_T("MyFrame"))

BEGIN_MSG_MAP(CMainFrame)
END_MSG_MAP()
```

> **Note**   One thing to keep in mind is that, as always, you can define whatever access levels (public, private or protected) you want for own class members. However, the DECLARE_WND_CLASS macro must be declared as public. If you declare it as protected or private, your project will not compile, because the ATL CWindowImpl::GetWndClassInfo function won't be able to access it.

If you open the Class View and click through the CMainFrame hierarchy, you'll see that quite a few functions are being inherited from the CWindowImpl and CWindowImplBaseT classes. One of those functions is the virtual function OnFinalMessage, which is called by ATL when a WM_NCDESTROY message is received. At this point, add the following virtual override to the CMainFrame class:

```
void OnFinalMessage(HWND /*hWnd*/)
{
  ::PostQuitMessage(0);
}
```

Now that you have a main frame window, open the ATLScribble.cpp file and add an include directive for the MainFrame.h file. Next, modify the _tWinMain function so that when finished, it appears as follows:

```
int APIENTRY _tWinMain(HINSTANCE hInstance,
                       HINSTANCE hPrevInstance,
                       LPSTR     lpCmdLine,
                       int       nCmdShow)
{
  _Module.Init(NULL, hInstance, NULL);

  CMainFrame mf;
  mf.Create(GetDesktopWindow(),
            CWindow::rcDefault,
            _T("My App"));
  mf.ShowWindow(SW_SHOWNORMAL);

  MSG msg;
  while (GetMessage(&msg, 0, 0, 0))
  {
    TranslateMessage(&msg);
```

```
    DispatchMessage(&msg);
  }

  _Module.Term();
}
Adding a View Window
```

As a checkpoint, you should be able to build and run the application. It doesn't do anything right now, but I find it helpful when following a long series of steps to test along the way. If the application doesn't build, you might want to either revisit the steps outlined previously or compare your code with that on the Web site for this book.

Now add a view class. Right-click in Class View to create yet another Generic C++ Class. This time, give the class a Class Name of CViewWin and specify its base class as CWindowImpl<CViewWin, CWindow, CWinTraits<WS_CHILD | WS_VISIBLE, WS_EX_CLIENTEDGE> >. Once again, answer Yes to the message box warning you that the CWindowImpl definition could not be found in the current project. Open the WinView.h file and add the following include directive:

```
#include "stdafx.h"
```

Then add the following declarations to the bottom of the class definition:

```
    DECLARE_WND_CLASS(_T("MyView"))

    BEGIN_MSG_MAP(CMainFrame)
    END_MSG_MAP()
```

Open the MainFrame.h file, add an include directive for the ViewWin.h file, and add the following member variable to the CMainFrame class:

```
public:
  CViewWin m_wndView;
```

The main frame is responsible for creating the view. Therefore, add the following entry (in bold) into the message map:

```
BEGIN_MSG_MAP(CMainFrame)
  MESSAGE_HANDLER(WM_CREATE, OnCreate)
END_MSG_MAP()
```

The OnCreate function then simply uses the m_wndView member variable you already defined to create the view window. Just add it to the CMainFrame class's definition.

```
LRESULT OnCreate(UINT uMsg, WPARAM wParam,
                 LPARAM lParam, BOOL& bHandled)
{
  m_wndView.Create(m_hWnd,
                   CWindow::rcDefault,
                   _T("MyView"));
  return 0;
}
```

The last thing you add before getting into the code that allows the user to draw on the client area is a WM_SIZE handler. Once again, add an entry into the CMainFrame class' message map and the actual function (both shown in the following code) to the class:

```
BEGIN_MSG_MAP(CMainFrame)
  MESSAGE_HANDLER(WM_CREATE, OnCreate)
```

```
 MESSAGE_HANDLER(WM_SIZE, OnSize)
END_MSG_MAP()
...
LRESULT OnSize(UINT uMsg, WPARAM wParam,
               LPARAM lParam, BOOL& bHandled)
{
 RECT r;
 GetClientRect(&r);

 m_wndView.SetWindowPos(NULL, &r,
                        SWP_NOZORDER | SWP_NOACTIVATE );

 return 0;
}
```

Handling mouse input

At this point, you've learned how to create a mainframe window and a view window. Now, you can start coding the specifics of your simplified Scribble application. The first thing you need to do is to write handlers for the WM_LBUTTONDOWN, WM_MOUSEMOVE, and WM_LBUTTONUP messages. These handlers enable the user to draw lines on the client area using the mouse. One point to insert here is that although this type of UI might seem very simple, it's important to realize that the basics learned here will be used in all your ATL Windows applications, regardless of complexity—especially in the area of UI response and message handling. To begin, add two POINT data members to the view class:

```
class CView :
...
protected:
 POINT m_startPoint;
 POINT m_endPoint;
...
```

Now, open the ViewWin.cpp file and initialize these two new members to –1 in the CWinView constructor.

```
CViewWin::CViewWin(void)
{
 m_startPoint.x = -1;
 m_startPoint.y = -1;

 m_endPoint.x = -1;
 m_endPoint.y = -1;
}
```

Next, add the handlers for the three mouse messages. Begin by adding the following entries to the CWinView class' message map:

```
class CWinView:
...
BEGIN_MSG_MAP(CMainFrame)
 MESSAGE_HANDLER(WM_LBUTTONDOWN, OnLButtonDown)
 MESSAGE_HANDLER(WM_LBUTTONUP, OnLButtonUP)
 MESSAGE_HANDLER(WM_MOUSEMOVE, OnMouseMove)
```

```
END_MSG_MAP()
```

...

First, code the CWinView::OnLButtonDown handler in order to keep track of the start point of a line. One thing to note here is that when handling mouse messages in MFC, you know that the lParam being passed to the handler contains a CPoint value indicating the client coordinates of the mouse at the time the mouse event occurred. Unfortunately, that is not the case with ATL. Here you need to manually extract the mouse coordinates using the very old-fashioned LOWORD and HIWORD macros.

```
LRESULT OnLButtonDown(UINT uMsg, WPARAM wParam,
                      LPARAM lParam, BOOL& bHandled)
{
 // Keep track of the beginning of the line
 // being drawn.
 m_startPoint.x = LOWORD(lParam);
 m_startPoint.y = HIWORD(lParam);

 return 0;
}
```

Next, in the CWinView::OnLButtonUP handler, reset the start point to –1 to indicate that no line is currently being drawn.

```
LRESULT OnLButtonUP(UINT uMsg, WPARAM wParam,
                    LPARAM lParam, BOOL& bHandled)
{
 // The user has stopped drawing, so initialize
 // the start point variable.
 m_startPoint.x = -1;
 m_startPoint.y = -1;

 return 0;
}
```

Obviously, the CWinView::OnMouseMove does the majority of the heavy lifting:

```
LRESULT OnMouseMove(UINT uMsg, WPARAM wParam,
                    LPARAM lParam, BOOL& bHandled)
{
 // If the user is currently drawing something...
 if (-1 != m_startPoint.x)
 {
  // Retrieve the current mouse coordinates.
  m_endPoint.x = LOWORD(lParam);
  m_endPoint.y = HIWORD(lParam);

  // Get the device context handle for drawing.
  HDC hdc = GetDC();

  // Use standard GDI calls to draw the line
  MoveToEx(hdc, m_startPoint.x, m_startPoint.y, NULL);
  LineTo(hdc, m_endPoint.x, m_endPoint.y);

  // Move the start point to end point so that
  // you don't waste cycles rewriting the same
```

```
    // part of the line over and over again.
    m_startPoint.x = m_endPoint.x;
    m_startPoint.y = m_endPoint.y;
  }

  return 0;
}
```

At this point, build and run the ATLScribble application. You should find that you could draw on the client area by holding down the mouse and moving it around (Figure 31-7).

Figure 31-7: Once you get the basics down, doing UI work in ATL isn't that difficult.

Adding menus

You just don't see too many Windows applications without menus. Therefore, in this section, I'll show you how to add menu support to an ATL application. The menu to be added enables the user to select from a choice of pen colors that will be used when drawing on the client area.

First, insert a menu resource. To do this, open the Resource View, right-click on the Menu folder, and select the Insert Menu option from the context menu. The new menu (IDR_MENU1) automatically opens in edit mode. Simply add a top-level menu of &Set Color with three child menu items: &Red, &Green, and &Blue. Note that the ampersands are optional and simply provide mnemonics for each of the menu options. Figure 31-8 shows the completed menu.

Because you load the menu in the _tWinMain function, open the ATLScribble.cpp file and add the following include directive:

```
#include "resource.h"
```

Now update the _tWinMain function to load the menu, and then pass the menu's handle to the CMainFrame::Create function:

```
HMENU hMenu = LoadMenu(_Module.GetResourceInstance(),
                   MAKEINTRESOURCE(IDR_MENU1));
mf.Create(GetDesktopWindow(),
        CWindow::rcDefault,
        _T("My App"),
        0,
        0,
        (UINT)hMenu);
```

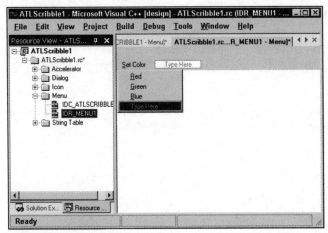

Figure 31-8: Visual Studio makes it a snap to add a menu to an application regardless of whether you're programming with MFC or ATL.

If you were to build and run the application, you would see that you now have a menu. Now, let's plug the menu options into some code. First, add a public `COLORREF` member variable called `m_color` to the view class. You use this variable to hold the currently selected user color.

```
class CWinView :
...
public:
 COLORREF m_color;
...
```

Initialize this value in the `CViewWin` class' constructor to black.

```
CWinView::CWinView(void)
{
 ...
 // Default the color to black
 m_color = RGB(0,0,0);
 ...
}
```

If you add the menu items and allow Visual Studio to set the resource IDs, then the IDs will have the form `ID_XXX_YYY` where *XXX* is the name of the top menu and *YYY* is the name of the menu option. Therefore, the Red menu option under the Set Color menu will have a resource ID of `ID_SETCOLOR_RED`.

At this point, add a handler for each of your three menu options into the `CMainFrame` class (shown here in bold). Notice the use of the `COMMAND_ID_HANDLER` as opposed to the `MESSAGE_HANDLER` that you've been using. As mentioned earlier in the chapter, command messages (such as menu commands) are handled via the `COMMAND_ID_HANDLER` while the `MESSAGE_HANLDER` is used for handling Windows messages. (Don't forget to also include the `resource.h` file at the top of the `MainFrame.h` file.)

```
class CMainFrame:
...
BEGIN_MSG_MAP(CMainFrame)
```

```
MESSAGE_HANDLER(WM_CREATE, OnCreate)
MESSAGE_HANDLER(WM_SIZE, OnSize)
COMMAND_ID_HANDLER(ID_SETCOLOR_RED, OnSetColorRed)
COMMAND_ID_HANDLER(ID_SETCOLOR_GREEN, OnSetColorGreen)
COMMAND_ID_HANDLER(ID_SETCOLOR_BLUE, OnSetColorBlue)
END_MSG_MAP()
...
```

Now, code the three CMainFrame menu handlers to update the CViewWin::m_color variable.
Set the three handlers to do the obvious work, and test again:

```
class CMainFrame:
...
LRESULT OnColorRed(WORD wNotifyCode,
                   WORD wID,
                   HWND hWndCtl,
                   BOOL& bHandled)
{
 m_wndView.m_color = RGB(255,0,0);
 return 0;
}

LRESULT OnColorGreen(WORD wNotifyCode,
                     WORD wID,
                     HWND hWndCtl,
                     BOOL& bHandled)
{
 m_wndView.m_color = RGB(0,255,0);
 return 0;
}

LRESULT OnColorBlue(WORD wNotifyCode,
                    WORD wID,
                    HWND hWndCtl,
                    BOOL& bHandled)
{
 m_wndView.m_color = RGB(0,0,255);
 return 0;
}
...
```

Finally, modify the CView::OnMouseMove function to use the newly selected user color. Here
I've reproduced that function with the changes you need to make highlighted in bold:

```
LRESULT OnMouseMove(UINT uMsg, WPARAM wParam,
                    LPARAM lParam, BOOL& bHandled)
{
 // If the user is currently drawing something...
 if (-1 != m_startPoint.x)
 {
  // Retrieve the current mouse coordinates.
  m_endPoint.x = LOWORD(lParam);
  m_endPoint.y = HIWORD(lParam);

  // Get the device context handle for drawing.
```

```
HDC hdc = GetDC();

// Create a solid pen with a width of 2 and
// the color specified by the user.
HPEN hPen = CreatePen(PS_SOLID, 2, m_color);

// Select the new pen into the device context,
// saving the old pen for later restoration.
HPEN hOldPen = (HPEN)SelectObject(hdc, hPen);

// Use standard GDI calls to draw the line.
MoveToEx(hdc, m_startPoint.x, m_startPoint.y, NULL);
LineTo(hdc, m_endPoint.x, m_endPoint.y);

// Move the start point to end point so that
// you don't waste cycles rewriting the same
// part of the line over and over again.
m_startPoint.x = m_endPoint.x;
m_startPoint.y = m_endPoint.y;

// Restore the old pen.
SelectObject(hdc, hOldPen);
}

return 0;
}
```

If you build and test the ATLScribble application now, you should see that you could now change colors to draw in any one of three different colors (four if you count the starting default color of black).

Summary

After an introduction to the ATL windowing classes and how message maps are implemented in order to control message processing, you learned how to write a basic, no-frills Windows application using ATL. After that, you then worked through a series of demos illustrating how to create frames and views, add and respond to menu events, and even work with modal dialog boxes and controls. What you should come away from this chapter with is the fact that ATL can be used for much more than just writing COM components, and that with just a bit of work, you can write full-blown Windows applications that are faster and more lightweight than their MFC counterparts. In fact, over the past two chapters, you've had an introduction to ATL and have learned how to create Windows applications using ATL. In the next chapters, you'll build on this by learning how to both source and respond to events.

✦   ✦   ✦

Eventing with ATL

*E*venting is one of the more obscure areas of COM technology. Many COM objects have no need for events. On the other hand, some objects — notably ActiveX Controls — make heavy use of events. The architecture of events is somewhat unexpected. So, too, is the way that you code events — both on the client-side and the server-side. Although the MFC and ATL both support events to varying degrees, the wizard support is minimal. Indeed, although the ATL wizards support events to a greater degree than the MFC wizards, the ATL wizards are notoriously inconsistent when it comes to events.

There is also a history of confusion in event terminology: For instance, an event interface is also called an *outgoing* or source interface. A *connection point* interface is associated with an event interface, but is not the same thing. The implementation of the event interface is called the *sink*. Confused yet? Worry not; all will be revealed. In this chapter, you'll consider exactly what events are, and the various choices you have for implementing them. These choices depend on whether your project is using attributes or not, and the degree to which you planned for supporting events when you used the wizard to generate the initial code.

What Are Events?

In the normal COM scheme of things, the client drives the communication between client and server. The client creates the server's COM object and makes calls into the object as it needs to. The object generally sits there passively waiting for calls to come in from clients.

What if your object needs to inform the client that something interesting has happened? For instance, a button control would want to tell the client when it has been clicked, or an object might be doing something in the background and want to inform the client when it's finished.

Suppose, for example, you have a COM object that is looking after a database. The object exposes an interface that includes a method to update the database indexes. This is a long operation, and the client doesn't want to block on the call waiting for it to complete. So the UpdateIndexes method starts the job and returns straight away. The client will want to know when the background-indexing job is finished.

You could address this by implementing some form of polling. The client could periodically call into some method on the object to see if the event had occurred, for example, to see if the button had been clicked or the background job finished. This would clearly be very inefficient.

Instead, suppose the object could call a method on the client. Then the object could call the method as soon as the conditions warranted it: when the button was clicked, or when the object was finished doing its background processing. For this to work, of course, it means that the client must expose a callback function for the server to call. Because the object and client live in the COM world, the correct way to do this is for the client to implement an interface that lists the method. Both client and object need to know about this interface: the client implements it, and the object calls into the client's implementation at a time when the object has finished updating its indexes. This is shown in Figure 32-1.

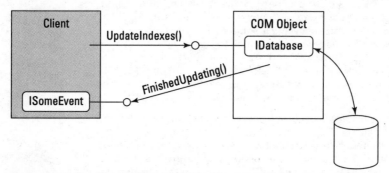

Figure 32-1: The client calls a method on the COM object, which calls the client's interface when the task is finished.

Before considering the code necessary for implementing events, suppose you have a simplified version of this client and server, where instead of firing an event, the server merely produces a MessageBox when it has finished updating its indexes. The object code might look like this (simplified and not completely robust):

```
void __stdcall DoUpdate(void*)
{
    Sleep(3000);    // Simulate doing some work.
    MessageBox(0,"Finished Updating Indexes", "Msg", 0);
}


STDMETHODIMP CDbObject::UpdateIndexes(void)
{
    // Create a thread to do the work,
    // so you don't block the client.
    DWORD tID;
    CreateThread(0, 0,
                 (LPTHREAD_START_ROUTINE)DoUpdate,
                 0, 0,
                 &tID);

    return S_OK;
}
```

The simple client code might look like this:

```
#import "..\DbServer\_DbServer.tlb" no_namespace named_guids
```

```
int _tmain(int argc, _TCHAR* argv[])
{
    CoInitialize(NULL);

    try
    {
        IDbObjectPtr p(CLSID_CDbObject);
        p->UpdateIndexes();

        cout << "Doing something else while the object works";
        for (int i = 0; i < 10; i++)
        {
            cout << ".";
            Sleep(1000);
        }
        cout << endl;
    }
    catch(_com_error& e)
    {
        cout << e.ErrorMessage();
    }

    CoUninitialize();
    return 0;
}
```

The Source Interface

An event interface is called an *outgoing* or *source* interface. It's *outgoing* because the method calls are outgoing from the object to the client, unlike a regular interface where the calls are incoming to the object from a client. It's called *source* because the object is the source of the calls. The client is the *sink* for calls on this interface. In a sense, the client is acting like a server, and the COM object is acting like a client.

Now for a plot twist. Normally, a COM object both defines and implements an interface, and describes and publishes the interface in its type library (originally, of course, in its IDL source file). Now, however, you have a situation where the client will implement the interface. So, where should the interface be defined? Logically, in the client's IDL file, but the client is not a COM server so it doesn't have an IDL file. The solution is a slightly asymmetric strategy: the COM object server will define the interface in its IDL file along with all the regular incoming interfaces. However, the object won't implement it. The client will implement it.

There's one final twist in the tale. Normally, the client reads (via #import, for instance) the server's type library to generate wrapper code for the methods implemented on the server. Now you're in a situation where the server needs to read the client's type library to generate wrapper code for the methods implemented on the client. However, as I just mentioned, the client doesn't have a type library. So the server reads its own type library (where the outgoing interface is described) to generate the wrapper code.

Wizard Support for Events

In Figure 32-2, you can see that I've added an ATL object via the ATL Simple Object Wizard (this is the actual demo project).

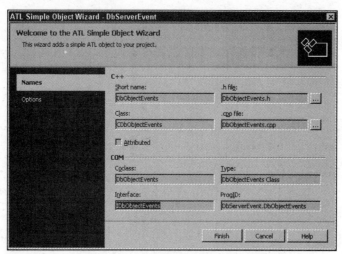

Figure 32-2: Standard ATL Simple Object Wizard dialog box with options selected for this particular demo application

The key point here is to click the Options tab, and then to select the Connection points checkbox (shown in Figure 32-3). (You'll learn about connection points shortly.)

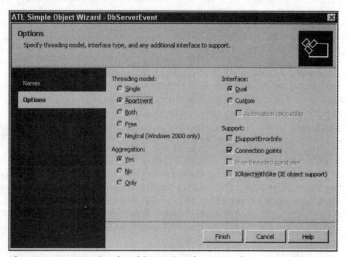

Figure 32-3: ATL Simple Object Wizard support for connection points

This generates almost all the necessary code, including the definition of an interface suitable for being designated an event interface, and code to flag this interface as an event interface. Exactly what code gets generated depends on whether you've chosen to use attributes in the project or not.

Event Interface Definition

If you create the code for a new COM object from scratch, you'd make it support connection points by choosing that option in the ATL Simple Object Wizard, as mentioned in the previous section. (Note that if you're still unsure of what a connection point is, I'll cover that in the next section, "Connection Points and IConnectionPoint.")

However, you might need to add this code manually after using the wizard to generate the initial object code. The following code fragments detail the required additional code.

For an attributed project, the definition (in C++) for an event interface looks like this:

```
[
    dispinterface,
    uuid("4E5C8AEC-0F6B-46A1-9451-FF8E3168AAA0"),
    helpstring("_IDbObjectEvents Interface")
]
__interface _IDbObjectEvents
{
    [id(1),
     helpstring("method FinishedUpdating")]
    HRESULT FinishedUpdating(void);
};
```

The corresponding code in the object class to define this as an outgoing interface looks like this:

```
[
    coclass,
    uuid("CB3F3AC4-DB2A-44C2-A2CC-8C024EA75617"),
    event_source("com"),
    ...
]
class ATL_NO_VTABLE CDbObject : public IDbObject
{
public:
    __event __interface _IDbObjectEvents;
    ...
};
```

The FinishedUpdating event is fired by the COM object whenever it deems appropriate. Note that there's nothing in the interface definition itself that tells you whether the interface is a source or sink interface. It can be either, depending on how it's used. Whether it's a source interface is determined by your particular object. For a nonattributed project, the event interface is defined in IDL like this:

```
[
    uuid(9D9FDBDE-0304-475B-9702-23A34CED0784),
```

```
        helpstring("_IDbObjectEvents Interface")
    ]
    dispinterface _IDbObjectEvents
    {
        properties:
        methods:
        [id(1), helpstring("method FinishedUpdating")]
HRESULT FinishedUpdating(void);
    };
```

Again, there's nothing in the IDL or the interface itself that tells you whether the interface is a source or sink interface. In this case, whether it's a source interface is determined by its entry in the `coclass` section of the IDL:

```
    [
        uuid(C3565BE9-5946-4DD6-A2C0-5DC56F254952),
        helpstring("DbObject Class")
    ]
    coclass DbObject
    {
        [default] interface IDbObject;
        [default, source] dispinterface _IDbObjectEvents;
    };
```

Note that you've specified that the `_IDbObjectEvents` interface is both an outgoing (source) interface and the default source interface. VB and scripting languages deal with only one source interface per COM object, so it's best to use the `default` attribute. Remember that the source object does not implement the source interface—it merely defines it through its type library. The client actually implements the source interface, having read the server's type library to find out the details of this interface.

You've specified the outgoing interface to be a `dispinterface`, because it's easier for a language such as VB or VBA to get event calls on a dispatch interface instead of on a custom interface, so that's all they support. If you're writing your own sink in C++ and you don't care about other clients, you can use a custom interface for improved performance. However, in most cases, events are relatively rare, so usually the performance isn't a big issue.

Connection Points and IConnectionPoint

Although I've mentioned the term *connection point* a few times, it bears defining at this juncture. You can think of a connection point as you would a socket in network programming. The way this works is that the client first implements an interface, which it plugs into the connection point. The component then calls the interface implemented by the client. In COM, these interfaces are defined as outgoing (or source) interfaces. In fact, as you saw in the definition of `_IDbObjectEvents` in the previous section, outgoing interfaces are defined in IDL via the `source` attribute.

```
    [default, source] dispinterface _IDbObjectEvents;
```

One way to easily remember these terms is to keep in mind that the interface is called an *outgoing interface* because it is the component that is calling the client. In addition, because the component is the source of the calls to the interface the term *source interface* is also appropriate. Another term that you'll hear frequently regarding connection points is *connectable object*. In ATL parlance, a connectable object is one that supports outgoing interfaces.

Although the COM object doesn't implement the source interface(s) it defines, it does implement a connection point for each of these source interfaces. Your source object will have exactly one connection point for each outgoing interface. Connection points are separate COM objects, but they're created by your object, not by CoCreateInstance, and typically implement only two interfaces: IUnknown and IConnectionPoint. The design works like this: The object needs to call into the client's implementation of the event interface. That means the object needs a pointer into the client's interface. How does the object get this pointer? The object offers a connection pointer interface for each source interface. The client calls into the object's connection point interface that corresponds to the event interface it implements. In this call, the client passes across to the object the interface pointer on its own implementation of the event interface.

The most important methods of IConnectionPoint are Advise and Unadvise. The client (sink) calls IConnectionPoint::Advise on the connection point object to establish the connection. The crucial parameter to Advise is the IUnknown pointer to the sink object that implements the event interface. The implementation of Advise stores this interface pointer in the connection point object. After that, the source object can fire an event by getting the interface pointer from the connection point object and calling a method on that pointer.

Advise returns a cookie—a DWORD with a unique value that represents this connection. To break the connection, the client calls Unadvise with the same cookie. This causes the connection point object to delete the associated interface pointer. It's vital for your client to do this when it no longer wants to receive events. Because multicasting is supported, it's possible for more than one connection to be made using the same connection point. When the event is fired, the source object has to call the correct method on each connection. If 20 objects have called Advise, when you fire the FinishedUpdating event, 20 calls to FinishedUpdating will be made, one for each interface pointer passed to Advise.

IConnectionPointContainer

COM objects can support more than one connection point. In order to do this, the source object must implement the IConnectionPointContainer interface. This interface allows the client object to obtain a connection point. IConnectionPointContainer is a simple interface, with only two methods:

✦ FindConnectionPoint returns a pointer to the connection point specified by the IID passed by the client object.

✦ EnumConnectionPoints returns an IEnumConnectionPoints enumerator that allows the holder to walk through all of the connection points supported by the source object.

The source object also maintains a collection of connection points that can be searched and enumerated via the methods in IConnectionPointContainer. Each connection point maintains a list of active connections, set up by calls to the connection point's Advise method and ended by calls to the connection point's Unadvise method.

In an attributed project, this code is largely opaque. However, for a nonattributed project, the declaration of the C++ object class would include all the necessary additions:

✦ IConnectionPointContainer in the object inheritance, and in the COM map

✦ A proxy class in the object inheritance that encapsulates the client's implementation of the event interface

✦ A connection point map listing all the connection points implemented by this object

Let's take a look at some code to see what I'm referring to.

```
class ATL_NO_VTABLE CDbObject :
    public CComObjectRootEx<CComSingleThreadModel>,
    public CComCoClass<CDbObject, &CLSID_DbObject>,
    public IConnectionPointContainerImpl<CDbObject>,
    public CProxy_IDbObjectEvents<CDbObject>,
    public IDispatchImpl<IDbObject,
                         &IID_IDbObject,
                         &LIBID_DbServerEventLib,
                         /*wMajor =*/ 1,
                         /*wMinor =*/ 0>
{
public:


BEGIN_COM_MAP(CDbObject)
    COM_INTERFACE_ENTRY(IDbObject)
    COM_INTERFACE_ENTRY(IDispatch)
    COM_INTERFACE_ENTRY(IConnectionPointContainer)
END_COM_MAP()

BEGIN_CONNECTION_POINT_MAP(CDbObject)
    CONNECTION_POINT_ENTRY(__uuidof(_IDbObjectEvents))
END_CONNECTION_POINT_MAP()

...
};
```

Note that this proxy class initially looks like this:

```
template <class T>
class CProxy_IDbObjectEvents : public IConnectionPointImpl<T,
  &__uuidof( _IDbObjectEvents ), CComDynamicUnkArray>
{
    //Warning--this class will be regenerated by the wizard.
public:
};
```

Later, you'll see how the wizard regenerates this class to encapsulate calls to potential client implementations of the event interface.

Sequence of Calls to Set Up an Event

The definition and firing of an event is sometimes called *sourcing an event*. The following sequence of steps should be followed to properly source events in ATL.

1. The client queries the source object for `IConnectionPointContainer`. That means all connectable objects (source objects) should implement `IConnectionPointContainer`. If an object doesn't implement `IConnectionPointContainer`, it suggests that it doesn't fire any events at all.

2. If the `QueryInterface` succeeds, the client passes `IConnectionPointContainer::FindConnectionPoint` the IID of an event interface it wants to receive. If the connectable object supports that interface, it returns a pointer to the connection point object for that interface. Alternatively, the client can call `IConnectionPointContainer::EnumConnectionPoints` to get an enumerator, so it can examine all of the supported connection points (and see whether it understands any of them).

3. If it receives a pointer to a connection point, the client calls `IConnectionPoint::Advise` on that pointer, passing an `IUnknown` pointer pointing to the mini-object that will actually receive the events. The client is responsible for storing the cookie returned by `Advise`.

4. At this point, the client receives events on the interface pointer it passed — the source object enumerates the connections and calls the appropriate method on each one.

5. When it wants to stop receiving events (such as before it shuts down), it calls `IConnectionPoint::Unadvise`, passing the cookie it stored previously.

Note that a client implements event interfaces for only those events the client is interested in. The server might fire several different types of events and therefore have several event objects, each implementing `IConnectionPoint`. Also, there may be several clients connected to any particular server event. The general pattern is shown in Figure 32-4.

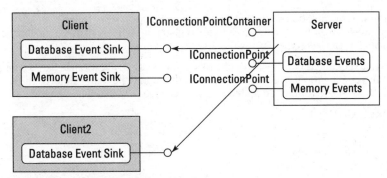

Figure 32-4: Using connection points

Nonattributed Server-Side Event Support

You've seen that you can add the additional connection point support to the object code either manually or by selecting the option in the Object Wizard dialog box. Recall, however, that the proxy class is only a skeleton at this stage. To complete the picture, you must generate additional code to fill in the details of this proxy class.

To get this additional code, you use a wizard in the server project to read the server's own type library to generate the proxy details. This is analogous to the #import directive used on the client-side to read a server's type library and generate proxy code.

For a nonattributed project, after the source interface is fully defined, compile the .idl file by right-clicking the .idl file in Solution Explorer and selecting Compile on the shortcut menu. This produces the type library. Next, right-click the object class in Class View, point to Add on the shortcut menu, and select Add Connection Point. This runs the Implement Connection Point Wizard, as shown in Figure 32-5.

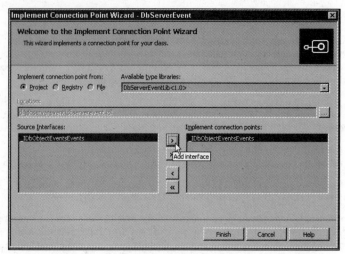

Figure 32-5: Running the Implement Connection Point Wizard

Note that if the wizard can't find a source interface in your type library that it considers you don't already have a proxy for, it will switch to the registry, and the Available type libraries list box will list all registered type libraries.

You might have to comment out the proxy class from the multiple inheritance list of your object class, and comment out or remove the connection point map entry to force the wizard to regenerate these entries and the detailed proxy class itself:

```
template<class T>
class CProxy_IDbObjectEvents :
   public IConnectionPointImpl<T,
          &__uuidof(_IDbObjectEvents)>
{
public:
   HRESULT Fire_FinishedUpdating()
   {
      HRESULT hr = S_OK;
      T * pThis = static_cast<T *>(this);
      int cConnections = m_vec.GetSize();

      for (int iConnection = 0; iConnection < cConnections;
           iConnection++)
      {
         pThis->Lock();
         CComPtr<IUnknown> punkConnection =
                        m_vec.GetAt(iConnection);
         pThis->Unlock();
```

```
        IDispatch * pConnection =
                static_cast<IDispatch *>(punkConnection.p);

        if (pConnection)
        {
            CComVariant varResult;

            DISPPARAMS params = { NULL, NULL, 0, 0 };
            hr = pConnection->Invoke(1, IID_NULL,
                LOCALE_USER_DEFAULT, DISPATCH_METHOD,
                &params, &varResult, NULL, NULL);
        }
    }
    return hr;
    }
};
```

As you can see, the proxy function `Fire_FinishedUpdating` simply iterates its list of connected clients and uses `Invoke` to call the client's implementation of the event interface method.

The final server-side piece of code is to trigger the event. Your much-simplified client and server object can now be updated to include event firing. On the server, you'd change the `MessageBox` to a call to the proxy `Fire_FinishedUpdating` method like this:

```
void __stdcall DoUpdate(void* p)
{
    Sleep(3000);
// MessageBox(0,"Finished Updating Indexes", "Msg", 0);
    CDbObject* pp = (CDbObject*)p;
    pp->Fire_FinishedUpdating();
}

STDMETHODIMP CDbObject::UpdateIndexes(void)
{
    DWORD tID;
    CreateThread(0, 0, (LPTHREAD_START_ROUTINE)DoUpdate,
                (void*)this, 0, &tID);

    return S_OK;
}
```

Attributed Server-Side Event Support

For attributed code, there is no exposed IDL for you to compile separately. Instead, you should make further use of attributes, specifically, the event-related attributes. The event-related attributes add code that uses the new .NET Unified Event Model. The Unified Event Model is designed to allow applications to use events in a way that minimizes the knowledge and dependencies that an object has on its clients and maximizes the object's reusability, and to do this consistently for native (non-COM) C++, COM, and managed classes. The elements of this model are listed in Table 32-1.

Table 32-1: The .NET Unified Event Model

Element	Description
Event source	An object that defines and contains events. You create an event source using the `event_source` attribute.
Event	A method within an event source that, when called, generates events. You define an event using the keyword `__event`. To *raise* an event means to *fire* it, by calling the event method.
Delegate	A class that can hold a reference to a method. A delegate class differs from other classes in that it has a signature and can hold references only to methods that match its signature.
Event receiver	Also called an *event sink,* this is an object that receives events. You create an event receiver using the `event_receiver` attribute.
Event handler	A method in an event receiver that receives events.
Hook	To hook an event means to associate (register) an event with an event handler. You associate a handler method with an event using the intrinsic function `__hook`. This will internally call `IConnectionPoint::Advise`.
Unhook	To unhook an event means to dissociate (deregister) an event from an event handler. You dissociate a handler method from an event using the intrinsic function `__unhook`. This will internally call `IConnectionPoint::Unadvise`.

Recall that the initial wizard-generated code for an object in an attributed project will already have included a declaration of the event source and event interface, like this:

```
[
    coclass,
    event_source("com"),
...
]
class ATL_NO_VTABLE CDbObject : public IDbObject
{
public:
    __event __interface _IDbObjectEvents;

...
};
```

Again, you can implement the `UpdateIndexes` interface method as before, except that instead of calling a proxy to the client's event interface method, you raise an event as shown in the following example:

```
void __stdcall DoUpdate(void* p)
{
    Sleep(3000);   // simulate doing some work
    CDbObject* pp = (CDbObject*)p;
// pp->Fire_FinishedUpdating();  // nonattributed approach
```

```
    __raise pp->FinishedUpdating();
}

STDMETHODIMP CDbObject::UpdateIndexes(void)
{
    // Create a thread to do the work,
    // so you don't block the client.
    DWORD tID;
    CreateThread(0, 0, (LPTHREAD_START_ROUTINE)DoUpdate,
                 (void*)this, 0, &tID);
    return S_OK;
}
```

Nonattributed Client-Side Event Support

Now that you have your server object happily firing events, you must turn your attention to the client. Recall that it is the client that implements the event interface. Also, the client must call Advise and Unadvise to connect and disconnect with the server object.

Given the same client as before, first make sure the #import is in the stdafx.h (the symbols it generates will be needed in several of your revised client files). You also need to rebuild the client in order to force the #import to re-read the server's type library and regenerate the TLH and TLI.

You could have asked for some (minimal) support for ATL in the client project when it was first created, but it's easy enough to add it now: just add these three lines to the bottom of the stdafx.h file (followed by the #import for the server's type library):

```
#include <atlbase.h>
extern CComModule _Module;
#include <atlcom.h>
```

Also, at the bottom of the stdafx.cpp file, add this line:

```
#include <atlimpl.cpp>
```

Next, in the client application .cpp file, declare a global instance of the CComModule class:

```
CComModule _Module;
```

Now add a call to the CComModule::Init and Term (do this just after the CoInit and CoUninit):

```
int _tmain(int argc, _TCHAR* argv[])
{
    CoInitialize(NULL);
    _Module.Init(NULL, GetModuleHandle(NULL));

    ...

    _Module.Term();
    CoUninitialize();
    return 0;
}
```

Now add a new class to implement the event interface. First, right-click the client project in Solution Explorer, and select Add ➪ Add class, and then a Generic C++ class. Name the class CEventHandler and derive this from IDispEventImpl. This is an ATL template class, and the template parameters should be something like this:

```
IDispEventImpl <0, CEventHandler, &DIID__IDbObjectEvents,
    &LIBID_DbServerEventLib, 1, 0>
```

Note that you can get the DIID and LIBID from the server's xxx_I.C file.

Next, you need to add a SINK map to the class CEventHandler by using BEGIN_SINK_MAP(...) and END_SINK_MAP. To the SINK map, add a SINK_ENTRY_EX macro for the event method FinishedUpdating, like this:

```
BEGIN_SINK_MAP(CEventHandler)
    SINK_ENTRY_EX(0, DIID__IDbObjectEvents, 1, \
                    FinishedUpdating)
END_SINK_MAP()
```

Add a prototype for the FinishedUpdating method. Remember that the function must use the __stdcall calling convention. You can find this function's signature in the .tlh file. Implement this function to do something obvious, like this:

```
HRESULT __stdcall CEventHandler::FinishedUpdating()
{
    MessageBox(0, "Finished Updating Indexes",
                "Event Received", 0);
    return S_OK;
}
```

Now you need to incorporate the EventHandler class within the client application. After instantiating the object, but before calling the method that triggers the server-side event firing, instantiate the client-side event handler class, and connect it to the object by calling Advise (or the IDispEventImpl wrapper DispEventAdvise). At the end, call DispEventUnadvise):

```
int _tmain(int argc, _TCHAR* argv[])
{
    CoInitialize(NULL);
    _Module.Init(NULL, GetModuleHandle(NULL));

    try
    {
        IDbObjectPtr p(CLSID_DbObject);
        CEventHandler eh;
        eh.DispEventAdvise(p);

        p->UpdateIndexes();

        cout << "Doing something else while the object works";
        for (int i = 0; i < 10; i++)
        {
            cout << ".";
            Sleep(1000);
```

```
        }
        cout << endl;

        eh.DispEventUnadvise(p);
    }
    catch(_com_error& e)
    {
        cout << e.ErrorMessage();
    }

    _Module.Term();
    CoUninitialize();
    return 0;
}
```

Attributed Client-Side Event Support

You could use the same client for both attribute-based and nonattributed server versions, because of course by the time the server is built, the use of source code attributes is no longer an issue. However, for the exercise, let's make use of attributes on the client-side also.

You need to add similar (but not identical) support for the ATL. First, add the following three lines to the bottom of the stdafx.h. Note that you don't (and in fact, can't) use CComModule in an attribute-based project:

```
#define _ATL_ATTRIBUTES 1
#include <atlbase.h>
#include <atlcom.h>
```

You also need this at the bottom of the stdafx.cpp file:

```
#include <atlimpl.cpp>
```

Next, in the client application .cpp file, import the server's type library, with one additional attribute: embedded_idl. This ensures that the event source type library is written to the .tlh file with the attribute-generated code preserved:

```
#import "..\DbServerAttEvent\_DbServerAttEvent.tlb" \
    no_namespace named_guids embedded_idl
```

To use attributes in a module, you need a module name attribute, as shown in the following example:

```
[ module(name="ClientModule") ];
```

The attributed equivalent of the client-side event handling class must be declared with the event_receiver(com) attribute. You offer a method to handle the event received. You also need to supply methods to hook and unhook the event (that is, to connect your event handling method with the server's connection point interface):

```
[ event_receiver(com) ]
class CEventHandler {
public:
    HRESULT HandleFinished()
```

```
        {
           MessageBox(0, "FinishedUpdating", "Event Received", 0);
           return S_OK;
        }

        void HookEvent(IDbObject* pSource)
        {
           __hook(&_IDbObjectEvents::FinishedUpdating,
              pSource, &CEventHandler::HandleFinished);
        }

        void UnhookEvent(IDbObject* pSource)
        {
           __unhook(&_IDbObjectEvents::FinishedUpdating,
              pSource, &CEventHandler::HandleFinished);
        }
   };
```

In `main`, unlike the nonattributed code, you don't use the `CComModule`. Instead of calling `IConnectionPoint::Advise` or `IDispEventImpl::DispEventAdvise`, you call the event handler class method to hook the event. Similarly, you use the following code to unhook the event:

```
   int _tmain(int argc, _TCHAR* argv[])
   {
       CoInitialize(NULL);
// _Module.Init(NULL, GetModuleHandle(NULL));

       try
       {
           IDbObjectPtr p(CLSID_CDbObject);
           CEventHandler eh;
//          eh.DispEventAdvise(p);
           eh.HookEvent(p);
           p->UpdateIndexes();

           cout << "Doing something else while the object works";
           for (int i = 0; i < 10; i++)
           {
               cout << ".";
               Sleep(1000);
           }
           cout << endl;

           eh.UnhookEvent(p);
//          eh.DispEventUnadvise(p);
       }
       catch(_com_error& e)
       {
           cout << e.ErrorMessage();
       }
```

```
//  _Module.Term();
    CoUninitialize();
    return 0;
}
```

At this point, you're done with the demo and you can build and run the application. Doing so will result in the output of the expected values and enforce your understanding of how to write client-side events in attributed ATL code.

Summary

You saw that events are a mechanism for establishing two-way communication between a client and a server. Although the architecture is unlike other areas of COM, it boils down to a fairly simple system. The server defines the event interface and publishes it in its type library. The client implements the interface and establishes the connection between the server and the client event implementation. The server has a proxy to the client's implementation. The event system is almost a micro version of the normal COM communication pattern, just in reverse.

When it comes to coding for events, it's easier to follow how the pattern is implemented if you don't use attributes (both server and client), but then, that's always true of attributes. Either way, if you trace and step through line by line, you'll find that the same `IConnectionPoint::Advise/Unadvise` mechanism is used regardless.

You also saw how the ATL comprehensively supports events—notably through such classes as `IDispEventImpl`. Finally, you learned about the Unified Event Model offered by .NET, and the extended keywords that are used to hook into this system. Continuing with our ATL discussion, in the next chapter you'll discover how to implement automation in your application using ATL.

✦   ✦   ✦

Automation with ATL

You've seen how the COM model, and specifically the underlying binary VTBL layout, allows components written in different source code languages to communicate with each other. The only requirement is that the language compiler can achieve the binary VTBL layout – and because this is essentially just a list of addresses, which is in turn just a list of integers, almost all compilers are capable of this. These languages are called *intimate clients* because once they've read the COM component's VTBL, they then have knowledge of the interfaces and properties the COM component exposes. Examples of intimate clients are languages such as Visual C++ and compiled Visual Basic.

However, some software is (increasingly) written in languages that cannot achieve this binary compatibility, simply because they are not compiled at all. Because these languages don't have the ability to directly acquire VTBL information about COM components, they are called *agnostic clients*. Examples of agnostic clients are scripting languages like VBScript and JScript and interpreted Visual Basic. Are these languages barred from using COM? Yes and No. Yes, they cannot cope with a VTBL, so they can't directly access a COM component's interfaces and properties. However, for a long time now, Microsoft has supported a higher-level layer on top of COM called *automation*.

In this chapter you'll see what the automation layer is, including the underlying mechanics represented by the `IDispatch` interface. I'll discuss the advantages and disadvantages of automation, and consider alternative ways to expose automation from a server. Finally, I'll explore alternative ways for a range of clients to use an automation server.

Introduction to Automation

Automation (formerly known as OLE Automation) is a COM protocol that allows COM objects to be used by clients that cannot use COM objects directly. At its simplest, automation provides a layer on top of the COM object to expose the object's properties and methods to clients that cannot use a VTBL or function pointers (such as clients written in scripting languages like VBScript or JavaScript). Later in this chapter I'll qualify this idea of a layer on top of COM, but for now the simplification will serve.

Since the early days, the terminology of automation has been heavily driven by VB develop-ment. In its early forms, VB was not a powerful development tool — it was good only for the front end, and had to connect to code written in other languages for any serious back-end processing. Also, in its early forms, VB couldn't talk directly to COM objects, hence the evolu-tion of automation. From VB6, VB is perfectly capable of all aspects of COM (with the excep-tion that VB objects must reside in a single-threaded apartment). However, other languages like VBScript are still in the same place that early VB used to be. There are two types of automation interfaces:

✦ *Dispinterfaces* are pure automation-only interfaces that do not offer a conventional COM VTBL. Functionality is exposed through an automation layer represented by implementing the four functions of the `IDispatch` interface.

✦ *Dual Interfaces* are interfaces derived from `IDispatch` (which is a COM interface), and therefore offer both a conventional COM VTBL as well as the strict automation func-tionality represented by the `IDispatch` functions.

I discuss both types of automation interfaces later in this chapter. Automation terminology includes two types of COM object exposed members:

✦ *Methods* are like the public member functions of a C++ class.

✦ *Properties* are named attributes of the object; they are like the data members of a C++ class. No COM object of any kind ever exposes its internal data members directly. Instead, you access these data members via `get` and `put` property functions. This level of detail is often obscured by the COM or automation runtime (such as the VB runtime or the Java virtual machine).

Ultimately, all COM objects, including automation objects, are accessed through a pointer to an interface. Interfaces expose only functions. The following example code shows how to set and get the `BatteryLife` property for a Robot object from a VB client. (You'll create the RobotServer project a bit later in the section "Creating an ATL Automation Server.")

```
Dim r As Object
r = CreateObject("RobotServer.Robot")

'Set a property
r.BatteryLife = 123&

'Get a property
bl = r.BatteryLife
```

Visual C++ does not hide the fact that setting or getting a property is in reality a function call. The following example code shows how to get and put the `BatteryLife` property for a Robot object from a Visual C++ client:

```
CRobot r;
r.CreateDispatch("RobotServer.Robot");
r.put_BatteryLife(123);
long bl = r.get_BatteryLife();
```

VARIANTs

Automation uses a self-describing data structure called a `VARIANT`. This structure contains two parts: a type field (`vt`), which represents the data type, and a data field, which represents the actual value of the data. The vt value governs the interpretation of the union, and values such as VT_I2, VT_I4, and so on are the constants that define valid data types. In other words, when you want to pass a parameter to an automation function, you pack your parameter data value into a VARIANT, and set its flag to indicate how the data should be interpreted. This mechanism supports the passing of parameters across different source code languages. In any automation communication, as long as both languages understand VARIANTs, and as long as you can pack your parameter data into VARIANTs, you can talk across the languages.

To simplify extracting values from VARIANTs, automation provides a set of functions for manipulating this type, and you should use these functions to ensure that all your code applies consistent coercion rules.

The point of VARIANTs is that the COM runtime DLLs (specifically the OLEAUT32.DLL) know how to marshal all the data types that can be packed into a VARIANT. Therefore, a significant benefit of using an automation (or automation conformant) interface is that you can hook into the standard marshaling code.

You should use the VARIANT type to specify variant data that cannot be passed by reference. The VARIANT type cannot have the VT_BYREF bit set. On the other hand, a variation on the VARIANT type, called a VARIANTARG, can be passed by reference. The variant types are defined in oaidl.h as indicated here:

```
struct tagVARIANT
{
 union
 {
  struct __tagVARIANT
  {
   VARTYPE vt;
   WORD wReserved1;
   WORD wReserved2;
   WORD wReserved3;
   union
   {
    LONGLONG llVal;          // VT_I8
    LONG lVal;               // VT_I4
    BYTE bVal;               // VT_UI1
    SHORT iVal;              // VT_I2
    FLOAT fltVal;            // VT_R4
    DOUBLE dblVal;           // VT_R8
    VARIANT_BOOL boolVal;    // VT_BOOL
    _VARIANT_BOOL bool;      // VT_BOOL
    SCODE scode;             // VT_ERROR
    CY cyVal;                // VT_CY
    DATE date;               // VT_DATE
    BSTR bstrVal;            // VT_BSTR
    IUnknown *punkVal;       // VT_UNKNOWN
    IDispatch *pdispVal;     // VT_DISPATCH
    SAFEARRAY *parray;       // VT_ARRAY
    BYTE *pbVal;             // VT_BYREF|VT_UI1
    SHORT *piVal;            // VT_BYREF|VT_I2
    LONG *plVal;             // VT_BYREF|VT_I4
    LONGLONG *pllVal;        // VT_BYREF|VT_I8
```

```
            FLOAT *pfltVal;            // VT_BYREF|VT_R4
            DOUBLE *pdblVal;           // VT_BYREF|VT_R8
            VARIANT_BOOL *pboolVal;    // VT_BYREF|VT_BOOL
            _VARIANT_BOOL *pbool;      // VT_BYREF|VT_BOOL
            SCODE *pscode;             // VT_BYREF|VT_ERROR
            CY *pcyVal;                // VT_BYREF|VT_CY
            DATE *pdate;               // VT_BYREF|VT_DATE
            BSTR *pbstrVal;            // VT_BYREF|VT_BSTR
            IUnknown **ppunkVal;       // VT_BYREF|VT_UNKNOWN
            IDispatch **ppdispVal;     // VT_BYREF|VT_DISPATCH
            SAFEARRAY **pparray;       // VT_BYREF|VT_ARRAY
            VARIANT *pvarVal;          // VT_BYREF|VT_VARIANT
            PVOID byref;               // VT_BYREF (Generic ByRef)
            CHAR cVal;                 // VT_I1
            USHORT uiVal;              // VT_UI2
            ULONG ulVal;               // VT_UI4
            ULONGLONG ullVal;          // VT_UI8
            INT intVal;                // VT_INT
            UINT uintVal;              // VT_UINT
            DECIMAL *pdecVal;          // VT_BYREF|VT_DECIMAL
            CHAR *pcVal;               // VT_BYREF|VT_I1
            USHORT *puiVal;            // VT_BYREF|VT_UI2
            ULONG *pulVal;             // VT_BYREF|VT_UI4
            ULONGLONG *pullVal;        // VT_BYREF|VT_UI8
            INT *pintVal;              // VT_BYREF|VT_INT
            UINT *puintVal;            // VT_BYREF|VT_UINT
            struct __tagBRECORD
            {
             PVOID pvRecord;
             IRecordInfo *pRecInfo;
            } __VARIANT_NAME_4;
          } __VARIANT_NAME_3;
        } __VARIANT_NAME_2;
      DECIMAL decVal;
    } __VARIANT_NAME_1;
};
```

Note   If you flag your interface with the `dual` or `oleautomation` attribute, you're telling the COM runtime that it can use standard marshaling for all the parameters for all the methods in the interface. That doesn't necessarily mean that the interface is an automation interface.

Note also that to flag an interface as automation-conformant doesn't mean that all parameters must be VARIANTs; it just means that the parameters must be either VARIANTs or any of the types that can be packed into a VARIANT.

The IDispatch interface

The IDispatch interface is the basis of the automation layer that sits on top of COM. IDispatch is itself a standard COM interface, derived from IUnknown. The purpose of IDispatch is to allow clients written in non-VTBL-capable languages to nonetheless use any properties or methods exposed by a COM object indirectly. Table 33-1 shows the main methods that the IDispatch interface exposes.

Table 33-1: IDispatch Methods

IDispatch Methods in Vtable Order	Description
(IUnknown methods)	QueryInterface, AddRef, and Release methods inherited from IUnknown
GetTypeInfoCount	Retrieves the number of type information interfaces that an object provides (either 0 or 1)
GetTypeInfo	Gets the type information for an object
GetIDsOfNames	Maps a single member and an optional set of argument names to a corresponding set of integer DISPIDs
Invoke	Provides access to properties and methods exposed by an object

The general sequence of events is:

1. Through documentation, an object-browser utility or the development environment, the author of the client application gets a list of the properties and methods exposed by a COM object. Often this documentation is supplied via the GetTypeInfoCount and GetTypeInfo methods of IDispatch.

2. The client author writes code to access these properties and methods, for example, r.BatteryLife.

3. The COM runtime support (such as the VB runtime or Java virtual machine) passes this BatteryLife property name to IDispatch::GetIDsOfNames, which takes in a string and returns a 32-bit value that identifies the property internally (called a DISPID), such as 99.

4. The runtime then passes this DISPID to IDispatch::Invoke, along with any parameters expected by this property/method in the form of one or more VARIANTs, for example, Invoke function number 99.

5. IDispatch::Invoke accesses the internal property or method specified by the DISPID (function number 99, in this case), and passes any parameters on to that property/method.

To better understand how the IDispatch interface works, consider a manual implementation of GetIDsOfNames:

```
STDMETHODIMP CRobot::GetIDsOfNames(REFIID riid,
                                   OLECHAR ** rgszNames,
                                   UINT cNames,
                                   LCID lcid,
                                   DISPID * rgDispId)
{
    HRESULT rc = S_OK;
    char funcName[50];

    WideCharToMultiByte(CP_ACP, NULL, rgszNames[0],
        -1, funcName, sizeof(funcName), NULL, NULL);
```

```
    if (1 != cNames)
        rc = E_INVALIDARG;
    else if (lstrcmp(funcName, "BatteryLife") == 0)
        rgDispId[0] = 1;
    else if (lstrcmp(funcName, "Speak") == 0)
        rgDispId[0] = 2;
    else
    {
        rgDispId[0] = DISPID_UNKNOWN;
        rc = DISP_E_UNKNOWNNAME;
    }
    return rc;
}
```

As you can see, this is little more than a mapping between a string and an integer. The client code wants to invoke a particular function (access a method or property) that the client knows the name of. The client passes in the name as a string to the component's automation code, which string-compares it against the property/method names that it exposes. If the automation code finds a match, it returns the corresponding property/method numeric identifier. A corresponding implementation of Invoke is shown in the following example:

```
STDMETHODIMP CRobot::Invoke(DISPID dispIdMember,
                            REFIID riid,
                            LCID lcid,
                            WORD wFlags,
                            DISPPARAMS * pDispParams,
                            VARIANT * pVarResult,
                            EXCEPINFO * pExcepInfo,
                            UINT * puArgErr)
{
// Determine which function to call based on the dispid.
switch (dispIdMember)
{
 case 1:    // BatteryLife Property, getting or setting?
 // Some clients get a property with either/both flags set.
 if ((DISPATCH_PROPERTYGET | DISPATCH_METHOD)
 & wFlags )
  {
  if (0 == pDispParams->cArgs)
   {
   pVarResult->vt = VT_I4;
   pVarResult->lVal = m_BatteryLife;
   return NO_ERROR;
   }
  else
   return E_INVALIDARG;
  }
 else if (DISPATCH_PROPERTYPUT == wFlags)
  {
  // There must be one parameter...
  if (1 != pDispParams->cArgs)
   return E_INVALIDARG;

  // and it must be a long.
  if (VT_I4 == pDispParams->rgvarg[0].vt)
```

```
    {
      m_BatteryLife = pDispParams->rgvarg[0].lVal;
      return NO_ERROR;
    }
  }
  else
    return E_INVALIDARG;

  case 2:      // ...etc.
    return S_OK;

  default: // dispid is not 1 or 2
    return E_INVALIDARG;
  }
}
```

If you follow the comments, you'll see that the code first determines which function to call based on the client-supplied DISPID. Having matched this number against your internal list of properties and methods, the code then works out whether the client is attempting to access a method or a property. If it's a property, is the client attempting to get or set it? Next, the code extracts the parameter values (if any) from the DISPPARAMS parameter and checks that these values are of the correct type. On the client-side, the code packs each parameter into a VARIANT, and then packs all the VARIANTs into a DISPPARAMS. In this way, you can use Invoke to pass any number and type of parameter to the target property/method.

The code can then perform the required functional operations as dictated by the method request, or read from or to your internal state members for the required property access.

 Note   You could perform this step by delegating to some exposed COM function in the normal way, and in this case your automation code would truly be a layer sitting on top of COM. However, you could also simply perform the required actions directly or by calling some noninterface functions, in which case your automation code does not represent a layer on top of COM as far as your COM object is concerned. This distinction is the difference between a dual interface (which offers an automation layer on top of COM) and a dispinterface (which offers automation access only).

Dispinterfaces

IDL defines dispinterfaces differently from standard interfaces. A dispinterface is not a description of a VTBL layout, but is instead a description of the properties and methods that can be called through IDispatch::Invoke. Important differences between a standard interface and a dispinterface include the following:

✦ A dispinterface does not require that a return type be an HRESULT. Therefore, return types can be error codes, method results, get properties, or anything else that can be represented by a VARIANT data type.

✦ There is no requirement that a dispinterface be immutable, because functions are not called through a VTBL, so you can add and delete, or reorder the properties and methods in a dispinterface even dynamically.

✦ Properties and methods in a dispinterface can be localized, which is particularly useful when these properties or methods take strings or dates as parameters.

✦ Method invocations are slower through a dispinterface than through a standard interface because you're going through the automation layer.

✦ The compiler cannot do as much static type-checking and name resolution as it can do with a standard interface (because you're packing all sorts of data into VARIANTs). This might increase the number of errors.

Dual interfaces

A dual interface is an interface that derives from IDispatch (which itself is derived from IUnknown). If you derive from IDispatch, there are two consequences: You have to implement all the IUnknown functions and all the IDispatch functions in the conventional COM manner, thereby exposing a conventional VTBL. Also, because you implement the IDispatch functions, your object can be used by clients that don't understand the COM VTBL. In other words, you have the best of both worlds (and also the limitations).

The advantages are:

✦ You can use the standard marshaling provided by the COM runtime, because these DLLs understand how to marshal all automation-conformant data types.

✦ Your object is usable by the widest range of clients — both COM VTBL-aware clients, and scripting clients whose runtime understands automation.

✦ Clients that can use the COM VTBL benefit from improved performance over an object that exposes only a dispinterface.

The corresponding disadvantages are:

✦ Although a dispinterface is not immutable, conventional COM interfaces are immutable, and because some of the clients of a dual interface will be dependent on the VTBL, it means that dual interfaces are immutable.

✦ If you use the standard marshaling, you have to be automation-conformant. That is, all parameters on all functions in your interface must be types that the OLEAUT32.DLL knows about.

✦ Scripting clients cannot call QueryInterface, and cannot therefore indicate the interface they want to use. The consequence of this is that they can only use the interface you flag as the default interface on the object.

ATL support for IDispatch

ATL supports IDispatch and dual interfaces through its template class IDispatchImpl. As you would expect, IDispatchImpl provides a standard implementation of the four IDispatch methods. You can verify this for yourself if you trace through the atlcom.h file — the significant code is inherited into IDispatchImpl from CComTypeInfoHolder. This is the definition of IDispatchImpl in atlcom.h:

```
template <class T,
          const IID* piid = &__uuidof(T),
          const GUID* plibid = &CAtlModule::m_libid,
          WORD wMajor = 1,
          WORD wMinor = 0,
          class tihclass = CComTypeInfoHolder>
```

```
class ATL_NO_VTABLE IDispatchImpl : public T
{
public:
 typedef tihclass _tihclass;
 STDMETHOD(GetTypeInfoCount)(UINT* pctinfo)
 {
  *pctinfo = 1;
  return S_OK;
 }

 STDMETHOD(GetTypeInfo)(UINT itinfo,
                        LCID lcid,
                        ITypeInfo** pptinfo)
 {
  return _tih.GetTypeInfo(itinfo, lcid, pptinfo);
 }

 STDMETHOD(GetIDsOfNames)(REFIID riid,
                          LPOLESTR* rgszNames,
                          UINT cNames,
                          LCID lcid,
                          DISPID* rgdispid)
 {
   return _tih.GetIDsOfNames(riid,
                             rgszNames,
                             cNames,
                             lcid,
                             rgdispid);
 }

 STDMETHOD(Invoke)(DISPID dispidMember,
                   REFIID riid,
                   LCID lcid,
                   WORD wFlags,
                   DISPPARAMS* pdispparams,
                   VARIANT* pvarResult,
                   EXCEPINFO* pexcepinfo,
                   UINT* puArgErr)
 {
   return _tih.Invoke((IDispatch*)this,
                      dispidMember,
                      riid,
                      lcid,
                      wFlags,
                      pdispparams,
                      pvarResult,
                      pexcepinfo,
                      puArgErr);
 }

protected:
```

```
static _tihclass _tih;
static HRESULT GetTI(LCID lcid, ITypeInfo** ppInfo)
{
 return _tih.GetTI(lcid, ppInfo);
}
};
```

Recall that by default, the ATL wizards generate attribute-based code. Also, by default, when you create an ATL object with the Object Wizard, the type of interface is set to be dual, and to derive explicitly from IDispatch:

```
// IRobot
[
    object,
    uuid("9913C8F7-CE4A-4C25-A112-6AFCC4201FD5"),
    dual,    helpstring("IRobot Interface"),
    pointer_default(unique)
]
__interface IRobot : IDispatch
{
};
```

Recall also that once you've added some members to this interface and built it, the ClassView pane will report IDispatchImpl as a base class for your coclass (see Figure 33-1).

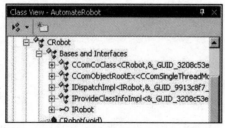

Figure 33-1: Default dual interface options

Alternatively, if you generate unattributed code, the ATL Object Wizard generates a coclass like this:

```
class ATL_NO_VTABLE CRobot :
    public CComObjectRootEx<CComSingleThreadModel>,
    public CComCoClass<CRobot, &CLSID_Robot>,
    public IDispatchImpl<IRobot, &IID_IRobot,
&LIBID_UnattRobotServerLib, /*wMajor =*/ 1, /*wMinor =*/ 0>
{
public:
...
```

```
BEGIN_COM_MAP(CRobot)
    COM_INTERFACE_ENTRY(IRobot)
    COM_INTERFACE_ENTRY(IDispatch)
END_COM_MAP()
};
```

The template parameters to IDispatchImpl are simply the interface, the interface IID, and the type library that describes the interface. Note that the COM map (which, recall, is the basis of QueryInterface for this object) includes IDispatch.

Creating an ATL Automation Server

So, now that you've seen the purpose of automation, the detailed job that IDispatch is designed to perform, and how ATL supports this, let's create an automation server with ATL. Using the ATL COM AppWizard, first create a complete default (DLL-based, attributed) hosting server called RobotServer. Next, add an ATL Simple Object, again with all the defaults (see Figure 33-2), and use the short name Robot.

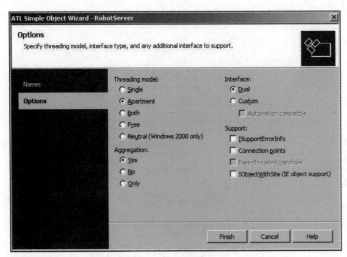

Figure 33-2: Default dual interface options

Don't be confused by the fact that that Automation compatible option is disabled; this applies only if you want a custom interface (an interface that doesn't derive from IDispatch), but you want the parameters to be automation-compatible anyway.

Add one property and one method to your IRobot interface: a property called BatteryLife of type long, and a method called Speak, which takes as input a BSTR. First, add the property (see Figure 33-3).

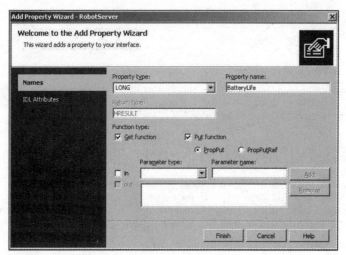

Figure 33-3: Adding an automation property

This results in the following additions to the interface:

```
    [propget, id(1), helpstring("property BatteryLife")]
HRESULT BatteryLife([out, retval] LONG* pVal);
    [propput, id(1), helpstring("property BatteryLife")]
HRESULT BatteryLife([in] LONG newVal);
```

This also makes the following additions to the `coclass` code:

```
STDMETHODIMP CRobot::get_BatteryLife(LONG* pVal)
{
    // TODO: Add your implementation code here
    return S_OK;
}

STDMETHODIMP CRobot::put_BatteryLife(LONG newVal)
{
    // TODO: Add your implementation code here
    return S_OK;
}
```

Note that the wizard doesn't generate any data members. Often, however, the exposed property is in fact an interface to some internal data member. Therefore, you should add a suitable private member variable to your `CRobot` class:

```
private:
    long m_nBatteryLife;
```

You should also initialize this variable (to say, 100) in the constructor. Then, you can implement your `get` and `put` property interface functions accordingly:

```
STDMETHODIMP CRobot::get_BatteryLife(LONG* pVal)
{
```

```
    *pVal = m_nBatteryLife;
    return S_OK;
}

STDMETHODIMP CRobot::put_BatteryLife(LONG newVal)
{
    m_nBatteryLife = newVal;
    return S_OK;
}
```

Adding an automation method is again very simple. In this example, you can add a method called Speak that takes one [in] parameter, a BSTR called bstrSpeech (see Figure 33-4).

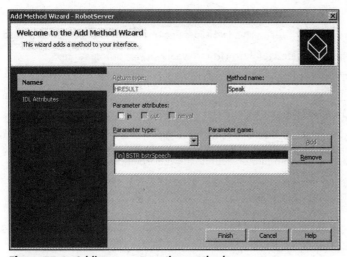

Figure 33-4: Adding an automation method

This generates the following entry in the interface code:

```
    [id(2), helpstring("method Speak")] HRESULT Speak(
[in] BSTR bstrSpeech);
```

It also adds this code in the coclass:

```
STDMETHODIMP CRobot::Speak(BSTR bstrSpeech)
{
    // TODO: Add your implementation code here

    return S_OK;
}
```

For the purposes of this example, implement this method to use MessageBox, as shown in the following code. In practice, though, it would not normally be realistic to rely on a user interface for your COM object.

```
MessageBoxW(0, bstrSpeech, L"Speech", 0);
```

Note   You actually use MessageBoxW, because the string part of a BSTR is wide string.

Once you've built the server, you can go on to experiment with a range of automation clients.

Automation Clients

If your COM object exposes a dual interface, there are two ways that a client can connect to it. If, however, a client is not VTBL-aware, it will still be capable of using automation access. In the following sections I'll explore different ways that a client can connect to a dual interface object, specifically:

✦ Using SmartPointer wrappers generated by #import

✦ Using COleDispatchDriver-derived wrappers generated by the MFC ClassWizard

✦ Using the scripting engine's support (from JavaScript) for automation

✦ Using the ATL support classes CComDispatchDriver, CComVariant, and CComBSTR

SmartPointer client

Just as you can use the #import directive to import a type library for a COM server, you can use #import for the type library of an automation server. In fact, there is no difference. So, the code in the following client should present no new information to the reader:

```
#import "..\RobotServer\_RobotServer.tlb" \
        no_namespace named_guids

int _tmain(int argc, _TCHAR* argv[])
{
    CoInitialize(NULL);

    try
    {
        IRobotPtr p(CLSID_CRobot);

        p->PutBatteryLife(123);
        long bl = p->GetBatteryLife();
        char buf[32];
        wsprintf(buf, "BatteryLife = %d", bl);
        MessageBox(0, buf, "Msg", 0);

        p->Speak(L"Hello World");
    }
    catch(_com_error& e)
    {
        MessageBox(0, e.ErrorMessage(), 0, 0);
    }
```

```
        CoUninitialize();
        return 0;
}
```

Given that this client-side code looks exactly the same as if the object were a COM object and not an automation object, what's the difference? The real answer to this question is that this client is not using automation at all. Even though the object exposes an automation interface, the #import-generated wrapper code is using the conventional COM VTBL part of the object's dual interface.

MFC wrapper client

One way to demonstrate true client use of automation is to use the MFC. The MFC ClassWizard can read the type library of an automation server (not any COM server, only automation servers). It generates wrapper code in much the same way as the #import directive does, except that it is automation wrapper code. Follow these steps to create an MFC automation client:

1. Create a new Win32 Application, called AutomateRobot. Make it a console application and add support for the MFC. This generates some minimal code, including an stdafx.h file with many of the core headers included (see Figure 33-5).

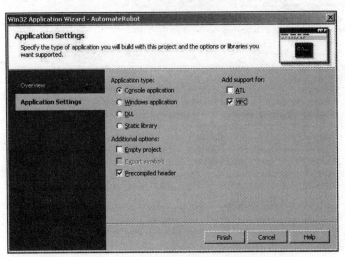

Figure 33-5: Creating a project that supports MFC

2. At the beginning and end of main (or _tmain), make calls to CoInitialize/ CoUninitialize. You'll do all your work in the else block.

3. Right-click the project in the ClassView pane, select Add ➪ Add Class, then Visual C++ MFC classes, and MFC Class from a TypeLib (see Figure 33-6).

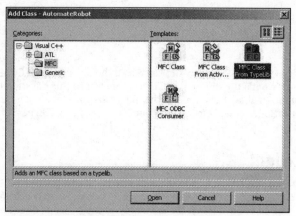

Figure 33-6: Adding an MFC class from a TypeLib

4. From the ensuing dialog box, select the `RobotServer` type library from the list, and select the `IRobot` interface (see Figure 33-7).

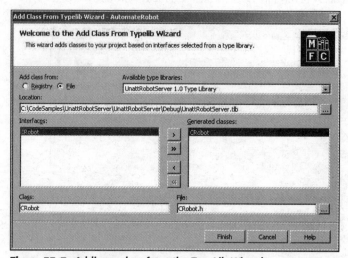

Figure 33-7: Adding a class from the TypeLib Wizard

This generates a wrapper class (strictly) to the automation interface:

```
class CRobot : public COleDispatchDriver
{
public:
 // Calls COleDispatchDriver default constructor
 CRobot(){}

 CRobot(LPDISPATCH pDispatch)
 : COleDispatchDriver(pDispatch)
 {}
```

```
CRobot(const CRobot& dispatchSrc)
: COleDispatchDriver(dispatchSrc)
{}

public:
 long get_BatteryLife()
 {
  long result;
  InvokeHelper(0x1,
               DISPATCH_PROPERTYGET,
               VT_I4,
               (void*)&result, NULL);
  return result;
 }

 void put_BatteryLife(long newValue)
 {
  static BYTE parms[] = VTS_I4 ;
  InvokeHelper(0x1,
               DISPATCH_PROPERTYPUT,
               VT_EMPTY,
               NULL,
               parms,
               newValue);
 }

 void Speak(BSTR bstrSpeech)
 {
  static BYTE parms[] = VTS_BSTR ;
  InvokeHelper(0x2,
               DISPATCH_METHOD,
               VT_EMPTY,
               NULL,
               parms,
               bstrSpeech);
 }
};
```

Notice that the code actually wraps an MFC helper function InvokeHelper, which itself eventually calls into IDispatch::Invoke on the server object.

5. Just before the _tmain function, insert the following include directive

```
#include "CRobot.h"
```

6. Locate the else block in the _tmain function and insert the following code. This code first instantiates a CRobot object, and then calls its CreateDispatch function. Upon success, the get_BatteryLife property is set, retrieved, and then displayed. Finally, the CRobot::Speak method is called and passed a value to display.

```
int _tmain(int argc, TCHAR* argv[], TCHAR* envp[])
{
 CoInitialize(NULL);
 int nRetCode = 0;
```

```
                  // initialize MFC and print and error on failure
                  if (!AfxWinInit(::GetModuleHandle(NULL),
                                                    NULL,
                                                    ::GetCommandLine(),
                                                    0))
                  {
                   _tprintf(T("Fatal Error: MFC initialization failed\n"));
                    nRetCode = 1;
                  }
                  else
                  {
                   CRobot r;
                   if (r.CreateDispatch("RobotServer.Robot"))
                   {
                    r.put_BatteryLife(456);
                    long bl = r.get_BatteryLife();
                    char buf[32];
                    wsprintf(buf, "BatteryLife = %d", bl);
                    MessageBox(0, buf, "Msg", 0);

                    r.Speak((BSTR)"Hello Automation");
                   }

                  }

             CoUninitialize();
              return nRetCode;
             }
```

7. You can now build and test your application, and you should see the anticipated message boxes indicating successful interaction with the Robot COM component.

If you want to verify that you're really doing automation here, set a breakpoint on any of the property/method calls and trace into the code. You'll see that you eventually get to the ATL-supplied IDispatch::Invoke (disassembly) proving that you are indeed going through Automation.

Now that you've seen how to access a COM object using Automation from a Visual C++ client, let's do the same thing from a scripting client.

HTML/JavaScript client

In this part of the exercise, you'll write a simple HTML page with very simple JavaScript code to automate your Robot server. Right-click on RobotServer in ClassView and select Add ➪ Add New Item, and then select an HTML page. After the <BODY> tag, insert an <OBJECT> tag for the Robot COM object. The easiest way to get this tag is to run up the OLE/COM object viewer, find the CRobot class in the tree list, and right-click the node to get a context menu. From this menu select Copy Object Tag to Clipboard, and then simply paste it from the Clipboard into the HTML file:

```
<OBJECT id=Robot1 classid=clsid:3208C53E-41AF-4841-A0D3-C162FB786FAF
VIEWASTEXT>
</OBJECT>
```

Within the object tag, set some attributes: a minimal width and height (because you don't want to see an object that doesn't have any visible representation):

```
<OBJECT id=Robot1 height=1 width=1
classid=clsid:3208C53E-41AF-4841-A0D3-C162FB786FAF
VIEWASTEXT>
</OBJECT>
```

Note In this demo, I'm using the HTML object tag to instantiate the COM object. However, you can also instantiate the object using script and the ProgId of the component. The following is how this would be done using JScript:

```
Robot1 = new ActiveXObject("RobotServer.Robot");
```

This script could then be placed in a function that is called in the page's onLoad function.

Next, insert a label BatteryLife and a text field. The user can type some value here for the BatteryLife property on the object:

```
BatteryLife: <INPUT id=Text1 type=text size=10 name=Text1>
```

You need a button to go with this. When the user clicks this button, you'll retrieve the value from the text box, put it into the object's BatteryLife property, and then get the BatteryLife property and report it.

```
<INPUT id=Button1 type=button value=Put/Get name=Button1
onclick="return Button1_onclick()">
```

Finally, use some simple JavaScript to call into the object via automation:

```
<script id=clientEventHandlersJS language=javascript>
<!--
function Button1_onclick()
{
    Robot1.BatteryLife = Text1.value
    alert("BatteryLife = " +Robot1.BatteryLife)
}

//-->
</script>
```

Save the file. Right-click in the editor window and select View in Browser. When the user clicks the Put/Get button, the value they have entered in the text box is passed to the object (see Figure 33-8).

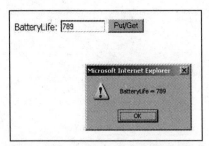

Figure 33-8: HTML/JavaScript test client

Using CComDispatchDriver

ATL provides a class called CComQIPtr, which is a smart pointer class for managing interface pointers. To simplify client use of the IDispatch interface, ATL provides the CComDispatchDriver class, which you can think of as a simplified specialization of the CComQIPtr class with a few additional helper methods that simplify the syntax required to call properties and methods using the IDispatch interface. CComDispatchDriver has an overloaded constructor that takes an IUnknown pointer argument and queries for IDispatch.

Similar to CComQIPtr<IDispatch>, CComDispatchDriver implements the necessary operator overloading that allows it to be used anywhere IDispatch* is required. When using CComDispatchDriver, you can call IDispatch methods directly using the overloaded indirection operator (->) or one of several simplified helper methods defined by the class, such as GetProperty, or PutProperty.

Let's see how you can use CComDispatchDriver to automate our Robot object. First create a Visual C++ Win32 Application project (not an ATL project). Set the options to a Console application, and check the ATL support box.

At the bottom of the stdafx.h file, although the wizard has included the main ATL header, atlbase.h, you need to add an include directive for the comdef.h file; otherwise you can't use classes such as _com_error.

In main, put the usual CoInitialize/CoUninitialize pair top and bottom. Also set up the usual try/catch block, and code the try block as follows:

```
try
{
 CComDispatchDriver p;
 HRESULT hr = p.CoCreateInstance(L"RobotServer.Robot");
 if (FAILED(hr))
  return 1;

 hr = p.PutProperty(1, &CComVariant(987));
 if (FAILED(hr))
  return 1;

 VARIANTARG v;
 hr = p.GetProperty(1, &v);
 if (FAILED(hr))
  return 1;

 long bl = v.lVal;
 char buf[32];
 wsprintf(buf, "BatteryLife = %d", bl);
 MessageBox(0, buf, "Msg", 0);

 p.Invoke1(L"Speak",
           &CComVariant(CComBSTR("Hello Automation")));
}
catch(_com_error& e)
{
 MessageBox(0, e.ErrorMessage(), 0, 0);
}
```

As you can see, the `CComDispatchDriver` class encapsulates a very simplified `CoCreateInstance`, and simple `PutProperty`/`GetProperty` functions. Also note that you can use the ATL `CComVariant` class to simplify your use of VARIANTs, and the ATL `CComBSTR` class to simplify your use of BSTRs. `CComVariant` wraps VARIANTs, not VARIANTARGs, so if you're expecting a return value — as you are in the case of the `GetProperty` — then you have to use `VARIANTARG` directly.

Now that you've finished with the client, simply build and test the project to see that this client also connects to and interacts with the COM object. At this point, you've learned quite a bit about building COM objects with dual interfaces and how to access their exposed methods and properties through Automation. Although knowing how to use Automation can be very advantageous, it's important to realize that creating COM objects with dual interfaces is not always the best thing to do. Let's now look at a couple of problems that dual interfaces cause so that you're better equipped to decide when and where to use dual interfaces and Automation.

Problems with Dual Interface and Automation

Although dual interfaces do provide the ability to have your cake and eat it too, they are generally very problematic. One problem that occurs when declaring multiple implementations of the same interface is that interapartment marshaling will only see a need to set up proxies for the first instance of a given interface. As an example, three dual interfaces present the client with three drastically different implementations of `IDispatch`. Another problem using dual interfaces is that you are limited to using only types that are supported by the automation-compliant types.

For theses reason (and more), it often advisable for developers to choose between creating VTBL-based components or `IDispatch`-interface components. The obvious benefit to the `IDispatch` interface is that it supports agnostic clients such as scripting languages. In this particular example, I'm using a dual interface solely for convenience. However, in a real-world application, I would normally choose one or the other.

Summary

In this chapter, you've seen how primitive high-level languages such as older versions of Visual Basic, and all versions of VBScript and JavaScript, cannot use the COM VTBL, but can use the automation layer supported by the COM runtime and the scripting engine.

The serious work of automation is done by implementing the `IDispatch` interface, and this can be done either side-by-side with a conventional COM VTBL (a dual interface), or instead of a VTBL (a dispinterface). Either way, all clients (both VTBL and non-VTBL) will be capable of accessing your object's functionality. The price you pay for automation is degraded performance and increased scope for errors (as a result of the explicit bypassing of type-checking through the use of VARIANTs).

In passing, you've seen a comparison between the VTBL-wrapper code generated by `#import`, and the automation-wrapper code generated by the MFC ClassWizard. You've also made use of the ATL support classes designed for automation — `CComDispatchDriver` and `CComVariant`.

✦　　✦　　✦

Introducing the WTL

In Chapter 31, you discovered that ATL can be much more than just a library for writing COM components; you can use the ATL windowing classes to write full Windows applications. The entire reason for that chapter was to get you thinking about whether the smaller, more efficient code produced by ATL outweighs giving up the comfort of the more familiar (and bloated) MFC when writing Windows applications. This chapter enriches that debate by looking at yet another template library.

In this chapter, I introduce a new template library, called the Windows Template Library (WTL), which provides a combination of the rich UI elements and architecture found in MFC with the template-based ATL. I'll start off with an overview, some history, and information on where to download it and the features it provides you. From there, I'll jump right into a demo application called, appropriately enough, HelloWTL. This gives you a good reference point to compare ATL and WTL because I provided an ATL version of that demo (HelloATL) in Chapter 31. After this demo, you will then produce a very simple version of the famed Scribble application using the WTL. When you've finished this chapter, you should be able to converse quite easily on the advantages and disadvantages of using the WTL and make an informed decision about whether or not it's right for your individual development needs.

WTL Overview and Features

The WTL is actually an extension of ATL, developed by the same ATL team, and shipped by Microsoft with the January 2000 Platform SDK. One interesting thing about the WTL is that it was actually an internal development tool used by Microsoft and was never supposed to ship. As a result, when the programming public discovered its existence, not only did Microsoft announce that it would not be supported and that a newer version would never ship, it was also rumored that the person responsible for its inclusion was fired. I personally spoke with the person responsible for bringing WTL out into the light of day and can tell you by virtue of his current position as a product manager for the both the MFC and ATL teams that rumors of his demise were greatly exaggerated.

In addition, not only is the WTL alive and well, but Microsoft has backed off its original renouncement of this fine development product and has publicly stated that it will continue shipping and is a supported product. Alas, all is not nirvana for us WTL fans, as it has also been stated that the WTL will have no formal documentation. All of which brings us to this chapter.

The WTL is an absolutely elegant library, which extends the ATL windowing classes by providing a lightweight framework for writing Win32 applications and controls, specialized views, GDI objects, and utility classes. Consisting of a relatively lightweight 750KB of headers, a few sample apps, and a Visual Studio WTL AppWizard, it compares very favorably with the 1MB of headers and implementation files required by ATL.

Now that you've read my opinion on the WTL, let's look at some of the features that this library provides you — especially in comparison to MFC.

✦ *C++ based* — I start with the most basic just to allay any fears that I'm throwing some newfangled scripting-like technology in here. Just like ATL, the WTL is a template-based C++ library that any competent C++ programmer should easily be able to learn.

✦ *Templated code* — As you learned in Chapter 30, when a library is templated, the resulting binaries tend to be much smaller and more efficient. As an example, a simple Hello World SDI application written with the WTL is less than 24KB. Compare that to the 440KB for the MFC (statically linked, release-mode) equivalent. Link the MFC dynamically, you say? That brings the application binary down to 24KB, but you still have to ship the 1MB of MFC binaries to support it. Therefore, if you're at all concerned with the size of your executables as well as the overall size of what you're shipping and your users are installing, then there's simply no comparison.

✦ *No interdependencies* — Because of the WTL's lack of interdependency, it can be freely mixed with straight SDK code.

✦ *No application model* — Obviously, I'm comparing this to the MFC reliance on its application and document/view framework. Anyone who has worked with MFC for any amount of time can tell you (and hopefully this is something you've learned throughout this book) that writing an MFC application and circumventing the built-in framework is not an easy task. With WTL, you do have a small, but functional framework. However, it's not forced on you and you easily write code oblivious to its existence.

✦ *Common Control Wrappers* — As you saw in Chapter 31, it takes some work to use any of the Windows common controls in your ATL applications. This is contrary to MFC, where all the controls are wrapped with thin C++ wrappers. Thankfully, the WTL team has done the same thing, and so working with common controls is very easy (a necessity for any medium-to-large-sized Windows application).

✦ *Print and Print Preview* — Like MFC, but unlike ATL, the WTL has support for printing as well as print preview.

Now that you've seen a short list of the features that WTL provides, let's look at the range of classes included with this library:

✦ *Standard UI controls* — These include the basic controls such as the edit box, list box, combo box, and button.

✦ *Windows Common controls* — As mentioned, the common controls are supported via thin wrappers. These classes include support for the list view, tree view, progress bar, and spin control.

✦ *Internet Explorer (IE) controls* — Included in these controls are things like the rebar, flat scroll bar, and date-time picker.

✦ *Command Bar support* — This includes the status bar and toolbar controls.

✦ *Menu support* — Not too many SDI or MDI Windows applications are written without the incorporation of some type of menuing system.

✦ *Update UI classes* — As with MFC, Update UI classes give you the ability to easily control enabling and disabling of your controls based on application-specific logic.

✦ *Common dialog boxes* — This includes the standard common dialog boxes — File Open, File Save/As, Print and Print Preview dialog boxes.

✦ *Property Sheet and Property Page classes* — The look and feel of property sheets may have changed in the MFC, but with WTL they still provide that familiar tab-like interface.

✦ *Frames and views* — Although you're not tied to frames and views as you are in MFC, you do have MDI frames, child frames, and views at your disposal for times when you do want a document/view application.

✦ *GDI* — This includes classes to control device contexts and GDI objects such as pens, brushes, and bitmaps that you learned about in Chapters 8 and 9.

✦ *Utility classes* — These include ports of MFC standards such as the `CPoint`, `CRect`, `Csize`, and `CString` classes.

Downloading and Installing the WTL

Note that this chapter's code was written with WTL 3.1 and although it does not ship with Visual Studio .NET, it can be downloaded from the Microsoft MSDN site (without requiring an MSDN subscription). To do that, simply point your browser to the following address:

```
http://msdn.microsoft.com/msdn-files/027/001/586/Search.asp
```

You should see the standard dialog box asking you whether you want to open the file from its current location or save it to disk. Select the Save to Disk option, select a destination folder, and save the file.

Once you've downloaded the self-extracting zip containing the WTL, simply run it. You will see the standard WinZip extractor dialog box (shown in Figure 34-1) that allows you to specify where you want it to copy the WTL files. Simply click the Unzip button once you've typed in the destination folder.

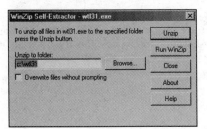

Figure 34-1: You no longer need to download entire bits of the Platform SDK in order to install WTL.

Once you've unzipped the WTL files into a folder of your choice, that folder will contain three different subfolders and a readme.txt file:

✦ *AppWiz folder*—This file contains a Visual Studio 6.0 AppWizard and *will not function* with Visual Studio .NET.

✦ *Include folder*—This folder contains all of the include files for WTL. You need to update your Visual Studio list of header file folders to search this folder.

✦ *Samples folder*—This folder contains four demo applications:

• BmpView, which displays a bitmap image

• GuidGen, a dialog-based application that generates GUIDs

• MdiDocView, a WTL equivalent of an MFC MDI application

• MTPad, an MDI WordPad-like application

✦ Readme.txt *file*—This file contains a packing list (list of distributed files), a *very brief* class overview, and a list of changes between versions 3.0 and 3.1 of the WTL.

Hello WTL Demo Application

Enough talking about how great this thing is; let's see it in action. The first demo application that I cover is the WTL equivalent of the simple HelloATL demo in Chapter 31.

Start by using the WTL AppWizard. Along with the standard choices of SDI, MDI, and dialog-based applications, the Wizard allows you to create something called a *multi-threaded SDI* application. Both Microsoft Internet Explorer (IE) and Windows Explorer have a special (and surprisingly little-known) option whereby running multiple instances actually results in a separate thread run from a single process that controls all *instances* of the application. The advantage is that far less memory is used because only one process actually exists. The multithreaded SDI option on the WTL AppWizard creates the template for just this kind of application.

You also have control over the views that are created. They can be generic CWindowImpl-based, or based on a form, list box, edit, list view, tree view, rich edit, or even HTML control. You can even choose whether to incorporate into your application a rebar (from IE), Command Bar (like Windows CE), toolbar, or status bar. Finally, your application can also host ActiveX controls and can even be a COM server.

At this point, create a new WTL AppWizard-generated application called HelloWTL. From the WTL AppWizard Step1 dialog box (shown in Figure 34-2), accept all the defaults and click the Finish button.

Now, build and run the application. You will see that you have a very standard Win32 application with a fairly regular frame and view, menu, toolbar, status bar, and About box. Although the basic menu items (Exit, View Toolbar/Status bar, and About) function, the other menu options do not. I'll show you how these work as you progress through the demo.

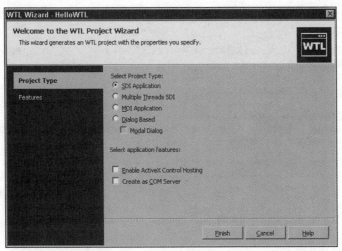

Figure 34-2: The WTL Application Wizard gives you many of the same application UI types that you're accustomed to getting with the MFC Application Wizard.

Now examine the code. First, note there is a standard ATL CComModule global object, initialized and terminated in the _tWinMain. Upon examining this function, and you see that the only other work that _tWinMain does is to initialize the common controls through a call to InitCommonControlsEx and call the global wizard-generated Run function (shown next).

```
int WINAPI _tWinMain(HINSTANCE hInstance,
                     HINSTANCE /*hPrevInstance*/,
                     LPTSTR lpstrCmdLine,
                     int nCmdShow)
{
  HRESULT hRes = ::CoInitialize(NULL);

  // If you are running on NT 4.0 or higher you
  // can use the following call instead to
  // make the EXE free threaded. This means that calls
  // come in on a random RPC thread.
  // HRESULT hRes = ::CoInitializeEx(NULL,
  //                                 COINIT_MULTITHREADED);
  ATLASSERT(SUCCEEDED(hRes));

#if (_WIN32_IE >= 0x0300)
  INITCOMMONCONTROLSEX iccx;
  iccx.dwSize = sizeof(iccx);
  iccx.dwICC = ICC_COOL_CLASSES | ICC_BAR_CLASSES;
  BOOL bRet = ::InitCommonControlsEx(&iccx);
  bRet;
  ATLASSERT(bRet);
#else
```

```
     ::InitCommonControls();
#endif

  hRes = _Module.Init(NULL, hInstance);
  ATLASSERT(SUCCEEDED(hRes));

  int nRet = Run(lpstrCmdLine, nCmdShow);

  _Module.Term();
  ::CoUninitialize();

  return nRet;
}
```

The Run function that follows creates the main frame window and a CMessageLoop object, calls ShowWindow on the main frame, and then calls CMessageLoop::Run on the CMessageLoop object. This in turn essentially just calls good old ::GetMessage and ::DispatchMessage.

```
int Run(LPTSTR /*lpstrCmdLine*/ = NULL,
        int nCmdShow = SW_SHOWDEFAULT)
{
  CMessageLoop theLoop;
  _Module.AddMessageLoop(&theLoop);

  CMainFrame wndMain;

  if(wndMain.CreateEx() == NULL)
  {
    ATLTRACE(_T("Main window creation failed!\n"));
    return 0;
  }

  wndMain.ShowWindow(nCmdShow);

  int nRet = theLoop.Run();

  _Module.RemoveMessageLoop();
  return nRet;
}
```

So far, nothing very special is going on here—just the standard window creation and message queue setup and processing—and that's just the way you want it. After all, the WTL is supposed to make things easier, not more difficult

Next, look at the CMainFrame class generated by the AppWizard. All the parent classes are in ATLFrame.h or ATLApp.h files generated when you installed the WTL. The main functionality comes from CFrameWindowImpl.

One thing to note here is the commandui support. Notice in the declaration of the CMainFrame class that one of its base classes is the CUpdateUI class.

```
class CMainFrame : public CFrameWindowImpl<CMainFrame>,
                   public CUpdateUI<CMainFrame>,
                   public CMessageFilter,
                   public CIdleHandler
{
...
```

This is the class that allows for the standard enabling and disabling of controls for a more intuitive user interface. The CUpdateUI is connected with an UPDATE_UI_MAP and eventually to OnViewToolBar and OnViewStatusBar functions in your derived CMainFrame class. These do the expected ShowWindow and SetCheck behavior as in MFC. In the following example, I have a CMainFrame class that has two commandui handlers: one for the toolbar and one for the status bar.

```
BEGIN_UPDATE_UI_MAP(CMainFrame)
  UPDATE_ELEMENT(ID_VIEW_TOOLBAR, UPDUI_MENUPOPUP)
  UPDATE_ELEMENT(ID_VIEW_STATUS_BAR, UPDUI_MENUPOPUP)
END_UPDATE_UI_MAP()
```

Aside from the CFrameWindowImpl and CUpdateUI classes, the CMainFrame is also derived from two other classes: CMessageFilter and CIdleHandler. The inheritance from CMessageFilter means that the class must implement a filter that weeds out messages before they are dispatched. An example would be filtering the way that certain keystrokes are handled. As the name suggests, the CIdleHandler is a class that is used when there aren't any messages in the queue.

Finally, both the derived view class (m_view) and a CCommandBarCtrl object (m_CmdBar) are embedded child members of the frame. Here's the entire class as generated by the wizard. Note the different message map entries. Message maps work the exact same way in WTL as they do in ATL, and are covered in Chapter 31.

```
class CMainFrame : public CFrameWindowImpl<CMainFrame>,
                   public CUpdateUI<CMainFrame>,
                   public CMessageFilter,
                   public CIdleHandler
{
public:
 DECLARE_FRAME_WND_CLASS(NULL, IDR_MAINFRAME)

 CHelloWorldView m_view;
 CCommandBarCtrl m_CmdBar;

 BEGIN_MSG_MAP(CMainFrame)
 MESSAGE_HANDLER(WM_CREATE, OnCreate)
  COMMAND_ID_HANDLER(ID_APP_EXIT, OnFileExit)
  COMMAND_ID_HANDLER(ID_FILE_NEW, OnFileNew)
  COMMAND_ID_HANDLER(ID_VIEW_TOOLBAR, OnViewToolBar)
  COMMAND_ID_HANDLER(ID_VIEW_STATUS_BAR, OnViewStatusBar)
  COMMAND_ID_HANDLER(ID_APP_ABOUT, OnAppAbout)
  CHAIN_MSG_MAP(CUpdateUI<CMainFrame>)
  CHAIN_MSG_MAP(CFrameWindowImpl<CMainFrame>)
 END_MSG_MAP()
```

```
BEGIN_UPDATE_UI_MAP(CMainFrame)
 UPDATE_ELEMENT(ID_VIEW_TOOLBAR, UPDUI_MENUPOPUP)
 UPDATE_ELEMENT(ID_VIEW_STATUS_BAR, UPDUI_MENUPOPUP)
END_UPDATE_UI_MAP()
};
```

The only significant function in the CMainFrame class is the OnCreate handler. This initializes the CComandBarCtrl object to attach the menu and load the command bar images (the icons on the menu). In effect, the CComandBarCtrl class converts a menu described by a menu resource into a toolbar, making it easier to associate the same command IDs and images for menu items and toolbar buttons. The frame then goes on to create a toolbar, a rebar, and a status bar. It then initializes the view. The final step is to add the frame's message filter and idle handler to the CComModule application object.

Message filtering is a technique to route a message between windows in your application after ::GetMessage pulls it off your queue, but before it gets processed with ::TranslateMessage and DispatchMessage function pair.

```
LRESULT OnCreate(UINT /*uMsg*/, WPARAM /*wParam*/,
LPARAM /*lParam*/, BOOL& /*bHandled*/)
{
HWND hWndCmdBar = m_CmdBar.Create(m_hWnd,
                    rcDefault,
                    NULL,
                    ATL_SIMPLE_CMDBAR_PANE_STYLE);

m_CmdBar.AttachMenu(GetMenu());
m_CmdBar.LoadImages(IDR_MAINFRAME);
SetMenu(NULL);

HWND hWndToolBar = CreateSimpleToolBarCtrl(m_hWnd,
                    IDR_MAINFRAME,
                    FALSE,
                    ATL_SIMPLE_TOOLBAR_PANE_STYLE);

CreateSimpleReBar(ATL_SIMPLE_REBAR_NOBORDER_STYLE);
AddSimpleReBarBand(hWndCmdBar);
AddSimpleReBarBand(hWndToolBar, NULL, TRUE);
CreateSimpleStatusBar();

m_hWndClient = m_view.Create(m_hWnd, rcDefault, NULL,
WS_CHILD | WS_VISIBLE | WS_CLIPSIBLINGS |
WS_CLIPCHILDREN, WS_EX_CLIENTEDGE);

UIAddToolBar(hWndToolBar);
UISetCheck(ID_VIEW_TOOLBAR, 1);
UISetCheck(ID_VIEW_STATUS_BAR, 1);

CMessageLoop* pLoop = _Module.GetMessageLoop();
pLoop->AddMessageFilter(this);
pLoop->AddIdleHandler(this);

return 0;
}
```

The view class simply derives from `CWindowImpl`, and the wizard generates one message handler for `WM_PAINT` with the usual TODO comment:

```
class CHelloWorldView: public CWindowImpl<CHelloWorldView>
{
public:
 DECLARE_WND_CLASS(NULL)

 BOOL PreTranslateMessage(MSG* pMsg)
 {
  pMsg;
  return FALSE;
 }

 BEGIN_MSG_MAP(CHelloWorldView)
  MESSAGE_HANDLER(WM_PAINT, OnPaint)
 END_MSG_MAP()

 LRESULT OnPaint(UINT /*uMsg*/,
                 WPARAM /*wParam*/,
                 LPARAM /*lParam*/,
                 BOOL& /*bHandled*/)
 {
  CPaintDC dc(m_hWnd);

  //TODO: Add your drawing code here.

  return 0;
 }
};
```

At this point, you make a single trivial change. Add code to the `OnPaint` to output the usual Hello WTL string.

```
LRESULT OnPaint(UINT /*uMsg*/,
                WPARAM /*wParam*/,
                LPARAM /*lParam*/,
                BOOL& /*bHandled*/)
{
 CPaintDC dc(m_hWnd);
 dc.TextOut(0, 0, "Hello WTL");
 return 0;
}
```

If you build and execute this application at this point (shown in Figure 34-3), you'll see that the application that took some considerable time and work with ATL takes nothing at all with the aid of the WTL AppWizard.

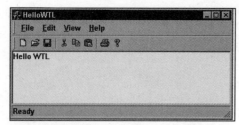

Figure 34-3: The WTL AppWizard lets you create lightweight applications as quickly as you do MFC applications.

In addition, don't forget all the extra goodies you get for free: a frame/view, cool menus, an About box, a toolbar and status bar (including show/hide functionality), and even commandui handling. "Yeah, but I get all that with the MFC AppWizards!" you might say. True, but now compare the sizes of the two executables and you'll see that with the WTL, you get all the UI niceties of MFC with none of its overhead in terms of runtime memory usage and binary file size.

WTL Scribble

Suppose you now want to emulate the ATL Scribble demo application from Chapter 31. To do that, create a new WTL SDI application called WTLScribble. Once the files have been created, add a handler for the view's WM_LBUTTONDOWN message. Your function should look like this when finished:

```
LRESULT OnLButtonDown(UINT uMsg,
                      WPARAM wParam,
                      LPARAM lParam,
                      BOOL& bHandled)
{
  return 0;
}
```

The message map entry should now look like this:

```
MESSAGE_HANDLER(WM_LBUTTONDOWN, OnLButtonDown)
```

Because you're using the ATL here, the wizard doesn't provide cracked messages in the way that the MFC does. WTL does supply a set of message-cracking macros, in atlcrack.h. If you examine this file, you'll see there is a macro for each Windows message. All you have to do is use the appropriate macro, and implement the handler with the corresponding signature. In addition, you need to use the BEGIN_MSG_MAP_EX macro instead of the usual BEGIN_MSG_MAP.

The new macro provides a way for cracked handlers to retrieve the current message and specify if the message was handled or not. This is because the cracked handlers don't have the Boolean argument of raw ATL handlers. Instead, BEGIN_MSG_MAP_EX defines an additional method, SetMessageHandled, for the purpose. As an example, look at the WM_LBUTTONDOWN cracker:

```
#define MSG_WM_LBUTTONDOWN(func) \
 if (uMsg == WM_LBUTTONDOWN) \
 { \
  SetMsgHandled(TRUE); \
  func((UINT)wParam, CPoint(GET_X_LPARAM(lParam), \
 GET_Y_LPARAM(lParam))); \
  lResult = 0; \
  if(IsMsgHandled()) \
  return TRUE; \
 }
```

Also note that the use of CPoint requires that you include the atlmisc.h header file. Therefore, you'll need to add include directives for both the atlmisc.h and atlcrack.h files at the top of your WTLScribbleView.h file. Next, manually change the CWTLScribbleView class' message map to the EX version, and add the following cracker macros and handlers. Last, because you're using the CPen, you must also include the atlgdi.h file.

```
BEGIN_MSG_MAP_EX(CHelloWorldView)
 MSG_WM_LBUTTONDOWN(OnLButtonDown)
 MSG_WM_LBUTTONUP(OnLButtonUp)
 MSG_WM_MOUSEMOVE(OnMouseMove)
END_MSG_MAP()

LRESULT OnLButtonDown (UINT flags, CPoint point)
{
 m_startPoint = point;
 return 0;
}

LRESULT OnLButtonUp (UINT flags, CPoint point)
{
 m_startPoint.x = m_startPoint.y = -1;
 return 0;
}

LRESULT OnMouseMove (UINT flags, CPoint point)
{
 m_endPoint = point;
```

```
CClientDC dc(this->m_hWnd);
CPen np;
np.CreatePen(PS_SOLID, 2, RGB(255,0,0));
HPEN op = dc.SelectPen(np.m_hPen);

if (m_startPoint.x != -1 )
{
 dc.MoveTo(m_startPoint.x, m_startPoint.y, NULL);
 dc.LineTo(m_endPoint.x, m_endPoint.y);
 m_startPoint.x = m_endPoint.x;
 m_startPoint.y = m_endPoint.y;
}

dc.SelectPen(op);
return 0;
}
```

To add simple menu/toolbar support for changing the color of the pen, just add a new menu called Color with three menu items: Red, Green, and Blue. Also add three corresponding toolbar buttons, and make sure they have the same IDs — this is normal behavior, after all. Code the command handlers to change a COLORREF member in the view. That's all you need to do to get the icons into the cool menu. Remember, the coolbar is created based on the menu IDs and any corresponding toolbar buttons found. Add entries to the view's message map, and the corresponding handlers, like this:

```
COMMAND_ID_HANDLER_EX(ID_COLOR_RED, OnColorRed)
COMMAND_ID_HANDLER_EX(ID_COLOR_GREEN, OnColorGreen)
COMMAND_ID_HANDLER_EX(ID_COLOR_BLUE, OnColorBlue)

LRESULT OnColorRed(UINT, int, HWND)
{
 m_color = RGB(255,0,0);
 return 0;
}

LRESULT OnColorGreen(UINT, int, HWND)
{
 m_color = RGB(0,255,0);
 return 0;
}

LRESULT OnColorBlue(UINT, int, HWND)
{
 m_color = RGB(0,0,255);
 return 0;
}
```

If you build the application at this point, you'll find that the cool menu and toolbar show up, but the messages don't get routed to the view class. That's because command messages originate at the frame class, so the cool menu/toolbar command messages are sent to the frame's message map. Because the ATL/WTL uses a somewhat different strategy for routing messages from one class to another from that used by the MFC, you must add this to the frame's message map:

```
CHAIN_MSG_MAP_MEMBER(m_view)
```

If you build and execute the application, you should see that you now have a full-blown Windows application, complete with menu and mouse handling (shown in Figure 34-4).

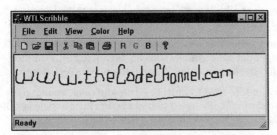

Figure 34-4: Simple Scribble application using the WTL

Is WTL Right for You?

As you can see, some things are a little different from the MFC, although you can see the logical extension from the ATL. However, what about the big picture? Serious developers shouldn't be too put off by a paucity of wizard support. On the other hand, cool menus are cool, but are they really worth changing from the MFC? Bear in mind that WTL is just ATL++, and ATL is the serious developer's tool of choice for anything COM-related. Is this enough of a reason to use it? After all, WTL is undocumented.

The bottom line is that WTL is just an (source code) extension to ATL, which brings up the question: What support do you need? Internally, Microsoft has been using early versions of WTL for years because it produces such small, efficient applications, and finally both the ATL/WTL team at Microsoft and the ATL/WTL community at large (especially DevelopMentor, http://www.develop.com) are all committed to continuing support for WTL.

The combination of ATL/WTL won't replace MFC overnight, and might never do so. However, many projects can be produced faster and run more efficiently, with much easier COM integration, by choosing ATL/WTL instead of MFC. I've been using the MFC since the very first version and therefore, it is usually my first tool of choice for almost any application. However, after discovering the WTL last year, I readily admit that I now favor the WTL for many projects, especially COM-related applications. Therefore, in making the decision as to whether or not WTL is right for you, I would simply recommend keeping an open mind, playing around with WTL, and making that decision on a project-by-project basis. After all, if preserving your investment in older technology were the only criterion, we'd all still be writing RPG applications.

Learning More About WTL

As I mentioned, the biggest (and really, the only) drawback to using the WTL is the lack of documentation. However, in today's Internet world, that is not nearly the death knell it once was for a technology. There are many sites (both professional and independent) that provide a huge array of demo applications, tutorials, and articles that will show you how to do just about anything you need to do in WTL. Here is a short list of my favorite resources:

✦ *The Code Channel*—Obviously, I'm a bit biased, because this is my site. However, www.theCodeChannel.com does provide a few WTL examples for you to start with.

✦ *DevelopMentor*—This company needs no introduction in the world of COM and ATL development as their name is all but synonymous with the technologies. Visit their Web site (www.develop.com) to find the largest online community of ATL/WTL developers.

✦ *CodeProject*—Among literally hundreds of C++ articles, this site (www.codeproject.com) also has a section devoted to WTL. Included in that section is an article specifically devoted to documenting the WTL class library.

Summary

This chapter started off by presenting a very broad overview of the WTL and where it fits into the whole MFC versus ATL development tool decision. Once I went over these basics, showed where to find and download the WTL, and then went over its features, I walked you through two demo applications. In the first demo (HelloWTL), you saw how easy it is to use the WTL AppWizard to create a fully functional Windows application. From there, the second application illustrated how to process menu messages and handle simple mouse input for a poor man's version of Scribble.

Like any full-blown development library, one could easily write an entire book on WTL. However, the focus of this book overall is Visual C++ and MFC. Therefore, I didn't want to stray too far from that topic. What I did want to do with this chapter is to simply open your eyes to other possibilities. After all, no one tool can solve every problem, and a combination of MFC and WTL knowledge gives you the best of both worlds when developing Windows applications.

✦ ✦ ✦

Programming with COM+

Building Stateful COM+ Applications

Although there are many books dedicated to COM+, this chapter and the next two chapters should be enough to get you started so that you can determine for yourself if you want to go further with this technology. Here you'll look at the essence of COM+ programming. You'll learn the most fundamental aspects of COM+ and expand into the critical design issues germane to scalable COM+ applications, and how they differ from other types of DCOM programs — all of which will prepare you nicely for the code-centric chapters on programming loosely coupled events and queued components that follow in Chapters 36 and 37.

I'll start out by discussing (and illustrating) how the COM components you learned how to create in COM and ATL chapters integrate into the COM+ world. From there, I'll discuss the different benefits that COM+ provides to COM components. Once that section is complete, you'll then learn the most important facet of COM+ development: state. You'd discover what it is, how it's set, and how it's maintained. Finally, the chapter wraps up with sections on the MTS Shared Property Manager, and how to reference and create objects with COM+.

COM+ and Standard COM Components

If you're reading an introductory chapter about COM+, I have to assume that you're new to the COM+ environment. To that extent, these sections focus on that all-important first step of integrating standard COM components into the COM+ world. You know by now that my standard technique is to teach through the illustration of demo applications and code snippets. Having said that, you'll begin by building a standard COM component. Once you've done that, you'll deploy and test the COM component under COM+. Then I'll introduce the advantages and disadvantages of integrating COM components into COM+.

Creating a standard COM component

To get started working with COM+, create a new ATL DLL project called Stateful. Do not specify COM+ support on the Application Settings tab, because in this particular demo you specifically want to test how a "normal" (pre-COM+) component operates within COM+. Once you've created your new project, add an ATL class to the project (via Project ⇨ Add Class). When the ATL Simple Object Wizard appears, specify Sum in the Short name field and leave the remainder of the fields' names as the defaults, as shown in Figure 35-1. On the Options tab, make sure that the dual interface option is checked because this component will also be used from script.

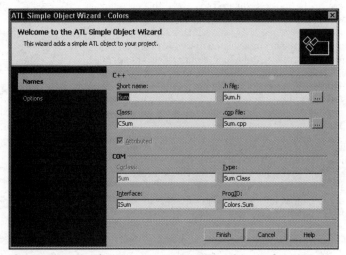

Figure 35-1: Simple ATL component to test using regular COM components in the COM+ environment

Note   Although dual interfaces do provide the ability to have your cake and eat it too, they are generally very problematic. One problem that occurs when declaring multiple implementations of the same interface is that interapartment marshaling only sets up proxies for the first instance of a given interface. As an example, three dual interfaces present the client with three drastically different implementations of IDispatch. Another problem using dual interfaces is that you are limited to using only types that are supported by the automation compliant types.

For these reasons (and more), it is often advisable for developers to choose between creating VTBL-based components or IDispatch-interface components. The obvious benefit to IDispatch interface is that it supports type-agnostic clients such as scripting languages. In this particular example, I'm using a dual interface solely for convenience. However, in a real-world application, I would normally choose one or the other.

Once you've created your Sum component, you need to add two methods to the interface. If you're new to ATL programming in Visual Studio .NET, methods can be added to ATL interfaces by opening the Class View, right-clicking the interface (ISum, in this case), and then selecting Add ⇨ Add Method.

The first method is called Add and takes three parameters—the first two of which are of type SHORT, called iOp1 and iOp2, respectively. The third parameter needs to be defined as retval and should be of type SHORT*. Name this parameter piTotal. Figure 35-2 shows the Add Method dialog box for this particular method.

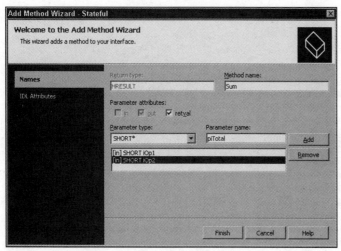

Figure 35-2: Defining a method for an ATL object

Now, add an additional method called Accumulate. This method defines two parameters. The first, named iValue, should be of type SHORT. The second, named piTotal, should be of type SHORT* and have the retval option selected.

After you've added the two methods, add a member variable to the CSum class called m_iTotal and initialize it to zero in the class's constructor. The following listing shows the C++ declarations and IDL for the Sum component in order to verify that you created your component, interface, and methods correctly:

```
// Sum.h : Declaration of the CSum

#pragma once
#include "resource.h"        // main symbols


// ISum
[
   object,
   uuid("087A1119-8D78-42BD-9175-4D120C445EDA"),
   dual,  helpstring("ISum Interface"),
   pointer_default(unique)
]
__interface ISum : IDispatch
{
   [id(1), helpstring("method Add")] HRESULT Add(SHORT iOp1,
```

```
       SHORT iOp2, [out][retval]SHORT* piTotal);
   [id(2), helpstring("method Accumulate")]
       HRESULT Accumulate(SHORT iValue,
[out][retval]SHORT* piTotal);
};


// CSum

[
   coclass,
   threading("apartment"),
   vi_progid("Stateful.Sum"),
   progid("Stateful.Sum.1"),
   version(1.0),
   uuid("05C99969-C6E4-457D-81EA-BF2CCF4FB8B3"),
   helpstring("Sum Class")
]
class ATL_NO_VTABLE CSum :
   public ISum
{
public:
   CSum() : m_iTotal(0)  {}

protected:
   int m_iTotal;

public:
   DECLARE_PROTECT_FINAL_CONSTRUCT()

   HRESULT FinalConstruct()
   {
      return S_OK;
   }

   void FinalRelease()
   {
   }

public:

   STDMETHOD(Add)(SHORT iOp1, SHORT iOp2, SHORT* piTotal);
   STDMETHOD(Accumulate)(SHORT iValue, SHORT* piTotal);
};
```

Now open the Sum.cpp file and locate the CSum::Accumulate member function. Once you've done that, modify it so that when finished, it looks like the following:

```
STDMETHODIMP CSum::Accumulate(int iValue, int *piTotal)
{
    if ( NULL == piTotal )
        return E_INVALIDARG;
```

```
    m_iTotal += iValue;
    *piTotal = m_iTotal;

    return S_OK;
}
```

Once you've finished with the `CSum::Accumulate` function, its time to modify the `CSum::Add` function.

```
STDMETHODIMP CSum::Add(SHORT iOp1, SHORT iOp2,
                       SHORT* piTotal)
{
    if ( NULL == piTotal )
        return E_INVALIDARG;

    *piTotal = iOp1 + iOp2;

    return S_OK;
}
```

Now, I'll discuss state data. The `Accumulate` method requires *object state data* (the `m_iTotal` member variable) whereas the `Sum` method uses only *transient state* data (stack variables). A bit later you're going to see both of these methods tested within the MTS runtime. For now, build your new DLL project.

Building a simple script client

At this point, you should have your ATL component built and ready to go. Here you'll use the language that allows you to test your component the quickest: VBScript. To do that, simply create a new script file called `SumClient.VBS` and modify it so that when finished it looks like the following:

```
' SumClient.vbs
'
' Simple COM Client VB Script

'Application Entry Point

'Create Sum Object
Set obSum = CreateObject("Stateful.Sum.1")
Total = 0

do
  'Set up menu
  Menu = "COM Client Menu" & vbCr & _
    "0 - Exit" & vbCr & _
    "1 - Accumulate a value" & vbCr & _
    "2 - Add two values" & vbCr & vbCr & _
    "Current Cumulative Total: "

  'Get selection
  Choice = InputBox(Menu & Total)
```

```
'Execute command
Select Case Choice
  Case "":
   'This interprets the cancel button as ' _
   'a quit request'
   Choice = "0"
  Case "0":
  Case "1":
   Value = InputBox("Enter a value to accumulate:")
   Total = obSum.Accumulate(Value)
  Case "2":
   Value1 = InputBox("Enter the first value to add:")
   Value2 = InputBox("Enter the second value to add:")
   MsgBox obSum.Add(Value1,Value2), 0, "Transient Total"
  Case Else:
   MsgBox "Bad choice"
 End Select
Loop While Choice <> "0"
'End of Application
```

You should be able to test your new component now. To do so, simply double-click the script in an instance of an Explorer window. In Figure 35-3, I've already run the application a few times, and I have an accumulated total of 42.

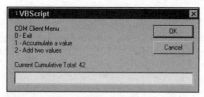

Figure 35-3: A little VBScript can be used to quickly test a COM component.

Integrating COM components into the COM+ runtime

This little COM component doesn't launch the space shuttle in terms of complexity. It does, however, give you a starting point. You now know that the Sum component works (as seen with VBScript client). Now, you need to test it with COM+. To do that, you need to create a COM+ application. Open the Component Services application (located in Programs ➪ Administrative Tools). As you can see in Figure 35-4, I've opened this application and expanded the folder detailing the system's COM+ applications.

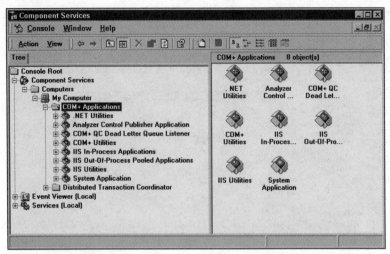

Figure 35-4: COM+ applications are created and managed through the Component Services tool.

Right-click the COM+ Applications folder and select the New Application option. You'll then see the first of several wizard dialog boxes. The first is simply a "welcome" message, so click Next to move forward. When queried as to whether you're installing a prebuilt application or creating an empty application, select the latter. This is because, although you have a DLL, you do not yet have anything that COM+ would recognize as an application. When the Create Empty Application dialog box appears, type the name **Stateful** and accept the defaults from that point forward. When you've finished, you should see that Component Services is now listing your new COM+ application amongst all the others.

Now, expand the `Stateful` application in the left-hand tree view to display its Components and Roles folders. From there, right-click the Components tree view entry, and select New Component from the context menu. Once again, you'll be welcomed to another COM+ wizard. Simply click Next to proceed. On the next dialog box, select the option to install a registered component, because obviously your `Stateful` component is registered (otherwise you would not have been able to use it from the VBScript). After the wizard builds the registered component list, locate and select the Stateful.Sum.1 component. Note that because the component is an in-process server (housed in a DLL), it will run in the `mtx.exe` runtime.

To test that you've created the COM+ application and added the `Stateful` component correctly, perform this little test. First, select the application's Components folder. Then select the Status View option from the View menu. Now, run the VBScript again and you should see that the COM+ status view has been updated to reflect the fact that a client has now activated the component (as shown in Figure 35-5). Note that neither server nor client had to be modified to accomplish this.

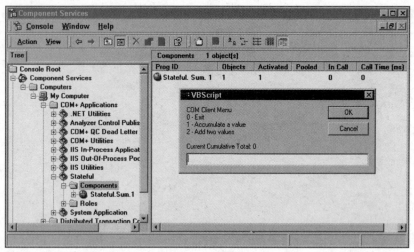

Figure 35-5: COM components can be added to COM+ without changing either the component or any of its clients.

Want to try a little DCOM/COM+? There's nothing to it. Right-click the `Stateful` application and then select the Export menu option. You'll get a warning because you imported the component and COM+ doesn't know anything about its interfaces. Ignore that and continue. When the Application Export Information dialog box appears, select the Application Proxy option and specify where you want the file copied. As an example, in my home office I have several machines all named after characters from *Les Miserables*. The machine I'm writing this book on is called JeanValJean. Because I wanted to be able to use my new application from a machine called Cosette, I simply supplied a value of `\\cosette\c\RemoteStateful`. Component Services then creates a client installer application in the path specified. I then went over to the Cosette machine and double-clicked the installer program (`RemoteStateful.msi`). This application installed the bits necessary for remote access to the `JeanValJean.Stateful` application. In order to test this, I simply copied the VBScript to Cosette and ran it. Voila! The Object and Activated counters on JeanValJean were both incremented. What has happened is that the running of the script on Cosette automatically invoked a DCOM connection to the COM+ system running on JeanValJean. Nothing could be easier.

There are two additional notes about building and testing components under COM+ on a single machine. First, COM+ server processes don't shut down immediately by default. You need to shut the application down explicitly by right-clicking the application and selecting the Shutdown menu option. If you forget to do this, you won't be able to rebuild your component because the DLL will be in use. The second problem has to do with COM registration. Remember that in Visual C++, you're creating a COM component that knows nothing about COM+. Therefore, when you build the component, Visual C++ will attempt to reregister the component as a standard COM component. You will then need to refresh the registry with the COM+ application configuration by right-clicking the computer in the Component Services Console and selecting Refresh All Components.

Security problems

If you are new to COM+, you are probably justifiably impressed with your accomplishments at this point. However, this little component has problems. One of these problems is security. Remember that your component is now running under a server process, which likely has a relatively powerful access token, as opposed to its previous home in the client process. Any time you start distributing components across process and machine boundaries, security concerns arise. It's difficult to decide what a client is allowed to do in a vacuum, and unless you are intimately familiar with the deployment environment's account structure, knowing who clients are doesn't really help you to decide what they should be allowed to do. As you'll see later on, COM+ supplies a powerful role system to shore up this security gap and help you sleep much better at night.

Transaction problems

An important topic related to non-COM+ specific components is that of *commitment control*, or *transactional behavior*. Simply put, this is the ability to define a group of functions as a logical set, such that if any one of those functions fails (for any reason) any work performed before the point of failure will be undone. It's important to note that if the component is not using transactions outside COM+, it probably won't miss them inside COM+. However, what *does* happen if you configure the non-COM+ component to use a transaction?

The answer is predictable, but it is not good. The problem is that the MS DTC (Microsoft Distributed Transaction Coordinator) keeps transaction-related statistics. If COM+ sees that your class requires a transaction, it will create a transaction for each object of that class when a method is called. If an object is destroyed quickly, DTC assumes the transaction is complete and commits it if possible. If an object hangs around past the transaction timeout deadline (set in the Component Services Console Computer Properties dialog box) without explicitly committing the transaction, the transaction will abort. This random behavior is hardly appropriate for applications requiring robustness of transactions.

You might want to try experimenting with automatic transactions on your Stateful component. To make your Stateful component transactional, simply right-click the component in Component Services Console and select Properties. In the Properties window, click the Transaction tab and select Requires a Transaction. Watching the transaction statistics display in the Component Services Console will enable you to track the commit and abort rate of your object's transactions. Deactivating your object within the transaction timeout (by quitting the VBScript client) commits the implied transaction, and maintaining the object longer (by leaving the client running) will abort the transaction. Although legacy components might appear to work acceptably within a transaction (as yours does), at least one component in a COM+ call chain should use the COM+ transaction facilities to ensure proper transaction completion behavior.

Scalability problems

As you have seen, COM+ has no problem using your COM+-oblivious component. The script process communicates with the COM+ server process without a hitch. The problems come when you try to use this component in a heavily utilized, high-performance environment. This component supplies no support for early deactivation or pooling. Because the component is not COM+-aware, COM+ cannot delete it during long intervals of inactivity. Indeed, doing so would most certainly break the stateful Accumulate method, because it relies on the object state m_iTotal value stored in the object's memory. About the only thing COM+ can do to improve the scalability of this object is to leave the server process running after it has been started (which it does within the timeout constraints set in the Component Services Console). The default inactivity period before a server is shut down is three minutes, but you can configure the application to remain running indefinitely.

Another problem is that each copy of your object maintains a copy of the total. This might not be appropriate in a multiuser server-based application. As you can see, maintaining stateful values has several weighty ramifications when designing COM+ components.

What would happen if you let COM+ know that your operations are complete? To do this, you need to get ahead of yourself just a little and add a bit of COM+-specific code (discussed in detail later in this chapter) to your application. At the end of each of the two ISum methods, just before the return, add the following code:

```
//Tell COM+ that your work is complete.
HRESULT hr;
IObjectContext * pOC;
hr = GetObjectContext( &pOC );
if ( FAILED(hr) )
    return hr;
pOC->SetComplete();
pOC->Release();
```

This is a boilerplate block of code that informs COM+ that your object has completed its task in full. Making this statement is, of course, a lie in the case of your component, and COM+ duly punishes such insubordination. Your object is never really done with its work until the client releases it. Why? Because the object is responsible for the state of the m_iTotal value and must remain in context as long as the client requires it. Try compiling this new version to see what happens. In order to work with the COM+-related MTS APIs and interfaces directly, you need to add the mtx.h header to your source and link against the mtx.lib and mtxguid.lib libraries.

Rebuild your component. Before testing the component, you will probably need to reregister it with COM+, because Visual C++ will register the DLL as an in-process server automatically after completing a successful build. To reregister your component, simply right-click the My Computer icon in the Component Services Console and choose Refresh All Components. Test the add function of your component. Works fine, right? Try executing the Accumulate routine two or three times. Not so good, huh? The Accumulate routine always returns the current value only.

To discover what's going on here, add a descriptive message box to your component's constructor, displaying Object Created. It should be something like this:

```
CSum::CSum ()
{
    m_iTotal = 0;
    MessageBox(    NULL,
                   _T("Sum Object Created"),
                   _T("Statful.dll"),
                   MB_OK );
}
```

Create a similar message in a destructor for the class. Build, reregister, and run your application again. Aha! As you can see, COM+ is snuffing your object between calls. Watching the status view of your package's component folder tells the tale. COM+ knows that there is one outstanding object. However, now that the object methods inform COM+ when they have completed an operation, COM+ feels free to delete the objects immediately upon return to the client. So you lose your total after each call. But, hey, the object is much more scalable now. If you could support 10 clients before, but the clients only used the object 10 percent of the time, you might be able to support as many as 100 clients now. This is because COM+ only maintains the number of objects needed to handle the *active* calls.

Note This example is designed to be demonstrative and is therefore necessarily trivial. This component has such a small memory footprint that it's probably just as much of a burden to create it over and over as it is to just leave it in memory. The important thing to gain from this example is how to enable COM+ to deactivate your components before the client is finished with them on operational (perhaps transactional) boundaries. Only careful testing under loads simulating real-world operation can tell you if your specific component can benefit from an early deactivation capable design.

COM+ and state

State consists of those elements that describe a particular object and its current condition in an object-oriented application. For example, your gas tank may be in the full state or the empty state. To be more generic, state consists of the values ascribed to relevant data items at a given point in time. In general, the values of a programmatic object's attributes describe its state.

Properly managing application state is one of the most critical aspects of COM+ application design. The great thing about the few restrictions that COM+ applies to your state model is that if you're designing a scalable server application and are not following these rules already, you probably should be. So your existing applications will experience relatively little impact or a great improvement in scalability, even if this entails a bit of extra work, when migrating to COM+.

Well-described objects often have several legal states. The launch object may have a Ready state, a Failsafe state, and a Fire state. Some state transitions on objects may be illegal, for example from Failsafe to Fire. Objects left in an illegal state are the leading cause of application failure. For example, it would be bad to have the Door attribute set to Open and the Ignition attribute set to TRUE. When it all boils down, no one really cares if your algorithm is wrong as long as the data it manipulates is always right. Reducing the total set of routines that can tamper with object state (for example, information hiding, or encapsulation) is, therefore, one of your most important software reliability tactics.

Types of state

State is a little like baggage — you can't just leave it lying around. You must carry it with you or check it somewhere safe. Some things, like your name, you keep around all the time. Other things, like your lunch, you only keep with you for a short while. Identifying the durability of a certain piece of state is an important step in establishing how that state will need to be managed in COM+. Although many state life-span variations exist, the three types that follow are very common.

Transient state

Transient state includes items that require only interim storage. Transient state is often maintained on the call stack. For example, method parameters and local variables constitute transient state. COM+ object methods invoked by a particular client always complete their execution in a sequential way, and so transient state requires no special handling. This is a form of *nondurable state* because it is not protected by a persistent storage mechanism.

Object bound state

Object bound state includes those elements of state tied to the lifetime of the object. Unfortunately, if you want to design an application platform that will support thousands of corporate users or tens of thousands of Web users, you can't very well maintain an object in memory for each user. Standard object attributes usually fall into the category of *semi-durable state*. Object state outlives the client's call, and in COM+ perhaps even the physical object, but not the logical object (the object that the client perceives). COM+ may dispatch various physical objects to service the requests of a client against a single logical object. You don't want to lose the information while the client is using the logical object, but in most cases you don't actually want to squirrel it away in a database to keep for all time either.

Durable state

Durable state is information that you maintain over long periods of time, often across several executions of an application. In many cases, durable state is data that you simply can't afford to lose. Usually this is the type of information that you carefully maintain in a database, and that you modify within a transaction and always back up.

State storage

So obviously, you should minimize your components' state as much as possible to reduce resource retention on the server. Not all objects can operate in the void of statelessness, however. So if you really need to build components that maintain state and yet require scalability, you need to select a mechanism for storing your durable and semi-durable state. The topics that follow present various possibilities for state storage and their respective trade-offs. The key factors that constantly play against one another are the burden of maintaining state and the burden of transmitting it. If you need state, your choices are to retain it or retrieve it from where it is stored. The next few sections examine various state storage options.

Client temporary

Client applications run on the client's computer. This is one of the big advantages of the whole client/server thing. When you add a client, you add another client processor to bear the load. If you're in the midst of trying to reduce the burden on the relatively few servers you have, it makes perfect sense to make the client keep track of any state the object might require. Client Web pages can maintain memory variables or standard HTML-style parameters to preserve needed state. Traditional clients can create memory structures to manage necessary information. This data can then be passed back to the COM+ object with each call. This approach works well for managing object (semi-durable) state. The advantages of client temporary storage are that the approach scales well and distributes the state maintenance burden to the client. The more clients, the more client machines there are to manage client state. Also, when a client crashes, it only takes out its own state. The drawback is that you will be required to pass necessary state data in with every method call. This can produce excessive call overhead, additional client code, and might not even be feasible in some cases.

Client persistent

Client systems are not generally within the protected circle of the corporate data center and are, therefore, rarely trusted with critical data-storage tasks. However, client preferences and other noncritical state information may be effectively stored persistently on the client machine. This state may be stored in the form of Web cookies, registry settings, or disk files among other methods. Client storage has the same basic pros and cons listed for client temporary storage, with the added feature of increased durability.

Server temporary

At this point you're probably wondering how to manage the necessary state of your components without slowing down the already lethargic Internet and without rewriting all your client code (as the two previous choices often require). Well, if you're just looking to maintain some client-specific object state between object activations, the MTS Shared Property Manager (SPM) may be your solution. The SPM is a high-speed repository for property data and is designed specifically to maintain shared object semidurable state. You could, of course, design your own system to retrieve state, but you'd have to have a pretty specific need to exceed the features supplied by the SPM. One of the first COM+ components you will build in this chapter will demonstrate use of the SPM. Alternatively, you could create a stateful object that COM+ must retain in memory until the object client releases it or the object itself concedes to be deactivated.

Server persistent

All the state management options discussed so far fail to meet the rigorous requirements and large storage capacity generally required of a significant enterprise application. For years, organizations have trusted their critical information to databases. Fortunately, COM+ integrates data access services into its runtime environment. COM+ supports pooled resources, such as database connections, which reduce the overall connection counts against the database and improve data access turnaround. Sophisticated data stores, such as databases, can also be enlisted into MTS transactions to provide robust data manipulation services that avoid inconsistent durable state (partially committed transactions, for example). Databases also have the significant advantage of distribution-supporting data access from various hosts in a network. The stateful objects and Shared Property Manager approaches discussed in the previous section instance data on a per server process basis, disallowing shared state across multiple servers. Of course, there is always a trade-off, and in the case of the database, it is performance, because databases are one of the most expensive data stores available.

As you can see, each of these state storage options has its place and may be useful in several scenarios. Which techniques will work best for you depends entirely upon your application.

COM+ Component Requirements

Now that you've explored the critical state management concerns of COM+, take a look at the more tangible COM+ physical component requirements. The following list presents the eight mandatory requirements of COM+ components:

✦ COM+ components require standard class objects with standard `IClassFactory` interfaces. Because COM+ controls object life span to enhance applications, scalability components cannot use unorthodox object creation techniques. Remember that COM+ intercepts all object creation requests and may perform any number of performance-enhancing shortcuts. Only COM+ directly invokes the class factory of a COM+ object.

✦ COM+ requires an `IClassFactory::CreateInstance` that returns one new object for each call. COM+ creates objects as its needs demand. `CreateInstance` methods that fail to produce precisely one new object with each call confound the lifecycle-management mechanisms employed by COM+. Singletons (produced by class factories that construct only one object and that return interface pointers to this single object over and over) are explicitly illegal.

✦ COM+ components must be implemented within a DLL with a `DllGetClassObject` routine that returns a class object. This DLL export is the routine through which COM+ gains initial access to component class factories.

✦ COM+ components require standard COM reference counting. COM+ can hardly manage object lifetimes if the standard `AddRef` and `Release` routines do not increment and decrement a reference counter once per call.

✦ COM+ components cannot aggregate with non-COM+ objects. Because COM+ intercepts method invocation in order to support several of its advanced features, all aggregate elements of a single logical object must be entirely within or entirely without the COM+ management infrastructure. This keeps subobjects from manipulating direct interface pointers to COM+ objects.

✦ COM+ components must support a complete `DllRegisterServer` implementation. The COM+ administration system manages components within applications down to the method level. The only way COM+ can effectively perform these administration tasks is to have access to `ProgID`, `CLSID`, `Interface`, and `TypeLib` information directly through calls to `DllRegisterServer`.

✦ COM+ components must use standard or type library marshaling. COM+ supplies no support for custom marshaling, and will never call a component's `IMarshal` interface. Interfaces using only automation types (typelib marshaling) can be marshaled by COM's `Oleaut32.dll` using type library information. Interfaces using an MIDL-generated proxy-stub DLL (standard marshaling) will also operate correctly under COM+.

✦ Components using standard marshaling must compile their IDL with `MIDL.exe` version 3.00.44 or greater using `/Oicf` switches, and link their proxy-stubs to `mtxil.lib` as the first library in the search list. Only components using standard marshaling will be concerned with this point.

As you can see, most plain-vanilla ATL components and all VB components meet the needs of COM+ structurally. The real trick is ensuring that your designs and implementation code meet the required, and strongly recommended, architectural guidelines of COM+.

Building COM+ Components

So now that you've dealt with the significant and critical design requirements of COM+, let's examine the implementation details. Here's the good news, the COM+ API only has two functions, `SafeRef` and `GetContextObject`. Of course, one of these functions returns a COM interface pointer that enables you to call several more methods, some of which return additional interfaces pointers and, well, you get the idea. So before you develop your first COM+-aware component, you need to get a handle on the various objects and interfaces available to COM+ constituents. The next discussion examines the nature of `IObjectContext`, the most important interface implemented by COM+, and `IObjectControl`, which is the only COM+ specific interface that a component may itself implement.

Context objects

Context is the stuff that gives you your bearings and makes the outcome of two executions of the same operation produce different results. Stateless components scale very well, but sometimes they need a little context: Something to tell them who's calling them and why, or if a transaction is active. For this reason, COM+ maintains a context object to shadow each COM+ object.

COM+ context objects are opaque and are accessed through methods of the IObjectContext interface. An object can retrieve an interface pointer to its context object's IObjectContext interface by calling the MTS GetObjectContext function. Table 35-1 provides a list of the IObjectContext methods.

Table 35-1: IObjectContext Methods

Method	What It Does
CreateInstance	Creates an object within the current context.
DisableCommit	Declares that the object's transactional updates are in an inconsistent state. (The object retains its state across method calls.)
EnableCommit	Declares that the object's transactional updates are in a consistent state. (The object retains its state across method calls.)
IsCallerInRole	Indicates whether the object's caller is in a specified role.
IsInTransaction	Indicates whether the object is executing within a transaction.
IsSecurityEnabled	Indicates whether security is enabled.
SetAbort	Aborts the current transaction. (The object can be deactivated upon return.)
SetComplete	Declares that the object's transactional updates can be committed. (The object can be deactivated upon return.)

Later in this chapter, you'll take a closer look at the CreateInstance and SetComplete functions.

Object control

What if you want to take advantage of the just-in-time activation and early deactivation features of COM+? In so doing, you agree to have your object deleted between method calls. Even better, what if you want to take advantage of object pooling by letting COM+ assign your object to whichever client happens to be requesting service currently? Both of these scenarios have a severe impact on object state. Deleting an object constitutes destroying its state, and reassigning an object constitutes handing one user's object state over to another user. For objects to operate correctly in this performance turmoil, they must either be stateless or be provided some way of saving and retrieving important state information persistently.

The IObjectControl interface is defined by COM+ and implemented by COM+ components. COM+ queries objects for IObjectControl and, if it is discovered, COM+ invokes the three IObjectControl methods at appropriate times during the object's lifecycle. Table 35-2 describes the three methods of IObjectControl.

Table 35-2: IObjectControl Methods

Method	When It Is Invoked
Activate	Called by COM+ when an object is activated, before any other methods are called on the object in the current context
CanBePooled	Called by COM+ to determine whether an object can be pooled for reuse
Deactivate	Called by COM+ when an object is deactivated, after which no other methods are called on the object in the current context

The stateful object example from the beginning of the chapter lost its state between calls when you enabled early deactivation through a call to SetComplete. As you can see, IObjectControl is the solution to your ill-functioning stateful object. Now you have a way to support early deactivation and just-in-time activation without losing state. The Activate call enables you to retrieve any needed state for client interactions, and the Deactivate call allows you to store any object state needed for later client calls. You might ask why the class constructor and destructor will not suffice. There are two specific reasons. First, some operations (such as accessing the object's context) cannot take place until after the object is completely constructed. These methods sidestep this issue by executing after construction and before destruction. The second and most important reason is that if the object supports pooling, it will be reused instead of destroyed and recreated.

Returning TRUE from CanBePooled informs COM+ that your object supports pooling. This enables COM+ to maintain a pool of objects that can be quickly dispatched to service client requests without the overhead of object construction and destruction. MTS versions 2.0 and earlier do not actually pool objects, but they still make the calls to IObjectControl as if they were doing it for future compatibility sake. COM+ actually implements object pooling. If you're interested in optimum scalability, you should try testing components that support early deactivation, just-in-time activation, and pooling. Only careful design and testing will uncover the optimal solution for a given component.

The Activate call wouldn't be much use without the benefit of context information. Being activated out of the blue doesn't help you understand who is calling and what state you might need to recover in order to perform the tasks requested. For this reason, most component designs use the Activate method as a queue to retrieve context information from COM+ (using GetObjectContext) and context-specific state information from wherever it may be stored.

Using Visual C++ to build COM+ components

ATL makes it easy to construct COM+-ready components. All the COM+ examples in the rest of this chapter have been developed using Visual C++ .NET and its associated ATL elements. Let's construct a basic ATL DLL that you can use to work through several of the examples that follow. Although not much is involved in constructing a COM+-ready ATL component, the ATL COM AppWizard takes care of the few details for you.

First, reconstruct the Stateful DLL, but this time, in the application settings dialog box, select the Support COM+ 1.0 option. If you maintain the same project and class names used in the previous example, you won't have to create a new COM+ application or modify the client application. It is also worth noting that Visual C++ .NET contains a performance feature that enables your build to flag certain DLLs for delayed (just-in-time) loading. This keeps the size of the application image in memory to a minimum and speeds up initial program load times. ATL links to the `mtxex.dll` (the MTS Executive) in this way, using the `/delayload` linker switch. Use of the `/delayload` switch requires helper functions to load the DLL on the fly. You can roll your own or link in the presupplied routines found in `delayimp.lib`, as ATL does.

Next, add a new ATL object to the project by right-clicking the project icon in the class view pane and selecting New ATL Object. Select the MS Transaction Server Component type and click Next. Give your class a name (like `Sum`) and then click the MTS tab in the ATL Simple Object Wizard Properties dialog box to configure MTS specific settings.

Selecting support for `IObjectControl` causes the ATL wizard to add interface support and starter code for all the `IObjectControl` methods. Selecting Can Be Pooled causes ATL to generate a `CanBePooled` method that returns `TRUE`.

After creating the class, you'll note that ATL adds a smart pointer attribute to reference the MTS `IObjectContext` interface. ATL adds code to initialize the pointer in the `Activate` method and release it in the Deactivate method. The generated code should look something like this:

```
HRESULT CSum::Activate()
{
    HRESULT hr = GetObjectContext(&m_spObjectContext);
    if (SUCCEEDED(hr))
        return S_OK;
    return hr;
}

BOOL CSum::CanBePooled()
{
    return TRUE;
}

void CSum::Deactivate()
{
    m_spObjectContext.Release();
}
```

Add the `ISum::Add` and `ISum::Accumulate` methods from the previous example. In your new class, you can replace the large `SetComplete` block of code with a simple call to `SetComplete` through the object context smart pointer. The `Activate` and `Deactivate` methods ensure that all other methods have free access to your MTS context object:

```
STDMETHODIMP CSum::Accumulate(int iValue, int *piTotal)
{
    if ( NULL == piTotal )
        return E_INVALIDARG;

    m_iTotal += iValue;
    *piTotal = m_iTotal;

    //Tell MTS that your work is complete.
    m_spObjectContext->SetComplete();

    //Return success.
    return S_OK;
}
```

Testing your new COM+ component should demonstrate the same functionality and problems that you experienced earlier.

Although you currently still lose state between calls, the object is now equipped with several ways to save and retrieve the m_iTotal state. The Activate method provides a way for your object to recover state before it is needed, and the context information provided by IObjectContext enables you to identify which client is calling. By the same token, the Deactivate method can be used to save the object state before it is destroyed. Or, as in your case, the total could be stored, and retrieved only when needed to improve performance. Your new multiuser COM+ object also needs to make sure that all users have access to the total. This task is easily solved using the MTS Shared Property Manager.

The Shared Property Manager

The need to save semidurable object state across multiple objects and activations is quite common. So common, in fact, that MTS provides a resource dispenser called the Shared Property Manager (SPM) for exactly this purpose.

The Shared Property Manager is instantiated up to once per MTS server process, providing all objects within the process access to shared state under its control. The SPM provides concurrency management to ensure that shared state elements are not corrupted by writes and reads from more than one object at a time. Shared properties are managed through named groups, reducing the potential for name collisions. Monolithic applications often make use of global variables when requiring shared state. The SPM solves the two biggest problems associated with global variables, access control, and global name space pollution.

SPM shortcomings

You need to keep several things in mind when designing components to utilize the SPM. Most important, the SPM is instantiated only once per server process. This means that any properties stored in the SPM are available to all components within the server process, and to no components without it. For this reason, it is generally a bad idea to share properties between components using the SPM. Should an administrator redeploy a component in another server process (application), the shared properties will no longer be shared, and each server process will maintain its own set of property data. Load balancing scenarios that allow clients to connect to the same class of object running on different computers present the same problem. A proper database is the most plausible solution when application-wide shared state is required.

SPM interfaces

Components using the SPM need to include the mtxspm.h header. This header defines three interfaces that provide access to the Shared Property Manager resources:

✦ ISharedPropertyGroupManager

✦ ISharedPropertyGroup

✦ ISharedProperty

The ISharedPropertyGroupManager interface provides access to the top-level SPM behavior, including named property group creation, retrieval, and enumeration. The only way to purge the SPM of any existing groups or properties is to shut down the server process in which the SPM is running. The ISharedPropertyGroup interface provides methods that enable you to create and retrieve properties by name or position within the referenced group. The ISharedProperty interface allows property values to be set and retrieved as variants.

Adding SPM features to a component

Now you can update your existing COM+ component using the SPM. Previously, the Stateful component maintained object state in an attribute. There are several problems with this approach. First, there is no way to share this information among the various objects that may be executing within your distributed multiuser application. This may be good or bad depending on the design, but for this example, assume you want all users to be able to add to the cumulative total. Totaling all sales by all salespeople for the day might work in this way. As discussed earlier, this makes the rash assumption that all clients will use a single COM+ server process for this class.

As soon as you make the total available to all objects in the COM+ process, you introduce synchronization problems. You cannot allow multiple objects to access the total simultaneously. You will also need to make sure that your total does not conflict with other property names in the shared namespace. As a final point, in making your component more scalable, you have sacrificed attribute persistence between calls.

The SPM solves all these problems by presenting a named group property store with built-in synchronization services for multithreaded access. By using the SPM to store your total, your new stateless Sum class will have no need for stateful attributes and has thus eliminated the m_iTotal property. The following shows an updated version of the Sum::Accumulate function:

```
STDMETHODIMP CSum::Accumulate(int iValue, int *piTotal)
{
 if ( NULL == piTotal )
  return E_INVALIDARG;

 //SPM, Group and Property interface pointers
 ISharedPropertyGroupManager * pSPGM = NULL;
 ISharedPropertyGroup * pGroup = NULL;
 ISharedProperty * pProp = NULL;

 //Get interface pointer to SPM
 m_spObjectContext->CreateInstance(
  CLSID_SharedPropertyGroupManager,
  IID_ISharedPropertyGroupManager,
  (void**) &pSPGM );
 if ( NULL == pSPGM )
  return E_FAIL;

 //Create or open the property group.
 BSTR bstrGroupName = SysAllocString( L"SumProperties" );
 long lIsoMode = LockMethod;
 long lRelMode = Process;
 VARIANT_BOOL fExists = VARIANT_FALSE;
 pSPGM->CreatePropertyGroup(bstrGroupName,
                  &lIsoMode,
                  &lRelMode,
                  &fExists,
                  &pGroup );
 SysFreeString(bstrGroupName);
 pSPGM->Release();
 if ( NULL == pGroup )
  return E_FAIL;
```

```
//Open the property.
BSTR bstrPropName = SysAllocString(L"Total");
pGroup->CreateProperty(bstrPropName,
                       &fExists,
                       &pProp);
SysFreeString(bstrPropName);
pGroup->Release();
if ( NULL == pProp )
 return E_FAIL;

//Update the total.
VARIANT vtTotal;
vtTotal.vt = VT_I4;
vtTotal.lVal = 0;
pProp->get_Value(&vtTotal);
vtTotal.lVal += iValue;
*piTotal = vtTotal.lVal;
pProp->put_Value(vtTotal);
pProp->Release();

//Tell MTS that your work is complete.
m_spObjectContext->SetComplete();

//Return success
return S_OK;
}
```

The shared property group manager

As illustrated here, three steps are commonly involved in using the SPM. The first step is to get an interface pointer to the ISharedPropertyGroupManager. Although it's perfectly acceptable to use CoCreateInstance in constructing the SPM, your example uses the context object's CreateInstance method. In the case of the SPM, both work fine. The details of IContextObject::CreateInstance are discussed in the following sections. Regardless of how you retrieve the ISharedPropertyGroupManager interface pointer, only a single instance of the SPM will ever be created for each process.

SPM property groups

The next step is to open the group of interest. Each SPM group has a unique name. Group names act a lot like a C++ namespace in that they partition the global space into named groups. Your group has been arbitrarily named SumProperties. Much like the CreateInstance call used to access the SPM, the CreatePropertyGroup call creates the group if it doesn't exist and opens it if it does, simplifying your program logic. One important point about your group is that you need it to maintain your total, even after your call completes and your object is deactivated. The Process release mode flag indicates that your group should be maintained for the life of the server process. The alternative is standard, which releases the group as soon as all outstanding group interface pointers are released.

SPM properties

The final step is opening the property and updating it. SPM properties are nothing more than named variants. One important aspect of the property update code is that it requires isolated access to the total property across two property calls. First, it needs to read the total, and then it needs to write it with the updated value. Allowing other objects to write to the total between these two calls would cause a loss of information. To solve this problem, you can open the group in LockMethod isolation mode. This locks the SPM at the group level for the duration of the method, providing exclusive access to the total during the read and write. The alternative is LockSetGet, which reduces group contention between components by locking at the property level, and only for the duration of successive get and put calls.

Note that you cannot trust the SPM to maintain state between client sessions, although it might on a busy system that never allows the server process to time out. Slow nights, weekends, a process crash, or any number of other things could conspire to terminate the server process and the SPM with it. The SPM is most certainly not a durable data store. State information that is durable or that needs to be shared across several servers should be stored in a database or some such distributed and reliable data store.

Referencing objects within COM+

Your non-COM+ component at the beginning of this chapter exhibited poor scalability, but no processing flaws. Unfortunately, many normal COM components will actually fail in some way when operating within COM+. The most common issue related to normal COM component failure is that COM+ manages object lifetimes in the COM+ runtime, where traditional component implementations allow the client to control the object's lifespan. Every object created within a COM+ server process is provided with a proxy object that acts as a front end to the actual object, and a context object that maintains information regarding the calling client and the call itself. This enables COM+ to intercept client calls, especially those to IUnknown, and then selectively delegate only those calls that are necessary. In situations where objects support early deactivation, COM+ may even release an object before a client has finished using it. What all this means is that the client really requires a connection to the COM+ proxy object, not the actual object itself.

This is not exactly a good thing! What happens when you give a client a direct reference to your object and then COM+ deletes said object after its current operation completes? The result is that the object is gone, and yet the reference you handed out behind the back of COM+ is still in the hands of the client. This means that you must not, I repeat, must not, return a COM+ object reference (interface pointer) to a client outside the current object context. The solution to this problem is the COM+-supplied SafeRef API:

```
void* SafeRef ( REFIID riid UNKNOWN* pUnk );
```

The SafeRef call enables an object to produce an interface pointer that is safe to pass to clients outside the current context. Failing to do this gives the client direct COM/DCOM access to the object, which of course foils most, if not all of the mechanisms of COM+, causing nasty fireworks. SafeRef works pretty much like QueryInterface, in that it takes the interface ID of the interface you want, the IUnknown of the object that you want it on (which must be the current object), and finally returns the safe interface pointer to that interface. Safe references must be released just as normal references are. Note that QueryInterface calls and SafeRef calls made on a safe reference always return another safe reference. The only serious complication possible here is that two nonequal IUnknown interface pointers may actually refer to the same object within the context of a COM+ object's method call (one to the safe reference and one to the actual object).

Creating objects within COM+

Another important weakness of non-COM+ components is that they often attempt to construct objects not configured to run within a COM+ package using CoCreateInstance. These objects will, of course, execute wherever the registry has them configured to execute. This might be okay, or it might be very bad. In general, after a method call enters the COM+ environment, it should stay there if the various benefits and rules of COM+ are to be maintained. COM+ has no control over components running outside the package environment. You may run across scenarios when external objects are required. If so, you must make sure that out-of-context referencing rules and other application-specific considerations are attended to.

So how do you create a new object within the current context? The answer to that question is by using your context object, of course. The IObjectContext interface supplies a CreateInstance method that operates like CoCreateInstance with the exception that it creates objects within the current context. The new object inherits the current activity (logical thread of control across COM+ servers), security settings, and possibly even the active transaction. Using the ITransactionContextEx CreateInstance method is much the same as the IObjectContext version with the exception that it enables the creator to control the transaction context of the new object.

Summary

The sample application developed in this chapter is at best trivial. Aren't you glad? You focused on building highly scalable, stateless COM+ components, and it was a snap. This is exactly what COM+ is all about. You write the business logic, and COM+ handles the high-end, main frame-style performance and robustness issues. If COM+ weren't easy to use, it would be far less valuable. The real trick is adjusting your brain to focus on matters of state. The most important things to take away from this chapter are the concept of state, behavior, and interface separation, along with the scalability guidelines of the COM+ system. This chapter covered the key concepts behind basic COM+ component development as well as the implementation issues related to IObjectContext and IObjectControl. Now that you've mastered the art of high-performance MTS component design, the next chapter shows you how to write some COM applications by starting with asynchronous event handling via loosely coupled events.

✦ ✦ ✦

COM+ and Loosely Coupled Events

In the previous chapter you learned how COM+ enables programmers to more easily develop componentized applications. However, once you decide to take the dive and start breaking your application into these distributable components to be dispersed throughout your network, there is still a very real challenge to deal with — asynchronous events. Simply put, almost any real component-based system requires its components to notify one another of events that transpire. One example would be a stock ticker component that needs to be updated when a given stock changes prices. Another example is a backorder fulfillment component that needs to know when certain parts have been received into inventory.

In this chapter, you will discover how COM+ loosely coupled events (LCE) and the COM+ Event Service enable you to easily incorporate asynchronous event notifications into your application. I'll begin by exploring the COM+ Event Service architecture and illustrating a simple demo application that fires an event and another application that receives notification of that event's firing. Once you've learned these basics, the chapter will illustrate some of the more advanced issues of programming the registering and unregistering of components, creating and applying event filters, and working with transient subscriptions.

COM+ Event Service

One common side effect of a distributed system is the problem with maintaining synchronicity between the different components. One such scenario would be an inventory control system where various modules, or components, would need to be made aware of when a SKU's (stock keeping unit) inventory level changes. For example, in any inventory control system you are also going to have a subsystem for handling backorders. This subsystem would need to know when a given SKU's inventory has been affected so that it can attempt to fulfill any outstanding backorders. Because it would not be efficient for the backorders subsystem to constantly poll the inventory data store for changes in inventory, there needs to be a means for the subsystem to know when certain SKUs have been updated.

As another example, let's take the case of a company that publishes articles on the Web. It would almost certainly have an application (a content update subsystem) to enable editors to update and add new content to the system. In addition, it might have other subsystems that need to be made aware of new content. Suppose the site has a Latest Updates page that needs to be updated each time an article is updated. In addition, I'll throw in the fact that the Home Page might need to be updated to reflect the very latest additions to the site. In this particular example, you'd want the content update subsystem to use a loosely-coupled means of broadcasting this change to the rest of the system so that it doesn't have to know about each subsystem that cares about new or updated articles.

So where does that leave you? You need an asynchronous, loosely-coupled means for one system to notify other systems that an event they have interest in has occurred. This is where the famed Observer pattern (as defined in *Design Patterns* by Erich Gamma, et al.) comes in.

The Observer pattern defines two actors, or participants, in this approach. The *publisher* (the inventory module) exposes a list the events that it can broadcast (publish) to the rest of the system. *Subscribers* (the backorders module) make known their desire to be notified of such events (subscribing). The two major benefits of this arrangement are the asynchronous nature of how this works and the decoupling of publisher and subscriber.

It's asynchronous because the subscriber doesn't continually poll or block on an event happening. It simply lets the system know (you'll see how shortly) that it is interested in an event's occurrence and how the system should notify it when that event occurs.

The decoupling occurs because there is a layer of abstraction between publisher and subscriber such that neither knows the details of how to communicate with the other. This enables the publisher to add events without coding for specific subscribers, and it allows the subscribers to code for events without worrying about specific semantics of interfacing to the publisher.

In essence, the COM+ Event Service is a feature first introduced with Windows 2000 that implements the Observer pattern to facilitate asynchronous eventing between the components of a distributed system. As you can see in Figure 36-1, the COM+ Event Service brings into play the COM+ catalog that is used as the go-between between publishers and subscribers. Simply put, the COM+ catalog is the underlying data store that contains COM+ configuration data.

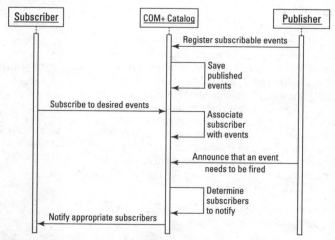

Figure 36-1: The COM+ catalog provides a layer of abstraction between event subscribers and publishers.

What are events?

So far, I've implicitly used the term *event* to refer a particular happening in a system, such as a new article being added to a Web site. At this point, it's important to realize that COM+ has a slightly different usage of this ubiquitous term. COM+ defines the term *event* to mean the actual notification (using a COM interface) from the publisher to the subscriber that something that subscriber cares about has occurred.

There is where the COM part of the equation comes in. The subscriber must implement a pre-defined COM interface (I'll explain this bit shortly) and, as such, act as a COM server to the publisher (the COM client). If you're at all familiar with COM, you'll recognize this as being a standard and straightforward means of having the publisher and the subscriber communicate with each other. If not, I strongly suggest reading Chapter 32, which covers eventing in COM/ATL.

To clear up another term, you'll recall that I referred to the COM+ Event Service as the layer of abstraction between publisher and subscriber and that its purpose is to decouple the two. It's this decoupling that gives way to the term *loosely coupled events* that you will hear so often with respect to the COM+ Event Service.

Now that you realize that an event in COM+ parlance is the call itself, it's important to understand that the act of calling this event is known as *firing an event*. If you look at Figure 36-1, you'll see that the first thing that happens is the publisher has to register itself with the COM+ catalog. This is done via a special system-provided class called the *event class*. As you'll discover when you get this chapter's demo application, the event class implements the interfaces necessary to enable the publisher to fire events. On the subscriber side, the subscriber is obliged to implement the event class in order to receive incoming notifications from the publisher of a data change.

A *type library* is then used to indicate to COM+ the specific interfaces and methods that the event class will expose. These defined event classes are then stored in the COM+ catalog via the COM+ Component Services snap-in or programmatically by the publisher.

The subscriber then indicates to the COM+ catalog which events it wants to subscribe to by providing and defining a *subscription* and passing it to the COM+ catalog. A subscription is a data structure that defines such things as the recipient of the event (the subscriber), the event class (defined and registered by the publisher), and which interface or method within the event class the subscriber is interested in. As with event classes, subscriptions can be manually defined by an administrator using the Component Services snap-in or they can be defined programmatically.

At this point, let's look a bit more at how events get fired. In order for the publisher to fire the event, it first calls the standard COM object creation function `CoCreateInstance` to create an instance of the event class. From there, when the publisher need only call the desired event method in order to notify subscribers that the published change has occurred.

When the publisher calls the desired event method, the COM+ catalog performs a lookup for all subscribers that have subscriptions naming the event class and event method used. For each subscriber naming the event class in question, the COM+ catalog calls the specified method. Now that you understand the COM+ Event Service's role in asynchronous event handling and the participants involved, let's look at some limitations and how they affect your system design and coding efforts.

COM+ Event Service limitations

At this point, you're probably thinking about how great this COM+ Event Service is and how it's going to help you in designing your distributed systems. You would be correct on both fronts. However, I would be remiss in my duties if I didn't also include some limitations to using this subsystem. This way, you're better prepared to take these caveats into account when designing your system and can design or code around these issues.

The first issue I'll bring up is that the subscription mechanism is not distributed. This means that if one developer creates a subscription on one computer, the rest of the network does not automatically know about that subscription. The reason for this is that there is no central repository of subscriptions for an entire network, or domain.

The generally accepted workaround to this limitation is to create all of your event classes and subscriptions on one central server. Unfortunately, that results in all notifications being emitted from one machine, which has the following drawbacks:

✦ If this central server is down, any part of your system that depends on these notifications will not work correctly.

✦ Defining all of the event classes and subscriptions on one machine is the antithesis of a load-balanced, efficient use of network resources.

✦ Performance degradation is a concern when the publisher is not on this central event server because the publisher would first have to remotely instantiate the event class on the server.

The second issue (and one that is easily overlooked until you fall victim to it) is that the notification mechanisms used by the COM+ Event Service are DCOM and COM+ Queued Components (which I cover in the next chapter). The problem is that these technologies weren't designed to accommodate what amounts to broadcasting information to multiple clients. Instead, both of these technologies were designed for one-to-one communications in which a single entity communicates with another single entity either synchronously (using DCOM) or asynchronously (using Queued Components).

Because of this underlying design, each subscriber needs to be notified individually. The result is that the delivery time increases in relation to the number of subscribers that need to be notified. Figuring out exactly how many subscribers your system can handle without becoming unusable is sometimes referred to as the *threshold of pain*. Defining this threshold tantamount to black magic and is a practical impossibility because doing so involves knowing individual factors such as the network topology, network traffic, CPU utilization on key machines (such as the event server), and so on. Therefore, you'll need to determine where the threshold of pain is by testing and benchmarking your specific system.

One workaround to this problem would be to write an *event broadcaster* of your own. This would basically mimic the datagram functionality found in NetBIOS and TCP/IP programming and would work like this. The event broadcaster would be a single (base) subscriber, responsible for receiving the events via DCOM or Queued Components and then sending the incoming data to all subscribers via a datagram.

Although this sounds like a bit of a pain — and it is — as you work through the examples in this chapter and start to get a feel for how useful this service is, you'll understand that the trouble you go through to implement your own event broadcaster is more than offset by the benefits derived from using the COM+ Event Service.

Event Service Demo

Now that you've received an overview of the COM+ Event Service and how publishers and subscribers define themselves and their intentions, let's see how this plays out in a demo application. In this demo, you will see how easy it is to use the COM+ Event Service by means of a simple application that fires events based on an article being added to a system. This demo will be three-step process involving the following:

1. Creating the publisher and defining it to COM+

2. Creating the subscriber and defining it to COM+. Remember that you can have as many subscribers as you wish, and that these steps can be repeated for each.

3. Creating the GUI application that will fire the event, which will cause COM+ to notify the subscribers to the event.

Creating the publisher

A publisher in the COM+ framework is really nothing more than a COM component that tells COM+ that it can source events. You'll see how to do that shortly, but you'll now create a simple COM component using ATL that will define the interface that all subscribers must implement.

Create a new ATL Project called WebSiteEvents. This project is named generically so you can get a feel for how you would name such a project. Even though this demo will only have a single event component and interface, it's certainly conceivable that this application played out in the real world would contain several multiple interfaces, and those interfaces would contain multiple methods. You'll see this as you continue through the demo. Click the Finish button to invoke the ATL Project wizard.

When the ATL Project wizard displays, click the Application Settings link to define the type of ATL project you will be working with. Leave the server type as the default of DLL. Because I am a long-time MFC developer, I almost always deselect the Attributes checkbox and then select the MFC Support option. If you're interested in attributed programming, especially with ATL components, I cover that in Chapter 30. In addition to the MFC option, also check the Allow merging of proxy/stub code option, as well as the Support COM+ 1.0 option. The first option is more of a convenience issue so that the proxy and stub code reside in the same DLL on the server. Once again, it's not urgent within the context of this discussion that you under-stand each of these options. However, they are all covered in Chapter 30 in the section enti-tled "Creating an ATL COM Application." Once you've selected the options I've described, click the Finish button to create your new ATL DLL.

Now select the Add Class option from the Project menu and select the ATL Simple Object template. When the ATL Simple Object Wizard displays (Figure 36-2), type in a short name of **ArticleEvents** and click Finish.

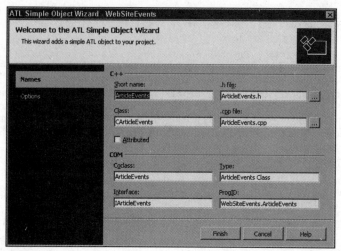

Figure 36-2: The ArticleEvents declaration as an ATL Simple Object.

Now, if you open the Class View, you will see that you have an interface called
IArticleEvents in your project. Right-click that interface and select Add ➪ Add Method.
This invokes the Add Method Wizard, where you need to define a method called NewArticle.
The first input parameter is called pbstrAuthor. To declare this parameter, first click the in
checkbox from the Parameter Attributes grouping, and then select the BSTR* item from the
Parameter Type combo box. Then type a Parameter Name of **pbstrAuthor** and click the Add
button. Follow this same procedure to create parameters named pbstrTitle and pbstrUrl.
Now, add one last input parameter named sCategory, but make this parameter a SHORT
(instead of a BSTR*). When you're finished, click the Finish button and then build the project.

Now, it's on to COM+. As you learned in the previous chapters, COM+ applications are created
via the Component Services snap-in, which can be found in your system's Administrative
Tools menu. When the Component Services snap-in displays, expand the tree view to display
first the Component Services item, then the Computers item, followed by the My Computer
entry. Under My Computer, you'll see the entry for COM+ Applications. First select that entry
and after right-clicking it, select the New Application option. Follow the wizard through
selecting the empty application option and a name of WebEventsApp. Accept all other
defaults.

At this point, you have an empty COM+ application. Now you need to add the publisher component to it. To do that, expand the COM+ Applications node, locate the WebEventsApp node, and expand it to see entries for Components and Rules. After selecting the Components node, right click it and select the New Component menu option.

This is a very important step—when the COM Component Install Wizard displays, first click the Next button and then click the Install new event class(es) button. When you do this, the wizard invokes a dialog box that enables you to select the DLL containing the new event class. Simply browse to the location of the WebSiteEvents DLL and select it. Figure 36-3 shows the ensuing dialog box once you've selected the DLL.

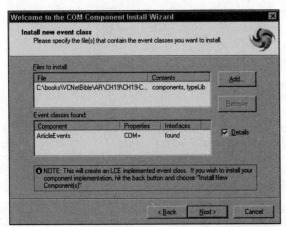

Figure 36-3: Selecting the component that defines the interface is the last step in defining a new event to COM+.

As you can see, adding event classes to a COM+ application is a simple act of clicking a button and specifying the DLL that contains the component and interface that define the event's interface. Click Next and then Finish to complete the creation of the event class. When you do this, you'll see results similar to those shown in Figure 36-4, where you can see that COM+ has successfully queried the component's vtbl and determined its interfaces and methods.

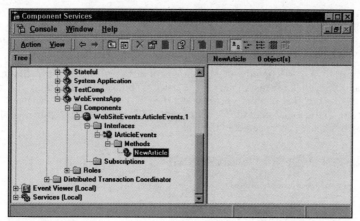

Figure 36-4: When an event class is added to a COM+ application, its interfaces and methods are found and listed.

Once you've defined the event class, you only have one task left to fully define the publisher. After right-clicking the newly-created component `WebSiteEvents.ArticleEvents` component, click the Properties menu option and then click the Advanced tab (Figure 36-5). The key field to concentrate on here is the Publisher ID field. The value you type in here is what you'll see when you create the subscription later. Remember that I said that when you create a subscription entry into the COM+ catalog, you are marrying a subscriber to a specific event class. For purposes of this demo, I used the value `WebSiteEventsPubId`. This value is also used by the publisher when it wants to create an instance of the event class in order to fire the event.

Creating the subscriber

As you'll see, creating the subscriber is very similar with just a couple of noted differences. To get started, create a new ATL project (you can add it to the current solution if you want to make the build easier) called `LatestUpdates`. As with the publisher, select the options for MFC support, merging of proxy/stub code, and support of COM+ 1.0.

When the project has been created, add an ATL Simple Object called `ArticleEvents` to the project, making sure that the `LatestUpdates` project is selected in the Solution Viewer. Because you are implementing the `ArticleEvents.IArticleEvents` interface, you'll need to add methods with the same signature as its methods. Therefore, add a method called `NewArticle` to the `LatestUpdates.IArticleEvents` interface with the same parameters you used in the previous section.

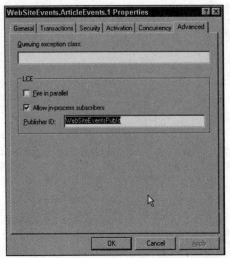

Figure 36-5: The event class's advanced settings are important because they include the publisher id needed by the subscriber.

As in all of COM, the difference between the interface definition (`ArticleEvents.IArticleEvents`, in this case) and the interface implementation (provided by `LatestUpdates.IArticleEvents`) is that the former is only a function signature and the latter contains the code to do something. Therefore, open the LatestUpdates project's `ArticleEvents.cpp` file and locate the `CArticleEvents::NewArticle` function. This is the C++ implementation of the COM interface called `NewArticle`. As mentioned before, this is all very difficult to define on the fly while teaching COM+. Therefore, if you're lost at this point, you'll probably need to read the COM chapters first (starting with Chapter 26) and then return here for a full understanding of everything that is going on.

In this demo application, you're only concerned with proving that this function is called as a result of another function being called (the event being fired). Therefore, modify the `CArticleEvents::NewArticle` function so that when finished it looks like the following:

```
STDMETHODIMP CArticleEvents::NewArticle(BSTR* pbstrAuthor,
                                        BSTR* pbstrTitle,
                                        BSTR* pbstrUrl,
                                        SHORT sCategory)
{
  AFX_MANAGE_STATE(AfxGetStaticModuleState());

  CString strAuthor = (LPCTSTR)_bstr_t(*pbstrAuthor, false);
  CString strTitle = (LPCTSTR)_bstr_t(*pbstrTitle, false);
  CString strUrl = (LPCTSTR)_bstr_t(*pbstrUrl, false);
```

```
CString strNewArticle;
strNewArticle.Format("NEW ARTICLE:\n"
  "Author: %s\n"
  "Title: %s\n"
  "URL: %s\n",
  strAuthor, strTitle, strUrl);
AfxMessageBox(strNewArticle);

return S_OK;
}
```

As you can this, this function simply formats a string to display the incoming data from the event notification. Finally, add the following include directive to the `ArticleEvents.cpp` file (as it defines the `_bstr_t` type) and then build the component.

```
#include <comdef.h>
```

Once the subscriber component is built, it will need to be added to COM+ as the publisher component was — this time with a COM+ application name of `LatestUpdatesApp`. Once you've created the application, add the ATL subscriber component to it. However, make sure to click the Install new components button (as opposed to the event class option).

Now, you simply need to add a subscription to the component. To do this, right-click the LatestUpdates component's Subscription folder and click the New Subscription menu option. After clicking the Next button to dismiss the welcome dialog box, you will see a dialog box like that shown in Figure 36-6.

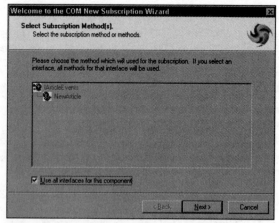

Figure 36-6: Select subscription dialog box

From the Select Subscription Methods dialog box, you can select the method(s) that will be subscribed to. Note that you have a few options here with regards to how you do that. One option is to select an interface, which will automatically include all of that interface's methods. This would be useful if the `IArticleEvents` had several methods—such as `UpdatedArticle`, `MovedArticle`, and `DeletedArticle`—that you wanted to subscribe to. In addition, clicking the Use all interfaces for this component option is useful if the event class exposes numerous interfaces that you're interested in. For example, the `WebSiteEvents` component—along with the `IArticleEvents` interface—could expose interfaces like `IUserEvents` that would contain methods called when new users register or de-register. Now you should see why, even when you think your application is going to be very finite, you should name your projects, components, interfaces, and methods as generically as possible, because it makes extending the system much easier. At this point, simply click the Use all interfaces for this component checkbox and click the Next button.

The next dialog box to appear is the Select Event Class dialog box shown in Figure 36-7. Here you are given the opportunity to select specific classes that you want to subscribe to. You can also click the Use all event classes that implement the specified interface checkbox. That way, if new event classes are introduced, your subscriber component will always be notified without you having to update it. Obviously, this might not always be desirable, and so the option is left to you. For this demo, select the WebSiteEvents.ArticleEvents.1 entry and click Next.

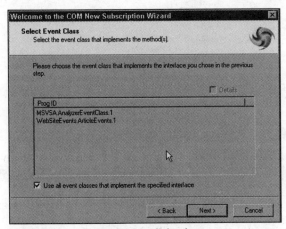

Figure 36-7: Event selection dialog box

On the next dialog box (Figure 36-8) you name the subscription. Because you selected the use all interfaces option earlier, give this subscription a generic name of `WebSiteEvent Subscriptions`. Select the Enable subscription immediately option so that you don't have to programmatically start the subscription. (You will see how to do that later in the chapter, but for now you'll do it the easy way.)

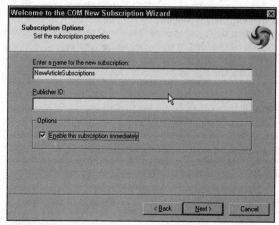

Figure 36-8: Naming the subscription and specifying a publisher id.

Once you're done, click Finish to complete the definition of the subscriber component. Now it's on to defining the code to test the event demo.

Firing a COM+ event

You've made it! At this point, you have a publisher of events and a subscriber to those events. Let's now code a simple application to gather input (to simulate a new article being added to the site) and fire an event with that information.

To do that, create a new MFC dialog-based application called `ArticleMaintenance`. Note that on this book's Web site, this main application, the publisher component and the subscriber component are all in the same solution to make building the entire solution a one-step process.

Once the project has been created, open the main dialog template and modify it so that when finished it looks like that shown in Figure 36-9.

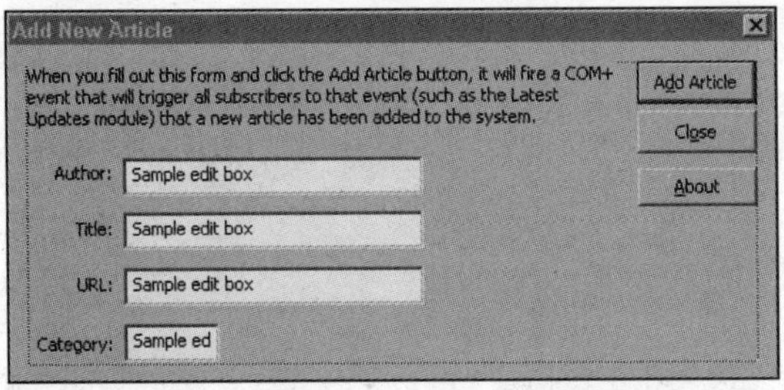

Figure 36-9: Demo dialog box to enter the new article that will be broadcast to all subscribers of this event.

For the four input controls, define the DDX variables as shown in Table 36-1.

Table 36-1: DDX Variables for Demo Application

Control	Member Type	Variable Name
Author	CString	m_strAuthor
Title	CString	m_strTitle
URL	CString	m_strUrl
Category	CString	m_iCategory

Once the dialog box is completed, it's time to code the firing of the event. To do that, first add the following COM initialization code just before the return statement in the dialog box's OnInitDialog function.

```
HRESULT hr = ::CoInitialize(NULL);
if (FAILED(hr))
{
  AfxMessageBox("Failed to initialize COM!");
}
```

Now add the following `include` directives to the top of the dialog box's implementation file. Note that here I'm using relative path names to the WebSiteEvent project's header files. I'm doing that for simplicity. It's a much better programming practice to add the folders to the project's include directories list and specify the header file without the hard-coded path name.

```
#include "..\WebSiteEvents\WebSiteEvents.h"
#include "..\WebSiteEvents\WebSiteEvents_i.c"
#include <comdef.h>
```

Add a handler for the dialog box's Add Article button and modify it as follows. The first thing the function does (after calling `UpdateData` to retrieve the dialog box's values) is to create an instance of the `IArticleEvents` interface (using the standard COM function `CoCreateInstance`). From there, the code converts the `CString` member variables representing the user input to `BSTR` values that can easily be passed via COM. Finally, the `IArticleEvents.NewArticle` method is called.

```
void CArticleMaintenanceDlg::OnBnClickedOk()
{
  if (UpdateData())
  {
    CWaitCursor wait;

    BOOL bSuccess = FALSE;
    HRESULT hr;

    CComPtr<IArticleEvents> event;

    hr = ::CoCreateInstance(CLSID_ArticleEvents,
      NULL,
      CLSCTX_SERVER,
      IID_IArticleEvents,
      (LPVOID*)&event);
    if (SUCCEEDED(hr))
    {
      BSTR bstrAuthor = m_strAuthor.AllocSysString();
      BSTR bstrTitle = m_strTitle.AllocSysString();
      BSTR bstrUrl = m_strUrl.AllocSysString();
      hr = event->NewArticle(&bstrAuthor,
        &bstrTitle,
        &bstrUrl,
        m_iCategory);
      if (SUCCEEDED(hr))
      {
        bSuccess = TRUE;
      }
    }
  }
}
```

Before you build the solution, you need to make a couple of minor alterations due to having multiple projects in the same solution. The first thing is to define the order of dependencies so that the projects are built in the correct order. To do that, select Project ➪ Project Dependencies. Select the `ArticleMaintenance` project and then click the `LatestUpdates` and `WebSiteEvents` projects. This tells Visual Studio that these two projects need to be built first. Next, open the Solution Explorer and after right-clicking the `ArticleMaintenance` project, click the Set as start-up project option. That's it; time to test.

Testing the COM+ Event Service

At this point, simply fire up the `ArticleMaintenance` application and enter some values. Figure 36-10 shows the results of running this application after providing it with information for an article available on my Web site.

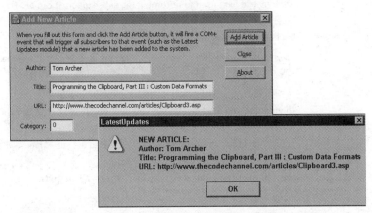

Figure 36-10: Example of asynchronous events using the COM+ Event Service.

One last point that I'll make here is that when you want to update the component code, you need to remember to stop the COM+ applications via the Component Services snap-in. To do that, simply select the application, right-click it to display its context menu, and select the Shut down menu option. Now that you know the basics of working with loosely coupled events and COM+, let's delve into some more advanced areas.

The IEventSubscription Interface

As you know, a subscription is an entity that, once created, resides within the COM+ catalog. However, I haven't yet discussed the fact that there are actually two different types of subscriptions: persistent and transient. Actually, the only subscriptions that live in the COM+ catalog are persistent subscriptions. I'll get into the distinction between persistent and transient subscriptions in the next section.

One thing to note is that regardless of whether the subscription is persistent or transient, the subscription itself is nothing more than a data structure containing the members needed to define a subscription and how it should be handled by the COM+ Event Service at runtime. Therefore, in order to better understand how subscriptions are handled, I've listed the members of the COM interface (IEventSubscription) to the COM+ subscription model in Table 36-2. Although most of these members, or properties, can be modified using Component Services, some can only be manipulated through the administrative methods supplied by the IEventSubscription interface.

Table 36-2: IEventSubscription Interface Methods

Method Name	Method Description
Description	Arbitrary text field used to document the subscription. It can be useful for your own documentation, but it cannot be used by the Event Service.
Enabled	Enables or disables the subscription.
EventClassID	Used to define the event class with which the subscription is associated. This is generally not used in favor of the InterfaceID property.
MachineName	The name of the machine on which the subscription resides.
MethodName	The name of the method that the subscription points to. This is relative to the InterfaceID property.
OwnerSID	Security identifier of the application that created the subscription.
PerUser	Takes a Boolean value, indicating that the subscription will only receive events if the user is identified with the OwnerSID property.
PublisherID	Identifies the publisher responsible for firing the event.
PublisherProperty	Probably the most likely method to be used when dealing with subscriptions, this method allows you to set a collection of properties in order to filter whether an event should fire.
SubscriberCLSID	The CLSID of the subscriber component. You would almost never touch this value because it is used by the event class in order to create the subscriber object.
SubscriberInterface	The COM IUnknown pointer on which the subscriber wants to receive incoming event calls.
SubscriptionID	Uniquely identifies a subscription within the event system.
SubscriptionName	The name given by the user for a subscription upon creation.

Before I talk about how to use the IEventSubscription interface, I will take a moment to discuss the types of subscriptions that you can create. At this point, there are two of them: persistent and transient. The basic difference between the two is that a persistent subscription survives across an IPL boundary. However, there are several other distinctions between the two subscription types:

✦ *Subscription creation* — Because persistent subscriptions actually reside in the COM+ catalog, they can be created either programmatically or via Component Services. Transient subscriptions, on the other hand, can only be created programmatically.

✦ *Mapping of registered events* — Persistent subscriptions map registered events to objects that are created automatically whenever an event is fired. However, transient subscriptions are a bit more dynamic in this regard in that they map registered events to specific interface pointers. Because of this, transient subscriptions are typically used when a currently running application wants to subscribe to a specific event dynamically, as opposed to a persistent subscription in which the mapping is more global and static in nature.

✦ *Components they work with* — Because persistent subscriptions are defined within the context of the COM+ catalog, they are always associated with configured COM components. Conversely, transient subscriptions can work with components that are either configured or non-configured. (Note that configured applications are those that have been registered in the COM+ catalog.)

✦ *Subscription longevity* — As mentioned previously, persistent subscriptions, by definition, reside in the COM+ catalog and therefore, exist across IPL boundaries. Transient subscriptions, on the other hand, are more of a dynamic entity and only exist in the scope in which they are created.

Working with Transient Subscriptions

In the previous demo, you learned how to use Component Services to register an event class and subscription, and even write a simple application to fire the event. However, that demo dealt only with persistent subscriptions. This demo looks at how you would perform the task of registering and unregistering transient subscriptions. One thing to also keep in mind is that whether you register a persistent or transient subscription, the act of firing the event and handling the event works exactly the same. In other words, the publisher and the subscriber should be abstracted from this knowledge.

Registering transient subscriptions

The first thing you need to see is how to register a transient subscription with the Event Service, because this task cannot be done via Component Services. To do this, simply perform the following steps:

1. Create an instance of a `COMAdminCatalog` object.

2. Use the `ICOMAdminCatalog::GetCollection` interface in order to retrieve a collection of the COM+ catalog's transient subscriptions.

3. Use `ICatalogCollection::Add` to add a new transient subscription.

4. Use `ICatalogObject::pub_Value` to assign the values discussed in the previous section regarding subscription properties.

5. Finally, save the subscription to the COM+ catalog using the `ICatalogCollection::SaveChanges` method.

Now, take a look at the following Visual C++ code to see exactly how this would work. This code can also be located on the book's Web site in a folder named `TransientSubscription`.

```cpp
HRESULT hr;
ICOMAdminCatalog* pAdminCatalog;

// retrieve the COM+ catalog object
hr = ::CoCreateInstance(CLSID_COMAdminCatalog, NULL,
                        CLSCX_SERVER,
                        IID_ICOMAdminCatalog,
                        (void**)&pAdminCatalog);
if (SUCCEEDED(hr))
{
 ICatalogCollection* pCatalogCollection;

 // allocate bstr for catalog name
 BSTR bstrCatalogName =
  ::SysAllocString(L"TransientSubscriptions"));

 // retrieve catalog collection for transient subscriptions
 hr = pAdminCatalog->GetCollection(bstrCatalogName,
                         (IDispatch**)&pCatalogCollection);

 // free bstr
 ::SysFreeString(bstrCatalogName);

 if (SUCCEEDED(hr))
 {
  ICatalogObject* pCatalogObject;

  // get new, initialized catalog object
  // (not in catalog yet!)
  hr = pCatalogCollection->Add((IDispatch**)&pCatalogObject);
  if (SUCCEEDED(hr))
  {
   // use the pCatalogObject->put_Value to set the
   // subscription values

   // when finished setting values, release catalog object
   pCatalogObject->Release();

   // save object into COM+ catalog
   LONG lResult;
   hr = pCatalogCollection->SaveChanges(&lResult);

   // check lResult for success
  }
 }
 pCatalogCollection->Release();
}
```

Unregistering transient subscriptions

Now that you've seen how to register a transient subscription, I will show you how to unregister a transient subscription. Although some of the setup work (such as instantiating the COMAdminCatalog object and retrieving the ICatalogCollection interface are the same, there are enough differences to warrant looking at a snippet of Visual C++ code to see how this is done programmatically.

```cpp
HRESULT hr;
ICOMAdminCatalog* pAdminCatalog;

// retrieve the COM+ catalog object
hr = ::CoCreateInstance(CLSID_COMAdminCatalog, NULL,
                        CLSCX_SERVER,
                        IID_ICOMAdminCatalog,
                        (void**)&pAdminCatalog);
if (SUCCEEDED(hr))
{
 ICatalogCollection* pCatalogCollection;

 // allocate bstr for catalog name
 BSTR bstrCatalogName =
  ::SysAllocString(L"TransientSubscriptions"));

 // retrieve catalog collection for transient subscriptions
 hr = pAdminCatalog->GetCollection(bstrCatalogName,
  (IDispatch**)&pCatalogCollection);

 // free bstr
 ::SysFreeString(bstrCatalogName);

 if (SUCCEEDED(hr))
 {
  // fill out collection
  hr = pCatalogCollection->Populate();

  if (SUCCEEDED(hr))
  {
   IEnumVariant* pEnumVariant;
   hr = pCatalogCollection->get__NewEnum(
   (IUnknown**)&pEnumVariant);

   if (SUCCEEDED(hr))
   {
    VARIANT var;
    VariantInt (&var);
    int nIdx = 0;

    while (S_OK == pEnuVariant->Next(1, &var, NULL)
    {
     ICatalogObject* pCatalogObject =
```

```
        (ICatalogObject*)var.pdispVal;
      if (/* compare to name you want to remove */)
      {
      hr = pCatalogCollection->Remove(nIdx);
      if (SUCCEEDED(hr))
      {
       long lResult;
       pCatalogCollection->SaveChanges(&lResult);
      }

      VariantClear(&var);
      break;
      }

      VariantClearn(&var);
      nIdx++;
     }
    pEnumVariant->Release();
   }
  }
  pCatalogCollection->Release();
 }
 pCatalogCollection->Release();
}
```

At this point, you've learned how to publish and subscribe to events, how to fire events, and how to programmatically define both persistent and transient subscriptions. Now, let's look at the final topic of this chapter: event filtering.

Event Filtering

With your simple example, even a popular Web site is generally only going to post 20 or so new articles per day. Therefore, the fact that COM+ is essentially broadcasting messages to all subscribers of the new article event detailing each new article doesn't exactly creating a crushing hardship for any network. However, what if you take this application to its natural conclusion and add events for all the things that someone monitoring the Web site would care about? For example, the site could fire events for news users registering, users un-registering, users posting messages to the various forums — even unique IP addresses connecting to the server. At this point, you'd probably want each subscriber to be a little more judicious in what it requests if it's not going to use all the data that it receives.

Let's say you have a site that defines an editorial calendar where a topic will be selected for each month for which you want to get as many articles as possible. If you had an articles submissions application where the user could enter their own articles, to be reviewed and posted later by site editors, it would be nice for the site admin to be notified that an article had been entered into the system that corresponded to the topic of the month. Now you can start to see scenarios where asynchronous events play an important part in distributed computing. Instead of changing the article submission application each month — always a bad idea — you could instead have a component that subscribes to the new article event, but filters on articles defined as being in a specific category.

The only question now is "Where does the filtering take place?" As stated, you certainly don't want to place a filter in the publisher because that would couple that code too tightly to a specific subscriber. Besides, a publisher might have many different subscribers, all of whom have different (possibly dynamic) filtering needs. You certainly don't want to put the event filtering logic in the subscriber because that would mean the subscriber would still incur the overhead of having to receive every notification of a given type before it could decide whether it even cared about that event. Not only does this waste the subscriber's resources, but also, in a network environment with a lot of events, it means needless network traffic.

Therefore, the only logical place to place a filter would be in the system that is actually firing the event to begin with — COM+. In this section, I'll first discuss how you can use the COM+ catalog to define a filter for a given subscription. By defining the filter in the COM+ catalog, you can relieve both the subscriber and the publisher from having to programmatically deal with the task of filtering out noise, or unwanted data. After that, you'll see how to programmatically add filter strings to the COM+ catalog. This is useful if you want to write an administrative application to use instead of allowing your users to use the Component Services snap-in.

Creating a filter string administratively

In this example, assume that your application wants to filter on a category. For simplicity (and because coding this bit doesn't add anything to the demo) I'll also assume that each category has a published, unique, numeric ID assigned to it.

To define a filter, first open Component Services and select the desired subscription that will have the filter applied to it and invoke its Properties dialog box. From there click the Options tab (shown in Figure 36-11).

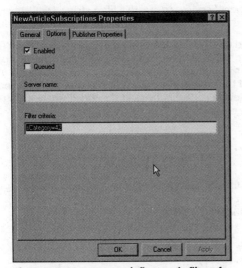

Figure 36-11: You can define static filters for each subscription via the Component Services.

From here, the options are fairly obvious. Simply specify the desired filter using a property and valid value as a name/value pair. A simple example would be if 42 is the ID of the category of the month. If you know that the parameter to the method for the category is called sCategory, the filter might be defined as follows:

```
sCategory=42
```

Because there will be times when your filtering won't be a cut and dried as simple equality test involving one parameter, COM+ includes support for the Boolean operators listed in Table 36-3 to aid in the definition of your system's filter strings.

Table 36-3: Filter Syntax

Operator(s)	Meaning
=, ==	Equal to
!=, ~=, <>	Not equal to
&	Boolean AND
|	Boolean OR
!, ~	Boolean NOT

Creating a filter string programmatically

Now that you've seen how to use Component Services to create a filter string, I will show you how to perform the same task using Visual C++ and the COM+ Event Service admin interface.

The first thing you need to do is to instantiate a IID_ICOMAdminCatalog interface. From there you retrieve the transient catalog as described in the previous section. Because the catalog publishes a property called FilterCriteria, you need only call the ICatalogCollection.put_Value method passing it the name of the property and the value for that property. In the following code snippet, I've bolded the relevant code that I've just described where a filter is being defined for articles matching the category 42.

```
HRESULT hr;
ICOMAdminCatalog* pAdminCatalog;

// retrieve the COM+ catalog object
hr = ::CoCreateInstance(CLSID_COMAdminCatalog, NULL,
                        CLSCX_SERVER,
                        IID_ICOMAdminCatalog,
                        (void**)&pAdminCatalog);
if (SUCCEEDED(hr))
{
  ICatalogCollection* pCatalogCollection;

  // allocate bstr for catalog name
  BSTR bstrCatalogName =
   ::SysAllocString(L"TransientSubscriptions"));

  // retrieve catalog collection for transient subscriptions
```

```
hr = pAdminCatalog->GetCollection(bstrCatalogName,
 (IDispatch**)&pCatalogCollection);

// free bstr
::SysFreeString(bstrCatalogName);

if (SUCCEEDED(hr))
{
BSTR bstrPropName = ::SysAllocString(L"FilterCritera"));

// notice the handling of the quotes for an embedded string
BSTR bstrValue = ::SysAllocString(L"sCatetory=42"));

VARIANT var;
var.vt = VT_BSTR;
var.bstrVal = bstrValue;

hr = pCatalogCollection->put_Value(bstrPropName, var);
// check hr for success

::SysFreeString(bstrValue);
::SysFreeString(bstrPropName);
}
}
```

Summary

In this chapter, you learned how COM+ addresses the issue of event notification via loosely coupled events and the Event Service. After learning the roles of the publisher and the subscriber components in the Event Service architecture, you then coded a demo application where you created an event interface, a subscriber to display a message upon receiving the event and a GUI application to fire the event. From there, you discovered some of the more advanced issues of the COM+ Event Service such as dealing with the IEventSubscription COM interface and using the COM+ Event Service admin interfaces to register and unregister transient subscriptions. Finally, you learned how to programmatically filter the subscriber's incoming events. At this point, you've learned quite a bit about using asynchronous event handling under COM+. However, one extremely important part of COM+ development and asynchronous events is the queueing. Therefore, I'll cover that in the next chapter.

✦   ✦   ✦

COM+ Queued Components

In the previous chapter, you learned about the COM+ Event Service and how it enables you to alert components and applications asynchronously when a particular programmatic event occurs that they've subscribed to. In this chapter, I'll wrap up the COM+ section with a look at Queued Components and how it enables you to provide support for disconnected users. I'll begin by looking at the advantages of queued components, and what the Queued Components architecture has to offer with regards to creating more robust, scalable, secure, fault-tolerant distributed systems. From there you'll see the rules for defining a COM component that will be used in the Queued Components framework and how to define a component as being queued within the Component Services application. Once you have a handle on these basics, you will then be presented with a demo application that, while simple in scope, effectively illustrates the basics of accepting user input and then sending that data to COM+, where it's queued until the client application can start up and receive the data.

Queued Components Overview

Most programmers like to just jump into code immediately. However, as an author, I have to temper my desire to do that with the fact that you might not be familiar enough with Queued Components to know if it's even correct for your application. Therefore, in this section I'll first present an overview of Queued Components — including the benefits it provides for distributed systems, the COM+ architecture behind its implementation, and finally some points to help you decide if this technology is right for you. Therefore, if you're already familiar with Queued Components, or simply want to jump into the code and "figure it out later," you can also proceed directly to the section entitled "Developing a Simple QC Demo" and return to this section later at your leisure.

Benefits of Queued Components

Before we get into the Queued Components architecture, let's briefly talk a bit about the benefits of using queued components, because that will help you understand why and how to develop your applications using this concept.

Over the past 10 to 15 years, the strategy of designing enterprise-level applications as singular, monolithic applications has gone the way of the do-do bird, being replaced by the concepts of componentized development, where the components are then distributed over a network or a group of networks (a WAN). However, although distributed computing has become the de facto standard in designing and deploying enterprise applications, one difficult decision facing software engineers is the decision of whether the system should be designed to be real time (synchronous) or queued (asynchronous). In making that determination, the following benefits of queued computing can be used as a guideline in making the best decision for your particular situation:

- ✦ Loosely coupled clients
- ✦ Disconnected applications
- ✦ More responsive applications
- ✦ Better resource use
- ✦ Message reliability and security
- ✦ Efficient server scheduling
- ✦ Easier to scale large applications

Loosely coupled clients

In a synchronous, or nonqueued, environment, one component of a distributed application being unavailable is a death knell to the overall system's ability to function, because each bit of interaction between the various components is serialized. This can obviously be problematic for systems where downtime is not only inconvenient, but also costs the company money. The reasons for a component being offline can range from a computer hardware problem where the machine is not on, or cannot communicate on the network, to situations where the network traffic is so heavy that attempts to communicate with the various distributed components time out before successful completion.

An application that uses the COM+ Queued Components service is abstracted from the need for all parts of a distributed system to be online in order for the system to function, because the communications between the components is actually done through COM+. The way this works is that applications send the data to COM+, which then queues the data until the intended target component is online and ready to accept data. As you can imagine, the ability to reduce dependency on component availability is one of the biggest advantages to using Queued Components.

Disconnected applications

A natural extension of not having the server and client tightly coupled is the fact that with queued components, disconnected applications are now a possibility. As an example, suppose you have an order entry system that can be run both locally (attached to the server through a local network) or remotely (on a salesperson's laptop). Because you can't guarantee that the salesperson will be connected to the server when the order is being entered, how can you programmatically deal with both scenarios? Obviously, you could have the code check the network status and save the data to be uploaded to the server later, or you could even turn on a flag such that the laptop version of the software always assumes a disconnected state. The problem with these approaches, however, is that the code now has to worry about whether or not it's connected. Queued Components allows you to write your applications in such a way that your code doesn't have to worry about checking for connectivity. This is because the data sent by the application is queued by COM+ (transparently to the application), and then relayed to the target component when a connection is made and the target is online and receiving data. Figure 37-1 illustrates the flow of information in a disconnected scenario.

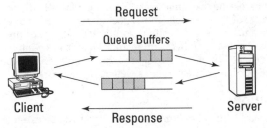

Figure 37-1: Disconnected scenario using the COM+ Queued Components service

More responsive applications

In a synchronous, or nonqueued, environment, a component that relies on other components must wait to be serviced — a component cannot call another component's methods and continue to do something else. The COM+ Queued Components service allows a component to make an outbound call and not have to wait to be serviced. Because components are not blocked after sending a request through the COM+ Queued Components service, they are free to return from a user-requested action in the case of a GUI application. This means better and faster user feedback. Obviously, this is a double-edged sword, however, because there are times when the source of a request will need to know the results of the request or even have data returned. I cover this and other common queuing concerns in the section entitled "Is Queued Components right for you?"

Improved resource use

In distributed, nonqueued environments, the server component persists in memory from the time it is created until the object is finally released. Obviously, in a serialized world, this can take an unknown amount of time, meaning that the server will need to block on the call to the client until that call either times out or completes. The problem is that this approach keeps components in memory for far longer than they need to be in comparison to a queued approach. With Queued Components, once the server has made the call — and once COM+ has queued the request and sent parameters — the server component's job is done as soon as the request is made, regardless of how long it takes the client to receive and process the request. Therefore, components can be freed from memory and can have any other associated resources freed in a much more efficient manner.

Message reliability and security

The COM+ Queued Components service is built on top of a proven queuing service — MSMQ (Microsoft Message Queue). MSMQ uses error detection and correction protocols to ensure that data is not lost, reordered, or duplicated. MSMQ also uses the MSDTC (Microsoft Distributed Transaction Coordinator) used by SQL Server and many applications to implement *two-phase commit* so that in the event of a failure during the process of sending a message (such as a server failure), the transaction (the act of sending the message) is rolled back (the effects of the transaction are undone). The message is then sent again at a later time when the server is up and functional. Lastly, MSMQ has built-in security services that can protect data from being viewed, altered in transit, or forged by unauthorized senders. However, you need to know almost nothing about MSMQ, because all of this is taken care of for you by COM+.

Efficient server scheduling

One often-overlooked advantage of queuing is that because a request for work is queued, you have more control over when that processing takes place. One example of this is that certain tasks can be prioritized over others according to application-specific parameters. For example, the processing required to fulfill a newly placed customer order naturally takes precedence over background tasks such as backorder fulfillment. In addition, resource-intensive work requested during peak system usage hours can be deferred until an off-peak period of server activity in order to lessen the burden on the server as well as the network as a whole.

Easier to scale large applications

With a nonqueued system, it is extremely difficult to know just how far it can be extended in terms of scalability (both users and data). However, with queuing it is much easier to load balance components across multiple servers because the components are abstracted from one another by COM+. Therefore, an individual component simply specifies which component it's attempting to communicate with. Where this component exists on the network is a job for the administrator to worry about and can either be controlled programmatically or through the Component Services application.

Defining Queued Components

At this point, I've gone over quite a laundry list of what Queued Components has to offer your system. Let's now look at how this service works, how to define a component as being queued, and the different components of the service on the COM+ side of things.

Creating and defining a component as queued

The process of creating a component varies only slightly from that of creating any other COM component. Using the prototypical remote order entry example, you might want to create a component called `InventoryOrder` with an interface called `ICreateOrder`. The `ICreateOrder` interface would then contain two methods (for purposes of this example) called `AddLineItem` (which takes as its arguments an item number, or SKU, and a value representing the quantity ordered) and `ProcessOrder`.

It's important to realize, however, that in order for a COM component to work in the Queued Components service, there are a few rules that it must follow:

✦ An interface cannot be queued if any of its methods are defined via the IDL as having the attributes `[out]`, `[in,out]`, and `[out,retval]`. This specifically relates to the inability to return data from a queued request and is something I'll cover in the "Is Queued Components Right for You?" section.

✦ Because the client and server component of a queued component might exist on different machines and run at different times, the data that is passed from the client to the component must be passed by value. This is an obvious restriction because passing by reference entails passing an address that is only understood within a given process (and that process may not necessarily exist when the server component is ready to process a client's request).

Once you've created a component that is to be queued, you simply need to mark it as queued. The three-step administrative process couldn't be easier:

1. Assuming that you're adding this component to a new COM+ application, not an existing one, you would create a new, empty COM+ application. This application acts as a surrogate process for the COM component. Chapter 35 explains how to create COM+ applications.

Note

As mentioned earlier, Queued Components uses the underlying queuing facilities of MSMQ. Therefore, you must install MSMQ in order to use Queued Components. One way to determine if you have MSMQ installed is to open the Component Services application. After expanding My Computer, you should see a folder for the system's defined COM+ applications. Because MSMQ uses the MS DTC in order to provide transactional support of messages, you should also see a folder entitled Distributed Transaction Coordinator. If you do not, MSMQ is not installed.

To install MSMQ, run the Add/Remove Programs applet from the Control Panel. When the applet is displayed, select Add/Remove Windows Components on the left-hand side of the dialog box. Depending on your installation, you might need to have your Windows CD available to complete this operation. When the Windows Component Wizard displays, select the Message Queuing Services option and then click the Next button to install MSMQ.

2. After the COM+ application has been created, mark the application itself as being queued. This is done by right-clicking the application and selecting the Properties menu option. From there, select the Queuing tab to see the options illustrated in Figure 37-2.

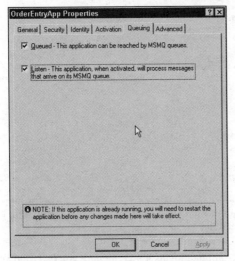

Figure 37-2: In almost all cases, you will select both the Queued and Listen options when marking a COM+ application as queued.

- The first option (Queued) must be selected for a queued component, and it simply states that client applications will communicate with this application via MSMQ.

- The Listen option is something you need to check only if your component will be using the standard Queued Components feature, which means that when the application is started, a server-side object is automatically created that reads in any messages intended for the application. You will almost always select both of these options.

3. Upon clicking the OK button, the Queued Component service will automatically create for your application an MSMQ queue of the same name as your chosen application name. This is the queue that will be used by MSMQ to route messages from the client to the server application's components.

To see this, open the Computer Management application, then expand the Services and Applications folder and within it the Message Queuing folder. By the way, this is another way to verify that a system has MSMQ installed. You should see four folders containing different queue types (outgoing, public, private, and system). As you can see in Figure 37-3, I've created defined a COM+ application named OrderEntry as being queued, and as a result the default queues have been created.

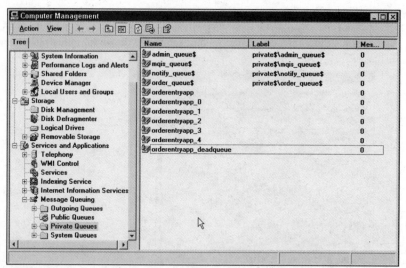

Figure 37-3: Several MSMQ queues are created by default when you define a COM+ application as being queued.

4. After you've marked the COM+ application as being queued, you can then add any number of COM components to that COM+ application and mark their interfaces as queued on a case-by-case basis.

To do this, select the desired component and then any interface that you want queued. From there, invoke that interface's Properties dialog box and click the Queued tab (see Figure 37-4). From there, click the Queued option and then the OK button. Note that if any method in the interface you want to mark as queued is not unidirectional, Component Services will not allow you to mark the interface as queued. It's an all-or-nothing proposition.

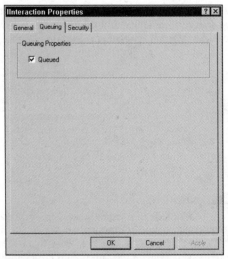

Figure 37-4: By specifying the Queued option, you are signifying that the component is designed to receive messages.

That's it on the server side. There's absolutely nothing from a code perspective that you need to explicitly do in order to mark a component as queued.

The client side of Queued Components

On the client side, things are even easier. In fact, the client doesn't even know that the component it's using is queued — hence the abstraction, and the reason that COM+ so easily facilitates systems needing to support disconnected users. Here's how it works from a Visual C++ application.

The client first calls the `::CoGetObject` to retrieve what amounts to a proxy for the desired component. Actually, what the client is receiving is a very special kind of Queued Component object called a *Recorder* object. However, it's important to realize that this `Recorder` object can be used just as if the client had a reference to the actual server-side component. The advantage of this is that the client code doesn't have to be written differently for a standalone versus a queued environment.

Once the client acquires the `Recorder` object, it can then call the desired methods of the server-side interface. However, each time the client calls a method, the `Recorder` simply buffers the call. The data is not sent until the client deactivates the object (either by explicitly releasing the object or letting it go out of scope). Using the order entry example, the client would call the `AddLineItem` method once for each line item to be added to the order. The client would then call the `ProcessOrder` method to signify that the order is ready for processing. Finally, the client would deactivate the object.

When the Recorder object is deactivated, the data is sent to the local MSMQ queue. When the client machine is connected to the server, MSMQ sends the data to the server-side queue for processing. This data flow is illustrated in Figure 37-5.

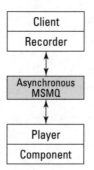

Figure 37-5: The Queued Components Recorder object acts as a proxy for the server-side component so that the client can use the component without worrying about whether the component is queued.

The server side of Queued Components

As with the Recorder component on the client side of things, the server side also has hidden components that aid in the process of making queued components function. Each queued COM+ application has defined for it a ListenerHelper and a Player. When a message is sent via MSMQ to a queue belonging to a given COM+ application, that application's ListenerHelper object reads the message. For each message read, the ListenerHelper object then creates an instance of the Player object and passes the message data to it.

The Player object is then responsible for opening the message and detecting which component needs to be created to handle the request. After the target component is created, the Player object translates the message into actual COM method calls to the component. Figure 37-6 shows how this intimate little dance between the different objects results in the component finally receiving the client's calls.

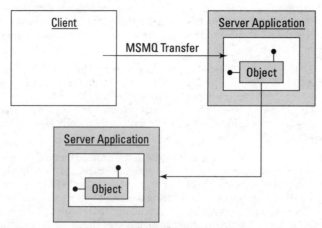

Figure 37-6: The server-side component is also abstracted away from the details of queuing so that it can be used in a queued or nonqueued environment without changing it.

That's really all there is to do on either side to get all the benefits listed in the section "Benefits of Queued Components." In fact, until now you've only seen the advantages to using queued components. Therefore, before I get too far ahead and look at this chapter's demo application, prudence would dictate that I step back and take a look at both the positives and negatives of queued components. In this next section, I'll detail some potential problems, or disadvantages associated with queuing so that you can decide for yourself when this is a good option for a given system.

Is Queued Components Right for You?

Because Queued Components is designed to ease the development of distributed systems, the first thing you have to consider when making a decision on using Queued Components (or MSMQ) is whether your application is truly a candidate for being a distributed system.

As I alluded to earlier, Queued Components has one very clearly documented (and logical) rule about how the queued interfaces of a component can be defined. The rule is that any communications with a queued component must be unidirectional. What I mean is that when you are designing your client application(s) and component(s), you need to be aware that the called will not be able to respond to the caller. This is logical because, by definition, a queued system indicates that the target server might not be available. Therefore, you could never depend on being able to make a call and receive return data. After all, doing that is the definition of a nonqueued system.

What you have to consider now is whether this is a major limitation of Queued Components and its applicability to your system. To answer that question, consider the types of information that a component would normally attempt to convey back to a calling client:

✦ Confirmation of data received

✦ Request for additional data

✦ Confirmation of tasks completed

✦ Need for lookup data

In the next sections, I'll discuss each item, giving examples of each, and then I'll address whether they can be accommodated with the scope of Queued Components.

Confirmation of data received

Confirmation of data received is the easiest issue to address. Using the order entry example, it would be very logical to assume that code should exist on the client to verify a return code from the component indicating that the order data had been received and is being processed. However, if you're thinking (and designing) like this, you're not putting yourself in the right mindset. Queued Components (and its underlying MSMQ queuing system) guarantee delivery of each message that gets queued. Once queued, at some point, upon connection to the server, the message will make its way to the server and eventually be processed. Therefore, the only return value you need with regard to an attempt to queue information is a value indicating whether the message was successfully queued. As you'll see in the demo application, you do receive this value from COM+.

Requests for additional data

One example of a server requesting more data would be a variation on the Challenge/Response security built into Windows NT. Using this mechanism, a client requests something. The server responds by challenging the client to identify itself in some way that helps to verify the client's authority to make the original request. The client then responds by sending the requested information, whereupon the server validates that information and carries out the requested task.

With this particular example, it would not be difficult to change the system's design to send all the necessary data to the component in the first call. In fact, if your application is truly a distributed application, and message queuing is the right alternative, you (as a component designer) would never know when the server component is going to receive the request. In other words, keep in mind that the whole concept of queuing is built on the precept that the client using it requests that a task be performed and then goes on about its business, knowing that while there's no guarantee of when the server will process the request, it will eventually. In fact, even if the component could respond to the client in this environment (say two hours later), how would the client understand the context of the component's response? The client would have already moved on and may not even be in the correct context any longer. Obviously, there are ways around this as well — you could pass an ID to the server and have it return that ID to identify itself, but the point is that this is not what queued components are about.

The workaround to this problem is simple: When designing components that are going to be queued, you need to keep in mind that all transactions are atomic. In other words, when a client calls a component's method, in order for it to perform a given task, the client and the component need to be designed in such a way that all the data that needs to be sent in order to carry out that task is sent in a single call.

Confirmation of task(s) completed

Once again, I will use the order entry component example. In a standalone application, when the client calls the ProcessOrder method, the order component would probably return some sort of value indicating that the order had been successfully processed. However, with Queued Components, you won't get that confirmation. One obvious reason is that by the time the server receives the order information and processes it, the client might not even be connected any more; and even if the client is still connected, will it be in a context in which it will understand the returning value?

Obviously, the issue of confirming the successful completion of work is an important one. However, because I'm talking about a distributed, queued environment in which a request for an asynchronous task was sent, the solution would be that the component responds to the client in the same asynchronous fashion. Designing a component (named, for example, ConfirmOrder) that would run on the client would address this issue.

The process flow would go as follows:

1. The client acquires a new order number from the system (you'll see how when you get to the demo).

2. The client then creates the OrderEntry component and retrieves its ICreateOrder interface.

3. The client calls the ICreateOrder.SetOrderNumber method, followed by calls to ICreateOrder.AddLineItem (for each line item), and finally a call to ICreateOrder.ProcessOrder.

4. The client keeps track of outstanding orders that have been submitted, but not verified as having been completed.

5. After the `OrderEntry` component has completed the processing of the order, it could then turn around, and using the same queuing mechanism, instantiate a `Confirmations` component and retrieve its `IConfirmOrder` interface.

6. The `OrderEntry` component then calls the `IConfirmOrder.SetOrderNumber` method followed by `IConfirmOrder.OrderCompleted`.

7. When the client reconnects to the server, it receives its messages for the `Confirmations` component (actually its encapsulating COM+ application) specifying which orders had been completed since the last time the machine had communicated with the `OrderEntry` component.

Need for lookup data

Another common misconception about using queuing with a distributed (and possibly) disconnected system is that of lookup tables (also known as master tables). In the order entry example, I've purposely kept things simple. However, obviously in a real-world, practical application, the client would need certain data from the server in order to validate the order. I'm referring to things like terms codes, tenders, and sales tax codes. In addition, most users of GUI applications are going to expect standard UI elements such as combo boxes and auto-fill controls such that they do not need to memorize all valid data combinations.

Even in a fully connected, yet distributed environment, you would not want to make round-trips to the server for each of these items because not only would performance on the client machine be poor (can you imagine fetching data from the server as you tab from field to field?), but also even a moderate number of users would produce such a tremendous amount of round-trips across the network that overall network performance would be adversely affected. The common workaround to this is to load key lookup tables on the client machines so that the validation and auto-fill features of the client would be performed without incurring network traffic.

However, what about larger tables such as items? Certainly any decent-sized company can't overload each salesperson's computer with their entire inventory. Once again, a little fore-thought into the design of the client goes a long way. In this case, it is quite common to have the salesperson download onto his laptop a subset of the inventory master table that represents the item information that is most likely to be needed. As a supplement, the salesperson would then take along a catalog of the company's items and would have to manually enter the information of any items that were not downloaded.

The last example of needing access to a lookup table is this: How does the salesperson get a unique order number if his machine is disconnected from the server? One very common way of answering this challenge is to design the system such that when the salesperson leaves the office, a block of unique order numbers is assigned for that PC. That way, these order numbers could be kept in a local table, and when the client connects to the server, the server would process the new orders. You could even go as far as designing the server to call a client-side component in order to automatically send down another block of allocated order numbers if the trip has been longer than expected or the salesperson had an exceedingly good sales day.

To queue or not to queue?

As a summary to this section, before getting too excited about the prospects of implementing queuing in your system, you should consider whether the system in question would work in an environment with the following traits:

✦ Communication is always asynchronous, with no guarantee of exactly when the requested task will be completed.

✦ There is no synchronous manner of reporting back the success or failure of a requested task.

✦ Calls to queued interfaces are limited to unidirectional communications.

✦ All data necessary to carry out a given request must be passed on a single atomic call.

As you've seen in this section, writing a distributed system — especially one that works asynchronously via queuing — takes a lot of planning in terms of the design of both the client and component. My advice would be that if you find the aforementioned items too restricting or simply impossible to live with for your system, it might not be a good candidate for queuing. Now let's look at a simple demo application that makes use of Queued Components.

Developing a Simple QC Demo

It's finally time to put what you've learned here to the test. In this section, you will write the component that I've referred to so often (OrderEntry) and its two main methods (AddLineItem and ProcessOrder). Obviously, you're not going to write a real order entry application. However, message boxes will be displayed from the component indicating successful retrieval of messages sent from the client application. In the case of the AddLineItem method, which takes as parameters the SKU and the quantity ordered, it will display that information. Then, when the ProcessOrder method is called, a simple message box detailing the order at that point will be displayed. Here are the steps that you'll go over in order to create this demo application:

✦ Write the OrderEntry component (using Visual C++ and ATL) and its interface with the aforementioned two methods.

✦ Create a COM+ application for the component, install the component into that application, and mark both the application and interface as queued.

✦ Write the client application using Visual C++.

✦ Test the component and client code.

Writing the Server-side Queued Component

At this point, invoke the wizard for an ATL Project called OrderEntry and select the following options:

✦ Uncheck the Attributed checkbox.

✦ Specify the Server type as being a DLL. You do this because, like most components, this test component will be housed in a DLL. In fact, when using Queued Components, your components must be inserted into a COM+ application. To do that, the component must reside in a DLL. After creating this component, you'll create the COM+ application that basically acts as a surrogate process for the component's DLL.

✦ Select the option to allow merging of proxy-stub code. This option is available for DLL projects only and is used because, by default, the proxy-stub code would be marshaling code contained in a separate DLL from the component.

✦ Select the Support MFC checkbox. This will be purely optional in your own applications. However, you need it here simply because the demo component uses some MFC-specific classes and functions such as `CString` and `AfxMessageBox`.

After you have chosen the settings described previously for your ATL component, click Finish.

Now add an ATL Simple Object with a short name of `CreateOrder`. This will create a public COM interface name of `ICreateOrder` and an implementing internal C++ class named `CCreateOrder`.

Once you've created the `ICreateOrder` interface, you can then add its methods via the Class View. Name the first method `AddLineItem` and specify two parameters. The first parameter should be defined as an input parameter, be of type `BSTR*`, and be named `pbstrSku`. The second parameter (also an input parameter) should be of type `SHORT` and named `sQuantity`.

As I've noted on more than one occasion, interfaces defined as queued cannot return values. Therefore, you might be wondering how it is that the Add Method Wizard can state that the method return type is HRESULT without letting us change it and this interface still works in the demo.

The fact is that in accordance with COM rules, all methods (except the three IUnknown methods) must return a value of type HRESULT. However, don't be misguided into thinking that you can simply return any value in place of an HRESULT. One of the main advantages of using Queued Components is that the component itself is completely unaware of whether it is being used in a queued environment. Therefore, even if you think this component will never be used in a nonqueued environment, it is good practice to code it as though it might be and to abide by COM rules with regard to returning the correct information in the HRESULT.

If you need more cajoling than that, think back on how many bugs you've had to fix because of another programmer's short-sightedness in deciding not to implement something correctly because "Nobody will ever use it like that."

Once you've created the `AddLineItem` method, modify the `CCreateOrder::AddLineItem` member function to display a message indicating the data that was passed to it. Remember to add an `include` directive for the `comdef.h` file (defines the `_bstr_t` type).

```
STDMETHODIMP CCreateOrder::AddLineItem(BSTR* pbstrSku,
                                       SHORT sQuantity)
{
  AFX_MANAGE_STATE(AfxGetStaticModuleState());

  CString strSku = (LPCTSTR)_bstr_t(*pbstrSku, false);

  CString strLineItem;
  strLineItem.Format("AddLineItem called:\n"
    "SKU: %s\nQuantity: %ld",
    strLineItem, sQuantity);

  AfxMessageBox(strLineItem);

  return S_OK;
}
```

This code is fairly self-explanatory. It simply declares a CString object on the stack and converts the incoming BSTR to a CString by first converting it to _bstr_t type and then casting that to an LPCTSTR type.

Once you've finished with the AddLineItem method, add a parameter-less method named ProcessOrder to the ICreateOrder interface. Then modify it as follows so that you can tell when it's been called by COM+:

```
STDMETHODIMP CCreateOrder::ProcessOrder(void)
{
   AFX_MANAGE_STATE(AfxGetStaticModuleState());

   AfxMessageBox("ProcessOrder has been called");

   return S_OK;
}
```

Once you've defined the ICreateOrder interface and its methods, you'll need to specify which interfaces are eligible to be queued. This is done via the IDL by simply attaching the QUEUEABLE attribute to the interface. Here's the beginning of my OrderEntry.idl file. (Notice the inclusion of the mtxattr.h header file that defines the QUEUEABLE attribute macro.) I've bolded the only two lines you'll need to manually change from what the wizard does for you:

```
#include "mtxattr.h"
import "oaidl.idl";
import "ocidl.idl";

[
   object,
   uuid(42363644-0245-40BF-95E4-50B472D9DE47),
   dual,
   helpstring("ICreateOrder Interface"),
   pointer_default(unique),
   QUEUEABLE
]
interface ICreateOrder : IDispatch{
...
```

Now, build the project, and using the Component Services, create an empty COM+ application named OrderEntryApp, and using what you learned in the "Defining Queued Components" section, mark it as queued. Once that is done, install a new component and through the wizard select the newly built OrderEntry.dll file. When you do that, COM+ will automatically resolve the names of the component's interfaces and the names of the methods and properties of those interfaces. In this case, you have defined only the single ICreateOrder interface. Therefore, mark this interface as being queued.

Now you need to write the client application to test the new queued component.

Writing a Queued Component Client Application

Now that you've finished with the server (component) side of things, it's time to write the client side. Because there are not administrative tasks on this end, this task is even easier.

Create a new MFC dialog-based project called OrderEntryClient. When you've created the project, open the project's main dialog resource template and modify it so that when finished it looks like that shown in Figure 37-7.

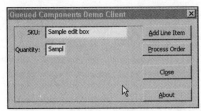

Figure 37-7: The data entered on this dialog box will be stored in a local MSMQ queue, and then sent to the server-side component.

After you've added the appropriate controls to the dialog template resource, add a DDX value variable of type CString called m_strSku for the SKU edit control. Next, add a DDX value variable of type int named m_iQuantity for the Quantity edit control.

Once you've finished with the dialog template, open the OrderEntryClientDlg.h header file and add the following include directives to the top of the file. The OrderEntry.h file contains the definition for the ICreateOrder interface, the OrderEntry_i.c file defines the IID_ICreateOrder structure, and the comdev.h file is a standard COM header file that defines the _bstr_t type you'll use shortly. Also, note that I'm using relative path names to the OrderEntry project's header files. I'm doing that for simplicity. It's much better programming practice to add the folders to the project's include directories list and specify the header file without the hard-coded path name.

```
#include "..\OrderEntry\OrderEntry.h"
#include "..\OrderEntry\OrderEntry_i.c"
#include <comdef.h>
```

Next, define a member variable for the COrderEntryClientDlg that will contain a pointer to the ICreateOrder interface:

```
protected:
  ICreateOrder* m_pCreateOrder;
```

Initialize the m_pCreateOrder interface pointer to NULL in the COrderEntryClientDlg class's constructor initializer list:

```
COrderEntryClientDlg::COrderEntryClientDlg(CWnd* pParent)
  : CDialog(COrderEntryClientDlg::IDD, pParent)
  , m_strSku(_T(""))
  , m_iQuantity(0)
  , m_pCreateOrder(NULL)
{
  m_hIcon = AfxGetApp()->LoadIcon(IDR_MAINFRAME);
}
```

Update the dialog box's OnInitDialog function to initialize COM and retrieve an ICreateOrder interface:

```
BOOL COrderEntryClientDlg::OnInitDialog()
{
 CDialog::OnInitDialog();

 ...

 HRESULT hr = ::CoInitialize(NULL);
 if (SUCCEEDED(hr))
 {
  hr = ::CoGetObject(L"queue:/new:OrderEntry.CreateOrder.1",
                     NULL,
                     IID_ICreateOrder,
                     (void**)&m_pCreateOrder);
  if (FAILED(hr))
  {
   DisplayHRESULTError(hr);
   m_pCreateOrder = NULL;
  }
 }
 else
 {
  AfxMessageBox("COM failed to initialize");
 }

 return TRUE;
}
```

As you're aware by now, you normally instantiate COM objects with a call to the ::CoCreateInstance or ::CoCreateInstanceEx functions or a call to a class factory's CreateInstance method. So why is the function calling the ::CoGetObject function?

This function is used to create a connection to the component. Actually, this function creates and connects the client to the Recorder component. As you read earlier, this object acts as a proxy in the component's stead. However, the key issue here is that the client application code has absolutely no idea that it isn't talking directly to the component itself. Such is the beauty of the Queued Components service and the reason why the ::CoGetObject function is used. In essence, this function acts as a layer of abstraction so that the client code doesn't have to worry about the details of how to connect to a component that might not even be available or how to deal with MSMQ (because this code might also be used in a nondistributed environment).

Because this function is so instrumental in making this whole thing work, look at the ::CoGetObject function a bit more closely. The first thing you probably notice is the strangely formatted string used as the first parameter. Actually, this string is really two parameters in one (delimited by a / character) and is called the component's *display string*, as shown in the following example:

```
queue:/new:OrderEntry.CreateOrder.1
```

The first part of the string (up to the / character) is called the *queue moniker*. A moniker is a COM+ object that takes a string argument and from that knows how to create and initialize another COM/COM+ object. As with all monikers, `ProgID` is associated with the queue moniker, and it is actually called with the information after the colon being passed as an initialization string. Figure 37-8 shows an example registry and the queue moniker `ProgID` entry in the `HKEY_CLASS_ROOT` husk.

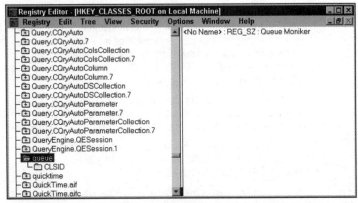

Figure 37-8: All monikers have a ProgID entry in the registry that enables the COM runtime to create the appropriate object.

As is the case with most functions that take a specially formatted string parameter, there are specific rules about what can be passed to the queue moniker. The most oft-used parameter is the `ComputerName`. This value is how you specify where the component resides on your network. As an example, say that the component was installed on a server called `MyBigBadXPServer`. If that were the case, the line would read as follows. (Note that the line is broken for book formatting reasons.)

```
queue:ComputerName=
MyBigBadXPServer/new:OrderEntry.CreateOrder.1
```

Now, when the queue moniker creates the queue object, it passes the value `ComputerName=MyBigBadXPServer`. It is then up to the queue object to know what to do with that information.

What happens if you simply omit the queue moniker? Because the queue moniker is used to activate MSMQ, the COM runtime would not know to use MSMQ, and would attempt to create the component for you. If the component were available on the local machine, the code would work. However, if the code were installed remotely, the call would fail.

Table 37-1 contains the other parameters you should be familiar with regarding the use of queue monikers.

The second part of the component's display string is the `new` moniker. As you can probably guess from the context of the call, this moniker is used to create the specified component and to access the specified method.

Table 37-1: Queue Moniker Parameters and Descriptions

Parameter	Description
AppSpecific	This is very similar to the "window word" that can be passed to a newly created window. It is completely up to the component developer to determine what information needs to be passed here. The only constraint you have is that the value must be of type unsigned integer.
AuthLevel	This value is used to specify the level of authentication that MSMQ is to use in verifying the message. Authenticated messages are digitally signed and require a registered certificate. Note that although you can alter the authentication level for a COM+ application through Component Services, this parameter seems to be ignored.
ComputerName	As you saw, this parameter is used to resolve to the actual server where the target component resides. If this parameter is omitted, Windows 2000 assumes that the component exists on the client (or local) machine.
Delivery	Used to determine which mode of delivery MSMQ is to use for the message (MQMSG_DELIVERY_RECOVERABLE or MQMSG_DELIVERY_EXPRESS).
EncryptAlgorith	This parameter enables the caller to specify the type of encryption algorithm being used. Valid entries are CALG_RC2 and CALG_RC4.
FormatName	Instructs MSMQ that a GUID is being used for the queue instead of the queue name. An MSMQ queue's GUID can be located by looking at its properties dialog box from the Computer Management snap-in.
HashAlgorithm	Defines which hash algorithm is used to encrypt the message. Any of the following are valid: CALG_HMAC, CALG_MAC, CALG_MD2, CALG_MD4, CALG_MD5, CALG_SHA, CALG_SHA1, CALG_SHAMD5, CALG_SSL3, and CALG_TLS1PRF.
Journal	This parameter specifies if a journal is to be used to track a message as it flows through a system. This value defaults to MQMSG_JOURNAL_NONE, which means no journal. You can track all messages by specifying MQMSG_JOURNAL. However, one really useful value is MQMSG_DEADLETTER, which allows you to track only messages that are sent to the dead letter queue.
Label	This value is for message tracking. For example, if you created a convention for labeling all your messages, it wouldn't be difficult to write an admin application that could provide information on the types of messages being routed to the dead letter queue.
MaxTimeToReachQueue	As its name implies, this value allows you to specify (in seconds) the amount of time a message can take in reaching its destination. Aside from a numeric value, you can also use the values LONG_LIVED or INFINITE.
MaxTimeToReceive	This value is slightly different from MaxTimeToReachQueue. Although that value is only concerned with how long the message takes in reaching the queue, this value is concerned with how long it takes the message to dequeue, or read out of the queue. Once again, the valid values are a numeric value indicating the time in seconds, LONG_LIVED or INFINITE.

Parameter	Description
PathName	This parameter allows you to fully qualify a path to the server queue (specifying both computer name and queue name) in the format `<server name>/<queue name>`.
Priority	This is one of the most important values in any distributed system. It enables the application to prioritize the outgoing messages so that the server can be used as efficiently as possible. If you don't specify a value for this parameter, the Priority setting for the queue is used.
PrivLevel	Used to define the messages privacy level. The valid values are `MQMSG_PRIV_LEVEL_NONE`, `MQMSG_PRIV_LEVEL_BODY`, `MQMSG_PRIV_LEVEL_BODY_BASE`, and `MQMSG_PRIV_LEVEL_BODY_ENHANCED`.
QueueName	Explicitly tells MSMQ which queue to use. If you don't specify this parameter (which the demo doesn't), the queue associated with the server application is used. Specifying both the `ComputerName` and the `QueueName` parameters is the functional equivalent of using the `PathName` parameter.
Trace	This value determines if the message gets traced as it moves from the client to its destination (the server application). The valid values are `MQMSG_TRACE_NONE` and `MQMSG_SEND_ROUTE_TO_REPORT_QUEUE`.

If the call to `CoGetObject` fails, a helper function is called that examines the passed `HRESULT` and displays the associated error message. At this point, add that helper function to the `COrderEntryClientDlg` class.

Note that I've inserted some of the standard errors that you might get from the `winerror.h` header file. If you run the application and receive an error stating "Unknown error occurred", that probably means that an `HRESULT` value was returned for which I do not have an `if` clause in this function. In this case, place a breakpoint at the beginning of this function, run the application in debug mode, and when the debugger stops execution at the breakpoint, inspect the `hr` variable. Visual Studio .NET has the ability to inspect `HRESULT` values and will display the exact string found in the `winerror.h` file. Therefore, if this happens and you want to catch that particular `HRESULT` error value, simply add it to this function:

```
void COrderEntryClientDlg::DisplayHRESULTError(HRESULT hr)
{
  if (MK_E_CONNECTMANUALLY == hr)
  {
    AfxMessageBox("Operation requires manual intervention");
  }
  else if (COMQC_E_APPLICATION_NOT_QUEUED == hr)
  {
    AfxMessageBox("Only COM+ Applications marked "
                  "\"queued\" can be invoked using "
                  "the \"queue\" moniker");
  }
  else if (MK_E_EXCEEDEDDEADLINE == hr)
```

```
   {
     AfxMessageBox("Object creating timed out");
   }
   else if (MK_E_NEEDGENERIC == hr)
   {
     AfxMessageBox("Moniker needs to be generic");
   }
   else if (MK_E_UNAVAILABLE == hr)
   {
     AfxMessageBox("The request operation is unavailable");
   }
   else if (MK_E_SYNTAX == hr)
   {
     AfxMessageBox("The display name param is invalid");
   }
   else if (MK_E_NOOBJECT == hr)
   {
     AfxMessageBox("Object could not be found");
   }
   else if (MK_E_INTERMEDIATEINTERFACENOTSUPPORTED == hr)
   {
     AfxMessageBox("Object does not support "
                   "required interface");
   }
   else if (ERROR_NOT_AUTHENTICATED == hr)
   {
     AfxMessageBox("auth");
   }
   else
   {
     AfxMessageBox("Unknown error occurred");
   }
 }
```

Before adding the event handlers of the buttons, make sure that you don't forget to uninitialize COM and release the hold on the ICreateOrder interface. Add a message handler for the dialog box's WM_DESTROY message and modify it as follows:

```
void COrderEntryClientDlg::OnDestroy()
{
  CDialog::OnDestroy();

  if (NULL != m_pCreateOrder)
    m_pCreateOrder->Release();

  ::CoUninitialize();
}
```

Now, add the following handler for the Add Line Item button. As you can see, the function first ensures that a valid ICreateOrder interface is present (in the form of the member variable, m_pCreateOrder). If it is, the function then retrieves the dialog box's values and after converting the SKU CString value into a BSTR, calls the ICreateOrder.AddLineItem method. If the method calls succeeds, a message will be displayed indicating that the request has been queued. If the method call fails, a call to DisplayHRESULTError will result in the displaying of the cause.

```
void COrderEntryClientDlg::OnBnClickedAddLineItem()
{
 ASSERT(m_pCreateOrder);
 if (m_pCreateOrder)
 {
  if (UpdateData(TRUE))
  {
   m_strSku.TrimLeft();
   if (0 < m_strSku.GetLength())
   {
    if (0 < m_iQuantity)
    {
     BSTR bstrSku;
     bstrSku = m_strSku.AllocSysString();

     HRESULT hr = m_pCreateOrder->AddLineItem(&bstrSku,
                                            m_iQuantity);

     if (SUCCEEDED(hr))
      AfxMessageBox("Your add line item "
                    "request has been queued");
     else
      DisplayHRESULTError(hr);
    }
    else
    {
     AfxMessageBox("You must enter a quantity "
                   "greater than 0");
    }
   }
   else
   {
    AfxMessageBox("Please enter a string to send "
                  "to the queued component.");
   }
  } // UpdateData will display its own error
 }
 else
 {
  AfxMessageBox("The ICreateOrder interface was "
                "never successfully obtained.");
 }
}
```

Finally, add a handler for the Process Order button and code it as follows. This function is
even simpler because it doesn't have to retrieve, convert, or pass any parameters. It simply
verifies that the m_pCreateOrder interface pointer has a value, and then uses it to call the
ICreateOrder.ProcessOrder method.

```
void COrderEntryClientDlg::OnBnClickedProcessOrder()
{
 ASSERT(m_pCreateOrder);
 if (m_pCreateOrder)
 {
  HRESULT hr = m_pCreateOrder->ProcessOrder();
  if (SUCCEEDED(hr))
```

```
        AfxMessageBox("Your process order request "
                    "has been queued");
    else
        DisplayHRESULTError(hr);
    }
    else
    {
    AfxMessageBox("The ICreateOrder interface was "
                    "never successfully obtained.");
    }
}
```

Now it's time to finally build and test your application!

Testing the Component and Client Code

You have arrived at the moment of truth — it's time to test the application. To do so, type in some test order information and click the Add Line Item button. Do this a couple of times and then finally click the Process Order button. You should see results similar to those shown in Figure 37-9.

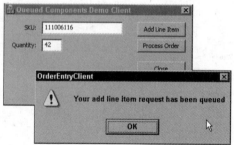

Figure 37-9: If everything works correctly, the fact that the server application isn't running won't stop the client from functioning properly.

Tip

If you receive an error trying to send the message, the problem might be that you are running in a Workgroup installation. For security to work, you must be running on a Windows domain. The way around this problem is simple.

From Component Services, right-click the COM+ application and select the Properties menu option. From there, click the Security tab and set the Authentication Level for Calls to None.

After clicking either the Add Line Item or Process Order buttons, and waiting a minute or two, you might be wondering where the message is from the server confirming that the message was received. The reason you don't see that message is that you haven't started the server application yet. I purposely didn't mention you needing this so that you can see that messages are truly being queued up for your offline server component.

At this point, switch to the Component Services tool and right-click your COM+ application. From the context menu, select the Start menu option. Depending on how impatient you were in getting your messages to display, you should now see something similar to what is shown in Figure 37-10.

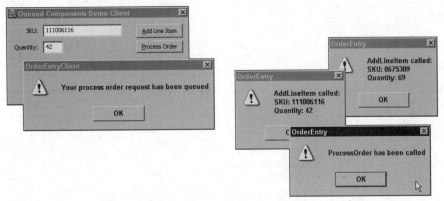

Figure 37-10: When the server application starts up, it begins to read in its queued messages and responds accordingly.

The next step in this exercise would be for you to deploy the server component to another machine on a network. After all, Queued Components aren't nearly as impressive (or useful) when the client and server both reside on the same machine. Obviously, I couldn't do that here because it would have been impossible to get a single screen shot showing both client and server if they ran on separate machines.

If you do not know how to package and install a COM+ component onto another machine, simply refer to the section in Chapter 35 entitled "Integrating COM components into the COM+ runtime." Once you've done that, you'll see that the DCOM required to make the connection between client and server is transparent to your application and it should run across the network the same as it does on a single machine.

Summary

In this, the last COM+ chapter, you began by looking at the advantages of queued components and what the Queued Components architecture has to offer with regards to greatly enhancing the capabilities of your distributed applications. From there you saw the rules for defining a COM component that are used in the Queued Components framework and how to define a component as being queued within the Component Services application. Once you had a handle on the basics, you then were presented with a demo application that while simple in scope, did effectively illustrate the basics of accepting user input and then sending that data to COM+ where it was queued until the client application started up, received the data, and displayed confirmation messages accordingly. At this point, you've completed your trek through the wondrous world of COM+, where you learned how to code stateful components, how to integrate asynchronous events into your system, and how to use queued components to more robust, scalable, secure, fault-tolerant distributed systems.

✦   ✦   ✦

ATL Server

Getting Started with ATL Server

In the previous Part, you learned about COM and ATL. In this Part, you will learn about a brand-new technology called *ATL Server*. A short definition of ATL Server is a set of extensions to ATL that enables C++ developers to more easily write Web applications that run on IIS servers. One thing to note is that although you certainly don't need to be an ATL guru to write ATL Server applications — and don't even need to know ATL at all in order to complete this first introductory chapter — you will need to be fairly proficient in ATL in order to take full advantage of the material covered in the next two chapters.

This chapter begins with a little history of server-side programming for the Web. This way, you'll come to realize why ATL Server was invented to begin with, which in my opinion generally aids in learning the technology itself. After you've read that, you'll look at the basic ATL Server architecture including *server response files* (SRF), *stencil processing*, and general runtime environment issues. Once you've gone through all this and know enough about ATL Server to at least talk about its purpose around the water cooler, you'll get your hands dirty with a simple demo application that will illustrate how easily ATL Server applications can be created using Visual Studio .NET. Finally, I'll wrap up this chapter with several code snippets that illustrate how to create an ATL Server application.

ATL Server Overview

ATL Server provides a way to produce dynamic HTML content for Web applications. By dynamic content, I mean the ability to adjust, alter, or generate HTML content on the fly depending on factors not known until runtime. For example, suppose you have an online store application and you want to display a special icon on Mondays that indicates that the customer is to receive a 10 percent discount on all merchandise on that day. Obviously, you wouldn't want to manually edit the HTML every Monday morning in order to add the icon, and then reverse that editing process at midnight. Using server-side logic (I'll discuss this bit shortly), you can write code that detects if the current day is Monday and automatically inserts the icon-related HTML tags if necessary. Therefore, the term *dynamic HTML* is defined as content that changes dynamically according to runtime circumstances.

Server-side processing history

ATL Server is just the latest in a long line of technologies meant to give the Web developer a means of writing server-side code. Like the technologies that came before it, ATL Server presents another evolutionary step in the direction of making this oft-difficult task easier. Let's take a look now at the early technologies that produce dynamic HTML for Web applications, and then I'll talk about what special advantages ATL Server provides.

Common Gateway Interface

The earliest technology that became popular for producing dynamic HTML content was the Common Gateway Interface (CGI). In its time, it was a phenomenal success because Web developers had been limited to HTML that could only display static text and images. Even today, many high-profile Web applications still rely heavily on CGI for a couple of reasons. First, some of these sites are extremely large and as such, it's easier to simply maintain the large legacy code base rather than undertake an entire rewrite. Second, many times these shops are unlikely to dump a proven technology that their entire programming staff has been working with for years for the promise of an unproven technology.

It's difficult to argue those points. After all, CGI is relatively easy and straightforward. I once spoke at great length with a very talented and experienced CGI programmer on this very issue and he intimated to me that what a lot of people don't realize is that if you can use a `printf` statement — and what C++ programmer can't? — you can write CGI code. Obviously, he was being a bit modest and certainly understating the difficulty. However, his point was that although CGI code and terminology may look foreign when you begin, it is a skill that can be learned very quickly, which is yet another reason that CGI remains a popular tool of choice among Web developers today.

However, CGI does have some major drawbacks. First, CGI applications are written in scripting languages and are, therefore, interpreted at runtime. As a result, they don't perform very well, and don't scale for the Windows operating system. This wasn't a major issue years ago when CGI was first introduced, because at that time applications were either Windows desktop applications or they were Web applications running on Unix servers. However, with Windows 2000 (and now Windows XP) gaining more and more acceptance in the marketplace as a bona fide Internet server, this once nonissue has become something of a showstopper. The fact that enterprise Web applications don't perform well on Windows platforms when written in CGI is leading many companies to search for alternate technologies.

Second, because CGI applications are written using scripting languages (such as Perl), programmers don't have the benefits of writing a system with a strongly typed, fully object-oriented language. The result is that CGI applications are typically not as robust or extendable as would be the case with systems written in languages such as C++ or Java.

Third, each call to a CGI application requires that a new process be launched. For enterprise-level servers, this can be extremely resource intensive. Add to that the fact that the process boundary means that database connections must also be established for each hit, and that can add up to far more load, when compared to the alternative technologies.

A fourth disadvantage of using CGI is that it provides no mechanism to maintain state across requests. As an example, if you're writing an on-line store or shopping cart, you will need to jump through a lot of hoops in order to maintain state across request boundaries.

Obviously, many people found these disadvantages to be too limiting and clamored for an alternative. That alternative came in the form of ISAPI.

ISAPI extensions and filters

After CGI, the next major breakthrough for Web developers was ISAPI, or Internet Service Application Programming Interface. Designed specifically for Windows servers, ISAPI offers a high-performance alternative to CGI because it's compiled native code rather than the interpreted CGI scripts.

However, once again, some drawbacks in this technology's design prevented it from becoming as widely accepted as it could have been. One such drawback (especially compared to CGI) is its steep learning curve. Specifically, ISAPI requires a fairly intermediate to advanced knowledge of multithreaded programming. Although you might be thinking "I know multithreaded programming and it's not that difficult," you know yourself that if you download just a few demo applications and articles from the Web, it doesn't take much to see that good multithreaded programmers are not that common. The simple fact is that this was a stumbling block for many developers, many of whom gave up before learning to effectively use ISAPI.

Another drawback to ISAPI is the lack of separation between static and dynamic HTML. As an example, ISAPI outputs both static HTML that never changes and dynamic HTML that does change. In larger applications this quickly becomes a maintenance headache.

Classic ASP

Classic Active Server Pages (ASP) — as opposed to ASP.NET — impacted Web development in a monumental way. It made developing dynamic HTML content easy, scalable, and robust and it did so by enabling two very different sets of programmers to write Web applications. Visual Basic developers were able to use a similar language called VBScript, and C++ and Java programmers were able to use JScript, or Java Script (now called ECMAScript).

However, once again, the biggest drawback to ASP has always been performance, because ASP script is interpreted and not compiled. Although ASP script offers an easy entry into dynamic HTML content creation without much of a learning curve, it simply doesn't offer the performance necessary to write an enterprise-level Internet or intranet application.

Introducing ATL Server

What developers needed was a technology with the learning curve of CGI, but the power and flexibility of ISAPI extensions. Enter ATL Server. As mentioned earlier, ATL Server extends ATL into the arena of Web development. It uses the ATL philosophy you learned about in Chapter 30 — write small, tight code, and only pay for what you use. For this reason, ATL Server applications are smaller than their ISAPI extension counterparts and execute with higher performance. Add to that the fact that ATL Server applications are written in C++, and you have a technology that merges the best of CGI, ISAPI, ASP, and C++.

In fact, one thing that you'll soon understand is that the ATL Server architecture is actually built using ISAPI extensions. This is what gives ATL Server its performance characteristics. However, with ATL Server, the multithreading issues that dissuade so many from using ISAPI to begin with are solved for you, and in most cases you won't have to think about them.

ATL Server helps you structure your Web applications by keeping static content in *server response files* (SRF, pronounced *surf*). The dynamic code and all programmatic logic then reside in a DLL, which is compiled to native code. This separates the static and dynamic HTML content, organizes the logic, and provides the performance of native code.

ATL Server architecture

The ATL Server architecture is pretty straightforward. Requests come in to the Web server with an .srf extension. IIS then dispatches the request to your application. This doesn't necessarily happen automatically—either you have to manually install the ATL Server DLLs, or let Visual Studio .NET deploy the application and take care of the details for you.

Your application then parses the .srf file and processes the stencil replacements. These are calls from the .srf file that are inside of double curly braces. The method calls are converted into calls that go directly into your ATL Server DLL. I cover stencil processing in more detail later in the sections "Stencil processing" and "Getting Started with ATL Server."

The application may make calls into the ATL Server services. These services offer things such as access to session state, caching, and cookies. The application then returns its response, which is then forwarded to the client. Figure 38-1 shows the ATL Server architecture.

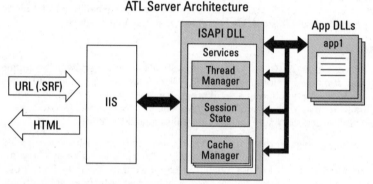

Figure 38-1: The ATL Server architecture

Environment support

Visual Studio .NET has support for ATL Server built in. As you'd expect, there's an ATL Server Wizard that helps you create your ATL Server project. There's also the traditional F5 debugging that C++ developers have come to rely on. In addition, it now offers support across servers and domain boundaries because you'll need this for enterprise applications.

An HTML editor is built in for editing .srf files. Don't get too excited, though, it's not an editor like FrontPage, but a simple implementation that offers bare-bones functionality.

One very powerful addition is that of deployment projects. If you've ever done much Web application development, you probably remember how painful it was to deploy all of the pieces. Everything had to be deployed just right in order for updates to perform correctly. And what's more, you almost always had to stop the Web server to do the update. Visual Studio .NET can create a deployment project that figures out where everything goes. Then, when it's time to deploy an update, you can let the deployment project do the dirty work— a single menu choice kicks it off.

Getting Started with ATL Server

Before you create your first ATL Server application, there are some prerequisites. You must install the Component Update, and you must have Visual Studio .NET installed.

In this section, I walk you through the creation of a simple ATL Server project and show you how it's organized. This will be the basis for all of your future ATL Server projects, so I'll take it slow.

Creating an ATL Server project

To create a quick ATL application, simply follows these steps:

1. From Visual Studio, select File ➪ New Project.

2. The New Project dialog box appears. After clicking on the Visual C++ Projects folder in the Project Types tree view, click the ATL Server Project template (shown in Figure 38-2).

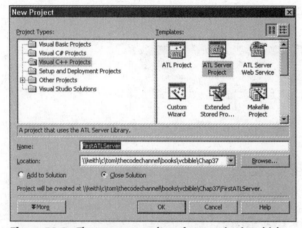

Figure 38-2: There are a number of categories in which you can set your project options.

3. Name the project FirstATLServer and click OK.

4. At this point, the ATL Server Project Wizard dialog box appears. As in the other wizards, this dialog box simply enables you to click on any of the tabs listed along the left side of the dialog box and further define your new project. You learn some of these more advanced settings in the next two chapters. For now, simply click the Finish button to create your new ATL Server project.

Building an ATL Server project

It's now time to build the project. Visual Studio makes it easy to build your ATL Server projects. The following steps outline this process:

1. Select Build ➪ Build Solution option. Notice that two projects are actually built — one called FirstATLServer and one called FirstATLServerIsapi. The FirstATLServer project represents the actual ATL Server application DLL, and it initially contains one request handler class for adding your code. This is where you'll do most of your programming. The FirstATLServerIsapi project represents the ISAPI extension DLL, and contains boilerplate code for ATL Server projects. You will seldom need to modify this project's files.

2. Once the project has been successfully built, the two DLLs and the .srf file are *deployed* — copied to the Web application's folder. This will be in your inetpub folder by default. For times when you want to have the Web application's files updated (such as when you update the .srf file), simply select the Deploy option from the Build menu.

3. Now it's time to run the ATL Server. As with any MFC project, simply select Build ➪ Start Without Debugging.

4. At this point, your default browser should start with the results shown in Figure 38-3.

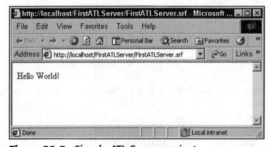

Figure 38-3: Simple ATL Server project

A quick tour of the files

None of this is very exciting — yet. However, it's important to understand the basics of ATL Server before moving onto the more advanced (and fun) stuff that lie ahead. At this point, you've created a fully working ATL Server application. However, if this is your first one, you're no doubt wondering what the deployment actually did and how a file with an .srf extension was executed in the browser. Let's look at those issues now. From Visual Studio, open FirstATLServer.h and note the following method:

```
[ tag_name(name="Hello") ]
HTTP_CODE OnHello(void)
{
  m_HttpResponse << "Hello World!";
  return HTTP_SUCCESS;
}
```

As you can see, this is pretty much straight C++ with the addition of the bits between the square brackets. These are called *attributes* and are new to Visual C++ .NET. Attributes are textual annotations to types that direct the compiler to insert code or modify the code in the generated binary file. As it turns out, attributes are integral to programming ATL Server applications. In this case, the `tag name` attribute directs the stencil processor (more on this later) to replace the `OnHello` method with the name Hello found within the `{{ }}` stencil marks in the `.srf` file. (This might seem strange at first, but bear with me, and it should all fall into place.) Lastly, the `HTTP_CODE` is simply a `DWORD` type that is defined in the `atlserr.h` header file

Now open the `FirstATLServer.srf` file and click the HTML tab (at the bottom of the editor window). You'll see the following:

```
<html>
{{// use MSDN's "ATL Server Response File Reference"
     to learn about SRF files.}}
{{handler FirstATLServer.dll/Default}}
  <head>
  </head>
  <body>
    This is a test: {{Hello}}
    <br>
  </body>
</html>
```

The two things that I want to draw your attention to are the handler DLL specification, and the `{{Hello}}` instance that calls the `OnHello` method. This is how incredibly easy it can be to generate content sent back to the client's browser. Obviously, in the real world not too many companies survive for long shipping copies of products that print out Hello World on the browser. However, as you'll soon see, the programming required to do the actual dynamic content creation is never much more difficult than this.

Stencil processing

As I mentioned earlier, `.srf` replacement tags are specified inside of paired curly braces like this:

```
{{ methods here }}
```

`.srf` files can have multiple request handlers — you can create more than one ATL Server DLL and use them from the same `.srf` file.

Replacement tags can have arguments. I cover this in more detail in the section "ATL Server Parameters."

SRF files offer simple control statements such as `if/else` and `while`. It's limited so that you will push your logic code into the native C++ DLLs.

ATL Server Parameters

One last introductory piece that I'll cover before I end this chapter is ATL Server parameters. There will certainly be times when you will want to pass parameters from a .srf file to an ATL Server handler. ATL Server makes functions in a DLL available to SRF files that IIS serves up. This is well and good for simple applications where a function simply generates something that is piped out to the HTTP data stream, but more complex functions require the passing of arguments. Suppose a user enters a pair of numbers on which your application must perform a calculation. If your choice is to build this part of the application with ATL Server, you need a way to pass the parameters into a calculation function. Yes, you could use session variables or cookies that are accessible from ATL Server applications, but this is poor design and consumes resources unnecessarily.

Single argument functions

For functions that take a single argument, it couldn't be easier. All you need to do is declare the argument in the function as a parameter. Suppose you have two functions — one that takes an invoice number (an integer type) and another that takes the customer name (a string type). Your code might look like the following:

```
HTTP_CODE ProcessInvoice(void)
{
  // Code here
  return HTTP_SUCCESS;
}


HTTP_CODE ProcessCustomer(void)
{
  // Code here
  return HTTP_SUCCESS;
}
```

You would simply modify these functions manually as you would any function in C++ to take the parameters that you need:

```
HTTP_CODE ProcessInvoice(int* pInvoiceNbr)
{
  // Code here, do something with *pInvoiceNbr
  return HTTP_SUCCESS;
}


HTTP_CODE ProcessCustomer(TCHAR* pszCustomer)
{
  // Code here, do something with pszCustomer
  return HTTP_SUCCESS;
}
```

For example, open the FirstATLServer.h file now and add the following two functions.

```
[ tag_name(name="ProcessInvoice") ]
HTTP_CODE OnProcessInvoice(int* pInvoiceNbr)
{
 m_HttpResponse << "Invoice number = " << *pInvoiceNbr;
 return HTTP_SUCCESS;
}
```

```
[ tag_name(name="ProcessCustomer") ]
HTTP_CODE OnProcessCustomer(TCHAR* pszCustomer)
{
 m_HttpResponse << "Customer = '" << pszCustomer << "'";
 return HTTP_SUCCESS;
}
```

Now, you need only supply the .srf tags that will result in these two functions being called. Note that you do not need to supply the quotes around the string value being passed to the ProcessCustomer function.

```
{{handler ATLServerParameter.DLL/Default}}
Calling ProcessCustomer: {{ProcessCustomer(Acme)}}
Calling ProcessInvoice : {{ProcessInvoice(6)}}
```

Now when you run the application, you will see results similar to those shown in Figure 38-4.

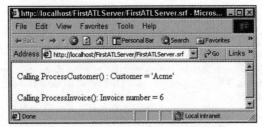

Figure 38-4: Passing single parameters to ATL Server functions is very simple and straightforward.

Multiple parameter functions

As easy as passing a single parameter to a function is, you'd think that passing multiple parameters would be as easy as delimiting each parameter with a comma. Unfortunately, it's not nearly so easy. In order to accommodate this requirement, you need to implement your own parsing function.

Similar to parsing command-line arguments in a C application, the parsing function receives a single string that contains the entire parameter list. One other thing to keep in mind is that any quotation marks that are typed in on the command line as the program is run will appear in the argument string as any other character. This may add additional parsing complexity in your applications at times.

Suppose you want to create a function that receives multiple integers from the .srf file. You must declare it as follows:

```
HTTP_CODE MyFoo(int *pnValueList)
{
    return HTTP_CODE;
}
```

You must also set an attribute that describes what parsing function you want to use as follows:

```
[ tag_name(name="Multiply" parse_func="parseMultipleInts") ]
```

```
HTTP_CODE OnMultiply( int *pnValueList )
{
    // Do something here
    return HTTP_CODE;
}
```

Parsing functions

Parsing functions receive three arguments and should be declared as follows:

```
HTTP_CODE parseMultipleInts( IAtlMemMgr *pMemMgr,
    LPCSTR szParams, int **ppDest );
```

Note that `**ppDest` is an integer and represents multiple integers. For multiple `short` or `DWORD` types, all you would need to do is change from an `int` to a `short` or `DWORD` such as the following examples:

```
HTTP_CODE parseMultipleInts( IAtlMemMgr *pMemMgr,
    LPCSTR szParams, short**ppDest );
HTTP_CODE parseMultipleInts( IAtlMemMgr *pMemMgr,
    LPCSTR szParams, DWORD**ppDest );
```

The `IAtlMemMgr` interface provides memory allocation functionality. You must allocate enough memory for the parsed arguments. Note that this memory will automatically be released for you. `szParams` is the argument string. As I mentioned in the previous section, `**ppDest` contains the parsed arguments. The next section explains what to do if the argument list you're expecting doesn't contain arguments that are all the same type.

The following function parses a list of integers. Although my example only takes two integers, I actually allocate enough space for 20 integers. You'll want to make an adjustment in this, depending on your use.

```
HTTP_CODE parseMultipleInts( IAtlMemMgr *pMemMgr,
    LPCSTR szParams, int **ppDest )
{
    // Use pMemMgr to allocate memory for ppDest, then parse
    // your parameter from szParams, and store them in
    // ppDest.

    size_t iAllocSize = 0;
    int nCount = 0;

    // Allocate the size of the single parameter
    // times 20 (you can't exceed 20 ints).
    iAllocSize = sizeof( int ) * 20;

    // Allocate memory in the memory manager, so that it may
    // be automatically freed later.
    *ppDest = (int *)pMemMgr->Allocate( iAllocSize );

    // Parse the input string.
    int iCommaPos; CString strRest, strData;
    strRest = szParams;

    // Look for parameters.
    while( ( iCommaPos = strRest.Find( "," ) ) > 0 )
    {
```

```
        strData = strRest.Left( iCommaPos );
        strRest = strRest.Right( strRest.GetLength() -
            iCommaPos - 1);
        ppDest[0][nCount++] = atoi( strData );
    }

    // If there's anything left, that's the last argument.
    if( strRest.GetLength() > 0 )
    {
        ppDest[0][nCount++] = atoi( strRest );
    }

    return HTTP_SUCCESS;

}
```

The .srf file that I used to call the Multiply function is as follows:

```
{{handler ATLServerParameter.DLL/Default}}
This is a multiplication test: {{Multiply(7,8)}}
```

Parsing parameters of unlike types

In order to parse parameters of unlike types, you're best off creating a data structure that can contain all of the parameters that you are expecting. For instance, if the first and fourth arguments are integers, and the second and third arguments are strings, the following data structure could be used:

```
typedef struct
{
    int nFirst;
    TCHAR szFirstString[60];
    TCHAR szSecondString[60];
    int nSecond;
} MYDATA;
```

The function would look as follows:

```
HTTP_CODE DoStuff( MYDATA *pMyData )
{
    // Use *pMyData->nFirst
    // Use *pMyData->szFirstString
    // Use *pMyData->szSecondString
    // Use *pMyData->nSecond
    return HTTP_SUCCESS;
}
```

The parsing function could then look as follows:

```
HTTP_CODE parseMultipleHelloParam(IAtlMemMgr *pMemMgr,
  LPCSTR szParams, stMultipleParam **ppDest)
{
    // TODO: Add your parameter parsing code here.
    // Use pMemMgr to allocate memory for ppDest, then parse
    // your parameter from szParams, and store them in
    // ppDest.
```

```
size_t iAllocSize = 0;

// Get the length of the single parameter. Reserve space
// for the trailing \0
iAllocSize = sizeof( MYDATA );

// Allocate memory in the memory manager, so that it may
// be automatically freed later.
*ppDest =
 (stMultipleParam*)pMemMgr->Allocate(iAllocSize);

// parse the input string, then
int iCommaPos = -1;
CString szRest, szData; szRest = szParams;

// look for the first parameter, nFirst
iCommaPos = szRest.Find(",");
if( iCommaPos > 0 )
{
    szData = szRest.Left( iCommaPos );
    szRest = szRest.Right( szRest.GetLength() -
        iCommaPos - 1);
    (*ppDest)->nFirst = atoi(szData);
}

// look for the second parameter, szFirstString
iCommaPos = szRest.Find(",");
if( iCommaPos > 0 )
{
    szData = szRest.Left( iCommaPos );
    szRest = szRest.Right( szRest.GetLength() -
        iCommaPos - 1);
    strcpy((*ppDest)->szFirstString szData);
}

// look for the third parameter, szSecondString
iCommaPos = szRest.Find(",");
if( iCommaPos > 0 )
{
    szData = szRest.Left( iCommaPos );
    szRest = szRest.Right( szRest.GetLength() -
        iCommaPos - 1);
    strcpy((*ppDest)->szSecondString, szData);
}

// look for the fourth (last) parameter, nSecond
 szData = szRest;
(*ppDest)->nSecond = atoi(szData);

return HTTP_SUCCESS;


}
```

Summary

ATL Server has a lot to offer. It has high performance, and doesn't have the multithreading headaches that writing ISAPI DLLs entails. It also enables C++ developers to leverage their existing skill sets, which paves the way for the creation of many new .NET Web applications. In this chapter, you not only learned the basic architecture of ATL Server, but you also created your first server application and learned the ins and outs of passing parameters to ATL Server functions. In the next chapter, you'll take this several steps further and learn how to create Web services using ATL Server. This is a very advanced topic, but as you'll soon see, learning how to do this is worth the effort in the benefits it provides.

✦   ✦   ✦

Creating Web Services with ATL Server

As you learned in Chapter 38, ATL Server gives you a quick way to develop high-performance Web applications using ATL and C++. In this chapter, you will see that it's also a great way to develop what are called *Web Services*. First, I'll go over what a Web Service is and the role it plays in today's Internet-driven marketplace. Then I'll go through the Simple Object Application Protocol (SOAP) because Web Services are built on this standardized protocol. Once I've done that, I'll drive home how to create Web Services by working through a series of demo applications, each one designed to illustrate something new regarding the development of writing Web Services with ATL Server.

Understanding Web Services

Before jumping into working with Web Services, I want to clarify exactly what they are and specifically resolve some ambiguity with other technologies with similar-sounding names.

I was lucky (brave?) enough to begin working with .NET several months before it was introduced at the July 2000 Microsoft PDC (Professional Developer's Conference) in Orlando, Florida. Before that time, if someone had asked me about services, I would have naturally thought of the daemon-like applications that run on Windows NT and Windows 2000.

Except for the fact that Web Services are also binary executables, there's almost no similarity between the traditional Windows NT/2000 services and Web Services. The former is an application that typically runs upon system startup and usually controls server-like functionality such as communications and database I/O. Web Services, on the other hand, exist for one specific purpose — they *provide remote functionality*.

Just so you don't get confused with yet another similar-sounding technology, I am not referring to the process known as *remoting*. Remoting is where a piece of code on one machine makes a call to a method that exists on another machine via something called a *proxy stub*. Therefore, the term *remoting* is a generic term and not specific to a particular task or goal.

Web Services, on the other hand, are *programmable bits of functionality accessible from potentially disparate systems*. As an example, suppose you have programmed a system that can validate credit card numbers and verify credit card purchases. If you provided a Web Service interface to your system, you could then sell this service to companies with software needing to access this type of functionality. With the fact that communication with a Web Service is done using the Web standards of XML and HTTP, your services would be available to more potential customers. With just a bit of thought, I'm sure you can start thinking of all kinds of services that you could begin selling using the Web Service architecture, which of course is the entire lure of Web Services. It promises to open up an entirely new industry where instead of simply thinking in terms of individual components, you also begin thinking of how to group these components in such a way as to provide services that can then be sold.

Now, this overall concept is hardly a new one. However, the Web Service architecture does provide some benefits over earlier technologies:

✦ They are easier to write.

✦ They are platform-independent.

✦ They work through firewalls.

Web Services are easier to write

Web Services are easy to develop because the .NET platform supports it natively — the plumbing is wired into the framework. To that extent, the Visual Studio ATL Server Wizard allows you to create a Web Service that provides a no-frills, but functioning, Web Service with a few mouse clicks.

On the surface, there appears to be almost no difference between an ATL Server project that's not a Web Service (such as those created in Chapter 38) and an ATL Server project that is a Web Service because the bulk of the implementation details are taken care of behind the scenes. However, there are a few differences that you should be aware of:

✦ Web Services have a SOAP handler attribute in the wizard-generated source code that causes Visual Studio to generate the code that handles all the details of making SOAP work.

✦ Web Service methods contain a method-level attribute (soap_method) that marks the method as one that can be called from an external source. Non-Web Service methods contain a method-level attribute (tag_name) if they are callable from the .SRF file.

The following two methods were copied from a default Web Service and a default non-Web Service methods, respectively:

```
// Default Web Service Method
[soap_method]
HRESULT HelloWorld(/*[in]*/ BSTR bstrInput,
                   /*[out, retval]*/
                   BSTR *bstrOutput)
{
  CComBSTR bstrOut(L"Hello ");
  bstrOut += bstrInput;
  bstrOut += L"!";
  *bstrOutput = bstrOut.Detach();

  return S_OK;
}
```

```
// Default Method From a non-Web Service
// ATL Server Project
[tag_name(name="Hello")]
HTTP_CODE OnHello(void)
{
 m_HttpResponse << "Hello World!";
 return HTTP_SUCCESS;
}
```

✦ A Web Service ATL Server project generates an `.htm` file that displays the Web Service methods, whereas a non-Web Service ATL Server project generates a `.SRF` file that makes calls into the project's DLL.

✦ A Web Service ATL Server project generates and maintains a `.DISCO` file. This is used as part of the discovery process when a caller queries as to the methods that a Web Service has exposed.

Web Services are platform-independent

One of the advantages of Web Services is platform independence. If you have already done credit card verification through services such as CyberCash or `Authorize.net`, you know that for these services to function properly, you need specialized components or mechanisms. In my own e-commerce development, I almost always used a COM component to do the credit card transactions.

The COM components I used normally did a lot of work to carry out their duties. First, they had to open sockets and make connections to the destination server where the verification and transaction took place. Then the data had to be transmitted. Of course, the data always had to be encrypted to prevent the exposure of sensitive customer information, especially the customer name, credit card number, and expiration date.

Obviously, this is not a very scalable solution if you have to interoperate several disparate platforms. Suppose the transactions could come in from Windows NT, Windows 2000, Unix, Solaris, and AS400 machines. How would a provider support the interaction with each one of these? The answer is that they probably wouldn't. There would probably be different mechanisms and entry points for the various systems.

Web Services are different. That is because their communication is based on open standards that are accepted industry-wide. The first standard upon which Web Services are based is HTTP. This workhorse of the Internet is available to virtually all operating systems and hardware platforms. On top of HTTP is SOAP, which is the envelope that contains the data, or *payload*.

Because Web Services are built around these two open standards, any operating system or hardware platform can implement them—and most do. This makes Web services platform-independent in the truest sense because all it takes is an implementation of two open standards.

Web Services work through firewalls

If you've ever done any COM programming and wanted to use those components over the Internet, you may be familiar with how difficult it is to get the components working. COM objects communicate using certain nonstandard ports (conceptual communications end points); as a result, COM objects require that devices like firewalls, which typically reside at the point where private networks connect to the Internet, need to be configured to allow the COM objects to communicate using their nonstandard ports. If you've been down this road, you know about the all but impossible task of getting a network administrator to open a port strictly for one application's usage. In today's virus-of-the-week world, who can blame them? You simply have to have firewalls (typically both software and hardware-based) to protect a private network that's connected to the Internet. It's a sad commentary on the way some people are, but it's a fact of life that we have to deal with. Having said that, it is the network administrator's job to protect the network and its resources and this usually means blocking certain ports from both incoming and outgoing traffic.

However, this is not a problem for Web Services, because they use HTTP as their transport protocol, and communicate via port 80, a well-known port that every significant Web server uses to receive and satisfy requests for data. As a result, firewalls don't block this port, which means that Web Services will almost certainly work through your firewall. You can't say that about those COM components or any other technology not based on HTTP.

Understanding SOAP

Although teaching the entire subject of SOAP is well outside the scope of a single chapter, it does help within the context of learning ATL Server to have at least a basic understanding of SOAP data packaging formats. Therefore, let's now get an overview of what SOAP is about and what it accomplishes, and take a look at deciphering what a SOAP data packet looks like.

For many years, application development involved a monolithic setting where a single computer was the only machine that a developer had to worry about. Most applications ran on a single computer. Even when a network came into play, the server was used only to share files — the application still tended to perform as a stand-alone application on each workstation.

However, networking standards evolved, and slowly file servers became application servers in a client/server architecture. This eventually evolved into n-tier processing where the different components of a single system were dispersed across multiple physical machines to improve scalability and performance. Through each of these phases of the software development evolution, the techniques and tools used to program applications changed, and programmers had to adapt. Now, the Internet has provided just the latest stage in that evolution. Not only are applications distributed, but also they can be distributed from one end of the earth to the other, housed on completely incompatible hardware and operating systems. It is not uncommon now for a client to request a system where the user interface components reside on machines in Hong Kong while the database being accessed is housed in multiple servers in Europe and the United States.

However, it's not just the physical distance separating these components that's the only problem. Various parts of the system might be composed of COM components, whereas other components are Enterprise Java Beans (EJB). There might even be different communications technologies in use, such as Object Request Brokers (ORBs) and different HTML schemes. What's a developer to do?

The plot really thickens when the computer platforms for each component of the distributed application can be incompatible. A Unix server could, for instance, contain the database, whereas a Windows server could contain the business logic. However, it's the marketplace that drives technology, not the other way around, and more and more companies are starting to see the benefits of such distributed, or enterprise applications.

Unfortunately, the obvious difficulties (putting it mildly) in designing and building such a system can either make your career (if you manage to succeed) or have you fantasizing about a career on the open highway driving your own semi 16 hours a day.

Thankfully, there is a framework that helps to tackle the myriad problems of enterprise application development head on. It is called SOAP (Simple Object Application Protocol) and it provides a standardized mechanism for disparate platforms to communicate with one another in a way. It is also a major part of the Web Service framework.

What Is SOAP?

So what is SOAP and just what does it accomplish that other transfer protocols don't? There are five key points to understanding SOAP:

- ✦ SOAP is a way to send messages across the wire.

- ✦ SOAP is simple to understand.

- ✦ SOAP is based on XML.

- ✦ SOAP works with any operating system.

- ✦ SOAP is based on standards.

SOAP is a way to send messages across the wire. One computer can use SOAP to send a block of data, for instance a billing record, to another computer. When using SOAP, both computers understand the protocol, and can send and receive the data using it.

The acronym SOAP starts with *simple*, and that's one of the key things it delivers. If you've ever worked with DCOM to communicate to remote servers, you know that DCOM is anything but simple — as a matter of fact it's pretty ugly.

SOAP is based on XML. The data that is carried in a SOAP package is always represented by XML. If you plan to do much with SOAP, you may want to take a look at the XML specification or do some reading and understand the basics of XML.

SOAP works with any operating system because it doesn't rely in any way on operating systems. It's a protocol on its own merit that dictates no hardware, operating system, or language specifications.

In terms of how SOAP compares to other transfer protocols, SOAP is built on standards, and therefore can easily be implemented by anyone. First, it relies on HTTP to send data across the wire. Second, it relies on XML to represent the data. And third, it relies on the SOAP specification so that every implementer will be in compliance and capable of communicating with all other implementers. Because SOAP has been accepted as Web standard by the W3C (World Wide Web consortium), you can get the various SOAP specifications from their site at http://www.w3.org/2002/ws/.

SOAP packages

SOAP data is sent in a well-organized manner as it goes across the Internet. This section shows you the hierarchy of SOAP packages.

Because all SOAP packages are sent within an HTTP message, the first part of a SOAP message is the HTTP header. Information in the section usually contains the domain name, the key word POST, the Content-Type specification, and other optional information.

After the HTTP header comes the SOAP envelope. This section contains the entire SOAP message. It's kind of like what's inside of the box that arrives at your doorstep. It's all of the important stuff you need (the actual data). The address label on the front of the box (the HTTP header) can almost always be discarded.

The SOAP envelope starts off with a SOAP header. This is different than the HTTP header. It doesn't contain information about the routing of the data (such as the domain name and the size of the content), but contains information related to the data, such as a transaction ID.

The SOAP body is also in the SOAP envelope after the SOAP header and contains the data. Let's briefly look at what has become the canonical example for illustrating SOAP data by examining a sample request and response packet used to transfer stock price information for a given stock symbol. I'll first show you the data so that you can see it uninterrupted and then afterward walk you through each element of that data to give you a better understanding of how the data for a SOAP packet is formatted. Let's start by looking at the SOAP *request packet* where the stock price for the stock symbol DIS is being queried.

```
POST /StockQuote HTTP/1.1
Host: www.stockquoteserver.com
Content-Type: text/xml; charset="utf-8"
Content-Length: 323
SOAPAction: Some-Namespace-URI#GetLastTradePrice
<SQ:Envelope
    xmlns:SQ="http://schemas.xmlsoap.org/soap/envelope/"
    SQ:encodingStyle="http://schemas.xmlsoap.org/soap/encoding/">
  <SQ:Body>
    <m:GetLastTradePrice xmlns:m="Some-Namespace-URI">
      <symbol>DIS</symbol>
    </m:GetLastTradePrice>
  </SQ:Body>
</SQ:Envelope>
```

The first element to look at is the SOAP header. You can easily spot this in a SOAP packet because it will extend from the POST command to the beginning of the data (defined by the Envelope element). As mentioned earlier, SOAP uses HTTP to send data. Therefore, you can see the first command here is the standard HTTP POST command where the SOAP request is being sent to the StockQuote server. The next line then shows the server URI (universal resource identifier) where the server resides. After that, the Content-xxx lines simply define the format and length of the data being sent. Finally, the HTTP SOAPAction header field (used only in request packets) can be used to indicate the intent of the SOAP request, and helps the SOAP server recognize what server to call. This value must be included when issuing a SOAP request.

```
POST /StockQuote HTTP/1.1
Host: www.stockquoteserver.com
Content-Type: text/xml; charset="utf-8"
Content-Length: 323
SOAPAction: Some-Namespace-URI#GetLastTradePrice
```

Now let's look at the SOAP data. SOAP messages always begin with a SOAP Envelope tag. From there, the xmlns attribute identifies the namespace, and the encodingStyle attribute identifies the serialization rules used in a SOAP message. This attribute may appear on any element, and is scoped to that element's contents, as well as any child elements that do not contain such an attribute themselves. Therefore, in this example, the specified encoding style is pertinent for the entire envelope. Note that this scope behavior is defined by XML standards. Also be aware that no default encoding is defined for a SOAP message. The following values for the xmlns and encodingStyle attributes are typically used with most SOAP data unless special formatting is required.

```
<SQ:Envelope
    xmlns:SQ="http://schemas.xmlsoap.org/soap/envelope/"
    SQ:encodingStyle="http://schemas.xmlsoap.org/soap/encoding/">
```

At this point, you finally arrive at the data — the Body element. This element simply signifies the operation being performed and any data to pass to that operation. In this example, the GetLastTradePrice function is being called, with a value of DIS being passed in as the expected symbol parameter:

```
<SQ:Body>
  <m:GetLastTradePrice xmlns:m="Some-Namespace-URI">
    <symbol>DIS</symbol>
  </m:GetLastTradePrice>
</SQ:Body>
```

Now take a look at what a SOAP response packet to the request could look like.

```
HTTP/1.1 200 OK
Content-Type: text/xml; charset="utf-8"
Content-Length: nnnn
<SP:Envelope
xmlns:SP="http://schemas.xmlsoap.org/soap/envelope/"
    SP:encodingStyle="http://schemas.xmlsoap.org/soap/encoding/">
  <SP:Body>
    <m:GetLastTradePriceResponse
    xmlns:m="Some-Namespace-URI">
      <Price>34.5</Price>
    </m:GetLastTradePriceResponse>
  </SP:Body>
</SP:Envelope>
```

Because this response packet shares many characteristics with request packet I'll only illuminate where the packets differ. The first thing you'll notice is that the HTTP header contains information indicating the success. Here you can see that a value of 200 is being returned to the caller. This is because SOAP follows the semantics of the HTTP status codes for communicating status information in HTTP. As a result, a 2xx status code indicates that the client's request, including the SOAP component, was successfully received, understood, and processed. If there is an error in processing, the SOAP server must issue an HTTP 500 error (Internal Server Error) and include information about the cause of the error (called a SOAP *fault*). From there, the remainder of the header specifies the content formatting and length information that you saw in the request packet. Finally, after the standard Envelope element definition, you can see that the Body element contains the return value for the originally requested stock symbol.

Although you should know that the ATL Server and the .NET framework do alleviate your need to have a complete understanding of SOAP, it's also important to at least have a basic grasp of the fundamentals of this all-important protocol because Web Services are built on

SOAP. If you're interested, or in need of further information on SOAP, the following Web resources should prove helpful:

✦ http://www.w3.org/tr/soap—Contains detailed information on the SOAP specification

✦ http://www.w3schools.com/SOAP/default.asp—A beginner-level tutorial on understanding and using the SOAP protocol

Now that you've had an overview of the SOAP protocol, let's get to work and create your first ATL Server Web Service.

Getting Started with ATL Server Web Services

In this section you'll get into the meat of ATL Server Web Services. First you'll create a Web Service, then you'll access it from an MFC-based Visual C++ program, and finally you'll see how Web Services created in Visual C++ can be used from ASP.NET.

Creating an ATL Server Web Service

At this point, create a new ATL Server Web Service project called MyFirstATLServerWebService. Once the ATL Server Project Wizard displays, click the Project Settings link (Figure 39-1).

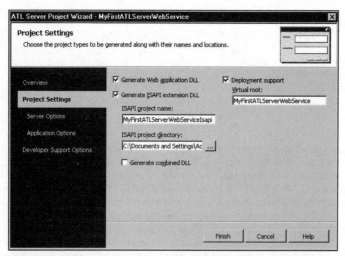

Figure 39-1: The ATL Server Project Wizard Project Settings page

Although there are several options that you'll learn about later in this chapter, the most important options I'd like to point out right now are the ones that determine the destination directories for both the project files and the deployment files. Obviously, the project files should go in a place that's easy for you to find and manage. Besides the location of the project files, you can specify the name of the virtual root to which the compiled project will be deployed. The virtual root will normally be created in your localhost folder unless you changed the settings of the deployment project so that the compiled files are deployed to another location (such as a live or development Web server).

The last thing you must do is click Finish. When you do this, all of the project files will be created. There are a number of files created, and Table 39-1 shows some of the files that will probably be new to you.

Table 39-1: Default Files for the MyFirstATLServerWebService Project

Project Folder	File Name	Description
Source Files	MyFirstATLServerWebService.cpp	This file defines the entry point for the DLL application and includes necessary boilerplate methods such as DllMain().
Header Files	MyFirstATLServerWebService.h	This file defines the ATL Server request handler class.
<Main Project Directory>	MyFirstATLServerWebService.disco	This is the file used to allow external applications to discover information about the Web Service.
	MyFirstATLServerWebService.htm	This file displays a nicely formatted description of the Web Service's operations.

The following is the boilerplate request handler code that the wizard generates (reformatted a bit to display properly on the printed page).

The first thing you should notice from this code is that the wizard creates a namespace called MyFirstATLServerWebServiceService. The System namespace is the root namespace for fundamental types in the .NET Framework. This namespace includes classes that represent the base data types used by all applications: Object (the root of the inheritance hierarchy), Byte, Char, Array, Int32, String, and so on. Many of these types correspond to the primitive data types that most programming languages define. When you write code using .NET Framework types, you can use your language's corresponding keyword when a .NET Framework base data type is expected.

```
// MyFirstATLServerWebService.h : Defines the ATL
// Server request handler class
//
#pragma once

namespace MyFirstATLServerWebServiceService
{
  // All struct, enum, and typedefs for your Web Service
  // should go inside the namespace.

  // IMyFirstATLServerWebServiceService - Web Service
  // interface declaration
```

```
//
[
 uuid("A6639212-7A3D-42CC-B434-33D537879666"),
 object
]
```

The next thing to notice is that the wizard creates an interface named `IMyFirstATLServer` `Web zServiceService`. The interface that is created is complete with `uuid` and IDL code. Even though the .NET framework takes much of this and hides it behind the scenes, ATL Server is much closer to the metal and keeps much of the implementation that's hidden in most .NET languages in plain sight.

```
__interface IMyFirstATLServerWebServiceService
{
 // HelloWorld is a sample ATL Server Web Service
 // method.  It shows how to declare a Web Service method
 // and its in-parameters and out-parameters.
 [id(1)] HRESULT HelloWorld([in] BSTR bstrInput,
                            [out, retval] BSTR *bstrOutput);
 // TODO: Add additional Web Service methods here.
};
```

The Web Service implementation comes next. It starts off with the `request_handler` and `soap_handler` attributes. These attributes specify the name and namespace of the request handler and determine that the underlying protocol is SOAP. This actually hides a great deal of the SOAP implementation. Instead of 50 or 60 lines of SOAP code, these attributes are used. The interesting thing, though, is that when you debug into this code, you can step into this SOAP code if you want (always a great way to learn the intricacies of just what's really going on).

```
// MyFirstATLServerWebServiceService - Web
// Service implementation
//
[
 request_handler(
  name="Default",
  sdl="GenMyFirstATLServerWebServiceWSDL"),
  soap_handler(
   name="MyFirstATLServerWebServiceService",
   namespace="urn:MyFirstATLServerWebServiceService",
   protocol="soap")
]
```

The `CMyFirstATLServerWebServiceService` class with its `HelloWorld` method makes up the last chunk of code in this file. The `HelloWorld` method simply takes a single string argument (actually a `BSTR` and not a native C/C++ string type), and returns a string (another `BSTR`). Your methods can take any number of arguments of any type. This includes binary types such as integers and doubles. The binary data types are converted to XML that will be transported inside of the SOAP envelope. This conversion is done behind the scenes without any effort on the part of the developer. As discussed earlier, converting the binary data to XML, and then having it contained in a SOAP envelope, makes the data platform-independent and also capable of going through firewalls.

```
class CMyFirstATLServerWebServiceService :
 public IMyFirstATLServerWebServiceService
{
public:
 // This is a sample Web Service method that shows
 // how to use the soap_method attribute to expose
 // a method as a Web method.
 [ soap_method ]
 HRESULT HelloWorld(/*[in]*/ BSTR bstrInput,
                    /*[out, retval]*/ BSTR *bstrOutput)
 {
  CComBSTR bstrOut(L"Hello ");
  bstrOut += bstrInput;
  bstrOut += L"!";
  *bstrOutput = bstrOut.Detach();

  return S_OK;
 }
 // TODO: Add additional Web Service methods here.
}; // class CMyFirstATLServerWebServiceService

} // namespace MyFirstATLServerWebServiceService
```

At this point, build the Web Service solution. Because the solution contains two projects (MyFirstATLServerWebService and MyFirstATLServerWebServiceIsapi) both projects will be compiled and a DLL generated for each.

Consuming a Web Service from an MFC application

Creating a Web Service is half of the equation; consuming it is the other. In this section you'll create a Visual C++ application that upon request connects to and communicates with the MyFirstATLServerWebServiceService Web Service, displaying the returned data to the user. To get started, create a new Visual C++ MFC dialog-based application named ConsumeMyFirstATLService with all of the wizard's default settings.

With the project created, update the dialog template to contain an edit control that will allow the user to enter data to send to the Web Service. Figure 39-2 shows the dialog box. (Obviously, you don't need to add the long-winded static control or About button because they don't impact your testing of the Web Service.)

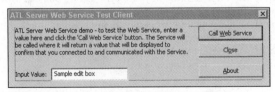

Figure 39-2: Client dialog template resource

Now, add a DDX `CString` variable to the dialog box for the edit control and name it `m_strInput`.

Now that the client side UI is set, the next step is to add a class that wraps the Web Service access. In order to do that, select the Add Web Service option from the Project menu. Figure 39-3 shows the dialog box that will then be displayed.

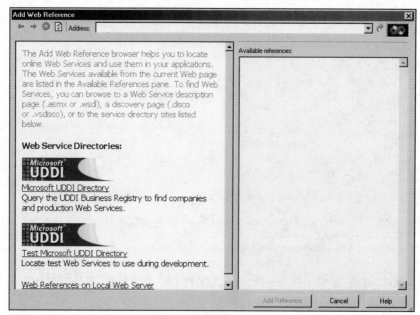

Figure 39-3: Adding a discovered Web reference

Assuming that you named your Web Service `MyFirstATLServerWebService` and deployed it to the default folder, you'll enter the following URL in the Address field:

```
http://localhost/MyFirstATLServerWebService/
    MyFirstATLServerWebService.disco
```

Now, either press Enter or click the Go button. At this point, the information about the Web Service you created earlier will be downloaded and displayed on the dialog box. An XML version of the Web Service Description Language (WSDL) contract will be shown, similar to what you can see in Figure 39-4. As you can see, it was determined from my settings that my host name is JEANVALJEAN, which is the computer name for my local machine. This is the machine that is running the Microsoft Internet Information Server (IIS) Web server.

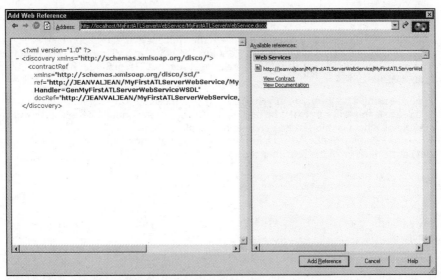

Figure 39-4: Resolved information from attaching to and querying a Web Service

The Web Services infrastructure is founded on communication via XML-based messages that comply with a published Web Service description. The service description is an XML document written in an XML grammar (WSDL) that defines the format of messages the Web Service understands. The service description serves as an agreement that defines the behavior of a Web Service and instructs potential clients in how to interact with it. The behavior of a Web Service is determined by messaging patterns that the service defines and supports. These patterns conceptually dictate what the service consumer can expect to happen when a properly formatted message is submitted to the Web Service.

For example, the request/response pattern associated with a remote procedure call (RPC)-style service would define which SOAP message schema to use for invoking a particular method. This pattern would also define the format that the ensuing response SOAP message will follow.

Another example of a messaging pattern is unidirectional interactions. This pattern is employed when a one-way communication is to take place. In this situation, the sender does not receive any messages from the Web Service, including fault messages.

The schemas that define the SOAP message formats can be defined internally to the actual Web Service description, or they can be defined externally and imported into the Web Service description.

In addition to message format definitions and messaging patterns, the service description also contains the address that is associated with each Web Service entry point. The format of this address will be appropriate to the protocol used to access the service, such as a URL for HTTP or an e-mail address for SMTP.

After clicking the Add Reference button, the reference will be added to the project. The first of these files, MyFirstATLServerService.h, contains the namespace and class that the main Visual C++ application can use to access the Web Service. The second file, MyFirstATLServerWebService.wsdl, contains the WSDL in XML format. (In fact, if you attempt to save this file with another name, you'll see that Visual Studio recognizes the type as an XML file type.)

If you are using a beta version of Visual C++ .NET, you can perform the following step. In the final release, this will surely not be needed. However, I'm including it here in case you are working on a beta version when you read this book. Open the MyFirstATLServerWebService.h file and place the following typedef (if not already present) at the bottom of the file (after the namespace closing brace).

```
typedef MyFirstATLServerWebServiceService::CMyFirstATLServerWebServiceServiceT<> \
CMyFirstATLServerWebServiceService;
```

Now open the ConsumeMyFirstATLServiceDlg.cpp file and add the following include directive:

```
#include "MyFirstATLServerWebService.h"
```

Finally, add a handler for the dialog box's OK button and code it as follows. The first thing you do is to call UpdateData to get the value typed in by the user to send to the Web Service. You then instantiate a CMyFirstATLServerWebServiceService object. After that, you allocate two BSTR values (one to hold the user's input value, and one to hold the value returned from the Web Service). After converting the user-supplied value from a CString to a BSTR (using the CString::AllocSysString function), you then call the Web Service's HelloWorld function that the wizard generated when you created the Web Service. After verifying the returned HRESULT value, you free the two BSTR values, and display the returned string.

```
void CConsumeMyFirstATLServiceDlg::OnBnClickedOk()
{
 if (UpdateData(TRUE))
 {
  CMyFirstATLServerWebServiceService Service;

  BSTR bstrReturn;
  BSTR bstrInput = m_strInput.AllocSysString();

  HRESULT hr = Service.HelloWorld(bstrInput, &bstrReturn);
  if (SUCCEEDED(hr))
  {
   CString strDisplay(bstrReturn);

   ::SysFreeString(bstrReturn);
   ::SysFreeString(bstrInput);

   AfxMessageBox(strDisplay);
  }
  else
  {
   AfxMessageBox("Error connecting to Web Service");
  }
 }
}
```

At this point, build the project and execute the application. Upon entering an input value and clicking the Call Web Service button, you should see results similar to that shown in Figure 39-5.

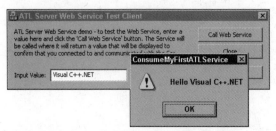

Figure 39-5: This application illustrates how to connect to and retrieve data from a Web Service from a Visual C++ application.

Summary

In this chapter, you learned about Web Services, what they are, and what role they play in developing today's Internet-capable, enterprise systems. After an overview of the architecture of this new technology, you then created a demo service using ATL Server and saw how to access that same service across the Web from a Visual C++ application. In the next chapter, you'll build on what you learned here and learn some of the more advanced usages of ATL Server, including a demo where you write your own shopping cart application.

✦   ✦   ✦

Writing ATL Server Applications

✦ ✦ ✦ ✦

In This Chapter

Writing a complete ATL Server application

Implementing tag handlers

Implementing style sheets

Using the CString class

✦ ✦ ✦ ✦

I n the past two chapters, you've had a pretty good overview of working with one of the most important enhancements to Visual C++ .NET — ATL Server. In Chapter 38 you learned how to create a basic ATL Server application, what role SRF files play, and how to define and call remote functions containing both single and multiple parameter signatures. Then in Chapter 39, you took this a step further and learned about writing ATL Server Web services and how to consume these Web services from an MFC application. In this chapter, I'll wind up this Part on ATL Server by coding a complete (and very practical) application that when invoked displays a random "tip of the day" message. In addition, you'll see this application built step-by-step, where each step represents a new bit of functionality added to the application. That way, it will be much easier if you want to refer back to this chapter when implementing a given feature, because each addition to the application resides in its own section.

Writing a Tip of the Day Demo

To get started, create a new ATL Server project named TipOfTheDay, accepting all the wizard defaults. However, before you build (or deploy) the solution, make sure that the Web server on your system is running. When Visual Studio .NET builds the solution for the first time, it contacts the Web server on your system, creates a new virtual root, and copies the solution's files to the new virtual root. If your system's Web server is not running, Visual Studio .NET will still attempt to deploy and will eventually time out. Your system may appear to hang while Visual Studio .NET is attempting to contact the Web server on your system. If you find that you mistakenly did not have the Web server running, you can cancel the build/deploy process and rebuild the entire solution by selecting Build ⇨ Rebuild Solution. Note also that when you build an ATL Server project it is automatically deployed. You can also deploy as a separate manual step (as an option on the Build menu).

Note   During various beta versions of Visual Studio .NET, I received errors when compiling my ATL Server projects that mostly centered around the fact that certain attributes could not be found (compiler error C2337). If you get these errors, simply add the _ATL_ATTRIBUTES to the project's preprocessor definitions. Although this does appear to be the default in the release build of Visual Studio .NET, knowing this can save you a lot of wasted time if you're working with a beta version.

Once you've built and deployed the project, you can run the application in two ways: from inside Visual Studio .NET, or directly from the browser. Run the solution from within Visual Studio .NET simply by pressing F5. When you press F5, Visual Studio .NET checks to make sure that the files (DLL and SRF files) are up to date, compares the local files with those on the Web server (and redeploys them if necessary), and finally starts up a copy of Internet Explorer that points to the solution's SRF file. The process may take anywhere from a few seconds to minutes depending on how fast your system is. The second way to run the solution is to point your browser to `http://localhost/TipOfTheDay/TipOfTheDay.srf` — note that you *must* include the name of the SRF file in the address. This should result in what you see in Figure 40-1.

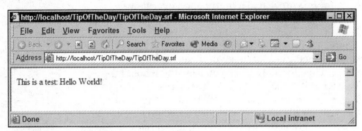

Figure 40-1: TipOfTheDay deployed site

Removing the wizard defaults

What the wizard produced for you is just a basic sample and pretty useless as far as the functionality you're looking for. Because the application will not be making use of the implemented Hello Handler, you need to remove all references to it.

To do that, open the `TipOfTheDay.h` header file in the `TipOfTheDay` project from the Solution Explorer. Remove the following lines from the `TipOfTheDay.h` header file:

```
// Here is an example of how to use a
// replacement tag with the stencil processor
[ tag_name(name="Hello") ]
HTTP_CODE OnHello(void)
{
    m_HttpResponse << "Hello World!";
    return HTTP_SUCCESS;
}
```

Now Open the `TipOfTheDay.srf` file. When you initially open the file Visual Studio opens it in Design view, you'll have to switch to HTML view to change the contents of the file accurately. Click the button marked HTML at the bottom of the design view window to switch to HTML view, and then remove the line with the `hello` token handler on it (the line appears between the `<body>` and `</body>` HTML tags).

```
This is a test: {{Hello}}
```

If you build the solution and deploy it again at this time, the application will still work correctly; it just won't do much of anything until you add some code to replace the wizard-generated code you just deleted.

Implementing tag handlers

You need to implement a handful of ATL Server tag handlers. The first thing the application needs is a `DisplayVersion` tag, which gives the application's title and version in a single string. The `DisplayVersion` tag is used in the content file's page title and header content. You also need a few tag handlers to load a random tip, `RandomTip`. You need tag handlers to get the details of the random tip: the tag names are `TipCategoryMajor`, `TipCategoryMinor`, `TipSource`, and `TipOfTheDay`. You also need to declare some member variables and a private method, and do some initialization. You also need some additional header files.

Let's get started. Open the `stdafx.h` file from the `TipOfTheDay` project. Under the `TODO` line, add the following `include` directives for the `comdef.h` and `msxml.h` files. The first `include` is needed for the `_bstr_t` and `_com_ptr_t` types. The second `include` is needed for XML support.

```
// TODO: reference additional headers your
// program requires here

#include <comdef.h>
#include <msxml.h>
```

Now, open the `TipOfTheDay.h` file from the `TipOfTheDay` project and under the protected section comment, add the member variables shown in the following listing. The first two variables define the major and minor category. You'll see what these mean shortly. The `m_bsTipOfTheDay` variable is obviously a `bstr` representing the string that will be displayed to the application. It's probably worth noting that you could easily make this application a quote of the day application as well. The `m_bsSource` variable represents the source of the tip or quote, and the `m_bInited` boolean flag is used to determine if the application has been initialized.

```
// Put protected members here

// category major: company, product, heading
_bstr_t m_bsCategoryMajor;

// category minor: division, technology, {optional}
_bstr_t m_bsCategoryMinor;

_bstr_t m_bsTipOfTheDay;

_bstr_t m_bsSource;

bool m_bInited;
```

Once the protected members variables have been added, you need to add only a single private method to make sure that the user has called `RandomTip` before accessing any of the `Tip*` tag handlers. To do that, add the `IsInited` method to the protected section of the `TipOfTheDay.h` file, like this:

```
inline bool IsInited(bool bShowInstructions = false)
{
  if (!m_bInited && bShowInstructions)
  {
    m_HttpResponse << "Call RandomTip before accessing "
```

```
                    "any Tip* Methods";
  }

  return m_bInited;
  }
```

In the same header file, add the following code to the ValidateAndExchange method under the TODO comment:

```
HTTP_CODE ValidateAndExchange()
{
// TODO: Put all initialization and validation code here
m_bInited = false;
m_bsCategoryMajor = "";
m_bsCategoryMinor = "";
m_bsTipOfTheDay = "";
m_bsSource = "Unknown";

// Set the content-type
m_HttpResponse.SetContentType("text/html");

return HTTP_SUCCESS;
}
```

Adding the DisplayVersion handler

The DisplayVersion tag handler writes the application name and version to the requesting response object's output stream. Insert the following code into the TipOfTheDay.h file after the ValidateAndExchange member:

```
[ tag_name(name="DisplayVersion") ]
HTTP_CODE OnDisplayVersion(void);
```

Now, add the following the function to the TipOfTheDay.cpp file:

```
HTTP_CODE CTipOfTheDayHandler::OnDisplayVersion(void)
{
m_HttpResponse << "Tip Of The Day ATL Server 1.0";
return HTTP_SUCCESS;
}
```

Adding the RandomTip handler

The RandomTip handler is used to load the Tips XML file and randomly get a tip to display to the requestor through the response object. For now, put in the stubs, and later you'll insert and examine the implementation of this method.

First, add the following code to the TipOfTheDay.h file:

```
[ tag_name(name="RandomTip") ]
HTTP_CODE OnRandomTip(void);
```

Now, insert the function into the TipOfTheDay.cpp file:

```
HTTP_CODE CTipOfTheDayHandler::OnRandomTip(void)
{
m_bInited = true;
return HTTP_SUCCESS;
}
```

Adding the TipCategoryMajor handler

The TipCategoryMajor handler writes to the response object stream of the requestor the Major Category for which the tip belongs. In the Tips XML file, the content of this field is optional. To do this, define the function as follows in the TipOfTheDay.h file:

```
[ tag_name(name="TipCategoryMajor") ]
HTTP_CODE OnTipCategoryMajor(void);
```

Now, insert into the function definition into the TipOfTheDay.cpp file:

```
HTTP_CODE CTipOfTheDayHandler::OnTipCategoryMajor(void)
{
 if (IsInited())
 {
  m_HttpResponse << static_cast<TCHAR*>(m_bsCategoryMajor);
 }

 return HTTP_SUCCESS;
}
```

Adding the TipCategoryMinor handler

The TipCategoryMinor handler writes to the response object stream of the requestor the Minor Category for which the tip belongs. In the Tips XML file, the content of this field is optional. Once again, here is the function declaration for the header file:

```
[ tag_name(name="TipCategoryMinor") ]
HTTP_CODE OnTipCategoryMinor(void);
```

And here is the function definition (add this to the TipOfTheDay.cpp file):

```
HTTP_CODE CTipOfTheDayHandler::OnTipCategoryMinor(void)
{
 if (IsInited())
 {
  m_HttpResponse << static_cast<TCHAR*>(m_bsCategoryMinor);
 }

 return HTTP_SUCCESS;
}
```

Adding the TipOfTheDay handler

The TipOfTheDay handler writes to the response object stream of the requestor the TipOfTheDay text that was specified for the tip in the XML file. This field is required in the XML file; otherwise you wouldn't have any tip to display. Notice that the name of the tag does not have to match the handling function. You may have also noticed that the call to IsInited passes an argument of true—this is so that if the RandomTip method has not been called, you can display an output string in the stream letting the developer of a content file know that it should be called. Add the following declaration to the header file:

```
[ tag_name(name="TipOfTheDay") ]
HTTP_CODE OnTipInfo(void);
```

Now, add the following function definition to the TipOfTheDay.cpp file:

```
HTTP_CODE CTipOfTheDayHandler::OnTipInfo(void)
{
```

```
if (IsInited(true))
{
 m_HttpResponse << static_cast<TCHAR*>(m_bsTipOfTheDay);
}

return HTTP_SUCCESS;
}
```

Adding the TipSource handler

The TipSource handler replaces the TipSource tag in the parsed file with the source of the tip. If the source is not specified in the XML file, an empty string will be written to the response stream and nothing will be displayed. Add the following declaration:

```
[ tag_name(name="TipSource") ]
HTTP_CODE OnTipSource(void);
```

Now, insert the following function into the TipOfTheDay.cpp file:

```
HTTP_CODE CTipOfTheDayHandler::OnTipSource(void)
{
 if (IsInited())
 {
  m_HttpResponse << static_cast<TCHAR*>(m_bsSource);
 }

 return HTTP_SUCCESS;
}
```

Updating the TipOfTheDay.SRF

Now that you've implemented most of the tag handlers, you need to update the TipOfTheDay.srf file to call them and display their results into the page. The following is what your updated TipOfTheDay.srf file should look like with the new handler usage and HTML (shown in bold). In the TipOfTheDay.srf file, you put the DisplayVersion tag in between the TITLE tags. You don't call RandomTip because you have yet to implement the handler completely and this way you can see what is generated if RandomTip is not called before using any of the other Tip* tags. You then make a table to house your Tip Of The Day information by displaying the CategoryMajor value in the upper left, the CategoryMinor value in the upper right, the Tip text in the middle, and the source underneath the Tip text.

```
<html>
{{handler TipOfTheDay.dll/Default}}
<head>
 {{// Set the title of the page with the
    component's title string}}
 <title>{{DisplayVersion}}</title>
</head>
<body>
 <table align="center" cellspacing="0"
  cellpadding="4" width="80%">
  <tr>
   {{// Display the random tip product
     and technology associations}}
   <td class="ProductTechnology"
    nowrap="true">{{TipCategoryMajor}}
```

```
      </td>

      <td> </td>

      <td class="ProductTechnology"
       nowrap="true" align="right">{{TipCategoryMinor}}
      </td>
    </tr>

    <tr>
     {{// Display the Tip of the day text
        information}}
     <td COLSPAN="3" class="TipInfo">
      {{TipOfTheDay}}
     </td>
    </tr>

    <tr>
     {{// Display the Source if any}}
     <td COLSPAN="3" class="Source" nowrap="true"
      align="right">{{TipSource}}
     </td>
    </tr>
   </table>
  </body>
</html>
```

Now build and deploy the application again. Once you've done that, you should see results similar to those shown in Figure 40-2. It's still boring, but you'll fix that shortly.

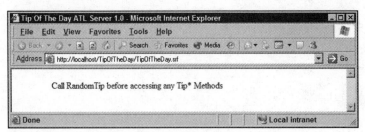

Figure 40-2: TipOfTheDay, with basic handlers implemented

Adjusting the look and feel

You have the working application, and it's in a table, but you can't tell that just yet. You can see from the code that you just implemented that you are using the class attribute. You should have a stylesheet that will give the generated page a look and feel. In this section, you will add a stylesheet to the TipOfTheDay.srf file and implement the stylesheet source.

In the Solution Explorer, right-click the TipOfTheDay project and select Add ⇨ Add New Item from the context menu. When the Add New Item dialog box is displayed, select Visual C++ Category on the left-hand side and then select Style Sheet from the Templates List view. In the Name field, type TipOfTheDay and click Open. A file will be added to your project called TipOfTheDay.css.

In the Solution Explorer, click the `TipOfTheDay.css` tree node. Then look at the properties window and set the `Content` attribute to True (Figure 40-3). Setting the `Content` attribute to True informs the project that this file needs to be added to the deployment package when it is built.

Figure 40-3: TipOfTheDay. CSS properties dialog box, with the Content attribute set to True.

Double-click the `TipOfTheDay.css` tree node to open the file and insert the following stylesheet information into that file:

```
/* Stylesheet definitions inserted into TipOfTheDay.CSS */
TABLE
{
  border:solid 1px black;
}

TD
{
  background-color:506C86;
  color:FFFFFF;
}
TD.ProductTechnology
{
  font-weight:bold;
}

TD.TipInfo
{
  background-color:infobackground;
  text-align:center;
  color:000000;
}

TD.Source
{
  background-color:506C86;
```

```
      font-size:xx-small;
    }

  TD.PageHeader
  {
    font-size:x-large;
    text-align:center;
  }

  A
  {
    color:FFFFFF;
  }
```

Next, you need to update the TipOfTheDay.srf file to use the new stylesheet. Insert the text in bold into the TipOfTheDay.srf file:

```
<html>
  {{handler TipOfTheDay.dll/Default}}
  <head>
   <link rel="stylesheet" type="text/css"
    href="TipOfTheDay.css">
    {{// Set the title of the page with the
      component's title    string}}
   <title>{{DisplayVersion}}</title>
  </head>
  <body>
   <table align="center" cellspacing="0"
    cellpadding="4" width="80%">
    <tr>
     {{// Display the random tip product
       and technology associations}}
     <td class="ProductTechnology"
      nowrap="true">{{TipCategoryMajor}}
     </td>

     <td> </td>

     <td class="ProductTechnology" nowrap="true"
      align="right">{{TipCategoryMinor}}
     </td>
    </tr>

    <tr>
     {{// Display the Tip of the day text information}}
     <td COLSPAN="3" class="TipInfo">
      {{TipOfTheDay}}
     </td>
    </tr>

    <tr>
     {{// Display the Source if any}}
     <td COLSPAN="3" class="Source"
      nowrap="true" align="right">{{TipSource}}
     </td>
```

```
    </tr>
   </table>
  </body>
</html>
```

Once you've inserted this code, build and deploy the solution. Once done, you should see results similar to those shown in Figure 40-4. It's not quite done yet, but it's coming along nicely.

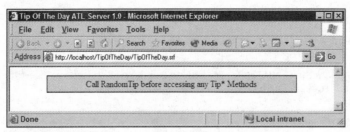

Figure 40-4: TipOfTheDay, with look and feel adjustments

Implementing a random tip of the day

Now that you have your tag replacement handlers implemented, an SRF file with a decent UI, and a UI with a look and feel, let's go back to your `TipOfTheDay.cpp` file and insert the implementation of `RandomTip` to load a tip from the Tips XML file and cache the values for the tip selected.

First, add another file to your project - an XML file that will be used to define the tip data. You are going to repeat the same exact steps you did for your CSS file, but instead you select the XML file type and name it `TipOfTheDay.xml`.

In the Solution Explorer, click the `TipOfTheDay.xml` tree node. Then look at the properties window and set the `Content` attribute to True (see Figure 40-3 for reference). As before, setting the `Content` attribute to True this will inform the project that this file needs to be added to the deployment package when it is built.

Now that you have your Tips XML file, double-click the `TipOfTheDay.xml` tree node and insert tips of your choice using the following schema, where `Tip` and its children should be repeated for each new tip.

```xml
  <?xml version="1.0"?>
 <Tips>
  <Tip>
   <CategoryMajor>ATL Server</CategoryMajor>
   <CategoryMinor>SRF Tags</CategoryMinor>
   <TipText>When commenting your files being
    used by your ATL Server, don't put tags in
    comments unless you mean to, as they will
    be processed by the associated ATL
    Server handler
   </TipText>
   <Source>Tom Archer</Source>
  </Tip>
 </Tips>
```

Now that you have an XML file with your Tip(s), you need to implement the core of the RandomTip tag handler. To do that, open the TipOfTheDay.cpp file and add the following lines of code to the source file below the stdafx.h include directive. The new include for time allows you to see the srand function so that your selected tip is as random as possible. The smart pointer declarations allow you to use the XMLDOM interfaces with ease.

```
#include "stdafx.h"
#include <time.h>          // need this to see the random function to get
a random tip

// Smart pointers that we will use when building the current random
tip.
_COM_SMARTPTR_TYPEDEF(IXMLDOMDocument,  __uuidof(IXMLDOMDocument));
_COM_SMARTPTR_TYPEDEF(IXMLDOMElement,   __uuidof(IXMLDOMElement));
_COM_SMARTPTR_TYPEDEF(IXMLDOMNodeList,  __uuidof(IXMLDOMNodeList));
_COM_SMARTPTR_TYPEDEF(IXMLDOMNode,      __uuidof(IXMLDOMNode));
```

Now scroll down to the RandomTip method implementation to insert the code necessary to load a tip and store its associated values. Right now your RandomTip implementation does nothing but set your initializing flag to True, so you need to add the code to open your TipOfTheDay.xml file. The first thing you need to do is create a XMLDOMDocument object using CreateInstance. (The XML DOM and using it from Visual C++ are covered more fully in Chapter 25.) Once you have an object, you can move onto the next step and attempt to load the XML file. Add the following bold code to the OnRandomTip method:

```
HTTP_CODE CTipOfTheDayHandler::OnRandomTip(void)
{
  HRESULT hr = S_OK;
  IXMLDOMDocumentPtr ptrTipsFile = NULL;
  hr = ptrTipsFile.CreateInstance(CLSID_DOMDocument);
  if (SUCCEEDED(hr) && ptrTipsFile != NULL)
  {
   // More implementation to come.
   ptrTipsFile=NULL;
  }
  m_bInited = true;

  return HTTP_SUCCESS;
}
```

After you have an XML object, you build the physical path to the TipOfTheDay.xml file using the new ATL CString class and the m_HttpRequest object.

You then try to load the list of XML Tips into the XML object. If you succeed you will move forward, and try to get a random tip and its contents. Add the following bold code to the OnRandomTip method:

```
HTTP_CODE CTipOfTheDayHandler::OnRandomTip(void)
{
  HRESULT hr = S_OK;
  IXMLDOMDocumentPtr ptrTipsFile = NULL;
  hr = ptrTipsFile.CreateInstance(CLSID_DOMDocument);
  if (SUCCEEDED(hr) && ptrTipsFile != NULL)
  {
   // build path to tip of the day xml file
   CString strPath;
```

```
m_HttpRequest.GetPhysicalPath(strPath);
strPath.Append("TipOfTheDay.xml");

// load document
VARIANT_BOOL vbLoaded = VARIANT_FALSE;
ptrTipsFile->put_async(VARIANT_FALSE);
hr = ptrTipsFile->load(_variant_t(strPath), &vbLoaded);
if (SUCCEEDED(hr) && vbLoaded == VARIANT_TRUE)
{
 IXMLDOMElementPtr ptrDocRoot = NULL;
 hr = ptrTipsFile->get_documentElement(&ptrDocRoot);
 if (SUCCEEDED(hr) && ptrDocRoot != NULL)
 {
  // More implementation to come.
  ptrDocRoot = NULL;
 }
}
ptrTipsFile=NULL;
}
m_bInited = true;
return HTTP_SUCCESS;
}
```

Next you need to get all the children of the root node from the XML document—these are the available tips. From the list of available tips you will get the number of tips, and select a random tip from the available tips using the rand method. Once you have the tip, you can finally get the attribute values of the tip for your associated Tip* handlers. Add the following bold code to the OnRandomTip method:

```
HTTP_CODE CTipOfTheDayHandler::OnRandomTip(void)
{
 HRESULT hr = S_OK;
 IXMLDOMDocumentPtr ptrTipsFile = NULL;
 hr = ptrTipsFile.CreateInstance(CLSID_DOMDocument);
 if (SUCCEEDED(hr) && ptrTipsFile != NULL)
 {
 // build path to tip of the day xml file
 CString strPath;
 m_HttpRequest.GetPhysicalPath(strPath);
 strPath.Append("TipOfTheDay.xml");

 // load document
 VARIANT_BOOL vbLoaded = VARIANT_FALSE;
 ptrTipsFile->put_async(VARIANT_FALSE);
 hr = ptrTipsFile->load(_variant_t(strPath), &vbLoaded);
 if (SUCCEEDED(hr) && vbLoaded == VARIANT_TRUE)
 {
  IXMLDOMElementPtr ptrDocRoot = NULL;
  hr = ptrTipsFile->get_documentElement(&ptrDocRoot);
  if (SUCCEEDED(hr) && ptrDocRoot != NULL)
  {
   IXMLDOMNodeListPtr ptrTipsList = NULL;
   hr = ptrDocRoot->get_childNodes(&ptrTipsList);
   if (SUCCEEDED(hr) && ptrTipsList != NULL)
   {
```

```
        long lTipCount = 0;
        hr = ptrTipsList->get_length(&lTipCount);
        if (SUCCEEDED(hr) && lTipCount)
        {
         IXMLDOMNodePtr ptrTip = NULL;
         // randomize and load tip of the day
         // seed random number generator
         srand( (unsigned)time( NULL ) );
         hr = ptrTipsList->get_item(rand()
             % lTipCount, &ptrTip);
         if (SUCCEEDED(hr) && ptrTip != NULL)
         {
          // More implementation to come.
          ptrTip = NULL;
         }
        }
        ptrTipsList = NULL;
       }
       ptrDocRoot = NULL;
      }
     }
     ptrTipsFile=NULL;
    }
   m_bInited = true;
   return HTTP_SUCCESS;
  }
```

Finally, you select the node you are working with for the current attribute from the Tip node.
You then get the attribute's contained value and store it into the associated member variable,
which a tag handler will later use to write the value to the page requestor. Add the following
bold code to the OnRandomTip method:

```
  HTTP_CODE CTipOfTheDayHandler::OnRandomTip(void)
  {
  HRESULT hr = S_OK;
  IXMLDOMDocumentPtr ptrTipsFile = NULL;
  hr = ptrTipsFile.CreateInstance(CLSID_DOMDocument);
  if (SUCCEEDED(hr) && ptrTipsFile != NULL)
  {
   // build path to tip of the day xml file
   CString strPath;
   m_HttpRequest.GetPhysicalPath(strPath);
   strPath.Append("TipOfTheDay.xml");

   // load document
   VARIANT_BOOL vbLoaded = VARIANT_FALSE;
   ptrTipsFile->put_async(VARIANT_FALSE);
   hr = ptrTipsFile->load(_variant_t(strPath), &vbLoaded);
   if (SUCCEEDED(hr) && vbLoaded == VARIANT_TRUE)
   {
    IXMLDOMElementPtr ptrDocRoot = NULL;
    hr = ptrTipsFile->get_documentElement(&ptrDocRoot);
    if (SUCCEEDED(hr) && ptrDocRoot != NULL)
    {
     IXMLDOMNodeListPtr ptrTipsList = NULL;
```

```
hr = ptrDocRoot->get_childNodes(&ptrTipsList);
if (SUCCEEDED(hr) && ptrTipsList != NULL)
{
 long lTipCount = 0;
 hr = ptrTipsList->get_length(&lTipCount);
 if (SUCCEEDED(hr) && lTipCount)
 {
  IXMLDOMNodePtr ptrTip = NULL;
  // randomize and load tip of the day
  // seed random number generator
  srand( (unsigned)time( NULL ) );
  hr = ptrTipsList->get_item(rand()
     % lTipCount, &ptrTip);
  if (SUCCEEDED(hr) && ptrTip != NULL)
  {
   IXMLDOMNodePtr ptrField = NULL;
   _bstr_t bsField;
   BSTR bstrText = NULL;

   bsField = "CategoryMajor";
   hr = ptrTip->selectSingleNode(bsField, &ptrField);
   if (SUCCEEDED(hr) && ptrField != NULL)
   {
    ptrField->get_text(&bstrText);
    m_bsCategoryMajor = bstrText;
    SysFreeString(bstrText), bstrText = NULL;
    ptrField = NULL;
   }

   bsField = "CategoryMinor";
   hr = ptrTip->selectSingleNode(bsField, &ptrField);
   if (SUCCEEDED(hr) && ptrField != NULL)
   {
    ptrField->get_text(&bstrText);
    m_bsCategoryMinor = bstrText;
    SysFreeString(bstrText), bstrText = NULL;
    ptrField = NULL;
   }

   bsField = "TipText";
   hr = ptrTip->selectSingleNode(bsField, &ptrField);
   if (SUCCEEDED(hr) && ptrField != NULL)
   {
    ptrField->get_text(&bstrText);
    m_bsTipOfTheDay = bstrText;
    SysFreeString(bstrText), bstrText = NULL;
    ptrField = NULL;
   }

   bsField = "Source";
   hr = ptrTip->selectSingleNode(bsField, &ptrField);
```

```
        if (SUCCEEDED(hr) && ptrField != NULL)
        {
         ptrField->get_text(&bstrText);
         m_bsSource = bstrText;
         SysFreeString(bstrText), bstrText = NULL;
         ptrField = NULL;
        }
        ptrTip = NULL;
       }
      }
     ptrTipsList = NULL;
    }
    ptrDocRoot = NULL;
   }
  }
  ptrTipsFile=NULL;
 }
 m_bInited = true;
 return HTTP_SUCCESS;
}
```

The final thing you need to do before you build and deploy is add the {{RandomTip}} tag to
the TipOfTheDay.srf file. Add the following bold lines to the TipOfTheDay.srf file:

```
<html>
<html>
 {{handler TipOfTheDay.dll/Default}}
 <head>
  <link rel="stylesheet" type="text/css"
   href="TipOfTheDay.css">
   {{// Set the title of the page with the
      component's title string}}
   <title>{{DisplayVersion}}</title>
 </head>
 <body>
  {{// See the TipOfTheDay}}
  {{RandomTip}}
  <table align="center" cellspacing="0"
   cellpadding="4" width="80%">
  <tr>
   {{// Display the random tip product
      and technology associations}}
   <td class="ProductTechnology"
    nowrap="true">{{TipCategoryMajor}}
   </td>

   <td> </td>

   <td class="ProductTechnology" nowrap="true"
    align="right">{{TipCategoryMinor}}
   </td>
  </tr>
```

```
      <tr>
       {{// Display the Tip of the day text information}}
       <td COLSPAN="3" class="TipInfo">{{TipOfTheDay}}</td>
      </tr>

      <tr>
       {{// Display the Source if any}}
       <td COLSPAN="3" class="Source" nowrap="true"
        align="right">{{TipSource}}
       </td>
      </tr>
     </table>
    </body>
   </html>
```

Make sure that the XML file you created earlier, TipOfTheDay.xml, is deployed to the Web server when you rebuild the solution. Confirm that the file will be deployed by clicking the TipOfTheDay.xml file in the Solution Explorer, and setting the value of the Content attribute to True if necessary, just as you did with the CSS file.

Once again build and deploy the solution to see where the application stands. You should see that the application is coming along very nicely and that you're almost done (see Figure 40-5).

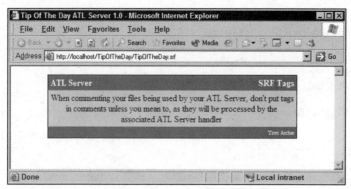

Figure 40-5: TipOfTheDay, with RandomTip implemented.

Introducing additional SRF tags

Server Response Files allow you to include other HTML files, text files, and SRF files to build up a page. When another SRF file is called, that file is parsed and any tokens found are processed. The resulting processed SRF file contents are injected back into the SRF file that included it, in place of the include tag. In this section, you will add a header and a footer to your SRF file. The header will be another SRF file, which will add a table bar with the version displayed in a large font. The footer will contain another table displaying the build that the project is for and how to contact me.

Adding a header

To add the header to the SRF file you first need to create the file and add it to your project. You are going to follow the same steps as you did for the TipOfTheDay.css and TipOfTheDay.xml files. Now, add a new SRF file to the project called Header.srf.

In the Solution Explorer, click the Header.srf tree node. Then look at the properties window and set the Content attribute to True (see Figure 40-3).

Now that you have your Header file, double-click the Header.srf tree node and insert the following code into it, between the <html> and </html> tags:

```
{{handler TipOfTheDay.dll/Default}}
<body>
<table width="100%" align="center">
 <tr>
  <td class="PageHeader">{{DisplayVersion}}</td>
 </tr>
</table>
<BR>
<BR>
<BR>
</body>
```

Adding a footer

To add the footer to the SRF file, you first need to create the file and add it to your project. You are going to follow the same steps as you have for the past three sections.

Add a new HTML page to the TipOfTheDay project called Footer.htm. In the Solution Explorer, click the Footer.htm tree node, and then set the Content attribute to True, as before.

Now that you have your Footer file, double-click the Footer.htm tree node and insert the following footer code, replacing all HTML code that the file contains:

```
<br>
<br>
<br>
<table width="100%" align="center">
 <tr>
  <td align="left" width="50%">VisualStudio .NET,
   ATL Server Example
  </td>
  <td align="right">Created By:
   <a href="mailto:tarcher@theCodeChannel.com">Tom Archer</a>
  </td>
 </tr>
</table>
```

Now that you have these new content files, you need to add code to the TipOfTheDay.srf file to have the ATL Server process and interject responses into the processed result. Add the following bold code to TipOfTheDay.srf:

```
<html>
<html>
 {{handler TipOfTheDay.dll/Default}}
 <head>
  <link rel="stylesheet" type="text/css"
   href="TipOfTheDay.css">
   {{// Set the title of the page with the
     component's title string}}
   <title>{{DisplayVersion}}</title>
 </head>
 <body>
 <!-- Header section-->
 {{include Header.srf}}

 <!-- Tip Of The Day section-->
 {{// See the TipOfTheDay}}
 {{RandomTip}}
 <table align="center" cellspacing="0"
  cellpadding="4" width="80%">
  <tr>
   {{// Display the random tip product
     and technology associations}}
   <td class="ProductTechnology"
    nowrap="true">{{TipCategoryMajor}}
   </td>

   <td> </td>

   <td class="ProductTechnology" nowrap="true"
    align="right">{{TipCategoryMinor}}
   </td>
  </tr>

  <tr>
   {{// Display the Tip of the day text information}}
   <td COLSPAN="3" class="TipInfo">{{TipOfTheDay}}</td>
  </tr>

  <tr>
   {{// Display the Source if any}}
   <td COLSPAN="3" class="Source" nowrap="true"
    align="right">{{TipSource}}</td>
  </tr>
 </table>
 <!-- Footer section-->
 {{include Footer.htm}}
 </body>
</html>
```

Now, build and deploy the project for the last time. When you do, you'll see that you have a very impressive application like that shown in Figure 40-6.

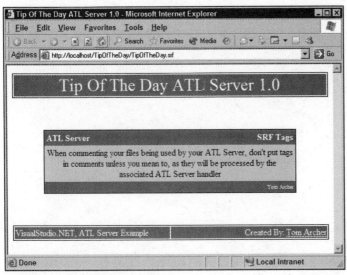

Figure 40-6: TipOfTheDay, final look

Summary

ATL Server applications are the next step for ISAPI. In the past, ISAPI extensions housed the logic, content, and UI. Now, ATL Servers provide the best of both worlds. They house only the logic and allow the some of the content and UI to be outside the DLL, which results in applications that can be more easily modified. The ATL Server approach is also a compiled solution that will give systems not running .NET an avenue for better performance in Web applications compared to using ASP. Microsoft has done well by making ISAPI development easier by implementing the Response and Request interfaces that ASP and ASP component developers are accustomed to, and also has provided rich abilities to external services through a compiled object.

✦　　✦　　✦

Programming .NET

Introducing .NET

Unless you've been living under a rock, you've no doubt at least heard of .NET and its promises to revolutionize the application development process, especially in the area of distributed, Internet-based systems. While the subject of .NET is a fairly broad one and can easily encompass an entire book, this chapter's intention is to give you a 10,000-foot view of this new platform, what it is, how it works, and what it provides for you as a developer. I'll start out with a brief description and benefits of .NET since it seems as though if you ask any two people for a definition of .NET, you get three answers. After that, I'll briefly cover what is entailed when you write, compile, execute, and deploy .NET solutions.

.NET Overview

As with anything sufficiently complex, there are several ways to define what .NET is. The simplest way is with a standard one-sentence blurb meant to highlight the more important facets of the framework. .NET is an architecture that enables the development and deployment of mission-critical enterprise applications. However, .NET is much more simply an architecture. It is made up of a range of compilers, tools, and even a runtime that encompass providing a consistent object-oriented programming model, the extinction of "DLL hell," multiple programming language integration, automatic memory and resource management, built-in type safety (at the runtime level), and exception handling and security. That was much more than one sentence, and although I threw out a bunch of buzzwords, if you didn't know what .NET was before, chances are you still don't. You see, the problem is that .NET has become so all-encompassing that defining it in a sentence — or two or three — can't be done. Therefore, I want to take a different approach to understanding just what .NET is and what it provides for you, the developer.

Developers are an especially picky and judgmental bunch when it comes to software. How often have you wondered aloud things like "Why can't I go online and easily find the information that I need? After all, the information is certainly 'out there,' but how can I search across a given category of information using the search criteria that I define?"

For example, suppose I want to search for a doctor in my area that specializes in a given area, is the gender I want, and accepts new patients. I wouldn't even know where to begin searching for that. If I'm lucky, maybe I can find the Web sites of doctor's offices that provide this information. However, even then, I'm limited to only that office's doctors, and the search criteria that that particular office defined. Most likely, I'm going to be restricted to going to each doctor's site (or egad!—calling them) and querying them individually.

Now there are some sites that provide a sort of centralized repository of data for certain industries. One example that I can think of off the top of my head is a well-known site for movies (www.imdb.com). This site not only has tons of information regarding movies, actors, writers, and just about everyone involved in the film-making process, but it also has cinema schedules posted and can be searched via zip code. However, even this sort of mechanism (shown in Figure 41-1) has severe drawbacks.

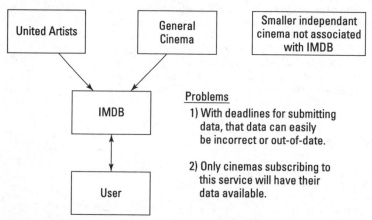

Figure 41-1: The existence of a middleman to overcome the lack of standards in the way companies store and publish data has several inherent drawbacks.

The first problem is that, because IMDB needs a lot of current movie showtime information in a timely and efficient manner, they impose deadlines with regards to the cinema chains submitting their information. As an example of this problem, recently we had a snowstorm in Atlanta that caused most of the cinemas around town to shut down. However, because the information on IMDB had been submitted to them at the beginning of the week, they still showed that movies were to be played that day. A quick browse of each cinema's site showed that they were closed for the day, but going to each individual site defeats the purpose of having an IMDB to begin with. A second problem is that although IMDB does list most major cinema chains, it doesn't list all cinemas, especially the smaller, independent ones. Therefore, not all cinemas in my area are going to be listed.

So what am I asking for then? I want a generic means of being able to search through an up-to-date category of data across all applicable data stores. That can't be done for two principal reasons.

First, there are no standards in place for the different companies to publish their information. Using the cinema example, each of these cinemas stores their data and publishes that data (including the means of querying it) in a different, proprietary manner. This need to have a consistent means of describing all types of data is the reason for the introduction of XML (eXtensible Markup Language), which is an important part of the .NET Framework. Second, developing the code and framework necessary to integrate the services necessary to tie together (at least logically) all these data stores so that they can all be queried) would be a huge undertaking.

This is where .NET comes in. Put simply, .NET is the means by which applications can publish and share information over the Internet through *services*. Note that, at the time of this writing, although you probably will be using .NET on a Windows-based machine there is nothing about .NET that is specific to the Windows operating system. In fact, the .NET architecture is designed so that its benefits and features (I'll discuss these shortly) can be realized by anyone wanting to leverage the Internet in order to reach the broadest customer base possible. At the epicenter of this framework is a runtime that is installed on top of your operating system — currently all 32-bit versions of Windows are supported. This runtime is responsible for delivering the following advantages to you:

✦ *Object-oriented, cross language class library* — The Base Class Library (BCL) provides a consistent, object-oriented set of classes to all .NET programming languages. If you've ever used class libraries such as the Microsoft Foundation Classes (MFC), the ActiveX Template Library (ATL), or the Windows Template Library (WTL), then you're familiar with having a class library at your disposal from a given language. However, you're also cognizant of the fact that once you start working in another language — it is very common for enterprise applications to be written in multiple languages — you must switch from one class library to another. However, with the .NET BCL, all the classes (and their methods, properties, and fields) are available to you regardless of what language you are using, as long as you're using a .NET language.

✦ *Run once, run always* — A common problem with distributed systems in Windows occurs when the components being installed for one system overwrite the versions of those same components that were required for other applications to run correctly. Because these components are generally distributed as DLLs, the problem is sometimes referred to as "DLL hell." .NET eliminates this problem by internally keeping track of the files (and their version numbers) needed by each application to run. This is stated when the application is first installed. Then, when another version of those files is installed for a different application, .NET stores these files in such a way that the first application's dependent files are not overwritten, thereby allowing both applications to run on different versions of the same files.

✦ *Consistent execution environment* — Because .NET executables only run under the .NET runtime, and there is only one .NET runtime, this means that when you build and execute an application under one version of .NET, it will run under all versions of .NET. Just look at the Win32 SDK and you'll find many examples of APIs that run differently under the various Windows platforms, and you can quickly see why this is a major improvement over the current system of Windows development.

✦ *Common Type System* — In conjunction with the CLS, .NET defines a Common Type System (CTS) that defines all the types supported by .NET and how these types are to be instantiated and managed. This means that all languages have access to the same types so that it is possible to pass data between modules written in different languages without having to convert data back and forth between the different formats supported by each language. In addition, because the runtime has control over the types (as opposed to each language), it can ensure things such as the correct number and types of parameters being passed to a given method.

✦ *Programming language integration* — As mentioned earlier, it is very common to see enterprise-level applications written using multiple languages. This has always been extremely difficult because each language has its own set of capabilities and limitations. Add to that the inherent complexities of sharing data between applications written with different languages and the nightmare of debugging such applications, and you'll definitely appreciate the fact that all .NET languages must conform to a standard that makes integration between code written in different languages much easier than ever before. Actually, there are a few specifications that I'll throw at you here.

Pursuant to the CTS defining all the types for the .NET Framework, the common language specification (CLS) then specifies a subset of these types that can be used for language interoperability. As a result, if you are writing code in a .NET language that is to be consumed by other languages, you will want to ensure that you only use types that are defined in the CLS.

To add to that, the common language infrastructure (CLI) allows applications written in multiple high-level languages to be executed in different system environments without the need to rewrite the application to take into consideration the unique characteristics of those environments. Part of this specification is the definition of a set of simpler types (compared to the CLS), collectively known as the "basic CLI types."

✦ *Memory and Resource Management* — Many die-hard C/C++ programmers are quick to dismiss this aspect because it always seems to imply a loss of programmer control. To those people, I would say this: Would it not be a wiser use of your time focusing on the problem domain instead of spending hours tracking down memory leaks because you forgot to free some memory at some point in the application? As software development has become increasingly expensive and time-critical, it is imperative to leave low-level tasks such as memory and resource management to the runtime and instead focus your efforts on writing better and more robust systems. To that extent, you'll never have to worry about memory and resource leaks again because .NET automatically tracks the allocation and freeing of objects and resources in the system. When an object or resource is no longer being used, it is scheduled for release, which is done behind the scenes by a background service.

✦ *Exception handling* — If you've programmed in Windows for any length of time, then you're already familiar with a wide range of choices of error handling. For example, some Win32 functions return an error code, and some return a value signifying that an error occurred, and then you have to call the Win32 `GetLastError` function to determine what that error was. When using COM, you have to handle `HRESULT` values. Finally, some APIs (parts of MFC) use exception handling. With .NET, there is only one error reporting system, exception handling, and it works across all .NET languages. In fact, .NET automatically catches COM errors and converts them into .NET exceptions. As any Windows developer can tell you, the most difficult and time-consuming aspect of software development is frequently the error checking. Now, with .NET, many of the problems associated with this work have been eliminated.

✦ *Greatly simplified deployment* — Unless you're shipping versions of Hello World, Windows applications are generally a pain to deploy. The more complex the application, the more difficult it is to deploy on the client's machines. In fact, this task has become so difficult in recent years that there are full-blown products (with their own built-in programming languages!) that are used to install Windows applications. Think about that for a second. You write something in C++, and someone else has to write another application just to install the thing. With .NET, there are no more registry entries to track, and there is no more need to create special folders for your components in order to ensure that your components are not overwritten by other applications.

✦ *Security* — The issue of implementing security has always been a very complex one and even in .NET it is still not easy. Although security is still not an easy topic to master, .NET does bring significant improvements in this area. To understand those advances, think of the fact that today security is based on user accounts. However, the problem with that is that this concept assumes that all code is equally trustworthy. In other words, the only thing that the security is providing is that it dictates what code you can run or not run based on who you are, but not on any characteristics of the code itself. This was fine in the past when you knew the origin of the code being executed.

However, with today's environment including code being downloaded from the Web, received as e-mail attachments, and run from Web page scripts, a different kind of security model is needed. To this extent, .NET introduces the concept of *roles,* where code is itself imbued with certain security characteristics that define how the system will interact with the code.

As you can see, .NET is many things, and now you can understand why it's impossible to answer the question "What is .NET?" very easily. In fact, I've just barely grazed the surface here in terms of highlighting the various .NET features. Let's now take a look at how you would go about designing and building an application to run under the .NET Framework. As you do that, you'll be able to more clearly see the features of .NET and how they work together to create an environment where application development is easier than ever before.

Choosing a .NET Language

In choosing a language, you need to keep in mind that to a certain extent it really doesn't matter which language you choose because they all have access to the BCL. The reason I hedge that a bit is that, although the BCL exposes a set of capabilities to all CLS-compliant compilers, it is up to the compiler teams to decide which features they want the users of that compiler to have access to. However, by and large, most languages have access to the same functionality 99% of the time, which is certainly much greater than ever before.

Having said that, another issue that dictates language choice is going to be personal style. There might be some members of your team who prefer writing code in C++ for the simple reason that C++ is the language that they have grown accustomed to using much of their careers. On the other hand, others might wish to use the Java compilers if that is their background. The key issue to remember here is that, because of a common type system, class library, and error-handling system, it really doesn't matter. All CLS-compliant languages are capable of easily interoperating as if one language were being used.

This can be a very tricky concept to master at first when you're coming from a more traditional background where each language definitely has its advantages over other languages. However, one Microsoft compiler team member once told me something that brought this point home. In .NET, compilers are really little more than syntax checkers. This is because all their functionality is now in the BCL. Therefore, picking a compiler is merely a means of deciding which syntax you like better. As an example of this, think of Visual Basic. Unlike C++, Visual Basic code is not case-sensitive. This includes method names and variable names. However, this is a programming language issue and has nothing to do with the runtime or any binary code. It simply comes down to a decision of whether or not you like that particular feature of the language.

The last point I'll make here is the concept of *managed code.* Managed code is an expression that refers to code that is written specifically to run within the .NET runtime. Therefore, although you can build managed code on any machine (and operating system) that hosts a CLS-compliant compiler, you need .NET on the client machine in order to execute it. Conversely, *unmanaged code,* which is created by a CLS-compliant compiler, does not require the .NET runtime in order to execute.

As of this writing, Microsoft has created four .NET languages: Visual C++ .NET, C# (pronounced C sharp), Visual Basic .NET, and JScript .NET. However, Visual C++ .NET is the only .NET compiler that can create unmanaged code. In fact, all of the demo applications in this book up to this point can be correctly referred to as unmanaged code. Starting with this chapter and extending to the end of the book, all sample code will be .NET managed code.

BCL and the System Namespace

Assume that you're coding your application. You can't even write a console version of "Hello World" without the BCL, so I'll assume that if you're writing a .NET application, you're going to be using this ubiquitous class library. Because the BCL is composed of literally hundreds of classes and thousands of methods and properties, there are entire books devoted to explaining how to program the specific areas of BCL (XML, Windows Forms, databases, and more). In fact, Chapters 43 and 44 cover two of those areas (COM interop and Windows Forms). However, what I want to do here is to outline some important concepts of the BCL and introduce the *system services*.

The classes of the BCL are split into *namespaces*. If you're new to namespaces, you can think of them simply as logical groupings of classes, types, and other namespaces. The namespace that you will be using the most as you program in .NET is the *System* namespace. In fact, the System namespace includes the Object class — the class from which all other .NET classes (including yours) are derived. This singly rooted class hierarchy is how .NET ensures you that every single class will have a minimum set of members and characteristics. Additionally, the System namespace includes classes for such basic tasks as garbage collection, exception handling, console I/O, and the various utility classes used to write applications. Included in those utility classes are classes for performing mathematical operations, as well as data conversion and date and time formatting.

Table 41-1 shows some of the BCL namespaces and classes that you will probably use quite a bit.

Table 41-1: BCL Namespaces and Classes

Namespace or Class	Description
System namespace	The root .NET namespace, this namespace contains the Object class and all the types used by every application. Almost any .NET application you'll ever write includes either this namespace or one of its nested namespaces.
System.Collections namespace	This namespaces contain the classes used for managing collections of objects.
System.Console class	As you can tell from the name, this class is used to read and write data to and from the console.
System.Activator class	This class contains the methods necessary to create types of objects locally or remotely, or obtain references to existing remote objects.
System.Reflection namespace	One of the most powerful concepts in .NET, reflection not only enables you to dynamically discover type information, but you can even create, save, and execute code at runtime!
System.GC class	The garbage collector (GC) keeps track of and reclaims objects that are allocated in managed memory. Periodically, the GC performs garbage collection to reclaim memory allocated to objects for which there are no valid references. This class is used to control that garbage collector.

Namespace or Class	Description
System.Windows.Forms namespace	This namespace contains the classes necessary for writing Windows applications within the .NET Framework. This includes classes for creating and managing forms, components, and the common dialog boxes.
System.Net namespace	As you can imagine, .NET contains a rich namespace that includes members for doing robust network communications.
System.IO namespace	Synchronous and asynchronous writing to and reading from data streams is accomplished with the members of this namespace.
System.Security namespace	This namespace includes the types necessary to incorporate or programmatically deal with security.

As mentioned, there are literally hundreds of BCL classes. I simply selected a few here to give you an idea of the breadth of functionality available to you. Basically, the BCL includes classes that allow you to do anything you can do in Win32, plus much more, and all using an object-oriented class library that is available to any .NET language. Although this chapter is simply an overview of the .NET environment, you'll discover how to code managed Visual C++ .NET applications using the BCL starting with the next chapter.

Building the Code

Once you've coded your application, it's time to build and then execute it. However, there's so much going on in these steps that is unlike anything in Windows, that I should delve into this step a bit more. I'll start out by exploring what gets created when you compile .NET source code and how that output is actually executed by the runtime. After that, I'll take a look at one of the more powerful concepts of .NET — the ability to dynamically discover type information and even save and execute code at runtime through something called *metadata*.

Microsoft Intermediate Language and the JITters

You might be surprised to find out that when you compile a .NET application on a Windows platform, the output is not a standard Windows portable executable (PE). Instead what is generated is an output that resembles assembly code. This code is called Microsoft Intermediate Language (MSIL). The way this works is that .NET compilers take source code as input and produce MSIL as output. MSIL itself is a complete language that you can write applications in; however, as with assembly language, you would probably never do so except in unusual circumstances. Because MSIL is its own language, each compiler team or vendor makes its own decisions about how much of the MSIL it will support. However, if you're a compiler writer and you want to create a language that interoperates with other languages, you should restrict yourself to features specified by the CLS.

The natural question at this point would be: Are .NET applications therefore interpreted like a script on a Web page? The answer is no. The MSIL that gets generated by .NET compilers is compiled into native CPU instructions when the application is executed for the first time by the .NET runtime. Actually, only the called functions are compiled the first time they are invoked to provide the most efficient means of runtime performance. After all, it wouldn't make for very good customer relations for an entire distribution system to compile upon its first invocation.

Figure 41-2 shows the steps involved in the process of compiling and then running a .NET application to bring into focus just what is going on and when.

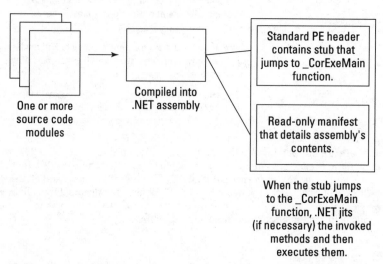

Figure 41-2: .NET applications are compiled into assemblies before they are run.

As you can see from Figure 41-2, there are several steps that come into play between compiling your code and having the .NET runtime recognize it and execute it correctly. The following is a brief outline of those steps:

1. Source code is written using one of the .NET languages: (managed) Visual C++, C#, Visual Basic, and so on.

2. The source code is compiled using the appropriate .NET compiler.

3. The .NET compiler outputs (or emits) the MSIL code and a manifest into a read-only part of the EXE. This file does have a standard PE (Win32-portable executable) header so Windows recognizes it as an application and loads it properly.

4. So far, nothing extraordinary has happened. However, here's the important bit: When the compiler creates the output, it also imports a function named _CorExeMain from one of the .NET runtime DLLs (mscoree.dll).

5. When the application executes, the operating system loads the PE, as well as any dependent DLLs. This includes the mscoree.dll, which exports the _CorExeMain function.

6. The Windows loader then jumps to the entry point inside the PE, which is put there by the .NET compiler. So far, this is standard protocol for any Windows application. However, because the operating system obviously can't execute the MSIL code, the entry point turns out to be just a small stub that jumps to the _CorExeMain function.

7. The `_CorExeMain` function then starts the execution of the MSIL code that was placed in the PE. However, because MSIL code cannot be executed directly (because it's not in a machine-executable format) the runtime first compiles the MSIL by using a just-in-time (JIT) compiler, also called a *JITter,* into native CPU instructions as it processes the MSIL. As mentioned earlier, JIT compiling occurs only as methods in the program are called for the first time. The compiled executable code is cached on the machine and is recompiled only if there's some change to the source code.

And that in a nutshell is how .NET applications are compiled and executed. The following outlines the different JITters that are (and will be) available to convert the MSIL into native code, depending on the circumstances:

✦ *JIT* — The default JITter is invoked each time an uncompiled method is executed for the first time. If you use the vacation plan analogy, this would be akin to a "pay-as-you-go" plan. Sometimes some of the earlier compiled code may be paged out of memory and therefore will need to be recompiled (or re-Jitted) when needed.

✦ *EconoJIT* — The *EconoJIT,* is specifically designed for systems that have limited resources. In fact, just before .NET started shipping, this JITter was removed from the desktop version of .NET and will only be available in the .NET Compact Framework. Examples of systems that would use the .NET Compact Framework are handheld devices, because they have relatively low resources (memory and hard disk space). The major difference between this JITter and the regular JITter is the incorporation of a concept known as *code pitching*. Normally, when a piece of code is compiled, it is then cached so that it executes without compilation the next time it is executed. However code pitching enables the EconoJIT to discard the compiled code if the system runs out of memory. The obvious benefit to resource-strapped systems is that the memory is then reclaimed and the system can continue running as efficiently as possible under those circumstances. However, the equally obvious disadvantage is that once the code for a particular method or group of methods has been pitched, that code has to be compiled again when invoked.

✦ *OptJIT* — The third type of compilation is called OptJIT. The OptJIT compiler was scratched from version 1 of .NET but is expected to be released in a future version of the .NET Framework. This JITter will allow third-party vendors to emit a subset of IL called Optimized IL (OptIL) and to have that IL compiled. OptIL is IL that includes instructions that enable the programmer to tell the OptJIT compiler how to optimize its output for certain tasks.

Assemblies and metadata

At the center of understanding how to program in .NET is the concept of an *assembly* and *metadata*. From a logical viewpoint, assemblies can be defined as physical files consisting of one or more portable executable files (DLL or EXE) generated by a .NET compiler. From a more structural standpoint, assemblies are the packaging of a *manifest* (more on this shortly), one or more modules, and, optionally, one or more resources. What assemblies bring to the party is the ability to semantically group functional units into a single file for purposes of deployment, versioning, and maintenance.

As I alluded to earlier, any DLL or EXE created with a .NET compiler is an assembly, although you might not realize that fact unless you're explicitly attempting to take advantage of some assembly-specific features such as versioning or deployment. In addition to EXEs or DLLs, .NET compilers allow you to create something called a *module*. A module is really a DLL (a file with a .netmodule extension) without a manifest. In other words, although logically it's still a DLL in terms of being a code module that is later used by other DLLs or EXEs, it does not belong to an assembly and must be added to an assembly in order to be used.

Manifest data

As the name implies, a *manifest* is a description of the assembly's contents. Within an assembly, a manifest can be stored in different ways depending on what type of .NET binary is being created. If the output being generated is an EXE or a DLL, the manifest is incorporated into the resulting PE. This is known as a *single-file assembly*. A *multifile assembly* can also be generated, with the manifest existing as either a stand-alone entity within the assembly or as an attachment to one of the modules within the assembly.

From a client's perspective, an assembly is a named and versioned collection of modules, exported types, and, optionally, resources. From the assembly creator's viewpoint, an assembly is a means of packaging related modules, types, and resources and exporting only what should be used by a client. Having said that, the manifest provides the level of indirection between the implementation details of the assembly and what the client is meant to use. Here's a breakdown of the information that gets stored in an assembly's manifest. Note that all of this information can be retrieved at runtime for the current assembly or any other loaded assembly:

✦ *Assembly name* — This is the textual name of the assembly.

✦ *Versioning information* — This value is a string containing four distinct parts that make up a version number. Included in these values is a major and minor version number as well as a revision and build number.

✦ *An (optional) shared name and signed assembly hash* — This information pertains to the deployment of assemblies.

✦ *Files* — Because assemblies can be multifile, this is a list of all files that exist in the current assembly.

✦ *Referenced assemblies* — When a .NET application references code or resources that exist in other assemblies, a reference to those assemblies is stored in the current assembly. This is how .NET keeps track of dependencies to help ensure that the files needed for the correct execution of an application are not accidentally overwritten or deleted.

✦ *Types* — All .NET types that will be used by an assembly are listed here.

✦ *Security permissions* — As mentioned earlier, with today's environment where code can be downloaded from many (possibly insecure) sources, security was a main concern for the .NET development team. This property of the assembly is actually a list of security permissions that are explicitly refused by the assembly.

✦ *Custom attributes* — Attributes are textual decorations of classes and members that define runtime characteristics. These attributes are then queried at runtime through a process known as *reflection,* the ability to query type information at runtime; it can even be used to dynamically generate, save, and execute code in memory. This property is a list of all custom attributes that the assembly programmer has added.

✦ *Product information* — Product information includes such standard items as Company, Trademark, Product, and Copyright.

So what exact benefits do assemblies provide? There are numerous benefits to the design, including the following:

✦ Packaging

✦ Deployment

✦ Versioning

Assembly packaging

As mentioned earlier, multiple modules can be packaged into a single physical file. The benefit here is one of performance. The reason is that when you create an application and deploy it using a multifile assembly, the runtime needs only to load the required modules. This has the effect of reducing the working set of the application.

Assembly deployment

Although it is convenient to think of assemblies as strictly a means of *application deployment*, this is a very limited view of their use. It's probably more accurate to view assemblies as a form of *class deployment* (much like a DLL in Win32), in which a single application can be made up of many assemblies. Because assemblies are self-describing (through the manifest), the easiest and most straightforward method of deployment is to simply copy them to the desired destination folder. Then, when you attempt to run an application contained in the assembly, the runtime queries the assembly's manifest as needed in order to load any external assemblies that are needed by the application.

In addition, the most common means of deployment is through *private assemblies* — that is, assemblies that are copied to a folder and that are not shared with other applications. The creation of a private assembly is the default and occurs automatically unless you explicitly make the assembly a shared assembly.

Assembly versioning

As mentioned earlier, one of the benefits of using .NET is that it helps to rid the world of "DLL hell." One of the means by which this is accomplished is that assemblies have built-in versioning. Note that Windows resource files have included the ability to define version information for years. However, the operating system has never been updated to enforce any versioning rules. It was always up to the programmer to enforce any needed rules regarding versioning. As a result, you'll find precious few Windows applications where version information is set, much less enforced.

As you saw in the previous section, the manifest includes versioning information for the assembly as well as a list of all referenced assemblies and the versioning information for those assemblies. Thanks to this architecture, the runtime can ensure that versioning policies are upheld and applications will continue to function even when newer, incompatible versions of shared DLLs are installed on the system.

Summary

Over the past 20 years of software development, I've seen more new products, paradigms, and architectures that were supposedly going to result in monumental productivity gains than I can possibly recount. However, having experienced firsthand IBM's SAA and Microsoft's DNA architecture — both of which were supposed to revolutionize how we programmed — I can tell you that .NET is the first architecture that I'm truly excited about. The benefits — especially realized by enterprise-level, distributed application's developers — of this system are far too numerous to expound on in a simple one-chapter introduction. However, hopefully this brief overview (as well as the next three chapters, which will show you how to code different applications in .NET) will encourage you to start looking seriously into this framework as a possible course of direction for your future development plans.

✦ ✦ ✦

Writing Managed C++ Code

In This Chapter

Creating a simple
managed C++ program

Using properties

Using delegates

Writing event handlers

The previous chapter had a brief overview of the virtues and benefits of using the .NET Framework to develop the next generation
of Internet-enabled software. However, we're all programmers here,
and although anything can look good on paper, we typically only
believe it once we code it. Therefore, in this chapter you'll dive into
using managed C++ to write .NET applications. Please note that this
is not an extensive foray into the subject of managed C++ programming because there are complete books on this subject. Rather, this
chapter's intention is to get you to the point where you can write
some basic managed C++ code and know some of the new language
features that managed C++ has to offer.

You'll start out by creating a standard Hello World console application so that you can quickly see what managed code looks like and
can ensure that your development environment is properly configured to both build and execute .NET applications. Once you've done
that, you'll move into learning about several important parts of the
managed C++ language. These features include using properties to
define smart fields and defining delegates to use for callbacks and
asynchronous event handling. As I said, we're programmers and want
to code above all else, so let's get to work!

Getting Started with Visual C++

If you're reading this book, you're probably a Windows developer, and
you are accustomed to writing full-fledged Windows applications complete with menus, dialog boxes, and controls. Therefore, although the
first application you'll code here will be a console version of Hello
World, you won't be spending a lot of time on it. Rather, my intention
is help you get a managed C++ application up and running to both test
your development environment and for you to quickly get an idea of
what managed C++ looks like.

Open Visual Studio and select File ➪ New Project. Notice that from
the New Project dialog box, you can create four different types of
managed C++ projects:

   ✦ *Managed C++ Application* — This option creates a stand-alone
     C++ application with support for managed extensions. This is
     the project type that will be used in the demos in this chapter.

✦ *Managed C++ Class Library*—As the name implies, selecting this project type results in the creation of a C++ DLL. Basically, it's the same as creating a managed C++ application project with the main difference being that the binary will be a DLL instead of an EXE.

✦ *Managed C++ Empty Project*—Almost all Visual Studio project types support the creation of an empty project. This is extremely useful if you're attempting to port existing code to a managed environment. Using this option, Visual Studio creates an empty project for you (one without files), but the project's make file contains all the necessary compiler and linker options needed to build a managed C++ application.

✦ *Managed C++ Web Service*—A *Web Service* is programmable application logic that is published (and accessed) using Internet protocols. Subscribers to these services, or client applications, then access these Web Services following a pattern similar to component-oriented software. An example of a Web Service would be if you wrote some code that validated automobile VINs (vehicle identification numbers). You could package this as a Web Service with your business model being that anyone that connects to and uses this service would pay some sort of fee.

Select the desired location of your new project, type a project name of HelloWorld, and click OK. At the time of this writing, the managed C++ projects do not include a wizard to specify additional project options. Therefore, once you type the name of the project and click the OK button, the project will be generated.

Take a look at the code to see just what a managed C++ application looks like—you'll probably be surprised to find that it is not that different than what you've seen throughout this book with plain old regular Visual C++ and MFC.

```
// This is the main project file for VC++ application project
// generated using an Application Wizard.

#include "stdafx.h"

#using <mscorlib.dll>
#include <tchar.h>

using namespace System;

// This is the entry point for this application.
int _tmain(void)
{
 // TODO: Please replace the sample code below with your own.
 Console::WriteLine(S"Hello World");
 return 0;
}
```

The first thing you should notice is the #using directive.

```
#using <mscorlib.dll>
```

In Chapter 41, I mentioned that .NET applications are bundled into assemblies, and that assemblies contain metadata that describes the assembly's contents. Therefore, the #using directive is what enables you to specify that you wish to import the metadata from a given assembly for use in your application. In this case, I am importing the main .NET assembly—mscorlib.dll—that among other things includes the definition for System namespace and the Console class that is used to output data to the standard output device. Including the #using directive in your code is analogous to importing a DLL into a standard (unmanaged) Visual C++ application.

From there, the second line of importance is the using namespace statement (not to be confused with the #using directive). As mentioned in Chapter 41, the classes and types defined in the BCL are semantically separated into distinct namespaces for easier use. There are two ways to then reference a BCL class or type. You can either fully qualify the entity with the namespace or you can specify to the compiler that you're using a given namespace in your code. In the latter situation, when the compiler encounters an unresolved class or type, it searches the namespaces you've specified that you're using (via the using namespace statement) and attempts to locate the class. If the compiler cannot resolve the reference to the class or type, it emits an error and does not produce an executable image of your application (compilation fails).

As an example, let's look at the Console class. This class exists in the BCL System namespace. If you do not include the using namespace statement, you would need to write your code in the following way in order to use the Console::WriteLine method:

```
System::Console::WriteLine(S"Hello World");
```

This could get quite cumbersome when dealing with classes that are buried several namespaces deep. Therefore, the using namespace statement allows for the following syntax:

```
...
using namespace System;
...
Console::WriteLine(S"Hello World");
...
```

The last thing I want to point out in this very simple Hello World application is the actual call to the Console::WriteLine method.

```
Console::WriteLine(S"Hello World");
Console.WriteLine(S"This is my first managed "
                  "C++ application!");
```

The only real things of note here are that the WriteLine method is obviously a static method (and therefore you do not need to instantiate the Console class) and the new S macro, which simply casts the supplied string to the .NET System::String type.

Although a few things here are new, this code is certainly readable by any intermediate-level C++ developer—which is obviously by design on Microsoft's part. Now, add a single line to the end of the _tmain function (just before the return statement).

```
Console::ReadLine();
```

This causes the application to pause for input. Otherwise, when you run the application from Visual Studio, a command-line prompt appears, displays the text, and then disappears without giving you much of a chance to see the output.

Once you've entered this single change to the demo application, build the application and execute it by pressing the F5 key (and indicating that you want to build the application, if queried by Visual Studio). Upon building and running your first managed C++ application, you should see results similar to those shown in Figure 42-1.

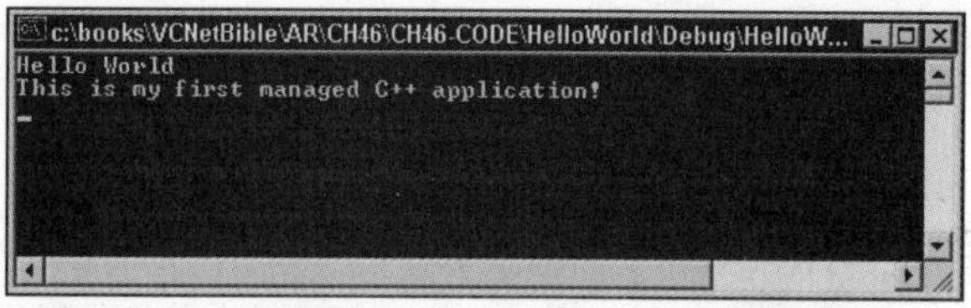

Figure 42-1: Creating a project using the Managed C++ Application project option results in a no-frills console application.

You've seen how to create the most basic managed C++ application possible. However, at least you know the basic syntax is going to be very similar to what you've always used with Visual C++ and MFC, and you've ensured that your .NET development and runtime environment are configured properly. Now take a look at some of the more advanced features of programming Visual C++ with managed extensions.

Properties as Smart Fields

Object-oriented programmers will tell you that a standard definition for a class is that it represents the encapsulation of data and the methods that work on that data. To that extent, it's always desirable to maintain a certain amount of isolation between a class's data and that class's clients such that clients never directly access a class's data. Much of the time, this is accomplished by defining *accessor methods*—methods that are used to retrieve and set the data values—so that the class designer can be assured that the data is being handled in a manner consistent with its design. It also allows the class designer a high degree of flexibility because the accessor method can simply return a value based on a value of the class's private member variables, it can perform a calculation, or it can even perform a query against a database.

In order to illustrate my point, let's look at an example where data would need to be isolated from direct client access. In this example, I have a class used to encapsulate (fashion) model data. Among the members of this class are three fields that are logically related—first name, last name, and alias.

Because many models prefer to be referred to by their alias (if they have one) then a good class design would be to have an accessor method for retrieving the model's name. That way, there are no mishaps where a client piece of code does not verify the existence of an alias before using the model's real name. This example would be programmed in standard (unmanaged) C++ and MFC as shown in Listing 42-1. Notice that the actual name fields are defined as `protected` and, therefore, not accessible from the client and that the accessor methods, `GetName` and `SetName`, are defined as `public`.

Listing 42-1: The Model program in standard C++

```
#pragma once

#include "stdafx.h"

class CModel
{
protected:
 CString m_strFirstName;
```

```
   CString m_strLastName;
   CString m_strAlias;

 public:
  CString GetName()
  {
   CString strModelName;

   if (0 < m_strAlias.GetLength())
   {
    strModelName = m_strAlias;
   }
   else
   {
     // For the sake of simplicity assume that
     // if you don't have an alias that you have a first name
     strModelName.Format("%s%s%s",
                         m_strFirstName,
                         ((0 == m_strLastName.GetLength()) ?
                         "" : " "),
                         m_strLastName);
   }

   return strModelName;
  }

  void SetFirstName(CString strFirstName)
  {
    m_strFirstName = strFirstName;
  }

  void SetLastName(CString strLastName)
  {
    m_strLastName = strLastName;
  }

  void SetAlias(CString strAlias)
  {
    m_strAlias = strAlias;
  }
 };
```

The client would then access the `CModel` name fields like this:

```
CModel* pModel = new CModel();
pModel ->SetAlias("Nicole Sheridan");
pModel ->SetFirstName("Fake");
pModel ->SetLastName("Name");
...
pModel->GetName(); // will return the alias Nicole Sheridan
```

As you can see, this code ensures that the problem domain rules associated with the `CModel` name fields are carried out correctly. However, managed C++ takes the concept of accessor functions a step farther as you'll now see.

Defining and using properties

Using accessor methods works well and is a technique used by programmers of several object-oriented languages, including C++ and Java. However, managed C++ provides an even richer mechanism — properties — that provides the same benefits as accessor methods and is much more elegant to code on the client side.

In managed C++, a property consists of the __property attribute and a method name preceded by either get_ or set_ to indicate either a getter or a setter method. Listing 42-2 shows Listing 42-1 rewritten using properties:

Listing 42-2: The Model program using managed C++

```
__gc class Model
{
protected:
 String* firstName;
 String* lastName;
 String* alias;

public:
 __property String* get_Name()
 {
  String* modelName;

  if (this->alias
  && 0 < this->alias->Length)
   modelName = this->alias;
  else
  {
    modelName = String::Format("{0} {1}",
      this->firstName,
      this->lastName
      );
  }
  return modelName;
 }

 __property void set_FirstName(String* firstName)
 {
   this->firstName = firstName;
 }

 __property void set_LastName(String* lastName)
 {
   this->lastName = lastName;
 }

 __property void set_Alias(String* alias)
```

```
   {
      this->alias = alias;
   }
};
```

At this point, you might wonder what this property attribute has accomplished for us. After all, the getters and setters in the `Model` class look very similar to the accessor member functions that were defined in the `CModel` class. However, you'll now see that the code on the client is much more elegant and efficient. Now the client simply accesses the class's getter and setter methods as though they were fields:

```
Model* pM1 = new Model();
pM1->FirstName = S"Laurie";
pM1->LastName = S"Wallace";

Model* pM2 = new Model();
pM2->Alias = S"Nicole Sheridan";
pM2->FirstName = S"Fake";
pM2->LastName = S"Name";

Console::WriteLine(pM1->Name);
Console::WriteLine(pM2->Name);
```

Note that the client no longer has to know that an accessor function exists for a given field because the client accesses a getter or setter as though it were a field. This makes the client less susceptible to changes made on the class side. By way of example, suppose you're using the standard method of accessor functions presented in Listing 42-1. When you design a given class, you need to decide which fields will have accessor methods and which will allow direct member (public) access. If, after client code has been written to use this class, you decide to replace a public field with an accessor method, you need to modify all client code accessing that member. In a sufficiently large and complex system, this is bound to lead to problems, because you're sure to overlook a few instances where the field was being used. Even if you have a nice source code documentation system, it's still going to require time that could be better spent on new development.

However, using properties enables the client to use the standard `lvalue=rvalue` syntax. That way, the class provider can change a given class member from a field to a property and the client source code won't change at all. It's just one more way the client is shielded from changes to the class. The only thing you would have to do is to recompile the client source code.

What the compiler is really doing

So, how does the compiler cause a call to a method when it appears that the client is simply setting a field value? To answer that, look back at the IL (intermediate language) generated for the calls to the Model class's properties. If you use a tool that ships with the .NET framework—ILDASM (IL disassembler)—and open the demo application (named `PropertyExample` in the `Chap42` folder on this book's Web site), you'll see the code shown in Listing 42-3. (Note that some of the lines have been broken for formatting reasons.)

Listing 42-3: The IL code for the Model class

```
.method public static
int32 modopt([mscorlib]
System.Runtime.CompilerServices.CallConvCdecl)
 main() cil managed
{
 .vtentry 1 : 1
 // Code size       103 (0x67)
 .maxstack  2
 .locals ([0] class Model pM2,
          [1] class Model pM1)
 IL_0000:  ldnull
 IL_0001:  stloc.1
 IL_0002:  ldnull
 IL_0003:  stloc.0
 IL_0004:  newobj     instance void Model::.ctor()
 IL_0009:  stloc.1
 IL_000a:  ldloc.1
 IL_000b:  ldstr      "Laurie"
 IL_0010:  call       instance void
   Model::set_FirstName(string)
 IL_0015:  ldloc.1
 IL_0016:  ldstr      "Wallace"
 IL_001b:  call       instance void
   Model::set_LastName(string)
 IL_0020:  newobj     instance void Model::.ctor()
 IL_0025:  stloc.0
 IL_0026:  ldloc.0
 IL_0027:  ldstr      "Nicole Sheridan"
 IL_002c:  call       instance void Model::set_Alias(string)
 IL_0031:  ldloc.0
 IL_0032:  ldstr      "Fake"
 IL_0037:  call       instance void
   Model::set_FirstName(string)
 IL_003c:  ldloc.0
 IL_003d:  ldstr      "Name"
 IL_0042:  call       instance void
   Model::set_LastName(string)
 IL_0047:  ldloc.1
 IL_0048:  call       instance string Model::get_Name()
 IL_004d:  call       void
   [mscorlib]System.Console::WriteLine(string)
 IL_0052:  ldloc.0
 IL_0053:  call       instance string Model::get_Name()
 IL_0058:  call       void
   [mscorlib]System.Console::WriteLine(string)
 IL_005d:  call       string
   [mscorlib]System.Console::ReadLine()
 IL_0062:  pop
```

```
IL_0063:  ldc.i4.0
IL_0064:  br.s        IL_0066
IL_0066:  ret
// end of method 'Global Functions'::main
```

Note the lines in bold (IL_0010, IL_001b, IL_002c, IL_0037, IL_0042, IL_0048 and IL_0053). As you can see, where the source code appears to be directly accessing Model member fields, the emitted IL is obviously generated to call the appropriate properties.

Note   If you've programmed in C#, you might be surprised to learn that you can directly call a getter or setter yourself:

```
pM2->set_Alias("Test Alias");
```

Although this generates a compile-time error in C#, it is perfectly legal in managed C++.

Specifying read-only, write-only and read/write properties

In Listing 42-2, you'll notice the Model::Name property was used to retrieve a value so that it could do the work of verifying if an alias existed for the model or not. Therefore, this property is obviously readable. However, because the property is used solely to determine which of two values to return to the client, this property would never be writable. As a result, I made the property read-only. How did I do this? By simply omitting a set_Name method. As a result, the following code results in a compile-time error:

```
// ERROR! This won't compile because the odel::Name
// property is read-only!
pM2->Name = "Alias";
```

You'll notice that the other three properties are all write-only. Once again, this is accomplished by virtue of set_ methods existing for each of these properties, but there are no get_ methods. As you can guess, you can also code both a get_ and a set_ method for a given property, and then the property is considered to be read/write.

Advanced uses of properties

So far, I've talked about properties being useful for the following reasons:

✦ They provide a level of abstraction to clients such that the client need not know if an accessor method exists for the member being accessed.

✦ They provide a generic means of accessing class members by using the standard object.field syntax.

✦ They enable a class to guarantee that any additional processing can be done when a particular field is modified or accessed.

The third item segues into an advanced usage of properties: the implementation of *lazy initialization*. Lazy initialization is an optimization technique where some of a class's members are not initialized until they are needed.

Lazy initialization is beneficial when you have a class that contains seldom-referenced members whose initialization consumes a good deal of time or resources. Here's an example of that. Suppose you have a modeling agency application that keeps track of all your models' salient information. When you load the record of a particular model, this application might retrieve current booking information from a database. However, what if you're on the road, and you just want to load simple bio information on a given model without needing to connect to a database and retrieve data? In this situation, you might have the data associated with the model's current bookings shielded by a property. That way, the application would not attempt to connect to the bookings table unless you specifically attempted to access this information.

As you've seen throughout this section, properties enable you to provide accessor methods to fields and an intuitive interface for the client where the client doesn't even have to know if accessor methods exist or not. For these reasons, properties are called *smart fields*. Now let's look at another new feature of managed C++ called delegates.

Delegates and Event Handlers

Another powerful addition to the (managed) C++ language is something called *delegates*. Delegates at their simplest are basically "safe" function pointers. By "safe," I mean that the runtime guarantees that a delegate points to a valid method, which further means that you get all the benefits of function pointers without any of the associated dangers that you would naturally be in risk of in standard C++, such as an invalid address or a delegate corrupting the memory of other objects. In this section, you'll look at delegates, how to define them, and the different programmatic challenges that they were designed to address. You'll also take a look at several examples of using delegates with both callback methods and asynchronous event handling. Let's begin by looking at how delegates are used with callback methods.

Using Delegates as Callback Methods

If you've programmed for any length of time in Windows, you know all too well the concept of *callback functions*. Callback functions enable you to pass a function pointer to a function so that the function being called can save the pointer and then call you back at a later time.

One example of this is how Windows enables you to enumerate all the top-level windows currently open on the system. Instead of reading through an array or collection, the way this works is that you call the EnumWindows Win32 API function, passing it a pointer to a function that you define. Windows then calls this function once for each open window, hence, the term *callback*. As I mentioned, callbacks serve myriad purposes, but the following are the most common:

✦ *Asynchronous processing*—Callback methods are extremely useful in asynchronous processing scenarios where the code being called will take a while to process the request. Typically, the scenario works like that shown in Figure 42-2. As you can see, the scenario starts off with a client making a call to a method, passing to it the callback method. The method being called starts a secondary thread and returns to the caller immediately. The newly created thread then goes about doing the work needed to fulfill the client's request and calls the provided callback function as needed. This programming style has the obvious benefit of allowing the client to continue processing without being blocked, or having to wait, on a potentially lengthy synchronous call.

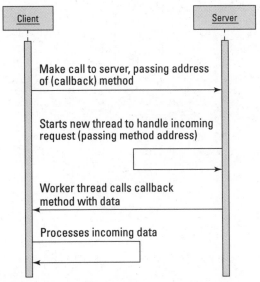

Figure 42-2: Callbacks are often used to facilitate asynchronous communications between two pieces of code.

✦ *Injecting custom code into a class's code path* — Not quite as prevalent as the asynchronous callback scenario, another common use of callback methods is when a class allows a client to specify a method that will be called to do custom processing. A perfect example of this is the Windows Listbox control. By default, this control enables you to specify a sort order of ascending or descending based on the items being inserted into the Listbox. Although this works 99 percent of the time, there are times when you will need sorting that is a bit more complex. For this reason, the Listbox control allows you to specify your own custom sort routine. This way, when the Listbox performs its sort (such as when a new item is inserted), it calls the callback function so that your code can then take control over the sorting algorithm used.

At this point, take a look at the example in this chapter's delegate demo application. In this example, you have a Library class that tracks each of the books (represented by a Book class) it has in its collection. In addition, you have a particularly voracious reader (BookReader class) that wishes to read all of the library's books. Assuming that there are quite a few books, you are implementing a callback function when this reader asks to read all of the library's titles.

First, create a managed C++ project called DelegatesExample. Once the files have been created, you need to add the following using namespace statement to support the ArrayList type that will be used to contain all of the Library class's Book objects.

```
using namespace System::Collections;
```

Next, add the Book class definition. Note that this simple class has only two fields of importance (Book::title and Book::author) and that you're making use of properties that you learned earlier in the chapter.

```
__gc class Book
{
public:
```

```
     Book(String* title, String* author)
     {
       this->title = title;
       this->author = author;
     }

protected:
   String* title;
   String* author;

public:
   __property String* get_Title()
   {
     return this->title;
   }
   __property void set_Title(String* title)
   {
     this->title = title;
   }

public:
   __property String* get_Author()
   {
     return this->author;
   }
   __property void set_Author(String* author)
   {
     this->author = author;
   }
};
```

Once you've coded the Book class, it is time to define the Library class. You'll do this piece-meal in order to go over the more salient points to this section. First, define this class with the following field and constructor. Note here that the Library::books member is of type ArrayList, which is simply a BCL class that implements an array. The constructor then instantiates three Book objects (specifying both book title and author) and adds them to the Library::books **array**.

```
   __gc class Library
   {
   public:
    Library()
    {
     books = new ArrayList();

     Book* b1 = new Book("Visual C++.NET Bible",
                         "Tom Archer & Andrew Whitechapel");
     books->Add(b1);

     Book* b2 = new Book("Inside C#",
                         "Tom Archer & Andrew Whitechapel");
     books->Add(b2);

     Book* b3 = new Book("The Career Programmer",
                         "Christopher Duncan");
```

```
    books->Add(b3);
    }

protected:
  ArrayList* books;
};
```

Aside from the `ArrayList`, this is nothing you haven't seen so far. Now you need to add the delegate definition. On the class side, this is done in two steps:

1. Define the delegate definition (that will be used as the prototype on the client side).

2. Provide a function that will be called by the client.

In Step 1, you simply decide the prototype of the callback function such that the client receives the information it is requesting. In this case, because the client wants to read all books, you simply provide a prototype that sends a `Book` object pointer as its only parameter. Add the following delegate definition to the `Library` class (noting the syntax of placing the `__delegate` keyword before the method definition):

```
public:
  __delegate void SendAllBooksCallback(Book* book);
```

Next, add a method to the Library class that iterates through the `Library::books` array, invoking the client's implemented delegate for each `Book` object found. As you can see from the `Library::SendAllBooks` signature, the client simply calls this method, passing to it a pointer of type `Library::SendAllBooksCallback`.

```
public:
  void SendAllBooks(SendAllBooksCallback* callback)
  {
    for (int i = 0; i < books->Count; i++)
    {
      callback(static_cast<Book*>(books->Item[i]));
    }
  }
```

Now for the client side, you'll just define a class called `BookReader` with two methods. The first method (`ReadAllBooks`) instantiates a `Library` object, instantiates a delegate of type `Library::SendAllBooksCallback`, and then calls the `Library::SendAllBooks` method (passing it the delegate).

```
void ReadAllBooks()
{
  Library* library = new Library();

  Library::SendAllBooksCallback* myCallback =
    new Library::SendAllBooksCallback(this,
      &BookReader::ReadBook);

  library->SendAllBooks(myCallback);
}
```

The second `BookReader` method is the actual callback method that will be called by the `Library` object for each book found in its `Library::books` array.

```
void ReadBook(Book* book)
{
```

```
      Console::WriteLine("Reading book {0} by {1}",
                          book->Title, book->Author);
    }
```

At this point, you're nearly done. Now, simply code the _tmain function to instantiate a BookReader object and call its BookReader::ReadAllBooks method. This source code in its entirety is shown in Listing 42-4.

Listing 42-4: Simple delegate example using managed extensions

```cpp
#include "stdafx.h"

#using <mscorlib.dll>
#include <tchar.h>

using namespace System;
using namespace System::Collections;

__gc class Book
{
public:
  Book(String* title, String* author)
  {
    this->title = title;
    this->author = author;
  }

protected:
  String* title;
  String* author;

public:
  __property String* get_Title()
  {
    return this->title;
  }
  __property void set_Title(String* title)
  {
    this->title = title;
  }

public:
  __property String* get_Author()
  {
    return this->author;
  }
  __property void set_Author(String* author)
  {
    this->author = author;
  }
};

__gc class Library
```

```
{
public:
 Library()
 {
  books = new ArrayList();

  Book* b1 = new Book("Visual C++ .NET Bible",
                      "Tom Archer & Andrew Whitechapel");
  books->Add(b1);

  Book* b2 = new Book("Inside C#",
                      "Tom Archer & Andrew Whitechapel");
  books->Add(b2);

  Book* b3 = new Book("The Career Programmer",
                      "Christopher Duncan");
  books->Add(b3);
 }

protected:
 ArrayList* books;

public:
 __delegate void SendAllBooksCallback(Book* book);
 void SendAllBooks(SendAllBooksCallback* callback)
 {
  Console::WriteLine(S"[Library::SendAllBooks] "
   "Using delegate object to send data to client");
  for (int i = 0; i < books->Count; i++)
  {
   callback(static_cast<Book*>(books->Item[i]));
  }
 }
};

__gc class BookReader
{
public:
 void ReadAllBooks()
 {
  Console::WriteLine(S"[BookReader::ReadAllBooks]"
   "Instantiating a Library object");
  Library* library = new Library();

  Console::WriteLine(S"[BookReader::ReadAllBooks] "
   "Creating a delegate object");
  Library::SendAllBooksCallback* myCallback =
   new Library::SendAllBooksCallback(this,
    &BookReader::ReadBook);

  Console::WriteLine(S"[BookReader::ReadAllBooks] "
   "Calling Library::SendAllBooks (passing delegate)");
```

Continued

Listing 42-4 *(continued)*

```
  library->SendAllBooks(myCallback);
 }

 void ReadBook(Book* book)
 {
  Console::WriteLine("Reading book {0} by {1}",
                   book->Title,  book->Author);
 }
};

int _tmain(void)
{
 Console::WriteLine(S"[_tmain] Instantiating a "
  "BookReader object");
 BookReader* pReader = new BookReader();

 Console::WriteLine(S"[_tmain] Calling"
  "BookReader::ReadAllBooks");
 pReader->ReadAllBooks();

 Console::ReadLine();
 return 0;
}
```

If you compile and execute this code, you will see the results shown in Figure 42-3.

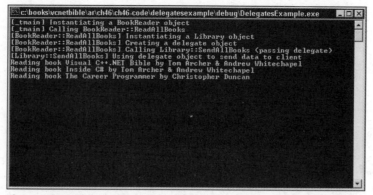

Figure 42-3: While C++ has always had the capability of using function pointers, delegates provide a safe means of doing so, thereby preventing common pointer problems associated with C++.

This little example would be even more realistic with two modifications:

✦ Instead of the `BookReader` object directly reading all of a given `Library` object's books, you could have the `BookReader` constructor take a `Library` object as a parameter to the `BookReader::ReadAllBooks` method. This is more realistic because it would mean that the reader would then have access to *n* number of libraries.

✦ An even better modification would be to also have a `Library::CheckIn` method. That way, instead of the `Library` blindly sending all its books to the `BookReader` object, it would impose a limit on the number of titles that could be checked out at any one time. Then each time the `BookReader` checks a book in, the `Library::ReadAllBooks` method would send another one out. This would be a more practical application of a delegate example. However, it would also entail you making this a multithreaded application — something you'll learn in the next chapter.

Summary

While Chapter 41 expounded on the importance of .NET in the next generation of applications, in this chapter you actually saw first hand a couple of the benefits of writing managed C++ code. You started out by creating a standard Hello World console application in order to get your feet wet and simply go over what managed C++ code looks like. It also helped to ensure that your development environment is properly configured to both build and execute .NET applications. After that, you then used two of the coolest innovations in managed C++: properties and delegates. Now that you've had a taste of some of the cool bits of .NET, let's move onto multithreaded programming within the .NET framework.

✦   ✦   ✦

Multithreading with Managed C++

As opposed to most programming languages used to write Windows applications, multithreaded support is not built into any of the .NET languages. This is because, as I mentioned, in Chapter 41, almost all functionality of the .NET languages exist in the .NET BCL (Base Class Library). This is done so that all languages have the same support for a given .NET feature. Having said that, though technically speaking multithreading is not a part of the managed C++ language, I feel that this very important topic is one that most programmers should be familiar with when learning how to program in .NET, regardless of their language choice. Therefore, in this chapter, I will cover the basics and even some intermediate to advanced issues regarding the aborting, scheduling, and lifetime management of threads. You'll also get into the topics of passing data to worker threads as well as synchronizing threads with the `System.Monitor` and `System.Mutex` classes.

Threading Overview

Multithreading allows an application to divide tasks into concurrently running units of execution such that each unit can work independently of each other. The result is more efficient use of both the system's resources and the user's time. However, if you're new to multithreaded programming, I'll throw out one caveat immediately: although adding multithreading capabilities to your systems can realize some fantastic gains, not every application is a good candidate for multiple threads. Therefore, it's important to realize that along with learning the syntax of multithreading, you must also understand when to use this powerful feature. To that end, I've included a section at the end of this chapter ("Multithreading Design Guidelines") to aid you in determining when creating multiple threads in your applications is the way to go. For now, start looking at how threading is implemented in the .NET framework.

Creating Worker Threads with the Thread Class

Because programmers like to see code first and talk about syntax second, let's look at a simple example of a multithreaded application using the .NET BCL with managed C++. To get started, create a project called `ThreadStart`. Once you've finished that, ensure that the main application file includes the following `#using namespace` statement:

```
using namespace System::Threading;
```

The `Threading` namespace includes the `Thread` class and `ThreadStart` *delegate* type definitions. If you've just jumped to this chapter without reading the previous .NET chapters, delegates are basically type-safe method pointers. Chapter 42 goes into goes into the subject of delegates in detail.

At this point, you'll define a class that will encapsulate your worker threads. You'll understand the need for a separate class shortly—as opposed to us simply starting a thread from the _tmain function. Therefore, define the class as follows:

```
__gc class CWorkerThread
{
}
```

You'll probably notice right away that even though this class is going to encapsulate your worker threads, the class does not derive from the BCL `Thread` class. The reason for this is simple. The BCL `Thread` class is defined as `sealed`, which means that it cannot be derived from. Therefore, instead of derivation, you need to use the concept of containment, which simply means to embed one component within another and to expose to any outside clients just the bits of the internally held class that you want them to have access to. To do that, add a `Thread` pointer member to your `CWorkerThread` class:

```
protected:
  Thread* m_pThread;
```

Next, add a constructor that will be responsible for instantiating the thread member.

```
CWorkerThread::CWorkerThread()
{
  m_pThread = new Thread(new ThreadStart(this,
    &CWorkerThread::ThreadMethod));
}
```

Here's where we'll take a bit of a time out to discuss how this works. The only parameter that the `Thread` class's constructor takes is a pointer to a `ThreadStart` delegate. As mentioned before, for the purposes of this conversation, a delegate can be thought of as simply a type-safe method pointer. To instantiate this delegate you simply need to pass it two parameters. The first parameter is a pointer to the class that contains the method that will be called as a result of the thread being started. The second parameter is then the address of the actual method. Therefore, you can tell from reading the thread instantiation line that you are creating a new thread and passing it a pointer to the `CWorkerThread` object as well as to a `CWorkerThread::ThreadMethod` method.

One thing that's important to understand is that a thread does not begin executing until you call the `Thread::Start` method. So that the user of your class can start the thread independently of instantiating the class, add a `Start` method like this:

```
void CWorkerThread::Start()
{
  // Start thread
  if (m_pThread)
  {
    m_pThread->Start();
  }
}
```

Finally, define the `CWorkerThread::ThreadMethod` method. It won't do very much at this point, because the goal is to have as basic a code example as possible in order to focus on the steps required to implement threading into your applications. Here you have a simple `for` loop that sleeps between iterations and prints out a message indicating progress:

```
void CWorkerThread::ThreadMethod()
{
 Console::WriteLine("[ThreadMethod] Thread initialized");

 for (int i = 0; i < 5; i++)
 {
  Console::WriteLine("[ThreadMethod] Thread Performing "
                     "task {0}",
                     __box(i+1));
  Thread::Sleep(500);
 }

 Console::WriteLine("[ThreadMethod] Thread finished working");
}
```

That's basically it. Now code the _tmain function to instantiate a couple of threads, add them to an array list, and then start each one:

```
int _tmain(void)
{
 CWorkerThread* pThread;

 for (int i = 0; i < 2; i++)
 {
  Console::WriteLine("[_tmain] Starting thread {0}",
                     __box(i));
  pThread = new CWorkerThread();
  pThread->Start();
 }

 Console::WriteLine("[_tmain] Finished creating threads");

 Console::ReadLine();

 return 0;
}
```

Running this application should result in what you see in Figure 43-1. Notice that just as you'd expect, once the threads have been started, the _tmain function carries on with its work and the worker threads then work independently of each other. (The entire code listing for this demo can be seen in Listing 43-1.)

Figure 43-1: Threads can be started in .NET with nothing more than the instantiation of the Thread object, the definition of the thread method that will do the work, and the calling of the Thread::Start method.

Listing 43-1: **Threads1.cpp**

```cpp
#include "stdafx.h"

#using <mscorlib.dll>
#include <tchar.h>

using namespace System;
using namespace System::Threading;

__gc class CWorkerThread
{
public:
   CWorkerThread();

public:
  void Start();

protected:
   void ThreadMethod();

protected:
  Thread* m_pThread;
};

CWorkerThread::CWorkerThread()
{
  m_pThread = new Thread(new ThreadStart(this,
```

```
      &CWorkerThread::ThreadMethod));
}

void CWorkerThread::ThreadMethod()
{
   Console::WriteLine("[ThreadMethod] Thread initialized");

   for (int i = 0; i < 5; i++)
   {
      Console::WriteLine("[ThreadMethod] Thread Performing "
         "task {0}", __box(i+1));
      Thread::Sleep(500);
   }

   Console::WriteLine("[ThreadMethod] Thread "
      "finished working");
}

void CWorkerThread::Start()
{
   m_pThread->Start();
}

int _tmain(void)
{
   CWorkerThread* pThread;

   for (int i = 0; i < 2; i++)
   {
      Console::WriteLine("[tmain] Starting thread thread {0},
         __box(i)");
      pThread = new CWorkerThread();
      pThread->Start();
   }

   Console::WriteLine("[_tmain] Finished creating threads");

   Console::ReadLine();

   return 0;
}
```

Passing Data to Worker Threads

In the first demo application (ThreadStart), you saw the basics of creating and starting a thread. In that demo application, the thread method simply looped five times, printing a message for each iteration through the loop. In this section, I'll talk about why the Thread class is sealed, why you can't pass data to a delegate, and how that overall design affects you in terms of passing data to a thread. When finished, you'll look at a simple demo application that illustrates this.

At first blush, you would think that to pass data to a thread, you simply inherit from the Thread class, add the needed data members, and off you go. However, as mentioned earlier, the Thread class is sealed and therefore cannot be derived from. The main reason for this design is that aggregation and interface implementation are generally thought of as "cleaner" solutions to implementing functionality. You saw an example of aggregation in the ThreadStart example. This interface model is used by Java, where you cannot derive a class from its Thread class, but instead must implement the Runnable interface (and its run method).

The second idea that might seem good at first is to pass data to the delegate. However, upon closer inspection you'll see that this idea won't (and shouldn't) work. The reason is that the ThreadStart delegate is used to wrap both an object pointer as well as the method that will be called upon thread invocation. Therefore, the ThreadStart delegate already provides a built-in mechanism for sending data to a thread. Having said that, you need only modify your demo application in one of two ways:

✦ One way would be to change the CWorkerThread constructor to accept parameters and have that data saved in member variables. The thread method will then have access to those variables when invoked by the .NET runtime.

✦ The second method would be to move the thread instantiation from the CWorkerThread class's constructor into a public method (named something like CreateThread) and have that method accept the needed data.

Let's see how that would look in code. This time, create a new project called ThreadData. Using the same CWorkerThread class as in the ThreadStart example, add the following two members. These two members will be used to track a thread's ID as well as the number of tasks to perform, respectively.

```
protected:
    int m_iThreadId;
    int m_nTasksToPerform;
```

Now, modify the constructor to initialize the m_iThreadId and m_nTasksToperform members. (The code change is shown in bold.)

```
CWorkerThread::CWorkerThread(int iThreadId,
                                int nTasksToPerform)
: m_iThreadId(iThreadId), m_nTasksToPerform(nTasksToPerform)
{
 // Create thread
 m_thread=new Thread(new ThreadStart(this,
   &CWorkerThread::ThreadFunction));
}
```

In the next modification to the code, change the CWorkerThread::ThreadMethod method such that it uses the passed date to control its for loop. As you can see, the __box statement is then used to convert an unmanaged type (an int, in this case) to a boxed type that the Console::WriteLine method will accept:

```
void CWorkerThread::ThreadFunction()
{
 Console::WriteLine("[CWorkerThread::ThreadFunction] "
   "Thread {0} has initialized to do {1} tasks",
```

```
    __box(this->m_iThreadId),
    __box(this->m_nTasksToPerform));

   for (int i = 0; i < m_nTasksToPerform; i++)
   {
    Console::WriteLine("[CWorkerThread::ThreadFunction]
     "Thread {0} Performing task {1} of {2}",
     __box(m_iThreadId),
     __box(i+1),
     __box(m_nTasksToPerform));

    Thread::Sleep(500);
   }

   Console::WriteLine("[CWorkerThread::ThreadFunction] Thread "
    "{0} finished working",
    __box(m_iThreadId));
  }
```

The last task you need to do here is to modify the _main function so that it calls the System::Random class to randomize the number of events that given thread must accomplish:

```
  int _tmain(void)
  {
   CWorkerThread* pWorkerThread;

   for (int i = 0; i < 2; i++)
   {
    Console::WriteLine("[_tmain] Starting thread {0}",
                       __box(i));

    System::Random* pRandom = new System::Random();

    pWorkerThread = new CWorkerThread((i+1),
      (int)Math::Round(pRandom->NextDouble()*10));
   }

   Console::WriteLine("[_tmain] Finished creating threads");

   Console::ReadLine();

   return 0;
  }
```

After you've finished coding these changes, build and run the application. You should see results similar to those shown in Figure 43-2.

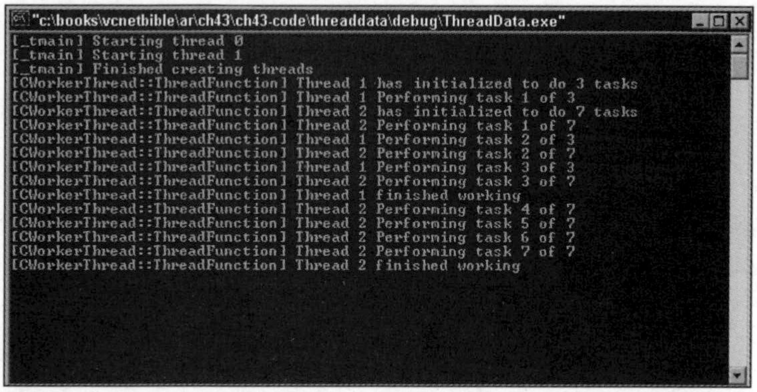

Figure 43-2: Passing initialization data to a thread is easily accomplished because of the way the ThreadStart delegate is designed.

The entire code listing for the ThreadData example can be seen in listing 43-2.

Listing 43-2: **ThreadData.cpp**

```cpp
#include "stdafx.h"

#using <mscorlib.dll>
#include <tchar.h>
#include <math.h>

using namespace System;
using namespace System::Threading;

__gc class CWorkerThread
{
public:
  CWorkerThread(int iThreadId, int nTasksToPerform);

public:
  void Start();

protected:
  void ThreadFunction();

protected:
  Thread* m_pThread;
```

```
protected:
  int m_iThreadId;
  int m_nTasksToPerform;
};

CWorkerThread::CWorkerThread(int iThreadId,
                             int nTasksToPerform)
: m_iThreadId(iThreadId), m_nTasksToPerform(nTasksToPerform)
{
  // Create thread
  m_pThread = new Thread(new ThreadStart(this,
   &CWorkerThread::ThreadFunction));
}

void CWorkerThread::Start()
{
  // Start thread
  if (m_pThread)
  {
    m_pThread->Start();
  }
}

void CWorkerThread::ThreadFunction()
{
  Console::WriteLine("[CWorkerThread::ThreadFunction] "
    "Thread {0} has initialized to do {1} tasks",
                     __box(this->m_iThreadId),
                     __box(this->m_nTasksToPerform));

  for (int i = 0; i < m_nTasksToPerform; i++)
  {
    Console::WriteLine("[CWorkerThread::ThreadFunction]"
      "Thread {0} Performing task {1} of {2}",
                       __box(m_iThreadId),
                       __box(i+1),
                       __box(m_nTasksToPerform));
    Thread::Sleep(500);
  }

  Console::WriteLine("[CWorkerThread::ThreadFunction] "
    "Thread {0} finished working",
                     __box(m_iThreadId));
}

int _tmain(void)
{
```

Continued

Listing 43-2 *(continued)*

```
CWorkerThread* pWorkerThread;

for (int i = 0; i < 2; i++)
{
  Console::WriteLine("[_tmain] Starting first thread");

  System::Random* pRandom = new System::Random();

  pWorkerThread = new CWorkerThread((i+1),
    (int)Math::Round(pRandom->NextDouble()*10));

  pWorkerThread->Start();
}

Console::WriteLine("[_tmain] Finished creating threads");

Console::ReadLine();

return 0;
}
```

Now that you know how to start threads and pass initialization data to them, take a look at managing thread lifetimes.

Managing Thread Lifetimes

There are many times when you will need to take control over the activity or lifetime of a thread. For example, you might decide to pause a thread and then resume that thread's execution. An example of this would be if you spun off a thread to do some processing and displayed a progress dialog box where the user could not only see the current work progress of the thread, but could also cancel the thread. This is a common feature in any situation where the task being performed by the worker thread will take a long time or consume a lot of resources. When the user clicks the Cancel button, you could pause the thread and display a dialog box asking the user to confirm aborting the thread. If the user confirms, you would terminate the thread. If the user declines, you would then need to resume the thread's execution. Another issue that I covered in this chapter deals with scheduling threads with regards to their priority. As you know, all threads are not created equal in terms of their importance. Therefore, I'll also cover how to set a thread's priority so that it runs according to the rules stipulated by your problem domain.

Pausing and resuming thread execution

Pausing a thread is simple enough, and is something you've already seen in the previous couple of examples. You need only call the `Thread::Sleep` method, passing it a value that indicates the amount of time the thread will be paused. Here are the two overrides of this publicly exposed method:

```
public: static void Sleep(int);
public: static void Sleep(TimeSpan);
```

The first version of the Sleep method takes as its only parameter the amount of time, in milliseconds, that the thread is to be paused. Here are a couple of examples of that implementation being called:

```
Sleep(500); // 500 milliseconds (0.5 seconds)
Sleep(5000); // sleep for 5 seconds
```

The second version of the Thread::Sleep method takes a TimeSpan object. This structure represents a time interval and can be instantiated in several ways.

```
// Initialize by specifying number of 100-nanosecond units
public: TimeSpan(__int64);

// Used to specify hours, minutes, and seconds
public: TimeSpan(int, int, int);

// Used to specify days, hours, minutes, and seconds
public: TimeSpan(int, int, int, int);

// Used to specify days, hours, minutes, seconds,
// and milliseconds
public: TimeSpan(int, int, int, int, int);
```

Personally, I can't see a use for a prototype where you can specify a value that includes days and milliseconds, but it's there in case you do. The following are valid calls to the Sleep method:

```
// Sleep for 50000 nanoseconds
Thread::Sleep(TimeSpan(500));

// Sleep for 5 minutes
Thread::Sleep(TimeSpan(0, 5, 0));

// Sleep for 1 day and 12 hours
Thread::Sleep(TimeSpan(1, 12, 0, 0));

// Sleep for 1 day, 1 hour, 30 minutes, and 30 milliseconds
Thread::Sleep(TimeSpan(1, 1, 30, 0, 30));
```

Now, the obvious question would be: How do I specify that a thread sleep "forever," or indefinitely? This is accomplished by using the Timeout class, where each member of this class is a constant that defines a different value. The value you're interested in here is the Timeout::Infinite member. Therefore, in order to pause a thread for an indefinite period of time, you would use the following line of code. This is the code you would use in the earlier example where you are pausing a thread until the user confirms its cancellation or resumption.

```
// Sleep indefinitely
Thread::Sleep(Timeout::Infinite);
```

One very important thing to notice about the Thread::Sleep method is that it is a static method, and therefore cannot be called with an instance of the Thread object. The reason for this is that the .NET runtime doesn't allow you to pause (via the Sleep method) any other thread except the currently executing one. Additionally, if a thread uses the Sleep method to pause itself, no other thread may resume that thread's execution.

As an example, look at the following code snippet. In this code, _tmain (operating in its own thread) starts a worker thread. The worker thread suspends execution via the Sleep method. During this time, the _tmain method itself sleeps (in order to give the worker thread enough time to begin working) and then attempts to resume the worker thread. However, if you plug this code into an application, you will receive the Threading::ThreadStateException shown in Figure 43-3.

```
void CWorkerThread::ThreadMethod()
{
 Sleep(5000); // sleep for 5 seconds
}
...
int _tmain()
{
 CWorkerThread* pThread = new CWorkerThread();

 pThread->Start();

 Thread::CurrentThread->Sleep(1000);

 // ERROR: This will cause an exception
 pWorkerThread->m_pThread->Resume();
 }
 ...
 }
```

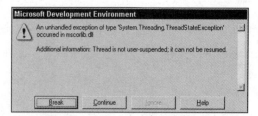

Figure 43-3: Only the thread calling Thread::Sleep to pause thread execution can call Thread::Resume to resume it.

Another way to suspend a thread is via the Thread::Suspend method. You might be wondering why two distinct methods exist to pause a thread. The reason is that there are some major difference between the Thread::Sleep and Thread::Suspend methods. The first difference is that although the Sleep method can only be called by the current thread, any thread can suspend any other thread via the Suspend method. The second main difference between the Sleep and Pause methods is that if one thread pauses another via the Pause method, it can then resume that same thread via the Resume method. Therefore, going back to the scenario I presented at the beginning of this section — where the code would pause a worker thread and present a confirmation dialog box in reply to the user's request to cancel an operation — this would actually be better accomplished via the Suspend method.

Note that once a thread suspends another thread, the first thread is not blocked. In other words, the call to Suspend returns immediately. In addition, note that regardless of how many times the Suspend method is called for a given thread, a single call to Thread::Resume will cause the thread to resume that thread's execution. You'll take a look at a demo application illustrating how to suspend and resume threads after this next section, which covers the issue of aborting threads.

Aborting threads

It only makes sense that if you can create, suspend, and resume threads, then you can also abort them. In .NET, this is accomplished via a call to the `Thread::Abort` method. Internally, the way this works is that when you call the `Abort` method, the runtime actually forces the thread's abortion by raising a `ThreadAbortException` exception. You might be wondering about what happens if the thread method has a `catch` block for that exception. Surprisingly, even in that case, although the `catch` block will be executed, the runtime will not pass control to that block. However, the thread will still be aborted nonetheless.

You should also realize that when the `Abort` method is called, the thread would not cease execution immediately. In fact, the documentation for the `Abort` method specifically states that "Calling this method *usually* terminates the thread." The reason for this is that the runtime only terminates the thread once it has reached what the documentation refers to as a "safe point." As a result, if your code is dependent on ensuring that the thread has been successfully stopped before it can continue with the next task, I suggest calling the `Thread::Join` method. The `Join` method is used to block the current thread until the specified thread is terminated. Finally, you should realize that once you call the `Abort` method, even if the method has not terminated, you can no longer perform any useful tasks with this method. In other words, there's no means of "unaborting" or continuing work with a thread once you call the `Abort` method.

Listing 43-3 contains the code for an example of how to call the `Abort` method. Notice that if you build and run this application, you will have similar results to that shown in Figure 43-4, where the `_tmain` function has called the `Abort` method, but the thread did not terminate immediately.

Listing 43-3: **ThreadAbort.cpp**

```
#include "stdafx.h"

#using <mscorlib.dll>
#include <tchar.h>
#include <math.h>

using namespace System;
using namespace System::Threading;

__gc class CWorkerThread
{
public:
  CWorkerThread(int iThreadId, int nTasksToPerform);

public:
  void Start();

protected:
```

Continued

Listing 43-3 *(continued)*

```cpp
  void ThreadMethod();

public:
  Thread* m_pThread;

protected:
  int m_iThreadId;
  int m_nTasksToPerform;
};

CWorkerThread::CWorkerThread(int iThreadId,
  int nTasksToPerform)
: m_iThreadId(iThreadId), m_nTasksToPerform(nTasksToPerform)
{
  // Create thread
  m_pThread = new Thread(new ThreadStart(this,
   &CWorkerThread::ThreadMethod));
}

void CWorkerThread::Start()
{
  // Start thread
  if (m_pThread)
  {
    m_pThread->Start();
  }
}

void CWorkerThread::ThreadMethod()
{
  try
  {
    Console::WriteLine("[CWorkerThread::ThreadMethod] "
     "Thread {0} has initialized to do {1} tasks",
                    __box(this->m_iThreadId),
                    __box(this->m_nTasksToPerform));

    for (int i = 0; i < m_nTasksToPerform; i++)
    {
      Console::WriteLine("[CWorkerThread::ThreadMethod]"
        " Thread {0} Performing task {1} of {2}",
                    __box(m_iThreadId),
                    __box(i+1),
                    __box(m_nTasksToPerform));
      Console::WriteLine("[CWorkerThread::ThreadMethod]"
        " Sleeping for 1 second to simulate work");
      Thread::Sleep(1000);
    }

    Console::WriteLine("[CWorkerThread::ThreadMethod]"
```

```
                " Thread {0} finished working",
                             __box(m_iThreadId));
    }
    catch(ThreadStateException* pe)
    {
      Console::WriteLine("Exception of type {0} caught",
        pe->GetType());
    }
  }
}

int _tmain(void)
{
  CWorkerThread* pWorkerThread;

  Console::WriteLine("[_tmain] Starting first thread");

  pWorkerThread = new CWorkerThread(1, 10);

  pWorkerThread->Start();

  Console::WriteLine("[_tmain] Sleeping for 1 second");
  Thread::CurrentThread->Sleep(1000);

  Console::WriteLine("[_tmain] Aborting worker thread");
  pWorkerThread->m_pThread->Abort();

  Console::ReadLine();

  return 0;
}
```

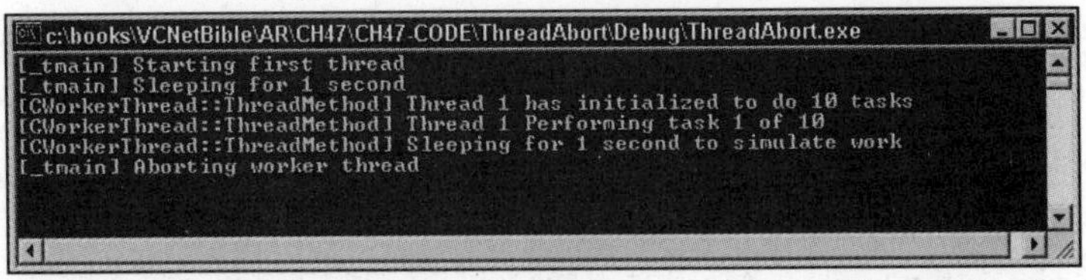

Figure 43-4: Although the Abort method generally causes the termination of a thread, it is not terminated immediately.

Putting it all together

Now that you know how to suspend, resume, and abort threads, let's put all this together to see how you would use this in a (semi-) practical application. This example (the source code is shown in Listing 43-4) starts a worker thread. It then displays the following menu:

```
"*** MENU ***
1. View thread's status
2. Pause thread's status
3. Resume thread
4. Quit
```

If the user selects the first option, they get a response that looks similar to this if the thread has been paused:

```
Thread status : 2 tasks of 10 tasks completed
Thread is currently SUSPENDED.
```

They get a message like this if the thread is currently executing:

```
Thread status : 2 tasks of 10 tasks completed
Thread is currently EXECUTING.
```

If the user selects to pause the thread, and the thread is suspended, a member variable of the CWorkerThread is updated to reflect that status, and a string is printed to the screen letting the user know that the thread was successfully suspended. Likewise, if the user chooses the "resume" option, the suspended thread (assuming it is suspended) is resumed, the CWorkerThread status member is updated, and a message is printed out letting the user know that the thread is now executing.

As you can see, from a logical point there is nothing overly complex about the example. However, it does give you an opportunity to see how easy it is to run a background thread while giving the user (or application logic) the opportunity to pause and resume the thread as needed. Once you've read Chapter 44 and learned how to write Windows Forms application, you'll then know how to apply this logic to GUI interfaces as well. Listing 43-4 has the code for this demo (ThreadSleep).

Listing 43-4: **ThreadSleep.cpp**

```cpp
#include "stdafx.h"

#using <mscorlib.dll>
#include <tchar.h>
#include <math.h>

using namespace System;
using namespace System::Threading;

__gc class CWorkerThread
{
public:
  CWorkerThread(int iThreadId, int nTasksToPerform);

public:
  void Start();
  void Suspend();
  void Resume();
  void Abort();

protected:
  void ThreadMethod();

protected:
  Thread* m_pThread;

protected:
```

```
    int m_iThreadId;

protected:
  int m_nTasksToPerform;
public:
  __property int get_TotalTasks()
  {
    return m_nTasksToPerform;
  }

protected:
  int m_iCurrentTask;
public:
  __property int get_CurrentTask()
  {
    return m_iCurrentTask;
  }

protected:
  bool m_bWorkCompleted;
};

CWorkerThread::CWorkerThread(int iThreadId,
                             int nTasksToPerform)
: m_iThreadId(iThreadId),
  m_nTasksToPerform(nTasksToPerform),
  m_iCurrentTask(0),
  m_bWorkCompleted(false)
{
  // Create thread
  m_pThread = new Thread(new ThreadStart(this,
                         &CWorkerThread::ThreadMethod));

}

void CWorkerThread::Start()
{
  // Start thread
  if (m_pThread)
  {
    m_pThread->Start();
  }
}

void CWorkerThread::Suspend()
{
  if (m_pThread)
  {
    m_pThread->Suspend();
  }
}

void CWorkerThread::Resume()
```

Continued

Listing 43-4 *(continued)*

```cpp
{
  if (m_pThread)
  {
    m_pThread->Resume();
  }
}

void CWorkerThread::Abort()
{
  if (m_pThread && !m_bWorkCompleted)
  {
    m_pThread->Abort();
  }
}

void CWorkerThread::ThreadMethod()
{
  for (int i = 0; i < m_nTasksToPerform; i++)
  {
    m_iCurrentTask++;
    Thread::Sleep(5000);
  }
  m_bWorkCompleted = true;
}

__gc class CMyApplication
{
public:
  CMyApplication()
  : m_pThread(NULL), m_bThreadPaused(false) {}

protected:
  CWorkerThread* m_pThread;

public:
  void Run();
public:
  String* ProcessMenu();
  bool ProcessUserOption(String* pstrResponse);

protected:
  bool m_bThreadPaused;
};

void CMyApplication::Run()
{
  m_pThread = new CWorkerThread(1, 10);
  m_pThread->Start();

  bool bUserQuit = false;
  do
```

```
  {
    String* pstrResponse = ProcessMenu();
    bUserQuit = ProcessUserOption(pstrResponse);
  } while (!bUserQuit);

  // CWorkerThread will check to see if still running
  m_pThread->Abort();
}

String* CMyApplication::ProcessMenu()
{
  String* pstrResponse;

  Console::WriteLine("*** MENU ***");
  Console::WriteLine("1. View thread's status");
  Console::WriteLine("2. Pause thread's statues");
  Console::WriteLine("3. Resume thread");
  Console::WriteLine("4. Quit");
  Console::Write("==>");

  pstrResponse = Console::ReadLine();

  Console::WriteLine("\n");

  return pstrResponse;
}

bool CMyApplication::ProcessUserOption(String* pstrResponse)
{
  bool bUserQuit = false;

  if (0 == pstrResponse->CompareTo("1"))
  {
    Console::WriteLine("Thread status : {0} "
        "tasks of {1} tasks completed",
      __box(m_pThread->CurrentTask),
      __box(m_pThread->TotalTasks));

    Console::Write("Thread is currently ");
    if (m_bThreadPaused)
      Console::WriteLine("SUSPENDED.");
    else
      Console::WriteLine("EXECUTING.");

    Console::WriteLine();
  }
  else if (0 == pstrResponse->CompareTo("2"))
  {
    this->m_pThread->Suspend();
    this->m_bThreadPaused = true;

    Console::WriteLine("Thread SUSPENDED!\n");
```

Continued

Listing 43-4 *(continued)*

```
    }
    else if (0 == pstrResponse->CompareTo("3"))
    {
      this->m_pThread->Resume();
      this->m_bThreadPaused = false;

      Console::WriteLine("Thread RESUMED!\n");
    }
    else if (0 == pstrResponse->CompareTo("4"))
      bUserQuit = true;

    return bUserQuit;
  }

int _tmain(void)
{
  CMyApplication* pApp = new CMyApplication();
  pApp->Run();

  Console::Write("Application finished. Press "
    "<Enter> to close window.");

  Console::ReadLine();
  return 0;
}
```

Working with Thread Priorities

You read earlier in the chapter that each thread is given a time slice, or an amount of CPU time, within which to perform work. You also read that in a preemptive multitasking environment, the CPU switches between threads automatically. However, this switching is far from arbitrary. When a thread is created it is associated with a priority level that indicates to the processor how it should be scheduled with relation to the other threads in the system. This priority level is defaulted to Normal (I'll discuss these settings in more detail shortly) for threads that are created within the runtime. For threads that are created outside the runtime, they retain their original priority setting.

A thread's priority can be set (and retrieved) via the Thread::Priority property. The value that you use with this property is of type Thread.ThreadPriority—an enum that defines the following values:

✦ Highest

✦ AboveNormal

✦ Normal

✦ BelowNormal

✦ Lowest

To illustrate how priorities can affect even the simplest code, I'll show you a couple of examples in which one worker thread "counts" from 1 to 10 and a second thread "counts" from 11 to 20.

First create a project called ThreadPriority. When finished, add a CWorkerThread class and a constructor that looks like the following:

```
CWorkerThread::CWorkerThread(int iStart, int iEnd)
: m_iStart(iStart), m_iEnd(iEnd)
{
  m_pThread = new Thread(new ThreadStart(this,
    &CWorkerThread::ThreadMethod));
}
```

As you can see, I've simply defined the constructor to take a start and end number. The constructor saves those two values and creates a thread using another member. Therefore, you'll need to define these members:

```
protected:
  Thread* m_pThread;
protected:
  int m_iStart;
  int m_iEnd;
```

Once you've defined these members, insert the following thread method into the CWorkerThread class:

```
void CWorkerThread::ThreadMethod()
{
  Console::WriteLine("Worker thread started");

  Console::WriteLine("Worker thread - counting slowly "
    from {0} to {1}",
    __box(m_iStart), __box(m_iEnd));

  for (int i = m_iStart; i < m_iEnd; i++)
  {
    for (int j = 0; j < 50; j++)
    {
      Console::Write(".");

      // Code to imitate work being done.
      int a;
      a = 15;
    }
    Console::Write("{0}", __box(i));
  }

  Console::WriteLine("Worker thread finished");
}
```

As you can see, I've used some nested loops in order to slow things down a bit. Otherwise, the threads would finish their work within a single time slice, which wouldn't be useful for looking at how changing thread priority affects thread execution.

Finally, instantiate two CWorkerThread objects and call their Start methods in the _tMain method. Once you've done that, build and run the application to see results similar to that shown in Figure 43-5.

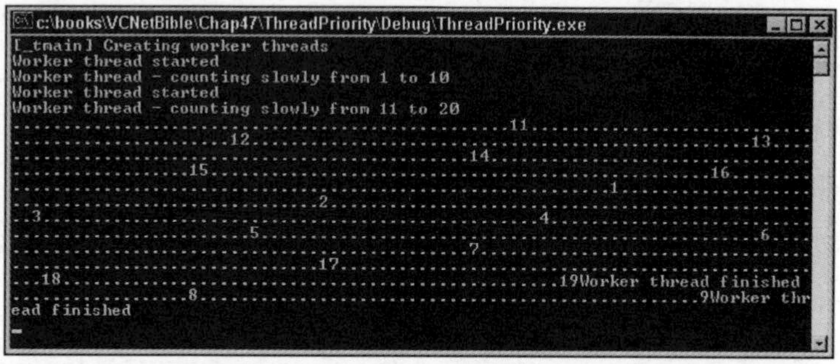

Figure 43-5: Without thread priorities, all of your worker threads will have equal rights to the CPU, which might not suit every occasion.

At this point, alter the _tmain function by setting the two thread object's priorities to ThreadPriority::Highest and ThreadPriority::Lowest, respectively. When you've finished, you should have code that looks like that shown in Listing 43-5.

Listing 43-5: **ThreadPriority.cpp**

```
#include "stdafx.h"

#using <mscorlib.dll>
#include <tchar.h>
#include <math.h>

using namespace System;
using namespace System::Threading;

__gc class CWorkerThread
{
public:
  CWorkerThread(int iStart, int iEnd);

public:
  void ThreadMethod();

public:
  Thread* m_pThread;

public:
  void Start();

protected:
  int m_iStart;
  int m_iEnd;
};

CWorkerThread::CWorkerThread(int iStart, int iEnd)
: m_iStart(iStart), m_iEnd(iEnd)
{
```

```
    m_pThread = new Thread(new ThreadStart(this,
      &CWorkerThread::ThreadMethod));
}

void CWorkerThread::Start()
{
  if (m_pThread)
  {
    m_pThread->Start();
  }
}

void CWorkerThread::ThreadMethod()
{
  Console::WriteLine("Worker thread started");

  Console::WriteLine("Worker thread - counting "
    "slowly from {0} to {1}",
    __box(m_iStart), __box(m_iEnd));

  for (int i = m_iStart; i < m_iEnd; i++)
  {
    for (int j = 0; j < 50; j++)
    {
      Console::Write(".");

      // Code to imitate work being done.
      int a;
      a = 15;
    }
    Console::Write("{0}", __box(i));
  }

  Console::WriteLine("Worker thread finished");
}

int _tmain(void)
{
  CWorkerThread* p1 = new CWorkerThread(1, 10);
  CWorkerThread* p2 = new CWorkerThread(11, 20);

  Console::WriteLine("[_tmain] Creating worker threads");

  p1->m_pThread->Priority = ThreadPriority::Highest;
  p2->m_pThread->Priority = ThreadPriority::Lowest;

  p1->Start();
  p2->Start();

  Console::ReadLine();
}
```

Now, build and execute this application to see the results as shown in Figure 43-6. As you can see, simply altering the `Thread::Priority` property can significantly change how your threads execute.

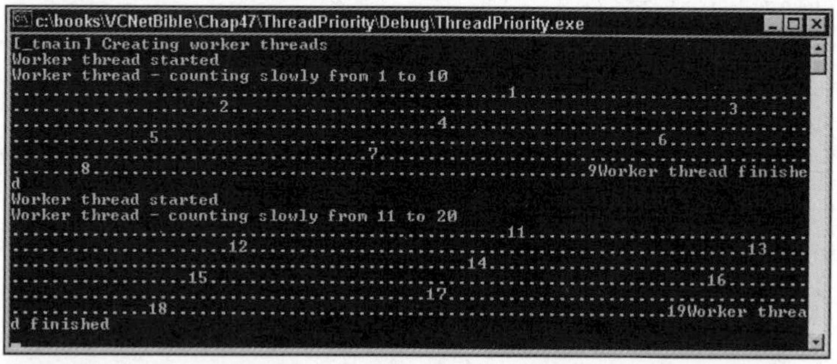

Figure 43-6: By setting thread priorities, you can assert some control over how your application's threads work in relation to one another.

One thing to keep in mind is that even though your code specifies a thread priority, it is the operating system (or runtime environment) that will ultimately use this value as part of its scheduling algorithm that it relays to the processor. In .NET, this algorithm is based on several factors, including the priority level that is defined for a thread as well as the process's *priority class* and *dynamic boost* values. The combination of these values is used to create a numeric value (0 to 31 on Intel processors) that represents the "true" thread's priority from the operating system's perspective. The thread having the highest value is the thread with the highest priority.

The last thing I'll say on the subject of setting thread priority is to use it with caution. It's fairly common for programmers new to multithreaded programming to do things such as setting their background threads to such a high priority that the thread containing the UI code doesn't get enough CPU time — ultimately resulting in a user interface that appears very slow and sluggish to the user. Therefore, unless you have a specific reason to schedule a thread with a high priority, it's best to let the thread's priority default to `ThreadPriority::Normal`.

Synchronizing Threads

One of the first problems that programmers new to multithreaded development get into is not realizing the importance of thread safety and synchronization. Think of it like this. When you're accustomed to writing single-threaded applications, you never have to concern yourself with issues of *state*. That is to say that a piece of code may be entered by more than one thread and in doing so, be in an invalid state. By way of example, when you go the local coffee shop you have to take a number to be waited on. Programmatically, this can be displayed with something as simple as a class that maintains a counter and upon being queried for one, releases and then increments that number.

```
__gc class CTicketDispenser
{
public:
```

```
    static int m_iNextTicket = 1;

public:
    __property int get_NextTicket()
    {
        return m_iNextTicket++;
    }
};
```

Although the exact implementation realized for the `CTicketDispenser::get_NextTicket` method would vary for each compiler, the result would be something along the lines of the flow shown in Figure 43-7.

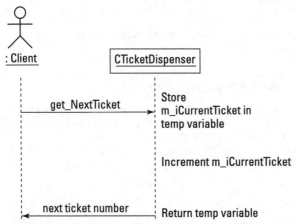

Figure 43-7: As long as only one thread ever calls this method, everything will run smoothly.

The problem with what you see in Figure 43-7 is that in a multithreaded environment hosted by a preemptive multitasking operating system, you are not guaranteed that a given thread will begin this method and complete its execution before another thread enters. As you can see in Figure 43-8, Thread #1 has entered the `CWorkerThread::get_NextTicket` method. The method immediately set a temporary variable to the value of the `CWorkerThread::m_iNextTicket` value (1 at this point). Precisely at this point, another thread enters the method (Thread #2). This second execution once again saves the `CWorkerThread::m_iNextTicket` value into a temporary variable (the value is still 1). Now even though the `m_iNextTicket` value will (correctly) end up with a value of 3, both threads will be returned the same ticket number! This is an example of what people mean when they say that code is "not thread-safe."

Although this example is greatly simplified, the point here is that anytime you have reentrant code that works with global variables, you must protect this code. That is where thread synchronization comes in. Let's now look at two techniques used to ensure that the integrity of your class data is protected when being used concurrently by multiple threads.

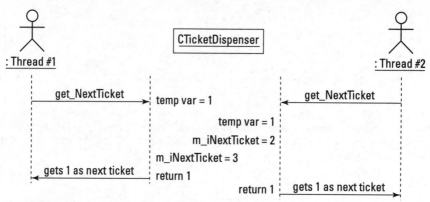

Figure 43-8: Even in very simple applications, concurrent threads can cause problems if the code was not originally designed to work with multiple threads.

Using the monitor class to protect code

To get started, create a project called `ThreadMonitor`. When the files have been created for you, open the `ThreadMonitor.cpp` file and add the following `TicketDispenser` class. Notice that the `CTicketDispenser::get_NextTicket` method has two `Thread::Sleep` method calls in it to emulate the delay the code (for 100 milliseconds) could reasonably expect to incur if it needed to retrieve the next ticket number from a database.

```
__gc class CTicketDispenser
{
protected:
  static int m_iNextTicket = 1;
public:
  __property int get_NextTicket()
  {
    int iNextTicket = m_iNextTicket;
    Thread::CurrentThread->Sleep(100);

    m_iNextTicket = m_iNextTicket + 1;
    Thread::CurrentThread->Sleep(100);

    return iNextTicket;
  }
};
```

Now, add the standard `CWorkerThread` class that you've seen a couple of times already:

```
__gc class CWorkerThread
{
public:
  CWorkerThread(int iThreadId)
    : m_iThreadId(iThreadId)
  {
    m_pThread = new Thread(new ThreadStart(this,
    &CWorkerThread::ThreadMethod));
```

```
      }

protected:
  int m_iThreadId;

protected:
  Thread* m_pThread;
public:
  void Start()
  {
    if (m_pThread)
    {
      m_pThread->Start();
    }
  }

  void ThreadMethod()
  {
    CTicketDispenser* pTicketDispenser
      = new CTicketDispenser();
    Console::WriteLine("[CWorkerThread::ThreadMethod] "
      "ID {0} gets ticket {1}",
      __box(m_iThreadId),
      __box(pTicketDispenser->NextTicket));
  }
};
```

Finally, modify the tmain function to spawn a few threads. Notice that here I include a pause to wait on the termination of those threads, and then print out the CTicketDispenser::NextTicket property:

```
int _tmain(void)
{
  for (int i = 1; i < 6; i++)
  {
    Console::WriteLine("[_tmain] Starting thread {0}",
      __box(i));
    CWorkerThread* pThread = new CWorkerThread(i);
    pThread->Start();
  }

  // Give your worker threads enough time to complete their
  //work.
  Thread::CurrentThread->Sleep(1000);
  CTicketDispenser* pTicketDispenser
    = new CTicketDispenser();
  Console::WriteLine("[_tmain] The current next "
    "ticket value is {0}",
    __box(pTicketDispenser->NextTicket));

  Console::ReadLine();
  return 0;
}
```

If you build and run this application, your results might vary, but they will approximate that shown in Figure 43-9, where you can clearly see that the results were not what the class designer would have intended. As you can see from my running of the application, three clients received a value of 1 and the other two clients received a value of 3, even though the final value is correctly noted as 6!

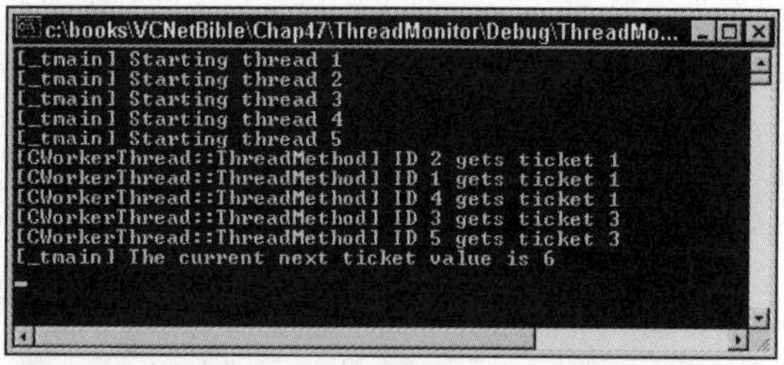

Figure 43-9: Code that involves an object's data being in an inconsistent state needs to be protected from multiple threads concurrently accessing it.

So how do you prevent these sorts of problems and make your code thread-safe? Take a gander at the Monitor class for help. The Monitor class is used to control programmatic access to class methods by granting a lock for an object to a single thread. The online documentation says that the Monitor object is analogous to *critical sections*. However, if you're familiar with the Win32 SDK implementation of critical sections, you'll soon see that although both techniques provide the same basic protection, there is one huge difference between the two.

The Monitor class is very easy to use and includes only a handful of public methods, including static methods to acquire a lock (Monitor::Enter) and release (Monitor::Exit) the lock. At this point, simply add the following calls at the top and bottom of your CTicketDispenser::get_NextTicket class:

```
__property int get_NextTicket()
{
  Monitor::Enter(this);
  ...
  Monitor::Exit(this);

  return iNextTicket;
}
```

Now if you build and run the application, you should see the same results as you did in Figure 43-9.

So why didn't the code work? As it happens, although a Win32 *critical section* is used to ensure that a block of code will be executed by only a single thread within a given process, the Monitor object doesn't quite work that way. The Monitor object only protects a single instance of another object's code. Therefore, adding a monitor didn't help in this case because you actually have five different CTicketDispensers objects. To solve this problem, and to see the Monitor object do what you want, make the following changes:

1. Move the instantiation of the CTicketDispenser object from the CWorkerThread::
ThreadMethod to the _tmain function. That way, you have only one CTicket
Dispenser object that is being used throughout the system:

```
int _tmain(void)
{
 CTicketDispenser* pTicketDispenser
   = new CTicketDispenser();
 for (int i = 1; i < 6; i++)
 ...
```

2. Modify the CWorkerThread constructor so that it takes a CTicketDispenser in its
parameter list:

```
CWorkerThread(int iThreadId,
              CTicketDispenser* pTicketDispenser)
: m_iThreadId(iThreadId),
pTicketDispenser(pTicketDispenser)
```

3. Add the CTicketDispenser member to the CWorkerThread class definition:

```
protected:
  CTicketDispenser* m_pTicketDispenser;
```

4. Modify the CWorkerThread::ThreadMethod method to use the m_pTicketDispenser
member object:

```
void ThreadMethod()
{
 Console::WriteLine("[CWorkerThread::ThreadMethod]
                    "ID {0} gets  ticket {1}",
 __box(m_iThreadId),
 __box(m_pTicketDispenser->NextTicket));
}
```

Now if you build and run this version (available on this book's Web site as ThreadMonitor
Working), you will see a correctly working application (shown in Figure 43-10).

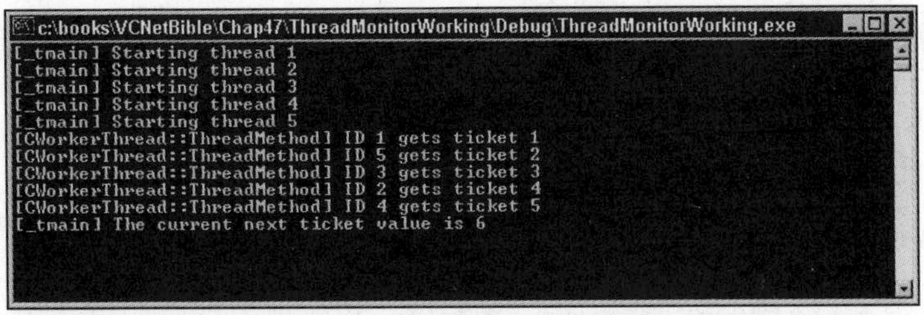

Figure 43-10: Monitor objects only work in protecting a block of code
for a single object instance within a single process.

Because Monitor objects can be very limiting, depending on your needs, I'll now look at
another synchronization class called a Mutex.

Synchronizing code with the mutex class

The `Threading::Mutex` class is the .NET equivalent of the Win32 `mutex` primitive. The mutex provides much the same basic functionality of a monitor object. However, mutexes are much slower because of their increased flexibility. The term *mutex* comes from *mutually exclusive,* and as the name implies, means that only one thread at a time can obtain a lock for a given block of code. However, the power of mutex is that it is system-wide. In other words, although a monitor object only works for threads within a given process, a mutex works across process boundaries. You can construct a `Mutex` object in one of four different ways:

✦ The first version initializes with default properties:

```
public: Mutex();
```

✦ In this version, the `bInitiallyOwned` value indicates whether the calling thread should own the mutex being created. Set this value to `FALSE` if your mutex is to be used across process boundaries.

```
public: Mutex(bool bInitiallyOwned);
```

✦ Add the `strMutex` name to the constructor so that you can name a mutex. This value is used to uniquely identify a mutex:

```
public: Mutex(bool bInitiallyOwned, String* strMutexName);
```

✦ The last parameter simply indicates (upon return from the mutex's creation) if the system granted the ownership to the calling thread. This value does not need to be initialized, because it will be set by the `Mutex` constructor:

```
public: Mutex(bool bInitiallyOwned,
              String* strMutexName,
              bool bOwnershipGranted);
```

Implementing this object in your code requires just a few simple steps:

1. First define a `Mutex` member object for the `CTicketDispenser` class. Make it a static member so that it is the mutex used for all code using this class definition. Here—because I used the default `Mutex` constructor—the _tmain thread will have ownership:

```
static Mutex* m_pMutex = new Mutex();
```

2. Next, add a call to the beginning of the `CTicketDispenser::get_NextTicket` method wait on the mutex lock. This method can either accept a time value that represents how long the code should wait to acquire the lock, or no parameters, which means to wait indefinitely:

```
__property int get_NextTicket()
{
 m_pMutex->WaitOne();
 ...
```

3. Finally, add a call to the end of the `CTicketDispenser::get_NextTicket` to release the mutex:

```
__property int get_NextTicket()
{
 ...
 m_pMutex->Close();
 return iNextTicket;
}
```

Now, if you build and run this application you will see the same results you had in the `ThreadMonitorWorking` example. Now that you know the basics of how to use threads in .NET, take a minute to look at what guidelines you should use in deciding if multithreading is the correct option for your code.

Multithreading Design Guidelines

Many programmers new to multithreading have one of two responses. They either want to immediately start using it in every application they write, or they don't want to touch it regardless of the possible benefits. Obviously, neither extreme is very practical. Therefore, in this section I'll look at some common scenarios in which threads can be used to improve your application, and some scenarios in which you're better off not using multithreading.

When to use threads

As a baseline, you should use threads when the results will be increased concurrency, simplified design, and better use of CPU time.

Increased concurrency

A number of years ago, I wrote a document retrieval system that accessed data from optical disks that were stored in *jukeboxes*. This system — typically used by banks — stored massive amounts of data with each jukebox holding 50 platters, and each platter holding hundreds of gigabytes of data. On the user's network, I stored a searchable index of the documents. However, when I found a match and determined the platter that it existed on, it would then take five to ten seconds to load that particular disk and find the requested document. Needless to say, users were not happy when the first beta version was a single-threaded application, because this wait for a disk to be loaded meant that user interaction with the system was blocked until the document was loaded. For Internet applications, most users accept delays of this magnitude. However, they don't accept such delays quite so easily for desktop applications.

Therefore, in order to allow continued user interaction with the system while I communicated with the jukebox hardware, I would spin off a worker thread to perform this task, thereby allowing the user to continue working. This thread would then notify the main thread when the document was loaded. Therefore, if you have independent activities that can be handled more efficiently with two separate concurrently running threads, then this is a good candidate for multithreading.

Simplified design

One popular means of handling complex systems (such as order entry/invoicing) is to split the system into subsystems where the subsystems communicate via queues and asynchronous processing. Using such a design, you'd have queues set up to handle the different events that transpire in your system. Instead of methods being called directly, objects are created and placed in queues where they will be handled. At the other end of these queues are server programs with multiple threads that are set up to "listen" for messages coming in to these queues. The advantage of this type of simplified design is that it provides for reliable, robust, and, most importantly, extendable systems. Therefore, although it's unusual that multiple threads will lead to a simplified design of a complex system, there are situations where this is true and you should take advantage of that.

Better use of CPU time

One design issue to look at is how a given thread is taking advantage of its time slice. In the document retrieval system example, the code I wrote to access the jukebox spent a great deal of time waiting on the hardware. Therefore, the thread itself wasn't really doing anything. Other examples of wait times include when you're printing a document, or waiting on other physical devices such as hard disk or DVD drives. In these cases, the CPU is not being used; therefore you should consider moving the work being done to worker threads that run in the background.

When not to use threads

As I mentioned earlier, it's a common mistake for those new to threads to attempt to deploy them in every application. Many times, forcing multiple threads into an inappropriate situation can result in overly complex system designs and difficult-to-maintain code. It can even result in code that is actually more inefficient than a single-threaded version. Therefore, give careful thought to the following situations where multithreading probably is not your best option.

Costs outweigh benefits

One of the most difficult aspects of writing a chapter on a subject such as multithreading is that its almost impossible to present the types of complex systems that cause the most problems. The reason for this is that it's easy to see multithreading done in a simple "get the next ticket" example and think that it's a relatively easy task to implement multithreading. Although conceptually this is true (because the language syntax for threading is simple), most applications needing multiple threads are quite a bit more complex than the types of examples that fit neatly in a chapter's pages. Therefore, I can only tell you that when you're designing a complete, real-world system (such as an accounting application or air traffic control system) you need to be cognizant of the fact that a great deal of time will be spent designing (and debugging) the multithreaded aspects of your system. As a result, you should make certain in such applications that the benefits derived from adding multiple threads to your system are not outweighed by the development costs.

You haven't benchmarked both cases

If you're new to multithreaded programming, it might surprise you to discover that the overhead required by CPU in thread creation, scheduling and context switching can actually result in code that runs slower than if you had left your application single-threaded. As a simple example, if you have to read three files from the same hard disk, spinning off three separate threads won't increase your application's efficiency because each thread is waiting on the same hard disk controller to do its work. Therefore, you should always benchmark both a single-threaded and multithreaded version of the task being done before launching into the time and cost of designing around a solution that might actually backfire in terms of performance.

Always default to a single-threaded design

When designing your systems, always respect the fact that including multiple threads in your system should not be the default when designing your systems. In other words, although multithreading can be a fantastic solution for some applications, you should carefully consider all options and the overall impact of benefits versus cost when making this all-important decision.

Summary

As you saw in this chapter, multithreading allows you to define multiple paths of execution that run concurrently in order to make the most efficient use of the processor's time and in some cases, simply a complex system's design. You learned that .NET supports the writing of multithreaded applications through the classes and types defined in the `System.Threading` namespace. With these classes and types, you discovered how to create threads, manage their lifetimes, and synchronize blocks of code to prevent objects from being accessed during times when their internal data is in an inconsistent state.

Hopefully, along with the syntax of multithreading, you learned that adding multiple threads to an application is not the right choice in all situations and can sometimes result in a system that is both more costly to develop and actually performs worse than its single-threaded counterpart.

Because a subject the magnitude of multithreading is one that should be covered in several chapters, or even an entire book, I strongly recommend that if you are new to multithreading, you follow up on the basics shown here with a lot of experimentation before attempting to design complex multithreaded systems.

✦   ✦   ✦

Working with Windows Forms

In the previous three chapters, you've seen an overview of the .NET system and what benefits it provides you, and you've written quite a few managed C++ demo applications. However, all the demos have been console applications. In this chapter, you're going to change that. In this chapter, you will discover the forms package — Windows Forms — that is used to write Windows applications under .NET. You'll start out with the basic, no-frills Windows Forms application that displays a message box when the client area is clicked. The next demo is an application that, upon the user's entry of an IP address, displays the DNS server's host name. While coding this application, you will learn how to dynamically create and position controls on a form and how to code and attach event handlers to those controls. Once you know how to work with forms and controls, the penultimate demo will illustrate how to add menus and menu handlers to your Windows Forms applications. Finally, in the chapter's last demo you will put everything you've learned together to create a simple image viewer application that makes use of several BCL classes to load and display images.

Building Your First Windows Forms Application

Although the subject of Windows Forms could easily encompass an entire book, this section will attempt to at least get you started using this extremely powerful forms package. As is my style, I won't waste a lot of your time postulating about how great I think Windows Forms is. Instead, I'll jump right into a series of demo applications so that you can see for yourself the types of applications that you can easily create using Windows Forms from your managed C++ applications.

Begin by creating a standard managed C++ project called `HelloWindows Forms`. Once you've created the project, you need to import the necessary assemblies to work with Windows Forms. To do that, locate the import of the `mscorlib.dll` assembly and add the following three `#using` directives (shown in bold) after that. As you can guess from the names, these assemblies provide the necessary support for displaying forms and drawing on those forms.

```
#using <mscorlib.dll>
#using <System.dll>
#using <System.Drawing.dll>
#using <System.Windows.Forms.dll>
```

Next, you need to specify the namespaces you want to use. Once again, locate the other using statements and add the following new statements (also shown in bold):

```
using namespace System;
using namespace System::ComponentModel;
using namespace System::Drawing;
using namespace System::Windows::Forms;
```

So far, so good. In order to create a Windows Forms form, you need to derive a form of your own from the System::Windows::Form class. This is simply enough to do. In the following example, the __gc decoration tells the .NET runtime that this class can be garbage collected:

```
__gc class MyForm : public Form
{
};
```

As you know, Windows applications must have an entry point named WinMain. Therefore, code a WinMain function whose prototype looks like the following:

```
int __stdcall WinMain()
{
}
```

Once you've defined the WinMain function, you can instantiate the MyForm object as follows (once again, note that this is just plain old C++ syntax here):

```
// Instantiate a MyForm object.
MyForm* pMyForm = new MyForm();
```

The last thing you do in the WinMain function is to invoke the static Application::Run method to create and display the form (as well as create the message pump for the window) like this:

```
// Create and display the form and
// start the message loop to control messaging.
Application::Run(pMyForm);
```

At this point, you could actually build and run this application, but it wouldn't do much at all; actually, it wouldn't do anything. Therefore, you should at least have something to look at so that you know that you didn't code this for nothing.

Add a constructor to the MyForm class that looks like the following. Here you're simply setting the Form object's title bar text and then adding an event handler so that when the form is clicked, a function is called (MyForm::OnClick). As you can see, in order to add an event to an object, you simply instantiate an EventHandler object, passing it the object that is being monitored for the event (MyForm, in this case) and the function to be called when that event is detected (MyForm::OnClick).

```
MyForm::MyForm()
{
    Text = "HelloWindows Forms Application";
    add_Click(new EventHandler(this, &MyForm::OnClick));
}
```

Finally, add the OnClick event handler to the MyForm class like this, so that when the form is clicked the application displays a textual message indicating that the event was caught, as shown in the following example:

```
__gc class MyForm : public Form
{
```

```
...
protected:
 void OnClick(Object *sender, System::EventArgs* e);
}
...
void MyForm::OnClick(Object *sender, System::EventArgs* e)
{
 MessageBox::Show("Hello Windows Forms!");
}
```

When you are finished, your code for HelloWindows Forms.cpp should resemble that shown in Listing 44-1.

Listing 44-1: **HelloWindows Forms.cpp**

```cpp
#include "stdafx.h"

#using <mscorlib.dll>
#using <System.dll>
#using <System.Drawing.dll>
#using <System.Windows.Forms.dll>

#include <tchar.h>

using namespace System;
using namespace System::ComponentModel;
using namespace System::Drawing;
using namespace System::Windows::Forms;

__gc class MyForm : public Form
{
public:
  MyForm();
protected:
  void OnClick(Object *sender, System::EventArgs* e);
};

MyForm::MyForm()
{
  Text = "HelloWindows Forms Application";
  add_Click(new EventHandler(this,&MyForm::OnClick));
}

void MyForm::OnClick(Object *sender, System::EventArgs* e)
{
    MessageBox::Show("Hello Windows Forms!");
}

int __stdcall WinMain()
{
  // Instantiate a MyForm object.
```

Continued

Listing 44-1 *(continued)*

```
    MyForm* pMyForm = new MyForm();

    // Create and display the form and
    // start the message loop to control messaging.
    Application::Run(pMyForm);

    return 0;
}
```

That's it! From here, you simply build and run the application to see your very first Windows Forms application (shown in Figure 44-1). It doesn't do much now, but it's a start, and you'll be adding some new resources right away.

Figure 44-1: To create a Windows Forms application, simply derive your own System::Windows::Form class, instantiate it, and pass it to the static Application::Run method.

Adding Controls to Windows Forms

Now that you know how to create a Windows Forms application and even add event handlers to it, you can take the next logical step and start adding some controls. In this demo, the user will be able to enter an Internet host name. Once they've done that, you'll use that host name and the System.Net namespace to retrieve the associated IP addresses. In the process of writing this demo, you will learn how to modify your System::Windows::Form derived class to include a text control, a button control, and a list box control. You'll also see how to add code to handle a button's click, and how to dynamically add items to a list box as a result of user interaction.

To get started with all this, create a new managed C++ application project called GetHostIps. Once you've created the new project, add the following #using directives and using namespace statements. Once again the additions to the Visual Studio–generated code are shown in bold:

```
#include "stdafx.h"

#using <mscorlib.dll>
#using <System.dll>
#using <System.Drawing.dll>
#using <System.Windows.Forms.dll>

using namespace System;
using namespace System::Drawing;
using namespace System::Windows::Forms;
using namespace System::Net;
```

Replace the _tmain function with a WinMain function. Then define a Form-derived class called MyForm and instantiate it in the WinMain function as follows:

```
#include "stdafx.h"

#using <mscorlib.dll>
#using <System.dll>
#using <System.Drawing.dll>
#using <System.Windows.Forms.dll>

using namespace System;
using namepsace System::ComponentModel;
using namepsace System::Drawing;
using namepsace System::Windows::Forms;
using namepsace System::Net;
__gc class MyForm : public Form
{
};

int __stdcall WinMain()
{
    // Instantiate a MyForm object.
    MyForm* pMyForm = new MyForm();

    // Create and display the form and
    // start the message loop to control messaging.
    Application::Run(pMyForm);

    return 0;
}
```

So far, this is the same code as the Hello Windows Forms example. However, things are about to change dramatically, starting with the addition of the form's controls. Begin by adding the following members to your MyForm class. As you can see, you're simply adding three controls of type TextBox (edit control), Button, and ListBox. The variable names should tell you each control's intended purpose. Nothing too difficult yet.

```
protected:
    TextBox *m_ptxtHostName;
    Button *m_pbtnGetIPAddresses;
    ListBox *m_plbxIPAddresses;
```

Once you've added those control members, add a parameter-less constructor to the MyForm class so that it can construct and initialize the form and its controls:

```
__gc class MyForm : public Form
{
...
public:
   MyForm();
...
```

Now, add the MyForm constructor code and start coding it. The first thing you do is set some form-level properties. As you can see in the following example, you're simply setting the form's caption (title bar text) and some form size attributes:

```
MyForm::MyForm()
{
   // Set the form's caption.
   Text = "Managed C++ Windows Forms App";

   // Set border style, turn off maximize button,
   // and set the form size.
   FormBorderStyle=FormBorderStyle::Fixed3D;
   MaximizeBox=false;
   ClientSize = System::Drawing::Size(300,200);
}
```

Now, add the following code to the constructor in order to instantiate the MyForm::m_ptxtHostName object and set its text, size, and location properties. This is the control where the user will enter the DNS host name.

```
// Create the host name text object and set its properties.
m_ptxtHostName = new TextBox();
m_ptxtHostName->Text="Enter desired DNS Host Name here";
m_ptxtHostName->Size = System::Drawing::Size(275,50);
m_ptxtHostName->Location = Point(5,5);
```

Once you've set up the text box, you still need to add it to the form in order for it to be displayed. Because the System::Windows::Form class contains a collection of controls called Controls that keeps track of all controls on the forms, you simply need to call that collection's Add method for this label:

```
// Add the label to the form.
Controls->Add(m_ptxtHostName);
```

After creating and adding the IP TextBox control to the form, you can then add the button:

```
// Now add a button control and set
// its relevant properties.
m_pbtnGetIPAddresses = new Button();
m_pbtnGetIPAddresses->Text = "Get IP Address(es)";
m_pbtnGetIPAddresses->Location = Point(5,60);
m_pbtnGetIPAddresses->Size = System::Drawing::Size(120,30);
```

Note that once again, to create a control, you need only instantiate a class's control member, and set the relevant properties. However, there's going to be something special about this particular form. Here you need to have an event handler so that when the button is clicked, a specified function is called. To do that, simply call the Button::add_Click function and specify the function that is to be called when the user clicks the button:

```
// Add a button handler function.
m_pbtnGetIPAddresses->add_Click(new
   EventHandler(this,&MyForm::ButtonClick));
```

As you can see, the `add_Click` function takes two parameters. The first is a pointer to the form and the second is the address of the event handler function. (You haven't coded the `MyForm::ButtonClick` function yet, but you will shortly.) Now add the button control to the form using the `Form::Controls::Add` method:

```
// Add the button to the form.
Controls->Add(m_pbtnGetIPAddresses);
```

You're almost there. Now, add the `ListBox` control and set its properties.

```
// Create the IP Listbox.
m_plbxIPAddresses = new ListBox();
m_plbxIPAddresses->Size = System::Drawing::Size(150,100);
m_plbxIPAddresses->ScrollAlwaysVisible = true;
m_plbxIPAddresses->Location = Point(130,60);
// Add the ListBox to the form.
Controls->Add(m_plbxIPAddresses);
```

Finally, the last thing to do is to add the `ButtonClick` method to the `MyForm` class as follows. Let's look briefly at what's going on. First, you're getting the `ObjectCollection` from the `ListBox` control. The `ObjectCollection` represents the items that are in the list box. From there, you call that object's `Clear` method to initialize the list box control's contents.

Once you've done that, you take the DNS host name entered by the user (`m_ptxtHostName`) and call the `Dns::Resolve` method. This method queries the currently configured DNS server for your TCP/IP network for the IP address associated with the specified host name or IP address. The method returns an `IPHostEntry` object, which contains the Internet host address information.

One of the members of the `IPHostEntry` object is the set of IP addresses associated with the host. This list can be acquired via the `AddressList` property (shown here) or the `get_AddressList` method. The `AddressList` is technically an array of `IPAddress` objects. Therefore, a simple `for` loop can be used to iterate through this array. From there, the `ListBox::ObjectCollection::Add` method is used to add items to the list box. Note that you're using the array object's `Item` property to get each specific IP address. You could have also used the `get_Item` method and passed as the only argument the index value of the desired IP address (`i` in this case). Finally, note that the `IPAddress` object's `ToString` is being used to get the textual representation of the IP address to insert into the list box.

```
void MyForm::ButtonClick(Object *sender,
                         System::EventArgs *e)
{
 ListBox::ObjectCollection* pItems =
  m_plbxIPAddresses->Items;
 pItems->Clear();

 IPHostEntry* IPHost = Dns::Resolve(m_ptxtHostName->Text);
 IPAddress* address[] = IPHost->AddressList;

 for(int i = 0; i < address.Length; i++)
 {
  pItems->Add((address->Item[i])->ToString())
 }
}
```

When you've finished, the code you typed should be the same as that shown in Listing 44-2.

Listing 44-2: GetDnsHost.cpp

```cpp
#include "stdafx.h"

#using <mscorlib.dll>
#using <System.dll>
#using <System.Drawing.dll>
#using <System.Windows.Forms.dll>

using namespace System;
using namespace System::Drawing;
using namespace System::Windows::Forms;
using namespace System::Net;

__gc class MyForm : public Form
{
public:
  MyForm();

protected:
  TextBox *m_ptxtHostName;
  Button *m_pbtnGetIPAddresses;
  ListBox *m_plbxIPAddresses;

protected:
  void ButtonClick(Object *sender, System::EventArgs* e);
};

int __stdcall WinMain()
{
  // Instantiate a MyForm object.
  MyForm* pMyForm = new MyForm();

  // Create and display the form and
  // start the message loop to control messaging.
  Application::Run(pMyForm);

  return 0;
}

MyForm ::MyForm()
{
  // Set the form's caption.
  Text = "Managed C++ Windows Forms App";

  // Set border style, turn off maximize button,
  // and set the form size.
  FormBorderStyle=FormBorderStyle::Fixed3D;
  MaximizeBox=false;
  ClientSize = System::Drawing::Size(300,200);

  // Create the Host Name text object and set its properties.
  m_ptxtHostName = new TextBox();
```

```
    m_ptxtHostName->Text="Enter desired DNS Host Name here";
    m_ptxtHostName->Size = System::Drawing::Size(275,50);
    m_ptxtHostName->Location = Point(5,5);

    // Add the label to the form.
    Controls->Add(m_ptxtHostName);

    // Now add a button control and set
    // its relevant properties.
    m_pbtnGetIPAddresses = new Button();
    m_pbtnGetIPAddresses->Text = "Get IP Address(es)";
    m_pbtnGetIPAddresses->Location = Point(5,60);
    m_pbtnGetIPAddresses->Size = System::Drawing::Size(120,30);

    // Add a button handler function.
    m_pbtnGetIPAddresses->add_Click(new
      EventHandler(this,&MyForm::ButtonClick));

    // Add the button to the form.
    Controls->Add(m_pbtnGetIPAddresses);

    // Create the IP Listbox.
    m_plbxIPAddresses = new ListBox();
    m_plbxIPAddresses->Size = System::Drawing::Size(150,100);
    m_plbxIPAddresses->ScrollAlwaysVisible = true;
    m_plbxIPAddresses->Location = Point(130,60);

    // Add the ListBox to the form.
    Controls->Add(m_plbxIPAddresses);
}

void MyForm::ButtonClick(Object *sender,
                             System::EventArgs *e)
{
  ListBox::ObjectCollection* pItems =
    m_plbxIPAddresses->Items;
  pItems->Clear();

  IPHostEntry* IPHost = Dns::Resolve(m_ptxtHostName->Text);
  IPAddress* address[] = IPHost->AddressList;

  for(int i = 0; i < address.Length; i++)
  {
    pItems->Add((address->Item[i])->ToString());
  }
}
```

Figure 44-2 shows the results of running this demo application and supplying a value of www.microsoft.com to discover all of that host name's IP addresses.

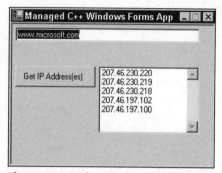

Figure 44-2: Using Windows Forms, you can dynamically create, set the properties of, and work with controls with a minimum of code.

Incorporating Menus in a Windows Forms Application

In this demo, you will lean how to add menus and menu event handlers to a Windows Forms application. I think that when you're finished you'll see that the steps used to perform these tasks are much the same as the steps needed to add controls and control event handlers. This consistency is one of the main reasons that developing software in .NET is so much easier than in previous development environments.

First, create a new managed C++ project called WindowsFormsMenuForm. As before, add the following #using directives and using namespaces statements:

```
#using <mscorlib.dll>
#using <System.dll>
#using <System.Drawing.dll>
#using <System.Windows.Forms.dll>

using namespace System;
using namespace System::ComponentModel;
using namespace System::Drawing;
using namespace System::Windows::Forms;
```

Now, add a class called WindowsFormsMenuForm and a constructor for that class as follows:

```
__gc class WindowsFormsMenuForm : public Form
{
public:
 WindowsFormsMenuForm();
}

Windows FormsMenuForm::WindowsFormsMenuForm()
{
}
```

Once you've added the `WindowsFormsMenuForm` class constructor, code the adding of the menu items and attachment of the menu items to event handlers. First, add the following line of code at the top of the constructor to set the title bar text:

```
Text = "Windows Forms Menu Application";
```

Now, create the top-level menu. You do that by first creating a local .NET `MainMenu` object:

```
MainMenu* pMenu = new MainMenu();
```

Once the `MainMenu` object is created, you can start adding menu items to it. Because most Windows applications have a File ⇨ Exit option, you can start there. Note that in the following code the `MainMenu` object (`pMenu`) has a collection of menu items (`MainMenu::MenuItems`) that have been added to it:

```
MenuItem* pFileMenu = pMenu->MenuItems->Add("File");
```

So now you have a top-level menu object (`pMenu`) and a File menu object (`pFileMenu`). As you probably guessed, you simply need to add the `Exit` item to the `pFileMenu` object. However, this time you want to specify an event handler that will be called when the user selects this option. (You haven't defined the `WindowsFormsMenuForm::OnExit` method just yet, but you will shortly.)

```
pFileMenu->MenuItems->Add("Exit",
  new EventHandler(this,&Windows FormsMenuForm::OnExit));
```

Now, add the Help and About menu options in much the same way as you just did the File and Exit menu options. (Once again, don't worry about the `WindowsFormsMenuFrom::OnAbout` method; you'll define it next.)

```
pFileMenu = pMenu->MenuItems->Add("Help");
pFileMenu->MenuItems->Add("About...",
                        new EventHandler(this,
                        &Windows FormsMenuForm::OnAbout));
```

You've created a local `MainMenu` object with two menu items (File and Help) that each have a single menu option (Exit and About, respectively). Now you need only tell the current `Form` object that this menu is the one to use:

```
Menu = pMenu;
```

Once you've finished coding the `WindowsFormsMenuForm` constructor, add the following event handlers. As you can see, they're fairly straightforward. The `OnExit` method calls the `Form` object's `Close` method (which causes the application to terminate), and the `OnAbout` method displays a message box indicating version information.

```
void WindowsFormsMenuForm::OnExit(Object *sender, EventArgs *e)
{
 // Simply call the Form object's pstrFileName Close method.
 Close();
}


void WindowsFormsMenuForm::OnAbout(Object *sender,
                                   EventArgs *e)

{
 // Display a message box as your about box
 MessageBox::Show("WindowsFormsMenu, Version 1.0",
               "About WindowsFormsMenu");
}
```

If you select the About menu option after building and running this application, you should see the same results as those shown in Figure 44-3.

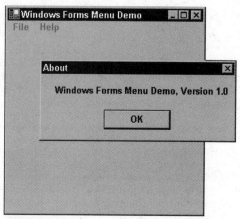

Figure 44-3: Adding menu items and attaching these items to form functions is accomplished with just a couple of lines of code.

The entire listing for this application can be found in Listing 44-3.

Listing 44-3: **WindowsFormsMenu.cpp**

```cpp
#include "stdafx.h"

#using <mscorlib.dll>
#using <System.dll>
#using <System.Drawing.dll>
#using <System.Windows.Forms.dll>

using namespace System;
using namespace System::ComponentModel;
using namespace System::Drawing;
using namespace System::Windows::Forms;

__gc class WindowsFormsMenuForm : public Form
{
public:
 WindowsFormsMenuForm();

protected:
 void OnExit (Object* sender, EventArgs *e);
 void OnAbout (Object* sender, EventArgs *e);
};
```

```
int __stdcall WinMain()
{
 Application::Run(new WindowsFormsMenuForm());
 return 0;
}

Windows FormsMenuForm::WindowsFormsMenuForm()
{
 // Set the title bar text.
 Text = "WindowsFormsMenu Application";

 // Create a top-level menu for your frame window.
 MainMenu* pMenu = new MainMenu();

 // Add a menu option to the File menu.
 MenuItem* pFileMenu = pMenu->MenuItems->Add("File");

 // Add the File menu items now that you have the File
 // item added. Notice that the event handlers for these
 // items are also specified as the items are added to
 // the menu.
 pFileMenu->MenuItems->Add("Exit",
                           new EventHandler(this,
                               &WindowsFormsMenuForm::OnExit));

 // Add another top-level menu option and its submenu.
 pFileMenu = pMenu->MenuItems->Add("Help");
 pFileMenu->MenuItems->Add("About...",
                           new EventHandler(this,
                               &WindowsFormsMenuForm::OnAbout));

 // Set the current Form object's pstrFileName menu
 // to the newly created menu.
 Menu = pMenu;
}

void WindowsFormsMenuForm::OnExit(Object *sender,
                                  EventArgs *e)
{
 // Simply call the Form object's pstrFileName Close method.
 Close();
}

void WindowsFormsMenuForm::OnAbout(Object *sender,
                                   EventArgs *e)
{
 // Display a message box as your about box.
 MessageBox::Show("WindowsFormsMenu, Version 1.0",
                  "About WindowsFormsMenu");
}
```

Writing an Image Viewer in Managed C++

In this—the chapter's last demo—you'll create a simple image viewer that allows the user to open and display an image stored on disk in JPG format. Along the way, you'll learn how to work with the File Open common dialog box, and discover how easy it is to load and display image files using the `Form::Bitmap` class. Get started by once again creating a simple managed C++ application project, this time called `ImageViewer`. Once the files for your new project have been created, add the following #using directives and using namespace statements:

```
#using <mscorlib.dll>
#using <System.dll>
#using <System.Drawing.dll>
#using <System.Windows.Forms.dll>

using namespace System;
using namespace System::ComponentModel;
using namespace System::Drawing;
using namespace System::Windows::Forms;
```

Now, create the main form class, `ImageViewerForm`, and the standard `WinMain` entry point:

```
__gc class ImageViewerForm : public Form
{
}

int __stdcall WinMain()
{
 Application::Run(new ImageViewerForm());

 return 0;
}
```

Add the following constructor to the `ImageViewerForm` class. The code is mostly the same as the constructor code used in the previous example, with the sole difference being the addition of a new File ➪ Open menu option (which I've bolded in this listing).

```
ImageViewerForm::ImageViewerForm()
{
  // Set the title bar text.
  Text = "Image Viewer";

  // Create a top-level menu for your frame window.
  MainMenu* pMenu = new MainMenu();

  // Add a menu option to the File menu.
  MenuItem* pFileMenu = pMenu->MenuItems->Add("File");

  // Add the File menu items now that you have the
  // File item added. Notice that the event handlers
  // for these items are also specified as the items
  // are added to the menu.
  pFileMenu->MenuItems->Add("Open...",
   new EventHandler(this, &ImageViewerForm::OnOpen));

  pFileMenu->MenuItems->Add("Exit",
```

```
    new EventHandler(this, &ImageViewerForm::OnExit));

    // Add another top-level menu option and
    // its pstrFileName submenu.
    pFileMenu = pMenu->MenuItems->Add("Help");
    pFileMenu->MenuItems->Add("About...",
      new EventHandler(this, &ImageViewerForm::OnAbout));

    // Set the current Form object's pstrFileName
    // menu to the newly created menu.
    Menu = pMenu;
}
```

Once you've added the code to the ImageViewerForm constructor to add the menu items, add the following event handlers:

```
void ImageViewerForm::OnExit(Object *sender, EventArgs *e)
{
  // Simply call the Form object's pstrFileName
  // Close method.
  Close();
}

void ImageViewerForm::OnAbout(Object *sender, EventArgs *e)
{
  // Display a message box as your about box.
  MessageBox::Show("This is version 1.0 of the Managed C++ "
                   "ImageViewer.  For the most up-to-date "
                   "version, please be sure and check "
                   "www.TheCodeChannel.com",
                   "About ImageViewer");
}
```

Now you come to the new stuff. The BCL includes an object that takes care of almost all of the drudgery associated with dealing with image files in a class called Bitmap. As you will see, this class, which resides in the System.Drawing namespace, couldn't be easier to work with. For now, add a member to the ImageViewerForm of type Bitmap*:

```
Bitmap *m_pImage;
```

Once you've done that, code the OnFileOpen event handler as follows. Note that to display a common file dialog box, you simply instantiate the OpenFileDialog object, set its Filter property (which filters which files are shown to the user by default), and display it using the OpenFileDialog::ShowDialog method. If the user selects a file, the OpenFileDialog::ShowDialog function returns a value of DialogResult::OK.

If the user did select a file from the File Open dialog box, the code requests the filename from the dialog object (pOpenFileDlg), instantiates a Bitmap object, sizes the form to the size of the image, and calls the Form::Invalidate method, as shown in the following example:

```
void ImageViewerForm::OnOpen(Object *sender, EventArgs *e)
{
  OpenFileDialog* pOpenFileDlg = new OpenFileDialog();

  pOpenFileDlg->Filter
    = "JPEG files (*.jpg;*.jpeg)|*.jpg;*.jpeg";
```

```
if (DialogResult::OK == pOpenFileDlg->ShowDialog())
{
 String *pstrFileName = pOpenFileDlg->FileName;

 m_pImage = new Bitmap(pstrFileName);

 AutoScroll=true;
 AutoScrollMinSize = m_pImage->Size;

 Invalidate();
}
}
```

As you learned in Chapter 8, calling the window's `Invalidate` method results in a `WM_PAINT` message being sent to the window. Because this is a Windows issue, and not specific to MFC, calling `Invalidate` on a .NET Windows Form does the same thing in .NET applications. Therefore, you need to override the `Form` object's virtual `OnPaint` method as follows so that you can display the image when needed.

Once you've verified that the `m_pImage` member has been set, all you need to do is to instantiate a `Graphics` object using the form's DC (device context) — very similar to what you learned back in Chapter 8 — and call the `Graphics::DrawImage` method, passing to it the `Bitmap` object and the position in the DC where you want the image displayed:

```
void ImageViewerForm::OnPaint(PaintEventArgs *e)
{
 if (m_pImage)
 {
  Graphics *pGraphics = e->Graphics;

  pGraphics->DrawImage(m_pImage,
                        AutoScrollPosition.X,
                        AutoScrollPosition.Y,
                        m_pImage->Width,
                        m_pImage->Height);
 }
}
```

When you finish this, your code should look like that shown in Listing 44-4.

Listing 44-4: **ImageViewer.cpp**

```
#include "stdafx.h"

#using <mscorlib.dll>
#using <System.dll>
#using <System.Drawing.dll>
#using <System.Windows.Forms.dll>

using namespace System;
using namespace System::ComponentModel;
using namespace System::Drawing;
```

```
using namespace System::Windows::Forms;

__gc class ImageViewerForm : public Form
{
public:
 ImageViewerForm();
protected:
 void OnPaint(PaintEventArgs *e);
private:
 //Event handlers for menu pFileMenu clicks
 void OnExit (Object* sender, EventArgs *e);
 void OnAbout (Object* sender, EventArgs *e);
 void OnOpen (Object* sender, EventArgs *e);

 //Your member variable for the image
 Bitmap *m_pImage;
};

int __stdcall WinMain()
{
 Application::Run(new ImageViewerForm());
 return 0;
}

ImageViewerForm::ImageViewerForm()
{
 // Set the title bar text.
 Text = "Image Viewer";

 // Create a top-level menu for your frame window.
 MainMenu* pMenu = new MainMenu();

 // Add a menu option to the File menu.
 MenuItem* pFileMenu = pMenu->MenuItems->Add("File");

 // Add the File menu items now that you have the File
 // item added. Notice that the event handlers for these
 // items are also specified as the items are added to
 // the menu.
 pFileMenu->MenuItems->Add("Open...",
                           new EventHandler(this,
                             &ImageViewerForm::OnOpen));
 pFileMenu->MenuItems->Add("Exit",
                           new EventHandler(this,
                             &ImageViewerForm::OnExit));

 // Add another top-level menu option and its submenu.
 pFileMenu = pMenu->MenuItems->Add("Help");
 pFileMenu->MenuItems->Add("About...",
                           new EventHandler(this,
                             &ImageViewerForm::OnAbout));

 // Set the current Form object's menu
```

Continued

Listing 44-4 *(continued)*

```
    // to the newly created menu.
    Menu = pMenu;
}

void ImageViewerForm::OnExit(Object *sender, EventArgs *e)
{
    // Simply call the Form object's Close method.
    Close();
}

void ImageViewerForm::OnAbout(Object *sender, EventArgs *e)
{
    MessageBox::Show("This is version 1.0 of the Managed C++ "
                     "ImageViewer.  For the most up-to-date "
                     "version, please be sure and check "
                     "www.TheCodeChannel.com",
                     "About ImageViewer");
}

void ImageViewerForm::OnOpen(Object *sender, EventArgs *e)
{
    // The OpenFileDialog is an encapsulation of the common
    // File Open dialog box.
    OpenFileDialog* pOpenFileDlg = new OpenFileDialog();

    // You can filter here just as you can with the standard
    // Win32 API or the MFC CFileDialog class.
    pOpenFileDlg->Filter
      = "JPEG files (*.jpg;*.jpeg)|*.jpg;*.jpeg";

// Display the File Open dialog box so that the user
// can select an image file to be opened.
// If user has clicked OK...
if (DialogResult::OK == pOpenFileDlg->ShowDialog())
 {
    // Retrieve the dialog box's pstrFileName FileName
    // property, which is the name of the file the user
    // selected to open.
    String *pstrFileName = pOpenFileDlg->FileName;

    // Now that you have a valid filename, set the
    // ImageViewerForm image member to an instantiation
    // of the Bitmap class using the filename.
    m_pImage = new Bitmap(pstrFileName);

    // Here I'm setting the form to scroll if the image
    // is too large to be accommodated. Note the setting of the
    // minimum size to the image size.
    AutoScroll=true;
    AutoScrollMinSize = m_pImage->Size;
```

```
  // Invalidate the form to cause a repaint.
  Invalidate();
 }
}

void ImageViewerForm::OnPaint(PaintEventArgs *e)
{
 // If you've loaded an image...
 if (m_pImage)
 {
  // Get the Graphics object associated with your
  // form's DC (device context).
  Graphics *pGraphics = e->Graphics;

  // Use the Graphics::DrawImage function to
  // draw the image.
  pGraphics->DrawImage(m_pImage,
                       AutoScrollPosition.X,
                       AutoScrollPosition.Y,
                       m_pImage->Width,
                       m_pImage->Height);

 }
}
```

Once you've built and run the ImageViewer application, selecting the Open menu option from the File menu should result in the common File Open dialog box being displayed, which allows you to search your folders for JPG files. Simply locate and select one to have the application load and display the image. Figure 44-4 shows an example of a young lady who I photographed recently.

Figure 44-4: Tasks that have always been problematic (such as loading and displaying images) are now built-in features of the BCL.

Summary

In this chapter, you learned a bit about Windows Forms through a series of demo applications. The first of these applications illustrated how to create a basic, no-frills Windows Forms application that displays a message box when the client area is clicked. The next demo was then an application that upon the user's entry of an IP address displays the DNS's host name. In the process of coding that particular demo, you discovered how to dynamically create and position controls on a form and how to code and attach event handlers to those controls. Once you knew how to work with forms and controls, the next demo illustrated how to add menus and menu handlers to your Windows Forms applications. Finally, the chapter ended with a demo application used for loading and displaying images. Although the knowledge you've accrued in these last four chapters on .NET won't make you a .NET guru overnight, hopefully these chapters and demo applications have shown you a bit of what can be done with managed C++ — enough to warrant fully exploring this wonderful and exciting new framework.

✦   ✦   ✦

Index

Symbols

Continued

Continued

Continued

G

Continued

Continued

Continued

Continued

Continued